D1187731

GAELIC PROSE IN THE IRISH FREE STATE

1922–1939

The author and publishers gratefully acknowledge financial support from

Foras na Gaeilge

and

the Boston College university research fund

Gaelic Prose in the Irish Free State

1922–1939

PHILIP O'LEARY

UNIVERSITY COLLEGE DUBLIN PRESS
PREAS CHOLÁISTE OLLSCOILE
BHAILE ÁTHA CLIATH

UNIVERSITY
OF
GLASGOW
LIBRARY

First published 2004 by
UNIVERSITY COLLEGE DUBLIN PRESS
Newman House
86 St Stephen's Green
Dublin 2
Ireland
www.ucdpress.ie

© Philip O'Leary 2004

ISBN 1 904558 13 5

All rights reserved.
No part of this publication may be reproduced,
stored in a retrieval system, or transmitted in any form
or by any means, electronic, photocopying,
recording or otherwise without
the prior permission of the publisher.

Cataloguing in Publication data available from the British Library

Typeset in Ireland in Plantin and Fournier
by Elaine Shiels, Bantry, Co. Cork
Text design by Lyn Davies
Printed on acid-free paper in England
by MPG Books, Bodmin,
Cornwall

Short Loan Collection

For Joyce

*

Contents

Acknowledgements

Many people on both sides of the Atlantic have offered me invaluable encouragement and assistance in the ten years I have been at work on this project. In Ireland, I would like to single out for thanks Angela Bourke, Gearóid Denvir, Margaret Kelleher, Declan Kiberd, Tomás Mac Anna, Proinsias Mac Cana, Nollaig Mac Congáil, Micheál Mac Craith, Alf and Fionnuala Mac Lochlainn, Nuala Ní Dhomhnaill, Gearóid Ó Tuathaigh, and Alan Titley. In addition, I must offer heartfelt gratitude to the staff of the National Library of Ireland, as well as to the staffs of the Central Catholic Library in Dublin, of the Dublin Corporation's Gilbert Library, and of the James Hardiman Library of the National University of Ireland, Galway. I will also thank here Joep Leerssen, who offered valuable advice on two continents. This book would never have appeared so promptly had it not been for my editor Barbara Mennell of UCD Press, whose intelligence, wit, and sheer good sense helped get us both through the process more or less sane.

In the United States, I would first like to thank my colleagues in the Irish Studies Program at Boston College, especially Brian Ó Conchubhair, Rob Savage, Marjorie Howes, and the late Adele Dalsimer, as well as Patrick Ford, the late John V. Kelleher, Tomás Ó Cathasaigh, and the late Harry Levin of Harvard University and the regular participants in Harvard's annual Celtic Colloquium. I hope this book will serve as a memorial, however inadequate, for those who have gone. My gratitude also goes to the staffs of the O'Neill and Burns Libraries at Boston College. On a more personal note, my parents have always supported my interests, and Joyce Flynn's contributions have been too varied and valuable to even try to acknowledge.

PHILIP O'LEARY
South Yarmouth, Mass.
March 2004

Abbreviations

AA	*Ar Aghaidh*
ACS	*An Claidheamh Soluis*
BÁC	Baile Átha Cliath
CA	*Capuchin Annual*
CB	*Catholic Bulletin*
COÉ	Comhlucht Oideachais na hÉireann
CS	*Connacht Sentinel*
CT	*Connacht Tribune*
CUS	Catholic University School
FG	*Féile na nGaedheal*
FL	*Fáinne an Lae*
FMR	*Father Mathew Record*
GR	*Garda Review*
IC	*Irish Catholic*
IF	*Iris an Fháinne*
IBL	*Irish Booklover*
IER	*Irish Ecclesiastical Record*
II	*Irish Independent*
IMN	*Irisleabhar Muighe Nuadhat*
IP	*Irish Press*
IR	*Irish Rosary*
IRA	Irish Republican Army
IRB	Irish Republican Brotherhood
IS	*Irish Statesman*
IT	*The Irish Times*
NLI	National Library of Ireland
NUIG	National University of Ireland, Galway
ODFR	Oifig Díolta Foillseacháin Rialtais
OS	Oifig an tSoláthair
QUB	The Queen's University of Belfast
SF	*Sinn Féin*
TCD	Trinity College, Dublin
TCNÍ	*Timthire Chroidhe Naomhtha Íosa*
UCC	University College Cork
UCD	University College Dublin
UCG	University College Galway
UI	*United Ireland*
UIrman	*United Irishman*

A WORLD TURNED RIGHTSIDE UP?

Had an early Gaelic Leaguer suddenly found himself transported to the mid-1930s, he would have been astounded at how many of his dreams had come true. He would see twenty-six of Ireland's thirty-two counties under native rule; his former movement colleagues in positions of authority in all branches of government from chief executive down; an educational system dedicated to re-Gaelicising the nation through the schools, schools in which all children took Irish as a major subject; and an entire state agency devoted exclusively to the publishing of books in what was now the country's first official language. Had he, on recovering from his initial euphoria, taken a more searching look into the soul of this new Gaelic nation, he may, however, have found cause for concern in the replacement of an earlier idealism and visionary excitement with the bitter partisanship and intransigence that too often characterised Irish political and cultural life in the Free State. These were reduced times, a less stirring age that Liam Ó Rinn ('Fear Faire'), who had worked for and lived through the great change, tried to define for his fellow Gaelic activists in a 1934 essay in *United Ireland*: 'The period in which we are now, from the year 1921 to 1950 or 1960 perhaps, will be considered in history as a period of preparation and transition as far as the Irish language is concerned. With all the work we have going on, in the schools, the army, the Gárda Síochána, and so on, teaching and learning, creating technical terms, translating acts of the Dáil and official orders, technical books and novels, we are only Gaelicising the country and fitting the language to the life our descendants will have soon when no one will be amazed by the language or think about it at all because it will be as natural as the air' (*UI*, 17/11/34).[1]

Ó Rinn's optimism here is striking. The glorious years of the Gaelic revival, when Irish people of all political and religious persuasions came together in inspired and inspirational fellowship to save the Irish language, restore the native culture, and ultimately fight for and win an independent Gaelic state may well have seemed like ancient history in 1934. The brief but vicious Irish Civil War of 1922–3 was, after all, only a decade in the past, and few of the bitter divisions that caused and were then exacerbated by that conflict had been meaningfully addressed by a new state struggling to establish its own validity both abroad and at home, to create a viable constitutional and institutional framework based on democratic and 'Gaelic' principles, and to deal with the problems of a small and poor agricultural state at a time of global political and economic instability.[2] Indeed Ó Rinn himself had seen the pro-Treaty Cumann na nGaedheal party, under whose administration he had worked since independence, rejected by the electorate in 1932, to be replaced by their erstwhile Civil War foes, the Fianna Fáil party of Éamon de Valera. Moreover, that electoral defeat was to drive some Cumann na nGaedheal supporters to flirt with fascism in the so-called 'Blueshirt' movement, a movement that had its violent counterpart on the republican side in the still active and powerful Irish Republican Army.[3] Former comrades in the language movement were to be found facing each other across this political and ideological divide, and, as we will see, deeply held beliefs about linguistic and cultural issues were to be infected by suspicions and even hatreds rooted in post-Civil War politics.[4]

Despite the charged and often sullen temper of the times, many continued to believe that under *any* native government the re-Gaelicisation of the country was a foregone conclusion. Thus in August 1922, the very month that saw the deaths of the Free State's two most important leaders, Arthur Griffith and Michael Collins, the latter shot in ambush by other Irishmen, and the consequent intensification of Civil War hostilities and reprisals, Ó Rinn ('L. Ó R.') could write in the pro-Treaty paper *Young Ireland*: 'Present-day Irishmen are especially favoured in that it is in their power to see a language being developed from what may be called the swaddling-clothes state to what we hope may be a state of the highest literary perfection . . . Irish is just beginning to find its way in the right direction and under the fostering care of a National Government those of us who have not yet reached middle age will probably live to see the language well within sight of the goal, when it can again take its place on the straight level with modern tongues and perhaps even surpass them' (*YI*, 12/8/22). With the Civil War still being fought, Éamon Ó Donnchadha wrote in the Gaelic League's official paper *Fáinne an Lae* in January 1923: 'The national language will grow as all ages of our youth are educated through Irish. To do that an Irish literature must be cultivated that will answer all the needs of life we will face from youth on. That growth will come naturally to the language and it will develop and grow in scope as it is extended in the educational affairs of the young. Learned people will gradually arise to compose an appropriate literature in it for their contemporaries.' (*FL*, 13/1/23).[5]

Three months later, in an essay in the *Irish Rosary*, Risteárd Ó Foghludha ('Fiachra Éilgeach') felt that so much progress was being made that even the deaths of the older generation of fluent native speakers could not hinder the ultimate triumph of the revived language. Having commented on the recent appearance of a number of books of various kinds in Irish, this author declared: 'All of those show, in spite of the grumbling of the mockers, that the reading and writing of the Irish language are daily progressing. It is doubtless true that there is no comparison at all between today's learners and the old-timers we are losing from one week to the next, but it is a great thing that we have as much of the true Irish in print before our pre-eminent Irish-speakers died' (*IR*, Apr. 1923, 308).[6] 'Maolmhuire' was even more enthusiastic in a 1928 essay in *An Tír*, writing: 'The seed planted in the Spring does not bloom until the heat of Summer comes. That is how it is with literature in Irish. We are gradually approaching the Summer of the literature, and it is a good omen for that season that there are so many good writers in the field who encourage us all that there will be a good heavy harvest ahead' (*Tír*, Aug.–Sept. 1928, 3).[7]

A senior movement figure who shared this view was Eoin Mac Néill, one of the founders of the Gaelic League in 1893, and a man who had experienced most of both the triumphs and the tribulations of the cultural and political revival as an editor, scholar, commander-in-chief of the Irish Volunteers before the Easter Rising of 1916, prisoner, Free State Minister of Education, and Irish representative on the abortive commission to adjudicate the disagreement over the border between the Free State and the six counties of Northern Ireland. In a 1930 essay in the New York Irish paper the *Gaelic American*, Mac Néill urged the creation of an Irish language department at the New York Public Library, writing: 'There is plenty of material already in print to stock such a department . . . and in Ireland the output of Gaelic literature is daily on the increase. Besides, the writers of Gaelic are now rising out of what we may call the academic stage and are producing work expressing the Irish mind of our time and quite original in character and experience.'[8]

Even some republicans, despite having plenty to lament and bewail after losing the Civil War, shared this positive outlook for the language and its new literature. For example, the left-wing Fianna Fáil supporter Donn Piatt wrote in his 1933 book *Stair na Gaedhilge* (The history of the Irish language): 'There is enough strength in the language, there is enough literature in it, there is enough nobility in it that it will be out of danger the day we have Freedom without danger, the day the most English thing in Ireland goes, the social system of the English, the capitalist system.'[9] One 'Dearcadh' had been more specifically interested in literature in an essay published in the IRA organ *An Phoblacht* seven years earlier, writing: 'We have reached that stage in the Gaelic movement at which literature is being produced: full-length novels, short stories in plenty, even literary criticism. It may be rough and ready literature, a little coarse for the thinly refined present-day reader, but it is real live literature. And day by day it grows stronger. In ten years shall we not easily have a book-case of good modern Irish literature, full of blood and freshness and exuberant strength?' (*An Phoblacht*, 5/3/26).

He was right, and it could have been a fair-sized bookcase if one were willing to define 'good' literature with some latitude.[10] Much of the credit for the provision of this literature must go to the Free State publishing agency An Gúm, which certainly got most of the blame for the quality of that literature. The policies and practices of the agency will be discussed in depth in chapter nine. Here we may simply note that despite the controversies in which it was always embroiled, An Gúm did fulfil its primary mission: the provision of a significant body of writing, original and translated, in modern Irish. For the first time ever, readers of the language were seeing a fairly steady stream of real books appearing in the shops of the major cities and towns at least, books quite different from the sporadically issued slender volumes – pamphlets really – that constituted the bulk of Gaelic prose in the days when the Gaelic League was the principal publisher in the language.[11] Writing in the Cumann na nGaedheal paper *The Star / An Reult* in 1930, Seán Ó Ciosáin, whose own work was published by An Gúm, spoke for many in his awareness of what the agency had accomplished: 'It was a courageous thing to found An Gúm, and despite all the obstacles that were in its way, there is no doubt at all that it is doing good work. For the first time since the Gaelic League was founded suitable books are being provided for the general reader. That is a great step forward, and it would be wrong for anyone at all not to give due credit to the people who had the courage and the vision to create this system' (*Star*, 1/3/30).[12] Indeed, it would be impossible to refute the boast made by 'An Sagart' in a 1937 piece in the Gaelic Athletic Association's quarterly *An Ráitheachán*: 'Gaelic has never been flung so broadly on the waters of the world during even our Golden Age' (*Ráitheachán*, Mar. 1937, 11).

One of the main issues at stake here was, of course, whether or not it would be possible for writers in the Irish language to make a living from their work, would, for example, be able to devote themselves to their craft in the same way as did successful Irish writers in the English language. The creation of a native state dedicated to a policy of re-Gaelicisation seemed to many to make what had long been a dream at least a possibility – and in the foreseeable future.[13] As early as May 1922, 'B. Ó F.' was challenging the readers of *The Plain People* to live up to the proud traditions of their past by supporting Gaelic authors: 'Why don't Gaels who have a good deal of money help contemporary writers of Irish? The majority of our writers cannot pay the price of printing a book – and there is no payment to be had for writing essays or stories. Irishmen used to be very famous before printing presses were created at all because of the number of books they wrote. But the writers of the old days could get help.' Interestingly enough, however, this author saw little prospect of significant state involvement in publishing: 'There are people who think that the rulers of Ireland will do everything to make literature and books available, but that is something they cannot do. They will not pay to make "literature" available.'

For 'B. Ó F.', the real hope was generous patronage from well-off cultural nationalists in the new state (*Plain People*, 21/5/22).[14]

Micheál Mac Ruaidhrí faulted An Gúm for not making a better effort to make potential readers aware of its books, and then continued: 'It is not enough to publish fifty or a hundred books a year. What's the use of publishing these books if they are left unbought and unread . . . What is the benefit to the nation of publishing many books if they stay in the possession of the publishers so long that they will be clean forgotten some time later on?' (*Tír*, Feb. 1930, 6–7).[15] Lecturing to the Dundalk branch of the revival organisation An Fáinne the following year, Peadar Mac Canna was reported as stressing that writers needed both financial and critical support, stating: 'If they did not help the writers of modern Irish, it would be futile for them to expect a great literature. It would benefit the writers if they themselves and their literary work were evaluated, for "a sage is not without fault"' (*Dundalk Examiner*, 31/1/31).[16] In a piece in the *Irish Press* in 1934, one of those writers, the novelist Maoghnus ('Fionn') Mac Cumhaill, pointed out that readers of Irish were expecting significant books from the handful of competent authors then at work and wondering why they weren't getting them. His answer, printed in boldface, was emphatic: 'The man who is able to write a book must get a bite to eat like everyone else. For that reason, he must go to the office in the morning and spend the day there on work hundreds are doing and hundreds can do' (*IP*, 26/11/34).[17] In a 1935 address to the Gaelic Society at University College Dublin, the Minister for Education, Tomás Ó Deirg, having announced that sales of original books in Irish rarely if ever exceeded 3,000 copies, while sales of translations ran to about 1,000 copies, conceded: 'Until 10,000 copies of a book could be sold, it was hardly worth while for Gaelic writers to undertake this work' (*CB*, Mar. 1936, 210).[18] Brian Ó hUiginn (Brian O'Higgins, 'Brian na Banban') approached the problem more whimsically in a 1923 story in *Irish Fun* in which the protagonist is offered two large cheques for work in Irish, only to then wake up! (*Irish Fun*, Dec. 1923, 165).[19]

For the young writer Art Ó Riain ('Barra Ó Caochlaigh'), money was less important than timely publication. In a 1924 letter to the Oireachtas Committee of the Gaelic League, he said he would decline prize money for his short stories in return for a chance to read the adjudicators' reports and see the work in print.[20] The following year, in an essay in *Fáinne an Lae*, 'An Buachaillín Rua' also stressed the importance for writers to see their work made available to the reading public: 'It is certain that literature in Irish will show no growth until the writers have a better opportunity of bringing the result of their thought and work out into the light of day. A good number of them must have written a good deal that they would give us if it were not for how costly the printing is and how restricted is the market for books in Irish' (*FL*, 14/3/25).[21] In 1926, the year An Gúm was founded, 'Proinnsíos

Tréan-Lámhach' was urging his fellow members of An Fáinne to support Gaelic authors as a national duty: 'It is clear to us that if Irish survives, most of the work will be done with books. No one writes a good book without getting some encouragement. The eyes of the public must be on him, he must get praise or fame, but even more than that, he must get the reward or remuneration. Royalties are the payment he gets, and the greater the sale of books the better it is for him' (*IF*, Apr. 1926, 14).[22] Sighle Ní Ghadhra went a step farther in a 1930 piece in *The Hearthstone*, urging Irish people to buy books in Irish whether they could read them or not: 'And for every three or four English books you buy, make sure to buy one in Irish – even if you do not know Irish! – You should encourage your own tongue. If you leave it to the savants and schoolchildren to buy Irish books, then, besides shirking your obligations as an Irishman, you are giving a set-back to the language' (*Hearthstone*, May 1930, 11).

One, albeit sporadic, source of financial and moral support for Gaelic writers was the prize money available through various literary contests. Traditionally, the most prestigious of these were the competitions sponsored by An tOireachtas, the Gaelic League's annual literary and cultural festival.[23] The festival was, however, suspended after the 1924 gathering and was not resumed until 1939, although the League did organise much smaller events with far fewer competitions in 1931 and 1932.[24] Other important literary awards during our period were those offered at major League *feiseanna* (festivals), the Aonach Tailteann prizes of 1924, 1928 and 1932;[25] An Gúm's special prize for a Gaelic novel in 1931;[26] a Department of Education prize for short stories in 1934;[27] a prize for short stories sponsored by the periodical *An Gaedheal* the same year;[28] an Irish government prize for a novel in Irish in 1937;[29] and Duais an Chraoibhín, a prize given in honour of Douglas Hyde beginning in 1936.[30]

Needless to say, no Gaelic author in his right mind could have expected to get rich from his work. Moreover, since most writers who chose to express themselves in Irish could also write in English, a language that was providing a decent livelihood to at least some of their literary compatriots, the decision to write in Irish was, in purely financial terms, a mistake. The Gaelic author who stayed with the language had to be motivated by much more than money, as Tomás Ó Máille pointed out in a 1926 editorial in *An Stoc*: 'It is, alas, true, that there is no good remuneration for writers of Irish. With regard to money, the Irish and English languages cannot be compared. There are a million speakers of English for every 500 speakers of Irish. Let us not be expecting money . . . money will not inspire the writers to the great work before them. Unless patriotism inspires them, and unless the condition Ireland is in prompts them to it, our hope for Irish will be hope in vain' (*Stoc*, Mar. 1926, 5).[31]

But it was precisely the condition Ireland was in at the time that frustrated so many Gaelic authors of even the highest patriotic commitment. Writers of

Irish may have been realistic enough to accept being unpaid. Being unread was a different matter altogether, and there was no more common complaint among writers at the time than the absence of any, much less a discerning, readership. Thus in a 1928 essay in *An Tír*, Aodh Mac Alastair conceded bluntly: 'After all that has been done for thirty-five years [the Gaelic League was founded in 1893] to teach our language to the people of this country, it can be said that we have so far failed utterly to make readers of Irish of most of the people who learned Irish' (*Tír*, Mar. 1928, 2).[32] Writing in the same journal the following year, 'Lorcán' stated: 'One of the things that most discourages us in Ireland today is the way the reading of the Irish language is neglected . . . The person who left the Gaeltacht, or who still lives there, is not, usually, a person who would buy and read books in Irish. The person who learned Irish, and did not get the teaching that would send him eagerly and greedily in search of more knowledge, cannot be considered a reader of the Irish language' (*Tír*, Mar. 1929, 6).[33] In a 1932 piece in *The Leader*, Seán Ó Ciarghusa ('Leac Logha') pointed out that Irish people could hardly be expected to purchase and enjoy books in a language they could only read with difficulty and incomplete comprehension: 'Only a small fraction of them have Irish, and they all have another language, English. Of the small fraction who have Irish, only a few of them can read it at all well. Another thing, a taste for the English language and a taste for literature in English have gone to the marrow in every group in the country, and they would not enjoy any other literature at present. Between this, that, and the other thing, let no one be surprised if whatever book in Irish is published is left unsold for a while – no, but for a long while. At any rate, let no one expect people to show any great eagerness for them' (*Leader*, 27/8/32).[34] Yet unless people made the effort to read work in Irish there could be no future for a genuine national literature for the newly independent nation, a point underscored by Micheál Breathnach, who was reported as saying in 1934: 'Unless there was a demand for Irish works, Irish authors would not write, and if there were no Irish books there would be no Irish literature' (*II*, 28/4/34).

William H. Irwine tried to look at the situation in a potentially positive light in the *Irish Rosary* in 1937: 'When the day comes that fifty per cent. of our schoolboys take up an Irish book to read the day after leaving school, the Irish language will be saved' (*IR*, May, 1937, 375).[35] One 'Fíbín' obviously felt that such a day was distant to the point of impossibility, writing in *The Leader* in 1939: 'Do Gaels boycott Irish? My own experience is that they do. I have had something to do with the marketing of Irish matter, both books and newspapers, and I found it very up-hill work. So up-hill was it that I never once got to the top of the hill. And I learned that the hottest Gaels were the coolest customers. I'm not in a position to take a census in the matter but I would almost bet that those who are best qualified to appreciate Irish literature buy least of it. I shouldn't be surprised, for instance, to learn that writers for the Gúm read very few Gúm books, never mind buying them' (*Leader*, 9/12/39).[36] One Gúm writer who both read carefully and reviewed thoughtfully the agency's publications was Liam Ó Rinn, who, in his 1939 book *Mo Chara Stiofán* (My friend Stephen), quoted, in translation, from a letter he had received from Stephen McKenna in which the famous Irish classicist had stressed the need for educated and demanding Gaelic readers: 'Therefore real writers need real readers . . . But it seems to me to be a new thing to put a great share of the work of remaking literature in Irish on the reader, given how much need there is for the writer to mould that literature without which the language cannot survive.'[37]

Some writers, however, wondered which of the two, writers or readers, was the catalyst for literary evolution and which was the consequence. With An Gúm on the scene for three years, the editor of *The Star* examined both sides of the question in some detail, writing of the Irish people: 'Few of them are familiar with books in Irish. For that reason, they find it difficult work to read one of them. There are barely a hundred people in Ireland who are able to read a piece of Irish as quickly as they would read a piece of English. The situation could not be otherwise. There are no papers in Irish except for a few little monthlies, and there are no books available. The people ignore the few books in Irish there are because their scarcity leaves everyone unaccustomed to read the like of them' (*Star*, 8/2/30).[38] Writing of the generic Gaelic Leaguer in the *Capuchin Annual*, Professor Liam Ó Briain of University College Galway stated: 'I think . . . that he is going to be replaced by another type: the young person who having learned to read Irish well at school and to speak and understand it pretty well, too, is going to either cast the language from him under the stress of earning his living, or is going to keep it up if it appeals to his intellect; who will read Gaelic books, go to Gaelic plays, etc. if he thinks them worth it. Quality, therefore, is the need of the future. The real mile-stones of our progress will be the outstanding books, plays, and translations . . . But they must be provided with an ever-growing and ever more instructed public' (*CA*, 1935, 137–8).

There can, of course, be no simple, unqualified answer to this question of whether readers or books come first in a linguistic and literary revival. The process is of necessity symbiotic and evolutionary, a fact to a significant extent obscured in the Gaelic movement by the extraordinary emphasis placed on literature from the very start of the revival. The roots of this emphasis are easy enough to trace. The Irish language, despite its marginalised status in the late nineteenth century, had a lengthy, varied, and rich tradition as Europe's oldest vernacular literature north of the Alps. Language activists were keenly aware of that tradition and eager to see it re-established in their own time. Meanwhile, however, they were faced with the unpalatable reality that English had become the nation's vehicle for literary expression and that, moreover, Irish writers of

English like Yeats, Synge, and later Joyce and O'Casey, were enjoying an international reputation and thereby validating English as a, if not the, legitimate voice of 'Irish' literature. Those in the movement with literary interests and ambitions – and there were many of them – were thus compelled, far before they were ready to do so, to challenge the legitimacy and subvert the reality of an 'Irish' literature in any language but Irish. Already in the last decade of the nineteenth century and the first decade of the twentieth, at a time when very few people could read any Irish at all, the creation of a modern literature in the language was put at the top of the movement's cultural agenda, a place it would hold throughout our period.

Indeed even with the Civil War still being fought, 'Sean-Ghaedheal' could write in *An Sguab* in March 1923: 'However much is said, however, it is my opinion that we can all agree about literature. As regards the Irish language, there is no more important or significant question. If the literature is good, the language is in no danger and the nation is in no danger. They will make progress automatically, and Irish will also be spoken better and more purely as a result' (*Sguab*, Mar. 1923, 119).[39] Four months later, Aodh de Blácam sounded a similar note in *Fáinne an Lae*: 'Let everyone understand that it is work in vain to revive the language of the Gaels as a poor, backward *patois* without learning, without literature. Unless we intend to create a fine, majestic literature in Modern Irish, it would be far better for us to give up the business and take up English and all the intellectual wealth to be found in it' (*FL*, 7/7/23).[40] In a paper read to a technical convention in Dublin in 1924, Éamon Ó Donnchadha urged well-educated Irish people to serve the nation by wielding a pen in the cultural crusade of Gaelicisation, and called on his audience 'to coax every educated intellect rising among us to write in Irish and to put new reading material and new storytelling into it that readers of Irish would find worth turning to from English and would continue reading from school age on' (*FL*, 21/6/24).[41]

Tomás Ó Máille used explicitly miltary imagery in 1926 to drive home the central role the writer would have to play in what D. P. Moran had once called 'the battle of two civilisations'. Commenting in *An Stoc* on the state of Gaelic writing in the western province of Connacht, he declared: 'It is said that the teachers are the soldiers of the Irish language. If so, the writers are the chieftains. If the writers choose to give direction to the Gaels, those with Irish will follow them. If the writers pay attention to their business and if they give direction and insight and pleasure to their readers as the writers of every language give their readers, the Irish language will not disappear. If the writers of Irish want, it will be dominant in Ireland. The day it is again dominant there will be an end to Anglicisation and West Britons in Ireland' (*Stoc*, Mar. 1926, 6).[42]

Cathal Ó Tuathail also had high ambitions for the new literature in a 1928 editorial in *An Tír* entitled 'Aiséirghe Gaedheal' (The resurrection of Gaels):

'No language at all will survive without literature supporting it. Literature is gradually growing in Irish. This new literature of ours is still like a child. It will grow by degrees as every living thing grows and it will improve with practice' (*Tír*, Apr. 1928, 4).[43] In 1930 Cearbhall Ua Dálaigh pondered the negative consequences of a failure to create a significant modern literature in Irish: 'It is this lack of literature that causes people to ignore Irish; it is what causes the laziness, and the lack of earnestness, and the apathy that have taken hold in people. If we were developing a great and important literature, you would be amazed how quickly the English-speakers of the country would take up Irish at once!' (*Nation*, 20/12/30).[44] The following year Muiris Ó Duibhir stressed that writers, at least, had better take up Irish at once if the language was to survive: 'The Irish language will not live on unless there is a great literature in it within twenty years' (*Ultach*, Aug. 1931, 5).[45]

As we shall see throughout this book, Gaelic writers had plenty of reason to know that their colleagues valued literature as an ideal far more than they did its mundane local creators. They must nevertheless have been simultaneously gratified by the exaltation of their craft by the movement and baffled as to how that craft could ever achieve the many and often contradictory goals that movement expected of it. Again and again in the statements quoted above, the reader will have noted how consistently, almost unconsciously, literature was conceived of not as high art, but as a very pragmatic tool, one that could repair national pride, protect and extend the language, and function as a pedagogical aid for language learners of all ages, particularly, of course, the young. For the Gaelic author in the Irish Free State, literature was not seen as a solitary pursuit of truth, but as a team sport in which he was expected to play his part in the push towards the goal of a Gaelic nation once again. That he must often have wondered just where he was supposed to line up, and why, only compounded the many difficulties faced by the author of any minority language in a bilingual society in which the lion's share of the prestige and profit accrue to the rival tongue.

Many in the movement believed quite sincerely that given the still threatened state of the language, particularly in the Gaeltacht or Irish-speaking area, the prime responsibility of the writer was to serve as a sort of amiable and accessible linguist, the keeper of rich resources of word, phrase, idiom, and outlook that could be doled out in manageable, even enjoyable doses in the form of straightforward stories, plays, essays, or poems. For these activists, literature was always and properly a subordinate ally of the language itself. This attitude was particularly evident in much of what passed for Gaelic book reviewing at the time. Thus, at the beginning of our period, in March 1923, 'C. M.' complained in his review of Nioclás Tóibín's novel *Róisín Bán an tSléibhe* (Fair Róisín of the mountain) that too many critics said much more about language than they did about literature, and then went on to do the same himself, concluding: 'But whatever might be said about the story, if you want the natural Irish of the people buy this book' (*Sguab*, Feb. 1923, 121).[46] For the majority of Gaelic critics not all that much changed over the years, so that towards the end of our period, in July 1937, we find M. Ó Floinn writing in his review of Pádhraic Óg Ó Conaire's *Éan Cuideáin* (Bird alone) in *An Gaedheal*: 'One could be hard enough on this book were it not for the excellence of the Irish in it – it will be forgiven much because of that' (*Gaedheal*, July 1937, 2).[47]

Indeed the frequent protests against this attitude by more sophisticated literary activists only underscore how widespread it was throughout this period. For example, in an unsigned note in *Fáinne an Lae* in 1926, the author lamented the absence of authentic critical standards in the reviewing of books in Irish, writing: 'For that reason we are often accustomed to be satisfied with books without any reason to be satisfied except that there is a certain amount of good Irish in them – books that would never be published if they were written in any other language' (*FL*, Aug. 1926, 4).[48] Séamus Ó Grianna, who, as we will see, regularly focused all his attention on the quality of the language in Gaelic publications, argued that this was a regrettable necessity of the times in a 1929 review of Seán Ó Caomhánaigh's *Fánaí* (Wanderer) in *Fáinne an Lae*: 'It should not be necessary, when one is reviewing a book, to discuss the kind of Irish that is in it. But because there is more than one kind of Irish, one must look at that side of the story' (*FL*, Apr. 1929, 4).[49] In his books column in *The Nation* in 1930, Pádraig Ó Catháin challenged his fellow critics to outgrow their obsession with linguistic fine points, asserting: 'And it is time for critics to stop talking about grammar . . . It is late in the day to condemn a book on grammatical grounds . . . The Christian Brothers' Grammar is a very poor argument to confute a budding O. Henry with; and the spectacle of the critic Canute-like forbidding the onward surge of simplification is not one to inspire in anyone's mind the comparison of martyrdom' (*Nation*, 6/9/30).[50]

Other writers were concerned that this perception of literature as a collection of texts produced for the benefit of language teachers had spread throughout the Gaelic movement. In a 1927 review of Pádraic Ó Conaire's *Brian Óg* for *Irisleabhar Muighe Nuadhat*, 'S. Ó H.' declared: 'Hitherto we would rarely get a novel in Irish that was worth calling a novel at all. At the very least, it must be admitted that there is a bit of childishness attached to some of them. They would not be read for the story in them, but only for the Irish to be learned from them. Hitherto the majority of the people did not care what was in a book if there was sweet and tasty pure Irish in it.' Having acknowledged that such a view of literature may have made sense 'when the Irish language was only being put back on its feet' (nuair nach raibh an Ghaedhilg acht dá cur ar a bonnaí arais), he added that readers of Irish should now expect more: 'The writers should remember that, and write books not only for the learners of Irish but for its readers, you might say, as well' (*IMN* 1927, 104).[51] 'G. de P.'

sounded a similar note in his 1931 review of another of Ó Conaire's books, *Fearfeasa Mac Feasa*: 'There is a fundamental weakness involved in much of the literature composed in Irish since the revival began. That literature was not written for the purpose of thoughts that were growing and erupting in the hearts of the authors. The authors were writing for the sake of the language itself, from a desire to practice it and spread it. People were writing who had little to say, except that they had the great good fortune to be Irish-speakers.' 'G. de P.' shared the belief of 'S. Ó H.' that to remain at this stage, however necessary it had been at one point in even the recent past, was now a real disservice to both the language and its literature (*Nation*, 11/4/31).[52] 'Oisín' agreed in a 1937 piece in the *Derry People*, and in doing so showed that this way of thinking was still alive. 'Oisín' first discussed the origins of the attitude: 'First of all, there were few people outside the Gaeltacht who were able to read or understand Irish. The people in English-speaking Ireland who read Irish were students or people who had a great interest in the language cause. These people were devoted, and they were ready to do anything at all for the sake of the Irish language or for the sake of their own knowledge of the language. If they saw anything at all in Irish, they would read it to improve their Irish and they would be satisfied with it.' He then went on to examine the effect of this utilitarian view of literature on the writers: 'But when they were writing Irish, many of them did not care whether they had a story to tell or not. They wrote in Irish and they wrote without a plot, without a subject. They were satisfied as long as it was good Irish' (*Derry People*, 20/2/37).[53]

One Gaelic writer who struggled to express his personal literary vision in this unfavourable intellectual climate was Pádraic Ó Conaire, and it is thus no surprise that it was in reviews of his work that two of the critics above lamented the lack of initiative in many of his contemporaries. It was also Ó Conaire, more than any other Gaelic writer, who raged against the expectation that writers turn out glorified language primers and who suffered the effects of that expectation on his own work.[54] In some of his best known essays in the early years of the Free State, Ó Conaire lashed out at what he dubbed 'the tyranny of the schoolchild' (*FL*, 12/5/23), the fact that writers were encouraged to sacrifice individual expression in the cause of language instruction. But Ó Conaire went much farther, pointing out that this insistence that literature be appropriate for pedagogical purposes would, as it did, effectively erase the distinction between writing aimed at schoolchildren and adolescents and that crafted for supposedly mature and sophisticated readers, a point also made by Séamus Ó Grianna in 1925: 'In English, there is literature and there are schoolbooks, and the two are not confused. The people interested in literature have *Hamlet*, and the children have "Ned put his leg in the tub." The same should be true in Irish, and the difference between what Father Peter [O'Leary] and people like him wrote and the literature of the great men who came before us should be recognised' (*SF*, 16/5/25).[55] Even before the creation of the new state, Ó Conaire was denouncing Gaelic philistinism, as he did in his 1920 essay 'Sgríobhnóirí agus a gCuid Oibre: An Easba Misnigh atá orra?' (Writers and their work: Is it lack of courage they suffer from?), where he wrote: 'The books were written for the young, they were published for the young – but the people in charge of the work made another mistake. You would think from looking at them and their work that there were nothing but children in Ireland, children with regard to intellect, no matter what age they were. They never considered that those children were growing up into men and women and that the same intellectual sustenance that had satisfied them when they were young would not satisfy them as they grew up.' Ó Conaire's analysis neatly unravels the chicken–egg dilemma of Gaelic readership discussed above. The books did come first in fair number. They were, however, designed to a large extent for the schoolchild – including what Ó Conaire dubbed 'the forty-year-old-child' (an páisde dhá sgór bliadhan) – and ignored the needs of the intellectual adults some at least of the schoolchildren would become in their reading habits.[56] Nor did the situation improve with independence. Indeed given the immediate need for a range of Gaelic textbooks and readers to implement the state's commitment to re-Gaelicising the nation through the schools, there was considerable pressure on writers to sacrifice personal ambitions to satisfy this large new market.[57] With a steady demand for Gaelic school texts and no real market for anything else in the language, it was understandable that publishers were reluctant to produce anything inappropriate for educational purposes.

It should, however, be noted that this obsession with the schools need by no means be seen as cynical or opportunistic. There was at the time a widespread belief that it was in the nation's classrooms that the most crucial battle of the cultural war against Anglicisation would be waged, a point unequivocally underscored by 'H. C.' in a September 1922 review in the *Connacht Tribune and Tuam News*: 'If the Irish language is to be saved it must be saved through the children, and in the schools. Whatever differences of opinion exist amongst us in Ireland to-day we are all agreed in accepting that proposition' (*CT*, 30/9/22). Diarmuid Ó Séaghdha agreed in the police journal *Iris an Gharda* in March 1923: 'It is the schools that will save or kill the Irish language' ('Siad na scoileanna a shábhalfaidh nó a mharbhóchaidh an Ghaoluinn) (*Iris an Gharda*, 19/3/23).[58] Moreover, Father Timothy Corcoran, SJ, professor of education at University College Dublin and, in the words of Adrian Kelly, 'the single most important individual impetus behind the Gaelicising of the schools'[59] asserted in an influential 1925 essay in the Jesuit journal *Studies* that the nation could be re-Gaelicised by the schools alone, 'even without positive aid from the home' (*Studies*, Sept. 1925, 387).

Given this conviction, it is hardly surprising that in a 1929 essay in the *Cork Weekly Examiner and Weekly Herald*, 'Gaedhilgeoir' could see the need for providing schoolbooks in Irish as both a sign of the movement's success and a challenge to its ongoing mission: 'More people are able to read Irish, particularly among the young, and unless there are suitable books, it will be difficult for them to improve their Irish much, and it is also difficult to spread the Gaelic spirit if the literary rubbish that comes from the cities of England remains dominant in this country' (*Cork Weekly Examiner*, 10/5/24).[60] An anonymous reviewer of Pádraic Ó Conaire's *Cubhar na dTonn* (The foam of the waves) in *An Stoc* in 1925, had reservations about the quality of the new schoolbooks coming on the market, though he hoped for improvement: 'Booksellers in Dublin are doing all in their power of late to try to provide the public with little books in Irish. Those who are getting most of the attention are the hosts of learners and children. The only thing that can be said about many of them is that the mill that is constantly grinding grinds both fine and coarse. Most likely the coarse will soon be winnowed from it and only the best will remain' (*Stoc*, Dec. 1925, 7).[61] Even as late as 1934, 'Droichead Átha', in an essay on 'Leabharlanna agus Leabhra Gaedhilge' (Libraries and books in Irish) in *An t-Éireannach*, could find the concentration on school texts both natural and acceptable, if not altogether satisfactory: 'Since the Gaelic League was begun around forty years ago, it is wonderful how many books have been written to help the language movement. We are hoping for a great modern literature as a result of this development. That is not what I want to discuss, but rather how important these books are for the learners of Irish. It is on these books that we depend almost entirely to teach the language in school' (*Éireannach*, 1/9/34).[62]

Most literary Irish-Irelanders lacked such philosophical detachment, and expressed their anger over the trivialisation of literature in the cultural revival. As early as June 1922, Liam Ó Rinn complained in *Young Ireland*: 'I would like to make clear that I am not at all satisfied with the kind of books in Irish that have been coming out lately, or perhaps I should say that I am not satisfied because a certain kind are not being published. Almost all of them are books for schools, books to teach Irish from. It seems to me we have enough of that kind.' Ó Rinn felt it was time to stop coddling those unwilling to put in the effort to learn the language, 'a crowd that will not be satisfied until someone thinks up a way of giving them Irish to drink from a bottle' (dream ná beidh sásta godí go gceapfar seift chun Gaedhilg a thúirt len' ól dóibh as buidéal) (*YI*, 10/6/22).[63] An anonymous critic in *An Branar* noted the quantity but was unimpressed by the quality of the school texts available in 1925, writing: 'Books in Irish have been quite plentiful of late and if their quality matched their quantity, we would be in good shape. Most of them are schoolbooks. Only a small fraction of them would merit any great praise even as schoolbooks' (*Branar*, Mar. 1925, 49).[64]

Once again, the foundation of An Gúm did not calm the fears of many Gaelic writers that serious literature was to have no significant standing in the new Gaelic order. In December 1927, Thomas F. O'Rahilly wrote in the Jesuit quarterly *Studies*: 'At present hardly anything is published in Irish except elementary school books of little or no value. Everyone seems to forget that schoolchildren are more influenced by what they read at home than by their school text-books. Likewise it seems to be forgotten that children must grow up, and that if they have no interesting books to read in Irish when they leave school, the Irish they have been taught at school will be quickly forgotten' (*Studies*, Dec. 1927, 563). Three years later, Violet Connolly was even more pessimistic on this subject in an essay in the same journal: 'So long as the official and unofficial measures to revive Irish stop short at the schools and universities and do not envisage the peculiar handicaps of this generation of writers, Irish literature must remain stunted and shallow – a wholly inadequate intellectual food for the nation' (*Studies*, Dec. 1930, 660). Seán Mac Amhlaoigh described and dismissed that inadequate intellectual sustenance in a 1931 essay in the *Dundalk Examiner*: 'Look at the state of writing in Irish at present. The idiom in the vast majority of the books that have been published in Irish for the past forty years is altogether too simple. The triviality and the childish speech is so prevalent in some of them that they would be a laughing stock if they had been written in any other language.' Mac Amhlaoigh insisted that while books of this kind had once served a purpose, their day was done: 'Books like this were very appropriate for learners of the language, but now that everyone in the schools has either a little or a great deal of Irish, more books of this kind will only bring disrespect on the language' (*Examiner*, 24/10/31).[65] Seosamh Ó Tallamhain added his thoughts on the topic in the same paper two months later: 'Most of the writers are serving the schoolchildren at present. Therefore the literary work that can be called literature or a weak attempt at literature is scarce' (*Examiner*, 5/12/31).[66]

Nor did the change of government after the Fianna Fáil election victory of 1932 make any real difference. The most thoughtful and detailed analysis of the state of Gaelic publishing in the 1930s was offered by León Ó Broin, himself a Gúm author, in his 1935 essay on 'Contemporary Gaelic Literature and Some of Its Paradoxes' in the *Capuchin Annual*: 'The teaching business has militated considerably in the past against the development of literature: writers have given up writing for teaching; others have tended to write down to the level of the learners, in other words to write school-readers. Psychologically and physically teaching is bad for writers. It stereotypes their minds, impoverishes their powers of description; tires them and causes them often to be peevish, dogmatic and hard. It is doubly bad for Gaelic writers because it brings them into daily contact with such distressing handicaps as the dialects and the need for a simplified spelling.' Ó Broin's attitude towards An Gúm as a corrective for this situation was, in retrospect, intriguingly ambivalent: 'An antidote to this tendency of the writers to be drawn into the teaching end of the language revival was provided in 1926 when an experiment was initiated by the Government for subsidising the output of general literature. For this experiment I know of no parallel in modern history outside Soviet Russia' (*CA*, 1935, 128).[67] In reality, market and not literary forces continued to set the publishing agenda, a disheartening fact addressed by Ó Broin himself in his 1938 piece on 'A State-Fostered Literature' in the *Irish Monthly*: 'The Gúm publications fall under two main heads, those that are described as Secondary School texts, and works of general literature. Up to the present there are 64 books in the first category, with an average sale of 1,600 copies each, and 358 in the second category, with an average sale of 480 copies each.' Moreover, Ó Broin noted that while 13 of the 64 textbooks had repaid their expenses, only five of the 358 other works had managed to do so. He continued: 'These figures speak eloquently for themselves. They show how valuable it is for an author to have his book put on the school list. Better still if his book is admitted to the school list and also appeals to the ordinary adult reader' (*Irish Monthly*, Feb. 1938, 126–7).[68]

Critics of the period at times went out of their way to compliment writers they felt had bridged this gap between the adolescent student and the adult reader. For example, in a review of Pádhraic Óg Ó Conaire's *Cóilín Ó Cuanaigh* in *Irisleabhar Muighe Nuadhat*, 'T. Ó C.' wrote of this saccharine children's story: 'It is a little story that was written for schoolchildren, but I swear that Cóilín's adventures will gladden and delight people who are not children' (*IMN*, 1924, 92).[69] Writing of Tomás Ó hAodha's story collection *An Figheadóir* in 1926, 'Séamus' declared: 'For the most part the stories are adventures, but adventures in which not only boys, but also grownups would take an interest' (*Sguab*, June 1926, 117).[70] Aindrias Ó Muimhneacháin ('An M. O.') wrote with far greater justification of Alín de Paor's novel *Paidí Ó Dálaigh* in 1933: 'It is a book that would satisfy and entertain everyone, whether young or adult . . .'. But he then added: 'and I would especially recommend that teachers make it available to their students' (*Camán*, 5/8/33).[71]

One can only imagine the frustrations and stresses endured by Gaelic authors attempting the all but impossible task of making an edifying and linguistically instructive school story and a serious literary work for adults share the same pages of a single book. Not surprisingly, they almost always failed. Just as predictably, they all but invariably did so by favouring the needs of the actual adolescent audience over those of the potential adult one.[72] As has been noted, no Gaelic author suffered more as a result of this tension than did Pádraic Ó Conaire, who wasted a great deal of his considerable talent serving the school market after independence. Indeed one of the sadder paradoxes of our period is that Ó Conaire was able to be a far freer, more adventurous, and more honest writer as an exile in London than he was living at home as the most widely recognised author in the national language in an independent Irish state.[73] But he was by no means alone in his fear of the tyrannical learner. In the preface to his 1938 local history *Stair na nDéise*, Art Mac Gréagóir confessed that he had almost yielded to that fear to the detriment of his work: 'When I was writing the book I went too far in the direction of simplicity lest I put in idioms that would discourage young people . . . When Liam [Ó Míodhacháin] read it, he changed my mind. He thinks that the ancient language of Ireland is too noble to treat unjustly in an attempt to make it suitable for the people who don't know it.'[74] Brian Ó hUiginn found a comic outlet for his frustrations with the extra-literary demands placed on the Gaelic author in a previously noted 1923 short story about an author to whom a woman offers twenty guineas for a play – one that would incorporate in a single work everything expected of a writer of Irish: 'A play in which there will be the Roman font and the Simplified Spelling and the old font as well; a play that will be simple enough for the learners of Irish, hard and complicated enough for the University students, interesting enough for the clerk in love and the farmer in a ditch, clear enough for the great scholars of Europe; a drama impossible for anyone to perform on a stage or read aloud' (*Irish Fun*, Dec. 1923, 165).[75]

It was, of course, challenges almost as impossible of achievement that An Gúm expected its authors to overcome. In the press release to the Gaelic journals announcing the birth of An Gúm, the state declared: 'An Gúm is especially involved with books thought to be suitable as textbooks in the Intermediate Schools. Apart from those, however, other books that were thought to have a particular value for learners of Irish could be accepted for publication' (*FL*, 27/3/26).[76] As we have seen, with time this second category came to be called 'general literature', but the change in title did not indicate a shift of focus. An Gúm long remained a branch of the Department of Education, its prime responsibility the provision of works of educational value, a responsibility evident in the department's *imprimatur* to be found in so many of An Gúm's books throughout our period: 'Approved for publication by the Department of Education under the Scheme [An Gúm] to assist with the publication of books in Irish suitable as textbooks in the Intermediate Schools' (Measta ag an Roinn Oideachais i gcóir foillsiúcháin fá'n nGúm chun cabhruithe le foillsiú leabhar i nGaedhilge atá oiriúnach mar théacsleabhra ins na Meán-Sgoileanna). Nor should it be thought that this seal of approval covered textbooks only. It also appeared in novels like Piaras Béaslai's *Astronár* (1928), Nioclás Tóibín's *An Rábaire Bán* (1928), Micheál Ó Gríobhtha's *Briathar Mná* and *Buaidh na Treise* (both 1928), Pádraig Ó Séaghdha's *Stiana* (1930), Aindrias Ó Baoighill's *An Dílidhe* (1932), and Tadhg Ó Murchadha's *An Cliathán Clé*; story collections like León Ó Broin's *Béal na hUaighe* (1927), Micheál Ó Gríobhtha's *Lorgaireacht* (1927), Art Ó Riain's *An Tost* (1927);

histories like An tAthair Mártan Ó Domhnaill's *Oileáin Árann* (1930) and Art Mac Gréagóir's *Stair na nDéise* (1938); biographies like An tAthair Benedict's *Lorcán Naomhtha Ua Tuathail* (1929); memoirs like Seán Joyce's *Eachtra Múinteora* (1929), Micheál Ó Conaill's *Cinn Lae: Fá Sgáth Sléibh' Eachtgha* (1937), and Peadar Ó hAnnracháin's *Mar Chonnac-sa Éire* (1937); or a folk collection like Peadar Ó Direáin's *Sgéalta na n-Oileán* (1929). Some of these books were perfectly suitable for adults, just as some of the books lacking this approval seem eminently appropriate as school texts. One must, then, wonder what criteria dictated whether a book was considered for school use, what ruled a title out for such purposes, and, most important from our perspective, what pressures Gaelic writers of the time felt to shape their work to meet such criteria and thus have a chance at that wider audience and the resultant greater sales.[77]

The blurring of the line between adolescent learners and adult readers worked against the development of a mature Gaelic literature in another way as well. Irish curricula at universities, where many of the next generation of writers and critics would be trained, were characterised by an emphasis on linguistics and literary history, their reading lists dominated by scholarly editions of earlier work – that of the seventeenth-century historian and poet Geoffrey Keating, for example – or by more modern works written for learners, not for people with a serious, not to say professional, interest in contemporary literature. In large part, this was, of course, a function of what was available, but it is worth noting that university authorities seem to have excluded from their syllabi most of what few modern Gaelic works of literary merit there were.[78] Thus, in the Department of Irish at University College Dublin in the 1933–4 academic year, the only contemporary prose title read by students in the general course was *Leabhar na Polainne*, Liam Ó Rinn's translation of a work by Adam Mickiewicz, while the only such title read by those in the honours course was Séamus Ó Grianna's novel *Caisleáin Óir*. Candidates for the MA degree read three contemporary writers: An tAthair Peadar Ua Laoghaire, Pádraic Ó Conaire, and Ó Grianna.[79] At University College Galway the same year, the only required contemporary prose was *Ceartlár Unága*, Eoghan Ó Neachtain's translation of Ridgwell Cullum's *Heart of Unaga*. Students working for the MA in Modern Irish ('Nua-Ghaeilge') read nothing later than the poetry of Raftery (*c.*1784–*c.*1835).[80] Things were considerably better at University College Cork, where the poet Tadhg Ó Donnchadha was professor of Irish. There, first-year students read Micheál Ó Siochfhradha's play *An Ball Dubh*, León Ó Broin's story collection *Béal na hUaighe*, Tomás Ó Criomhthain's *Allagar na hInise*, Pádraig Ó Siochfhradha's story collection *An Baile Seo 'gainne*, Art Ó Riain's novel *Lucht Ceoil*, and Seán Ó Ciarghusa's story collection *Geantraighe*. Second years at Cork read An tAthair Peadar Ua Laoghaire's novel *Niamh*, Ó Criomhthain's *An t-Oileánach*, Ó Grianna's story collection *Cioth is Dealán*, Pádhraic Óg Ó Conaire's novel *An Fraoch Bán*, Seán Ó Ciarghusa's novel *Onncal Seárlaí*, and Seaghán Mac Meanman's story collection *Indé agus Indiu*. Third-year assignments included Pádraig Ó Séaghdha's story collection *An Buaiceas*, Muiris Ó Súileabháin's *Fiche Blian ag Fás*, Mac Meanman's story collection *Fear Siubhail*, An tAthair Pádraig de Brún's translation of Corneille's *Polyeucte*, and Seosamh Mac Grianna's story collection *An Grádh agus an Ghruaim*. The MA syllabus included 'detailed study' of the writings of An tAthair Peadar, Pádraig Ó Siochfhradha, and Pádraic Ó Conaire.[81] One must, however, wonder how the universities could ignore works like the plays, stories, and essays of Micheál Mac Liammóir; the novels of Seán Ó Caomhánaigh and Éamonn Mac Giolla Iasachta; or the plays of Piaras Béaslaí or Gearóid Ó Lochlainn.

Building on my previous book *The Prose Literature of the Gaelic Revival, 1881–1921: Ideology and Innovation*, this study will attempt to bring alive, through a wide range of manuscript and primary sources, the trials and triumphs of the Gaelic literary movement in the first two decades of Irish independence. And that range of primary sources was wide indeed, as genuine and practical enthusiasm for the language in the new state led to Irish columns, essays and reviews appearing not only in the expected Gaelic and Irish-Ireland periodicals, but also in state publications for the police, army, and civil service; in the major daily papers; in various provincial weeklies – notably, but not exclusively those bordering Gaeltacht areas; in magazines published by schools and universities; in religious periodicals; and the list goes on. Moreover, given the size of the Gaelic market, few if any writers could turn down a paying assignment regardless of the source, so one on occasion finds the work of established authors in curious places.

My starting date of 1922, the year the Free State officially came into existence as the result of the Anglo-Irish Treaty of 1921, should need no explanation. My closing date is a bit more problematic. The Irish Free State technically ended on 29 December 1937, when the new constitution adopted by the Irish people in referendum came into effect. I have, however, chosen 1939 as my closing date for a variety of reasons. First of all, 1939 saw the revival of the national Oireachtas after a hiatus of 15 years. The Oireachtas had been, and would soon be again, the most important cultural event in the Gaelic calendar, a festival that inspired and rewarded all of the significant Gaelic writers who were to appear in the future. This year also saw the publication of *Idir Shúgradh agus Dáiríre* (Half-joking, half-serious), the first book by Máirtín Ó Cadhain, the most accomplished Gaelic prose writer of the modern era, as well as Liam Ó Rinn's *Mo Chara Stiofán*, a book many in the movement at the time felt was the most mature and challenging literary work that had thus far been written in the language. On the wider Irish scene, the death of Yeats in 1939 sharpened the focus of Gaelic intellectuals on the younger, often bilingual, generation of Irish writers they hoped to recruit for the cause. And, needless to say, 1939 also brought the Second World War, Irish neutrality, and the consequent partial isolation of the country from European and world affairs. In many ways then, 1939 had much in common with 1922 as a year of more than ordinary hope and anxiety for the Irish nation as a whole as well as for the Irish language and those committed to its revival.

In fact, our entire period was an ambivalent time for those in the language movement. In some ways, they had come farther than even in their heart of hearts they had ever thought they would. In that first flush of independence, many in the movement saw the new challenges as incentives to even greater accomplishment. Thus in a 1922 essay in *The Free State*, 'M. Ó T.' pleaded for Irish unity so that the nation could take on the daunting tasks ahead: 'We have to restore the Irish language, and only few realise what a gigantic duty it will be to restore a language which has for generations been used only by a few peasants, which most of us learn as we would learn French, which has no literature in modern times, and a completely archaic vocabulary. We have to Gaelicise the next generation . . . We have to create a native literature, art, and learning, and how many people have we who are equipped for the task?' (*Free State*, 11/3/22). But volunteers there were, willing both to start the job and accept that they wouldn't see it finished, an attitude given forthright expression by the veteran activist Feardorcha Ó Conaill ('Conall Cearnach') the same year in *Fáinne an Lae*: 'It [modern prose in Irish] will come in the end, but that might take us fifty years. Every single writer of the present day is doing spadework, clearing the way for the famous writers to come later on. The only question is whether the language will be saved. If it is, it is certain that a Gaelic Turgenev and a Gaelic Pushkin will be born, although they have not yet been born' (*FL*, 13/5/22).[82] Indeed there were those like Liam Ó Liatháin who relished their role as pioneers envisioning a linguistic promised land they would never enter. Writing in *Irisleabhar Muighe Nuadhat* in 1924, Ó Liatháin celebrated the language's potential: 'Irish is a new language among the languages of Europe. It is the Rip Van Winkle among languages. It bears the mark of antiquity . . . But we must put the freshness and the strength of youth in it, stretch and bend its old limbs, and put the red blood running in its veins again. We must develop a brand new literature in it. Not only that. But we must, at the same time, establish a brand new civilisation of our own in this country' (*IMN* 1924, 6).[83] Micheál Mac Liammóir shared this optimism, although in a 1922 essay in *An Sguab* he also sounded a cautionary note, declaring that if writers of Irish could create 'a true literature for the people instead of trivial, worthless foolishness, who knows but the day would yet come that Ireland will be among the most cultured and learned nations in Europe' (*Sguab*, Nov. 1922, 29).[84]

With time, however, such optimism faded in face of the hard economic, social, and cultural realities of nation building. Writers in particular had, as we have seen, a good deal to worry and complain about as their work was manipulated and marginalised to serve non-literary agendas, a process that resulted in the publication of far too much of the 'trivial, worthless foolishness' Mac Liammóir had warned against in 1922. Despite all their frustrations, however, a group of committed and often cantankerous writers soldiered on, their creed, at once idealistic and clear-headed, summed up by Éamon Ó Donnchadha in a previously cited 1924 lecture in Dublin: 'Time has carved out a great wide gap between the old Gaelic world and the modern world of today, but the two worlds can be reconciled and brought together in literature in Irish by one who understands them both and has an innate sense of the art of literature' (*FL*, 14/6/24).[85] The attempt to answer these questions of how to bring a time-hallowed Gaelicism (*Gaelachas*) alive again in the modern world and what constituted a distinctively Gaelic literary sense were to dominate Gaelic prose literature in the Irish Free State, with the debate often taking on an aura at once familial, confident, claustrophobic and smug.

Before we continue, however, a few practical issues have to be addressed. All quotations from Irish originals in the text, except in a very few instances duly noted, are my own English translations, kept as literal as is feasible. The original Irish text is, however, always provided. Short Irish phrases are often incorporated in parentheses in the text itself; longer passages are in the notes. Since some of the fiercest contemporary controversies dealt with issues of dialect and orthography, I have, apart from silently emending obvious typographical errors and inserting an 'h' in place of the Irish *ponc* or dot above a letter to indicate lenition, left all Irish passages as I found them. Where I have used and referred in the notes to texts reprinted in the standardised orthography, I have always gone back to check the original for the spelling actually used in the quotations. With regard to Irish personal names, I have tried to balance accuracy and consistency, favouring the former. Once again, personal names are left in the form those who bore them preferred and have not been standardised. The Anglicised form of names is given on first usage when writers regularly used both the Gaelic and Anglicised versions of their names, and in the case of those writers like Hyde, W. P. Ryan, Father Dinneen, and Ernest Blythe far better known under the Anglicised form, that is what is used throughout. Pseudonyms have a long history in Gaelic literature. In our period, competitors in literary competitions like those of the Gaelic League's *Oireachtas* and civil servants for whom it was inappropriate, or foolhardy, to take sides in public controversies regularly had recourse to such pen names. Using the standard Gaelic reference works as well as my own research, I have identified many but by no means all of the writers behind the pseudonyms. If known, the given name of the person using a pseudonym will be provided when he is first mentioned, and thereafter will be the form used. In a few instances, however, where a pseudonym became universally accepted, it will frequently be used in alternation with the author's real name. Translation of pseudonyms usually leads to absurdity and will therefore be avoided.[86] Titles of books will always be given in the original, with English translation added at first occurrence.

In *The Prose Literature of the Gaelic Revival*, I regularly used the term 'Gael' to denote a person committed to the revival of Irish. I felt comfortable doing so because that is what such people proudly called themselves. However, in the years of the Free State, claims to this title were, as we shall see, contested. Moreover, it was at this time that the term 'Gael' itself took on those connotations of insularity, intolerance and fanaticism with which it has been burdened, often enough justly, ever since. For these reasons, I have not used the term quite as freely in this book as I did previously, although I also realise that the alternatives – 'revivalist', 'activist', 'Irish-Irelander' – are both awkward and imprecise. I am also uncomfortable with the term 'Gaelic' as in 'Gaelic literature'. I fully accept the prior claim of writing in Irish to the title 'Irish literature', but to so use it for a more general audience can only cause confusion, and the circumlocution 'literature written in Irish' soon becomes tiresome. Therefore, in the interest of clarity and concision, though with some misgivings, I have regularly referred to that literature here as 'Gaelic'.

ONE

MAIMED FROM THE START

DEBATES WITHIN THE GAELIC LITERARY MOVEMENT IN THE NEW STATE

In December 1929, Séamus Ó Grianna, as editor of *Fáinne an Lae*, shared with his readers a recent gratifying dream:

> There was not a tuft from the time you left the Gaeltacht behind on which there was not a schoolteacher lying, with his advanced certificate lying on his breast . . . As for the people from An Mug [i.e. An Gúm], not a man of them was left alive. As for the 'Education' people, some of them were lying . . . on the hillsides with their blood 'putting a nicer colour on the mountains'. A puny wretch who would not reach your knee, a Civil Servant, who was a champion of the Roman font, came along and a big, red-headed gallowglass from Fanad spat at the poor man and killed him (*FL*, Dec. 1929, 5).[1]

Later the same month, the outraged Executive Committee of the League removed Ó Grianna from the editorial chair, this time for good.[2] Ó Grianna managed in this short paragraph to touch on most of the issues that were agitating and dividing the language movement at the time. More important, his dire fantasy involved what were, after all, self-proclaimed, usually sincere, often even zealous allies in the cause of re-Gaelicising the newly independent state, underscoring in lurid fashion the bitterness and personal animosity that permeated so many aspects of Irish life long after the dumping of arms by the 'Legion of the Rearguard' ended the Irish Civil War in May 1923.

Ó Grianna was by far the most outspoken and acerbic polemicist active at the time, one utterly convinced of the justice of both his cause and his methods, as he made clear in *An Phoblacht* in July 1931:

> Then of course I am bitter. They are always accusing me of having just the one tune, that is constantly talking about the Gaeltacht . . . and however much I anger the pot-bellied fools whose heads are in the air because they have a tiny little bit of 'Irish', however much I do that, that's how I prefer it (*An Phoblacht*, 4/7/31).[3]

His aggressive sarcasm seems often to have infected those he drew into the argument on the other side, as when in July 1931 one 'Sliabh Beaghain' wrote in *An Phoblacht*:

> If Máire is an acute, sharp-sighted person and if what he says is true, let us cast away the Irish language. To the devil with the country, with the language, and with the customs of our race. What a waste of time it will all have been up to now. All who died for our sake would have been suffering from delusions. Let us invite England to retake the country at once (*An Phoblacht*, 27/6/31).[4]

Such disillusionment and bitterness were widespread in the wake of the Civil War. As early as 1922, in a letter to the composer Geoffrey Palmer, Lil Nic Dhonncha expressed her disgust with the current climate within the language movement: 'Feeling, too, is very bitter all round and it is terribly painful working amicably in the Connradh [Gaelic League] with people you despise and anathemize [*sic*] in every respect.'[5] In 1924, Donn Piatt offered an amusing outsider's perspective on the current level of collegiality within the language movement in a story entitled 'Na Néalladóirí' (The cloud-watchers) in the University College Dublin journal *An Reult*. A Martian brings two UCD students with him to discuss Irish with Martian linguists, but the squabbling of the students scandalises their hosts:

> The two spoke about the Roman type, the Gaelic type, and simplified spelling, and they did not agree on a single question. They spoke about 'Gaodhluinn' and 'Gaeluinn', about 'Gaedhilg', 'Gaedhealg' and 'Gaedhilge', and they did not forget 'Gaelge' or 'Dublin Irish' . . . and the peaceful Martians were open-mouthed, gaping at them (*Reult*, May 1924, 94–8).[6]

Three years later, 'Eimer' was more down-to-earth in a similar assessment of the contentious tendencies of language activists: 'If Irish speakers were a little less wrapped up in their own world and a little bit more sympathetic, tolerant, and friendly with the rest of us would they not be a better advertisement for the Irish language and Irish interests in general' (*Leader*, 8/10/27).

Of course, there was often little enough tolerance within the movement itself. Doubtless with Ó Grianna's *Fáinne an Lae* in mind, an anonymous front-page contributor to the pro-Free State government weekly *The Star* lambasted the Gaelic League as 'the prey of political hangers-on, victims of obscure phobias, nursing imaginary grievances, exploiting their attachment to Irish in an effort to make financial capital of their devotion' (*Star*, 30/3/29).[7] Writing in the same paper two months later, the scholar Thomas F. O'Rahilly attacked 'fanatics who are dialect-mad and whose love for Irish consists in hating the Irish of their neighbours' and 'designing people with vested interests who are not above using the fanatics for their own ends, ignoramuses who lay down the law about this or that matter in connection with Irish, charlatans who batten on Irish as flies on jam' (*Star*, 25/5/29). The Aran-born Micheál Ó Maoláin wrote in the same spirit from the other side of the political divide in *The Nation* in 1931:

> I myself heard a speaker giving out at a meeting of An Fáinne members in Dublin in this manner. 'When the last native speaker is dead, the Chairman of An Fáinne will get up and say "We'll make progress now."' And perhaps he'd be right, because the "new Irish" will not succeed or prosper while there is one of the other group above ground' (*Nation*, 10/10/31).[8]

Time might eventually begin healing the wounds such attacks were constantly reopening, but not soon enough for more broadminded Gaels like Aodh de Blácam, who lamented in February 1935: 'We distrust one another, and pursue our own enthusiasms, in brilliant little sects, yet to one another's destruction' (*Irish Monthly*, Feb. 1935, 131).

In retrospect, it can seem that the battles were so bitter because the stakes were so low or, perhaps more accurately, so peripheral to the cultural war as a whole. Certainly the two specific issues that provoked the most animosity – and ink – throughout the period are now long settled and largely forgotten. In the first two decades of the independent state, however, the related questions of orthography and typeface were argued with a ferocity that could divide families and friends, and drive would-be sympathisers away from the revival in amazed disgust.[9] For many years before independence, various scholars and writers had wrestled with the challenge of writing a twentieth-century language in an orthography that had ceased evolving with that language almost three hundred years earlier. Perhaps the most influential of those seeking to reconcile speech and spelling were Shán Ó Cuív (i. e. Seán Ó Caoimh, in the traditional spelling he wished to replace), Liam Ó Rinn, Thomas F. O'Rahilly, and Piaras Béaslaí, all of whom argued for a so-called 'simplified' spelling of the language, illustrating their theories with their own publications and, briefly, with the Munster-based journal *Glór na Ly* (edited by Ó Cuív in 1911–12). In the days before independence there was not, however, any central agency with the power and resources to investigate and ultimately impose any significant reform.

With independence, the new state had that kind of clout. Moreover, civil servants working with Irish, most notably Colm Ó Murchú, Tomás Page, and Liam Ó Rinn in the new parliament's translation department, felt the pressing need for a less cumbersome orthography to get through their enormous workload as they moulded the language to suit a range of entirely new topics and contexts.[10] Others believed, with equal sincerity, that a change in orthography would lead to chaos, Anglicisation of the language, or both, as traditional spellings, with the etymologies they preserved, were dropped or mutilated by those with an inferior grasp of the language and its history.

The font issue was contested just as fiercely. One side insisted on retention of the traditional 'Gaelic' font ('an cló Gaelach') introduced for the printing of Irish by Queen Elizabeth I in 1571. Their opponents, many again involved in the daily business of writing, translating and publishing Irish for the new state, stressed that the language could be taught more easily, printed more efficiently, and published more economically in the 'Roman' font (an cló Rómhánach) with which virtually all Irish people – and all Irish publishers – were already familiar. The resistance the reformers faced, the often vituperative and personal nature of that resistance and their response, and the foot-dragging and inconsistent caution with which the state came to grips with the problem provide us with an invaluable awareness of the real and deeper forces rending the language movement at the time.[11]

Those forces will be examined in greater detail in this book. Here it need only be said that those engaged in controversies over spelling or font saw themselves holding key, threatened lines in a broader campaign. Their belief that significant compromise would start the dominos tumbling helps explain the otherwise disproportionate ferocity with which both sides looked at those with different views. By far the most unyielding in this debate were those who felt most besieged – the champions of traditional spelling and font. The passion of many of these people was further excited by their continuing and profound opposition to the legitimacy of the very state whose civil service was pushing through the changes they so dreaded, a civil service whose avenues to improved social and economic mobility and job security were denied them because of their political convictions.

At any rate, politics, patronage, and patriotism were potent forces fuelling opposition to what Seán Mac Eachain in 1923 dubbed 'the manufacture of Gaelic monstrosities' in orthography and typeface (*Leader*, 21/4/23). A decade later, Seán Ua Ceallaigh ('Mogh Ruith') sneered at those who favoured a reformed spelling and the Roman font:

> In a word, practically everyone is against them except the covert enemies of our native speech, the sprinkling of weaklings ever ready to doff the cap to patronage, and the time-servers who think less of the well-being of the language than of the notoriety to be derived from the advocacy of a fad (*CB*, July 1934, 614).

Seaghán Mac Meanman resorted to abuse pure and simple, calling those who favoured the Roman characters 'invertebrates' (*ACS*, 15/8/31). And there were literally scores of similar pronouncements throughout the period.[12]

Furthermore, in addition to these individual expressions of outrage, several of the most influential journals, among them *An Stoc*, *An t-Éireannach*, and the *Garda Review* came out in favour of the traditional font. Also, those in favour of retaining *an cló Gaelach* organised themselves in an attempt to compel the state to change its policy in this regard. In September 1928, a mimeographed letter over the signatures of Pádraic Ó Conaire and Séamus Ó Grianna was sent to prominent revival figures, asking them to sign a petition in opposition to the Roman characters. The text of the letter read in full:

> We have decided to ask the people who are recognised and famous as writers or scholars of the Irish language to help us oppose the attack made by the Government in order to thrust the Roman type down our throats, without permission, without consultation.[13]

This appeal met with immediate and impressive support. Among those who signed were Father Dinneen, Seosamh Mac Grianna, Seán Ua Ceallaigh, Risteárd Ó Foghludha, Seán Mac Maoláin, An tAthair Pádraig de Brún, Pádhraic Ó Domhnalláin, Tomás Ua Concheanainn, Micheál Ó Maoláin, Seán P. Mac Énrí, and Peadar Mac Fhionnlaoich. It was Mac Fhionnlaoich who took the next step, moving at the annual conference of the Gaelic League in 1928 that the League itself go on record in opposition to the government's policy concerning the new font. The motion was passed, though an amendment opposing the purchase of *any* books in the *cló Rómhánach* was defeated (*Tír*, Oct. 1928, 5).[14] With the assumption of power by de Valera's Fianna Fáil party in 1932, *an cló Gaelach* was temporarily reinstated for government use, but the issue continued to elicit strong emotions throughout the 1930s.

Proponents of orthographic and typographic reform were far less dogmatic than were their adversaries. For them, the real issue was pragmatic, not patriotic. In an April 1923 essay on 'The Simplification of Irish' in the *Irish Independent*, An tAthair Seoirse Mac Clúin wrote:

> One set of characters is sufficient; only one, therefore should be used. The Roman characters will, apparently, crush out the Gaelic in the struggle for existence. It may be urged in their behalf that they involve less expense and less trouble for the printer . . . If the Roman type is more convenient, it should be used to the exclusion of the other. The question is merely one of expediency (*II*, 31/3/23).

Five years later, 'Typograph' was even more dismissive of the emotional arguments of his opponents. Welcoming the government's decision in favour of the Roman font, 'Typograph' wrote that now Irish would have access to the same range of printing options as did English and continued:

> But all the logic, all the science, all the commonsense in the world will not weigh one iota with the cranks. If Hugh O'Neill was in charge of the National Army to-

> day, these Rip Van Winkles would urge him to use the same weapons as he used at the Yellow Ford . . . Anyone who heeds them is worse than themselves (*Freeman*, 18/8/28).

The quizzical detachment of those outside the movement was captured by a *Dublin Opinion* satirist in 1924 in a limerick entitled 'It Didn't Peaghdha!': 'A man by the name of Ó Sheaghdha [*sic*] / Signed a cheque, and it took half a deaghdha, / "Life is short," then said he; / So I'll try now to be / Patriotic in some other weaghdha' (*Dublin Opinion*, Aug. 1924, 211).

There were, however, some voices of moderation on these issues. For example, in 1928, Cathal Ó Tuathail, the editor of *An Tír*, lamented the bitterness of the debate and argued that while he favoured the Roman font for practical reasons, there was room for compromise and a future for both typefaces based on the personal choices of individual writers (*Tír*, Aug.–Sept. 1928, 1). 'Laighneach' agreed, writing in *The Leader* in October 1928:

> I do not see why the two types should not live on peaceably side by side. If people could live in perpetual indignation, there would not be much hope in this direction; but the most enraged anti-Romanite must cool down sometime, and when they have all cooled down and ceased to evoke crass opposition, even convinced Romanites may sometimes see fit to publish books in Gaelic characters and *vice-versa* (*Leader*, 24/11/28).

One 'convinced Romanite' open to such.compromise was Liam Ó Rinn, who in August 1928 argued that with some reforms rooted in the Gaelic manuscript tradition itself, *an cló Gaelach* could have an important, if not pre-eminent, role in Gaelic publishing in the future (*Freeman*, 18/8/28). As a practical if redundant expression of this spirit, Domhnall Ó Mathghamhna and Shán O Cuív published books in which all the material appeared in both fonts![15]

Half-way measures were anathema to Diarmuid O Murcu [*sic*], the champion of 'Eeris', a radically simplified form of the language developed by one 'Dr Panini' (probably O Murcu), 'Irish Scholar, Philologist, Educationist (BA 1st Hon. MA 1st Hon., Ph.D., Diploma certifying immunity to word superstition, "blas" – complex, dialectitis and other forms of quackery.'[16] In effect, his system not only simplified Irish orthography using the Roman font, but also radically transformed the grammar and syntax of the language in an effort to eliminate virtually any linguisitic obstacle for the learner. O Murcu, who prepared 'Eeris' versions of several texts to illustrate the virtues of the system, could boast: 'Through the Eeris method, everyone, even a foreigner, can acquire a working knowledge of Irish in about a week.'[17] O Murcu found few converts for 'Eeris', most Gaels agreeing instead with a columnist for *The Leader* who wrote in 1939: 'Our own view about "Eeris" – the creation of standardised simplified Volapuk Irish that never was heard on land or sea – is that it is an imbecile proposal' (*Leader*, 2/9/39).

Among the sensitive points 'Panini' touched in his campaign was one far more basic and important to the language than superficial conventions like orthography and typeface. Debating 'Eeris' with 'Panini' himself in the pages of *An Tír* in 1934, 'Cnuasaire' pronounced the whole project a Munster plot, and declared that the best 'cure' for his opponent's 'sickness' was for him 'to come right now and spend a month in Conamara and another month in Donegal' (*Tír*, Jan.–Feb. 1934, 5).[18] Provincial rivalries had always existed in the revival as speakers of the three major dialects of Munster, Connacht, and Ulster Irish sought to advance their own brand of the language or complained about the preference being shown another dialect by the Gaelic League or by a particular journal or publisher. Indeed there were separate journals catering to the speakers of each of the dialects: *Glór na Ly* and *An Lóchrann* in Munster; *An Connachtach*, *An Chearnóg*, *An Stoc*, and *Ar Aghaidh* in Connacht; and *An Crann* and *An t-Ultach* in Ulster, to name the most important that appeared between the beginning of the revival and the 1930s. Independence exacerbated these rivalries by raising the stakes. Now, Irish would be taught in all the schools of the Free State, requiring the recruitment of new teachers and inspectors and the writing or translating and publication of a wide range of new textbooks. Moreover, with state support – most notably in the form of An Gúm – Gaelic authors saw the prospect of something resembling a career opening up for them. And young Irish speakers looked forward to the possibility of a very appealing permanent and pensionable position in the new civil service as the state attempted to realise the vision of a Gaelic nation that had led to its creation. In this new order, preference for one dialect or discrimination against another counted in very practical terms, and was nosed out with a paranoia born of civil war.

Most of that paranoia was directed at those who used Munster Irish – whether native speakers or learners. Munster Irish had long been seen as having a special status among the dialects. In part this perceived distinction was due to the fact that some of the earliest and most influential writers of Irish were from Munster – among them An tAthair Peadar Ua Laoghaire, Father Patrick Dinneen, Tadhg Ó Donnchadha ('Torna'), Risteárd Ó Foghludha ('Fiachra Éilgeach'), Pádraig Ó Séaghdha ('Conán Maol'), Pádraig Ó Séaghdha ('Gruagach an Tobair'), Pádraig Ó Laoghaire, Father Richard Henebry, Séamus Ó Dubhghaill, Pádraig Ó Siochfhradha ('An Seabhac'), and Shán Ó Cuív, to name several – or had learned and so favoured the Munster dialect – writers like Piaras Béaslaí, Colm Ó Murchú ('Taube'), and Liam Ó Rinn, the last two members of the translation department of the Free State Dáil, one of the earliest and, in linguistic terms, most important and potentially influential or intrusive branches of the new civil service, depending on one's linguistic allegiances. Moreover, the perceived political connection between Munster Irish and the new state was real. Although himself an Ulsterman, Ernest Blythe had learned his Irish in West Kerry, and several of the leading figures in post-independence Irish politics had been members of the Gaelic League's contentious stronghold of Munster Irish in Dublin, the Keating Branch.[19] Among future leaders who were branch members were Cathal Brugha, Seán Ua Ceallaigh, Piaras Béaslaí, Richard Mulcahy, and Michael Collins, all of whom, with the exception of Brugha and his biographer Ua Ceallaigh, supported the 1921 Treaty with Britain.

In this light, it should hardly be surprising that champions of other dialects could see a Munsterman, if not under every bed, at least in every cushy chair in a government office, busy advancing the unjust prerogatives his dialect already enjoyed. Speakers of Ulster Irish were most vocal in their sense of linguistic disenfranchisement, and they had a point. Six of the nine counties of the traditional province of Ulster were not under the jurisdiction of the new state, and of the three counties that were, Donegal, the only one with a significant population of native speakers, was as remote from the central authority in Dublin as it possibly could be. So keenly did the Ulster speakers take to heart their marginalisation that in 1927, in alliance with activists from County Louth on the Ulster border, they set up Comhaltas Uladh as an all-but autonomous affiliate of the Gaelic League and commenced publication of their own journal, *An t-Ultach*.[20] While these developments heightened the profile of Ulster Irish and its speakers, in the long and even medium run one could argue that this independence could at times degenerate into a partition that further lessened the influence of Ulster Irish among those shaping language policy in the Free State.

Of course there was no way the Northerners would go quietly into second-class citizenship as long as they had Séamus Ó Grianna in their corner and eager to take on all comers. In a letter to the editor of *Fáinne an Lae* in February 1925, Ó Grianna, calling on the aid of Connacht, quite literally declared war on the Irish of Munster:

> Open 'Fáinne an Lae' to the dialects so they can fight the battle in God's name. It is nothing but foolishness for us to say that this battle is not ahead of us, or that we have nothing at all to fight over. There are people who say that there isn't any difference at all among the dialects. Not so. The Irish from Conamara to the Rosses of Donegal is not the same kind as there is in the province of Munster. They are not a single language. And the person who says they are is a fool (*FL*, 21/2/25).[21]

In an essay in *An t-Ultach* the same month, he put the blame on Munster for forcing the war, writing: 'The people of Munster are like the English in other ways beyond their sounds. They are trying to do away with our Irish language' (*Ultach*, Feb. 1925, 1).[22]

He repeated the battle cry later the same year, declaring in *Fáinne an Lae* in October:

> The war of the dialects must take place. And in God's name let us fight that fight as real Gaels should. The dialect of the northern half of Ireland is not the same as the dialect of Munster. They differ from each other in every way. They don't have the same accent, they don't have the same sounds, they don't have the same grammar, they don't have the same idioms, they don't have the same thoughts, they don't have the same spirit or the same structure.

His conclusion to this diatribe was coyly disingenuous: 'I won't say which of them is better or which of them is worse' (*FL*, 31/10/25).[23] Time only sharpened his suspicions, so that in 1932 he was warning the readers of the Dundalk *Examiner* that they should be ready to resist the machinations of the Munstermen, who were 'partitionists in their hearts' (partitionists i n-a gcroidhe): 'Every Ulsterman and every person throughout the country who understands what Irish is or who wants to see Ireland free and Gaelic, should prepare themselves for this fight' (*Examiner*, 16/7/32).[24] Of course Ó Grianna saw an obvious solution to this distressing state of conflict. Speakers of Munster Irish could simply surrender in face of the greater antiquity, authority, and beauty of the language as spoken in Donegal:

> It would settle most of this business about a standard if we were to go back to the Irish that existed before there was any difference at all among the dialects. It is not possible to oppose this idea when this old Irish is still alive among thousands of people (*An Phoblacht*, 30/10/25).[25]

Ó Grianna had vocal allies in his campaign to expose the intrigues of the Munster speakers. Irony was the rhetorical weapon of choice for A. Ó Domhnaill, who wrote in *An t-Ultach* from the Rosses of Donegal in 1935 to offer tongue-in-cheek tribute to the Munstermen: 'They have done great work. For half a century they have convinced the rest of Ireland that they have Irish' (*Ultach*, Feb. 1935, 8).[26] Far more strident was Seaghán Mac Meanman, who in 1930 claimed that the Roman font was part of a Munster plot hatched by civil servants of 'The Irish Free State – or the Munster Free State, I should say' (Saor-Stát na hÉireann – nó Saor-Stát na Mumhan ba cheart domh a rádh): 'They were Munstermen, and they wanted to trample the good Irish of the Ulstermen and the Connachtmen under their feet, and spread the broken and gapped "Irish" of Munster throughout Ireland . . . If they succeed, there is an end to the tongue of the Gaels' (*Tír*, July 1930, 12).[27] Two years later, in a letter to *An Camán*, he was all but rabid on this point, seeing the proposed publication of An tAthair Peadar Ua Laoghaire's translation of the Bible as a ploy to make Ua Laoghaire's Munster Irish a national standard:

> I don't want to see Irish die, but I would a thousand times prefer for the language to be dead than for the dialect that is more like bad Latin in the mouth of a person with a lisp than it is like Irish to be a standard in the country (*Tír*, July 1932, 4–5).[28]

Amazingly enough, he was not the only activist at the time willing to go off that particular deep end. In a 1929 letter to the *Irish Independent*, one 'Stocaire' asserted: 'Personally I should prefer to see the Irish language dead and buried than to see Gaoluinn [Munster Irish] adopted as the language of the nation' (*II*, 3/1/29).[29]

Propaganda bred paranoia for Ulster writers, who began to believe their own dire analyses. For example, in 1928 Mac Meanman wrote in *The Nation* that

> the Munstermen in the service of the Free State hate, despise, and loathe the Ulstermen. The Ulstermen who stood against the Old English and the New English longer than any another group of people in Ireland! . . . The poor Ulstermen, six of whose counties were sold so that it would be easier to control and pacify the three that were kept (*Nation*, 28/4/28).[30]

Ó Grianna had already called attention to a conscious plot to destroy Ulster Irish in an essay in *Sinn Féin* in 1925, although he did not, surprisingly, link it to Munster:

> It distresses all of us in the province of Ulster to see that what annoys and angers people on this side of the Boyne who are supposedly saving the Irish language is to hear that there is a part of the country in the province of Ulster where the people still have only Irish, a fact that should be a source of joy. I couldn't help hearing people rejoicing that the government of the Six Counties was a great help in killing Irish in the North (*SF*, 30/5/25).[31]

The previous year, one 'Smidic', in an open letter to Ó Grianna in the same journal, saw Free State complicity in this treachery: 'And Máire, do you know what I often could not help hearing? That there are very few Irish speakers south of the Boyne who don't want the border to last until the Belfast Government can kill the language in the province of Ulster' (*SF*, 29/11/24).[32]

While the intemperance of such insinuations and attacks provoked some protests, at least one Munster writer, Seán Ó Ciarghusa, welcomed the potentially positive effects of elevated adrenaline levels among the Gaels that could result from the kind of dialect war waged by Ó Grianna and his allies. Writing in *An Sguab* in 1923, Ó Ciarghusa declared: 'Fighting is better than loneliness, and I myself don't mind seeing or hearing controversy among the authors of the North and the South to see whether the clash of the tongues would awaken the readers of Irish from the deep sleep they are in' (*Sguab*, Aug. 1925, 147).[33]

Given the prominence their dialect has enjoyed in Ireland for the past half-century or so, it is striking how low a profile speakers of Connacht Irish maintained throughout this war over words. Even in articles welcoming Cumann Liteardha Mhic Éil, a literary society for speakers of Connacht Irish in Dublin, the Mayo-based journal *An Chearnóg* was proud, but restrained:

> We have more writers of Irish than has any other province, and yet the Irish of our province is dying. Why? Why is the Irish of Munster forcing our own Irish out of the schools? It doesn't matter why. It's the remedy we want and we have it at last. The remedy is the MacHale Literary Society (*An Chearnóg*, Jan. 1924, 1).[34]

'Taidhbhse Dhubhaltaigh Mhic Firbhisigh' was even more generous in a 1927 essay in *An Stoc*. Having insisted that books in Connacht, not Munster, Irish be used in Connacht schools, he added: 'I don't say that with disrespect for Munster Irish. I have great respect for it in its proper place, that is, in the province of Munster' (*Stoc*, Feb. 1927, 5).[35] In general, Connacht activists maintained this positive approach, eschewing provincial and personal animosities while extolling the excellences and advantages of their own dialect. For instance, a correspondent in *The Blueshirt* saw Connacht Irish evolving naturally into the national standard as the result of the work of Aranman Micheál Ó Maoláin and his Coiste na bPáisdí, an organisation that sent urban children to the Conamara Gaeltacht:

> But if Micheál and the other Connachtmen who are helping him succeed, there is no doubt that a solution will be found for the standardisation of Irish . . . Young people from Cork and Kerry and the Decies will be going to Connacht and they will take away the Connacht dialect, and that dialect will be mixed with the Munster dialect and they will soon settle that disastrous question that has been causing trouble and doing harm to the cause of the Irish language for the past forty years (*Blueshirt*, 11/5/35).[36]

Not surprisingly then, unless caught in the crossfire, Connacht speakers managed to avoid the worst of the acrimony involved in this debate. As we have seen, Ó Grianna regularly enlisted the Connacht dialect as an albeit subordinate Northern Irish ally in his jeremiads about Southern degeneracy and subterfuge. More strikingly, an anonymous reviewer of Connachtman Máirtín Ó Cadhain's translation of Charles Kickham's *Sally Cavanagh* in the Cork journal *An Muimhneach* urged his readers to make the effort to savour Ó Cadhain's Conamara Irish: 'The Connacht dialect is in it, and therefore, Munster people will not understand much of the speech in it, but they will have a chance to get to know the excellence of the speech they have in the west' (*Muimhneach*, Dec. 1932, 4).[37] Liam Ó Rinn, a learner who favoured

Munster Irish, came to believe that in all probability Connacht Irish would ultimately become the preferred national standard.[38] Indeed the only really negative comments on Connacht Irish appear in Piaras Béaslaí's satirical one-act play *Cúigeachas*, in which the protagonist is a bigoted Kerryman contemptuous of Conamara Irish. His daughter's Connacht suitor pretends to be from County Clare (in Munster) and extravagantly imitates the Kerry dialect. At curtain, the father learns that he himself had actually been born just on the 'wrong' side of the Connacht border. Despite the play's light comedy, Béaslaí, Liverpool-born but a master of Munster Irish, took as his theme the serious danger of linguistic provincialism at a time when all dialects of Irish were threatened by English.[39]

Many in the movement, speakers of all dialects, shared his concern and called for Gaelic unity in face of the common foe. For example, in a 1926 letter to the *Irish Independent*, an anonymous speaker of Munster Irish wrote:

> But why should either dialect [Munster or Connacht] be studied to the exclusion of the other? The day that one perishes will see the death-bed of the other. It is criminal ignorance on the part of anyone to depreciate Irish simply because it happens to be Munster or Connacht or Ulster. 'Ní neart go cur le chéile' [There is no strength without co-operation] rather than 'divide and conquer' should be the war-cry of every genuine Gael at the moment (*II*, 3/11/26).[40]

Virtually identical views were expressed in a July 1935 editorial in *An t-Éireannach*:

> It is shameful in a country as small as ours, whose Irish is as weak as it is, it is shameful to say that Gaels would be divided from each other in the cause of the language. You would think from the talk there has been of late about Connachtmen, Munstermen, and Ulstermen that every one of the dialects of Irish was a foreign language and that it was their duty to treat it with contempt. It is likely that some of them would prefer to speak English than to have it said that they would speak in the dialect of any other Gaeltacht (*Éireannach*, 6/7/35).[41]

Similar calls for a more temperate allegiance to one's native or preferred dialect were heard with some frequency throughout the 1920s and 1930s. Even Ó Grianna could have moments of moderate reflection, as when, having noted in a 1928 column in *Fáinne an Lae* that some readers had been surprised by his critical comments on a book in Ulster Irish, he asserted: 'It is high time for us to realise that Ireland is greater than any of her provinces, and to judge a book on how good or how bad it is, no matter where it comes from' (*FL*, Apr. 1928).[42] Needless to say, he didn't always follow his own advice in this regard.

It is, perhaps, not surprising that Munster writers felt most secure in making a concession like that from a May 1923 contributor to *An Sguab* who wrote:

> It happens that we ourselves have Munster Irish, but anyone who has independent opinions and is not narrow-minded must admit that none of them, Munster Irish, Connacht Irish or Ulster Irish, are better than the others in any way. There are good things in every one that are not to be found in the others, but there is no doubt that there is too much talk and too much nonsense going around concerning provincialism and dialects (*Sguab*, May 1923, 147).[43]

By far the most effusive Munster exponent of alliance across artificial dialectal borders was Tadhg Ó Donnchadha, who wrote in his preface to *Ceol na Mara* (The music of the sea), a reader for schoolchildren by the Conamara *sean nós* singer and writer Máire Ní Ghuairim:

> From cultivating the dialects the blooms will soon come. The work is underway before our eyes day by day, and it will succeed with the help of God. We notice a magic or something particularly pleasing in every one of those 'rivers' [i.e. dialects]. The magic of courage in that of the North; the magic of manliness in that of the South; the magic of femininity in that of the West. A person would not be long working with our new literature until he would see that, and the language is the richer for all of them.[44]

Predictably, Ulster writers were more wary about yielding even an inch of what they believed was their linguistic and moral high ground on this issue. Nevertheless, in July 1939, Niall Ó Searcaigh addressed a warning to both native speakers and learners in *An t-Ultach*:

> For goodness sake, friends, consider the enemy you both have, English. And don't let it be said of you after your deaths that you did not have enough sense to stand shoulder to shoulder. And that, instead of trying to write books in Connacht Irish and things in Munster Irish, you were fighting over nothing (*Ultach*, July 1939, 4).[45]

No one, however, summed up the fundamental fallacy underlying the debate over dialect better than did Myles Dillon, who was quoted in 1929 as saying 'that there were only two dialects worth talking about – bad Irish and good Irish' (ná raibh ach dhá chanamhaint ann gur fiú trácht ortha – droch-Ghaedhilg agus Gaedhilg mhaith) (*II*, 20/3/29).

An article of faith for many who saw the dialect squabble as a serious waste of energy and resources was that a national standard for the language would evolve from the dialects naturally over time. The point was made forcefully by an anonymous writer in the *Weekly Freeman* in March 1923:

> It is the writers who make a literary language of a spoken language. The dialect that is written most and best, that is always the dialect that serves as a literary language in every country. And that's how it will be with us in Ireland, if the language isn't put to death with rules to keep writers from writing their own language (*Weekly Freeman*, 31/3/23).[46]

Two months later, Liam Ó Rinn developed this idea in a discussion of the need for a literary standard for the language:

> It is already evolving. Every good writer wants to write in a way that everyone will understand, and so he chooses the speech that everyone will understand and he avoids obscurity (*UIrman*, 19/5/23).[47]

Writing in the *Irish Independent* in 1931, Diarmuid Ó h-Almhain saw Dublin as the alembic from which the new standard would emerge, a prospect that probably united most speakers of all dialects in outraged dismay:

> Although there are regions in Ireland in which Irish is habitually spoken, it is unlikely that there is any place where it is spoken more with real feeling than in the city of Dublin, however anglicised a city it is, and however far from the Gaeltacht. People from Connacht, Munster, Ulster and Leinster who don't rely on a single dialect of the three we have – all of them associating with each other in this city, and the dialect of his choice on the lips of every one of them. As a result of that, a new dialect is gradually evolving – 'the Dublin dialect' (*II*, 21/4/31).[48]

Other Gaels took a more interventionist approach to the question. In a 1923 essay in *Studies* that provoked a good deal of debate, the German Jesuit Gustav Lehmacher wrote of the student of Irish:

> Then suddenly he is brought face to face with the fact that nowadays a literary Irish language does not exist, that learned Irishmen must take their language from the farmers and fishers of the sea-coast, that everyone must go off and discover a Ghaedhealg féin [his own Irish] (a Ghaedhilg féin, a Ghaedhilge féin, a Ghaodhluinn féin, as the case may be), that there is no question of a language which imposes itself on all and is an exemplar which all must follow (*Studies*, Mar. 1923, 27).[49]

While few if any accepted what seems to have been his preferred solution – 'to go back in style and pronunciation to Early Middle Irish' – Lehmacher's call for immediate scholarly involvement in the establishment of a national standard touched a chord. In his response to Lehmacher's essay, Tomás Ó Máille, the Connacht scholar and founder-editor of *An Stoc*, wrote:

> It is to be regretted that the tendency of Irish writers for the past six or eight years is rather in the direction of going away from a standard than approximating to anything like uniformity. If the principal Irish writers of all the provinces were to meet and to agree to leave out of their writings, as far as they knew how, anything obviously dialect or local, the problem would be in a good way towards being solved (*Studies*, Mar. 1923, 41).[50]

All of these linguistic skirmishes, however acrimoniously contested, were peripheral to the real issue troubling and challenging the language movement throughout the 1920s and 1930s. The new state was committed to re-Gaelicising the nation as quickly as possible, and this was perhaps the one goal of the Free State administration with which their republican opponents were in full agreement, although they were predictably critical of many of the methods adopted for its realisation. The Gaelic League, from which so many prominent figures on both sides of the political divide had learned their patriotism, proclaimed in a new constitution in 1925 that its *raison d'être* was 'to restore Irish throughout all of Ireland, so that it will be a free and Gaelic country again' (an Ghaeilge a chur faoi réim arís ar fud Éireann uile ionas go mbudh tír shaor Ghaelach í athuair).[51] The problem was, of course, what, in practical terms, it meant to be *Gaelach*. Was it possible to be an Irish person (*Éireannach*) without being a 'Gael'? Were words like *Gael* and *Gaelach* purely linguistic terms or was the whole concept of *Gaelachas* (Gaelicism) more complex and elusive? Was it definable at all? Many at the time were more than willing to try to frame such a definition – and often to try then to impose it on their fellows whether they agreed with it or not.

For some, the concept of *Gaelachas* was an exclusionary test of membership in the genuine Irish nation. In April 1924, Seán Ua Ceallaigh editorialised in the *Catholic Bulletin*:

> The Irish nation is the Gaelic nation; its language and literature is the Gaelic language; its history is the history of the Gael. All other elements have no place in Irish national life, literature, and tradition, save as they are assimilated into the very substance of Gaelic speech, life and thought. The Irish nation is not a racial synthesis at all; synthesis is not a vital process, and only what is vital is admissable in analogies bearing on the nature of the living Irish nation, speech, literature, and tradition (*CB*, Apr. 1924, 269).[52]

In an April 1931 editorial in the *Dundalk Examiner*, the author echoed D. P. Moran's two civilisations theory from the early days of the revival:

> There should not be any difficulty in explaining *Gaeleachas* and everything it involves. We all understand that there are two kinds of culture struggling for

dominance in Ireland at present – the culture of the Gaels and the culture of the English. The English still have the upper hand, and *Gaelachas* is everything that is needed to put an end to the sway of the English over the mind and soul of all the people of Ireland (*Examiner*, 11/4/31).[53]

'Uíbh Ráthach' echoed this position in *An Claidheamh Soluis* the following year, proclaiming:

> There must be a single civilisation in the country and not two as there are now . . . When the the Gaels again have the land of their ancestors and our people have the local manufactures started up again, and one culture – the true Gaelachas – then God's blessing will be on us and his hand with us (*ACS*, 20/2/32).[54]

Addressing the Clare Feis in June 1934, Pádraig Ó Siochfhradha declared that the goal of Irish-Ireland had to be 'the re-establishment of the Gaedheal again with his traditions and his ideals in complete supremacy in his native land. That is the logical destiny of the Gaedheal' (*Clare Champion*, 9/6/34).[55]

In fact, in a January 1930 editorial in *An Stoc*, the usually judicious Tomás Ó Máille urged Gaels to cultivate intolerance as a virtue, writing of Irish people with a weak sense of national identity: 'If this people grows accustomed to Liberalism and Tolerance, two ways in Ireland to say slavery, neither the Irish language nor *Gaelachas* will be bothering them much' (*Stoc*, Jan. 1930, 6).[56] If, given the political climate of Europe at the time, a reader feels uneasy with such sentiments, he has cause. In November 1926, *Fáinne an Lae* published an excerpt from a long letter sent from Rome by an anonymous correspondent in which the author equated the faith of true Gaels, whom with irony he called fools, with that of Italian *Fascisti*: 'That kind of faith held by a certain group of people who want a free and Gaelic Ireland is called *Gaelachas*. The same kind of faith is called *Facismo* in Italy' (*FL*, Nov. 1926).[57] It was certainly this kind of thinking that could inspire an editorial like that on 'Gaelicism and Democracy' in *An Camán* in 1933:

> Within these free Gaelic organisations forces can be evolved to put pressure on value systems that have grown in and grown up through the period of the conquest and that, in their tangled briar-like forms, still hamper development. Gaelic pressure around and about these things and Gaelic pressure alone, will eventually bend or break them to the national will (*Camán*, 12/8/33).

Fortunately, others in the movement rejected simplistic and rigid dichotomies and the intolerance they generated for a more fluid and evolutionary definition of both Irish nationality and 'the national will'. Few, however, questioned movement orthodoxy about what cultural, if not ethnic, strain would be paramount in that definition. In September 1923, a correspondent in the *Derry People* wrote:

> Now, the term 'Gaelic' in its primary significance simply means Irish. But it may also be understood to imply a recognition of the fact the predominant, if not overwhelming strain in the composition of the Irish nation is Gaelic or Celtic.

Acknowledging that 'the Ulster Scot is probably of purer Celtic race than say, a Wexfordman', he argued that the culture that had been attractive enough 'to assimilate the Dane and the Anglo-Norman, and the Firbolg and the new-comer of recent times' would be able to 'weld all Irishmen into a national brotherhood'. He concluded: 'Now let us get rid of misconceptions as to what is implied in this term. It does not mean that full privilege of citizenship will be confined to those of pure Gaelic blood, for no such persons exist to-day' (*Derry People*, 8/9/23). In June 1930, Frank Gallagher editorialised on 'The Common Name' in *The Nation*, a paper that supported de Valera's Fianna Fáil party:

> For good or ill the Irish nation is the present Irish people. Them, all of them, must the true nationalist serve . . . In the nature of the case he must win control for the majority, but it is simply as a majority that he must bring it to victory, not because it is preponderantly Catholic, not even because it is Gaelic (*Nation*, 28/6/30).[58]

In an important essay on the writers of the Blasket Islands in *Bonaventura* in 1937, Thomas Barrington lashed out at 'the rabid traditionalists who have done more than anyone else to discredit all traditionalism', stating: 'They have tried to associate Gaelicism in the public mind with bigotry, bad manners, and insularity' (*Bonaventura*, Summer 1937, 121).[59] It was, doubtless, such 'rabid' Gaels who provoked the future Gaelic scholar David Greene, himself a Protestant, to tell his fellow delegates at a meeting of the inter-university Irish society An Comhchaidreamh in August 1938 that 'he thought that less self-consciousness was needed. When they could discuss Gaelic literature without being obsessed with the idea of Gaelicism, a greater advance would have been made' (*Cork Weekly Examiner*, 6/8/38). Blunt in his insistence that such a great advance was much needed was 'Droighneán Fionn', who wrote in *An t-Ultach* in 1929:

> I am going to say things that many Gaels will not like. It will, I fear, be said that I am not a Gael. That could be true and I am not going to deny it . . . I am not covetous in that way. To tell the truth, I am far from certain 'what a Gael is.' When I see some of the people on whom that name is hung, it reminds me of something like what the Frenchman said about men and dogs: 'The more I see the Gaels, the more I love the English' (*Ultach*, [Feb.] 1929, 2).[60]

The debate over who was or was not a Gael continued throughout the period. And the distinction was an important one, as is clear from a short piece by Liam Ó Raghallaigh in the *Irish Press* in 1932: 'I am a Gael. Isn't that a noble thing? A Gael in my heart, a Gael in my mind, a Gael from Gaelic ancestors stretching from time immemorial. I am a Gael, and I am boasting of it. I challenge the whole world to outdo the Gaelic race' (*IP*, 30/9/32).[61] Were, however, the terms 'Gaedheal' and 'Éireannach' ever interchangeable? One 'P. Ó C.' certainly felt that at the time he was writing, in 1927, many 'Éireannaigh' had no legitimate claim to the title: 'None of them are Gaels whose mind is not full of love for Gaels, for Gaelic culture, and for knowledge about Gaels' (*Lóchrann*, Jan. 1927, 109).[62] Daniel Corkery was in agreement in his review of León Ó Broin's biography of Charles Stewart Parnell in 1937, writing: 'Gaedheal and Éireannach are used as synonyms. It hardly makes for clarity' (*Ireland To-Day*, June 1937, 77). On the other hand, Pádraig Ó Duilleáin sidestepped the issue in a 1926 essay in the London journal *Guth na nGaedheal*, equating the Gaels not with all Irish people, but with 'good' Irish people:

> If the individual is a disciple of the Gaelic League, a believer in its principles, and a wholehearted supporter of its mission, he is a 'good' Irishman. If he is not a Gaelic Leaguer, although he may be a 'good' man in the abstract, a 'good' Catholic, a 'good' Protestant, a 'good' politician of any party you like, and a lot of other good things as well, he is not a 'good' Irishman (*Guth na nGaedheal*, 1926, 2).

For Liam Ó Rinn, an Irishman, however 'good', was not necessarily a Gael, although that unpalatable fact was not necessarily all that bad:

> Since the English language came to Ireland, there is all the difference in the world between an Irishman and a Gael. Sometimes, the Irishman is far better than the Gael. There are good Irishmen, Irishmen who were raised in English-speaking Ireland, and who would put their lives at risk for their country, and there are Gaels who were raised in the Gaeltacht who would sell their souls for money (*UIrman*, 30/7/32).[63]

Worth noting here is that the decisive factor in the definition of a Gael is ultimately linguistic, although clearly implied is that linguistic differences had generated a profound cultural divergence between Irish-speaking Ireland (the Gaeltacht) and English-speaking Ireland (the Galltacht). Another writer who rejected out of hand any attempt to see meaningful ethnic differences between the Gael and the Éireannach was 'Foreign-Named', who wrote to the editor of *Honesty* in 1925:

> At one point, however, I am at issue with you, and that is in your somewhat ready assumption that the Irish divide themselves naturally into two races – Gaels and

'West Britons': the one consisting of the unmixed descendants (apparently) of the early inhabitants; the other, those of the various colonists who have come to, or been thrust upon, Ireland in the past. To the first seems to be ascribed all those virtues which will yet make of Ireland a power of world-wide influence, while the second would seem to be accused of passing their days in thinking out new methods of sabotage of National aspirations (*Honesty*, 24/10/25).

Actually, while there was a great deal of suspicion of those who actually deserved the name of 'West Britons' – the term coined by D. P. Moran for Irish people who looked to England for their political, cultural, and aesthetic standards – for the most part those influential in the language movement avoided ethnic essentialism as a means of defining who was or was not a Gael. The majority opinion seems to have been that the title could be earned.[64] In a 1924 essay on 'An Stát Gaedhealach' (The Gaelic state) in *An Sguab*, León Ó Broin conceded: 'The people who are in Ireland at present are not Gaels but a mix of Gaels, Scandinavians, Normans, English, Scots, Welsh, and others.' But he went on to argue that ethnic purity was irrelevant with regard to what he clearly saw as a question of personal cultural allegiance:

> We have as much right to call ourselves Gaels – those of us who speak Irish and believe in Gaelic nationality – as has the man yonder to call himself an Englishman, he in whom there is the blood of Britons, Romans, Angles, Saxons, Jutes, Danes, and Normans, not to mention the blood of the French, the Irish, and the Scots. Therefore, if there are few – if any – 'Gaels' alive today, we say that we are Gaels because the Irish language and the civilisation of the ancient Gaels are not altogether dead among us (*Sguab*, 5/31/24).[65]

Writing in *An t-Éireannach* in 1935, 'R. F.' stated that while not all Irish people were Gaels, they could choose to live a life that merited the title:

> Every Irish person today should ask himself this question: what is the state of everything connected with *Gaelachas*. We are Gaels or we are anglicised. That's all there is to say. A person cannot say he is a Gael if he is half involved in Gaelic affairs and at the same time half lost in the slough of despond, that is in the filth of the perverse traits of the English (*Éireannach* 16/3/35).[66]

For 'C.', writing in *An Muimhneach* in 1933, the decision to become a Gael involved some very serious life choices, as he insisted that to earn the title one had not only to make a serious and sustained effort to master the language, avoid all but Irish games and dances, and purchase only Irish-made goods, but was also obliged to marry an Irish speaker! (*Muimhneach*, Jan. 1933, 21 and 30).[67]

No less an authority than Douglas Hyde, one of the founders and the first president of the Gaelic League, weighed in on this question in January 1926. Speaking over the air on the first broadcast of an Irish radio station, Hyde, himself a Protestant and of mixed ethnic stock, offered an optimistic evolutionary solution to the whole Gael / Éireannach debate:

> The time is coming quickly when a young man without Irish will not only be unable to say he is a Gael, but also to say he is an Irishman; for no Irishman will be an Irishman (except, perhaps, on the far side of the miserable Border) who doesn't have some command of the language of his ancestors (*FL*, 9/1/26).[68]

And in what must have been a startling challenge at the time, 'D. P.' in 1927 told readers of *Irish Freedom* that an Irish sailor had told him of encountering three black men from Barbados who were speaking a language he could not understand. When the sailor questioned their Irish surnames, one of them, Tomás Mac Cárthaigh, confronted him with the words: 'We are Gaels, but are you an Irishman?' (Gaedhil is eadh sinne, ach an Éireannach tusa?). Hearing the sailor's affirmative answer, Mac Cárthaigh was scornful: 'Huh! . . . You calling yourself an Irishman and not knowing Irish. I don't believe you're an Irishman at all' (*Irish Freedom*, Feb. 1927, 3).[69]

Was, then, language the absolute essence of *Gaelachas*? Obviously, few would deny its enormous importance in defining *an aigne Ghaelach* (the Gaelic spirit or mind).[70] For instance, in his 1934 book *Prós na hAoise Seo* (The prose of this century), Shán Ó Cuív asserted:

> Each race has its own way of thinking, and scholars of the mind say that language is a kind of mirror of the mind, and that it reveals to us the way the people who speak it think . . . And it could be proved that the people who speak Irish have their own way of thinking as well. We call that way of thinking the Gaelic mind.[71]

The politician most responsible for realising this vision through the schools after the change of government in 1932 was Tomás Ó Deirg, de Valera's Minister for Education, who told a gathering of the Catholic Truth Society in Tuam, County Galway in 1936:

> It is no wonder at all that it is in the national language that we most feel the mind and the character of this country of ours, for it is the national language that gives us the clearest insight into the mind and character of the people. The national language is the medium that gives us insight into the heart and soul of our people, and from shaping the character and outlook of the nation, it also shapes the character and mind of the people themselves(*IP*, 29/6/36).[72]

For many, however, language alone, despite its importance, was not enough to define, much less validate *Gaelachas*. This point was made forcefully by Seán Mac Lochlainn in a 1925 letter to the *Irish Independent*: 'It is not for the language *per se* that Gaelic revivalists are fighting, but for all that it means and has meant, morally, socially, and nationally in the history of Ireland' (*II*, 2/10/25). Cormac Breathnach went farther in an article on 'Gaedhilg agus Gaedhealachas' (The Irish Language and *Gaelachas*) in *Inis Fáil* two years later:

> There are people who say and who believe that the Irish language and *Gaelachas* are the same because they think that it is not possible for one who has Irish on his tongue not to have *Gaelachas* in his heart. Although I accept the opinion that one cannot be a Gael without the Irish language, I do not agree that the *Gaelachas* that is natural for a Gael is in the heart of everyone today who has some Irish . . . The Irish language without *Gaelachas* is a soulless thing (*Inis Fáil*, Dec. 1928, 43).[73]

In a 1938 essay in the *Irish Independent*, one 'Conchubhar' also argued that the mere possession of the Gaelic language did not make one a Gael. 'Conchubhar' conceded that many had learned to speak, read, and write Irish 'splendidly' (go feilmeata), but had failed to embrace *Gaelachas*. For 'Conchubhar', the lesson taught by jazz-loving, movie-going Irish speakers was self-evident: 'The language is only part of *Gaelachas*, and if the soul is more important to us than the body, shouldn't the soul of *Gaelachas* be more important to us than its body, or shouldn't they at least be of equal importance to us' (*II*, 11/11/38).[74] The same idea was given more succinct expression by P. S. O'Hegarty ('Sarsfield') in a 1936 essay in *The Leader*: 'Irish will come into its own when we realise that Gaelicisation of the mind must precede Gaelicisation of the larynx' (*Leader*, 18/7/36).[75]

That suggestion brings us, of course, back to where we started – in search of a definition of *Gaelachas*. That definition eluded many in the movement throughout the 1920s and 1930s, none of whom was franker in his admission of failure than was 'Sliabh Bladhma', who wrote in *An Gaedheal* in 1935:

> There are many things that I revere or enjoy and like to think of as essentially Gaelic. Much more of what I feel to be Gaelic is very hard to define. When I look at Gaelic life, history, literature, the difficulties of full or exact definition are too great for me.

He did, however, offer an excuse:

> In regard to Gaelicism, with which we are immediately concerned, my own main and final reason for not trying to sum it up is that I look upon it as something which is ever growing . . . It is not something completed and definite (*Gaedheal*, 16/2/35).[76]

Others were more willing to shroud their confusion in platitudes, as did, for example, the anonymous contributor of an essay on 'Iolsgoil na h-Éireann / A Gaelic University' that appeared in *Sinn Féin* in 1924:

> The Iolsgoil they aim at is to be Gaelic with the Gaelicism of the traditional Gael – speaking the language of the Gael, teaching patriotism and studying the realisation of the destiny God has in mind for our Nation and race (*SF*, 19/7/24).

Time did not clear the fog, as is evident from a 1938 piece by 'Oisín' in the *Derry People*:

> Sometimes I am not certain that we all have the same understanding of the word 'Gaelachas'. In my opinion what it means is the Gaelic system and the national outlook with which Gaels want to replace the Anglicised civilisation that there is in this country at present (*Derry People*, 27/8/38).[77]

One point on which there was considerable agreement was the notion that *Gaelachas* was deeply rooted in the Irish past and most accessible through a study of the language, beliefs, traditions and cultural expressions from that past. For the editor of the *Clare Champion*, writing in 1929, Irish was most valuable as a link to ancient qualities in danger of being lost:

> The mind, the environment, the policy, the customs, the ideals, the beliefs of the Gaels, operating throughout a long series of centuries, framed and moulded the speech of the Gael. What follows? That the Gaelic tongue is now in its turn the one reliable index to the Gaelic mind, the Gaelic character, the entire Gaelic past . . . Only by the perpetuation of that speech can the ideals, characteristics, and distinctiveness of the Gael be perpetuated. Let it die out wholly, and we break with our past (*Clare Champion*, 28/12/29).

Perhaps no one better expressed this obsessive identification of *Gaelachas* with the past than did Cormac Ó Cuileannáin in a 1935 essay in the *Cork Weekly Examiner*, where he wrote of 'the authentic nationalist' (an náisiúntaidhe ceart):

> Indeed he is not a revolutionary, nor a maker of new laws. He stands on the side of the OLD THINGS. He is a preserver. He is a conservative by nature. There is no group of people in the country who deserve that name more than the people who champion *Gaelachas*. Their goal is to defend and to preserve and to perpetuate the old faith, the old language, the old Christian literature, the old culture, and the old traditions (*Cork Weekly Examiner*, 16/3/35).[78]

A more balanced conservatism was that of Liam Ó Buachalla. Addressing a group of university students in Galway, he spelled out his position at some length:

> Of course, when Gaelic culture is discussed, some of us are accustomed to shake our heads or to begin laughing. Many believe that bringing Gaelic culture back is the same as bringing back everything connected with the old civilisation of the country. Indeed there is a great deal, including laws, customs, and other things, that would be worth bringing back at once; the country would be better and nobler for them. There is much else that could not be brought back. But we must get an accurate knowledge of those ancient things; we must go back to them with the necessary inspiration so that the appearance, shape, and flavour of *Gaelachas* will be on the store of wisdom we bring back (*Irisleabhar*, 1934–5, 31).[79]

If they could not define *Gaelachas* with precision, many in the movement felt the best solution was to spread the net as wide as possible, drawing in any aspect of Irish tradition and culture that could give insight into the putative national psyche. The most articulate exponent of this approach was Pádraig Ó Siochfhradha, who wrote in a wide-ranging 1925 essay on 'Gaelachas' in *An Lóchrann*:

> Other things are necessary besides the language itself, though intimately related to it, in order to give a person a Gaelic appearance and manner, that is, he must be filled with the folklore, with the culture and the philosophy and the spirit of the Gaels who came before him . . . It is by means of those things and by means of the Irish language that a child is made into a Gael. He is not a Gael without them – not even an Irishman. For a person who learned Irish and did not come to know the other things through it and with it, Irish would be nothing but a layer of skin he would be constantly shedding. The Irish language itself would not give him the mental sustenance or satisfaction a person's mind needs and it would not take hold on his nature nor his intellect, and the Irish language would not be seated on the golden throne in his soul (*Lóchrann*, Nov. 1925, 1).[80]

He returned to the subject in an essay with the same title in the Enniscorthy *Echo* in 1931, an essay characterised by his bitterness at the disillusioned loss of popular commitment to *Gaelachas* that marked the post-Civil War decades:

> Outside of a small number of Gaels, no other group in Ireland has reached the state of nationality. It is irrelevant how many Englishmen or 'Irregulars' or 'Staters' any person in this country has killed. He is not a Gael as a result of that unless he chooses to speak Irish and unless he is full of the knowledge and the culture of his race and his country (*Echo*, 2/5/31).[81]

S. B. Ó Donnchadha offered a similarly comprehensive vision of *Gaelachas* in the University College Cork journal *The Quarryman*, writing:

> What is the meaning of Gaelachas? To bring the noble language of the Gaels into common use and to permanently establish the National Culture and all that goes with it in the hearts of the students. A treasured part of that culture are the Gaelic customs – the Gaelic dances, the Gaelic music and the National games (*Quarryman*, Mar. 1936, n.p.).[82]

But without a doubt the most authoritative expression of this loose interpretation of *Gaelachas* was that issued by the Gaelic League itself in 1925: 'What is understood by *Gaelachas* is the practice of the Gaelic language, culture, folklore, games and dances, and having Irish freedom as a national goal.' In his essay announcing and discussing this proclamation, Cormac Breathnach stressed that the League intended the definition to be challenging but not exclusive: 'Any Irish person at all who is in favour of full *Gaelachas* as the Executive Committee explained it and who does his best to put it into practice as much as he can should be reckoned a true Gael' (*Camán*, June 1931, 7).[83]

In practice, however, this understanding of *Gaelachas* as a commitment to far more than the language alone was to provoke one of the most divisive, destructive, and ultimately futile debates within the Irish-Ireland movement of the time. To put it bluntly, while there were many genuinely devoted to both Gaelic sports and native dances, a fair number of people were delighted with a broad definition of *Gaelachas* because they found it far easier and more enjoyable to dance reels or chase a hurling *sliotar* or a football than to learn, much less master, the Irish language. Predictably enough, exaggerated claims for the centrality of sport and dance in the preservation and expression of *Gaelachas* were common in the nationalist press of the time. For instance, in 1933 Art Mac Ganna, the vice-president of the Irish Dancing Commission, wrote in his preface to *Ár Rinncidhe Fóirne: Ten Irish Figure Dances*:

> Irish dancing and Irish games are accepted as being complementary to the Irish language revival; from the social point of view it may be said that Irish dancing has been the spearhead of the struggle for the re-establishing of a distinct Gaelic culture and civilisation. It follows, therefore, that the propagation of Irish dancing is a matter of great moment, and its regulation and control secondary only in importance to the revival of the language itself.[84]

Gaelic games were accorded an equal prominence by 'Celt', who, writing on the Tailteann Games in *Honesty* in 1928, declared:

> Aonach Tailteann should similarly help the return of our approaching manhood to those sports, pastimes, and bodily ideals with which it has ever been associated, and which area is as vital to our national well-being and security as a distinctive tongue is essential to our national identity. While we are striving to restore the Irish mind, should we not try simultaneously to rebuild Irish muscle? (*Honesty*, 5/5/28).[85]

A further development that moved sport to the top of the cultural agenda was the increasingly close co-operation between the Gaelic League and the Gaelic Athletic Association (Cumann Lúthchleas Gaedheal), a co-operation that culminated in the GAA's assumption of responsibility for publishing the League organ in 1933, when *An Camán* became the official publication of both organisations, much to the detriment of the specific programme of the League.[86] The new priorities are clear in an editorial note on 'foreign dances' addressed to the Free State authorities by Seán Ua Ceallaigh in October 1933:

> We advise them to remember that the only effective remedy is the redevelopment of the native games and music that helped to maintain the spirit of the people through penal days, famine, and evictions; and we ask them to co-operate with and, if necessary, stimulate GAA and Gaelic League to put these in the place of decadent alien attractions adapted, for the most part, to the emotional needs of a decaying Lutheran world that like the dances, clings together in the great pagan cities of its decline (*Camán*, 28/10/33).

We will hear a good deal more rhetoric in this distasteful vein below.

Fortunately for the revival itself, there were many activists who, whatever their opinion about dances or sport, insisted that the language had to remain at the heart of the crusade to re-Gaelicise the nation. Pádraig Ó Briain ('Manannán') was, as usual, biting on this point in his regular column in *An Phoblacht* in April 1936:

> The language is the tool of the mind; dancing is just a pastime. The people who play Gaelic sports are not allowed to watch or to play English sports, but there is no ban on their speaking and using and promoting the English language as much as they want (*An Phoblacht*, 11/4/36).[87]

In a 1930 essay in *The Star*, Liam Ó Rinn ('Coinneach') memorably dubbed the obsession with native dancing 'Gaelachas na gCos' (*Gaelachas* of the feet) (*Star*, 19/4/30).[88] But he was by no means the first to attack the 'Feet Gaels'. As early as April 1924, León Ó Broin had lashed out at those who practised the peripheral at the expense of the essential:

> People think that it is a sign of Anglicisation to wear a dress suit or to carry a walking stick, not to mention anything else. It is a great wonder that we are not told to use our fingers instead of knives and forks. Isn't the argument the same? This cursed fondness for *Gaelachas* that is not *Gaelachas* – ignorance and lack of civilisation, that is all there is to it (*FL*, 19/4/24).[89]

The editor of *The Kerryman* was disgusted by the ersatz patriotism of many so-called 'Gaels', writing in March 1924: 'Talk against foreign games from a person who does not know his own language nor care about it is nothing but nonsense. Isn't language more important than a game? We are sick of much of the patriotism that we hear' (*Kerryman*, 8/3/24, supplement).[90] Most succinct in his dismissal of the claims of the Feet Gaels was Seán Ó hUadhaigh, who wrote in the London journal *Guth na nGaedheal* in 1936: 'A language is not revived by the use of the feet, either on the dancing-floor or on the football field' (*Guth na Gaedheal*, 1936, 34).

The preferred weapon of the Feet Gaels in their campaign to advance their specific hobbies was the ban. Such prohibitions were nothing new to the GAA, which had from its foundation in 1884 forbidden its members to play or attend 'foreign' or 'garrison' games like soccer, rugby, and cricket.[91] Enforcement of that ban continued throughout our period, and with the closer links that developed between the GAA and the Gaelic League at the time, the League found itself, to the distress of some of its members, offering official support for the ban as a key defence of *Gaelachas*. Joint committees of Irish-Ireland societies were formed as early as 1927 'to consolidate the national forces', with all members of the Gaelic League expected to join the GAA and vice-versa, and members of both organisations committed to promoting Irish dancing (*Honesty*, 31/12/27). This alliance culminated at the Ard-Fheis (annual convention) of the League in Belfast in 1931, a meeting at which a resolution was passed that members who had any involvement with non-Gaelic games or dances could not serve on any League committees.

Many sincere activists felt such restrictions on personal choice were both necessary and beneficial. Joseph Hanly bordered on paranoia with regard to this topic in his 1931 book *The National Ideal*, writing:

> In our weakened and perilous condition, foreign games, foreign music, foreign dancing, foreign food and foreign clothing contribute, each in its own way, towards our permanent national enslavement, just as effectively as abandonment of the national language or wilful subordinated allegiance to a foreign power.[92]

P. J. Devlin sounded a similar note of alarm in the mid-1930s as he defended the GAA ban in his book *Our Native Games*:

> There has always been a conflict raging between native and alien ideals, and the policy of peaceful penetration has become more destructive of nationality than open aggression. Sinister influences, working on native weakness, have always been enticing men from the ranks of national endeavour, and these ranks must protect themselves.[93]

The provision of such protection might require extreme measures, a situation viewed with equanimity by the editor of *An Camán* in an April 1933 piece on 'Individual Liberty and False Broad-mindedness':

> The ideals aimed at by these organisations [i.e. the GAA and the Gaelic League] are the suppression of foreign games and foreign culture, to be supplanted by the native brand – the regeneration of a complete nationality. These issues are so broad that individual freedom within the organisations must be sacrificed in the interests of the principles at stake (*Camán*, 29/4/33).

This mindset was to spawn a shoal of motions, resolutions, and rules at meetings of the GAA and of the Gaelic League itself, all attempting to regulate the leisure pursuits of those in the movement. Particularly intrusive were bans on all foreign dances, affecting as they did both genders, rural and urban dwellers, and people of all ages and levels of physical fitness. Needless to say, advocates of these prohibitions were unmoved by appeals to personal liberty, preferring instead to stress duty to the national cause for which some had suffered so much. At the 1927 convention of the GAA in Tipperary, the organisation passed a resolution that Irish dances should hold 'premier place' at all social events organised by GAA clubs, and one representative went farther, calling it 'a terrible slur on the Irish people to see Irish boys and girls dancing imported dances from London, Paris, and Timbuctoo. It was a pity the men of Easter Week died for half of them.'[94] 'Lugha Lámha Fada' also appealed to history to drive home his point in a 1931 essay on 'Gaodhalú na h-Óige' (The Gaelicisation of the young) in the short-lived GAA periodical *An Ráitheachán*:

> Another thing you should not be involved with at all is foreign dances. We are all hard on Diarmuid Mac Murchadha because he is the one who invited the English to come to Ireland. We call him 'English Diarmuid', but the Irishman, no matter who he is, who favours foreign twitches and the customs of the English is another 'English Diarmuid' (*Ráitheachán*, Dec. 1936, 58).[95]

Such overblown rhetoric seems, however, to have repelled more people than it convinced. As early as March 1923, Seán Mac Eachainn, writing in *The Leader* on 'Sense, Nonsense and the Gaelic Ideal', was warning would-be

Gaels that cultural extremism would only marginalise the movement at just the moment a real re-Gaelicisation project could begin in earnest under a native government:

> The Gaelic League is rapidly becoming as academic and out-of-touch with the popular taste as the Royal Irish Academy. The average person regards the Gaelic League much as he regards the Total Abstinence Society or the Third Order of St Francis. He may want to learn some Irish, but he does not want to be tied down by vows to shut his ears to tickling foreign music or to sit with a long face when the band strikes up a one-step. Naturally, he comes to regard membership of the Gaelic League as a form of penance (*Leader*, 24/3/23).

In an essay in *The Land* two months later, 'M. J. Mac M.' expressed identical reservations about the mean-spirited dogmatism of influential voices within the League, writing of the organisation:

> To-day it is in danger of becoming a spent force before its work is completed. This is largely because it persists in maintaining a very rigid and narrow outlook . . . Cant of this sort must be ruthlessly swept away. Heaven knows we are very much on a par with other races, and if we do not keep ourselves free from demoralising imported influences by the strength of our national character, we shall certainly never do it by means of artificial barriers (*Land*, 12/5/23).[96]

This debate came to a head in the year or so before the League's 1932 Belfast Ard-Fheis. Leading the attack on the organisation's authoritarians was *The Star*, a paper that had often locked horns with republicans in the language movement, particularly during Ó Grianna's editorship of *Fáinne an Lae* in the late 1920s. In a blistering attack in March 1930 entitled 'Kilts and Jigs', the editor argued that it was now the job of the state to preserve and restore the language and that the League had, at any rate, made itself largely irrelevant:

> But a thing that talks even more definitely against it is the fact that it always was something of a breeding-ground for cranks. From an early stage it added to its language propaganda the policy of encouraging step-dancing, piping, Gaelic football and the wearing of kilts, and what have been called Queen Maeve costumes . . . The Gaelic League, as a result of the national importance with which it invested matters which were of no real consequence in themselves, developed in many of its members a peculiar outlook which made them aggressive, narrow, and self-righteous. That had its advantages when the supporters of the language were in the wilderness. Nowadays freakishness is something which should be avoided (*Star*, 29/3/30).[97]

In the same journal the following month, Liam Ó Rinn coined his 'Gaelachas na gCos' phrase and then went on to expose a mindset he found deeply disturbing:

> God gave us ten commandments and the Church gave us six, but God and the Church left us our free will . . . But the League had to go farther than God and the Church and therefore, after coming up with some other commandments for us, it decided to take our free will from us. 'Fulfil all these commandments or you will not be allowed to learn Irish' . . . A new kind of religion was established with Oliver Cromwell as invisible head of it! O holy Cromwell, pray for us so that we do not give in to the children of Beelzebub, that is, the children of Waltz, Fox-trot, Soccer, Rugby, Guinness, Power, Short Skirts, Beethoven, and Courting on the Stairs (*Star*, 19/4/30).[98]

Mac Giolla Bhríde (William Gibson, Lord Ashbourne), the aristocratic and cosmopolitan Protestant president of the League, provoked a good deal of controversy when he put the repudiation of such intolerance at the top of his agenda in the final year of his presidency in 1933. Speaking at a League *comhdháil* or conference in Spiddal, County Galway in May of that year, Mac Giolla Bhríde declared that the organisation's mission was 'to strengthen the mind of the people and instil in them the spirit of independence, and to do that by reviving our national language and putting it into effective use from one end of Ireland to the other.' However, he saw that work being undermined by the vocal fanaticism of some members: 'I notice that there is a danger that the League is becoming more restrictive every year. Motions are passed year after year against many things, and the amount of freedom left to League members grows less with each year' (*Tír*, May, 1933, 4).[99] In an interview with 'Cormac' in *An Tír*, Mac Giolla Bhríde said that while the League had once stood for Irish freedom, 'today anyone would think that the League was out to put an end to freedom altogether through the motions passed against this thing and that thing' (*Tír*, Aug. 1933, 3).[100]

'Cormac' himself was one of Mac Giolla Bhríde's strongest allies on this issue, writing in the Sept.–Oct. 1933 issue of *An Tír*:

> The majority of the Gaels are truly tired of that little group of people who can't do anything better than pass 'resolutions' and come up with 'rules', so that, through their 'motions' and 'rules' they have a way to keep people who are not in the League out of it and to expel people who are in the League (*Tír*, Sept.–Oct. 1933, 3).[101]

The threat to freedom was also very much on the mind of 'Labhraidh Loingseach', who in 1933 contributed an essay entitled '*Gaelachas* – a Hodge-podge' ('Gaedhealachas – Práchas') to *An t-Ultach* in which he wrote:

> The understanding some people have of *Gaelachas* is strange. If you don't do this, if you don't support that rule, if you do something like that, you are not a 'Gael', and you are not on the side of *Gaelachas*. I think that the Gaelic League has far too many rules . . . Gaelic Leaguers would like us to have a free and Gaelic country again: Thanks be to God that that is still an unfulfilled desire for them, or I would prefer to live somewhere else than in that free and Gaelic country, for I reckon there would be little freedom in it (*Ultach*, Aug. 1933, 5).[102]

Not surprisingly, these debates outlasted Mac Giolla Bhríde's presidency and continued to plague those who saw the obsession with marginal concerns dissipating the movement's vitality and appeal at a critical opportunity. In a 1935 piece in the *Irish Independent*, Risteárd Breathnach lamented the inability of Irish-Irelanders to focus on the real challenges facing them and wrote of the language:

> It must be shown that it doesn't belong to one group rather than another; that people who play rugby have as much right to it as people who play Gaelic football; that it can be spoken at a dance as well as at a céilí [Gaelic dance] – in a word, that it is the language of the Gaelic nation, and no one has the right to say who will speak or who will cultivate it (*II*, 25/6/35).[103]

Francis Shaw, the future Jesuit and Celtic scholar, shared this concern in a lecture to members of the Literary and Historical Society at University College Dublin:

> Historical Gaelic culture was substantially free from narrow insularity, was broadminded, tolerant, and liberal. The modern movement was largely concerned with matters which, if they had anything to do with culture, were but on its fringe – games, dancing, and other amusements. The modern Gael failed to take into account that if Gaelic culture had not been interrupted, Gaels of the present day, in their way of life and thought, would resemble far more Irishmen of to-day than they would Irishmen of the sixteenth century (*II*, 30/1/36).

More than a few Irish-Irelanders were, however, worried about just what might get in if the doors of the movement were left open and unguarded. In a June 1938 piece on the GAA ban and Gaelic League support for it, 'Osruidhe' wrote:

> The worst thing is the amount of nonsensical talk about something that isn't worth a straw, all of that talk of course through the English that we are all supposedly so sick of, while the people who don't care about the Irish language and all it involves mock the Gaels (*Leader*, 4/6/38).[104]

These intra-Gaelic disputes were not always all that amusing. Many in the movement may have been troubled by the obsession with 'national' pastimes like sports or dancing, but outsiders, whether sympathetic or sceptical, were more likely to be scandalised and even disgusted by the hatred of things 'foreign' that motivated that fixation and prompted an outburst like the one that follows from 'Cimarron' in 1933:

> The civilisation that dominates Irish life is diseased. It is foreign. Gomorrah-like. Miasmal. The antithesis of everything Gaelic. Everything truthful. Everything manly. Tumble it down. To-morrow. Seize and maintain that mood of revolt. Interpret it in action (*An Phoblacht*, 30/12/33).

Nothing seemed more 'Gomorrah-like' or 'miasmal' to cultural nationalists than did jazz, denunciations of which were regular throughout our period. Jazz was the target of one of the League's 1933 resolutions, when the organisation's executive committee unanimously approved Peadar Ó Máille's motion that the national radio station be censured for broadcasting any jazz at all, since such music was 'against Christianity, against learning, and against the spirit of nationality' (i gcoinnibh Críostuidheachta, i gcoinnibh léighinn agus i gcoinnibh spiorad na náisiúntachta) (*Camán*, 16/12/33). The following year, Mohill, County Leitrim started an aggressive campaign against jazz, in which the local Gaelic League branch took the lead, inspiring an anonymous rhymester to write 'Follow the Lead of Mohill', which began: 'Unnatural syncopation has got into the people's feet, / And disturbed the soothing rhythm of an Irish-Ireland beat' (*Camán*, 13/1/34).[105]

Most of the criticisms of jazz by Irish-Irelanders did not, however, focus on the aesthetic aspects of the new music.[106] Instead, jazz was rejected on cultural, moral, and racial / racist grounds as 'the music you would hear at a cattle show' (an gleo a chluinfeá ag taisbeántas eallaigh) (*Ultach*, June 1927, 1); 'the frenzied music of blacks and pagans' (ceol mire na ndubhach agus na bpágánach) (*Tír*, June 1928, 4); 'weird tribal dances' from 'darkest Africa' (*IC*, 24/2/34); 'the negroid wrigglings and insipid croonings which are part of the jazz germ's deadly work' (*Camán*, 28/4/34); '"hot nigger jazz", a perverted, decadent music, a music far more appropriate . . . for a debauched, thieving, wanton nation than for the Irish nation' (saobhcheol meathta, ceol gur oireamhnaighe go mórfhada . . . do náisiún ainsriantaidhe, bradach, gáirseamhala ná do náisiún na hÉireann) (*AA*, Nov. 1935, 3); 'that timehonoured pastime of the niggers and jungle natives' (Dundalk *Examiner*, 23/4/38); or 'a reversion to unbridled paganism' (*Gaedheal*, 2/2/35). The accompanying dances were, if possible, worse: 'jungle and pagan dances to jazz music' (*Honesty*, 28/12/29); 'the barbaric dance of the black pagans of Africa' (damhsa bharbardha Phágánach dubh na h-Aifrice) (*Ultach*, Mar. 1928, 5); 'nigger dances' (*II*

24/8/28); 'vulgar and suggestive importations' (*Camán*, 21/1/33); 'nigger importations, which are certainly more flesh than spirit or art' (*CS*, 26/5/31). In *An Chearnóg* in February 1924, 'Mac Dara' said the foreign dances and music, 'impure, obscene dances, and music that was composed in Hell' (damhsaidhe neamhghlana, gársamhla, agus ceól a ceapadh i n-Ifrinn), were the best example he could find of the sorry state of the nation's culture, adding: 'If the mothers of the country knew what a foreign dance was, they would prefer to see their daughters stretched out dead at their feet before they would allow them to go into a place like that.' For this writer, jazz dances were not just a sin against God, but a crime 'against the Gaelic mind and against the Irish soul that Pearse died to save' (in aghaidh an intinn Ghaedhealaigh, agus in aghaidh anam na h-Éireann a fuair an Piarsach bás le n'a shábháil) (*An Chearnóg*, Feb. 1924, 4).[107] Writing in 1928 in *The Leader*, 'Sagart' painted an even more lurid picture of 'dance-halls all over the land where the semi-nude children of the martyrs jazz till the small hours of the morning' (*Leader*, 28/4/28).

It should be obvious from the number and nature of these denunciations that jazz, however noxious, was only a conspicuous symptom of an even more insidious disease. In a 1932 essay on 'The Secret Ireland', the editor of *Outlook* wrote:

> On the one hand is jazz and jazzy infidelity, on the other is the rural life, austerity, and the Gaelic ideal. Now, the one belongs to a decadent Pagan civilisation. The other receives its form from Catholic civilisation and it seems to us that Catholic civilisation cannot revive if all its works in Ireland are abandoned (*Outlook*, 19/3/32).

This intimate link between *Gaelachas* and Roman Catholicism will be examined in greater detail below, but first we need to get a better sense of the worldview the Gaels believed jazz to represent.

In a January 1925 essay in the short-lived Cork monthly *An Birín Beó*, W. F. Stockley asserted:

> The Irish language is to be the uniting power in an Ireland that is not composed of jazz barbarians, cinema loafers, sniggerers who have not the brains to be anything, and all the riff-raff who think they are English, up-to-date, and who are beneath the notice of the English that count (*Birín Beó*, Jan. 1925, 8).[108]

Seán Ua Ceallaigh reminded readers of *An Camán* in a front-page editorial in 1934 supporting the Leitrim anti-jazz crusade that jazz was just one aspect of a much larger threat, writing:

> The jazz ague is but part of the decadent imperial epoch, and in fighting against one of the poisoned tentacles of imperialism we can only hope to succeed

> ultimately and completely by destroying the imperial monster itself. Fight jazz because it is pagan, but remember that jazz has many allies in other forms of pagan influence, not the least of which is that craven, serf-like spirit inherent in the anti-Irish Irishman (*Camán*, 6/1/34).[109]

And at the very end of our period, 'S. Ó M.' sounded an apocalyptic note in the University College Galway annual *An t-Irisleabhar* for 1939–40: 'I nevertheless think that it will be an admission by the people of Ireland themselves that their time as a nation is past the day they are always out for "jazz" and "swing" and the like' (*Irisleabhar*, 1939–40, 31).[110]

In one of the many diatribes against jazz, this one by 'Delta' in the *Irish Rosary* in 1927, anti-semitism took its place beside racism in the author's mind: 'The character of this jazz music is faithfully reflected in the jazz dances, which seem to have been borrowed or adopted from the negroes and popularised by the Jews' (*IR*, Feb. 1927, 155). This journal, run by the Dominican Order, provided a forum for anti-Semites on several occasions in our period, and unfortunately this attitude was not a nasty idiosyncrasy of one religious magazine. In the London Gaelic periodical *Guth na nGaedheal* in 1923, Edward Lynam wrote ominously in his essay 'An Island Race':

> Now far more than ever she was before, Ireland is accessible, and even attractive, to immigrants, – immigrants of the undesirable kind, and a steady though quiet migration from eastern Europe to the north and west has been going on for four years, and will increase (*Guth na nGaedheal*, 1923, 15).

In a 1934 letter to *An t-Éireannach*, an anonymous correspondent used this issue of Jewish immigration to invoke traditional stereotypes and to play on nationalist concerns about contemporary popular amusements:

> Since Jews were expelled from Germany, they have come to this country in droves, and now there are thousands of them in Dublin, and not only are they there but they have a firm grip on much of the commerce and many of the shops. They own almost all the theatres and the cinemas (*Éireannach*, 8/12/34).[111]

The most disturbing example of anti-semitism within the language movement itself is the essay in the scholarly Gaelic journal *Humanitas* by the then nineteen-year-old Cearbhall Ua Dálaigh, a future Chief Justice and President of Ireland and member of the European Court. Writing of the Nazi youth movement, Ua Dálaigh stated: 'They want to smash forever the power of the Jews and the power of the Americans; they want Germany to be a stronghold and a beacon of knowledge between America and Asia . . . What the German wants, he gets' (*Humanitas*, Mar. 1930, 26–8).[112]

If the crude racism and anti-semitism of some in the Irish-Ireland movement was very much an ugly sign of the times throughout the world, Gaelic attitudes towards women, as given explicit expression in words, were more specific to post-independence Ireland. After the significant and often highly visible participation of women like Maud Gonne, Constance Markievicz, and Helena Moloney in the armed struggle, and Norma Borthwick, Mary Butler, Éibhlín Nic Niocaill and Úna Ní Fhaircheallaigh (Agnes O'Farrelly) in the language movement, women were much less involved in Irish public life after the founding of the state. Indeed, as has been pointed out by several scholars, one of the chief roles allotted them was as the mother, wife, or sister of martyred rebels, roles occupied, for example, by Mrs Pearse, Mrs Thomas Clarke, and Mary MacSwiney respectively.[113] This development, one that was to culminate in de Valera's new constitution of 1937, was, of course, the result of conscious decisions by those in power, particularly the veteran Gaelic activist de Valera himself, rather than of any natural or logical evolution. Several influential Irish-Irelanders turned their minds and pens to the question of women's place in a new Gaelic order during the years leading up to the 1937 constitution. In his 1923 book *The Gaelic Commonwealth: Being the Political and Economic Programme for the Irish Progressive Party*, William Ferris, a chaplain in the Free State Army, wrote: 'In normal times, when men are not afraid to be manly, the first duty of a woman is to be womanly and both by word and example to prevent her weaker sisters from being unsexed either politically or industrially.' Apparently, one powerful 'unsexing' agent was the vote, a right promised women in the Easter 1916 Proclamation of the Irish Republic. According to Ferris, 'It is most undemocratic that Irish womanhood should be dragged into the turmoil of politics without being in any way consulted about it. The women of Ireland should hold a referendum as to whether or not they wish to have the franchise foisted upon them.'[114]

One important Gaelic writer who had given the matter a great deal of thought was Father Patrick Dinneen. Among his papers in the National Library of Ireland is a lengthy essay in English on the rights, and more particularly the duties, of women. The essay, labelled by the Library 'Queen of the Hearth – essay on womanhood in fifteen sections' – is undated, but was written after the First World War. Dinneen died in 1932. Excerpts from this unpublished piece make clear how much de Valera's Constitution was a document of its time and place. Dinneen stressed that

> the hearth and not the public platform is the proper sphere of woman's labours and the proper scene of her triumphs. Therefore, we must . . . regard the Parliamentary franchise as a step in a direction full of danger and which it would be difficult to retrace . . . Woman warms to the hearth by the fervour of her spirit she grows chill in the atmosphere of Parliament or the polling booth . . . She is the queen of the hearth but a perturbed and perturbing spirit in the arena of public debate.[115]

Not surprisingly then, Dinneen saw little need for women to pursue higher degrees: 'Women are not intended by nature for the prolonged study of serious subjects and if they violate nature's laws they must pay the penalty.'[116] Again anticipating de Valera's Constitution, Dinneen declared:

> External duties which even remotely tend to draw the mother from her true empire, the hearth, should be regarded with suspicion . . . The dignity and responsibility of motherhood in the family should belong to one who is free from external cares and wholly devoted to her domestic duties.[117]

Doubtless aware that many women at the time, even those most devoted to hearth and family, might find his argument as flawed as his rhetoric was condescending, Dinneen went on the offensive in his section on 'The Spirit of Rivalry':

> But we have an instinctive loathing for a plague of pseudo-Amazonian fury. We detest the race of pygmy martial women that jostle us in the streets, that make night hideous with their brawls, that violate the sacred sanctity of home life, that engage in unequal contests with men. With [*sic*] shrink with horror from the unsexed woman.[118]

De Valera's Constitution, approved by Dáil Éireann on 14 June 1937 and by the people of the Free State in plebiscite on 1 July 1937, took effect on 29 December 1937. It would have pleased Father Dinneen. In the first section of Article 40, all citizens, 'as human persons', are guaranteed equality before the law, but the section continues: 'This shall not be held to mean that the State shall not in its enactments have due regard to differences of capacity, physical and moral, and of social function.' 'Social function' was the crux here, as becomes evident in Article 41, that dealing with the family. Section 2 of that article reads as if it had been written by Dinneen: 'In particular, the State recognises that by her life within the home, woman gives to the State a support without which the common good cannot be achieved.' Section 2 continues: 'The State shall, therefore, endeavour to ensure that mothers shall not be obliged by economic necessity to engage in labour to the neglect of their duties in the home.'[119]

In the very month the people went to the polls to approve or reject the Constitution, Aodh de Blácam praised the vision from which de Valera's document had evolved in an essay in the *Irish Rosary*, lauding 'Gaelic culture as the effective channel of Catholic wisdom in society':

> Above all we have the parochial life which safeguards nations. Never let it be broken up by high industrialism, the unemployment of masses of workers by

anonymous and soulless companies, or the transference of young womanhood from the home to a degrading machine-room (*IR*, July 1937, 529).

That de Valera's views were believed to have the sanction of a higher law is evident from the 1938 book *Teagasc Morálta na h-Eaglaise* (The moral teaching of the church) by An tAthair Pádraig Mac Giolla Cheara, who, in his section on the fourth commandment, wrote: 'Although women are allowed to work and hold jobs outside the house, the duty imposed on them by natural law is to look after the housework and to care for the children.'[120]

Terence Brown has argued that in the first decades of independence Irish-Irelanders employed as 'an ideological weapon' what he terms 'the vision of national fragility'.[121] This vision was given its most explicit contemporary expression by Tomás Ó Deirg in a 1936 lecture to the Catholic Truth Society in Tuam, County Galway: 'We are just a small race of people, four million of us or so, cast onto a little island out in the middle of the great sea with hundreds of millions of English speakers on all sides of us' (*CS*, 30/6/36).[122] We have seen above how concern about jazz, cinema, paganism, distant and never-to-be-seen Africans,[123] and persecuted refugee Jews could degenerate into paranoia about the very survival of a distinct Gaelic culture. For many Gaels, the world was a very scary place, one in which eternal vigilance was mandatory. At times, that vigilance gave rise to associations pledged to identify, expose, and expel corrupting agents from abroad. The most notable of such organisations, ones that pre-dated the foundation of the state, were the various vigilance societies set up to fight 'evil' literature. Concern about pernicious reading matter seems, if anything, to have grown among many sections of the Irish population after independence, doubtless because it was felt that now something concrete and effective could be done about it. Few Irish periodicals of the time failed to denounce 'imported, denationalising filth' (*Leader*, 11/2/28); 'feasts of filth and unashamed parades of profligacy' (*Honesty*, 16/5/25); 'dirty, rotten things that give off a foul stench' (rudaí salacha lobhtha a bhfuil boladh bréan asta) (*FL*, June 1928, 7); 'poisonous literary rubbish imported from abroad' (*IR*, Mar. 1925, 232); 'this trashy, noxious, and demoralising reading matter' (*Leader*, 9/3/29); 'the rubbish and filth of a foreign tongue' (drabhfhuigheall agus salachar teangan iasachta) (*FL*, 4/7/25). As might be expected, Catholic periodicals were prominent in this crusade against bad books and papers, with the *Irish Rosary*, run by the Dominicans, who had founded Ireland's first vigilance society in 1911, taking the leading role.

By no means, however, was the Catholic press exceptional in its concern about questionable reading matter, especially that imported from England. Fulminations against such publications were a staple in *The Leader* throughout our period, with the most frequent contributor on the topic being Father Dinneen, who wrote in March 1922:

> There is no bad knowledge like knowledge of bad reading, for it is possible to read bad books without anyone knowing, and those kinds of books are plentiful around us, and it is not just the books that are bad, some of the papers are as well, especially some of the weekly papers (*Leader*, 4/3/22).[124]

Another contributor to *The Leader* who shared this perspective was 'Dromard', who in May 1928 conjured up a powerful image from the Irish past to condemn such 'literature:'

> The new Soupers are the imported papers. Taking advantage of the division in the national ranks as their predecessors took advantage of the Famine, they are pushing themselves into Catholic homes throughout the country (*Leader*, 19/5/28).

One 'Corcasiensis', identified as 'a well-known clergyman', linked the purveyors of questionable literature with a more recent set of English villains: 'Long ago this damnable flood of filth should have been excluded. What is it, but the Black and Tans in a more insidious guise? Shall we be silent while our Queen of high romance is robbed of the proud jewel of morality?' (*II*, 10/7/26).[125]

For those in the language movement itself, the emphasis tended to be on the linguistic / cultural rather than the denominational / moral aspect of this threat from imported publications. For example, when in June 1928 Séamus Ó Grianna weighed in on the issue with an essay on 'Droch-Litridheacht' (Evil literature), he stressed the Englishness rather than the paganism (or Protestantism!) of the imports:

> We have the English language. We had great respect for it. Now we are lamenting the state to which it is bringing us . . . Tone, God's blessing on his soul, said that England was the source of all evil in Ireland. As long as we have respect for England and the language of England, we might as well try to kindle a fire with water as think that we could turn our backs on bad writings (*FL*, June 1928, 7).[126]

Ironically, Ó Grianna was forced to defend himself against a charge by 'Niamh Cinn Óir' and 'A. Ó D.' that a story about a spoiled priest in his collection *Cioth is Dealán* would, in the words of 'Niamh', drive 'the noble Gaelic thoughts' (na smaointe uaisle Gaedhealacha) from a reader's mind (*Ultach*, June 1927, 3). In a vigorous defence, Ó Grianna said that not only did priests and nuns read his work with pleasure, but he himself had read it aloud to his mother on the advice of a priest who had told him 'if there is a word or a line or a page in it that you would feel diffidence or shame about reading to her, draw the blue pencil through it' (*Ultach*, Lá Fhéil Eoin, 2).[127]

Fortunately, not all interested in writing in Irish at the time saw Ó Grianna's mother as the court of infallible final appeal on questions of faith, morals, and literary accomplishment. Pádraic Ó Conaire had, of course, long insisted on the necessity for imaginative and creative freedom for the writer, a cause he continued to champion in our period in essays like 'Writers under the Free State' (Lucht Peann faoin Saorstát), 'Books and a Way to Get Them' (Leabhra agus Bealach lena bhFagháil), and, most notably, 'Truth and Falsehood in Literature' (An Fhírinne agus an Bhréag sa Litridheacht). Among his allies at the time was Donn Piatt, who wrote in 1929:

> The person who sets out to be a writer in Ireland must have leave to examine and tell the naked truth. Let him not avoid the ugly thing, if it is necessary to examine it . . . In a word, let the writer always tell the truth about the Irish no matter how bitter it is. But don't let the truth cause him to lose hope. To be human is to be flawed. The Irish are human beings. They have all the evil inclinations of the human being and all the good qualities of the human being (*Ultach*, June 1929, 5).[128]

The fact that many in Ireland at the time, and later, did not wish to face this fact, and that they often saw little difference between objectionable books and periodicals and challenging works of literature, was, of course, what made the question of censorship so contentious from the earliest days of the state.[129] It was the Catholic press, and most forcefully the *Irish Rosary*, that once again took the lead in urging the state to provide a legislative barrier to what they had so long denounced as a 'flood' of evil imported publications. The more intemperate, D. P. Moran among them, urged concerned citizens to take more direct action and applauded when they did so.[130] In a February 1927 editorial in the *Irish Homeland*, we read:

> We are glad to note that in several centres, piles of imported filthy papers have been seized and burned. We hope it may not long be necessary to have such action taken by groups of citizens, and that the import of such vile rags shall be prohibited by law. But until the law is in existence, we hope that responsible Catholics will take every step necessary to save our youth from the blighting, degrading influence of foreign corruption (*Irish Homeland*, Feb. 1927, 2).

The editor returned to the subject a few months later: 'It is unfortunate, indeed regrettable, that people of this land who wish to save their children from the direct and indirect evil of filthy imported papers are forced to contravene the civil code, but we would ask who is responsible?' (*Irish Homeland*, June 1927, 1).

While the focus on morality is hardly surprising in the passages cited above, the lack of any serious or sustained interest in the cultural and especially the linguistic implications of widespread Irish consumption of imported reading material is striking. There were, however, exceptions to this trend. In a 1925 editorial on 'Dríodar Léightheoireachta' (Trashy reading) in the *Irish Independent*, the author argued that language activists should take a particular interest in the movement to ban objectionable publications:

> For the relationship between the two causes is so close that they should proceed together as allies. However successful the new movement is, the more suitable will be the soil for the propagation of the Irish language. And, on the other hand, the Irish language is the best protective barrier – we won't say the only protective barrier – that in the end keeps us safe against this destructive flood that is threatening the mind of the nation (*II*, 2/5/26).[131]

John O'Toole agreed, explicitly linking language and morals in his June 1926 essay 'The Battle with Bad Books' in the *Irish Tribune*:

> There would not seem much meaning in the restoration of the Gaelic language to a godless, secular people. Our long Past since St Patrick's time would seem meaningless to a neo-pagan set of folk who felt no spiritual connection with it. Friends of the language, then, should be more earnest than all others in organising resistance to the tide of bad writings (*Irish Tribune*, 8/6/26).

On the whole, those involved with the language movement, however earnest or committed to their faith, did not play a disproportionately prominent role in the organised resistance to bad literature or in the organised pressure for state censorship.[132] For example, while Father Lawrence Murray could write in *An t-Ultach* in 1928 that the government should avail itself of the emotion aroused by the murder of the Free State Justice Minister Kevin O'Higgins to pass a censorship bill,[133] Shán Ó Cuív had argued more dispassionately in an editorial in *Fáinne an Lae* two years before that censorship was a tricky proposition. Ó Cuív believed there was a need to enact a law 'to prohibit the sale of the rubbish that comes in to us from England daily' (chun cosc a chur le díol an drabhaíl a thagann isteach chughainn ó Shasana i n-aghaidh an lae), but warned of the potentially deleterious consequences of such legislation: 'That is an old question that has been debated for years, but it is difficult to come up with a word that would prohibit printed filth and that would not prohibit other printing at the same time' (*FL*, 20/2/26).[134] An exception to this trend was Pádhraic Ó Domhnalláin, who in an editorial in *Fáinne an Lae* in 1924, seemed to find reading itself the problem:

> The Irish people were wiser and more discerning when they were reading only a few books – and those few good. That and their own folklore . . . sustained them so that they were the better for it and so that its effect on them was obvious as a result.

He then urged that close attention be paid to the books Irish schoolchildren were reading: 'It seems to us that the sifter must be used on many of the textbooks that are in use in the schools of Ireland at present. Who would say that many of the ones available are suitable for young Gaels?' (*FL*, 8/11/24).[135]

The idea that language would be far more efficacious than law was, however, the preferred position of Irish-Irelanders in the debate about how best to defend the country's moral, intellectual, and cultural borders against assault from abroad. There was nothing new in this idea. The belief in the language as a protective barrier against outside threats had been advanced by writers as different as An tAthair Peadar Ua Laoghaire and Pádraic Ó Conaire in the years leading up to independence. Now, however, with native control of the educational system and all the rest of the state apparatus, language activists and other Irish-Irelanders felt that they had the opportunity to construct that sheltering wall of words. In an essay on 'Dangerous Reading – Some Remedies' in *Iris an Ghárda* in October 1923, the Lazarist priest Father J. S. Sheehy wrote:

> I have one great and comprehensive means to suggest, in conclusion, as a rampart against all this vile writing of our day . . . All this wretched literature is dumped on the shores of Ireland by stepsister England. It is done with ease; because, alas, we are almost anglicised – many of us, I fear, completely so. All of us who have the energy, especially the young – ought to study the 'Dear old Tongue' which enshrines the mind and soul of Ireland, as it is the most manifest and effective expression of Irish Nationality (*Iris an Ghárda*, 15/10/23).

Writing in *Irisleabhar Muighe Nuadhad* the following year, Liam Ó Liatháin said geography offered no hope for Ireland; rather 'the Irish language is the only protective shield we have, the only rampart against the enemy. Even America, however great its power, is part of the English Empire. For it has no culture except the culture of the English' (*IMN*, 1924, 9).[136]

Some in the movement wanted the linguistic wall to be very high and very thick, agreeing with 'Pot Still', who wrote in 1926: 'We, Irish, need to be so desperately in earnest to save our language that we have no room in our affections nor in our tastes for anything aesthetically or artistically foreign' (*Leader*, 27/11/26). Arguing for the negative in a 1930 debate in *An Tír* on the motion that Gaels were 'too provincial in the outlook they had on the affairs of the world, and that they would be better off if they took more interest in what the other nations of the world had to teach' (ró-oileánach sa dearcadh bhí aca ar chúrsaí an tsaoghail, agus go mb'fheairrde iad dá gcuiridís breis suime sa teagasc atá le fáil ó náisiúin eile an domhain), Seosamh Mac Cormaic asked:

> What does Europe have to offer us that we do not already have? . . . We have often been accused of being too insular, too narrow-minded, of not wanting to have any

viewpoint on things outside the four corners of Ireland. But if that was so, what did we lose as a result of that? Even if we did remain insular, we are far better off for it, for we succeeded in avoiding the pagan civilisation of the continent (*Tír*, May 1930, 8).[137]

As we saw in the introduction to this book, there were, however, many Gaels who knew that the lessons to be learned from the world outside – even from Britain – were not invariably pagan or pernicious. Moreover, those in the movement interested in the richer aspects of European and world culture and eager for their compatriots to experience them were quite properly concerned about the willingness – even eagerness – of some nativists to dig and hide in linguistic bunkers, in the process compelling their fellow citizens to take shelter from what they may not have even perceived as a threat. This concern was given memorable expression by James Devane in his 1937 book *Isle of Destiny: The Clash of Cultures*, where he warned:

> It is not improbable that there will develop in the Irish Free State a racial culture – soured and embittered by a fanatical mission to reconstruct a purely native civilisation out of the Gaeltacht, spurning the great pagan cultures and the noble secular culture of Christian Europe, and on the religious side maintaining an insular, ultramontane Jansenist Catholicism, with none of the glow and warmth of the great Catholic tradition of Europe.[138]

On the other hand, Seoirse Mac Niocaill, while aware that such charges were being advanced by enemies of the movement, felt they were groundless, telling a Gaelic League audience in Dublin in 1925 that

> English had shut them out from European culture – it had been the greatest barrier between them and the moving life-thought of Europe that ever existed. By the aid of Irish, which was full of life, and vigour, and energy, we had the finest opportunity that any of the European nations ever had in placing ourselves in the very forefront of European culture, life, and activity (*II*, 28/10/25).[139]

Gárda Superintendent Éamonn Ó Ríoghardáin was of like mind, writing in the *Garda Review* in January 1934:

> The revival of the Irish language we are very often told, will erect a barricade between ourselves and the outside world, and will cut us off from the culture and civilisation of Europe. The answer to this contention is to be seen in every country in Europe which possesses a language of its own. The history of our own country contradicts it in unmistakable terms. The Irish-speaking Ireland of the seventeenth and eighteenth centuries was in much more vital and intimate contact with the continent of Europe than the English-speaking Ireland of the nineteenth and twentieth centuries (*GR*, Jan. 1934, 221).[140]

This kind of confident openness to the outside world may explain why language activists seem, in general, to have been considerably less worried about Communism than were many of their compatriots, people like Capt. Francis Mac Cullagh, who, in a 1933 essay, told how 'the baleful glare of the blood-red comet of Paganism . . . turns crimson the illimitable snows of Muscovy' (*CA*, 1933, 225–32). Typical of a more confident Gaelic attitude was an essay by 'Cormac' that appeared in 1933 in *An Tír*: 'The people of Ireland never yielded to England in matters of religion; they will not now yield to the anti-Christian philosophy of Russia' (*Tír*, Apr. 1933, 6).[141] Indeed, the most vociferous Gaelic critic of 'Bolshevism' was the idiosyncratic 'Dr Panini', who wrote in the introduction to his *Irish Up-to-Date / Eeris (Eire + is)*:

> An educated Catholic democracy, not necessarily a Gaelic-speaking democracy, will prove a real barrier against Bolshevism, etc., which love [sic] the darkness of ignorance. Bolshevism propagates ideas which by its methods of propaganda can easily overcome the language barrier, but which find effective resistance alone in minds trained to think.

He followed this statement with a list of 'imperfect mediums, etc.' in the Irish language as spoken that kept people from clear thinking and thus susceptible to Communist infiltration![142]

Several far more influential language activists took a moderate and balanced approach to the Soviet system, as did, for example, Shán Ó Cuív, who wrote in his essay 'An Saol sa Rúis' (Life in Russia) that

> Russia is no heaven on earth, but rather an ordinary country in which people have to live like people in every other country, and not every change that has occurred for the past while has been a change that benefited the people.[143]

Liam Ó Rinn was more sympathetic with the Russians in the preface to *Dánta Próis* (Prose poems), his book of translations from Turgenev. Ó Rinn began by noting the existence of 'certain people who have accepted the sanctity of private property as a principle and who therefore hate the attempt being made by the people of Russia to manage their own affairs contrary to that principle'. He saw such people trying to convince others 'that the people of Russia are semi-barbarians' (gur daoine leath-bharbartha na Rúiseánuigh).[144] Ó Rinn's concern about the arrogance of some capitalists was shared by others in the language movement, for whom soulless materialism was the real enemy, whether clad in Communist or capitalist ideology. For example, in his essay 'De Theoranta na Sochaidheachta' (Concerning the Limits of Socialism), the Jesuit Micheál Mac Craith acknowledged the abuses of 'the system of private / selfish industry' (cogairse tionnscail na leithileach) and continued:

> Every day the ordinary people are being made aware how necessary it is to put restrictions on the very wealthy so that it can be said without fear not only do the people not want general socialism, but that they do not need even a partial form of socialism.[145]

The one outside influence that virtually no one in the language movement wanted to bar from the country was that of the 'Holy Catholic Apostolic and Roman Church . . . the guardian of the Faith professed by the great majority of the citizens', as de Valera put it in Article 44, section 2 of the 1937 Constitution that recognised 'the special position' of that church.[146] A central tenet of the linguistic and cultural faith of many was that Catholicism and *Gaelachas* were inextricably intertwined in the Irish character.[147] In an anonymous 1923 essay in *Irisleabhar Muighe Nuadhad*, the author felt the point was almost too obvious to need development:

> The intimate connection between the Irish language and the faith is clear to everyone, and therefore there is no need to refer to that question. If the language goes, the faith will be in danger. The spirit of infidelity is in the English language (*IMN*, 1923, 61).[148]

Writing the following year in the *Mungret Annual*, the journal of the Jesuit secondary school of that name, An tAthair Gearóid Ó Nualláin expanded on this idea in an exegetical essay on the Gospel of John:

> Esteem for the Faith, respect for the Virgin Mary, reverence for Saint Patrick, love for Jesus Christ – all of these things are in the Irish language; they are firmly interwoven, tightly wrapped up and bred into the spirit of the Irish language. But the English language involves altogether different qualities.

He then laid out the stark consequences of his argument:

> An Irishman, however excellent, who does not support the Irish language is supporting the English. It is clear to the world that the Englishman is against God and against the Faith, so that the Irishman who acts like an Englishman must either be blind or an enemy of the Faith and of the God of Glory (*Mungret Annual*, 1924, 154).[149]

For 'T. Ó R.' (probably Toirdhealbhach Ó Raithbheartaigh), *Gaelachas* and Catholicism were, as cultural terms, synonomous: 'If a new literature is to be written in Ireland, to be true literature it must be Gaelic. That is the same as saying that it must be Catholic' (*Ultach*, Dec. 1927, 7).[150] In an editorial in the 1933–4 issue of University College Galway's *University Annual*, Éamon de

Bhaldraithe went so far as to imply that only Catholics could be true Irishmen, never mind Gaels:

> Even in Ireland, it is now necessary to show clearly where we stand. We should not hesitate to do so, or to point out to those not so sure, and to others who think differently that we are first of all Catholics and Irishmen afterwards, and that we have no use for those who think otherwise however good Irishmen they may claim themselves to be (*University Annual*, 1933–4, 12).

It was the celebration of two events of enormous importance to Irish Catholics that inspired some of the most fervent expressions of this belief that Gaelic culture was inherently Catholic. The first was the centenary of Catholic Emancipation in 1929, an occasion that prompted the following reflection by Feargal Mac an Bháird in *An Tír*:

> It was the Irish language, after the grace of God, that was the strongest ally that the Faith had after the defeat of the Gaels . . . The language is a protective shield for the Faith and for Nationality. Ireland would probably not be a Catholic country today were it not for the Irish language. It is the Irish language that has fired the spirit of the Faith in the hearts of the Gaels for fifteen hundred years and that will keep that Faith strong and powerful as long as a word of that language is spoken in Ireland (*Tír*, July 1929, 16).[151]

The second event was even more stirring because of its international significance. The year 1932 marked the 1500th anniversary of the traditional date of the start of St Patrick's mission to Ireland, and the Church decided to celebrate the event by holding the Eucharistic Congress in Dublin that year. Irish Catholics seized on the occasion not only to demonstrate their unflagging loyalty to Rome, but also to take their place on the world stage as citizens of a newly independent Catholic state. For Catholics involved in the language movement, it was also essential that their co-religionists from around the globe be made aware of the culture that validated that independence, a culture they saw as permeated by Catholicism for a millenium and a half. Muiris Mag Uidhir felt the Gaels had successfully made the point during the Congress, writing in an essay entitled 'Ainm na hÉireann i nAirde i Measc Náisiún an Domhain' (The name of Ireland exalted among the nations of the world):

> The whole world now knows that Ireland is a Catholic country, and that it is a country that has its own national language, a language that was spoken at all times to praise and give thanks to God . . . There is no danger to the Faith in Ireland if the Irish language survives safe (*Tír*, July 1932, 1).[152]

More succinct was Riobárd Ó Faracháin in a 1932 essay on 'An Creideamh i gCúrsaí Litridheachta' (The faith in literary matters): 'But I will not finish this essay without saying this: let us remember that the most Gaelic part of our mind is the part in which Catholicism is most intense' (*Outlook*, 23/1/32).[153]

For several important Gaelic writers, this link between language and creed was a central theme in their life and work. Art Ó Riain, one of the two winners of An Gúm's 1931 prize for a novel, has the pious protagonist of *Lucht Ceoil* say to a German friend: 'Remember that the faith is so intimately interwoven in the life of the Gaels that it would not be possible for it not to be found in everything they do.'[154] This note is sounded even more strongly in his 1926 story 'Radharc na Fírinne' (A vision of the truth), reprinted in his 1927 collection *An Tost agus Scéalta Eile* (The silence and other stories), a collection of which 'P. de B.' (probably Pádraig de Brún) wrote in his review for *Irisleabhar Muighe Nuadhat*:

> There is one trait for which I would like to offer him special congratulations, and that is the way he has woven Catholic philosophy into the stories . . . We find this especially welcome because it has been brought roughly to our attention of late that there is a danger of the new literature in Irish being immersed in the trough of squalor because of its following the slippery trail of the English language (*IMN*, 1928, 97).[155]

Seán Ó Ruadháin, who shared the prize with Ó Riain, offered his most fervent endorsement of the link between Irish and Catholicism in the 1940 issue of *Irisleabhar Chnuic Mhuire / Knock Shrine Annual*: 'There is probably no other living language with which piety and faith are more involved than with Irish as it is spoken daily' (*Irisleabhar Chnuic Mhuire*, 1940, 98).[156] This theme underlies much of his prize novel *Pádhraic Mháire Bhán, nó an Gol agus an Gáire* (Pádhraic Mháire Bhán, or weeping and laughter):

> But the Gael has one inheritance that he himself does not understand, and that is strong faith and firm hope. Anyone who has that is rich although it be his lot in life to go from house to house seeking alms, and the person without it . . . may the God of Glory help him.[157]

Séamus Mac Conmara, a young seminarian who died at the age of 27 in 1936, was the winner of another important Gaelic prize, Duais an Chraoibhín, for his posthumously published 1939 novel *An Coimhthigheach* (The stranger). Not surprisingly for a language activist who was also a student for the priesthood, Mac Conmara was emphatic that Irish was a language that over the centuries had been molded into a medium specifically and singularly Catholic. He devoted an entire 1933 essay entitled 'The Glory of God and the Honour of Ireland' (Glóire Dé agus Onóir na hÉireann) to the subject, proclaiming:

> In the two things bound together in the Irish language movement – the culture and the folklore that we need to establish a new nation, and the Irish language as a depository for that culture – we feel one quality above all. That quality is the extraordinary kinship they have with the Catholic faith. That kinship is so strong that you could say that it is not a quality but rather a fundamental and essential element.

Equally predictable was the prophylactic role he saw the revived language serving:

> What I am recommending is that we have a new means to protect ourselves, a strainer or a filtering device that would, you could say, stop the material that is bad and allow through the material that is good. But that is precisely what the Irish language would do if we had it. There above is the Irish language, our defensive shield against the outside world.[158]

In his novel, which will be discussed in more detail later in this book, the protagonist, an unjustly defrocked Gaelic priest, is an explicit Christ-figure, who at the book's end enters the Cistercian monastery of Mount Melleray in County Tipperary.

There was, however, no greater champion of Catholic *Gaelachas* among Irish-language writers than Peadar Ó Dubhda, for whom building institutional links between the Church and the language movement was a lifelong mission. In October 1936, he began a bilingual crusade to draw the attention of language revivalists and other cultural nationalists to the necessity of linking language and faith if both were to survive in the hostile climate of the time. Writing in Irish in *An t-Éireannach*, he declared: 'Patrick bound our language and our Christianity into one seamless system, and the saints and scholars knotted them together during the fifteen hundred years that came after that' (*Éireannach*, 10/10/36).[159] In a piece in English in *The Leader* published on the same day, he wrote: 'Look at the godless world around threatening us on every side, and see if there is any more lasting barrier we could set up than our Faith and our language in one' (*Leader*, 10/10/36). The following month, he expanded on this idea in the same journal:

> And now, dear reader, it's easy to tell of what real value the language can be to us. First, it is the surest and most lasting safeguard of our Christianity. Secondly, it is our cultural medium as a separate race, and a steriliser of the poisonous drugs that come to us through a tongue that is not ours and imposes a modern pagan civilisation on us (*Leader*, 7/11/36).

Many scholars have discussed how, while never suffering anything that could be called persecution, Protestants found themselves progressively marginalised in the cultural life of newly independent Ireland.[160] Certainly sincere Protestant language activists such as Douglas Hyde, Ernest Blythe, Ernest Joynt, Seán Beaumont, Úna Dix, and George Ruth must have found sentiments like those cited above hurtful, however much they may also have understood them. It was, then, an act of real generosity for Ruth to state at a 'Protestant Convention' in Dublin's Mansion House in May 1922:

> There are people here who have done great work for the Irish language and for Irish nationality in the Gaelic League and in other movements in Ireland. They know well how friendly the Gaels always are towards them. Now when we will not be divided from each other because of politics, I do not see any reason for discord or disunity between Protestants and Roman Catholics. We are all Irish; we are all Gaels (*An t-Eaglaiseach Gaedhealach*, June 1922, 4).[161]

Not all would agree, however, and Protestant nationalists had to hear and read derogatory comments about their co-religionists and their faith on a regular basis throughout our period.[162] For example, Father Lawrence Murray offered an uncompromisingly sectarian interpretation of contemporary linguistic and cultural debates in a 1932 address to Ard-Scoil Uladh in Belfast:

> I believe that there is something bigger in this fight the Gaelic League is making than a fight between two languages. The League is trying to keep the ancient civilisation of our country alive. It is a fight between the civilisation Patrick began in Armagh and the civilisation Martin Luther began, a civilisation that still exists, and whose fruits we see even today (*Tír*, Oct. 1932, 11).[163]

A few years previous, in a 1928 essay on 'Leigheas ar Olcaibh Fearachasacha na hÉireann' (A remedy for the economic ills of Ireland), 'R. Mac E.' had seemed more broad-minded, writing: 'I do not set down anything against any faith at all here; I have no concern with the way anyone at all worships; I do not oppose any faith as a sacred faith.' But his underlying theme was that Ireland was 'a Gaelic Catholic nation' (náisiún Gaedhealach Catoiliceach), which now suffered under 'a kind of economy that grows out of the gospel Calvin propagated' (modh fearachasach fhásas as an tsoiscéal a scaip Calvin) (*Tír*, June 1928, 6).[164] In 1934, the editor of the *Catholic Bulletin* was adamant in his insistence that Irish Protestants were inherently alien:

> Right down from the days of Elizabeth, our people rightly deemed that one term in Irish, *Sacsanach*, does excellently well as a label for English and for Protestant. They sensed the two elements of alien and apostate influence as being one in their whole essence and purpose: and they have the same true sense of the facts today.

That essence and purpose was, needless to say, baneful:

> What the Irish people as a whole have always felt is that the Irish language, in our Catholic people's history, has always been a strong safeguard of the treasury of the Faith; and that in Ireland the language and the literature of England is shown, by its whole developed record, to be in substantial and close alliance with Protestant ascendancy, arrogance, and aggression (*CB*, Nov. 1934, 871).

The editor was here responding to an essay in *Studies* by Aodh de Blácam, in which the author had explored the complexities of 'Anglo-Irish' identity and history, and stated: 'The upshot of all this is that to identify *Catholic* with *Gael*, as it is bad religion, so it is bad history. It is a sort of Irish Nazi-ism' (*Studies*, Sept. 1934, 439). Others shared de Blácam's distaste for such dismissals of Protestants from full participation in the Gaelic nation on merely sectarian grounds. For example, in a 1928 piece in the *United Irishman*, Peadar Mac Fhionnlaoich chastised a speaker at the annual conference of the Catholic Truth Society for calling the Free State 'a Catholic State' (Stát Catoiliceach):

> We want a Republic for all of Ireland. And, since there are many people in Ireland who are not Catholics, we want no law or rule that will impose on them any more than on anyone else. It will be a Catholic State in the sense that the majority of the people will be Catholic. And they will have their proper rights. We will not go farther than that. Rome will not be allowed to interfere with us any more than will the English (*UIrman*, 3/11/28).[165]

In a letter to *An t-Éireannach* in 1934, 'Cothrom na Féinne' took Séamus Maguidhir to task for using the expression 'the English Faith' (an Creideamh Gallda) to refer to the religion of Wolfe Tone, Robert Emmet, 'and many others who suffered death for the "dear dark-headed one"' (agus a lán eile nach iad a d'fhulaing bás ar son 'an ceann dubh dílis'):

> If Tone were alive at present, would he have an English faith? He would have to listen to a Catholic hymn being played in Croke Park, although it would be a game for the whole nation that was going on. Although I am a Catholic myself, I have great respect for every Gael, whatever about his faith. There is a great division between faith and nationality, and the sooner everyone understands that the better (*Éireannach*, 7/3/36).[166]

It was inclusive generosity of this kind that enabled Protestants like Hyde, Joynt, Blythe, and Beaumont to see the language as a national ideal that could unify Irish people of all religious persuasions, including those north of the new border. Joynt was lyrical on this point in an essay addressed to fellow members of An Fáinne in the group's journal in 1922: 'There is, however, another nationality beyond political nationality. We, members of An Fáinne, understand that spiritual nationality is the most enduring and firmest nationality.' The central cohesive force in this spiritual identity open to all Irish people was the language, the advancement of which unified members of An Fáinne in the most profound way: 'Perhaps it would be no harm to say that our *fáinne* [ring] and the wedding ring have the same meaning. It is symbol of a bond between us, "until death do us part"' (*IF*, Aug. 1922, 12).[167] But there were also, as we have seen, Catholics in the movement who shared this non-sectarian vision, among them the Belfast-born Ailbhe Ó Monacháin, who wrote in the *Irish Press* in February 1937:

> The Gaelic League has attracted more Protestants than any other national movement since the United Irishmen: and a Protestant Gaelic Leaguer is not as a rule a sleepy one. Protestants join the Gaelic League because it is there, and there only, that they find sincerity, pride, dignity, and a pleasant, natural, national social life (*IP*, 25/2/37).[168]

Following all the controversies discussed above with emotions ranging from partisanship through bemusement and on to disgust was one group of Irish people who never questioned their *Gaelachas*, and who often felt that, however insular the country as a whole was or should be, they and theirs were stranded on neglected islands within or just off the island of Ireland. These were, of course, the people of the Gaeltacht, whose champions argued not only for the legitimate political, social, and economic rights of those living in Irish-speaking areas, but for the acceptance of the Gaeltacht as the most important element in a resurgent Gaelic nation. In practical terms within the cultural revival, such an acceptance meant the primacy of the native speaker of Irish in all aspects of the campaign of re-Gaelicisation. Leading this crusade was a new breed of native-speaking intellectuals, writers, and activists, quite different from those who had been prominent in the years before independence. Previously, those native speakers who came to the attention of the public were for the most part either priests like Fathers Ua Laoghaire, Dinneen, Henebry, or Sheehan; people who had risen to the genteel middle class through the meritocracy of the British civil service and the teaching profession – men like Pádraig Ó Séaghdha ('Conán Maol'), Peadar Mac Fhionnlaoich, Séamus Ó Dubhghaill, Tomás Ó hAodha, and Eoghan Ó Neachtain – or often illiterate tradition-bearers and folklore informants like Amhlaoibh Ó Loingsigh, Micheál Mag Ruaidhrí, or Tadhg Ó Conchubhair. Now, however, as a result of an increased, even aggressive self-confidence, born largely of Gaelic League propaganda and support, increased educational opportunities, the zeal of the independence struggle, and the founding ideology of the new state, native-speakers were emerging with much higher expectations and much less patience than most of their predecessors. Believing what they had been hearing for years about the centrality of the language in the project of reconstructing a distinctive Gaelic civilisation, native speakers were ready to step forward to demand the leadership roles that seemed to them theirs by right.

By far the most fervent exponent of this position was Séamus Ó Grianna, whose rise to prominence offers a textbook example of the path so many native-speakers followed at the time, with initial recognition through the Gaelic League leading to third-level education at St Patrick's College in Drumcondra, Dublin, involvement in the fight against first Britain and then the Free State, acclaim as a Gaelic man of letters, editorship of a Gaelic journal, and steady access to more than one forum for the promulgation of his cultural agenda. Ó Grianna had begun to advance the cause of the native-speaker before independence, most notably in a debate with Piaras Béaslaí in the pages of *Misneach*. It was, however, only after the foundation of the Free State and his subsequent conviction that the rulers of that state were hypocritically denying the primacy of the native speaker, particularly the native-speaker from Donegal, in the interests of a deracinated and sterile 'official Irish' (*Gaeilge oifigiúil*), that he decided to expose and combat his real and imagined foes with all the imposing linguistic and rhetorical resources at his command.

His tactical weapon of choice was irony, as in essay after essay he presented himself as 'an insignificant person from the Gaeltacht' (duine suarach as an Ghaedhealtacht) (*FL*, 16/12/22), 'a timid, simple-minded person' (uasgán) (*FL*, 14/2/25), 'a rough, crude rustic who was raised in a thatch-roofed hut in the Rosses' (dóirnéalach garbh glas a tógadh i gcró ceann-toigheadh ins na Rosaibh) (*Ultach*, Feb. 1932, 6).[169] On occasion, his tone was one of feigned resignation, as in the open letter to 'Brighid' (Seán Mac Maoláin) he published in *Fáinne an Lae* in April 1922:

> I have been in despair about the Irish of the province of Ulster for a long time . . . People will not care about our Irish at all from now on, nor about that of Munster, or Connacht. Dublin Irish will be the thing from now on. And indeed, that is a wretch leading the pack. Wooden-legged Irish is not a bad nickname for it, but the wooden leg is approaching us (*FL*, 8/4/22).[170]

But his usual strategy was as simple as it could be – all-out assault, no prisoners taken. In a July 1924 piece in *Sinn Féin*, he sarcastically accused some who had learned the language of wishing it and its native speakers dead to protect their own status: 'Isn't it difficult for us to admit that the rough, crude rustic has Irish and we do not . . . But they are going are the Gaels. And it is a going with no return. Our seven curses go with them and with their sounds and their idioms' (*SF*, 2/8/24).[171] He repeated this accusation in a scathing 1927 essay in the *Catholic Bulletin* prompted by the so-called 'Cleggan Disaster', a tragedy off the Galway coast that claimed the lives of several Irish-speaking fishermen:

> If the native speakers had a way to make themselves heard, it would be difficult for the scholars and the authors and the professors to keep the high status that they have. It is better to let them die of hunger than to give them the opportunity to make laughing stocks of us . . . the miserable little Mickies and Johnnies and Timmies . . . It would not take much to have me put my seven curses on them (*CB*, Dec. 1927, 1305–6).[172]

In another open letter to 'Brighid' the same year in *Fáinne an Lae*, he disingenuously asked how a native speaker could ever expect to be taken seriously in any discussion of the language:

> Native speakers! For God's sake, have a bit of common sense now. To think that we are going to imitate the simple-minded people of Donegal and Conamara, and most of them with no more 'culture' than a dog. My dear woman, there are some of them who don't have a word of English (*FL*, 29/11/24).[173]

In a 1927 letter to the literary historian and critic Muiris Ó Droighneáin, Ó Grianna claimed he had been driven to take up the pen by the drivel he saw being produced in the name of Gaelic literature by learners of the language:

> I had no intention at all of writing anything at all when I was young. I thought (and still think) that I didn't have it in me to create significant literature. But when I saw the kind of Irish that was being written, some of it by the people who had barely learned the 'first book', I thought I would show them the difference between 'Irish' and Irish.[174]

In 1928, Ó Grianna used the subject of one his rare positive book reviews in *Fáinne an Lae*, Thomas O'Rahilly's *Measgra Dánta*, as the occasion for a declaration of war on those learners he saw attempting to claim the language as their own as a means of advancement in the new state:

> I don't like saying something like this about people who are doing their best. I would not say it either if it were not that I see with my own eyes the day coming when the native speaker will have to take on the people who learned their Irish, when he will have to fight a hard and ardent battle in defence of the inheritance that was left him (*FL*, July 1927, p.5).[175]

More typical was the review of a secondary textbook he wrote for the same journal a few months later, in which he launched a withering attack on the anonymous author's linguistic inadequacies:

> If we are not serious about the Irish language, why in the name of Ireland, in the name of our ancestors, in the name of the truth, in the name of decency, and in the name of God, why don't we let it die in peace and not be dribbling over it as we are. It is bad enough that we can be told that we let it die. But is not the way we are butchering it a thousand times worse? (*FL*, Nov. 1927, 8).[176]

It was, of course, such attacks on learners of the language, often singling them out by name or leaving no doubt about whom he had in mind, that finally resulted in Ó Grianna's removal from the editorial chair at *Fáinne an Lae*. Matters came to a head with his February 1928 front page editorial assault on the educational policies and policy makers of the Free State. Already dismissed and re-hired once in 1929, Ó Grianna saw his tenure as editor of the League journal come to its definitive end in December of that year with the publication of the extraordinary editorial with which this chapter began. Yet despite this setback, he had no intention of declaring a truce, much less calling off the war, and thereafter his volleys were fired from a range of publications, among them those of the League, over the next decades. For example, in a letter to the editor of *An Claidheamh Soluis* in 1931, he sneered at those Gaelic 'scholars' who, having learned the language, saw themselves superior to the mere native speaker:

> Any simpleton at all can stimulate the Phagocytes. But there isn't a power on earth to make a person a native speaker. Swallow that, big man with big degrees and little Irish. There is not a doctor in the world that could put the edge on your tongue that is on mine, unless that Russian who is working on the monkey glands could. Perhaps if the glands were taken from an old Gaeltacht person and put into you it would do you good (*ACS*, 24/10/31).[177]

In another gibe at the universities the following year, Ó Grianna dismissed the Irish taught and spoken there as mere 'rubbish' (gramscar) to a native speaker, and continued:

> I don't know whether they think what they have is 'Gaelic Culture'. Perhaps they do. It is said that the black crow thinks it is white . . . I don't know whether there was ever any other language on earth as fine as Irish. Or any other language whose salvation was entrusted to the kind of dunces and frauds who are making a living out of the Irish language (*Ultach*, Feb. 1932, 6).[178]

And in a sardonic piece on 'An Dóigh le Gearr-Scéal do Scríobhadh' (The way to write a short story), Ó Grianna's worldly-wise 'Doppelgänger' offers him the following advice:

> Don't God and the world both know that literature does not grow in the Gaeltacht? Of course none of those people have English. They don't have a degree. None of them teach in the university . . . Have sense. The Gaeltacht is finished. No one pays it any attention now (*Examiner*, 28/12/35).[179]

While 'Máire' was doubtless unique in the savagery of his indignation, a combustible blend of linguistic, cultural, political, and class sensitivities, as well as in his gift for satire, he was by no means the only Gaelic writer of the time to hold these views. One of those to whom some of his fiercest open letters were addressed was the novelist Seán Mac Maoláin. Although himself a learner of the language, Mac Maoláin had earned Ó Grianna's respect and gone on to enlist enthusiastically in his cause, answering Ó Grianna's letters with a series of his own in the Gaelic press.[180] For example, in a letter to 'Máire' in *Fáinne an Lae* in January 1924, Mac Maoláin blasted 'the new Irish' (an Nua-Ghaedhilg), writing:

> When there was nothing to be gained from the Irish language it used to be said that the only ones who spoke it were the people out in the hills and on the coasts out west. Now that the world has changed a bit, we are being told that the Irish of the hills is not up-to-date enough (*FL*, 12/1/24).[181]

Reviewing Ó Grianna's *Micheál Ruadh* two years later, Mac Maoláin was predictably delighted to find an Irish book written the way an Irish book should be written. Dismissing the work of those Gaelic writers raised in English-speaking Ireland or dealing with the life of English-speaking Ireland, as lacking 'the proper Gaelic flavour' (an blas ceart Gaedhealach), Mac Maoláin declared:

> Thus if anyone wants to get a story in Irish that has the true flavour of the Irish language, and is as it were steeped in *Gaelachas*, let him get a story written by a Gaeltacht person in the Gaeltacht about the people of the Gaeltacht (*Ultach*, Aug. 1926, 2).[182]

A native-speaking writer who met all these criteria was Seaghán Mac Meanman, and, not surprisingly, he was also a committed advocate of the primacy of the native speaker. Reviewing Brighid Ní Dhochartaigh's *Comhrádh cois Teineadh* (Fireside conversation) in *Sinn Féin* in 1924, Mac Meanman claimed that a reader would recognise at once that the author was a native speaker, unlike many Gaelic scholars 'who didn't hear and didn't learn the language until they were stooped in the shoulders and stumbling with a cane' (nach gcualaidh a's nár fhoghluim an teangaidh go rabh siad ag crupadh ins na guailiseachaibh a's ag tuitim ar a mbata) (*SF*, 10/5/24).[183] Mac Meanman's bemused contempt for much of the Irish used by learners of the language inspired his 1936 play *Peinsean Shean-Mháire Ní Ruadháin*, in which the comedy arises from the mutual incomprehension of an elderly native speaker and a civil servant with 'Dublin Irish', including the memorable line 'You – You – have a big good income! Poultry is – is – profitable' (Tá – Tá – good income mór agat! Tá – Tá poultry profitable). The opinion of the locals is summed up by a neighbour of the title character: 'But your Irish is great nonsense!' (Acht is mór an pléiseam do chuid Gaedhilge!)[184]

Seosamh Mac Grianna shared many of his brother's ideas about native speakers and learners, but in general expressed them with more tact, as he did in a 1924 essay on the need for Gaelic writers to be as accomplished as Irish writers in the English language: 'They must come into the world in the Gaeltacht or at any rate they must suck the milk that will nourish in them the spirit of the Gael' (*Ultach*, May 1924, 5).[185] Two years later, in an essay on 'The Gaelic Renaissance and Its Fruits', he discussed the necessity for Gaelic writers to bridge 'the chasm between the eighteenth and twentieth centuries, vast and volcanic', and saw the solution in the self-conscious native speaker:

> To me it seems that a writer from the Gaeltacht can easily link the past with the present, dress the new thoughts in the old language. He must have the Irish outlook, an outlook modified since the landing of Strongbow, but never changed (*An Phoblacht*, 16/7/26).

With time, however, his attitude hardened, as he began to see native speakers representing a virtually distinct nationality from that of their English-speaking compatriots:

> I am a Gael, born and reared in the Gaeltacht, and living now in Dublin. There are hundreds, thousands like me in the city. We have a language of our own, our own outlook and tradition. Here we are in exile, as much as a Palesman would be in Paris or Moscow. Rather cruel, is it not, ye men of the Pale? But add to it that we are exiles in our own land . . . It is unlikely now that the Gaeltacht and the Pale will ever make a happy blend (*IP*, 1/3/32).[186]

By the time he wrote his famous essay on Pádraic Ó Conaire, published in 1936, he sounded more and more like his older brother. Discussing Ó Conaire's allegorical story of language revival 'Aba-Cana-Lú', he asked:

> Was it not possible that Pádraic knew then that the Irish language was going, and that the day would come when the only thing left would be an Anglo-Irish parrot with broken Irish as a sign that the noble old tongue had ever lived?[187]

In 1934 and 1935, *An t-Ultach* published a series of uncompromising essays on this topic by 'An Dóirnéalach' under the general title 'Béarlachas agus Ciotachas' (Anglicism and clumsiness), in one of which he wrote sarcastically:

> It is, of course, a great advantage that the new Irish is weaning itself from the speech of the *Gaeltacht*. It would never succeed or prosper, if it remained tied to the speech of the rabble who have no proper upbringing. But, unfortunately, it cannot do that without weaning itself altogether from the Irish language as it always was until recently (*Ultach*, Jan. 1935, 1).[188]

A few months later, he dropped sarcasm for blunt abuse:

> And the truth is that the 'new Irish' is a thing without merit,
> without life, without soul. It hasn't the slightest resemblance
> to real Irish except the resemblance the scattered skeleton of
> a corpse has to the healthy, sound body of a living person
> (*Ultach*, Easter 1935, 6).[189]

It would take a chapter, if not a book itself, to cite and discuss all the often vitriolic variants of this position. Here a few examples from both native speakers and fluent learners who supported them will have to suffice to give some sense of how widespread and passionately held was this belief in the absolute primacy of the native speaker in the language and cultural revival. As we have seen, this belief could veer into paranoia, as when 'Tadhg Gaedhealach' called in 1923 for 'An Association for the Defence of the Irish Language' (Cuallacht Cosanta na Gaedhilge)

> to defend the language and its characteristics against the traitors who are out after it; from the people who would break and rend it and who would tear it apart and not leave strength or vigour in it; the people who would leave it without any heat in blood or skin, but would leave it to us in a slovenly, mean condition, without a heart or a pulse of its own (*Sguab*, July 1923, 192).[190]

The following year, Máighréad Ní Annagáin sparked a debate with Gearóid Ó Lochlainn in the pages of *The Leader* with her harsh review of the lack of *Gaelachas* she noted in the productions of the Gaelic drama group An Comhar Drámaidheachta. In one essay, she anticipated Mac Grianna's view of the native speaker as having a distinct nationality from those in the Pale, writing:

> It does not necessarily follow that because one has learned Irish one has acquired the Gaelic mentality; this has to be born in one. If a person speaks French it does

> not necessarily follow that he is a Frenchman or has the French outlook and temperament, and there are a good many people about Dublin who can speak Irish after a fashion, but to us real Gaels they are foreigners, as we, the Gaels of the bog, the mountain, and the shore, are, and I am afraid will always remain, foreigners to them (*Leader*, 6/12/24).[191]

Writing on '"An Gaedhilgeoir Duthchais" agus "An Gaedhilgeoir ó'n gCliabhán"' ('The Native speaker' and 'the Irish speaker from the cradle') in 1927, 'Úna Bhán' suggested criminal penalties for learners who wrote flawed Irish:

> I myself think that there should be a law to throw anyone at all who would 'write' a book without knowing the language well himself into prison until his bones would rot. It is bad enough that the language is dying, but it would be much better to let it die a natural death than to *kill* it as is being done at present.

This author's definition of a native speaker created a new elite within those born to the language:

> My own opinion is that it is not right to call anyone at all a 'native speaker of Irish' except for the one whose usual speech was Irish until he was grown up, and not only that, but I would not say that he is a proper native speaker unless he used the language after that every time he had the chance, and, in addition to that, unless he spent a while each year among Irish speakers in a place where he would not have to speak any English (*FL*, Nov. 1927, 3).[192]

In a brief column in *Honesty* in December 1929, 'Súil i n-Airde' wrote of Free State civil servants in a manner worthy of 'Máire' at his most paranoid. This author believed that while most in the government were simply apathetic about the plight of the Gaeltacht and the emigration of native speakers, those in the Department of Education and An Gúm were positively delighted by the decimation of the Irish-speaking population. He pictured an employee of An Gúm 'jumping with joy . . . because he sees that there will not be a single true Irish-speaker left to bother him' (ag léimrigh le h-áthas . . . mar chíonn sé ná beidh aon fhíor-chainnteóir Gaedhilge fágtha chum chur isteach ná amach air), and reported overhearing an inspector from the Education Department saying, 'It is a long time since I read anything that made me happier than the census' (Níor léigheas le fada aon nidh a chuir níos mó áthais orm ná an móráireamh) (*Honesty*, 7/12/29). The Aran-Islander Micheál Ó Maoláin used irony against upstart learners attempting to usurp the place within the movement that should properly belong to native speakers. In a 1935 piece in the *Irish Independent*, he blasted 'The Official Language' (An Teanga Oifigeamhail), and continued:

> Something that always amazes me is how easy it is for people who were not born with Irish to write books in that language. Some of them are able to put books on the market every other month. 'Irish while you wait', you could say. As for readers, that question does not trouble them at all, and why would it? There is plenty of money it seems (*II*, 9/7/35).[193]

Two years later, Ciarán Mac A' tSaoir offered readers of *An t-Ultach* a tongue-in-cheek Orwellian reaffirmation of this position:

> The person who says that it is right to pay any attention at all to the people who have Irish has neither sense nor reason. The whole world should know now that it is not possible for a person to have any understanding of Irish at all if he can converse in it. No one who can speak a language understands it. But the person who has Irish and who cannot speak it will converse in some other language and the Irish will be gathered up and stored away in his skull, getting stronger every day (*Ultach*, July 1937, 1).[194]

The blend of envy, fear, contempt and legitimate wounded pride that characterised the attitude of many of the native speakers and their allies toward learners and their brand of Irish is perhaps best captured in the second stanza of the poem 'An Ghalltacht fá dTaobh Damh' (English-speaking Ireland around me) by 'Sgreigeas Fheachla' published in *An t-Ultach* in June 1937:

> I see only the English language churls / or the crowd with the improved new Irish, / In habit, in state, in coach, in house, / Every buck going around in his motor car. / Every rich inspector with English and with Irish / Or a hodgepodge with which to converse. / And the poor heroes weak on the deer's bed / And the rabbit in the house of the lion (*Ultach*, June 1937, 6).[195]

Needless to say, those who had learned Irish at considerable sacrifice and with considerable effort for idealistic and patriotic reasons were not about to let themselves be dismissed in so cavalier a fashion from the movement to which they had devoted their lives. The danger of a new, linguistic civil war erupting was pointed out by 'Lagan' while the actual Civil War was still being disastrously waged. Writing in *The Leader* in November 1922, he asserted:

> Latterly, and notably since An t-Athair Peadar's death, the native speaker is declaring an ambition to be, so to say, an Irregular in literature . . . There is no need to go into details. Anyone who reads the Irish newspapers is aware what the native speaker let loose with a pen in his hand can do (*Leader*, 25/11/22).

'Liam' offered a satirical picture of one such Gaeltacht literary terrorist at work in his 1922 essay 'The Gaeltacht Oracles', describing the response of an old Gaeltacht woman on hearing a timid learner try to address her in Irish:

> This was to the sean-bhean [old woman] like the sound of the trumpet to the war-horse in Scripture. She would draw herself up to her full height, with arms akimbo, throw a glance of anticipated victory over her shoulder at the audience . . . as if to say, 'See me crush this presumptuous worm', and then proceed to annihilate the luckless wight with a fluent torrent of Gaelic. With a feeble 'Ní thuigim' [I do not understand] and a wan smile, he would slink away, abashed and discomfited, amid the smiles and guffaws of the audience, while the sean-bhean, left in possession of the field, looked after him with a smile of derision and pity (*II*, 15/9/22).

Pádraic Ó Conaire, who, if not a native speaker in the strictest sense, had spoken the language since childhood, used the occasion of a 1924 essay on Joseph Conrad to rebut the 'false opinion' (an bharamhail bhréagach) that only a native speaker could create true literature in a language, writing:

> No matter what race he comes from, the form and the innate quality of the Irish language is in the speech of everyone whose ancestors lived in Ireland over, say, the past three hundred years, even if English words come out of his mouth . . . It is that false opinion of which I am speaking that has for a long time done the most harm to the writing of the Irish language. Let it henceforth lie in the grave with Conrad.[196]

Conrad was also in Father Dinneen's mind when he wrote in 1925:

> Let us not listen to those who say 'no one except a native speaker, an Irish speaker from the cradle on, can compose literature in Irish'. Do not yield to talk of that sort. The death occurred the other day of a Pole who had written powerful novels in English although he didn't speak English until he was an adult (*Leader*, 11/4/25).[197]

The same year as Dinneen's piece appeared, 'Aodh' published one of a series of essays in the *Catholic Bulletin* in which he urged learners to muster up the courage to face 'the fellow obsessed with "native speech"' (giolla na cainnte 'dúthchais') and his obscurantism:

> There will be outcry and tumult around your ears for every word that these 'natives' don't find 'native'; and unless you feel the strength in yourself to ignore all of that, the noise and the commotion and the terrible cries, and work on paying it no heed, you would be better off not to begin, but to stay quietly at home. Until you can convince yourself that that these 'natives' are nothing but kernes and lackeys and camp-followers, without knowledge, without understanding, without instruction, you have no business thinking about adapting Irish to the present (*CB*, Feb. 1925, 171).[198]

It was also in 1925 that a generation of new readers encountered Father John M. O'Reilly's *The Native Speaker Examined Home: Two Stalking Fallacies Anatomized*, first published in 1909 and now available in its second edition. O'Reilly had shown some courage in his criticism of the cult of the native speaker in the first decade of the century; he was even braver in re-affirming that criticism in the heated ideological climate of the early Free State. That reaffirmation was, however, seen by some as a salutary intervention in the often acrimonious debate then under way. For example, in his review in the *University Annual* of University College Galway for 1925–6, 'Cuillin' welcomed the book: 'While we do not agree with some of his conclusions, we must admit that his arguments are sound, and that his protest against the over-prominent place held by the native speaker is to a large extent justified' (*University Annual*, 1925–6, 57).[199]

In 1928, Father Lawrence Murray, the influential founder and first editor of *An t-Ultach* – that favourite forum of the Donegal native speakers – weighed in on those like himself who had learned the language, arguing that the salvation of the language would have to come from English-speaking Ireland, and not from the Gaeltacht:

> My own opinion is that not much literature will come from the Gaeltacht – that not enough will come, at any rate, to save the Irish language. There are not all that many native speakers now, and most of them are too poor to think about literary questions. The people of the Gaeltacht haven't seen much of the world.

And he urged young learners to remember that that other learner, Patrick Pearse, had faced the same objections two decades before, and 'if the mockery of the critics of that time had taken away Pearse's courage, we would be reading a different story about the history of Ireland today' (dá mbainfeadh magadh lucht léirmheas na h-uaire sin an t-uchtach de'n Phiarsach, bhéadh a mhalairt de scéal le léigheadh indiu fá dtaobh de stair na hÉireann) (*Ultach*, Nov. 1928, 3–4).[200] The following month in the same journal, 'An Droighneán Fionn', who also identified himself as a learner, took on the native speakers, including Ó Grianna, head-on. Having acknowledged his appreciation of Ó Grianna's writing, he continued: 'But "Máire" is neither the Gaeltacht nor the Irish language' (Acht ní h-í 'Máire' an Ghaedhealtacht 'nó an Ghaedhilg). For this author, what was essential was 'to save the Irish language for the WHOLE nation' (an Gaedhilg a shábháil do'n náisiún AR FAD), and for this reason learners with literary talent were, with all their faults, of critical importance:

> And if what we, who have learned Irish as a foreign language because of the love we had for it and for the country, have is insipid and wretched, will it not reveal to those who follow us the faults we had so that they will be able to avoid them . . .

> That is what we are asking for ourselves, native speakers! We are far from expecting that we will ever write as if we were native speakers. Now! Don't be hard on us! We are only trying to help you. Help us! (*Ultach*, Dec. 1928, 3).[201]

It is also worth noting that 'Fear na Blagaide' had taken Ó Grianna to task more severely in an essay in *The Leader* earlier that year. This author blasted 'Máire' for both the content and the tone of his attacks on learners in *Fáinne an Lae*, in the process raising the obvious point, one much favoured by learners throughout this debate, that native speakers had done nothing of their own to earn that honour:

> It is up to the Coisde Gnótha to prevent people like 'Máire', who never had to make any sacrifice for the language, which they have acquired by an accident of birth, from using the official organ of the Gaelic League to discourage non-native speakers from trying to speak in the national language (*Leader*, 26/5/28).[202]

In a letter to *An Tír* the following year, Tomás Mac Ruaidhrí made his point with a caustic cynicism worthy of Ó Grianna, as he attacked 'foolish people' (daoine dí-chéillidhe) in the language movement:

> If they are allowed to have their way, the native speakers will be on one side, and they are the only ones whom everyone should respect, and it is to them alone every penny in Ireland should go. And again, if those foolish people are allowed to have their way, the people who learned Irish will be on the other side altogether. They will not have leave to speak out loud in the presence of the native speakers, or to do anything but constantly find ways to keep the native speakers in certain places in the positions they got nicely and easily because of the work the learners of Irish did (*Tír*, Mar. 1929, 12).[203]

Maoghnus Ó Domhnaill, who although born of native-speaking parents in Annascaul, County Kerry just east of Dingle, was himself a learner, used similar sarcasm to criticise the arrogance of some native speakers in a 1932 editorial in *An Claidheamh Soluis*:

> But there is now a danger that one or two of the native speakers think that there is some kind of saintliness or divinity connected with themselves with regard to the Irish language . . . They think that no one but themselves has the right to be involved with the Irish language and they ridicule the people who are trying to learn it. Their bodies will not stay five feet aloft above the ground like the body of Mohammed, and it will do the people of Ireland no good to go on pilgrimage to them in the hope of bringing home a little scrap of *Gaelachas* (*ACS*, 23/1/32).[204]

In an April 1929 letter to *An Tír*, Seosamh Ó Dálaigh had gone even farther: 'I say to someone who can do nothing but mock the person who didn't speak Irish at the start of his youth that he is an enemy of our country and of our language' (*Tír*, Apr. 1929, 12).[205]

More philosophical in his concern about the potentially disastrous consequences of this split in the movement was Seosamh Ó Tallamhain in his two-part essay on 'Scríbhneoireacht' (Writing) in the *Dundalk Examiner* in 1931. Rejecting the notion that a learner could never capture the Gaelic spirit, Ó Tallamhain wrote:

> Any two Irish people have the same nature, whether Irish or English is their native language. Therefore, if the English-speaker succeeds in mastering Irish and if he has any talent for writing, I would say that someone like him can compose and write literature in Irish (*Examiner*, 5/12/31).[206]

Not surprisingly, B. P. Ó Nualláin, later famous as 'Flann O'Brien' and 'Myles na gCopaleen', was more sardonic in his criticism of the exclusionist native speakers in an October 1932 essay:

> But there is a certain group that seems to hate and think little of anyone who learns Irish . . . If these new cultural aristocrats had power, they would not allow anyone to put pen to paper to reveal his thoughts. Their tune is that it is not right for anyone except the native speaker to write anything. If there is a position to be filled it is, of course, a revolt against the civilisation and culture of Ireland to give it to anyone but a native speaker no matter what other qualities he lacks (*Tír*, Oct. 1932, 3).[207]

Writing in the *United Irishman* in 1933, Liam Ó Rinn noted that learners were often more committed to the language than were native speakers, 'something that is no surprise since a person does not easily part with a thing he gets as the result of hard work' (ní nach ionadh ó thárla ná scarann duine go bog leis an rud a gheibheann sé de bharr dian-tsaothair). Ó Rinn felt the best course for such learners was to simply ignore the carping negativism of some native speakers:

> If the people of the Gaeltacht do not want to extend Irish as it should be extended, we cannot make them do it . . . If the good example of English-speaking Ireland has not inspired them to do it I fear that nothing else will. What we in English-speaking Ireland should do is to take a firm and steadfast vow in our hearts to revive the Irish language in English-speaking Ireland, whether that Irish is good or bad – whether it is an ugly jargon or the opposite – and no matter what the Gaeltacht does or does not do (*UIrman*, 7/1/33).[208]

Tomás Breathnach was in at least partial agreement with Ó Rinn, writing in a 1937 essay:

> There are other people to be found from whose speech it is clear that they want to put a gag in the mouth of anyone who does not have Irish from the cradle on, and who are of the opinion that his like should not under any circumstances be allowed to attempt to write the language.

But, having conceded that most learners would never achieve the linguistic mastery of the native speaker, Breathnach continued:

> Let us continue speaking Irish, even if it is broken, halting Irish, and we will carry the day . . . Great credit is due to anyone who has the courage and the perseverance to learn Irish, and it is neither fitting nor proper for anyone to denigrate such a person because of how broken his Irish is . . . 'Praise the young and they will develop' and there is nothing better that the people with the pure Irish and the bitter words could do than to follow that advice (*Bonaventura*, Autumn 1937, 193–4).[209]

Tomás P. Ó Siadhail developed this idea at length in a speech to the second *Comhdháil* of An Comhchaidreamh, the organisation of Irish-speaking university students and graduates, meeting in Ros Muc in the Conamara Gaeltacht in 1937. Having argued that the future 'Great Literature in Irish' (Ard-Éigse sa Ghaedhilg) would most likely emerge from English-speaking Ireland, he continued:

> At any rate, I do not agree in any way whatsoever with the opinion about the question held by certain people, that is, that no one but the native speaker should write Irish. 'Clear out of our pools' is the welcome this crowd gives the young writer from English-speaking Ireland who attempts to put his thoughts on paper in Irish. These people must be made to understand that no one particular group in this country has sole right of possession over the language or over writing in the language.

Ó Siadhail's guiding principle was forthright, generous, and optimistic: 'Every Irish person is a native speaker *in posse*' (Is cainnteoir ó dhúthchas *in posse* gach Éireannach) (*AA*, Oct. 1937, 7).[210]

In fact, many on both sides of this debate were fair, willing to acknowledge the real and potential contributions of those of a different linguistic background and to forego debating points in favour of compromise for a common cause. Most serious learners of the language, many of whom had spent considerable time in the Gaeltacht, were too honest not to admit the enormous debt they owed and would continue to owe native speakers as they worked to perfect their acquired Irish. Doubtless Riobárd Ó Druaidh spoke for the majority when he wrote in his editor's preface to Fearrgus Ó Nualláin's *Laidean tré Ghaedhilg I* (Latin through Irish I):

> The Irish speakers of the Gaeltacht are, no doubt, an instance of the survival of the fittest. Their language, as spoken by the natives, bears the unmistakable stamp of a dialect evolved by a highly cultivated aristocratic caste . . . It is not to be expected that the extension of spoken Irish can mean the imparting to multitudes of the purity and idiom, the grave strength and richness which mark the native spoken Irish of the generation now all too quickly passing away.

Having argued that most speakers of any language rely on 'a more or less debased jargon which serves them quite well for ordinary purposes', Ó Druaidh continued:

> There is really no need to be uneasy about the quality of Irish of the future. If Irish is going to survive as a spoken tongue, it will follow the lines of other languages. There will be a conventional *koine dialekte* of absolutely neutral quality; there will be layers on layers of specialised jargon more or less hideous; and there will be a highly-cultivated dialect, the inheritor of the traditions of the present Gaeltachd, confined to those who have the time, the inclination, and the ability to evolve artistic forms in speech and in writing.[211]

León Ó Broin, himself one of the most accomplished and literarily gifted learners of the language, believed that a glimpse of Ó Druaidh's golden future was already available in the best work of contemporary native speakers. In a 1939 review of *As na Ceithre h-Áirdibh* (From all points of the compass), a collection of stories by several authors, Ó Broin wrote:

> It demonstrates very vividly a fact which has tremendous bearing on the future of Gaelic literature. I refer to the ease with which the literate native speaker can write Irish of good literary quality and style. This he can do almost without guidance, for, in the spoken language he has a highly polished vehicle of expression that only needs to be written naturally, as he speaks it, to make its appeal (*Irish Monthly*, Apr. 1939, 289).[212]

Writing in August 1924, Éamonn Mac Giolla Iasachta, the editor of *An Sguab*, paid a similar tribute to the Irish of the native speaker, but insisted that learners were also essential to the revival:

> And which group is most important in the final analysis? If it were not for the learned Irish speakers the learners would not be able to learn at all, and without the learners of Irish it would be just as well for the other group to give up the work at

> once. There is no strength without co-operation; that is all there is to it, and let us understand that (*Sguab*, 31/8/24).[213]

'Noel' offered readers of *The Leader* a more self-effacing vision of such creative collaboration between native speakers and learners in 1928:

> We cannot do without the native speaker. Neither can we afford to lose the crowd which happens to be non-native. They are the whiskey and whatever else that go to make a punch. However, if I could safely feel tomorrow that a strong literature, in the drama, novel, short-story, poetry, was safe in the hands of a group of native-speakers having a broad outlook, a deep intelligence and a revivalist soul, I would lead the non-natives from the stage to applaud in the gallery (*Leader*, 11/2/28).[214]

Seán Ó Ciosáin, another learner who broke new ground in Gaelic fiction, though content to acknowledge the importance of the native speaker, was less willing to yield his place on the national stage, writing in 1930:

> If Irish is a living language – and we are often black in the face from trying to convince the enemies of the language of that – we must understand that it must evolve, and that we should not always be tormenting ourselves about how Old Peats Teaimí in the west of the Dingle Peninsula would express certain thoughts in Irish. It is not that I am saying that we should not pay great attention to that same old man, but it is not right to go overboard in the matter (*Star*, 1/3/30).[215]

Having discussed the deficiencies of the native speakers of her own time in a 1937 essay in *The Leader*, Eithne Ní Bhroin expressed her own preference for the work of 'the scholars and the literary men' (na scoláirí agus na fir liteardha), but then suggested a key role for native speakers in any future Gaelic renaissance: 'The native speaker will be there as a defender of the living language. These two groups will write fine big books worthy of being called "literature"' (*Leader*, 28/8/37).[216]

In a gracious tribute to the most recalcitrant spokesman for the native speakers, 'A. Ó D.' praised Ó Grianna's 1926 story collection *Cioth agus Dealán* and then added:

> And the learners of Irish, and after all is said and done, most of us are learners, will find in it the vigour and the beauty of living Irish as it is still spoken in the Donegal Gaeltacht as well as an acute and pleasing description of the ordinary life of the people (*IMN*, 1927, 102).[217]

Some native speakers were willing to reciprocate. Even the pontifical Ó Grianna was prone to the odd lapse into fallibility with its accompanying act of charity, as when in 1928 he looked back on the pre-Treaty and pre-Civil War golden age of the Gaelic League, rhapsodising:

> The spirit of nationality was like yeast in the Gaelic League. That yeast set a process in motion. The air was quivering in those years and you would think that even the tiniest match would set it aflame. Native speakers and learners repected each other. Both groups often beholden to each other. And both respecting Ireland. The day the Gaels were defeated that spirit left the Gaelic League. It will come back when the people of Ireland think that it is not for the sake of philology or folklore that Irish should be cultivated, but for the sake of Ireland a nation (*FL*, Aug. 1928, 1).[218]

Moreover, even in the midst of one of his most bitter debates in defence of native speakers, he could on occasion write or speak in a more inclusive and even welcoming manner. In a May 1925 review of Brighid Ní Dhochartaigh's *Seamróg na gCeithre nDuilleóg* (The four-leafed shamrock) in *An Sguab*, he stated that one could and should overlook the simplicity of the book's Irish, keeping in mind the audience for which it was written:

> Then children in English-speaking Ireland will find this book useful. To tell the truth, it is easier to begin with a little book like this than with the complicated Irish of the native speakers. Castles are built in stages, and that is also how languages are learned. Therefore, we should be grateful to the teachers who write books of this kind (*Sguab*, May 1925, 356).[219]

In a June 1927 essay in *Fáinne an Lae*, he accepted without reservation one of the learners' main arguments against the arrogance of the native speaker:

> It is a source of joy for a person to have had Irish from his childhood on, but it is not a source of pride. Not a single one of us had any control over his coming into the world where he did. You were not asked whether you wanted to see the light of day in Rathmines nor was I asked whether I wanted to see it in the Rosses of Donegal.

He then continued in a vein that would trouble few if any committed learners: 'When I speak about the people of the Gaeltacht I think of them in this way. They have Irish. It is they who do. And they must be used to spread the language throughout Ireland' (*FL*, June 1927, 1).[220] In another essay in the same journal in 1929, he was emphatic in his acceptance of the learner as an ally, writing:

> There are thousands of decent, virile people in the country – people who didn't get Irish at their mother's knee but went back to the Gaeltacht every chance and opportunity they got and learned it. People without envy in their hearts. People

> who are grateful and who give thanks that there is a Gaeltacht. There are thousands of these in the country and it is a good thing that there are (*FL*, Apr. 1929, 5).[221]

And in 1930, he actually paid tribute to those who had worked to acquire the language: 'It is a good thing to learn Irish. The people who learned it have done fine work' (*IF*, May, 1930, 1).[222] It should, of course, be noted that none of these gestures of compromise had the rhetorical punch of his more usual condemnations of learned Irish and its uppity speakers, and that none yielded anything but a sort of affiliate status to those not born to the language. Moreover, given that such gestures were likely to be followed shortly by one of Ó Grianna's more typical jeremiads, it is difficult to see how those on the other side could take them all that seriously.[223]

Learners may have found more comfort and encouragement in the temperate statements of other advocates of the primacy of the native speaker. Particularly generous was the veteran writer and activist Peadar Mac Fhionnlaoich, who was twice president of the Gaelic League, from 1922 to 1925, and again from 1933 to 1940. For example, in a piece in *Sinn Féin* in January 1925, he responded to a charge that the League had at a recent conference 'ignored' the Gaeltacht with a spirited defence of those who had learned the language:

> It moved me to admiration, as I am sure it did many others, to hear all our affairs (some of them of a very critical nature) discussed during a whole day in good Irish. I say good Irish deliberately though there were possible exceptions. Let it be granted that most of the speakers did not get the language at their mother's knee and that it was wanting in niceties of blas [accent] and phrasing. What then? Must the Irish people wait until they are born once again to an Irish-speaking mother before they may venture to speak Irish? And is it any offence to speak imperfect Irish until they are able to improve it? (*SF*, 24/1/25).

Later that same year, he went even farther, writing that he was convinced the language would be revived from Dublin, not the Gaeltacht:

> The Gaeltacht will, of course, be used . . . The native speakers of Irish will be used to get the accent and correct usage of the language, as well as to get whatever amount of the old literature they still remember. But a new dialect and a new literature will be created, and it is in Dublin that that will be done (*An Phoblacht*, 30/10/25).[224]

We can, perhaps, leave the last words of peace and reconciliation with two writers whose anonymity obscures their own linguistic origins. Writing in *An Tír* in 1928, 'Sliabh na mBan' lamented this discouraging split in the movement:

> Incidentally, many people have caused trouble between the Gaeltacht and English-speaking Ireland, and many are doing so now, even if they themselves do not know it . . . In the name of the Irish language and in the name of good sense, let these two sides of us understand each other, and let the language not be lost between us (*Tír*, July 1928, 4).[225]

The following year, an anonymous contributor to *Fáinne an Lae* echoed this complaint, declaring:

> Now it is a great shame and a lack of vision to attempt to divide those involved with the Irish language into two groups and to set them at each other. Anyone at all who understands the situation knows that Irish cannot be saved without the Gaeltacht. And another thing: without English-speaking Ireland. Both groups are necessary. Irish would be of little use to Ireland if it were to stay out in the bog back behind the hills. And the people of English-speaking Ireland will be of little help unless they go back and take up the Irish that is in the bog and make the most of it. The two groups are as necessary as are his hands and his head for a person (*FL*, Mar. 1929, 1).[226]

Unfortunately, such calls to common sense were all too often drowned out by more strident battle cries as both sides tried to adjust to, if not seize control of, a situation that had changed so utterly in so short a time in the wake of independence and civil war. A language long dismissed as a mark of servility was now both prized as a national treasure and seen by many as a sure guarantor of status, opportunity, and social mobility. Not surprisingly then, the now more confident native speakers wanted to step down from their isolating ideological pedestals and into the classrooms and government offices of the new Gaelic state, while the increasingly confident learners were just as eager to step up from reading books to writing them, from memorising rural idioms and proverbs to shaping a modern language for a modern people. Echoing Ó Grianna's militant imagery in his dismissal of what he saw passing for Irish in the Free State, Aodh Ó Dochartaigh issued an ominous warning to readers of *An t-Ultach* in 1935: 'The battle is approaching us. And the people of the Gaeltacht will have to let the country know about their contempt for this filthy refuse' (*Ultach*, Jan. 1935, 5).[227] The bitterness that battle created was to poison most if not all of the debates to be examined in this study. The first front would be the rural heartland itself, a topic to which we may now turn.

TWO

THE REAL AND BETTER IRELAND

RURAL LIFE IN GAELIC PROSE

'There is nothing in this world as nice or as Gaelic as a truly Gaelic true Gael speaking truly Gaelic Gaelic about Gaelic Gaelic.'[1] Many readers will doubtless recognise this excerpt from the speech of a noble Gael to an audience of 'Gaelic Gaels of the Gaelic line' (Gaeil Ghaelacha de shliocht Ghaelach) at the Corca Dorcha *feis* in 'the middle of the Gaeltacht' (lár na Gaeltachta) in Brian Ó Nualláin's brilliant 1941 parody *An Béal Bocht* (The poor mouth). Few, however, may realise just how keenly Ó Nualláin was in tune with the temper of many in the Gaelic movement of his time. One wonders, for example, whether he had read An tAthair Mártán Ó Domhnaill's panegyric of Inis Meán in his 1930 book *Oileáin Árann*:

> The true Gaelic speaker will find too short the time he spends among people who are truly Gaelic, not only about Gaelic, but in every way. But with the help of God, we will get a chance to come back to Inis Meán and to spend a little while among the people of this island in the Gaeltacht of Gaeltachts.[2]

Humour was the furthest thing from Ó Domhnaill's mind in this passage. He was in dead earnest that true *Gaelachas* had to be sought in its natural habitat, those areas in which the language had been preserved in unbroken succession since the arrival of the Gaels in Ireland.

By no means was this a minority or extreme position. For those who championed the native speaker as the only possible saviour of the language and native culture of which it was the vehicle, logic demanded that they elevate the Gaeltacht into a site of mandatory pilgrimage for those wishing to begin the long process of attaining authentic *Gaelachas*. Paeans to the Gaeltacht, 'the most precious treasure in Ireland' (an seoid is luachmhaire i nÉirinn) (*FL*, 15/9/23), were a regular feature of the Gaelic intellectual landscape of the time. For example, in a 1926 essay on 'An Ghaeltacht' Cormac Breathnach wrote:

> There are in the Gaeltacht – and there alone – special things, such as the culture and civilisation and folklore and true genius of the Gaelic race. These are things that are interwoven with the language; indeed, they are the life of the language, and the person who does not absorb them with the language is felt to be lacking something; for although he has Irish, he does not have the Gaelic character. That character can only be engendered and nourished in the Gaeltacht (*FL*, Dec. 1926, 1).[3]

Writing on 'The Gael and the Gaeltacht' in The *Irish Ecclesiastical Record* the following year, Brother Philip developed this idea more tendentiously:

> Yet nobody knows this land who does not know the Gaeltacht, and certainly anyone knowing it will realise that it and it alone is the true Ireland, separated from Britain in matters mental and spiritual by a chasm wider far and deeper than the sea that divides their shores . . . The Gaeltacht represents the last stronghold of the Gael and his native civilisation (*IER*, Aug. 1927, 143–4).

Seosamh Mac Grianna felt that the gap between Gaeltacht and Galltacht could only be bridged by English-speaking Irish people willing to acknowledge their own second-class citizenship in the Gaelic state to which they aspired. In a combative 1932 letter to the editor of the *Irish Press*, Mac Grianna asserted of his fellow native speakers from the Gaeltacht: 'We know that we are the absolute right when nationality becomes the standard . . . For, whoever hauled down the British flag from Dublin's towers, we are the nation' (*IP*, 1/3/32).[4] Cormac Breathnach sounded a similar note in *Fáinne an Lae* in December 1926:

> And who are the people of the Gaeltacht? Noble descendants of Gaels who have been living in poverty suffering the oppression of Foreigners for hundreds of years . . . They are people who have the only foundation on which it would be possible to build a Gaelic state (*FL*, Dec. 1926, 1).[5]

Having discussed the long struggle for independent Irish nationhood in the University College Galway journal *An t-Irisleabhar* in 1936, Máirtín Ua Flaithbheartaigh continued:

> This Gaelic nation is, therefore, alive, but if so, it is in the Gaeltacht that it is alive. Its territory is narrow, but its qualities are strong. The Gaeltacht is the only part of this State worth serving if what the people of Ireland have in mind is to revive the Gaelic nation. If Ireland were unified tomorrow and if she were free from shore to shore, she would have no right to call herself a nation if she did not have the Gaeltacht. The nation's right of inheritance is in the Gaeltacht alone (*Irisleabhar*, 1935–6, 14).[6]

The Jesuit E. Cahill stressed the spiritual as well as the cultural centrality of the Gaeltacht for the Irish nation, in the process invoking a familiar metaphor:

> The people of the Gaedhealtacht . . . are the warm repositories of the old Irish Catholic tradition . . . Hence, the people of the Gaedhealtacht, besides being amongst the very best of the Irish race physically and morally, are of incalculable importance to the future of the Irish nation. Besides, the old Catholic Irish tradition of the Gaedhealtacht, where alone the Irish Catholic tradition now lives, is one of the nation's best bulwarks against the materialism of the English-speaking world by which it is surrounded.[7]

For the Conamara novelist Pádhraic Óg Ó Conaire, the nobility of the people of the Gaeltacht was an article of faith assserted in every one of his seven novels, six of which appeared between 1922 and 1939. Typical is the tribute found in *Solus an Ghrádha* (1923):

> There now are the descendants of the true Gaels whose ancestors Cromwell drove from the smooth fields of Meath . . . But they settled here at the edge of the sea and among the hills and they established the Faith and the Gaelic Civilisation that the plunderers failed to destroy. Yes, they settled here, and they kept the Faith and the noble qualities of the Gaels alive and strong; and a person who will not spend a while by the shore and the hills at the edge of the sea in the west is a person ignorant of the good qualities of the Gaels.[8]

There were, however, dissenting voices. For example, in a 1935 essay in *The Leader*, 'Dubliner' took sharp exception to a recent piece in the *Irish Press* praising a plan to send Dublin children to the Gaeltacht, where they would experience 'the real nation' and get to know the 'truly Irish' people who lived there:

> The phrases 'truly Irish' and 'real nation' are good examples of the wholly unjustifiable elevation of native Irish speakers above a modest 97 per cent of Irishmen . . . The Gaeltacht certainly possesses culture of a kind – culture which all simple, kindly country-dwellers have. The wisdom of proclaiming this, however, as 'a culture higher than anything that exists elsewhere' is more than doubtful: it has not produced great painting, great sculpture or great drama, to mention but three forms of artistic expression which flourish during periods of high culture (*Leader*, 17/8/35).[9]

James Devane was in complete agreement in an essay in *Ireland To-Day* the following year in which he blasted 'Four Irish Myths':

The Gaeltacht myth is the most dangerous of all. For it contains half a truth and it appeals to one of the most dangerous passions – national chauvinism. The Gaeltacht myth relates that there was once a great civilisation in this land distinguished by commerce, crafts, science, the arts, architecture, an uniform, organic and fertile life. Somehow or other – like those phantom cathedrals and cities of the old Celtic legends – all vanished away, and simple peasants of Connemara and fishermen on the western sea-board are the trustees of all that inheritance. If Ireland is ever to come to anything it must abandon Europe, eschew everything foreign to this land, and at the humble hearth of Connemara crofters, light the torch which will guide the path to our pristine splendour. That is a myth. It reduces the civilisation of the Celt and Gael to the level of a farmyard patois; a culture of the cabbage-patch (*Ireland To-Day*, June 1936, 15–16).[10]

As we saw in chapter one, others critical of the orthodox glorification of the Gaeltacht pointed out that even if its residents were the trustees of the Gaelic inheritance, they owed that honor to accidents of history and geography, a fact underscored by Thomas F. O'Rahilly in his contribution to a forum on the language in the Jesuit quarterly *Studies*. O'Rahilly wrote 'that the great bulk of these native speakers of Irish have kept the language, not through any love of it or through any feeling of patriotic pride, but almost solely because they could not help it' (*Studies*, Mar. 1923, 39). Éamonn Mac Giolla Iasachta of *An Sguab* expanded on this idea in 1925, writing of Gaeltacht people:

The reason they did not abandon Irish as the other people of the country did was that Cromwell and his breed never attacked them. And the reason they did not was because they did not think it worthwhile. There was no plunder for them to take in the place . . . It was the poverty, therefore, that saved Irish in the Gaeltacht (*Sguab*, Mar. 1925, 300).[11]

Not all Irish-Irelanders would have shared such concerns about Gaeltacht poverty. Indeed for some of the movement's ideologues, the very virtues for which the people of the Gaeltacht were so regularly extolled were rooted in the endemic and often dreadful destitution of isolated Gaeltacht areas. Writing in *Timthire Chroidhe Naomhtha Íosa* in 1934, the Jesuit S. Ó Curraidhín offered a romantic, pietistic view of Gaeltacht life:

It is a hard life the people of Conamara have. Hard indeed. They must be ploughing and digging their bit of land from dawn to sunset; always ploughing and fighting a raging sea to win a bite to eat . . . But they have one thing that modern civilisation rarely does, a treasure that, alas, it is not possible for land however fine or money however much to buy – peace of soul in God (*TCNÍ*, July 1934, 161).[12]

This link between destitution and virtue was made explicit by Micheál Ó Gríobhtha in his 1937 story 'An tSrúill' (The sea), in which a stranger explains to a Gaeltacht man how lucky he is: 'The poverty in this district is like a fortification around you to keep the evil of the world far away from you. Virtue is still here; the occasion of sin is not.'[13] For An tAthair P. Eric Mac Fhinn, the spiritual wealth of the Gaeltacht more than compensated for its material poverty. Having discussed the many hardships the characters must endure in Séamus Ó Grianna's 1924 novel *Caisleáin Óir* (Castles of gold), he concluded: 'He has little doubt that it is happier for the Gaels with whom the life of the saints stayed, living from hand to mouth, or even in famine and hardship, as fishermen in Donegal, than for those who found glory in the courts of Europe' (*An Róimh*, Summer 1925, 38).[14]

The narrator of Seán Ó Ciosáin's 1935 story 'Móna' also felt that despite – or perhaps because of – the myriad hardships of their lives, the people of the West Cork Gaeltacht had a saner view of life than did their more educated, comfortable, and introspective urban compatriots:

> In a way I envy them – they have so straightforward a mind. Without a doubt they have their own troubles. Always watching the weather for that is what most sends misfortune or the opposite their way – always wrestling with some hardship, but nonetheless without any complexity of mind. Everything is black and white to them, unlike intellectuals who have twenty shades for every colour.[15]

An even more naive expression of this patronising primitivism can be found in an essay by Séamus Mac Cuaige in *Gearrbhaile*, the magazine of St Joseph's College in Ballinasloe, County Galway, in which the author offers the following rhapsody:

> Although most of the people in that area are poor, they are never gloomy or troubled; they are cheerful and joyful the whole day long. It is my opinion that there is not a group of people under the sun who are as happy as those poor people. They don't complain or anything like that, but are always altogether satisfied with the lot God assigned them (*Gearrbhaile*, Jan. 1927, 5).[16]

Mac Cuaig's Gaeltacht is, in effect, merely an exaggerated version of Éamon de Valera's rural Gaelic utopia as described in his famous St Patrick's Day radio address to the diaspora in 1943:

> That Ireland which we dreamed of would be the home of a people who valued material wealth only as a basis of right living, of a people who were satisfied with frugal comfort and devoted their leisure to things of the spirit; a land whose countryside would be bright with cosy homesteads, whose fields and villages

would be joyous with the sounds of industry, the romping of sturdy children, the contests of athletic youths, the laughter of comely maidens; whose firesides would be the forums of the wisdom of serene old age.[17]

Now regularly – and unjustly – cited as an occasion for parody, de Valera's vision was very much in the Gaelic mainstream of the 1920s and 1930s.[18] Frugal self-reliance was the emphasis in the parliamentarian Micheál Óg Mac Pháidín's 1930 panegyric of the Gaeltacht person in *The Star*:

> The Gael of the Gaeltacht is not a greedy man. He does not want to be a fat, churlish man of means. He is content with moderation. If he has his little patch of potatoes and oats coming along nicely unaffected by the blight, he is at his ease that year. If he has a good heap of potatoes, a stack of dry turf, and the rent and the taxes paid, there is not a man in Ireland less worried (*Star*, Dec. 1930).[19]

For Aodh de Blácam, on the other hand, rural Gaelic life had a transcendant importance de Valera would have very much understood. Writing in the *Irish Rosary* in 1937, the very year the people of the Free State voted in referendum to accept de Valera's new constitution for the state, de Blácam declared:

> You may praise up an abstract society in which justice and charity meet; but when you have the people of a parish going to Solemn High Mass on the feast of the patron, and giving the rest of the day to wholesome social jollity, then in such a pattern you have the Catholic brotherhood embodied, visible, persuasive. That is what I mean by Gaelic culture as the effective channel of Catholic wisdom in society (*IR*, July 1937, 529).[20]

The idea that the life of such rural parishes in the Gaeltacht was the most – if not the only – appropriate subject for literature in what was at the time still very much a rural language had, therefore, strong appeal on both practical and ideological grounds. Even so urban and urbane a Gael as 'Fear Faire' could appreciate the importance of rural life in Irish society:

> Rural Ireland is Irish Ireland . . . We do not forget that cities, as centres of learning and commerce, have a vital place in comprehensive nationhood. Yet in all lands, especially in Ireland, the countryside is the part in which the springs of racial strength flow (*CB*, June 1938, 554).[21]

Indeed Tomás Ó Gríobhtha saw the Gaelic Irish as an inherently rural people:

> The Gael is by nature given to the rural life. He likes it; it suits him. It is the best and the noblest life. There is nothing better than the man living the appropriate life,

> that is, having enough land to support himself, livestock and resources to match; free from debt and uncleared loans, and living to God's satisfaction and esteemed by his neighbors. That is without any doubt the life of a noble person (*Star*, 12/4/30).[22]

According to the editor of *An Muimhneach*, literature in Irish had always been a literature of the countryside. In a sharply anti-urban 1933 piece on unemployment, the editor asserted:

> The Gael always had a heartfelt hatred for the false civilisation of the town. It is the innocent life of the countryside that is revealed in his own literature. He liked to commune with mysterious nature in the loneliness of the country and to philosophise in his own mind about all the wonders opening out around him. That raised his mind to the all-powerful God (*Muimhneach*, Mar. 1933, 56).[23]

The man who would become the most influential Irish literary critic of his time, Daniel Corkery, hoped that writers of Irish would return to their rural loyalties, rejecting what he saw as a specious cosmopolitanism in favour of 'the qualities of nationality' (tréithe na náisiúntachta) and 'the qualities of the faith of the people' (tréithe creidimh na ndaoine). Writing in 1924, Corkery argued:

> But now the Renaissance is gone – dead – and therefore those two notes are coming back again to every literature in Europe and America. As an indication of that, you could call the best literature that has been created in our own time 'Regional'. It is the mind of the common people that is of greatest concern in literature of that kind (*FMR*, Nov. 1924, 242).[24]

Needless to say, those common people, if native and natural speakers of Irish, would be farmers and the families of farmers. Máiréad Ní Ghráda, who would go on to become one of the most adventurous and accomplished dramatists in Irish, and one who by no means limited her focus to rural life, could argue in a 1935 essay that the Gaeltacht was, and should remain, the heartland of Gaelic literature: 'The Gaeltacht must not be neglected. There is no growth in store for literature in Irish unless it is rooted in the soil native to it' (*II*, 11/10/35).[25] In a 1937 editorial piece in the Galway monthly *Ar Aghaidh*, An tAthair Eric Mac Fhinn blasted those who criticised Gaelic writers for concentrating on rural themes, arguing that those writers had little choice since it was only in the countryside that the Irish language was in everyday use. He then went on to discuss what he saw as the real motivation behind those dismissive of rural life as literary subject:

> There is an English word that well fits the defenders of that philosophy – the word 'snob', a word that, as far as I know, cannot be translated into Irish or any other

language, and that an English writer defined as 'a person who reveres contemptible things and shows that reverence in a contemptible way' (*AA*, Oct. 1937, 2).[26]

This attack was both unfair to those thoughtful and well-intentioned critics eager for the language to test its capabilities and probably unnecessary, given that most Gaelic writers and critics seem never to have questioned the primacy of rural themes in the new Gaelic literature. The problem was not, of course, the rural subject or theme in itself, but rather the crude and unsophisticated way that subject or theme was developed, a point stressed by Mac Giolla Bhríde in a 1929 review of Micheál Mac Liammóir's story collection *Lá agus Oidhche* (Day and night):

> There is still a great need for many books that deal with the life of the people in Ireland. I hope that the writers of these books do not forget something very important in my opinion; that is: that it is not enough to provide readers of Irish with the same kind of reading always. There is, for example, one life, the quiet, simple life of the Gaeltacht, and there are many things yet to be written about that life instead of constantly saying the same things about it. It does not matter how quiet and simple the life of the people in the Gaeltacht is, it is possible for a gifted writer to find enough material in it to write essays and stories that will be remembered for a long time (*Tír*, Nov. 1929, 7).[27]

Unfortunately, there were few genuinely first-rate writers producing even fewer memorable books in Irish on rural life at this time. Most seem to have been content to suppress whatever aesthetic judgment they had in order to celebrate that 'quiet simple life' of the Gaeltacht. The reasons for this abdication, in addition to sheer lack of literary ability on the part of some, was primarily ideological. If the Gaelic West, the soul of the emergent nation, was threatened, the duty of the good nationalist was to defend it, particularly against the misconceptions, whether ignorant or malicious, of those who had no first-hand experience of the Gaeltacht. Speaking through the narrator of his 1939 novel *Ceol na nGiolcach* (The music of the reeds), Pádhraic Óg Ó Conaire made explicit his sense of mission in setting the record straight, describing the people of the Conamara Gaeltacht as 'people . . . who never got justice from writers, who thought they had the proper insight. Much that has been written about them was written with exaggeration and mockery. Speech was put into their mouths that their minds never thought of.'[28] Alan Titley has argued persuasively that the principal theme of the traditional Gaeltacht novel in Irish, what he calls 'the communal Gaeltacht novel' (an t-úrscéal pobail Gaeltachta), is 'the change of life . . . the new life bursting in on the old life, and the old life always a stone's throw from us in some past time that we can never seize hold of' (an t-athrú saoil . . . an saol nua ag fáscadh reatha ar an seansaol, agus an seansaol fad urchair méaróige i gcónaí uainn in aimsir chaite éigin nach bhfuil breith riamh againn air).[29] But if this sense of inexorable change and the elusive existence of an always just passed golden age is a, if not the, thematic core of the Gaeltacht novel, the prime motive of this genre is the celebration of a people and a lifestyle whose like, in Tomás Ó Criomhthain's famous phrase, will never be seen again.

As might be expected, so universally accepted a creative impulse soon evolved into a thematic nexus in its own right, so that Gaelic novelists, story writers, and dramatists often seem to have felt that they had fulfilled their mission by merely putting admirable Gaeltacht characters and their ways and customs before their reading or viewing audiences. Certainly some critics seem to have judged their efforts by that criterion, as when in his review of Seaghán Mac Meanman's *Indé agus Indiu*, Colm Ó Frighil's highest praise was for the author's ability to deal sympathetically with Gaeltacht life:

> There are not many writers in the province of Ulster who want to take on the task of writing a book, but of the few there are, Seaghán Mac Meanman is the writer who best reveals the life of the people in the Gaeltacht in a simple and natural way (*Tír*, Nov. 1929, 5).[30]

And even so well read a critic as Shán Ó Cuív could praise Séamus Ó Dubhghaill's *Beartín Luachra* (A little bundle of rushes) for being little more than 'a true picture of rural life in south Kerry during the author's youth' (fíor-pheictiúir ar shaoghal na tuatha i gCiarraidhe theas le linn óige an ughdair).[31] Moreover, as we will see below, many Gaelic critics of the time valued the famous Blasket Island autobiographies as highly, if not more so, as anthropological studies than as literature – if they even saw a clear distinction between the two with regard to writing from and about the Gaeltacht. Brian Ó Nualláin would, of course, parody this attitude in *An Béal Bocht*, but he was already taking aim at it as early as 1933 in 'Aistear Pheadair Dhuibh' (The journey of Peadar Dubh), in which the Gaeltacht characters ask their priest why God had created them for a life of such unceasing misery, only to be answered: 'It wasn't God who did the creating, but Parthalán Mac an Dubhda, the writer, and Feidhlimidh Ó Casaidhe, the poet – two Dubliners.' Ó Nualláin's protagonist sets out for the capital with his shotgun, deals with the guilty littérateurs, and introduces normalcy to his Gaeltacht townland: 'There are shops on the bog now, and one can get a bus ticket, a cigarette, and the daily mail there. There are ordinary people on that bog today' (*Inis Fáil*, Mar. 1933, 64).[32]

It was not, however, ordinary people that the Gaels expected or wanted to find in the Gaeltacht. The literary efforts by novelists, story writers, and dramatists to capture the life of the noble and unique people of the Gaeltacht before it passed away forever will be discussed in more detail below. Before doing so, however, we should take an overall view of the image of Gaeltacht people developed by the language movement over the years, particularly in light of how the Gaels were attempting to at once refute negative stereotypes and offer in their place a more appropriate and inspirational alternative. First of all, those in the movement regularly stressed the physical hardships and lack of resources and amenities in the Gaeltacht, challenges that would break the spirit of a lesser people. Well aware of the stereotype of the shiftless and lazy Irish, cultural nationalists confronted those distortions with their own depictions of the ceaseless industry necessary to merely survive in such an environment. No one rejected the stereotype more forcefully than did Seán Joyce ('Loch Measca') in his 1929 memoir *Eachtra Múinteora* (A teacher's story of adventure):

> Not only were the Irish-speakers of this country poor, but they were held in contempt by the rich and the learned folk with the Latin, who did not know what want, hunger, and thirst were, but who would say that the Irish-speakers were a lazy lot. The Irish-speakers of the West are not lazy, but rather lively, active people, far-seeing and clear-minded, who earn their daily bread honestly with the sweat of their bones.[33]

In his 1938 story 'An Truisle' (The stumble), one of their own, Ros Muc-born and bred Colm Ó Gaora, painted the following picture of a group of Conamara people going to the curragh races on one of their rare days off:

> There were men from every direction going rapidly along the road. They were half-stooped and their legs half-bowed, as if they were crippled – from the hard work of the year. They carried one shoulder high – the right shoulder on one, or the left shoulder on another. A person would know from looking at them whether they worked left or right-handed from the shape of that shoulder. The hard work with the loy or the pulling of the baskets put them in that condition. The women had a slow, stiff walk. You would think that they were thinking that they were under a burden even today.[34]

The brutal hard work expected of women in Donegal was described by Ó Grianna in *Caisleáin Óir*:

> It was a winter morning. The snow that had been on the ground for a week was beginning to thaw. A vicious, bitter wind was coming in blasts down from Errigal and going to the heart of the three women who were wading along through the snow on their way to An Clochán Dubh with little bundles of stockings on their backs. Caitlín Chonaill's head was almost touching her feet with the age and the load together.[35]

Such hard work was consistently linked with high-mindedness or spirituality, an association very much in keeping with the de Valerian rural vision. By no means was this connection always left implicit, as is clear from the comments of An tAthair Cainneach in a 1925 essay on 'Obair' (Work):

> Work was first put on the human race as penance; but it turns into a pleasure and a blessing for the person who sticks to it willingly. It does his mind and his body good; his health is better for it; his mind is nobler for it; neither sorrow nor anxiety can get at him as long as he gives his full attention to the job in hand (*Branar*, May 1925, 139).[36]

Certainly this was the dominant though by no means exclusive way of thinking about the hardships of Gaeltacht life in the 1920s and 1930s. Physical suffering earned the spiritual consolation of both individual virtue and communal solidarity.

Of course no Catholic Gael ever believed that good works alone brought deliverance here or hereafter. Faith was imperative, and the deep and unquestioning piety of the Gaeltacht was stressed by virtually every writer who spoke of the region and its people. In a 1935 review of Robin Flower's English translation of Tomás Ó Criomhthain's *An t-Oileánach*, John J. M. Ryan wrote: 'The world into which *The Islandman* leads us is a world of faith, of boundless trust in God, and of thankfulness for His help and protection amid the hardships and difficulties of a precarious existence' (*IR*, Jan. 1935, 73). 'M. Ó R.' sounded a similar note in his 1938 review of Pádraig Ó Gallchobhair's *Cáitheamh na dTonn*. He began with a rebuttal of Gaeltacht stereotypes, and then explained the more authentic perspective this book would provide:

> This book would awaken your mind and your thoughts about everything that is noble and good in the nature of the Irish speakers by the sea. A person would notice the simplicity, nobility, and the love they have for God – their gratitude to him is greater when they have much to complain about (*AA*, June 1935, 3).[37]

This faith was nothing generic or non-denominational, but an intense devotion and loyalty to the clergy, liturgy, and rituals – including a rich store of apocryphal and local folk practices – of the Roman Catholic Church. Muiris Mag Uidhir underscored this point in a 1930 essay on 'Saoidheacht Ghaedhealach' (Gaelic culture): 'Gaelic culture survived despite the tyranny of Foreigners. Faith and Nationality were interwoven with each other, with the language as a golden thread binding them together always' (*Tír*, Mar. 1930, 1).[38] Micheál Ó Maoláin developed this idea with regard to his native Aran Islands in a 1939 essay in *Irisleabhar Chnuic Mhuire / Knock Shrine Annual*:

> I do not think that there is any other place in Ireland where they have as much reverence and love for the Blessed Virgin – although there is much of both in every part of the country – than they do in the Aran Islands. Of the three islands, Inis Meán has to be given pre-eminence . . . I do not think that five minutes ever passed in the life of a person from Inis Meán without the name of Mary being mentioned by him in a prayer or in some blessing (*Irisleabhar Chnuic Mhuire*, 1939, 52).[39]

Innocence and sincerity were seen as particularly widespread virtues in these encomia of Gaeltacht life. In a 1926 piece entitled 'Mo Shiubhalta' (My travels), 'Tadhg Gaedhealach' wrote of Achill Island in Mayo: 'Here and in places like it is the most precious seed for this nation and for the whole world if we want to bring back the simple, innocent life' (*Sguab*, Feb. 1926, 27).[40] In a 1936 review of An tAthair Pádraig Mac Giolla Cheara's *Páidín Mac Giolla Bhuidhe as Bun-Throisc*, 'M. Ó R.' made clear that these virtues were by no means the monopoly of Mayo: 'The main thought that would run through the reader's mind is the simplicity, wisdom, and innocence hidden in the people of the Gaeltacht' (*AA*, July 1935, 7).[41]

It was, moreover, these personal virtues that made possible the kind of idealised 'local organic community' that almost all writers saw as the basic social unit of Gaeltacht society and that so captivated outside observers, including those who midwived the Blasket autobiographies. It was, for example, this sense of a coherent and caring community that most struck Seán Mac Maoláin on his first visit to the Donegal Gaeltacht, as he recalled in his 1969 autobiography *Gleann Airbh go Glas Naion* (Gleann Airbh to Glasnevin):

> However much I liked the beauty of the countryside, I did not like it more than I did the people themselves and their ways. Young and old, the people of the townland were like one big family, and they were as good to each other as would be the members of any family anywhere.[42]

Aindrias Ó Baoighill developed this idea with examples at the start of his 1939 novel *An tAiridheach* (The caretaker), set in the Donegal Gaeltacht:

> The inhabitants of Mín an Fhéidh are kind, honest people. Rarely does one hear of any two of them acting in an unneighbourly fashion toward each other. When life treats one of them harshly, the rest help him . . . They do a hundred other good turns of the same kind from one end of the year to the other; but no one hears any mention of that willingness to help, and they would prefer that neither I nor anyone else be talking about it.[43]

If so, they must have been seriously annoyed by many of their literary champions, who repeatedly called attention to their merits in depiction after depiction of an all but pre-lapsarian Gaeltacht. So seductive could this idyllic vision be that even a writer like Seosamh Mac Grianna, who knew far better from personal experience just how human and flawed Gaeltacht people were, could momentarily fall under its spell, as he did in the following passage on the men of Ros Cuain in *An Druma Mór* (The big drum): 'And to give them their due, no matter how assertive they were, no man at all was boasting that he had a better house, or better land, or more wealth than another man. They looked at the virtues a person was born with, and the virtues he developed as he matured.'[44]

While the more ethically satisfying – and debatable – exaltations of the Gaeltacht as free of class divisions may have had great initial appeal to contemporary readers, particularly those in cities, far more important in cultural and literary terms was the recurrent tribute to Gaeltacht conservatism, the tenacious preservation of *all* elements of the national heritage through the centuries. It was primarily for this almost instinctive conservatism that the people of the Gaeltacht had earned the gratitude and admiration of cultural nationalists, those Irish people for whom such a veneration for the past was an article of their national faith. Cormac Ó Cuileannáin gave this idea a specifically Catholic nuance in a previously quoted 1935 essay in the *Cork Weekly Examiner*:

> The real nationalist – the person who longs for a Gaelic Ireland, is a pillar of the faith. Indeed he is not a revolutionary, nor a maker of new laws. He stands on the side of the OLD THINGS. He is a preserver, he is a conservative by nature. There is no group of people in the country who deserve that name more than the people who champion Gaelachas. Their goal is to defend and to preserve and to perpetuate the old faith, the old language, the old Christian literature, the old culture, and the old traditions (*Cork Weekly Examiner*, 16/3/35).[45]

An tAthair Seoirse Mac Clúin agreed in an essay on 'An Bloscaod Mór' (The Great Blasket) in his 1924 collection *Róisín Fiain na Mara* (The wild little rose of the sea). For Mac Clúin, the only way the Irish could escape drowning 'in the foul stream of John Bullism' (i mbréansruth Seán-Buidheachais) was by turning instead to 'the worthy wine of the old spirit' (fíon fiúntach na seanaspride) that was to be found in its full strength and purity only in the Gaeltacht.[46]

The following year, Seán Ua Cadhla rooted 'Sean-Aimsireacht' (Old-fashionedness), 'education according to ancestral heritage' (oideachas do réir dúthchais) in his phrase, firmly in the rich oral culture of the past – and of the western Gaeltacht:

> What is meant by old-fashionedness is the things that used to be talked about when people were brought together to visit and talk by the fire in the long winter nights

> long ago . . . Good talk and wit are at present to be found nowhere in Ireland except in the Gaeltacht (*FL*, 4/7/25).[47]

In March 1932, the editor of *Outlook* developed this idea in an essay entitled 'The Secret Ireland':

> If we save the Gaeltacht, we can hope to bring back those traditions [i. e. 'habits of thought which belonged to the Gaelic tongue when it was universal'] to the whole country. We can hope to build up a national culture such as Ireland would have possessed if there had been no anglicisation; that is, the culture of the medieval mind . . . Only those who know the Gaeltacht personally can understand the charm and richness of any unanglicised society.

It is, however, striking that this author also argued that 'it is important that we not get into the habit of regarding the Gaeltacht as a different Ireland' or as 'a kind of museum' (*Outlook*, 19/3/32).[48]

For most in the movement, however, the Gaeltacht was to remain very much a place apart – or above – the anglicised Ireland of the twentieth century. Writing in *Bonaventura* in 1937, Thomas Barrington saw the Blasket autobiographies as guidebooks to lead the Irish people back to the good Gaelic life:

> The islands present a way of going back to the Gaelic life of the past, a living and an easy way . . . This little island of fishermen has climbed to a certain measure of fame because it is united in loving three good things: Catholicism and traditionalism and courage. Will Ireland ever climb to fame in like manner? (*Bonaventura*, Summer 1937, 123).

It was as a term that encapsulated all of these ethnic, moral, and cultural virtues that the *Irish Press* in 1933 extolled 'Sean-Aimsireacht' as an inspiration both immediate and sustaining for the newly independent state, at the same time carefully rescuing the term from the perverse, navel-gazing connotations it had developed under foreign influence:

> That word 'old-fashionedness' is a trick of the English, because they think that if Gaels feel shamed by it, they will have little hesitation in rejecting their language and their ancestors . . . The Gaelic nation is at present so weak that it cannot be rescued without going back to the life that was. That is the same as saying that the new Gaelic nation will have to be nourished on 'old-fashionedness' until it is able to act (*IP*, 10/10/33).[49]

Not all Gaels felt such a need to explain or defend their fidelity to the old values. For them, Séamus Ó Grianna was, as was so often true, the spokesman, as when in a speech on 'Long Ago' (Am Fadó) to Dáil Chonnacht in Dublin in November 1924, he compared Irish life past and present and concluded 'that it would have been delightful to be alive long ago' (go mb'aoibhinn bheith beo ins an am fadó) (*FL*, 29/11/24).[50]

Many Gaelic intellectuals stressed that a significant component of what had made life in the past so delightful was still to be found in the rich folklore of the Gaeltacht. And even more important, that folklore had preserved much of what had made life in the past so Gaelic, a point to which writers returned again and again throughout this period. For many, the principal appeal of oral tradition was linguistic, based on the conviction that the very best of the sacrosanct *caint na ndaoine* was to be found therein. For example, in 1924 Caitlín Nic Ghabhann explained the purity of Gaeltacht Irish to readers of *Iris an Fháinne* in the following terms:

> It amazes them, when they go to the Gaeltacht, to find out that the man of the house, who is not able to read Irish, or English either perhaps, speaks flawless Irish . . . It is the storytelling and the singing by the fire that kept Irish pure, uncorrupted, during the past centuries, when it was left uncultivated (*IF*, Mar. 1924, 31).[51]

Two years later, the editor of *An Lóchrann* lamented the lack of knowledge of and interest in folklore among the young, and continued:

> But let us take care that what they will have will not be an Irish that is a new language, carrying only grammar and spelling and pronunication but divorced from history, from beautiful speech, from the folklore of thousands of years and from a fellowship of temperament and understanding with the people from whom we have come (*Lóchrann*, Aug. 1926, 68).[52]

The folklore journal *Béaloideas* was regularly praised as an extraordinary linguistic resource, as it was by 'R. Mac M.' in 1934:

> And there are people, people in search of pure Irish – no insignificant number – and I suspect that many of them do not know that 'Béaloideas' is a fountain of real Irish, and that the person who would slake his thirst there from time to time would no longer have to be a speaker of weak Irish (*IP*, 20/11/34).[53]

Seán Ó Ciarghusa agreed in *The Leader* in 1936, declaring of the folklore collected in *Béaloideas*: 'It must be cultivated in Ireland because the Irish is better and purer in the folklore than it is in the books as yet' (*Leader*, 15/8/36).[54]

While never downplaying the potential linguistic significance of oral tradition, many Gaels stressed that folklore had preserved something every bit as essential as an uncorrupted language; it had protected through the ages the uncorrupted national soul, the *Gaelachas* that made the Irish a separate and significant people. Commenting on a 1928 meeting of the Irish Folklore Commission, Father Lawrence Murray wrote:

> We fear that the majority who are speaking about nationality and *Gaelachas* do not understand the relationship that exists beteen these things and folklore – that it is not possible to re-Gaelicise the country without bringing back the folklore and the culture that goes with it as well. The old stories, the old songs, old prayers, the proverbs, they reveal to us the mind and the traits of the ancient Gaels; and if we want to be truly Gaelic and have the proper Gaelic outlook, we must be immersed in the old folklore (*Ultach*, Mar. 1928, 4).[55]

In 1938, Eoin Mac Néill, one of the most important intellectual leaders in the language revival movement from its very inception, wrote in an article entitled 'The Meaning of Folklore / We Are Witnesses of the Rebirth of Our National Tradition':

> For hundreds of years invaders fought to destroy that distinctively Irish outlook on life in order to kill the Irish nation. They came perilously near succeeding. They broke the tradition. But it still lingers, and in our own day we have lived to see the turn of the tide, the re-birth of the Irish national tradition which is the spinal cord of Irish nationality. Hence, the value of folklore, the inspiration of national consciousness, and the medullary matter of literature (*II* 26/9/38).

In 1929, one of the most active and distinguished members of the Folklore Commission, the veteran Gaelic writer Pádraig Ó Siochfhradha, argued that the study of folklore was necessary to put the substance and soul into the schoolroom Irish being learned in the Galltacht: 'Therefore if we have only the cold words of Irish, it is a thin and exhausted kind of *Gaelachas* that we will have as a result.' Ó Siochfhradha stressed that native folklore could add to a mere academic mastery of the language 'the history of the mind of the people whose language it was for thousands of years . . . things that evolved from the language and are part of its equipment and its beauty, and without which it would be a poor, bare, ruined thing.' Then, after listing the myriad genres and practices that comprise Irish folklore, he challenged his readers with the question, 'Could anyone think that we would have *Gaelachas* without those things?' (*FL*, Sept. 1929, 1).[56]

A few in the movement were bold enough to answer that question in the affirmative, doubtless agreeing in principle with Aodh de Blácam's 1924 assertion that 'never will Europe return to the folk mind' (*Studies*, Mar. 1924, 73). As early as March 1922, the Holy Ghost priest Raghnall de Brún developed this idea at some length in the University College Dublin journal *An*

Reult in an attack on the obsession of some with what he called 'Meadhon-Aoiseachas' (Medievalism):

> We suffered from mental servility. There were two ways of doing everything, the Gaelic way our ancestors practiced before us and the English way. We had no initiative in literature. No matter what subject matter we had, there was only form in which it would be proper to tell it – the form used by the *seanchaí* [storyteller]. If it was not in that form, the whole story was nothing but Englishness and it was said that the person who composed it was assisting John Bull in the anglicisation of the country (*An Reult*, Mar. 1922, 51).[57]

Father Dinneen expressed his reservations about the fascination with folklore in more reserved tones in the souvenir programme for the 1928 Aonach Taillteann, writing: 'It is well worth our while to preserve and revive the old customs and the old practices. But we must move with the times and do that preserving and reviving in a way that conforms to the life we are living.'[58] Seán Ó Ciarghusa developed a similar point in a 1928 essay on translation:

> Without a doubt, there are many things in the English language that would be useful to us, and particularly all the knowledge that language was gathering while the poor Irish language was a fettered prisoner. We go to English for that knowledge and for any other things in it that Irish does not have. But for the things that do not belong to English but rather to Irish, namely, the Irish language itself and all the poetry and Fenian lore and the good humour and the folklore of the Gaels, for them let us go to the place where they are, that is, the Gaeltacht and the Irish language itself.[59]

Two of the most prolific and in different ways influential Gaelic writers of the period also expressed their concern about the preeminent position assigned to folk material by some revivalists. As was so often true, it was Liam Ó Rinn who formulated his scepticism most clearly in a review essay subtitled 'Béal-Oideas agus Litríocht' (Folklore and literature) in 1934:

> That word 'folklore' sometimes disgusts me ... The old storytelling always reminds me that the Irish language is on its deathbed, that it is dying along with the old people of the Gaeltacht. In my mind I equate the committed group who are collecting the folklore with the antiquarians who gather little remnants to enable them to have some insight into the worlds and the civilisations that have been covered with grass or sand since time immemorial.

For Ó Rinn, any attempt to rejuvenate Gaelic culture in the twentieth century with an infusion of traditional folklore was as ludicrous as it was misguided:

'After all has been said about folklore, it is as dry and withered as old age itself; like old age again, woe to the one who would be expecting to find a source of hope in it. I feel in my bones that there is not and never will be any growth in it' (*UI*, 8/11/34).[60] Peadar Ó Dubhda expressed similar ideas more bluntly in 1937:

> We have not really begun yet, and I'll tell you why. We're too much attached to the 'Béaloideas' idea that is being shouted about and talked about and written about so much during the last seven or eight years, a mania that has taken hold on the Gaelic movement to the detriment of the Gaelic movement.

Ó Dubhda concluded his essay with a question – 'What's wrong?' – to which he replied: 'A surfeit of Béaloideas, that's what's wrong' (*Gaedheal*, Nov. 1937, 8).

Ó Rinn and Ó Dubhda were, of course, townies, coming to folk material very much as outsiders. For this reason, their critique probably lacked the impact of that advanced by Seosamh Mac Grianna, a man who claimed of an 'Anglicised bourgeois' opponent in another debate within the movement: 'He cannot answer my statement, because I know what folk-culture is, and I know how much folk-culture there is' (*Irish Workers' Voice*, 18/3/33). That Mac Grianna had a profound respect for that culture in its living context is evident from, for example, his introduction to his brother Séamus's collection of stories learned from their father about the local legendary hero Micheál Ruadh Ó Baoighill, or from his 1932 essay in *An Camán* on 'Sgéalta na nDaoiní' (The stories of the people): 'I think that it would be worth our while to make use of the stories of the people in the new literature that we are going to create for the Gaels of the future.' Indeed he went on to say that as he thought about these folk narratives he realised 'that the Gaels had a full education without a book, without a pen' (go rabh oideachas iomlán ag na Gaedhil, gan leabhar, gan pheann) (*Camán*, 6/8/32).[61] What troubled him, however, was that those ignorant of that culture were attempting to manipulate it for their own, albeit often well-intentioned ends, a concern he romanticised in *Mo Bhealach Féin*:

> But I could not imagine some of Colm Cille's prophecy being recited anywhere else except at a turf fire in a company in which everyone understood everyone else, with the immense shadow of the hills outside, and the Great Sea lashing the dappled crags, and that old pilgrimage route over yonder and the fierce loneliness of the world above the bed of the saints.[62]

Elsewhere, however, he was more aggressive concerning the abuse of traditional material by those for whom it was either vocation or avocation rather than an element of lived experience, as in his 1933 letter to the editor of the *Irish Press*: 'As a Gael, I am interested in the destruction of folklorists' (*IP*, 19/4/33).

For the majority of Gaels at the time, however, the inextricable link between native folklore and resurgent *Gaelachas* was yet another article of the national creed. For example, in an essay on 'Béal-Oideas agus Breall-Oideas' (Folklore and foolish lore), An tAthair Raghnall Mac Suibhne from the Congregation of the Holy Ghost saw native folklore as a defensive barrier against an empty cosmopolitanism, writing:

> There is not a book or a treatise that is more full of nationality than is folklore, especially in Ireland. One sees in the old stories the Gaelic mind and the refinement of true *Gaelachas*. One sees the distinctiveness of Gaelic nationality as that nationality was created by God and before it was corrupted by the English . . . If the revival of folklore endures, *Gaelachas* is in no danger (*Humanitas*, June 1930, 30).[63]

The playwright Annraoi Saidléar sounded the same note in a 1932 review of Pádraig Ó Siochfhradha's *An Seanchaidhe Muimhneach* (The Munster storyteller):

> The references, the images, the thoughts, the dreams, the proverbs, these expressions from the Gaeltacht are the marrow and bone in the Irish language itself. It is they that make Gaels a race apart, that reveal the distinctiveness – that strong support of nationality – that separates Gaels from a race whose references, dreams, and thoughts are not the same (Enniscorthy *Echo*, 12/3/32).[64]

Caitlín de Bhaldraithe was in agreement in an essay in the *Irish Rosary* later the same year:

> It is in the folklore, in the proverbs and in the poetic epigrams that the temperament and the mind of the Gaels and the wisdom and the philosophy of the people who went before us are revealed to us. It is not known who composed most of the poetic epigrams, but we do know that the opinions of our ancestors and their philosophy are in them (*IR*, Sept. 1932, 674).[65]

Most Gaelic intellectuals had high hopes for what a renewed interest in that folklore could inspire in their compatriots. Certainly there was a widespread belief that while folklore should be studied seriously, it should not be seen as a purely academic discipline. Pádraig Ó Siochfhradha was insistent on this point in a 1929 essay on 'Feidhm an Bhéaloideasa chun Gaedhealachais' (The significance of folklore for *Gaelachas*), declaring of folklore:

> Like the language and history it is a living thing that must be used daily for it to survive at all. The natural use of the three of them is for people to know them. They aren't to be put into a glass case, nor locked up in a museum, as would be done with the dead remnants of the craftwork our ancestors did (*FL*, Sept. 1929, 1).[66]

In 1935, the Central Branch of the Gaelic League passed unanimously a resolution criticising what was seen as an inappropriately elitist attitude on the part of those in charge of the Irish Folklore Commission. The resolution read:

> That we have no confidence in the people who have been mentioned as members of the Folklore Commission because of the kind of work they do; that we think it better to work the scheme for the benefit of the Irish language among the people than to work it for the benefit of the professors (*IP*, 18/1/35).[67]

In a 1938 piece in the *Irish Independent*, the professor of Irish at Maynooth, An tAthair Donnchadh Ó Floinn, expressed similar views, writing:

> I fear that all our collectors are not free from this taint of scientific snobbishness. They may collect much, but they will miss what they should strive above all else to reach – the Gaelic. The abuse of folklore is when it disjoins humanity from the dry bones of science, when it 'clasps the cold body and foregoes the soul'. It cannot have been the intention of those who founded our Folklore Commission that it should exist only in order to supply scholars at home and abroad with data for abstruse speculations. Its main aim was and is, and must be, the re-establishment of spiritual continuity with our past (*II*, 28/9/38).[68]

No one, of course, denied that the first step had to be to collect the material as quickly as possible, an initiative made imperative by Gaelic awareness of how quickly and irrevocably that material was passing away with the elderly native speakers who had preserved it. Central to virtually all discussions of folklore in our period were laments for the dying oral culture of the Gaeltacht, laments that degenerated into a form of cliché Máirtín Ó Cadhain was later to blast as 'the Delargyesque lament, the medieval dirge (ólagón) that is sucking every strand of hope out of the race'.[69] A few examples should suffice here to catch the tone of this *ólagón* and the sense of urgency that it inspired, the awareness, in James Delargy's own words from 1938, that 'in recording the tradition of the past from old country people, we work at times with death at our elbow' (*II*, 27/9/38). In the circular issued by The Irish Folklore Commission in 1927, the newly founded organisation appealed to potential supporters to act before it was too late:

> The folklore that our ancestors had is dying with the old people who are leaving us daily. There will not be an opportunity to collect and preserve it for the nation unless the work is done in our time and in the next ten years.[70]

Despite the greatly increased collection effort undertaken by the Folklore of Ireland Society (later the Irish Folklore Commission), many Gaels felt they were engaged in a race against time, for, as the anonymous eulogist of the *seanchaí* Seán Mór Mac Guill wrote in 1936: 'The storytellers are slipping away from us day by day' (Tá siad ag sleamhnughadh uainn lá ar lá mar sgéaluidhthe) (*Éireannach*, 2/5/36). Perhaps nowhere is this characteristic elegiac note for the passing of the native lore and its carriers sounded more poignantly than in the brief preface Henry Morris ('Feargus Mac Róich') wrote for *Oidhche Áirneáil i dTír Chonaill* (A night's visiting in Donegal), his 1924 collection of sixteen stories from the Donegal Gaeltacht:

> The cover of night is coming down black and dark on the art of storytelling in Donegal. Although the number of Donegal people who have Irish from the cradle is still large and plentiful, they no longer have the art of storytelling as did their ancestors from time immemorial.[71]

In his English language editorial in the first issue of *Béaloideas* in June 1927, Delargy announced: 'The aim of our Society is a humble one – to collect what still remains of the folklore of our country' (*Béaloideas*, June 1927, 5).[72] There was, of course, nothing at all humble about this ambition, but fortunately the society could count on a significant percentage of those involved in the language revival as committed allies. Nor was this idea of the need for wide-scale and systematic collection of folk material new to Delargy and his associates in the Folklore Society. In 1923, an anonymous correspondent in the *Weekly Freeman* praised the efforts of Gaelic Leaguers in Clare to involve schoolchildren in the collection of folklore. Anticipating the later Schools Folklore Project administered by the state, this writer urged that the Clare initiative be expanded nationwide: 'It would be a fine thing if every county in which Irish is still alive would follow the example of County Clare' (*Weekly Freeman*, 27/10/23).[73] Two and a half years later, 'Tadhg Gaelach', inspired by a recent visit to the Dingle Peninsula, urged his fellow Gaels to set to work preserving native folklore while there was still time:

> I am afraid that it will be too late when these people governing us understand the preciousness of the jewel that is hidden in the Gaeltacht. Discerning people should be sent to search and collect from people everywhere in which Irish has stayed alive; and should stay collecting and collecting and filling books from them (*Sguab*, May 1926, 87).[74]

The founding of the Folklore of Ireland Society and its journal *Béaloideas* was universally applauded among the Gaels, with An tAthair Mártan Ó Domhnaill, for example, offering his gratitude for the new interest in native traditions in his 1930 book *Oileáin Arann*:

> The pity is that so much of the folklore and so many of the old stories of our country have already been lost. And although that is true, it is a source of joy and hope for us that there is a group, however small, who have a real interest in folklore and who are endeavouring to preserve it forever and therefore to save the amount of it that it is possible to find.[75]

The veteran language activist and folklorist Henry Morris stressed the importance of this work for all in the movement in a 1934 broadcast from Radio Athlone, declaring:

> Our language, our history, and our folk-lore are all complementary to one another, and our knowledge of each will be helped by a study of the others. The preservation of our folk-lore is therefore a national work and should so be regarded by the Government, by educationalists, by literary men, and by all who have the higher interests of the country at heart (*Teacher's Work*, Oct. 1934, 93).[76]

To encourage more popular involvement in the preservation of folklore, competitions were held, prizes offered, and subsidies provided. Most prestigious among the competitions were those of the Oireachtas.[77] Local *feiseanna*, popular throughout the period, also on occasion sponsored such competitions. More steady and substantial support for folklore collection also became available during the period. First of all, the League decided to use some of the £2,000 bequeathed to it by Edward Martyn to encourage and support the collection effort.[78] Moreover, in 1937, the state, in addition to the considerable financial support for the collection of folklore provided through the schools, granted the Irish Folklore Commission £125 'to publish more folklore material and to sell it cheaply' (chun breis adhbhair béaloideasa a chur i gcló agus a dhíol go saor) (*IP*, 11/2/37).

Several Gaelic journals also did their share by offering prizes for folk material submitted to them. For example, in August 1926, *An Lóchrann* urged young readers to collect and send in folklore, and offered book prizes for the best submissions (*Lóchrann*, Aug. 1926, 68). In 1931, the journal began to offer prizes for *dinnseanchas* or place-name lore (*Lóchrann*, Apr. 1931, 4). *An t-Ultach* announced its prizes for folklore in December 1926, having received the money to finance the competitions from the Folklore of Ireland Society (*Ultach*, Dec. 1926, 9). More modest were the competitions sponsored by *An Stoc*, which, like *An Lóchrann*, offered books as its monthly prizes (*Stoc*, Jan. 1927, 4). Even the *Garda Review* was involved in this effort, offering unspecified prizes for folklore submissions in 1928 (*GR*, June 1928, 602).[79]

Publication, not prizes, was, of course, the most important benefit that Gaelic journals offered the Gaelic writer, and, with the notable exception of *Humanitas*, virtually all Gaelic journals throughout this period published folk material in varying amounts. Nor did the appearance of *Béaloideas* have a serious effect on the volume of folklore published elsewhere. *An Lóchrann*, which had given pride of place to traditional material since its foundation in 1907, continued that commitment. Indeed in May 1926, the year before the Folklore of Ireland Society came on the scene, the journal announced that it intended to create an archive of its own (*Lóchrann*, April-May 1926, 46).[80] No journal welcomed folklore submissions more warmly than did *An Stoc*, whose editor Tomás Ó Máille wrote in the October 1924 issue:

> Let old songs be sent to us, old stories, lore dealing with the Fianna or any other old sayings . . . There is also plenty of traditional lore dealing with places here and there throughout the country that has not yet been put on paper in English or in Irish. Things like that must be written down while they can be gotten. Go at it, writers (*Stoc*, Oct. 1924, 4).[81]

While not all Gaelic journals were quite so enthusiastic about publishing large amounts of folklore, all of them – from *An t-Ultach* to the *Garda Review* – saw such publication as an integral part of their mission to propagate authentic *Gaelachas* to the emergent nation.

Furthermore, even leaving aside *Béaloideas*, which published 27 substantial issues between 1927 and 1939, the Gaelic journals of the time served readers interested in folklore very well. Of course, it was also true that folklore, of which there was such a ready supply, served the editors of these journals equally well. In February 1933, Father Lawrence Murray suggested to readers of *An t-Ultach* that the journal's recent inclusion of so much folklore was to compensate for a lack of other satisfactory submissions (*Ultach*, Feb. 1933, 2). Whatever motivated the editors of these journals, they published an extraordinary range of traditional material of all kinds. Not surprisingly, folktales were a particular favourite, with offerings by many of the best-known Gaeltacht writers of the period – among them Tomás Ó Criomhthain, Peadar Ó Direáin, Tadhg Seoighe, An tAthair Pádraig Eric Mac Fhinn, Seán Mac Giollarnáth, Peig Sayers, and Muiris Ó Súileabháin – appearing in various journals. Ó Criomhthain was especially prolific, publishing tales in *An Lóchrann*, *An Phoblacht*, *Timthire Chroidhe Naomhtha Íosa*, and the Enniscorthy *Echo*. Both the brother and sister of 'Máire' and Seosamh Mac Grianna contributed traditional tales to *An t-Ultach*, as did Eibhlís, the sister of Muiris Ó Súileabháin, to *An Lóchrann*; Seán, the son of Tomás Ó Criomhthain, to *An Sguab*, *An Lóchrann*, and the Cork *Weekly Examiner*; and Micheál Ó Gaoithín, the son of Peig Sayers, to *An Stoc*. Two writers who would make enormous literary contributions after 1939 began their publishing careers by submitting folk stories. Máirtín Ó Cadhain published tales in *An Stoc* in 1929 and 1930 and in *Béaloideas* in 1930 and 1936, as well as a song in *An Stoc* and miscellaneous lore in *Béaloideas* in 1935. The poet Máirtín Ó Direáin had tales in *An Stoc* in 1931 and in *Ar Aghaidh* in 1937, as well as a piece on Christmas customs on his native Aran Islands in *Ar Aghaidh* in 1936 and one on Midsummer bonfires in the *Irish Press* the following year. Among the less expected writers who published folktales in journals of this period were the Galway professor of French Liam Ó Briain, whose contribution appeared in *An Stoc* in 1924, and Úna Bean Uí Dhíosca, a story from whom was published in *Béaloideas* in 1937.[82]

Folk material also appeared – at times rather intrusively – in various works of Gaelic fiction of the period, as well, as we will see, in the Blasket Island autobiographies. For example, there is a good deal of information about traditional crafts and farming practices in Éamonn Mac Giolla Iasachta's 1927 novel *Cúrsaí Thomáis* (Thomas's affairs). Such material plays an even more important role in Seán Ó Ruadháin's *Pádhraic Mháire Bhán*, where it on occasion threatens to disrupt the narrative line.[83] Diarmuid Ua Laoghaire actually interpolated several folktales into the plot of his 1934 historical novel *An Bhruinneall Bhán* (The beautiful fair-haired maiden),[84] as did Pádraig Ó Gallchobhair ('Muirghein') in his 1934 works *Caoineadh an Choimhighthigh* (The Stranger's Lament), 'Draoidheacht Mara' (Magic of the sea), and 'Céile Sheáin Mhóir' (Big Seán's wife), the last two dealing with mermaid lore.[85]

In addition to playing a secondary role in works like these, folktales and other traditional material were the primary focus of a fair number of books in this period. Among these collections of folk stories for adult readers were An tAthair Seoirse Mac Clúin's *Binn is Blasta* (Sweet and tasty) (BÁC: Brún agus Ó Nóláin, Teór., 1922), Father Lawrence Murray's *Pota Cnuasaigh* (A pot for cooking miscellaneous things) (Dún Dealgan: n.p., 1923), Séamus Ó hEochaidh's *Sceulta Mhícil Uí Mhuirgheasa ó'n Rinn* (The stories of Micheál Ó Muirgheasa from Ring) (BÁC: COÉ, 1923), Henry Morris's *Oidhche Áirneáil i dTír Chonaill* (1924), Séamus Ó Grianna's *Micheál Ruadh* (1925), Peadar Ó Direáin's *Sgéalaidhe Leitir Mealláin* (The storyteller of Lettermullen) (BÁC: COÉ, 1926) and *Sgéalta na n-Oileán* (The stories of the islands) (BÁC: C. S. Ó Fallamhain, Teo., i gcomhar le hOS, 1929), Tadhg S. Seoighe's *Sgéalta Chois Teallaigh* (Fireside stories) (BÁC: COÉ, [1929]), Pádraig Ó Siochfhradha's *An Seanchuidhe Muimhneach* (BÁC: Institute Béaloideasa Éireann, 1932), Éamonn Ó Tuathail's *Scéalta Mhuintir Luanaigh* (Dublin: Irish Folklore Institute, 1933), Seán Mac Giollarnáth's *Peadar Chois Fhairrge* (BÁC: ODFR, 1934) and *Loinnir Mac Leabhair agus Sgéalta Gaisgidh Eile* (Loinnir Mac Leabhair and other heroic tales) (BÁC: ODFR, 1936), Conchubhar Ó Muimhneacháin's *Béaloideas Bhéal Átha Ghaorthaidh* (The folklore of Ballingeary) (BÁC: ODFR, 1935), Douglas Hyde's *Ocht Sgéalta ó Choillte Mághach* (Eight Stories from Kiltimagh) (BÁC: COÉ for Cumann le Béaloideas Éireann, 1936), Micheál Ó Tiománaidhe's *An Lampa Draoidheachta agus Naoi Scéalta Eile* (The magic lamp and nine other stories) (BÁC: ODFR,

1935) and Kenneth Jackson's *Scéalta ón mBlascaod* (Stories from the Great Blasket) (BÁC: An Cumann le Béaloideas Éireann, 1939), collected from Peig Sayers. Story collections for which no date of publication was provided include An tAthair Tomás Ó Cillín's *Artúraidheacht 'Thír-An-Áir'* (Arthurian lore from 'The Land of Slaughter') (BÁC: COÉ, n.d.) and Domhnall Ua Murchadha's *Rann-Scéalta, Scéalta Gearra, agus Paidreacha Áluinne* (Yarns, short stories, and beautiful prayers) (n.p: n.p., n.d.).

As the title of this last book indicates, compendia of miscellaneous folklore were also published in this period. Notable among these collections were Cormac Ó Cadhlaigh's *Slighe an Eólais* (The road to knowledge) (BÁC: Brún agus Ó Nóláin, Teór., n.d.), Pádhraic Ó Domhnalláin and Tomás Ó Raghallaigh's *Bruth-Fá-Thír* (Flotsam and jetsam) (BÁC: M.H. Mac Ghuill agus a Mhac, Teo., 1923), An tAthair Donnchadh Ó Donnchadha's *Seanchas an Chreidimh* (The traditional lore of the faith) (BÁC: M.H. Mac Ghuill agus a Mhac, 1923), An tAthair Pádhraic Mac Aodha's *Leabhrán Urnaighthe na Ceathramhan Ruaidhe* (The little Carraroe prayerbook) (BÁC: Séamas Ó Dubhthaigh agus a Chomh, Teór., 1933), Diarmuid Ua Laoghaire's *Saothar Bliana* (A year's work) (BÁC: ODFR, 1935), and Domhnall Ua Murchadha's aptly-titled *Sean-Aimsireacht* (Oldfashionedness) (BÁC: OS, 1939), a collection that includes, among other things, stories, prophecies, fairy lore, weather prognostications, and superstitions about card-playing. Book-length collections of proverbs were also popular at the time, with readers able to choose among Thomas F. O'Rahilly's scholarly bilingual *A Miscellany of Irish Proverbs* (Dublin: Talbot Press, 1922); Cormac Ó Cadhlaigh's *Eagna an Ghaedhil* (The wisdom of the Gael) (BÁC: Brún agus Ó Nóláin, Teór., 1925), which also offered explanations of many of the proverbs found in *Slighe an Eólais*; Pádraig Ó Siochfhradha's *Seanfhocail na Muimhneach* (The proverbs of Munster people) (Corcaigh: Cló-chualacht Seandúna, 1926, originally published in 1916); Henry Morris's *Seanfhocla Uladh* (Ulster proverbs) (BÁC: Muinntir Ch. S. Ó Fallamhain, Teo., i gcomhar le hOS, 1931), with variants and explanations of the proverbs; *Macallaí ó'n bhFrainc: Corra Cainnte, Ráidhte agus Sean-Fhocail i bhFraincis agus i nGaedhilg* (Echoes from France: Idioms, sayings, and proverbs in French and in Irish) (BÁC: COÉ, [1936]), a compilation by a Sligo Ursuline nun of 274 French idioms and 88 proverbs with their Irish equivalents; and Ális Ní Dhuibhir's *Míniú na Sean-Fhocal* (The explanation of the proverbs) (Dublin: National Correspondence College Press, 1938), a collection of 658 of 'the choicest proverbs in the language – with a full explanation of each'.[86]

There were, in addition, several important collections of local lore of various kinds. Seán Ó Dálaigh ('Common Noun') discussed in detail aspects of life in the Corca Dhuibhne Gaeltacht of West Kerry in his *Clocha Sgáil* (Quartz stones) (BÁC: Muinntir C.S. Ó Fallamhain i gcomhar le hOS, 1930) and *Timcheall Chinn Sléibhe* (Around Slea Head) (BÁC: ODFR, 1933).[87] This area was particularly well served by its writers, for Tomás Ó Criomhthain also wrote an account of all the place names of the Blasket Islands in *Dinnsheanchas na mBlascaodaí* (The place-name lore of the Blaskets) BÁC: ODFR, 1935),[88] and Pádraig Ó Siochfhradha provided detailed historical information on the places and place names of his home area in his *Tríocha-Céad Chorca Dhuibhne* (The baronies of the Dingle Peninsula) (BÁC: COÉ, 1939). Connacht writers who produced works of local history, traditions, customs, and folkways were Peadar Ó Concheanainn with his *Inis Meadhon: Seanchas agus Sgéalta* (Inis Meán: Traditional lore and stories) (BÁC: ODFR, 1931), Colm Ó Gaora with his *Obair is Luadhann nó Saoghal sa nGaedhealtacht* (Work and toil, or life in the Gaeltacht) (BÁC: ODFR, 1937),[89] and Séamus Mac Con Iomaire with *Cladaigh Chonamara* (The shores of Conamara) (BÁC: OS, 1938). Mac Con Iomaire wrote his book while recuperating in hospital in America, a fact that prompted a scathing criticism of Irish government inaction on emigration from Tomás Ó Máille in his preface.[90]

The value of these collections – and of the folk material published in the journals – will often seem suspect to the trained folklorist. Collectors were often cavalier about what is now accepted methodology. While we frequently find explicit claims of *verbatim* fidelity and careful identification of sources in the journals, we also encounter again and again such comments as 'I do not think that that story was ever in print yet; I heard it from an old person at home' (*IMN*, 1926, 27);[91] 'I don't have the names of the people from whom I heard these stories, but I heard them in Chois Fhairrge' (UCG *University Annual*, 1927–8, 6);[92] 'this is a little traditional anecdote I heard from an old person who is close to ninety' (*Star*, 12/4/30);[93] 'that is a story I got from an old man who lives here' (*Stoc*, Dec. 1930, 8);[94] and 'I got this information from an old woman in the neighbourhood' (*AA*, July 1938, 6).[95] At times, this lack of scholarly precision was due to the circumstances of collection, as Father Lawrence Murray, having identified his informant for a tale as Johnny Shéimisín (Ó Dónaill), continued that he had written the story 'word for word as he told it – as well as I could write it' (focal ar fhocal mar d'innis sé é – chomh maith a's chuaidh agam é a scríobhadh) (*Ultach*, Aug. 1930, 6).[96] But at other times, collectors seem to have been unaware of the importance of detailed field notes, so that a writer like An tAthair P. Ó Roithleáin could on occasion be relatively meticulous, and at other times provide no useful information at all on his sources or methodology.[97]

Nor were the authors of full-length collections necessarily more scrupulous. For example, while Seumus Ó hEochaidh, Henry Morris, Seán Mac Giollarnáth, Douglas Hyde, and Kenneth Jackson showed varying degrees of professionalism in their collections from the period, writers like Seoirse Mac Clúin, Peadar Ó Direáin, and Tadhg S. Seoighe seem to have felt free to revise and reshape their sources where they thought necessary.[98] Liam Ó Míodhacháin carried this process a step farther, using traditional models as the basis for a modern-day fantasy that takes its hero from Ring to the moon to Manhattan before he wakes to find the whole escapade a dream.[99] Even a veteran folklore enthusiast like Conchubhar Ó Muimhneacháin may have touched up some of the material in *Béaloideas Bhéal Átha Ghaorthaidh*, in a concluding note to which he thanks all the *seanchaidhthe* who had 'helped' him, but names none of them, a rather startling confirmation that Irish folklorists at this time usually saw their informants as voices of their community rather than as conscious narrative artists working with traditional forms and materials.[100]

To try to impose some consistency and professional criteria on the somewhat anarchic fieldwork of enthusiastic amateurs, as well as to ensure the authenticity of the *Gaelachas* embodied in the lore being collected, several writers offered practical advice on how to go about the task. The most detailed outline of how folklore should be collected appeared in the first several issues of *Béaloideas*. In June 1927, Delargy wrote: 'The collector should record material *verbatim*, retaining *all* peculiarities of dialect and making no "corrections"' (*Béaloideas*, June 1927, 6). But *Béaloideas* was not alone in its concern for accuracy and scholarly standards in the collection of folklore. In the same month that Delargy issued his first set of guidelines for would-be collectors, *An Lóchrann* offered similar advice to those engaged in this work: 'Let them write down the story or anything else just as the person says it, whether it is right or wrong, nicely done or sloppy.' *An Lóchrann* insisted that collectors include detailed information on their informants (*Lóchrann*, June 1927, 151).[101] In 1932, Shán Ó Cuív told readers of the *Irish Independent* interested in collecting folklore on their summer holidays that 'above all the most important thing is to accurately repeat the old person's speech' (fíor-aithris ar chaint an tseanduine, sin é an rud is tábhachtaí ar fad) (*II*, 1/7/32).[102] Lecturing in 1934, Domhnall Ó Grianna felt compelled to state what one would think would have been a self-evident caveat: 'No one who does not have a proper knowledge of the local Irish should be allowed to begin collecting folklore anywhere' (*II* 19/4/34).[103]

It was not until 1937, however, with the publication of Seán Ó Súilleabháin's *Láimh-Leabhar Béaloideasa* (Handbook of folklore), that amateur folklorists were given detailed practical guidance on how to approach their task scientifically. Delargy welcomed this handbook in the preface he wrote for it:

> This booklet – the first of its kind in Irish – will be a source of inspiration and a fountain of information and advice for collectors of folklore, for the scholars of the language and the literature, and for those of the Gaelic race who have not abandoned the thing that was once the heritage of the whole nation – 'The Traditional Lore of Ireland'.[104]

Ó Súilleabháin himself added a section entitled 'Comhairle do'n Bhailitheoir' (Advice to the collector) enjoining the collector, among other things, to write down all material available, to write that material down *verbatim*, never to 'correct' the informant, and always to record as much information as possible about the informant. In addition, he included a sample of the informant fact-sheet used by collectors working for the Folklore Commission, and instructed his readers to send what they gathered to the Commission at University College Dublin.[105] The body of the booklet then set out the extraordinary range of traditional material to be sought – from the practical details of home and farm life to folk medicine and proverbs to belief in supernatural beings and occurrences.[106]

A different kind of practical advice was offered by writers aware that informants were not always eager to share their lore with outsiders. This problem was dealt with comically in Seán Ó Ciarghusa's 1929 story 'Iarsma an Uilc' (The result of evil), where an idealistic student of folklore in search of 'the fountain of True Irish' (tobar na Fíor-Ghaedhilge) and 'the fountain of true traditional lore' (tobar an fhíor-sheanchais) is taken in by a manipulative and materialistic old Gaeltacht woman;[107] in Micheál Ó Siochfhradha's 1930 stories 'An Turus' (The journey) and 'An Corp' (The body), in both of which locals invent lore to dupe naive collectors from the Galltacht;[108] and in Seán Ó Conchubhair's 1935 story 'An Bailightheóir Béaloidis' (The folklore collector), about the misadventures of a pompous and irascible collector from Dublin (*Gaedheal*, Sept. 1935, 2).[109]

Folklore collectors were also the target of one of Brian Ó Nualláin's early satires, 'Ceist na Gaedhilge / Béal Idiots / Sean-Scéal ó Shean-Lad' (The question of the Irish language / Oral idiots / An old story from an old lad), in which the collectors bind and beat an old man to force him to provide them with a parodic bogus folktale. Ó Nualláin's piece concludes:

> But let there be no confusion, reader, while a drop of spirits remains at the bottom of a glass, those men will not give up this noble work. If you are a grey-haired person or an aboriginal eighty year old, don't think you can run or hide from them. And when they come, have a story ready for them, or if you prefer, two excuses [lit. two half-stories], for two excuses are the same as one story. Have that and you are in no danger (*Blather*, Oct. 1934, 32–3).[110]

A more serious approach was taken by Tomás Bairéad in his 1936 story 'Folach na Fiannaidheachta' (The concealment of lore about the Fianna) in which the collector, a teacher in a Gaeltacht area, finds little sympathy or support for his efforts from many of the local people.[111] Máirtín Ó Cadhain offered a poignant depiction of such indifference to the talents of a local *seanchaí* in his 1939 story '"Fóide Cnapánacha Carracha Uachtar an Bhaile"'

('The rugged, rocky land of the top of the townland'), where the old man's talents are only recognised by his neighbours after he wins acclaim at the Oireachtas in Dublin.[112]

To avoid such pitfalls, Seán Mac Lochlainn ('Muirbheach Lúigh de Mil') told readers of *An t-Éireannach* that the would-be collector would have to be as crafty as his would-be informants: 'This collecting of folklore is an art in itself – in particular how to question the storytellers. Often the direct question is not at all appropriate. One must tack, circle around – take the storyteller from the windward side, you might say' (*Éireannach*, 5/1/35).[113] The previous year in the same journal, 'Gréasuidhe Pholl a' Chlaidhe' (possibly An tAthair Eric Mac Fhinn) confronted the thornier issue of whether Gaeltacht informants should be paid for their contributions, suggesting, in effect, that folklore transmission be a kind of workfare for native speakers on the dole (*Éireannach*, 8/12/34).[114] For another anonymous correspondent in *An t-Éireannach*, there was nothing cynical or greedy in an informant's expectation of compensation for his lore, such payment being a matter of simple justice: 'Although the storytellers of the Gaeltacht are liberal and generous with their folklore, I myself do not think it is right or proper to be sucking folklore from them without giving them some payment for it' (*Éireannach*, 9/5/36).[115]

Educators of the time were eager to include folk material in their curricula, as is clear from an April 1925 editorial praising the Folklore Commission in the professional journal *The Teacher's Work: A Practical Journal of School Progress and Efficiency*:

> For our thousands of teachers, in particular, what is most necessary is a provision of handy materials drawn from the best and purest streams of traditional folk-tales. Such stories, chosen above all as vehicles of finely imaginative exposition and of conversation, should everywhere be made available for placing on the lips of the many tens of thousands of pupils in all our schools . . . The value to teachers of such repositories is beyond any and every estimate (*Teacher's Work*, Apr. 1935, 281).[116]

Of course the most extensive and signficant contribution primary school teachers and students alike made to the preservation of national folklore was the so-called Schools Collection of 1937–8 (July 1937 to December 1938). This scheme, carried out in some 5,000 schools with the co-operation of the Department of Education and the Irish National Teachers' Organisation, was to produce 1,126 bound volumes amounting to half a million pages.[117] Moreover, 'some six hundred of the teachers became correspondents of the [Folklore] commission, replying to over a hundred questionnaires on specific topics of folklore and traditional culture over the years'.[118]

Other Gaels wanted to bring the art of the *seanchaí* to adult audiences. In a 1925 piece on the theatre group An Comhar Drámaidheachta, Éamonn

Mac Giolla Iasachta praised recent productions, but called for more Irish music in the theatre and then continued:

> We wonder, also, whether the audience would not like for there to be a seanchaí or a storyteller telling a story during the interval now and again. Bringing a breath of the Gaeltacht, as much as is possible, into the theatre would benefit both actors and the rest of us (*Sguab*, Nov. 1925, 464).[119]

Seeking an even wider audience, Aindrias Ó Muimhneacháin suggested that given the difficulties of producing Gaelic drama on the radio on a regular basis, the state station should turn its attention to broadcasting performances by *seanchaithe* (*Gaedheal*, Aug. 1935, 5).[120] The radio authorities seem to have been listening because broadcasts of folk material became a fairly regular feature of Irish radio. The most important programme on folklore was Seán Ó Súilleabháin's long-running 'Béaloideas' series for schoolchildren (see, for example, *IP*, 29/3/38); but there were also lectures by the likes of Séamus Ó Grianna (*II*, 20/12/27); Delargy (*II*, 5/3/29); Hyde (*II* 26/3/29); Pádraig Ó Siochfhradha (*II*, 5/11/29); and Pádhraic Ó Domhnalláin (*II*, 22/4/30) in Irish, and by Liam Gógan (*IP*, 1/5/36) in English. Even more important were broadcast performances by *seanchaithe* like Amhlaoibh Ó Loingsigh (*IP*, 11/12/35); Maitias Ó Luasaigh (*IP*, 2/4/36); and the writer Nioclás Tóibín (*IP*, 23/12/36).

For many Gaels, however, it was the potential influence of folk material on the imagination of writers like Tóibín that was most exciting, for they saw in the extraordinary richness of Irish oral tradition a virtually inexhaustible source of indigenous models, motifs, and metaphors from which the creators of the new Gaelic literature could draw in their own work. Doubtless the most famous expression of this idea is that found in Delargy's editorial in the inaugural issue of *Béaloideas* in June 1927: 'We think that whatever literature is henceforth written in Irish will be nothing but a mediocre, insipid, insignificant thing unless it is Gaelic and unless it is rooted in the literature and the folklore of the Irish language' (*Béaloideas*, June 1927, 3).[121] But there was nothing either extreme or idiosyncratic in Delargy's assertion here. Nor was he the first to express such ideas in this period. Writing in *The Leader* in April 1925, T. Ó hÉigeartaigh saw the influence of folklore as giving the new Gaelic literature a moral edge over writing in other languages. In an absurdly laudatory review of 'Fionn' Mac Cumhaill's *Maicín* – he claimed 'there is nothing in any language more excellent'! – Ó hÉigeartaigh wrote:

> The superiority of books in Irish as mental food and entertainment, appears to come from the fact that all Irish writers, worthy of the name, draw their treasure from a rich mine, *viz.*, the old Gaelic traditions, manners and customs. The fountain at which they drink contains pure, fresh, sparkling water. A noble and elevating

> influence follows the reading of such writers as a natural consequence (*Leader*, 11/4/25).

Addressing readers of *Iris an Fháinne* the following year, Peadar Mac Fhionnlaoich had more purely literary concerns in mind when he wrote of the importance of the native oral tradition for the modern Gaelic writer: 'Gaels had little to learn about stories or storytelling, and it would be foolish for us to be following the Anglo-Saxon style of storytelling. It is better by far for us to "follow closely the fame of our ancestors"' (*IF*, Apr. 1926, 24).[122]

Nor was Mac Fhionnlaoich the only major Gaelic writer to espouse such views. Among the most eloquent champions of the literary potential of folklore was Pádraig Ó Siochfhradha. Preaching to the converted at a meeting of the Folklore of Ireland Society at University College Dubllin in February 1930, 'An Seabhac' was reported as saying:

> There was a great need for it [folklore] to give colour and flavour to the the speech of this new group rising up in Ireland, and to be a benefit and a source and an inspiration in literary and artistic and dramatic affairs and other such things for this race of ours henceforth, as it was a part of the life of the soul and intellect for our ancestors hitherto (*FL*, Feb. 1930, 2).[123]

Shán Ó Cuív was no less forceful than Delargy or 'An Seabhac' in his commitment to this idea in *Prós na hAoise Seo*, writing:

> It is on that folklore that the new literature should be based, on that and on the work of the poets and the prose authors who went before us, and until we have good examples of the folklore from every region in the Gaeltacht, we will not have made a proper start at cultivating the language in literary affairs. Folklore will be a support for us and a link with the prose and poetry of our ancestors.[124]

A few Gaelic writers more specifically interested in the stage saw the folk tradition as a potentially rich source of diverting and impeccably native plot lines, characters, and themes. In a 1936 piece on 'Drámaí do'n Aos Óg' (Dramas for the young), one 'Truagh' argued:

> There are certain qualities associated with every literary movement in the world, and it is those qualities that distinguish them from each other. Now those qualities must be found in every genre of literature that is cultivated in a particular area if that genre is in harmony wih the dominant literary movement in that area. Those qualities are to be found in folklore, because in folklore one finds the mind of the people who cultivate the literature being expressed in the simplest way from the point of view of culture. Therefore, dramas based on folklore are in harmony with the literary movement in Ireland (*Enniscorthy Echo*, 12/9/36).[125]

Playwrights had understood and practised this principle for years, and even the annual Dublin Feis included in its 1931 programme a play performed by an Irish-speaking school 'into which the great folk-lore of our country infused an influence that gives us a foretaste of what its influence will be in our coming literary advance' (*Camán*, July 1931, 3). This idea seems to have been particularly popular in Dundalk, where it was advanced in a lecture to the local branch of An Fáinne by Cathal Ó Tuathail in December 1930, and by Peadar Ó Dubhda following a lecture in the town by Delargy in 1938. Ó Dubhda argued that unless living folklore were brought to the Irish people, preferably in dramatised form, 'in fifty years they would still be worshipping Greta Garbo and Mickey Mouse'.[126]

What, then, did those creative writers who turned to this material do with it? First of all, doubtless in response to the heightened awareness of just what genuine folktales were and how they should be collected, printed, and appreciated, there were far fewer examples of the kind of 'short story' so common earlier in the revival that was little more than a slightly reworked oral narrative passing as original fiction. Stories like 'Fionn' Mac Cumhaill's 'Díth na Céille' (Senselessness) (*FL*, 13/10/23); 'An Drochrud' (The evil thing) by 'Taobhnóg' (*Ultach*, Mar. 1925, 7–8); Éamon Ó Tuathail's 'An t-Iasgaire agus an Bársóir' (The fisherman and the nag) (*Ultach*, Aug. 1929); the anonymous 'An Bhaintreabhach is a Mac' (The widow and her son) (*Teacher's Work*, Mar. 1933, 58) are very much exceptions in this period. Of course, this is by no means to say that writers of the time did not try to exploit folktales as a source of plots, or more important, as validation of the native authenticity of their work. Ngúgí Wa Thiong'o has written of how African writers working in European languages 'preyed' on folklore in order 'to make the borrowed tongues carry the weight of our African experience'.[127] In many ways, it could be argued that even Irish writers working in the native language of the country were tempted on occasion to 'prey' on traditional material to make the language they were reviving carry the weight of a real or idealised Gaelic experience. This rather schizophrenic expression / exploitation of native lore was given appropriately ambiguous formulation by Eoin Ó Searcaigh in *Iris an Fháinne* in 1924. Having stressed the need for the Gaelic writer to have 'native Irish' (Gaedhealg ó dhúthchas), a mastery of 'caint na ndaoine', 'writing ability' (buaidh na scríbhneoireachta), and, perhaps most important, 'the Gaelic mind' (an aigne Ghaedhealach), Ó Searcaigh continued: 'The writer of Irish who wants to give his readers literature will find things in the old stories that will give his work finish and beauty if used properly' (*IF*, Nov. 1924, 15–16).[128]

In practical terms, few writers of the period, with the possible exceptions of Seosamh Mac Grianna, Séamus Ó Grianna, and, at the very end of the period, Máirtín Ó Cadhain, were able to strike the kind of balance Ó

Searcaigh suggested was necessary.[129] For the most part, those writers who turned to traditional material took the easy way out, looking for little more than serviceable plot lines or colorful characters. Doubtless they were further encouraged in this regard when their efforts won praise, as did those of Tomás Ó hAodha, of whose collection *An Figheadóir*, Pádhraic Ó Domhnalláin wrote in 1926:

> Plots are abundant and plentiful in that part of North Munster. The author takes some of those plots, carries them off, and gives his fancy clear sailing on the sea of the imagination. He tacks here and there when he wants, and he proves that he is able to handle the boat as neatly as the best of the old natives (*An Phoblacht*, 2/7/26).[130]

A more adept practitioner of this appraoch than Ó hAodha was Seaghán Mac Meanman, of whom Nollaig Mac Congáil has written 'he puts knowledge about it [i.e. the "Hidden Ireland" of his stories] before us in the same way he got it from his teachers, namely the storytellers, the legitimate heirs of the oral tradition'.[131] Certainly in the two story collections he published during this period, *Fear Siubhail a's a Chuid Comharsanach agus Daoine Eile* (A travelling man and his neighbours and other people) (1924) and *Indé agus Indiu* (Yesterday and today) (1929), which he identifies in his preface as the continuation of the earlier volume, Mac Meanman was explicit in his claim that these books contained nothing but 'a handful of stories from the bag of a travelling man' (mám sgeulta as mála fir siubhail) and that all of them had some basis in fact.[132]

While it may not, therefore, be true to say that creative writers of the 1920s and 1930s were either eager or resigned to leave folklore to the folklorists, it is a fact that their sense that native oral tradition and the people who had shaped it were passing away before their very eyes inspired them to focus their attention on the lives and experiences of those people rather than more specifically on the elements of the lore they had preserved. A significant number of the stories inspired by this awareness were, of course, intended as no more than ephemeral light reading. On occasion, however, a story of this sort could go beyond the merely innocuous to gentle satire. Thus, political issues are touched on in 'An Gréasaidhe Luipreacháin' (The leprechaun cobbler) by 'Sean-Ghaedhilgeoir' (*CT*, 21/4/23); in 'Dole Sheáin' (Seán's dole) by Pádhraig Ó Fatharta (*AA*, Sept. 1935, 6); and 'Ceol Comhachtach' (Powerful music) by Seán Ó Maoláin (*Ultach*, June 1939, 4–5), in the last of which a bigoted Ulster Unionist buys a cow that will only give milk when it hears the Irish national anthem being sung in Irish! Rural snobbery was the target of light satire in 'An Pearasól' (The parasol) by 'D. Ó D.', in which the pompous wife of a farmer uses her newly acquired parasol to restore the dignity she feels she has lost by marrying beneath her (*Far East*, July 1936, 152–3).[133]

A minority of the writers committed to rural themes were willing to offer a more challenging and even disturbing analysis of country and Gaeltacht life.[134] For example, Pádhraic Ó Domhnalláin ('Darach Mac Eibhir') paints a grim picture of the life and death of a greedy and dishonest Mayo shopkeeper in 'An Mhallacht / Sgéal Fíor' (The curse / A true story) (*FL*, 1/9/23). Equally bleak is 'Máire' by 'An Sgurach Fásta', a moody account of the death of a miserly and unneighbourly woman living alone (UCG *University Annual*, 1923–4, 7–8). Rural violence was also, as we will see below, an important theme in fiction at the time. Perhaps the most disturbing tale of this kind from the period is Peadar Ó Domhnaill's 'An Feall a d'Fhill' (The treachery that came home), in which the crew of a turf boat attacks and drowns men in a curragh whom they mistake for their enemies in a feud. Soon after, the man in charge of the turf boat is himself drowned, prompting the following authorial conclusion:

> The man who drowned the O'Malleys without giving them time to repent, neither he himself nor his son got time to repent when they were drowned in the same harbour. The God of Glory was looking down on them and he struck them a blow as sudden as the one they themselves had struck on the men who had not deserved it (*TCNÍ*, Sept. 1937, 211–12).[135]

Other offbeat stories include 'Tórramh Sheana-Dhonnchadh' by 'Mathúin', a bit of a black comedy involving three rogues who play a trick with the corpse at a wake so that the mourners will flee, leaving them the food and drink (*FMR*, Aug. 1929). Seán Ó Ciosáin's 'Cad Dubhairt an File?' (What did the poet say?) tells of the initially successful attempts of an obsequious Gaeltacht man to sponge drinks from some language students or 'Fine Days' (Laetheanta Breághtha), so-called for their tendency to make excessive use of this not always appropriate phrase), and of their subsequent disgust with and rejection of him.[136] A similar sort of sycophantic begging on the part of Gaeltacht people – this time their target being a local man who has returned from Australia – is depicted in Pádhraic Ó Domhnalláin's 'An Chónra' (The coffin).[137] More edifying is the picture of Gaeltacht people offered by Etáis Ní Chnáimhín in 'Brighid nó an Bhean a Tréigeadh' (Bríd, or the woman who was deserted), the story of a mysterious 'gentlewoman' (bean uasal) who arrives in a village to live alone, befriend the children, and win the respect of the adults despite her aloofness. One day the only literate woman in the village reads to a friend a newspaper account that shocks them both so that they burn the paper. What they have learned is that the enigmatic woman was confined for twenty years to a mental asylum from which she had escaped (*Tír*, Dec. 1930, 6–8).

An ongoing sub-genre of the Gaelic short story dealt in various ways with Gaeltacht people come home for either a visit or for good from America.

Given the enormous number of Irish, and particularly Gaeltacht people who had emigrated to the United States, and the importance of their financial support for those they left behind, this interest in the 'returned Yank' was altogether natural on the emotional as well as on the pragmatic level. Moreover, with emigration itself a continuing crisis challenging both the state and the language movement throughout this period, it is hardly surprising that emigrants would figure importantly if ambivalently in the prose literature of the movement. While some cultural nationalists appreciated the financial and political support provided by the Irish abroad, others were far less impressed with the sacrifices made by the emigrants. Indeed, in June 1928, one 'Faugh-a-Ballagh' all but pronounced them cowards and traitors in an essay entitled 'Love of Country!' in *Honesty*:

> Have we, the sons of such sires, the same love for Ireland to-day? Is the emigrant ship a noble and courageous act towards the memory of such martyred sires who suffered so much for faith and fatherland? Is there any necessity for emigration? Is there any excuse for such desertion of our country? None whatever (*Honesty*, 30/6/28).

The same idea was expressed more succinctly by Tomás Ó Máille in a 1928 editorial in *An Stoc*: 'It is often said that it was the finest of the Gaels who go across the sea. That is not our opinion nor the substance of our story, but rather that the finest of the Gaels are those who stay home to stand up for justice for Ireland' (*Stoc*, Dec. 1928, 4).[138] In 1924, Pádhraic Ó Domhnalláin, the editor of *Fáinne an Lae*, spoke of the 'shame' (*náire*) of young Irish people 'deserting' (*tréigean*) their country and warned: 'If they continue this haste, the government will have to stop them' (*FL*, 30/8/24).[139]

The motivation behind such an apparently callous attitude to those who were leaving was doubtless concern about the terrible rate of emigration that independence had done nothing to reduce. The editor of the *Dundalk Examiner* faced up to this unpalatable truth in an essay on 'An Imirce as Éirinn' (Emigration from Ireland) in Oct. 1930:

> Everyone whom this question troubled thought that the solution to it would be at hand as soon as the Irish got authority in the running of the country. It was, of course, thought that the Children of the Gaels would no longer be obliged to go across the sea to make a living . . . Everyone who held that opinion was deceived, for instead of Emigration from Ireland slowing, it has increased for six or seven years (*Examiner*, 4/10/30).[140]

This note of angry frustration is evident in editorials and essays throughout the period. For example, *An t-Éireannach*, which saw itself, with justification, as the voice of the Gaeltacht, returned to this theme again and again, stressing that the Gaeltacht people who left their country did so under duress. For instance, in a May 1936 editorial in the paper, we read:

> Cromwell banished the Gael to mountain and to marsh. But the little Cromwells who are in the world now will not leave him on mountain or marsh: they are banishing him from the mountain and banishing him across the sea – over to the devil's house, a place that his fathers before him refused to go, but that he cannot refuse now (*Éireannach*, 2/5/36).[141]

Few could, and with so many loved ones in the United States and so many others hoping to go there, it is no wonder that we find an intense – and ambivalent – interest in 'The New Island' (*An t-Oileán Úr*) on the part of both Gaeltacht people and the writers who chronicled their lives. Some of those writers, eager to stem the flow of emigration, drew the attention of their countrymen to the problems rather than the promises of life in America. For example, writing from New York City in 1926, Séamus Mac Con Iomaire, the author of *Cladaigh Chonamara*, painted a grim picture of conditions in America for readers of *An Stoc*: 'I don't have much time, working from dawn to dusk. That's the way it is for everyone here, constantly competing, always running as if their skin was on fire' (*Stoc*, Nov.–Dec. 1926, 7).[142] For Micheál Ó Baoighill, writing in *An t-Ultach* in 1931, the focus was on the many Irish who failed to achieve prosperity and were ground down and debased by the rat-race:

> How many people did America ever make rich? Very few. But it is many a person it killed or put on the road to ruin. I am certain that if there were at present a bridge across the great sea there would be thousands of Irish people hurrying over, but as they are, they do not have a penny (*Ultach*, Feb. 1931, 3).[143]

Writers of fiction were also interested in the narrative and thematic possibilities of the hardships of American life for the Irish emigrant. In Peadar Mac Fhionnlaoich's 1922 story 'Pádraig', a man returns home from the United States to a brother who is at first overjoyed to have him back. Soon, however, the returned Yank begins to drink heavily, cursing and otherwise abusing his brother, who then dies of a broken heart, after which the Yank himself dies penniless and unlamented (*FL*, 29/7/22). Interestingly enough, Father Dinneen offered a transposal of these fraternal roles in his 1928 story 'An Bheirt Dhearbhráthar' (The two brothers) in which a rich Yank returns home dressed shabbily. His brother rejects him until he learns of his wealth, but by this time the Yank, disgusted, goes back to America where he leaves his entire fortune to an order of nuns! (*Leader*, 14/7/28).[144] A hardness of heart similar to that of Mac Fhionnlaoich's coarse Yank is implicit in the emigrant children of the protagonists in Seán Ó Dálaigh's 1930 story 'Is Giorra Cabhair Dé ná an Doras' (God's help is closer than the door) and Criostóir Mac Aonghusa's 1936 story 'Cladóir' (Shore-dweller), in both of which the children of poor Gaeltacht people emigrate, succeed, and then forget their parents altogether.[145] In Micheál Ó Baoighill's 1930 story 'An Choigchríoch' (The foreigner), an Irish emigrant is murdered by a bar-room gambler and card cheat in the Klondyke (*Ultach*, Oct. 1930, 7–8), while in Peadar Ó Concheanainn's 1929 story 'Séamas Ó Riain ar Thóir Saidhbhris' (Séamus Ó Riain in search of wealth), the emigrant gets home safely, but only after a run-in with a corrupt foreman costs him his job and cures him of his infatuation with the American dream (*Stoc*, Jan. 1929, 6 and 8). Less lurid was 'An Baineadóir' (The reaper), a story by 'Díoltóir Brat' that ran as a serial in *An Gaedheal* in 1936. The protagonist of this story, delighted to be home for good, tells his neighbours that even those who succeed in America want only to return to Ireland (*Gaedheal*, Mar. 1936 to June 1936). The protagonist of S. Ó Mealláin's 'An Filleadh' (The return) having failed to entice his mother to join him in America realises the error of his ways and returns home never to leave again (*Hibernia*, June 1939, 14–15).

Neither stress, poverty, corruption, injustice, nor violence was the greatest danger that the United States held for the Gaelic Catholic emigrant, at least according to a fair number of the writers whose stories appeared in *Timthire Chroidhe Naomhtha Íosa*. The basic premise underlying these stories was outlined by Father P. Doyle in a 1930 essay on 'The Fate of the Irish Emigrant' in another Catholic periodical, the *Irish Rosary*: 'You can save your soul in America. Indeed you can save it anywhere if you are determined to do so. But everywhere and for everyone the work of salvation is not easy, and I think it is safe to say that going to America is not the same as taking a short cut to Heaven' (*IR*, July 1930, 502). It certainly wasn't for the emigrant characters in stories like 'Cosamhlacht a Mháthar' (His mother's likeness) by 'T. Ó C.' (*TCNÍ*, Dec. 1923), 'Scéal' (A story) by Eibhlín Ní Ghairbhfhiaich (*TCNÍ*, Sept. 1925), 'An t-Amhránaidhe' (The singer) by Gobnait Ní Luineacháin (*TCNÍ*, June 1929), 'Daille' (Blindness) by Cáit Ní Éaluighthe' (*TCNÍ*, Dec. 1929), 'An Deoraidhe' (The exile) by Brighid Ní Cheallacháin (*TCNÍ*, Dec. 1930), 'Cúiteamh na Maighdine' (The virgin's reward) by 'M. Nic A.' (*TCNÍ*, May 1932), 'An Filleadh' (The return) by S. Ó Curraidhín, S. J. (*TCNÍ*, Jan. 1935), 'Lorg an Fhoirtiúin' (The mark of fortune) by Caitlín de Barra (*TCNÍ*, Dec. 1936), or 'Ag Filleadh Abhaile' (Returning home) by Brighid Bodhlaeir (*TCNÍ*, July 1937).[146] The general thematic tone of these stories can be summarised with a quote from the earliest of them, 'Cosamhlacht a Mháthar' by 'T. Ó C.:'

> As with hundreds of others, Pádraig was not long gone from the clean, pious air of his native townland until he was gradually ceasing to practice his faith. He was, of

> course, doing nothing but yielding to the spirit of the country, the spirit of indifference in spiritual things.[147]

In this story, it is a vision of his mother's face seen when he is burgling a house that brings him to his senses and inspires him to return to pious Catholic family life at home. The protagonist of Séamus P. Ó Mórdha's 'Díoghaltas' (Vengeance), coming from Montana intent on killing the man who had gunned down his Donegal-born father in a saloon there, is also saved from this crime by the memory of his dead mother's piety (*Hibernia*, July 1938). The young man in Pádhraic Óg Ó Conaire's 'Bean agus –' (A woman and –) does not return to Ireland, but memories of his mother keep him on the straight and narrow in the United States (*Standard*, 22/6/29). In most of these stories, however, the protagonist does make it home either reformed or susceptible to reformation, although in Brighid Bodhlaeir's 'Ag Filleadh Abhaile' further assistance is needed after the emigrant's return. Having lived rough in the Klondyke, her protagonist has lost his faith and only attends church because everyone else does. One day as he sets out to go fishing, his sister, unbeknownst to him, sews a Sacred Heart medal onto his coat. At sea, his boat is swamped, but he is saved to reform before dying mere days later – in a state of grace of course.[148]

It was, however, comedy rather than pathos that dominated Gaelic depictions of Americans, whether native-born or returned emigrants. The 'Stage Yank' had a venerable history in revival literature, and continued to flourish throughout the 1920s and 1930s and indeed beyond. In part, these comic treatments were rooted in a real concern about the influence American, and particularly Irish-American, visitors to Ireland could have on Gaeltacht people, a concern made explicit by M. Mac Aodhagáin in a 1932 essay on 'An Ghaedhilg agus an Ghaedhealtacht' (The Irish language and the Gaeltacht):

> Another group that is doing great harm to *Gaelachas* in the Gaeltacht is the Yanks . . . They come home dressed-up, Anglicised, independent, financially well-off, having great respect for America and little understanding of and even less respect for their native land. . . . 'What good did Ireland ever do me?' says the stylish hussy in a dialect that would make a sea urchin want to puke (*IMN*, 1932, 11).[149]

Mac Aodhagáin pretty neatly catalogues the characteristics of the Stage Yank in this passage: flashy clothes, conspicuous wealth, ignorance, bombast and a distressing accent. It was a stereotype Gaelic authors would play for all it was worth, as did 'Tréan-Dorn' in his 1924 sketch 'An Ponncán agus an Giolla' (The Yank and the servant): 'If you see a fleshy, well-fed man, wearing odd, multi-coloured clothes, a road-map sticking out of his pocket, big, round, horn-rimmed glasses on him, looking all around and taking up the whole street, you can guess where he is from' (*II*, 4/8/24).[150]

For some writers, it was American boastfulness that was most distasteful. In Cormac Mac Cárthaigh's serialised 1932–3 story 'Cúrsaí an Bhreithimh' (The judge's affairs), we get the following description of the Yank:

> He had everyone in the neighbourhood deaf with accounts of the country yonder – the way everything is done there, even boiling cabbage – this wretch here could not catch up with them over there in a hundred years. Then the amount of money to be had, the fine jobs without having to be out in the frost or in the rain, in the mud or on the bog (*Muimhneach*, Dec. 1932, 13).[151]

In León Ó Broin's comic sketch 'Punncáin ag Lorg Eolais / Ag Taisteal na h-Eorpa' (Yanks seeking knowldege / Touring Europe), one of a pair of gauche American tourists in Dublin boasts of her interest in the Irish language: 'I intend to spend three days in Trinity College where those beautiful old manuscripts are – you know, the ones Douglas Hyde and all the other old natives wrote – and I will not go home until I understand them' (*II*, 5/11/29).[152]

Given this belief that many if not most Yanks were pompous braggarts, it was only natural that Gaelic writers delighted in creating situations in which such characters could get their humiliating come-uppance. For example, in Séamus Mac Confhada's 1929 story 'An t-Éireannach Bhí i Meiriocá' (The Irishman who was in America), a New Yorker in the window of a tall building being stared at by an Irishman tells the visitor – whom he calls 'Paddy' – that these buildings are nothing but stables in comparison to some in the city, only to be answered by the Irishman: 'Ah . . . I knew well that they were only stables when I saw the ass's head sticking out of the window' (*Stoc*, Nov. 1929, 2).[153] In Seán Ó Cearbhaill's 'Bhí an t-Éireannach Gasta go Leor Dó' (The Irishman was quick enough for him), a blowhard Yank visiting Dublin, having heard his driver tell him how long it took to build Dublin Castle and the Customs House, says they would have been put up in next to no time in America. When they pass the General Post Office, the driver acts surprised, claiming it hadn't been there earlier that morning![154] A macabre twist on this theme was provided by Séamas Ó Séaghdha in his 1938 radio play *An Taoile Tuile* (The flood tide), in which three men, one a boastful returned Yank, are caught in fog while fishing off the Kerry coast. Their salvation depends on the timing of the turning tide, and the Yank, with his imposing watch, pontificates on their situation, only to find that he has failed to take daylight savings time into account. All are then apparently drowned (*Bonaventura*, Summer 1938, 101–9).

Other tales involve the misadventures of Irish characters in the New World. One of the oddest stories of this sort is Seán Ó Ciarghusa's 'An Nathair Nimhe agus an t-Éireannach' (The poisonous snake and the Irishman), in which a young Irishman whose legs have been amputated in America gets work as a snake charmer in a circus, on the principle that snakes can't harm people from Ireland. During his show, a snake lunges at him, seems baffled, and slinks away in fear. The young man is made a hero until people find the serpent's tongue(!) in his wooden leg. Despite feeling that they have been duped, they pass the hat and send him home (*FL*, 9/8/24).[155] Irish-American provincialism is lightly spoofed in Séamus P. Ó Mórdha's 'Citizen de Chuid a' Domhain' (A citizen of the world). Set in 'The Franklin Hotel' on 112th Ave. [*sic*] in New York, the story tells of how the narrator has met a man who claimed to be a true citizen of the world, above national pride and petty politics. When, however, he hears someone insult County Cavan, he pummels the offender and is arrested, prompting the following reflection by the narrator: 'A citizen of the world! I looked down the street. I saw my poor citizen between two constables who were bringing him with them to the barracks because he had the mettle to stand his ground for the honour of Breifne' (*Ultach*, May 1938, 2–3).[156]

There were also a fair number of plots in which emigration to America plays a role. The most famous of these is doubtless Ó Grianna's *Caisleáin Óir*, in which after remaining faithful to his Donegal sweetheart for many years and through many adventures in the American West and the Yukon, the protagonist returns to find her a careworn and overworked old woman, on whom he turns his back. Desertion is also the fate of a young woman in Micheul Ó Cinnfhaolaidh's 1922 story 'Cuimhne an Fhraoich Bháin' (The memory of the white heather) (*Green and Gold*, Dec. 1921–Feb. 1922). The deserted woman is the protagonist of the 1934 story 'An Feitheamh Fada' (The long wait) by 'Guaire Sona' (*New Irish Magazine*, Dec. 1934, 55). In one of Seán Ó Ciarghusa's 'Trí Scéalta Grádha' (Three love stories), a woman returns to Ireland in search of a husband, only to have a man jilt her when he finds that she lacks the kind of wealth Yanks are supposed to have. She tells him bitterly that if she were rich, 'it is not here towards Ireland I would turn my face' (ní annso ar Éirinn thiubhrainn m'aghaidh). She goes back to America 'without a man, without a farm' (gan fear, gan feirm) (*Sguab*, May 1926, 88). Perhaps the most interesting story of this sort was Seán Mac Maoláin's 'Ar Airgead an Amaidighe' (On the fool's money), in which an emigrant who has become wealthy as a bootlegger in New York brings his Québecoise wife to Ireland on their honeymoon. In Glendalough, he meets the young woman he had loved before leaving home in the company of the husband she had met and married in England. Both are well off and settled, but the author makes clear they should have stayed home and married each other (*Ultach*, Dec. 1936, 4 and 16). The only happy ending to any of these love stories involving Yanks occurs in Annraoi Saidléar's one-act play *Oidhche sa Tabháirne* (A night in the tavern), performed by an Comhar Drámaidheachta at the Peacock Theatre in November 1937, in which the returned emigrant is able to thwart the plans of his fiancée's father to marry her to a fifty-year-old farmer, to restore a farm to its rightful owner, and to marry his long-time love.[157]

It should also be noted that this man is not the only decent returned Yank in the Gaelic literature of this period. Politics provides the point of contrast between the Yank and his Irish neighbours in Seán Ó Dúnaighe's 1923 story 'An Ponncánach' (The Yank), in which a rather arrogant American who had initially fled Ireland after killing a soldier stands up to an Ascendancy woman after a performance of the early revival play *An Dochtúir* (The doctor), telling her the day of her class is over and the day of the Gael has arrived (*Sguab*, Sept. 1923, 230–2).[158] Religion forms the bond in Máire Nic Giolla Sheanáin's story 'Mian Shighle' (Sheila's desire), where an aunt come home from America brings her niece to the Eucharistic Congress in Dublin, a trip the girl thought she could never make because she had given all her own money to the missions (*TCNÍ*, June 1932, 129–31). Another well-off Yank returns to Ireland in 'An Deoraidhe' (The exile) by 'T. Ó C.', but he has come back to live gratefully in the homeland he had once scorned (*Dundalk Examiner*, 28/11/31). More active cultural service was provided by the returned Yank in Séamus Maguidhir's 1936 piece 'An Muirthead' (The Mullet). Maguidhir has high praise for this American, a man described as a Gael and a fluent Irish speaker who spends much of his time at home in Mayo in search of native lore.[159]

Needless to say, most Gaelic fiction dealing with Irish country life dealt with the lives of garden-variety Irish people, rather than with those of the more exotic returned Yanks, whether penitent, pompous, or patriotic. Stories dealing with rural society were, as we have noted, standard fare in the Gaelic journals, and also comprised the majority of the work in collections like Tomás Ó hAodha's *An Figheadóir* (n.d.), Nioclás Tóibín's *Oidhche ar Bharr Tuinne agus Scéalta Eile* (A night on the waves and other stories) (n.d.), Seaghán Mac Meanman's *Fear Siubhail a's a Chuid Comharsanach agus Daoine Eile* (1924) and *Indé agus Indiu* (1929), Séamus Ó Grianna's *Cioth is Dealán* (Shower and sunshine) (1926), Séamus Ó Dubhghaill's *Beartín Luachra* (1927), Seosamh Mac Grianna's *An Grádh agus an Ghruaim* (Love and dejection) (1929), Micheál Ó Siochfhradha's *Seo Mar Bhí* (How it was) (1930), Seán Ó Dálaigh's *Clocha Sgáil* (1930) and *Timcheall Chinn Sléibhe: Aistí agus Scéalta* (1933), Tomás Bairéad's *An Geall a Briseadh* (The promise that was broken) (1932) and *Cumhacht na Cinneamhna* (The power of fate) (1936), Micheál Ó Gríobhtha's *Cathair Aeidh* (Caherea) (1937), An tAthair Casáin's *An Londubh agus Scéalta Eile* (The blackbird and other stories) (1937), Séamas Maguidhir's *Dhá Chrann na Marbh* (The two trees of the dead) (1939), and Máirtín Ó Cadhain's *Idir Shúgradh agus Dáiríre* (1939).

Rural society also furnished the backdrop for many of the Gaelic novels of the period, including some that will be discussed in chapter four. Among such novels set wholly or partly in the countryside were 'Fionn' Mac Cumhaill's *Tusa a Mhaicín* (You, laddy) (1922), *Maicín* (Laddy) (1924), and *Na Rosa go Bráthach* (The Rosses forever) (1939); Pádraig Ó Siochfhradha's *Seáinín, nó*

Eachtra Mic Mí-Rialta (Seáinín, or the adventure of an unruly lad) (1922) and *Caibidilí as Leabhar Mhóirín* (Chapters out of Móirín's book) (1934); Pádhraic Óg Ó Conaire's *Mian a Croidhe* (Her heart's desire) and *An Fraoch Bán* (The white heather) (both 1922), *Solus an Ghrádha* (Love's light) (1923), *Seoid ó'n Iarthar Órdha* (A gem from the golden west) (1933), *Éan Cuideáin* (Strange bird) (1936), and *Ceol na nGiolcach* (1939); Séamus Ó Grianna's *Caisleáin Óir* (1924); Éamonn Mac Giolla Iasachta's *Cúrsaí Thomáis* (1927) and *Toil Dé* (God's will) (1933); Micheál Ó Gríobhtha's *Buaidh na Treise: 'Cogadh Gaedheal re Gallaibh'* (The triumph of strength: 'The war of the Irish with the Foreigners') (1928); Nioclás Tóibín's *An Rábaire Bán* (The dashing fairhaired fellow) and *Róisín Bán an tSléibhe* (both 1928); Pádraig Ó Séaghdha's *Stiana* (1930); Seán Ó Ruadháin's *Pádhraic Mháire Bhán* (1932); Seán Ó Ciarghusa's *Bun an Dá Abhann* (1933); Seán Ó Dúnaighe's *An Crann Cuilinn* (The holly tree) (1933) and *Inghean an Ghearaltaigh* (n.d.); Diarmuid Ua Laoghaire's *An Bhruinneall Bhán* (1933); Pádraig Ó Gallchobhair's *Caoineadh an Choimhighthigh* (1934); Diarmuid Ó hÉigeartaigh's *Tadhg Ciallmhar* (Sensible Tadhg) (1934); Tadhg Ó Rabhartaigh's *Mian na Marbh* (The wish of the dead) (1937); Aindrias Ó Baoighill's *An t-Airidheach* (1939); Ciarán Ua Nualláin's *Oidhche i nGleann na nGealt* (A night in the Glen of the Madmen) (1939); and Seosamh Mac Grianna's *An Druma Mór* (1969).

Rural life was also by far the most common subject of Gaelic plays throughout the period, a situation Seán Ó Ciarghusa found entirely natural, writing in 1939 of Mícheál Breathnach's rural comedy *Cor in Aghaidh an Chaim* (Trick for trick):

> I do not think I have ever seen a play I liked more for subject matter, acting, and everything else. I have long said that there is dramatic material in the Gaeltacht, and potential dramatists as well, and that nothing has to be made up to make the material suitable for the stage. 'Trick for Trick' and Micheál Breathnach prove my point (*Leader*, 16/3/29).[160]

That not all critics agreed with Ó Ciarghusa is, however, evident in a 1938 review in *The Leader* by 'N.' (doubtless Nuala Moran): 'We must admit we are heartily tired of the cabin scene with the dresser and the check table-cloth, and the *Bean a'Tighe* cutting the bread for the *Fear a'Tighe* and the neighbours dropping in for a chat, and all the rest of it' (*Leader*, 26/2/38). Sadly, this little catalogue of setting, characters, and plot elements summarises a fair number of the plays in Irish staged in Dublin and elsewhere in this period, including more than a few of the offerings of An Comhar Drámaidheachta. Among the new, original rural plays for adult audiences performed, published, and/or broadcast in the 1920s and 1930s were: Pádraic Ó Conaire's *Caitlín na Clúide* (Kathleen of the chimney-corner) (n.d.), An tAthair Éamonn Ó Dochartaigh's

Dréacht Grinn / Eibhlín S'Againn (A humorous piece / Our Eibhlín) (*FL*, 24/3/23), Pádraig Ó Bróithe's *Réidhteach na Ceiste* (The answer to the question) (1925), Seán Ó hÓgáin's *An Fheilm* (The farm) (1926) and *Smacht* (Control) (1933), Criostóir Ó Raghallaigh's *Dúthracht* (Zeal) (1927), Shán Ó Cuív's *Troid* (Fight) (1927), Micheál Ó Gríobhtha's *Bean an Bhrait Bháin* (The woman in the white cloak) (1928), Annraoi Saidléar's *Misneach* (Courage) (1928) and *Oidhche sa Tábhairne* (1937), Séamus de Bhilmot's *An Casán* (The path) and *Múchadh an tSolais* (The extinguishing of the light) (both 1931), León Ó Broin's *An Sgríbhinn ar an mBalla* (The writing on the wall) (1931), Micheál Mac Liammóir's *Oidhche Bhealtaine* (The eve of May Day) (1932), Micheál Breathnach's *Cor i nAghaidh an Chaim* (1932) and *Tart* (Thirst) (1939),[161] Diarmuid Ó Súilleabháin's *Cliamhain Isteach* (A man who married into the farm) (1933), Brian Ó Cianaidh's *Gníomhartha Lae 'san Gaedhealtacht* (A day's doings in the Gaeltacht) (*Ultach*, June and Aug. 1933), Máire Bean Mhic Ghránnda's *Dráma Beag / Caraid Iosagáin* (A little play / The friend of little Jesus) (*Ultach*, Dec. 1933), *Cóiriú na Leabthan* (Making the bed) adapted by 'Caoilte' from a short story by Pádraig Ó Siochfhradha (see *Mungret Annual*, 1934, 92), Pádraig Ó Gallchobhair's *Lorg an Phóitín* (The effect of moonshine) (1934), Séamus Ó Séaghdha's *Leigheas an tSlaghdáin* (The cure for a cold) (1935) (see *IP*, 31/10/35) and *An Taoide Tuile* (The flood tide), Máiréad Ní Ghráda's *An Udhacht* (The will) (1935), Máirtín Ó Cadhain's *An Phléasc* (The explosion) (1935),[162] B. N. Lóiste's *Cathal faoi Ghealltanas* (Cathal pledged) (1936), An tAthair Pádhraic Mac Aodha's *An Broc Dubh* (The black badger) (1936) and *Peadar a' tSléibhe* (Peadar of the mountain) (1937), Seán Mac Thorcail's *Slis den tSean-Mhaide* (A chip off the old block) (1936), Máire Ní Éigeartaigh's *Ar Lorg na Gaedhealtachta* (In search of the Gaeltacht) (1936) (see *IP*, 13/5/36), William P. Ryan's *Feilm an Tobair Bheannuighthe* (The farm of the holy well) (1936), Stan O'Brien's *Ag Iarraidh Mná* (Seeking a wife) (1936) (see *IP*, 6/2/36), Aodh Ó Cathaláin's *An Ridire Bóthair* (The knight of the road) (1936) (see *IP*, 19/11/36),[163] Muiris Ó Súileabháin's *Oidhche thar Oidhcheannta* (A night of nights) (1936) and *Uisce Casachtaigh* (Cough water) (1938) (see *IP*, 19/6/36 and 16/2/38), Aoife Taafe's bilingual *Féirín na Sidhe* (The gift of the fairies) (1936) (see *IP*, 2/1/36), Seaghán Mac Meanman's *Cad Chuige nach dTabharfainn?* (Why wouldn't I give?), *Peinsean Shean-Mháire Ní Ruadháin*, and *Athrughadh Intinne* (A change of mind) (all 1936), and Tomás Luibhéid's *Biorán Suain* (a sleep charm) (1937).

The majority of these plays were comedies, with matchmaking and marriage a favourite theme. But in the midst of all the cabin kitchens, elderly bachelors, dowry debates, and *poitín*, one also finds more original and intriguing country plays. For example, de Bhilmot's *Múchadh an tSolais* deals with a former seminarian's loss of faith and his rage at the passivity of his poor fisherman father in the face of a system that has enabled a local gombeen man to grow rich at his neighbours' expense. He sets off to attack the merchant, but is unable to get at him in his large, well-lit house. Instead, he cuts off the man's electricity, thereby causing the deaths of some fishermen who were guiding themselves by the light from the house. The play ends rather predictably with his remorse and bitter realisation that the God whose existence he had denied was watching over the men his own actions had killed.[164] The drowning death of a fisherman father sets in motion the tragic events of An tAthair Pádhraic Mac Aodha's *An Broc Dubh*. The man's son swears the sea will never get him as it did his father. Instead, he falls victim to *poitín*, eventually dying drunk on a hillside, after which his mother loses her wits. Also of interest in this play is the discussion at the forge in the second act, a discussion that ranges over contemporary issues such as the redistribution of unused estates to landless people in towns and cities as a cure for unemployment, and the restriction of foreign imports into Ireland.[165]

Máirtín Ó Cadhain's *An Phléasc* was based on a real Conamara tragedy, the June 1917 explosion of a mine that killed nine men who had found it washed ashore and hadn't known what it was. Of interest is Ó Cadhain's interpretation of the men's interest in the object as rooted in greed, as one of them makes clear in the third scene:

> You would leave that behind you on the sea. Well, it is easy to see that you are a fool. How do you know that there isn't a chest inside it, and that we wouldn't make our fortune out of it? By Christ, there must be some wealth in it with the shell they put on it. Perhaps they stash the gold they put on the ships from England to America now in those (*Macalla*, 1983, 8–9).[166]

Ryan's *Feilm an Tobair Bheannuighthe* (Dúndealgan: 'An Sgrúduightheoir', 1936) is a verse play of ideas, in which the author wrestles with many of the same questions that obsessed him in his novels *Caoimhghin Ó Cearnaigh* (1910) and *An Bhóinn agus an Bhóchna* (1915–16). In the play, a Dublin-based intellectual returns to his parents' farm at their request after his brother's emigration to America. Back home, he immediately begins to preach *Gaelachas* and socialism to his uncomprehending neighbours, offering them his vision of a just, green, and Gaelic utopia.

Perhaps the most forthright rural play of the period from a purely ideological point of view was Brian Ó Cianaidh's *Gníomhartha Lae 'san nGaedhealtacht*. Ó Cianaidh seems to have taken at their word those who believed the Gaeltacht offered all the Gaelic playwright needed, for his play is nothing but a series of scenes depicting everyday events in the area, including, inevitably, a match being made. That Ó Cianaidh was on to something here was proved when he won first prize with this one-acter at the 1933 Belfast Feis.

No depictions of Gaeltacht life from this period were, however, to have and hold such a fascination for readers of Irish as did – and still to some extent do – the three so-called Blasket Island autobiographies: Tomás Ó Criomhthain's *An t-Oileánach* (1929), Muiris Ó Súileabháin's *Fiche Blian ag Fás* (1933), and Peig Sayers's *Peig .i. A Scéal Féin* (1936). And to these one could add Ó Criomhthain's *Allagar na h-Inise* (Island cross-talk) (1928) and Sayers's *Machtnamh Seanamhná* (An old woman's contemplation) (1939). Moreover, it is important to note that translations into English of *An t-Oileánach* and *Fiche Blian ag Fás* were also published in our period, that of the former in 1937, that of the latter the same year the book appeared in Irish. As a result, almost immediately the Gaeltacht autobiography became the keystone of the evolving canon of writing in Irish.[167] In fact, the literary production of this tiny island off the Kerry coast was so startling in both its quantity and quality that it led Thomas Barrington to a hyperbolic dismissal of the literary work of all the rest of the country in a 1936 essay in the *Irish Rosary* entitled 'Fishermen and Literature': 'The output of this island of poverty-stricken fishermen only serves to underline the fact that Gaelic letters in the rest of Ireland is dead, dead as a doornail' (*IR*, July 1936, 521). The satirical monthly *Dublin Opinion* paid a more light-hearted tribute to the islanders' literary triumphs on the cover of its June 1933 issue with a cartoon labelled 'The Literary Wave Hits the Islands', a cartoon that showed every nook, cranny, and cave of the Great Blasket filled with people furiously scribbling or typing while a curragh pulls away laden with rolled manuscripts.[168]

There can be no doubt that the publication of *An t-Oileánach* was a milestone in the Gaelic movement, recognised as such in both the early reviews and in the later reviews on the appearance of Robin Flower's English translation, as well as by the first prize for 'Prós Samhlaoidheachta' (Imaginative prose) the book was awarded at the 1932 Aonach Tailteann, and the stamp with which the state later honoured the author.[169] Cearbhall Ua Dálaigh saw it as a book that enabled Gaels to hold their heads high in literary company. Writing in 1931, he declared: 'People are reluctant to praise books in Irish for fear that the man yonder would jump at them and would say that they were nothing but worthless rubbish. But I am not afraid to defend "The Islandman" in front of the world' (*CB*, May 1931, 505).[170] Contemporary enthusiasm for the book led to some very large claims, as when in an obituary column on Ó Criomhthain in *The Leader*, Seán Ó Ciarghusa wrote: '"An Seabhac" said that "The Islandman" was the best book that had come out of the Gaeltacht. I would say that it is the best book that has come out of Ireland in our time' (*Leader*, 20/3/37).[171] Struck by the freshness and originality of the book, Eoin Mac Néill made a claim whose apparent conviction could not mask his ambivalence about how to assess the work in meaningful critical terms, an ambivalence that has been shared by many others over the years. Mac Néill wrote: 'It knows no external standard of comparison and no external standpoint' (*Star*, 24/8/29). One 'M. D.' seems to have agreed, writing in his review for *An Stoc*: 'This is the best book in Irish I have read for a long time, and a book whose like cannot be found' (*Stoc*, Dec. 1929, 6).[172]

Indeed some critics seem to have felt that Ó Criomhthain's book transcended mere literature altogether. In a 1935 review of the English translation, a work he called 'a priceless boon upon those who are not sufficiently versed in Irish to read the book in the original', John J. M. Ryan proclaimed: 'The world into which "The Islandman" leads us, is a world of faith, of boundless trust in God, and of thankfulness for His help and protection amid the hardships and difficulties of a precarious existence' (*IR*, Jan. 1935, 73). A student author, Micheál Mac Eochaidh, writing in *The Clongownian* in 1931, offered Ó Criomhthain as a role model for an emergent Gaelic nation:

> Freedom is dawning on us at long last and it is long overdue. But we will not have freedom, the full light of freedom, until the spirit of the Islandman, the faith of the Islandman, the language of the Islandman, and the indomitable hope of the Islandman are firm and fast in the mind and the heart of the Gaels (*Clongownian*, 1931, 42).[173]

There were, however, a few dissenting voices. For example, in a 1931 lecture to a convention of secondary school teachers, Micheál Breathnach praised Ó Criomhthain's Irish, but then went on to criticise the book itself: 'But of course anyone at all would grow tired after reading some of it because it is the same thing page after page, with little happening and few changes of scene . . . A good book, without a doubt, but let us not go overboard with the praise' (*Dundalk Examiner*, 25/4/31).[174] Ernest Blythe also had his reservations, writing in 1933:

> It is the best An Gúm has done and I don't think that there are more than a couple of books in modern literature in Irish better than it. Nevertheless, it is not a masterpiece . . . It will not be among the classics of the Irish language . . . It must, therefore, be admitted that there is nothing in Tomás's book but ordinary stuff that will have no lasting effect in literary affairs (*II*, 4/4/33).[175]

Even more negative was Seán Ua Ceallaigh ('Mogh Ruith') in his review of Séamas Ó Searcaigh's *Nua-Sgríbhneoirí na Gaedhilge* (New writers in Irish) in 1933, where he called *An t-Oileánach* 'perhaps the most over-rated book, despite its somewhat unique nature, ever issued from the Irish press' (*CB*, Jan. 1934, 55). One 'Ceannfaolaidh' developed his objections to *An t-Oileánach* at length in a 1934 piece in *An t-Ultach*. This writer was particularly upset by Ó Criomhthain's winning the Aonach Tailteann prize for the book, blasting both the prize committee and the prize winner at length:

> They saw literature . . . in *The Islandman*. Not only that, but they made the book into the standard and the foundation of Literature. Was it not the greatest book in modern Irish? Was it not comparable with any contemporary literature in English or in Irish?

For this critic, the book was nothing more than 'the narrative of an old man who has a good memory and a philosophy so simple and common that it should not be called a philosophy . . . As a narrative it is not high literature, and there is no imagination in it at all' (*Ultach*, Nov. 1934, 6).[176]

One must wonder whether it was primarily his linguistic obsession that caused Séamus Ó Grianna to be so dismissive of Ó Criomhthain's earlier book *Allagar na h-Inise*. In his review for *Fáinne an Lae*, 'Máire' does begin with high praise for the author's (Kerry) Irish, but goes on to wonder why some of the book was ever published: 'I don't understand why some pieces in this book were published. Even less do I understand why it is thought that they are literature.' Noting that the state, through An Gúm, had funded the book and that 'An Seabhac' had helped 'cobble' it together, Ó Grianna scoffed: 'But I would like to say this much to them: They can spend the money on cobbling, but they will never succeed in convincing the public that they are making shoes.' One of the more curious and disturbing elements of this review is the condescending tone this champion of the native speaker adopted towards this native-speaking author, calling him 'an old man from the Blaskets talking about fertilising potatoes or the price of an ounce of tobacco' (seanduine as na Blaisgéidí ag cainnt ar leasughadh phréataí nó ar luach unsa tobaca) (*FL*, Feb. 1929, 3).[177] Maoghnus Ó Domhnaill argued in 1932 that *Allagar na h-Inise* was a better book than *An t-Oileánach*, writing of the latter: 'There is a story in *The Islandman*, but there is little literature in it.' For Ó Domhnaill, the problem was that it was university people, with little personal knowledge of the Gaeltacht or indeed little real appreciation of literature, who had so inflated the reputation of *An t-Oileánach* at the expense of Ó Criomhthain's earlier work: 'And we find it strange that people who are supposedly familiar with literature from all over the world and a couple of other places as well have so little understanding concerning well-written books and literature' (*ACS*, 14/5/32).[178]

Muiris Ó Súileabháin's *Fiche Blian ag Fás*, despite high praise in an introductory note by E. M. Forster for the English translation by Moya Llewelyn Davies and George Thomson, received a considerably more reserved welcome from the Gaels than did *An t-Oileánach*. By far the most positive assessment was that by 'Kerryman' in a 1933 review that began: 'So far as Gaelic literature is concerned, "Fiche Blian ag Fás" is a portent. The Gaeltacht is finding its voice.' For this critic, the voice it had found in this book was a major one indeed, as he called Ó Súileabháin 'a man likely to leave as big a mark on Gaelic literature as Fr. O'Leary and to leave behind him an output of bigger and more vital work' (*UIrman*, 13/5/33). Even Seán Ó Faoláin, who, as we will see, was beginning at this time to distance himself from the Gaelic enthusiasm of his youth, could write of Ó Súileabháin's book on the occasion of its winning the O'Growney Prize from the Irish Academy of Letters in 1934: 'This book is a sign of the new world that is arising in Ireland, and a sign also of the link there is between the world of our own time and the old world that is slipping away from us. "Twenty Years A' Growing" is a root of the new sprout' (*II*, 6/12/34).[179]

Those who did not like the book pulled no punches in their reviews. Alluding sarcastically to Forster's comment that *Fiche Blian ag Fás* was like 'the egg of a sea-bird – lovely, perfect, and laid this very morning', Seán Ua Ceallaigh lambasted the book:

> We have read it, and we regret to say, with a steadily flagging interest varied with intervals of nausea. So that our readers may sniff the odour of this reputed sea-bird's egg, represented to the public as almost affording a feast of Kerry Irish at its best, we propose to examine it in some detail from the standpoints of grammatical form, idiom, diction, and let typical passages from the translation convey its tone and spirit and general character.

Ua Ceallaigh then went on to blast the dialogue ('punctuated by offensive expectoration and repeated invocations of the Prince of Darkness'), 'the myriad blunders that disfigure every page of the work', the orthography ('literary vandalism'), and the examples of *Béarlachas*, to attempt a catalogue of which, he said, 'would require a whole issue of the *Bulletin*'. His conclusion was that instead of being the egg of a sea bird laid this very morning, the book was 'an artificial egg chockful of the rank meat for which John Bull's intellectual appetite eternally craves' (*CB*, July 1933, 562–73). Looking back on Ó Súileabháin's work in both its Irish and English incarnations in 1936, Éibhlín Nic Ghráinne offered a startling justification for her distaste for the book:

> *Fiche Blain ag Fás* is written in the old convention of the Anglo-Irish school, of Carleton and Banim, of showing the Irish 'peasant' and his queer ways to the English-speaking world outside . . . Looking without prejudice at the two books *Fiche Blian ag Fás* . . . and *Twenty Years A-Growing*, and comparing them, the truth appears, in spite of protests, that the translation's the thing. For the English version reaches the great reading public of England and America, and it bears the necessary hall-mark, the prestige of an English publishing house.

Nic Ghráinne also turned Forster's praise against the book as a work of Irish art, arguing that

> literature that is built up on a standard like this rings false. It gains its effect by creating surprise, as E. M. Forster admits, in the mind of the reader who belongs to an alien culture, but the Irish reader feels no such wonder and is interested only in the story for its intrinsic value (*Dublin Magazine*, Apr.–June 1936, 96).

Peig seems on the whole to have attracted less attention at the time, despite its winning the prestigious Gaelic literary award Duais an Chraoibhín. As was often the case, Liam Ó Rinn found an important and original perspective from which to welcome the book. Having commented on Sayers's language, including her use of 'many of those little phrases especially related to women's work' (mórán de sna habairtí beaga bhaineas go speisialta le hobair bhan), he continued:

> That reminds me that we have virtually no books from the women of the Gaeltacht, a fact that means we are left with too much masculinity in published Irish – it would be better off if there would be some of the delicate trace of the female mind in it. And that is probably why I like 'Peig' so much.

Behind this dated language, Ó Rinn had an interesting notion of what the strengths of this 'female mind' (*aigne bhanda*) were: 'Women usually prefer to talk about people rather than things . . . I would say that they are right. The poor animal called a person is far more interesting than anything in the whole world outside of it' (*UI*, 18/7/36).[180] Several other writers also commented on the value of Sayers's feminine perspective on Gaeltacht life, but none as insightfully as Ó Rinn.[181] A negative and patronising note was sounded by 'An Stad' in 1936: 'Indeed, one almost fears that the success of this, her first effort, may prompt her to recall and record more, and they not so well worth it. However, her editors may be depended on to guard her against that, I expect.'[182]

One of the problems contemporary critics had with these books was the whole question of genre. What kind of writing were they? What were their authors trying to do? And for what audience? The difficulty was compounded by the fact that all of the Blasket books were very much revival projects, inspired, midwived, and edited by enthusiastic outsiders with cultural agendas of their own.[183] By no means do I intend to disparage the work of Brian Ó Ceallaigh and Pádraig Ó Siochfhradha with Ó Criomhthain, George Thomson with Ó Súileabháin, or Micheál Ó Gaoithín and Máire Ní Chinnéide with Sayers.[184] Nevertheless, with so many different minds shaping these books for an audience with its own expectations of what the Gaeltacht would say and how it would say it on finding its own voice, we can hardly be surprised if contemporary Gaels were at times as confused as they were delighted when they heard that voice speak.

In an undated letter to an unidentified correspondent, Ó Criomhthain himself wrote that he had told his story 'exactly as I lived my life' (laomdireách amach mar do chuireas an saoghal digheam) and asserted that, in effect, he had no choice: 'I have no story about any two people in the world. Therefore, if a person who is writing his own story has to go seeking help from the story of everyone, that will divert him from his own story, and he won't have his own story or that of anyone else.'[185] For some in the movement, however, Ó Criomhthain would be more valuable as the voice of a people rather than the voice of a living, independent, in many ways idiosyncratic individual. This was certainly the attitude of Pádraig Ó Siochfhradha, who wrote in a brief editorial preface to *Allagar na hInise*: 'This book is a voice from the Gaeltacht – that Gaeltacht that has been mute, weak, powerless to express itself or plead its own case to make the outside world concerned about rescuing it.'[186] It should be no surprise then that some insisted on reading him as, in Riobárd Ó Faracháin's phrase, 'a member of the tribe speaking on behalf of the tribe' (duine de'n treibh ag labhairt thar cheann na treibhe) (*Outlook*, 9/1/32). From this point of view, Ó Criomhthain and the other Blasket writers became amateur anthropologists. It was certainly as such that Maoghnus Ó Domhnaill judged Ó Criomhthain when he wrote of *An t-Oileánach* in 1932:

> It is no harm to make the life of the people of the island known to English speakers in other countries, and here in Ireland itself. The majority of the people of this country are blind to the fact that the like of it exists at all, and in some way it will delight them as would some of the books written about the remote regions of the earth (*ACS*, 14/5/32).[187]

An tAthair Mac Fhinn saw a similar significance in Ó Súileabháin's book:

> And there is a deep understanding of the life of the Gaeltacht to be found in the book . . . It is a coherent book that anyone at all – from Galway to Berlin – who wants to get to know the life and the people to whom the living Irish language belongs will want to read (*AA*, Aug. 1933, 5).[188]

For 'E. Nic Gh.', reviewing *Peig* for the *Dublin Magazine*, the book's primary importance seems to have been as a treasury of folk belief:

> There are many other native speakers of Irish, still living, who like Peig have inherited the seanchuidhe's craft and whose lore indicates the riches of that literary tradition . . . Because this inherited store of literary tradition is transmitted orally, it is no less literature than the written word turned into the more lasting mould of manuscript or of print. It is the nucleus of the literature of modern Ireland (*Dublin Magazine*, Jan.–Mar. 1937, 94).

This critic raises two important and interlinked points here: the appreciation of a special literary quality in *Peig*, and the virtual interchangeablity of Peig herself with many others of her generation in the Gaeltacht as the creator of the book. Very little attention was paid at the time to the literary accomplishments, techniques, or styles of the Blasket authors. In effect, there seems to have been a belief that the Gaeltacht was rife with undifferentiated literary geniuses all sharing in some sort of collective Gaelic consciousness for the edification of the rest of the nation. Nowhere is this curiously ambivalent attitude more evident than in Eoin Mac Néill's glowing review of *An t-Oileánach* for *The Star*:

> The writer of this book is what they call a 'peasant'. He is just a typical specimen of the farming and fishing population of our Western islands and forelands . . . As things are, this book is a novelty and a wonder, but I am not going to flatter the author. I am confident, from what I know, that here in Connemara, or in Aran, or in many another part of our Western islands and forelands, others could be found in the same way of life as Tomás, capable of producing literature of equal interest and merit, with a similar command of language, a similar power of description, a similar facility of writing live dialogue (*Star*, 24/8/29).

In his review of *Peig*, Pádraig Ó Cléirigh also saw the author pretty much as a generic resident of the Gaeltacht, asserting that one of the book's greatest virtues, one that it shared with the other Blasket works, was 'that that literary peasant has been overthrown, and the normal, human person who actually is in the Gaeltacht has been put in his place' (go bhfuil an peasant liteardha úd bainte dá bhonnaibh agus an duine gnáth daonna atá dáiríribh sa Ghaedhealtacht curtha 'na ionad) (*II*, 30/7/37). A sharp dissent from this patronising view of the Blasket authors was registered by 'M. D.' in his review of *An t-Oileánach* for *An Stoc*:

> Tomás Ó Criomhthain is a man of whose like not many are left. He has a good understanding and a big heart, and he is level-headed. I have probably met people like him, but none of them could have written a book like this, nor any book at all. It is because of that that we should be very grateful to Tomás (*Stoc*, Dec. 1929, 6).[189]

There was, then, at least a little discussion of the individual personal and literary qualities of the Blasket authors. In his review of *An t-Oileánach* for the *Irish Rosary*, 'D. P.' called it 'the first book that will endure' from the presses of An Gúm, and went on to praise Ó Criomhthain as 'a natural stylist' with 'keen observation and the power of sincere self-revelation' (*IR*, Sept. 1929, 720).[190] Thomas Barrington also awarded pride of place to Ó Criomhthain in 'Telescope and Memory', his 1937 study of the three major Blasket books in *Bonaventura*. Of *An t-Oileánach*, he wrote:

> This is a wonderful book, without doubt the greatest that has come out of Ireland this many a year. The style is spare but enhanced by a kindly irony. The story is told with austerity. Sentimentalism is shunned like a plague. It has tremendous power because of this simplicity. It strives to create no literary effect. It is a plain, unvarnished telling (*Bonaventura*, Summer 1937, 116).

Barrington was far less taken with Ó Súileabháin's work, which he found 'musical' but lacking in depth, and marred by 'his worst faults: occasional sentimentalism and easy moralising'. Having praised Peig for her 'considerable craft' and a style 'clear as crystal', Barrington nevertheless felt her book lacked 'something of the absorbing interest of the other two autobiographies' (*Bonaventura*, Summer 1937, 117–18). Many of these observations will strike even today's reader, blessed with over sixty years of critical reflection and simple hindsight, as pretty much on target.

In the opening paragraph of his 1936 review of *Peig*, Liam Ó Rinn offered a provocative explanation for why some Gaels found the work of Ó Criomhthain and particularly Ó Súileabháin troubling:

> The Gaelic world was greatly stirred when 'The Islandman' and 'Twenty Years A' Growing' were published. Indeed there are people who still have not recovered from the fit of anger that seized them because Muiris Ó Súileabháin, out of sheer innocence, told the truth about the people of the Gaeltacht, that is, that they are not little clay and plaster saints, nor pseudo-aristocrats, but ordinary people as have come down from the time of Adam on (*UI*, 18/7/36).[191]

In the manuscript of *An tOileánach*, Ó Criomhthain made clear that it was his intention to provide an absolutely accurate picture of island life:

> Long ago, after telling a story the storyteller used to say – that's my story, and if there is a lie in it, so be it. This is my story, and there is not a lie in it – nothing but the truth. I would think it a fine thing for every student in Ireland and abroad to have the book in his hand.[192]

But that was just the problem. Many in the movement did not want students of whatever age to learn some of the lessons in Ó Criomhthain's book, and thus the text as it first appeared in print after having been edited by Pádraig Ó Siochfhradha is quite different from the text Ó Criomhthain had produced. The question of the censorship inflicted on *An tOileánach* has attracted a fair amount of scholarly attention.[193] What is of interest to us here is what these alterations tell us about the intellectual climate of the time, in particular with regard to the ideological construct of the noble Gaeltacht native speaker that Ó Criomhthain's book did so much to encourage and underpin. What obviously distressed Ó Siochfhradha most about Ó

Criomhthain's original text was its relatively frank treatment of sexuality, and he therefore removed any earthy references and anecdotes concerning Tomás's interest in the opposite sex, an interest Tomás tells us began when he was fifteen, 'and a person could say that it was quite early for anyone so young to be cocking an ear towards young women' (agus díarfeadh duine gur luath an gnó d'aon duine có óg sion a bheith a cocáil a chlúasa a d'-treó óig-bhan). Moreover, his curiosity about women seems to have been reciprocated. In one episode cut by Ó Siochfhradha, Tomás and his friend 'the King' strip to bathe at a well, only to notice they are being watched by 'a trio of big young women and their bodies and faces watching us' (triúar alpachán dóig-mhná ⁊ a g'corp ⁊ a n'aghaidh a féachaint orainn). His friend runs into the sea, but Tomás stays put, 'and this thought occurred to me, why should it be myself that is frightened of them instead of the other way around. I thrust my hands over a certain part of my body, and remained standing straight-up there to spite them' (⁊ do rioth an machtnamh-so chugham, cad é an bonn do bhí le mé-fhéin do thógaint sgéith roampa-sion seachas iad-féin. Do bhuaileas mo bhosaibh trosna air bhall áiraighthe do'm chorp, ⁊ d'fhannas am choilsheasamh gan cor do chur díom mar olc ortha). Two of the young women turn away, but one stays put and jokes about his being dry now. He responds that only one side is dry, 'but that I would have to turn my rear end to the sun for a while more, and since you have not managed to see any strange sight from this side of me, perhaps you'll find it different when I turn my rear end to you' (ach go g'caithfhainn mo thón do thabhairt tamall eile le gréin, ⁊ ó anuair nár rángaigh leat aon phictiuir stróinséartha d'fheisceint ó'n dtaobh-so dhíom, b'fhéidair ná beidhfeá mar sin anuair a thabharfhead mo thón leat).[194]

In a later episode, Ó Criomhthain is alone when he encounters a group of six women, who, however comely, would have had no place in de Valera's rural utopia. At first, Tomás fears the women have designs on him: 'What I feared most was that the six would join together to take off my trousers, but it did not occur to them to do that' (Sé faitígheas is mó do bhí oram, go gcuirfheadh an seisear le chéile chuin mo bhríste do bhainnt díom, ach níor buaileadh na n'aiginne sion do dhéannamh). Instead, however, they put on an unexpected show for him:

> The upshot was that the clothing on the six brats would not have cost much, and whatever weariness I felt went from me, for the six were going at each other often, and no sooner were they standing than their arses were in the air, and very often a part of their bodies to be seen that the sun had not shone on before that until this time.[195]

In addition to cutting these accounts of sexual behaviour, Ó Siochfhradha also removed or toned down references to drunkenness among the islanders or to fights, particularly when women were involved in either activity.

While learning of Gaeltacht sins and shortcomings from the pens of writers who had never – or only recently – left their home places was a new experience for those in the language movement reading the Blasket books, they should already have learned a good deal about the flawed humanity of Gaeltacht people from many other sources since the start of the revival, and those flaws continued to draw the honest and critical attention of Gaelic writers throughout our period. Indeed the exposure of the individual and social failings of their own real or imagined community had always been and would remain a central thematic focus of Gaelic novelists, story writers, and dramatists.

No single social institution received so much or such varied literary treatment as did marriage, involving as it did match-making, family alliances, generational strife, and social status. One 'Thespis' expressed his awareness of both the importance of the subject and the frequency with which it had been treated superficially in a review of An Comhar Drámaidheachta's 1928 production of Diarmuid Ó Súilleabháin's *Cliamhain Isteach*:

> The whole matter of match-making in Ireland is a standing joke for dramatists and story-tellers, particularly in English. It is time the mistake was pointed out. A complementary mistake is to picture, or talk of, love as being the grand ruling passion in rural Ireland. It may be the grand, but isn't the ruling, passion. I don't know that that is a misfortune either. – Marriages in Ireland don't seem to be unhappier than anywhere else, to put it no stronger, and the 'made' matches seem to turn out as happy as the love ones (*Leader*, 14/4/28).

Despite the reservations of 'Thespis', matchmaking and marriage were frequently seen as either standing jokes or ruling passions in literary works about rural Ireland. Certainly there was a plethora of plays, stories, and episodes from novels that dealt comically, even farcically, with these social conventions. Among comic stories dealing with courtship and marriage were Nioclás Tóibín's 'An Grádh agus an t-Airgead' (Love and money),[196] 'Do Cheannsughadh Mná' (Taming a woman) by 'Mial' (*Sguab*, Nov. 1925), 'An Cleamhnas' (The match) by 'M. Ó C.' (*Stoc*, Apr. 1930), 'Pósadh Shimeóin' (The marriage of Simeon) by 'Esther' (*Lóchrann*, July 1930), 'Saoghal na nDaoine / Bainis Dhomhnaill Bháin' (The life of the people / The wedding of Domhnall Bán) by Eoin Ó Searcaigh (*Dundalk Examiner*, 20/9/30), and 'Cleamhnas Mhicil Úna' (The match made for Micheál Úna) by Máirtín Ó Direáin (*AA*, June 1936, 2–3).

With regard to the other abuse of the love theme criticised by 'Thespis', that of elevating love to the 'grand ruling passion' of Irish rural life, no writer indulged himself more regularly than did Séamus Ó Grianna, whose allegiance to a cloyingly romantic understanding of love was to characterise his treatment of the subject throughout his lengthy and prolific career. An tAthair Seán Ó Gallchóir offers the following succinct summary of the romantic love plot in *Caisleáin Óir*, a summary that could apply equally well to the plot of eight of his novels and what Ó Gallchóir estimates as around one hundred of his stories:

> This love is powerful – as if it were a disease. It is chaste, sentimental, romantic. The conditions of life cause them to separate from each other . . . At the end of the story, love does not bloom. The story of their love comes to a joyless and sad end.[197]

Ó Grianna also manages to weave a virtually identical romantic tragedy into the novel as a subplot when the protagonist's friend Micheál Dubh tells his own tale of heartbreak, including the following description of his last evening in the company of his sweetheart:

> I have had trouble and sorrow and life's oppression ever since as a result of that same night, and yet despite all of that, I would do it all again and again for one more night like that night, to get one more look at those clear, dark-blue eyes, to get to take those fair, slender, elegant fingers in my hand, to get one kiss from her sweet little mouth that was as cold as an icicle and as red as a rowan berry.[198]

Yet even in Ó Grianna's fiction, a more pragmatic, not to say cynical, attitude towards love is the one that prevails in this vale of tears. A view of courtship as a grimly materialistic transaction is central in *Caisleáin Óir*,[199] as well as in three stories in *Cioth is Dealán*, in one of which, 'Anam a Mháthara Móire' (The soul of his grandmother), the narrator's grandmother explains these facts of life in the Donegal Gaeltacht:

> Himself and the miller's daughter Nábla had been engaged to each other for years. Everyone thought that they would have each other. But things turn out as they are destined to, not as people think they will. The Fair-haired Miller was sitting pretty at the time, with the means to give his daughter a good dowry. And it was not empty-handed that a man had any business going to ask him for Nábla.[200]

Of course, Ó Grianna was by no means alone in his treatment of marriage as an arrangement involving the exchange of property, cattle, money, and the promise of security and / or prestige, rather than as a relationship having its origins in love. In Diarmuid Ó Súilleabháin's 1928 play *Cliamhain Isteach*, a well-meaning widower wants to provide security for his daughter by making a good match for her, but the daughter finds the whole process degrading: 'The money! And you would sell me for money? My grandfather did not sell my mother for money when you got to marry her; and if she were alive, I would not be sold for money.'[201] While the bargaining over her dowry is predictably crass, the play ends happily with the father realising his mistake and allowing her to marry the penniless IRA man she loves. Annraoi Saidléar's 1937 play *Oidhche sa Tábhairne* also ends well when a daughter threatened by her parents with marriage to a miserly 50-year-old farmer ready to revoke the lease he has on their property holds out long enough for her fiancé to return from America to save the day. A happy ending of a more hard-headed (and hearted) sort is found in Seaghán Mac Meanman's 1936 play *Athrughadh Intinne*, in which the daughter initially resists her parents' efforts to marry her to a widower with four children, but is then swayed by her mother's description, in the man's presence, of his assets, including two cows ready to calf, a heifer in calf, eight calves, and a Government bull. When the young woman learns that a neighbour has her eye on the man, she accepts him, with a clear-eyed awareness of just what she is doing: 'Well, Biddy won't get the chance. I'll take him myself! The best man is the man who is never empty-handed and who never lacks money!'[202]

Novels in which the more sordid side of matchmaking is explored include Seán Ó Ruadháin's *Pádhraic Mháire Bhán*, Seán Ó Ciarghusa's *Bun an Dá Abhann*, Éamonn Mac Giolla Iasachta's *Toil Dé*, Ciarán Ua Nualláin's *Oidhche i nGleann na nGealt*, and Séamas Mac Conmara's *An Coimhthigheach*. Mac Giolla Iasachta has one of the characters in his novel lash out at this concept of marriage as transaction in the person of 'those farmers who buy and sell their children like beasts' (na feirmeoirí úd a dhíolann a's cheannuigheann a gclann ar nós beithidheach).[203]

It is, however, in the Blasket books themselves that we get the most vivid and personal expression of what this custom meant for those who lived with and by it. One of the most memorable chapters in *Peig* is the one titled 'Cleamhnas agus Pósadh' (Matchmaking and marriage) in which the young Peig tries to figure out which of the three men come to visit is the one destined to be her husband, thinking: 'Everyone of them was too good a man for me if I were seven times better than I was.' Asked by her father whether she will accept the man and move to the Great Blasket with him, she replies succinctly: 'I know nothing at all about the people of the Island . . . but you know them well, and what you want is what I want. I will go wherever you tell me.'[204] The marriage takes place a few days later, and Sayers seems never to have regretted her decision. There was a bit more romance in Ó Criomhthain's life, for he fancied a young woman from Inis Mhicileán, only to be overruled on practical grounds by his sister, who argues the case before their parents: 'She spelled out to the two old people the obligation involved for the person who would not marry a neighbour but rather would bind himself to another group far from home and from whom there would be neither help nor assistance to be had on the day of need.'[205] The parents agree, and week later the pair are married, and, as he tells us himself in *An tOileánach*, Tomás expresses his sense of loss through the song he chooses to sing at the party after his wedding, the tragic 'Caisleán Uí Néill nua an Bean Dubh ó'n Sliabh' (O'Neill's castle, or the black-haired woman from the mountain).[206] Ó Súileabháin was never personally involved in such matchmaking on the island, but he was well aware of the rules of the game, as he makes clear in the following passage in which a man discusses the good fortune of a neighbour in finding a good husband: 'He has plenty of land, and it is the best land; he has hundreds of sheep on the hills, not to mention the money he has saved.'[207]

It is also worth noting that a few writers acknowledged that there was resistance to this system on the part of some. For example, in the 1923 'Sgéilín' (A little story) by 'Fionn', a young woman rejects a match with a 40-year-old farmer despite his having 'a fairly big farm of good land, and the best cattle in the county' (feirm resiúntach mór de dheagh-talamh, agus an t-eallach do b'fhearr sa gcondae), as well as little interest in the size of her own dowry. She leaves the would-be matchmaker in little doubt as to her feelings on the matter: 'Séamus Ó Colmáin . . . if you think that I would marry a lame man like Mr. Ó Murchadha, you're wrong. You would be better off doing nothing than doing a bad deed' (*Land*, 28/4/23).[208] The protagonist of Gráinne Ní Mháille's 'I nDiaidh Gréine Siar' (Following the setting sun) is estranged from his father after he rejects an arranged match and marries a woman he loves (*IC*, 23/2/29). In *Machtnamh Seanamhná*, Peig Sayers tells of how two women – a man's wife and a woman who had loved him and lost – engage in a violent confrontation over him.[209] To avoid such a dire situation, some ran away. Ó Criomhthain tells us in *An t-Oileánach* of a Dunquin woman who slipped away to the Blaskets to avoid an unwanted marriage, only to later marry a man more to her own liking. Ó Criomhthain seems to have found her behaviour baffling: 'Although they were a pair of men with nothing either good or bad to distinguish them, look how the girl chose one easily.'[210] In 'Fionn' Mac Cumhaill's *Na Rosa go Bráthach* (1939), a woman elopes with her chosen partner rather than wait for an older sister to marry.[211]

The problems that troubled at least some marriages, even in the Gaeltacht, were the focus of other Gaelic writers of this period. Micheál Ua Conláin's 1923 story 'Giolcach dhá Bhriseadh' (A reed being broken) is the tale of a cold and tyrannical husband and father who only realises the evil he has done after the death of his wife (*IF*, July 1923, 32–4). Seán Ó Ciarghusa's 'Trí Scéalta Grádha' offer grim views of the financial aspects of Irish rural marriage, including the role of money in marital breakdown, the baneful effect of deceit within marriage, and the possibility of insanity as the result of an unhappy union.[212] Niall Ó Domhnaill's 'Fealltamhnas i gCineadh' (Treachery in a race) deals with a woman's wretched marriage to a drunkard who has come to detest both her and their children, and who now lives a dissolute life in Scotland. We learn, however, that some of the blame for the state of the marriage lies with the wife's sister, who has turned the wife against her husband when he is away on seasonal work. Determined to reform, the man returns home, where in the meantime the wife has died after becoming lost in a snowstorm. In revenge, her brother strikes the husband down with a blackthorn stick and then clubs him to death (*Ultach*, Dec. 1930, 1–4). Seán Ó Dálaigh's '"Mian Mic a Shúil"' (The desire of her eye) is a variant on the evil stepmother motif in which a man finally asserts his control over his malicious second wife. God then punishes the woman for her behaviour, the punishment taking the form of her first child's being born one-eyed.[213] In 'Nighean Róise' (Rose's daughter) by 'Lorcán', a strong farmer's daughter marries a hired hand and is thereafter ostracised by her family for 13 years (*Tír*, Apr. 1933, 9–12).[214] In 'Dhá Chrann na Marbh' (1939) by Séamus Maguidhir, we have another cruel and selfish stepmother who marries a brutal and drunken man. Neither of them feels any remorse when she drives his children from his house.[215] The thought of sharing a house with her son's new wife forces a mother to leave home for the Galway poorhouse, dying on the way, in León Ó Broin's 1929 story 'Peig Sheáin Ruaidh' (Seán Ruadh's Peig) (*Inis Fáil*, Dec. 1929, 24–6). Such tensions between daughter and mother-in-law are at the heart of Pádhraic Óg Ó Conaire's 1936 novel *Éan Cuideáin*, in which the wife is a Quebécoise woman whom the son has married in Montréal, while in Tomás Bairéad's 1932 story 'Rún na Mná Duibhe' (The secret of the black-haired woman), a mother would actually be happier to see her son dead than following the sinful path of his father, who had deserted her.[216]

Nowhere in Gaelic fiction were marital problems explored more frankly than they were in Úna Bean Uí Dhíosca's 1932 novel *Cailín na Gruaige Duinne* (The brown-haired girl). The marriage in question here is not a true Gaeltacht marriage, but rather a union between a university-educated young urban woman of Protestant background and the Gaeltacht man with whom she falls in love while in the area to learn Irish. Whatever movement idealism she has is snuffed out by the brutal and treacherous reality of her husband, who drowns her beloved pet dog, all but ignores her during her pregnancy, and is ultimately betrayed to his death during the Civil War by his equally distasteful brother. After the drowning of the dog, she leaves him, the first marital breakdown in modern Gaelic fiction, preceding by 15 years the better-known example that made Séamus Ó Néill's *Tonn Tuile* (Flood tide) something of a sensation in 1947.[217]

One of the movement's taboos that Ó Rinn felt Ó Súileabháin and Sayers had violated involved mention of the fondness of some Gaeltacht people for strong drink, particularly *poitín*.[218] And he could certainly have added Ó Criomhthain to his list of offenders here.[219] The islanders of all three books relish the chance to get well and truly drunk on those rare occasions that money and availability come together for them. For example, Ó Criomhthain offers the following description of the consequences of a night's drinking in Dingle: 'I had a reason to be vexed: the boat that was with us had gone home and the crew of my boat was utterly useless, three brothers of them drunk, another man in prison, two others that after a whole day I still had not seen.'[220] Island women join in the revelry at a wedding feast described in *Allagar na h-Inise*:

> People began pressing punch on them until they were quite tipsy. They headed up the king's road, a woman falling, another getting up, two singing, two crying, and although the road was level and without obstacles, they were not making any progress, for they were going up a while and down a while.[221]

Ó Súileabháin offers the following picture of men at the Ventry *naomhóg* (currragh) races: 'One man and then another called for a gallon again and again until they were blind drunk . . . It was not long now that the songs started all over the house, and they were flushed with the drink as is usual with the likes of them.'[222] Sayers summed up the situation with a succinct sentence on the people of Dunquin, where she herself was raised: 'All of them had a cursed fondness for a drop.'[223]

Drink was also treated matter of factly or comically by other Gaelic writers of the period in stories like 'Mar Baisteadh Maidhc' (How Mike was baptised) (*Lóchrann*, July 1926) and 'Glóire Bhaile an Phludaigh' (The pride of Baile an Phludaigh) (*Lóchrann*, Nov. 1926) by Micheál Ó Siochfhradha; 'An Cailín Seo agus an Cailín Údaidh Eile' (This girl and that other girl) (1929) by Seaghán Mac Meanman; 'Seán Ó Murchadha agus an Poitín' (Seán Ó Murchadha and the moonshine) (Enniscorthy *Echo*, 30/5/31) by Seán de Buitléir; the anonymous 'An t-Sealg' (The hunt) (UCG *University Annual*, 1930–1); and Ailbhe Ó Monacháin's 'Mar Chuaidh Páidín de'n Ól / Dearmad Ádhmhal' (How Paddy gave up the drink / A lucky mistake) (*CT*, 15/7/33). Mac Meanman's narrator sings the praises of whiskey in his story:

> It does not matter what priest or minister says, there can be nothing nicer on a table in the evening than a quart bottle full of golden whisky . . . If you look through the bottle at the light you will see the amber clouds around the shores of Í Breasail and the Land of Youth, and the golden rays that come eastwards from the sun when it is going into the sea.[224]

Not surprisingly, *poitín* and the usually comic attempts to suppress it feature largely in the stories written by police officers for the *Garda Review*, stories like 'An Cleasaidhe agus Fuisge na Nodlag' (The trickster and the Christmas whiskey) by Seán Ó Móráin of the Corofin barracks in County Clare (Dec.

1935); 'Ag Tóruigheacht Poitín Dom agus Mé im Shuidhe Air' (I was searching for *poitín* and sitting on it all the while) by S. Ó Gnímh of the Clifden, County Galway barracks (Nov. 1936); or 'Fear Bréige ag Déanamh Poitín agus Caora ag Feadghaíl' (An imitation man making poitín and a sheep whistling) by Sergeant Tomás Ó Foghludha of the Killorglin station in Kerry (Apr. 1937).

It was not, however, just priests, ministers, and civic guards who worried about the effects of strong drink on Gaeltacht life. Temperance was a consistent and recurrent theme in the Gaelic drama and fiction of this time. Two tragic plays of the period, Pádraig Ó Gallchobhair's *Lorg an Phóitín* (1934) and An tAthair Pádhraic Mac Aodha's *An Broc Dubh* (1936) depict the dire consequences of alcoholism. The temperance message is delivered more lightheartedly in B. N. Lóiste's comedy *Cathal faoi Ghealltanas*, in which the roguish protagonist initially manages to evade through trickery the obligations of the temperance pledge he had taken from a priest, only in the end to take the pledge in earnest.[225] Among stories that dealt with the tragic consequences of alcohol abuse were '"Tiocfaidh an Bás i Lár na h-Oidhche"' (Death will come in the middle of the night) by 'A. Ó F.' (*TCNÍ*, Sept. 1922); 'Cár Imigh Fiacha na mBróg?' (Where did the price of the shoes go?) by Father Dinneen (*Leader*, 18/8/23);[226] 'Dileasg' (Dulse) by 'Guaire' (*Stoc*, March and Apr. 1926); 'An Crúisgín Folamh' (The empty little jug) by 'Muiris na Móna' (*The Cross*, Nov. 1931); 'Lomadh na Luain Ort' (May you be totally destroyed) by Seán Ó Dálaigh;[227] 'An Stiléara' (The moonshiner) by Tomás Bairéad;[228] 'Seáinín Ó Frighil' by An tAthair Seán Ó Siadhail (*IR*, Dec. 1933); 'Billí na Beorach' (Billy of the beer) by 'Liam Liath' (*Gaedheal*, Dec. 1936); and the anonymous 'Toradh na Dílseachta agus na Foighde' (The result of loyalty and patience).[229] A temperance message is also implicit in Tomás Ó hAodha's comic story 'Eachtra Nóta Deich bPúnt' (The adventure of a ten-pound note) (*FL*, 15/12/23); Seaghán Mac Meanman's comic story 'An Cheud Mheisge agus an Mheisge Dheireannach' (The first drunkenness and the last drunkenness);[230] and Father Dinneen's 'Dómhnall agus Tomás' (*Leader*, 7/1/28).

Gaelic novels at the time that included temperance among their themes were Micheál Ó Gríobhtha's *Briathar Mná* (A woman's word) (see p. 79), Seán Ó Ruadháin's *Pádhraic Mháire Bhán* (see p. 273), Diarmuid Ua Laoghaire's *An Bhruinneall Bhán* (see pp. 157–8), Tadhg Ó Rabhartaigh's *Mian na Marbh*, Séamas Mac Conmara's *An Coimhthigheach* (see pp. 8, 15–16, 20), and Pádhraic Óg Ó Conaire's *Ceol na nGiolcach*. Nowhere is the message clearer than in the mini-sermon a debauched Donegal father delivers to his son in the slums of Glasgow in Ó Rabhartaigh's novel:

> Oh, Cathal, my son [lit. brother], it is the most cursed habit any young man ever took up. The drink is the source of every evil, and it is I who knows that, alas! . . . My advice to you, my son, is to keep away from the drink. If you knew what the drink

did to me, my son, you would not allow one drop of it into your throat throughout your life.[231]

In Ó Conaire's novel, Marcas Ó Loideáin, a prosperous Conamara man, convinces a neighbor to ban *poitín* at his son's wake, a major break with the prevailing social conventions. For Ó Loideáin, his opposition to *poitín* is rooted in a sense of local and national shame about what drink can do to his people:

May I not leave here if I am not stricken with shame when I read the *Connacht Champion*: people fighting and drunk coming home from funerals, throwing stones, and the odd one of them using a dagger! There is no need for us to blame England for this, nor is there is any need for us to be waiting for Home Rule to put an end to it either.[232]

Writing in the *Irish Monthly* in April 1933, Margaret Gibbons wondered whether writing from and about the Gaeltacht was giving Gaelic readers a false picture of life there:

Another aspect, by the way, of this prevalence of folk-tale, fool-tale, and 'good story' from the Gaeltacht (above all the good story), is to give the casual student a distorted view of the native character – to send him away with the impression that the Gaeltacht residents are all tricksters, cheats, liars – the girls false, the men cynical (*Irish Monthly*, Apr. 1933, 196).

Gibbons was not entirely off base here, for Gaelic writers often did show a willingness to look at the darker side of Gaeltacht life. For instance, violence – personal, not patriotic – figures in a fair number of Gaelic stories and novels in this period. On occasion, as in Micheál Ó Gríobhtha's 1928 novel *Buaidh na Treise* or Mac Grianna's *An Druma Mór*, that violence is presented in a heroic light. More frequently, however, the emphasis is on the brutality and shame of such violence within the native-speaking community itself. Stories in which this kind of violence figures include An t-Athair Casáin's 'Gleann an Uaignis' (The glen of loneliness);[233] Peadar Mac Fhionnlaoich's 'An Fiadhach' (The hunt);[234] Pádhraic Ó Domhnalláin's 'Dubhshlán Fear Éireann!' (A challenge to the men of Ireland!) and 'Clú an Pharóiste' (The fame of the parish);[235] Seaghán Mac Meanman's 'Tús Sgéil as an Leabhar Thuas' (The beginning of a story from the above book); and 'Oidhche Mhór i bhFad ó Shoin' (A great night long ago);[236] Micheál Ó Siochfhradha's 'Loch an Pheidléara' (The peddlar's lake);[237] Seán Ó Dálaigh's 'Lomadh an Luain Ort;'[238] Séamas Maguidhir's 'An Béacudán' (a headless otherworld being) (*Éireannach*, 25/4/36); and Gearóid Ó Meachair's 'Díoghaltas na Mara' (The revenge of the sea) (*Blackrock College Annual*, 1936, 33–8). Violence is narrowly avoided in Liam O'Flaherty's 1924 story 'Fód' (A sod), about turf-cutting rights (*Dublin Magazine*, May 1924, 882–3); and in Micheál Ó Maoláin's 'An Braithlín' (The sheet), in which the discovery that a goat not a neighbour stole the missing sheet of the title prevents the situation from going beyond insults (*FL*, Nov. 1927–Mar. 1928).

Novels in which violence plays an important part include 'Fionn' Mac Cumhaill's *Tusa a Mhaicín*, which tells of deadly sectarian violence in Donegal as well as fighting at weddings;[239] Éamonn Mac Giolla Iasachta's *Cúrsaí Thomáis*, in which we find brutality, murder, and violent revenge, involving at one point the narrator himself;[240] Pádhraic Óg Ó Conaire's *Éan Cuideáin*, in which a Conamara man back from Canada is forced to engage in a bloody fight as soon as he returns home;[241] the same author's *Ceol na nGiolcach*, in which there is an attempted rape by a man who is later murdered by a Galway prostitute;[242] and Ciarán Ua Nualláin's detective novel *Oidhche i nGleann na nGealt*, where rural greed leads to attempted fratricide.[243] A story about the actual commission of such a crime is told by one of the characters in An tAthair Pádhraic Mac Aodha's play *An Broc Dubh*, in which a mysterious travelling woman relates how her own husband had been killed by his brother in a brawl in a *síbín* or illegal drinking house.[244] Violence also figures in the Blasket books. Both Ó Criomhthain and Sayers tell of fights involving women, Ó Criomhthain in *Allagar na h-Inise* and Sayers in *Machtnamh Seanamhná*.[245]

Gaeltacht greed and its consequences were the focus of several other works in Irish during this period. Leaving aside the many stories, novels, and plays about arranged marriages in which this theme was central, we find rural greed and selfishness at the heart of works as different as Ciarán Ua Nualláin's farcical story 'Cúrsaí Báis!/ Sean-Scéal Suairc Soilbhir Sruth-bhriathrach Seafóideach Siamsamhail Scannruightheach Scaolmhar Scléipeach Saothamhail Suimeamhail So-léighte' (Matters of death! / A pleasant, cheerful, flowingly worded, nonsensical, amusing, frightening, timid, hilarious, learned, interesting, easily read old story) (*New Irish Magazine*, Aug. 1934, 43–4); Máiréad Ní Ghráda's 1935 comedy *An Udhacht*;[246] and Cearbhall Ua Dálaigh's tragic 1931 story 'Sobal Sneachtaidh' (Heavy snow) (*Nation*, 10/1/31). This seems, however, to have been a delicate subject for the Gaels, many, if not the majority, of whom were, as we have seen, committed to a mythology of Gaeltacht otherworldliness. At any rate, while we find an unseemly eagerness for the death of a wealthy American relative depicted in Pádhraic Óg Ó Conaire's *Seoid ó'n Iarthar Órdha*,[247] and theft referred to in Séamas Mac Conmara's novel *An Coimhthigheach*,[248] and, in the form of grave-robbing, in Tadhg Seoighe's 1925 story 'Adhlacadh agus Aiséirghe Shean-Mhícil' (The burial and resurrection of Old Michael),[249] it is in the Blasket books, whose authors were more removed from revivalist pieties, that this unedifying aspect of Gaeltacht life is most forthrightly depicted.[250] In *Allagar na h-Inise*, Ó

Criomhthain speaks of a man's theft of another's *naomhóg*, as well as of the occasional theft of turf.[251] Ó Criomhthain also speaks in the same book of the islanders' avid interest in sea-wrack, even though they are aware that valuable items only float ashore after terrible disasters at sea:

> 'How do you know that ship would not strike against the rock and give you your fill as the *Quabra* did', said Micheál, 'so that we lived for three years because of it.' 'But ships like that do not always strike when there is need of them', said Micil.[252]

Muiris Ó Súileabháin offers a similar picture in *Fiche Blian ag Fás*, in which men toss their caps in the air with joy on seeing wrack approaching the island:

> On the following day, you would think it a fine thing to look down on the shore and the beaches, great banks of boards here and there, and the *naomhóg* that got the least of the catch had over a hundred boards. – By God, a man said, the war is a good thing. – Indeed, man, another man said, if it lasts this island will be a Land of Youth for us.[253]

Invidious class distinctions and the accompanying snobbery are the focus of several works at this time. Needless to say, an easy and frequent target of criticism on this account was the 'gombeen man', the shopkeeper who exploited his neighbours to enrich himself.[254] Some writers, however, took on the more troubling task of examining class bias among ordinary Gaeltacht people themselves. The subject is at times treated comically, as in Micheál Ó Siochfhradha's story 'Mar Baisteadh Maidhc'[255] or Seaghán Mac Meanman's play *Cad Chuige nach dTabharfainn?*[256] More frequently, writers focused on the distasteful and even destructive aspects of Gaeltacht class consciousness. In this light, Micheál Ó Gríobhtha's story 'Criostíona' still has some relevance for today's Ireland in its depiction of bias against Travellers, or 'tinkers' as they are called in the story.[257] Other stories critical of such snobbery include Seaghán Mac Meanman's 'Bláthach Préataidhe agus Salann' (Buttermilk, potatoes, and salt),[258] Séamus Ó Grianna's 'Sagart Éamoinn Sheáin Óig' (The priest of Éamonn Sheáin Óig, i.e. the son of Éamonn Sheáin Óig who was going to become a priest),[259] and Máirtín Ó Cadhain's 'Culaith le Cois' (An extra suit).[260] In Ó Grianna's story, the snobbery is associated with the ability to educate a son for the priesthood, a connection that is also developed in Ó Grianna's novel *Caisleáin Óir* and in Pádhraic Óg Ó Conaire's *Ceol na nGiolcach*. The degrading effect of these attitudes is evident in Seán Ó Ruadháin's *Pádhraic Mháire Bhán*, where in one scene social distinctions assert themselves even among men working on a public relief project:

> One man with a bottle of milk, one with a bottle of tea, and a man who had to eat his bite of bread dry. The men who had flour bread were not shy or afraid, and they

> began eating in front of all who were there, as if they were showing off . . . but there were more there who only had bread made with Indian meal, and that itself made with water, and more again who were dependent on boxty [bread made from potatoes], and they hid while they ate.[261]

An effective corollary of this snobbery was Gaeltacht gossip and backbiting, the often quite malicious agent of class awareness and social control. Tomás Ó Criomhthain at times seems to revel in the sharp tongues of his neighbours in *Allagar na h-Inise*, although to be fair his emphasis is far more on wit than on cruelty or intimidation.[262] Gossip was treated comically by Micheál Ó Siochfhradha in his story 'Ciall Cheannaigh' (The teachings of experience),[263] and by Seán Mac Thorcail in his 1936 play *Slis de'n tSean-Mhaide*, in which a neighbour's malicious lie almost prevents a couple's marriage.[264] Again, however, most Gaelic writers of the period chose to explore the more painful aspects of rural backbiting, as did Mac Giolla Iasachta in *Cúrsaí Thomáis*,[265] Ó Gríobhtha in *Briathar Mná*,[266] Ua Laoghaire in *An Bhruinneall Bhán*,[267] Mac Conmara in *An Coimhthigheach*,[268] and Seán Mac Maoláin in his story 'An Drabhlas' (Debauchery) (*Ultach*, Apr. 1939, 1–2).

A few Gaelic writers of the time focused their attention on the non-human inhabitants of the Irish countryside, in the process creating a sub-genre of animal stories in the language that continues to the present. By far the most accomplished among those writing fiction of this sort was Liam O'Flaherty, whose 'An Fiadhach' (The hunt) and 'Bás na Bó' (The cow's death) were hailed by the editor as a Gaelic publishing event when they appeared in the issues of *Fáinne an Lae* for 27 June and 18 July 1925 respectively.[269] Others who used animals as protagonists in their stories were A. Nic Ghiolla Iasachta in 'Riobaillín' (Little tail) (*Standard*, 8/6/34); O'Flaherty's brother Tom in 'Bás an Ghainéid' (The gannet's death) (*Éireannach*, 22/2/36); An tAthair Casáin in 'An Londubh';[270] Micheál Ó Siochfhradha in 'An Bhainirseach 's a Mac' (The female seal and her pup) (*Bonaventura*, Winter 1938, 107–10); and Máirtín Ó Cadhain in 'Leathtromadh na Cinneamhna' (The oppression of fate).[271] Of these writers, only Ó Siochfhradha comes close to matching the dispassionate distance that makes O'Flaherty's many stories about animals in Irish and in English so memorable. His brother's story, told by a first person narrator watching the bird's death, ends: 'By the power of the book, it almost made me cry' (Dar brígh an leabhair, is beag nár bhain sé deor asam). An tAthair Casáin's story is a cloyingly sentimental tale of birds mating and nesting. Ó Cadhain, still an apprentice in his first collection, gives the robin that is the protagonist of his story emotions that seem altogether too human.[272]

Where human beings were involved, three major themes from earlier Gaelic fiction and drama continued to hold the interest of writers at this time. Gaeltacht cleverness, the ability of native speakers to outwit authority figures, was a ready source of humour, although this theme lost a bit of its appeal after independence, when the authority figures became the agents of a native state. Indeed in virtually all of the works in which trickery is central, the dupes remain the time-tested ones, the Royal Irish Constabulary in Pádhraic Óg Ó Conaire's *Mian a Croidhe* (1922), Micheál Ó Maoláin's 'An Chaora Bhearrtha / An Seáirsint' (The sheared sheep / The sergeant) (*FL*, 15/3/24) and Seaghán Mac Meanman's 'Bláthach Préataidhe agus Salann' (where the policemen are all from Munster!); a bailiff in Ó Maoláin's 'Mar Bualadh Bob ar an mBáille' (How a trick was played on the bailiff) (*Nationality*, 13/6/31); a Protestant minister in Ó Ruadháin's *Pádhraic Mháire Bhán*; and a member of the gentry in Micheál Óg Mac Pháidín's 'Gearrán Phadaí na hInnse' (Paddy of the Island's gelding) (*Tír*, Mar.–Apr. 1934). Gaeltacht people themselves are the victims of a trickster who disguises himself as a beggar woman in 'Bean Déirce' by 'Gath Gréine' (*An Phoblacht*, 23/6/28). In Seaghán Mac Meanman's 1936 comedy *Peinnsean Shean-Mháire Ní Ruadháin*, the butt of the humour is a Free State pensions officer who insists on speaking an incomprehensible brand of 'Dublin Irish'. Seeing her pension about to be reduced because of her income from poultry, the elderly protagonist exclaims: 'You don't have a spark of sense! It was in the prophecy that the Gael would weep over the grave of the Foreigner, and it is true. I won't get a red penny!'[273]

The second important theme continued from earlier revival prose was emigration. As noted above, this social problem was a major concern for language activists throughout the first two decades of the native state, and creative writers of Irish shared the movement's perspective on emigration as an injustice inflicted on the people of the Gaeltacht, an idea given bitterly forceful expression by An tAthair Liam Ó Beirn in 1934:

> Some of us are all right – dogs with a piece of meat. The (English) world would be better off, and we ourselves would be also, if the rest of us would make our living in America. Let us clear out on the advice of the sensible people![274]

Pádraig Ó Gallchobhair expressed a similar anger the same year in an authorial intrusion into his novel *Caoineadh an Choimhighthigh*: 'The world was not shared out fairly! Fine lads heading off with no clear destination and churls who would not soil their mouths talking to poor people going around with all they needed!'[275] This sense of injustice is developed in the anonymous 1925 story 'An tAthrughadh' in *Fuaim na Mara*, the school journal of Coláiste Mhic Phiarais in Galway. In this story Aranmen have long talked of the change (*athrughadh*) they expect to come after the English are driven out, but even after independence they have to leave the country. For the protagonist, the Free State flag he sees as he emigrates means nothing at all: 'The new flag came before his eye again. A bitter laugh came from his lips. At last the Great

Change [i.e. emigration] had arrived for him' (Tháinig an bratach nuadh faoi n-a shúil arís. Bhris gáire searbhasach ar a bhruasaibh. 'Sa' deireadh bhí an t-Athrughadh Mór [.i. an imirce] chuige) (*Fuaim na Mara*, 1925, 69–72).[276] Other anti-emigration stories include An tAthair S. Ó Curraidhín's 'Na Cnuic Ghlasa' (The green hills) (*TCNÍ*, Nov. 1935), An tAthair Seán Ó Siadhail's 'An Cinneamhaint' (Destiny) (*IR*, Sept. 1933), and Séamus P. Ó Mórdha's 'An Bonn Airgid' (The silver medal), *Hibernia*, Aug. 1939, 20–1.

Emigration is also, of course, an important theme in Gaelic novels of the period like Ó Grianna's *Caisleáin Óir*, Ó Ruadháin's *Pádhraic Mháire Bhán*, and Ó Rabhartaigh's *Mian na Marbh*. So prominent in the Gaelic consciousness was concern about emigration that Father Dinneen could conclude a 1926 essay on Virgil's *Georgics* with a brief sermon on the subject:

> There is not a country under the sun more beautiful or richer than Ireland. Lately and for a good number of years, there have been quarrels going on among us, so that we have neglected the cultivation of the land and grown dissatisfied with our native land, and the young have wanted to abandon it. It is high time for us to stand by it and make use of it and reject quarrelling and conflict.[277]

The third ongoing theme in Gaelic fiction and drama at this time involved what was presented as the true native attitude towards belief in the otherworld. As had been true from the very beginning of the revival, while superstitions of all kinds were regularly found in folklore collected with any degree of professional competence, such superstitions were all but invariably debunked in the creative literature, with any characters believing in them portrayed as gullible and ludicrous.[278] Leaving aside fairy plays for children like those written by Sinéad de Valera, Micheál Mac Liammóir, and Micheál Ó Gríobhtha,[279] exceptions to this sceptical treatment of the otherworld were, predictably, stories based on oral tradition like 'Eachtra Mhuiris Uí Chonaire' (Muiris Ó Conaire's adventure) and 'An t-Athrach Bréige' (The false change) by Micheul Ó Cinnfhaolaidh (*Green and Gold*, Mar.–Apr. and Sept.–Nov. 1923, respectively), 'An tAirgead Croise' (The two-shilling piece) by 'Gaedheal Glas' (*Weekly Freeman*, 29/3/24), 'Píobaire an Bhrianaigh' (O'Brien's piper) by 'Seachránuidhe' (*An Reult*, May 1924), 'An Sprid Muice' (The ghostly pig) by Seán Ó Dúnaighe (*Green and Gold*, Nov. 1924–Mar. 1925), 'An Teacht thar n-ais' (The return) by 'Móin Ruadh' (*Cork Weekly Examiner*, 6/5/33), 'Triúr faoi Chómhnra' (Three carrying a coffin) by 'Úna' (*Éireannach*, 20/10/34), 'Teach a Raibh Taidhbhse Ann' (A house in which there was a ghost) by Peadar Ó Dubhda (*Dundalk Examiner*, 16/3/35), 'Sidheóga ag Gabháil Thart / Eachtra san Iarthar' (Fairies going past / An adventure in the West) by Peadar Ó Domhnaill (*IP*, 31/10/35), and 'Deimhniú an Sgéil' (The confirmation of the story) by Piaras Béaslaí.[280]

In a few stories writers used the supernatural in more original ways, as did Nioclás Tóibín, whose 1923 story 'An t-Aon a h-Art' (The ace of hearts) deals with the tragic consequences of three wishes that have been magically granted (*Sguab*, Aug. 1923); or Seaghán Mac Meanman, who built his 1924 story 'Tús Sgéil as an Leabhar Thuas' around the folk superstition about the *cingcíseach*, one born within the Pentecost triduum, such a person being fated to kill, be killed, or both.[281] Seosamh Mac Grianna leaves us in doubt as to whether it is an apparition or a guilty conscience that leads to the suicide of the protagonist in his 1924 story 'Taisgidh an Úcaire' (The fuller's treasure) (*IF*, Nov. 1924). León Ó Broin drew on the supernatural to provide a macabre atmosphere for his 1932 story 'Cruitín an Chóta Dubh' (The hunchback in the black coat).[282] In Liam Ó Rinn's 'Oidhche Shamhraidh' (A summer's night), a man scoffs at what turns out to be a tragically prophetic dream (*Branar*, June 1925). The 1936 story 'Mallacht na Baintrighe' (The widow's curse) by Tomás Ó Flaithbheartaigh, brother of Liam, deals with the death of a man cursed by a widow for cutting off her donkey's ear because the beast was eating his crops (*Éireannach*, 15/2/36).

Three playwrights made creative use of supernatural beliefs in their work. In Máirtín Ó Cadhain's play *An Phléasc*, an old woman has premonitions of disaster, premonitions borne out when the mine the local men have found explodes. In An tAthair Pádhraic Mac Aodha's *An Broc Dubh*, the dire omen is the black badger of the title, although Mac Aodha never manages to incorporate belief in the badger's significance into the plot of the play, and in effect simply lets the idea drop as the action develops. Tomás Luibhéid's play *An Biorán Suain* (BÁC: ODFR, 1937) deals unapologetically with the supernatural, based as it is on the belief in fairy changelings, although in this case there is a happy ending.

As is often true, Tomás Ó Criomhthain gives us a clearer insight into the more complex, ambivalent, at times even pragmatic Gaeltacht attitude to that otherworld that lacked the sanction of Christian orthodoxy. Speaking of a new baby in one of the island houses, he reports in *Allagar na h-Inise*:

> Well, whatever customs have died out with them, the customs concerning the Good People [i.e. fairies] have not, and therefore two elderly women had to be found for the night so that the infant would be there in the morning. There was a big fire. There was food and drink. The two watcher-women got a pipe apiece and tobacco to put in them – and knowing them as I do, the cost that resulted from the two pipes was greater than the money spent on the child's baptism.[283]

A similar ambivalence is found in the 1927 story 'An Diabhal Bán' (The fairhaired devil) by 'M. Ó F.', in which a weird white hare is believed to have caused the death of a Gaeltacht man. The parish priest tells the narrator that he is sure there is a natural explanation, although he doesn't know what it is. The narrator, taking no chances, urges his readers to avoid the creature, believed to be the devil, if ever they visit the area (*IMN*, 1927, 54–8).

Usually, however, there is no such ambivalence in the Gaelic creative work of the period. Again and again, 'supernatural' occurrences are shown to have entirely natural causes, usually to the comic discomfiture of those gullible enough to be amazed or terrified by what they think they have seen.[284] In *Fiche Blian ag Fás*, Ó Súileabháin tells of how he himself was frightened twice in the same night by mysterious apparitions of altogether mundane origin, and he draws the conclusion at the heart of so many similar stories from this time: 'Look now, I said, that the person without patience is to be pitied, and it is my opinion that this is how fairies are made for many on this island.'[285] Among the myriad examples of such stories are 'Tadhg Ó Nualláin agus an Sprid / An Bob nár Bualadh' (Tadhg Ó Nualláin and the spirit / The trick that was not played) by Pádraig Ó Bróithe (*II*, 16/9/22); 'Seán gan Eagla' (Fearless Seán) by Lughaidh de Róiste (*Irish Fun*, Oct. 1922); 'An Sprid ar Phort na Dothra' (The spirit on the bank of the Dodder) by Micheál Ó Gríobhtha (*II*, 5/3/23); 'Baba Shéamuis agus a Scéal / Ar Cuire ag Caraid' (Baba Shéamuis and her story / Visiting a friend) by 'E. Ó N.' (*II* 5/11/23); 'Molly Dhamanta, an Bhean Feasa' (Damned Molly, the wise woman) (*Leader*, 22/12/23) and 'Billeóga Té agus Cártaí' (Tea leaves and cards) (*Leader*, 29/12/23), both by Father Dinneen; 'Fear Misnigh' (A brave man) by León Ó Cinnéide;[286] 'An Sean-Duine san Osbuideul / Sgeul an Taidhbhse' (The old man in the hospital / The story of the ghost) by 'Sean-Ghaedheal' (*II*, 13/7/25); 'Ag Fiadhach Spride' (Hunting a spirit) by Seán Ó Ciarghusa (*Sguab*, Aug. 1925); 'An Lao Biata' (The fatted calf) by Tomás Ó Mannacháin (*Stoc*, Nov. 1925); 'An Taidhbhse' (The ghost) by Pádhraic Ó Domhnalláin;[287] 'Seán Aerach agus an Sprid' (Light-hearted Seán and the spirit) by 'Seán Aerach' (*II*, 19/7/28); 'An Sprid do Theich le na h-Anam / Tinneas-Fiacal Bréige' (The spirit who fled for its life / A fake toothache) by 'Siobhán' (*II*, 13/8/28); 'Taidhbhse an Bhuachalla Bháidhte' (The ghost of the drowned boy) by Liam Seán Mac Cáisleáin, in which a Yank is the dupe (*An Phoblacht*, 12/1/29); 'Ar Lorg Troda' by Pádraic Ó Conaire;[288] 'An t-Airseoir' (The Devil) by An tAthair Gearóid Ó Nualláin (1938), in which a priest is the trickster;[289] and 'Taidhbhse ó'n Fharraige' (A ghost from the sea) by Ailbhe Ó Monacháin (*Ultach*, May 1938), in which the 'ghost' turns out to be a lobster loose in a house. In addition, Father Dinneen's 'Molly Dhamanta, an Bhean Feasa' and 'Billeóga Té agus Cártaí' debunk the powers of 'wise women' (*mná feasa*), with the protagonist of the former apparently based on the famous Biddy Early of County Clare (*Leader*, 22/12/23; 29/12/23). Superstitions were also treated with skepticism in Aindrias Ó Baoighill's novel *An Dílidhe* (The orphan) and 'Fionn' Mac Cumhaill's *Na Rosa go Bráthach*.

However jaded they were about the otherworld of traditional folk belief, Gaelic writers – particularly but not exclusively those contributing to Catholic periodicals – seem to have accepted without question the possibilty of more orthodox miraculous interventions in human life. For example, such miracles form the plot and point of virtually all of the pious little anecdotes that comprise Brian Ó hUiginn's collection *Scéalta na Maighdine Muire* (Stories of the Virgin Mary) (BÁC: Brian Ó hUiginn, [1939]). Other stories of this sort in which the divine or saintly figures of Catholic belief – including Irish mothers – and the holy places and articles associated with them change the course of human life include 'Aon Aibhé Amháin' (One Ave) by An tAthair Pilib Ó Duinneacháin (*Irisleabhar Lorcáin Naomhtha*, Nov. 1922); 'An Bhean a Tháinig' (The woman who came) by 'S. Ó H.' (*Sguab*, Dec. 1925); 'Múr Rós' (A heap of roses) by S. Ó Tiománaigh (*TCNÍ*, Mar. 1926); 'Athrú Sheán Uí Chonaill' (Seán Ó Conaill's transformation) by 'Máilleach Chois-Fhairrge' (*TCNÍ*, Dec. 1927); '"A Naomh Ióseph, a Phátrún an Deagh-Bháis, Guidh Orainn"' (O St. Joseph, patron of a good death, pray for us) by An tAthair R. de Nais (*TCNÍ*, June 1928); 'Nodlaig an Athair Máirtín' (Father Martin's Christmas) by Gráinne Ní Mháille (*Standard*, 28/12/29); 'Glaodhach Ola 'san Oidhche / Díoghaltas Dé' (A sick call in the night / God's vengeance) by 'Bebo' (*II*, 11/4/30); 'Triúr Feirmeóiridhe' (Three farmers) by Conchubhar Ó Deasmhumhan (*TCNÍ*, Sept. 1930); 'Luach-Shaothair an Aifrinn' (The reward for Mass) by Seán Ó Caoimh (*Standard*, 5/12/31); 'Aifreann Dé' (God's Mass) by 'Ciarraidheach' (*TCNÍ*, July 1932); 'Breac Beannuighthe Thobar Mhichíl' (The blessed trout of St Michael's well) by Seán Ó Dálaigh;[290] 'Míorbhuilt Thurais Naoimh Breandán' (The miracle of St Brendan's pilgrimage) by Máire Bhreathnach (*TCNÍ*, Oct. 1936); and 'Siúbhán an Phuirt' (Siúbhán of the harbour) by An tAthair Seán Ó Siadhail (*IR*, Jan. 1934). An interesting variant on this theme can be found in 'An Tigh Aerach' (The haunted house) by Gárda Muiris R. Ó Cuisín of the Store Street station in Dublin, a story in which the spirit of a dying woman helps the police to solve a crime (*GR*, Aug. 1935). God was not to be trifled with in works of this kind. When a boy skips Mass to go on an outing at sea, he is drowned (*IC*, 5/11/36).

A few writers managed to do something a bit more original and interesting with this sort of material. For example, there is a conflict between folk and orthodox belief in the 1933 story 'Iompódh an Chlóca' (The turning of the cloak) by the Capuchin An tAthair Casáin. An old woman tells the narrator of how when trapped in a fairy mist she had saved herself by turning her cloak inside out. He is at first impressed, but then remembers that she had also mentioned saying the Rosary, and realises that it was that act of devotion that had rescued her (*CA*, 1933, 220–3). Such conflict occurs again in Seán Ó Dálaigh's 1933 stories 'An Sagart agus an Amhailt' (The priest and the phantom) and 'Garsún agus an Sluagh Sidhe' (A boy and the fairy host). In the former, a priest bests a spirit with a Christian blessing and a display of the Host, while in the latter he drives off the fairies with a benediction. Unusual here is that these traditional supernatural beings are presented as actually existing.[291] That access to such spiritual power as was exercised above must be earned is clear from Siobhán Ní Chonchubhair's 'An Leas ar Cháirde' (The benefit put off), in which after a life of sin a rich man wants to make sure he will have a priest with him at the end. He therefore locks one in his library, but when he is dying the priest cannot be found, although he insists he never left the room in which he was confined (*FMR*, May 1929).

A more mundane but far more vital and sustaining aspect of Gaeltacht religious faith was the people's ability to see their lives, however difficult or tragic, as part of God's larger plan. Nowhere is this faith expressed more eloquently than in Art Ó Riain's 1926 story 'Radharc na Fírinne', in which the narrator, an Irishman returned home from England financially triumphant but spiritually bankrupt, reflects on what he has learned from the powerful faith of Irish country people:

> All creation yields to the will of that Director: the sound of the ferocious sea, the murmur of the little waves in the lake, the terrible sound of the thunder, every one of them is under His control. It is to Him that the music of the universe is sung, and the stars of heaven are silent when he raises His hand. Only the human being spoils this chorus, with the same word that destroyed it in the beginning: *Non Serviam*![292]

Few, if any, characters in the literature by and about Gaeltacht people at this time seem ever to have been tempted to such Luciferean – or Joycean? – rebellion. Rather, in story after story and novel after novel, country people submit unquestioningly to the will of God (*Toil Dé*), whatever sacrifice it might demand of them. Cormac Ó Cadhlaigh felt this Christian resignation was among the noblest traits of the Gael, writing in his 1925 book *Eagna an Ghaedhil*:

> If there is one quality of the Gael beyond any other that is worthy of praise, that quality is the trust and confidence he always has in the God of Glory, praise to Him forever. Whatever hardship or whatever trouble befalls him, hope is strong in his heart because he understands that the Omnipotent King is above him protecting him and preserving him.[293]

Dómhnall Ó Conchubhair expressed an identical faith in his poem 'Dé Bheatha Toil Dé' (Welcome to the will of God), of which the penultimate stanza reads:

> Every injury that happens comes for our benefit / If we but have patience and perseverance because of it: / For the most generous God will reward us enough /

> For on earth – as in the Kingdom of Glory, /Welcome to the will of God, and may it be done.[294]

For 'Oisín', this unquestioning acceptance of the will of God was 'the rule and the story of their lives' (riaghal agus sgéal a mbeatha) for Gaeltacht people:

> What is in the mouths of these people shows that they don't want much in this world and that they are willing to accept whatever God puts before them. 'God's will be done.' I would say that that is the rule and the story of their lives. Hardship, hunger, death itself do not matter; if they have bad luck, they do not complain. What is always said, no matter how hard their situation, is 'God's will be done' (*Derry People*, 25/9/37).[295]

The importance of this belief as a source of strength and solace for the Blasket Islanders is most evident in the two books by Sayers, where, in the face of one tragedy after another, she never loses her faith:

> We were poor people who knew nothing of the prosperity or the vanity of the world. We accepted the sort of life we were living; we did not expect a different one. God, praise be to Him always! gave us help. It is often we noticed that the Holy Supreme Master was favourable to us, for it is many a squall and storm that overtook our people on the sea, and from which there was no escape except with His help.[296]

And while always more dispassionate than Sayers, Ó Criomhthain sought comfort for the drowning death of his son by seeing it as the will of God.[297]

Once again, examples of this belief in Gaelic creative work of the period are too numerous to list, although it is worth noting that it provided the actual title for at least three Gaelic stories, the anonymous '"Toil Dé Indé is Indiu is a Choidhche"' (The will of God yesterday, today, and forever) (*TCNÍ*, Jan. 1932); '"Céad Fáilte Roimh Thoil Dé!"' (A thousand welcomes to the will of God!) by An tAthair S. Ó Curraidhín (*TCNÍ*, Dec. 1934); and 'Ba Toil Dé É' (It was the will of God) by Séamus Maguidhir;[298] as well as for Éamonn Mac Giolla Iasachta's novel *Toil Dé*.[299] Other novels in which this kind of resignation was thematically significant were 'Fionn' Mac Cumhaill's *Tusa a Mhaicín, Maicín*, and *Na Rosa go Bráthach*; Ó Grianna's *Caisleáin Óir*; Micheál Ó Gríobhtha's *Buaidh na Treise*; Pádraig Ó Séaghdha's *Stiana*; Art Ó Riain's *Lucht Ceoil*; Aindrias Ó Baoighill's *An Dílidhe*; Seán Ó Dúnaighe's *An Crann Cuilinn* and *Inghean an Ghearaltaigh*; Alín de Paor's *Paidí Ó Dálaigh*; Pádraig Ó Gallchobhair's *Caoineadh an Choimhighthigh*; Úna Bean Uí Dhíosca's *An Seod Do-Fhághala* (The unobtainable jewel); Seán Mac Maoláin's *Éan Corr* and *Iolar agus Sionnach*; and Séamas Mac Conmara's *An Coimhthigheach*.

Plays in which the authors refer to this belief include Micheál Ó Gríobhtha's *Bean an Bhrait Bháin* and *De Dhruim na hAille* (Over the cliff); and An tAthair Pádhraic Mac Aodha's *An Broc Dubh* and *Peadar an tSléibhe*.

It was usually in the face of terrible tragedy such as the loss of husband, wife, or child that the Gaeltacht people of these works sought meaning and coherence in God's often incomprehensible design. But on occasion it was God's will to grant joy, as in 'Gleann na Léime' (The glen of the leap) by 'Bean Rialta' (*TCNÍ*, June 1926), where a young girl is enabled to learn the Catholic religion and save her father's soul; or 'Pádhruic Ó Meachair' by 'Máilleach Chois Fhairrge' (*TCNÍ*, Sept. 1928), where a young man who has lost his faith in New York and stopped writing home dies in a state of grace after having a letter sent to his mother to inform her of his repentance. In the anonymous '"Toil Dé Indé is Indiu is a Choidhche"' (*TCNÍ*, Jan. 1932), God helps a successsful doctor come to terms with his son's priestly vocation, while in 'Beirt Dhrithár' (Two brothers) by An tAthair Seósamh Mac Giobúin, He gives a woman the wisdom to accept the fact that her son has no such vocation and that she should be proud of him as a doctor: '"Yes indeed", she said, "God's will is not the same as human will, but His holy will always has a good end"' ('Seadh, go deimhin,' a deireann sise, 'ní mar a chéile toil Dé agus toil an duine, ach is maith an chríoch a bhíonn ar A Naomh-Thoil choidhche') (*FL*, July 1929, 6).

A few writers offer a more original perspective on this pious Gaeltacht acceptance of God's will. The concept of *toil Dé* is, for example, used ironically by Séamus Ó Grianna in 'Grásta ó Dhia ar Mhicí' (God's grace on Mickey);[300] and by León Ó Broin in 'An Bhrighdeach' (The bride);[301] and for comic effect by An tAthair Gearóid Ó Nualláin in 'An Hata' (The hat);[302] by 'M. Ua C.' in 'Is é Dia an Réidhteoir is Fearr' (God is the best arbitrater) (*FMR*, Dec. 1928); and by Micheál Breathnach in 'Daoine Gaoithe' (Blowhards). Writing of his narrator's propensity for attracting the attention of such tedious people, Breathnach writes:

> No matter where I am, the 'blowhards' find me, and what I have now decided is to yield my will to the will of God in the matter in the hope that He will not be too hard on me on the Judgement Day considering what I am suffering in this life.[303]

Far more defiant was the mother in M. Ní Rodaighe's 'An Mharthainn Phádraic' (St Patrick's charm), who refuses to find the notion of *Toil Dé* a consolation for the death of her son in the War of Independence (*Gaedheal*, 15/12/34).

In a challenging 1924 essay in *An Sguab* on the need for Irish unity, an essay in which he defended the rights of Ulster Protestants, Aodh de Blácam suggested that God's will was a force that demanded the active involvement of human beings rather than their passive resignation: 'It is not right for us to set God's gifts against each other, but rather have them helping each other. The person who disparages God's gifts in his brother does not fulfil the will of God in himself' (*Sguab*, 31/8/24).[304] Writing in the same journal the following year, 'Tadhg Gaedhealach' was more explicit on this point, stating of Gaeltacht people: '"Leave it to God", they say about everything. Perhaps that is their greatest fault, that too much is left to God. The other teaching has to be brought home to them, that is, that "God likes to get help"' (*Sguab*, June 1925, 373).[305] Far more radical was Tom O'Flaherty, who, in his 1934 English-language story 'Going Away', has his narrator reject an old woman's appeal to God's will as an explanation for her daughter's emigration:

> 'The good God almighty has no more to do with it than one of those hens resting on that pole . . . There is nothing for her here and even if you only had herself and you could give her the place maybe it would be better for her to go.' 'Sure I don't know', she whimpered. 'Some people say everything is God's will.' I did not reply.[306]

And the Gaeltacht activist and soon-to-be major literary figure, Máirtín Ó Cadhain, lashed out at such fatalism in a 1937 piece in *An Gaedheal* prompted by the dreadful deaths of young migrant labourers from Achill Island in a bothy fire in Scotland, asserting that when native speakers of Irish became aware of their inherent worth and strength, they would fight to bring about their own salvation (*Gaedheal*, Oct. 1937, 12).[307]

Diarmuid Ó Doibhlin has written:

> The strongest characteristic that I notice in modern literature in Irish in the early years is the constant celebration in it, north and south, in the Blaskets and in the Rosses, a regular, constant celebration of aspects of the Gaelic world – a world that had, in spite of everything, endured, in spite of the tyranny of the English and the neglect of the Irish, in spite of the national schools, in spite of poverty, emigration and famine.[308]

Despite their awareness of some failings – even serious ones like those noted above – Gaelic authors of our period were all but unanimous in their celebration of the virtues of Gaeltacht people. Again and again in the prose literature of the 1920s and 1930s, we find paeans to their steadfastness, integrity, generosity, and above all uncorrupted *Gaelachas*. For several writers, most notablyPádhraic Óg Ó Conaire, these qualities were most effectively highlighted by introducing into a novel or story outsiders, people who went to the Gaeltacht with either biased, or at best neutral, attitudes about what they expected to find there, only to be won over heart and soul by the innate nobility of the people they met. For example, in Ó Conaire's 1922 novel *Mian a Croidhe*, the bewitched outsiders are a French painter and her husband;[309] in *An Fraoch Bán* (1922), a group of Dublin university students; in *Solus an Ghrádha* (1923), a Dublin doctor and the Dublin engineer with whom she falls in love on the Aran Islands; and in *Seoid ó'n Iarthar Órdha* (1933), an English gentleman whose life is saved by a young Conamara woman. It is, however, this young woman, returned from a stay at a prestigious convent school in Dublin and courted unsuccessfully by the Englishman, who perhaps best expresses the attitude of the outsider in Ó Conaire's early novels:

> I would certainly like to take a trip throughout the world. But that is all. I would prefer the loneliest glen in the West to the most beautiful place in any country in the world. I myself think that there are no people under the sun of Heaven like those poor, kindly people who live at the edge of the shore and in hollows in the hills, even if they are not without their own faults. That does not matter. Humanity and decency are in their blood.[310]

Moreover, Ó Conaire was not the only writer of the time to use this device of the outsider. For the protagonist of Úna Bean Uí Dhíosca's *Cailín na Gruaige Duinne*, a first visit to the Gaeltacht dispels the bigoted misconceptions of her family and convinces her of the dignity of her own nation and its language:

> Until that moment I probably did not really believe that our own language was still being spoken by some of the people of Ireland. It surpassed anything you ever saw! Wasn't that the proof that Ireland was a nation apart? Could we not give the lie to the crowd who would say otherwise? . . . I understood that the people of Ireland were not wild animals as my uncle had said.[311]

Writing specifically of the work of Séamus Ó Grianna in his ground-breaking study *An tÚrscéal Gaeilge*, Alan Titley dissects the schizophrenia at the heart of much of what was written about the Gaeltacht in our period (and after), stating:

> In a very simple way altogether *Bean Ruadh de Dhálach* and *Le Clap-Sholus* reveal the contradiction that made two halves, not only of Máire's desires, but of the ideal of Irish-language activists in general, who sought spiritual salvation among a poor and wretched class that they were never willing to go near except in the bright light of the summer. That is to say, without pulling any punches, the wretched, lost organic community was always a linguistic ideal only, and not a social or cultural (in the broadest sense) ideal, nor an ideal for a way of living or life.[312]

The most famous – and parodied! – lines in twentieth-century Gaelic prose are doubtless those from the final chapter of *An t-Oileánach*:

> I wrote precisely about many of our affairs from a desire that they would be remembered somewhere, and I tried to describe the temperament of the people around me so that there would be an account of us after we were gone, for there will never be our like again.[313]

On one level, all Gaelic writers of this time accepted the truth of Ó Criomhthain's awareness here. Even Gaeltacht-born writers knew in their heart of hearts – as did, for example, Ó Grianna, Pádhraic Óg Ó Conaire, Seán Ó Ruadháin, Pádraig Ó Siochfhradha, and later Máirtín Ó Cadhain – that they could never really go home again. But on another level, they and their Galltacht-born comrades in the movement yearned to believe that such a home continued to await them. The solution for many to this psychic dilemma was to try to stop – or even turn back – the clock, to create in their stories, novels, and plays, a fictional Gaeltacht in which with the turn of a page the like of the splendid and irreproachably Gaelic forebears from whom they had descended could be seen, met, and emulated again and again. Brian Ó Nualláin analysed the potential pitfalls of this sort of literary escapism with his usual scrupulous and acerbic wit in one of his columns in *The Irish Times* in 1943:

> Of course, leaving home is the first preliminary to literary work. You then write nostalgic stuff about the grand old place where you were born and which you left because you could not bear the sight of it. Our Gaelic writers are particularly all of that breed.[314]

An Béal Bocht, set in the most wretched and thoroughly Gaelic imaginary Gaeltacht of them all, was his parodic wake-up call to all of that nostalgic breed for whom dreaming and writing had become a single activity. Unfortunately, despite the devastating precision of his satire, the likes of those devoted to what Myles called 'the peasant drool and absurd postulates of what we may dub Modern Irish literature'[315] were to be seen with barely diminished frequency for a good while to come.

THREE

BRINGING MOHAMMED TO THE MOUNTAIN

NEW DIRECTIONS IN GAELIC PROSE

> If Irish is not a suitable language to teach and to express every art, however high, every thought however noble, it is not really right to preserve it. And it is useless to spend time or money on it, since it is destined to die. And if so, it would be more fitting, more sensible and humane, to let the poor thing die in peace, and not to be shaking it, and bothering it in its last days. But it is able to handle every task it could be given and to fulfil its duty if it gets a fair chance. And it will not die. May God not let it die (*An Phoblacht*, 30/11/29).[1]

Thus Pádraig Ó Briain summed up the challenge and the stakes facing contemporary Gaelic writers. Similar views were expressed again and again throughout the 1920s and 1930s. For example, writing in the first issue of *An t-Ultach* in January 1924, Eoin Ó Searcaigh issued the following challenge to his colleagues in the movement: 'We must show everyone that the Irish on the tongues of the people is able to handle the usual affairs of today's world just as English does in England, French in France, German in Germany, Spanish in Spain, and Italian in Italy' (*Ultach*, Mar. 1924, 5).[2] Eoin Mac Néill demanded a similar effort in his preface to An tAthair Seoirse Mac Clúin's *Róisín Fiain na Mara* in the same year: 'If you want Irish to be alive, put it to work, exercise it, and yourself, vigorously, do not leave it peacefully sleeping, take it out on the street, make it work, do not let it shrink from any kind of work that is useful to the Irish people.'[3]

In a 1932 review of Seán Ua Ceallaigh's *Taistealaidheacht* (Travel), 'E. R.' argued:

> If Irish is to be our usual language, it must be cultivated so that it will be suited to the affairs of the great world, including writing, education, and commercial affairs. Up to now, little effort has been made, and not much worth mentioning has been done to deal with things relating to the great world through Irish (*IMN*, 1932, 102).[4]

When a serious effort was made to tackle this task, it could provoke as much amazement as approval, as is evident in the delight with which 'T.W.' welcomed the appearance of the journal *Humanitas* in 1930:

> *Humanitas* is one of the few Irish journals which does not concern itself with the propriety or necessity of using Irish to convey ideas. It proceeds from and not to these harassing advocacies, and for that alone it would have deserved well of its country. But it does more, it plunges into that sea of literature which is forever beating on the shores of time. It brings Irish into those depths where Mona Lisa learned to smile (*Star*, 12/4/30).

Some critics at least felt that it was intellectual laziness that kept the Gaels, readers and writers alike, from exploring such promising depths. For instance, in 1925 one 'Aodh' wrote:

> Many Irish-speakers are odd people. They don't like trouble or work of any sort, but they particularly dislike reading anything penetrating or difficult. Unless they see and grasp everything nicely and easily and satisfactorily, without work, without effort, they get angry at once, angry and amazed . . . 'Fat iz he dhrivin' at at all?' they say! As if he must be mad or out of his senses in some way since we don't understand him! (*CB*, Apr. 1925, 379–80).[5]

Liam Ó Rinn agreed that the problem was not with the language itself but with those ignorant of its proven potential, writing in the *Irish Statesman* in 1929:

> Many who know no Irish, or who have acquired a *bó óg* [young cow] knowledge of it from out-date primers, think it is merely a low-down patois fit only for the expression of the most primitive ideas, and they vastly exaggerate the difficulty of providing such literary, scientific, etc. symbols as are lacking. In both respects they are grotesquely and fantastically wrong. Although but a learner of the language, I have never had any difficulty in discussing even ultra-modern ideas in Irish, and seldom have I had to use any terminology more technical or up-to-date than that used by an Irish-speaking farmer or fisherman. Indeed, I have not even availed of the hundredth part of their vocabulary. Hence, to my mind, to develop the language means simply to use it (*IS*, 14/12/29).

For others, the problem was not lack of initiative, but lack of nerve. Among those who believed that before Gaelic authors could face the wider world they would have to face the narrower minded was Micheál Mac Liammóir, who wrote in 1924:

> We must not close our eyes to anything at all. We must be constantly searching. Why do we tremble before false gods, the fools and the Philistines? Why do we bow

> down to the prejudiced judgment of the ignorant rabble, to the hypocrisy of the butchers and the bakers? (*Sguab*, Sept. 1924, 173).[6]

A similar sense of ubiquitous intellectual intimidation underlies the comments of Donn Piatt in his 1929 essay 'Ireland and European Culture': 'Our language is permitted as long as we keep it for exchanging the time of day in, and only read folk-lore in it. We must not develop it fully' (*Honesty*, 14/9/29).

A major problem was not just that Gaelic writers were afraid of the new, but, as we have seen, that so many of them and their readers were so comfortable with the old, with the rural Gaeltacht settings and themes that had been the staple of writing in Irish from the beginning of the revival. For example, in the 1924 essay cited above, Mac Liammóir stated that the Gaelic writer would make no progress adapting the language to the demands of a world radically different from that of the traditional Gaeltacht, unless he or she were able 'to forget for a little while the potatoes and the sods of turf and little Nora going to the well and Pádhraic Óg milking the cows and old Brighid weeping with the Rosary in her hand and the noble, gentle priest going down the dewy boreen' (*Sguab*, Sept. 1924, 173).[7] Mac Liammóir's catalogue of worked-out country motifs is devastatingly on target, and to have forsaken these topics would have rendered more than a few Gaeltacht writers of the time all but mute. The more perceptive of even native-speaking authors seem, however, to have shared the concern that prompted his sardonic outburst. Writing in *An t-Ultach* in 1924, Seosamh Mac Grianna posed the question, 'What is wrong with us?' (Goidé tá d'Easbaidh orrainn?), and answered with a series of suggestions as to how the state of Gaelic literature could be improved. Among his proposals was 'don't allow uninteresting rubbish to be put in print' (ná leig broc gan suim a chur i gcló), a prohibition he developed at some length:

> This commandment forbids us to give any help at all to books like 'Prátaí Mhíchil Thaidhg' [Michael Tim's potatoes] and 'Ag Séideadh agus ag Ithe' [Breathing fast and eating], and 'Cloch Cheann Fhaolaidh' [Clochaneely] in which there is neither significance, nor juice, nor sap. It commands us, when someone puts something in Irish he knows no one would read if it were in English, to attack that person and to flay him to the bone and not to read his ranting, so that fear would not let him do any more harm (*Ultach*, May 1924, 5).[8]

Every bit as iconoclastic was 'Bricriu', who in 1935 wrote of Gaelic writers of short fiction:

> But wouldn't you think from all their stories that there was nothing worth talking about in Ireland outside the Gaeltacht? Their whole attention was on the life of the Gaeltacht . . . And they stuck to that way of doing things so that I have often said

> that Irish would never be considered as the usual language of the country until the writers forgot the Gaeltacht altogether and turned their faces to the towns (*Ultach*, Aug. 1935, 5).[9]

Micheál Ó Maoláin ('Giolla 'n Mhagadh') could favour the literary claim of his adopted Dublin over that of his native Aran, writing in *An t-Éireannach*: 'The only trained writer, you know, is the man who lives in a city or a town. If we are to have a literature in Irish, the townsmen must get themselves ready to work and begin producing' (*Éireannach*, 27/2/37).[10] Micheál Ó Siochfhradha stressed the need for such urban Irish-speakers to turn their attention to the stage as soon as possible, writing of Na hAisteoirí in *An Reult* in 1925: 'What we need most is original plays, in Irish, about modern life – for example, plays that will illustrate contemporary urban life, or the intellectual life, or what is going on in the great world' (*Reult*, June 1925, 45).[11] But perhaps most typical of the attitude of even those in the native speakers' camp sensitive to the need for the language to expand into the cities was the reaction of Father Lawrence Murray, who while not himself raised with the language was a consistent champion of those who were. Reviewing Peadar Ó Dubhda's *Cáith agus Grán*, a collection most of whose stories were set in Galltacht towns, Murray conceded:

> We need writing like this in Irish, for the life of the people in the towns of this country is not like the quiet, simple life of the people of the Gaeltacht; and, unfortunately for us, it could be that more people take interest in writing of this kind (*Ultach*, Feb. 1930, 5).[12]

Writers from the Galltacht, eager to see the language come to terms with the life they themselves knew best, rarely had such reservations. For many, a new brand of Irish taking root and evolving in the cities and towns of English-speaking Ireland would mean the salvation of the language. And while this was to remain a minority view throughout our period, it was one that inspired its adherents with a growing confidence and sense of their own key role in the revival. In 1923, an anonymous contributor to *Irisleabhar Muighe Nuadhad* wrote: 'If Irish spreads at all, it will spread out throughout the country from the cities and in particular from Dublin. And it will change so greatly that the Irish speakers of today will scarcely be able to understand it in, say, a hundred years' (*IMN*, 1923, 59).[13] In a speech to UCD's Cumann Liteartha na Gaedhilge (Gaelic literary society) in 1937, the society's president, Tomás Ó Siadhail, stated:

> If we are to have high culture in Irish in this century I would say that it will come from the place presently called English-speaking Ireland. It is my opinion that there is and has been for a few years now more intellectual and spiritual vitality in

English-speaking Ireland. If it were not for how much interest the people of English-speaking Ireland take in the Gaeltacht, little would be heard from it at all (*Comhthrom Féinne*, Jan. 1937, 17–18).[14]

The Galltacht writers who undertook the challenge of making Irish at home in the cities and towns of English-speaking Ireland knew they would hear more than a little from their Gaeltacht counterparts. They also knew that one of the greatest barriers in the way of bringing living Irish to the Galltacht was one of the greatest treasures of the Gaeltacht, the extraordinary wealth of folklore that had inspired and continued to inspire much of the creative prose being written in Irish at the time. Those who sensed the threat to healthy literary development represented by a slavish and sterile obsession with the folk tradition were ready to follow the earlier lead of Pearse and Ó Conaire and take the offensive. In his favourable 1936 review of *Cois Life*, Seosamh Ó Torna's collection of urban stories, Liam Ó Rinn, himself one of the true pioneers of contemporary urban fiction in Irish, chided his fellow Gaelic authors for their failure to move beyond tired old settings, subjects, and themes:

> Irish-language authors in general are too given to painting rural life for us. It is a new thing for us to have an author who loves the city streets and looks at the country only as the city dwellers look at it. I am sick of fishing and farming matters, and I would say that rural people themselves are sick of accounts of them, that they far prefer stories in which the constantly changing life and the lights of the cities are dealt with (*UI*, 4/7/36).[15]

The Dundalk-born and bred Peadar Ó Dubhda was another Gaelic author keen to see the life he himself lived given voice in the language he had learned and to which he had dedicated his life. Focusing specifically on the need to attract young readers of Irish, he wrote in 1937:

> We have not really begun yet, and I'll tell you why. We're too much attached to the 'Béaloideas' idea that's being shouted about and talked about and written about so much during the last seven or eight years, a mania that has taken hold on the Gaelic movement to the detriment of the Gaelic movement . . . Can you imagine any Irish girl of, say, twenty or twenty-two, who smokes her cigarette with her cup of tea before rising from the dinner-table and who takes out her little mirror and powder-puff before going out, hoping to entertain herself or her friends during the next twenty or thirty years with 'Éamonn a' Chnuic,' or 'Good Morrow, Fox, Pray What Is That You're Eatin',' or the 'Cailín Ruadh' or 'Táimse 'mo Chodladh' – songs she learned to sing at the branch-classes a few years ago? (*Gaedheal*, Nov. 1937, 8).

Such calls for the language to go boldly where it had rarely if ever gone before involved an act of faith in its ability to do so, a faith that not all felt they were able to share, at least in the short term. For example, writing on 'Terms in Irish' in 1923, León Ó Broin asked:

> Is it [terminology] not the most urgent question of the moment in the Irish language world – at least it should be. Personally, I am convinced that it is the most important, and unless it is speedily attended to, will cause endless bother, and perhaps result in maiming the language for us (*Leader*, 13/1/23).

In an essay in *Humanitas* in 1930, Daniel Corkery argued: 'It is possible for a language to be too close to the soil. I would say that the Irish language, as it is spoken, especially in those areas where the schools of literature had ceased to function in the eighteenth century, is too close to the soil' (*Humanitas*, June 1930, 5–6).[16]

Far more common than such reservations and worries were declarations that the language was, even then, if not entirely ready to handle all the challenges the contemporary world could offer, at least ready to be made so. Speaking to members of An Fáinne in 1922, Pádraig Ó Dálaigh summarised the task before those who would make Irish the daily language of a modern nation:

> Irish is now going through the mill of this new world, and it must be arranged and adjusted so that it will be suited and appropriate for every necessity with regard to the affairs of today's world . . . Old words will have to be sought out and new words invented or stolen; all the dialects must be mixed together as would be done with milk in a vat, and, after a while, the cream taken from them and the churning done, and after turning and mixing them well, taking the butter to ourselves as the language of all Ireland (*Misneach*, 27/5/22).[17]

Never does he reveal any doubt that this work could and would be done – in his own generation. Lecturing in Dublin two years later, Éamon Ó Donnchadha made this confidence explicit: 'And if Irish suited the Irish person, if it was once enough of a language for him for all the demands he made of it, it should suit him now if it is broadened and twisted to suit the new world.' Ó Donnchadha acknowledged the job would not be easy, but he also believed it would be accomplished, at least in part, in his own time:

> Time has cut a great wide gap between the old Gaelic world and the new world of today, but the two worlds can be reconciled and brought together in Irish-language literature, by the person who understands them both and is a literary artist by nature (*FL*, 14/6/24).[18]

Reviewing Dinneen's dictionary in 1928, Father John M. O'Reilly conceded a persistent pessimism about the capabilities of the language:

> There is a feeling abroad, chiefly and most notably among the folk themselves, but also, of course, among our 'learned' superior crowd – to which latter it gives great satisfaction and comfort – that Irish is merely a folk language, fit to do duty for mountaineers and villagers, but utterly incapable of anything higher, anything scientific or progressive.

For O'Reilly, Dinneen's *Foclóir Gaedhilge agus Béarla* provided the 'swiftest and most deadly answer' to any such misconceptions (*CB*, Mar. 1928, 321).[19]

While many Gaels doubtless wished they could share such optimism, they were too aware of the actual linguistic and cultural state of the nation to be able to convince themselves that the situation could be changed all that quickly, even given the brains and zeal of the committed young. For example, in 1922 Feardorcha Ó Conaill wrote that he was a bit startled by the eagerness with which some writers took on 'everything under the sun' (gach uile rud faoi'n ghréin) in Irish, arguing: 'I don't think that the proper prose will come until Irish is in general use throughout Ireland, in the cities, in the tram, in the theatre, in the schools, in the colleges, among the people selling and buying at the market.' Ó Conaill reckoned that this linguistic expansion would take at least fifty years, and in the meantime, 'all of today's writers are doing spadework, clearing the way for the famous writers to come in future' (obair láighe atá ghá dhéanamh ag gach aon sgríobhnóir an lae indiu, ag glanadh an bhealaigh roimh na sgríobhnóirí tásgúla atá le teacht amach annseo). For him, the important task of the present generation was simply to save the language, for 'if it is saved, it is certain that a Gaelic Turgenev and a Gaelic Pushkin will be born, although they have not been born yet' (má sábháiltear, is cinnte go mbéarfar Turgénef Gaolaoch agus Púiscín Gaolach, cé nár rugadh fós iad) (*Misneach*, 13/5/22).[20]

A similar awareness that the linguistic Promised Land was not for his own generation underlay Shán Ó Cuív's argument in his 1936 pamphlet *The Problem of Irish in the Schools*, where he wrote:

> It will take a long time to secure the use of Irish as the ordinary medium of intercourse in the highly complex life of a city like Dublin. That, however, is the objective of the language movement, and the daily use of Irish in the simple forms of life is the first step in the attainment of that objective.[21]

Seán Ó Catháin was also aware of the difficulties facing those trying to rush Irish into the twentieth century, writing in a 1937 review of Ó Cuív's essay collection *Deora Áthais agus Dréachta Eile* (Tears of joy and other essays), a book he felt made an important contribution to proving the language's capacity and flexibility:

> The charge is often made that Irish cannot be moulded or adjusted for the questions of today. There is some truth to that, in that Irish, as it is spoken today – the speech of the people, as is said – is not fit for the questions of this time. But it is a mistake to say that it cannot be made fit.

Ó Catháin was confident that the language's past history of engagement with a wide range of topics was adequate proof of its future capacity: 'Philosophers say that it is not possible to argue against what happened, and note that history, philosophy, medicine, astronomy, and theology were discussed in simple, clear Irish up to five hundred years ago' (*TCNÍ*, July 1937, 165).[22]

For some Gaels eager to hear their compatriots discourse again in Irish on such an array of topics, the problem was the havoc wrought on the language's resources by that centuries-long silence. Writing in the University College Cork journal *Éarna* in 1924, A. Ó Raithile (probably Alfred O'Rahilly, later president of the university) acknowledged: 'A language which for centuries has been in suspended animation cannot suddenly be made a vehicle for modern scientific theories.' (*Éarna*, Mar. 1924, 53). Liam Gógan was more optimistic in an essay in *An Reult* the same year, stating:

> And literature in Irish has no reason or excuse for being so thin and tired except for a lack of words, and therefore, or as a result of that, a lack of thoughts . . . The words for the most part exist if one seeks them, finds them, and uses them. From those many useful words will grow a noble, energetic literature rather than a literature of fools and churls (*Reult*, May 1924, 20–2).[23]

Joseph Hanly wanted to expedite this process, calling the expansion of the Irish lexicon 'a great and national task'.[24] One writer wrestling with that task was Tomás Ó Cléirigh, who wrote in the preface to his *Aodh Mac Aingil agus an Scoil Nua-Ghaedhilge i Lobháin* (Aodh Mac Aingil and the school of modern Irish in Louvain:

> As long as the Irish language was suppressed it had little connection with the life of the nation. It lost status so that it needed to deal only with matters of farming and fishing. As a result, we are behind because of a lack of words appropriate to today's world, and Mac Aingil and those like him had many words and expressions that would be useful now and that could be put into service for the whole country.[25]

Virtually nobody with a serious interest in the language at this time denied that there was a pressing need to expand its capacity to deal with an intimidating array of topics that it had never previously needed to address. There were, however, fundamental differences regarding where the new vocabulary required was to come from. The minority position was that Irish could most quickly catch up with other modern languages by tapping into the linguistic resources those languages had themselves evolved over time to meet the very challenges now troubling the Gaels. Perhaps the most forceful advocate of this approach was one 'Cnoc Sídhe Gamhna', who wrote in *Irisleabhar Muighe Nuadhad* in 1925: 'It is a sign of strength for a language that it can draw in words it needs and bring them into line with its own laws. It is no sign of weakness to be aware of a shortage of words, but rather a sign of vitality and life' (*IMN*, 1925, 65).[26] The classicist George Thomson believed the Irish language's lack of an extensive specialised vocabulary could be seen as a latent strength, writing in the preface to his Gaelic edition of Euripides' *Alcestis* in 1932:

> As for technical terms, it is my opinion that Irish is in good shape, in literary matters at any rate, for having so few of them. If some term is lacking, the meaning must be conveyed smoothly and honestly with simple speech, something that will benefit the teacher and the student both; but if too many of them are available, it is too easy for us to conceal a lack of knowledge behind learned speech.

But when such new terms were essential, Thomson argued that Irish should follow the lead of the other European vernaculars:

> I thought it best to take what I had to invent from Latin, as do English, French, and many other languages, than to go back to Old Irish to seek them, for it seems to me that it is more important that they be easily comprehensible than that they be in a form of pure Irish.[27]

Caitlín Nic Ghabhann sought a middle ground between Thomson's embrace of foreign sources and the linguistic nativism he rejected, writing in 1924:

> We must draw on English and other foreign languages. That stands to reason. Irish has not been cultivated for hundreds of years . . . Hundreds of words must be brought into Modern Irish to make it suitable for modern life. That is precisely the danger. That is why we should be careful and on guard. That is why we should make our early writings available and why everyone who intends to add to literature in Irish should make a study of them (*FL*, 26/4/24).[28]

'P. de B.' (possibly Pádraig de Brún) agreed in a 1925 review of *Bunús na h-Eoluíochta* (The basis of science) by Tomás Mac Conraoi and Éamon Ó Donnchadha:

> Where a suitable Irish word exists they have not rejected it; but where it is possible only by permitting scientific inexactitude or by accepting a cumbersome

> circumlocution to get a native equivalent, they have freely taken the foreign word and given it a Gaelic garb. That way lies progress. Every modern language follows the same course (*II*, 17/8/25).[29]

Most Gaels were, however, less ready to compromise on this point, feeling as they did that the language contained adequate seeds for healthy indigenous growth, and that indiscriminate introduction of exotic elements might well produce a freakish hybrid. In 1929, Liam Gógan introduced his serialised 'Foclóir na hArdshaoirse agus a Cómhcheárd: Irish-English Dictionary of Architecture and Allied Arts' in the *Teacher's Work* with the following reflections:

> The ideal in Irish terminology ought to be to make Irish what it might have been had there been no conquest, and this can only be achieved by drawing inspiration from the language itself, as it is spoken and as it has been written from 1200 AD onwards. Most of our terminological failures are due to the fact that the new words are not racy of the soil and this, in turn, is due to the absence of study of the language itself in evolution from its earliest known manifestations (*Teacher's Work*, Dec. 1929, 45).[30]

In 1922, *An Sguab* announced in its inaugural edition a contest for the best Irish versions of expressions like 'Stop Press', 'Trespassers Will Be Prosecuted', 'Great Clearance Sale', etc., a contest in which Micheál Mac Liammóir took the second prize (*Sguab*, Oct. 1922, 18). The new journal was here following the lead of the Oireachtas, which had run competitions for 'téarmaí' with some regularity from 1899 to 1920.[31] This approach seems, however, to have had its day, and contests made little contribution to the expansion of the language's resources. Yet, even without hope of reward or recognition, some writers continued to compile lists of words they had resurrected, borrowed or coined. For example, in 1923, Éamon Ó Donnchadha offered Irish-speaking readers of the *Irish Independent* a series of terms to assist them in the use of the telephone (*II*, 10/5/23). In 1927, an anonymous contributor published in *An Stoc* 'Téarmaigheacht na Meadhon-Ghaedhilge' (The terminology of Middle Irish), a list of words for modern or technical activities 'that were formed when there was no break or gap in the Irish language' (a rinneadh nuair nach raibh briseadh ná beárnadh ar an nGaedhilge) (*Stoc*, Apr. 1927, 5),[32] the same principle that guided Gógan in his 1929–30 compilation of architectural terms noted above. In March 1932, the *Garda Review* began a series that ran for years under the title 'Téarmaí Oifigeamhla / Official Translation into Irish of Technical Police Terms'. The linguistic demands of another profession were served by Éamon Ó Donnchadha, who in 1935 published his booklet *Gluais Matamaitice* (A mathematical glossary) (BÁC: Brún agus Ó Nualláin, Teóranta, [1935]). The needs of urban office workers and civil servants who wished to transact their business in Irish were addressed in Pádraig Ó Bróithe's *Gaedhealg 'san Oifig / Irish in the Office: Office Dialogues with Pronunication and Translation* (Dublin: Powell Press, n.d.).[33] For members of the public interested in corresponding with civil servants in the first official language, there was *Titles (in Irish and English) of Civil Service Posts / Teidil (i nGaedhilg agus i mBéarla) Phostanna san Stát-Sheirbhís* (n.p.: n.p., 1938). Among the titles Gaelicised therein were 'caretaker of British military cemeteries' (airigheach roiligí saighdiúirí Briotáineacha) and 'female cleaner and bothy woman' (banghlantóir agus bean bothaighe). Even Máirtín Ó Cadhain felt such work was worth time taken from his Gaeltacht and republican activism and creative writing. In 1937–8, he put together a list of some two hundred colloquial or technical expressions for which he provided Irish equivalents. Among the phrases he Gaelicised were 'I will make minced meat of you', 'the preservation of neutrality means the sacrifice of comforts', 'get a move on, will you', and 'Ireland is a creditor country while England is a debtor'.[34]

Needless to say, a major source of new terminology was the state. In September 1922, with the Free State not even officially in existence yet, the government created Rannóg Aistriúcháin an Oireachtais (The translation division of the Parliament) to prepare translations into English of laws enacted in Irish, and, far more frequently, translations into Irish of laws enacted in English. Given an enormous body of texts involving the most complicated and up-to-date subjects, staff members like Liam Ó Rinn, Tomás Page, Colm Ó Murchú, and Risteárd Ó Foghludha performed near miracles to keep pace with the legislative agenda of the new administration. Their work was singled out for particular praise by 'Critic' in 1932:

> They are modestly and expeditiously accomplishing tasks which the most learned of our scholars could not make a shot at . . . The translation staff are every week turning out documents in which matters that no speaker or writer of Irish ever tackled before are efficiently dealt with.

He regretted, however, that their work was too little known:

> It is a pity that city dwellers and others requiring a wider vocabulary and a more varied command of phrase than satisfies the fisherman of the Gaeltacht do not make a habit of occasionally reading the Irish versions of the statutes, and that teachers of urban schools do not dip into them (*UIrman*, 10/9/32).[35]

More immediately accessible was the work of An Coiste Téarmaíochta (The terminology committee) in the Department of Education. Set up in late 1928, this group was in our period to publish word lists dealing with history and geography (stair is tíreoluidheacht) (1928), grammar and literature (gramadach is litridheacht) (1930), science (eoluidheacht) (1932), music (ceol) (1933), commerce (tráchtáil) (1935) and games (cluichidheacht) (1938). Throughout, it was guided by what we may call a nativist methodology, stressing that compound words be made from words already in the language; that compound words be formed by joining prefixes and suffixes to existing words; that foreign words brought into Irish be Gaelicised; and that words be revived from Old and Middle Irish, with their meanings adjusted if necessary.[36]

For the most part, however, readers were far more likely to learn necessary new terminology from the books, essays, and articles – some heavily glossed – in which many Gaelic writers tried, aptly or absurdly, to expand the capacities of the national language. The seriousness with which most of those writers took the responsibility imposed on them by their choice of material is exemplified by the comments of Seán Ua Ceallaigh in the preface to his travel book *Taistealuidheacht no Cúrsa na Cruinne*:

> Needless to say there are many uncommon words and names that an author comes across on a great journey like that, and there is nothing like them in Irish yet because of how little use has been made of our native language for a long time. I took counsel with the cleverest Irish-language writers in my acquaintance concerning those words and names, and the result of our deliberations is here, for better or worse.[37]

Among the words he uses in his text and defines in his glossary are a mix of borrowings, neologisms, and coinings from native roots, among them 'camufláiste' (camouflage), 'leigheas creidimh' (faith-healing), 'polaibhog' (polliwog), 'ricseagh' (rickshaw), 'samhladóir' (camera), and 'sciatha sneachta' (snow-sheds).

In a 1926 piece on 'The Carnegie Rural Libraries', the Jesuit bibliographer Stephen Brown, having identified himself as a Gaelic Leaguer and a strong supporter of the revival, wrote:

> And here is the dilemma with which we are faced. Is all reading of books in the English language to be combated as anglicising in its influence? If so you must cut out from the reading, not merely of the peasantry and working classes, but of all classes, all science and learning, even popular science, all technical works, philosophy, and anything of a philosophical nature, including political economy, sociology, psychology, citizenship, all literary criticism and modern literary work, all history, civil and ecclesiastical, travel, and descriptions of foreign countries, modern questions of all kinds. Why? Because of those kinds just mentioned, no literature exists in the Irish language at present (*IR*, Jan. 1926, 67).

But not all agreed with this bleak assessment. There were, in fact, some who felt the workers were well ahead of the worriers in this regard. For example, a regular Gaelic columnist for the *Connacht Tribune*, impressed by the lectures sponsored by the Galway branch of the Gaelic League, wrote a few months before Brown's essay appeared:

> There are very knowledgeable people throughout Ireland who think that it is not possible to discuss science and other difficult questions like it through Irish, but if these people were present listening to the lectures, they would understand that the language of the Gaels can be bent and spun and twisted to express every thought, however deep, and every science, however new, as well as any other living language and better than a good number of them (*CT*, 10/10/25).[38]

Among the lectures held in Galway and subsequently published with glossaries in the *Connacht Tribune* were talks on medicine and astronomy by Seán P. Mac Éinrí (*CT*, 3/3/23 and 7/2/25);[39] on 'Nádúr an Damhna' (The nature of matter) and on radio by Seán Óg Mac Éinrí (*CT*, 18/4/25 and 13/2/26); and on chemistry by Tomás Dilliún (*CT*, 16/1/26). And these were just a few of the topics treated, more often than not, knowledgeably and accessibly in Irish during the 1920s and 1930s. Interested Gaels could find essays on everything from astronomy (*II*, 23/4/23; 2/5/23; 30/4/24; 29/11/24; 20/12/29; 10/12/30; 6/11/33; 20/11/34; 29/4/35; and 10/1/36; *Leader*, 9/7/27; 16/7/27; *IP*, 19/8/32; *UI*, 8/9/34; *Irisleabhar Chorcaighe*, 1936, 77–9); to relativity (*II*, 8/7/24, *FL*, 3/10/25); sea turtles (*IP*, 6/4/32); and television (*II*, 3/9/27; 28/1/28; 7/8/28; *Leader*, 4/4/36 to 25/4/36; 5/8/39).[40] Particularly active in this regard were three regular anonymous contributors to the *Irish Independent*: 'Ceannabhán', 'Sean-Éireannach', and 'Taistealuidhe'.[41] Liam Ó Rinn also played a leading role in expanding the intellectual range of the language. In addition to his formal essays, he regularly used his book reviews in *United Ireland* as the occasion for discussing an impressively diverse range of subjects. For example, he turned a September 1934 review of H. J. Stenning's *Creation's Doom* into a discussion of the state of contemporary science (*UI*, 8/9/34), a review of J. R. Ackerley's *Hindoo Holiday* into an overview of Ghandi's India (*UI*, 24/11/34), and a review of J. Ellis Barker's *New Lives for Old: How to Cure the Incurable* into a commentary on homeopathic medicine (*UI*, 27/4/35).

Topics of a new sort were also beginning to appear in a handful of books written in Irish at this time.[42] For example, in 1922 Seán Ó Cuirrín published his *Uimhrigheacht* (Arithmetic) (BÁC: COÉ). Caitlín Nic Ghabhann's geography text *Tír-Eolas na hEorpa* (The geography of Europe) (BÁC: COÉ,) appeared in 1923, to be followed by another textbook by her, *Eolaidhe na Cruinne: Leabhar Tlacht-Eolais* (A guide to the globe: A geography book) (BÁC: Brún agus Ó Noláin, Teor.) the next year. In 1927, an anonymous nun from the St Louis convent in Monaghan published *Cuirp-Eolas* (Physiology)

(BÁC: M.H. Mac Ghoill agus a Mhac), a work that included a four-page glossary. In 1928, Éamon Ó Donnchadha's *Uimhríocht* (Arithmetic) (BÁC: Muinntir C.S. Ó Fallamhain, i gcomhar le hOS) appeared, as did Séamus Ó Duirinne's *Eachtra na Nádúire* (The adventure of nature) (BÁC: M.H. Mac an Ghoill agus a Mhac, Teor., 1928), a short natural history textbook of which the author boasted: 'There is no technical language here; there is not a word in it that is not in use in the Gaeltacht.'[43] A more serious and important work on nature was Séamus Mac Con Iomaire's *Cladaigh Chonamara* (The shores of Conamara), a compilation of facts and lore dealing with the coastal biota of Conamara written by the author in America, where he had emigrated as a young man. Among the information the native-speaking Mac Con Iomaire provides are the names of 43 kinds of seaweed. Of broader scope was Liam de Lása's *Fotha Feasa* (A foundation of knowledge) (BÁC: COÉ, n.d.), a general science textbook with an accompanying glossary for the many technical terms introduced by the author. Those interested in the science of human behaviour could turn to *For-Oideas Aigne-Eolais do'n Aos Léighinn* (An overview of psychology for students) (BÁC: COÉ, [1932]) by 'Siúir' (Sister), an illustrated text directed at teachers and rich in new terminology. That the clerical author never lost sight of the spiritual side of human nature is clear from the book's concluding lines: 'It is a great consolation to the teacher in the end that he will not be judged by the effectiveness of his lessons, nor the result of examinations, but by how he helped children to reach the Kingdom of their Eternal Father.'[44] Four years later, another anonymous nun, this one from the Ursuline Convent in Sligo, offered pupils *Eoluidheacht don Scoláire Óg* (Science for the young student) (BÁC: ODFR, 1936). Gaelic humanists were offered more challenging fare in George Thomson's *Tosnú na Feallsúnachta* (The beginning of philosophy) (BÁC: ODFR, 1935), a work the author intended as an introduction for the general reader to early Greek thought up to the time of Plato. For the more musically inclined, there was *Teagosc-Leabhar na Bheidhlíne* (An instructional book for the violin) by Treasa Nic Ailpín and Seán Ó Cuirrín (BÁC: Brún agus Ó Nóláin, Teor., 1923), while those of a financial bent could consult Cormac Ó Cadhlaigh's *Cuntaisíocht* (Accounting) (BÁC: Brún agus Ó Nóláin, n.d.).

Readers of Irish interested in armchair travel could turn to a handful of books on far-flung places, the most ambitious being perhaps Seán Ua Ceallaigh's *Taistealuidheacht no Cúrsa na Cruinne*, the account of his round-the-world trip in 1923 as a Republican propagandist and fund-raiser, with particular focus on his experiences in the United States, Australia, and, to a much lesser extent, India. The same year saw the appearance of Liam Ó Rinn's more intellectual account of a sojourn in Paris as *Turus go Páras* (A trip to Paris). Four years later, Micheál Ó Murchú republished as *Litreacha ó'n bhFrainnc* (Letters from France) (BÁC: ODFR, 1935), essays that had originally appeared in the *Irish Independent*. In 1936, An Gúm published Seosamh Mac Grianna's *An Bhreatain Bheag* (Wales) (BÁC: ODFR, 1937), and his travels in Wales would, of course, also be central in *Mo Bhealach Féin*. Among the many travel or informational pieces on foreign places that appeared in journals of the period, some of the more important or intriguing were 'Rudaí a Deirtear Thall a's Abhfus / Cathair O. Henry' (Things said here and there / O. Henry's city) (on New Orleans) by 'Ceann fá Eite' (*II*, 1/11/22); Micheál Breathnach's essay on Haiti, 'Poblacht na bh-Fear n-Gorm / Tír na Sléibhte' (The black men's republic / The land of the mountains) (*II*, 7/7/24); Peadar Ó Dubhda's 'Turas Gaedhilgeoir go Lourdes' (Irish-speakers' trip to Lourdes) (1929);[45] the essays on Germany Tomás Ó Cléirigh published in *Seoidíní Cuimhne* in 1937; or León Ó Baoighill's 'Talamh na hÉigipte / A hÁilleacht agus a Draoidheacht' (The land of Egypt / Its beauty and its magic) (*II*, 29/10/37).

Literary criticism was one discipline in which Gaelic authors took an understandably keen interest. Writing in *Fáinne an Lae* in 1923, 'D. Mac E.' (= 'Darach Mac Eibhir' = Pádhraic Ó Domhnalláin?) argued that it was perhaps premature to expect any really sophisticated criticism in the language, but conceded that his Gaelic colleagues didn't seem troubled by that fact:

> And it is a bit early yet for Irish-speakers to assume the mantle of criticism in literary affairs. It is said that a craft that has not been learned is an enemy. Today's readers of Irish scarcely remember that proverb. Every living one of them is a critic! (*FL*, 15/9/23).[46]

Reviewing Séamus Ó Searcaigh's *Nua-Scríbhneoirí na Gaedhilge* more than a decade later, 'L. Mac G.' indicated that not all that much had changed:

> As for the opinions he has about the works he discusses, we should remember that criticism is still just beginning in Ireland, and especially that it is very difficult to give any proper judgment on a writer in his own lifetime. Therefore, one should not expect an infallible judgment from any critic, but rather welcome whatever opinion he has if he shows that there is any fairly credible foundation for it. That is how criticism will be developed and literature will be cultivated (*IMN*, 1934, 91).[47]

Patience did wear thin for some literary Gaels, who saw no significant improvement in this genre. In a 1935 essay on 'Irish Literary Criticism' in *The Leader*, 'Celt' offered a troubling explanation for the lack of serious attention paid to new books in the language:

> I believe the regular reviewers are well enough disposed towards Irish, and that if they don't review Irish books, the reason is that they can't read them. That, after

> twenty five years working of the National University, is, if true, deplorable: but we have to take things as we find them. Irish does not seem to be taken seriously by anybody who matters except the Government and the Gaelic League (*Leader*, 2/11/35).

In a 1932 article on 'Léirmheas Liteardha / Is Fearr an t-Imreas ná an t-Uaigneas' (Literary criticism / Fighting is better than loneliness), Shán Ó Cuív, one of the few serious Gaelic critics, offered another suggestion about why there was so little informed discussion of literature in the language:

> But with regard to the Irish language, no proper start has yet been made to have a debate in Irish itself on literary matters. The great authors are silent. Some of them are creating a new language, and most likely others think they themselves are creating great literature. Perhaps they are, too, except that the readers of that great literature are not lucky enough to recognise it. But at any rate all of them are too busy to reveal their thoughts about literature, if they do have any thoughts about it (*II*, 13/12/32).[48]

There was, however, nothing new in his suspicion that would-be Gaelic critics might not have all that much worthwhile to say about literature if they chose to express themselves on the subject. Writing in *Iris an Fháinne* in 1926, Proinnsíos Tréanlámhach focused on the lack of sophistication and literary training evident in the work of contemporary Gaelic critics:

> At present, a book usually only gets praise or lukewarm praise: something negative is said one time in a hundred, no matter how much it is required. This is incomprehensible when we remember that almost everyone who understands the situation is of one mind about how bad some of the Irish being written today is. If there is any use at all for critics, they should be able to tell us which books are any good and which are not . . . After giving this question a good deal of thought, it would seem to me that an ignorance of the rules concerning good writing or good style is to blame for almost all of these faults (*IF*, Apr. 1926, 10–11).[49]

Others, while admitting and deploring this ignorance, set it in the context of the arrested development of the language. In a 1933 essay in *The Leader*, 'Celt' described Gaelic discussions of literature as more akin to 'vivisection' than criticism, and wrote of those attempting the task:

> They have practically no precedents to guide them. They have very little of the terminology of criticism to help them in pronouncing judgement. They themselves are not professional critics at all and cannot be expected to be other than awkward and self-conscious in trying to fill the role (*Leader*, 16/11/35).[50]

Tomás Ó Deirg agreed with this view when he answered critics of An Gúm in an address to the Munster Feis in Killarney the same year:

> I would like to see a reasonable criticism done on the work that is published; but I would hope for help from the criticism and not censure. Perhaps the greatest difficulty with regard to Irish-language criticism is that we lack an established literary standard (*Tír*, Sept.–Oct. 1933, 6).[51]

Another of the handful of thoughtful Gaelic critics, Aodh de Blácam, argued in 1925 that 'Irish literary criticism is feeble because it is not in the Gaelic tradition' (*Dublin Magazine*, Feb. 1925, 441). The need to remedy that deficiency was in the forefront of the mind of 'Craiftine' when he wrote in *An Gaedheal* in 1937: 'We need a native scheme of criticism. For that we must forthrightly face the fundamental qualities of the native literature, and not allow any foolish softness or foolish sentimentality to stop us' (*Gaedheal*, Jan. 1937, 3).[52]

That 'Craiftine' understood the nature and extent of the challenge is evident from even a cursory glance at what passed for criticism in Irish at the time. On one side stood those reviewers for whom any negative comment on a book in the language was an act of treachery.[53] On several occasions in our period we find writers expressing what would seem to be the self-evident truth that Gaelic books might from time to time fall short of perfection. Thus, in a 1930 review we find S. S. Ó Cathasaigh suggesting apologetically, 'It is probably not right to disparage any book at all in Irish in the world as it is. But nonetheless one must stand up for the rights of the language' (*Stoc*, Jan. 1930, p. 5).[54] In a piece in *Humanitas* the following year, Liam de Róiste was less amenable to compromising critical standards, writing of literature in Irish:

> It was a spoiled little disorderly pet. Up to now writings in Irish have not been judged by any standard at all that would put them on an equal footing with the writings of other modern languages, and because of that, it is very difficult to arrive at any accurate and reasonable assessment of modern literature in Irish from the beginning of the revival on (*Humanitas*, Mar. 1931, 27).[55]

In 1937, Myles Dillon was disgusted with the disingenuous praise that often greeted creative work of all kinds in Irish:

> Who has not sat miserable during the performance of Irish plays and Irish musical items which were disgraceful in every particular, only to join at the conclusion in the chorus of praise? That must come to an end. If an Irish book is silly or dull or badly written, there is no use in pretending that it is not so, although one has to beware of discouraging where only encouragement is needed. In other spheres of activity standards are high, and they are likely to be higher. The standard in regard to Irish should be the highest of all (*Ireland To-Day*, Feb. 1937, 24).

The other major grouping of Gaelic critics held a diametrically opposite view of their task, one whose criteria were neatly lampooned by Donn Piatt in *An t-Ultach* in 1931:

> How is criticism done in the Island of the Saints? That is easily told. You throw up a penny. If it lands with the hen up, you will find fault with the book. Now, open this book anywhere and read on until you find (a) a typographical error (b) a mistake in spelling (c) a dialect you don't like (d) genuinely bad Irish (e) 'bad Irish' according to your own opinion. Write a review on the faults then, and there you have it. If the harp comes up, praise the book and compare it to Dante or something else you never read. IF IT IS A FRIEND OF YOURS WHO WROTE THE BOOK, KEEP THROWING PENNIES UNTIL THE HEN COMES OUT ON TOP (*Ultach*, July 1931, 3).[56]

All too often it seems that this might as well have actually been the methodology of the average Gaelic critic. An obsession with orthography, dialect issues, and a rigidly enforced if vaguely defined linguistic purity – all comments on these questions being illustrated with direct quotes that often comprise the bulk of the alleged 'review' – characterise much of what passed for literary criticism during the 1920s and 1930s, a trend whose ultimate sterility was indicted by Aodh de Blácam in 1924:

> To-day no Irish is printed save what will pass a drastic and even pedantic criticism. If the same standards were applied to the writing of English very little of what is printed in that tongue would appear. In consequence, matter has been wholly sacrificed to grammar and style (*Studies*, Mar. 1924, 65).[57]

'Róisín Dubh' was more specific in a 1929 essay in *An t-Ultach*: '"There isn't much that is good in the story, but the Irish is excellent. There are plenty of idiomatic expressions on every page of it." There you have the most common review of new books in Irish' (*Ultach*, Nov. 1929, 2).[58] Indeed in 1923, one major Gaelic literary figure, Pádraig Ó Siochfhradha, could devote most of his review of an early novel by another, Pádhraic Óg Ó Conaire, to issues of language, orthography, and typography, saying all but nothing about the book's literary value (*An Chearnóg*, May 1923, 4).[59] It was doubtless with this kind of 'criticism' in mind that 'S. Ó D.' humorously suggested in a 1929 piece in *The Star* that the best thing that would come from the standardisation of Irish orthography would be the silencing of a whole school of Gaelic critics fixated on this issue. But then, in more serious vein, he went on to say that doing away with such incompetent reviewers would

> pave the way for the development of a criticism in Irish, an important branch of literature which cannot be built up by the invention of technical terms but must

> grow out of the effort made by conscientious writers to express the feelings evoked in them on considering the literary products of other minds (*Star*, 16/11/29).

In 1938, Ciarán Ua Nualláin raged that as long as the Irish in a book was good, many Gaels would praise a work 'the like of which a black storyteller in Borneo would be ashamed to tell' (go mbéadh náire ar scéalaidhe ghorm i mBornéó a leithéid a ársaidhe). From this perspective, he argued, Father Dinneen's dictionary was the finest book ever written in the language because it was full of good Irish (*Hibernia*, Sept. 1938, 29).

Obviously, much of this linguistic criticism was driven by the same provincial rivalries we have encountered so often in the course of this book. And, once again, disputes over regional or other loyalties often led to personal animosity and vituperation. Father Lawrence Murray, himself no half-hearted partisan of Ulster Irish, deplored this tendency in an editorial in *An t-Ultach*:

> Some of the critics are not willing to give an opinion about a piece of writing without first finding out what province the writer is from. There are other people who are of the opinion that it would be far better for the Irish language to die than that the people who have learned Irish would begin writing books. Few people make an attempt to criticise a book as is done in the literature of other countries. Ignorance of the simple general rules regarding criticism is to blame for all these faults (*Ultach*, Nov. 1928, 3).[60]

Actually, it was a fundamental principle of a non-literary sort that inspired many of these Gaelic 'critics', one identified in 1928 by 'Aengus', who claimed that the motto of Gaelic reviewers was

> Do not allow anyone, except for me and my friends, to have character, intellect, intelligence, spirit, or courage. It is we who have all knowledge; it is we who are right; anyone who does not agree with us should not be associated with; he is an enemy to the Irish language and to *Gaelachas* (*Tír*, May 1928, 3).[61]

Amazingly enough, a fair number of reviews were even worse than those motivated by patriotic suppression of the critical faculty, querulous linguistic scrupulosity, or provincial or personal animosity. For example, the anonymous critic of Seán Ó Ruadháin's *Pádhraic Mháire Bhán* in *An Muimhneach*, dedicated a full two thirds of his review to a single lengthy quote (*Muimhneach*, Dec. 1932, 4). On occasion, when reviewers did venture an opinion, they left their readers no better off than they would have been with a pastiche of such quotes. For example, in 1931, the anonymous critic of Seosamh Mac Grianna's *Eoghan Ruadh Ó Néill* for *An Camán* commented:

> It is customary to write a few words about new books to let the public know that their like is on the market. If it is a good book, and particularly if it is a book from the pen of an author already known for his storytelling, there is no need to say more (*Camán*, Oct. 1931, 3).[62]

With such inanities passing for literary insight, it is little wonder that Micheál Ó Maoláin could write of one such review in 1923: 'You would have learned just as much – or perhaps more – by going and looking in the window of any bookshop' (*FL*, 22/12/23).[63]

Fortunately, a few contemporary Gaelic critics were beginning to move beyond such benedictions, blasts, and banalities at this time, either in individual essays like Uaitéar Ó Finn's 'An Reachtabhrach mar Fhile' (Raftery as a poet) (*Reult*, May 1924, 36–44); Micheál Mac Liammóir's 'Lucht Ealadhna agus an Tír-Grádh' (Artists and patriotism), 'An Misneach Nua sa Litríocht' (The new courage in literature), and 'Triúr Sgríbhneoirí i Nua-Litríocht na Rúise' (Three writers in modern Russian literature) [Pushkin, Turgenev, Chekov] (*Sguab*, Sept. 1923, 233–4; Sept. 1924, 172–3; and *FL*, Mar. to July 1927, respectively);[64] Aodh de Blácam's 'Cosc ar Deagh-Scríobhadh' (A hindrance to good writing) (*FL*, 8/12/23); Daniel Corkery's 'Stair Litríocht na Gaoluinne' (The history of literature in Irish) (*FL*, 17/3/23);[65] Tadhg Ó Donnchadha's 'Meathphuir' ('Metaphors') (*Éarna*, Dec. 1923, 27–35); Seosamh Mac Grianna's 'Goidé Tá d'Easbaidh orainn?' (*Ultach*, May 1924, 5–6); 'Smaointe ar Nua-Litridheacht na Gaedhilge agus an Saoghal Mór' (Thoughts on literature in Irish and the great world) by 'M. Nic Ph.' (UCG *University Annual*, 1926–7, 15–16); Cearbhall Ua Dálaigh's 'Scríbhneoirí agus a Stíl' (Writers and their style) (*II*, 3/6/29); Micheál Breathnach's 'Sgríbhneoirí na Nuadh-Ghaedhilge / Filidheacht, Prós, agus Drámuidheacht' (Modern Irish writers / Poetry, prose, and drama) (*Dundalk Examiner* (18 and 25/4/31);[66] 'An t-Athair Peadar Ó Laoghaire' by 'An Chorcaigheach' [*sic*], (UCG *University Annual*, 1931–2, 40–2);[67] Tomás Ó Coipingéir's 'An Aisling: A hÁilleacht is a Fuirm' (The vision poem: Its beauty and its form) (*II*, 10/4/33) or his 'Dólás Filíochta: Saothar Aodhagáin Uí Rathaille' (The sorrow of poetry: The work of Aodhagán Ó Rathaile) (*II*, 20/3/33); An tAthair Seán Ó Siadhail's 'Seathrún Céitinn: File agus Stairidhe [Geoffrey Keating: Poet and historian] (1570–1650)' (*IR*, Apr. to July 1933); Proinnsias Ó Cinnéide's 'Prós Litríocht na Gaedhilge – An Riocht Atá uirthi Anois' (Prose literature in Irish – Its condition now) (*II*, 15/4/36; *IP*, 22/4/36); Máirín Ní Mhuirgheasa's 'Filíocht Ghaedhilge an Lae Indiu' (Contemporary poetry in Irish) (*IP*, 29/2/36, 2/1/37, and 9/1/37); 'An t-Úrsgéal sa Nua-Litríocht' (The novel in modern literature) by 'Carraig' (*Gaedheal*, May 1937, 3); 'Nua-Litridheacht na Gaedhilge' (Modern literature in Irish) by 'Éamon a' Chnuic' (*Leader*, 18/9/37); Seán Ó Ciarghusa'a 'Saothar an Athar Peadar/ An Ceacht is Mó Atá le Baint As' (The work of Father Peter / The greatest lesson to be learned from it) (*IP*, 11/9/39); or in reviews that went beyond the brief publication notices so common at the time, reviews of the sort written by 'Aengus' for *An Tír*, by Seán O Catháin for *Timthire Chroidhe Naomhtha Íosa*, by Cearbhall Ua Dálaigh for the *Irish Press*, or by Liam Ó Rinn for journals like *The Star*, the *United Irishman*, and *United Ireland*.[68] In addition, there was a fair degree of sophistication in much of the critical writing that appeared in *Irisleabhar Muighe Nuadhat* throughout the period, and particularly in the lively contributions to the short-lived *Humanitas* from writers like the editor, Pádraig de Brún, and Daniel Corkery.[69]

Even more encouraging was the appearance of full-length books in Irish on literary topics. The earliest and most ambitious of these was An tAthair Seoirse Mac Clúin's *An Litríocht: Infhiúcha ar Phrionnsabail, Fuirmeacha agus Léirmheastóireacht na Litríochta* (Literature: An examination of the principles, genres, and criticism of literature) (BÁC: Brún agus Ó Nóláin, Teor., [1926]), a work that tries to isolate the sources of literary creation as well as to discuss the various genres from poetry to criticism. Throughout, Mac Clúin asserts an Arnoldian view of literature as a criticism of life and shows a clear distaste for propaganda or for writing that focuses on the ugly, morbid, or immoral, an aberration of which he sees far too much in the work of modern authors like Zola, O'Flaherty, and Patrick McGill. These two points come together in his belief that the critic has a moral obligation in this decadent age:

> If our days have any importance, if our lives are more than merely passing the time, what will we say about the person who praises them and makes himself a high-priest of paganism in front of the populace. If anything is true with regard to this question, it is that the critic is a very important person; that he has a responsibility . . . We used the word 'high-priest' a little while ago. Without a doubt the critic should be a high priest; but for that a sanctified life and a pure heart are necessary, and the goal of picking out the noble thought and deed. Indeed, it is not a bad preparation, in addition to other things, to read a chapter of the New Testament daily (pp. 216–17).[70]

Doubtless the most controversial aspect of Mac Clúin's work was the degree to which he relied on English literature for his illustrative examples. In a review of *An Litríocht* for *Studies*, 'Omikkron' faulted Mac Clúin for 'the foreign appearance and the anglicised tinge' (an dreach alltair, an dath gallda) that his choice of examples gave the book, and urged Mac Cluin to turn his back on Arnold, Saintesbury, Hazlitt and their like; to immerse himself in the native tradition for ten years; and then to write – as he inevitably would – a very different book (*Studies*, Dec. 1926, 675–6). 'A. Ó D.' agreed in *Irisleabhar Muighe Nuadhad*, praising the book highly, but questioning Mac Clúin's dependence on English examples, and faulting him for not drawing on native roots when coining new technical terms (*IMN*, 1927, 100–1). Writing in *Fáinne an Lae*, 'Brian Dubh' expressed identical reservations, but also pronounced the book 'a milestone on the road to rescuing the Irish language' (cloch mhíle ar bhóthar tárrthála na Gaedhilge) and urged all his readers to get a copy (*FL*, Nov. 1926, 3).[71]

While no such intellectual ferment can be ascribed directly to Mac Clúin's treatise, the book did have some important successors in the field of Gaelic criticism, all of them more in line with the 1937 demand of 'Craiftine' for 'a native scheme of criticism'. In 1931, Críostóir Ó Raghallaigh published *An Léirmheastóir* (The critic) (BÁC: Brún agus Ó Nualláin, Teor., 1931), setting out his motives in the preface:

> When I was putting this book together, what I wanted was to discuss, in simple Irish, the writings of certain writers of Irish in the expectation that the interest of the reader in our own literature would be awakened and that readers would be given help to recognise and assess good literature.

Readers were not, however, to expect a comprehensive or rigorous analysis: 'For the most part what is in this collection is bits of Irish I myself liked, and therefore one will notice little negative comment in the opinions I have expressed about them' (p. iii).[72] The body of the text consists of passages from 17 authors followed by a general and pedestrian discussion of each. In the final section of the book, Ó Raghallaigh asks readers to identify and comment on anonymous passages.

More substantial was Séamus Ó Searcaigh's *Nua-Sgríbhneoirí na Gaedhilge* (BÁC: Brún agus Ó Nualláin, Teor., 1933), although once again his target audience was secondary school students:

> I know that I have acted boldly in writing a book on the modern writers of the Irish language. I know that none of those writers alive today will be satisfied with what I have said about his literary work. But I did not undertake putting the book together from a desire to satisfy the authors but rather from a desire to help the young who will have to study their work. I hope that I have not done an injustice to any author. If I have, I did not do so out of malice, but from a lack of perception (pp. 5–6).[73]

In the second edition of the book, published within a year of the first, Ó Searcaigh included a stylistic analysis of specific passages ('léirmheas ar stíl ghiotaí próis') as well as exercises ('obair le déanamh') 'to give students practice in discussing an author's style' (le cleachtadh a thabhairt do mhic léighinn ar chur síos ar stíl ughdair) (p. 5).[74]

Adult readers could turn to Shán Ó Cuív's *Prós na hAoise Seo*, a study of 15 contemporary Gaelic writers. For Ó Cuív, familiarity with a writer's work alone was an inadequate basis for full appreciation, as he makes clear in his preface:

> Because of my acquaintance with them, I had a gauge to assess their work not possible for one who never saw them with his own eyes and who never heard their voices and who knew nothing of their intellectual ability or the qualities in them by nature and training and the lives they had lived, except for what he would get from the writings they left behind (p. 5).[75]

Throughout the work, Ó Cuív stresses the central significance of those writers who were native speakers, stating:

> We are fortunate to have their writings to defend ourselves against the writing that will arise out of the new world now present when learners of Irish are more numerous than the people who speak the language naturally. That new world is a great danger to the language (p. 11).[76]

Of writers who learned the language, he includes only Pearse and Donnchadh Pléimeann in his discussion, and he pronounces his friend An tAthair Peadar Ua Laoghaire 'the major prose author of this century' (príomh-ughdar próis na haoise seo) (p. 14).[77]

More substantial than Ó Cuív's booklet was Muiris Ó Droighneáin's *Taighde i gComhair Stair Litridheachta na Nua-Ghaedhilge ó 1882 anuas* (Research towards a history of Modern Irish literature from 1882 on) (BÁC: ODFR, 1936), a history of modern literature in Irish from the first appearance of *Irisleabhar na Gaedhilge* on. Ó Droighneáin divides his study into three periods – 'Ré na dTosnuightheóirí' (The period of the beginners) (1882–92), 'Ré na gCainnteoirí Dúthchais' (The period of the native speakers) (1892–1903), and 'An Aimsir Seo' (The present) (1903 on) – with separate discussions of poetry, prose, and drama. The book concludes with a section entitled 'Saothar na Sgríbhneoirí' (The work of the writers), a series of brief biographical and bibliographical essays on 118 writers, followed by a list of the works of several dozen more. While Ó Droighneáin regularly quotes the opinions of others from essays and reviews, he clearly sees himself as a chronicler rather than a critic, adhering closely to the guidelines set out by his mentor Tadhg Ó Donnchadha in the book's preface:

> The business of the literary historian, as he discusses a particular period, is to number the authors of that period, and give an account of their lives, along with the legacy they left us. And in addition some account of the greatest 'movement' that happened in literature during that period. When the historian goes beyond that all he has is subjective opinion, and the world knows that 'there are no fewer opinions

than there are men'. Everyone will have his own opinion no matter what the historian says. And the person who wants an opinion, let him read the literature for himself and form his own opinion of it. Isn't that why literary history is written? (p. 2).[78]

One Gaelic writer never reluctant to express an opinion on any subject literary or otherwise was Seosamh Mac Grianna, whose lengthy essay on Pádraic Ó Conaire gave its title to his 1936 collection *Pádraic Ó Conaire agus Aistí Eile* (Pádraic Ó Conaire and other essays). While the essay tells us at least as much about Mac Grianna as it does about its subject, it does offer some provocative insights into the work of Ó Conaire. Another Gaelic writer who devoted a significant amount of attention to the work of an illustrious predecessor was Séamus Ó Searcaigh, whose biography *Pádraig Mac Piarais* (Patrick Pearse) (BÁC: OS, 1938) included a lengthy chapter on 'An tUghdar' (The author).

There was a fair amount of writing in Irish on the Gaelic tradition in poetry, in particular poetry written in the eighteenth century. There can, of course, be little doubt that much of this interest was inspired by Daniel Corkery's seminal classic *The Hidden Ireland: A Study of Gaelic Munster in the Eighteenth Century* (1924). It was, for example, to correct what he saw as Corkery's ignorant and unjust neglect of Ulster poetry that Mac Grianna in 1925 wrote the essays that were published as a booklet the following year under the title *Filí gan Iomrádh* (Poets without fame). Mac Grianna also delivered a series of lectures on Ulster poets at Coláiste Bhríde in Ométh in the summer of 1925, lectures that were subsequently published in *Pádraic Ó Conaire agus Aistí Eile*. The year 1925 is also the date Ó Droighneáin suggests for Séamus Ó hAodha's *Aodhagán Ó Rathaille* (BÁC: COÉ, n.d.), an edition of the poet's work preceded by introductory essays on Ó Rathaille and the poems. By far the most active and important scholar of the poetry of the eighteenth and nineteenth centuries was Risteárd Ó Foghludha ('Fiachra Éilgeach') who produced editions with commentary of the poetry of Tadhg Gaelach Ó Súillebháin (1929), Seán Clárach Mac Domhnaill (1932), Pádraig Phiarais Cundún (1932), Donnchadh Ruadh Mac Conmara (1933), Liam Ruadh Mac Coitir (1937), Liam Inglis (1937), An tAthair Conchubhar Ó Briain (1938), Eoghan an Mhéirin Mac Cárthaigh (1938), and Liam Dall Ó hIfearnáin (1939).[79] Others who wrote on this topic were Toirdhealbhach Ó Raithbheartaigh in his *Máighistrí san Fhilidheacht* (Masters of poetry) (BÁC: ODFR, 1936), 1932) and, more significantly, Piaras Béaslaí in the two volumes of *Éigse Nua-Ghaedhilge* (Modern Irish poetry) (BÁC: COÉ, 1933). In his review of the second volume of *Éigse Nua-Ghaedhilge* for the Enniscorthy *Echo*, the playwright Annraoi Saidléar showed his appreciation of the real advance in Gaelic criticism represented by Béaslaí's informed and perceptive readings of his texts:

> This is something new for a critic who discusses literature in Irish. High praise or harsh abuse are the usual thing, and often they are foolish. But Piaras has a measuring stick and he measures the poetry of every one of the writers accordingly (*Echo*, 14/10/33).[80]

The most erudite, versatile, and enterprising critic writing in Irish at this time was, without a doubt, Liam Ó Rinn. In addition to his many insightful reviews and essays on literary matters, he also in 1939 published *Mo Chara Stiofán*, the memoir of his friendship with the Irish classicist Stephen McKenna. His summaries of conversations and correspondence with the polyglot and urbane McKenna both in Ireland and after the latter's emigration to England range over literary and cultural topics as diverse as African-American spirituals (p. 29), Yoga (pp. 31–3), Buddhism (pp. 89–90), the work of James Joyce (pp. 65–6), the role of translation in the language revival (pp. 52–3, 56–8, 87, 98, 121–2, 125–6, 153, 165), and socialism (p. 139). To deal with these sometimes startling subjects, he applied the same imaginative and flexible approach to the coining of new words that he had brought to his reviews, attributing much of what he thought about the subject to what he had learned from McKenna:

> He would say that, since the style of growth for Irish was not entirely settled as is the style of growth for English, it would not be difficult for us to shape Irish as we wish. His constant complaint was that whatever tendency Irish had toward foreign influences was a tendency toward English influence, and, instead of resisting that, we follow the trail of English as if it were 'the standard for all humanity' (p. 36).[81]

Throughout the book one is aware of how vigorously these two progressive Gaelic intellectuals rejected the stultifying rigidity and lack of imagination that characterised much of what then passed for literary debate in Irish, particularly on the part of those obsessed with their own definitions of *Gaelachas* and *cainnt na ndaoine* (pp. 63–4, 82, 84, 102–4, 122, 176–7). For both of them, the greatest failing among contemporary Gaelic writers was their lack of either thought or cultivated technique. Ó Rinn quotes McKenna on this point:

> It seems to me that writers of Irish are squandering great gifts or good gifts through lack of thought. I imagine them to be like a man who wants to marry a noble woman. When he goes to her to win her for himself, he brings with him, in addition to the full power of his intellect and all the magic of his character, the stubbly beard that has been growing for a week and the collar and handkerchief that have not been washed for three months (p. 107).[82]

McKenna used another startling comparison to make the same point, telling Ó Rinn:

> Thoughts are what we lack most, thoughts and a strong, powerful style; clarity, variety, fire; keeping the reader fully awake and paying attention to the speech. In my opinion, the majority of advertising posters are better as writing than the majority of the classics. Look at them! Direct speech that hits you in the eye and goes into your brain, and stays in your memory, and rings in your dreams, and lures the money out of your pocket (p. 114).[83]

Above all, what was essential for the pair was that Irish have a fully contemporary modern prose literature.

To help would-be writers meet this challenge, Ó Rinn wrote *Peann agus Pár* (Pen and paper) (BÁC: OS, 1940), a practical manual of the writer's craft modelled, as he himself tells us, on books like Flora Klickmann's *The Lure of the Pen*, Basil Hogarth's *The Technique of Novel Writing*, Michael Joseph's *Short Story Writing for Profit* and *How to Write a Short Story*, and G. Lanson's *Conseils sur l'art d'écrire* (Advice on the art of writing). Ó Rinn warned young writers willing to break new ground in Irish that they would face the carping negativism of purists, but he was even more concerned about the lack of modern exemplars and of a tradition of rigorous but sympathetic criticism in the language:

> The work writers of Irish will have to do is harder for the fact that we still have no great modern literature, and therefore they have nothing available to help them like what is available in so many ways for the apprentice writer of English. There is, for example, no one to judge their first efforts (p. 34).[84]

In effect, Ó Rinn was here trying to train the artist to be his or her own first and best, if not only, critic until the arrival of the proper school of Gaelic literary criticism that he himself, McKenna, Béaslaí, and a handful of others were striving to call into being.

In *Mo Chara Stiofán*, Ó Rinn underscores McKenna's awareness that any movement of Gaelic authors would require a more sophisticated and discerning readership, on the principle that 'proper writers' (scríbhneoirí cearta) need 'proper readers' (léitheoirí cearta):

> The reader we want and so crucially need must be trained . . . until he is so good that he will be delighted (conditionally) precisely because of the difficulty involved in what is new: Let him not, O let him never, on pain of mortal sin, let him never on any terms, sniff and say, 'objectionable: hard language'. Let him say, with a loud laugh, 'Thanks be to God, here is something to sharpen our minds;' let him be eager to come to grips with what is new and strange, and hard to understand (pp. 174–6).[85]

Such readers are, of course, rare in every language, and given how small was the audience to begin with for work in Irish, McKenna's project was an ambitious one. The solution he and Ó Rinn envisioned was to start by simply creating readers of any kind by providing in Irish a wide range of subject matter in a wide range of styles and registers. Ó Rinn quotes McKenna in characteristically provocative mode on this topic as he called for

> something far more important at present than any kind of literature that is written with a capital L and that is mentioned with hushed breath, that is, good stuff to read about the things the ordinary civilised people of the twentieth century want to be reading about. Literature is the preserve of gods and academics and in this age what makes a language is more like the language of newspapers, and there must be a good share of nonsense in it, and not magical nonsense, mind, nor the nonsense of superstitions or old country stories, but Garvicery and the like . . . The Irish in which there would only be Dante would damn itself; Charles Garvice is my choice of the two (p. 50).[86]

Ó Rinn returned to this point in *Peann agus Pár*, writing:

> When that blessed word 'literature' is said, many people think first of Homer and Dante and Shakespeare and Dostoevsky. If we had four like those, they would be a splendid gift from God, but alas! stars of their splendour are rarely seen in the depths of the literary sky. As we lament their absence, however, let us ask ourselves whether they are the sort of authors who will clear the road for us and solve our problem. We must admit what everyone knows, namely, that it is not the pre-eminent authors that most people in any country like. If we had a Gaelic Shakespeare, we would need a Gaelic Edgar Wallace also (pp. 7–8).[87]

Ó Rinn's belief that there was a real and immediate need for engaging and even trivial reading material in Irish was fairly widely shared, although not all were quite so enthusiastic about the prospect. For example, writing in the London journal *Guth na nGaedheal* in 1933, Liam Ó Domhnaill was condescending in his assessment of the literary tastes of modern readers:

> They think the fairy legends are foolish and incredible, and at the same time they eagerly read stories that make no sense at all. Most people make use of a book as they would make use of a magic sleep needle – to put themselves to sleep (*Guth na nGaedheal*, 1933, 14).[88]

The majority of Gaels seem, however, to have shared the more open-minded approach of Micheál Breathnach, who wrote in 1922:

> Look for yourself at how swept away the [the young] are by the 'Buffalo Bills' and the 'Sexton Blakes', although there is nothing in them but bad English and no credibility. It would, most likely, be bold of me to recommend to writers of Irish to imitate 'Buffalo' and 'Sexton', but the sooner that is done the better the chance that Irish will triumph over English (*II*, 10/8/22).[89]

In 1935, Ciarán Ua Nualláin, one Gaelic writer who was to produce pioneering work in both humorous essays and detective fiction, called for assistance in the endeavour:

> We are asking too much of the ordinary person and showing that we do not have an understanding of human nature if we ask him to buy and read books for the sole reason that they are in Irish, without asking ourselves whether he would read them if they were in English. It is clear that if he had books in Irish as interesting as books in English are, he would read them (*II*, 6/7/37).[90]

A rather unlikely advocate of diverse recreational reading matter in Irish was Séamus Ó Grianna, who wrote in his 1928 review of *Geantraighe*, Seán O Ciarghusa's collection of comic sketches:

> Until very recently, little was written except for learners of Irish. There must be a bit more progress. Every kind of thing in which people have interest must be written. Stories must be written that will be read as I read *Geantraighe* – sitting and smoking my pipe and not thinking at all about the fact that the stories were written in Irish (*FL*, Oct. 1928, 8).[91]

'Grafán' urged his fellow writers to produce more work of just this kind in a 1932 essay:

> It is reading matter for the public that we want. There is too much discussion of literature, that is if that discussion blinds us with regard to the provision of things that will help make a normal living national language of Irish (*IP*, 22/1/32).[92]

One Gaelic writer who answered this call was Micheál Ó Gríobhtha, who, in the preface to his escapist adventure novel *'Go mBeannuighthear Dhuit:' Eachtra thar Eachtraíbh* ('Hail Mary:' An extraordinary adventure) (BÁC: COÉ, [1925]), claimed he wrote the book to satisfy a friend's request for a Gaelic *Deadwood Dick*. Ó Gríobhtha continued:

> Although it was bold of me to attempt the like, I decided to do my very best to try to create a story in which there would be adventures and a lively narrative, and evil and good; I set out to create a story that a reader would not put down until he

had read half of it. I don't know whether I have succeeded; the reader is the judge (p. 3).[93]

Reviewing the book for *Fáinne an Lae*, 'B. Ní Fh.' pronounced it a success in precisely those terms, claiming that she could not put it down (*FL*, 21/11/25), while 'C. L.' (probably 'Cloch Labhrais', i.e., Seán Ó Ciarghusa), writing in *An Sguab*, stated: 'Without mincing words, the story is a Gaelic "Deadwood Dick"' (*Sguab*, Nov. 1925, 478).[94] Ó Gríobhtha certainly managed to pack plenty of action into the eighty pages of a story that takes his Irish narrator / protagonist from New York City to the gold camps of the Wild West to the mean streets of Rio de Janeiro in a search for a hated enemy. Edification finds its place alongside excitement, however, as the narrator foregoes his long-planned vengeance on hearing his mother say the Hail Mary in an adjacent room and then returns to the Catholic faith from which he had lapsed.[95]

Seán Ó Ciarghusa, the author of the collection so highly praised by Ó Grianna, created a tale every bit as stirring and improbable as Ó Gríobhtha's, but more comical, in his 1930 novel *Onncail Seárlaí* (Uncle Charlie) (BÁC: Muinntir C.S. Ó Fallamhain Teor., i gcomhar le hOS, 1930), in which the blustering title character tells his young nephews about his travels through the Yukon and Dawson City on his way to the North Pole and encounters with terrifying polar bears, villainous sailors, and folk-singing Eskimos.[96]

Another novel with a setting full of adventurous appeal was 'Fionn' Mac Cumhaill's *Sé Dia an Fear is Fearr* (God is the best man) (BÁC: COÉ, [1928]), which, with Seán Óg Ó Caomhánaigh's *Fánaí* (Wanderer) (BÁC: Muinntir Alex Thom agus Comh. Teor., i gcomhar le hOS, 1927) and a fair number of stories for children in *Our Boys*, was among the few literary works from the period set mostly in the American West.[97] Mac Cumhaill takes his young protagonist Naos Óg from his native Donegal Gaeltacht to Scotland and thence to America for adventures with cowboys and near death from thirst in the desert. As in Ó Gríobhtha's *Go mBeannuighthear Duit*, the story ends in exemplary fashion with Naos a priest visiting the grave of a former sweetheart who had died a nun in a remote western convent.

Ó Caomhánaigh's *Fánaí*, the story of an Irishman living and working in North Dakota in the second decade of the twentieth century, is of special interest as the only novel in Irish to run foul of state censorship in this period. A detailed account of the controversy occasioned by the novel on its first publication by An Gúm as a book suitable for use in secondary schools has been provided by Tadhg Ó Dubhshláine in his essay 'Scéal Úirscéil: *Fánaí*, Seán Óg Ó Caomhánaigh, 1927' (The story of a novel: *Fánaí* by Seán Óg Ó Caomhánaigh, 1927). What is most noteworthy about this whole episode is not, however, the intervention of the censors, but rather how little the novel was changed as a result of that intervention, and on how many of the rigorous and detailed objections raised by Dublin's diocesan censor An Gúm followed the author's wishes in the end.[98] Alan Titley has dismissed *Fánaí* as primarily 'an adventure novel softened by a flaccid love story' (úrscéal eachtraíochta arna mhaothú ag scéal bog ballnascúil grá),[99] and most of the plotline consists of a straightforward blend of far-fetched adventure and sentimental romance. The protagonist, Seán Ó Lonargáin, falls in love with the beautiful daughter of his ranch-owner boss, marries her in secret, is treacherously and savagely beaten by his enemies, loses his memory of all that happened before the beating, undergoes an operation that brings him to himself again, and is able to see his enemies punished before he is reunited with his now landed wife and their young son. The scenes of courtship and kissing that so troubled the censor at the time of the book's publication are almost comically tame now, particularly if we remember that one result of that courtship is that Seán is able to convert his beloved to Catholicism! There is, however, one scene that remains troubling and earns Ó Caomhánaigh the distinction of being among the first to introduce the question of sexual violence into Gaelic fiction. A villainous foreman whose brusque proposal of marriage has been refused by the woman Seán later marries, attacks the woman who has turned him down:

> There was no relenting in the struggle between them. He felt no shame. He was not used to women refusing him . . . With all the strength she had, she struck him in the teeth with her two fists. He just smiled sarcatically at her efforts. He made another rush to subdue her. She screamed (p. 19).[100]

Fortunately her scream brings Seán, whose presence saves her from what she calls 'a degrading evil fate' (drochaoide úiríseal) (p. 21).

A few Gaelic writers attempted another genre popular with young readers at the time, and one whose adventures required no exotic settings. Imported periodicals had made Irish children familiar with the stories of derring-do and high principle set in English public schools, and some Irish authors thought the genre could and should be Gaelicised. Indeed Pearse himself had taken the lead here with his serialised story in English, 'The Wandering Hawk' (1915–16). There were a good number of such stories in Irish in the bilingual magazine *Our Girls / Ár gCailíní*, which offered a prize for the best story received in several categories, one of which was 'school stories' (*Our Girls*, Mar. 1931, 136). Judging from the number of works of this kind published in the journal's short run of a little over two years, this sort of thing had a genuine appeal for the readership. Curiously, the Christian Brothers magazine *Our Boys* did not run such stories, relying instead on a regular supply of patriotic historical tales, detective stories, and westerns in both Irish and English.

Schoolboy readers of Irish could, however, follow the adventures of their own sort in Tadhg Ó Murchadha's *An Cliathán Clé* (The left wingback) (BÁC:

OS, 1932). Set in a fashionable Dublin boarding school, the novel offers the usual mix of mischief, athletic prowess, and high-spirited but principled 'manliness'. We have a night-time rush on a motorcycle through the streets of Dublin, the defeat and winning over of the school bully, and a deep underlying affection for the school and what it represents. There are also, however, a few surprises. First of all, while the protagonist is pictured reading Pádraig Ó Siochfhradha's *Jimín Mháire Thaidhg*, his favourite fare is English school stories, and not much else. Second, of all the masters, the most stiff and least popular is the Irish teacher. And third and most striking, while there is a passing reference to hurling, the game of preference and status for these young Gaels is rugby, although track is also popular. In fact, one could argue that the only thing really Irish about the book is the language in which it is written, a point made by 'Léightheoir Comhthrom' in his review for *Timthire Chroidhe Naomhtha Íosa*: 'There is scarcely any trace of nationality to be seen in the spirit of the students in the story' (Is beag má tá rian náisiúntachta le feiscint sa sgéal i meon na macléighinn) (*TCNÍ*, Aug. 1932, 188).

Several writers at this time expressed their interest in seeing detective stories become a Gaelic genre. For example, in a previously cited essay on the need for light reading in Irish, Ciarán Ua Nualláin gave pride of place to stories of this kind. Having noted the enormous popularity of the genre in Ireland, he continued: 'You would, therefore, think that there would be hundreds of these being written in Irish. You would think that to lure the public to read books in Irish there would be more of them than of any other sort' (*II*, 6/7/37).[101] Two years later, the *Irish Press* published the texts of several radio talks on detective fiction by Liam S. Ó Brolcháin, prefacing the first instalment with the following comments:

> An Gúm is translating detective stories into Irish – and no two people are of the same mind whether this effort should be praised or blamed. There are, however, few people who understand the history of the detective story or who have thought a bit about its characteristics, even though the story of detection is the kind of literature in greatest demand at present (*IP*, 8/5/39).[102]

A good number of mystery and detective stories, translated and original, were made available to readers of Irish at this time. And while of the full-length books virtually all were translations of writers like Arthur Conan Doyle, A. E. W. Mason, and F. W. Crofts, Gaelic storywriters put their own squad of sleuths to work on the streets of Dublin. The first to cultivate the genre in this period was An tAthair Seoirse Mac Clúin, who created a duo reminiscent of Holmes and Watson with his detective (braitheadóir) Séamas de Barra and his narrator / sidekick Antoine Ó Briain. The pair first appeared in 'Díoghaltas na hOidhche' (The vengeance of the night) in *An Sguab* in

October 1922; and returned to the same journal in 'Cionntach?' (Guilty?) (Jan.–Feb. 1923); 'An Diamond Buidhe' (The yellow diamond), this one told in the third person (Apr. 1923); 'Seósán Mac Seaca, Duine-Uasal' (Seósán Mac Seaca, gentleman) (Aug. 1923); 'An Guthán Bréagach' (The fake telephone) (Nov. 1923); and 'Fé Sholas an Lasáin Sin' (By the light of that match) (Dec. 1923). De Barra solves his crimes through acute observation and astounding Sherlockian deductive reasoning that amazes all concerned, particularly the official police investigator Mac Clúin provided as an appropriately obtuse foil.

Micheál Ó Gríobhtha's gumshoe in the three stories that comprise *Lorgaireacht* (Detection) (BÁC: Muinntir Alex Thom agus Comh., i gomhar le hOS, 1927) is Toirdhealbhach Ó Briain, who wins the confidence of and is hired by the head of the Gárda detective division, Oisín Mac an Iarla. Like Mac Clúin, Ó Gríobhtha was obviously influenced by the Holmes stories, as his detective collects seemingly trivial clues, breaks codes, and resorts to disguises. Of interest in the stories is the emphasis on the foreign origin or non-Free State residence of most of the criminals – Scots, returned Yanks, and, in the final episode, Northerners – and the care taken to recreate a detailed and credible Dublin setting. In fact, it was the very success with which Ó Gríobhtha reproduced his English models in Irish that troubled one reviewer, who complained:

> The Irish in it is good, but nevertheless I never read a more foreign story. There is nothing in it but how unfortunate people are intensely pursued by law enforcement people: but it isn't even good as a detective story because many things happen in the story that do not happen in the real world. It is a shilling shocker that a school boy would find in the shops in England any day of the week (*An Phoblacht*, 21/4/28).[103]

Two serialised detective stories about private investigators also appeared in magazines during this period. The longer of them by far was the anonymous 'Sgéal Nua Bleachtaire / Eachtra an Oileáin' (A new detective story / The adventure of the island) that ran in the *Cork Weekly Examiner* from July to Oct. 1931. The other, 'Lorgaire i nGan Fhios Dó' (A detective unbeknownst to him) by 'Díoltóir Brat', was published in three short parts in *An Gaedheal* from August to Oct. 1936. The hero of An tAthair Gearóid Ó Nualláin's 'An Sgathán' (The mirror) is the Gárda detective Muiris Ó Mathghamhna, who, in a dramatic confrontation worthy of Hercule Poirot, unmasks the villainy of an English criminal. Much of the deductive reasoning in the story hinges on the criminal's misreading of a clock he consults by looking at its reflection in a mirror (*IMN*, 1928, 51–62). The same author's 'An Taidhbhreamh' (The dream) is set in Paris and has no Irish connection at all. There is, however, a fair bit of anti-semitic stereotyping in this tale of a wealthy Jewish agent in the service of Germany whose house the French police allow to be robbed by a thief who has helped them to uncover the agent's treachery (*IMN*, 1931, 9–32). Irish policemen are the heroes of N. A. Icerg's 'Muileann Dé' (God's mill) (*IMN*, 1932, 14–23), where the murderer is an Ulsterman hiding in Cork; in Art Ó Riain's 'Scéal an Cheannphuirt' (The superintendant's story) (*Bonaventura*, Spring 1938, 50–6), where the adventure takes place for the most part in Belgium; and of Gárda P. Tóibín's 'An Dúnmharbhughadh Bréagach' (The fake murder) (*GR*, Mar. 1939, 479–82), in which a man falsely accused of murder is absolved through clever, detailed, and dogged police work that reveals how the 'murdered' man had committed suicide by means of a complex mechanical device in such a way as to implicate a hated rival in love. Pádhraic Ó Domhnalláin's mystery story 'Cérbh é an Gaduidhe?' (Who was the thief?) was set on a train journey from Conamara to Dublin in 1829 (*IP*, 12/6/39).[104]

Detective stories were also a staple of the bilingual magazine *Our Boys* (including its Irish-language supplements *Ár mBuachaillí* and *An Gaedheal Óg*). Schoolboy sleuths are also the heroes of Liam Domonaí's 'Taidhbhsí na Seana-Chaisleáin' (The ghosts of the old castle) in the school magazine *The Rock*, a story in which the boys help the Gárdaí catch foreign murderers hiding in Ireland (*Rock*, Summer, 1937, n.p.). Detective stories were one of the prize categories in the contest run by *Our Girls*, but few of the magazine's readers seem to have been interested in the genre.

The two most substantial Gaelic efforts in this direction occurred at the end of the period with Ciarán Ua Nualláin's *Oidhche i nGleann na nGealt* (A night in the Glen of the Madmen) (BÁC: OS, 1939) and Seoirse Mac Liam's *An Dorus do Plabadh* (The door that was slammed) (BÁC: OS, 1940), a novel which, despite its publication date, has an author's preface dated December 1937 in which Mac Liam tells how he came into the 'facts' of this story. Ua Nualláin's novel is a rather dark study of rural greed and arranged marriage as a source of economic strife within families. His detective, Parthalán Mac Mórna, manages to thwart a man's intricate and long meditated plot to kill his own brother to prevent being ousted from the family homestead on that brother's marriage. Playing on local superstitions involving Gleann na nGealt, the would-be killer also plans to pervert profound religious convictions by pretending to be at death's door in order to send his brother for a priest and then ambush him in a lonely spot in the glen. Covering all contingencies, he painstakingly prepares, in advance, an insanity defence for himself. Mac Mórna was to return in the four stories that make up Ua Nualláin's collection *Eachtraí Pharthaláin Mhic Mórna* (The adventures of Parthalán Mac Mórna) (BÁC: OS, 1944).

Set in 1912, *An Doras do Plabadh* features another Holmesian investigator, Peadar Ó Dubhghaill. Throughout the novel, Mac Liam gives us detailed and specific references to the Dublin geography and street scene, and discusses urban affairs with no trace of linguistic self-consciousness.[105] Among the locales his sleuth visits is the city morgue, a setting sketched with clinical precision and detachment (pp. 169–70). While Mac Liam's hero is very much in the tradition of the outsider willing to play fast and loose with police procedure in time of need, he also shows an unusual awareness of official restraints and sensitivities (p. 205). At the novel's close, the coroner's jury gives a judgement the detective – and we readers – know to be inaccurate, but having himself unravelled all of the conflicting and at times agonising motives of those involved, Ó Dubhghaill decides that, in this case at least, the truth is best left unspoken until years have passed and those involved have died (p. 295). *An Doras do Plabadh* is a competent and engaging mystery / suspense novel, still one of the finest of the kind we have in Irish.

A few writers explored the comic potential of the crime genre. Gearóid Ó Lochlainn's 1923 play *Na Gaduithe* (The thieves) (BÁC: ODFR, 1935) depicts two would-be Sherlocks attempting to pin several bank robberies on two guests staying at a hotel. After a series of farcical misunderstandings, it is revealed that the two 'guests' are themselves investigators, and a young woman one of them is courting is a police officer. One of the real villains turns out to be a man masquerading as a German professor come to Ireland to study Irish and collect folklore.[106] The crime in Pádraig Ó Bróithe's 'An Péas-Ghaduidhe ó Londain / Imtheacht an Ama' (The policeman-thief from London / The passage of time) is initially ascribed to a pickpocket from London, but turns out to be the result of confusion on the part of the Irish protagonist (*II*, 14/11/23). In Art Ó Riain's 'Seóirse ar an dTóir' (George on the trail), a young man who explicitly identifies himself with Sherlock Holmes overhears a conversation that he interprets as the plotting of a murder. After wasting a good bit of time, effort, and money, he learns that what he had heard was entirely innocuous (*Inis Fáil*, Dec. 1928, 13–19). The hapless detective in Tomás P. Ó Siadhail's 'Imtheachta "an Tec"' (The adventures of the 'Tec') is a schoolboy whose obsession with crime fiction is manipulated with farcical effect by his classmates (*Rockwell Annual*, Aug. 1932, 47–50). Brian Ua Nualláin ('Myles na gCopaleen') created his own quirky Holmes in 'Eachtraí Shearluic' (The adventures of Sherlock). Myles's Holmes, who plays Irish tunes on his fiddle, is consulted by a client claiming to be Oisín in search of the Fianna. Recognising Dr Moriarty in disguise, Holmes and Watson bundle him off to the Grangegorman mental hospital in a turf cart, only to be themselves institutionalised as the story ends (*Blather*, Dec. 1934, 77). In one of his very first literary efforts, 'Árdúghadh Céime "Speisialta"' (A 'special' promotion), An Gárda Pádraig Ua Maoileoin narrated the comic tale of how Gárdaí capture an international criminal wanted throughout Europe (*GR*, Apr. 1939, 577–8).

'Marbhán' by 'Conán' is a detective story set in the year 2000 and dealing with the attempts of an underground royalist group to subvert the political system of an Irish-speaking 32-county Irish Republic, attempts thwarted by the protagonist of the title (*CT*, 25/3/33). This was by no means the only Gaelic work set in an imagined future. Seán Ó Ciarghusa's play *Díbeartaigh ó Shean-Shasana* (Outcasts from old England) takes place in 2025, when the Irish language has been so successfully restored that a group has been founded to revive English in Ireland.[107] León Ó Broin's comic one-act play *Sprid na Sean-Laoch* (The spirit of the old heroes) (*Sguab*, Nov. 1925, 467–9) opens in 1975 in 'a remote corner of the Phoenix Park' (cúinne iargcúlta de Pháirc an Fhionnuisge) and involves a conversation between statues of Lord Nelson, Daniel O'Connell, and Fr Theobald Mathew, and two French-speaking county council workers! The statues, which have been removed from O'Connell Street to the Park, complain about their demotion and about the general decline in Dublin's social mores. At the end, the workers demolish the statue of Nelson.[108] In Pádraic Ó Conaire's 1926 story 'Páipéar a Fristadh [*sic*] i mBosga / 1926 agus 1966' (A paper that was found in a box / 1926 and 1966), a public official reads a copy of a 1926 *Connacht Tribune* to citizens of Galway in 1966, all of whom are astounded by the conditions in which their ancestors had lived (*CT*, 29/5/26). The title of Brian Ua Nualláin's comic 'Díoghaltas ar Ghallaibh 'sa Bhliadhan 2032!' (Vengeance on the English in the year 2032!) is perhaps self-explanatory. Myles takes us to an entirely Irish-speaking Dublin where his narrator is able to dupe an English tourist into delivering an abusive tirade in Irish thinking he is just asking directions (*IP*, 18/1/32).

An Irish-speaking Dublin of the future is also the setting for another of Ua Nualláin's comic stories, 'Teacht agus Imtheacht Sheán Bhuidhe / Iarsma an Bhéarla / Cuireadh ar Phlátaí Ceoil é!' (The coming and going of John Bull / The remnants of the English language / Let it be put on record), in which a search of all Ireland is able to turn up no more than a handful of old men able to speak a heavily dialecticised brand of English (*IP*, 13/6/32). Seosamh Ó Torna's 'Cheithre Bhuille an Chluig' (Four o'clock) offers a picture of a different sort of Gaelic utopia. A man returns to Dublin after a year in Africa to discover 'a new world in Ireland' (saoghal nua in Éirinn). There is no crime, no vice, no deception or trickery, no smoking or drinking, no police force or army. The only tax inspectors are at work to ensure that people don't overpay the government, and Mountjoy Jail is now a monastery. There is, however, an underground movement of the erstwhile wealthy and powerful attempting to reintroduce vice for their own financial benefit. The startled narrator learns that the whole world is now similarly reformed, all being explained by a recent discovery that Einstein was wrong, that space is straight, not curved, so people should be straight, not crooked. In the end, all anticlimactically turns out to have been a dream, but Ó Torna's story, with its nicely detailed descriptions of the new Dublin, is one of the more imaginative and engaging Gaelic stories of this period (*Bonaventura*, Spring 1938, 94–5).

It is certainly of interest that none of these stories of the future is at all concerned with fantasies of scientific or technological progress, focusing instead on questions of cultural and social evolution.[109] Science fiction in the generally accepted sense was nowhere near as popular among the Gaels, whether translators or authors of original fiction, as was the crime / mystery genre. We have only An tAthair Micheál Mac Craith's brief sketch 'Cuairt ar an nGealaigh' (A visit to the moon) (*FL*, 17/3/23), his slightly more substantial 'Eachtra Fuirne' (The adventure of a group of people) (*FL*, 15/12/23 and 15/3/24), Art Ó Riain's 'Aisling' (A vision) (*FL*, Oct. 1927, 6), and Seosamh Ó Torna's 'Duinneall' (*Bonaventura*, Spring 1938, 70–5). Ó Torna's story is by far the most interesting of these. His protagonist is a country boy who, having come to the city to work with machines, becomes increasingly mechanical himself ('Duinneall is a compound of *duine* [person] and *inneall* [machine]):

> As a result of his constant contact with every kind of machine, something I hardly dare mention happened. A damnable transformation happened in the man's heart and mind. His free will slipped away. His intelligence hardened. The talent for poetry ebbed and the light of faith and love that he had darkened. Mechanism overwhelmed the humanity in him. As the Gaelic qualities were submerged, the characteristics of the machine took their place. At last, one could not believe he was either a person or a machine, but rather something in between.[110]

And, according to Ó Torna's narrator, this new hybrid is becoming ever more numerous:

> The customs of your ancestors will be crushed under foot by fashionable Duinneall. Drama and music will be forbidden you by mechanical Duinneall. Statesman Duinneall will take away your freedom. The pick of the Duinnealls – Duinneall the Soldier – will take out your guts. And to make things even worse, Duinneall the Philosopher will not leave you your spiritual soul.[111]

'Aisling' was not Ó Riain's only attempt at this genre. His 1927 novella *An Tost* (BÁC: Muinntir Alex Thom i gcomhar le hOS, 1927) is divided into five sections, set in 1914, 1916, 1921, 1938 and 1975. In the two sections set in the future, the protagonist is the Irish government's 'Minister for Air Travel' (aire um Aer-Thaisdeal) to whose lot it falls to defend the nation against the combined threat of England and Japan, eager to occupy the country for strategic purposes. In the period just before hostilities erupt, the Irish president declares neutrality:

> This war has nothing to do with us . . . and we want nothing to do with it. We are announcing to the whole world, and particularly to the countries that are fighting, that we are not and will not be on any side as long as we are not attacked. If Irish people have any sympathy with any side or if they hate any side, it is best for them not to express that sympathy or hatred. A closed mouth, zealous work, and trust in God – that is my advice to you (p. 33).[112]

Soon, however, Ireland is driven to surrender its neutrality for an alliance with 'the two Americas' (an dá America), a move that fails to stave off an invasion by the English and Japanese. After the occupation of the country and the torture of the heroic protagonist with a laser-like device, the nation is liberated by a joint Irish and American rescue operation flown in in enormous American aircraft ('oll-longa Ponncánacha'). Having survived to see the rescue effected, the protagonist dies from the abuse he has suffered. Ó Riain's tale is noteworthy for, among other things, its creation of the kind of futuristic devices that are the stock-in-trade of much science fiction – the laser gun, the huge aircraft, and coin-operated pay radios on the street.[113]

There were also, in addition to the westerns and the swashbuckling tales like *Go mBeannuightear Duit* and *Onncail Seárlaí* noted above, a handful of Gaelic stories with unexpectedly exotic settings. Liam Ó Rinn's 'Alimec' (*UIrman*, 9/6/23) is an Aladdin-type story in which an Arabic shepherd's discovery of a magic ring leads to a career of adventure and wealth before the man learns that there is more to life than money, status, or power. An tAthair Gearóid Ó Nualláin's 'An Hata' (The hat) is a comic story of lovers' misadventures set for the most part in the south of Germany, where the Irish protagonist has gone to learn about the publishing industry.[114] A grimmer note pervades Pádraic Ó Conaire's 'Beirt ar Oileán' (Two men on an island) (*FL*, 21/6/24), in which sailors off the coast of Australia find a note in a bottle telling of the travails of a shipwrecked pair. The letter's author says he has come to hate his partner and believes he will murder him unless they are rescued soon. The ship heads for the location indicated in the letter, and arrives to find a lunatic sitting beside the grave of his comrade. Shipwreck, treachery, and violence also provided the plotline for Ó Conaire's 'Sgéal ó "Spágach"' (A story from 'Flat Foot') and its continuation 'Ar an Muir' (On the sea) (*Óglach*, 25/4 and 9/5/25). In Diarmuid Ó Duibhne's 'Micheál Mac Coill, Mairnéalach' (Micheál Mac Coill, Sailor) (*Standard*, 26/1/29), a shipwrecked man and his friend fight off hostile natives to escape from a volcanic island in the Indian Ocean. Africa is the setting for at least six stories in Irish in this period: 'An Gaedhilgeóir' (The Irish speaker) (*Róimh*, Summer 1925, 21–2), the tale of a heroic missionary by 'Cathal;' 'Gaisge an Oifigigh Óig' (The heroism of the young officer) (*Óglach*, 16/8/24) by Pádraic Ó Conaire, a tale of how an officer in the French Foreign Legion finds his courage in a bottle of champagne buried in the sand; 'An Fad-Radharcán' (The telescope) (*TCNÍ*, Mar. 1929, 3–5) by An tAthair Raghnall Mac Siubhlaigh, another story of the missions, this one a comic account of how a priest tricks a native chief into sparing his life by performing 'miracles' with a telescope; 'Duine Uasal ar Lorg Eolais / Eachtra a Bhain leis' (A gentleman seeking knowledge / An adventure that happened to him), in which an African chief proves himself more honourable than his European counterparts (*II*, 12/5/30); 'Díoghaltas Upthacha' (Upthaca's revenge) by Seán Mac Gabhann (*Lóchrann*, Mar. 1930, 7–8), in which an English big-game hunter is cursed by an African servant he has insulted and is later killed when a hippopotamus tramples his tent during the night; and Seán Ó Cuirrín's 'Beirt Dhéiseach' (Two men from the Decies), in which an Irish emigrant living in South Africa joins a pagan cult, but is eventually restored to his senses and his faith through memories of home with its Gaelic virtues.[115] Additional Gaelic works with far-flung settings include 'An Clog Greanta ar an gClabhar / Scéal a Bhain leis' (The engraved clock on the mantlepiece / A story concerning it) by 'Aonghus', in which a man in Germany is threatened by wolves (*II*, 9/12/22); 'Mac Seoin ar Stailc thar Lear / Turas Traenach' (Johnson on strike abroad / A train journey) by 'S. de B.' (*II*, 13/8/23); León Ó Broin's 'An Rún' (The secret) (1932), a story of embezzlement and murder that takes place in Vienna;[116] An tAthair Casáin's 'An Seirbhíseach Fóghanta Dílis' (The good, faithful servant), an edifying tale of religious rebirth set in Italy;[117] and Gearóid Mac Gofraidh's 'Ar Lorg na Saoirse' (In search of freedom) (*Gaedheal Óg*, 25/3/39), an adventure story for boys set in Siberia and dealing with Russian politics. Freezing cold is also the challenge for the hero of 'Reoidhte, Dar Mh'Anam!' (Frozen, by my soul) by 'An M. O.' (*Standard*, 1/8/31), although his near death experience in the Arctic turns out to have been only a dream. The Irish protagonist of Micheál Ua h-Eibhrín's comic 'Cúis Báinidhe do Naomh Peadar' (A cause of rage for St Peter) (*Standard*, 30/3/29) wanders even farther afield, tending the Golden Gate while St. Peter takes a break!

Other Gaelic writers favoured esoteric themes over exotic settings to provide their readers with a change of pace from the standard Gaeltacht fare. For example, ghosts are central characters in Gearóid de Paor's Dublin story 'Ar Phort na Canálach' (On the canal bank) (*Nation*, 2/11/29) and in Pádraig Ó Bróithe's play *Réidhteach na Ceiste* (The answer to the question) (BÁC: ODFR, 1931), in which a young woman being forced into a marriage by her mother dies of a heart attack when she is urged to elope by the man she really loves, a man we later learn has died elsewhere at the very moment he was supposedly speaking with her.[118] Micheál Mac Liammóir's story 'Ceól Éigipteach' (Egyptian music) (*Sguab*, June 1923, 177–80) deals with a young man's eerie vision of ancient Egypt experienced in a Grafton Street cafe, while his 'Aonghus Ó Cruadhlaoich' (*FL*, 15/12/23) is a tale about the demonic possession of a young Irish intellectual and mystic.[119] A more whimsical treatment of visions of the Orient was offered by Piaras Béaslaí in 'Tram an Taidhrimh' (The dream tram) (*Branar*, May 1925, 105–12), in which a prosaic Dublin clerk dreams of lording it over a harem in Teheran only to find he has fallen asleep on the Rathmines tram. Spiritualism, parapsychology, and even a seance figure in Gearóid Ó Nualláin's story 'An Sprid' (The spirit), whose main character is a Dublin professor and student of Madame Blavatsky.[120] Seosamh Mac Grianna's 'Dhá Chroí Cloiche' (Two hearts of stone) (*Humanitas*, June 1930, 11–14) is a parable of cowardly lovers and the power of art to reveal truths, however bitter.[121] A professor's fascination with hypnotism is the subject of Micheál Ó Cionnfhaolaidh's comic 'Cleas na Meisirearachta (The hypnotism trick) (Dundalk *Examiner*, 12/11 to 3/12/32), while B. N. Lóiste's 'Cleasaidheacht na gCos' (The trickery of the feet) (*IR*, July 1935, 520–3) is an interesting account of the delusions of a man awakening from an anaesthetic after surgery.

It was, however, neither murder nor mysticism, the enigmas of the elsewhere or the elsewhen, that many Gaels were keenest to read about in their own language. For the residents of cities and towns who had learned Irish and the many native speakers who now made their homes in places like Dublin, Cork, Galway or even London, these rather ordinary urban places they knew best were the real new frontier for Gaelic prose. Needless to say, most were also aware that, as with any pioneering venture, writing in Irish about city life would involve coming to terms with some very real problems, problems underscored by Cearbhall Ua Dálaigh in a 1931 essay on 'Nua-Litridheacht na Gaedhilge, 1920–1930:'

> We can, perhaps, write novels that will deal with the life of the Gaeltacht today, but it is obvious that many of the books that deal with the life of the city will fail altogether. It is a fact that in the case of the novel the virtue and the power of the book are firmly bound up with the speech of the people themselves. And since it so happens that the people of the cities have up to now not condescended to conduct their affairs in Irish, it would not be possible that what authors write will ring true (*CB*, June 1931, 609–10).[122]

Compounding this very real linguistic difficulty was a fairly widespread ideological distrust of the urban condition, a naive ruralist bias rooted in part in the romantic nationalism of nineteenth century Europe by which the Irish movement had been so predictably and profoundly influenced. We find again and again throughout the 1920s and 1930s the same kind of formulaic denunciations of city life that had been common since the beginning of the Gaelic Revival and that of course figured so prominently in Éamon de Valera's famous 1943 St Patrick's Day broadcast. Indeed in a 1932 essay entitled 'Ar

Ais chun na bhFearann' (Back to the land), 'Uíbh-Ráthach' anticipated both de Valera's concern and his rural utopianism:

> The ambition that the young people have in this new civilisation of ours is extraordinary . . . The result is there to be seen, the towns and the cities are growing, but it is obvious that it is not a healthy growth . . . When Gaels once again have the lands of their ancestors, and have the local manufactures going, and our people have a single culture – true *Gaelachas* – then God's blessing will be on us and his hand will be aiding us (*ACS*, 20/2/32).[123]

For those Gaels suspicious of the city, among its greatest dangers was its dreadful, disorienting flux, bustle and chaos, a point underscored by 'Deoraidhe' in an essay on London in UCG's *University Annual*:

> All the people, young and old, coming and going without stop or pause. Everyone having his own business, the light of battle in the eyes of the men and the women. For it seems that there is a great bloodless battle going on always in their minds and in their hearts . . . Even the little children cannot help being old before their time; the light deserts their young eyes, and the laughter their poor hearts, for the great city, like a merciless giant, is always around them and its discordant roar is in their ears (*University Annual*, 1922–3, 6).[124]

Aodh de Blácam developed this idea in near apocalyptic terms in 1935:

> We see the European urban civilisation going down to-day in corruption of body and mind, in merciless warfare, and in unbelief. It is the price of a wrong philosophy, a wrong set of values. Only 'green' Europe, the peasant lands behind the big cities, promises to live on after the ruin . . . The Gaelic civilisation, with its princes who were just strong farmers, its proud houses that were just great farmhouses (like that of Odysseus in Ithaca) was overthrown, but the race holds to the old idea still; it is not spoilt yet (*CA*, 1935, 257).

Even those Gaelic writers most fascinated by the excitement, diversity and potential for innovation that the city represented could on occasion seek relief from its loneliness, alienation, and transience in comforting stereotypes. For example, in his later years Pádraic Ó Conaire came increasingly to sing the praises of a vagabond life in the open air in contrast to the stifling regimentation he saw imposed on those living in cities. That this was not just a romantic conceit to generate engaging – and marketable – newspaper columns is clear from the following ideas for further development jotted down in one of his notebooks at the time: 'The Census / Showing the wretched condition of the country. I'm not thinking of the size of the population, but of the emigration to the town and the life there. The decay of the human being in the city. / Specialisation.'[125] Seosamh Mac Grianna, whose many unresolved conflicts were the source of both his creative impulse and his continuing contemporaneity,[126] was particularly ambivalent about urban life. While, as we will see, he wrote a good deal about the city and even at one point proclaimed himself a Dubliner (*Leader*, 19/5/34), he could also speak as an unreconstructed, even bigoted ruralist. For example, in his 1936 essay on Ó Conaire, he discusses in lurid terms the effect of life in London on the young man newly arrived from Conamara:

> And the person who went through London . . . through the smoke and the fog that challenge the glorious sun – through thin, gloomy, silent people with no flesh and blood on their bones nor thought in their minds; the person who saw the great river that once had water in it and a shine on its surface – the person who saw it and it thick with filth and the air above it thick with filth . . . the person who saw deference for the law and neglect of heritage – the person who saw adoration of the deed and contempt for the mind that enhances the deed; to make a long story short, the person who was in London understands the mental anguish that does not find peace until the grass of the grave gives it peace.[127]

He returned to this theme the following year in *An Bhreatain Bheag*, claiming that the Celts – among whom he included the French – built better cities than did the English, but that the English were more at home in the urban setting than were the Celts. It was, however, in *Mo Bhealach Féin*, through the symbol of a pigeon trapped in an urban boarding-house that he most memorably expressed his contempt for the constrictions of city life:

> One night as I was going up to bed, thinking deeply, I found a pigeon perched above my window. It was like a messenger from another world, an expansive world in which there were shadows and danger, a world that would lure you like a music you would hear both far from you and near to you, the world of the fairy host . . . Perhaps it was nature, perhaps it was nurture, but the first thing I did was to make an attempt to catch that pigeon. That was when the room felt confined. It was so confined that the pigeon would have smashed his bones to pieces in it had I not opened the window. It gave a long swoop over across the street . . . That long swoop that was as noble as a wave has stayed in my mind ever since and a lump of sorrow with it (p. 15).[128]

Gaels suspicious of the city dwelt on the old paradox of the cold impersonality of a place in which so many persons made their lives. Describing the citizens of Washington DC in his story 'Draoidheacht na Gaedhilge,' Tadhg Saor Ó Séaghdha wrote: 'They often had my head spinning from watching them going by; and you would never ever hear one of them greeting another. Another thing I noticed also was that none of them wanted to smile.'[129] In his 1937 novel *Mian na Marbh*, Tadhg Ó Rabhartaigh depicted Glasgow through the eyes of a Gaeltacht emigrant as a place devoid of any meaningful community despite its superficial social opportunities:

> The place was alive and busy with people and all of them in a hurry, coming and going every which way. All kinds of people were here, from the greyhaired person to the child, each one with his own troubles. Young boys and girls passing Cathal, talking and laughing and joking . . . It would be nice to be home tonight . . . and wouldn't it be nice to be listening to his mother's pleasant conversation, instead of to this terrible noise roaring in his ears from morning to midnight! (pp. 78–9).[130]

Nor was Dublin any more congenial, as Pádhraic Ó Domhnalláin stressed in his 1935 essay 'In Ospidéal' (In hospital), in which he wrote of a sick friend: 'I didn't know that he was sick at all. But your next-door neighbour could be at death's door, perhaps, in Dublin, and you wouldn't know it. There is no aloofness like the aloofness of Dublin!'[131] And similar descriptions of town or city as a bleak and alien place can be found in novels as diverse as Ó Grianna's *Caisleáin Óir* (p. 174); Tóibín's *An Rábaire Bán* (pp. 46–7, 127–8), where the cities in question include Cork and Waterford; Ó Ruadháin's *Pádhraic Mháire Bhán* (p. 251); Mac Maoláin's *Éan Corr* (pp. 82, 181); and his *Iolar agus Sionnach* (pp. 16–17), where the city is eighteenth-century Paris.

Reviewing Aindrias Ó Baoighill's novel *An Dílidhe* (The orphan), an anonymous critic claimed that one of the book's virtues was that it painted an accurate picture of the psychological difficulties urban life caused those coming to the city from rural areas. 'C.' wrote: 'The author describes well life in the city and how lonely the man from the country often is there' (*Lóchrann*, Apr. 1931, 4).[132] There was a fairly widespread consensus at the time that if the city was an unwholesome environment for its natives, it was a particularly dangerous place for the growing number of country and Gaeltacht people migrating there in the illusory hope of greater economic and social opportunities. Moreover, as An tAthair Pádraig Mac Giolla Cheara argued, most of this suffering was in vain, for the promises of a more prosperous and fulfilling life in the city were rarely realised:

> The crowds are silent in Dublin, and there is not a street corner on which you can stand without meeting men and women begging. It seems to me that the country people are much given to coming to the city, and that is a great pity. If they are poor in the country, there is seven times more poverty ahead of them if they are left on the street of the town relying on charity (*Dundalk Examiner*, 27/2/32).[133]

Given such a view of what the city could do to naive country people, especially those from the Gaeltacht, one can hardly be surprised at the uncompromising position espoused by Maoghnus Ó Domhnaill in a 1931 editorial in *An Claidheamh Soluis*. Writing of rural people, he proclaimed:

> They should be kept far away from the cities because the cities make puny, worthless creatures of them. The best of the country people are in the Gaeltacht . . . The country people should be protected from the cities, and we should start with the Gaeltacht (*ACS*, 12/12/31).[134]

Father Dinneen, despite a strong ruralist bias, tried to be more objective in his assessment of the city. For example, writing in 1927 on 'An Tuaith nó an Chathair mar Ionad Machtnaimh' (The country or the city as a place for thought), he argued that the confusing diversity and bustle of urban life precluded serious meditation on the human condition:

> In the city, the crowds of people are going this way and that; every person having his own worries. There is every sort of person there: the poor person, the rich person, fools, sensible people, cheats, honest folk. A person would think that it would be easier to think deeply about the human race and himself in particular. But that is not how it is. The crowds go past, but you do not understand their affairs and you never will.

What the city does provide, however, is the essential raw material and intellectual resources for such meditation in a more conducive setting: 'It is a good and profitable thing that there are cities; but one should on occasion abandon the city and get away from its noise' (*FL*, Dec. 1927, 3).[135] In the same year, Dinneen could pay fulsome tribute to the decency and friendliness of Dubliners: 'The people of Dublin are not surpassed by those of any other city for honesty, for civility, for kindness' (*Leader*, 29/10/27).[136]

Others took a wryer view of this hackneyed town / country dichotomy. In Máiréad Ní Ghráda's 1939 story 'Sos Comhraic' (Truce), an IRA volunteer from Dublin rhapsodises about the beauties of nature, only to be warned by a country colleague to cease his 'constant babbling' (síor-ghligínteacht) lest he fall into a boghole.[137] In Pádhraic Ó Domhnalláin's story 'An Lánamhain Óg fá'n Tuaith' (The young couple in the country), such misadventures befall a young couple from Dublin come to the country to live out a rural idyll. After frazzling themselves and both scandalising and entertaining their neighbours with such farcical mistakes as buying a flock of roosters instead of hens, they sell the farm and return to the city for good.[138]

For many Gaelic authors, however, the city was neither a stereotypical den of iniquity nor a necessary evil to be exploited and fled. It was, or had become, home. In his 1937 essay 'Sa gCathair Dom' (In the city), a piece he presents as a letter to a Galway farmer, Tomás Ó Cléirigh begins with a trite anti-urban outburst:

> Ugh! The hard flagstones and the pains that came into my feet because of them, and worse than even that the damned squealing and screeching of the trams. I cannot understand how the educated people of the city put up with such barbarity, since I am certain that noise like it is not heard on this side of the gates of Hell. I recently heard that money is involved and I believe it, for money is the root of all evil.

Nevertheless, after a short time in the city, he has begun to change his mind: 'Yet despite all that, I like the city very much, and as for the people of the city, I never grow tired of watching them.'[139] Caitlín Nic Ghabhann could wax lyrical on the appeal of her native city, writing in 1925: 'Let us look at Dublin Bay now – and at the half-circle of lights around it – south, east, and north. . . . Would you not think it was Tir na nÓg in front of you instead of Dublin – a magical city instead of a mundane capital city!'[140] And that most urbane of urban Gaels, Liam Ó Rinn, was inspired by the beauty of Paris to a reflection on the endless fascination of city life everywhere:

> In my opinion a city never looks better than when the streets appear to be ablaze from all the lamps and the people are walking around talking and laughing brightly and merrily. You see a half-dark street and light shining from houses and shops here and there in it. Down the street with you cautiously and timidly. You feel as if there were a mystery there . . .[141]

Many Gaels were eager to explore that mystery, and there was a good deal of writing about urban life, both fiction and non-fiction, throughout the 1920s and 1930s. Following a tested precedent in Gaelic language instruction, an anonymous contributor to the *Irish Independent* offered readers a series of dialogues illustrating how the language could deal with typical situations of everyday urban life such as buying clothes (6/7/31; 3/8/31); dealing with servants (20/7/31); shopping for groceries (3/8/31); or going to the horse races (26/10/31).[142] We also find many vignettes or pen sketches of the urban scene, like those written by Seán Ó Ciarghusa for *The Leader* on topics such as 'urban wonders' (iongantaisí cathrach), the scenic and historical attractions of Dublin (2/12/33); a religious mission in the city (3/3/34); the Irish Hospitals Sweepstakes (10/11/34); urban social patterns (27/4/35); traffic jams (6/7/35); and bookies (4/11/39).

The most import urban sketches were, however, those by Seosamh Mac Grianna published in the *Irish Press* in 1932 and 1933.[143] Among these essays were 'Ceoltóirí na Cathrach' (The musicians of the city) (19/1/32),[144] 'Bacaigh na Cathrach' (The beggars of the city) (24/2/32), 'Cad a Chruinnigheas Sgaifte?' (What gathers a crowd?) (14/4/32), 'An Saoghal ins na Bocht-Sráideanna' (Life in the poor streets) (9/6/32), 'Gasraí na bPáipéar' (The newspaper boys) (12/7/32), 'Glór Daonda na Cathrach' (The human voice of the city) (12/9/32), and 'Ag Siubhal na Sráideann / An Chathair Istoidhche' (Walking the streets / The city at night) (5/1/33). Mac Grianna could be sensitive to the beauty and diverse vitality of the city:

> There is poetry in the city. It is nice in the day and beautiful by night. Walking the street, I think about the fact that I am passing the poor and the rich, the lord and the merchant, the worker who is at the foundation of the world, the talker, the poet, the gambler, and the thief. I pass weeping and laughter, love and hate.

In such a mood, he could see the city as simultaneously 'full of strife' (achrannach) and 'significant' (éifeachtach), as 'a habitation snatched from the deadly tranquillity of the world. The heart of a district and a district's blood and sickness and cure. A nest in the middle of a desert; light in the darkness; a voice far off in the silence of the night' (*IP*, 5/1/33).[145] Yet never did he lose his fundamental, almost instinctive, revulsion for city life, a revulsion given its most memorable expression in *Mo Bhealach Féin*, but present in these brief sketches as well:

> Poverty and wealth are within a footstep of each other in Dublin. Turn to your right or your left off of the finest streets and you are in the midst of the poor streets – the 'slums'. The city is like an apple of which three quarters is rotten (*IP*, 9/6/32).[146]

Other pictures of the poverty and accompanying degradation of the urban environment can be found in Ernest Joynt's 'Lonndain Shasana san Oíche' (London at night) (*FL*, 22/9/23); 'Anró' (Hardship) by 'Guaire', with its dismal focus on the 'smoke and dirt' (smúid agus salachar) of the Dublin slums on a dreary day (*Stoc*, Jan. 1926, 6); Áine Ní Riain's 'Tuirse Cléibh a's Croidhe' (Weariness of breast and heart), a moody and effective evocation of the isolation and loneliness of a married woman whose husband has been badly injured in an accident, of an old person dying in a hospital, and of a solitary woman looking back with regret on a young suitor she had rejected (*FL*, Jan. 1928, 3); Tomás Ó hIceadha's 'Garsún an "Mhacalla"' (The boy who sells *The Echo*), dealing with a Cork paperboy whose life is characterised by 'misery, poverty, hunger, destitution, hardship . . . outside and at home' (aindeise, bochtaine, ocras, dealbhas, cruadhtan . . . amuigh agus i mbaile) (*Lóchrann*, Feb. 1930, 7);[147] Máire Ní Chuill's 'Tráthnóna Fliuch sa Chathair' (A wet afternoon in the city), also set in Cork (*Lóchrann*, Mar. 1930, 8); the anonymous 'Cois na Life' (By the Liffey), with its emphasis on the poverty, hypocrisy, and lack of both Christianity and *Gaelachas* in modern Dublin (*FL*,

Dec. 1930, 5–6); Seán de Barra's 'An t-Olc 's an Mhaith' (The evil and the good), a series of vignettes showing the variety of life in the city, among their subjects a prostitute and a foul-mouthed woman staggering from a pub (*Camán*, 1/7/33); or Máire Ní Chonaill's perceptive 'Plód-Tighthe na Cathrach' (The slums of the city) (*Redemptorist Record*, Sept.–Oct. 1937, 31 and 39).[148] In León Ó Cinnéide's 'Na Cluig' (The bells), the emphasis is on the loneliness of a pensive young man from Mayo lodging in Dublin's Eccles Street (home of Joyce's Leopold Bloom) (*Stoc*, Jan. and Feb. 1926).[149]

Descriptions of destitution and degradation were a regular feature of Gaelic short fiction dealing with city life at this time. And while on occasion this focus on privation was softened through sentimentality or appeals to religion, the impression left by many of these short stories was of the city as a brutish, degrading, and heartless environment. Thus in 'Ceo an Chroí' (The heart's mist), Tomás Bairéad paints a grim picture of poor urban youths scrounging in the trash bins from a train.[150] The demeaning influence of poverty was also a theme in Bairéad's 'Cáit a' Mheadhon Oidhche' (Midnight Kate) and 'Costas an Ghirrfiaidh' (The cost of the hare). In the former, a story An Gúm omitted from subsequent editions of the collection in which it appeared, and that Liam O'Flaherty himself found offensive,[151] a woman suspected of being a prostitute because of her noctural wanderings is found to be actually in search of food in trash bins. In the latter, set in the mid-nineteenth century, prison is seen as a desirable alternative to the cold and hunger of cities and towns in winter.[152] In 'Truaghán Mná' (A miserable woman), his account of a woman's descent into beggary, Riobárd Ó Faracháin offered the following bleak view of life for the urban poor:

> She was born in the shadow of hunger; she was raised in a narrow, dirty house. The air she would suck into her lungs did her no more good than harm . . . Famine – filth – hardship – those were the things that were conferred on her.[153]

Máiréad Ní Ghráda focused on the misery and shame of a farmer come to Dublin with high hopes only to fail miserably in 'Uabhar an Fhir Déirce' (The beggar's pride) (*Bonaventura*, Autumn 1938, 171–9). In Brighid Ní Dhochartaigh's *Seamróg na gCeithre nDuilleóg*, a resident of the Donegal Gaeltacht goes so far as to place much of the blame for their plight on the sufferers themselves, offering the following explanation for urban poverty:

> There is not a city in the world without poverty like that in it, because every kind of person is gathered in it; people who are too lazy to work and who would far prefer hunger and need to exerting themselves in any way at all. Other people who want to earn a livelihood, but who cannot find work or pay; other people who prefer thievery and treachery to doing an honest day's work.[154]

'Sgéal Gearr: An Chathair' (A short story: The city) by 'An Stócach' begins with a grim picture of urban misery, but goes on to focus on the vitality of the city:

> The life, also, that was in the city; it was alive; there was always something going on in it . . . Crowds of people strolling, ceaselessly coming and going . . . at night, the lights putting an amber shine on everything and changing the appearance of the place so that you would think that it was an otherworld city (*AA*, May 1931, 3, 7).[155]

An odd perspective on urban poverty is to be found in Seán Ó Muimhneacháin's 'An Uaisleacht' (Nobility), in which a beggar woman is injured by a car driven by the son of a lawyer who then refuses to pay her the court-awarded compensation. The story ends with her lamenting the passing of 'the old blood of the gentry' (sean-fhuil na n-uasal) as she stands at the door of Lady Rathgar's house 'looking down proudly on the citizens of Dublin' (ag féachaint anuas go h-uaibhreach ar bhurgaibh Átha Cliath) (*CA*, 1931, 135). More curious still is 'Is Beannuighthe Iad na Boicht' (Blessed are the poor) by 'Ranji'. The narrator of this story, a civil servant in charge of pensions, is led by a St. Vincent de Paul worker to the slum dwelling of a once well-off family now living in proud destitution. When he arrives, the devout wife has died, leaving her husband his own peculiar consolation: 'She has at last received what she asked for and wanted; she was responsible for everything . . . From the day we were married . . . she was always praying to God that we would be poor before we died' (*Sguab*, Sept. 1925, 436–7).[156]

For some writers, the city was a centre of temptation, a place where traditional values were under constant and often insidious assault. For example, in Micheál de Paor's 'Aer an tSaoghail' (The pleasures of the world), a young woman comes to Dublin from the country, starts going to dances, and stops wearing her religious medal because it shows through the thin material of her fashionable new dress. Soon she also stops going to confession, begins to daydream through Mass, and falls in with a crowd who mock her Catholic faith. One morning at Mass she dreams of her mother, who is at the very moment praying for her in a rural church, and is as a result inspired to amend her life (*TCNÍ*, June 1924, 4–6). It is fear of just such influences that causes a mother in Seán Mac Meanman's 'Rothaidhe an tSaoghail' (The wheels of destiny) to keep her daughter from a snobbish convent school where she would learn to wear high heels and scorn her own origins.[157] The protagonist of Niall Ó Domhnaill's 'Léigheann agus Dúthchas' (Learning and heritage) was apparently not lucky enough to have so vigilant a parent. A native speaker who has gone to university and become a professor, he comes to regret having rejected his heritage, but also realises that the damage he has done is irreparable and that he is now trapped in the superficial, impersonal, and pretentious life he has made for himself (*Ultach*, June 1930, 1–2).[158]

Others who surrendered to the seductions of the city committed more dramatic and/or criminal offences. In Riseárd Ó Corcoráin's 'An Geall Deiridh!' (The last bet!), an inveterate gambler is considering suicide when he sees a bit of newspaper with the name of a long-shot horse on it. He rushes to a pawnshop to pawn the gun with which he had been going to kill himself, only to be shot dead by the pawnbroker, who, having been robbed previously, is taking no chances now. The following day's paper reports this 'justified killing' (marbhú dlisteanach), as well as the victory of the long shot at 200–1 (*FL*, 18/11/22). A murder is plotted, though not actually committed, in Liam Ó Rinn's 'Smaoineamh Contabharthach' (A dangerous thought), in which a young man schemes to acquire a rich uncle's wealth (*Star*, 13/4/29). In 'An Seomra Láidir' (The strong room) by 'An t-Iubhar', a bank treasurer who wants his son to get a job with him locks what he believes to be a dishonest clerk in the vault, only to discover later that he has suffocated his son instead (*Ultach*, Apr. 1931, 2–3). Equally treacherous is the murder perpetrated in Gearóid Ó Lochlainn's 1926 play *Deireadh an Leabhair* (The end of the book), in which a man gets vengeance by giving his enemy a book with poisoned pages![159] The urban crime is theft in 'Sgreadadh na Long' (The screeching of the ships) by 'Éibhlín' (*An Phoblacht*, 2/9/33) and 'Goid ó Ghaduidhe' (A theft from a thief) by 'Bricriu' (*Ultach*, Mar. 1934, 6–7). The dangers for pedestrians in an increasingly motorised Dublin were the subject of several stories in the period, among them Ó Muimhneacháin's 'Uaisleacht', Ó Riain's 'Scéal an Cheannphuirt,' and Colm Ó Laoghaire's 'Fann agus Tuirseach' (Weak and weary) (*Gearrbhaile*, 1937, 39–40).

Other social problems associated with urban life were treated, often with surprising honesty, by several writers during this period. Predictably, the abuse of alcohol, if not alcoholism itself, as a response to poverty and stress is a theme in many Gaelic stories about the city, but we also find suicide addressed by León Ó Broin in 'Ag Stracadh leis an Saol', 'Ocras na hIntinne' (The hunger of the mind), and 'Is Fearr le Dia na Mná' (God prefers women), all from his 1929 collection *Ag Stracadh leis an Saol agus Scéalta Eile*, and by Brighid Ní Dhochartaigh in *Seamróg na gCeithre nDuilleóg*.[160] Prostitution is dealt with seriously in 'Sgreadadh na Long' by 'Éibhlín', in 'Cáit a' Mheadhoin Oidhche' by Tomás Bairéad, and in *Ceol na nGiolcach* by Pádhraic Óg Ó Conaire; and comically in 'An Strainséar sa Seomra Beag' (The stranger in the little room) by Pádraic Ó Conaire (*CS*, 3/8/26). The protagonist of Nioclás Tóibín's 'Teoiní agus Tighthe Lóistín' (Tony and lodging houses) is apparently a kept man at story's end, and when his parents meet him by chance in Youghal:

> The woman – a woman who seemed to be getting on in years – was approaching them. There was a man with her – a fine young man. He had a little dog in his arms.

> They looked at him. It was Tony . . . There arose between Tony and his family that loathing and hatred that separated them until death.[161]

Urban sexual violence plays a role in Micheál Ó Gríobhtha's 'Cról', where a man's evil intentions are thwarted by the canine hero of the title.[162] León Ó Broin and George Thomson both dealt sympathetically with the issue of illegitimacy. In Ó Broin's 'Is Fearr le Dia na Mná', an unwed pregnant woman is driven by intolerance to give birth alone in a field in winter, while in Thomson's 'Éirí an tSaoil' (Success in life), he details the consequences of motherhood for an unwed woman hoping to find a husband, and in 'An Leanbh Tabhartha' (The illegitimate child), he depicts the courage of an unwed mother unwilling to surrender her child for adoption.[163]

The marriage problems of city couples are the subject of Mac Liammóir's 'An Fear-Chéile' (The husband) (*FL*, Jan. 1927, 5); Peadar Ó Dubhda's 'An Toil 's an Taithighe' (The will and the habit);[164] Donn Piatt's 'An Aisling ar Imthigh Dhá dTrian dí le Sruth' (The dream of which two thirds went for nought) (*An Phoblacht*, 15/4/33); and Seán Mac Maoláin's 'Taisce Dhomhnaill Dhuibh' (The treasure of Domhnall Dubh).[165] The first two are comic treatments of this theme, the last two serious, although in Mac Maoláin's story the woman manages to foil the machinations of a man who wishes to marry her for money and then flee to Scotland after the ceremony if he finds there is not enough of it.

There were also a few more favourable depictions of the city. For example, there were at least two pieces extolling the peace and beauty of St Stephen's Green as an urban oasis (*II*, 14/2/24 and 24/8/25). 'Fionn' Mac Cumhaill's 'Sráid Grafton' (Grafton Street) offers an amusing and light-hearted description of young men and women shopping, courting, seeing and being seen in Dublin's most fashionable street (*FL*, 24/5/24). 'Noel' introduced readers of the *Irish Independent* to some of Dublin's eccentric characters in 'Daoine Greannmhara a Bhuail liom / Aistighil na Cathrach' (Amusing people I've met / The drollery of the city) (*II*, 27/5/29), while in 'Idir Am Luighe agus Am Éirighe' (Between bedtime and rising), Peadar Ó Dubhda shows the variety and appeal of urban nightlife.[166] Seán Ó Carra provides a comic treatment of the antics of some who had enjoyed one aspect of that nightlife, the pub scene, in 'Oidhche' (Night) (*Irish Storyteller*, Aug. 1935, 23 and 25). Ciarán Ua Nualláin offered a comic perspective on the discrepancies among the public clocks of the city in 'Cluig Phuiblidhe / Níl Siad ar Aon Intinn fá'n Am i gCathair Átha Cliath' (Public clocks / They are not in agreement about the time in the city of Dublin) (*II*, 9/8/39).

The stresses and self-doubts experienced by priests were treated in a few works. Seán Ó Faoláin explored a seminarian's inner struggle to reconcile the claims of human love and missionary vocation on the eve of his ordination in

'Prendergast' (Éarna, June 1924, 12–16). And in 'Na Trí Righthe' (The three kings) (*IMN*, 1925, 35–41), An tAthair Gearóid Ó Nualláin offered an honest picture of the spiritual malaise of two priests and a layman whose marriage has failed, although his recourse to a miraculous simultaneous rebirth experience for all three on the eve of the Epiphany may strike modern readers as unduly facile. Loss of faith was also at the thematic core of Liam Gógan's unpublished 1925 one-act play *An Saoghal Eile* (The other world), in which the ghostly return of a friend convinces a group of students of the reality of the supernatural realm.[167]

By far the most substantial work in Irish dealing with the challenges and rewards of a priestly vocation was Séamas Mac Conmara's 1939 novel *An Coimhthigheach*. Mac Conmara's protagonist is a priest who has served time in an English prison for theft and has been suspended from the exercise of his sacramental duties. He comes as an unknown stranger to Newry to begin a new life. Much of the novel is predictably concerned with the efforts of the townspeople, including the family with whom he lodges, to solve the mystery surrounding this pious and kindly newcomer. When it is learned that he has been in jail, most of the people turn on him, refusing to visit him even when he falls seriously ill. Never does he complain or grow angry, and in his stoic endurance one character sees a reflection of the sacrifice of Christ: 'If it is not blasphemous of me, I often imagine that if a person could get to know Christ, what he would find out is that Ó Muirthile is not unlike him' (p. 133).[168] By novel's end we learn that his sufferings are all due to his refusal to violate the seal of the confessional. Moreover, he is exonerated by the written confession of the man who committed the theft for which he was jailed, and wins the respect of the very townspeople who had previously shunned him. With his full priestly prerogatives and responsibilities restored to him, he decides to forsake the world that has so mistreated him and enter the monastery at Mount Melleray, not as an escape, but rather as a reward for his fidelity and patience: 'He realised that this was the reward God had promised him for the terrible sacrifice he had made for his sake – a reward not of this world and that the dull-witted people of this world would not be able to understand' (p. 204).[169] While one could wish that Mac Conmara had further humanised his clerical hero by giving him more of the self-doubts and failings that vex the 'dull-witted people' that most of us so often are, *An Coimhthigheach* represented a real advance for Gaelic fiction at the time in its willingness to at least raise, in a serious and sustained manner, the question of the potential isolation and loneliness of priests ministering to a population that could only with great difficulty understand the nature and challenges of their vocation.

The kind of world Mac Conmara's priest so willingly leaves is the setting for Gearóid Ó Lochlainn's one-act play *Bean an Mhilliúnai* (The millionaire's wife) (BAC: Clódhanna Gaedhealacha, 1923) in which the author explores the debasing effects of unscrupulous business practices on those who use them. Ó Lochlainn's protagonist, Proinnsias Ó h-Artagáin, is a wealthy manufacturer who views with contempt all progressive social theories that would in any way restrict his ruthless methods. Social Darwinism is the code by which he lives and thrives:

> Business is war . . . and cleverness and money are the weapons used in that war. The person who does not understand how to make use of those two instruments is struck down without pity or mercy. It would be just as well for the person who would allow charity or pity to divert him from advancing his business to give up the game altogether! (p. 8).[170]

The climax of the play occurs when a man whom he has ruined through the use of methods strictly legal but morally questionable arrives at his home to kill him, only to spare his life because of his wife's goodness and her rejection, to her husband's face, of his worldview and practices. Moved by her passion, Ó h-Artagáin rather improbably sees the error of his ways and offers his victim and would-be killer a just and reasonable business proposition that will enable him to remain solvent. In some ways, however, the play raises more questions than it answers. Is Ó Lochlainn here condemning the capitalist system as then practiced or merely its worst excesses? Are we to see Ó h-Artagáin's act of generosity as a sign of genuine reformation or merely as a ploy to placate his naive and squeamish wife? His condescending final speech is suggestive, as he responds to her apology for confronting him so firmly: 'Of course I have nothing to forgive you for, dear. Between ourselves, you understand, I wouldn't say but that you were more or less right!' (p. 30).[171]

Other writers focused on the more mundane tension and alienation of urban life, themes that of course remain every bit as relevant today. In the anonymous 1934 story 'Brionglóid' (A dream), the rigidly puritanical protagonist is haunted by a recurring dream of falling farther and farther behind. In the end, his dream is quite literally realised when he falls and is killed trying to catch a train he is late for.[172] Obviously such stresses would be easier to manage and overcome if one lived in a supportive, communal environment. But meaningful community is precisely what is rarest in several of these sketches and stories of the city. For example, in 'Lonndain Shasana san Oíche', Ernest Joynt offers the following stereotypical picture of urban isolation:

> There is no loneliness like the loneliness I feel when I am alone among the many thousands on the bright streets of the Great Babylon. Then I am – it seems to me – just a little drop, as you would say, in the middle of the ocean, without friend, without comrade, without an acquaintance anywhere near me (*FL*, 22/9/23).[173]

'An Staic Chearnógach' (The square post) by An tAthair Gearóid Ó Nualláin and Fearrgus Ó Nualláin deals with the dehumanising drudgery of office work and the depressing subservience of clerks in ways reminiscent of Joyce's 'A Little Cloud' and 'Counterparts',[174] while Micheál Ua Conláin's 'Bean i gCeist' (A woman in question) tells the story of an old millionaire who looks back on a life that has left him 'the soulless magician with money' (an draoi airgid gan aon anam) and who envies a fellow office-worker from his youth who had sacrificed position and prospects for love (*FL*, 31/5/24). In 'Seán Óg' and 'Draoidheacht na Gaedhilge', Tadhg Saor Ó Séaghdha shows Irish protagonists wrestling with loneliness in London and in Washington respectively. London is also the place where the Donegal Gaeltacht heroine of Brighid Ní Dhochartaigh's *Seamróg na gCeithre nDuilleóg* feels most lost and miserable: 'But despite all the wonders Caitríona's heart among the strangers was lonely and sad . . . They were all sullen, unnatural people.'[175] It should, however, be noted that at least one Gaelic writer, 'An Gath Gréine', was able to spoof this hackneyed view of urban life, with the following introduction of his comic story 'Fáilte' (Welcome):

> A person who spends his life working around the city, that's the one who will take interest in the story I am going to tell him. It is not for country people, for it will be nothing new to them. I am a person who was born and raised in the city, a place where we have to get to know a person before we speak to him. We cannot be friendly with a stranger, either, until someone arrives who knows the two of us and will introduce us to each other. If you are a stranger or an outsider my boy, avoid the city and turn your face to the country! (*An Phoblacht*, 22/9/28).[176]

Nor was 'An Gath Gréine' the only Gaelic writer to see the comic potential of the city. For example, in his 1923 story 'Tríopais do Bheirt' (Tripe for two), Seán Ó Ciarghusa used the classic Dublin backdrop of the Moore St. markets for his farcical account of two young brothers bashing each other with tripe while some of the market women join in with predictable results (*FL*, 31/3/23). The humorous aspects of romance in the city were developed in Ernest Joynt's '"An Rud Badh Mheasa Leat ná Do Bhás – "' ('What you think is worse than your death –') (*Reult*, May 1924, 23–32); León Ó Broin's 'Firín an Uachtair Oidhre' (The little ice-cream man) (*Lóchrann*, Mar. 1926, 33–4); Seán Ó Siadhail's 'Eachtra Sheáinín, Dligheadóir' (The adventure of Johnny the lawyer) (*IR*, May 1934, 391–5); Pádhraic Ó Domhnalláin's 'Dhá Litir' (Two letters);[177] Tomás Bairéad's 'Imnidhe an Ghrádha' (Love's anxiety);[178] and Micheál Ó Gríobhtha's 'An Teine Chnámh' (The bonfire) (1937).[179] There are intriguing twists in a few of these stories. Ó Siadhail's Dublin protagonist is a happily unmarried attorney pursued by women. He accepts a dinner invitation from one of his female admirers when he learns that a United States senator from New York will be among her guests. That senator turns out to be a woman, and, perhaps impressed by this new example of female accomplishment, the lawyer reconsiders his ideas about women and marries his hostess for this soirée. In Bairéad's story, a young male office worker is beset by romantic tribulations, including a possible breach of promise action. In the end, he seems to have been bested in love by a policeman who allows his girlfriend's publican father to violate licensing laws. Ó Gríobhtha's story, while set in the Gaeltacht, offers a satiric perspective on romantic infatuation when the female protagonist, a middle-class snob educated in England and fixated on sentimental novels, learns the hard facts of love in the real world.

The shady side of urban life was treated comically by 'Fionn' Mac Cumhaill in 'Ar Lorg Taisme: Eachtra na Sráideann' (Looking for an accident: An adventure of the streets), in which a man ponders getting himself hit by a car to procure the money he needs to pay his landlady (*IP*, 18/12/31); by León Ó Broin in 'Fear na Beirte Ban' (The man with two wives) (1932), in which a shifty lawyer tries to get on the good side of the new Irish civil service;[180] and by B. N. Lóiste in 'Seic an Chúitimh' (The compensation check), in which three neighbours fake a road accident involving one as driver, one as victim, and one as witness (*IR*, Oct. 1935, 765–8). Ó Broin seems to have enjoyed poking fun at what could have been sensitive topics in the emergent state. Certainly Free State politics and pieties were viewed with a whimsically jaundiced eye in stories like 'Mairg a Phósfadh' (Woe to the one who would marry) and 'Troid na gComharsan' (The neighbours' fight), the former of which gently satirises the Gaelic League and An Fáinne, while the latter offers a wry take on the whole question of Gaelicisation and even uses the national anthem for humorous effect.[181] That Ó Broin was entirely at his ease with both urban life and comedy is evident from others of his stories from the period like 'Óg-Bhean i gCruadh-Chás / Na Sáil-Arda Údan' (A young woman in a predicament: Those high heels), in which an ultra-fashionable young woman catches one of her high heels in a tram track in the middle of College Green (*FL*, Feb. 1927, 3); 'An Ganndailín' (The little gander) (1929), set on a tram;[182] or 'Sgéal na Gamhna Buidhe' (A drawn-out story [lit. The story of the yellow calf]) (1932), a tongue-in-cheek story about a tax inspector.[183]

Writers trying to make a career in the city were the subject of three comic stories in Irish. In Niall Ó Domhnaill's 'Éifeacht i bhFuagraí' (Significance in advertisements), a short story writer suffering from block is inspired to write a tale of female fixation on movie stars only to be reminded of his own former infatuation with Dolores Del Rio (*Ultach*, Autumn 1930, 2–3). Micheál Ó Siochfhradha's 'Mise Imeasc na n-Ughdar' (Myself among the authors) tells of how the narrator makes himself a name in Gaelic Dublin's literary circles by his attacks on other writers and his posing as a native speaker: 'It was a "secret" among them that I was a "native speaker" – something that was not true – but that put my reputation out of danger of attack by inquisitive people' (*Lóchrann*, July and Aug. 1931).[184] Seán Mac Maoláin's 'Teine na Bothóige' (The fire in the cabin) (1939) is about two young Dublin clerks of Gaeltacht origin who, having published stories, decide to write novels. After a series of misadventures on Christmas holiday in the Wicklow Mountains, they both end up burning their rejected manuscripts (*Ultach*, Dec. 1939, 1–3).

Miscellaneous humorous depictions of life in the city include Seán Óg Ó Caomhánaigh's 'Fé Smacht Mná' (Under a woman's control) (*Land*, 2/6/23); Brian Ua Nualláin's 'Siubhlóid' (A stroll) and 'Ceól' (Music) (*IP*, 4/7/32 and 24/8/32) – the former a still pointed satire on the exercise craze – and his 'Rath agus Mío-Rath' (Success and misfortune) (Enniscorthy *Echo*, 22/12/34); An tAthair Casáin's 'Ró-Dhéanaighe' (Too late) (*CA*, 1932, 186–8); and Seán Mac Maoláin's 'Sagart Saoitheamhail' (A peculiar priest) (*Ultach*, Feb. 1933, 1–3). Other examples of the comic treatment of urban subjects in Gaelic short fiction include Seán Ó Laoghaire's 'An Fear a Bhearradh É Féin na Luighe ar Fhleasc a Dhroma' (The man who used to shave lying on the flat of his back) (*II*, 10/4/22); 'An Bhean Tuaithe sa gCathair / An Pílear Mór ó Bhaile an Bhrocháin' (The countrywoman in the city / The big policeman from Baile an Bhrocháin) by 'Uachtar Ard' (*II*, 17/5/22); Seosamh Ó Maoláin's 'Fionn agus Féasóg' (Fionn and a beard) (*Irish Fun*, Feb. 1924, 223); 'Ar Lorg Oibre san gCathair / Eachtra Greannmhar' (Looking for work in the city / A funny story) by 'S. Ó F.' (*II*, 6/4/25); 'An Sean-Duine agus an Garsún / Sceul Nua-Aimseardha' (The old man and the boy / A modern story) by 'Goibhniú' (*II*, 7/1/26); Diarmuid Ó Duibhne's 'Sean-Sheumas so againn-ne / Cúrsaí na Cathrach' (Our old Séamas / City matters) (*II*, 1/3/27); 'Lanamha Óg ag Lorg Tighe' (A young couple looking for a house) by 'Seathrún' (*II*, 27/7/28); León Ó Broin's 'Aoibhinn Beatha an Ghárda' (A guard's life is delightful) (*GR*, Dec. 1929, 60–1); and Pádhraic Ó Domhnalláin's 'Beagnach Mall / An Fear a Raibh Mío-Ádh air' (Almost late / The man with bad luck) (*II*, 15/4/35).

There were also a fair number of stage comedies with urban settings, a few of them among the most successful Gaelic plays of the period.[185] The action of Shán Ó Cuív's *Niamh Chinn Óir* (Niamh of the golden hair) (BÁC: Máire Ní Raghallaigh, 1929) centres on a young Dublin wife's desire to get her hair fashionably bobbed as her friends have done, an idea that scandalises her husband: 'May it not be long until they are bald. Every foolish one of them trying to make a young man of herself! Soon they will begin wearing trousers!' After a quarrel, she agrees not to cut her hair, a fortunate choice because she is able as a result to land the role of the legendary Niamh Chinn-Óir in a television ('telebhisiún') play on ancient Ireland ('an sean saoghal i nÉirinn') to be performed in Dublin for broadcast in New York.[186] The father in Micheál Mac Liammóir's comic play *Lúlú*, performed at Taibhdheac na Gaillimhe in 1929, is a contemporary Galwegian plagued by two headstrong modern daughters for whom he is eager to find husbands so that he can have some peace.[187] León Ó Broin's *Siamsa Gaedheal* (A Gaelic amusement), the protagonist of which is a high-ranking Gárda official, deals farcically with courtship and a breach of promise suit, while his *Rogha an Dá Dhíogh* (A choice between two evils) is about the apprehension of a bank robbing con-man who has ingratiated himself with an upper middle-class family.[188] His most successful urban comedy was *An Clósgríobhaí* (The typist) (BÁC: ODFR, 1936). In this play, produced by An Comhar Drámaidheachta in the Abbey Theatre in 1929, a fashionably dressed young confidence woman who has stolen a letter of reference from a country girl she has already outsmarted, goes on to hoodwink a pair of Dublin advertising men who are themselves pretty much scam artists.

While Máiréad Ní Ghráda's *An Grádh agus an Gárda* (Love and the guard) (BÁC: ODFR, 1937) is set in a small town in Clare, one of the protagonists is a Dublin medical student who is in trouble for kicking a policeman when drunk and who sends a friend to impersonate him on a visit to family friends in Clare so that his teetotalling aunt will not disinherit him. When the aunt is herself fined for reckless driving, she comes to hate the Gárdaí and is thus delighted when she eventually learns what her nephew has done so that all ends well. Comic mixups are also at the heart of Pádraig Ó Bróithe's urban one-acter *Cinnte* (Certain) (BÁC: ODFR, 1937), in which a man very much alive is believed dead, in part because his letter to his sister rebutting the rumour is intercepted by a postman jealous of what he thinks is a rival writing to his sweetheart. The play ends predictably with several weddings. The anonymous 1939 radio play *Sardines nó Ceart na mBan* (Sardines or women's rights) satirises feminism as 'The Association of Women against Men' (Cumann na mBan i n-aghaidh na bhFear), a group that dissolves when most of its members marry and a previously 'liberated' wife – one of her acts of revolt being to serve her husband the sardines he detests – comes to see the error of her ways and the man's true worth (*Ultach*, June 1939, 1–2).

Piaras Béaslaí had, of course, been writing clever and stageworthy plays for Na hAisteoirí since the 1910s, and he continued this work in our period, with two of his full-length comedies from this time having town or city settings. *Blúire Páipéir* (A bit of paper) (BÁC: ODFR, 1938), performed by An Comhar Drámaidheachta in the Peacock in 1936, is both a courtship farce and a satire on pseudo-intellectuals and pseudo-artists. One of the male protagonists, a self-proclaimed cosmopolitan man of letters, says that he will only produce his as yet unperformed plays in Paris, and not in petty and provincial London or Dublin. His condemnation of the Irish capital includes a dig at Béaslaí's own company, An Comhar Drámaidheachta: 'There is a little group in Dublin who keep the fame to themselves, and are jealous of anyone else who is clever. A new author cannot get justice' (pp. 22–3).[189] Later in the play, another man offers a humorous view of literary criticism as a method of satisfying personal grudges (p. 46). *An Fear Fógraidheachta* (The advertising man) (BÁC: ODFR, 1938) was performed by An Comhar Drámaidheachta in the Peacock in 1934. It deals farcically with a young man's botched attempts to use the tricks of the American advertising trade to win his uncle a wife.[190]

While it is doubtless in these comic works – and in particular in the plays of Ó Broin and Béaslaí – that urban life was written of most naturally and least self-consciously by Gaelic authors of this period, there were others who were able to use Irish to deal with Galltacht settings and new topics in a manner that was honest, matter-of-fact, and convincing. Micheál Ua Conláin's 'An t-Ádh' (Luck) tells of a businessman who has his pocket picked at the races. In the wallet is an important though as yet unread letter setting up an appointment with friends to discuss a commercial venture. He has information that the project will lead to the ruin of all involved, but without the letter does not know where to meet his associates to warn them. In terrible anxiety, he returns home to find the assembled friends waiting for him at this, the agreed meeting place (*IF*, Aug. 1922, 31–4). In the peculiar tale 'Eachtra i n-Amharclainn i mBaile Átha Cliath' (An adventure in a theatre in Dublin) by 'Fionn', the narrator meets a young woman sitting by herself and crying in a theatre. She claims to be frightened by the soldiers in the audience, particularly the Australians. He escorts her home, but when she reaches the door she summons a man inside to attack him. The narrator then awakens from what has all been a dream (*Land*, 12/5/23). In Micheál Mac Liammóir's 'An Turas' (The journey), a fashionable young French woman on a train leaving Paris is bemused by her fellow passengers, among them some boorish English people (*FL*, Oct. 1926, 5–6). Moodier and more subtle is 'Leabhar do Léigh Sí' (A book she read) by Cearbhall Ua Dálaigh, a pen portrait of the quiet daily life and satisfactions of an urban homemaker (*Nation*, 5/4/30). In 'Reilig' (Cemetery), Tomás Bairéad gives mordant insight into the obscure world of an obituary writer for a city newspaper.[191]

Some writers chose to set their work in the one urban milieu in which Irish was naturally spoken, the social network that grew up around the language movement itself. On occasion, this decision seems to have been prompted by a lack of confidence in the capacity of the language to deal convincingly with the life of English-speaking Ireland. At other times, however, it seems to have been due merely to an author's personal familiarity with or involvement in the world of Gaelic activism. A few of the stories set in this environment deal with romance among Gaelic Leaguers, as do 'Fionn' Mac Cumhaill's 'An tAscath' (The soldier) (*FL*, 11/11/22); Micheál Breathnach's 'An Chéad Taom den Grádh / "Galar Caillte, Cráidhte"' (The first fit of love / 'A dreadful, painful sickness') (*II*, 24/5/22); Pádraig Ó Bróithe's 'An Gaedhilgeoir agus an Fáinne / Cormac ag Lorg Mná' (The Irish speaker and the Fáinne / Cormac seeking a wife) (*II*, 2/6/22); Sorcha Nic Mhuiris's 'An Sean-Sgeul agus Crot Nua air / Beirt ó'n gCathair' (The old story in a new guise / A pair from the city) (*II*, 28/12/23); 'An Cailín Donn' (The brown-haired girl) by 'Lorcán' (*Tír*, May 1933, 9–11); Conchubhar Ó Coileáin's 'Ní Neart go Cur le Céile' (There is no strength without co-operation) (*Camán*, 10/2/34); Máirtín Ó Direáin's 'Sgéal Grádha / "Cruinniughadh na Beirte"' (A love story / 'The gathering of the pair') (*CT*, 22/2/36); and Riobárd Ó Faracháin's 'Súile Stróinséar' (A stranger's eyes) (*Bonaventura*, Autumn 1938, 166–76). Other stories set in urban Gaelic circles include An tAthair Gearóid Ó Nualláin's 'Cúig Phíosaí Óir' (Five pieces of gold);[192] S. Ó Gríbhthín's 'Lá Mí-Fhortúnach' (An unfortunate day), a comic tale set in Croke Park during an All-Ireland football final between Kerry and Kildare (Enniscorthy *Echo*, 28/11/31); León Ó Broin's 'Mairg a Phósfadh'; 'Nighean Róise' (Rose's daughter) by 'Lorcán' (*Tír*, Apr. 1933, 9–12), in which a chance meeting at the dancing competitions of the Dublin Feis is the catalyst for bringing a father and daughter together after more than a decade of estrangement; Pádhraic Ó Domhnalláin's 'Deágh-Nodlaig?' (A good Christmas?); and Máirtín Ó Direáin's 'Cúpla!' (A couple!), about the love affair between the editor and sub-editor of an Irish-language labour movement newspaper (*IP*, 27/3/39).[193]

There were also a few attempts to introduce the language into settings alien, if not actively hostile, to it. For example, Micheál de Paor's 'Ar Mhalairt Aigne' (Of a different opinion) is set among English speakers in a fashionable Dublin hotel, and has as its central character the snobbish wife of an English colonel (*IF*, Mar. 1924, 27–9). There were also a handful of Gaelic stories about Anglo-Irish 'Big Houses' and their Ascendancy owners.[194] In 'Síol nár Fhás' (A seed that did not grow) (*IMN*, 1927, 69–73) by 'L. Mac Ph.', the frivolous Oxford-educated son of a landlord is on the verge of being enlightened and converted by the faith of a dying old retainer when he gets a telegram telling him that he has won a bundle of money on a horse race. His reflections on class, creed and colonialism just before his visit to the old servant are of interest:

> On one side of him were nobility and power and wealth and pride, and on the other side, poverty and lowliness, torment and piety. He had often already insulted in deed and thought that class of rustics. Why were they not like the people from whom he was descended, the people of England? Why were there not vigour and energy and progress in them? . . . Why would they not establish industries and great cities, and make themselves a force in the world? Only with regard to their faith were they zealous, with regard to that faith that, in his opinion, was keeping them useless, ineffective . . . a rustic rabble, they would disgust one (p. 70).[195]

Etais Ní Chnáimhín merely used a Big House setting to provide atmosphere for a ghost story in 'Taidhbhsí / "I nGleann Scáile an Bháis"' (Ghosts / 'In the valley of the shadow of death') (*Standard*, 12/9/31).

For most Gaelic writers interested in the subject, the emphasis was, however, as much on the debility and decline of the Ascendancy as on its arrogance. In 'Uaigneach?' (Lonely?), Pádhraic Ó Domhnalláin's protagonist is the last member of a family of renegade Gaelic Catholics who became Protestants and Anglicised themselves for social advancement. This man now lives alone in his decaying ancestral home in a fantasy world of dinner parties, elegant balls, and vice-regal visits (*FL*, May 1928, 5). A similarly embittered and unbalanced man living in a similarly decaying Big House represents the end of another Ascendancy line in Ó Domhnalláin's 'An Leaghadh' (The melting away),[196] while in Tomás Bairéad's 'Mná Chaointe na Linnseach' (The keening women of the Lynches), the final heir is a pampered lap dog, the family having destroyed itself through its own selfishness and corruption.[197] The only positive picture of a member of the Ascendancy is found in 'Dualgas' (Duty), one of Seán Ó Ciarghusa's brief comic anecdotes from various periodicals, in which a Resident Magistrate is presented as 'a generous, princely, Gaelic [i. e. down-to-earth] man' (fear fial, flaitheamhail, Gaedhealach), whose generosity lands him in trouble with a Customs and Excise official.[198]

Other writers brought the language to the English-speaking and predominantly Unionist northeast of Ulster, perhaps motivated by the sort of optimism voiced by Aodh de Blácam, himself a convert to Catholicism, in 1924: 'If I am right . . . the mark of the nation, the mind of the Gaels is to be found equally in the Protestantism and the Catholicism of Ireland' (*Sguab*, 31/8/24).[199] We get several Gaelic essays on Belfast in this period, among them 'Taobh Thall den Teorainn / Domhnach Dom ann' (Across the border / A Sunday I spent there), an oddly seedy picture of a Sabbath in the city by 'Guaire' (*FL*, 21/2/25); Seán Mac Maoláin's rather idealised view of Catholic West Belfast in 'Oidhche Shathairn ar Bhóthar na bhFál' (Saturday night on the Falls Road), with its emphasis on the piety of the residents as they flock to confession (*Ultach*, Nov. 1927, 5); Peadar Ó Dubhda's 'Chun Glóire a Ríogh agus Onóra a dTíre!' (For the glory of their king and the honour of their country!), a tongue-in-cheek view of the Orangemen's Twelfth of July celebrations in 'Tír na gCréag' (The land of the Craigs);[200] Séamus Ó Néill's 'Oidhche Shathairn i mBéal Feirsde' (Saturday night in Belfast), a lively and generally sympathetic look at his adopted city on both sides of the sectarian divide (*Éireannach*, 11/8/34); and his 'Fear ag Feadalaigh / An Saoghal i mBéal Feirste' (A man whistling / Life in Belfast), with its focus on the city's pavement artists, street musicians, and poor (*Éireannach*, 23/2/35). On the other hand, Seán Ó Ciarghusa's 'Naomh Pádruig i gCarsonia / An 12adh Lá' (St Patrick in Carsonia / The twelfth day) paints a stark picture of frightened nationalists eager to leave Belfast before the Orange parades of the twelfth of July (*Sguab*, Aug. 1923, 215–16).[201]

Short stories set in the North include Seán Mac Maoláin's 'Sgéilíní ó Bhéal Feirsde' (Little stories from Belfast), a series of amusing and not particularly sectarian anecdotes about Orangemen (*IF*, Aug. 1922, 10–11); Séamus Ó Néill's 'Brón na Máthara / Géar-chás Nualann is a Mic' (The mother's sorrow / The crisis of Nuala and her son) (Dundalk *Examiner*, 13/8/32); Tomás Bairéad's 'Saibhreas na gCon' (The wealth of the greyhounds), in which working-class people in Belfast seem to treat their greyhounds better than they do their children;[202] 'Rún a Chroidhe' (The secret of his heart) by 'Lorcán', a story of hidden and thwarted love and treachery among young office workers in Belfast (*Tír*, Feb.–Mar. 1933, 9–11); Ó Dubhda's 'An Dá Sheift' (The two tricks), a comic tale of the duping of an Orangeman;[203] and Maighréad Nic Mhaicín's 'Scilling' (A shilling). The last is the most interesting and accomplished of these works. Nic Mhaicín depicts the exploitation of female factory workers in Belfast, both on the job and at home, culminating in the confused rebellion of one of them against the humiliation of having to wait in line to receive a miserly Christmas bonus from her employer.[204]

Personal tastes and interests were explored by other writers interested in making the language a vital part of their own daily lives. For example, 'Rás nach Raibh ann ach 'san Aigne' (A race that only occurred in the mind) by 'M. Ó F.' is the tale of a thrilling motor race that all turns out to have been the dream of a man who nodded off in church (*IMN*, 1924, 43–5), while horse racing was the subject of Peadar Ó Dubhda's 'Séadna (ar an aimsir seo)' (Séadna [at this time]), in which An tAthair Peadar Ua Laoghaire's hero returns as a successful gambler,[205] and of Donn Piatt's comic 'Och, Ochón, An Rása Mór!' (Alas, alas, the big race!) (*IP*, 7/11/32). The sport of choice was golf in Micheál Breathnach's 'Golf – An Chéad Chluiche' (Golf – the first game) (*FL*, 19/9/25), Micheál Mac Donnchadha Pléimeann's 'Golf' (*Blackrock College Annual*, 1935, 115–18), and Seán Ó Ciarghusa's 'Golf,' in which the author urges fellow Gaels to reclaim the game from Anglicised snobs.[206]

Seán Ó Fearchair's 'Eachtra Oidhche' (A night's adventure) (*Gaedheal Óg*, 31/8/39) is an adventure story for boys involving airplanes, a modern invention first introduced into Gaelic writing by Peadar Ó Dubhda in *Ar Lorg an tSeanchaidhe* (On the trail of the storyteller) in 1915. Ó Dubhda continued to produce innovative and imaginative fiction for the young during this period in works like *Lá na Cúirte* (The day of the court) (Oméith: Lucht Choláisde Bhrighde, [1924]), in which the narrators recounting a day's work at a court house are ordinary objects such as an umbrella, a penny, and a walking-stick. Most of the humour in these little comic pieces has its origin in the meticulous but naively clueless accounts of objects, people, and procedures offered by the narrators. Nioclás Tóibín also used unconventional narrators – a monkey, a donkey, a dog, a blackbird, a lemon, and an engagement ring – in his collection of stories for children *Ár gCúrsaí Féin* (Our own affairs) (BÁC: Brún agus Ó Nualláin, Teor., [1937]).

A more serious look at childhood was Micheál Mac Liammóir's 'Sgannradh' (A fright), a well-crafted story in which a game gone wrong creates real terror for a little boy (*FL*, 22/7/22). Present-day readers will be more troubled by Peadar Ó Dubhdha's story 'An Bonn Malluighthe' (The cursed coin), whose central character is a Jewish antique dealer. While there is nothing explicitly anti-semitic about the story, and while the protagonist has an educated and sympathetic Irish friend, there is reference to the Jew's sharp business practices and his greed, and in his friend's final comment on him he is linked with Judas through a reference to thirty pieces of silver.[207] Downright startling for its boldness at the time, was George Thomson's previously noted story 'Éirí an tSaoil', the story of an Irishwoman who, having been driven from home as an unmarried mother, goes on to become the head of a major feminist organisation in Britain and receives an MBE from the king for her accomplishments. However, though written some time between 1926 and 1934, the story was not published until 1988.

In addition to individual stories dealing with urban life, there were also several important collections of such works: León Ó Broin's *Árus na nGábhadh agus Sgéalta Eile* (The house of the dangers and other stories) (BÁC: Cló Oifig Uí Mhathghamhna, 1923); *Béal na hUaighe agus Sgéalta Eile* (The mouth of the grave and other stories) (BÁC: Muinntir Alex Thom agus a Chomh. Teor., 1927), *Ag Stracadh leis an Saol agus Scéalta Eile* (1929), and *An Rún agus Scéalta Eile* (1932); Seán Mac Maoláin's *Ceannracháin Cathrach* (Poor urban creatures) (BÁC: ODFR, 1935); Seán Ó Ciosáin's *Sgéalta Cois Laoi* (1935); Seosamh Ó Torna's *Cois Life* (1937); and Riobárd Ó Faracháin's *Fíon gan Mhoirt* (Wine without dregs) (BÁC: OS, 1938). Virtually all of the stories in Ó Broin's collections have been discussed above, but it should be noted that not all readers in his own time found them worthy of notice. Reviewing *Ag Stracadh leis an Saol* for *An t-Ultach*, 'P. Ó D.' (most likely Peadar Ó Dubhda) wrote:

> The author has attempted to put the ugliest aspects of human life into literature in Irish – in a couple of the stories. He makes use of that material that writers of English like O'Flaherty use when they want to give something pleasing to the perverse-minded readers in London. I would say that these stories are an insult to the humanity and the Christianity of the people of Ireland.

'P. Ó D.' was particularly disgusted by the collection's title story about the suicide of a frustrated Gaelic writer whose retelling of the tale of Diarmuid and Gráinne had been rejected by an editor as 'a bit smutty' (roinntín gársúil). This man has unwittingly wed a woman already married, and is ignored even when he does publish because of his reputation for immorality. The suicide has left instructions that his corpse should not be buried in 'this cursed country or in any other country' (sa tír mhalluighthe seo nó i n-aon tír eile), and the narrator of the story complies by pushing the body back into the sea in which the writer had drowned himself. For 'P. Ó D.,' this sort of despair was not 'a quality of the Gael' (tréith de'n Ghaedheal) (*Ultach*, Nov. 1929, 2).[208]

Mac Maoláin's *Ceannracháin Cathrach* seems to have occasioned no such reservations on its publication. In fact, in his review for *Timthire Chroidhe Naomhtha Íosa*, An tAthair Seán Ó Catháin explicitly distinguished Mac Maoláin's treatment of the city from that of the 'dung beetles' (priompalláin), those Irish writers of English who were obsessed with the sordid side of urban life (*TCNÍ*, Sept. 1935, 213–14). 'M. Ó R.' agreed in his review for *Ar Aghaidh*, stating of the stories in the collection:

> Almost all of them are set in the back streets of Dublin. But that does not mean that they lack the flavour and the idiom of the Gaeltacht . . . When the writer gives an account of the people of the back streets, he does not give an account of only their bad behaviors – he gives a natural account of them and that is a good thing for it takes the flavour of the Anglicised writers from his account (*AA*, Sept. 1935, 8).[209]

Praising Mac Maoláin's originality in *The Father Mathew Record*, An tAthair Micheál wrote 'the mantle of Pádraic [Ó Conaire] has fallen on Seán if it has fallen on anyone among writers of Irish' (gur thuit fallaing Phádruig [Uí Chonaire] ar Sheán má thuit sé ar aoinne ameasc sgríobhnóiri Gaedhilge), and declared of this particular volume: 'That is a sign that Irish is turning to the towns where it will be necessary to graft it to new roots. The most noteworthy book that has come from An Gúm for a long time' (*FMR*, Aug.–Sept. 1935, 411).[210] Two of the stories in *Ceannracháin Cathrach*, 'Dhá Aisling' (Two visions) and 'Brianaidh na mBréag' (Brian of the lies) have as protagonists Gaeltacht people who have come to Dublin to escape the poverty of the West. In the former, the son of a Gaeltacht woman now living in the capital is killed when hit by a car. A road accident is also important in 'Moldaí agus Gobaí', although here it is the comic litigious consequences that provide the plot. In 'Cor de Chuid na Cinneamhna' (A twist of fate), the author depicts the almost ant-like quality of tenement life in the slums, but even here he transcends the usual anti-urban stereotype through his recognition of the humanity and vigour of the poor, a recognition that can see the loving side of a mother given to drink. Mac Maoláin's most Ó Conairesque story is 'Maighréad na Milseán' (Margaret of the sweets), in which the owner of a sweet shop in Dublin, having been swindled out of her life savings by a con-man with whom she has fallen in love, loses her mind and has to be committed to an asylum.

The most engaging story in Seán Ó Ciosáin's *Sgéalta Cois Laoi* is 'An Bheirt Intleachtóirí' (The two intellectuals), in which Frank O'Connor and Seán Ó Faoláin are satirised. Also of interest, however, are 'An Fear do Bhuail Umam i Montréal' (The man I met in Montreal), an Ó Conairesque tale about a character who claims to have met Trotsky in Canada; 'An Múinteoir Gaedhilge' (The Irish teacher), another comic story, this one about a greedy and hypocritical teacher of Irish; 'Móna', noted above in the discussion of Gaelic stories about the Ascendancy; and 'Eachtra an Mhála' (The adventure of the bag), in which Irish-speaking friends go to the movies and enjoy listening to Negro spirituals as well as that bugbear of the time, jazz.

There are only four stories in Seosamh Ó Torna's *Cois Life*, one of which, 'Sinnsear Cloinne', will be discussed later with works dealing with the War of Independence. 'Oidhche Churtha an Chluig Siar' (The night for turning the clock back) offers a generally objective picture of the vitality of the city, as well as of its impersonality and social inequities. For example, the author describes crowds waiting outside the Theatre Royal:

> There was a crowd of people all over the place, some of them coming out after the end of the first performance, and more waiting in a long line for the doors to reopen. There was a poor girl wearing a shawl singing 'Gráinne Mhaol' to them. At the same time, the attorney's wife was putting on her gloves after searching for her ticket. When the song stopped, Michael saw the hand reaching out to him. He slipped a sixpence piece into the hand without even looking at it (p. 71).[211]

The influence of Pádraic Ó Conaire is evident in 'Spré Ghráinne Ní Aichir' (The dowry of Gráinne Ní Aichir), in which an increasingly deranged and despised woman tries to kill the man she believes has jilted her. More original is 'Mar d'Fhág Seán Ó Néill Lána de Bhál' (How Seán O'Neill left Wall Lane), a story in which the author seems explicitly to reject literary naturalism. Having sketched a quick picture of urban poverty, he immediately comments:

> There are writers and you would think they like nothing better than to be giving a detailed account of people who would be in a similar situation. But if you yourself, brother, had ever been an object of pity, having lost your courage and with no hope of relief, you would not want to bring up those matters again. I will let the story pass (p. 35).[212]

What is most striking about this story, however, is how closely this urban Gael adheres in it to the stereotypical dichotomy between the idyllic life enjoyed by country people and the degrading existence endured by city-dwellers. Ó Torna's protagonist is finally able to realise his dream of moving his family to the country when he writes to and receives help from a relative he has seen in an American movie, and the story ends with a celebration of his new rural, or perhaps more accurately suburban, life.

Reviewing Ó Faracháin's *Fíon gan Mhoirt*, an anonymous critic praised the collection as 'a very important book' (leabhar ana-thábhachtach) because 'it is written from a modern Dublin mind and about contemporary life in the town' (is ó intinn nua-shaoghalta Bhleácliathach agus ar bheatha an lae indiu san mbaile mór atá sé scríobhtha), but added that, despite the author's 'polished and fluent' (snasta líomhtha) Irish, several of the stories were mere sketches or outlines ('scáil sgéil') rather than finished works (*GR*, Mar. 1939, 476).[213] He was right on both counts. Several of the stories are flimsy and/or, like 'An Cárta Nodlag' (The Christmas card) and 'Urlabhra' (Speech), heavily and uncritically influenced by O. Henry and his surprise endings. But all deal with urban life, in particular middle-class urban life, from the inside with no linguistic self-consciousness. Three of the stories, 'An Mhúscailt' (The awakening), 'Pilib an Cheoil' (Philip of the music), and 'Urlabhra', have as protagonists professional or classical musicians. In 'Pilib an Cheoil', a young musician leads a strike against the wishes of his fiancée's father, who is also his boss.[214] 'Imtheachta Chlub na gCleasaidhthe' (The proceedings of the tricksters' club) has as its main character an Irishman with a passion for American gangster films, a passion that has led him to assume a rather startling would-be Chicago accent with accompanying underworld lingo though he has never visited the United States. Ó Faracháin's most original and effective work is 'An Feall Gránna' (The ugly betrayal), a frame story in which a struggling writer uses a friend's moving tale of love gone wrong as raw material for his own fiction. The friend tells of meeting a young woman he had once known and admired, but who has now become a prostitute. He takes her home out of kindness, only to be seen by his fiancée's brother, who leaps to sordid conclusions about the pair and tells his sister, putting an end to the engagement. All eventually ends happily if improbably – O. Henry again! – when the former fiancée reads the protagonist's story (in Irish of course), realises the misunderstanding, and goes on to marry the man she had unjustly rejected. In a final ironic twist, the writer-protagonist shows the lukewarm acceptance letter he had received from the editor who published the piece:

> If it were not for how little time was left, it would not be published at all. If you cannot write anything but nonsense that no one could find credible, we will get someone else who will do the job for us. In God's name, try to write stories that could happen. Charles Garvice has died, and we don't want any heir to him (pp. 45–6).[215]

The single most substantial and important work of fiction in Irish with an urban setting was Art Ó Riain's 1932 novel *Lucht Ceoil*, one of the two novels, the other being Seán Ó Ruadháin's *Pádhraic Mháire Bhán*, that won An Gúm's prize for a novel in Irish first announced in 1929 and awarded in 1931. Critics were virtually unanimous in their praise of Ó Riain's accomplishment. Writing in *Irisleabhar Muighe Nuadhat*, one 'S.' proclaimed: 'It is a novel of which we have few of its like in Irish. It is the life of the city and the life of the people who live in and near it that is revealed in it. This is the book for the person who wants to get to know that life' (*IMN*, 1933, 62).[216] An tAthair Eric Mac Fhinn was even willing – more or less – to overlook Ó Riain's Galltacht origins and his preference for the Roman font, writing in *Ar Aghaidh*:

> This book is the nicest example – if it were not for the foreign font – that has yet been seen of Dublin Irish. I am by no means mocking here, but dead serious. You would know in some way that it is not a Gaeltacht person, like 'Máire' or Pádraic Ó Conaire, who wrote the book, but that does not mean that it is not a nice story in its own way (*AA*, Mar. 1933, 7).[217]

The story is certainly an eventful one. A young Irish journalist named Barra Ó Caochlaigh (Ó Riain's pen-name) returns from London, where the pernicious fogs have damaged his health, to take up lodgings in the home of a woman deserted by her alcoholic husband. When he finds a dead man with his landlady's stolen jewels in his pocket, he is arrested, tried, convicted, and imprisoned for robbery, though acquitted of murder for lack of evidence. Released after two itinerants who had witnessed the crime testify to his innocence, he is still unable to find work in Dublin and has to return to England, where for a while he makes a living as a church musician and busker until he meets Athanasius, an extraordinary and idealistic English rebel and leader of what we would probably now call either a cult or a commune. Athanasius, whose headquarters are on an island stronghold in the middle of a river, helps Barra to stand up to his despicable employer, a Jewish money-lender whom Athanasius beats up, and then to resist the authorities who come to arrest them both for this assault. Fleeing to Dublin in the aftermath, Barra is welcomed by the daughter of his former landlady, and the novel ends happily with their marriage and the entrance into a Carmelite convent of the landlady's other daughter, a brilliant musician and previously snobbish social climber who has now seen the light.[218]

Looking back on the novel after sixty years, Alan Titley has praised the credibility of Ó Riain's protagonist and offered an intriguing reading of the novel as an indictment of both unbridled capitalism and of corporatism, an indictment rooted in the author's own fervently orthodox Catholicism.[219] It is striking that while the novel is concerned exclusively with city life and modern issues – the Gaeltacht, for example, is irrelevant throughout – Ó Riain regularly denounces the materialistic and irreligious ethos of his time, building on, but going well beyond, traditional condemnations of urban alienation and corruption. Not surprisingly, it is the counter-cultural champion Athanasius who voices most forcefully this aspect of Ó Riain's philosophy:

> Look, lad . . . The human race will be headless altogether within a hundred years if it continues as it is. Show me anyone who thinks for himself at present. No one

> does . . . A hundred years ago, when a craftsman was making things with his own two hands, he had to put his own sense and understanding to work. You could see the result of that. There was some personality involved in the fruit of his labour, something that showed you that a *person* made it . . . I used to be told, when I was at school, that the human race is always learning, that every generation that comes has more knowledge than the generation before it. Nonsense, lad! Perhaps it used to be like that, but that was a long time ago (pp. 192–3).[220]

But Ó Riain could never be satisfied with the secular humanism of Athanasius, however sincere and courageous. It is religion, not rebellion, that causes him to reject that modern materialism he sees as the source of loneliness, suffering, and violence. This thematic strand in the novel emerges most clearly in chapter 43, 'Aithrighe agus Leor-Ghníomh' (Repentance and atonement), in which Ó Caochlaigh goes to the Cistercian monastery of Mount Melleray in County Waterford. Ó Riain makes his point with a strikingly contemporary simile:

> It was wonderful how the thoughts were awakened and stirred in me during those two days. At times I would think that the monastery was a heaven on this earth, the peace was so deep and the prayers so common there. At other times, it was clear to me that the monks were invincible heroes, and that there was some power emanating from them, a power that was having an effect on the world unbeknownst to it – just like that room of enormous power that I saw by the Shannon once, a quiet room in which only one man was working; but he could provide light to all of Ireland, or leave the country in darkness, as he wished (p. 269).[221]

Ó Riain had explored these ideas earlier in 'Eagna na hÓige' (The wisdom of youth) (*FL*, 6/9/24), 'Lucht Cnoc' (Hill people) (*FL*, 27/12/24), and 'Radharc na Fírinne' (*FL*, Sept. 1926). In all of these stories, what Ó Riain saw as the soulless commercial ethos of a possible new Ireland was condemned for its subversion of traditional values rooted in faith and family. For example, in 'Radharc na Fírinne', an Irishman who has achieved enormous worldly success in England returns home to sneer at Irish lethargy and entrepreneurial backwardness. Eventually, of course, he sees 'radharc na fírinne' on encountering the simple but profound faith of a poor countrywoman, and, in an explicit rejection of Stephen Dedalus's personal and artistic credo, he accepts with true humility his place in God's scheme. As he looks at bustling factory workers after his return to England, he further realises that it is frantic modern western individualism and not reverent Irish communitarianism that is most truly aberrant and ultimately morbid.

A vision of this kind leads in *Lucht Ceoil* to the conversion of the landlady's drunkard husband, who dies at Mount Melleray after writing a confession in which he admits that it was he who committed the robbery and killing for which Ó Caochlaigh was tried, and then schemed successfully to throw the blame on the innocent man. And it is also a similar new understanding of Christianity, one inspired by the death of her priestly brother, that leads the sister of Ó Caochlaigh's fiancée to forsake her brilliant musical career to become a cloistered Carmelite nun.[222]

It should, however, be stressed that Ó Riain's was no mere loyalty to the institutional Church and its clergy. His narrator offers the following trenchant if generous character analysis of the worldly, successful, and self-deluded English parish priest who dismisses him from his post as a church musician when he sees him busking in ragged clothes:

> I had an intense desire to ask him what kind of clothes the Apostles wore or what professions they had, but I restrained myself. Everyone must yield to his handicap, and Father Harfleur's only handicap was excessive respectability, and even that for the good of his people, in his mind (p. 217).[223]

Ó Riain was a genuine Catholic radical who, however narrowly traditional his faith and however marginal his philosophy in the Ireland of his time, offered a coherent, consistent and cogent critique of modern western values and trends.

Lucht Ceoil was, then, innovative and significant for far more than just its setting, and it is a shame that this still engaging and readable novel has not been reprinted. Ó Riain was not, however, alone among Gaelic writers in his willingness to offer a thoughtful individual perspective on new and challenging issues. We will see in more detail in chapter four how, despite Maurice Goldring's claim that Irish nationalists were suspicious of 'isms' as un-Irish,[224] several writers used historical fiction to comment on political and social issues of their own time. For example, in *Stiana*, Pádraig Ó Séaghdha explores several concrete solutions to contemporary problems, alluding to the possibility of transferring Gaeltacht people to better holdings in the Midlands (p. 94), offering strong support for the co-operative movement (pp. 93–5), and arguing for the sort of economic protectionism for Irish industry that would soon be implemented by de Valera's Fianna Fáil party on their assumption of power in 1932 (pp. 114–22).[225] In its frequent references to the importance of native institutions, the novel offers a clear if implicit rejection of the policy of an independent Irish state that was at the time adopting and/or adapting much of the British colonial apparatus already in place, an apparatus Ó Séaghdha depicts as inherently corrupt and anti-Irish.

Úna Bean Uí Dhíosca used her 1932 novel *Cailín na Gruaige Duinne* to advance her pacifist thesis that Irish national aspirations could be most fully and permanently achieved by engaging the opposition with a principled and uncompromising campaign of non-violent resistance. It should, however, also be noted that in this novel she deals honestly and forthrightly with the sensitive subject of marital breakdown, fifteen years before Séamus Ó Néill made this a central theme in his much better known novel *Tonn Tuile*. Dix depicted an incipient if inchoate feminist awareness behind her protagonist's decision to leave her brutish Gaeltacht husband and go to live in a YWCA in Belfast:

> I do not say that it was right of me to leave Michael, but I put the blame on the state Irish life was in. I little thought the day I married Michael that the day would arrive that I would curse him. But like many others in Ireland at that time, especially the women, I was not in my right mind. It had become painfully clear to me that if I stayed with Michael I would lose my mind altogether. It is not that I said that to myself, but something was driving me from him (p. 91).[226]

Equally honest is her portrayal of the woman's post partum depression, a mental state that causes her to ignore her baby and even to consider killing the child:

> It would give me a heartfelt fright to look at the window, because an intense desire would come over me to throw myself out if I could reach it. The child would send me into black fits of weeping. One time they thought I would commit some evil deed if they left the child with me . . . I had to suffer the worst mental conflict ever imposed on a person. I lay there like a stone statue, but every hair on my head was standing, the skin of my head was stretched like the skin of a drum, there was a numbness in me from head to foot, and a weird feeling in my blood. The demon that was in me began goading me – 'Smother him; put your two hands around his neck and take away his breath; that will give you relief' (pp. 93–4).[227]

Seosamh Mac Grianna, who had no reservations about claiming allegiance to at least two other 'isms' – Communism and agnosticism (*Irish Workers' Voice*, 18/8/33) – evolved his own personal brand of existentialism in *Dochartach Duibhlionna* (Melancholy Doherty) (BÁC: Cú Uladh, 1925), in which a man who has killed his father tells his story to a priest on the eve of his execution. In many ways, the protagonist of this novella is the quintessential Mac Grianna hero – a man bitterly dissatisfied with the world as it is, convinced that he is truly exceptional in his capacity for love, for crime and for artistic vision, and more than a little paranoid. From the very beginning, he sees himself as the greatest sinner who ever lived:

> O! father, did any other of the descendants of Eve do the deed I have done? . . . No. No. Isn't it strange that fire does not come from Heaven and burn the world on which I am walking. Stay away from me, father, are you not afraid of the demons and devils that are in my body? Are you not afraid that your hand will wither to the shoulder if you lay it on me? (pp. 3–4).[228]

He has, however, at the same time partially convinced himself that his father deserved his death for his snobbish and materialistic contempt for his son's intellectual and aesthetic sensibility. Tempted to commit suicide by drowning himself in a lake, he resists, but not for reasons of morality, much less Catholic morality. Rather, he feels the water itself would reject him as unclean:

> The lovely appearance left the lake. Gloom – murkiness – piercing cold came over it. Angry little choppy waves began rising from it. It did not want me at all; it put on an angry appearance for fear that I would be thinking of soiling its innocent water with my cursed bones (pp. 18–19).[229]

The novella ends ambiguously as the narrator considers the possibility of redemption, but, still convinced of his own singular depravity, he is motivated at least as much by fear as by remorse or love as he makes his plea for the Virgin's intercession:

> Perhaps, father, my fate is not that bad. Isn't it said that the Lamb of God takes away the sins of the world, the heaviest and blackest of them? There are strong fires in Purgatory. Perhaps it is not sinful of me to be thinking that they would clean the stain before Judgment Day. O loving Mary, from the mouth of Hell I implore you, defend me from your terrible Son (p. 20).[230]

Liam Lillis Ó Laoire has pointed out that Mac Grianna's obsession was always with people on the margin or at the limits, an observation that certainly applies to the main character of *Dochartach Duibhlionna*.[231] In *Mo Bhealach Féin*, Mac Grianna is, of course, his own protagonist, a stranger in the strange land that he found the Anglicised Ireland of his time. The narrator is keenly aware of his uneasy position 'between two traditions' to use Declan Kiberd's phrase, identifying himself on the very first page of the book as 'the principal poet of the Gaels in this twentieth century, in the time of the Resurrection' (rígh-éigeas na nGaedheal ins an ficheadh céad seo, i n-aimsir na hAiséirghe). The central irony throughout *Mo Bhealach Féin* is, however, just how little effect the national resurrection set in motion in 1916 has had on those who profess to be its apostles, the Irish 'nationalists' of the new dispensation, how culturally blind and trapped they remain and how oppressive is the intellectual regime they have perpetuated:

> After going around half of Ireland, the journey brought nothing into my head but constriction. I was in prison. Being within the borders of the country was just like being in my little room here. I went to bed despondent, and was visited by dreams that something different was in store for me immediately (p. 59).[232]

Whatever those great expectations might be, Mac Grianna did not believe they would be advanced by any of the political, economic, or social movements of the 1920s or 1930s. His narrator flirts with but ultimately rejects a series of fashionable 'isms', not because he sees them as antithetical to his Gaelic nature, but because he finds them stifling to his humanity. Republicanism, institutional Gaelicism, Communism, celticism, and even Marcus Garveyism all fail to satisfy his need for a vision of life at once 'significant' (éifeachtach) and 'poetic' (filiúnta), two terms he seems to have at times used almost interchangeably.[233] His principal objection to all of these philosophies was that to enjoy the security and certitude that all claimed to offer, one had to surrender one's individual vision and creative potential. And for Mac Grianna such a surrender was unthinkable:

> My journey was done. I was proud. If anyone were to ask me why I had made that walk, I would be hard put to answer him. It was my own way. It strengthened my mind and hardened my body. It had substance. It was difficult. And devils could never bring me to do the little, easy thing . . . All of life is behind the little screen of words we put on it, and there is a different sanity on that side and this, here where we only expect convention and counsel, like blind people guiding each other. I would rather walk in the dark than be blind (p. 159).[234]

Perverse, paranoid, prophetic, and exasperating, Mac Grianna's is a startlingly modern if frequently discordant voice in the chorus of Gaelic writing in his time.

Unfortunately, that voice was to be silenced shortly after it had its authoritative say in *Mo Bhealach Féin*. Mac Grianna ended that book with a stirring challenge to his enemies and an optimistic vision of his own future mission:

> I do not know where I will go next, but I do know that the wonders will come to me without my expecting them. The great world is full of poetry for the person able to understand it, and the well will never run dry. And as long as I live I will be guiding the children of the Gael to this well (p. 178).[235]

Yet within a few short years, he broke off his novel-in-progress *Dá mBíodh Ruball ar an Éan* (If there were a tail on the bird) in apparent despair: 'The well ran dry in the summer of 1935. I will write no more. I did my best and I do not care' (p. 317).[236] Mac Grianna was later to tell visitors who came to see him in the asylum in Letterkenny where he spent the last decades of his life that he had 'put a tail on the bird', but if he did so, none of that additional work has survived.[237]

More's the pity, because what we do have of *Dá mBíodh Ruball ar an Éan* is a characteristically original and provocative contribution to the evolution of

Gaelic prose into a medium fully capable of expressing all of the concerns and nuances of contemporary life. The narrator, a journalist named Maghnus Mac Giolla Bhrighde, is another of Mac Grianna's existential outsiders, a man whose life's course has been determined by his 'secret mind' (*méin rúin*):

> It was that secret mind that caused me never to succeed in life. It was that same mind that caused me to expect for years that I would be standing above the crowd. Sometimes I was a hero, sometimes I was a saint, and sometimes I was a poet, and often I was a fleeting, shapeless desire that was as untameable as the wind (p. 231).[238]

But it is the writer Cathal Mac Eachmharcaigh who is Mac Grianna's true *alter ego* in the novel. In one of his diary entries, Mac Eachmharcaigh recalls asking a friend a question hauntingly relevant for Mac Grianna himself: 'Did the world always betray art so that you lost your art for a while, so that you were for a spell as if in Hell?' (p. 271).[239]

The third principal character in the book is Liam Ó Ceannfhaolaidh, the leader of Laochra na Saoirse (The warriors of freedom), an extremist political group with a vague but ominous right-wing ideology:

> The Warriors of Freedom never bothered with the people who were out of work. In their opinion, these people were sick, and should be put in prison under the eyes of 'work doctors'. It was their view that Communism was coming and that a friendly partnership would have to be formed among the people who were working and who were in charge of what was worthy in the country (p. 249).[240]

The organisation functions with a Machiavellian ruthlessness that is even willing to have its own members killed to create public sympathy. Disgusted by what he has learned about the group, Mac Giolla Bhrighde comes to see his opposition to it as a battle between himself, 'a strong, ardent, daring, Gaelic man' (fear láidir teith dosgaidheach Gaedhealach), and Ó Ceannfhaolaidh, 'a thin-necked, useless, emotionless, Anglicised man' (fear caol-mhuineálach beag-mhaitheasach fuar-intinneach Gallta) (p. 300). Also opposing the Laochra is Eighneacháin Mac Lochlainn, a former member of the party but now an elected representative of the Dáil as well as Minister for Finance. Mac Lochlainn is every bit as devious as the Laochra themselves, and, having convinced the party he could best serve its interests by winning high office in the government, he now plans to smash the organisation by seizing its assets. The novel breaks off before we find out whether Mac Lochlainn succeeds and at what cost to himself, the state, or the movement, but even in its truncated form it confronts in a creative and original manner the troubling question of the relationship between constitutional and conspiratorial politics in the Ireland of the 1930s, a question of enormous significance at a time when the authority of the new state was being challenged by the right-wing Blueshirts on one side and by the uncompromising republican IRA on the other.

No Gaelic writer of the time, including Mac Grianna, was more interested in the novel's potential as a forum for discussing and advancing ideas and theories than was Éamonn Mac Giolla Iasachta (Edward McLysaght). Generating those ideas never seems to have been a problem for Mac Giolla Iasachta. Perhaps best known for his *Irish Family Names* (1957), he was also at various times a Free State senator, chairman of the Irish Manuscripts Commission, Keeper of Manuscripts at the National Library of Ireland, and Chief Herald of Ireland. In addition to his novels in Irish and English, he wrote other works in English on genealogy and social history, including, from our period, *Short Study of a Transplanted Family* (1935) and *Irish Life in the Seventeenth Century* (1939). In the 1920s, however, his principal loyalty was to the Irish language, as he made clear in a 1924 essay in *An Sguab*: 'The national faith I have is just the faith that Éamon de Valera proclaimed five or six years ago – that I would prefer Ireland under English domination with Irish being spoken in it to Ireland free and Irish dead.' And it was to advance his personal version of the Gaelic agenda that he entered politics: 'I find politics altogether hateful. If I am in the Senate of the Free State, I am there to strike a blow for the Irish language if I can' (*Sguab*, Nov. 1924, 209).[241] In his 1925 election manifesto, he proclaimed: 'I have been in the Senate for three years, and I would dare to say that I have done my best to advance the cause of the Irish language throughout that time. The Irish language was always my first concern in the Senate' (*FL*, 22/8/25).[242]

Perhaps the most significant way in which he served the language was by using it to discuss important ideas about which people cared in novels that mature and intelligent people could read with pleasure. He had begun to use fiction as an intellectual forum in his 1919 novel *The Gael* (Dublin: Maunsel, 1919), a book he dedicated to his son Fergus with some reservations, writing that he found it 'strange' (*ait*) to honour the monoglot Irish-speaking boy with a book in English. In his next two novels – the last he would write – he rectified this situation, turning to Irish for the development of his ideas on the political, social, and cultural life of his country in the immediate post-independence period. Although he published the first of these novels, *Cúrsaí Thomáis*, under the pseudonym 'M.', one contemporary critic for *An Stoc*, having stated he had no idea of the author's identity, was able to see parallels between this book and *The Gael*:

> It is very interesting altogether how the author describes the life and work of the Farmer in Ireland in this part of the book. Indeed I have hardly ever read in any novel so good and truthful an account of farming matters except, perhaps, for Seamus O'Kelly's *Wet Clay* and *The Gael* by McLysaght (*Stoc*, Feb. 1928, 3).[243]

In a review of *The Small Fields of Carrig*, E. O'Clery's English translation of *Cúrsaí Thomáis*, an anonymous critic stressed that even more important than the author's intimate and profound knowledge of rural life was the originality and even daring with which he approached his material:

> Very few of the much-boomed works, English or German, which are selling now by the hundred thousand, have a fraction of the insight and observation shown in this superficially artless story of the thoughts and adventures ofThomas MacGuinness. This is not to say that Edward MacLysaght is a Dostoevsky, but his book begins a new chapter in Irish literary history, because it shows how perfectly the Irish language may be adapted for a novel in the modern style (*Nation*, 1/3/30).[244]

Writing from the vantage point of sixty years after the book's publication, Alan Titley praised Mac Giolla Iasachta for the thoughtful critique of capitalism and class hierarchy implicit in *Cúrsaí Thomáis*, stating: '*Cúrsaí Thomáis* is one of the very few novels in Irish, and Irish novels of any kind, in which you become aware of the nobility of work and the dignity of labour.'[245]

The narrator of *Cúrsaí Thomáis* returns to County Clare from North America with a friend who has inherited a farm and is determined to work it successfully. While Mac Giolla Iasachta uses the novel to preach his gospel that the small farmer must be the true backbone of the nation, and while he devotes a good deal of space to the accurate and sensitive depiction of rural customs, social patterns and labour practices, he also discusses subject matter quite alien to most of the Gaelic fiction of his time. And although at one point the narrator explicitly denies that he is in any way an intellectual or a philosopher, he regularly raises weighty issues like ethnic identity, religion, and sexuality. Not surprisingly, discussions of ethnicity and ethnic stereotyping focus predominantly, though not exclusively, on the Irish. For example, the narrator ponders Irish reticence concerning the deeper emotions and intimacy:

> However much I speak my mind on every other question, I restrain myself when affairs of the heart are in question. Indeed that is a custom that the Irish have, as do the French, and for that matter, all the Latin nations most likely, how given we are to be open and talkative about the usual affairs of our lives and at the same time how reticent we are about the important things and the profound things that concern our inner side (p. 92).[246]

More surprising is Mac Giolla Iasachta's unconventional approach to Catholicism and the Catholic clergy in the novel. The narrator's friend and employer, Stiofán Mac Conmara, attributes his own heterodox Catholicism to his long residence in America, where he saw few priests and stopped attending Mass. He does not, however, feel any shame about having lapsed from formal practice of his faith, and is even willing to engage the parish priest in vigorous debate on the subject. In a more traditional work of Gaelic fiction, that debate could only end with the triumph of the priest and the repentance of the sinner. Mac Conmara does not yield an inch.

Even more troubling to some than this sympathetic portrayal of a sincere and articulate non-practising Catholic was Mac Giolla Iasachta's frank treatment of sexuality in the novel. Both illegitimacy and prostitution are discussed, as is – for the first time in fiction of the revival – abortion. Commenting on the public denunciation of a pregnant unmarried woman, Mac Conmara exclaims: 'Believe me, it won't be long until the likes of Cathleen will not have children if there is a danger that they will be made into public warnings as was done to her. And then we would be as bad as the rest of the world' (p. 87).[247] Moreover, at a time when virtually all Gaelic writers dealt with love in the most numbingly saccharine, stilted and disembodied manner, Mac Giolla Iasachta's honest treatment of sex was all but revolutionary. After fathering an illegitimate child, Mac Conmara learns that his partner was part black: 'There was a drop of black blood in her. She had a black child. I was a madman when I saw him. She told me that she would commit suicide, and she drowned herself the same night' (p. 89).[248] Although he tries to follow a more traditional code of sexual morality, Mac Aonghusa regularly finds himself tempted in the company of women to whom he is attracted:

> But at the same time I felt an energy and a vigour in me and a desire to advance a bit in life, and in particular a desire to be close to her throughout the day from morning to night – I do not say throughout the night because I do not think there were any bad thoughts about her in my mind, although that desire was doubtless back there: I was a young man of course (p. 144).[249]

Temptation reaches its peak when he finds a former girlfriend a prostitute in Dublin and seeks shelter in her room: 'I was a little bit nervous. But I remembered how my affairs were at that time, and, another thing, Peg was a very good-looking woman, wearing nothing but a nightgown. I was a young man' (p. 215).[250] He does resist the temptation, but one can imagine readers of the time wondering what a nice Gael like Tomás was doing in a place like that.

Needless to say, Mac Giolla Iasachta's daring shocked some of his colleagues in the language and literary movement, among them the critic for *Studies*, 'S. Mac M.', who, having praised the narrator's understanding of rural life, went on:

> But Tomás is not satisfied without imitating that vile set, the filthy, shameless writers who are at present plentiful . . . There is a sharp complaint to be heard from time to time in this country of ours about bad books from England, and, of course,

> there is reason for it. But it is time for us to pay good attention to the books that will be published at home from here on . . . I would far prefer to praise the book than to find fault with it; I have no choice this time, however, except to say that I hope the day is far from us that another Gaelic book like this is published (*Studies*, Sept. 1928, 497–8).[251]

The reviewer for *An Stoc* agreed that Mac Giolla Iasachta was to a large extent following the literary fashion of Anglo-Irish authors in his treatment of questionable material, and particularly in his recreation of Dublin's 'Monto' red-light district, but he was also aware that *Cúrsaí Thomáis* represented a real step forward for Gaelic fiction as a novel that adults could read without a full suspension of their critical faculties:

> I recommend that readers of *An Stoc* – except for the boys and the girls – get this book. Thanks be to God – if it is not a sin for me to say it in this case – a book is available at last that is not suitable as a school book (*Stoc*, Feb. 1928, 3).[252]

Writing of the book in *The Leader*, Liam de Lása wondered whether the Irish language in itself could have a prophylactic effect on the transmission of sexual themes:

> Frankly, 'tis a modern novel. There are coarse things and repulsive things in this new book, but we do not see them as we do the same things in English. Somehow, the Gaelic dress hides their nakedness. We have much in it of the sexology and psycho-analysis and psychopathy that make up the English novel, but no bawdy writing or deliberate dwelling on nasty things, as we find in sensational novels, of nymphs and red skies across the water. The Irish book is clean and wholesome; its realism, frank and uncompromising, paints vice only to excite the utmost horror and loathing, and sympathy for the victims.

De Lása pronounced the book 'a fine sustained piece of literature' (*Leader*, 7/1/28). 'Mac' went even farther in his defence of the book in the *Irish Rosary*, a journal that could never be accused of a lack of vigilance in defence of moral standards, warning Mac Giolla Iasachta that 'he must brace his nerves for a shower of scurrilous abuse from yokels who are incapable of understanding his book' (*IR*, Dec. 1927, 957–9). The reviewer for *The Nation* agreed, writing of the English translation of the novel: '"The Small Fields of Carrig" is a candid and very human story, although it may not please some of those who expect to find nothing in Irish literature except what is within the comprehension of children' (*Nation*, 1/3/30). Most fulsome in his support for the novel was 'T. Ó R.' (perhaps Toirdhealbhach Ó Raithbheartaigh), who called the novel 'by far the best book that has been written since the Gaelic League began' (an leabhar is fearr i bhfad dár scríobhadh ó thosaigh Connradh na Gaedhilge), and continued:

> Not only is no other writer of Irish worthy of comparison with him, but to my knowledge no novel in English has come out in Ireland for the past two years that is near it . . . Perhaps this book is the start of the Irish language Renaissance (*Ultach*, Dec. 1927, 7).[253]

Most encouraging about this novel at the time was that it was the mature ideas even more than the adult urges of its characters that made it inappropriate for the schoolchildren to whom most Gaelic writers of fiction were directing their work.

In *Toil Dé*, Mac Giolla Iasachta turned his attention to contemporary political and social issues. Reviewing the book for *United Ireland*, Liam Ó Rinn argued that it was a less well-crafted work than *Cúrsaí Thomáis*, more of an intellectual treatise than a finished work of fiction, but he also acknowledged:

> Many people will read *Toil Dé* with pleasure. It is a very honest effort to give us a genuine novel in Irish . . . Another quality I almost forgot is the diversity in it: farming, politics, war, love, the life of poor people (every person fully alive and drawn accurately), a rugby competition, a vamp, the Dáil, the Senate etc. A novel that deals with our own time so closely that it would not be possible to set it in any other time (*UI*, 7/7/34).[254]

More negative was 'Carrig', who wrote of the novel in 1937: 'The book has no thought or philosophy as a base. It does not create nor does it attempt to create for us any ideas of its own concerning the affairs of human life or the affairs of the country' (*Gaedheal*, Aug. 1937, 8).[255]

It must have been didacticism rather than philosophy that 'Carrig' missed in the novel, for the book is full of important ideas about the nature and future evolution of an independent Irish state. The central conflict in the novel concerns the efforts of an educated, well-off, and landed Roman Catholic father and son to define their identity and assert their national allegiance during the War of Independence and the Civil War. The newly radicalised father, Máirtín Mac Cárthaigh, expresses his solidarity with the rebels quietly and indirectly, as does his New Zealand-born wife, but his son Diarmuid joins and fights with the IRA, and after the Treaty sides with the Free State out of admiration for and loyalty to Michael Collins. His fiancée, Anna Bhreathnach, on the other hand, supports the anti-Treaty forces, and it is worth noting that while Mac Giolla Iasachta in his accounts of their arguments clearly sees that logic is on Diarmuid's side, he allows Anna to make some telling emotional appeals to patriotism and courage (pp. 180–1, 184). On the other hand, he seems to have been using Anna's die-hard republicanism as emblematic of the kind of dangerously impulsive and radical 'women's politics' (poilitidheacht na mban), of which many at the time were, as we saw in chapter one, fearful, and which was represented most prominently by Maud Gonne, Countess Markievicz, Mrs Tom Clarke, and Mary MacSwiney (pp. 184, 294). Certainly the compromise that Diarmuid and Anna reach to make possible their marriage will to all intents and purposes silence this perceptive and articulate young woman, as Anna surrenders if not her principles, at least her advocacy of them: 'But look, lad, we don't want to hear a word about politics ever again. Let us cast it away as a subject of interest. I am sick of it. I will spend the rest of my life mending your stockings if you want' (p. 306).[256] Startingly, Diarmuid's mother, another intelligent and forceful woman, applauds this decision: 'As sure as there is grass growing in Ireland, femininity is stronger than politics in Anna' (p. 308).[257] Perhaps Mac Giolla Iasachta himself found this compromise unduly facile, but, like many other Irish thinkers at the time, was unable to offer one more satisfying or convincing in the wake of civil war. At any rate, he had recourse to an equally implausible *deus-ex-machina* ending that enabled him to avoid exploring the complex and contradictory challenges of a marriage between the Free Stater Diarmuid and the die-hard Anna by having the former fall to his death after an accidental slip at the Cliffs of Moher. The novel then concludes with Anna going to live with her dead fiancé's parents, a conclusion that inspires the following flight of didactic optimism from the author:

> Let us leave them like that: if they are not a happy household, they are a close household, a household working together and not surrendering to the despair that afflicts them. And of course, we should not lose our courage because a single person, or two or three, however likeable, however good, have gone from us. Thank God, Father Fergus was right: there are good men, and good women too, in Ireland still; and plenty of work for them to do in the rebuilding of Ireland (p. 314).[258]

In effect, *Toil Dé* is a rather schizophrenic novel, a work primarily interested in political and cultural ideas in the chapters leading up to the Civil War, and then focusing on personal and romantic concerns thereafter. But even though we can fault Mac Giolla Iasachta for his inability or unwillingness to face the consequences of the Civil War divisions and hatreds, we should appreciate just how much of value he does have to say about 'the rebuilding of Ireland'. Some of the points he raises seem to have been pet issues of his own, like the need for Irish shipping (p. 49), the ugliness of glass-encased funeral wreaths (p. 149), Irish neglect of historical monuments (p. 159), and the disadvantages of adopting summer time (pp. 161–2). But far more important issues were also addressed in the novel, among them several familiar from *The*

Gael and *Cúrsaí Thomáis*. For example, once again Mac Giolla Iasachta affirms his belief that a productive and enlightened rural population should be the foundation for the new state and that that population required leadership from those more prosperous and better educated. Throughout the novel, Máirtín Mac Cárthaigh is motivated by a keenly felt sense of *noblesse oblige*, an awareness of what can only be called a vocation to improve the lives of those around him. It is for this reason that he urges Diarmuid to study agriculture:

> If you intend to continue farming, I will be needing something more than an energetic workman. What I myself lack is knowledge of the art of tillage and so on. You will have to get a degree and bring home knowledge of the latest methods. I am aware of my ignorance and I am trying to improve things here (p. 187).[259]

This belief in an ascendancy of service is central to the thinking of the Mac Cárthaigh family with regard to both social class and national identity. For example, Diarmuid is disgusted by the apostasy of the well-off, whether of Anglo-Irish or of native Gaelic stock:

> According to themselves, they were not of the Gaelic nation – that was their story ten years ago before the new order was established in Ireland at any rate. They had contempt for the Gaels who did the ploughing and harrowing for them to keep them on top. You would think that this mindset would be unnatural in one of old Gaelic stock although it would be understandable in one of English background, but it is hard to recognise the Gael from the Anglo-Irish person among the Irish gentry (p. 48).[260]

The problem is not, then, primarily one of ethnicity, but rather of allegiance. Speaking in his own voice on the post-independence departure of many members of the landed establishment, 'both native and Anglo-Irish' (*idir Ghaedheal a's Gall*), Mac Giolla Iasachta was explicit on this point:

> That group was truly Anglicised in their minds, but even so they called themselves Irish despite the hatred they had for the Gaels of Ireland. I would not deny that they also loved Ireland, in their own way: a local love like the love the English have for their own county. They were Englishmen in their minds and hearts, and that love was, in the end, only a love for the fine wide fields they had in Ireland, for the hunting, for the shooting, for the fishing, and for all the sport they could have in it (p. 208).[261]

Predictably, Mac Giolla Iasachta's bridge over what he called 'the divide between the gentry of the country and the common people' (deighilt uaisle a's maithe na tíre ón gcoitchiantacht), the bridge that would allow the gentry to share again in their own national heritage, was *Gaelachas*:

> The reign of the landlords in Ireland was absolutely over . . . They had not learned their lesson fully, however. They did not hate the children of the Gael as much perhaps as they had before they were driven out, but they failed entirely to understand the goal and the energy behind the insurrection and they were always blind to the meaning of *Gaelachas* (pp. 208–9).[262]

Needless to say, the members of the Mac Cárthaigh family learn Irish and devote themselves to the re-Gaelicisation of their country, with Diarmuid dreaming of founding a progressive Gaelic school modelled on Pearse's Sgoil Éanna (pp. 192–3).

Also of interest is Mac Giolla Iasachta's continuing independence in his treatment of the Catholic Church and its clergy. Máirtín Mac Cárthaigh at one point finds himself trying to explain his nationalism to a snobbish priest, who exclaims: 'I do not know what is happening to the world at all. The richest and the most respectable people in my parish siding with the rabble!' (p. 79).[263] Another priest angers Mac Cárthaigh's wife by his refusal to hear the confessions of Irish-speakers in their own language (p. 85). Even more significant is the criticism of sectarian education implicit in Máirtín's warning to Diarmuid that Church authorities will never allow him to run his school along the progressive lines he projects (pp. 192–3). And it should also be noted that Diarmuid, despite the opposition of a priest, decides to attend Trinity College instead of the National University (pp. 195, 211–12).

Like Mac Giolla Iasachta himself, Máirtín Mac Cárthaigh enters the new Irish Senate, where he refuses any party affiliation and finds himself increasingly isolated and ineffectual. He soldiers on, however, inspired by a vision that few of his colleagues in that turbulent and embittered time would have found either feasible or congenial:

> However slight his interest in the ordinary work of the Parliament, there was one question outside agricultural affairs in which Máirtín took a great interest: he wanted there to be true friendship between Ireland and England, a friendship based on parity of respect, as was proper when two ancient, independent nations were in question (pp. 248–9).[264]

When he finally delivers his long pondered major speech on this subject in Irish, all who understand him are impressed and influenced, but for the majority of the senators 'the precise, knowledgeable sentences being spoken so forcefully by Máirtín Mac Cárthaigh were like the jargon of a black man from the ends of Africa' (p. 255).[265]

Though no other Gaelic writer of the time wrote of politics with the ambition and scope of Mac Giolla Iasachta, several did turn their attention to the often less than edifying debates of their own day. In addition to the stories dealing with the contemporary scene by León Ó Broin and Art Ó Riain discussed above, we have a few satirical pieces on politics in our period. Father Dinneen offered a comic picture of a politician starved for attention in 'An Chuma i n-ar Leigheasadh Domhnall' (How Domhnall was cured) (*Leader*, 12/1/29), while C. B. Mac Séamuis lampooned the dilatory nature of parliamentary procedures in 'I dTír Áirithe / Cuirtear Coimisiúin ar Bun / Fabhail-Sgéal Beag' (In a certain country / A commission is established / A little fable) (*II*, 5/6/39). Colm Ó Gaora's story 'An tÓráididhe Gasta' (The clever orator) satirises the fervent Irish anti-communism of the period. A member of an organisation opposed to the ill-treatment of donkeys inadvertantly uses the word 'comrade' and thus draws on himself the wrath of the right-thinking.[266] Utterly farcical was the anonymous 'Gradam an Mhaighistreach' (The master's grandeur) (*Standard*, 4/7/31), where an insulted servant takes advantage of his would-be politician master's riding an elephant at a circus to cause him embarrassment. More serious were Aodh de Blácam's political allegory 'Ar Thóir Róisín / Fáithscéal Úr-Dhéanta' (In search of Róisín / A contemporary fable) (*FL*, 15/3/24), and 'An Cailín nár Thuig File' (A girl who did not understand a poet) by 'L. Mac G.', a tale of what the author saw as the ongoing Free State repression of anti-Treaty republicans in 1931 (*An Phoblacht*, 29/4/33).

Politics *per se* doesn't seem to have provided much inspiration to Gaelic playwrights. Peadar Ó Dubhda's *Margadh Sheáin / Dráma Beag de'n Togha Mór* (John's bargain / A little drama of the general election) is a brief skit dealing with the general election of the previous year (Dundalk *Examiner*, 28/1/33). Considerably more ambitious was Séamus de Bhilmot's allegorical play *'Grádh Níos Mó'* ('Greater love') (BÁC: OS, 1947).[267] Set in an unspecified foreign capital, the play dramatises the events surrounding the invasion of the country by its old colonial occupier using as pretext a border dispute. De Bhilmot raises several intriguing issues in the play, among them the need for the newly independent state to assert its rights in the eyes of the world, the moral dilemma of targeting civilians in modern total warfare, and the question of what price one should be willing to pay for victory in such a conflict. The leader of the nation, a hero of the independence struggle, is disgusted by the indiscriminate nature of modern combat and resists allowing his troops to use gas, even when they are in danger of being overwhelmed in their defence of the capital. At one point, a gardener debates the morality of just following orders. Acknowledging that it is the duty of soldiers to obey their superiors, he continues:

> But who gave the orders? Professional soldiers who have spent their lives with plans for death and blood. But now, when their plans are useless what do they do? . . . They go behind the army and inflict death on the women and children of the soldiers. War! A glorious fight for your country! And those people think that there are no exceptions . . . that they can get people to carry out their terrible orders. They think that it is as easy for a person to change his character as it is to change his clothes (pp. 35–6).[268]

And, with a startling appeal to the example of Pearse, who had surrendered in Easter 1916 rather than bring further suffering on Dublin's civilians, the leader himself again rejects the use of gas for his beleaguered troops, fails in an attempt to destroy the factory producing it, and, facing a crucifix in the moments before his death, exclaims: 'You stood alone once. You will understand my story. You will understand it' (p. 43).[269]

With this work by de Bhilmot we have in many ways come full circle, for if in the early 1920s there was real concern about whether Irish could address the rapidly changing and complex affairs of the present, we find in this play a mature and forthright exploration of momentous questions that were to convulse Europe and the rest of the world in the immediate future, from the time of the Second World War to today's headlines from the Middle East, Africa, the Balkans, and Afghanistan, not to mention the north of Ireland itself. De Bhilmot was, of course, building on the accomplishments of a host of other Gaelic pioneers, from Pearse and Pádraic Ó Conaire, through Béaslaí, Mac Grianna, Ó Broin, W. P. Ryan, Art Ó Riain, Úna Bean Uí Dhíosca, George Thomson, Máiréad Ní Ghráda, and Liam Ó Rinn to name just a few. That so many of those achievements were ignored in their own time and have been long forgotten since is hardly the fault of writers who took on the hard work of bringing the Irish language into the mainstream of contemporary Irish life. Writing in 1920, two short years before the creation of an independent state would put unprecedented demands on the creativity and adaptability of what was to become the officially recognised national language, Colm Ó Murchú ('Taube') summed up the daunting challenge facing the Gaelic author in this new Irish order:

> There are only two things to be done if we want Irish to be our national language again – to bring Irish forward three hundred years or to put the world back that amount of time. It's not hard to make out which of those two things will be done. As with Mohammed and the mountain long ago, this world is too firmly established, and I'm afraid that it is Irish that will have to move forward if it wants to make contact with it. Now literature is the road Irish will have to take in that movement forward. Literature is the soil in which Irish will grow until it has made up the amount of growth necessary, and literature is also the sieve through which will be sifted every new thing that comes and has to come into the language during that growth (*IF*, Aug. 1920, 12).[270]

In the face of apathy, misunderstanding, and even active opposition, a surprising number of Gaelic writers answered that call, in the process bringing Ó Murchú's Gaeilgeoir Mohammed a good deal closer to the modern mountain than most would have imagined possible when they set out with him on the journey.

FOUR

'WELLSPRING OF NATIONALITY'

THE GAELIC WRITER AND THE IRISH PAST

For the advanced nationalists who comprised the vast majority of those involved in the language movement, the meaning of their country's history was clear. In the words of Helena Concannon, the historian and wife of Tomás Ua Concheanainn, Irish history revealed

> how it came about that a little nation, single-handed – and single-hearted – has been able to do such great deeds for God and humanity, and how wonderfully that nation has been preserved through sufferings and combats unparalleled, to do like deeds for the same causes in the years to come (*Studies*, Mar. 1922, 142).

Caitlín Nic Ghabhann put the same idea in the mouths of ancestral spirits speaking to the citizens of the Free State in her 1925 history of County Dublin, *Mágh Ealta Éadair*:

> Take courage. This ancient Gaelic Nation for which thousands have died will always be a Gaelic Nation. The country that stood its ground for nine hundred years against the enemies you have seen coming against it will stand its ground to the very end. Awaken your courage, my children![1]

For many at this time, particularly those who accepted Michael Collins's view of the Anglo-Irish Treaty of 1921, the survival of that Gaelic nation was now all but assured, depending only on the proven courage and determination of the Irish themselves. Writing shortly before his death in 1922, Collins proclaimed:

> We shall have complete freedom for all our purposes. We shall be rid completely of British interference and British rule. We can establish in its place our own rule, and exactly what kind of rule we like. We can restore our Gaelic life in exactly what form we like. We can keep what we have gained and make it secure and strong. The little we have not yet gained we can go ahead and gain.[2]

While those who rejected the Treaty would doubtless have argued that much, not little, remained unwon, they too had to be aware that the course of Irish history for what Yeats had called 'the seven heroic centuries' had been changed beyond recognition. It is, then, hardly surprising that many at the time may have felt that history as they had always conceived it had come to an end with stunning rapidity, and that they themselves had helped to achieve the culmination of almost a millennium of national aspiration and heroic self-sacrifice. In effect, the Irish people of the 1920s and 1930s believed they were battle-tested, first-hand authorities on the most important period in the history of their nation, the period that had finally brought to coherence and consummation virtually all that had gone before.

This proud obsession with the immediate past could, of course, obscure or distort a proper understanding of the events of more remote periods in Irish history. Throughout these two decades, writers not infrequently chided their countrymen for their ignorance of the full sweep of the national past, often in terms not all that different from those heard at the beginning of the Revival. Writing in the *Weekly Freeman* in 1923, T. F. O'Rahilly blasted what he called 'the prevalent disease of ignorance' among the Irish, stating: 'They were probably the most ignorant people in Western Europe, and of nothing were they more ignorant than of their own past history' (*Weekly Freeman*, 17/11/23). Pádraig Mac Suibhne agreed, asserting in *Irisleabhar Muighe Nuadhat* in 1929:

> There are no people on the face of the earth less knowledgeable about the traditional lore and history of their country than the people of Ireland. There are great lessons in every bit of it if one but comes to understand them (*IMN*, 1929, 58).[3]

In 1934, the editor of *An t-Éireannach* asked:

> How many people take the least interest in the history of the country after they turn their backs on school or college? And even more shameful, how many people are there who know a bit or a lot about history, but whose knowledge is a dry, dead thing – a thing without juice or sap? Could not the people of the country be brought to take a keen interest in the history of the country; and, by degrees, could they not be brought to feel how beautiful, splendid, and noble their own country is? (*Éireannach*, 30/6/34).[4]

On the whole, however, most Gaels at this time probably agreed with 'Ballybricken' when he wrote in 1926 that

> to-day the student of history is far better placed than he was in the past, and if the Irish-Ireland Movement had accomplished nothing else beyond all that it has done to turn the minds of the Irish people to the subject of their history and given the

> incentive, which it undoubtedly has done, to the writing of history as well as to its study, it would deserve well of future generations (*Honesty*, 13/2/26).

An Gúm put historical research and writing on its agenda quite early, announcing in July 1930:

> To assist with the publication of books other than novels in Irish, the Department of Education is offering a certain number of special grants of £150 to £250 apiece to authors who will write books on specific subjects under the following headings provided that the subjects be approved by the Department:
>
> (1) A history of some recent political or social movement;
>
> (2) A biography of a famous Irish person;
>
> (3) A study of a particular aspect or a particular period from the history of literature in Irish (*Lóchrann*, July 1930, 7).[5]

In effect, however, most of the government's publishing in the field of history was directed at the schools and colleges, and, as we will see, the state provided a good number of history textbooks, original and translated, during this period. The reader interested in the past who wanted something more than a traditional textbook was nowhere near so well served by An Gúm, a point raised by Séamus Ó Néill in his 1936 review of Tomás Ó Cléirigh's *Aodh Mac Aingil agus an Scoil Nua-Ghaedhilge i Lobháin*, one of the rare serious works of history the agency published: 'It is good that Tomás Ó Cléirigh wrote this book in Irish. It is a pity that An Gúm does not set people who know how to do the job to writing books of this kind' (*Examiner*, 8/8/36).[6]

If the amateur historian could find little to read about Irish history, he would have been able to hear a fair amount on the subject. In addition to sponsoring competitions on history at the Oireachtas and at local *feiseanna*, Gaelic League branches continued their longstanding policy of holding regular lectures on historical topics. This commitment was spelled out in the League's schedule of activities for 1929 under the heading 'Stair (History)': 'To teach the history of the country. To have lectures on that material in English, if necessary, for the primary classes' (Stair na tíre a mhúineadh. Léigheachtaí a bheith ar an ádhbhar sin i mBéarla más gádh é, do na bun ranganna) (*Honesty*, 21/9/29). Most branches seem to have taken this programme seriously, with the London branch, for example, initiating a series of brief weekly lectures in Irish history after every language class at its Ard-Scoil in 1935.

The League was by no means the only Gaelic organisation to sponsor such lectures. It was, for example, the Dublin branch of An Fáinne that sponsored one of the lectures upon which Nic Ghabhann's *Mágh Ealta Éadair* was based. In 1924, the Cork branch of the same group hosted, among others, Seán Ó Ciosáin, who addressed the members on 'Stair na hÉireann: An Innsint

Gaolach nó an Innsint Gallda' (Irish history: The Gaelic version or the English version) (*Cork Weekly Examiner*, 30/12/24). An Cumann Gaedhealach, the student Gaelic society of University College Dublin, also included history lectures on its program, as when Máirín Nic Dhiarmada addressed her fellow students on 'Na Mná i Saoghal na h-Éireann Fadó' (Women in Irish life long ago). Nic Dhiarmada offered an unapologetically feminist reading of her sources:

> Here is how I understand the story. The condition of women was not altogether identical to the condition of men. If one of them was dominant it was the men. But the men did not keep any power to themselves; they only kept the reputation of power. They did not want to take privileges from the women, but they thought it a fine thing to let the whole world know that it was they who had the authority. Nevertheless they liked to bestow luxuries on their wives when they were quiet and mild-mannered. They thought little of the intellect of women and of their honesty, and therefore they kept the power to themselves, and I tell you that the world has changed little from then to now (*IP*, 16/12/31).[7]

Members of the Catholic Truth Society might not have found Nic Dhiarmada's lecture all that edifying, but they could have heard more congenial talks on Irish history under the auspices of their own organisation.[8]

Many Gaels saw the new technology of radio as an even more powerful medium to bring national history into the home itself. Shortly before the inauguration of the national broadcasting service 2RN (later Radio Éireann), Pádhraic Ó Domhnalláin wrote in an editorial in *Fáinne an Lae*:

> The Government of the Free State is about to begin broadcasting. Let them remember the Irish language, the history of Ireland, Irish learning . . . It is the clever, fluent broadcaster who will teach the masses in future, like the storytellers of Ireland in olden times (*FL*, 20/6/25).[9]

Early the following year, the director of the new station, Séamus de Chlanndiolúin, seems to have taken Ó Domhnalláin's appeal to heart, announcing a series of weekly lectures in Irish based on Eoghan Ó Neachtain's history textbook *Stair-Cheachta* (*FL*, 27/2/26). History lectures were broadcast – in both Irish and English – with some regularity thereafter. And throughout the 1930s the station periodically sought new ways to incorporate history into its programme schedule, as when the director issued a notice to Gaelic writers seeking lectures that could be tied in with commemorative occasions (*Ultach*, June, 1935, 6).

Another new medium whose extraordinary popularity in Ireland both troubled and intrigued the Gaels was the cinema. Many, while deeply concerned about the influence of imported English and American films, recognised the potential of the movies to educate the masses in both the facts and, more important, the spirit of Irish history. Both of these reactions are evident in the comments of an anonymous contributor to *An Phoblacht* in 1933:

> There are only two cures for the movies: – to drive them out altogether (and we would not lose much), or to get Gaelic pictures in which there would be the culture and nationality and spirit of our country. And we have so much material: the variegated and vigorous history of our people, the life of the Gaeltacht and the city, the beauty of the countryside, and the mind of the Gaels (*An Phoblacht*, 29/4/33).[10]

Five years later, Éinrí Mac Éamoinn made a similar plea for Irish historical films:

> Our history is another sphere in which there is ample scope for the production of films of real Irish interest. The colourful personalities of the past make fine material. The story of our Faith, the Mass-rock and sagart aroon – these are the themes for native pictures (*Leader*, 16/4/38).

Colm Ó Domhnaill set his sights higher, writing in *Comhthrom Féinne* on the aesthetic potential of Irish history as subject matter for the screen:

> It is possible to get material for a better film than 'Catherine the Great' or 'The Chess Player' from our own history. Why not show a film of 'The Battle of Clontarf' and the contention that preceded and followed it? It would have to be as good as Lang's 'Nibelung'. In the attack on Limerick and the blowing up of the arms at Ballyneety there is material that would be fitting for Eisenstein himself (*Comhthrom Féinne*, June 1934, 48).[11]

Gaels also hoped that Irish history would be the focus of more traditional forms of cultural expression. Drama was one genre that many felt had been too long neglected. Having seen B. N. Lóiste's historical play *Inbhear Náile* (St Náile's estuary), an anonymous reviewer lamented: 'It is a pity that we do not have more dramas like this – dramas based on the history of the country, both lay and ecclesiastical history' (*TCNÍ*, Dec. 1936, 285).[12] Underlying such frustration was a sense of just how much Gaelic playwrights might accomplish with the treasure trove of material available to them. Impressed by a 1928 production of Pádraig de Brún's translation of Sophocles' *Oedipus Rex* at Maynooth, Aodh de Blácam wrote:

> It is a cause for pride for those at the College how well this wonderful drama was translated and produced – and heard! I hope that it will inspire someone to take material for a drama from the history or the literature of Ireland, so that we will yet

> see kings and saints represented on the stage in a dignified and imposing manner (*IMN*, 1928, 48).[13]

By far the most fervent in his belief in the historical drama as an inspirational force was Liam Ó Drisceóil, a student at Mount St Joseph's College in Roscrea, County Tipperary, whose prize-winning essay on 'An Dráma mar Chabhair do'n Ghaoluinn' (Drama as an aid to the Irish language) was published in the school magazine *An Fiolar* in 1933. Ó Drisceóil proclaimed:

> There is material for drama in every bit of the history of Ireland. If, for example, a drama based on Benburb were produced on stage, and if we were to hear again Eoghan Rua Ó Néill inciting his soldiers . . . Or if we were to hear the battle cry of the Wild Geese at Fontenoy . . . the memory of our fathers before us would be brought home to us, and few would not hate the rabble who use English – and even better there would be awakened in our hearts love for the beautiful language native to Patrick, Brigid, and Colm Cille (*Fiolar*, 1933, 25).[14]

Other Gaels shared his belief in the educational potential of historical drama. Writing in *An Muimhneach* in 1933, 'S. Ó R.' argued:

> The learned and the learners would get most use out of the drama. The history of our country would be seen brought to life again; they would see the ancient culture of the Gaels; and they would hear the sweet Irish being spoken from the stage with sweetness and accuracy, with [proper] accent and in abundance (*Muimhneach*, Apr. 1933, 75).[15]

Some, however, were quick to point out the challenges of historical drama, challenges only made more daunting if the plays were directed at young audiences. For example, writing in 1927, Liam Ó Rinn explained why it was so difficult to write credible plays on historical topics:

> We know how people alive now speak and what they would be most likely to do and say in this or that kind of situation, and how they would say it. We have knowledge and experience of the 'atmosphere' of the world as it is now, but we do not yet have enough knowledge of the events of the time that is gone to imagine for ourselves the 'atmosphere' or 'atmospheres' of that time (*Freeman*, 10/9/27).[16]

The Gaelic League committee that under the chairmanship of Aindrias Ó Muimhneacháin compiled the pamphlet *An Gaedheal agus an Rádió* was so aware of the difficulties of historical drama that it offered the following advice to would-be Gaelic practitioners of the genre:

> It is not a good idea to choose a historical drama from the old times because something like that cannot be produced without clothing and furnishings relevant to the time period of the drama itself to convey that unfamiliar world to the audience.[17]

One simple way around this problem was to simplify the plays themselves down to a bare, easily followed, and engaging minimum. This approach was put into practice in our period with short original musical plays ('mion-drámaí ceoil') and even shorter musical skits ('gníomh-amhráin') acting out the lyrics of songs. Both of these sub-genres were discussed by Tomás Mac Eochaidh in *Láimh-Leabhar Drámaidheachta* (A drama handbook), a practical manual published by the Western branch of Cumann Drámaidheachta na Sgol in conjunction with its annual festival in Galway in 1938. Explaining the difference between them, Mac Eochaidh wrote:

> For the musical skit you provide a song in which an adventure or a story is being narrated, and you illustrate that story as well as you can. For the short musical play, you yourself compose the story or the adventure, and then you provide the songs that best suit and illustrate the story to the audience. You can only put one song into the musical skit; there is no limit to the number of songs that can be put into the short musical play – but they must all have some connection with the plot of the drama.[18]

Mac Eochaidh stressed that history was a logical source of original plot lines for the *mion-drámaí* and for songs with which to accompany them or on which to base *gníomh-amhráin*. Moreover, he seems to have put his theories into successful practice at the 1938 festival in Galway, where his own *mion-dráma ceoil* dealing with Patrick Sarsfield, *Fairíor nach ar son na hÉireann* (Alas not for Ireland) won first prize in its category, and his *gníomh-amhrán*, *Donnchadh Bán*, was singled out for praise by Gearóid Ó Lochlainn and Frank Dermody.[19]

The historical novel was a genre with whose conventions many readers of Irish were already familiar and comfortable through the work of both English language authors like Scott and Canon Sheehan and the few Gaelic writers such as Peadar Ua Laoghaire and Patrick Dinneen who had tried their hand at it. Furthermore, historical fiction constituted a fair percentage of the work being translated under the auspices of An Gúm. One can, therefore, understand the Gaelic disappointment with how little writers of Irish had accomplished in this area since the beginning of the Revival. This frustration is evident in the words of an anonymous contributor to the *Irish Rosary* in 1923:

> Many of late are saying that it is tough work for the writer of Irish who wants to compose stories for us about things that happened in Ireland according to history, stories of the kind that Walter Scott and R. L. Stevenson wrote about the Scottish

> lowlands and Standish O'Grady and that noble woman Miss McManus wrote in English. It is without doubt tough work, but we must have a little bit of patience (*IR*, Feb. 1923, 140).[20]

Even a writer sceptical about the possibilities of bringing history alive on the stage could urge Gaelic authors to attempt the feat on the page. Liam Ó Rinn, whose reservations about historical drama were noted above, wrote in 1934:

> The bare, cold facts of history are not much help to us to imagine for ourselves the ancient adventures as they looked long ago to the people who took part in them or who saw them, or who heard them talked about soon after they happened. The novelist comes and he puts flesh on the skeleton. He breathes life into it, and he makes it possible for us to live through the whole story as if we were alive as it happened. Indeed there are many people whose only knowledge of history is what they got out of historical novels and dramas (*UI*, 29/9/34).[21]

Underlying all these various laments and exhortations was the sense that Irish history at this crucial point in the nation's destiny was a presence powerfully felt but little understood. As M. Ó Floinn put it bluntly in a 1937 review of León Ó Broin's biography *Parnell*: 'It must be admitted that the history of Ireland is still unwritten' (*Gaedheal*, Sept. 1937, 10).[22] Liam Ó Rinn was in general agreement, writing in 1932:

> It is an old complaint of mine that we still do not have the history of Ireland in Irish. We only have a few trivial little books of history in our own language, and I think half of those are translations from English (*UIrman*, 23/7/32).[23]

In a 1930 review of the first part of Peadar Ua Laoghaire's *Aodh Ruadh*, 'C. O'S.' confronted Gaelic scholars with their failure in this regard:

> And I have a question for contemporary scholars of the Irish language. Why is there not to be found from them a good, accurate account of the two great Hughs, a biography in which there would be new material from the manuscripts and so forth that have emerged from hiding in Spain, in Ireland, and in England during the time that has passed since Ó Cléirigh first composed the original book? That is something that readers sorely need. No praise is due to Irish scholars that there is not at this point in time a series of books available in the new manner and in the new spirit on Gaelic heroes (*Dublin Magazine*, July–Sept. 1930, 70).[24]

Many in the movement wanted more of that modern method and spirit and less of the traditional heroic biographical approach from the hoped-for new school of Gaelic historians. For example, in 1932 Maoghnus Ó Domhnaill asserted:

> The history of the country has still not been written properly, and it will never be written properly until the people have all the information, for although we hear plenty of talk about battles and movements we do not understand the life or the character of the ancient Gaels or the thoughts that were in their hearts . . . The battles and the movements were like the surface of the water that was being stirred and disturbed by the storm, but as for the things that were under the water itself, as for the things that the common people felt and the life they lived, we are almost blind to them (*ACS*, 6/2/32).[25]

Such an obsession with strife and violence was the major flaw for which one 'C. S.' faulted An t-Athair Pádraig Mac Giolla Cheara's history primer *Scéal na h-Éireann* (The Story of Ireland):

> The name on the book is 'The Story of Ireland' and if the story of Ireland is only war, wrangling, and trouble, Father Patrick has given us that story. But it was not like this, there is another side to the story, and he does not discuss that side at all . . . Therefore, after having read the book, children would think that what we are accused of by the enemies of our country is true, that we were always wrangling and fighting (*Studies*, Sept. 1924, 486).[26]

The new state, through its first Minister for Education Eoin Mac Néill, apparently agreed, setting out the following guidelines for the teaching of history in its programme for the National Schools:

> In general, the periods of our history which are more inspiring should be more specially dwelt on. Military events should be kept in their proper perspective, and be subordinated to the religious, social, industrial, literary, and artistic records of the people (*Nation*, 17/12/27).

The following year, the editor of the professional journal the *Teacher's Work* urged those responsible for implementing the new programme to take the responsibility seriously, stating: 'Wars, treaties, national alignments all have their reasonable claim to attention. But the other, the more human and usual things, have a superior claim' (*Teacher's Work*, Mar. 1928, 261). That the change to a more balanced treatment of history in the classroom was resisted by some is evident from the comments of Micheál Ó Donnchadha in a 1932 piece sharply critical of the way the subject was taught in Irish schools:

> I myself thought for a while that the people who were in the world long ago had nothing to do except to be shooting and killing each other from one end of the year to the next; I never thought that there were women at that time, nor children, nor workers, nothing but kings and soldiers . . . The scholars (and the teachers also, I

> fear) take more interest in matters of war than they do in matters of peace and commerce (*II*, 10/11/32).[27]

Many Gaelic writers had no doubt about the nature of those 'more human and usual things' that were 'better calculated to lead to pride of country'. Calls for what we would now call social and cultural history were common throughout this period. As early as 1922, M. Diolún (Myles Dillon) saw promising new developments in the teaching of Irish history, writing in the UCD journal *An Reult*:

> Until recently, history as it was taught was the story of the kings who came to rule the country, and about the battles they fought, the day of their birth, the day of their death, and so on. But usually an attempt is now made to interpret for the new world the old world, both noble and common, their customs and their deeds and their thoughts, affairs of war and affairs of peace (*Reult*, Mar. 1922, 57).[28]

Writing on 'Stair na hÉireann' (Irish history) in 1928, an anonymous contributor also downplayed the importance of political and military history, claiming that there were at least two other aspects of the national past every bit as important: 'the history dealing with the work and civilisation of our nation – art, culture, and architecture' (an stair a bhaineas le saothar agus sibhíaltacht ár náisiúin – ealadha, cultúr agus foirghníomhacht) and 'history dealing with the possession of the land' (stair a bhaineas le seilbh na talmhan). This writer obviously felt that the teaching of this kind of Irish history would provide just the sort of inspiration the state's new programme envisioned: 'With that kind of history being taught, the children would understand the high rank Ireland once achieved, and the importance involved with our national language and with our ancient way of life' (*Tír*, Oct. 1928, 8).[29] An tAthair Eric Mac Fhinn agreed, writing on 'Béaloideas' (Folklore) in 1936:

> The most important part of history – and the part that is least referred to in the usual books about the history of Ireland, in the nineteenth century, say – is the life of the people of the country: their customs, their thoughts, the things they liked, the way they lived – even the little foolish things that would remind the exile of the days of his youth. Those things are to be learned from the oral narration of the old (*AA*, Feb. 1936, 4).[30]

Moreover, according to 'An Dálach' in a 1939 essay on 'Béaloideas / Oighreacht na Sean-Aimsire' (Folklore / The inheritance of the past), this was precisely the sort of knowledge suppressed by the traditional focus on statecraft in the teaching of history:

> There are many aspects of the life of the nation that are not clear to the person who writes an account of political matters alone. The mind and character of the people who kept the precious folklore alive is not clear to him. The philosophy that was behind the traditional lore and the indefatigable spirit of the Gael is not clear. He did not understand that the heritage of the race is more lasting than the foolish little things in which he himself took an interest (*II*, 7/3/39).[31]

It was this 'precious folklore' that provided the principal source from which Gaelic writers interested in history drew the material with which they fleshed out the traditional outline of the nation's past, following a principle laid down by Peadar Mac Fhionnlaoich in 1935: 'Folklore informs us, not only about the bare events of history, but about the mind and heart and thoughts of all who came before us' (*Éireannach*, 6/4/35).[32] The most vocal champion of this approach was James Delargy. Writing in *Studies* in 1936, he pronounced Irish folklore 'the State Papers of a forgotten and neglected people', and continued:

> Written sources dealt in the main with the history of the nation and its leaders, and it was necessary to seek a wider field for research in order to know and understand the life lived by the ordinary people in both town and country. There were many questions of importance to the student of social history, none of which could be answered satisfactorily by any historian – but the answers were to be found, not in books, not in manuscripts, but on the lips of poor people living in many parts of the country (*Studies*, Sept. 1936, 399).[33]

Many agreed. For example, in his *Aistí ar Litridheacht Ghréigise is Laidne*, Father Dinneen defended Livy's use of folklore in his history of Rome, and implied that such material would also be helpful to Irish historians:

> Many readers gave credence to those stories; and their being at the very beginning greatly enhances the story, for those of them that did not happen were composed through love for the Roman Republic and to teach the common people. There are stories like those dealing with other countries and with Ireland as well.[34]

One Gaelic writer who had already made use of such stories was Caitlín Nic Ghabhann, who wrote in the preface to *Mágh Ealta Éadair*:

> There is nothing more lasting – nor more reliable, in its own way – than folklore. Stories about the ancestral land are told by the fire, generation after generation. They are added to, or taken from, but the substance of the stories remains unchanged. Sometimes, the stories are proved true.[35]

Pádraig Ó Siochfhradha readily acknowledged the important role folk tradition played in the compilation of his authoritative survey of place names on the Dingle Peninsula, *Triocha-Chéad Chorca Dhuibhne* (The cantreds of Corca Dhuibhne) (1939). Speaking of his experience in his native West Kerry, he wrote in the preface to the book:

> The people to whom I read my lists had a very great interest in them, and for them the amount of history and traditional lore that were awakened by the memory of the names was like bringing the dead alive from the grave. It was brought home to me that the history and life of the ordinary rural people in the townlands is one aspect of folklore that is worth searching for and setting down in writing and preserving as knowledge for every generation to come.[36]

The Gaelic author interested in exploring the potential range of such material could turn for guidance to Seán Ó Súilleabháin's *Láimh-Leabhar Béaloideasa*, which included a separate section on 'Seanchus Stairiúil' (Traditional lore dealing with history) and referred to historical questions in all of its sections and subsections.

Among other writers who drew explicitly on folklore sources in their treatment of national, and more particularly local, history were Father Lawrence Murray in his work on Oméith and southeastern Ulster;[37] Domhnall Ua Murchadha in his *Sean-Aimsireacht*; the authors of both famous and less well-known Gaeltacht autobiographies, people like Tomás Ó Criomhthain, Peig Sayers, and Niall Mac Giolla Bhríghde; writers of regional fiction like Séamus Ó Grianna and Seaghán Bán Mac Meanman;[38] and Domhnall Ó Súilleabháin, who concluded his 1936 biography of Daniel O'Connell with a chapter entitled 'An Conallach sa mBéaloideas' (O'Connell in the folklore).[39]

Needless to say, the use of folklore as historical source had its dangers – dangers that not all avoided at all times. For example, in his *Oileáin Árann*, An tAthair Mártan Ó Domhnaill seems reasonably aware of the potential unreliability of the traditional sources on which he draws throughout the book, but in practice is almost invariably willing to accept the credibility and accuracy of traditional stories about the islands' 'saints', for example, just as he subscribes to the pseudo-historical scheme of early Irish history set out in *Lebor Gabála Érenn* (the so-called 'Book of Invasions').[40] At any rate, Ó Domhnaill would have been a far more trustworthy historian had he followed the approach outlined by the editor of the *Teacher's Work* in 1931:

> The school treatment of Irish folklore has to be far more cautious than the handling of local facts illustrative of general history. Folklore anywhere is a thing requiring delicate handling. The expert workers in Irish folklore have as yet given very little attention indeed to the school uses of their work. Only their wide

> knowledge can give any real guarantees as to the kind of folklore that can be used in schools, and as to the limitations and positive aspects of that use. That inspectors should press on teachers, as yet without any form of expert guidance and instruction, the handling of folklore in schools is an inconsiderate absurdity (*Teacher's Work*, 7/8/31).[41]

Absurdity of any kind was, of course, something Gaelic writers of history wished to avoid, and the more thoughtful among them acknowledged that the best way to do so was to strive for high standards of intellectual rigour and objectivity. That standards of that kind had all too often been absent from what Irish history had been written by Irish people in the past was too evident to ignore. In an unsigned 1926 review of Arthur Young's *A Tour in Ireland*, the critic (perhaps the paper's editor León Ó Broin) conceded:

> It is not until recently, for whatever reason, that we applied ourselves to examining Irish history scientifically and tough-mindedly. As proof of that, we need only look through our bookcases at home. Where are those big, famous volumes commonly seen in the bookcases of people of learning and culture in other countries? We have a half-dozen or a dozen books about which we can say with a certain amount of confidence that there is true information on the history of our ancestors in them, and not fables and lists of resounding battles. Those books were written recently.

The writer then goes on to list the authors of that handful of worthwhile books, naming Eoin Mac Néill, Edmund Curtis, Alice Stopford Green, and Douglas Hyde, all of whom wrote most if not all of their work in English (*FL*, Sept. 1926, 1).[42]

In 1925, one 'Giraldus' had looked to the day when sound Irish history would be written in Irish. Reviewing *Fir Mhóra na hÉireann* (Great Irishmen) by Éamonn Mac Loingsigh and Aindrias Ó Baoighill, he wrote: 'The reading of a little book of this kind encourages one to hope that some day we may have in Irish and from an Irish hand some attempt at a critical and impartial study of the problems of Irish history' (*IBL*, Apr. 1925, 26). The real challenge facing the would-be objective Gaelic historian was not, however, the assessment of sources or the mastery of proper methodology. As was true in so many areas of Irish national life at this time, the crux of the issue was ideological. Could a writer deal with the national past in a way that would be both properly edifying – even inspiring, as the state's guidelines for the teaching of history mandated – and intellectually rigorous? Séamus Ó Searcaigh confronted this question head-on in a 1928 lecture to the Catholic Truth Society:

> A new interest is now being taken in Irish history, but I fear that while that may be so, rarely is a true picture of the past put before scholars. You would think from

> many of the history books that are to be found that our ancestors had none of the failings of the human race, that they were people who spent their lives devoutly and piously, that most of them were saints who gave themselves up entirely to God. Doubtless there were saints among them, but there were people in every age, as there were in every other country, who did not obey God's commandments. I think that the proper goal for the historian is to give a picture of the past that includes both good and bad (*Tír*, Nov. 1928, 8).[43]

Writing in 1933, 'Tyrone' agreed, but saw the Irish tendency to idealise the national past as a reaction to colonial misrepresentations:

> The history of Ireland has naturally yet to be written. For a long time the English enemy, who had the ear of the world, circulated against us and against our ancestors the vilest propaganda . . . So we too took refuge in propaganda and pictured the native Gael, or the Celt as he was not too accurately called, as a person possessing the virtues and the genius of an archangel. The true facts of Irish history still remain to be presented and true appreciation of the Gael and of his possibilities still remains to be made (*UIrman*, 29/4/33).[44]

Maoghnus Ó Domhnaill had developed this idea with a striking image seven years earlier when he wrote that 'both groups of historians, those who are hostile and those who are friendly to Ireland, have always been placed in the position of war correspondents when dealing with Irish history' (*An Phoblacht*, 29/10/26).[45]

An optimistic – or perhaps better, facile – solution to this dilemma was offered by Ó Searcaigh in a lecture to Irish-speaking civil servants in 1930. Ó Searcaigh first reminded his audience that all 'sensible' (*céillidhe*) people accepted 'there were good qualities and bad qualities in the Gael as there were in every other race' (go raibh droch-thréithe agus deagh-thréithe sa Ghaedheal mar bhí in gach cineadh eile) and that it was the historian's job 'to put the good and the bad together so that we would see the Gael as he was' (an mhaith is an t-olc a chur le chéile ar dhóigh go bhfeicfimís an Gaedheal mar bhí sé). The trick was that seeing the Gael as he was could apparently be in itself inspirational. Ó Searcaigh continued: 'It is not the historian's goal to improve the modern world nor to awaken filial piety in the mind of the young, nor to write down a sermon on the wickedness of the past. All of those things will come as a result of his work if the mind of the reader is inclined to what is noble and good, but not because it is the goal of the historian, but rather because of the truth of the picture he has presented' (*Tír*, June 1930, 9–10).[46]

Not all found this balance between pietas and impartiality so easy to strike. One of the two major principles underlying the interest of the Gaels in history was that the study of the national past should inspire a fervent patriotism, that it should, in the words of Conchubhar Ó Coileáin, awaken 'the spirit of nationality in its readers, especially in the young' (sprid na náisiúntachta i lucht a léighte, san aos óg go mór-mhór) (*Camán*, 2/12/33). Few would have disputed Maoghnus Ó Domhnaill's view that history was 'the wellspring of nationality and of loyalty to the Irish language' (foinnseacha na náisiúntachta agus na dílse do'n Ghaedhilg), or that it was like 'the golden stream the prophet saw long ago flowing westwards from the horizon and adorning and gilding the lands' (an sruthán óir a chonnaic an fáidh fadó ag scéidh anoir ó imeall na spéire is a dhein na dúithchí a mhaisiú is a órdhadh) (*FL*, 5/12/31). The author of the 1924 *Irish Independent* editorial on 'Uaisleacht na hÉireann' (The nobility of Ireland) certainly agreed, writing:

> It is from history will come to us again the confidence and that national hope that were alive in Ireland when the national language was commonly spoken in the country. Let us give our young students accurate knowledge of the golden age of faith and learning, when our native land was respected throughout Europe. For the salvation and the uplifting of the nation today are in the revival of the spirit that was alive in Ireland at that time (*II*, 5/8/24).[47]

Like most authors of school histories, Father Dinneen saw the instilling of patriotism as being among his chief goals when he wrote *Scéal na hÉireann don Aos Óg* (The story of Ireland for the young) (1932):

> The reading and examination of that story ought to interest the schoolchildren; it will inspire them to patience, to generosity, to charity; it will inspire them to bravery and to courage; to loyalty to their native land and to the teaching of the saints.[48]

That such inspiration was not to be limited to children is evident in thoughts expressed by Liam Ó Rinn the same year. Ó Rinn, the most sophisticated and perceptive Gaelic literary critic of this period, claimed that he himself preferred history that stirred the blood to that which merely satisfied the mind:

> It is no good paying attention to the 'letter' of history and not paying attention to its 'spirit' . . . A tasty lie that will inspire the people to love their country is better than an insipid truth that will leave them West Britons (*UIrman*, 26/11/32).[49]

Some Gaels were quick to point out that in using the teaching of history to shape patriotic citizens, Ireland would only be following the general practice of modern Western education. Writing on such teaching in 1932, Toirdhealbhach Ó Raithbheartaigh asserted: 'History is almost as important as the Irish language itself. History is one of the cornerstones of Nationality, as it is in England, in Germany, in France, even in the United States'

(Dundalk *Examiner*, 17/9/32).[50] Others, however, felt that given Ireland's long history of colonial oppression, history should be understood, shaped, and wielded as a weapon in the national struggle. Seosamh Mac Grianna spoke most forcefully for this group when he wrote in *Léigheacht ar Crois-Bhealaigh i Stair na h-Éireann / Turning Points in Irish History*, a pamphlet in English published by anti-Treaty Sinn Féin in 1924:

> The changing epochs of Irish history through the centuries have a precious lesson for the true patriot. We find the Irish people asserting their nationality again and again since the conquest, proving that the race is indestructible. We find that however much the race wandered in the stress and storm of defeat and oppression, they always returned to the idea of complete separation from England.[51]

It was this reading of Irish history that caused 'Gréasuidhe Pholl a' Chlaidhe' (perhaps an tAthair Mac Fhinn) to write of elderly Conamara people in *An t-Éireannach* in 1934: 'Reading history makes the old people tremble, particularly those among them who did not get much education, for they are afraid the day will come when that son of theirs will have to go out for the country' (*Éireannach*, 8/12/34).[52]

The country to be gone out for was the same for all Gaels: Pearse's independent Gaelic state, an Ireland 'not free merely, but Gaelic as well; not Gaelic merely, but free as well'. Writing in 1923, 'Austin' doubtless spoke for the vast majority of his compatriots when, invoking history, he said their goal was the building up of

> a Gaelic-speaking, Gaelic-thinking Ireland, an Ireland that will be worthy of herself, worthy of the glory of the days when she led the world in civilisation and culture, worthy of those heroes of olden times whose ancestry is lost 'mid the grey mists of history's dawn (*II*, 8/10/23).

It was the cardinal tenet of the Gaelic creed that a free Ireland that was not Gaelic was a monstrous and sterile hybrid doomed to national extinction, even if it were somehow to retain its own political institutions. From this perspective, it was the inculcation of true *Gaelachas* rather than simple patriotism that was the goal of the history teacher. Or perhaps better, true modern Irish patriotism had to be rooted in and imbued with a conscious and explicit spirit of *Gaelachas* if it was to protect the extraordinary recent gains for which so many had suffered so much. To read Irish history from any but the Gaelic perspective could lead only to profound misunderstanding and worse, as an anonymous writer explained in the anti-Treaty paper *Éire* in 1923:

> Irish history written from a non-Gaelic point of view produces the impression of a chaos of unbridled ambition and greed, amidst savage aborigines . . . What the Gael

> fought for, namely, National Freedom, and the abiding fact of Irish nationality struggling against guile, violence and bribery is all carefully concealed (*Éire*, 15/12/23).

Joseph Hanly agreed, writing in the *National Ideal* in 1931:

> Even by writers who meant well, Irish history by English-minded people has been, with exceptions, one long tale of national suppression. Until recent times it was biassed, in most instances, by political and religious influences, and by neglect of 'The Hidden Ireland'.[53]

And in the same year, Shán Ó Cuív wrote:

> It has often been said – and truly – that we would be blind to the history of Ireland until the Gaelic side would be available to us. As long as we were relying on the other side, the side written by foreigners who did not understand the mind of our people and who gave their own interpretation to everything they saw, we could not give a true judgment on any thing that happened in this country since the Foreigners got the upper hand (*II*, 6/11/31).[54]

That Hidden Ireland – the real Ireland of unbroken tradition – had no more uncompromising champions at this time than the brothers Séamus Ó Grianna and Seosamh Mac Grianna. Writing in 1931 on the question 'An Sábhólthar an Náisiún Gaedhealach?' (Is the Gaelic nation being saved?), Ó Grianna emphasised that any attempt to do so had to be grounded in an understanding of what that nation was and what it had always stood for:

> Now the person who will write the history of Ireland as it should be written has much to learn, and in addition to that, he will have to sweep out of his way the cobwebs woven by fools who thought they knew history. And above all, he will have to understand the difference between nationality and freedom (*An Phoblacht*, 25/7/31).[55]

Mac Grianna went out of his way to blast such Anglocentric 'fools' (*amadáin*) in the preface to his *Na Lochlannaigh* (The Vikings). Condemning as failures virtually all previous attempts at writing Irish history, he then isolated the causes for those failures, the most important among them being an inadequate command of the Irish language and an inability to see the world from the perspective of 'an aigneadh Ghaedhealach' (the Gaelic mind). Moreover, he was willing to push the stakes even higher for the would-be Irish historian: 'If the author is not from the Gaeltacht, it is difficult for him to have any understanding of the kind of Gaels who lived a thousand years ago.'[56]

Defining himself elsewhere as 'a Gael, born and reared in the Gaeltacht', Mac Grianna wondered whether most English speakers in Ireland even cared about the distinction between nationality and independence articulated by his brother, writing of himself and his fellow Gaeltacht natives in 1932:

> We know we are the absolute right when nationality becomes the standard, but how often have we been heard to say it? It is not slavishness that keeps us silent, for we have no such thing as the inferiority complex. But we feel that the politics of the Pale are superfluous and lacking in sanity, and one of its most dangerous symptoms is that we are left out entirely. For, whoever hauled down the British flag from Dublin's towers, we are the nation (*IP*, 1/3/32).

The following year, Mac Grianna identified himself in *Irish Workers' Voice* as a proletarian, a Communist, and an agnostic, as well as a native Irish speaker, but his reading of Irish history remained constant:

> There has been no revolutionary movement in Ireland since Eoghan Ruadh O'Neill. Eoghan Ruadh would at least have taken the first step in the direction of revolution by making a Gaelic Ireland free. Once a nation, we could go forward abreast of international evolution. We failed to become a nation, and have been doomed to imperialism ever since. All risings in Ireland since were quarrels between imperialists – 1782, 1798, 1848, 1867, and 1916 (*Irish Workers' Voice*, 18/3/33).

The brothers were not alone in their belief that the history of English-speaking Ireland had little if any meaning for the real Irish nation. Writing in 1925, Donn Piatt stated:

> I believe that I lost many a mark at school because I could not take any interest in some of 'Irish History'. I never took an interest in the history of the English in Ireland, and I would not bother my head with the people who became 'more Irish than the Irish themselves' – if there is any truth in that . . . But I never heard the name of an O'Byrne or an O'Toole being mentioned without my heart beating faster. Those were the right people – the people who stood for freedom (*An Phoblacht*, 14/8/25).[57]

It is, by the way, interesting to see how flexible a Gaelic historian could be when attempting to absolve an Anglophone patriot of the original sin of his linguistic origins. In his biography of John Mitchel, an English-speaking firebrand much admired by Séamus Ó Grianna as well, Niall Ó Domhnaill has his hero admit that his own people were 'Irish people' (Éireannaigh) but not 'Gaels' (Gaedhil), while also claiming that he felt a powerful allegiance to 'the ancient nation of the Gaels' (sean-náisiún na nGaedheal). Doubtless it was this allegiance that Ó Domhnaill saw as enabling him to become one of the three most committed opponents of English rule in all of Irish history, the other two being the impeccably Gaelic Seán Ó Néill ('Seán an Díomais') and Aodh Ruadh Ó Néill.[58]

Writers like Ó Grianna, Mac Grianna, and Piatt were very close to positing their own version of the 'Two Nations' theory of recent revisionist Irish history. As Nollaig Mac Congáil has pointed out, Mac Grianna regarded the people of the Gaeltacht and the people of the Galltacht as virtually separate species.[59] Indeed at the beginning of *Mo Bhealach Féin*, published in 1940 but written in the early to mid 1930s, he refers to Gaeltacht people as 'in an absolutely foreign country among the Anglo-Irish' (ar an dubhchoigchrích imeasg na nGall-Ghaedheal).[60] And in his 1932 letter to the *Irish Press* quoted above, he states:

> It is unlikely now that the Gaeltacht and the Pale will ever make a happy blend. I think you are all prepared to admit that we are a nice people, and will not think us unreasonable if we do not wish to become merged in the English-speaking world of which you are a part (*IP*, 1/3/32).

Such a view explains his division of Irish history into two distinct periods in *Léigheacht ar Crois-Bhealaigh i Stair na h-Éireann*:

> The history of Ireland falls naturally into two epochs, Ireland free and Ireland enslaved. With the first period we will not deal at any considerable length. It was an age of prosperity, of unshackled natural development. But a true and detailed knowledge of the period of subjection is very valuable to us. We live in its latter end; we are its children. A thorough understanding of it will give us a wisdom which will help us in our task of putting an end to it forever.[61]

In the years after he wrote these words in 1924, what writing on history Mac Grianna himself did – most notably in the books *Eoghan Ruadh Ó Néill* (1931) and *Na Lochlannaigh* (1938) – was concerned for the most part with his first period above. Moreover, he seems with time to have lost the optimism that believed that a study of 'the period of subjection' could help put an end to it. Other writers, however, continued to see an immersion in *Gaelachas* as a way to give the Irish a deeper and more authentic understanding of their past, in the process bringing to an end the nation's long period of political and intellectual servitude. Writing in 1924, 'Niall Mór' heralded the regenerative power of *Gaelachas* for a resurgent people:

> There was a power stronger than any politics behind it. That power was the Irish language and the spirit it awakened throughout Ireland. It has only brought us

> half-way so far. It will bring us the whole way to Freedom's harbour as soon as Gaelic Ireland takes control, that Gaelic Ireland that was defeated during the time of Eoghan Ruadh Ó Néill and Patrick Sarsfield (*Ultach*, July 1924, 4).[62]

It was all but axiomatic among Gaels that a truly Gaelic history of Ireland could only be written in the language of Gaelic Ireland. There was, of course, nothing new about this belief. Writers from the beginning of the Revival had insisted that Irish had to be the language of Irish history. In fact, the perceived need to restate this principle could be seen as a sign of how little impact the Revival had made in certain areas of Irish intellectual life. At any rate, writers in the 1920s and 1930s made sure that no one could claim they were retreating on this point. In 1923, a reviewer of Seamus MacManus's *The Story of the Irish Race* stated categorically: 'The reader is left uninformed of the all-important fact that without a thorough knowledge of the Irish language no adequate knowledge of Irish history is attainable' (*CB*, June, 1922, 402).[63] In 1925, Caitlín Nic Ghabhann simply dismissed English language sources in *Mágh Ealta Éadair*: 'I did not bother much with the history books that were written in English only – some of them that I skimmed through were not reliable, others for the most part dealt with the life of the English in this country.'[64] Writing in 1926, An tAthair Seán Mac Craith said of the Irish language: 'It is so intimately bound up with the history of the country – you must have it to properly understand the true story of Ireland' (*FL*, 8/5/26).[65] Joseph Hanly was in full agreement, writing in 1931:

> History in any other than the national language is less than half the tale. The English language, as a medium of Irish history, restricts, confuses, and obstructs investigation in every direction, but particularly in the more vital aspects – interpretation, age, and traditional Gaelic history, without Gaelic culture, distinctive Gaelic ideals, and Gaelic mentality is but a sterile imposition . . . True history, local and national, must be compiled by Young Ireland, from original sources, in its natural medium, the language in which Irish history and tradition were made.[66]

Hanly's final point here could, of course, create a problem, for a significant amount of Irish history had been made by Irish people who spoke and wrote English, as did, for that matter, Hanly himself. Those like Mac Grianna, Ó Grianna, and Piatt might argue that the history such people made was of secondary significance in any proper scheme of Irish history, but even they must have felt the inadequacy of such a response. Other writers saw other obstacles in the way of a more widespread use of Irish as the principal medium for the study and writing of Irish history. Addressing the New Ross, County Wexford branch of the Gaelic League on 'the older history of Ireland' in 1931, Liam Gógan 'expressed his regret that it was still inopportune to do so in the national language' (Ennsicorthy *Echo*, 21/3/31). Gógan didn't seem to have offered a specific reason why the use of Irish in such a context would be problematic, but Art Mac Gréagóir was more forthright in the preface to his *Stair na nDéise* in 1939. Claiming that he did not want to be 'one of the people who are extinguishing the Irish language' (ar cheann de sna daoine atá ag múchadh na Gaedhilge) and was convinced 'that it is more beneficial and appropriate to give an account of the people of the past in the language they used in the past' (gur deise agus gur oireamhnaighe cunntas do thabhairt ar lucht an tsean-shaoghail sa teangain do bhí aca sa tsean-aimsir), he admitted that this decision would considerably restrict his potential readership:

> Is it not a disappointment and is it not a pity that this book is of no use to the great majority of the people who would best understand the Irish in it, that is, the country people who heard Irish as a living language from their youth? Haven't the people with Irish had a strange education when a book in Irish must be translated to English so that good speakers of Irish could get any benefit from it?[67]

Pádraig Ó Siochfhradha claimed in 1939 that 'anyone with a serious interest in things relating to the folklore and history of the country has a knowledge of Irish by this time' (éinne go bhfuil suim dáiríribh aige i neithe a bhaineas le béaloideas is le stair na tíre tá eolas ar an nGaedhilg fán am so aige).[68] But Gógan and Mac Gréagóir, who were writing for a popular audience, experienced the linguistic reality of the situation differently.

One obvious way to bring Irish history at least into the classroom as quickly as possible was to translate suitable texts available in English, and a fair number of such translations appeared in the 1920s and 1930s. Among them were *Sceul Ár dTire*, Liam Ó Rinn's 1923 translation of A. B. Ochiltree Ferguson's *Our Country's Story* (BÁC: COÉ, [1923]); the Gaelic version of a cathechism-like quiz book published by the Christian Brothers as *Stair na hÉireann: Ceist is Freagra* (The history of Ireland: Question and answer) (BÁC: M.H. Gill agus a Mhac, 1927); *Stair na hÉireann*, Micheál Breathnach's translations of two volumes by Father John Ryan, *Ireland from the Earliest Times to AD 800* and *Ireland from AD 800 to AD 1600* (BÁC: Connradh na Gaedhilge, n.d.); and Gearóid Mac Spealáin's translation of the four books of James Carty's very popular text *A Class-Book of Irish History* (BÁC: Muinntir C.S. Ó Fallamhain, Teor., 1936–8).

But the real need was for original histories of the nation in the national language, and the following such works appeared in our period: *Laochra Gaedheal* (The heroes of the Gaels) (BÁC: ODFR, 1936 [1922]) by Tomás Ua Concheanainn and his wife Helena, the latter a trained historian;[69] Séamus Ó Fallamhain's *Gearr-Stair .i. Gearr-Aithris ar Dhaoine Cáileamhla i Seanchas na hÉireann* (A short history, i.e., A short account of famous people in Irish history) (BÁC: COÉ, [1922]); Proinnsias Ó Súilleabháin's *Sgéal na h-Éireann i gCóir Páistí Scoile* (The story of Ireland for schoolchildren) (BÁC: COÉ, Teor., [1922]); Micheul Ó Cionnfhaolaidh's *Eolas ar Éirinn* (Information about Ireland) (BÁC: Muinntir Dollard, 1923), a school geography text in which the material on most counties is accompanied by a story about a famous person from its history;[70] Micheál Mac Énrí's *Sár-Laochra Éireann* (The great heroes of Ireland) (BÁC: Brún agus Ó Nóláin, [1924]); Pádraic Ó Conaire's *Eachtraí Móra ó n-Ár Stair* (Great adventures from our history) (BÁC: Taisceadán Ádhbhar Léighinn do Sgoileannaibh Éireann, [1924]); An tAthair Pádraig Mac Giolla Cheara's *Scéal na hÉireann* (1924); Micheál Ó Maoláin's *Taoisigh Éireann* (Irish leaders) (1924); Éamonn Mac Loingsigh and Aindrias Ó Baoighill's *Fir Mhóra na hÉireann* (Sráid Bhaile Dhúin Dealgan: Preas Dhún Dealgan, 1925); Ó Maoláin's *Inis Ealga: Stair Bheag na h-Éireann i gCóir an Aosa Óig* (Inis Ealga [Ireland]: A little history of Ireland for the young) (BÁC: M.S. Ó Maoláin , Foillsightheoir Oideachais, n.d.); Proinnsias Ó Súilleabháin's *Stair na h-Éireann ó Aimsir Naoimh Pádraig go dtí an Lá Indiu* (The history of Ireland from the time of St Patrick to the present) (BÁC: Alec Thom agus a Chuid, Teor., n.d.); Séamus Ó hIfearnáin and Tadhg Ó Breacáin's *Tír Eolas agus Stair na h-Éireann* (The geography and history of Ireland) (BÁC: COÉ, n.d.); Father Patrick Dinneen's two-part *Scéal na hÉireann don Aos Óg* (BÁC: Brún agus Ó Nualláin, Teor., [1932]); Séamus Ó Grianna's *Feara Fáil* (Men of Ireland) (Dún Dealgan: Cló-Lucht 'An Scrúduightheoir', 1933); Micheál Ó Siochfhradha's two-part *Stair-Sheanchas Éireann* (The history of Ireland) (BÁC: COÉ, n.d.); Micheál Breathnach's *Cúrsaí na hÉireann ó Thosach go dtí Cath Chionntsáile* (Irish affairs from the beginning to the Battle of Kinsale) and *Cúrsaí na hÉireann ó Chath Chionntsáile go dtí 1921* (Irish affairs from the Battle of Kinsale to 1921) (BÁC: Brún agus Ó Nualláin, Teor., n.d.); and Aodh Mac Dhubháin's *Stair na hÉireann (ó Chath Chionntsáile anall go dtí Foillsiú na Bun-Reachta, 1937)* (The history of Ireland {from the Battle of Kinsale to the publication of the Constitution, 1937}) (BÁC: Brún agus Ó Nualláin, Teor., 1939).[71]

What is most striking about these books, besides their almost exclusive focus on the classroom, is that so many of them present Irish history in Carlylean terms as a series of biographies of great men. The pattern was set early by Tomás Ua Concheanainn and his wife Helena, who structured *Laochra Gaedheal* around the lives of Cormac Mac Airt, St Patrick, St Colm Cille, Brian Bóruma, Ruaidhrí Ó Conchubhair, Art Mac Murchadha Ó Caomhánaigh, Silken Thomas Fitzgerald, Seán an Díomais Ó Néill, Aodh Ó Néill, Aodh Ruadh Ó Domhnaill, Eoghan Ruadh Ó Néill, Patrick Sarsfield, Wolfe Tone and Daniel O'Connell. The exact same heroes, without any alteration whatsoever in the list or its order, formed the basis for Ó Fallamhain's *Gearr-Stair*, Mac Énrí's *Sár-Laochra Éireann*, Mac Loingsigh and Ó Baoighill's

Fir Mhóra na hÉireann, and Ó hIfearnáin and Ó Breacáin's *Tír-Eolas agus Stair na h-Éireann*. Micheál Breathnach concluded the second volume of his *Cúrsaí na hÉireann* with biographies of all on the list above from Aodh Ó Néill to O'Connell, but added Swift, Grattan, Emmet, Davis, Mitchel, Parnell, Pearse, and Connolly. Micheul Ó Cionnfhaolaidh, constrained by the division of his *Eolus ar Éirinn* according to county, nonetheless managed to include brief stories about Cormac, Colm Cille, Brian Bóruma, Art Mac Murchadha Ó Caomhánaigh, and Sarsfield. To the canonical roster he added Cú Chulainn and Fer Diad (Louth), Medb and Ailill (Mayo), Fionn Mac Cumhaill (Kerry), Saint Brigid (Kildare), Cormac Mac Muireadhaigh (Tipperary), Ó Súilleabháin Bhéara (Cork), Laurence O'Toole (Dublin), Henry Joy McCracken (Antrim), Jem Hope (Down), Michael Dwyer (Wicklow), the Pikemen of 1798 (Wexford), and Thomas Francis Meagher (Waterford). Ó Grianna included all of the usual names in his *Feara Fáil*, omitting only Ó Conchubhair, Silken Thomas, and O'Connell, while adding Cú Chulainn, Diarmaid Mac Murchadha, Edward Bruce, Emmet, Mitchel, and Pearse. In his *Eachtraí Móra ó n-Ár Stair*, Pádraic Ó Conaire omitted from his discussion Cormac, Ó Conchubhair, Mac Murchadha Ó Caomhánaigh, Silken Thomas, and Tone, and added the 'Manchester Martyrs' of 1867, the men of 1916, and Anne Devlin, the only woman – with the exceptions of the legendary Medb and Brigid – to appear in any of the rolls of honour.[72]

The decision by so many of these writers to read Irish history as a succession of heroic biographies was a conscious one. Tomás Ua Concheanainn and his wife Helena, who first compiled what became the standard biographical framework on which to build the nation's history, wrote in *Laochra Gaedheal*:

> But it is the absolute truth to say that the men who fought for Ireland never failed to leave many heirs after them. As soon as a hero was laid low, one person and then another of his race or of his own stock was ready to stand strong in the gap of danger.[73]

Séamus Ó Grianna developed this point in greater depth in 1927:

> You often hear people talking about the people of Ireland and saying: 'The mass of the people always have their hearts in the right place, but the leaders sell them out.' I myself think that the mass of the people never had their hearts in the right place and never will. Any time Ireland performed any great feat at all, she did so because there was one great man who followed his own counsel and made the mass of the people submit to him (*CB*, Sept. 1927, 960).[74]

The editor of the *Father Mathew Record* was in full agreement, writing in 1937:

> There is no need for a person to spend any time studying the history of Ireland to understand that people shaped it and not policies . . . It was Byron, I think, who taunted us by saying 'The Irish dearly love a lord.' I would yield to him, but I would say that we bowed to the lordship of mind and soul as often as we did to the title. It would be easy to mention names that would illustrate how certain political leaders gripped the imagination of the people so that they were remembered for more than a hundred years (*FMR*, Mar. 1937, 131).[75]

Even the author of the most substantial book of Gaelic literary criticism in the period, An tAthair Seoirse Mac Clúin, wrote of history in his *An Litríocht*:

> How can a reader have a worthy, vital opinion unless there is a vital life in the pages of the book, and the vital forces of the human heart? It will not be said that the best possible history is in The *French Revolution* by Carlyle . . . but isn't the story intensely powerful? And do the great characters not rise up before us with vigour and vital force?[76]

At any rate, contemporary critics seem to have found little problem with the approach, perhaps agreeing with 'E. de B.' (Ernest Blythe), who wrote in a 1923 review of Ó Cionnfhaolaidh's *Eolas ar Éirinn*:

> The author understands this important point i.e. that it is best to link the history of any age written for the young with the name of some great person who lived and worked in that age, for example, Colm Cille, Brian Bóruma, Eoghan Ruadh Ó Néill, etc. (*FL*, 22/9/23).[77]

It is possible to gain some insight into the mindset of the authors who produced these textbooks by examining their treatment of three turning points in Irish history: the usurpation of power by Brian Bóruma in the first decade of the eleventh century, the mass political movement created by Daniel O'Connell in the nineteenth century, and the Anglo-Irish Treaty and subsequent Civil War of the immediate past. Brian's seizure of power from the Uí Néill king Máelsechnaill mac Domnaill had troubled Gaelic historical writers from the start of the Revival. Those working in the aftermath of a civil war were, not surprisingly, even more uncomfortable with an act that could be seen as both an affront to duly constituted authority and a confirmation of the prejudices of those enemies of the new nation who wanted to see and present the Irish as violent and divided from very early on in their history. Tomás Ua Concheanainn and his wife Helena took the direct approach in *Laochra Gaedheal* by simply acknowledging Brian's fault: 'After this Brian thought that he would depose Máelsechnaill altogether. In order to bring that about he did something it was not right to do, and he must be censured for doing so.'[78] That painful admission out of the way, they went on to praise the reign of Brian in traditionally lavish terms. Séamas Ó Fallamhain was a bit vaguer in his condemnation of Brian in *Gearr-Stair*:

> Brian was arrogant, and he was not content to remain as he was. He wanted to be High King. He fought with the people of Connacht and with the King of Leinster, and at last the High King, Máelsechlainn, had to submit to him in the year 1002.[79]

Micheál Mac Énrí admitted Brian's 'voracious desire for the High Kingship' (saint chum na h-Árd-Ríoghachta) in *Sár-Laochra Éireann*, and traced the baneful influence of his action on later rulers.[80] Still, however, he devoted most of his account of Brian to the splendour and beneficence of his reign. In *Stair-Sheanchas Éireann*, Micheál Ó Siochfhradha has Máelsechnaill yield to Brian for noble reasons, 'from a desire that Gaels would not be fighting with each other' (d'fhonn ná beadh Gaedhil ag troid le n-a chéile). Nevertheless, after praising Brian as 'a very good High King' (Árd-rí an-mhaith), he writes of the rulers who followed him:

> They saw that Brian made High King of himself through violence, and that he had no other legitimate claim. They understood that they themselves did not need any legitimate claim if they had the strength. That is how the provincial kings began fighting with each other and plundering the country to see which of them would be High King.[81]

Some writers were more evasive. In *Fir Mhóra na hÉireann*, Mac Loingsigh and Ó Baoighill concede Brian's ambition, but present Máelsechnaill as acquiescing in the transfer of power. Proinnsias Ó Súilleabháin depicts the situation as an abdication on the part of Máelsechnaill. In *Tír-Eolas agus Stair na h-Éireann*, Ó h-Ifearnáin and Ó Breacáin say nothing at all about the usurpation. Both Ó Grianna and Breathnach, on the other hand, present Brian's move in an entirely positive light. Ó Grianna emphasises the incessant internal strife that had made it possible for the Vikings to gain a foothold in Ireland in the first place, and then portrays Brian as the man of destiny come to free his nation: 'The man who was needed came. Brian Bóruma took control of the country as High King, and the others submitted to him.'[82] Breathnach makes explicit this notion of Brian as a pioneer nation builder: 'What he set as a goal for himself was to bind and consolidate the tribes of Ireland together into one strong nation.'[83]

O'Connell presented less of a problem for these writers. His monumental importance in Irish history could hardly be ignored, thus his inclusion in the standard litany. But there was also a widespread consensus at the time that the constitutional nationalism to which he had devoted his political life had failed.

Irish freedom had been won by those of the physical force party. The Gaels had another and even more important objection to the Irish-speaking O'Connell – his championing of the English language as the sole medium for public discourse in modern Ireland. Once again Ua Concheanainn set the tone by criticising O'Connell for both an excessive faith in parliamentarianism and for his repudiation of the Irish language. On the whole, however, there seems to have been a grudging respect and even affection for O'Connell among these writers. No reference whatsoever is made to his discouragement of the language in the textbooks by Ó Fallamhain, Ó h-Ifearnáin and Ó Breacáin, Mac Énrí, Ó Súilleabháin, or Ó Siochfhradha. Mac Loingsigh and Ó Baoighill simply censure him for failing to set a good example by speaking Irish at his monster meetings. Breathnach, while critical of O'Connell's attitude to the language, nevertheless praises him for winning Catholic Emancipation, for giving the people a renewed courage, and for teaching them how to organise effectively. In the end, perhaps the best summary of the attitude of these Gaelic historians to O'Connell was that offered by Ua Concheanainn:

> There is not one of us who will go to the great cemetery of Glasnevin and who will look at the great memorial monument in the shape of a round tower over his grave whose heart will not be stirred in his breast and who will not say to himself that the faults of the heroic warrior will be forgotten and his great deeds and his great exploits will remain in the memory of Gaels forever.[84]

Such magnanimity was a great deal more difficult to generate with regard to the vitriolic debates concerning the Treaty and the bloody tragedies of the Civil War. Most of the textbook writers simply took advantage of their scheme of organisation to end their studies with O'Connell, thereby avoiding discussion of the recent past altogether. Even Ó Grianna, a staunch anti-Treaty republican, was able to remain silent on the events leading to the Civil War by ending *Feara Fáil* with Pearse. Those writers who did bring their work up to the present did so with caution. In his *Stair na hÉireann ó Aimsir Naoimh Pádraig go dtí an Lá Indiu*, Proinnsias Ó Súilleabháin ended with the Treaty and the setting up of separate parliaments in Dublin and Belfast, but made no reference to the Civil War, instead concluding the book with a patriotic exhortation to his student readers. Micheál Breathnach provided a fairly neutral account of the debate on the Treaty in Dáil Éireann, identifying prominent figures on both sides of the controversy. He did not deal with the Civil War, although a comment made on the new government's work for the language revival makes his allegiance clear: 'Since the Irish Free State was founded (1922) our own Government has done much to revive the Irish language.'[85] Dinneen was less evasive, offering the following even-handed assessment of the Treaty: 'That treaty puts Ireland in the same position as Canada, except that certain ports would be available to the British fleet in peacetime and the whole coast during a war.'[86] Micheál Ó Siochfhradha was in general agreement, writing that, through the Treaty, 'the Irish people succeeded in achieving a good share of their freedom' (d'éirigh le muinntir na hÉireann cuid mhaith dá saoirse do bhaint amach), but that it was not 'a treaty without fault' (connradh gan locht) because of the clauses dealing with partition, the oath of loyalty to the British crown, and English retention of naval bases on Irish soil. Ó Siochfhradha was also fairly objective in his account of the events leading to the Civil War, a catastrophe whose dire results he passionately condemned:

> It is difficult to calculate the evil result that came of this unfortunate fight. A split beyond healing was caused among the group most loyal to Ireland. A seed of spite and suspicion was planted among Gaels; many of the best men in the country were killed and were shot in the Civil War, and in the destruction that happened incalculable damage was done to the goods and the business of the country.[87]

A less controversial subject for study, one virtually all Gaels believed should form an important element in school curricula, was local history. One practitioner of this sub-genre, An tAthair P. Ó Roithleáin, who wrote frequent essays on the history of County Galway for *The Connacht Sentinel* in 1930 and 1931, felt that this was an aspect of their own past the Irish had shamefully neglected: 'It is true to say that it was the stranger who showed us how respectful we should be towards history and towards historical places around us (*CS*, 3/6/30).[88] The inspirational effect on Irish students of such subject matter, taught properly, was its principal value for Liam Ó Rinn, who wrote of such students in 1932: 'They will feel as it were a stream of history running through them and that it is their duty and a natural thing for them to cling firmly to everything involving their own country' (*UI*, 23/7/32).[89] 'Sean-Éireannach' felt that the provision of good local histories should precede any attempt to produce an authoritative national history. Reviewing Nic Gabhann's *Mágh Ealta Éadair*, he asserted:

> It is often said that it is a pity that we do not have a Gaelic history. A history that would tell, in the national language, the story of Ireland for the Gaelic nation itself. To be sure, certain scholars have done specialised work, but it is likely that the popular history in Irish will not be written until rural history, or local history, has first been studied. On that foundation, a true national history will perhaps soon be constructed (*II*, 25/5/26).[90]

To assist teachers interested in bringing such potent educational material into their classrooms, St Joseph's College in Ballinasloe, County Galway in 1929 published *Scéim agus Ceistiúchán le h-Aghaidh Stair Paráiste* (A scheme and a questionnaire for parish history), a booklet with sections on place names, language, archaeology, ballads, folklore in general, etc. There were also, of course, practical guidelines for the collection of local oral tradition about the past in Seán Ó Súilleabháin's *Láimh-Leabhar Béaloideasa* (1937).

The response to this call for local histories was sporadic and uncoordinated until de Valera's minister for education, Tomás Ó Deirg, hired An tAthair Micheál Ó Flannagáin to oversee the preparation of a series of county histories, with Ó Flannagáin himself writing the original texts in English for translation into Irish.[91] The only volume to appear in the 1930s was *Ros Comáin* (Roscommon) (BÁC: OS, 1938), but other works were published later dealing with Monaghan (1940), Carlow (1940), Kerry (1941), and Sligo (1944). Ó Flannagáin also prepared manuscripts on Cork, Dublin, Donegal, Mayo and Wexford, but none of these works was ever published.[92] Other book-length local histories were Nic Ghabhann's *Mágh Ealta Éadair* (1925); Ó Domhnaill's *Oileáin Árann* (1930); Peadar Ó Concheanainn's *Innismeadhain* (1931); Micheál Ó Conaill's *Cineál Féichín agus Síol Anmachadha* (BÁC: Máire Ní Raghallaigh, 1932); Seán Ó h-Ógáin's *Conntae an Chláir: A Tríocha agus a Tuatha* (County Clare: Its cantreds and its population groups) (BÁC: OS, 1938); and Art Mac Gréagóir's *Stair na nDéise* (1938).[93] In his preface, Mac Gréagóir stressed his commitment to the truth, yet even he acknowledged that he was willing to be quite flexible at times, for example regarding oral traditions concerning local saints.[94] Most of his colleagues writing on their home areas seem to have been much less troubled on this score than was he, freely incorporating legendary material as sound history.[95] Essays on local history also appeared with some regularity in newspapers and journals. And of course a good deal of local history can be gleaned from the various Gaeltacht autobiographies.

Of course, textbooks, however influential, comprised but a small percentage of Gaelic writing on history in the 1920s and 1930s. There was also a considerable body of work, factual and creative, on both Irish history in general and on specific periods and important characters. Beginning in September 1936, the *Teacher's Work* serialised Micheál Ó Ceallaigh's 'Ceachtanna Staire' (History lessons), a quick outline accompanied by study questions that started with the Celts and ended with the Norman Invasion and its immediate aftermath (*Teacher's Work*, Sept. 1936 to May, 1937). Irish history of a later period was treated by Peadar Ó Domhnaill in his serialised translation of an unidentified source as 'Stair na h-Éireann' in the Enniscorthy *Echo* in 1931, beginning with the issue for 19 September. Ó Domhnaill's history started at the time of Aodh Ó Néill and Aodh Ruadh Ó Domhnaill. In 1923, Peadar Mac Fhionnlaoich provided readers of *Sinn Féin* with an overview of the history of Ulster from the days of Cú Chulainn to 1921 (*SF*,

29/12/23). Cearbhall Ua Dálaigh dealt with a less tendentious subject, 'Bailtí na h-Éireann: A bhFás agus a Meath' (The towns of Ireland: Their growth and their decline), in 1931 (*Nation*, 7/2/31). One Irish city, Dublin, was the subject of an 'operetta' in Irish at the 1931 Dublin Feis, a work for which no text seems to survive, but which, judging by comments in *An Camán*, must have spanned centuries: 'We never witnessed a more artistic blend of Pagan and Christian sentiment, of Gaelic and sacred music, of folk and classic drama' (*Camán*, July 1931, 3).[96] A more substantial play on the history of Dublin was Micheál Mac Liammóir's *The Ford of the Hurdles: A Masque of Dublin*, performed at the Mansion House during Civic Week in September 1929. However, although Mac Liammóir wrote his programme note in Irish, the text of the pageant was entirely in English.[97]

The biographical approach to history favoured by the textbook writers was also practiced by writers on historical topics of general interest for an adult readership. For example, *Timthire Chroidhe Naomhtha Íosa* published many saints' lives in this period, as well as a series of biographies of Irish missionaries from the early medieval period to more modern times under the general title 'Laochra na Misiún' (Heroes of the missions) in 1930, most of them the work of the Jesuit S. Mac Stiopháin. The same journal ran a series on 'Mairtírigh na hÉireann' (Irish martyrs) commencing in January 1934 and concluding in January of the following year. The author was Seán Ó Catháin, SJ. Ursuline nuns martyred during the French Revolution were the subject of an essay by 'MA' in the 1932 edition of *Naomh Ursula*, the magazine of the convent school of that name in Thurles, County Tipperary. Saints' lives in Irish were a regular feature of the 'Nead na Gaedhilge' (The Irish language nest) column of the Passionist Fathers' monthly magazine *The Cross* in the early 1930s. Most of these were the work of 'Muiris na Móna', whose two series 'Ár Naoimh i gCéin' (Our saints abroad) and 'Naoimh na hÉireann' (Irish saints) ran in the magazine in 1930 and 1934–5 respectively.[98] In addition, a series of pamphlets on various saints, many of them Irish, commenced publication in 1936.[99] Younger readers were also introduced to 'Éireannaigh Cháiliúla' (Famous Irish people) in a series that ran in *An Gaedheal Óg* in the first half of 1939.[100]

Writing in 1924, Móirín a Cheavasa presented an overview of Celtic history in Continental Europe that Irish readers may well have felt was all but identical with the history of their own dealings with the English:

> The finer fibred, more spiritual, complex, beauty-loving Celtic nations, in spite of all their astonishing bravery, were unable to withstand the unimaginative, but cunning and unscrupulous Romans, half barbarians as they were in all but military ability and organisation (*Éire*, 3/5/24).

Had those readers wished to learn more about those kindred nations, they would, however, have been disappointed. Gaelic knowledge of the Celts remained at the most rudimentary level throughout the period. Indeed two writers, Liam Gógan and Cearbhall Ua Dálaigh, thought it worthwhile to write on the most basic question of all: 'Who were the Celts?' (Cérbh iad na Ceilt?)[101] While few went much beyond that, on occasion interest in ancient history could surface in unexpected places, as when in 1925 the journal of the Free State Army, *An t-Óglach*, ran four essays comparing the military tactics of the Celts with those of the Romans under the general title 'Anso is Ansúd 'sa Seanchas' (Here and there in history). The most informed discussion of the Celts in Irish in this period appeared in the lengthy preface to the edition of Book IV of Caesar's *De Bello Gallico* prepared by Séamus Ó Ciardha and Domhnall Ó Conalláin (BÁC: COÉ, n.d.), a preface that included sections on 'Na Galliathaigh' (The Gauls) 'Teanga, Litridheacht agus Oideachas na nGailliathach' (The language, literature, and education of the Gauls), 'Creideamh agus Déithe na nGailliathach' (The religion and the gods of the Gauls), and 'Coras Polaitidheachta agus Comhdhaonna na nGailliathach' (The political and social sytem of the Gauls). Of course in the absence of knowledge grounded in sound research, Gaelic notions of the Celts could be given free rein, as when Cluad de Ceabhasa proclaimed the ancient Irish 'the First Republicans of Europe' (*An Phoblacht*, 20/11/25).[102]

The Gaelic treatment of the early history of Ireland itself was not all that much more informed. There was, as we have noted, a persistent disposition to accept without question the pseudo-historical framework of early Irish history derived from the twelfth-century text *Lebor Gabála Érenn*. We find Tomás Ua Concheanainn and his wife Helena treating the arrival of 'our ancient ancestors the Milesians' (ár sean-sinnsir Clann Mhíleadh) as fact in the first volume of their *Seoda na Sean* series for young readers in 1924; Breandán Mac Énrí accepting the historical existence of the Fir Bolg in 'Cuairt Siar go Dún Aengus / Rian na bhFear mBolg' (A visit west to Dun Aengus / The trail of the Fir Bolg) (*II*, 9/9/29); 'C. Ó C.' offering a basic recapitulation of the medieval scheme in 'Gabhála Éireann' (The invasions of Ireland), serialised in *An Lóchrann* in February 1930; and Pádraig Ó Bolguidhir basing a 1931 history lecture to An Fáinne on the same source (Enniscorthy *Echo*, 26/12/31).[103] Even writers sceptical of the scheme were reluctant to let it go. Writing in 1938 on the occasion of the Irish Texts Society's publication of the first volume of R. A. S. Macalister's scholarly edition of *Lebor Gabála*, 'Sliabh Bladhma' claimed:

> There may not be any formal history, as we generally regard it, in the *Leabhar Gabhála*, yet much of it, I think, is far from being invention or fancy. Some of it, carefully considered, would harmonise with esoteric and more or less mystical traditions of a distant past of humanity (*Gaedheal*, Feb. 1938, 1).

One writer who tried to make the connection between *Lebor Gabála* and such 'esoteric traditions of a distant past of humanity' was Domhnall Ó Mathghamhna, who, in an appendix to *Inis Atlaint* (Atlantis), his translation of Plato's *Critias*, pondered whether the Fomorians of *Lebor Gabála* could have been Atlanteans. Of *Lebor Gabála* itself he wrote:

> The account that the ancient authors give of every invasion of Ireland deals with events that doubtless happened; but they happened so long ago that they only remained in the memory of the people in a vague way, like dreams.[104]

There were, of course, those in the Gaelic movement more interested in facts than dreams. By far the most academically accomplished of them was Eoin Mac Néill, the pre-eminent authority on early Irish history at this time. However, with the exception of his March 1932 essay 'Eoghanachta Mumhan' (The Eoghanachta of Munster) in *An Reult*, his scholarly writing in this period was done in English. Liam S. Gógan, who worked in the National Museum of Ireland, used both languages to educate his countrymen about Irish antiquities.[105] Less scholarly were essays by Peadar Mac Fhionnlaoich on 'Stailc Ocrais sa Sean-Shaoghal' (Hunger strikes in the past) (*Sinn Féin*, 17/11/23),[106] by Cearbhall Ua Dálaigh on 'Sean-Dhlighthe na h-Éireann' (The ancient laws of Ireland) (*Nation*, 26/4/30), by 'D. Ó M.' on cromlechs (*IP*, 29/12/32), by Seán Óg Ó Ceallaigh on 'Gabháil Chine agus Roinnt na Talmhan' (The capture of people and the division of land) (*An Phoblacht*, 20/1/34), and by Conchubhar Ó Ruairc on 'Feiseanna na Sean-Aimsire' (Festive gatherings of ancient times) (*Standard*, 18/6/37).

As we saw above, the major saints of early Christian Ireland attracted the attention of some writers. There was, for example, a serialised biography in Irish of Patrick in *Our Boys* in 1927 and 1928, and in 1932, the 1500th anniversary of the saint's mission to Ireland was commemorated by essays from Pádhraic Ó Domhnalláin in the *Irish Press* (17/3/32) and by Father Dinneen in the *Capuchin Annual* (pp. 101–8).[107] 'A. Ó C.' recreated several episodes from the life of Patrick in 'Seacht Míreanna' (Seven scenes) (*Standard*, 12/3/37). The national saint was also the subject of two stories derived from folk tradition, Tadhg Ua Séaghdha's 'Craosach Dearg' (Ravenous) (*Éarna*, July 1923, 19–25), and Séamus Maguidhir's 'Mairthean Phádraic' (Patrick's sustaining prayer) (*Éireannach*, 11/4/36). In addition, 'St Patrick before the High King of Tara' formed one scene of three in a pageant involving 250 people staged at Feis Charman in New Ross, County Wexford in 1932 (Enniscorthy *Echo*, 9/7/32). Colm Cille was the subject of a serialised biography in *Our Boys* in 1928, as well as of an essay by Maoghnus Ó Domhnaill in the Enniscorthy *Echo* (12/9/31), and by Eoin Ó Searcaigh and Séamus Ó Néill in the *Irish Independent* (8/6/34 and 16/10/36, respectively). More substantial was

B. N. Lóiste's *Inbhear Náile* (BÁC: ODFR, 1936), a play in four scenes set on the eve of Colm Cille's exile from Ireland. There were also plays about Brigid and St Feichín. *Brighdín*, a 45-minute radio play by Peadar Ó Dubhda, was broadcast in 1934 (Dundalk *Examiner*, 30/6/34), and Máiréad Ní Ghráda's *Muire na nGaedheal* (The Mary of the Gaels) in 1937 ('Radio Programmes', *IP*, 3/7/37). Máirín C. Nic Ghiobúin's *Feichín Fobhair: Dráma um Mhíorbhailt* (Feichín of Fore: A drama about a miracle) (BÁC: ODFR, 1936) depicts the Westmeath saint performing several miracles and closes with his vision of future Irish missionaries serving in Asia.[108] The experiences of the first generations of Irish Christians also provided the subject matter for Peadar Mac Fhionnlaoich's 'Cnoc Maolruanaidhe', the tale of a holy man who loses everything he has through sin;[109] for Art Mac Maga's 'Laoch Chríost' (Christ's warrior), the story of a king's son in Connacht who, having been ordered to drive out the first Christians in the province, instead converts and eventually becomes a priest (*TCNÍ*, Dec. 1924, 7–10); and for the anonymously authored 'Tearman' (Sanctuary), in which an eighth-century abbot shelters the man who had killed his brother and plundered his monastery (*Standard*, 14/9/29).

The scholars as well as the saints of early Ireland attracted Gaelic interest at this time. For example, W. P. Ryan published a lengthy serialised essay on 'Príomh-Éigeas na hÉireann: Johannes Scotus Eriugena' (The principal philosopher of Ireland: Johannes Scotus Eriugena) in 1924 (*FL*, 15/3 to 17/5/24).[110] Others interested in this field of study were the Jesuit Micheál Mac Craith, who included an essay on Petrus de Hibernia, the Irish teacher of St Thomas Aquinas, in his 1928 collection *Deora Drúchta Camhaoire*;[111] 'Taistealaidhe', who discussed a letter from the Irish scholar Dungal to Charlemagne concerning a solar eclipse (*II*, 5/7/27); and the Capuchin An tAthair Eláir, who wrote on Duns Scotus in *Bonaventura* (Autumn 1937, 128–35). The eighth-century religious reform movement Céilí Dé and its leader Oengus were the subject of a 1924 essay in *Sinn Féin* by Peadar Mac Fhionnlaoich (*SF*, 17/5/24).[112] Pádhraic Ó Domhnalláin discussed pre-Columban Irish journies to the New World in his essay 'An tOileán Úr' (The New Island i.e. America) in 1935.[113]

Other Gaelic writers turned their attention to secular figures in early Irish history, with particular interest focusing on Cormac Mac Airt. Cormac Ó Cadhlaigh provided a detailed and scholarly summary of the principal texts dealing with this legendary third or fourth century king in *Cormac Mac Airt* (BÁC: Muinntir Alex Thom i gcomhar le hOS, 1927). Two years previously, A. Ó Céileachair had published a much more naive essay on the king in the Cork journal *An Birín Beo*, an essay in which he treated his sources uncritically as straightforward history (*Birín Beo*, Jan. 1925, 6). Henry Morris ('Feargus Mac Róigh') included a folk tale about Cormac entitled 'An Dóigh a Chuaidh Cormac Mac Airt un na bhFlaitheas' (How Cormac Mac Airt went to

Paradise) in his 1924 collection *Oidhche Áirneáil i dTír Chonaill*, and there were also stories about Cormac for young readers in *Inis Fáil: Sgéalta faoi Árd Righthe na h-Éireann* (Ireland: Stories about the High Kings of Ireland) by Tomás Ua Concheanainn and his wife Helena, and in the fourth volume of Séamus Ó Grianna's *Sraith na Craobhrua* (The Red Branch series).[114] For children who preferred their history with pictures, *Our Boys* in 1937 commenced serialisation of the long-running comic strip 'Sgéal Chormaic Ulfhada, Árd-Rí Éireann, AD 227–67' (The story of Cormac Ulfhada, High King of Ireland, AD 227–67), all of the captions for which were in Irish.

Other stories set in early Ireland were the anonymously authored 'Sgéal Chonaill Ghulban' (The story of Conall Gulban); Captaen R. Ó Foghludha's 'Conus do h-Ainmnigheadh "Currach an Laoigh" agus "Tobar na Leamhnachta"' (How the Marsh of the Calf and the Well of the New Milk were named) (*Óglach*, Oct. 1927, 105–7); and Séamus Ó Néill's 'Saoghal Guill' (The life of Goll) (*Dundalk Examiner*, 26/9/31). In April 1923, *An Chearnóg* commenced a lengthy serialisation of 'Mac-Ghníomhartha Thaidhg Uí Ghrádaigh' (The boyhood deeds of Tadhg O'Grady), a wonder tale by 'Líam' [*sic*] set vaguely 'long ago, before the Foreigners set foot on Irish soil' (ins an am fadó, sul ar chuir na Gaill cos ar thalamh na hÉireann) (*An Chearnóg*, Apr. 1923, 1). And in May 1933, Taibhdhearc na Gaillimhe staged *Bóramha Laighean*, a play on the so-called 'Leinster Tribute'. This was not, however, a new play, but rather one 'written in the early days of the Gaelic League by Seana-Sheán Ó Conchubhair, a Gaelic teacher who gave the best years of his life working for the language.'[115]

Gaelic thinking about the Viking era of Irish history was dominated by the figure of Brian Bóruma. Leaving aside his importance in the textbooks, we find several lengthy essays on him in this period. In the 1928 volume of *Irisleabhar Muighe Nuadhad*, An tAthair Seosamh Mac Ruaidhrí extolled Brian as the equal of Charlemagne, as the destined unifier of his nation, and as the saviour of European Christianity from the Viking captivity. Needless to say, Mac Ruaidhrí's view was that Máelsechnaill soon became an acquiescent and loyal subordinate to Brian (*IMN*, 1928, 1–5). An t-Athair Pádraig Mac Giolla Cheara wasn't quite so effusive in his essay 'Brian Bóroimhe – Aoine Chéasta, 1014' (Brian Bóruma – Good Friday, 1014) in 1930, but he did defend Brian's usurpation as the necessary act of a visionary nation-builder (*An Phoblacht*, 19/4/30). In 1937, the London Feis sponsored an essay contest on 'Aontughadh na hÉireann fé Bhrian Bórumha' (The unification of Ireland under Brian Bóruma). The winning effort by Donnchadh Ó Flannagáin, serialised in *Féile na nGaedheal* in 1937 and 1938, predictably stressed the endemic Irish disunuity to which Brian had put a temporary halt, treating the usurpation as an unfortunate but unavoidable step in the unification process.[116]

By far the most ambitious work on Brian and his reign was Seosamh Mac Grianna's *Na Lochlannaigh*. In *Léigheacht ar Crois-Bhealaigh i Stair na h-Éireann*, Mac Grianna had followed the orthodox line that saw Brian as a national hero, but after doing the research for *Na Lochlannaigh*, he was much more sceptical about Brian's claim to this role as national liberator. Instead, he focused his efforts on rehabilitating the reputation of the Ui Néill king Máelsechnaill, a man he felt had been treated even more unjustly by historians than he had been by Brian. While the Ulsterman Mac Grianna was willing to concede that Brian did have a legitimate claim to the High-Kingship, what troubled him was the consistent disparagement of Máelsechnaill the Northerner in favour of Brian the Southerner, a millennium-old slander he set out to correct in this book:

> Máelsechnaill the Great was a better man than any of them, and he has not been forgiven for that for nine hundred years. But the person who will give his just due will admit that he was as capable a soldier as Ireland ever raised, and that perhaps she never raised another like him.[117]

In his reading of the Battle of Clontarf, it was the timely and courageous intervention of Máelsechnaill rather than the leadership of the elderly Brian that won the day.[118]

In a perceptive review of *Na Lochlannaigh*, Tomás Ó Floinn praised the book for its originality and style, but added, 'As a historical account of the time of the Vikings in Ireland, this book is not worth considering' (*Gaedheal*, Apr. 1938, p, 7).[119] Ó Floinn saw it instead as a provincial propaganda tract designed to exalt Máelsechnaill at the expense of Brian. An Gúm seems to have also had reservations, refusing to pay the author the higher rate it offered for researched historical work.[120] Although he was angered by this decision and called attention to the research he had done for the book, he probably should not have been surprised. Discussing Mac Grianna's historical work, Pól Ó Muirí has written:

> There is an importance to Mac Grianna's outlook on history. Perhaps it would be more proper to say that he did not write history books, but rather a personal account of history. I believe that we see in these books an attempt to explain Irish history from the perspective of the people of the Gaeltacht.[121]

From this perspective, we can see Mac Grianna in *Na Lochlannaigh* resurrecting an heroic past as yet another indictment of a miserably inadequate present, a notion he himself makes explicit in the book when, having referred to Domhnall Mac Muircheartaigh's overland portage of a fleet of ships to fight a battle against the Vikings, he draws a stark lesson for his own time:

> This was as effective a deed as it is possible for human beings to do, and it lets us know that whatever our ancestors lacked in knowledge or equipment, they were mighty men, and that we ourselves are nothing but puny creatures that tailors make look better and whose brains are kept functioning with papers.[122]

Other works published on Brian during this period were a folktale dealing with his son Murchadh that appeared in *Béaloideas* (June 1936, 108–16); Micheál Ó Gríobhtha's 'An t-Ubhall Óir' (The golden apple), a lengthy tale set at Brian's court at Kincora shortly after his victory over the Vikings of Limerick in 977, but having very little to do with historical matters;[123] Pádraig Ó Siochfhradha's short play *Cath Cluana Tarbh* (The Battle of Clontarf), dealing with the king's death;[124] and Pádhraic Ó Domhnalláin's 'Bí i do Thost' (Be quiet), a story that opens in the West of Ireland just before the Battle of Clontarf and concludes with the Irish victory there. Among the most courageous of these Western warriors is an abbot whose modesty about his deeds gives the story its title.[125]

By far the most important creative work on the Viking age in Ireland was Piaras Béaslaí's play *An Danar* (The Dane), a work that won a gold medal at the 1928 Aonach Tailteann and was first performed at the Abbey Theatre in February of that year. Set near Dublin in the tenth century, the play focuses on conflicts between Christianised Vikings in Ireland and those who have maintained their traditional paganism. The protagonist, Olaf, is a pagan in love with the devout Christian daughter of the local Norse king, against whom he leads a failed revolt to restore the old ways. One would expect Béaslaí to endorse those in the play who agree with the sentiments expressed by a Gaelicised Christian Viking:

> Woe to the person who stays a foreigner in the country in which he was raised. It is not in Scandinavia but in Ireland that we and even our fathers were born. We live among the Irish, we have had dealings with them for centuries, and we are the better for it. We had much to learn from them. It is no wonder we respect them.[126]

But Béaslaí was confident enough as a dramatist to allow the doomed and heroic Olaf to have the best and most seductive lines, however wrong-headed. After Olaf is led off to execution, one of the king's officers rejoices that things can now return to normal in words curiously reminiscent of the final scene of Synge's *The Playboy of the Western World*: 'It is a good thing we are finished with that mad schemer. We will have the old settled life from now on, as it was before Olaf interfered with us.' The king's daughter, shaken by his fearless and unrepentant defiance, answers another officer's dismissive comment that it is the saints and heroes who cause all the world's troubles with the simple lament: 'May God have mercy on their souls'.[127]

The following four tumultuous centuries inspired considerably less Gaelic interest than might have been expected. In particular, the campaigns of the Normans in Ireland were largely ignored by Gaelic writers of the period. In 1939, Taibhdhearc na Gaillimhe produced *Síol Cómhraic (Dragon's Teeth)*, a play by Jeremiah Murphy (Diarmuid Ua Murchadha) and Tomás Ó Máille dealing with the events surrounding the Leinster king Diarmuid Mac Murchadha's bringing of the Normans under 'Strongbow' to Ireland and the latter's marriage to Diarmuid's daughter Aoife.[128] Pádhraic Ó Domhnalláin's story 'Freagra an Danair' (The Dane's answer), set in Dublin as Diarmuid and 'Strongbow' approach in 1170, is interesting in that it depicts the Norse Dubliners as proud and courageous fighters, and their leader as 'the last brave king who was over the Foreigners of Dublin' (an rí cródha deiridh a bhí ar Ghaill Átha Cliath).[129] The West was the setting for two stories dealing with this period. Séamus Maguidhir recounted a tale of Cathal Croibhdhearg Ó Conchubhair in his 'Fánaidheacht i gCondae Mhuigheo' column in *An t-Éireannach* in 1936 (*Éireannach*, 26/9/36), and Seosamh Mac Grianna published a story in English about Ruaidhrí Ó Conchubhair's son Cathal Mór in the *Irish Press* in 1931 (*IP*, 7/11/31). Tomás Ó Máille provided the facts about the eleventh-century Gaelic chieftain in Scotland on whom Shakespeare's *Macbeth* – 'the version of the English' (innsean na Sasanach) – is based in 'Macbeathadh mac Finnlaich' (UCG *University Annual*, 1925–6, 19–21).

The most important work in Irish dealing with this period was the Discalced Carmelite An tAthair Benedict's *Lorcán Naomhtha Ua Tuathail* (BÁC: Muinntir C.S. Ó Fallamhain, Teor., i gcomhar le hOS, 1929), a biography of the archbishop of Dublin, Laurence O'Toole. The book is a frustrating mix of sound scholarship and naive hagiography, as the author draws on research into medieval charters, pontifical documents, annals, land rolls, and canonisation records, but at the same time accepts his subject's many miracles at face value. One anonymous critic neatly identified its major failing, wondering whether An tAthair Benedict was trying to write a 'history' (*stair*) or a 'story' (*sgéal*), and continuing:

> If this book is considered as a story, I would say that there is too much information about the history of that age . . . But if it is an authoritative 'life', it must be judged accordingly. Sometimes, Father Benedict erects historical castles on slender evidence; at other times, he cannot conceal his own opinion from us (*Star*, 26/10/29).[130]

For the thirteenth and fourteenth centuries we have four short stories. Pádhraic Ó Domhnalláin's 'An Éiric' (The retribution) offers a stark look at intra-Gaelic treachery and violence involving the Ó Conchubhair and Ó Raghallaigh families in Connacht in 1244, while his 'An Cíos' (The tribute) tells of similar rivalries between the Norman Burke and Gaelic O'Flaherty families in the following century.[131] Niall Ó Domhnaill's 'Tóraidheacht Mhuireadhaigh Uí Dhálaigh' (The pursuit of Muireadhach Albanach Ó Dálaigh) deals with the exile of this famous poet (*c.*1180–*c.*1250), driven from Ireland to Scotland for his intolerable arrogance (*Ultach*, Dec. 1937, 5, 8–9). Peadar Ó Dubhda's 'Bás an Bhrúsaigh' (The death of Bruce) presents the death of Edward Bruce and the defeat of his army in 1316 as the result of English treachery.[132]

Éiric Fhuilteach (Bloody retribution), a play by Jeremiah Murphy, 'assisted by Tomás Ó Raghallaigh' and produced at Taibhdhearc na Gaillimhe in 1938, dramatised the events leading to the death of Art Mac Murchadha Ó Caomhánaigh in the first decade of the fifteenth century.[133] In 1934, the same theatre had also produced Frank Dermody's *Ceart agus Cúiteamh* (Justice and retribution), a full-length dramatisation of the famous case in which a mayor of Galway named Lynch hanged his own son as a murderer and in the process gave the English language a new verb. The play was translated into English by the author as *Mayor Lynch of Galway* and performed in Galway in that language the following year.[134] Improbably enough, a UCG student writing as 'In Loco' had some fun with this gruesome episode in a story in the university's rag week magazine *The Wind Bag (An Bolgán Béiceach)*. 'In Loco' has the hanged young man return to Galway to claim his rightful place. He had escaped death by having Dermot Mac Murrough hanged in his place, and is now hoping to have a Hollywood movie made of his adventure. Among those mentioned in this harebrained trifle are Fionn Mac Cumhaill, Shaw, and Edward VIII's Mrs. Simpson (*Wind Bag*, 1937, 5). Annraoi Saidléar's 1934 play for children *Éibhlín Talbóid* is set in 1417 in Dublin Castle, where the niece of the English Viceroy John Talbot has become Gaelicised and in the end rather implausibly converts her uncle to the cause and leads him away from the Castle to join the Irish rebels in the nearby mountains.[135]

Some familiar Gaelic literary figures also produced fiction set in the fifteenth century. Niall Ó Domhnaill's 'Urchar Uí Dhomhnaill' (O'Donnell's shot) deals with rivalries between the O'Donnells and the O'Neills in the Northwest in mid-century (*Ultach*, Dec. 1936, 5–6, 15–16); while his 'Oidhche Ruadh Leitir Chatha' (The red night of Leitir Chatha) tells of strife among the O'Neills themselves and conflicts between them and the O'Donnells during this same period. In the latter story, Eoghan Ó Néill makes clear he would rather be fighting the English than his fellow countrymen, and the author concludes the tale with a final image of the futility of such internecine bloodshed.[136] Pádhraic Ó Domhnalláin's 1935 story 'Rí Bréige' (A false king) is set in 1487 and deals with the Fitzgeralds' decision to ally themselves with the House of York and to support the claims of the Yorkist pretender Lambert Simnel.[137] On a more intellectual note, in 1934 Tomás Ó Raghallaigh published an essay on 'Tadhg Óg Ó hUiginn: Árd-Ollamh Éireann agus Alban' (Tadhg Óg Ó hUiginn: Chief learned poet of Ireland and Scotland) (*IP*, 16/7/34).

By far the most striking of the works dealing with this century was Seosamh Mac Grianna's 'Creach Chuinn Uí Dhomhnaill AD 1495' (Conn Ó Domhnaill's plundering raid AD1495) (1929). In this story the poet Feardorcha Mac Aodhagáin, feeling slighted by his Mac Domhnaill patron in Antrim, goes to Conn Ó Domhnaill in Donegal with a scheme to get vengeance. He enrages Ó Domhnaill with his praise of his home place and thereby provokes the Donegal leader to attack and plunder his original patron. When asked by his defeated foe for the reason behind the slaughter, Ó Domhnaill replies with imperturbable arrogance, 'Strength of hand' (Treise lámh).[138] Informed of the poet's treachery and asked for mercy by Mac Domhnaill's wife, Ó Domhnaill pledges to hang the offender, grants her request, and then sets out to once more wreak havoc on his fellow Gaels. Moved by 'a passion in his heart for which there was not room in that province' (racht ina chroidhe nach rabh farsaingeach ins an chúigeadh sin aige), he calls to his eager men at the conclusion: 'Warriors, there is another plundering raid ahead of us. We will travel Ireland from sea to sea. Left face; to Desmond [in Munster].'[139] However proud of his native county of Donegal, Mac Grianna was hardly in this story condoning insolent, unmotivated violence or any sort of Social Darwinian intra-Gaelic imperialism. Rather, he was once again confronting the readers of what he believed to be the much diminished Ireland of his own time with a more vital and extravagant Ireland whose people strove to live a life at once *éifeachtach* (significant) and *filiúnta* (poetic).[140] In this story, he again makes explicit the contrast between magnificent past and mediocre present, writing of the people of Ó Domhnaill's time: 'The people who lived at that time were above all generous. They did not have the pettiness of mind that the little crowd today have, but their black was black and their white white.'[141]

Given its importance, the stature and appeal of its major figures, and the fact that it had attracted so much Gaelic interest earlier in the Revival, the relative paucity of historical writing on the sixteenth century is somewhat puzzling. There was, as we have seen, a fair amount in the textbooks, all of which included Seán an Díomais Ó Néill, Aodh Ó Néill, and Aodh Ruadh Ó Domhnaill in their catalogues of seminal personalities in Irish history. Apart from the textbooks and An tAthair Peadar Ua Laoghaire's two-part *Aodh Ruadh* (1929), a modernisation of Lughaidh Ó Cléirigh's *Beatha Aodha Ruaidh Uí Dhomhnaill* (The life of Aodh Ruadh Ó Domhnaill) originally serialised in the *Cork Weekly Examiner* from 1905 to 1908, we have only a few essays, a handful of stories, and two plays, only one of which was published. Essays on the Battle of Kinsale (1601) appeared in the Mount Melleray annual *An Sléibhteánach* in 1923 and in *Fáinne an Lae* (6/9/24), the former by Pádraig Ua Flathamháin, the latter by Pádhraic Ó Domhnalláin. 'Duibhlinn' wrote of

Aodh Ruadh Ó Domhnaill's escape from Dublin Castle at Christmas of 1591 (*IP*, 3/2/33), a subject on which Risteárd Ó Foghludha provided further information a few days later (*IP*, 14/2/33). In addition, there was a piece on the 'Flight of the Earls' (1607) by Diarmuid Breathnach in 1935 (*II*, 12/9/35). Gráinne Ní Mháille was the subject of articles by Seán Ó Cathasaigh in *An Stoc* (March and Apr. 1929); and by Séamus Maguidhir in *An t-Éireannach* (14/12/35). A campaign by Aodh Ó Domhnaill in County Galway was the topic of an anonymous essay in the *Connacht Tribune* (17/1/31); the battles in Connacht between the O'Flahertys and the Burkes were dealt with by Gearóid Ó Laidhigh in 'Stair na bhFlaithbheartach / An Cogadh Millteach leis na Búrcaigh' (The history of the O'Flahertys / The terrible war with the Burkes) (*IP*, 2/8/32); the treachery of English rulers was discussed by Pádhraic Ó Domhnalláin in 'Réim na dTúdrach / Galldú na h-Éireann / Cleasa a Feidhmigheadh' (The reign of the Tudors / The Anglicisation of Ireland / Tricks that were used) (*II*, 22/9/38); Seosamh Mac Grianna wrote of the scholar Maoghnus Ó Domhnaill in 'An Peann ar Scáth an Chlaidhimh / Mánus Ó Domhnaill agus *Beatha Cholm Cille*' (The pen in the shadow of the sword / Maoghnus Ó Domhnaill and The life of Colm Cille), (*FL*, Jan. 1929, 7–8); and Máirtín Ua Flaithbheartaigh published a lengthy serialised piece on poets and their aristocratic patrons in *Ar Aghaidh* (Feb. to Sept. 1939). Perhaps the most original essay about the period was Seán Ó Cróinín's 'Sean-Chogadh Economuíochta / 300 Blian ó Shoin' (An old economic war / 300 years ago), finding parallels between English interference with Irish trade in 1663 and the so-called 'Economic War' between Ireland and England in the 1930s (*IP*, 21/4/37).

Seosamh Mac Grianna dealt with the disagreements that arose concerning the final resting place of Seán Ó Néill in his 1929 story 'Dúil gan Fháil' (Unattainable desire), ending with a stirring vision of the dead leader united with the Gaelic pantheon of Fionn, Oisín, and St Patrick.[142] Máire Ní Churráin's 'Pósadh Mhaghnuis Uí Dhomhnaill' (The marriage of Maoghnus Ó Domhnaill) treats Maoghnus's plan to betray to the English the sole Geraldine heir, a man who had earlier converted to Protestantism in an attempt to have his inheritance restored to him by Queen Elizabeth (*Mother and Maid*, 27/2/32). Pádhraic Ó Domhnalláin's 'Airgead an Abba Bháin' (The white [Carmelite] abbot's money) (1935) tells of how an abbot said to be closely related to Aodh Ruadh Ó Domhnaill tricks some Elizabethan marauders, leaving them to die of starvation on an island.[143] 'An Croch' (The gallows), a tale set in Tipperary in 1511, was taken down by Micheál Ó Dubhshláinge from Tomás de Búrca and published in its present form in *Timthire Chroidhe Naomhtha Íosa* by An tAthair S. Ó Dúinríogh (*TCNÍ*, Feb. 1936, 42–3). And in 'Oibreadh Intinne' (Mental work), Niall Ó Domhnaill recreated a dream in which the narrator sees a vision of future Ó Néill–Ó Domhnaill solidarity

(Dundalk *Examiner*, 18/2/39).[144] The two plays from this period set in the sixteenth century were *Bean nó Spré?: Dráma ar an Sgéal Grádha mar gheall ar Fhínghín Mac Cárthaigh agus Eibhlín Nic Chárthaigh sa bhliain 1588* (A Wife or a dowry?: A drama dealing with the love story about Fínghín Mac Cárthaigh and Eibhlín Nic Chárthaigh in the year 1588) by 'Peigín', serialised in *An Lóchrann* commencing in November 1931; and the anonymous *Oidheadh an tSíodaigh* (The violent death of Silken Thomas), a play on the short-lived 1534 revolt of 'Silken Thomas' Fitzgerald, performed at Maynooth on St Patrick's Night in 1938 (*IMN*, 1938, 85).

The seventeenth century exerted a much greater fascination on Gaelic writers, perhaps because they saw in its welter of incessant conflict and shifting alliances involving native Irish, Old English in Ireland, Ascendancy, Cromwellians, Royalists, Jacobites, and Williamites, a reflection of their own unsettled time with its baffling interactions among Free Staters, Republicans – constitutional, 'slightly constitutional', and physical force – socialists, ex-Unionists, and Northern nationalists and loyalists of many kinds. At any rate, the period inspired a surprising quantity and variety of writing on historical subjects in the 1920s and 1930s. There was, for example, an essay by Seán P. Mac Énrí on the activities of the Irish in Continental Europe (*CT*, 14/11/25); one by Leift. Seán Ua Maolchatha on 'Cogadh Chromuell i gCo. Tiobraid Árann' (Cromwell's war in Tipperary) (*Óglach*, Apr.–June 1928, 94–113); one by 'T. Ó R.' on the Confederation of Kilkenny leader Éimhear Mac Mathghamhna (*Ultach*, Mar. and Apr. 1932); one by Diarmuid Breathnach on 'Briseadh na Bóinne / Rí Liam agus Rí Séamus' (The defeat at the Boyne / King William and King James) (*II*, 15/7/35); and one on the Battle of Aughrim by the novelist-poet-playwright-to-be Eoghan Ó Tuairisc in his school annual *Gearrbhaile* in 1939 (pp. 6–15, 24).

There was also a heightened Gaelic interest in the cultural history of this period, with essays in Irish on Flaithrí Ó Maolchonaire, the archbishop of Tuam, by An t-Athair P. Ó Roithleáin in (*CT*, 21/6/30), and by Tomás Ó Cléirigh (*IP*, 24/3 and 8/6/32); other essays by Ó Cléirigh on Aodh Mac Aingil (*IP*, 11/11/31), on Giollabhrighde Ó Eoghusa (*IP*, 28/1/32), and on the Four Masters (*II*, 2/9/32); other pieces on the Four Masters by Domhnall Ó Grianna and Eoin Ó Searcaigh (*II*, 18/10/27 and 10–11/4/36 respectively), and by Seosamh Mac Grianna (*Camán*, 18/6/32); an article by 'S. M.' on the theologian Luke Wadding (*IP*, 9/7/36); essays on Keating by Domhnall Ó Cearbhaill (*II*, 23/4/22), by M. C. Mac Confhormaoile (*Irisleabhar Chumann na gCéimithe i gCorcaigh / Cork Graduates' Club Annual* 1932) and by An tAthair Seán Ó Siadhail (*IR*, Apr. 1933, 289–91); an article by 'An Dubhdach' on Piaras Feirtéar (*II*, 10/9/28); a piece on Dáibhidh Ó Bruadair by 'P. B.' (doubtless Piaras Béaslaí) (*II*, 28/1/32); essays on the story behind Tomás Láidir Ó Coisdealbha's famous song 'Una Bhán' (*IP*, 3/10/34 and 11/10/34);[145] on Pilib

Ó Súilleabháin by 'Móin Ruadh' (*II*, 27/11/36) and on the scientist Robert Boyle (*II*, 26–27/12/38); and an essay by Seán Mac Maoláin on Maoghnus Ó Domhnaill (*IP*, 1/3/31). In addition, there was a general survey of 'Litridheacht na h-Éireann ó 1600–1650' (Irish literature from 1600–50) by Pádraic Mac Suibhne (*IP*, 31/3/32). By far the most impressive contribution in this area was Tomás Ó Cléirigh's 1936 study *Aodh Mac Aingil agus An Scoil Nua-Ghaedhilge i Lobháin*, an expansion of his 1926 MA thesis in the National University of Ireland.

Several Gaelic authors wrote short stories set in the seventeenth century, among them 'Uaimh an Áir' (The cave of slaughter) by 'Pádraic', a tale of Gaelic vengeance on Cromwellians in Donegal told to the author by an old man who insisted it was true (*Cork Weekly Examiner*, 2/6/23); 'An Faraire Beag' (The little sentry) by 'Sliabh gCrot', a story about a heroic young martyr at the Siege of Limerick (*Sguab*, 31/8/24); Pádraic Ó Conaire's comic tale of James II, 'Spórt an Rí' (The king's sport) (*CS*, 12/1/26); and Pádhraic Ó Domhnalláin's 'Oidhre an Léighinn' (The heir of learning), a story in which the scholar Dubhaltach Mac Firbisigh defends a young woman against a drunken English soldier at the cost of his life, and his 'An Torc Fiadháin' (The wild boar), a tale of how local people kill a land-grabbing Cromwellian officer in Connacht.[146] Ó Domhnalláin was by far the most prolific of the creative writers working on this period. His 1935 collection *Oidhre an Léighinn* contains, in addition to the title story noted above, 'An Fealltóir!' (The traitor!) (pp. 41–5), a fictional account of how French ineptitude and treachery cost the Irish victory at Aughrim; 'Rinnce na Bóinne' (The Boyne dance) (pp. 75–8), a contemptuous picture of a lavish dance held in Dublin by the sottishly over-confident James II just two weeks before his cowardly flight from the battlefield at the Boyne; and 'Cé Mharbhuigh é?' (Who killed him?) (pp. 108–10), a story of how the Irish took vengeance in 1717 on a man who had betrayed them at the Siege of Limerick.[147] In addition, in 1939 he published 'Mallacht an Fháidhe / Baintighearna na Creige / Iongantas a's Eagla' (The prophet's curse / The widow of the crag / Surprise and fear), a story set during the Williamite War in which a tragic prophecy is borne out, leading to the end of a noble family (*II*, 1/5/39).

Ó Domhnalláin also included in *Oidhre an Léighinn* a story based on the theme from this historical period that Gaelic writers of fiction seem to have found most compelling: the terrible price the Irish of the seventeenth century, in particular the clergy, paid for their loyalty to the Catholic faith. In Ó Domhnalláin's 'An t-Easbog Malluighthe' (The accursed bishop), originally published in the *Catholic Bulletin* in 1927, the Cromwellian general Ireton dies raving mad of plague, haunted by the vision of the Bishop of Emly whom he had had executed (*CB*, Jan. 1927, 58–60). In Eibhlín Ní Allagáin's 1928 story 'An tSeilg' (The hunt), a priest is killed by Cromwellians while saying Mass, having refused to join his congregation in flight without first finishing the ceremony (*TCNÍ*, June 1928, 12–14). In his 'Tobar Mhuire' (Mary's Well), Séamus Maguidhir retells a story he had heard ten years before about a priest in Mayo betrayed to Cromwellians and hanged by them (*Éireannach*, 9/5/36). Tomás Bairéad's 'Ciarán Cathach' (Curlyheaded Ciarán) involves the slaughter by Cromwellians of virtually an entire congregation at an outdoor Mass, one of the few survivors being the title character, who goes on to enter the priesthood.[148] Another short tale of the slaughter of a priest by Cromwellians was incorporated by Peadar Ó Dubhda into his 1937 novel *Brian*.[149] Priests narrowly escape death at the hands of Cromwellians in the anonymous 'Togha Ádhmhar' (A lucky choice), in which a sister's love for her priestly brother so impresses a judge that he frees the condemned man (*IMN*, 1923, 43-46); and S. Ó Tiománaigh's '"Seáinín na Sagart" nó Ciúin Tráth na h-Oidhche' ('Seáinín of the Priests' or the quiet time of the night), in which a renegade Catholic priest-hunter is duped, allowing his prey to escape (*TCNÍ*, Mar. 1925, 8–9).

There were six plays from the 1920s and 1930s set in this period, four of them of some significance. The other two were An Bráthair M. S. Ó Flaithfhile's *Neart agus Ceart: Dráma Beag do Leanaibh Scoile* (Might and Right: A little play for schoolchildren) (*Our Boys*, 13/10/27), set during the Cromwellian wars, and Tomás Mac Eochaidh's 'little musical drama' (ceol-dráma beag) about Patrick Sarsfield, *Fairíor nach ar son na hÉireann* (Alas not for Ireland), performed at Féile Chumainn Drámaidheachta na Scol in Galway in 1938.[150]

A more substantial drama was Tomás Ó Raghallaigh's *Eachdhruim an Áir* (Aughrim of the slaughter) (Gaillimh: Ó Gormáin, Teach na Clódóireachta, 1932), a play in which Sarsfield and the French general St Ruth appear, but whose central conflict involves an English nobleman whose love for an Irish woman causes him to side with the Irish. Mistakenly believing his cousin to have been murdered by an Irish soldier, he turns against his new allies and is wounded by an Irishman who sees him, also mistakenly, as a traitor.[151]

Micheál Ó Gríobhtha's 1935 play *De Dhruim na hAille* (Over the cliff) (BÁC: ODFR, 1935) is set in northeastern Ulster in 1641. As the play opens, both Protestants and Catholics are feverishly discussing among themselves rumours they have heard concerning sectarian atrocities. While the Catholics are presented as trusting in God and entirely non-violent, the Protestants fall under the sway of Parthalán na Carraige, a savage bigot who at various points hangs an innocent young man and then prohibits his burial, desecrates a set of Rosary beads, and tries, without success, to force his Catholic grandmother to curse the Pope. On his orders, all the local Catholics are driven to their deaths over a cliff, but shortly thereafter he himself, having proved a coward, is killed by an English officer disgusted by his treachery. Noteworthy in the play is the fact that the English try, albeit ineffectually, to thwart the bigot's plot, and that not all Protestants are taken in by him. One of these decent Protestants has the play's final lines: 'O Parthalán of the Rock, you have gone over the cliff; but I am certain that the dwelling place for your soul tonight is not the same as that of the papists' (A Pharthaláin na Carraige, táir imthighthe de Dhruim na hAille; ach bíodh orm nach ionann árus anocht dot anam-sa agus d'anmain na bpápairí) (p. 68). Reviewing the play for *Timthire Chroidhe Naomhtha Íosa*, Seán Ó Catháin stressed the relevance of its message for the present:

> The idea behind this drama, that the two groups will get along together if they are left alone and not incited against each other, is as true today as it was three hundred years ago. And it is to be feared that the question of the split will never be settled until that is understood (*TCNÍ*, Oct. 1935, 225).[152]

Máire Ní Chinnéide's *Scéal an Tighe* (The story of the house) (BÁC: OS, 1952) was performed in the Peacock Theatre in 1938. The play opens with a prologue set in a house in present-day Dublin, and then shifts to the setting of the play proper, the same house in the latter half of the seventeenth century. A young woman submits to her father's wish that she marry a French aristocrat for financial reasons. When her Irish lover asks her to elope, she agrees, but their plan is discovered and the lover is wounded by her brother. Her father, brother, and husband-to-be put the wounded Irishman on board a ship bound for South America, and the arranged marriage goes ahead. The woman, believing her lover dead, wastes away and dies. The epilogue, again set in the present, shows a young man and woman from these same ill-fated Irish families about to marry and so right the ancient wrong in the same house in which it had been perpetrated.

The fourth significant play set mostly in this century, though never published, seems to have been the most ambitious, if not successful. Séamus de Bhilmot's *Casadh an Rotha* (The turning of the wheel), performed by An Comhar Drámaidheachta in 1929, begins with a prologue in which St Brendan the Navigator speaks of America. The first act then moves to the Battle of Kinsale, where, according to Frank O'Connor's sarcastic review for *The Irish Statesman*, the cause is lost 'we are led to understand, through the treachery of a returned Yank' (*IS*, 26/10/29). The rest of the play deals with the fortunes of the informer's descendants in American exile, ending with the avenging of the centuries-old act of treason by a heroic young Irish airman, who has apparently flown the Atlantic solo from Kinsale.[153]

Pádraic Ó Conaire's historical novel for young readers, *Brian Óg*, was serialised in *The Irish Review of Politics, Economics, Art and Literature* in 1922 and 1923 as *Brian Óg na n-Éacht* (Young Brian of the feats), and published as a book in 1926 (BÁC: COE, n.d.). The novel opens in 1690 in a seminary in

Lisbon, where several young Irish students are enrolled. The protagonist, Brian Óg Ó Dálaigh, soon realises his vocation is as a patriot, not a priest, and he returns to Ireland on a smuggling ship to serve James II. Throughout the novel, Ó Conaire makes clear, however, that Brian's devotion is to Ireland and not to the English king whose uniform he wears and who is invariably portrayed as an obtuse and cowardly buffoon. The story ends with Brian and a group of like-minded Irish soldiers watching James leave the country and swearing that henceforth their fight will be for Ireland and Ireland alone.[154]

Commenting on Seosamh Mac Grianna's 'Creach Chuinn Uí Dhomhnaill' in a 1930 review of Mac Grianna's collection *An Grádh is an Ghruaim*, 'T. Ó R.' praised the author's honesty and ability to bring Irish history to life, but continued:

> I think that the author did not have enough scope or space here . . . I would like to see the man who did 'Creach Chuinn Uí Dhomhnaill' have an opportunity to have a great pile of paper under his hand. He could make a classic historical novel (*Tír*, Mar. 1930, 3).[155]

At this very time Mac Grianna was trying to write just such a novel, publishing the first bit of it as 'Beatha Eoghain Ruaidh Uí Néill' (The life of Eoghan Rua Ó Néill) in *Fáinne an Lae* in November 1929. The full novel was published by An Gúm in 1931. Breandán Delap has succinctly analysed the novel's shortcomings, including its excessive reliance on J. F. Taylor's 1924 biography *Owen Roe O'Neill*.[156] Nollaig Ó Muraile has discussed the ambivalence at the core of the work: Mac Grianna's inability, or unwillingness, to decide whether he is writing a reliable traditional biography or a successfully engaging work of fiction.[157] Nor were contemporary readers blind to the author's ambivalent intentions in the book, as is clear from the comments of 'S. Ó C.' in his 1931 review: 'Although there is an account of history in it, one could hardly say it is a work of history. It is a story based on history' (*II*, 6/10/31).[158] Yet despite these serious failings, the book does tell us a great deal about how this most influential Gaelic writer on historical topics in the 1920s and 1930s viewed the national past and its lessons for the present. Mac Grianna's fascination with Eoghan Ruadh was both longstanding and complex. As Nollaig Mac Congáil has noted, Mac Grianna believed that with the death of Eoghan Ruadh began 'an Anglicised period in Irish history' (ré ghallda i stair na hÉireann),[159] and most critics have focused, correctly, on Mac Grianna's insistence on Ó Néill's impeccable *Gaelachas*, his proud awareness of being a member of one of the most unyielding of all Irish families. Mac Grianna's own dedication to the book confirms this reading: 'I dedicate this book written by a Gael about a Gael to "the beautiful, ancient, noble descendants of Cobhthach Caoilmbreagh"'.[160] However, despite this inward-looking dedication, the novel itself consistently presents Ireland under Ó Néill as evolving into a confident European nation centrally involved in the affairs of the wider world:

> But there came with the years what he had hoped for long ago; messengers were coming from Charles of England seeking peace, and messengers were coming from the east from the Pope and Rome. Ireland was a part of Europe in the eyes of nations at last.[161]

Throughout, Ó Néill and his officers are depicted as cosmopolitan polyglots, as well as men of action. Moreover, unlike the colonisers and Anglo-Irish bound to their mother country England in a stultifying dependence, Ó Néill and his followers, drawing on a sophistication rooted in wide experience of the world, are able to conceive of Gaelicism as a dynamic and inclusive force in Irish life: 'I have no better name than a human devil for the person who puts a boundary between the people of Ulster and Leinster and who also does not call us all Irish people.'[162] Elsewhere in the novel, Ó Néill explicitly includes in his vision of the new nation those members of the Old English families in Ireland [i.e. Catholics of English descent] willing to embrace *Gaelachas*, and, even more importantly, those Protestants in the North ready to make that same commitment. Unlike all previous Gaelic writers on history, Mac Grianna rejected a facile identification of Irishness with Catholicism. And while he could hardly ignore Ó Néill's own devotion to the Church, he once again set that allegiance in a European context,[163] and allowed his protagonist to express doubts about the political wisdom and sincerity of the Pope, about Cardinal Rinnucini, his envoy in Ireland, and about the conservative, self-serving Catholic leadership of the Confederation of Kilkenny.[164] For the Ó Néill of Mac Grianna, the fight is one for the nation first, and only then, and in a limited way, for the Faith. Therefore, he can see the Ulster Protestants as potential allies in the only true Irish cause worth fighting for: 'There are Protestants living in the Province of Ulster, and some of them will be there after the war, no matter how long it lasts. What if we were on the same side with them when Cromwell came over.'[165]

Writing in 1924 of the battles fought by Eoghan Ruadh, Mac Grianna stated: 'The importance of this war is in the lessons which we can learn from it, for our own guidance at the present day.'[166] In this novel, more than in any of his other works on Irish history, he was using his reading of the past to focus and vindicate his critique of the present. He posits an evolving, generous, and properly assimilatative *Gaelachas* as the generative force that could fashion a new Irish nation from the ethnic divisions and hatreds spawned by colonialism, and he defines the enemy as those who pay lip service to such an independent nation while doing all in their power to negate the very cultural and social initiatives that would justify that nation's claim to a separate existence.[167]

Unfortunately, the author's own unresolved ambivalences and lack of any intellectual, much less ideological, consistency blunt the impact of his originality. Mac Grianna seems in the end unable to sustain the consequences of his analysis, and instead falls back on a traditional account of Ó Néill's heroism that entirely undercuts the original and provocative reading of the past he seems to have been striving to formulate in this book.[168] Ó Néill's final campaign is thus diminished to little more than a traditional test of manhood and ethnic superiority, with the actual outcome – including, presumably, the vision in which Eoghan has come to believe – altogether secondary:

> Whether Ireland is lost or not, whether the generations to come lived in subjugation or freedom, there was a greater fight than that to be settled that day. Fate was there at the Siur, watching how the testing of manhood would go. It was up to him to prove that neither Siur nor Shannon would see, nor bard would ever sing in the misty ages to come, that a churl of Cromwell's people was a better man than the choicest royal warrior of the descendants of Niall. He stood there . . . and he was not a countryman or a man of faith or a man dedicated to the happiness of the human race, but a fighter and a Gael waiting for the attack that would test nature and his training.[169]

Yet despite all its many faults, Mac Grianna's *Eoghan Rua Ó Néill* offers the most signifcant and challenging commentary on Irish history of any work written in Irish in the first half-century of the Gaelic Revival.

Mac Grianna also wrote a novel on the eighteenth century rapparee or outlaw Redmond O'Hanlon, but this work, *Réamonn Ó hAnluain*, was twice rejected by An Gúm and never subsequently published.[170] Two other Gaelic novels set in the eighteenth century did, however, appear in the 1920s and 1930s. Micheál Ó Dochartaigh's *Creach Bhaile an Teampaill* (The plundering of Baile an Teampaill) (BÁC: ODFR, 1930) was published posthumously, its author having died in 1917. The story opens in Mayo around 1740 and depicts the arrogance, greed, and cruelty of the local Yeomen towards their Catholic neighbours, these injustices invariably tolerated by the ruling authorities.[171] Seán Mac Maoláin's 1938 novel of the 1798 Rising, *Iolar agus Sionnach* (Eagle and fox) (BÁC: ODFR, 1938) is notable for its setting in the northeast of Ulster.[172] Also of interest is Mac Maoláin's honest presentation of the suspicion harboured by Catholic Gaels for the Presbyterian leadership of the United Irishmen, a wariness that persists despite the almost instinctive Gaelic hatred of the English enemy (pp. 56–8, 125). In addition, the author explores in passing the stultifying effect of long-term colonial subjugation on the oppressed by noting the timid conservatism of Catholic Gaels content to luxuriate in tales of past glory, but unwilling to risk what meagre gains they have made for the prospect of genuine freedom. Despite these promising flashes of originality and the author's care to underscore the non-sectarian radicalism of the United Irishmen (pp. 16–18, 56, 139, 148), Mac Maoláin seems much more at home in his accounts of the bigotry of the Yeomen and the brutality they inflict on the Gaels, brutality that provokes a desire for violent and intimate revenge in the oppressed. The novel ends with a defeat the author seems to see as all but destined and the flight into permanent exile of the surviving leaders (pp. 182, 226).[173]

'Fionn' Mac Cumhaill's novel *An Dochartach* (O'Doherty) (Dundalk: Dundalgan Press, n.d.) deals with the eventful and melodramatic post-Rising life of a veteran of the '98. Seósa Ua Dochartaigh had been at the age of twenty a leader of the movement in Donegal. After the defeat, he goes to sea, where he soon assumes command of a ship after the captain's death. In the West Indies, he visits a slave market and is disgusted by everything he experiences there. Just as he is about to leave, he sees a young white woman put up for sale, an atrocity that moves him even more than had the auctioning off of the blacks. He buys her for an exorbitant price and immediately frees her. Back in Dublin, he accidentally and implausiby meets the woman's parents and sets off again to rescue her in a new ship with an English crew. On the way home the crew mutinies and throws Ua Dochartaigh overboard. The leader of the mutineers then claims the young woman from her parents, who had promised her hand to her rescuer. Needless to say, Ua Dochartaigh survives and after untold suffering is rescued by an Irishman in a curragh and returned home. He goes in disguise to the young woman's wedding feast, reveals his identity, and saves her. The British imposter is later killed by his own crew when he cannot provide the rewards he has promised them. Clearly, for Mac Cumhaill the past was not a subject for serious analysis, but merely a pretext for exotic settings and outlandish situations.

Short story writers overwhelmingly focused on three topics from the eighteenth century: the 1798 Rising, the actions of patriotic outlaws, the so-called Whiteboys and rapparees, and the sufferings of the Catholic people and their clergy under the Penal Laws. Micheál Ó Dochartaigh's posthumously published 'Bliadhain na bhFranncach' (The year of the French) (1930) details the injustices inflicted on the local people after the defeat at Ballinamuck in 1798, including the attempted rape of a young woman, who kills her attacker, a British soldier, and later escapes with her family to Spain.[174] Other stories of the '98 are Seán de Buitléir's 'Loch Garman i 1798' (Wexford in 1798) (Enniscorthy *Echo*, 26/12/31); the anonymous 'Mághnus Ó Domhnaill / Eachtra Gaisceamhail i 1798' (A heroic adventure in 1798) (Dundalk *Examiner*, 22/10/32); Pádhraic Ó Domhnalláin's '"Ní Abróchad"' ('I will not say');[175] L. Mac Giolla Phádraig's 'Gársún na Gruaige Finne' (The fair-haired boy) (*Gaedheal Óg*, 16/3/39); Peadar Ó Dubhda's 'Ar Chapall an Ríogh' (On the king's horse);[176] Séamus Maguidhir's 'Mairtir Óg na Muaidhe' (The young martyr of the Moy), and 'Dáithí na Miodóige' (Dáithí of the Dagger).[177]

Other stories with rapparee protagonists were Pádhraic Ó Domhnalláin's 'Ar Fud an Domhain' (Throughout the world);[178] Ó Domhnalláin's 'Carraig Mhic Fhaltair' (Walters' Rock);[179] Seosamh Mac Grianna's 'An tSiolpach' (The rugged man) (Enniscorthy *Echo*, 4/12/33); Peadar Ó Dubhda's 'Réamonn Ropaire' (Redmond the rapparee); and his 'Coiléir, an Ropaire' (Coiléir the rapparee);[180] and Domhnall Ua Murchadha's 'An Broiceallach Ua Buachalla' (The sturdy Buckley).[181] Stories about the 'Whiteboys', members of rural secret societies who attacked the persons and property of landlords and their agents, were P. Ó Roithleáin's 'Sean-Chroch na Gaillimhe in aice le Móiní na gCiseach, Aimsear na "mBuachaillí mBán"' (The old gallows in Galway near Móiní na gCiseach, the time of the 'Whiteboys') (*CT*, 24/11/34); and Séamus Maguidhir's 'Dhá Chrann na Marbh' (The two trees of the dead).[182] There were also three folktales dealing with the Whiteboys published in *Béaloideas*: 'Diarmuid Ó Laere', collected from the Ó Síothcháin family on Cape Clear Island (Dec. 1935, 125–6); and 'Na Póil is na Gaibhne (Na Carabhat agus na Seana-bheastaí)' (The police and the blacksmiths (The Cravats and the Old Vests), and 'Carabhat agus Sean-Bheastaí' (Cravats and Old Vests), two stories from Pádraig Ó Milléadha's 'Seanchus Sliabh gCua' (The traditional lore of Sliabh gCua) (Dec. 1936, 178–81).

By far the most popular subject for short fiction among writers interested in this period was the repression suffered by Catholic Gaels and their clergy under the Penal Laws. Particularly common were stories in which the priest and sometimes most or all of his congregation are butchered during a clandestine outdoor Mass being celebrated on a so-called 'Mass Rock', many of which are still pointed out in the Irish countryside, and one of which Seán Ó Cuirrín apostrophised in 1937:

> O Mass Rock! You saw bloody slaughter, plundering, and oppression all being inflicted on poor Gaels. You saw those in distress being devastated and the feeble being laid low; but in spite of the danger of death they faced, you felt beside you the blessed priest with his tortured people, and they speaking to the God who came down to them on your surface (*Bonaventura*, Summer 1937, 135).[183]

Thus we find stories like Eithne Ní Chumhaill's 'Aifreann ar Chnoc Ghort a' Choirce' (Mass on the hill of Gortahawk) (*TCNÍ*, Sept. 1924, 14–16); Pádraic Ó Conaire's 'An tAifreann Binn 'Ghá Rádh' (The melodious Mass being said);[184] Fachtna Ó hAnnracháin's 'Carraig an Aifrinn' (The Mass rock) (*Standard*, 30/3/34); Seán Ó Cuirrín's 'Carraig an Aifrinn', based on the song 'An raibh tú ag an gcarraig?' (Were you at the rock?) (*Bonaventura*, Summer 1937, 135–8); Seán Ó Duibhne's 'An Sagart Óg Ó Domhnaill / Sgéal a Bhaineas le Aimsear na nDlighthe Peannaideacha i nÉirinn' (Young Father O'Donnell / A story dealing with the time of the Penal Laws in Ireland) (*Ultach*, June

1934, 6–8); Séamus Maguidhir's 'Aifreann na Geine' (Midnight Mass) (*Éireannach*, 21 and 28/12/35); and Peadar Ó Dubhda's 'Caisleán Dhúin Mhathghamhna' (The castle of Dún Mathghamna).[185] There were also tales of priest hunters like Aingeal Ní Chuaigh's 'Bláth Bán an Chnuic' (The white flower of the hill) (*TCNÍ*, Sept. 1924, 5–9); Micheál Ua h-Eibhrín's '"Ní mar Síltear, Bítear"' (Things Are not What They Seem) (*Standard*, 11/5/29); Séamas Mac Conmara's 'An Sagart Bréige' (The false priest) (*TCNÍ*, Aug. 1935, 182–6); the Jesuit A. Ó Conaill's 'An Stróinséara: 1740' (The stranger: 1740) (*TCNÍ*, Jan. 1936, 18-29); and Séamus Maguidhir's 'An t-Athair Mághnus Mac Suibhne' (Father Mághnus Mac Suibhne) and 'Pluais an tSagairt' (The priest's cave) (*Éireannach*, 23/5/36 and 30/1/37). A dream in which he sees a massacre at a Mass in Penal days inspires the protagonist of 'Callshaoth agus Imeagla' (Trouble and terror) by 'C. Au M.' to admiration of 'the things my ancestors suffered for their Faith' (nidhthe d'fhuiling mo shinnsear ar son a gCreidimh) (*CA*, 1930, 97–9). A similar dream causes a young woman tempted to skip Mass on a rainy day to leap from bed and head for church in Camilla Ní Chuinn's 'An Taidhbhreamh' (The dream) (*IR*, Nov. 1937, 847–8).

Miscellaneous stories dealing with the eighteenth century include Pádhraic Ó Domhnalláin's 'An tSochraid' (The funeral) (1927), a tale of smuggling on the Galway coast in 1792;[186] Tomás Ó Mannacháin's 'Madadh Chaisleáin Dún Baile' (The dog of Dún Baile castle) (*Stoc*, Oct. and Nov. 1928), a story of robbery and violence set in an inn; P. Ó Roithleáin's '"Peadar na Sgrap" / Aimsear na nDlighthe Peannuideacha i gCinn Mhara' ('Peadar of the scraps' / The time of the Penal Laws in Kinvara) (*CS*, 22/11/32); and Ó Domhnalláin's 'Corn an Fhealltóra' (The traitor's goblet) (1936), a story of Wild Geese heroism at the Battle of Malplacut in 1709 (Enniscorthy *Echo*, 16/5/36). There were also stories about eighteenth-century Gaelic poets like Mac Grianna's 'Codladh an Mháighistéara' (The master's sleep) and 'Séamas Mac Murchadha', both about Peadar Ó Doirnín;[187] and Domhnall Ua Murchadha's 'Cearbhall Ua Dálaigh' and 'Gliocas Aodhgáin Uí Rathghaile' (The cleverness of Aogán Ó Rathaille), both tales from oral tradition.[188]

Although Gaelic essayists seem to have found less inspiration in the eighteenth century than did the creative writers at this time, some interesting – and surprising – work appeared.[189] For example, there were biographical essays on Edmund Burke and the United Irish leader Henry Joy McCracken, the former, by Dinneen, appearing in *The Father Mathew Record* (Feb. 1929), the latter by R. Ó Bruadair in *An t-Ultach* in 1933 and 1934 (*Ultach*, Nov. 1933 to Sept. 1934). Pádhraic Ó Domhnalláin wrote on the parliamentarian Henry Grattan in 'Pairliment Ghratan agus na hÓglaigh' (Grattan's Parliament and the Volunteers) (*Camán*, 24/9/32), and on 'An-trom na dTighearnaí' (The oppression of the landlords) (*CB*, Jan. 1933). In 1931, *An Phoblacht* published Séamus Ó Grianna's account of the 1798 capture in Loch Swilly of Wolfe Tone

(*An Phoblacht*, 20/6/31), a man many saw as the father of Irish republicanism and whose lengthy autobiography was translated into Irish by Pádraig Ó Siochfhradha (BÁC: ODFR, 1932). Tone was also the subject of a 1932 essay by Séamus Ó Néill (*IP*, 3/8/32). Other essays on the '98 include D. Ó Foghludha's 'Muirtí Óg / Laoch Crodha de Chine Gaedheal' (Young Muirtí / A brave hero of the Gaelic race) (*II*, 24/8/33); Colm Ó Ciarghusa's '"Talamh Beannaighthe" [Blessed land]: "Croppies' Acre"' (*IP*, 15/11/34); and '1798: Na Franncaigh i gCill Alaidh' (1798: The French in Killala), a translation by 'Mac Casnaidh' of an eyewitness account of the French landing that had originally appeared in the *Dublin Penny Journal* in 1833 (*IP*, 7/11/38). Activity of a more dubious patriotism was the subject of the anonymous essay 'Smuglaeracht ar Chóisde An Iarthair / An Fáth a Bhí Leis, agus an Chaoi in a nDeintí é' (Smuggling on the West Coast / The reason for it and how it was done) (*CT*, 13/12/30), and of 'Ar Thóir na mBairillí / Saor Thrádáil i nIarthar Chiarraighe' (Chasing the barrels / Free trade in West Kerry) by 'P. Ua S.' (*IP*, 2/7/34). Séamus Ó Maolchathaigh in 'Eachtra an Athar Nioclás Ó Síthigh' (The story of Father Nicholas Sheehy) (*Bonaventura*, Winter 1939–40, 129–38), and Tadhg Óg Mac Carthaigh in 'An t-Athair Ó Síthigh / Mairtír de'n Ochtmhadh Aois Déag' (Father Sheehy / A martyr of the eighteenth century) (*II*, 25/1/34) dealt with the familiar theme of clerical suffering under the Penal Laws in their accounts of this Tipperary priest hanged and beheaded in 1766. The heroism of Wild Geese fighting in Europe was the topic of 'Ar Pháirc an Chatha ag Fontenoy' (On the field of battle at Fontenoy) by 'Oirche' (*IP*, 9/1/32). Essays of wider scope were Seán Ó Mocháin's 'Saoghal na nGaedheal san Ochtmhadh Aois Déag' (The life of the Gaels in the eighteenth century) (*Stoc*, June, July–Aug. 1927) and two anonymous essays for young readers: 'Na Stíobhaird' (The Stuarts) (*Our Boys*, 18/3/37), and 'Éire san 18mhadh Aois' (Ireland in the eighteenth century). In the latter piece, the Anglo-Irish, 'that group Lecky calls the Irish people' (an dream úd ar a dtugann Lecky muinntir na hÉireann) are dismissed as nothing but

> a miscellaneous crowd of 'the litter of every foreign sow', 'treacherous wild boars' who subdued Gaels under great subjection and who inflicted tyranny and oppression on 'the descendants of kings, the sons of Míl, fierce dragons and heroes' (*Our Boys*, 15/4/37).[190]

Essays focusing on the cultural life of Gaelic Ireland in the eighteenth century include pieces on Turlough O'Carolan by Tomás Ó Cléirigh (*II*, 17/12/23) and Donn Piatt (*II*, 3/2/33); on Aogán Ó Rathaille by Gearóid de Paor (*IP*, 21/1/32); on Eoghan Ruadh Ó Súilleabháin by Diarmuid Ó Briain (*IP* 26/8/32, with a letter in response from Dinneen, 31/8/32); on Liam na Buile Mac Suibhne by Pádraig Mac Suibhne ('Suibhneach Meann') (*II*,

5/12/32); on the background to *Caoineadh Airt Uí Laoghaire* (The lament for Art O'Leary) by Shán Ó Cuív (*II*, 27/1/33); on the blind poets Séamus Dall Mac Cuarta, Liam Dall Ó hIfearnáin, and Raftery by 'Liam Dall' (*II*, 3/4/33); on Riocard Bairéad by Tomás Ó Raghallaigh (*IP*, 11/1/34); on poets from West Cork by Diarmuid Ua Mathghamhna (*II*, 2/2/34); on the poets of the eighteeenth century in general by 'T. Ó M.' (UCG *University Annual*, 1926–7, 29–33, 43); and on the so-called 'hedge schools' by Conchubhar Ó Ruairc (*Standard*, 17/6/38).

Gaelic dramatists also made less use of eighteenth-century material than did writers of fiction. By far the most significant Gaelic play set in the period was Piaras Béaslaí's *An Bhean Chródha* (The brave woman) (BÁC: ODFR, 1931). Set near Bandon in County Cork, the play shows the title character, a young Protestant woman named Máiréad de Barra, coming to an awareness of the Irish side of her heritage and arranging to meet with the local rapparree leader Domhnall Ó Mathghamhna, a man with whom she falls in love but then later lures into a deadly trap. Distraught by what she has done, she throws herself on the dying man's sword in expiation. Despite the melodramatic plot line, the play deals with serious issues seriously and from an original perspective. For example, the playwright dramatises the difference between the bigoted descendants of Cromwellians, who feel only contempt for the Irish, and the more perceptive Protestants, aware of and ambivalent toward their own mixed heritage. One of the latter group, the landlord, who as magistrate is in charge of the hunt for the rapparree, says to an English soldier and one of the local Protestants:

> It is true that I know this district. I was born and raised here, and my family is rooted firmly in the soil of the country. I spent years abroad, and the Gaels have no love for me because I took part with the enemy – with the cause of God, I meant to say – but I understand them better than does any English captain or any butcher from London (p. 27).[191]

Later, Máiréad contests with Domhnall the right of her people to consider themselves Irish: 'But those people of English descent were born in Ireland also. They breathed in the same air; they saw the sun shining on the same plains.' Domhnall is willing to concede that right, but only on his own terms, terms to which he feels Máiréad has already consented through her actions: 'But my hope is greater looking at you, Máiréad – at you who were raised among the Foreigners. You are a sign of the new world in Ireland. You extended your hand to me. The Gaelic blood in you triumphed over the foreign blood' (p. 82).[192] Needless to say, the play's subsequent tragic ending proves his optimism premature, but through Máiréad and Domhnall, Béaslaí at least suggested a way out of the bi-polar ethnic rigidity that entraps most of the characters in the play. Also worth noting is Domhnall's belief that his place is not in heroic exile among the Wild Geese, but rather at home in Ireland, even though he knows he will never be able to realise a fraction of his patriotic vision before his inevitable capture and death:

> Why should I stand by this poor wretched country? I have no chance for glory or authority here; I have no hope of doing significant things that will benefit the people. There is nothing but hardship and poverty here. But there are forces stronger than reason. My heart would not allow me to abandon this country and to leave the land to the foreign churls who took it from us. If I cannot drive them out, I can make their lives miserable (p. 60).[193]

Other plays dealing with the betrayal of a rapparee were *Máighréad Ní Cheallaigh* by 'Eibhlín', serialised in *An Phoblacht* from 17 June to 1 July, 1933; and *Díolta faoi n-a Luach* (Sold for less than his worth) by Séamus Ó Néill, serialised in the Dundalk *Examiner* from 19 June to 17 July 1937. In the former, a bilingual play in three scenes, the title character tells the English about the plans of the rapparree Domhnall Ó Caoimh, a man she has tricked into believing she loves him. After discovery of her treachery, Ó Caoimh kills her and then escapes. In the latter, a young woman plots with her miserly father to sell out the rapparree Séamus Mac Murchadha after she comes to believe he is courting someone else. When he confesses his love and proposes to her on the night appointed for his arrest, she tries in vain to warn him. Perhaps most interesting in this play is the flawed character of the highwayman himself, a rather pompous and conceited man more interested in profit than patriotism and ready to end his campaign and flee Ireland as soon as he is married. Yet despite his personal delusions, he has an acute and unsentimental awareness of the diminished world in which the native Irish live: 'Don't you know that noble and lowly mean nothing now. We are all slaves. Lords, earls, we have all been in the slough of misery since the English defeated us.'[194] Séamus Ó hAodha's play *Giolla an Amaráin* (The unfortunate fellow) won a prize at the 1939 Oireachtas and was performed as a one-acter in the Abbey Theatre the same year. Set in Newfoundland, the play dramatises the life there of the poet Donnchadh Mac Conmara, best-known as a writer for his song 'Bán-Chnoic Éireann Óigh' (The fair hills of Ireland) and for his long poem 'Giolla an Amaráin', but also notorious for his opportunistic shifts in religious allegiance. Despite his disgust with himself as a spoiled priest and a ne'er-do-well, Ó hAodha's Donnchadh is a fervent Irish patriot. The song 'Donnchadh Bán' provided the subject for Tomás Mac Eochaidh's short 'musical drama' (*ceol-dráma*) of that title staged at the schools' drama festival in Galway in 1938, and *Caoineadh Airt Uí Laoghaire* inspired Mac Eochaidh's *Clais an Aifrinn* (The Mass gully) the following year.[195] Máirtín Ó Cadhain claimed that he wrote a play for Taibhdhearc na Gaillimhe on another Gaelic poet, Tomás Láidir Mac Coisdealbha, the author of the famous love song 'Úna Bhán', but that An Taibhdhearc rejected the play, which was later lost.[196] In addition, a translation by Micheál Ó hAodha of a piece originally by Tomás Ó Sionoid was staged as an outdoor pageant in Wexford in 1938. The pageant involved dramatic scenes interspersed with patriotic songs about the 1798 Rising (Enniscorthy *Echo* (20/8/38).[197]

Reviewing Niall Ó Domhnaill's biography of John Mitchel, Seán Ó Catháin wrote:

> There is hardly any period in the history of Ireland less studied today than the nineteenth century. No one likes a story when there is nothing in it but sadness and gloom and constant defeat in battle. And after getting religious emancipation at the beginning of the century, what else happened but famine, emigration, the depopulation of the country, and the insignificant Fenian rising in 1867, and then the growth and decline of the worthless 'Party' (*TCNÍ*, Dec. 1937, 278).[198]

Yet this catalogue of misery – with the exception of the parliamentary campaign of the Irish Party – provided plot and theme for an impressive body of Gaelic writing in the 1920s and 1930s. There were no fewer than eleven novels, dozens of stories and essays, two full-length biographies, and nine plays dealing with the nineteenth century.

As we will see, however, Gaelic interest in the period was quite selective. There were, for example, only two plays on Robert Emmet, Pádraig Ó Meadhra's *Riobárd Emmet* (Aonach Urmhumhan, Muinntear an 'Guardian', 1937), a play for schoolchildren, and Seán Ó Longáin's *Ríobárd Emmet* (BÁC: Brún agus Ó Nualláin, Teor. [1937]), a play also directed at the young, and described by its author as partially based on an English original.[199]

There were no creative works whatsoever on O'Connell or his campaigns for either Catholic Emancipation or Repeal of the Union with Great Britain, nor was there anything on his rivals in the Young Ireland movement or their failed revolt in 1848. What we have in Irish on O'Connell, apart from the textbooks discussed above and Domhnall Ó Súilleabháin's biography, are essays by Cearbhall Ua Dálaigh and Diarmuid Ua Laoghaire in the *Irish Independent* (8/7/29 and 11/6/29, respectively), and by An tAthair Eric Mac Fhinn in *Irisleabhar Muighe Nuadhad* in the centenary year of Emancipation. The occasion of the Mac Fhinn piece may explain its conciliatory tone: 'Whatever judgment is made on the work of Daniel O'Connell, Gaels find his name sweeter than that of any other leader at all in the time since the death of Brian Bóruma' (*IMN*, 1929, 12–21).[200] There were also several pieces on the Liberator by Dinneen, all of which defend O'Connell against those who sought to denigrate his importance in Irish history (see, for example, *Standard*, 9/2/29; *Standard*, 18/5/29, 15/6/29, 22/6/29, and 6/7/29; *IP*, 16/6/32). On the Young Irelanders, there was Tadhg Ó Donnchadha's 1931 essay '"Éire Óg" agus an Ghaedhilg' ('Young Ireland' and the Irish language) in the London journal *Guth na nGaedheal* (1931, 27–30), biographical pieces on Thomas Davis by P. Ó Séaghdha in *Iris an Gharda* (26/3/23) and by Máirtín Ua Flaithbheartaigh (*IP*, 14/12/36), a piece on Thomas Francis Meagher 'of the Sword' by P. Ó Caorainn in *An Sléibhteánach* (1922–3, 94–9) and by Cearbhall Ua Dálaigh in *The Irish Press* (22/10/32), and Niall Ó Domhnaill's full-length biography *Beatha Sheáin Mistéil* (The life of John Mitchell) in 1937. While intent on emphasising the patriotism and vision of Mitchell, Ó Domhnaill did offer a fairly balanced view of O'Connell's contribution to the national movement and acknowledged that the English language had played an important role in the radicalisation of Irish politics in the nineteenth century.[201] He also defended, altogether unconvincingly, Mitchell's consistent support for slavery during his years in exile in the United States.

The Home Rule movement under Charles Stewart Parnell was ignored by Gaelic writers, with the very large and notable exception of León Ó Broin's *Parnell: Beathaisnéis* (Parnell: A biography) (BÁC: OS, 1937), the most accomplished and scholarly Gaelic biography to appear in the first half century of the Revival. One contemporary critic, M. Ó Floinn, found the book to have 'an Anglo-Irish flavour' (blas Anglo-Irish) (*Gaedheal*, Sept. 1937, 10), a criticism rejected out of hand by Seán Ó Catháin, who boldly said that Ó Broin's work reminded him 'that Parnell did more for Ireland than any Irishman (Gaedheal) before him or since, with the exception of Daniel O'Connell alone' (*TCNÍ*, Oct. 1937, 237).[202] Ernest Blythe found the book the best yet written on Parnell, but was a bit more temperate in his praise of the leader himself:

> Parnell was not a Gael in his heart or in his mind. He was not a Gael by blood or by upbringing. But nevertheless, no one should consider him a foreigner who happened to take the side of the Gaels in the new fight that was beginning when he was coming of age (*II*, 8/6/37).[203]

The three areas of nineteenth-century Irish history that obsessed Gaelic writers at the time were the land issue – the abuses of landlordism, evictions, agrarian resistance and violence, etc. – the Great Famine of 1845 to 1850, and the physical force republicanism of the Fenians and their successors. For example, all eleven of the Gaelic novels set in the nineteenth century deal in varying ways with the issue of the ownership and control of land, as do more than twenty stories and four of the plays.

The heroine of Nioclás Tóibín's 1923 novel *Róisín Bán an tSléibhe* (BÁC: COÉ, 1923) is a young woman of mixed Irish–English ancestry who sees her background as 'a bit of Irish history' (beagáinín de stair na h-Éireann) and no disgrace to her. As the plot develops and Róisín experiences the snobbery of the English and their contempt for the Irish and comes to understand the injustice on which the landlord system is based and the fraud by which it is maintained, she increasingly identifies with the Gaelic element in her heritage. She also falls in love with a young man who has been among the leaders in a violent and successful attempt to stop an eviction and who is later convicted for the death of one of the bailiffs. In a conclusion that strains probability, she aids her fiancé to escape from Clonmel jail and ultimately gets both a husband and her threatened inheritance.

Séamus Ó Grianna included a harrowing eviction scene in his *Caisleáin Óir*, in which a dying old woman's last moments are spent by the side of the road watching bailiffs unroof her house and arrest her son for attacking them. In another scene, Ó Grianna showed how the poor could see an arranged marriage, even against a young woman's will, as an acceptable sacrifice to forestall eviction. Land issues also play an important role in the early chapters of Seán Ó Ruadháin's *Pádhraic Mháire Bhán*, with its depictions of landlord and bailiff tyranny, the inadequacy of state relief schemes, and the hope offered by the United Irish League.

Rural injustice provides the motivation and justification for the exploits of the patriotic smugglers who are the protagonists of Micheál Ó Gríobhtha's 1928 adventure novel *Briathar Mná* (BÁC: Muinntir C.S. Ó Fallamhain, Teor., i gcomhar le hOS, 1928), set on the Clare coast in the years from 1808 to 1814. For Ó Gríobhtha's Gaels, hatred of the law is inbred. Ó Gríobhtha dealt with these themes at greater length in *Buaidh na Treise* (BÁC: Muinntir C.S. Ó Fallamhain, Teor., i gcomhar le hOS, 1928), a novel with the telling subtitle *Cogadh Gaedheal re Gallaibh* (The war of the Gaels against the Foreigners). Class and ethnic divisions are at the heart of this story set in Clare in the first quarter of the nineteenth century. The bigoted English widow of an enlightened landlord poisons her son's mind against his Irish tenants, among them the novel's protagonist, Feargal Ó Lochlainn.[204] The son's obsession with imposing loyalty to the Crown on his tenants exacerbates the tension between himself and Ó Lochlainn, who, even in exile in America, devotes himself to preparing for the day he will face his rival. Their climactic fistfight becomes Ó Gríobhtha's simplistic symbol of ethnic conflict:

> So much interest was taken in the matter that all sides were blinded by the importance they felt to be in it. The Gaels thought that if Feargal won there would be an end forever to the oppression of the landlords; and the Foreigners thought that if Seon won there would be an end to the bad manners and the insubordination of the Gaels (p. 173).[205]

Naturally, Ó Lochlainn thrashes his opponent, and the significance of his victory is underscored by his winning the hand of a woman of mixed Irish–English ancestry who was also being courted by his rival. At the conclusion of the novel, however, Ó Lochlainn's awareness that the system is unshaken even if its local representative has been drubbed leads him to emigrate again, this time with his new fiancée.

Tóibín's *An Rábaire Bán* (BÁC: C.S. Ó Fallamhain, Teor., i gcomhar le hOS, 1928) also focuses on class divisions. The poor young protagonist of the title falls in love with the well-off daughter of a landlord. Their relationship is threatened by the machinations of another landlord, a conniving and dishonest man who wants the woman for his own son. Having decided to emigrate, the protagonist sets off on a ship that sinks, leading to his *deus-ex-machina* rescue and return to Ireland, where, in another improbable twist of the plot, the seemingly insuperable class obstacles are surmounted, or, perhaps better, simply glossed over, and he is able to marry his landed sweetheart.

In his meandering novel *Bun an Dá Abhann*, Seán Ó Ciarghusa was every bit as sensitive to the ethnic and class implications of property ownership (pp. 179, 187), but much less optimistic about, or even interested in, the possibilities of reconciling the two groups contesting the land in the nineteenth century. For Ó Ciarghusa, the divide between Catholic Gaels and the Protestant Ascendancy was deep and unbridgeable. Early in the novel, he makes explicit the link between faith and fatherland (p. 24), and this identification of necessity leaves Protestants 'the others' (an chuid eile) (pp. 26–7, 30, 198). At the core of the novel is a fierce battle waged to prevent an eviction, a battle that leads to the conviction and imprisonment of several local men. These events radicalise the previously apolitical tenants, who greet the fighters as heroes on their release.[206] The local Protestants (Gaill) are notably absent from the celebration. Ó Ciarghusa is willing to acknowledge that there were some broadminded Protestants (p. 339), and he also deals with the issue of class divisions among the Catholics themselves (pp. 91–2). In the final analysis, however, the world of this novel is marked by antagonism between those of Gaelic and English descent, an antagonism for which there could be but one satisfactory resolution: 'It is my prayer that there will be no strife nor cause of strife between Gaels and Foreigners in a while for there will be no Foreigners to take part in such' (p. 351).[207]

Agrarian unrest and violence during the so-called 'Tithe War' of the 1830s over the payment of taxes by Catholics to support the clergy of the established Church of Ireland were important issues in Pádraig Ó Gallchobhair's novel *Caoineadh an Choimhighthigh.*[208] The novel also pictured the Royal Irish Constabulary responsible for maintaining the status quo as drunken and lazy, and presented emigration as yet another injustice rather than as an escape. Resistance to that status quo was the subject of Diarmuid Ua Laoghaire's *An*

Bhruinneall Bhán (The fair-haired maiden) (BÁC: ODFR, 1934), in which the title character leads an aggressive but non-violent campaign against the landlord system, a system presented as legalised theft. Ua Laoghaire provides her an explicit anti-imperialist rationale for her beliefs: 'Isn't it a terrible tragedy for many people and for most of the nations of the world that they cannot take care of their own business and their own nation, and not be interfering with other people and other nations, and supposedly "bringing them to religion!"' (p. 54).[209] Faced later with the sexist disparagement of a landlord, she retains leadership of her movement and refuses all compromise with her opponents, offering a vision of the very different Ireland she would create were she in control of the nation's destiny: 'If I were ruling the nation, the first thing I would do would be to gather all the scoundrels together, and drive them into a pen, and shackle them, so that they could be recognised as well as controlled' (p. 237).[210] In the meantime, she has won the authority to set fair rents for at least this one community. Unfortunately, the potentially radical thrust of the novel is blunted by its facile avoidance of the question of violence,[211] its explicit moralising on the vices of the rich and the virtues of the poor,[212] and its anti-climactic conclusion with the heroine's marriage.

Úna Bean Uí Dhíosca's *An Seod Do-Fhághala* (The unobtainable jewel) (BÁC: ODFR, 1936) opens in 1802 on the Clare–Kerry border at the River Shannon. Bartlaí Ó Séaghdha is the leader of a group of local volunteers and a man with a passionate hatred of England rooted in his experience of an eviction. Ó Séaghdha sees violence as the only hope of salvation for an Ireland God seems to have forgotten, and is thus doubly distraught when Áine Ní Dhomhnaill, the woman he loves, enters a convent in the belief that she can best serve her country through prayer. Eventually he abducts her from the convent, but regrets his action and seeks and receives her forgiveness just before their boat is capsized on the Shannon.

The novel transcends this melodramatic plotline because of the author's exploration of more profound thematic questions. For example, Ó Séaghdha offers the following anti-imperialist reading of British colonial history:

> Theft and treachery and plunder, that is what goes on under the noble flag of Britain . . . You are indeed respected by other marauders, but hundreds of curses are rising up against you from every country in which you have set foot – in Africa, in Asia, and in Europe (p. 87).[213]

Later, O Séaghdha engages in a trenchant debate over the conflicting claims of disinterested patriotism and a desire to right individual grievances as motives for Irish resistance to English rule, a question that was to exercise many important Irish writers of both languages, among them Liam O'Flaherty and Peadar O'Donnell, with regard to the War of Independence. The author also explored in some depth an even more profound theme, the idea that obsession with the things of this world, whether material possessions or love, is the greatest danger threatening humanity. She first introduces this question with her contrast between the peace of the convent and the greed, selfishness, and violence of the world outside. Greed is represented in the novel by Nélus Ó Domhnaill, the odious, traitorous father of Áine. Selfishness and violence characterise Ó Séaghdha, who, despite his patriotism, is blind to Áine's spirituality and unwilling to allow her to live her life according to her own wishes and values. Áine's understanding of this central theme gives the novel its ambiguous title, when she says to Bartlaí:

> Do you remember the story of that man in the gospel, the man who found the precious pearl? He sold all he had to buy the pearl. It is the same with me. Do the same thing and it will bring solace to your heart. Throw away everything that comes between you and doing the will of God, and you also will have the precious pearl (p. 115).[214]

Aindrias Ó Baoighill's *An t-Airidheach* (BÁC: OS, 1939) also deals with the fundamental injustice of the landlord system. Not surprisingly there is resistance and violence. In addition, Ó Baoighill included widespread emigration among the effects of this oppression: 'Was it any wonder that the young people were in such a hurry leaving – leaving oppression and tyranny?' (p. 150).[215]

In 1932, Seán Ó Ciarghusa called for plays in Irish about Gaelic Big Houses and strong farmers.[216] While he did not see his wish fulfilled on the stage, a few novelists, among them himself, Diarmuid Ua Laoghaire, and Úna Bean Uí Dhíosca wrote fiction dealing with the strong farmer class. That class was also all but apotheosised in Diarmuid Ó hÉigeartaigh's *Tadhg Ciallmhar* (Sensible Tadhg) (BÁC: ODFR, 1934). This novel, which opens in West Cork in 1780, chronicles the steady rise in fortune of the title character Tadhg Ó Síothcháin and his family until his death in 1862. A contemporary critic complained of the novel's distance from reality: 'This Tadhg of Diarmuid's is so sensible that he is almost an "automaton", and his life is so calm and smooth that you could say that Diarmaid found "Utopia" in the book, wherever that may be outside the covers of the book' (*FMR*, Aug.–Sept. 1935, 411).[217] But a lack of verisimilitude is among the least of this novel's shortcomings. Tadhg is not so much a country Gael as a Catholic proto-capitalist with a view of life the strictest Social Darwinist could commend and a work ethic that would make the smuggest Puritan proud.[218] At various points in the novel, he deals with profiteering local shopkeepers and moneylenders – whose activities are never questioned, much less condemned – develops a sharp business sense of his own, and aggressively advances the social standing of his children, making one a priest, another a doctor, and marrying a daughter to the son of a former English army captain named Samuel Hicks. In addition, while Irish is the language of his home, he takes care that his children be taught English, and he himself regularly speaks that language with those who know it. More troubling is the fact that when his brother, with whom his parents are living, is evicted, the brother and parents go to live with a sister. The text merely states that Tadhg was unable to do anything about the eviction, but never explains why (p. 129). Even Tadhg's virtues can seem self-serving: his nationalism is conservative and safe, his religion pietistic when not merely perfunctory, his reading predictably and often narrowly focused on self-advancement. Although the novel spans the period of the Great Famine, there is virtually no mention of it; it certainly does not ripple the smooth flow of Tadhg's social progress. Indeed one could think that the author was ashamed of those of Tadhg's contemporaries improvident enough to starve to death in the 1840s. All in all, *Tadhg Ciallmhar* is a remarkable embodiment of the dark side of de Valera's dream of rural Ireland as 'the home of a people living the life that God desires that men should live'.

Short fiction dealing with the issues of landlordism and native resistance to it was a staple in Gaelic periodicals of the period, and various authors offered a satisfyingly varied range of perspectives on that subject. Among such stories were Gearóid Ó Nualláin's 'Tighearna an Tailimh' (The landlord);[219] 'Droichead na mBan' (The bridge of the women) by 'Ranji' (*Sguab*, Aug. 1925, 411–13); and Séamus Ó Ceallaigh's 'An t-Each ar Mhuin an Mharcaigh' (The horse on the rider's back) (*Stoc*, Sept. 1925, 2–3). Peadar Ó Dircáin published two stories on land issues in the 1920s, 'Dúthaigh Sheoigheach' (The Joyce Country) (*Stoc*, June 1926, 2) and 'Gliceas Pílear' (A peeler's cleverness) (*Stoc*, Dec. 1929, 7), in the latter of which a man who has killed a landlord escapes to America where he lodges in the house of a black man. He sends letters home to his wife, one of which is read by her brother, a police sergeant, who goes to America to arrest him only to be shot dead by the fugitive with a gun he has been loaned by his black friend, a man treated throughout as trustworthy, generous, and successful. Séamus Ó Grianna's 'Faoi na Fóide is Mé Sínte' (Myself stretched out under the sods) depicts the extraordinary courage of a man who helps a sick neighbour who has been evicted.[220] Séamus Ó Dubhghaill presents a landlord in a more favourable light in 'Baile na Scairte / Siopa na Croise' (Baile na Scairte / The shop at the crossroads) in which a man returned from America sets up a shop, becomes a bailiff, and plots to steal a neighbour's land, only to be repudiated by the new landlord, 'a manly, noble youth' (ógánach uasal fearamhail).[221] While set during the Land War of the nineteenth century, Seaghán Mac Meanman's 'Peadar Fhéidhlimidh na nDartán' (Peadar the son of Phelim of the clods) is more interested in the despicable niggardliness of a recent widower and new husband than in any larger political issues.[222] The same author's 'Mícheál Chordáin' is a more typical account of landlord excesses and tenant vengeance, although the utter lack of any clear political ideology on the part of the characters leaves one wondering whether politics in the usual sense of the word has any relevance at all for them.[223]

Interest in the subject continued unabated among Gaelic storywriters in the thirties. In 'An Tighearna' (The landlord), Donn Piatt told the story of a former clerical student educated in Portugal who returns home in 1876 to lead a resistance against the land system and beats to death a landlord during an attempted eviction (*Ultach*, Dec. 1930, 8–9). Deadly violence also occurs in the same author's 'Cath na gCreachach Garbh / An Talamh i Seilbh Gaedheal' (The battle of Na Creaga Garbha / The land in the possession of Gaels), recounting the successful resistance to an eviction in County Louth in 1876 (Dundalk *Examiner*, 10/9/32). A similar result is achieved without bloodshed in 'Mar Scaipeas an Ceó' (How the fog scatters) by 'Loth' (*IMN*, 1931, 85–8). In Cormac Mac Cárthaigh's 'Cúrsaí an Bhreithimh / Sgéal Leanamhna' (The affairs of the judge / A serial story), a family emigrates to New York during the Land War to avoid living with the constant spectre of eviction (*Muimhneach*, Dec. 1932, 12–14). An eviction is thwarted through trickery in Pádhraic Ó Fínneadha's '"Briseann an Dúthchas –" / Mar a h-Imrigheadh Cleas ar na Báillibh' ('What's bred in the bone –' / How the bailiffs were tricked) (*CT*, 11/2/33), and, temporarily, by force in the anonymous 'Nuair a Las na Teinte ar Árd na Coilleadh' (When the fires were lit on Árd na Coilleadh).[224] 'Seaghán a' Mála' (Seán of the sack) by 'Móin Ruadh' tells of an Irishman in the English army stationed in Macroom who gives bullets to local men with which they kill a tyrannical landlord. All involved are transported, but at story's end the protagonist is back home, a tramp (*Cork Weekly Examiner*, 26/5/34).

Penal transportation following agrarian resistance is also central in two folk tales about the famous County Waterford 'outlaws' published in *Béaloideas* under the title 'Na Conairigh' (The Connerys) (*Béaloideas*, Dec. 1936, 181–4). Séamus Maguidhir recounted the exploits of an agrarian rebel in 'Donnchadh Brúin' in 1935 (*Éireannach*, 2/11/35), and told the story of Captain Boycott the following year (*Éireannach*, 7/11/36). Tomás Bairéad's 'Costas an Ghirrfhiaidh' (The cost of the hare) depicts the deceit and injustice of the landlords and the judicial system they controlled.[225] Considerably more involved were the two stories on the period Shán Ó Cuív included in his 1937 collection *Deora Áthais agus Dréachta Eile*. 'Pluais an Mhóránaigh' (Moran's cave) opens with the kidnapping of a landlord and his daughter to keep them from aiding their candidate in a parliamentary election in the 1830s. They are hidden in a cave, the explanation of the tragic origin of whose name comprises the bulk of the tale.[226] In 'Bean fé Bhrón' (A sorrowful woman), a Clareman unable to make his rent sees his only cow siezed by a bailiff, who is found shot dead a week later. Despite his claim that he was being held captive by a group of armed men at the time of the killing, he is convicted and condemned to death. His wife goes to Dublin, pleads his case to the Viceroy, and wins commutation of his sentence to penal exile. On the day he is to be transported, another man confesses his guilt and the Clareman is freed.[227]

A decent RIC sergeant appears in 'An Sáirsint Óg' (The young sergeant), Seán Ó Duinnín's tale of the Land War in Kerry. The sergeant in a panic stabs a man at a rally to be addressed by Parnell and then, disguised, visits the victim every day and brings a doctor for him from Cork. The dying man forgives his killer, who then tends the man's broken-hearted mother until she dies in his arms (*Bonaventura*, Spring 1939, 134–8). There was no sentimentality in Séamus Maguidhir's 'Bánughadh Bhaile an Mhullaigh' (The depopulation of Baile an Mhullaigh) published the same year. Maguidhir set out to illustrate how the system of landlordism corrupted all those involved in it. A kindly landlord is replaced by a coercive one whose viciousness provokes an attack on him. As a reprisal, the landlord displaces an entire community. Even worse, however, his vengeance is misdirected, for the people actually responsible for the violence have successfully placed the blame on their innocent fellow countrymen. Maguidhir ends the story with a powerful appeal that the injustices of the past – apparently even those committed by Irish people against each other – not be forgotten until they are redressed.[228]

Plays dealing with the land agitation were Seán Ó hÓgáin's *An Fheilm* (The farm) (1926), Micheál Ó Siochfhradha's *An Ball Dubh* (The black spot) (1927), Domhnall Ó Conchubhair's *Conncas* (Conquest) (1932), and Eoghan Mac Giolla Bhrighde's *I n-Aimsir an Mháirtínigh* (In the time of Martyn) (1935). While landlordism is a central concern of Ó Siochfhradha's play, it is even more involved with the inner workings of a group of Fenians after the failed revolt of 1867 and so will be discussed below. Never staged, indeed obviously never meant to be, Domhnall Ó Conchubhair's two-act *Conncas* is a murkily allegorical dramatisation of the struggle for the land in the nineteenth century.[229] More theatrically effective was Ó hÓgáin's *An Fheilm* (BÁC: OS, 1962), a play first produced at the Abbey Theatre in December 1926. Set in 1880, the play paints an unedifying picture of Irish country people as it reveals the conflicts that arise when a man expresses his willingness to take the farm of an evicted neighbour, a man his wife had once loved. The would-be land grabber and his wife quarrel over his plan, his argument being that the other man's family had taken land under questionable circumstances in the past. She warns him that violence might ensue, particularly given the recent return from America of the other man's brother-in-law. This returned emigrant urges his sister's husband to take violent action, an idea the latter rejects as sinful. Taking matters into his own hands, the brother-in-law breaks into his enemy's cottage with a group of masked men and forces him, on his knees, to renounce his claim to the disputed land. At this point the man to be evicted rushes in, struggles with his brother-in-law, and is accidentally shot. The raiders flee, leaving the man to die without a priest since the land grabber is now afraid to leave his house to get one.

A debate over the efficacy and morality of violence against the landlord system is also central in Mac Giolla Bhrighde's *I n-Aimsir an Mháirtínigh* (BÁC: ODFR, 1937), a play based on actual events that occurred in the Rosses of Donegal.[230] In this play, An Sagart 'ac Pháidín (Father McFaddin), despite his own rage at the threatened eviction of one of his parishioners, counsels patience and non-violence: 'Easy, easy! I am afraid that you will spill blood yet. Dear friends, this will not do the job. You must be patient. That is the teaching of the Holy Church' (p. 21).[231] Elsewhere in his address to his people, the priest is, however, much more militant in his view of the situation, and the more seditious sentiments in his speech are taken down in shorthand by an Irish informer. The priest is forced to go into hiding, pursued by a zealous police officer named Martyn, who finally traps him while he is saying Mass. Once again, an t-Athair Mac Pháidín tries to calm those eager to defend him against the police, but a riot erupts, in the confusion of which the priest escapes to go on the run, a situation whose historical resonances are not lost on the local people: 'Alas! He is like the priests in Penal times – on the run and with a good reward to be had by the person who would betray them' (p. 43).[232] Grieved by police harassment of his people, the priest surrenders himself. In the final act, the evicted family has been able to get their cottage back with the help of their neighbours, and Mac Pháidín has been freed, although those involved in his earlier rescue have been sentenced to long prison terms. The play ends with a stirring speech from the priest about the coming resurgence of the Gael and the fall of the English and the landlords.

While the Famine was not the principal subject of any of the Gaelic historical novels, it provided the background for a fair number of short stories. In most, the emphasis was predictably on the sufferings and horror of that watershed catastrophe in Irish history. Tragic stories of this kind include León Ó Broin's 'Sgáil an Ghorta' (The shadow of the Famine) (*An Chearnóg*, Mar. 1923, 1–2); Seosamh Mac Grianna's 'An Tráth-Dheilbh' (The time of destitution) (later retitled 'Ar a' dTráigh Fhoilimh' [Destitute]) (*Ultach*, Dec. 1925, 6–7, 10); Tomás Ó Criomhthain's 'An Bhean Chráidhte' (The tormented woman) (*FL*, Oct. 1930, 3); P. Ó Roithleáin's 'Liam Ó Rúnaigh / Tionnóint de'n Droch-Shaoghal' (Liam Ó Ruanaigh / A Famine tenant) (*CT*, 17/11/34); 'Eachtra ar an nDroch-Shaol' (A story of the Famine), a folktale collected by James Delargy from Seán Chormuic Í Shé (*Béaloideas*, June 1935, 79–80); the Jesuit S. Ó Curraidhín's 'Ocras / Scéal Aniar' (Hunger / A story from the West) (*TCNÍ*, Mar. 1935, 53–6); Séamus Maguidhir's 'An Droch-Shaoghal' (The

Famine) (*Éireannach*, 18/1/36); and Seán Ua Cadhla's 'Scéal Cradhscail ó'n Droch-Shaoghal' (A terrible story from the Famine).[233] By no means should these short works be seen as generic tales of unjust suffering. Most of the writers offered individual and interesting, if not profound or original, insight into what the Famine meant to those who experienced its horrors. For example, Mac Grianna's Famine story is perhaps the finest piece of short fiction he ever wrote in its stark description of a dying man carrying the corpse of his brother to the grave only to die himself after burying him. Unforgettable is his picture of the protagonist with a corpse bound to his back jostling to reach a cauldron in a feeding station:

> Cathal took her place, and he put the wooden cup he had in over the mouth of the cauldron. Thereupon the corpse on his back was grabbed from behind and he was pulled roughly out from the cauldron. He stumbled five or six steps and fell.[234]

Equally wrenching is the man's reluctance to throw dirt on his brother's uncoffned face and the story's bleak, impersonal conclusion. Séamus Maguidhir's story revolves around the question of whether starving people have the moral right to steal food. A man who does so is turned in to the authorities by his own father, though he is eventually acquitted on a legal technicality.[235] Seán Ua Cadhla focused on the psychological impact of the trauma of widespread starvation and disease on those affected:

> At that time the people throughout the district were so afraid and terrified and horrified and irrational through lack of food and through the awful sickness that afflicted them as a result that if they met each other on the road, they did not have the courage to greet each other; nor, not surprisingly, would anyone take any interest in what his neighbour was doing (*Gaedheal Óg*, 12/10/39).[236]

Famine as the result of political decisions was one of the themes of Ó Broin's 'Sgáil an Ghorta', in which a European war in some indefinite historical period causes food shortages and high prices even in County Galway, 'on the edge of the world' (ar imeall an domhain).

Some writers focused their work on the question of Souperism, the practice, widely believed at the time to have been quite general during the Famine, of forcing Catholics to renounce their faith as a condition of receiving food aid. Stories of this kind are Máire Eibhlín Ní Ruithléir's 'Cnoc an Dúin' (The hill of the fort) (*TCNÍ*, Sept. 1923, 8–9); 'Faoisdean Cheallacháin' (Ceallachán's confession) by 'C. Au M.' (*FMR*, Jan. 1931, 178–9); An t-Athair Benedict's '"Is Mór idir na hAimsirí"' (There is a great difference between the times) (*Fiolar*, 1936, 7–13); and Micheál Ó Gríobhtha's 'Sciúrd, An Peata Sionnaigh' (Sciúrd, the pet fox).[237] Of particular interest in the story by 'C. Au

M.' is the author's view that God was testing the fidelity and resolution of Irish Catholics through the Famine, which he refers to as 'the life God sent to the Irish, testing them and seeing whether it would be loyalty or cowardice, strength or weakness, that would be revealed in their faith'.[238]

'Brighde agus na Buachaillí Bána' (Bríd and the Whiteboys) by Eibhlís Ní Shúilleabháin, the sister of Muiris Ó Súileabháin, is a curious story in that while set in the Famine, its real subject is the Whiteboys, here presented in a very negative light (*Lóchrann*, Nov. 1931, 5). Even more startling are two comic stories set during the Famine. In Peadar Ó Mearáin's 'Sionnach Calastairn' (Calastarn's fox), a Mayo trickster sneaks into a priest's house where a relief committee is distributing tickets for grain. The man says that if he isn't allowed a generous share then and weekly thereafter, he will bring all his neighbours in the same way he had entered. He is bribed and leaves happy (*An Chearnóg*, Feb. 1924, 7–8). Cáit Ní Mhaoir's 'An Torramh Bréagach' (The sham wake) is a black comedy in which a man convinces his mother to play dead so that neighbours will give them food and money. During the 'wake' he prods the 'corpse' with a needle, whereupon she leaps up, sending the mourners into a panicked flight. Son and mother then lock the door and enjoy their gains (*Hearthstone*, Apr. 1930, 299).

Neither of the plays from the period dealing with the Famine, Dinneen's *Teachtaire ó Dhia* (A messenger from God) (BÁC: M. H. Gill agus a Mhac, n.d.), and Séamus de Bhilmot's *Baintighearna an Ghorta* (The lady of the Famine) (BÁC: OS, 1944), produced at the Abbey Theatre in 1938, confronts the painful issues raised by the event, choosing instead to dramatise miracles of faith. In Dinneen's play, set in 1847, the wife of a farmer sees beggars as 'teachtairí ó Dhia' and treats them with great generosity, much to the disgust of her husband. Her munificence, and his disapproval of it, continue throughout the Famine. One day the husband returns home to find his storerooms empty. A beggar woman then enters, and the wife offers her the family's last calf and turnips. The woman sends her husband to the storeroom, which he finds miraculously replenished. The husband immediately repents of his selfishness, and the beggar identifies herself as St Brigid, her rags falling away to reveal the habit of an abbess. She blesses the woman and her progeny forever. De Bhilmot's play, set at Drumcliff in County Sligo in 1847, also juxtaposes faith and generosity – this time that of a parish priest – with niggardliness, here that of several middle-class Catholics. The play opens with the priest thanking his impoverished parishioners for providing him with the money to buy back a statue of the Virgin stolen from the church in 1798. He tells his people to put their faith in Mary to save them from famine. The priest is later criticised for his misuse of the money of the sick and starving by a man who offers to buy the statue. Needless to say, the priest refuses, and the stranger is subsequently exposed as Satan. Shortly thereafter, a beautiful woman appears in the vicinity giving out bread, and the priest notices the statue is missing. The woman is, of course, the Blessed Virgin herself, who says she will save the parish because of the faith of the priest, who appears at the end with a virtual halo around his head. In this play de Bhilmot makes all of the arguments used against the priest seem logically irrefutable, but allows him to triumph through the strength of his unshakeable faith alone.

It is, perhaps, somewhat surprising that there was not more Gaelic literary interest in the nineteenth-century physical force movement that gave birth to the Irish Volunteers (later the Irish Republican Army) who were to go on to win national independence. I have found only five stories and one play on the Fenians, and a single story and play dealing with the violent splinter group 'The Invincibles'. The stories are Aindrias Ó hAnglainn's 'Uaigh Mhichíl' (Michael's grave) (*Éarna*, Mar. 1922, 26–9); Pádhraic Ó Domhnalláin's 'An Gabha Nua' (The new blacksmith);[239] 'Páid Óg agus Troid na Saoirse / Eachtra Nodlag' (Young Pat and the fight for freedom / A Christmas story) by 'Seana-Pháid; Shán Ó Cuív's 'Caint agus Gníomh' (Talk and action);[240] and Séamus Ó Dubhghaill's 'Bliain na bhFíníanach' (The year of the Fenians).[241]

Micheál Ó Siochfhradha's *An Ball Dubh* (BÁC: Muinntir C.S. Ó Fallamhain, Teor., i gcomhar le hOS, 1927) centres on a powerful dramatic debate about the justification for deadly violence in the national cause after the debacle of 1867. In 1869, a British army officer and Kerry landlord needs more money and plans to clear his estate of tenants. He is warned against this course of action by a friend who both objects on moral grounds and warns of the reprisals such wide-scale evictions will almost certainly provoke from secret societies, including the defeated but still organised Fenians. In an especially vicious speech, the landlord says he will willingly evict the tenants himself. Financial difficulties are not the only problem vexing this man. He is also concerned that his half-Irish daughter is in danger of going native, a fear that would be greatly exacerbated if he knew of her love for the brother of the local Fenian leader, himself a rebel as well. The Fenians, well aware of the landlord's ruthlessness, discuss how to deal with him. In the central thematic debate of the play, the Fenian leader insists that patriotic principle must take precedence over personal grudges, however justified. He therefore rejects random retaliation against specific individuals. The majority of his men disagree, arguing that English oppression of Ireland and landlord oppression of individual Irishmen and women are two sides of the same coin. The leader, stung by the accusation that he can stand on principle because his own holding is not threatened, puts the issue of the landlord's fate to a vote, at the same time forcing the others to confront the crucial question of when deadly violence can be justified even in a just cause:

> When is it right to inflict death? What is the correct rule? What is the correct law? Brothers, because it is so severe, because it is so noble, because it is so lasting, it is not right to use it [the death penalty] except against the most severe and most noble and most lasting danger – the rule for it is necessity – necessity that has gone beyond control and beyond cure and beyond the sway of law (p. 45).[242]

His plan is to confront the landlord directly and straightforwardly and demand that he forego the evictions.

Convinced that the conditions for deadly violence have already been met, and aware, moreover, that they would have no chance against the authorities in an open contest, the men determine to hold a lottery to decide who is to carry out the landlord's execution. The paper with the black spot is drawn by the lover of the landlord's daughter. After the landlord is killed, the rebel sneaks into his house to confess to his fiancée what he has done and to tell her he plans to flee somewhere where he can try to come to terms with his ambivalences, his guilt, and his despair. Aware the house is surrounded by soldiers, she tries to detain him, but he leaves and is killed. The play ends with her praying for his soul.

Both the story and the play about the Invincibles focus in heroic mode on the vengeance the organisation exacted on the informer James Carey, whose revelations had led to the execution of those responsible for the 1882 Phoenix Park murders of the English Chief Secretary and his Under Secretary. In these works, both by Donegal writers, the main character is Pádraig Ó Domhnaill, the Donegal man who carried out the execution of Carey. In Niall Ó Domhnaill's long story 'Ar Scáth na Croiche' (In the shadow of the gallows), a strong contrast is set up between the cowardly and social-climbing Carey and the patriotic and self-sacrificing Invincible Joe Brady, whose distaste for the bloody work before him is underscored by the author. Also stressed is Carey's contempt for his comrades on the basis of social class, his paranoia that they will betray him, his cowardice before the police, and his hypocritical appeals to Irish patriotism in the court and later on the ship taking him into a supposedly safe exile. In contrast to Carey, the men whose death he has ensured, and in particular Brady, face their enemies with courage and integrity. Pádraig Ó Domhnaill, the man chosen by the American Fenians to execute Carey, is not happy with the assignment, but accepts it as his duty, an acceptance rooted in his sense of the many just grievances of both his nation and his homeplace in the Rosses. Confronted by Ó Domhnaill on board the ship taking him to South Africa, Carey reaches for his gun, but is beaten to the draw by his opponent, who then shoots him quite methodically in front of his wife. The story ends with an account of the pride and dignity with which Ó Domhnaill himself faces the scaffold.[243]

Eoghan Mac Giolla Bhrighde's play *An Fealltóir* (The traitor) (BÁC: OS, 1939) opens in Donegal where a police raid forces Ó Domhnaill to flee into exile in America. Before leaving Donegal, he engages the local schoolmaster in the by now familiar debate about the justification for violence in the national movement. The master also warns Ó Domhnaill about informers, receiving the prophetic response: 'There are always traitors; but, even so, there are still men to take vengeance on them, and by my conscience! it is a heavy retribution that will be taken from the traitors this time' (p. 21).[244] The second act shows Carey in prison, duped by the police and his own paranoia into his act of treachery. The third act, set aboard ship, has Carey boasting about his patriotism and cursing traitors and informers. Confronted by Ó Domhnaill, who offers him an even break in a gunfight, Carey tries to cheat and is shot by Ó Domhnaill, who then fires twice more into his body, hoping his end will serve as an example to others tempted to treason. In the final scene of the play, he explains to Carey's widow that he was merely carrying out her husband's own judgment on informers. He concludes:

> I only did my duty. I well know what is in store for me. If so, it is pride, not shame, I will feel when I go up on the scaffold. The treacherous Carey left a heavy stain on the reputation of Irishmen, but perhaps that stain won't be so black and ugly when it is washed with the blood of an O'Donnell (p. 51).[245]

There were also several miscellaneous historical stories about the nineteenth century written in Irish during the 1920s and 1930s, among them Tadhg S. Seoighe's 'An Gaduidhe Ó Floinn' (O'Flynn the thief) (*Stoc*, Aug. 1925, 5–6), a tale of a highwayman set around 1870; Diarmuid Ó Murchadha's 'Norburg na Sainnte' (Greedy Norburg) (*FMR*, Apr. 1929, 94-95), in which the notorious hanging judge's greed is used to trick him into freeing a man; Pádhraic Ó Domhnalláin's 'Nimh do'n Mhadadh' (Poison for the dog), about a trick played on a Protestant by a Bianconi car driver;[246] Tomás Bairéad's 'An Crochadóir nár hÍocadh' (The hangman who was not paid), dealing with grave-robbing in nineteenth-century Dublin;[247] Seán Ó Ciarghusa's 'Eachtra Ara / Scéal a h-Innsigheadh fá Rud a Tharla / Gaolta ag Faire' (A driver's adventure / A story told about something that happened / Relatives on the watch) (*II*, 31/5/39), also about grave-robbing; and Séamus Maguidhir's 'Ba Toil Dé É' (It was God's will), although this story, despite its early nineteenth-century setting, does not deal with any events of historical significance.[248]

Gaelic writers of non-fiction had, on the whole, less to say about the nineteenth century than did their creative counterparts. There was, of course, a significant amount of oral tradition dealing with local historical issues to be found in the Gaeltacht autobiographies, in particular the three books from the Blasket Islands[249] and in the various works on local history like Nic Ghabhann's *Mágh Ealta Éadair*, Ó Domhnaill's *Oileáin Árainn*, Ó Domhnalláin's *Conamara*, Mac Gréagóir's *Stair na nDéise*, and the county history *Ros Comáin*. The only significant individual essay on agrarian issues was, however, 'Bualadh Charraige Seabhac' (The fight at Carraig Sheabhac), a factual account by 'Naoise' of an incident in the tithe agitation (*IMN*, 1922, 10–14).

Even the Famine inspired less investigation than one might have expected, although we do find the anonymous 'Caisleán an Chlocháin / Mar d'Fhás an Baile / Bliadhan an Ghorta' (Clifden castle / How the town grew / The year of the Famine) (*CT*, 6/12/30); Cáit Ní Dhuibhir's 'An Gorta, 1847: A Chúis is a Thoradh' (The Famine, 1847: Its cause and its result) (Enniscorthy *Echo*, 16/5/31); and Pádhraic Ó Domhnalláin's 'An Tighearna agus an Gorta' (The landlord and the Famine) (*CB*, Mar. 1933, 257–9). Ní Dhuibhir insightfully discussed the effect of the Famine on the psyche of Irish country people, writing:

> If a person who lived before the Famine were to walk up and down throughout Ireland at present he would say that it was not the same race at all. The joy and the fun have gone out of the people. They are not as welcoming to strangers as they were, for in the Famine they were afraid of them, and they would not let them in at all. That fear and avarice got bound up in them and it is difficult to to drive them out.[250]

And in his 1931 travel book *Taistealuidheacht*, Seán Ua Ceallaigh, after a visit to India, discussed the endemic famines there as the result of British imperialism, comparing the Indian situation to that of nineteenth-century Ireland, while acknowledging that the Indians had suffered even more than his own countrymen.[251]

Gaelic writers of this time seem to have done very little research on the Fenians. 'C. Ua D.' (Cearbhall Ua Dálaigh) wrote on 'Ionnsuidhe na bhFíníní ar Chanada / An Lá do h-Oscladh Tigh Pairliméide Ottawa' (The Fenian invasion of Canada / The day the Paliament building in Ottawa was opened) in the issue of the *Irish Press* for 4 Aug. 1932. One 'F. B. L.' published an essay on John O'Leary in the the annual Gaelic journal published by UCG, of which O'Leary had been an alumnus (*Irisleabhar*, 1933–4, 16–20); Domhnall Ua Murchadha gathered some oral traditions regarding the movement in his *Sean-Aimsireacht* in 1939; and Micheál Óg Mac Pháidín published a piece on '"Dóchas na hÉireann" / Long na bhFiann i mBáighe Dhún na nGall / Dílseacht Sean-Iascairí' ('Erin's Hope' / The Fenian ship in Donegal Bay / The loyalty of old fishermen) the same year (*II*, 13/4/39). The only Gaelic essay dealing with the movement in general was, however, Riobárd Ua Duinnín's 'Na Fíníní' (The Fenians), the panegyric thrust of which should be obvious from the following excerpt:

> Praise for ever from Gaels to the Fenians of Ireland! Better men than they never lived! It is unlikely they ever will. Pure, steadfast Christians, wise, knowledgeable

men, good loyal Gaels, bold, manly enemies – those were the Fenians (*IMN*, 1938, 58–60).[252]

Miscellaneous essays on nineteenth-century topics include Peadar Ó Direáin's 'An Saoghal i Leitir Mealláin / Ceithre Fichid Bliadhan ó Shoin' (Life in Lettermullen eighty years ago) (*Stoc*, Aug.–Sept. 1926 to Feb. 1927); and Pádhraic Ó Domhnalláin's 'An Naoú Aois Déag' (The nineteenth century), an essay on the century in general marked by a naive acceptance of the steady 'progress' of the age and an ambivalent attitude towards racist European imperialism.[253] There was also a fair amount of biographical writing in Irish at the time, the most substantial works of this kind being Niall Ó Domhnaill's biography of Mitchell, Domhnall Ó Súilleabháin's biography of O'Connell, and León Ó Broin's ambitious life of Parnell. In addition, there were essays on Irish America, including Pádhraic Ó Domhnalláin's 'Lá Maoidhte Saoirse Stát Mheiriceá / An Troid a Rinne na Gaedhil / Bunú Cabhlaigh Thall' (American Independence Day / The fight the Irish made / The founding of the navy over there) (*IP*, 5/7/38); M. Ó Dubhghaill's 'Comhartha Cuimhneacháin / Státaí Aontaighthe Mheiriceá / Gaedhil i gCogadh Saoirse' (A memorial / The United States of America / Irish in the War of Independence) on Irish involvement in the Revolutionary War (*II*, 17/3/39); Annraoi Saidléar's 'Pilib Ó Siorradáin' (Philip Sheridan) (Enniscorthy *Echo*, 26/9/31), a biographical piece on the Irish-born Union general in the American Civil War; Séamus Ó Mórdha's 1939 essay on the same man, 'Pilib Ó Sioradáin: Ceann-Feadhain de Phór Bhreifne' (Philip Sheridan: A leader of Breifne stock) (Dundalk *Examiner*, 9/9/39); and an essay on John England, the Cork-born first bishop of Charleston, South Carolina (*Irisleabhar Chorcaighe*, 1936, 34–9).

Essays on the cultural history of nineteenth-century Ireland include pieces on Raftery by 'M. Ó D.' (*II*, 8/2/32) and by Máire Ní Ghuairim (*IP*, 8/5/33); on Peadar Ó Conaill, 'lexicographer and scholar' (foclóiridhe agus fear léighinn) by 'Guardal' (*IP*, 12/4/32); on Micheál Mac Suibhne by Aodh Mac Dhubháin (*II*, 28/6/32); on Pádraig Phiarais Condún by Shán Ó Cuív (*II*, 13/9/32); on Tomás Ruadh Ó Súilleabháin by Tomás de Bhál (*II*, 13/2/33); on the Carlow-born scientist John Tyndall (*II*, 30/11/38); and on the National Schools by Father Dinneen (*IP*, 26/2/32).

In the diary kept during his imprisonment in 1921 and published as *Machtnamh Cine* (BÁC: ODFR, 1933), Peadar Ó hAnnracháin recalled the pride of his fellow prisoners in what their generation had done for their country: 'There are some here who do not believe that any generation of Gaels did half as much as they themselves have already done! But isn't it a good thing for people to believe in themselves' (p. 15).[254] This pride and the resultant confidence were shared by most Gaelic writers, more than a few of whom had, during this brief but momentous period in the national struggle, helped shape the history that would later be their subject in novel, story and play. Breandán Delap has argued that a perhaps unavoidable obsession with the stirring events of their own time kept many writers from seeing the creative potential of other periods of the nation's past. Delap writes: 'The historical process was alive and active at the beginning of this century [i.e. the twentieth], and as a result the novelists of the time rejected the strangeness of the history of remote times.'[255] That at least some Gaelic writers were able and willing to look beyond the event horizon of their own time and recreate more remote periods in Irish history should be clear from the foregoing discussion. But Delap is right in underscoring how powerful was the attraction for Gaelic writers of the tumultuous time through which they had just lived. No fewer than ten novels, thirteen plays, and dozens of short stories were written in the 1920s and 1930s on the period between the Easter Rising of 1916 and the end of the shooting phase of the Irish War of Independence in July 1921. So common were works dealing with these five glorious years that Liam Ó Rinn could wonder whether writing of the recent past was not too easy an option for the Gaelic author. Discussing one of the stories in Seosamh Ó Torna's 1936 collection *Cois Life*, Ó Rinn stated with a trace of exasperation:

> Another thing: Despite the story's being fairly unusual, I took a dislike to it because it dealt with Easter Week and the fight against the Black and Tans. I thought it was too easy to compose a story of that kind since life is full of adventures in a time of struggle (*UI*, 4/7/36).[256]

Delap has questioned whether such works about the immediate past should be regarded as historical writing at all, suggesting instead that they fit better into a genre the Spanish call *Episodia Nacional*, a piece of writing dealing with 'historical events that happened close to the time of their writing' (eachtraí stairiúla a thit amach in gar d'am a scríofa), particularly events contemporaneous with the author's own lifetime.[257] In Delap's view, this genre allows the writer to comment with greater apparent distance and thus objectivity on ideas and movements of the present under the guise of recreating the past. But isn't that what most good historical writers do anyway, regardless of how remote in time is their setting? The opportunity to express himself forcefully on the present was certainly the motive for Seosamh Mac Grianna's or even Peadar Ua Laoghaire's fascination with the past. Moreover, with a few notable exceptions, the vast majority of the historical works we have discussed or will soon discuss were, as Ó Rinn implied in his comments on the story by Ó Torna, far more involved with events than ideas. The most striking of those exceptions set in the 1916–21 period were the novels *Stiana* (BÁC: Muinntir C.S. Ó Fallamhain, Teor., i gcomhar le hOS, 1930) by Pádraig Ó Séaghdha, *Cailín na Gruaige Duinne* by Úna Bean Uí Dhíosca, and *Toil Dé* by Éamonn Mac Giolla

Iasachta. All three of these works lead up to the Rising, and those by Dix and Mac Giolla Iasachta go on through the War of Independence, and all are novels dealing with ideas of immediate relevance to the time in which they were written. It should also, of course, be remembered that those Gaelic authors who wrote of this period thought they were writing about history. Indeed virtually all of them, like the majority of their fellow citizens, saw the War of Independence as not just history, but as the most crucial moment in Irish history.

For Gaelic writers interested in history the twentieth century pretty much began in 1916. Of the years before that date we have only Seán Mac Maoláin's 'Eachtra Shéamuis Sleamhain' (The story of sly Séamus) (*FL*, 4/11/22), a comic story about a Belfast detective who steals some papers he thinks will link the Gaelic League to the Kaiser's war effort, only apparently to puzzle himself to death trying to decipher the drawing of a house intended to illustrate a language primer; León Ó Broin's 1929 story 'Cúrsaí Toghacháin' (Election events), a tale of electioneering and dirty politics in pre-Rising Dublin that recalls Joyce's 'Ivy Day in the Committee Room';[258] *Stiana* by Pádraig Ó Séaghdha; Máirtín Ó Cadhain's '"Idir Shúgradh agus Dáirire"' (Half joking, half serious), a story about class divisions and social snobbery among the Irish Volunteers and their youth wing the Fianna in Conamara;[259] and Seosamh Mac Grianna's novel *An Druma Mór* (The big drum), a work completed and submitted to An Gúm in 1930 or so but not published until 1969. Of the novels, *Stiana* spans the late nineteenth and early twentieth centuries and deals with resistance to the landlord system and the corrupt police and legal machinery that maintained it. *An Druma Mór*, like Mac Grianna's 1924 short story 'Leas agus Aimhleas' (Benefit and harm) (*Ultach*, Oct. and Nov. 1924), depicts conflicts among different factions of Catholic nationalists in the Donegal Gaeltacht as the growing strength of Sinn Féin after the Rising threatens and eventually overwhelms the influence of the Ancient Order of Hibernians, the organisation to which most of the local men have owed a long allegiance.

Much of the beginning of the novel is devoted to the rivalries within the community concerning the big drum that heads the annual St Patrick's Day procession, the great event of the year for local nationalists.[260] Of particular interest to Mac Grianna was the psychology and motivation that drives the would-be leader of his people. His protagonist Proinsias Bheagaide, described in a striking, ironic passage as a blend of Mohammed, Columbus, and Aodh Ruadh Ó Néill, has some rudimentary political sense and understanding of how to manipulate his followers, but his primary motive for seeking the leadership is to assert his manhood and prove that he is truly *éifeachtach* by siezing control of the drum from the AOH and thereby dividing the community into two hostile factions. Mac Grianna drew the obvious parallel between this local row and the Irish Civil War and its aftermath:

> Two groups opposing each other is a strange thing and something to think about, particularly two groups that know each other well. It would be useless to say to either of them that the other side was right at all, however slightly . . . And the better the two groups know each other, the more zealous they are against each other . . . When a quarrel like that is in progress, it would make you think that Christianity was just a poet's dream, and that whatever reason we were out on earth for, it is natural for us to be doing our absolute best to subjugate each other (p. 118).[261]

In the end, both the drum that has been the symbolic expression of power and status in the community and the AOH that has dominated local politics for decades have been rendered irrelevant by the march of history. Or have they? The novel concludes with an outsider, an IRA officer, trying to understand these Gaeltacht people, perplexed by their unquestioned belief that all politics is local, but unsure, as was Mac Grianna himself of course, whether their profound parochialism is a source of strength or weakness.

There were no novels from the 1920s and 1930s set exclusively during Easter Week 1916, although the Rising does figure prominently in Mrs Dix's *Cailín na Gruaige Duinne*. There were, however, a play and a good number of stories, all but one fairly straightforward accounts of heroic sacrifice and death.[262] Gearóid Ó Lochlainn's 1937 play *An t-Eirighe Amach* (The rising) dramatises an elderly Fenian's heroic death after his son's failure to serve in the Rising. Other works of this kind were Pádraig Mac Gabhráin's 'An tSean-Mhallacht; an Sean-Fhuath; an tSean-Fhuil' (The ancient curse; the ancient hatred; the ancient blood) (*Irisleabhar Lorcán Naomhtha*, Nov. 1922, 12–15); 'An Gaodhal' (The Gael) by 'T. Ó C.' (*IMN*, 1922, 38–9);' 'Óglach Éireann agus a Mháthair / Sgéal i dTaobh Éirighe Amach na Cásgadh' (An Irish Volunteer and his mother / A story about the Easter Rising) by 'Brian na Múrtha' (*Óglach*, 15/5/26); 'Colm ó Chonnamara' (Colm from Conamara) by 'Mac Dara' (*CB*, May, 1928, 521–6); Nóra Ní Bhroin's 'Ceann d'á Bhuadhaibh' (One of his virtues) (*An Phoblacht*, 21/3/31); Micheál Ó Baoighill's 'An Dá Namhaid' (The two enemies) (*Ultach*, May 1931, 1–3); Máiréad Ní Raghallaigh's 'An tSean-Bhean Bhocht' (The poor old woman) (Enniscorthy *Echo*, 12/9/31); Liam Ó Murchadha's '"Dulce et Decorum Est – "' (*Outlook*, 12/3/32); Tomás Ó hAilpín's 'Ar Son a Thíre' (For his country) (*Gaedheal*, 22/12/34); and 'Leacht' (A monument) by 'W.' (*Bonaventura*, Winter, 1939–40, 139–43). The bitterness following the suppression of the Rising figures in 'Baile na mBréag' (The town of the lies) by 'Eibhlín', in which a defeated rebel smashes his rifle in frustration (*An Phoblacht*, 3/6/33). The hope that had inspired the revolt is the focus of Shán Ó Cuív's 'Luan Cásga' (Easter Monday), in which a mother blesses her volunteer son as he sets out to fight.[263] A far more original perspective on the Rising was provided by Mórag Ní Néill in 'An Fhuinneog' (The window). In this story, the patriotic daughter of a well-off Anglo-Irish family worries that her fiancé, a soldier in the British army, will have to fight the rebels, in whose ranks her own brother is serving. The fiancé is among those ordered to attack the position held by her brother's company. She informs the brother of the British intentions, and in the attack her fiancé is killed, leaving her stricken with both grief and guilt.[264] There are no such mixed emotions in the protagonist of Máiréad Ní Ghráda's 'An Crann' (The tree). In this story a young man who has gradually lost the patriotic fervour his grandmother had tried to instil in him with the story of her husband's hanging by the English outside his own door, remembers his pledge to her that he would fight for Ireland's freedom when he sees the Irish seizure of the GPO on Easter Monday.[265]

The sole comic story about the Rising was Seán Ó Ciarghusa's 'Gaedheal gan Cam' (A straightforward Gael), in which a young Irishman living in London in 1916 tells his landlady and her daughter that he is going to join the army. They naturally assume he means the British army, and are delighted and proud, particularly since, as an Irishman, he could have avoided service. They learn the truth from a picture of him in a newspaper accompanying an account of the Rising. Clearly, from the sabre cut on his cheek, he has acquitted himself with courage against the British.[266]

The most substantial piece of non-fiction in Irish dealing with the events of Easter Week 1916 was Peadar Mac Fhionnlaoich's *Bliadhain na h-Aiséirghe – 1916* (The year of resurrection – 1916) (BÁC: Coiscéim, 1992), originally serialised in *An t-Éireannach* from 7 Sept. 1935 to 12 Sept. 1936. While willing to give some credit to the accomplishments of nineteenth-century constitutional nationalists, Mac Fhionnlaoich was unyielding in his insistence that it was the physical force movement epitomised by the Rising that had finally won what independence had been won. He was, however, willing to criticise not only Eoin Mac Néill for countermanding the order that the Rising commence throughout the country on Easter Sunday, but also the by then sacrosanct figure of Pearse, who he felt had surrendered prematurely (pp. 75–6). Other interesting points discussed with honesty in his work are the looting that broke out during the week (pp. 79–81), the questioning of the Rising's legitimacy by individual volunteers (p. 199), the firing by volunteers at unarmed RIC men who had surrendered (p. 218), and the patriotism and true Gaelicism of some Protestant nationalists (p. 220). Other essays on 1916 include 'Oidhche na Gaoithe Móire / An Luigheachán' (The night of the big wind / The ambush) by 'Caitlín', dealing with the fight led by Thomas Ashe at Ashbourne, County Meath (*II*, 2/10/24); 'Éirghe-Amach na Cásca / Deich mBliadhna ó Shoin' (The Easter Rising / Ten years ago) by 'Goibhniú' (*II*, 6/4/26); 'Micheál Ó Maoláin, I.C.A.' by Liam Ó Briain (*IP*, 10/5/32); 'Teach an Phiarsaigh i Rosmuc Thiar i gConnacht / Céad Uachtarán na Poblachta' (Pearse's house out west in Conamara / The first president of the Republic) by Colm Ó Gaora (*IP*, 15/8/32); 'Treoraidhe na nOibridhthe' (The leader of the workers [James

Connolly]) by Máirtín Ó Direáin (*IP*, 8/5/37); and 'Ionnsuidhe fé Dhún an Airm' (An attack on the the Magazine Fort) by Seán Ó Briain (*IP*, 25/1/38).

The only work dealing exclusively with the period between 1916 and the beginning of the War of Independence in January 1919 seems to have been Ailbhe Ó Monacháin's 'An Sean-Mhálaidh Ní Ghuidhir' (The old Molly Maguire) (*Ultach*, May 1938, 5–7), in which the Volunteer narrator goes on the run to a safe house in Munster. There he meets an old man known as a supporter of John Redmond ('Molly Maguires' being the term used for supporters of Redmond by his foe William O'Brien). This old Fenian has, however, renounced the parliamentary leader because of his speeches urging Irishmen to enlist in the British forces in the First World War, but is too proud to let his neighbours know of his change of heart. Inspired by the Rising despite his distrust of Sinn Féin, he tells some young men where they can find hidden Fenian gunpowder, thanking God that he has been 'able to give a little help to you in the fight; the last fight with the help of God' (in-inmhe cuideadh beag a thabhairt dibh-se san troid; an troid deireannach le cuideadh Dé).

The War of Independence itself inspired six novels, in addition to four more in which it figures with varying degrees of prominence, eleven plays, and a plethora of stories. In the earliest of the novels, 'Fionn' Mac Cumhaill's *Tusa a Mhaicín* (You, Maicín) (BÁC: COÉ, [1922]), published only a year after the war with the British had ended, the protagonist is an IRA leader tracked by cruel and greedy spies, the most vicious of whom ultimately die sordid deaths at each other's hands. The novel ends with a cryptic prophecy about the protagonist's future involvement in a civil war. Near the end of Seán Ó Ruadháin's *Pádhraic Mháire Bhán*, the title character, whose many prior adventures provide the main plot of the book, becomes an IRA officer who leads his men in a major, very bloody, and highly successful ambush on the British forces in Mayo, an ambush that leaves him badly wounded.[267] A more thoughtful and troubling perspective on the guerilla warfare that came to characterise the War of Independence was offered by Éamonn Mac Giolla Iasachta in *Toil Dé*. While acknowledging the necessity for guerilla tactics with all their frequent savagery, and even justifying the recourse to intimidation as an appropriate strategy for the outmanned and outgunned IRA, Mac Giolla Iasachta made no attempt to romanticise the conduct of the war on either side. Needless to say, Mac Giolla Iasachta was not suggesting any moral equivalence between the two sides. His Black and Tans are appropriately drunken, violent, and bestial, although he also concedes them a sort of impulsive courage.

Alín de Paor's *Paidí Ó Dálaigh* (BAC: COÉ, [1933]) tells the story of a boy who out of respect for his mother's wishes does not join the local Fianna, much to the scorn of his friends. Instead, he agrees to serve the cause by working as an undercover agent for the IRA. Perhaps the most interesting aspect of the novel is its sympathetic treatment of at least some members of the Royal Irish Constabulary.[268] For example, while condemning the anti-national bias of the majority of constables, de Paor is willing to indicate the more personal reasons why a young man might join the force (pp. 27–9, 70). He also describes the ambivalence of many constables concerning their more aggressive role as agents of British control after the Easter Rising. One such decent RIC man is the father of Paidí's best friends, a man whose own wife calls the IRA 'the best of the lads' (plúr na mbuachaillí) (p. 89) and worries that she and her sergeant husband will end up as traitors to their own people. At one point de Paor describes the RIC as brave Irishmen, however misguided: 'The police were Irishmen, and the fact that they were in the pay of the enemy did not diminish their courage. It is a pity that the light of patriotism was not poured into their hearts in time!' (p. 120).[269] The sergeant hates the thought of facing his countrymen, but when the time comes, he does so, fighting bravely as do all his comrades, until he is killed in an IRA ambush made possible by information that Paidí has provided. The dying man forgives both the boy and the rebels: 'There is no need to repent . . . You couldn't help it . . . I was on the wrong side' (pp. 145–6).[270] Never does the sergeant's family condemn the IRA. And despite his grief and guilt, Paidí himself goes on to serve the cause until he also dies a hero's death in combat.

Another novel that offered an original reading of the War of Independence was Peadar Ó Dubhda's *Brian* (BAC: ODFR, 1937). The protagonist, enraged by the savagery of the Black and Tans, a force presented as worse than the pagan persecutors of the early Christians (pp. 29–30), comes to long for blood vengeance, believing the British can only be defeated by means of their own treacherous and brutal tactics. Putting his plan into execution, he disguises himself and tracks and kills a spy, after which he goes on the run, at one point attending a Mass where he hears his deed condemned by the priest as murder. Guilt, as well as the harrowing sufferings he is forced to endure while on the run, unhinges his mind, causing a state of amnesia in which he conveniently remains throughout the Civil War. Moreover, Ó Dubhda's shift in emphasis from a novel dealing with political and military issues to a love story coincides with the approach of the Truce in July 1921, once again enabling him to avoid a direct confrontation with the complexities and compromises that followed the war and led to the Treaty.[271] One should not, however, too quickly fault Ó Dubhda for lack of insight or nerve. For example, elsewhere in the novel he discusses the enervating effect of long colonial oppression on those who suffer under it, offering the following explanation of the opposition to the IRA he admits existed during the war:

> It is certain that it was not worthwhile for any man on the green land of Ireland to stir hand or foot for some of the people of this country, but at the same time, those who did not agree with us could be forgiven. Understand that seven hundred years

of slavery lie behind their ignorance, and it is none too easy to drive that out in a couple of months or a couple of years. These people will be all right after a while when they see those with the old spirit in them (pp. 104–5).[272]

Seán Mac Maoláin's *Éan Corr* (Odd man out) (BAC: OS, 1937) also raised some interesting questions about the war. The narrator is a young Gaeltacht woman who, despite her patriotism, is troubled by violence, even in a just cause. She comes under the influence of a woman whose years in America and wide reading of Irish history have made a fervent nationalist, and she is converted to the cause. The principal male character in the novel is an alcoholic ex-soldier in the British army who volunteers to help the IRA but is rejected because of his drinking problem and past service with the enemy, a service he swears had nothing to do with love for the Empire, but for which he feels no shame. At one point, for example, he tells of how his life had been saved by a British comrade – with Irish blood on his mother's side it may be added! In the end, he dies heroically, his 'good soldier's death' (bás deagh-shaighdiúra) inspiring and radicalising the local Gaeltacht people.[273]

In his review of the novel, An tAthair Seán Ó Catháin focused on Mac Maoláin's depiction of the courage of this ex-soldier as the most original and important aspect of the book, pointing out that many like him had joined the British armed forces because they believed their doing so would further the cause of Home Rule (*TCNÍ*, Sept. 1937, 213). But Mac Maoláin raised other significant points as well. For example, he notes the initial indifference of many of the Gaeltacht people towards the national cause, but traces their lack of commitment, not to cowardice but to an undeveloped historical perpective and lack of political awareness, the results of years of colonial servitude. Also of interest is Mac Maoláin's picture of the socially ambitious young woman who flirts with and eventually spies for the enemy. While her actions seem to lack any political motivation whatsoever, her shopkeeper father is vehemently opposed to Sinn Féin, and the author elsewhere hints at the possibility that local people could betray the rebels (pp. 128–30).

So strong was the dramatic appeal of the War of Independence that many writers used it as a stirring backdrop for stories in which the actual conflict was of no real significance. Works of this sort include Úna Ní Chuidithe's 'I gCoinnibh na nGall' (Against the English) (*Éarna*, Mar. 1922, 23–5); Sorcha Ní Neachtain's 'Páidín Ó Domhnaill' (*Stoc*, Aug.–Sept. 1924, 1 and 5); Seán Ó Dúnaighe's 'Tárló na Nodlag' (The Christmas incident) (*Green and Gold*, vol. 6, no. 21 [1926]); León Ó Broin's 'An Gé Balbh' (The mute goose), in which the author at the end deftly gives the story a comic connection with the war;[274] An t-Athair Casáin's 'Duine de'n Mhuinntir Bheag so' (A member of this little community);[275] and Brighid Ní Dhochartaigh's novel *Seamróg na gCeithre nDuilleóg*. The war also provided a thrilling stageset for Diarmuid Ó

Duibhne's *Cliamhain Isteach*, a play about arranged marriage in which the happy ending betrothal of a young woman to a penniless IRA man is made possible by her father's conversion to the cause. The most skilful at working the war into a plot with which it had no intrinsic connection was Piaras Béaslaí. In his 1928 comedy of mistaken identity *An Fear as Buenos Aires* (The man from Buenos Aires), he makes his protagonist an IRA man who slips into a strange house to escape pursuit and then must pretend he is the Spanish-speaking businessman his 'host' has been expecting. The detectives on the street outside are no real threat, but serve to ensure that he stays in the house long enough for all the comic complications of his masquerade to be explored.[276]

Of the stories in which the war was central, there were predictably a large number that depicted glorious death for the cause. Works of this sort were Donnchadh Ó Floinn's 'An Tarna Sgéal' (The second story) (*Reult*, Mar. 1922, 40–1); Pádraig Ó Coisdealbha's 'An Lil Bhán' (The white lily) (*Irisleabhar Lorcán Naomhtha*, Nov. 1922, 21–2); An t-Athair Micheál Mac Siomóin's 'Ó Thíorghrádh go Creideamh' (From patriotism to faith) (*Inis Fáil*, Nov. 1924, 4–5); Caitlín Ní Bhuachalla's 'Bás an Ógláigh' (The death of the Volunteer) (*Reult*, May, 1924, 72–4); 'Páid a' Chóta' (Pat of the coat) by 'Seachránaidhe' (*Branar*, Mar. 1925, 26–33);[277] An Bráthair Finghin's 'Iomchur na Croise' (The carrying of the cross) (*Éarna*, Dec. 1925, 32–3); 'Glaodhach na Mara Iartharaighe' (The call of the western sea) by 'S. M. i nGaillimh' (*TCNÍ*, Dec. 1926, 5–8); Gráinne Ní Mháille's 'Breitheamhnas Aithrighe' (Penance) (*Standard*, 5 and 12/10/29); Pilib Ó Muineacháin's 'An Leitir' (The letter) (*Outlook*, 16/1/32); Séamus Ó Néill's 'Ar Son na hÉireann' (For Ireland) (*Ultach*, Dec. 1932, 6–8); Máiréad Ní Dhonnchadha's '"Is Treise Dúthchas ná Oileamhaint"' (Nature is stronger than nurture) (*CS*, 2/5/33); 'Méirleachas in Aghaidh an Dlighe' (Villainy against the law) and 'Aghaidh-Fheidil Dubh' (The black mask) (*An Phoblacht*, 27/5/33 and 22/7/33) by 'Eibhlín'; the anonymous 'Ní'l Grádh is Mó' ('There is no greater love');[278] Liam Ó Droma's 'Oidhche Dúinn go Doiligh Dúbhach' (A hard, gloomy night for us) (*Irisleabhar Chorcaighe*, 1936, 63–4); and Maoghnus Ó Domhnaill's 'Muiris'.[279]

Surprisingly, there were more comic stories dealing with the war than there were tales of patriotic martyrdom. Among such stories involving humour were 'An Pléascán' (The explosion) by 'Seachránaidhe' (*Reult*, Mar. 1922, 15–22);[280] Donn Piatt's 'Eachtra na Cloinne Buidhe' (The story of the Orangemen) (*Irish Fun*, Oct. 1922, 91 and 93) and 'Bob do Bhualadh' (Playing a trick) (*Irish Fun*, Mar. 1923, 198–9); Aindrias Mac Aodhgáin's 'An Dúilí-Dealg' (a kind of children's toy) (*Reult*, May, 1924, 50–6);[281] Peadar Mac Fhionnlaoich's 'An Tír Tarraingire agus an Bealach Chuice' (The promised land and the way to it) (*SF*, 20/12/24) and 'Taidhbhse Eile' (Another ghost) (*SF*, 14/2/25); S. Ó Maoláin's 'Léine ar Iaraidh' (A missing shirt) (*Irish Fun*,

Oct. 1925, 106); Pádraic Ó Conaire's 'Contúirt: Marcas Maol agus a Chuid Cleas' (Danger: Bald Marcas and his tricks) (*CS*, 15/12/25); Micheál Breathnach's 'Seilg an Ghasraidh' (The pursuit of the band of men);[282] Seán Ó Ciarghusa's 'Liaimín';[283] Peadar Ó Dubhda's 'Luigheachán gur Theip Air' (An ambush that failed);[284] Micheál Ó Siochfhradha's 'Glóire Bhaile an Phludaigh' (The glory of Baile an Phludaigh), 'An t-Éitheach' (The lie), and 'Ceol nár Chleachtamair' (A music we did not rehearse);[285] Micheál Ua h-Eibhrín's 'Ar Son na Saoirse' (For freedom), *Standard*, 13/7/29; Cearbhall Ua Dálaigh's 'Fear na Féasóige' (The bearded man) (*Nation*, 19/7/30); Seaghán Mac Meanman's 'Bláthach Préataidhe agus Salann' (Buttermilk, potatoes, and salt) (1931);[286] 'Duine Marbh ar Thóir na dTans!' (A dead person in pursuit of the Tans!) by 'Neans' (*An Phoblacht*, 12/8/33); Micheál Ó Gríobhtha's 'An Sprid' (The spirit);[287] Tomás Ó Maolcraoibhe's 'Na Rialacháin go Deire' (The regulations to the end) (*Garda Review*, Feb. 1937, 350); Ailbhe Ó Monacháin's 'Mo Chéad Chuairt ar an Ghaedhealtacht' (My first visit to the Gaeltacht) (Dundalk *Examiner*, 17/9/38); and Pádhraic Ó Fínneadha's 'Is Fearr Stuaim ná Neart' (Good sense is better than strength).[288]

Again, stories of this sort tend to follow a predictable pattern, often best summarised by the title of Ó Finneadha's story above, a tale like so many others in which the British turn out to be at least as obtuse and gullible as they are cruel and treacherous. There were, however, occasional embellishments to the formula. For example, S. Ó Maoláin's 'Léine ar Iaraidh' is the story of an ambush in which the IRA have been ordered to take no prisoners. After a bloody firefight, the surviving Black and Tans surrender, and the IRA officer is unable to carry out his original intention, because of 'something honest in the soul of the Gael that does not allow him to inflict on the English the rough treatment they deserved' (rud éigin cneasta a bhíon i n-anma an Ghaedhil ná leogann dó an íde a thuill siad thabhairt do sna Gaill riamh). Instead he strips and releases the prisoners. One of the British officers thought dead turns out to be alive and is taken to hospital, where a doctor orders him washed. In the process, a shirt the filthy patient thought he had long lost is found glued to his skin, much to his delight: '"By all that I have ever seen! That's the shirt I lost in the Great War. It's been on me ever since," said the Englishman with satisfaction.'[289] In 'Glóire Bhaile an Phludaigh', Micheál Ó Siochfhradha, who seems to have taken particular satisfaction in skewering sacred cows, tells the story of a group of strutting and pompous 'patriots' who form a band, leaving a dozen or so genuine rebels to do the more dangerous work. After a drinking binge, they brawl among themselves and end up leaving the movement. The story's conclusion casts a remarkably jaundiced eye on the facile patriotism of those afraid to take any real chances: 'Only a dozen stuck with the soldiering. Some of them were killed. A hundred were at his funeral – marching.'[290] Black humour characterises 'Na Rialacháin go Deire' by the policeman Tomás Ó

Maolcraoibhe, a tale about a sergeant in the Black and Tans who is known as a stickler for regulations and who is killed in an IRA ambush. As he falls, his uniform cap tumbles off, only to be retrieved by a soldier of whom he has been particularly critical, who replaces it on the corpse with the words 'the regulations to the end, Sergeant' (na rialacháin go deire, a Sháirsint).

There were also several stories dealing with the role the underground Sinn Féin courts and the IRA played as the legitimate agents of justice in the countryside as the people boycotted the institutions of the colonial state. Stories of this sort were Seosamh Ó Maoláin's 'Bricíní Arís' (Minnows again) (*Irish Fun*, July 1924, 54 and 70); Peadar Mac Fhionnlaoich's 'An Báillidhe' (The bailiff) (*SF*, 10/1/25); Tadhg Ó Murchadha's 'Aighneas an Tobair' (The dispute over the well) (*TCNÍ*, Dec. 1939, 81–8); and Shán Ó Cuív's play *Cúirt na Dála* (The Dáil court), a comic piece about a miser getting his comeuppance from a wise and witty republican judge.[291]

Stories dealing specifically with women's involvement in the republican cause were An t-Athair Gearóid Ó Nualláin's 'Sála Salacha' (Dirty heels) with its heroine a patriotic woman who sees herself as a Judith who dupes an English Holofernes to save her IRA husband;[292] Brighid Nic an Iomaire's 'An Dochtúirín' (The little doctor) (*Our Girls*, Oct. 1931, 344 and 346); Caitlín Ní Niallaigh's 'Ar Son Róisín Dubh' (For Róisín Dubh), and 'Peig' by 'S. M.W.' (both in *Our Girls*, Oct. 1932, 262–3); and the first of Shán Ó Cuív's 'Eachtraí Scríobhneora / Trí Neithe a Chorraigh a Chroidhe' (A writer's adventures / Three things that stirred his heart) (*II*, 6/10/32). More troubling were Tomás Bairéad's 'An Dath a d'Athraigh' (The colour that changed), in which the heads of female collaborators are shaved,[293] and Colm Ó Gaora's 'An Díoghaltas' (Vengeance), in which the father of a young Gaeltacht woman who elopes with a British soldier burns all her things and lives for vengeance. He is finally able to kill the soldier in London, but then spends the rest of his life in a madhouse.[294]

There were also dozens of stories dealing with the war that are less easy to characterise, among them 'Taidhbhse an tSaighdiúra' (The soldier's ghost) by 'An Sionnach' (*FL*, 1/7/22); An t-Athair Gearóid Ó Nualláin's 'An Chrois' (The cross) and 'An Díomhaointeas' (Idleness), the latter with a protagonist modelled on Michael Collins;[295] Ó Nualláin's 'An Dúnmharbhú' (The murder);[296] 'Cúram an Chroidhe Ró-Naomhtha do'n Tír-Ghrádhthóir' (The Sacred Heart's care for the patriot) by 'S.' (*TCNÍ*, Sept. 1923, 5–6); Liam Ó Rinn's 'An Gníomh' (The deed) (*UIrman*, 24/11/23); the anonymous 'An Gheit do Baineadh as an gCaptaen / Eachtra Linne na nDubhchrónach' (The fright the captain got / An adventure of the Black and Tan time) (*Óglach*, 13/9/24); Peadar Mac Fhionnlaoich's 'An Brathadóir' (The traitor), one of several stories in which informers are of importance (*SF*, 18/10/24), his 'Píléar an Cheoil' (The musical peeler) (*SF*, 1/11/24); and his 'An Spíodhaire Anall'

(The spy from abroad) (*SF*, 24/1/25); Seosamh Ó Maoláin's 'Prátaí na Poblachta' (The potatoes of the Republic) (*Irish Fun*, Dec. 1925, 145 and 160); Seán Ó Ciarghusa's 'Séamuisín na hEórnan' (Little Séamus of the barleycorn) (*Sguab*, June, 1926, 106–9, 111–12); Séamus Ó Grianna's 'Faoi na Fóide is Mé Sínte;'[297] 'Blaic an Tean nár Ró-Dhubh / Castar na Daoine ar a Cheile' (The Black and Tan who wasn't too black / People meet) by 'Rio' (*II*, 13/8/26); Seaghán Mac Meanman's 'Tuilleadh Duilleog Amach as Leabhar Radaire' (More pages from a stroller's book) and 'Ná Leig Sinn i gCathuigh-thibh nó i n-Achrann' (Lead us not into temptation or strife);[298] Micheál Ó Siochfhradha's 'An t-Éitheach';[299] 'Sráid na n-Iongantas' (The street of the wonders) by 'F. Mac E.' (*Star*, Nov. 1930, 61); Mac Meanman's 'Duilleoga Amach as Leabhar Radaire' (Pages from a stroller's book);[300] Tomás Ó Muireadhaigh's 'Cúis Troda' (Reason for a fight) (*Comhthrom Féinne*, 9/12/31); Tomás Bairéad's 'Teach Ósta na dTans' (The Tans' hotel) and 'An Balbhán Bocht' (The poor mute);[301] Ailbhe Ó Monacháin's 'Dúthchas' (Heritage) (*Ultach*, June and July 1932); 'An Breacadh ar Bhlascaoid Mhóir' (Daybreak on the Great Blasket) by 'Eibhlín' (*An Phoblacht*, 20/5/33); the anonymous 'Cluiche Cárdaí agus Cluichí Eile' (A game of cards and other games), set on Bloody Sunday in 1920 (*AA*, Oct. 1933, 1–3); Seán Ua Néill's 'Na Geabhtaí Druidthe' (The closed gates) (Dundalk *Examiner*, 25/11/33); Seán Mac Maoláin's 'Sgéal Saoitheamhail' (An entertaining story) (Dundalk *Examiner*, 29/12/34); and his 'An Fear Faire' (The watchman);[302] Antoine Ó Monacháin's 'Oidhche Éachtach' (An extraordinary night) (*Éireannach*, 21 and 28/12/35); Seosamh Ó Torna's 'Sinnsear Cloinne' (First-born);[303] Shán Ó Cuív's 'Malairt Smaointe' (A change of mind);[304] Caoimhghín Mac Cnáimh-sighe's 'Uchtach Stócaigh' (A young man's courage) (*Our Boys*, 10/6/37) and 'Sgéalaidheacht' (Storytelling) (*Our Boys*, 19/8/37); Micheál Óg Ó Gríobhtha's 'Ór agus Ár' (Gold and slaughter) (*Our Boys*, 14/10/7); Pádruig Ó Cruadhlaoich's 'Aithrighe an Spíodóra' (The spy's repentance) (*Our Boys*, 28/10/37); Piaras Béaslaí's 'Deimhniú an Sgéil' (The proof of the story), featuring a ghost returning to vindicate an IRA comrade's application for a pension;[305] Colm Ó Gaora's 'An Ruathar' (The attack) and 'An Píobaire Dall' (The blind piper);[306] Riobárd Ó Faracháin's 'Braighdeanas' (Captivity);[307] Domhnall Ó Cinnéide's 'Buaidh na n-Óglach' (The Volunteers' victory) (*Our Boys*, 17/2/38); the anonymous 'Móin agus Piléir!' (Turf and bullets!) (*Our Boys*, 16/3/38); and the anonymous '"Níl Scaradh ag Aoinneach Léithe"' ('No one wants to part from her') (*Ultach*, Mar. 1938, 4–6). The War of Independence was also the subject of seven of the stories in Máiréad Ní Ghráda's 1939 collection *An Bheirt Dearbhráthar agus Scéalta Eile*: the title story, 'Sos Comhraic' (A truce), 'An Spiadhaire' (The spy), 'Cam' (Crooked), 'An Cúiteamh' (Retribution), 'An tSochraid' (The funeral), and '"Is Treise an Dúthchas ná an Oileamhaint"'.

Several of these stories merit further comment for the original perpectives they offer on the period. One of the two main characters in An tAthair Gearóid Ó Nualláin's 'An Chrois' is a quintessentially noble Gaelic rebel eager to carry his cross for Ireland. The other, however, is a vicious drunkard willing to spread rumours about his wife and a fellow volunteer, a man who dies rescuing him from danger he has foolishly courted in a ploy to win glory for himself. Seaghán Mac Meanman's 'Ná Leig Sinn i gCathuighthibh nó i n-Achrann' offers a sardonic look at the career of an Irish traitor who is never found out and goes on to become a wealthy politician. Tomás Bairéad's 'Teach Ósta na dTans' also deals with a spy, this one working for the IRA. In a rather macabre O. Henryish twist, he is killed by the IRA and then given a hero's funeral by the British: 'On the day of the funeral, there was an English flag on O'Rourke's coffin just as on all the other coffins. And the people who did not salute it were beaten!'[308] The death of a suspected spy at the hands of the IRA is also the subject of Ailbhe Ó Monacháin's 'Dúthchas', the victim this time being a young Palatine Protestant volunteer who is court-martialled and executed. In a later raid, the IRA learns that the Protestant's mother was the spy, and that he had died to protect her. The story ends with an apology and a tribute from the IRA: 'A wreath was placed on Seoirse's grave with a card on which was written: "In loving memory of a loyal son, and as a token of grief from his old comrades."'[309]

Mother and son also figure in Micheál Ó Siochfhradha's 'An t-Éitheach', in which a volunteer finds himself unable to fulfil his mission to inform a comrade's mother of his death. Politics, not death, disrupts a family in Seosamh Ó Torna's 'Sinnsear Cloinne', a tale of how the son of an anti-national rich man repudiates his father's self-serving conservatism to follow the radical example of the father's impoverished, idealistic brother. At one point, the young man, now an IRA officer, leads a raid on his father's house to order him to join the boycott of loyalist businesses in Belfast. At story's end, the young man and his uncle are proud and happy, while the father, despite his wealth, is broken and miserable. The focus is on the relationship between siblings in Maoghnus Ó Domhnaill's 'Muiris'. Believing his brother has failed in his duty against the enemy, a man takes his place and is killed, an apparent validation of the folk belief in the *bean sí* (banshee) introduced earlier in the tale. In Shán Ó Cuív's 'Malairt Smaointe', the tension is between a wounded IRA officer and a patriotic farmer embittered at how little has been gained from the War of Independence in contrast to the obvious benefits won through the land agitation. More cynical was the social satire of '"Níl Scaradh ag Aoinneach Léithe"', a story that opens with a young man reading a letter from the British administration to an old farmer denying him state aid. At story's end, the same young man, now an IRA veteran and a bureaucrat in the Irish civil service, writes a word-for-word identical letter to the same old man.

The most original Gaelic writer of fiction on the war was Máiréad Ní Ghráda.[310] The title story of her collection *An Bheirt Dearbráthar* tells of the jealousy of a volunteer over his brother's winning away his fiancée, a woman who had been pledged to him in an arranged match. This jealousy grows to a hatred that leads him to betray his brother to the Black and Tans. In '"Is Treise an Dúthchas ná an Oileamhaint"', the emotional transformation of the protagonist is regenerative, as a snobbish Irish emigrant who has succeeded in London and returns to show off to his countrymen discovers that in the Ireland of 1921 he is just another 'Paddy' in the eyes of the authorities. When he intervenes to save an Irishwoman being threatened by a British soldier, a struggle ensues in which the soldier is accidentally shot dead with his own gun. The final line of the story underscores the protagonist's patriotic change of heart:

> His heart was beating rapidly and there was a ringing in his head, and there was a stitch in his side, but his spirits were high, and there was happiness in his heart the like of which he had not felt there for a long time.[311]

The most original of her stories is 'An tSochraid', in which she offers an unusual perspective on the war through the eyes of a young RIC man from Ulster at a comrade's funeral.[312]

The most important work of non-fiction dealing with the period was *Tús agus Fás Óglach na hÉireann, 1913–1917* (The beginning and growth of the Irish Volunteers, 1913–17) (BÁC: ODFR, 1936), Liam Ó Rinn's 1936 translation of Colonel Maurice Moore's personal history of the rise of the Irish Volunteers, a work never published in the original English. The most significant original work in Irish on the war was Tomás Ó Máille's brief posthumously published memoir of his active service in Conamara, *An t-Iomaire Ruadh* (The red ridge) (BÁC: COÉ, 1939). 'Q. 195' told of the experiences of Irish prisoners of war in English jails in 'Luan Cingcíse, 1917 / Gáir Chatha i bPríosún' (Whitmonday 1917 / A battle cry in prison), *IP*, 29/5/39). There was a brief biographical essay by Shán Ó Cuív on George Clancy, the mayor of Limerick murdered by Black and Tans (*II*, 15/4/32); one by Seán Ua Ceallaigh on Cathal Brugha (*IP*, 1/4/33); one by 'Cianán' on the martyred Cork mayors Tomás Mac Curtain and Terence MacSwiney (*Irisleabhar Chorcaighe*, 1936, 27-30); and one on MacSwiney by Ruaidhrí Mac Munna (*IP*, 26/10/34). By far the most ambitious biography by a Gaelic writer at this time, Piaras Béaslaí's two-volume *Michael Collins and the Making of a New Ireland* (1926), was, however, in English.[313]

Several of the plays set in the period have already been discussed. Both Béaslaí's *An Fear as Buenos Aires* and Ó Duibhne's *Cliamhain Isteach* merely use the war as a backdrop, while Ó Cuív's *Cúirt na Dála* deals comically with the dispensing of republican justice. In León Ó Broin's play of criminal activity *Rogha an Dá Dhíogh*, the war is important only in providing a mysterious background for a Gárda detective who turns out to have been an undercover agent for the IRA rather than the Black and Tan he was suspected of being.[314] Two other plays, Antoine Mac Suibhne's skit *Mar Gheall ar Shaighdiúr Óg* (Concerning a young soldier) (*An Phoblacht*, 30/7/32) and Pádhraic Mac Aodha's *Peadar an tSléibhe* (Peadar of the Mountain) (Gaillimh: Ó Gormáin agus a Chomh., 1937) feature Irish characters opposed to the activities of the IRA. In the former, a man scandalises his fiancée with his criticism of the rebels as 'fools' (*amadaigh*) unable to see how futile is their struggle against the might of the Empire. In Mac Aodha's play, it is a father who is contemptuous of the cause for which his son is fighting.[315] Yet when the Black and Tans raid his home and beat him up, he refuses to divulge the son's whereabouts, and later the son's death in action seems instrumental in bringing him back to the Catholic faith he had lost. Two of the characters in Micheál Breathnach's *Draoidheacht Chaitlín* (Kathleen's enchantment) (BÁC: ODFR, 1932) are also dismissive of the IRA. Like so many other Irishmen, they served with the British in the First World War, and one is now with the Crown forces in Ireland. Trying to get information, this soldier plays on the jealousy his former comrade feels towards an IRA leader who stole his fiancée while he was at the front. Tempted to inform, the jilted lover sees a vision of Ireland as a beautiful woman in chains who invokes the spirits of his heroic rebel ancestors from Kinsale to the time of the Fenians. As a result of this *aisling*, he refuses to give information even under threat of death and eventually dies heroically, his death quickly avenged by the IRA. An Irish informer is a major character Pádraig Ó Bróithe's *An Fobha: Mion-Dráma Oireamhnach do Bhuachaillí Scoile* (The raid: A short drama suitable for schoolboys) (BÁC: Brún agus Ó Nualláin, Teoranta, [1938]). At play's end, the informer is captured by the IRA and led off for questioning, but there is no mention of his ultimate fate. Another three plays dealing with the war seem never to have been published. *Ar Son na hÉireann* (For Ireland), considered for production at Taibhdhearc na Gaillimhe in 1933, was described by a columnist for the *Connacht Sentinel* as 'an original and stirring drama in seven scenes dealing with the Anglo-Irish and Civil Wars' (*CS*, 17/10/33).[316] Micheál Ó Séaghdha's *Gníomh* (A deed), performed by An Comhar Drámaidheachta in 1939, seems, to judge from the brief summary included in the review in *Ar Aghaidh*, to have been reminiscent of Sean O'Casey's *The Shadow of a Gunman* (*AA*, Jan. 1939, 3). Micheál Breathnach's *'Briseann an Dúthchas'* ('What's bred in the bone'), performed at Taibhdhearc na Gaillimhe in 1939, deals with an initially unpatriotic father coming to embrace the Republican cause for which his son has died, giving his own life heroically as a result.[317]

Both of the most serious and challenging plays set in the period call into question the violence so often taken for granted, when not explicitly glorified, in creative literature dealing with the War of Independence. Moreover, in both plays a prisoner is executed by men who have come to know him, a plot device better known from Frank O'Connor's 1931 story 'Guests of the Nation', but probably just as familiar to Irish readers from the wrenching true account of a similar execution in Ernie O'Malley's *On Another Man's Wound* (1936). In Gearóid Ó Lochlainn's *Na Fearachoin* (The fierce warriors) (BÁC: OS, 1946), set near Dingle in County Kerry, a young man of Unionist background is urged to spy on the IRA by a friend with whom he served in the British army in the First World War. Rejecting the friend's comparison of such an action with wartime spying on the Germans, the young Kerryman points out that he himself is Irish, an awareness the implications of which grow on him as the play progresses. Of particular interest here is Ó Lochlainn's dramatisation of the protagonist's ambivalent status – unable to betray the land of his birth to the British, but simultaneously distrusted by his countrymen for reasons of class, creed, and political affiliation. His ambivalence is shared by his father, a Home Ruler who is disgusted by the violence of both the IRA and the Black and Tans, and by his sister, in love with an IRA leader but loyal to her unionist principles. When this rebel leader is brought wounded to their house, the family is forced to choose an allegiance, and they do so by sheltering him. Increasingly radicalised, the protagonist goes further and tears up his British commission. Shortly thereafter, his old army comrade is captured by the IRA and held as a hostage, and when the Black and Tans capture, torture, and murder a rebel, he is executed. This entire scene is marked by considerable sensitivity, all involved, including the prisoner, playing out their roles with courage and dignity. The IRA men are deeply troubled by what they have done on the orders of their commander, though in the end they accept the execution as necessary, as does, apparently, the victim himself, to whose courage his killers pay tribute. As the play ends, the protagonist joins the IRA, a decision his father reluctantly accepts before leaving for Scotland with his daughter. The family's sense of itself as Irish is now beyond doubt. Father and daughter will come home to Kerry, where she will marry the IRA commander.[318]

Micheál Ó Siochfhradha's one-act *Deire an Chuntais* (The end of the account) (BÁC: ODFR, 1932) was also set in Kerry during the Black and Tan terror. The entire action of the play focuses on the 'Guests of the Nation' scenario, with two fairly affable British prisoners being held by the IRA. These two hostages are quietly patriotic and when offered what they feel are dishonourable conditions for their release, they refuse without hesitation. It is clear throughout that Ó Siochfhradha feels the ordinary soldiers on both sides are victims here, trapped by the 'cold military rules' (rialacha fuara airm) one of the IRA captors identifies as the cause of the impending tragedy. Unfortunately for all concerned, those rules are far more powerful than mere good will. The foes part with mutual respect – both sides doing what they sincerely see as their duty – and the British go off to die resigned, generous, and free of shame or hatred, one of them offering a philosophic forgiveness to one of his captors:

> You did your best for us – more than your best. Do not feel any regret. You stood by your duties and we stood by ours. There is an unjust duty on one of the sides. It doesn't matter which side now, but we will meet in that place where no one has to attend to a duty that is wrong (pp. 30–1).[319]

The dictates of perceived duty and political allegiance determined with extraordinary predicability how Gaelic writers would treat the Civil War of June 1922 to April 1923. For those who accepted the 1921 Anglo-Irish Treaty, with whatever doubts and reservations, the war was a tragic mistake. This reading of the conflict was brought home – quite literally – in the stories, some of which were written while the fighting was still raging, in which Irishmen accidentally cause the death of their own close relatives, or in which other Irish people must come to terms with those of their countrymen who have killed their loved ones. For example, Pádraic Ó Conaire, who saw the war as a time when the Irish were 'gripping each other's throats, killing each other and murdering each other more spitefully and more fiercely than the English had killed either of them for a couple of hundred years' (*CS*, 28/8/26),[320] wrote two pieces of this sort: the July 1922 sketch 'Beirt Chara' (Two friends) about two comrades fighting on opposite sides, one of whom is killed, the other badly maimed (*Free State*, 20/7/22) and the 1924 story 'An Sáirsint' (The sergeant), in which the tragedy is narrowly averted when a sergeant in the Free State army prevents a soldier from shooting a fleeing member of the anti-Treaty forces, a man who when captured turns out to be the sergeant's brother (*Óglach*, 10/5/24).[321] The two brothers in 'An Luigheachán' (The ambush) by 'Brandubh' are not so fortunate, each being killed by the other in an ambush and their bodies taken to a house that turns out to be that of their parents (*FL*, 5/5/23). In Máiréad Ní Ghráda's 'An Díthreabhach' (The recluse), the title character loses his mind after killing his own son in the war; and in her 'Máthair an tSaighdiúra' (The soldier's mother), a woman unknowingly shelters the anti-Treaty fighters who have killed her Free State soldier son, but does not betray them even after learning what they have done.[322] In León Ó Broin's 'Beo Bocht Bacach' (Alive, poor, and lame), the emphasis is on the tragic irony of the death of an old Fenian who had been beaten by supporters of the British during Easter Week, had lived to see the Crown forces depart after the War of Independence, and has now been killed by stupid chance in a Civil War ambush (*An Chearnóg*, Feb. 1923, 4–5). Micheul Ó Cinnfhaolaidh's 'Tar Éis an Chatha' (After the battle) held out some hope of reconcilation. In this story, a soldier comes across a wounded foe – Ó Cinnfhaolaidh never lets us know which side either is on – and they converse. Neither's heart is in the fight, but the healthy soldier acknowledges that there is one person he hates, the man who had killed his father with a stone. In a flash of artillery fire, he recognises the wounded man as his father's killer and wonders whether he should shoot him or leave him to die in an approaching fire. In the end he does neither, instead taking the other on his back and running from the flames (*Green and Gold*, Sept.–Nov. 1922, 214–17).

Both plays with Civil War settings, León Ó Broin's *An Mhallacht* (The curse) and Séamus de Bhilmot's *An Casán* (The path), deal with the unintentional killing of relatives or friends.[323] Ó Broin, who served in the Free State army, also worked the scenario from 'Guests of the Nation' into his play. Of two brothers-in-law involved in the execution of two British captives in the War of Independence, one, now with the Free State, unwittingly kills the other, a republican sniper, during the Civil War. What is most interesting about this short play is the insistence on the part of the sniper's wife that the earlier execution, however justified at the time, has left this curse of blind violence on those who carried it out:

> We forgot about the wives of those two, that they had mothers and families mourning them and giving a thousand curses on the ones who snatched them from them forever. That curse is still on us. The curse of the blood of the men and the curse of the keening of the women.[324]

And in lines reminiscent of O'Casey, one of the women exclaims: 'Colm will leave me tomorrow or the day after tomorrow to fight for Ireland. Why is Ireland so voracious, so impatient that she must devour the best men, that she cannot let this generation go.'[325] In de Bhilmot's play, a land-obsessed farmer with two sons fighting on opposite sides in the Civil War disgusts one with his greed and pettiness and accidentally shoots the other dead trying to protect his holding from his enemies. As a result, he now has no one who wants the land for which he has so thoroughly dehumanised himself.

Writers with anti-Treaty convictions presented the war very differently, as a continuation of the centuries-old struggle for full independence. In this view, those Irish who accepted the Treaty were simply England's proxies against their own countrymen. In their short propaganda play *Saoirse no Suaimhneas?* (Freedom or peace?) (1922), Seosamh Mac Grianna and Séamus Ó Grianna depicted the Civil War as presenting an unambiguous choice between traditional heroism and fidelity to one's word and comrades on the Republican side and self-serving treason on the Free State side.[326] Peadar Mac Fhionnlaoich captured this sense of betrayal, as well as the weary but unbowed spirit of anti-Treaty republicanism in his 'Mo Bhuachaillí Féin' (My own boys) (*SF*, 15/11/24):

> I did not, however, think that the Volunteers were earnest in the fight, particularly at the start of the excitement. They had no desire to fight. They defended themselves and that was it. And they knew well that the English were behind the Staters, thousands of them there in the Park and at the Curragh waiting patiently to see whether there would be any need for them to intervene. The fight was lost but the cause was not.[327]

The courage of those who stayed true to or were won over by that cause was the subject of stories like 'Laochas Máthar' (A mother's heroism) by 'Fínghíneach' (*An Phoblacht*, 22/12/34); Mac Fhionnlaoich's 'Sasnach "Damanta"' (A 'damned' Englishman) (*SF*, 22/11/24); Nóra Ní Bhroin's 'Ceann d'á Bhuadhaibh' (One of his virtues) (*An Phoblacht*, 21/3/31); and 'An Sasanach Gaodhlach' (A Gaelic Englishman) by 'Éibhlín' (*An Phoblacht*, 13/5/33). Mac Fhionnlaoich's 'Eachtraí an Óglaigh' (The Volunteer's adventures) (*SF*, 4/10/24) deals with the 1922 shooting of Michael Collins, whose role in the lead-up to the Civil War is sharply criticised by one of the characters, while in the same author's 'An Sean Chaisleán' (The old castle) (*SF*, 27/9/24), the Civil War provides the setting for a ghost story. In 'Mion-Gháir Shéamuis Uí Bhroin' (The chuckle of Séamus Ó Broin) by 'Colm' (*An Phoblacht*, 15/7/33), patriotic songs bring a wavering volunteer back to his proper republican loyalties in the early days of the fighting.

Occasionally, a writer managed to put propaganda aside when writing of the war. In 'Bás Phadna' (The death of Padna) (*Star*, 15/2/30), Seán Ó Ciosáin tells of the bitterness against republicans that drives an Irish Catholic veteran of the British army to join the Free State forces. Tomás Bairéad's sympathies were more with the other side in the previously mentioned 'An Dath a d'Athraigh', in which an ex-RIC man won to the cause of independence fights with the anti-Treaty forces until, disgusted by all the bloodshed, he gives himself up, only to be executed – illegally it seems – by Free State soldiers. In 'An t-Oifigeach' (The officer), Máiréad Ní Ghráda, who had worked for Ernest Blythe when he was a minister in the Free State government, painted an unflattering portrait of a corrupt Free State officer too self-important and snobbish to see his own Irish-speaking mother who has come to ask him to protect her from eviction.[328] The only comic story set during the war was Cearbhall Ua Dálaigh's 'Ag Beirbhiú Putóige na Nodlag' (Boiling the Christmas pudding) (*Nation*, 8/3/30), a stereotypical satirical treatment of the sort of food anti-Treaty volunteers had to eat on the run.

On the whole, however, it seems that most Gaelic writers, like the authors of the textbooks discussed above, preferred to remain silent on the Civil War, doubtless sharing the discouragement of An t-Athair Seoirse Mac Clúin, who wrote on the occasion of the funeral of a fallen soldier in the Civil War:

> My grief that we have come to that, that reason and argument and moral authority have been cast aside, and that the cowardly gun is the judge seated in the judgment seat; that people are bowing to it and worshipping it, and it a high god.[329]

Nor is it any wonder that Micheál Breathnach could write of the war in his 1966 autobiography: 'I do not intend to discuss the harm the Civil War did nor the evil consequences it left behind. I would rather draw a big black curtain down on that period and put it out of my memory altogether if I could.'[330]

Six counties in the north of Ireland were still, of course, under British rule after the War of Independence, and two literary works from the 1930s deal with the situation there. 'Buaidh an Mheisnigh' (The triumph of courage) (*Tír*, Aug. to Dec. 1932) by 'Conall' depicts the brutality of the Crown forces in their attempt to suppress the IRA in the North in late 1922. Maighréad Ní Chanainn's *Faoi Bhrat na Saoirse* (Under the flag of freedom) (*Ultach*, Nov. 1934, 1–2, 8) is an allegorical play of the crudest kind in which a young woman named Róisín begins in chains under a Union Jack and ends under a tricolor, proud, free, and wearing a crown on which is written 'Ulster'. Her salvation is the result of heroic action on the part of her fiancé, an IRA man who had been 'asleep' through her sufferings.[331]

One issue on which Irish-Irelanders of every political persuasion could agree was the language and the need for its revival. Therefore it is hardly surprising that we find some writers turning their attention to the history of Irish and particularly the reasons for its decline. The most important such work in our period was Donn Piatt's *Stair na Gaedhilge*,[332] but there were also essays on language shift from the seventeenth century on by Lughaidh Mac Séadna (*II*, 18/1/35) and in the years following the Famine by Shán Ó Cuív (*II*, 8/9/31). More encouraging were the books and essays that appeared on the history of the revival movement itself, for these recalled to the Gaels not only the considerable progress that actually had been made, but also the zestful spirit of shared purpose in a shared cause they could only hope to experience again. The most significant contributions to the history of the movement in our period were Douglas Hyde's two books *Mise agus an Conradh* (Myself and the League) (BÁC: OS, 1937), his account of his involvement with the League from its foundation to 1905, and *Mo Thuras go hAmerice, nó Imeasg na nGaedheal ins an Oileán Úr* (My trip to America, or among the Gaels in the New World) (BÁC: ODFR, 1937), his record of a fundraising trip to the United States in 1905–6; Muiris Ó Droighneáin's *Taighde i gComhar Stair Litridheacht na Nua-Ghaedhilge ó 1882 anuas*, and Sister Mary Vincent's study *An tAthair Peadar Ó Laoghaire agus a Shaothar*.

Among essays in Irish on the history of the Gaelic movement are 'Ceist na Gaedhilge / Súil Siar ar Staid na Teangan / Obair na Sgoileanna' (The question of the Irish language / A look back on the state of the language / The work of the schools), a report on a lecture by Hyde to Cumann Gaelach na Stát-Sheirbhíse in 1928 (*II*, 2/11/28); 'Óige an Chonnartha / Féachaint Siar ar an Sean-Aimsir / Sgéal Craoibhe / Oíche Aighnis agus Oíche Thórraimh' (The youth of the League / A look back at the old times / The story of a branch / A night of argument and a wake night) by 'Dún Buidhe' (*II*, 25/4/32); 'Oireachtas 1900 / Ard-Rúnaí Nua an Chonnartha' (The Oireachtas of 1910 / The League's new chief secretary) by Shán Ó Cuív (*II*, 27/5/32); 'An Connradh i dTosach a Réime' (The League at the start of its career) by Seán Ua Ceallaigh (*IP*, 21/4/33); 'Tosach na Drámaidheachta / I Magh Chromtha do Léirigheadh an Chéad Chluiche!' (The beginning of the drama / The first play was performed in Macroom!) (*IP*, 18/6/34) and 'Ar an gCéad Oireachtas' (At the first Oireachtas) (*IP*, 23/2/38), both by Aindrias Ó Muimhneacháin; 'Ceithre Litreacha / Seadairí Gaedhilge an Lae Indé' (Four letters / Yesterday's champions of the Irish language) (*IP*, 18/6/36); Toms Mac Muiris Ruaidh's 'Mór-Shaothar ár Sagart ar son na Gaedhilge' (The great work of our priests for the Irish language), *IC*, 8/4/37; the anonymous 'Stair an Oireachtais / An Chéad Tionól Riamh' (The history of the Oireachtas / The first gathering ever) (*IP*, 17/11/38); and 'Bliain a' Chogaidh Mhór / Oireachtas Mór agus Stairiúil / Ar Bhruach Léinlocha an Aoibhnis' (The year of the Great War / A great and historic Oireachtas / On the banks of the delightful Lakes of Killarney) by Seán Tóibín (*II*, 7/11/39).[333]

Pioneers of the movement who were the subject of essays in Irish include Philip Baron (*IP*, 26/4/32); Archbishop John MacHale of Tuam (*Sléibhteánach*, 1924–5, 126–9; *IP*, 10/11/31; *IP*, 11/11/37); Eugene O'Curry (*An Phoblacht*, 11/7/31; *IP*, 1/5/33); Denis Fleming (Donnchadh Pléimeann) (*II*, 3/5/32); Father Eugene O'Growney (*II*, 17/4/29; *IP*, 5/9/38); William Rooney (*II*, 13/5/26; 20/4/29); Michcál Breathnach (+1909) (*II*, 20/9/37); and Séamus Ó Dubhghaill ('Beirt Fhear') (*II*, 31/5/32).[334] In addition, Micheál Ó Maoláin gave a series of radio lectures on movement figures in 1939, reports of which were published in the *Irish Independent* (27/11/39, 4/12/39, 11/12/39, and 18/12/39); Tomás Bán Ua Concheanainn delivered a lecture in Galway on Connacht's role in the revival, focussing on the contributions of MacHale and Father Ulick Bourke (reported in *II*, 20/3/28);[335] and the *Irish Press* ran a five-part series on the origin and development of the Gaelic League's summer colleges (*IP*, 16/5, 20/5, 30/5, 15/6 and 23/6/36). 'D. Ua C.' used a review of Tadhg Ó Donnachadha's index to *Irisleabhar na Gaedhilge* to provide a short overview of the journal and its significance (*IP*, 11/6/36).

While Gaelic interest in the past focused almost exclusively on Ireland, there was from time to time some writing in Irish on the history of other places. The most comprehensive of such works was Laoise Ní Dhubhgáin's *Aistí ar Stair na hEorpa* (Essays on the history of Europe) (BÁC: Brún agus Ó Nualláin, n.d.), a collection of six essays, the first three of which deal with the Protestant Reformation in Germany, the fourth with the Catholic Counter-Reformation, the fifth with the Thirty Years War, and the sixth with the Treaty of Westphalia that ended that conflict.[336] Material from the Bible was reworked by An tAthair Peadar Ua Laoghaire, whose *Sgéalaidheachta as an mBíobla Naomhtha* (Stories from the Holy Bible) and *Sgéalaidheacht na Macabéach* (The story of the Maccabees) were published posthumously, the former in seven parts between 1922 and 1925, the latter, based on Josephus, in two parts in 1925 and 1926. An t-Athair Seán Ó Siadhail's *Aistí Soisgéalacha* (Essays relating to the Gospels) (BÁC: ODFR, 1937) provided a scholarly discussion of the New Testament gospels and included a chapter in which there was some discussion of the linguistic situation in Biblical Palestine. In *Beatha Íosa Críost* (The life of Jesus Christ) (BÁC: Comhartha na dTrí gCoinneal, 1929), Pádraig Ó Baoighealláin and Pádraig de Brún endeavoured to provide a coherent chronological life of Christ translated from the Greek New Testament. Two books in Irish dealt with the French Revolution: Seosamh Ó Laochdha's *Muirthéacht na Frainnce* (The French Revolution) (BÁC: Muinntir C.S. Ó Fallamhain, Teor., i gcomhar le hOS, 1930), a work in which no mention was made of Wolfe Tone or any Irish connection; and William Gibson's *Gregoire agus Iom-Chlódh na Frainnce* (Gregoire and the turn about in France) (BÁC: An Tír, [1932]).

Among essays in Irish on the history of countries other than Ireland were George Thomson's vivid and dramatic preface to his translation of three dialogues by Plato (1929)[337] and his 'Megiddo: An Chéad Chath 'sa Stair go bhfuil Cunntas Cruinn Againn Air' (Megiddo: The first battle in history of which we have an accurate account) (*Óglach*, Dec. 1931, 51–2); 'Stair na hEorpa' (The history of Europe) by 'T. A. Mac D.', serialised in *Our Boys* in 1930–1; the serialised 'Startha as an Sean-Tiomna' (Stories from the Old Testament) (1933) by 'Molaga' (*TCNÍ*, Jan.–July, Sept.–Dec. 1933); the anonymous 'Beatha Íosa Críost' (The life of Jesus Christ), serialised in *The Standard* in Dec. 1929; Father Dinneen's 'Páis agus Bás Íosa Críost' (The passion and death of Jesus Christ), serialised in *The Father Mathew Record* in 1934; and Séamus Ó Searcaigh's biographical essay 'San Tomás d'Acuin' (Saint Thomas Aquinas) (*IR*, Feb. 1934, 118–20). Other religious figures discussed in Irish were St. Nicholas (by Nioclás Tóibín, *IP*, 23/12/38) and Pope Gregory the Great (by Liam Ó Briain, UCG *University Annual*, 1925–6, 43–5). Seán M. Ó Fiathacháin had a broader focus in his 'Na Pápaí agus Oideachas ins na Meadhon-Aoiseanna' (The popes and education in the middle ages) (*Hibernia*, May 1937, 11). Ancient Rome was the subject of an article by 'D. Ó M.' (*II*, 22/8/32), who also wrote on the destruction of Pompey (*IP*, 2/2/33), the Emperor Nero (*IP*, 22/1/34), and Attila's threat to Rome in the fifth century (*IP*, 26/6/33). There were pieces on French history by Pádhraic Ó Domhnalláin (*II*, 29/10/23 and 12/12/39); by 'Taistealaidhe' (*II*,

16/8/27); by Máiréad Ní Ghráda (*II*, 5/10/33); and by M. Ó Dubhghaill (*II*, 5/9/38). London's Great Fire of 1666 was the topic of a 1935 essay by Peadar Ó Domhnaill (*IP*, 5/9/35), while 'Sagart do Bhíodh san Astráil' (A priest who used to be in Australia) and Risteárd Ó Foghludha informed readers of the same paper about the history of the Catholic Church in that country (*IP*, 28/6/32 and 13/7/32, respectively). On a more martial note, the Thirty Years War was the subject of a 1928 essay by 'Fear Taistil' in the *Irish Independent* (31/5/28), while Séamus Ó Néill discussed the origins of the First World War in the same paper a decade later (*II*, 30/9/38). Particularly interesting is Diarmuid Ó Conchubhair's 'Leis na Fearaibh Gorma' (With the black men), an essay dealing with English colonialism in Nigeria, including Irish involvement in that enterprise (*Catholic University School Annual*, Summer 1939, 22–4).

There were also a handful of historical stories with non-Irish settings, among them Seán Ó Caoimh's 'Gleann na nDeór' (The vale of tears), dealing with the life of Lot after the destruction of Sodom and Gomorrah (*Standard*, 26/12/31); 'Clódius na mBan' (Claudius the womaniser) by An tAthair Gearóid Ó Nualláin and Fearrgus Ó Nualláin, set in Rome in 62 BC;[338] Pádhraic Ó Domhnalláin's 'Napóleon agus an Fealltóir' (Napoleon and the traitor), about a Breton who betrays his people to the French;[339] Ó Domhnalláin's 'Bás Mharat' (The death of Marat);[340] 'Ionnsaighe agus Cosaint / Baile Rheinfelden' (Attack and defence / The town of Rheinfelden), a story of the Thirty Years War by 'Siubhlóir' (*II*, 27/11/30); Eanraoi Ó Gráda's serialised 'Na Ceóltóiridhe Óga' (The young musicians) (1933), set vaguely in Florence 'long ago' (*fadó*); Máiréad Ní Ghráda's 'Maoineach na Maighdine Muire' (The darling of the Virgin Mary) (*Bonaventura*, Autumn 1938, 135–44); and Tomás Bairéad's '"An Chláirseach Bhinn"' ('The sweet harp'), an O. Henryish story of the fickleness of women set at some indefinite period in the Scottish past.[341]

There were also at least seven stories dealing with the battlefields of the First World War: Pádhraic Ó Domhnalláin's 'An Sgréachóg' (The screech-owl) (*FL*, 17/2/23); An tAthair Gearóid and Fearrgus Ó Nualláin's 'Togha agus Rogha' (Pick and choice);[342] three comic sketches, 'Eachtra Oidhche sa Chogadh' (The story of a night in the war) by 'Saighdiúir' (*II*, 15/2/27), 'An Mac a Bhí Caillte / Sgéilín ó'n gCogadh Mór' (The son who was lost / A little story from the Great War) by An tAthair Seán Mac Cuirtín (*Inis Fáil*, Easter 1927, 28–30), 'Seift Learaidhe' (Larry's scheme) by 'Cú Chulan' (Dundalk *Examiner*, 13/2/32); 'Cródhacht an Dochtúra / Scéal ón Chogadh Mhóir' by 'Seathrún' (The doctor's courage / A story from the Great War), in which none of the characters are identified as Irish (*IC*, 22/10/36); and 'An Dochtúir Óg' (The young doctor), the tale of the death of a heroic priest in Flanders in 1916 by Seosamh Ó Seachnasaigh (*IMN*, 1938, 62–3).

The only two historical plays with non-Irish settings both dealt with the life of Christ. León Ó Broin's *An Oíche Úd i mBeithil* (That night in Bethlehem)

(BÁC: OS, 1949) is a nativity play with an interesting anti-imperialist perspective on the Roman occupation of Palestine.[343] Séamus de Bhilmot also offered a political reading of New Testament events in his play of Holy Week, *''San Am Soin, –'* ('In that time –') (BÁC: OS, 1944). de Bhilmot presents Barabbas as a Jewish patriot who advises Christ, who he wishes was willing to lead his people against the Romans. His view of Christ as a potential political threat is shared by the Romans, who see him as far more dangerous than Barabbas.[344]

There can be no doubt what lesson Gaelic intellectuals and writers wanted to find in Irish history, a lesson outlined by Pádraig Ó Siochfhradha in 1938:

> The Gaels in Ireland had the five elements or ingredients that comprise full nationality – (1) A population of a single heritage and a single blood .i. unity of race. (2) A population with a single language – the Irish language that was the only common language for the whole race. (3) A uniformity of memory and tradition with regard to history, culture, and custom (*Bonaventura*, Autumn 1938, 12).[345]

The fact that Irish, as opposed to Gaelic, history painted a far more complicated and less satisfactory picture was, however, too obvious to ignore. As a result, Gaelic writers of the 1920s and 1930s, like their predecessors, saw the need for unity and the tragic persistence of discord as the fundamental theme of much of the nation's history. Moreover, this awareness was exacerbated by the Civil War, the subsequent vitriolic and occasionally violent controversies in the Free State, and the ongoing and increasingly intractable reality of Partition in the six counties of Northern Ireland. Ironically, as we have seen, some writers contributed to the divisions they simultaneously bewailed. For example, Seosamh Mac Grianna was only the most forceful and articulate to insist that the only Irish history of any real significance to the nation was the history of Gaelic Ireland, and that those of non-Gaelic descent unwilling to assimilate themselves into that culture and history were of no relevance to the land of their birth. Other writers, primarily but not exclusively Catholic clerics, repeated a theme that had persisted in historical writing in Irish from the beginning of the Revival, the conviction that Irish nationality was inextricably interwoven with Roman Catholicism. We have seen how this identification was particularly widespread in writings dealing with the seventeenth and eighteenth centuries, how it shaped the Gaelic reading of the Great Famine, and how it surfaced again and again in the creative works about the freedom struggle from 1916 on, with their heroic priests, self-sacrificing mothers, devout volunteers, and patriotically inspired penitents. Indeed Caitlín Nic Ghabhann seems to have believed that religious affiliation, and not ethnicity, culture, or language, was *the* defining characteristic of Irish nationality, writing in her history of County Dublin in 1925: 'If the English had followed the old faith, or if the Irish had accepted the new faith, in all probability there would be a different story to be told about Dublin – and about Ireland.'[346]

Yet even those writers like Mac Grianna and Nic Ghabhann who seem to have been disposed to define genuine Irish nationality in fairly narrow and exclusive ethnic or sectarian terms agreed unequivocally with the Gaelic consensus that disunity was the recurrent cardinal sin of the Irish people throughout their history, what Tomás Ó Criomthain referred to as 'the usual habit of the people of Ireland to always be divided among themselves when there was anything decent to be had by her.'[347] Dissenting voices were all but non-existent, although we do find 'Sean-Ghall' proclaiming in the Civil War year of 1923:

> 'Check your authorities', is wise counsel. If you do you will laugh at 'dissension' as being responsible for Bruce's defeat, or of 'discord' being more common among the Irish than among the English, Scotch, Spaniards, French, or Italians (*CB*, Aug. 1923, 555).

Maoghnus Ó Domhnaill went even further in his essay 'The Myth of Irish Disunity' three years later:

> The history of Ireland does not reveal any greater tendency to faction and dissension than that to be found in feudal England, or in Germany before the accession of Frederick the Great. Our fatalistic belief in the impossibility of unifying Ireland is largely based on a false reading of our national history. The sooner that we get it out of our heads that Irish civil strife throughout the ages was the result of a bad national trait, rather than the fruits of an English policy, the better for the nation (*An Phoblacht*, 19/11/26).[348]

However tempting such a reading must have been, the vast majority of those Gaels interested in history seem to have found it to a great extent an exercise in wishful thinking, agreeing instead with the views expressed by Art Mac Gréagóir in 1938:

> History teaches us a lesson appropriate for the events of this time. Look at the harm the hatred and needless fights have done from time to time. If people great and small would ponder that, it would help them to be patient amd generous with each other.[349]

It was certainly impossible to blame the English for fomenting the internal dissensions that, as Mac Grianna showed in *Na Lochlannaigh*, facilitated the Viking conquests of the ninth and tenth centuries.[350] And whatever surreptitious role the English played in promoting and/or exacerbating conflicts among the Irish themselves, few Gaelic writers in the 1920s and 1930s were willing to absolve their countrymen of a good share of the blame for that dissension, whether as conscious catalysts or as unwitting dupes of the colonial overlord. For that reason, disappointment over sincere differences of opinion and disgust over betrayals of people and principles were, as we have seen, one of the most common thematic strands running through Gaelic historical writing of the period. Nowhere is this sense of Irish inability to overcome internal division in face of an external enemy more clear than in Mac Grianna's assessment of the situation confronting Eoghan Ruadh Ó Néill: 'The person who could keep the men of Ireland united at this time could tie a knot around sand.'[351] Or, as the fiancée of the rebel in Mrs Dix's *An Seod Do-Fhághala* concisely and memorably sums up this theme: 'The servants of God would have won if it were not for the jealousy that the leaders felt towards each other.'[352]

One issue that had divided sincere and patriotic Gaels in the past and that, as we have seen, continued to do so with even more troubling implications in the new native state was the question of if, when, and how violence could be justified in the cause of national liberation. Most Gaelic creative writers who dealt with the armed struggle against the English – and most writers who worked with historical topics did focus disproportionately on the various physical force movements – offered an uncritically heroic view of nationalist violence against a traditional enemy who had never hesitated to use force brutally and indiscriminately whenever threatened. Violence was so regular and unquestioned a feature of these historical works, particularly those set during the War of Independence, that the killing of the enemy could even at times be handled with macabre humour. A few writers, however, took advantage of their wartime settings to examine the whole question of violence as an agent of political change. We have, for example, seen the misgivings and reservations about even what is accepted as unavoidable deadly force in plays such as Ó Broin's *An Mhallacht*, Ó Lochlainn's *Na Fearachoin*, and Ó Siochfhradha's *An Ball Dubh* and *Deire an Chuntais*. Likewise, the often dreadful ramifications of guerilla warfare were debated in Mac Giolla Iasachta's *Toil Dé* and detailed in Ó Dubhda's *Brian*. No one, however, wrote more passionately or courageously on this question than did Úna Bean Uí Dhíosca (Mrs Elizabeth Rachel Dix), whose *Cailín na Gruaige Duinne* offered a response both patriotic and pacifist to the bloody events leading to national independence. Mrs Dix's commitment to non-violence was both lifelong and unwavering. During the Civil War, she wrote to *The Separatist* to challenge the views of one 'M. E.' that only force could successfully overcome force. Identifying herself as a member of the 'Irishwomen's International League', Dix asked, 'Is "M. E.'s" idea of standing fast against wickedness to imitate it?' (*Separatist*, 9/9/22). Three years later, in a letter to the editor of *Fáinne an Lae*, she returned to this theme, reaffirming her repudiation of violence and her belief in 'the power of truth' (cómhacht na fírinne). Arguing that by shedding blood the IRA had brought a 'curse' (*mallacht*) on the country, she continued:

> If we had a leader like Gandhi in Ireland, it would not be long until the world saw the wonderful, miraculous strength of the spiritual power of a nation that stands bravely for its rights and puts its trust in God as did the Irish when they fought without weapons for their Faith (*FL*, 26/12/25).[353]

A decade later, in a letter to the editor of *An t-Éireannach* prompted by an inter-university debate in Galway on the question of the international arms race of that time, she turned the attention of her readers to their own country:

> As for Ireland, we did not have an army at the time of Daniel O'Connell, and was not the spirit that was in the nation wonderful and was not the victory wonderful, a victory without evil consequences? Do we not have four armies in Ireland at present, and are they a source of courage for us? The smaller the army a nation has, the better and safer it is. An army is no shield, but a portent of bitter disaster. Our trust is in the sword of light – **the spirit of the people** (*Éireannach*, 9/3/35).[354]

She also championed the cause of spiritual over physical force in *An Seod Do-Fhághala*, but it was in *Cailín na Gruaige Duinne* that she offered her most extensive analysis of the whole question of violence as an appropriate means to a laudable end. The protagonist of this novel, a young Protestant woman of Unionist stock who has become an Irish nationalist, first voices her pacificism in an argument with her family concerning the First World War:

> I did my best not to think about the war, but I failed. Every time I had the courage to say it I said that the war was absolutely against Christianity, and anyway, it had nothing to do with Ireland. I was at odds with every member of my family.[355]

Despite her conversion to the cause of Irish freedom, she is every bit as discouraged by the Irish recourse to violence to achieve freedom as she was by the mass slaughter engaged in by the major world powers in the trenches of Europe. Simultaneously inspired and dismayed by the actions of Pearse in Easter Week, she ponders:

> In a way he was right, but as I understand the matter now, he was not entirely right. If we want to make a sacrifice for our dear little country, that is a fine thing, and good will come of it, but if we sacrifice other people against their will, in addition to the good, bad blood and malice and hatred will pour forth from Hell as a result. If Pearse and his fellow Gaels had sacrificed themselves for Ireland without setting

in motion a bloody war between the English and the Irish, we would not be in the slough of despond as we are at present.[356]

Her belief was that there was 'a natural organic growth to national independence' (fás nádúrtha planda faoi'n saoirse náisiúnta) that would come to fruition in time without armed intervention. Although she later, unlike her husband, accepts the Treaty, she is clear that both sides share the blame for the Civil War: 'However bad was the war of the Irish against the English, the war among the Irish was seven thousand times worse. What good is it to cast the blame on one side only? The blame was on the two sides.'[357] By the novel's end, she has followed her political rebirth with a religious conversion to Catholicism, but remains unwavering in her commitment to non-violence. Nor does she see her principles as a convenient or cowardly refusal to face facts and take sides, believing instead that pacificism offers 'a more noble way to advance the welfare of our Mother Ireland' (slighe níos uaisle chun leas ár Máthar Éire do chur chun cinn) (pp. 101–2).

Breandán Delap has argued that the Gaelic historical novels written in the 1920s and 1930s were fatally marred by their authors' 'xenophobic ignorance' (aineolas seineafóibeach).[358] There can be no denying that many of those writers should – and could – have known a great deal more about the periods they were trying to recreate. It is, however, more problematic to indiscriminately charge them with xenophobia, since, with the exception of the Vikings, the only foreigners who play any meaningful role in their work are the English. Anglophobia would, then, be a more appropriate accusation. It was perhaps a concern about such sterile ethnocentrism that caused Shán Ó Cuív to urge Gaelic teachers and writers of history to explore the interactions between Ireland and the outside world:

> From the time of St Patrick on, and from the centuries before that, there was little going on with regard to which people from Ireland did not have some connection with other countries. When history is taught, that should be remembered in order to awaken the interest of the students in their own country and to link the history of this country with the history of those other countries in such a way that people would better understand what history is (*II*, 15/7/32).[359]

But even in their treatment of the traditional foe, some of these writers managed to break out of traditional modes of thought. One of the most intriguing developments to be found in Gaelic historical writing at this time was an embryonic if inchoate awareness of Irish solidarity with other colonised peoples, although it is often difficult to distinguish between a more sophisticated and progressive anti-imperialism and old-fashioned Brit-bashing.[360] The latter impulse certainly seems dominant in Peadar Ó hAnnracháin's curse on British soldiers in *Machtnamh Cime*: 'Is it not a great pity that they could not be strangled now. Hasn't God given them a long leash, considering all the injustices they have inflicted on much of the human race.'[361] Less clear is the ideology behind Pádraig Ó Séaghdha's *Stiana* (1930), whose protagonist feels an almost instinctive hatred for the English, but also sympathises with other peoples who have suffered under imperial rule. Moreover, as the novel ends he is off to the East Indies in the service of a native prince, where he will be able to employ his expert marksmanship in his ongoing battle with Empire. In the words of his new employer,

> the sound of your bullets will be in the ears of the enemies of your ancestors, and you will be like a thorn in their flesh. There will be terror in face of your shot and it will be said that there is magic in your hand. Instead of Stiana, you will be called Nana Sahib, and Nana Sahib will be in the people's mouths.[362]

Equally ambiguous on the question of anti-colonial solidarity was Seán Ua Ceallaigh, who in *Taistealuidheacht* could combine racist descriptions of blacks with shock on first seeing racial segregation in the United States, sympathy for oppressed aboriginal people in Australia, awareness of Australian prejudice against Asians, and condemnation of the imperialist manipulation of famine in both Ireland and India.[363]

Much more forthright and consistent in his anti-imperialism was Peadar Mac Fhionnlaoich, a man who would have had little trouble believing the worst about English intentions anywhere on the globe. In *Bliadhain na hAiséirghe*, he offered a quick outline history of English imperialism in the nineteenth century: 'During the same time England was getting more and more powerful and dominant throughout the world, invading weak nations and seizing their countries; adding ridge to ridge and field to field in the Great Empire.'[364] We have already noted the anti-imperialist sentiments expressed by Beartlaí Ó Séaghdha in Mrs Dix's *An Seod Do-Fhághala*, and similar views were also voiced by the IRA leader in Ó Lochlainn's *Na Fearachoin*, a man who sees the Irish struggle as part of a larger global movement for justice and liberation:

> We do not know what the end of the story will be for the human race. Perhaps we will always be fumbling ahead of us like poor, foolish, blind creatures. But the day there are not men who will stand and fight against evil and injustice, the human race is damned for good.[365]

And in the opening scene of León Ó Broin's *An Oíche Úd i mBeithil*, two Roman soldiers debate the rationale for imperialism, one arguing:

> We do not know any way to establish peace except to take freedom from a person when he reveals his dissatisfaction with something, with hunger, for example, or with heavy taxes, or with an attempt to smother in his heart the love he has for his own gods.[366]

Perhaps the best example of the confused state of Gaelic – indeed of Irish – thinking on this subject was Pádhraic Ó Domhnalláin's 1930 essay 'An 19adh Aois' (The nineteenth century). Marked throughout by an uncritical acceptance of the 'progress' made during the century, the essay discusses white imperialism as an expression of 'the European ingenuity and wisdom that united the world' (stuaim agus gaos Eorpach a d'aontaigh an domhan). And while Ó Domhnalláin begins his discussion by stressing that this expansion was made possible by European advances in weapons of mass destruction, he continues:

> It must, however, be said that it is not entirely by the sword that Europeans raised themselves from the bottom to the top of the world. The virtue that is a part of their culture helped them to do it. It was understood that they had qualities of leadership, that they had talent beyond a talent for fighting, and that many accepted them and their administration for that reason.[367]

Clearly Irish ambivalence about the nation's status, whether full partner in the developed world or recently liberated colony united in sympathy with the oppressed, did not begin with membership of the European Community.

The potential of history to clarify, if not resolve, ambivalences, to provide a shared ground on which Irish people of different traditions could meet, was another important theme raised, though never adequately developed, by a few Gaelic writers at the time. For example, reviewing Pádraig Ó Siochfhradha's translation of Tone's autobiography in 1932, one 'Léightheoir Comhthrom' wrote that it would do readers good 'to spend a while in the company of Tone at present, with a bit of despair and disunity afflicting us in Ireland' (i láthair na h-uaire seo agus iarrachtín éadóchais agus easaontais ag goilleamhaint orainn annso i nÉirinn, tamall a chaitheamh i gcomhluadar Tone). But there was more than a hint of avoidance, if not downright escapism, in his explanation of why this was so: 'It is better for us to look far back than to be remembering and grumbling about what happened in the years just gone by' (*TCNÍ*, Oct. 1932, 236).[368] Shán Ó Cuív was more specific, writing in an essay on 'Aondacht na hÉireann' (Irish unity) in 1937 that it was the cultural, not the political, history of the nation that offered hope for reconciliation:

> The roots of the present division are firmly planted in the history of Ireland and the history of England. There was never true political unity in Ireland . . . We did,

> however, have a unity other than political unity. We had a language and customs and a civilisation that made Ireland a distinct country.

For Ó Cuív, that past cultural unity could lead to a future political unity, 'when the day comes on which all of the people of Ireland, north and south, boast of Ireland and say with pride that they are Irish' (nuair a thiocfaidh an lá 'n-a mbeidh na daoine go léir i nÉirinn, theas agus thuaidh, ag maoidheamh a hÉirinn agus á rá le bród gurab' Éireannaigh iad). Left unexplored, of course, was the price to be paid for such cultural assimilation by 'people who are not of the old faith . . . nor of Gaelic descent' (daoine nách den tsean-chreideamh . . . ná de shliocht na nGaedheal).[369] An unwillingness to face this question could lead to rather startling lapses in logic, as when one 'Ceól' asserted in 1935 that 'one may have a Gaelic outlook on life and art, or one may have an English outlook, but a position between the two is artistically an impossibility', but then went on to express the pious aspiration that a proper reading of Irish history could engender 'that mutual understanding that will one day raze the walls erected by political and religious bigotry' (*Gaedheal*, 2/2/35). One who saw himself attempting to do just that was Art Mac Gréagóir, who wrote in the preface to *Stair na nDéise*:

> History teaches us a lesson appropriate to the affairs of the present. Look at the harm the spite and the needless fights have caused from time to time. If people great and small would ponder that, it would help them to be patient and charitable towards each other.[370]

All thinking Irish people of Mac Gréagóir's day and since have tried, with varying degrees of patience and charity, to envision an Ireland broad enough to encompass the little houses of Belfast's loyalist Shankill Road and the Big Houses of the former Ascendancy. For those involved in the Gaelic movement, there was the additional challenge of reconciling the legitimate, and in any case inescapable, demands of cultural diversity with the urgent duty to preserve a cultural continuity rooted in the Irish language and spanning two millennia of the nation's history, what Máirtín Ó Cadhain was to memorably call 'two thousand years of that foul sow that is Ireland' (dhá mhíle bliain den chráin bhréan sin arbh í Éire í).[371] That the majority of Gaelic writers on the Irish past took no real risks in an attempt to balance this equation may disappoint but probably should not surprise us. Rather we should recognise the honesty and courage of the few who did try to imagine an Ireland not merely Gaelic, but Irish as well; not merely Irish, but Gaelic as well.

FIVE

'REBUILDING TARA IN OUR MENTAL WORLD'

THE GAELIC AUTHOR AND THE HEROIC TRADITION

> You should have seen Cuchulain playing tennis with the gentry and ladies of the Bon Ton suburb. He learnt the whole art and skill of the game in ten minutes, and straightway beat the Champion of all Ireland six–love, six–love, and six–love.[1]

Unfortunately, Gaelic literature of the Free State period offers nothing to match this marvellous image from Eimar O'Duffy's 1926 novel *King Goshawk and the Birds*. While Irish writers in the English language like Yeats, James Stephens, Eva Gore-Booth, O'Duffy, Austin Clarke and Flann O'Brien resurrected, albeit in very different ways and from very different motives, the heroes of early Irish literature, their Gaelic colleagues for the most part seem to have been uneasy, at times even evasive, about this aspect of their literary heritage. This is not, of course, to say that they were not alert to and on occasion willing to exaggerate the significance of that heritage. For example, in 1922, Father Paul Walsh wrote in a review of Rudolf Thurneysen's *Die Irische Helden und Königsage*, a scholarly volume for which an Irish government under serious financial pressure had provided a subsidy: 'The saga literature of Ireland should be one of the glories of the nation. No country in Western Europe possesses a body of ancient tales and stories comparable to that which has come down to us in our ancient manuscripts' (*IER*, Feb. 1922, 219). Seán A. Ó Cuineáin shared this opinion of the nation's early literature, writing in the same year: 'There is nothing at all in the ancient literature of western Europe worthy of comparison with the ancient literature of the Gaels' (*II*, 31/8/22).[2] Lecturing the Dundalk branch of An Fáinne on *Táin Bó Cúailnge* in 1930, An tAthair Mac a' Bháird widened the scope of reference: 'It is the opinion of famous scholars that there is nothing in the literature of the world that surpasses that epic' (*Dundalk Examiner*, 8/3/30).[3]

Yet at the same time, there was a painful sense that most Irish people, including most Gaelic intellectuals, were largely ignorant of that language and its literature, and, worse, were willing to cede its creative reshaping and revival to Irish authors working in English. Writing in 1925, Muiris Ó Catháin identified this ignorance as a mark of post-colonial servility:

> If the Irish people bear one mark of conquest more striking than any other, it is that the majority of them are ignorant of the beautiful ancient literature of their country. Not only are most people ignorant of it, but even what knowledge of it some of our fine Anglo-Irish writers have is corrupt. For, since they don't understand the language in which it is written, they can only know it through questionable translations of little, scattered, random bits (*Branar*, Apr. 1925, p.63).[4]

Less pessimistic was 'Sliabh Bladhma', who in 1934 urged his fellow Gaels to actively explore and reclaim cultural territory they ignored at their own peril:

> But possibly we could all make much more of Tara . . . in our mental and imaginative life. Things I read and hear makes [*sic*] me wonder at times if that mental and imaginative sphere is as rich or carefully cultivated as it ought to be. Even our poets seem seldom or never to give their imagination play. . . . Altogether, in prose and poem, we have material for a noble re-building of Teamhair [Tara] in our mental world. It is a fascinating task, and the spiritual profit is great (*Gaedheal*, 1/9/34).

Needless to say, Gaels were not unappreciative of the important work being done at this time by Celtic scholars worldwide, some of them, like Eoin Mac Néill and Osborn Bergin, alumni of the language movement itself. In his scholarly and well-informed 1933 book *Gaedhealachas i gCéin* (Gaelicism abroad), William P. Ryan discussed in some detail the work done by foreign academics in this area. Native scholars were, however, beginning to meet their responsibilities, and the ancient literature was the focus of serious attention in Gaelic journals such as Maynooth's *Irisleabhar Muighe Nuadhad* or those associated with the National University like *Lia Fáil: Irisleabhar Gaedhilge Ollsgoile na hÉireann*, *An Reult: Irisleabhar na h-Ollscoile*, the journal of the Gaelic Society at University College Dublin, and *An t-Irisleabhar, Ollsgoil na Gaillimhe*.[5]

Nonetheless, as the quotes above should suggest, the focus of Gaelic activists was on the intellectual and spiritual transformation of the Irish people, or at least that vast majority of them not utterly lost to Anglicisation. From the very beginning of the language movement, there had been a profound suspicion of individuals and institutions whose interest in the Irish language and Irish culture was purely or principally academic. One recalls, for example, the scorn heaped by the Gaels on Trinity's Robert Atkinson at the turn of the century.[6] And even after independence, few concerned Gaels were willing to forget their suspicions of what they perceived to be an elitist and self-serving scholarly establishment.[7] For example, in 1930 Liam Ó Rinn argued that editors should focus their efforts on providing scholarly texts of the originals with accompanying modern Irish translation for the interested and informed Gaelic layperson. In his opinion, until such work was done, the ancient texts would mean little if anything to the ordinary educated speaker of Irish:

> If books in Middle Irish are not being bought, it is the editors who should usually be blamed. They edit these books for scholars, for people who examine the old bones of the Irish language, for people who often take no interest in the beauty and the elegance of the ancient prose . . . They [the early tales] are nothing but lumber to him [the reader of modern Irish], and that will be so as long as the scholars rely on the gods of high learning and pay no heed to the common person (*Star*, 15/3/30).[8]

It was doubtless concerns of this kind that in 1939 inspired 'Bricriu' to ask and to suggest an answer in the affirmative to the question 'Are Irish Scholars Snobs?' (*IP*, 2/11/39).

What Gaelic activists wanted was for native scholars to use their learning to enrich contemporary Irish reality by restoring to the nation an authentic and accessible sense of its own past.[9] Such was obviously the thinking behind the 1924 Oireachtas competitions for essays about the Ulster and Fenian Cycles as well as for 'a plan that would show how to explain and teach Old Irish through Modern Irish' (sanas a thaisbeánfadh cionnas an tSean-Ghaedhilg do mhíniú agus do mhúine thríd an Nua-Ghaedhilg).[10] For those of scholarly bent, the first task would be to get the manuscript material catalogued, edited and published. For example, in 1931 Joseph Hanly asserted that 'the recovery, editing and publication of this Irish manuscript literature is a work of supreme national importance'.[11]

For many, however, what was of even more pressing importance was to make the early literature available to the broadest possible audience through the immediate provision of competent modern Irish versions – translations – of the full range of earlier Irish literature. This had been a perceived need from the very outset of the language revival, and there is a fair bit of repetition in Gaelic calls for such modernisations in the years of the Free State. For example, reviewing Tomás Ó Máille's *Mac Dathó* in 1925, An tAthair Pádraig de Brún wrote:

> But would it not be right, in this day and age, to translate the ancient tales directly from Old Irish to Modern Irish? The people's ignorance of them is shameful, and shameful as well is the fact that scholars have not done this work. Modern Irish literature will never achieve either beauty or breadth until students know the subject matter and the flavour and the artistic sense of the tales (*Dublin Magazine*, Jan. 1925, 434).[12]

Liam Ó Rinn devoted several of his literary columns in the *United Irishman* and *United Ireland* to this question in the mid 1930s, writing, for instance, in 1933:

> As long as it continues to be translated into English, the literature of our ancestors will have no influence at all on contemporary literature in Irish, and it will mean no more to speakers and writers of Irish than do the bones of old Latin or Sanscrit, things covered with the dust of the ages with nobody interested in them except for erudite scholars thousands of miles removed from the mind and heart of ordinary people (*UIrman*, 1/7/33).[13]

In his lengthy review of the Blasket Island autobiographies in 1937, Thomas Barrington issued a similar call to his countrymen and women to immerse themselves in 'Gaelicism', writing:

> The only way to do it is by (literally) unlocking the storehouses of tradition. There are rooms piled high with manuscripts in Trinity College, the Royal Irish Academy, and in many other great libraries. These manuscripts enshrine Gaelic Ireland's best thought . . . We treat this literature with very distant respect. Much of it has been published, of course, in the original Middle Irish and with an English translation. It is, therefore, of little use to anyone who wishes to do his Gaelic reading in modern Gaelic . . . The reader of English literature has been catered for by many 'popular' re-tellings. But for the reader of modern Gaelic – hundreds are turned out from the schools every year – for him there is nothing. Hence Gaelic Ireland is as stagnant as the most evil-smelling puddle.

Barrington's focus is clear from his conclusion: 'Perfect scholarship is not called for, but simply versions that the general reader can read, understand, and get enthusiastic about' (*IR*, July 1936, 524).

The possible result of such enthusiasm was central in the thinking of 'D. P.', who in his review of Osborn Bergin and Richard Best's edition of *Lebor na hUidre* in 1929 wrote:

> A competent modernisation of such old classics as these could retain the style and interpret the spirit of the originals far better than English translations: and yet we have no modern-Irish *Táin*! If the work of Messrs. Best and Bergin urges somebody to supply the want, its influence will be doubly felt – and not less in creating the new literature than in renovating the old (*IR*, Sept. 1929, 718).

Seosamh Mac Grianna agreed. Having admitted that he had never read the *Táin* in the original, he urged Gaelic scholars and writers to ensure that such ignorance would be all but impossible in the future:

> The first thing that is necessary is to publish the ancient literature in modern spelling and with no explanations in English. Then to privilege it over every other kind of education in schools and in colleges, among priests and professors and writers.[14]

Several writers suggested that the encouragement and publication of such modernisations would provide a far more worthwhile mission for An Gúm than did the provision of translations, the vast majority from English. For example, in 1930 'B. Ní M.', a regular columnist for *The Star*, expressed the hope

> that soon there will be published in Irish the tales and the essays and the bits of literature that have been published in the past twenty years in foreign periodicals, for example, in *Revue Celtique*, in *Zeit[schrift] für Celt[ische] Phil[ologie]*, and in *Silva Gadelica*. It would be far more appropriate and far more sensible to prepare modern versions of the ancient tales than to translate the nonsense that passes for literature today (*Star*, 22/2/30).[15]

However, when writers did attempt work of this kind, they quickly found themselves very much on their own, with few if any generally accepted models to follow, and virtually no consensus on how the work should be approached. Again, there was nothing new here, and writers of the 1920s and 1930s pretty much re-fought without resolution the same linguistic and ideological battles familiar from the turn of the century on. Perhaps the sole point on which there was no debate was the conviction that only through the medium of Irish could one arrive at an authentic understanding and appreciation of Irish literature. For instance, in one of his essays calling for Gaelic modernisations, Ó Rinn was dismissive of the versions available in English: 'An English translation of those things gives us nothing but English and an English style' (Ní thugann aistriú Béarla ar na nithe sin dúinn ach Béarla agus stíl Bhéarla) (*UIrman*, 24/6/33). By 1937, the editor of *An Gaedheal* could declare – prematurely – that the need for such unsatisfactory linguistic expedients was a thing of the past. Reviewing Cormac Ó Cadhlaigh's *An Fhiannuidheacht* (The Fenian Cycle), he declared:

> From now on there is no need for us to rely on the English versions of Standish O'Grady, Eleanor Hull, Joyce and their like to understand the Fenian material. And I am not faulting their works, but they are translations of the ancient stories and often they do not give an accurate understanding, but rather the unreliable opinion of the translator (*Gaedheal*, Feb. 1937, 2).[16]

What is of significance here is the notion that the rendering of Old or Middle Irish into modern Irish is somehow not a translation, that there is an all but transparent syntactic and lexicographic equivalence between the earlier and modern forms of the language.

However tempting and ideologically satisfying this view must have seemed, those engaged in the process could only wish their task was so simple. Like any translator, the moderniser of an early Irish text had choices to make, the first involving the question of the nature and degree of fidelity to the original that could or should be achieved. This issue had also perplexed Gaels from the start of the revival, and writers were no closer to its solution in the 1920s and 1930s. Writing in 1929, Liam Ó Rinn urged An Gúm to undertake an ambitious programme of modernising the early literature

> to edit and interpret in modern Irish our ancient literature from the beginning of the Middle Irish period on, and to translate into modern Irish (when necessary and to the extent necessary, keeping the translation very close, as it is said – in order to preserve the medieval atmosphere) (*Star*, 17/8/29).[17]

This was also the approach recommended by the writers' group Cumann na Scríbhneoirí when they proposed to Dáil Éireann that the government help fund the writing and publication of 'the literature of Old Irish put into modern Irish' (litríocht sean-Ghaedhilge curtha i nua-Ghaedhilge), such versions to follow the original 'as closely as possible' (chó dlúth 's is féidir don leagan bunaidh) (*FL*, 29/4/22). 'E. Ó N.' agreed in his 1929 review of Bergin and Best's edition of *Lebor na hUidhre*:

> If this sort of literature amused our ancestors should we not make some effort to become acquainted with it? Why not modernise it? It should be put in a modern garb, using the current oral and literary Irish and avoiding anything in the nature of re-telling or re-casting. Some uncalled-for liberties have been taken with older texts in recent years and the result has not been a success, to say the least of it (*II*, 19/8/29).

Commitment to such a rigorous methodology seems, however, to have been seen as mere pedantry by Seán Ó Cathasaigh, who published serialised extracts from the *Táin* in the Galway weekly *Ar Aghaidh*. For this writer the ancient literature was enlisted as a weapon in the entirely contemporary battle then raging in the Free State between native speakers and learners of the language:

> It is not an exact translation of the ancient text word for word. The author's intention is to make the ancient story available to present-day Irish speakers. They have a far better hereditary claim on that story than do the scholars who talk and write about that ancient story in English. And the author could not care less about those scholars or their ilk if his own people, the native speakers of Irish, enjoy his work.[18]

In some ways words were the least of the problem. A more obvious and unpalatable difficulty concerned what Ó Rinn called 'the medieval atmosphere' (atmosféir na meán-aoise). Writing in support of Ó Rinn's views, 'Londonach' deliberately skirted the issue, referring to the need to provide, in addition to full modernisations, 'adaptations, retellings, for those to whom the authentic stuff would be meat too strong' (*Star*, 24/8/29). Such 'strong meat' had been routinely left off the table by Gaelic modernisers from the days of An tAthair Peadar Ua Laoghaire, and there was no real debate about the need to bowdlerise ancient texts to render them suitable reading matter for the proper bourgeois Catholic nationalists, not to mention the schoolchildren, who comprised the bulk of the readership for a substantial percentage of Gaelic books in the years of the Free State. For example, the well-known authors of two of the most extensive modernisations from the early literature in this period both acknowledged, without apology, that they had altered their originals when they felt it necessary for moral reasons. In his preface to *Rudhraigheacht* (The Ulster Cycle), Seán Ua Ceallaigh wrote:

> Some of the speech of Úathach had to be left out, as had to be done another time with some of the deeds of Clann Tuireann after their fight in the Eastern World. Even in our world, we would not be allowed to publish in a schoolbook everything the soldiers did after the war in South Africa, for example, or during the great wars throughout Europe over the centuries. There is a great deal of bad conduct in the camps behind the battlefields.[19]

In like manner, Pádraig Ó Siochfhradha stated in the preface to his version of *Tóraidheacht Dhiarmada agus Ghráinne* (The pursuit of Diarmaid and Grainne): 'I left two or three things out of the text so that the story would be more suitable to be read in classrooms.'[20] Tomás Ó Máille went further, writing in the preface to his *Mac Dathó*:

> As will be clear to the reader at first glance, I have not made a direct translation from the Middle Irish but have told it as a tale as it would be told now. I followed the ancient story closely in places (the dialogue); in other places I changed it greatly.[21]

Needless to say, his divergences from the text are not random. He eliminates Conall's sucking dry of Mac Dathó's enormous cooked pig as well as Cet's transfixing of Celtchar's testicles with a spear when the latter invades his territory.

The fact that the early literature required some sort of active mediation – linguistic or ethical – to make it comprehensible and/or palatable to twentieth-century Gaels was a real problem. When one cuts through the high-flown generalities, one finds three vaguely defined but widely accepted reasons why Gaelic activists wanted the ancient literature rescued from both academics and (Anglo-Irish) artists. The first was the belief that a genuine experience of this literature could provide an essential link in the re-fashioning of the cultural continuity of the Gaelic nation that Gaelic intellectuals saw as uniquely their mission in the new state. However fuzzily understood, the existence of such a continuity was an article of faith, as Muiris Ó Catháin asserted in 1925:

> However far back from us is the period of the ancient literature, there is something in that literature that shines down through the ages to us. We notice certain traits in it that are commonly felt more clearly than they can be understood in isolation (*Branar*, Apr. 1925, 64).[22]

Recalling the frustrations of his own days as a schoolteacher in the 1910s, Séamus Ó Grianna focused on the practical aspect of this question in typically uncompromising terms, asking in *Saoghal Corrach*, the second volume of his autobiography: 'When will we see the day that no student in Ireland will be allowed to look at Shakespeare or Cicero until he first learns the *Táin*, the Fenian lays, and the medieval literature?'[23] It is also worth noting that all of these writers shared what we would now call a thoroughly nativist reading of the early literature, although none expressed this view more forthrightly than the Dublin policeman D. Ó Riagáin, who wrote of the *Táin* in the *Garda Review*:

> It is Ireland's *Iliad*. It comes down to us from the middle of the 'La Tène' period. The marks of paganism or the marks of polytheism are abundant in the *Táin*. Its main cast of characters derive from the Tuatha Dé Danann. The *Táin* owes virtually nothing to any other country other than Ireland itself – it is a thoroughly native literature (*GR*, Nov. 1937, 1350).[24]

The second major reason for active Gaelic interest in the early literature was more purely literary. Lamenting the many faults of the new Irish literature in a review of Seán Ua Ceallaigh's *Trí Truagha na Scéaluidheachta* (The three sorrows of storytelling) in 1930, 'Eala na Laoi' complained of the 'shabby' (*suarach*) and 'childish' (*leanbhaidhe*) quality of most modern literary work in Irish. His cure was for writers to immerse themselves in early Irish literature 'in which there are distinguished literary traits, including beauty of speech and depiction and artistic form' (''n-a bhfuil árd-thréithe litríochta, idir áilneacht cainnte agus pictiúracht agus déanamh ealadhanta') (*FL*, July, 1930, 3). An tAthair Seán Ó Catháin was in full agreement, writing in 1935:

> There will not nor can there be any real value to the work of a writer who does not know the literature that preceded him. I call that literature that preceded him 'ancient literary memory', and I say that even if he should be a learned and clever person, the person who has not been schooled in that ancient memory is wasting his time if he tries to compose literature (*TCNÍ*, June 1935, 130)[25]

An anonymous author expressed vigorous support for this opinion in a rather improbable forum for the discussion of serious literary issues, writing in *Our Boys* in 1937: 'The foundation of the new literature is to be found in the ancient literature, and unless the new structure is erected on that foundation, it will only be an alien growth' (*Our Boys*, 13/5/37).[26] According to Liam Ó Rinn, Stephen McKenna shared this opinion of the educational and aesthetic potential of the early literature:

> He thought that it was well worth their while for writers to study it, not to imitate the style and phrasing, but to encourage themselves to develop a Gaelic style of their own, to fashion new phrases as concise as the ancient ones by following native models, so that they would have a protective barrier against Anglicism, so that they would have the ancient authors as an intellectual resource and a source of inspiration just as English-language writers have Shakespeare, Milton, and many other authors.[27]

Joining in the widespread criticism of An Gúm's translation scheme, Seán Ó Ciarghusa argued that the language hardly needed to import literary models it already had – in embryo at least – in its own tradition. Discussing the whole question of translation, Ó Ciarghusa wrote: 'The types of literature that we lack are to be found or there are at any rate guideposts for them in ancient Irish if we had the sense to seek them out, or to teach the young people of the Gaeltacht to seek them out.'[28]

Other writers agreed, but focused more specifically on language itself, seeing Old and Middle Irish as the unimpeachably authentic source to be mined for new words, images, and stylistic models. For instance, in a 1929 essay, Liam Ó Rinn wrote:

> If the ancient literature is given to us – in close translation that retains the ancient flavour of the nobility of the middle ages – the influence of the ancient literature will work on the new literature in such a way that it will not be rife with jargon as is much of the English that is being written, and also in such a way that our writers will be moved to use concise and incisive language and to fashion powerful and illuminating compound words, each one of which will be almost a picture in itself (*Star*, 31/8/29).[29]

Seán Ó Catháin was also of this opinion, as is clear from his 1925 review of Tomás Ó Máille's *Mac Dathó*, in which he urged scholars to study, edit, and publish the early literature, and continued:

> Were that done, those cultivating the language would become acquainted with and knowledgeable about the mind and the traits of our ancestors and also about the nature of Middle Irish literature. It is also likely that the modern language

> would benefit from weaving into it words and idioms, both useful and beautiful (*IMN*, 1927, 105).[30]

For those who shared this opinion the older forms of the language also provided a way out of the divisive and sterile battles over dialect. In his contribution to a 1923 debate on the possibilty of the state's sponsoring or even imposing a national standard for the language, Liam Gógan argued that such a standard would have to have its basis in Old Irish (*FL*, 20/1/23). In a lecture at University College Dublin six years later, the Celticist Father Francis Shaw was in general agreement, stating that a true standard could only evolve naturally, but that in the meantime it was essential that older forms of the language be studied closely for guidance. According to the correspondent for *An Tír*, Father Shaw said

> that it was his opinion that this question would be settled more quickly if writers of the Irish language were ready to accept the prose of the ancient literature as the standard for the literary language instead of accepting the standard of a particular dialect (*Tír*, Apr. 1929, 3).[31]

Exasperation with those unwilling to follow such a course of action is evident in an anonymous 1925 essay in the *Irish Rosary*: We have plenty of fanatical Gaels, who foam at the mouth if you decline to accept any of their pet theories and illusions, but who cannot be persuaded to study the literature which is enshrined in the older forms of the language (*IR*, May 1925, 388).

Unfortunately, for others the study of the earlier language and literature could, as we saw in chapter one, open yet another front in the dialect war, as when in his 1927 review of Ua Ceallaigh's *Trí Truagha na Scéaluidheachta* (The three sorrows of storytelling), Ó Grianna sneered: 'And I hope I will be forgiven what I said when I read the book: "There are four sorrows of storytelling", I said. "Munster Irish in the mouth of Cú Chulainn is the fourth sorrow, and it is the greatest sorrow"' (*FL*, Sept. 1927, 8).[32] Perhaps the most forceful champion of the idea that modern writers of Irish should master earlier forms of the language before submitting their work to the public was the German Jesuit Gustav Lehmacher, who, in a 1923 symposium in *Studies*, suggested a radical solution to the dialect debate: 'Would it be possible to go back both in style and pronunciation to Early Middle Irish?' (*Studies*, Mar. 1923, 31).[33]

It was, however, the third major motive for involvement with the early literature that most excited those Gaels working with it. There was all but universal agreement at the time concerning the inspirational potential of the heroic tradition properly understood. For example, writing in 1938 'Sliabh Bladhma' proclaimed:

> I do not think that Pearse and O'Grady had any particular theories as to the remote original Cuchulainn or the nature of the Irish mind that first shaped the saga ... For each of them the saga was just something that stirred imagination and heart, that exalted the inner life ... And such enkindled imagination (in the true sense), such interior exaltation, are deep necessities of us all at Bealtaine and in every season. The Cúchulainn epic would be little if we could not illustrate it in our own lives and Ireland's in a new way (*Gaedheal*, May 1938, 2).

In *An Fhiannuidheacht*, Cormac Ó Cadhlaigh was explicit about his didactic purpose in this work:

> What I set out to do, in the first place, was to gather and to bring together and to arrange all the Fenian material, both lays and tales, in such a way that it would be easy for the student to find them all together in one book and so that he could learn and understand from reading them what nobility and what heroism was native to our Gaelic ancestors and what thoughts they had inspiring them and urging them on to live a noble life.[34]

The anonymous author of an essay on 'The Work of Fianna Éireann' in the souvenir programme for an Easter Week commemoration at Pearse's St Enda's School in April 1922 doubtless had his audience of Ireland's potential future leaders in mind when he wrote:

> Our work in Ireland is a work of restoration, but it is something more. We must link up the life of Ireland to-day, and of the future, with the life of that Ireland that gave us the the Cúchulain Sagas and the Stories of Fionn and the Fianna. The Ireland that is pictured in our older literature was a land of kingly men and queenly women whose lives were strangely beautiful and noble, people who knew how to use life and how to sacrifice it when need arose. They had a fine perspective of things, ample and generous, the breadth of view and the depth of feeling without which no nation has ever risen to greatness.

One of those most active in making versions of the early tales accessible to young readers, Tomás Ua Concheanainn, left no doubt as to why he had undertaken this work, writing in the preface to *Eamhain Macha / Cú Chulainn agus Ridiri na Craoibhe Ruaidhe* (Eamhain Macha / Cú Chulainn and the knights of the Red Branch):

> There is not a girl or a boy in Ireland who should not have some knowledge of those stories, for it cannot be truthfully said that any Gael, whoever he or she may be, who does not know the ancient stories of the Red Branch, has a proper education or upbringing.[35]

Other modernisers and critics were every bit as insistent that this work was not to be seen as escapist costume drama, that the ancient literature still had important lessons to teach, some of them of entirely contemporary relevance. In his preface to *Trí Truagha ne Scéaluidheachta* in 1932, Ua Ceallaigh presented his originals as illustrative of the kind of needless tragedy that results from suspicion, irresponsibility, and rash action, failings none of which were in short supply in the very year independent Ireland saw an edgy if successful transfer of power between two political parties born in civil war a mere decade earlier. Ua Ceallaigh concluded his preface:

> Mochaomhóg cursed Lairgnéan, the king of Connacht, because his queen took from the saint his beloved birds, that is, the four children of Lir, and they died as a result . . . In the same way, Cathbad the druid cursed Emain because the sons of Uisnech were killed there, and he also said that neither Conchubhar nor anyone of his race would ever hold Emain from that kin-killing to the day of judgment. Ruadán cursed Tara later. We still feel the effects, and it is incumbent on us to think about that.[36]

In his 1935 preface to *Rudhraigheacht*, Ua Ceallaigh drew, however improbably and unconvincingly, a more specific lesson about the historic indivisibility of the Irish nation from the Ulster Cycle and other early tales, writing:

> It is a pity that there has not of late been the same fellowship between Ulster and Corca Dhuibhne. However long the situation lasts, we have in our own time allowed foreigners to cut the friendship that was bound when Brian Bóruma, his son, and his son's son were buried in Armagh.[37]

In an essay on 'Fianna Glan-Áilne Gaedheal' (The beautiful, pure Fianna of the Gaels) in *The Clongownian* the previous year, Séamas Ó h-Éamhthaigh offered Fionn's men as all-encompassing cultural and moral exemplars:

> Let us therefore embrace the Fenian lore. Let us embrace it as material for stories, as educational material, as material for drama. What we can learn from it is not insignificant. Courage, nobility of mind, true friendship, virtuous heroism – those things are the harvest to be reaped by us today, the harvest that is the fruit of that little seed that was put in the earth long ago when it was springtime in a splendid Ireland (*Clongownian*, 1934, 131).[38]

An tAthair Tomás Ó Cillín provided a succinct statement of this idea when he quoted a *seanchaí* in the preface to his *Artúraidheacht 'Thír-an-Áir'*: 'Fenian lore and devilry were never in the same house.'[39] In *An Fhiannuidheacht*, the most active harvester at work at this time, Cormac Ó Cadhlaigh, drafted

Fionn and the Fianna into the band that stalked with Cú Chulainn through the GPO on the summons of Pearse in 1916.[40] While equally entranced by the martial and moral splendour of the ancient heroes, Seosamh Mac Grianna believed their major role in the salvation of the nation was as yet unplayed, writing in *Na Lochlannaigh*:

> The spirit and the deeds of Cú Chulainn strengthened Pearse, and perhaps the truth and the nobility and the beauty of the Fenian Cycle will strengthen the Gaels some time in the future, and we will forego treachery and want no one to even imagine us capable of falsehood.[41]

As is evident from some of the statements above, several commentators were eager to enlist the warriors of old as allies in contemporary political battles both within the Free State itself and with the traditional English foe. Perhaps predictably, it was the republicans, outnumbered by the actual Irish people then living, who found this appeal to the illustrious – or imaginary – dead most tactically promising. In a stirring piece entitled 'Súiste Ghuill agus Bachall Phádruig' (Goll's flail and Patrick's crozier) in 1928, Séamus Ó Grianna wrote of one of the dialogues between Oisín and Patrick in the compilation *Acallamh na Senórach* (The colloquy of the ancients):

> The person who composed this story understood the outlook the Fianna had, the outlook Ireland had when it was worthy to be called a country. When it was high-minded, proud, fierce and unafraid to look any country straight in the eyes. At that time Ireland relied on Goll's flail . . . The men who stood firm against [the English] all believed in the flail. Hugh O'Neill, Hugh O'Donnell, all the way down to Cathal Brugha (*An Phoblacht*, 7/4/28).[42]

The republicans were not, however, allowed to present themselves as the sole legitimate heirs of Cú Chulainn and Fionn. Even the most extreme supporters of the Treaty settlement were aware of the inspirational value of the heroic period as depicted in the early literature. Arguing that the nation needed to reject the

> mania of Fianna Fáil and its Left Wing allies – the obsession, born of the slave mind, that nothing national existed before the British came, and that the war with them can never come to an end because without the British to hate and fight there would be no Irish nationalism,

'T. P. G.' presented what he called 'an excellent corrective, and one which I hope the Blue Shirts will adopt when returned to power'. His proposal was no less than 'the public recognition of Tara in the nation's life': 'It should be invested with all the trappings to which its historic and glorious past entitle it. It should be reverenced as the centre of the Irish nation's life during the golden age of our race' (*UI*, 28/4/34).[43]

What enabled this transformation of bloody-minded, hard-drinking pagans into ethical exemplars for a conservative Catholic state was Gaelic ignorance – doubtless often wilful – of the real ethos of the heroic literature. Ambivalence reigned throughout the period on questions as basic as the historicity of the protagonists of the early tales. If some suspension of disbelief was required here, that was no problem whatsoever for many, who seem to have followed the principle set forth by an anonymous writer in *An Sguab* in 1926: 'If the ancient Irish were so noble that they invented Cú Chulainn, we should be noble enough to believe that he existed' (*Sguab*, Feb. 1926, 33).[44] Certainly Séamus Ó Ceallaigh took for granted the historical existence of Cú Chulainn, Fionn, *et al.* in his 1932 series 'Heroes of the Gael' in *An Camán*,[45] as did An tAthair Mac a' Bháird in the lecture cited above, and T. H. Nally in his 1922 book *Aonach Tailteann and Tailteann Games: Their Origin, History, and Ancient Associations*. Moreover, a belief in Cú Chulainn as a real person runs through all of Peadar Ó Dubhda's many references to the hero in his essays and stories set near his native Dundalk.[46] In addition, school texts like Micheál Ó Siochfhradha's *Stair-Sheanchas Éireann: Cuid 1: Ó Thús Aimsire go 1609 AD* and Pronnséas [*sic*] Ó Súilleabháin's *Stair na h-Éireann ó Aimsir Naoimh Pádraig go dtí an Lá Indiu* presented the heroes of the early literature as historical personages.[47] On the other hand, there were, of course, many who shared the more sophisticated understanding of the early tales expressed by S. Ó Scoiligh in remarks on the Ulster Cycle in *Irisleabhar Muighe Nuadhad* in 1932:

> It is difficult for us to have any confidence in folklore or in history that is so old, since the most discerning truth is rarely in the mouths of the masses. Perhaps there once was a man long ago by the name of Cú Chulainn who did many heroic deeds, but it is certain that no man alive could do the things claimed for him. At any rate, it is likely that there was a man of his sort who did much for his Province and that his deeds of valour were a topic of conversation among the people and everyone added his bit to them until in the end it was thought that he was a giant (*IMN*, 1932, 52).[48]

A larger leap of faith was required to clear the hurdle of the paganism and sheer bad manners of the ancient warriors, and some balked at the prospect. For example, reviewing Ó Cadhlaigh's *An Fhiannaidheacht*, 'S. Ó C.' (probably either Shán Ó Cuív or the Jesuit Seán Ó Catháin) wrote:

> I do not entirely agree with the author when he praises the virtues of the Gaels as they are to be found in the stories. It is true that the Fianna always valued

> manliness and courage and loyalty. But as I understand the stories, those were 'natural' virtues. They had no understanding of Christian virtues like humility and patience and gentleness . . . Therefore, I do not think it is right to pay attention to the 'morality' of the stories and to forget the paganism that is in them (*Studies*, Dec. 1937, 680).[49]

This was, however, a distinctly minority view. Most Gaels seem to have convinced themselves, perhaps by an act of the will, that Celtic savagery was not unmitigatedly savage and that Celtic – or at least Irish – paganism was not all that pagan. At any rate, the laudable far outweighed the loathsome in all Gaelic assessments of the heroic literature at this time. Writing in 1926, Muiris Ó Catháin stated: 'We admit that there are barbaric qualities in the ancient literature, but it seems to us that on every page there are also refinement and nobility' (*FL*, Aug. 1926, 1).[50] With regard to the more specifically theological difficulty, Ella Frances Lynch could write in a piece on 'Gaelic Culture' for the *Irish Rosary* in 1929: 'Even the ancient Gaelic paganism with its high-minded folk thought and peasant wisdom, stands out in shining contrast with the sordid degeneracy of modern paganism' (*IR*, June, 1929, 439). Muiris Ó Catháin developed a similar idea the same year, although his emphasis was on parallels between Irish heroic literature and the Old Testament:

> The fundamental idea behind all these opinions of mine is that there is a startling similarity between certain things in the ancient mythological literature and in the Ulster Cycle and certain very important things in the ancient stories of the Old Testament . . . Is it, therefore, possible that with regard to some of the qualities in our ancient literature they are vestiges of the stories of the old true religion – the religion of the Old Testament? (*Camán*, 30/12/33).[51]

Writing in *Irisleabhar Muighe Nuadhad* a decade earlier, Liam Ó Liatháin had simply melded ancient Irish paganism and ancient Irish Christianity into a single source of moral uplift: 'We must develop in ourselves the integrity and the nobility of the Fianna, and the gentleness [*sic*!] and courage of Cú Chulainn, and must fix firmly in our hearts that old faith that Patrick taught us' (*IMN*, 1924, 6).[52] Perhaps most startling of all is the transformation wrought on Cú Chulainn by W. P. Ryan in his 1925 English-language poem 'Cúchulainn:'

> You taught the real Earth is spirit pure,
> That men are spirit-children on her breast,
> That Life's a grand experimental tour
> For ends unmanifest.

> And last, Ó son of Lú [Cú Chulainn], the light's mystic Source,
> You routed all the fell foes of the race:
> Pride, hatred, lust, despair. You cleared man's course
> For thought and growth and grace.[53]

A problem confronting those Gaels more interested in artistic than behavioural models was the extravagance and chaotic nature of the early literary corpus as we have it. For once, some critics at least faced this hard truth head-on, as did 'P. B.' in 1927: 'Let it be admitted . . . that they [the early tales] have their faults. Those who know the Homeric poems will appreciate Homer's wonderful measure, in comparison with the exaggerations of our story-tellers' (*IER*, June 1927, 666). Appealing to the same standard in 1929, Séamus Ó hÁinlighe praised the *Táin* as 'the noblest and most extraordinary, not only of the tales of Ireland, but of the great stories of Western Europe', before going on to admit that 'the Homer or the Virgil never came to refine that great literature, to tie together the disjointed bits, to sort out the complexities and to bestow on his descendants the finished epic of the Celtic world' (*IMN*, 1929, 34).[54] Seán Ó Catháin was more specific in his criticism of the aesthetic failings of the early literature when he reviewed Micheál Mac Liammóir's play *Diarmuid agus Gráinne*:

> There is often no unity in the ancient tale. A person's deeds are not based entirely on his personality, and often they don't correspond with his nature. The 'deus-ex-machina' – *geissi* [supernatural injunctions], magic, or deities – such things overwhelm people in such a way that they are but 'playthings of the gods' (*TCNÍ*, May 1936, 115).[55]

Ó Catháin returned to this idea in his review of Peadar Ó Dubhda's novel *Brian*, calling attention to the novel's disjointedness and identifying this lack of narrative and stylistic coherence as a persistent fault running through Irish literature from the beginning:

> The longest tales in the Fenian Cycle and in the Ulster Cycle are but short stories tied together. The Irish never, it seems, bothered with revealing the development of character. And that left their tales lacking unity except for the fact that all the adventures happened to the same hero (*TCNÍ*, Nov. 1937, 261).[56]

Writing in 1934 with *Duanaire Finn* (The poem-book of Fionn) in mind, 'Sliabh Bladhma' called on his fellow Gaelic intellectuals to confront and solve this problem:

> I wonder if one of our experts could arrange and mould a selection of the earliest lays into a connected work. This sort of service was rendered in Finland by Dr Elias

> Lonnrot, a Northern, early 19th century Dr Hyde, and the result is the loose-fitting but distinctive and often charming epic, the 'Kolevala' (*Gaedheal*, 6/10/34).[57]

For at least one Gaelic commentator, the fact that such work had not been previously accomplished was yet another consequence of the disastrous disruption of Irish cultural life caused by English colonialism. Writing in 1938, Seán Ó Ciarghusa asked:

> How do we know that the age of the Gaelic Shakespeare or Dante is not in our past rather than in our future? If justice had been properly established in Ireland since the time of the *Táin*, who will say that the stories and adventures in the *Táin* would not long ago have been woven together into a single beautiful poem; a poem that would be worthy of comparison with the *Iliad* or the *Comedia* or with the dramas of Shakespeare? (*Leader*, 5/11/38).[58]

As we will see below, a few Irish writers did undertake such a task of compilation and synthesis with the intention of providing a reasonably coherent and consistent narrative. None of them achieved anything comparable to the scope and success of the *Kalevala*, and for most Gaels the lacunae and contradictions of their sources remained an obstacle to be lamented rather than an opportunity to be exploited. Their failure of imagination in this regard is particularly obvious when one thinks of the originality and creative zest with which Yeats, Stephens, Clarke, O'Duffy and O'Brien recast what they found and supplied what they didn't in their refashionings of the early tales. Indeed for Stephens, the gaps, inconsistencies, and weird juxtapositions of his sources became their primary fascination for a modernist author, as he indicated in a letter to his agent James Pinker in 1918. Writing of sections of what was to become the novel *In the Land of Youth* (1924), Stephens was rhapsodic:

> In the matter of the tales which I have been lately sending you, however, they are easily the best things I have ever written, and the treatment, in each case, is so modern that modernity itself is put out of date by it. Forgive me if I brag a little. I have fallen on real treasure-trove, from the story-teller's point of view . . . .[59]

Facing the same treasure trove the Gaels seem to have been more intimidated than intoxicated. Certainly they set their creative sights far lower than did Stephens. In fact, for many, interest extended little farther than the collection and publication of some of the considerable mass of heroic, particularly Fenian lore still alive in the Gaeltacht. The odd Ulster or Fenian tale[60] was published in collections like Henry Morris's *Oidhche Áirneáil i dTír Chonaill*,[61] Seán Mac Giollarnáth's *Loinnir Mac Leabhair agus Sgéalta Gaisgidh Eile*,[62] or Conchubhar Ó Muimhneacháin's *Béaloideas Bhéal Átha an Ghaorthaidh*,[63] or in Gaelic journals or the national newspapers[64] – the most important journal in this regard being *Béaloideas*. Tomás Ó Máille, the editor of *An Stoc*, urged his readers to collect Fenian material to be published in the magazine and then sent on to Carl Von Sydow for his projected comparative study of Irish and Scandinavian literature (*Stoc*, Nov. 1924, 4), and the 1932 festival that advertised itself as the Oireachtas offered a first prize of £15 for 'four unpublished stories about the Red Branch or the Fianna or both together (between 7,000 and 10,000 words)' (ceithre cinn de sean-sgéalta {nár cuireadh riamh i gclódh} ag baint leis an gCraoibh Ruaidh nó leis na Fianna nó an dá chuid le chéile {eadar 7,000 agus 10,000 focal}).[65] Of course, for many Gaels the preservation of such heroic lore was more than a mere academic task, as is obvious from Niall Ó Domhnaill's 1930 description of old Donegal people telling stories of Fionn:

> What was left of the Fianna was in that mountain cottage that night. Yes, and their time had passed. They were oppressed, and fate lay heavy over them. But Oscar was again in the battle of Gabhra; Goll was in torment on the sea rock, still challenging Clann Baoisgne; Diarmaid was fleeing with Gráinne and they were sheltering for the night in Broinn-na-Sliabh; Oisín lost Niamh-Chinn-Óir yesterday, and tonight Feidhlimidh Rudhraighe shared his depression (*Ultach*, Apr. 1930, 2).[66]

Rather startlingly, other Gaels were willing to get some at least of their heroic reading matter second, third, or even fourth hand through translations of work by Standish James O'Grady. In our period his *Finn and His Companions* and *The Coming of Cuchulain* were both translated to a favourable Gaelic critical reception, the former by Micheul Ó Cionnfhaolaidh in 1923, the latter by An tÁthair Tomás Ó Gallchobhair in 1933.[67] Of course, we should also remember that O'Grady was admired by Seosamh Mac Grianna as well.[68]

On a more ambitious scale, several Gaels did, as we have seen, provide modernisations and/or summaries of the more important heroic tales. From the Ulster Cyle we find Seán Ua Ceallaigh's fairly free retellings of the main tales in *Rudhraigheacht* and of the three stories known collectively as *Trí Truagha na Scéaluidheachta*;[69] the summaries of Ulster Cycle tales for young readers published by Tomás Ua Concheanainn and his wife as *Eamhain Macha: Cú Chulainn agus Ridirí na Craoibhe Ruaidhe*; and Ó Máille's free recreation of *Scéla Mucce Meic Dathó* (The story of Mac Dathó's pig) as *Mac Dathó*, a version in which he developed a bit the character of Mac Dathó's wife and considerably expanded the final anticlimactic episode of the tale involving Fer Loga.[70] But there was more. Tadhg Ó Baoighill's version of *Táin Bó Cúailnge* from *The Book of Leinster* and related stories like *Fled Bricrend* (Bricriu's feast) ran in *An Claidheamh Soluis* from 21 November 1931 to the paper's demise in May 1932. Ó Baoighill combined plot summaries with modernisations of the odd passage, although even in his modernisations he tended to leave many words as he found them, explaining them in a glossary. Pádraic Ó Conaire summarised three of the more famous stories about Cú Chulainn as well as a few Fenian stories in *Eachtraí Móra ó n-Ár Stair*, a book for schoolchildren.[71] Schoolchildren were also the audience for Séamus Ó Grianna's series of booklets published under the general title *Sraith na Craobhrua*, volumes IV to VI of which included Ulster and Fenian Cycle material;[72] the anonymous series of brief retellings published in the 'Do'n Aos Óg' column of the *Irish Independent* in 1927 and 1928;[73] and the anonymous retellings of Ulster and Fenian Cycle tales published in *An Gaedheal Óg* in 1938 and 1939.[74] In addition, Micheul Ó Cionnfhaolaidh's school geography *Eolas ar Éirinn* included a modernisation of the 'Pillow Talk' prologue to the *Táin* in the section on County Mayo, and a brief summary of Cú Chulainn's fight with Fer Diad in the one on County Louth.[75] Pádhraic Ó Domhnalláin offered a version of *Aided Con Roí* as 'Díoghaltas' (Vengeance) in *Na Spiadóirí agus Sgéalta Eile*, and another of a story about Medb as 'Mochean Mheidhbhe' (Medb's welcome) (*IP*, 9/8/32). Several of the central episodes of the life of Cú Chulainn were retold in modern Irish, among them his killing of his own son in a version by Peadar Mac Fhionnlaoich (*An Phoblacht*, 14/5/26); his chivalric fight with Fer Diad by Séamus Ó Grianna in 'Cúchulainn i nDeabhaidh Lainne' (Cú Chulainn in a fight with swords);[76] and his heroic death against overwhelming odds by Seán Óg Ó Ceallaigh (*IP*, 12/11/34). Cait Ní Dhonnchadha retold a section of *Serglige Con Culainn* (The wasting sickness of Cú Chulainn) and the beginning of the *Táin*, as well as stories about Cú Chulainn's first taking of arms, his getting his heroic name, his education with Scáthach in Scotland, and his death, in the *Cork Weekly Examiner* in 1934 and 1935.

The significance of Seán Ó Cathasaigh's modernisation of the *Táin* has been obscured by the fact, first of all, that it was published in brief monthly instalments in *Ar Aghaidh*, and, second, that after running from November 1938 to August 1939, it did not appear again until June 1952, after which date it continued to its conclusion in November 1959. Thus, while Ó Cathasaigh submitted the entire text as his MA thesis at University College Galway in 1943, few readers of Irish would have been aware that there was a full modern version of the *Táin* available in the language. In the preface he wrote for his thesis, Ó Cathasaigh spelled out his intention in undertaking the task:

> My intention at first when I was publishing excerpts from the *Táin* in *Ar Aghaidh* was to make available as simple a version as possible so that any old-timer would understand it if he just had a little glossary that would solve the obscurities of the past for him. That was my intention when I was preparing it as a thesis after that.

And while he felt that he might not have done full justice to the beauty of his original, he was in no doubt that his work would serve an important purpose:

> The Irish language alone is the appropriate vestment for the *Táin*. This version probably benefits from the extent to which I left some of the flavour of the past in it; and, in addition, it will do no harm to the Irish of today to weave a bit of Old Irish through it.[77]

In keeping with this aim, Ó Cathasaigh provided readers of *Ar Aghaidh* with 'a glossary or little dictionary that explains some words, the majority of which were once in the Irish language but which the average Irish speaker no longer has today' (sanasán nó foclóir beag, a mhínigheas roinnt focla a raibh a munáite [*sic*] sa nGaedhilge tráth ach nach bhfuil ag an ngnáth-Ghaedhilgeoir i láthair an lae indiu).[78] On the whole, he met his linguistic challenge with mixed success. For example, he admits that he was not always able 'to put a finished vestment on the old version' (culaith shlachtmhar a chur ar an sean leagan). In particular, he had difficulty – as have all translators of the text – with the archaic verse passages usually referred to as *rosca*.[79] Moreover, at times he failed to sufficiently update the language of the original, a failure that must on occasion have frustrated the 'old-timers' who were his ideal readers.

With regard to the questions of decorum the text presented, Ó Cathasaigh was quite daring for his time, portraying Cú Chulainn's distorted appearance when in his *ríastrad* or warrior frenzy with appropriately grotesque accuracy, noting explicitly that the noblewomen of Ulster expose 'their breasts . . . and their bosoms and their chests' (a gcíocha . . . agus a n-uchta agus a n-urbhruinne) to the young Cú Chulainn when he returns in a rage after his first warrior exploits, and retaining the many references to Medb's extravagant sexuality. Furthermore, he renders accurately the humiliating punishment Cú Chulainn inflicts on Láiríne when they meet in single combat:

> Cú Chulainn rushed at him, and he ground and rubbed him between his hands, and he shook him and he squeezed him, and he bound him and he crushed him and he shook him so that he discharged all his excrement so that the ford was coated with his shit and so that the air in all directions was befouled with his dirt.[80]

For the Fenian material, we have in addition to the previously noted scholarly synthesis of the cycle in Ó Cadhlaigh's *An Fhiannuidheacht*,[81] Douglas Hyde's edition of *An Agallamh Beag* (The little colloquy) with facing modern Irish translation in *Lia Fáil* (1927, 79–107); Micheál Breathnach's analysis in *Prós na Fiannaidheachta* (The prose of the Fenain cycle) (BÁC: COÉ, n.d.) with many extensive illustrative passages adapted from the originals; Tadhg Ó Donnchadha's scholarly edition and discussion of *Filidheacht*

Fiannaigheachta (Poetry of the Fenian cycle) (BÁC: COÉ, [1938]);[82] and his school text *Ór-Chiste Fiannuíochta* (A treasure-chest of literature about the Fianna); *Fianna Éireann* (The Fianna of Ireland) by Tomás Ua Concheanainn and his wife Helena (BÁC: Brún agus Ó Nóláin, Teor., n.d.); Máiréad Ní Ghráda's retellings of four Fenian tales in *An Giolla Deacair agus Scéalta Eile* (The difficult lad and other stories) (BÁC: COÉ, [1936]); Diarmuid O Murcu's [*sic*] *Bodaire n Coota Lachtna* [*sic*] (The churl in the grey coat), a version of the tale in 'Eeris' (Blaaclia [*sic*]: Bruun agus O Nualaen, Teor. [*sic*], [1935]); a tale entitled 'An Bhean Achrannach' (The quarrelsome woman) in Micheál Ó Colmáin's *In Óige an tSaoghail: Sean-Sgéalta Gaodhalacha* (In the youth of the world: Old Gaelic stories) (Baile Átha Cliath: Cló na gCoinneal, [1924]); and another on 'Oisín i dTír na nÓg' (Oisín in the Land of the Young) in Shán Ó Cuív's *Sgéalta ón Radio* (Stories from the radio) (BÁC: ODFR, 1931); Ó Siochfhradha's edition, in slightly updated orthography, of *Tóraidheacht Dhiarmada agus Ghráinne* (BÁC: COÉ, n.d.), and *Tóraidheacht an Ghiolla Dheacair* (BÁC: Comhlucht Oideachais na hÉireann, Teor., n.d.);[83] and *Diarmuid agus Gráinne, An Giolla Deacair, Bodach an Chóta Lachtna* (BÁC: An Preas Náisiúnta, [1939?]), as edited by Pádraig Ó Canainn. In addition, retellings of Fenian stories in modern Irish appeared with some frequency in daily and weekly papers in our period.[84] There was also what we might now consider a set of crib notes for the Fenian Cycle, a volume entitled *Cnámha Sgéil na Fiannuíochta* (Plot summaries of the Fenian cycle), prepared by the National Correspondence College.

Ó Cadhlaigh had earlier turned his attention to the King Cycle in his *Cormac Mac Airt* (BÁC: Muinntir C.S. Ó Fallamhain, i gcomhar le hOS, 1927), and in 1939 published *Guaire an Oinigh* (Guaire the generous) (BÁC: OS, 1939). Tomás Ua Concheanainn and his wife Helena offered their versions of some of the tales concerning Cormac and Niall Naoi nGíallach in *Inis Fáil / Sgéalta faoi Árd-Righthe na h-Éireann* (BÁC: Brún agus Ó Nóláin, Teor., n.d.), a work that incorporated material from his series 'Seoda na Sean' (Treasures of the ancients) in *An Stoc* in 1925.[85] From the Mythological Cycle, the story of the Children of Lir was particularly popular. In addition to the versions in which it appeared as one of 'Trí Trua na Sgéaluíochta', several variants of it were published separately: Seumas Ó Súildhubháin's *Clann Lir de Thuatha Dé Danann* (The children of Lir of the Tuatha De Danann) (BÁC: COÉ, 1923); Micheál Ó Colmáin's *Clann Lir* (BÁC: Cló na gCoinneal, 1932); Diarmuid O Murcu's *Clann Lir in Eeris* (BÁC: C. J. Fallon [1935]); and Pádraig Ó Bróithe's *Clann Lir agus Inghean an Árd-Ríogh: Dhá Scéal* (The children of Lir and the daughter of the high king: Two stories) (BÁC: Brún agus Ó Nualláin, [1936]). There was also a lengthy anonymous modernisation of 'Oigheadh Chlainne Tuireann' (The violent death of the children of Tuireann) that ran in *An Camán* from 24 September to 19 November 1932.

Among miscellaneous modernisations and retellings we have 'A. Ó M.'s' 'Talland Étair (Iarsma de Sgeul Fáindigheachta [*sic*])' (The siege of Howth {A remnant of an ancient tale}) (*Ultach*, Mar. 1927, 6–7; modernised excerpts from *Tógail Troí* (The destruction of Troy) by 'Ógh-Réir' (*FL*, Dec. 1927, 3) and by 'M. M.' (*ACS*, 31/1/31);[86] a couple of passages from Julius Pokorny's *Historical Reader of Old Irish* put into modern Irish by 'E. Ó N.' in *An Stoc* in 1930 (*Stoc*, May 1930, 11; Dec. 1930, 9); an anonymous modernisation of a bit from *Féilire Óengusso* (The martyrology of Aengus) (*Féile na nGaedheal*, Nov. 1931, 8); Muiris Ó Droighneáin's 'Bás Cheallaigh (as *Silva Gadelica*) / Tar Éis an Chatha' (The death of Ceallach {from *Silva Gadelica*} / After the battle) (*Ultach*, Nov. 1933, 1–2); and Séamus Maguidhir's summary of *Cath Maige Tuiredh* (The battle of Moytura) in his regular 'Fánaidheacht i gContae Mhuigheo' column in *An t-Éireannach* (19/9/36). The most extensive modernisation of non-literary material from our period involved John of Gaddesden's medical text *Rosa Anglica*, the edition of which by Winifred Wulff for the Irish Texts Society, was the basis for Liam Ó Rinn's modern Irish version that began a lengthy serialisation in *United Ireland* in the issue for 2 May 1934.

A handful of Gaels saw more challenging and exciting potential in the heroic tradition. For example, Cormac Ó Cadhlaigh, Joseph Hanly, and Micheál Ó Siochfhradha stressed the role the early literature should have played and could still play in the evolution of Gaelic drama, Hanly writing:

> No original literature in the world offers more scope for dramatisation than the Irish. Every story of the great Ulidian cycle can be dramatised. The 'Táin Bó', which is recognised as the greatest epic matter north of the Alps, is drama by its very nature. The conversations between St Patrick and Oisín are the essence of dramatic art.[87]

Ó Siochfhradha developed this idea in greater detail:

> The Táin is all but a full-fledged drama: Meadhbh, dissatisfied in Cruachan as she counts her wordly wealth – the messengers in being refused by the king of Cuailnge at his court – the gathering of the hosts by Meadhbh – the great cattle raid. There is a powerful dramatic strain there as there is in all the tales for the bards used to recite them before the kings, and there is no great distance between a performance by a single man and a performace by a group (*Reult*, June 1925, 42).[88]

Ó Cadhlaigh hoped that *Guaire an Oinigh*, his own compilation of stories about the Connacht king, would inspire his more creative contemporaries to undertake the task of bringing legendary figures like Guaire alive again on the page or stage: 'If some writer is now prompted to write a novel or a play about Guaire based on the stories about him here, that would be one positive result from the research that was done to compile them.'[89] Less convincing perhaps is Niall Ó Conghaile's suggestion that *Tochmharc Emire* (The wooing of Emer), the stories of Deirdre and Diarmuid and Gráinne, or 'Oisín i dTír na nÓg' were ideal subjects for musicals (*Éireannach*, 28/7/34).[90] A dissenting voice was that of the anonymous critic who reviewed the Galway premiere of Micheál Mac Liammóir's *Diarmuid agus Gráinne* for the *Irish Independent* in 1928. Having noted that 'stage versions of the heroic legends are not, it is true, as much in favour as they were in the early years of the dramatic movement', suggested a reason:

> But patriotic enthusiasm, though it may move mountains, will not, of itself, produce good drama, and it is only the bare truth that the vast majority of these experiments, however lofty the intention that inspired them, were from the point of view of the spectator a weariness to the flesh (*II*,19/11/28).

Other Gaels wanted to seek more up-to-date spectators, resurrecting an earlier suggestion by Seán Ó Caomhánaigh that episodes from the early literature be made into feature films. Among those sharing this opinion were Tadhg Ó Donnchadha, who saw the heroic tales as an antidote for the sordid paganism ('an phágántacht agus an bréantas') of the English and American film industries (*Gaedheal*, 23/3/35);[91] Aughuistín Breathnach, who felt that such films would have to be in colour to do full justice to their sources (*Tír*, Feb. 1930, 4); and Micheál Ó Maoláin, who saw movies based on the sagas as a curative for the Anglicisation promoted by imported screen fare (*ACS*, 8/8/31). 'J. A. P. was even more enthusiastic, writing in the army journal *An t-Óglach* in 1926:

> A film version of the story of Deirdre could infinitely outdistance in beauty anything that has ever been staged; the great figure of the Hound of Ulster would inspire countless millions, and outer world would learn that Ireland has a folklore that cannot be eclipsed (*Óglach*, 18/9/26).

Moreover, at least one film buff, James Wall, felt such screen adaptations would not be all that difficult, writing in an essay on 'Films from Sagas' in the *Irish Independent*:

> The manuscripts provide full details of costume and custom to facilitate the producers. The sets and scenery have been provided by Nature. Maeve's armies might still march across virgin country from Connaught, and Cuchallain [sic] might again hold the Ford, almost without camouflaging a single cottage or blackening out an electric pylon (*II*, 28/4/37).

And, perhaps in response to the many translations of English detective novels issued by An Gúm in its early years, one 'Ogma', himself a member of the Gárda Síochána, wrote in the *Garda Review*:

> Personally I have encountered several excellent examples of the crime detection story in ancient Irish literature; but there is only one – and not one of the best – that I am able to give without going to original sources not at present within my reach.

The story to which he refers concerns Cú Chulainn's sword, now in the possession of Socht, a hostage of Cormac Mac Airt at Tara (*GR*, Jan. 1931, 239).[92]

When we turn, however, to what genuinely creative uses Gaelic authors put these sources, there is little enough to boast of. The Ulster Cycle seems to have inspired only four stories and four plays. The general tone of Nioclás Tóibín's 'Conall Cearnach ar Chnoc Cailbhre' (Conall Cearnach on the hill of Calvary) should be clear from its conclusion:

> It is said that there was a representative there from every nation on earth and that Conall was the representative of the Gaels – that race that has ever since remained loyal to Christ and that will in all likelihood remain so forever.[93]

Peadar Ó Dubhda's 'An t-Ógánach Ceann-Órdha' (The golden-headed youth) is, on the other hand, the Gaelic recreation that most closely – although to be honest not all that closely! – approaches the wit and invention of works by some of the Anglo-Irish writers. Ó Dubhdha has his narrator fall asleep and dream of Cú Chulainn returning to modern-day Dundalk. There he first does battle with a motor car – a Ford he is told – prompting his incredulous reply: 'Ford? I killed Ford with a jab of the *ga bulga*!' ('Giolla an Átha? Mharbh mise Giolla an Átha le sucadh de'n gha bolg!') After several other misadventures, he goes to a theatre where he delights in the hijinks of 'Micí Luchóg' (Mickey Mouse), and later attacks the screen in pursuit of the villains in the feature film. Needless to say, he is throughout discouraged by the degeneracy – physical, moral, and linguistic – of those he meets in the town.[94] Comedy is also the keynote in the anonymous story 'Éire i nAimsir Mhéidhbhe' (Ireland in the time of Medb) in the 1933–4 issue of the UCG *University Annual* and in Caoimhghín Ó Góilidhe's story 'Eadaragallamh le Pádraig' (An interview with Patrick) from the *Cork Weekly Examiner*. In the former, a UCG undergraduate dreams a professor takes him on a walk through the Irish past, while in the latter, a reporter sent to interview St Patrick in Heaven gets an earful about his boastful countrymen: 'We are tormented by Cú Chulainn reciting the *Táin* to us and by Oisín and all his boasting about Niamh and by Keating giving out the *Forus Feasa* all the time' (*Cork Weekly Examiner*, 12/3/38).[95]

It had long been hoped that Gaelic playwrights would bring the ancient heroes alive again on stage. Such was certainly the view of Geraldine Dillon, a member of the board of Taibhdhearc na Gaillimhe, who, having dismissed Synge's *Deirdre of the Sorrows*, a translation of which An Taibhdhearc had performed, as 'unfinished and full of faults' (neamh-chríochnuithe agus é lán de lochtaí), continued: 'Is it not a pity that so many of the Fenian stories of Ireland are being destroyed! When will someone write a good heroic play? Here is a wonderful opportunity for the new writer' (*IP*, 8/9/32).[96] Of the plays that were written in our period, *Tochmharc Eimhir*, was produced at Feis Charman in Wexford town in May 1934.[97] *Connla*, presumably based on the tale of Cú Chulainn's killing of his son of that name, was produced at Carndonagh on the Inishowen Peninsula in Donegal in June 1937,[98] and *An Táin Bó Cuailgne* was performed as a musical drama at the convent school of St Ursula in Thurles, County Tipperary, on St Patrick's Day, 1932. The last was an intriguing production in three scenes. The first portrayed the 'pillow talk' of Medb and Ailill from the *Book of Leinster* text; the second a feast at the home of Dáire in Ulster; the third Medb's meeting with the prophetess Fedelm; the fourth the Connacht court at Crúachan; the fifth the combat between the foster-brothers Cú Chulainn and Fer Diad; and the sixth, inexplicably and anachronistically, Medb and Ailill 'rejoicing and revelling in the royal household, with the ancient flag of Ireland above her, that is the emblem of the sun against a blue sky' (ag déanamh gáirdeachais agus pléaráca sa Rígh-theaghlach, agus bratach ársa na hÉireann ós a cionn, .i. suaitheantas gréine ar ghorm spéire) (*Naomh Ursula*, 1932, 69). None of these plays was ever published.

Far more important was Micheál Ó Siochfhradha's three-act *Aon-Mhac Aoife Alban* (The only son of Aoife of Scotland) (BÁC: OS, 1938), produced by An Comhar Drámaidheachta at the Peacock Theatre in March 1937 under the direction of Cyril Cusack.[99] While no masterpiece, it is an interesting interpretation of the tale and one that seems more stageworthy than most Gaelic plays of the time. Ó Siochfhradha was at pains to point out his sources for costumes, weapons, etc.,[100] and adhered fairly closely to his original. Moreover, his deviations from that original are consistent in that all tend to heighten the nobility of his characters and the tragedy of their fate. Thus he eliminated the deceitful and sexual aspects of Cú Chulainn's victory over Aoife and sentimentalised their relationship, in particular by softening her character. He also had Aoife rather than Scáthach give Cú Chualainn the *ga bulga*, the deadly spear that disembowelled his opponents, delayed Conlaoch's journey to Ireland until his twenty-first year, sanitised the account of the *ríastradh* and the effects of the *ga bulga* (doubtless in part for practical reasons of staging), and, most important, had Cú Chulainn fight the young man with no idea who he really was. Predictably enough, Ó Siochfhradha, unlike Yeats in *On Baile's Strand* (1904), seems to have lacked the nerve or the ability to recreate the vivid and unsettling blend of pathos and buffoonery that characterises his original.[101]

In addition to these plays, one of the 'three episodes' in a pageant produced at Feis Charman in New Ross, County Wexford in 1932 involved 'the Red Branch heroes at their games of skill at Emhain Macha' (Enniscorthy *Echo*, 9/7/32).[102] Needless to say, dialogue probably didn't play much of a role in an outdoor spectacle of this kind, so it is debatable how 'Gaelic' the pageant was. This question is even more relevant with regard to the 'Gaelic' ballets 'Íde Con Culainn' or 'The Doomed Cuchulain', choreographed by Sara Payne, with costumes by Anne Yeats, and first performed at the Father Mathew Hall in Dublin on 13 November 1937 (*IP*, 13/11/37);[103] and a piece based on the Deirdre story with choreography by Forrest and music by Éamonn Ó Gallchobhair. There can, however, be no doubt of the cultural nationalism that motivated many of those involved in this new venture, as Dr Ethna Byrne made clear in her 1938 essay on 'Our National Ballet':

> We are working for a truly Irish Ireland, all trying to build up Gaelic everything – drama, opera, music, everything Gaelic, everything our own. We are endeavouring to establish a really Gaelic culture. Now a National Ballet, a purely Irish art, is tremendously important (*Leader*, 12/11/38).

There were two plays based on *Orgain Denna Ríg* (The destruction of Dinn Rígh). *Buaidh na Fírinne* (The virtue of truth) by Seósa Ní Chathail was serialised in *An Lóchrann* from February to April 1931. *Maon: Úrchluiche dTrí nGníomh* (Maon: An original three-act play) (Baile Átha Cliath: Connradh na Gaedhilge, 1924) by Seosamh T. Ó Ceit won first prize for an original play at the 1920 Oireachtas. The play, which features the use of a chorus to introduce its second and third acts and which highlights the love of Scoiriath and the protagonist Maon (Labraid Loingseach), was written in verse and never produced.[104]

An tAthair Tomás Ó Ceallaigh's Gaelic opera *Sruth na Maoile*, based on the tragic story of the children of Lir with music by Geoffrey Molyneux Palmer, was produced in the Gaiety Theatre in Dublin in 1923 and again at the Theatre Royal Hippodrome, Winter Gardens, Dublin in August 1924.[105] In the context of the political bitterness of the time, it is hardly surprising that the opera failed to fire the popular imagination, losing a hefty total of £165 15*s*. 4*d*. in its brief run.[106] Undaunted, Ó Ceallaigh and Palmer decided to try again, this time with a comic opera about Diarmaid and Gráinne. Initially, Ó Ceallaigh had hoped the work would be in Irish, but eventually Palmer's ignorance of the language meant that Ó Ceallaigh wrote his libretto in English.[107] From his letters to Palmer at the time, it is clear that Ó Ceallaigh was profoundly discouraged by the Civil War, but still hoped that Irish-Irelanders had not lost their sense of humour:

> Of course, Conán (the ill spoken) must be kept true to character. I'm giving him a song in the first scene. I must warn you that it's all going to be absolute burlesque – ancient and modern ideas mixed up hopelessly. It's time we had a laugh.[108]

The opera, eventually titled *Grania Goes*, was never either performed or published.[109]

Indeed the Fenian Cycle in general inspired far less creative work than might have been expected at this time. Perhaps the most interesting experiment was Aodh de Blácam's 'Draoidheacht an Óir / Scéal a Bhaineas le nár nAimsir Féin' (The enchantment of gold / A story dealing with our own time) (*Green and Gold*, Christmas 1923–Mar. 1924, 314–19). In this tale a Belfast man leaves a party in Dublin with thoughts of the Fianna running through his head. The kilted cabby he hails in Stephen's Green turns out to be Caoilte Mac Rónáin, who has come from the Hill of Allen, 'where the Fianna of Ireland are in a deep sleep awaiting the day they will be called back to Ireland' (áit a bhfuil Fianna Éireann 'na suan trom fá néallta codlata ag fuireach le lá a ngairme ar ais go hÉirinn). Caoilte informs the narrator that Fionn had awakened three years earlier and had set out to discover 'why the centuries are slipping past with nothing heard from our people' (cén fáth go bhfuil na haoiseanna ag sleamhnú thart gan tásc nó tuairisc ó nár gcineadh). Caoilte now asks the narrator to help him track down the missing Fionn, who turns out to have been somehow bewitched by the degeneracy of the modern age and is now living in Rathfarnham as 'Síomón Stráinséar', a vicious and anti-Gaelic miser. All ends happily when Fionn is recognised by his hound Bran. As they look over Dublin from the hills, Caoilte answers Fionn's question as to the whereabouts of Oscar and Oisín, in the process drawing the story's lesson for the narrator, and us: 'Look . . . How many people are there in all those houses down there? And how do we know which of them is Oscar and which Oisín, and they bewitched like Fionn and not knowing that they are of Fionn's people.'[110]

Characters from the Cycle appear along with students and staff from Coláiste na Rinne in 'Cuaird Aesoip' (Aesop's visit), a comic tale by Seán Ó Catháin serialised in his 'Do Gheinealach Focal Anso' column in *An Sguab* beginning in February 1926. These columns consisted of original humorous stories full of antiquarian words resurrected and glossed in notes at the end. Fenian characters also appear, though not in central roles, in 'An Mhiúil' (The mule), a comic story by Micheál Ó Gríobhtha in which there is a radio broadcast of a camogie match between two teams from the otherworld. The Fenian characters, along with St Patrick and Medb, are merely noted as being in attendance.[111] Oisín helps mortals win a hurling match in Seán Mac Maoláin's 1935 story 'Iomáin Thráigh Uaimh an Deirg' (The hurling on the Strand of the Red Man's cave) (Dundalk *Examiner*, 18/5/35 and 25/5/35).

Ciarán Ua Nualláin tried his hand at one of his brother Brian's specialties in his tale 'Ais-Éirghe Fhinn Mhic Chumhaill' (The resurrection of Fionn Mac Cumhaill), a story in which an IRA man discovers the dormant Fianna in a cave and ponders whether he should wake them to drive out the English. In the end he lets them sleep on, thinking it would be an act of 'devilry' (diabhlaidheacht) 'to give another life to a group whose day was done' (saoghal eile a thabhairt do dhream a thug a ré), and unsure of whether their return would be an unmixed blessing: 'How would I know that the Fianna were as civilised and friendly as they were famed for being?' (Cár bhfios damh go rabh na Fianna chomh sibhialta agus chomh carthannach agus bhí cáil ortha a bheith?) (*IP*, 6/1/36). More serious in intent – though perhaps more ludicrous in effect – was Domhnall de Róiste's 'An Rud do Chonnaic Oisín Domhnach na Comhdhála' (What Oisín saw on the Sunday of the Congress), in which Oisín is in awe when St Patrick brings him to a Mass at the Phoenix Park during the Eucharistic Congress of 1932 (*IP*, 14/11/32).

There were also several dramatic treatments of Fenian material. Visitors to Aonach Tailteann in 1928 could enjoy what was clearly intended to be an inspiring pageant featuring the young Fionn winning command of the Fianna.[112] Entertainment rather than edification was the aim of *Tóraidheacht an Ghiolla Deacair*, a 1939 pantomime by Diarmuid Ua Murchadha and Seán Ó Neachtain at the Taidhbhdhearc. Of this work, the programme informs us that 'by the magic of pantomime the stage is enabled to behold these ancient warriors in contact with circumstances which belong even to the twentieth century.'[113] The Cycle also inspired three published plays:[114] *Goll Mac Móirne* by 'M. G.', serialised in *Ar Aghaidh* from Dec. 1932 to Feb. 1933; *Buaidh an Ultaigh* (The triumph of the Ulsterman), Séamus Ó Néill's first important play, serialised in *An t-Ultach* from November 1933 to February 1934; and, by far the most significant and successful of all the reworkings of ancient material in this period, Micheál Mac Liammóir's *Diarmuid agus Gráinne: Dráma Trí nGníomh* (BÁC: ODFR, 1935). Ó Néill's play is based loosely on *Cath Fionntráigh* (The battle of Ventry), although as a good Ulsterman the playwright attributes the Fenian victory to the timely intervention of a young hero from the North. The work was premiered in Belfast in December 1934 and revived by An Comhar Drámaidheachta in the Peacock in December 1936.[115]

Mac Liammóir's play was the inaugural production of Taibhdhearc na Gaillimhe in August 1928. Mac Liammóir himself co-directed the play with Hilton Edwards, designed the set and the costumes, and played the role of Diarmaid.[116] The work was revived in the Gate Theatre in Dublin in 1933 and at the Taibhdhearc in 1936. It was also translated into English for performance at the Gate. With *Diarmuid agus Gráinne* Gaelic critics knew they were seeing something very different and far better than their usual fare. For example, Ernest Blythe was ecstatic after seeing the Galway premiere, declaring: 'I have seen a great many Irish plays put on the stage, but I have never seen anything so well done as the production of "Diarmuid agus Gráinne" in Galway' (*Freeman*, 8/9/28). Writing of the play on its publication in 1935, 'Sliabh Bladhma' stated: 'The drama intensifies the conviction that the Fionn-saga, old as it is, is perenially new and alive, and has riches we have not yet realised' (*Gaedheal*, Apr. 1936, 1). In his review of the play in *Timthire Chroidhe Naomhtha Íosa*, Seán Ó Catháin commended Mac Liammóir for successfully meeting what he identified as the two central challenges facing adapters of the early literature: the tales' lack of coherent narrative and aesthetic structure, and their paganism (*TCNÍ*, May 1936, 115–16). And Séamus Ó Néill had high praise for Mac Liammóir in his review in *An t-Ultach* the same year:

> Micheál Mac Liammóir is not afraid to draw on 'simile' or 'metaphor' and that is the way I prefer it . . . You will feel the true spirit of antiquity in this play. The author understood properly how intimate was the link at that time between the life of the people and the wonders of creation (*Ultach*, Feb. 1936, 3).[117]

It is, however, worth noting that both 'Sliabh Bladhma' and Ó Néill felt it necessary to defend Mac Liammóir's Irish against expected attacks from the native speakers' camp.

Diarmuid agus Gráinne is a much more coherent, artistically crafted, and technically sophisticated play than was usual on the Gaelic stage of the time. On the whole, Mac Liammóir was faithful to the plot of his original, but he added his own intriguing psychological and aesthetic touches throughout. He dedicated the play to Máire Ní Chaoimh, who he says had suggested the subject to him, calling *Tóruigheacht Dhiarmada agus Ghráinne* 'the only story that has come down to us from antiquity in which there is an element of satire and which at the same time deals with love, beauty, and death' (an t-aon sgéal amháin tháinig anuas chugainn ó'n tsean-aimsir a raibh mianach an aoir ann agus san am chéadna a bhain leis an ngrádh, leis an áilleacht agus leis an mbás). All of these elements can be found in Mac Liammóir's interpretation of the tale. In particular, love is presented in the play as an overwhelming and dangerous force and one beyond human control, as Gráinne makes clear in act two:

> The black wind from the north is not stronger than my desire. The green waves of the sea leaping on high under the light of the moon are not stronger than my desire. There is nothing under the sun, Diarmaid, that is as strong as my desire (pp. 66–7).[118]

Mac Liammóir does, however, seem to see women as more willing victims, and therefore ultimately agents, of this power than are men. Speaking to Aonghus shortly after Gráinne's outburst just quoted, Diarmaid exclaims:

'She came of her own will, Aonghus, of her own fierce will. A strong will in a beautiful woman . . . isn't that stronger, Father, and isn't that more terrible, than anything else under the sun' (p. 70).[119] Throughout this play, in which fate hangs heavy and supernatural intervention is always at hand, one of the most ominous elements is the personality of Gráinne herself. At several key moments in the action, Mac Liammóir stresses her disturbing, even frightening, smile (*meangadh*), the ironic and knowing glint in her eyes. Fionn shares his uneasiness about Gráinne with Diarmaid, Oisín, and Goll in act one: 'There is a heavy load on my heart because of the beauty of this woman. She holds her head proudly and if her voice is soft and gentle, isn't the whole world's worth of mockery and scorn to be seen in her eyes' (p. 36).[120] And when Gráinne later urges Diarmaid to carry her away, he tries to escape from her: 'Release me, Gráinne. Although your body is as sweet as honey, it is a poisonous sweetness, and I see the flash of poison in your eye' (p. 51).[121]

Nor does Mac Liammóir suppress the sexual tension of his original, at one point in act two having Gráinne both sneer at Diarmaid's reluctance to sleep with her and flirt seductively with a man from the otherworld in his presence. When Diarmaid engages this man in mortal combat, Gráinne watches 'with a strange, half-joyful, half-fearful smile on her lips' (agus meangadh beag aisteach, leath-áthasach, leath-eaglach ar a béal) (p. 108). Again, when Fionn and Diarmaid make peace and Diarmaid comments that he feels their friendship will have been strengthened by past adversity, Gráinne looks on with a smile (*meangadh gáire*) (p. 133). After Diarmaid's death she goes to Fionn, and the stage directions tell us: 'The hatred leaves her face to be replaced by a look half desperate, half contemptuous' (Imigheann an fuath dá haghaidh agus tagann féachaint uirri atá leath-éadóchasach, leath-fhonóideach). Then having asked Fionn what he is holding in his arms and being answered ('Golden-haired Gráinne' (Gráinne Chinn-óir), she says – and unfortunately there is no stage direction indicating her tone – 'Not she! Not she! Don't you see?' (Ní hí, ní hí! Cé nach bhfeiceann tú?) With a gesture towards Diarmaid's corpse she concludes: 'Gráinne is – there' (Tá Gráinne – annsin). Thereupon the play ends with the following tableau:

> Fear comes into the eyes of Fionn. He wraps the cloak around her. They go out together. Diarmaid stretched out in the middle of the stage, and the men of the Fianna on their knees around him in a half-circle. Silence (pp. 157–8).[122]

At several points in the play Mac Liammóir introduces masterful bits of stage business, perhaps most memorably Fionn's careful drying of his hands after allowing the water that could have saved Diarmaid to seep through them (p. 157). He also creates original dialogue that reveals much about the psychological makeup and motivation of his characters. Particularly effective in this regard is the scene between Gráinne and Fionn in act two where each berates the other for selfishness or treachery, but where each is genuinely hurt by accusations he or she knows to be just and true (pp. 80–7). In his review of the play Seán Ó Catháin took Mac Liammóir to task slightly for his dialogue, which he found 'often too extravagant' (ró 'árd-nósach' go minic) (*TCNÍ*, May 1936, 116). But even in its occasional excesses, the very opulence of Mac Liammóir's language, the vivid sensuality of his imagery, contributes to the play's unity of mood and effect, its brooding, at times almost decadent atmosphere. Mac Liammóir's characters are no moral paragons, nor is theirs the healthy outdoor world usually associated with tales of the Fianna, but more than any other writer of his time, Mac Liammóir succeeded in bringing an ancient tale startlingly alive for an audience of twentieth-century adults.[123]

Why was he so alone in this success given how much interest and pride in the heroic literature there was in Gaelic circles? The easiest explanation is, of course, that he was by far the most gifted writer who drew on this material. But there weren't even that many failures, as most creative writers simply looked elsewhere for artistic inspiration. Several reasons for this avoidance suggest themselves. First of all, Gaelic authors, for all their claims to be the sole legitimate heirs of the Irish literary tradition, may have been at heart intimidated by the bold achievements in this area of their Anglo-Irish predecessors and contemporaries. With writers like Yeats and Stephens in the field, the Gaels may well have been reluctant to invite comparison. Furthermore, with the exception of Mac Liammóir, Gaelic writers seem to have been too much in awe of their cultural heritage to attempt the kind of ironic handling of heroic sources that was in the 1920s and 1930s characteristic of reworkings of the material by authors of Catholic background working in English like Clarke, O'Duffy, or O'Brien.

Secondly, it seems that there was in this period a growing ambivalence about heroic violence itself, particularly among Gaelic authors who aligned themselves with the Free State during the Civil War and its aftermath. We have, for example, seen how three playwrights in our period, León Ó Broin in *An Mhallacht* (1927), Micheál Ó Siochfhradha in *Deire an Chuntais* (1931), and Gearóid Ó Lochlainn in *Na Fearachoin* (1938),[124] used the plot made famous by Frank O'Connor in 'Guests of the Nation' (1931), to question the glory of war and the nobility of discipline and duty.

Thirdly, with regard to the Ulster Cycle at least, many Gaels may have felt a bit edgy about a heroic pantheon whose field of activity fell for the most part outside the boundaries of their own state. This sense that the Free State's claim to northern heroes had in some way been compromised by Partition may also help explain the greater Gaelic interest in the Fianna after the foundation of that state.

Finally, although this point may seem to contradict some of what has been said above, it is clear that for many in the movement their own recent history had been more fabulous and inspiring than anything in the ancient literature. By far the favourite subject of Gaelic authors in the 1920s and 1930s was, as we have seen, the courage, nobility, and self-sacrifice of those who fought for national independence in what David Hogan called 'the four glorious years' from 1917 to 1921. This belief that Ireland's true heroic age was the immediate past is given clearest expression in a story of the Easter Rising by Peadar Mac Fhionnlaoich, a writer who had himself in 1914 published *Conchubhar Mac Nessa: Stair-Sheanchas Curadh na Craobhruaidhe* (Conchubhar Mac Nessa: The history of the heroes of the Red Branch), a book of retellings of Ulster Cycle tales.[125] In the title story of his 1924 collection *An Cogadh Dearg*, the protagonist is a young man whose patriotism has been nourished by his reading of the Fenian tales. By the story's end, however, he has himself taken the field against the foreign invader, and as a result 'he doesn't think as much of the exploits of the Fianna as he once did; he says that the exploits that happen in our own time are greater.'[126]

With all these conflicting doubts and questions – not to mention the ever-present challenge of actually mastering the language of the early sources – it should perhaps be little wonder that most Gaels were willing to leave buried, even as they praised, the troublesome and troubling legends of the national past.

SIX

FLAWED, FAILED, FORGOTTEN?

THE QUESTION OF TRANSLATION

'I worked for An Gúm for three and a half years. What I remember is that it was as if I were in a prison, with my keepers making use of the rules of the prison in every way possible to insult and degrade me and to make me miserable' (*UIrman*, 10/9/32).[1] Thus Seosamh Mac Grianna summed up the brief period in which he had produced no fewer than eleven translations for An Gúm. The bitterness of his brother Séamus against An Gúm was even more profound, as he felt that working for the agency, for which he produced six translations between 1934 and 1940, had actually impaired his physical, psychic, and linguistic well-being. Writing in 1941, he stated: 'For a year after that there was a dizziness in my head and my back was hunched. There were cramps in my fingers and I was losing my sight. And my Irish was broken, bruised, and gapped' (*Ultach*, Jan. 1941, 1).[2] While these two brothers were notoriously and vociferously cranky, their view of An Gúm's translation enterprise was widely shared in their own time, and seems to have become the accepted wisdom ever since.[3] The general attitude was perhaps best expressed by Máirtín Ó Cadhain, who had himself translated a novel and a short story for An Gúm in the 1930s, when he wrote: 'Most of the work done by An Gúm . . . was translation, preponderantly from English. Many have commented on the futility of it.'[4]

Before we rush to the judgment that An Gúm's project was flawed from the start and doomed to failure and oblivion, we should, however, examine more closely the context in which the translation policy was formulated, the debates it engendered, and the successes it enjoyed in its own time and on its own terms. There was certainly nothing new in the idea that Gaelic writing might benefit from a judicious infusion of translated work as the language and its literature were being revived and recreated in the first decades of this century. The question had been debated with insight and even passion by some of the leading Gaelic intellectuals of the period,[5] and a working consensus at least had been reached so that translations were published in book form and appeared regularly in virtually every Gaelic journal both before and immediately after independence. In addition, there were specific and successful competitions for literary translation at the national Oireachtas from 1912 on,[6] and various journals also offered prizes for this kind of work. To a great extent, therefore, An Gúm was merely building on this pre-existing consensus when it made translation part of its publishing agenda from the start. Moreover, at a meeting on 22 Sept. 1927, An Gúm decided to sponsor its own contest for translation.[7] This competition was announced in the *Irish Independent* for 9 Feb. 1928 and drew 51 entries, including some from the best-known Gaelic writers of the time, among them Ó Grianna, Micheál Ó Siochfhradha, Seán Mac Meanman, Seán Óg Ó Caomhánaigh, and Peadar Ó Dubhda.[8]

The controversy provoked by An Gúm's increasing reliance on translation was not, however, merely the logical continuation of the debate begun earlier in the Revival. Neither was it, as was so often true in the years of Saorstát Éireann, a re-invention of the wheel, as writers rehashed arguments and refought battles without apparently realising how much of what they were saying had already been said, often far more originally, articulately and honestly, by their predecessors in the movement. The foundation of the Free State and its aggressive commitment to re-Gaelicising the nation, particularly through the schools, had, as we have seen, created a new linguistic and literary situation that was to rapidly shift translation from the dilettantish periphery to the dead-serious core of the debate about what the new literature in Irish was to be and do.

In the early years of the Revival, translation was pretty much a personal pastime, with individual writers amusing themselves by putting into Irish whatever caught their fancy. Needless to say, both ideological camps of the period, the nativists and the progressives as I have called them, had their say on the question, though it is perhaps a good indication of how secondary a concern was translation that some of nativist bent, like Fathers Dinneen and O'Leary, whom we might have expected to be most suspicious of it, were among its earliest practitioners. Apparently even nativists, while they could and did draw attention to the potential danger of translation on a wider scale, in particular from English, felt that danger was so slight at the time that they themselves could court it.

The progressives were in general more consistent on this issue. Writers like Pádraic Ó Conaire saw translation as one way – though never the most immediate or obvious – to introduce Gaelic readers to the wider literary and cultural world beyond the Irish Sea, or perhaps better the English Channel. This view of translation as a means of bringing Irish speakers out of the provincialism imposed on them by Anglicisation remained a key element in the progressive programme throughout the 1920s and 1930s. Ó Conaire himself wrote in 1922:

> True literature will never be created to order, but it is nonetheless possible to do a great deal with regard to it. But there is a kind of literature or literary work, and people can be put to work on it – for example, translations from every foreign language (*Free State*, 8/4/22).[9]

Many shared Ó Conaire's belief that translation was necessary to recharge Gaelic intellectual and literary energies. In 1922, Liam Ó Rinn ('L. Ó R.'), writing on 'Gádh le hAistrúchán / Nochtadh Anama an Náisiúin' (Need for translation / Expressing the soul of the nation) in the *Irish Independent*, stated:

> Let us not belittle books translated from foreign languages. If it were not for them we would not know that the French or the Spanish or the Chinese were not some kind of beasts. We have no monopoly of beauty and nobility. None of the civilised races of the earth is without some particular beauty in its literature. In order for us to experience it, we must put the books in which it is found into Irish. It will enrich and strengthen Irish (*II*, 10/3/22).[10]

Writing in 1930, one 'Criomhthann' provided an optimistic and cosmopolitan rationale for systematic and large-scale translation into Irish:

> A sign of the vitality of a language is the way it is able to put its own stamp on material that is in another language . . . There are few things more necessary to put vitality into the new literature in Irish than good translations of the work of the great authors in other countries (*Tír*, June 1930, 12).11

One of the more ambitious Gaelic translators, S. Labhrás Ua Súilleabháin, who published a full version of *Macbeth* in 1925, rooted his apologia for the task in just such a belief. Moreover, he was quite explicit about the changed circumstances in which the Gaelic translator was then working:

> At the particular stage which has now been reached in the cultivation and spread of our own language, I feel that the value of this phase of literary development – the translation of foreign classics – cannot well be over-estimated. In a little while, it is our hope, we shall be Irish-speaking, Irish-reading. We have at the moment, in the desks of all our National Schools, the boys and girls who will be the future writers of a new and vigorous school of modern Irish literature, and who will be the leaders of Irish thought. The avenue along which they will guide that literature which they will create must be determined to a great extent by the sources of information and cultural development which are available to them in the national language through which they are now being educated. Is it not a duty to present to them, in translation from the ancient, medieval, and modern classics, sources of inspiration which, while in no way adulterating their distinctively national outlook, cannot fail to be of value towards the attainment of that end which the whole nation has in view?[12]

Despite his prolixity, Ua Súilleabháin here raises two key issues, one empirical and the other merging into ideology, that were to define the ground rules for the new debate about translation in the Free State. Like all interested in the revival of the language in the 1920s and 1930s, he recognised that the Gaelicisation of Irish education initiated by the new government had changed the Gaelic literary scene in radical and challenging ways. The schools were now producing thousands of graduates per year at least potentially capable of reading work in Irish if such work was available and appealing to them. One of the earliest commentators to draw attention to these changed circumstances was James O'Grady, who wrote in 1922: 'This is a case where quantity will matter more than quality, a fact which should not induce contempt in the high-brow . . . We must start right away with translations of modern authors into Irish' (*YI*, 2/9/22).[13]

The shortage of appealing reading matter only worsened with time, and proponents of translation were driven to exasperation by what they saw as their opponents' pig-headed blindness to reality. In 1933, Ernest Blythe, the single most influential figure behind the original decision to make translation a central element in the work of An Gúm, declared: 'I do not see any other way to make enough books in Irish available in English-speaking Ireland and in the Gaeltacht for the young people who would be able to read them except to proceed with translation' (*II*, 28/3/33).[14] The following year, a writer in *The Blueshirt* was in full agreement: 'We understand that there is propaganda going around to put a stop to translation, but until there are educated writers available, we will have to go on with translation' (*Blueshirt*, 29/12/34).[15] León Ó Broin, the secretary of An Gúm's Publication Committee and himself a fairly prolific translator, stressed this same point concerning the absence of publishable manuscripts in Irish in his defence of the agency's translation policy in his autobiography *Just Like Yesterday*. Pointing out that when An Gúm was founded 'there was also a vast scarcity of reading matter, for books in Irish, other than elementary school texts, were regarded as economic monstrosities', he claimed that with the exception of some stories by Pádraic Ó Conaire, 'little in the nature of original writing came in otherwise, and that fact compelled us to turn to translations on a large scale sooner than we might otherwise have done.'[16]

In a 1929 editorial on 'The Need for Translation' in *The Star*, Micheál Mac Suibhne tried to give some idea of the magnitude of the challenge facing An Gúm. Having estimated that for all different tastes to be served in Irish some 2,000 novels in the language would be needed, and that Irish writers were then producing two or three good novels and four or five mediocre ones a year, Mac Suibhne worked out the maths and then held out some hope:

> At the rate of eight good and second-rate novels per annum it would require 250 years to collect 2,000 Irish novels. But while we are likely to have a very small group

> of people capable of writing original novels of any value, it should not be impossible to find within the next eight or ten years as many as a hundred translators who could in the course of twelve months give us very good Irish versions of three or four foreign novels each (*Star*, 17/8/29).[17]

Given such daunting projections and challenges, it is no wonder that Tomás Ó Deirg, the Fianna Fáil Minister for Education in whose department An Gúm was based, lashed out at the agency's critics in 1933:

> What choice do we have other than translation? Should we greatly diminish the number of books we are publishing now, and rely on the occasional worthwhile book of original composition that we get now and again in order to bring the new literature in Irish into being? (*Tír*, Sept.–Oct. 1933, 6).[18]

Many opponents of wide-scale translation would have answered Ó Deirg's rhetorical question in the affirmative, for they were by no means convinced that the potential supply of good original writing in Irish was so limited. In fact, the notion that An Gúm's emphasis on translation suppressed the creative instincts of a whole generation of would-be Gaelic novelists, story writers, and dramatists was the principal article of faith underlying the criticism of the policy and practices of the agency in the 1920s and 1930s, and ever since.

The most forceful advocates of this view were the brothers Ó Grianna, both of whom felt their genius had been thus stifled, and one of whom, Seosamh, had a legitimate case. But they were not alone in their opinion. Many other writers, most but not all native speakers of the language, accused the government through An Gúm of ignoring new Irish work in favor of translation from abroad.[19] For example, writing in 1931, Annraoi Saidléar complained:

> We have too strong a leaning towards translation ... Translation is a good thing, but let us understand that it is only a stopgap. I fear that writers who have creative talent will turn to translation as an easy way to make easy money. Some of them have already done so. It is a bad sign. The other tender young plant will be killed unless we are far kinder to it (Enniscorthy *Echo*, 8/8/31).[20]

Writing the following month, Peadar Ó Dubhda lamented:

> It is said that many of the best writers and the best creators of stories have been working on translation for a while. This is a great pity, for it is certain that that will affect the literary talent they already have. It would be far better for the literature of the language to allow these men to work on original composition and to pay them for it (*Ultach*, Oct. 1931, 4).[21]

Liam Ó Rinn seems to have shared some of Ó Dubhda's reservations, writing in 1932:

> If our Gaelic writers are always working on translation, there is a great danger that whatever talent for original writing they have that has not already been stifled will atrophy altogether. Their minds have long been shaped by the work of translation so that they soon will not be able to do any other kind of work, even if they try (*UIrman*, 22/10/32).[22]

Less restrained was the anonymous critic for *An Gaedheal* who accompanied his glowing welcome for the publication of *Peig* with a blast at An Gúm's translation policy:

> Isn't there a great difference between it [*Peig*] and the heap of rubbishy translations that come to us from An Gúm? Would it not be far better to put aside for writers from the Gaeltacht some of the money that is spent on a futile enterprise? If that were done, original stories would not be as scarce as they are (*Gaedheal*, Aug. 1936, 4).[23]

These writers were, in effect, challenging a frequent assumption of those in favour of the translation policy, the belief that translation plays an important role in the normal evolution of a national literature. This belief was given forthright expression by 'W. L.' in a 1927 review of An tAthair Benedict's translation of the autobiography of St Theresa of the Child Jesus: 'If a modern Irish literature is to be built up, there must, side by side with original work, be a continuous effort to translate into Gaelic books of world-repute like this biography' (*II*, 3/1/27). Micheál Mac Suibhne agreed, writing in 1929 that 'almost all great modern literature owed its origin to a period of translation from foreign masterpieces, and we suggest that nothing better could happen our Irish writers than to go to school for a while in this way' (*Star*, 12/10/29). Liam Ó Rinn stressed that the creation of a vital national literature would be a gradual process and one in which translation had a major role to play:

> I would advise the people who say that there is a great deal of unreality in the work of translation to have patience. Rome was not built in a day, nor have I ever heard that a national literature grew in a single decade . . . It is an enormous task to reshape a language that was neglected for three hundred years so that it would be able for the work that the normal civilised languages of Europe do, and that in such a way that one would not notice any artificiality or unreality in the way it would do the work (*UIrman*, 15/7/33).[24]

For proponents of the policy, translation was, then, a necessary recourse given the current state of the Irish language and its literature, especially at a time when the number of potential readers was exponentially outpacing the number of potential writers. Once again, Ó Rinn stressed that translation on a large scale was to be no more than a temporary expedient in the development of the new Gaelic literature, writing in 1934:

> It is amazing how much translation is being done, but that does not mean the language is growing out of the native force that is in it. It is merely like the doctor's cure for the sick child or the assistance of foreign engineers to create large projects for a small country so weak after oppression that it would be too difficult for it to do anything worthwhile on its own. (*UI*, 24/2/34).[25]

Equally convinced of the necessity of wide-scale translation at this stage, but more concerned about its potential dangers, was Seán Ó Ciarghusa, who, in a long serialised essay on translation in the *Catholic Bulletin* in 1927, wrote:

> I fear that there are people who would say that there is no benefit for the Irish language, but rather the opposite, in translation. That harm rather than good will come of it. I am not sure, but I think that we must translate whether I like it or not or whether it is good or bad for us or the Irish language because we have no choice.[26]

Most Gaels who gave any thought to the question were more optimistic, believing that in addition to exposing Gaelic authors and readers to the wider world, translation could offer some very practical and immediate benefits to the language and its literature. On the most basic level, many felt that translation could provide the quickest solution to a problem that had bedevilled the revival movement from the start, that is the lack of an adequate and generally accepted vocabulary with which to discuss that wide range of modern subjects on which the language had been all but silent for three centuries.[27] Writing in *The Father Mathew Record* in 1935, the Capuchin An t-Athair Micheál credited An Gúm's translation programme for much of this progress: 'One thing that this scheme of the Government's does is that it translates many technical terms that we lack in Irish, and the children will have all these terms naturally' (*FMR*, Jan. 1935, 62).[28]

For others, the judicious practice of translation did more than merely extend the word-store of the language. It could also teach aesthetic lessons, helping the would-be Gaelic author to discover a subject and develop a style. While at the time unenthusiastic about translation *per se*, Micheál Breathnach did, in a 1931 lecture to secondary school teachers, stress the practical benefits of the craft: 'Translation will do good by putting vigour and strength into the language and giving our writers an example of the kind of literature that is being written in other languages, but apart from that it offers no benefit'

(*II*, 8/4/31).[29] In a thoughtful piece on the whole question of translation in 1932, Seán Ó Ciosáin focused on what writers could learn from the practice: 'Translation is a good device to teach the craft of writing to the young writers if they have a talent for writing. We all know that Shakepeare spent long years reworking old dramas before he composed a drama of his own invention' (*IP*, 19/3/32).[30]

Many Gaelic intellectuals believed translation would offer even greater benefits to the language and its literature as those doing the work took on more sophisticated and challenging texts. In a review of the first part of An tAthair Peadar Ua Laoghaire's *Sgéalaidheachta as an mBíobla Naomhtha* (Stories from the Holy Bible), Liam Ó Rinn wrote:

> I do not think that we will have any literature that we can compare with the great literatures of the world until we have examples in our own language from which to learn the craft, that is, translations of some of the great noble works and of many of the works that are not so great or so noble (*YI*, 9/12/22).[31]

In a lengthy 1926 review of Ua Súilleabháin's translation of *Macbeth*, 'Aodh' was quite critical of individual points in Ua Súilleabháin's work, but had high praise for what he saw him as trying to do:

> Mr O'Sullivan has done one thing, and that is a splendid thing: He has broken new ground – in Ireland! He has shown that it is time for us, however late in the day, to rise above the literary level we have maintained for so long and aim at something higher, to see whether at long last we can at least hope to some day achieve the literary level of the world in which we live (*CB*, Feb. 1926, 215).[32]

Three years later, one 'D. P.' praised the work of An tAthair Pádraig de Brún in similar terms for the same reason. Reviewing de Brún's translation *Oidiopús i gColón* (Oedipus at Colonus), 'D. P.' wrote:

> Why is it that Dr Browne's work of infusing new ideas into Gaelic literature has not been acclaimed as a much-needed service nobly done? The reason, I think, is that while the service in itself was long overdue, the brilliant manner in which it was rendered was far in advance of what we in our day could have hoped for or expected. The fact is Dr Browne is far ahead of his time (*IR*, Aug. 1929, 636).

Many Gaels wanted more than high challenge and inspiration from translation, believing that such work could provide Gaelic writers with proven models for kinds of writing, even whole genres, that for various reasons had never been developed in Irish. Seán Ó Ciarghusa underscored this point in his essay on translation for the *Catholic Bulletin*: 'Another benefit that comes from translation is that it sometimes remedies a deficiency in a language' (Tairbhe eile thagann de bhárr tionntuighthe, go ndeineann sé easnamh bhíonn ar theangain do léigheas uaireannta).[33] Ó Ciarghusa had drama in the forefront of his mind here, and this was, as we will see later, the non-native genre that virtually all Gaels felt could benefit from a judicious recourse to translation. Other intellectuals drew attention to a wide range of kinds and registers of writing that Gaelic authors should begin to cultivate through an apprenticeship in translation. For example, in an essay entitled 'An t-Aistriúchán' (Translation), Cearbhall Ua Dálaigh wrote in 1930:

> The Irish language has become rusty from being out in the air and the bad weather so long. We will not be able to set it to work as we wish without some translation. It is a long time since the standard learned subjects have been treated in Irish, and that is why it is clumsy and crude today. There is great need of translation; let books of philosophy, history, art, and learning be translated into Irish, as well as books of stories, adventures, and poems. Let us have them all, and more if possible (*Nation*, 29/11/30).[34]

There were, however, those who felt that even such obvious and important benefits were overshadowed by the dangers inherent in wide-scale translation. Many believed that An Gúm's emphasis on translation was not only unnecessary, but also unnatural in that it threatened to abort what had been a slow but steady growth in the quantity and quality of Gaelic writing since the beginning of the Revival, an evolutionary process they believed was certain to continue and ramify, especially as more native speakers were properly educated and took their rightful place in the intellectual and literary life of the nation. Writing in 1931, one such native speaker, Seosamh Mac Grianna, analysed what he felt were the assumptions underlying An Gúm's work:

> There is no literature in Irish worth reading.
> We have no Gaelic writer worthy of being called a writer.
> Everything of any value is across the Irish Sea.
> It is easier to find readers for bad Irish than for good Irish.
> There are twenty men who cannot write literature who can translate (*IP*, 13/11/31).[35]

And one can sense the exasperation behind the words of Peadar Ó Dubhda in 1931:

> I would say that whoever first thought of advancing our literature through translation had the same warped notions as the people who try to learn music through opera. Neither of these things will grow from the exotic (*Ultach*, Dec. 1931, 3).[36]

Just as emphatic on this point was Cathal Mac an Bháird in a 1932 essay on 'Leabharthaí agus Léightheoracht' (Books and reading):

> Many books in Irish have been issued by the Government of late, but most of them are only translations from English and other languages. In my opinion, literature never grows out of translations, and these books now being issued do not benefit the language throughout the country. If the Irish language grows at all, it will have to do so naturally, and as I see it, there is nothing at all as unnatural as hearing or reading a story in Irish when that story is set in London, Berlin, or in the capital city of France (*GR*, Feb. 1932, 285).[37]

Exotic settings were for many Gaelic intellectuals the least of the problems that flowed from An Gúm's translation policy. Virtually all opponents of the scheme stressed the danger to the language of widespread translation, particularly from English, although some, like Stephen McKenna, would make an exception for the work of Irish writers of English.[38] Such a fear of rampant *Béarlachas* (Anglicism) had, of course, been at the heart of Gaelic suspicion of translation since the days of Fathers Henebry and Ua Laoghaire. The remarkable expansion in the amount being brought into Irish from English could only exacerbate this concern. Even a proponent of translation like Liam Ó Rinn regularly chastised writers for lapses into *Béarlachas*, although it should be noted that he was every bit as hard on creative writers guilty of a similar linguistic or imaginative deficiency.[39] Another proponent of translation, Seán Ó Ciarghusa, was less confident. Having acknowledged his reservations about renderings from English 'lest the Irish language be corrupted' (ar eagla truaillighthe na Gaedhilge), he admitted that there was no avoiding such translations, but that both writers and readers should be alert to the attendant dangers:

> We must all, therefore, writers and readers that we are, understand the craft or art of translation so that we can recognise and avoid Béarlachas . . . If the Irish language is worth saving, let it be saved in its purity and its authenticity. We have enough of the English 'Brogue' without adding a Gaelic 'Brogue' as well.[40]

And in one of his first forays into public controversy, Máirtín Ó Cadhain in 1930 blasted the translation of *Dr Jekyll and Mr Hyde* by Feardorcha Ó Conaill ('Conall Cearnach'), writing:

> It is easy to recognise that this translation is *Béarlachas* – out and out Béarlachas from start to finish . . . I do not think that there is a bit of dialogue from the beginning of the book to the end that is proper native Irish . . . This translation is like putting homespun cloth on a black man and then pretending he is an Aranman (Stoc, Apr. 1930, p 4).[41]

Nor was linguistic corruption the only danger. In the 1920s and 1930s it became, as we have seen, the core dogma of the Gaelic creed that there was such a thing as *Gaelachas*, that it could be defined with some precision, and that it was under relentless assault from enemies both external and internal, malicious and misguided, and thus in dire need of protection. Those of nativist bent were the most insistent and impassioned adherents of this view, with Séamus Ó Grianna as their most vocal and acerbic spokesman. But most progressives also shared the commitment to *Gaelachas*, even if they were far less clear about its nature and less convinced of its fragility. In such a climate, wide-scale translation, the deliberate, state-sponsored infusion into the language and its literature of foreign ideas, images, and attitudes was bound to be controversial. For some, the dangers they saw as inextricable from this aspect of translation might simply be too great to risk.

Seán Ó Ciarghusa raised this question of the danger of corruption both ethnic and ethical – the two terms were often well-nigh synonomous in some Gaelic circles at the time – in his 1927 essay, arguing that the greatest threat posed by translation was

> the philosophy of the first language being entirely different from the philosophy of the second language, – Foreign instead of Gaelic, Pagan instead of Christian. Translation from the like of that is poison in the veins of the second language and no one knows how far the effects of its swallowing that poison will go.[42]

Daniel Corkery, while acknowledging that translation had a role to play in the development of a native literature, nonethless urged caution, stressing that indiscriminate borrowings from the literature of other cultures could threaten precisely those qualities that would make that native literature native:

> I am not unwilling to accept translations from other languages. But I am unwilling to put standards from another literature above the standards we already have in our literature . . . If, as a result of our misunderstanding of those translations, we neglect the native manner; if we imitate them; if we bring into Irish the pseudo-dignity of which the whole world is weary, we will have little chance of writing classics in it [Irish] (*Humanitas*, June 1930, 6).[43]

Seosamh Mac Grianna wrote in similar vein in 1931:

> Now there is no harm in translating a German book or a French book or an English book into Irish. Nor is there any harm in a German or a Frenchman or an Englishman coming to Ireland to live. But if all the Germans in Germany or all the Frenchmen in France or all the Englishmen in England come to Ireland to live, no Irishman at all will have a place in his native land (*IP*, 3/12/31).[44]

In a lecture to a student organisation at University College Galway in February 1936, Máirtín Ua Flaithbheartaigh drew the attention of his listeners to the special dangers translation posed for new readers of the language in the Gaeltacht, which he called the only true home of 'the birthright of the nation' (ceart oighreachta an náisiúin):

> When the Department of Education distributed books in the Gaeltacht, the books were no bad thing, but it did harm the young people who were reading about and absorbing the traits of peoples and places that they did not understand in an Irish with which they did not identify. Gaelic learning is not the better for the translations (*An t-Irisleabhar* [UCG], 1935–6, 19).[45]

And in a 1939 books column in the *Cork Weekly Examiner*, an anonymous critic stated:

> It is true that a great load of books have now been translated from English over a long period, so that one would say that we are smothered by Anglicism [Sasanachas]. There is nothing in these books but foreign customs and a foreign spirit (*Cork Weekly Examiner*, 7/1/39).[46]

There was nothing abstract or hypothetical about this concern. Those voicing such fears had specific translations in mind, for An Gúm had quickly issued a fairly large number of publications, with translations far outweighing original work. For instance, in its report for 1936, An Gúm revealed that of the books it had published to date, translations accounted for 82 of the 100 novels, 54 of the 95 plays, and seven of the 13 biographies. Its total output of translations at this time was 214 titles, of which 170 were from English (*Bonaventura*, Summer 1937, 174).[47] When one considers that in all probability a fair percentage of Gaelic versions of Continental titles were actually based on English-language versions of those works, one gets an even clearer sense of the magnitude of the problem.[48] Nor was that all. Even more distressing than the sheer quantity of titles drawn from English was what many perceived to be the lamentable quality of more than a few of those books.[49] Nativist or progressive, suspicious of translation or supportive, critic after critic heaped abuse on what An Gúm was actually producing, dismissing the bulk of the publications as 'trivial little books in English' (leabhra beaga suaracha Béarla) (*Guth na nGaedheal*, Féile Pádraig 1935, 14); 'books entirely unworthy of the attention of Irishmen and women' (*Irish Freedom*, Aug. 1936, 4); 'the moribund English-language literature of the last century' (litríocht Bhéarla leath-mharbh na haoise atá caite) (*UI*, 8/2/36); 'mere translations or imitations of an inferior kind of sensational English literature' (*CB*, Apr. 1936, 346); 'third-rate English novels' (*Leader*, 12/12/36); 'stupid translations which had an Anglicised or

American outlook' (Dundalk *Examiner*, 26/3/38); or, flatly, 'British imperialist trash' (*An Phoblacht*, 9/7/32).

We have already noted the nationalist grounds on which such translations were criticised, but there were also sound practical reasons for questioning the wisdom of translating so many English titles. However they felt about the fact, Gaelic intellectuals and activists knew that all literate Irish people could read English, and so would presumably prefer to read books written in that language in the original. From this perspective, An Gúm's provision of so many translations from English was quite simply a waste of time and scarce resources, a point underscored time and again by critics of the agency. For example, an anonymous reviewer of Seán Mac Maoláin's translation of E. C. Bentley's detective novel *Trent's Last Case* argued:

> It is a famous story, and many a person has read it. Why, then, translate it into Irish? Although the truth is bitter, this much is true – and it will remain true for a while – that the ordinary person, the schoolchild for example, will not read a story in Irish if he can easily lay his hand on the original story in English (*TCNÍ*, Nov. 1934, 262).[50]

Similarly, in his review of *Oileán an Uathbháis*, Proinnsias Ó Brógáin's translation of the English suspense novel *Island of Terror* by 'Sapper', one 'E.' wrote in 1938:

> The people who like the terrifying 'thriller' will be delighted by this book. It is an attempt, most likely, to get the flighty young reading Irish, but I myself don't think that the attempt will succeed, because the same young are more likely to read a book of the sort in English and it is very easy to get it. It is a pity for writers of Irish to be wasting time with translations of this sort (*Bonaventura*, Spring 1938, 213).[51]

Some apparently saw the problem as even more serious. Addressing a 1938 Gaelic League convention on a motion from the London branch calling for more translations from Continental languages and fewer from English, Micheál Ó Maoláin said 'that if officials who approved of some of the translations were in any other country they would be sent to jail' (*II*, 23/4/38).

How accurate was the perception that most of An Gúm's translations were of second-rate English titles? As we have seen, there exist publication records that do indeed confirm that a disproportionate percentage of An Gúm's translations were from English, although to be fair there were also some intriguing versions of work from other languages as well. Thus we find An tAthair Pádraig de Brún's translations of Sophocles, Euripides, Plutarch, and Racine; Domhnall Ó Mathghamhna's versions of several classical texts;[52] as well as George Thomson's translation of Plato;[53] Cormac Ó Cadhlaigh's of Caesar;[54] versions of Turgenev's 'prose poems' by Liam Ó Rinn;[55] of stories by Tolstoy and Pushkin by An tAthair Gearóid Ó Nualláin;[56] *Gearrscéalta Tcheckov: Cuid a hAon* (The short stories of Chekhov: Part one) and *The Cherry Orchard* translated by Maighréad Nic Mhaicín;[57] plays from Spanish translated by Tomás Ó hEighneacháin and Máirtín Ó Cadhain;[58] a Gaelic *Pinocchio* in the Irish of Pádraig Ó Buachalla;[59] a handful of titles from German;[60] Gearóid Ó Lochlainn's translations of Ibsen's *Enemy of the People* and of *Hercules* by another Norwegian playwright, Adolf Recke;[61] and a large number of Gaelic renderings of stories, plays, and the odd novel from French by many different translators, of whom Risteárd Ó Foghludha ('Fiachra Éilgeach') was probably the most prolific.[62] All such translations were, however, merely exotic exceptions to the English rule.[63]

The next question is whether all or most of the English titles given a Gaelic incarnation were ephemeral and / or trashy. Some certainly were not. For example, we have Gaelic versions of Shakespeare's *Macbeth* (tr. Labhrás Ua Súilleabháin) and *Coriolanus* (tr. Liam Ó Briain),[64] as well as of books like Bunyan's *Pilgrim's Progress* (tr. Ernest Joynt);[65] Scott's *Ivanhoe* (tr. Seosamh Mac Grianna) and *The Talisman* (tr. Niall Ó Domhnaill); Emily Brontë's *Wuthering Heights* (tr. Seán Ó Ciosáin); Dickens's *David Copperfield* (tr. Seán Ó Ruadháin) and *A Tale of Two Cities* (tr. Seán Mac Maoláin);[66] Eliot's *Silas Marner* (tr. Aindrias Ó Baoighill); four of Conrad's novels or novellas, *The Nigger of the 'Narcissus'*, *Typhoon*, *Amy Foster*, and *Almayer's Folly* (tr. Seosamh Mac Grianna); Jack London's *The Call of the Wild* and *White Fang* (tr. Niall Ó Domhnaill and Tadhg Ó Curnáin respectively); and individual stories by Hawthorne (trans. Pádraig Ó Bróithe).[67] Two things stand out here. In the first place, with the exception of Conrad, these are safe, schoolroom classics. We find Irish versions of none of the modern masters of the English language – no Woolf, Forster, Lawrence, Hemingway, Fitzgerald, Stein, or Faulkner. In the second place, even what classics there were were far overshadowed by books and authors long forgotten, the sort of writers alluded to by Seamus Heaney in his poem on the language revival, 'A Shooting Script':

> Then voices over, in different Irishes,
> Discussing translation jobs and rates per line;
> Like nineteenth century milestones in grass verges,
> Occurrence of names like R. M. Ballantyne.[68]

One can add to Heaney's R. M. Ballantyne, names like F. W. Crofts,[69] W. H. Davies,[70] J. S. Fletcher,[71] H. Rider Haggard,[72] A. E. W. Mason,[73] Helen Mathers,[74] Eden Phillpotts,[75] Captain Mayne Reid,[76] and W. Clark Russell,[77] all of whom An Gúm made available to readers of Irish.

Many Gaels felt that it wasn't their job to worry about the state of contemporary English fiction or to sort out the Conrads from the Phillpotts. For them, the logical solution to the problem was to avoid translation from English to the greatest extent possible. In a 1935 review of three translations from An Gúm, Seán Ó Catháin wrote:

> I have often recommended in these pages that the Publication Committee try to make available translations from languages other than English. If the goal the Committee has set itself is to provide books that will lure people to reading Irish, translating books in English is of little use (*TCNÍ*, Apr. 1935, 91).[78]

According to Liam Ó Rinn, Stephen McKenna was in full agreement on this point, having told Ó Rinn 'I would prefer that our writers translate from any language at all except English when they want to put true literature into Irish' (gur maith liom go n-aistreodh ár scríbhneoirí ó theangain ar bith ach an Béarla nuair a bheadh fonn orthu fíor-litríocht a chur i nGaeilge). But interestingly enough, unlike the 'G. B.' quoted previously, he felt that high English literature was much more of a threat to the language than was the ephemeral general and escapist writing from which he believed the language would be compelled to draw heavily for the foreseeable future.[79]

The problem, of course, was how to put into practice a more cosmopolitan translation policy. There was no lack of good will here, for the demand for translations from languages other than English was both consistent and insistent throughout the period. For example, in 1930, Séamus Ó Casaide, the editor of the *Irish Book Lover*, asked: 'Is it not time, and high time, for us to have the major books of French, Latin, German, Spanish, and so on available in Irish? You writers who are working on books, can't you see the gaps in the wall?' (*IBL*, May–June 1930, 65).[80] Three years later, Ó Rinn devoted a thoughtful column to this question under the title 'Saothrú na Gaedhilge / Teangmháil leis an Eoraip / Aon-Teangachas in Obair Aistriúcháin' (The cultivation of the Irish language / Contact with Europe / Monolingualism in translation work), in which he wrote:

> It will do ourselves and the Irish language good to become acquainted with the people of Europe, with their customs, their mind, their heart, and their soul, through translation. There is a great deal of literature throughout Europe that has never been translated into English, and it would be better for even what there is available in that language to come to us through our own language with our own native colouring on it (*UIrman*, 22/7/33).[81]

Donn Piatt had developed this last point in some detail the previous year in *An Phoblacht*, seeing Irish reliance on English translations of foreign work as a mark of cultural servitude: 'As long as we depend on English editions of anything – which France does not, Spain does not, Catalonia does not, Germany of course does not, we are still in the bog, still an intellectual province of England' (*An Phoblacht*, 30/7/32). By far the most ambitious in his ideas about the future of Gaelic translation was Ernest Blythe, who offered the following vision in 1936:

> Indeed things should be so arranged that a translation of every outstanding new book published – French, German, Italian, Spanish, Dutch, Swedish or Polish – would appear in Irish at least as soon as in English. To this end a fair number of young Irish writers should be encouraged and assisted to master a Continental language (*II*, 28/12/36).[82]

Other writers, doubtless just as eager to escape Piatt's bog, were more specific in their hopes as to how translation could help. There were, for example, specific calls for translation from German (*IMN*, 1930, 89); Russian,[83] Old Norse,[84] Spanish (*Rockwell Annual*, 1929, 46), and Yiddish (*UIrman*, 19/8/33). In addition, many stressed the need for Gaelic versions of Greek and Roman classics, a fair number of which were, as we have seen, provided at the time. Indeed in his *Laidean tré Gaedhilg*, Fearrgus Ó Nualláin saw translation from the classics as the best corrective for the obsessive linguistic provincialism of the time:

> Literary art finds its natural expression in dialect. Scientific expression makes inevitably for a *koine dialekte*; it is conventional, not artistic; it is analytic, not organic; it is complex, not composite; it will not be deterred from using a word or phrase because such a word or phrase was never heard in use among the speakers of its own parish, or even its own province. Translation from the classics will probably have more effect than anything else in evolving a standard dialect in Irish.[85]

More pragmatic were the regular calls for the translation of plays for the new Gaelic stage. Throughout the 1920s and 1930s, An Comhar Drámaidheachta in Dublin, and after 1928 Taibhdhearc na Gaillimhe in the west, were struggling to build up both a repertoire of plays and an audience of loyal playgoers for theatre in Irish. With a mere handful of original scripts available and no real prospect of a meaningful increase in that number in the immediate future, both groups, as well as Gaelic League branches and local companies, turned with varying degrees of enthusiasm to translation to lure and hold an audience. As early as 1925, an anonymous contributor to *An Branar* wrote: 'We would like to recommend to An Comhar that they hire two or three people with a wide knowledge of European literature to make out a list of suitable plays in English, French, Spanish, etc. and then to get them translated' (*Branar*, Apr. 1925, 99).[86] One 'Óganach' offered a compelling ideological argument for the translation of plays, claiming that given the lack of 'native examples' (somplaí dúthchais) and the urgent need to break 'the grip of English' (greim an Bhéarla), translations were the only available means to put the language on stage at once (*FL*, 19/2/25).[87]

Risteárd Ó Foghludha was equally pragmatic in a rather testy defence of his own efforts in this area the same year:

> The work must be kept going from month to month, but no one will bother with translation or with adaptation as soon as we have enough good original Irish plays on hand. Until then, grumbling is not what Irish speakers should be giving us, but work, something, as we know, that many of them find distasteful (*FL*, 18/4/25).[88]

León Ó Broin, himself both an original playwright and a successful translator of plays, agreed, urging those Gaels interested in the theatre to seek out stageworthy scripts wherever they could be found, and arguing that translation, for the moment at least, offered the best hope for such scripts.[89] With fledgling Gaelic dramatists in mind, he wrote in *Fáinne an Lae* in 1926: 'I would, however, advise them not to put together an original play until they have translated or read carefully and thoughtfully a good number of foreign plays.' And he offered the following advice concerning where those plays could be found: 'We must go in search of good foreign plays: plays in German, French, Italian, etc.' According to Ó Broin, only if the potential translator were ignorant of these languages should he or she turn to plays in English (*FL*, Dec. 1926, 4).[90] The most influential figure in Gaelic theatre in the 1920s and 1930s, playwright, translator, producer, director, and actor Gearóid Ó Lochlainn, knew from experience that there was no way to avoid translation, nor did he believe there was any reason to. Ó Lochlainn wrote in 1929:

> To be sure we should assist our Gaelic dramatists and give primacy to their work if it is any good at all. There are, however, few of them at the moment, and therefore we will be dependent on a good number of translations to fill out the year's schedule for a long time still.

For Ó Lochlainn, this situation was by no means disastrous: 'But even if an abundance of original plays in Irish were available, it would be right always to leave some room on the schedule for translations of worthwhile plays from other countries. Competition leads to excellence' (*Star*, 20/7/29).[91]

The advent of radio only made the need for Gaelic performance pieces more acute, for many realised that even what few Gaelic plays existed were not appropriate for broadcast. In its 1936 report *An Gaedheal agus an Rádió*, the Gaelic League discussed the provisional role of translation in the creation of radio drama:

> In order to fill the gap so that we will have enough suitable original plays in Irish, there is no harm in translating plays from other languages . . . Of course that will only be a stopgap until we have suitable original plays of our own.[92]

Most succinct on this whole question was Seán Ó Ciarghusa, who wrote in 1925: 'We must "go on the stage" although we have no plays for it except translations' (*Sguab*, Feb. 1925, 277).[93]

Others, however, were less sanguine, and dissenting voices were raised, especially when, as not infrequently occurred, an evening's bill of Gaelic drama consisted entirely of translations. In a 1924 essay on 'Contemporary Literature / The Growth of Irish Drama', 'Theo' declared:

> At this stage, I should think that translation of the dramatic masterpieces of foreign countries is to be deprecated. This process will have the effect of unfavourably, if not ruinously, influencing the development of an Irish theatre on purely national lines (*Leader*, 20/12/24).

Micheál Breathnach agreed, writing in 1926: 'I would not hold it against An Comhar to give us one from abroad, or two, perhaps, if they were under pressure, but I would say they went too far when they filled the entire programme with the work of the man yonder.' Moreover, Breathnach knew exactly what was wrong with what he saw as indiscriminate reliance on translation:

> Another thing, none of the three plays accorded well with the spirit and mind of Gaels. The Foreigner who would come to Dublin and would go to a performance by An Comhar hoping that he would see the National Drama of Ireland would be baffled and disappointed, for all there was of *Gaelachas* the other night was the language itself (*FL*, Nov. 1926, 1).[94]

Seoirse Ó Broin was in full agreement, stating categorically in a published debate with León Ó Broin, Ó Lochlainn, and Liam Ó Briain: 'It is my opinion that however much translation is done, however much dramatists rely on the work of the foreigners, however much the person yonder is imitated, so much weaker will be the growth of Gaelic drama itself' (*Star*, 27/7/29).[95] 'Glúndubh' was more moderate in his comments after attending the first Féile Dhrámuíochta na Sgol (Schools' drama festival): 'It is not right to hinder a dramatist from searching for material wherever he wishes, but along with that freedom come duties. He should not go abroad in search of material until the Nation is strong and truly Gaelic' (*Éireannach*, 23/6/34).[96] In an editorial provoked by An Taibhdhearc's production of Aodh Mac Dhubháin's translation of R. C. Sherriff's First World War play *Journey's End*, the *Irish Press* warned of the dangers of such translation before the Gaelic soul of the nation had been restored to its full vigour, concluding with an unexpected variant of an arch-nativist theme: 'But the goal of the work of the Irish language is not for us to have our own language to express a foreign mind. It would be seven times better for us to keep our own mind uncorrupted and to cast away the Irish language' (*IP*, 7/9/31).[97]

This debate at times grew quite heated among those most concerned, so that we read in a May 1930 report in *The Star*:

> I hear that there is a bloody and merciless war on among the people in charge of Taibhdhearc na Gaillimhe, because – if what I hear is true – the majority of the Committee think that it is foreign, that it is barbaric, to translate any foreign plays at all (*Star*, 3/5/30).[98]

One 'Ball Geal' went even further in an attack on An Comhar Drámaidheachta in 1932:

> Instead of making an effort to get Irish plays and produce them, they supported a propaganda that aimed at killing nationality. Insipid foreign dramas that never appealed to Irish sentiment were staged, and, what was worse, were accepted as contributions to the literature of drama, though they will never be utilised as an asset to revive national drama in Ireland (*Leader*, 5/11/32).

On purely pragmatic grounds, however, such an extreme position was untenable, and the majority of Gaelic theatre enthusiasts welcomed plays from the wider world with little hesitation. For some, the primary justification for translation was that it provided would-be playwrights with proven models to study and emulate. Thus in 1931, 'C.' wrote in a review of An Comhar Drámaidheachta's production of a Chekhov play translated by Mac Liammóir:

> There is no doubt at all that it is good sense for the people of An Comhar and every other group of their sort to put foreign dramas on stage for, if they are well produced, they will provide an excellent pattern for dramatists, inspiring them to do their best (*Leader*, 9/5/31).[99]

Translations were even more important from the point of view of the audiences Gaelic theatre companies were so eager to attract. Without them, it is hard to see how potential playgoers could ever have expected to see much new at all in any given season. Not surprisingly then, it was the audience that was foremost in the minds of many of those interested in theatre in Irish when they thought about the whole question of translation. For example, in a 1931 piece in which he acknowledged he was attacking 'the territories of the angels' (críocha na n-aingeal), Tomás Ó hEighneacháin, himself a translator of plays from the Spanish of Sierra and Quintero, wrote in the *Irish Independent*:

> It is the audience that An Comhar Drámaidheachta must think of most, and they must produce dramas that the majority of them will like. If there are not more original dramas being produced, the reason is that the public far prefer good foreign dramas to clumsy native dramas (*II*, 11/12/31).[100]

That he had a valid point is evident from a 1933 audience survey conducted by An Comhar Drámaidheachta in Dublin. Asked to name the three plays produced by An Comhar they had most enjoyed and would most like to see again, audience members gave pride of place to three translations: the Gaelic versions of *Le Bourgeois Gentilhomme* and *Les Fourberies de Scapin* by Molière, and *She Stoops to Conquer* by Goldsmith.[101]

At any rate, translations, some of them quite interesting, unexpected, competent, and apparently stageworthy became a staple of the Gaelic theatre throughout our period. Irish-speaking audiences were able to see and hear, in some cases before their English-speaking compatriots, plays by Molière, Chekhov, Gogol, Ibsen, Adolf Recke, G. Martinez Sierra, Eugene O'Neill, Sacha Guitry, Henri Ghéon, S. and J. Alvarez Quintero, Carlo Goldoni, Eça de Queiroz,[102] and George M. Cohen, as well as a selection of Anglo-Irish plays by Goldsmith, Shaw, Yeats, Synge, Gregory, Lennox Robinson, Paul Vincent Carroll, and T. C. Murray.[103]

In a 1934 piece in *An t-Éireannach*, 'Droichead Átha' posed a question that had long puzzled some on the literary side of the language revival:

> Why are the principal treasures of Welsh literature not translated to Irish. It would be no wonder that there would be a kind of mutual bond and sympathy between their literature and our own, for it is the spirit of the Celts that is expressed in both of them (*Éireannach*, 1/9/34).[104]

Doubtless the most striking proof of the superficiality of Gaelic awareness of cultural developments in Wales was the absolute silence in Irish literary circles with regard to the work of two major artists who were reshaping Welsh literature at precisely this time. I have found no references at all in Gaelic periodicals to the work of Kate Roberts, while Saunders Lewis seems to have been known solely as an ultra-nationalist militant.[105]

If linguistic and cultural misunderstandings continued to plague Irish relations with fellow Celts, and in particular with the Welsh, Irish interest in the closer Celtic kin in Scotland became warmer, better informed, and more actively reciprocal in the 1920s and 1930s. To be sure, there were still those who seemed to believe that their discovery of a shared Irish-Scottish Gaelicism was newsworthy. In a 1923 review of An tAthair Gearóid Ó Nualláin's translation of three stories from Scots Gaelic, one 'C. M.' wrote:

> The Gaelic people here in Ireland should know that they have friends abroad, that we should renew our friendship with them, that they can help us in this fight for the Irish language and that we can help them. Is not Irish our shared language – are we not both Gaels? (*Sguab*, Mar. 1923, 121).[106]

In 1934, Sorcha Ní Ghuairim could see a sign of hope in the strong Irish representation at the Mòd in Inverness:

> It proves that the Gaels of Ireland and Scotland are getting acquainted and learning about each other, and that they are not denying their relationship with each other. And why would they? Are we not one and the same? It is my hope that it will not be long until the two Gaeltachts get a better acquaintance with and knowledge of each other, and that the day will come when each of them will be working as one for the heritage of the Gaels, language, music, and all that goes with them (*Éireannach*, 3/10/36).[107]

On the other hand, some Irish Gaels, while sympathetic with their Scots kinfolk in the cause, insisted that Ireland take the leadership role in any partnership. In 1936, A. Parsons wrote:

> It would be cruel, as well as ungenerous, to crow over Scotland when the darkness is descending over her national culture, but it is well within the bounds of possibility that Scottish students may before long be compelled to come to Ireland to learn their national language (*II*, 14/9/36).

Siobhán Ní Shúilleabháin developed the idea at some length the following year:

> There is no doubt that our efforts and our success here are having, and will have, a great influence on the minds and policy of the Scottish Gaedheals. Many of them have studied the language development in Ireland closely. They look to us to blaze the trail to Gaelic nationhood. They point out that we have freedom of action, and the necessary resources at our command (*Leader*, 16/9/37).

Some Gaels drew the attention of their colleagues to literature in Scots Gaelic. Reviewing John Lorne Campbell's *Duain Ghaidhealach mu Bhliadhna Thearlaich / Highland Songs of the Forty-Five* for *Béaloideas*, 'G. Ó M.' (Gerard Murphy) wrote: 'Study of Scots Gaelic literature and ways of life, because they are so akin to the literature and ways of life of Irish Gaeldom, should be regarded as an essential part of this cultivation of our past' (*Béaloideas*, June 1937, 146–7). On the whole, however, what discussion there was of that literature remained quite uninformed throughout this period. In his 1933 history of the Irish language, Donn Piatt encouraged the Irish to read more about Scotland and more in Scots Gaelic, suggesting the journal *Scottish*

Gaelic Studies as a good place to start. This was no new interest on Piatt's part, for as early as 1924 he was telling the readers of *An t-Ultach* that they should read Scots Gaelic literature and that the fact that that literature was published in the Roman font was no excuse for ignoring it (*Ultach*, July 1924, 3).[108] Writing in the same year, Tomás Mac Neacail argued that Scots Gaelic offered Irish readers a unique chance to experience something new, a literature that was unimpeachably Gaelic without being Irish:

> Of late, when the mark and savour of English is on everything, it is good thing that there is a truly Gaelic literature that is, moreover, not Irish and in which the Irish person will find new ideas and a broadening of knowledge (*FL*, 26/4/24).[109]

In a 1930 lecture to the Dundalk branch of An Fáinne, Cathal Ó Tuathail suggested that material from Gaelic Scotland could offer Irish language theatre companies a native alternative to the exotica of translations and urban settings (*Dundalk Examiner*, 20/12/30).

To help Irish readers interested in discovering this literature, various Irish periodicals published notices or reviews of work in Scots Gaelic. The goal of many of these pieces seems to have been to convince the Irish that they *could* read the work of the Scots. In a 1924 review of a collection of poems from Scottish manuscripts, 'S. de R.' (Seoirse de Rút / George Ruth) explained: 'I have thought it best to give examples from the most interesting volume in order to show how possible it is for Irish Gaels to appreciate it [Scots Gaelic]' (*Eaglaiseach Gaedhealach*, Dec. 1924, 331). Similarly, in a review of Séamus Mac Leoid's *Cailín Sgiathanach* (A maid of Skye) the same year, 'Cuala' acknowledged the challenge the book presented the Irish reader, but offered encouragement as well: 'There is fine Gaelic in this book, although some of the speech is a bit difficult to understand for the person who has not studied the Gaelic of Scotland. Even so, any Irishman would understand the gist of the speech' (*Éire*, 19/4/24).[110] Both Peadar Mac Fhionnlaoich and Cormac Ó Cadhlaigh pondered the possibilities of a more radical step to enable a thriving literary relationship between the two languages. Writing in 1936, Mac Fhionnlaoich called for Irish and Scots Gaels 'to accept a common denominator for all the dialects of spoken Gaelic still left to us, and unite our forces against the ever oncoming flood of *Galldachas* that threatens to overwhelm us' (*II*, 19/9/36). During the Celtic Congress in Edinburgh the following year, Ó Cadhlaigh chaired a meeting of Irish, Scots, and Manx delegates to discuss issues of common concern, a meeting that agreed to the following proposal: 'At the next congress it would be worth while to convene a small conference to study the possibility of uniting the Gaelic of Ireland and Scotland for literary purposes' (*II*, 17/7/37). Clearly, the Manx were very much peripheral players in this scheme, which came to nothing anyway.

More significant than such expressions of solidarity were the contributions in Scots Gaelic itself that appeared in Irish periodicals in the 1920s and 1930s. It is, perhaps, not surprising that Scots Gaelic folktales as well as reviews of collections of such tales were to be found in *Béaloideas* with some regularity in the 1930s.[111] But there was far more. In addition to his generally exhortatory English essays in *Bonaventura*, Ruaraidh Erskine (writing as Ruaraidh Arascan is Mhairr) also published articles in Scots Gaelic in the same journal. Other writers who contributed Scots Gaelic essays to *Bonaventura* were 'Le Petit Blanc', who wrote on the difference between Scots and Irish *céilithe* (social evenings) in spring 1938, and 'Abrach', who published a bilingual essay on the decline in the number of native speakers of Scots Gaelic and on the activities of An Cumann Gaidhealach the same year (*Bonaventura*, Autumn 1938, 177–8).[112]

Among the more intriguing Scots Gaelic contributions to Irish periodicals at this time were the reviews by Calum Mac Gilleathain of Peadar Ó hAnnracháin's *Mar Chonac-sa Éire* and Pádraig Ó Siochfhradha's *Tríocha-Céad Chorca Dhuibhne* in *Ar Aghaidh* in 1938 and 1939 respectively.[113] Mac Gilleathain also published an essay in Scots Gaelic on the shared Gaelic heritage of Ireland and Scotland in the 1938–9 issue of UCG's *An t-Irisleabhar* (*Irisleabhar*, 1938–9, 18–19). In all probability, this Calum Mac Gilleathain – the brother of Somhairle Mac Gilleathain, the most prominent Scots Gaelic poet of this century – was the Reverend Mac Gilleathain tentatively identified by Éamon Ó Ciosáin as the writer who, under the pen-name 'Fraoch Geal', published more than thirty essays in *An t-Éireannach* between 1935 and 1937.[114] Nor was he the only Scots Gaelic writer who contributed to *An t-Éireannach*. We also find an occasional anonymous piece,[115] as well as a letter in Scots Gaelic on the church by Alasdair Mac Eachainn (18/4/36), and two essays sent from South Africa by Donnchadh Mac Dhunléibhe, in which he pointed out how much more enlightened were language policies there than in Scotland (13/2/37 and 27/2/37).[116]

While the average reader of Irish at the time would probably not have been able to read a piece in Scots Gaelic with enough ease to really enjoy the experience, those with a serious and informed interest in language and literature could. At any rate, it is clear that there was no perceived need for translation from Scots Gaelic,[117] and the most substantial example of such work in the period was An tAthair Gearóid Ó Nualláin's *Trí Sheoda ó Alban* (Three jewels from Scotland), a booklet that offered Irish versions of three tales from the 1907 collection *Na Daoine Sidhe is Uirsgeulan Eile* (The fairy people and other stories), edited by Úna Inghean Fhir na Páirce.[118] The other Celtic languages presented a different challenge, one that would require extensive translation if their literatures were to have any effect on writing in Irish. Some Gaels were willing to accept that challenge, as was, for example, Aodh de Blácam, who wrote in 1924:

> It would be natural for us to take an interest in the literature of the Celts in addition to the literature of Ireland. I would recommend to the educational authorities in Ireland to distribute Celtic books in the schools. I would recommend to writers of Irish who are translating the classics of the world into Irish to take up the principal stories of Wales and put the adventures of King Arthur and others into Irish. The Celtic books would be more amenable to Irish than, for example, the books of the Teutonic peoples, and in addition Irish readers would enjoy them (*FL*, 31/5/24).[119]

Most Gaels, however, stepped back from the daunting linguistic and literary work such translation would entail. There was startlingly little Gaelic interest in translation from the Celtic languages throughout the 1920s and 1930s, with even the comparative riches of contemporary Welsh literature being all but ignored. The most forthright call for such translation was the one we have already noted from 'Droichead Átha' in 1934. Few seem to have found his argument convincing, or at least convincing enough for them to learn enough Welsh to do the job. No book-length works at all were translated from Welsh during this period. Instead, we find just the odd poem or story. The most active translators of verse were N. A. Icerg, whose work appeared in *Irisleabhar Muighe Nuadhad* from 1932 to 1934,[120] and Tadhg Ó Donnchadha, whose commitment to translation from Welsh was longstanding and whose work was published in *Óige*, *The Capuchin Annual*, most notably and regularly in the UCC scholarly journal *Éarna*, and in *Humanitas*. Ó Donnchadha also published translations of three stories from the Welsh of Gwynn Jones ('Fionn Mac Eoghain') in the *Cork Weekly Examiner* in 1922.[121] Daniel Owens's 'Rhy Debyg' (Too similar) appeared in the Irish of Tomás Ó Cléirigh as 'Iomrall Aithne' ('Mistaken Identity') in 1930 (*Humanitas*, Sept. 1930, 27–30), and the same author's 'Het Siôn Jones' in a version by 'A. Ó C.' as 'Hata Sheáin Jones' (John Jones's hat) in 1936 (*Standard*, 30/10/36).[122] No Welsh plays were translated into Irish in these two decades. With regard to Breton, there was nothing written in the 1920s or 1930s to match the work of Ó Donnchadha, who had included Irish translations of relevant Breton texts in his insightful and informative essays on Britanny twenty years earlier. Indeed Ó Donnchadha himself seems to have largely ignored the Bretons at this time, and no one took his place to discuss and translate Breton literature for an Irish audience. The only translations from Breton I have found from this period are a brief scene (scene 18) from the play *Buez Sant Patrice* (*The Life of St. Patrick*), and a folktale, 'An Píobaire ón Sliabh' (The Piper from the Mountain).[123] Manx language and literature were all but invisible in Gaelic periodicals at this time. Hyde edited and translated into Irish the song 'An Fionnadairí' (Manx *Fenadyree*, according to Liorish Juan Y Kelly's 1866 Manx–English dictionary *Fockleyr Manninagh as Baarlagh*, 'a satur, wild man of the woods, elf', derived from *fenee*, 'invaders, wild Irish') in the UCD journal *An Reult* (Mar. 1922, 1–5, 22).

In effect, a reader of Irish in the Free State with an interest in contemporary Celtic literature was no better off than his counterpart of thirty years earlier. To be sure, those more linguistically accomplished – or perhaps simply more persistent – could learn a good bit about Gaelic Scotland in Scots Gaelic, but it seems fair to wonder how many took the trouble. Readers wanting to experience in Irish the Welsh writing about whose abundance, riches, and relevance to their own literary situation they were on occasion instructed had to make do with random snippets of verse and the odd short story. The Celtic realms of Brittany, Cornwall, and Gaelic Man remained as mysterious to the vast majority of Gaels as they were to their English-speaking countrymen. The question of language was, of course, the crux for those trying to build any such alliance, as Tomás Mac Con Fhada had stressed as early as 1924, when he reminded readers of *An Stoc* that 'Celtic' was a linguistic, not an ethnic, category: 'There is no Celtic race, but there are Celtic peoples or Celts; that is to say, peoples who speak Celtic languages and have Celtic customs' (*Stoc*, Nov. 1924, 1).[124] And, as had always been true, until the Gaels faced the implications of that question, any meaningful cultural collaboration between the Irish and the other Celts would have to remain not even an ideal, but rather a pious and inconsequential aspiration.

As is so often true in discussions of Gaelic literature in this century, the question again arises: What went wrong? Why did the entire translation initiative end up epitomising frustration and futility for so many writers and readers of Irish at the time? For once, the problem was not a naiveté with regard to the challenges the project entailed nor an unwillingness to face them. Translation was one issue to which a good deal of serious thought had been devoted from the earliest days of the Revival, and the writers of the Free State period had no excuses for ignorance of the ambiguities and difficulties of the task before them. Nor did they seek any. For example, in 1933 Liam Ó Rinn offered an insightful if intimidating list of hurdles to be cleared by the would-be translator:

> I have already said that the work of translation is hard work . . . It is not possible to lay down any rules for it. The rule that would be appropriate in one place will only ruin the work in another place. It is not enough for the translator to have a good knowledge of the two languages, unless he can bend his own mind until it is at one with the mind of the original author. He must have some degree of poetic and artistic talent. It rarely does the trick to translate a phrase word for word. The simplest phrases in the world must often be twisted and turned so that they will have a natural as well as a vivid literary appearance and so that they will fit in with the phrases before and after them (*UIrman*, 29/4/33).[125]

Writing in *Ar Aghaidh* in 1935, 'G. Ó M.' went so far as to say,

> Of course it is harder to translate a book into Irish than it is to write an original book in Irish on the same subject. The finer is the book itself with its own garb on it, its trunk, its bones, and its body, both flesh and blood, the harder still is it it to translate (*AA*, Dec. 1935, 1).[126]

And in his serialised essay on translation for the *Catholic Bulletin*, Seán Ó Ciarghusa included in his list of the 'dangers' (*baoghail*) of translation one with which 'G. Ó M.' would identify:

> One of the dangers is that the translator may be a craftsman and not an artist . . . and that he is often a bungler as well who merely puts a cloak of the second language on the body of the first – work that is of no benefit to the form or the body of the second language.[127]

The question of how faithful or free a translation should be, raised by all three of the writers above, was for obvious reasons the one that most concerned Gaels interested in the subject. Those worried about foreign, especially English, contamination of the language and its ethos through translation were bound to question whether that threat would be lessened if the literal hold of the original were loosened. Those more sensitive to literary and artistic issues pondered whether the greater scope for creative expression of the essence of the original outweighed the possibility that such freer adaptation might give a dishonestly distorted experience of the source text. On the whole, however, both groups seem for their own quite different reasons to have arrived at the same basic solution, so that rigorous adherence to the letter of the original was the most common failing chastised by critics in reviews of An Gúm's translations.

In 1930, Liam Ó Rinn, himself a translator from three languages into Irish, urged his fellow writers to eschew literal translation in favor of what he called 'close plagiarisation' (*dlúth-phlagiarization*). His suggestion was that the 'translator' should read twenty or so lines from the original, put down the book, recreate those lines in good Irish from memory, and then consult the original again for revision, always being careful not to lose the 'freshness' (*friseáltacht*) of the first effort. Ó Rinn wrote:

> If you try to be too exact, you will betray the spirit of the original work (and the spirit that is in the word is nobler than the word itself), and your attempt will be displeasing to the reader – and to the original author also, if he understands Irish (*Star*, 8/3/30).[128]

Ó Rinn returned to this idea the following year in his travel book *Turus go Páras*, suggesting that Gaelic writers would do better to concentrate on adaptation (*cur-in-oiriúnt*) rather than translation (*aistriú*). He continued:

> There are different kinds of translation . . . and if a person cannot do a close translation without making something more insipid than lemonade of the finest Burgundy in the original work, it would be better for him to try adapting the original work.[129]

Another prolific translator, Seosamh Mac Grianna, agreed, writing in 1931:

> If you were to sit down and read a book in English or French and think about it in your mind and in your heart, and then write it out in Irish in the way that you thought that its style and its theme and its passion would be best understood by a Gael, you would make a good translation (*IP*, 3/12/31).[130]

An anonymous author of the 'Im' Leabharlainn Dom' (In my library) column in *Timthire Chroidhe Naomhtha Íosa*, a column in which brief reviews of translations were a regular feature, called for even greater freedom, writing in 1934: 'It is the job of the translator to consider the words until the words leave his memory and the original thoughts alone stay with him, and then to express those thoughts in his own Irish words.' Concerned primarily that the 'translator' catch the spirit and to the extent possible the style of the original, this writer conceded: 'All things considered, is not the work of the translator difficult?' (*TCNÍ*, Aug. 1934, 189).[131] This was a point to which Ó Rinn returned repeatedly in his many reviews of translations, writing in August 1934, for example: 'The cause of much of the difficulty involved in translating a book is that, because the work he is doing is called translation, the translator must break his heart trying to translate the froth as well as the substance' (*UIrman*, 5/8/33).[132]

In practice, what was often meant by 'free renderings' was the 'Gaelicisation' of the original in question, its being provided with an Irish, frequently Gaeltacht setting, and a Hibernian cast of characters. In his introductory note to his translation of Sophie de Ségur's *Les Malheurs de Sophie* as *Aindeise Shiobhán* (Siobhán's misery), Cormac Ó Cadhlaigh wrote: 'In this translation, the names of people and places and songs were changed so that the stories could be given a Gaelic look.'[133] Thus Sophie became Siobhán; Camille, Cáit; Lambert, Tadhg; and Madeline de Fleurville, Éibhlín Ní Shúilleabháin. This approach was particularly common in the translation of plays, doubtless in part as a response to the audience's perceived resistance to hearing characters who could not know the language speak Irish on stage. Shán Ó Cuív identifies his play *An Bhean ón dTuaith* as 'a retelling of . . . *La Vieille Cousine* by Émile Souvestre ('aithinnsint . . . ar *La Vieille Cousine*, a chum Émile Souvestre');[134] León Ó Broin turned Tristan Bernard's *L'anglais tel qu'on le parle* into a comical comment on the Irish linguistic scene as *Labhartar Béarla Annseo* (English is spoken here);[135] and Máiréad Ní Ghráda wrote of her play *An Uadhacht* (The will) that she had found 'the original idea of this play in Puccini's opera

"Gianni Schicchi"' (bun-smaoineamh an dráma seo i gceol-dráma le Puccini, 'Gianni Schicci' [*sic*]).[136] And there were many others. That this approach was understood and appreciated is clear in the comments of one 'Fear Feasa' in his 1923 review of Nioclás Tóibín's Gaelicisation of a French original as *An Dubh 'na Gheal* (Black as white, i.e. Bamboozled), an adaptation he thought avoided 'foreign form and colouring' (deilbh agus dath na h-iasachta) in favour of 'a truly Gaelic colouring' (an dath fíor-Ghaedhealach) (*Sguab*, Aug. 1923, 222).[137]

But again why, after all this thought, debate, effort, and expense, were Gaels left with such a generally undistinguished and unimaginative library of translated work, the vast majority of which came from the language they were all striving to supplant. The answer was both simple and all but universally known and understood at the time. Unlike most people in the English-speaking world, all Gaelic writers were bilingual.[138] Few, however, had any mastery of languages other than English and Irish – often itself recently enough acquired for many – or any prospect or intention of learning any well enough to translate from them. In a letter to *United Ireland* in 1934, one 'X. Y. Z.' criticised both An Gúm's project and Ó Rinn's support of it on precisely these linguistic grounds, writing: 'I know of few people who have enough French or German or Spanish either to do any authentic translation, and the few who do have some slight knowledge of some language do not have enough Irish' (*UI*, 17/3/34).[139] Four years earlier, Micheál Mac Suibhne, the editor of *The Star*, had offered a pessimistic estimate of the pool of potential translators available to An Gúm who were competent in languages other than English:

> Although it pays translators at a much higher rate than a British publisher would pay for the turning of continental works into English, it has only a comparatively small band at work. Of these not more than half a dozen are able to translate from French, and not another half dozen from all the other European languages taken together (*Star*, 19/7/30).

This situation drove one anonymous contributor to *United Ireland* to share the near-heresy of an earlier anonymous writer that 'the most important thing is the publication of a copious and constant stream of translations from English'. Commenting on this statement, this correspondent wrote:

> I have been advocating this point ever since the Gúm was established and my principal reason for that was that most of our national teachers and others who are native speakers of Irish have no knowledge of any other language and if translation were confined to the works of Continental writers those who have the work of translation on hands would be very little removed from mere students of Irish with weak construction and limited vocabulary (*UI*, 28/4/34).[140]

All things considered then, it is perhaps surprising that we have even what few isolated, quirky, and uneven translations of European literature that we do have from this time.[141]

There was, moreover, a fair amount of both variety and imagination in the sorts of things even those limited to English alone were calling for and trying to provide. We find Gaels advocating increased translation in such areas as popular science and general information,[142] children's literature,[143] science fiction,[144] light reading of all kinds,[145] religious works, including the Bible,[146] an encyclopaedia,[147] challenging contemporary non-fiction,[148] and detective stories. The last of these sub-genres is of particular interest, not only because of the number of crime stories brought into Irish at the time, but also because there were significant and revealing differences of opinion concerning this source of translation. For many at the time, Irish versions of mystery novels like *At the Villa Rose*, *The Cask*, *The Kang-He Vase*, *Island of Terror*, or *Trent's Last Case* epitomised just about everything that was wrong with An Gúm's project, an opinion still held by some who see a Gaelicised Sherlock Holmes as emblematic of the eccentric hybridity of the whole enterprise. These were novels originally written in English, widely available in Ireland already, occasionally of dubious literary merit, and rooted in a British, often imperialist, worldview. For others, however, they were a powerful and plausible lure to win readers, particularly young ones, for the language. As Liam Ó Rinn said of crime novels: 'If you are tired and you want to pass a few hours pleasurably and aimlessly, there is no better way than to pick up one of them, the offspring of the mind of Edgar Allan Poe' (*UI*, 22/12/34).[149] Reviewing *Teach na Saighde*, Pádraic Mac Giolla Bríghde's translation of A. E. W. Mason's *The House of the Arrow*, an anonymous critic wrote in 1937: 'In this case, the Irish is excellent – so easy and charming that it made the present reviewer read several chapters for the language alone, and then the story gripped him and he became a crime fan, or whatever readers of this stuff are called' (*CB*, Sept. 1937, 719).

In addition to its inherent interest, mystery fiction could offer significant literary lessons to the Gaelic translator and would-be creative writer. First of all, this kind of fiction was rooted in a narrative that was clear, coherent, and ultimately credible, qualities sorely lacking in the plots of most original Gaelic prose at this time. Stephen McKenna saw even greater potential in translated detective stories, suggesting to Ó Rinn that Gaelic writers could learn about more than just plot structure and pacing from the genre. In a letter to Ó Rinn in 1930 he stated that detective stories deal with 'a side of life that should be brought into Irish in some way for the sake of the language itself' (taobh den saol ba cheart a thabhairt isteach sa Ghaeilge ar chuma éigin ar mhaithe leis an teangain féin).[150] While he himself did not specify just what this 'side of life' was, An tAthair Micheál offered his own suggestion in a 1935 essay, in the process answering those who felt that in its focus on the sordid the detective novel could be a corrupting force: 'I think I now understand why Gaelic authors translate books in English of the kind called detective stories. The reason, I think, is that there are no other clean and moral novels apart from them' (*FMR*, Oct. 1935, 483).[151]

A few Gaels looked forward to the day when contemporary writing in Irish would itself be found worthy of translation into other languages. That breakthrough had in fact already begun with the translation of Pearse's work by Pearse himself and by Joseph Campbell, as well as with the publication in 1922 of Julius Pokorny's German versions of stories by Pearse, Ó Conaire, and Pádraig Ó Siochfhradha as *Die Seele Irlands*. In 1929, E. O'Clery published *The Small Fields of Carrig*, his translation of Éamonn Mac Giolla Iasachta's *Cúrsaí Thomáis*.[152] Pádraic Ó Conaire's work was made available to readers of English in three volumes, *The Land of Wonders* (1919), *The Woman at the Window* (1921), and *Field and Fair* (1929), the first two translated by Éamonn Ó Néill, the third by Cormac Breathnach. Of course, as we have seen, the most heralded translations from Irish during this period were those of the Blasket autobiographies: Tomás Ó Criomthain's *An t-Oileánach* (1929), translated by Robin Flower as *The Islandman* in 1934, and Muiris Ó Súileabháin's *Fiche Blian ag Fás*, translated by George Thomson and Moya Llewellyn Davies as *Twenty Years a-Growing*, both the Irish and English versions appearing in the same year of 1933.

There were, however, mixed feelings concerning such efforts. Some shared the pride of Cearbhall Ua Dálaigh, who proclaimed, 'Let the world know that we are rising' (Bíodh fhios ag an saoghal go bhfuilimíd ag éirghe), and continued, 'translation to English will not make people avoid the Irish, but rather the opposite, in my view' (ní chuirfidh an t-aistriú go Béarla leisce ar dhaoine chun na Gaedhilge acht a mhalairt, dar liom) (*Nation*, 29/11/30). It was certainly in these terms that *An Claidheamh Soluis* welcomed the news that Flower planned to publish a translation of *An t-Oileánach*: 'It is no harm to let English speakers in other countries and here in Ireland itself know about the life of the people of the island' (*ACS*, 14/5/32).[153] On the other hand, reviewing *Fiche Blian ag Fás* in both its Irish and English versions, Éibhlín Nic Ghráinne raised what remains a central question no less troubling and no closer to solution today than it was more than half a century ago:

> The book-of-the-month may bring royalties (and they are not to be scorned), but to our struggling Gaelic literature much harm is done by concurrent translation. An English version published simultaneously with the original in our present state of letters dwarfs the original and puts it in a secondary place at once; it raises a false standard (*Dublin Magazine*, Apr.–June 1936, 96–7).

Was An Gúm's entire translation project a misguided effort to raise another equally false standard? In retrospect, it is, as usual, easy to pass judgment, to pronounce An Gúm's work in this area seriously flawed at best. But was that work a total failure? Far more research needs to be done before an even approximately definitive answer to this question can be given, but there are facts and cues enough to enable us to begin to try. In the first place, An Gúm, using translation, did fulfil its mission to significantly increase the amount and variety of reading matter available in Irish, an accomplishment to which León Ó Broin drew attention in 1935, writing: 'It must be remembered that more Irish books were published in the last eight years than probably in the whole of the preceding three centuries' (*CA*, 1935, 122). There was, in fact, no 'probably' about it, and translation comprised the majority of those new books. Secondly, An Gúm put those books into circulation. A 1937 essay by 'An Sagart' reported that An Gúm's 300 publications to that date had sold a total of 250,000 copies (*Ráitheachán*, Mar. 1937, 11).

What we do not know, of course, is how many copies of any individual translation were ever read.[154] Nor is it easy to ascertain what effect reading – or even more important, actually translating – any of these books had on those involved. Certainly, Séamus Ó Grianna, his brother Seosamh, and Máirtín Ó Cadhain would lead us to believe that any such effect was altogether harmful, but whatever Séamus picked up from Canon Sheehan or Ó Cadhain from Charles Kickham, one can still wonder whether Seosamh learned nothing at all from Conrad or Peadar O'Donnell. Subsequent critics like Alan Titley, Máirin Nic Eoin, Breandán Delap, Máirtín Mac Niocláis and Pádraig Ó Siadhail have in general dismissed the notion that Gaelic writers benefited from their work for An Gúm,[155] but a more rigorous comparative study of the relationship between translated and original work in the period is needed before any final judgments can be passed. On this point we are, then, left with a conventional perception but no conclusive proof of the failure of the translation project.

Finally, has the project been forgotten, other than as a convenient symbol of a period of Gaelic writing now generally – and to some extent appropriately – dismissed as stagnant and unadventurous? Until quite recently, there was certainly little increase worth mentioning since the 1930s in the foreign literature available to readers of Irish, and one could argue that this dearth of lively and challenging translations, the fact that translation remained largely, as it had been before 1926, a literary hobby for dilettantes, was the most distressing result of the uncritical rejection of what An Gúm was trying to do in the years of the Free State. We may well reject the answers the writers of this period found for the quesions they raised, but we should not forget the questions themselves nor the high seriousness and integrity of those who asked them at a time when many, in the words of 'An Sagart', believed that 'Gaelic had never been flung so broadly on the waters of the world' (*Ráitheachán*, Mar. 1937, 11).

SEVEN

'THE TRAIL OF THE SERPENT'

THE GAELIC MOVEMENT AND IRISH LITERATURE IN ENGLISH

In a 1924 speech to the Gaelic League of London, Caitlín Nic Ghabhann called attention to what she saw as an insidious fifth column betraying the Irish cultural revival from within, telling her audience that 'every Irishman who writes in English is working for England' (*Féile na nGaedheal*, Nov. 1924, 6). There was, in fact, nothing idiosyncratic or unduly extreme at the time about either her opinion or her rhetoric. In this same year Pádhraic Ó Domhnalláin linked 'writers who won honour and fortune from the "Celtic Note" (sgríbhneoirí a bhain onóir agus airgead amach as an 'gCeltic Note') with Orangemen, earls, and Free State senators as the vanguard of those trying to deny Irish its proper primacy in the new Ireland (*FL*, 19/7/24). In a 1932 essay entitled 'Gaedhilg *v.* Béarla' (Irish *v.* English), the playwright Annraoi Saidléar went even further, asserting: 'Every word of English that is spoken, read, or written is an enemy of the Irish language' (Namhad do'n Ghaedhealg seadh gach focal Béarla a labhartar, a léightear, a scríobhtar) (Enniscorthy *Echo*, 16/1/32).

There was, therefore, some urgency in Pádraig Ó Siochfhradha's 1936 assertion that there was no longer room for compromise on the question of a writer's linguistic allegiance. He argued that all writers of English in Ireland were a threat to *Gaelachas*, adding: 'Anything that is done in English belongs to Anglo-Ireland, cultivating and making a "tradition" for it and giving it various kinds of beauty and culture and perpetuating its status as part of the nation.' For 'An Seabhac', the time had come for writers to make a definite commitment one way or the other:

> Let us make it clear to them that half-way houses are nonsensical and pointless, that their only choice is to stay with English and Anglo-Ireland or to go over to Irish altogether and to nationality as a result. Let them understand that one cannot be a Gael unless he goes with the latter entirely (*Ráitheachán*, Sept. 1936, 17).[1]

Given the virulence with which the Gaels routinely attacked each other over such a wide range of controversies within their own movement, it should come as no surprise that they had little respect for their literary compatriots who had allied themselves with the language most Irish-Irelanders saw as their bitterest enemy.[2] What is, however, unexpected is that the Gaels paid less attention of any kind to Irish writers of English at this time than they had in the period prior to independence, particularly in the pages of *An Claidheamh Soluis* under Pearse's editorship in the first decade of the century. Of course, as is clear from the statements quoted above, there was nothing benign about this relative neglect, and at regular intervals we find prominent Gaels reformulating one of the most stable tenets of the movement's creed, one dating back to the very beginning of the revival. At a 1922 meeting of the Irish Texts Society, the officers were keen to clear up any possible misunderstanding of the organisation's mission:

> The necessity for the adoption of some definite term for the existing literature in the Irish language was then discussed, and it was suggested that this, and this alone, truly constituted Irish literature. Anglo-Irish literature or the literature in English or in any other language other than Irish relating to Ireland should not be designated Irish literature – a term which it was essential to use free from ambiguity (*IBL*, April–May, 1922, 167).

There was certainly no ambiguity in the mind of Tadhg Ó Donnchadha when in a 1923 review of a book of translations from Irish into Welsh he took pride in the fact 'that the Gaels of Ireland have a message for the great world outside' (go bhfuil teachtaireacht age [*sic*] Gaedhil na hÉireann don domhan mhór amuigh), and left no doubt as to the proper linguistic medium of that message, asserting

> that it is in the native language that that message will be composed and polished. It is through the native language and through that alone that we can turn back on ourselves and capture the mind of our ancestors to give a new *entwickelung* [*sic*] or direction to the heritage of learning and literature we have gotten from them (*Éarna*, July, 1923, 41).[3]

It was again this ancestral bond that was foremost in the thoughts of Ó Donnchadha's brother Éamon the following year when he wrote:

> It is in Irish alone that one finds a coherent and genuine account of the lore of our ancestors. It is in the literature of Irish alone that one gets a sense of the mind and the spirit of our race, that mind and spirit that accompanied every generation of them one after the other (*FL*, 7/6/24).[4]

Just how widely shared was this belief is evident from an address delivered by P. Bourke to the Gaelic Society of Trinity College, still very much an Ascendancy institution, and reported in *An t-Eaglaiseach Gaedhealach*. Arguing that the relationship between the Anglo-Irish literary movement and the Gaelic revival was that of shadow to substance, Bourke was dismissive of the lasting national significance of Irish writers in the English language:

> There are a few rare and outstanding exceptions in which the English words were infused with Irish sentiment, but how can any two languages be supposed to be equally rich, happy, forcible in expressing the moods, temper, idiosyncrasies, peculiarities of a people to whom the one is the native organ of expression which has grown with them, changed with them, is of them and by them, and the other the reverse of all this (*Eaglaiseach Gaedhealach*, July–Aug. 1924, 282).

In a letter to the *Irish Statesman* the following year, 'T. O'R' wondered whether the term 'Anglo-Irish literature' meant anything at all, writing:

> To give anything more than a nebulous definition of what has been called 'Anglo-Irish literature' is impossible, for the reason that there is no clear line of demarcation between it and the rest of English literature, of which it forms a small part (IS, 31/1/25).[5]

Michael Tierney, a University College Dublin academic with whom the Gaels did not always see eye to eye, was thoroughly orthodox on this point, writing in *The Star* in 1929:

> Now it is undeniably true to say that the life and character of the Irish nation in history, whether in good or evil circumstances, have continued to find their truest expression in the native language of Ireland. Their truest, if not almost their only continuous expression; for you will find the real Ireland of to-day more truly expressed in the autobiography of a Blasket fisherman than in that of George Moore, just as in the Eighteenth Century it was more truly expressed by Eoghan Rua Ó Súilleabháin than by Goldsmith. The speaker of the native language still gets close to the heart of Irish life; the speaker of English, even though born and bred in Ireland, belongs to some cosmopolitan movement and expresses something alien even when he thinks of Ireland (*Star*, 17/8/29).

For the more optimistic – or deluded – in the movement, this problem seemed on the way to solving itself with the natural withering away of a hothouse exotic Anglo-Irish literature in the bracing new climate of resurgent *Gaelachas*. In his previously quoted address to the Trinity College Gaelic Society, P. Bourke declared of the so-called Irish Literary Renaissance:

> But the movement is dying, as it was bound to die; it did not draw life from the people; it was not of the earth, fresh, spontaneous, wholesome . . . It was in other aspects too divorced from the facts of real life to make any lasting impression. It stood in many respects in a parasitical relation to the Celtic Revival, it was limited by being forced to use English to express Irish ideas. It has been confused by many people with the Revival itself, but the progress of time has drawn a line of clear demarcation between the substance and the shadow (*Eaglaiseach Gaedhealach*, July–Aug. 1924, 283).

Writing of Yeats and the Irish Academy of Letters in 1933, an anonymous contributor to the Dundalk *Examiner* stated:

> Is it not a sorry story that that man and his fellow mountebanks do not understand that their time is past in this country, and that the young people who are rising up now will have nothing good, bad, or indifferent, to do with their antics or their prizes for 'literature!' (*Examiner*, 4/2/33).[6]

Aodh de Blácam, who was one of the Gaelic critics most open to Irish writing in English, believed that while 'Anglo-Irish' literature, a literature he saw as written by Anglicised people of Irish birth for English audiences, would 'go on just as long as English literature, of which it is a branch', 'Anglo-Gaelic' literature, 'works written by Irishmen for Ireland', was probably doomed – and soon:

> If the Gaelic Revival sweeps the next generation, in the next wave of progress, as I expect, the national literature will come to be written mainly or wholly in the national language, which is best fitted, after all, to express the subtlety and strength of the Irish mind, and carries a flavour of history and racial feeling that is its claim upon us (*IP*, 25/3/37).[7]

Many if not most Gaels could face the demise of so-called Irish literature in English with equanimity. Indeed many felt that the loss of such a literature was no loss at all. Particularly dismissive was 'Oisín', who wrote in 1939:

> I do not say that the new books in Irish are better than or as good as the books being put out in French or in English, but they are ten times better than the foolishness that passes for new literature by writers of English in this country (*Derry People*, 25/2/39).[8]

For many of his colleagues in the movement, the most important failings of this literature were moral. It was 'bad' literature in a very real sense. This view was especially common among the Catholic clergymen who played such a prominent role in the revival. In 1923, the Lazarist priest Father J. S. Sheehy offered readers of *Iris an Gharda* some literary advice:

> For those who cannot get a mastery of the Irish language, Anglo-Irish writers should be preferred who treat of Irish history, poetry, archaeology, and other Irish subjects with sympathy and love. But even here I would utter a word of warning. Some of those Anglo-Irish writers are a source of danger, those, I mean, of what is called the 'Theosophical and Decadent School'; I mention no names. But these writers are frankly pagan (*Iris an Gharda*, 15/10/23).

In 1935, the Jesuit Seán Ó Catháin invoked the authority of an eminent Gaelic author from the past to reinforce his criticism of the moral laxity of Irish writing in English:

> Keating once compared a certain group of writers to the beetle, that filthy bug that spends its life on the dungheap. Those [the writers condemned by Keating] make a habit of leaving human beauty and nobilility aside and meticulously displaying whatever filth and baseness there is. We know that there are Irishmen like that at present . . . That literature was, of course, composed in English (*TCNÍ*, Sept. 1935, 213).[9]

Yet despite all this sound and fury, hostility towards Irish writers of English was often tempered, as it had been from the earliest days of the revival, by an awareness – usually grudging, almost always anxious – of their popular and aesthetic successes. For instance, in 1922, Robert Lynd rejected the view that the growth of an Irish literature in English had been in any way a misfortune for the native culture, stressing instead the crucial role Irish writers of English had played in nurturing a national spirit through catastrophic times:

> The great thing was that the language should be handed down to the whole of the Irish people. As things were this could only have been done during the last century by having a literature in English as well as a literature in Irish (*IBL*, Apr.–May, 1922, 161).[10]

'Niall Mór' made the same point from a different perspective in 1924, stating: 'The attempt made by the people in the nineteenth century who tried to reveal the life of Ireland in their stories in English was far more successful than what we have done in our own language so far' (*Ultach*, July 1924, 4).[11] Aodh de Blácam was willing to go even further in a piece on 'Gaelic and Anglo-Irish Literature Compared' the same year, conceding:

> In the matter of literature, however, the Gaelic revival has been comparatively a failure, and this reacts upon the movement as a whole by reason of learners of Irish still having to depend upon the English language for reading matter and intellectual sustenance (*Studies*, Mar. 1924, 64).[12]

In succinct agreement was 'Droighneann Donn', who in 1928 commented sourly: 'Anglo-Irish literature is far ahead of literature in Irish although that is not saying all that much' (*Ultach*, Dec. 1928, 3).[13] Others were not so flippantly dismissive. In a thoughtful piece in *An Lóchrann* the same year, 'Tadhg' faced the unpalatable facts:

> The little bits or the little books that have been composed over the past thirty years are not worth talking much about in comparison with the worthwhile books that are to be found in English. As for substance and size, beauty and finish, they cannot be compared with the English-language books that are being written by Irish people, and being eagerly read by Irish people (*Lóchrann*, Feb. 1928, 5).[14]

As our period drew to a close in 1939, some Gaels seem to have been considerably more confident about the ability of the new literature in Irish to hold its own or better against its more widely acclaimed counterpart in English. Among such true believers was 'Seán', who proclaimed:

> We will take yesterday first, and there are big names that count for much in modern English literature in the scale against us: Wilde, Moore, Shaw, Yeats, Canon Sheehan! This much I am free to admit, and against whom we have only Pádraic Ó Conaire and Father O'Leary to put up . . . In a comparison of the Gaelic and Anglo-Irish writers of to-day I have fair hope that an impartial and unbiased judge would give the verdict in favour of our Gaelic writers . . . I have made the assertion, challenge it who will, that the Gael can at last stand up to the Gall here at home as far as literary craftsmanship is concerned. In the last twenty years at least a few Gaelic books have been written which will stand the test of time, while I do not know of one book written by an Anglo-Irish writer that will be read in a generation from now (*Leader*, 10/6/39).

However satisfying and strategic such confidence may have been, its connection with the cultural reality of the time was tenuous at best. Few judges, especially if they were at all impartial or unbiased, would or could have agreed with 'Seán'. Indeed the rather grudging acknowledgement of the popular and artistic appeal of Anglo-Irish authors noted above *could*, on occasion, merge into an acceptance of the validity of their work as a genuine if always subordinate component of the literature of the nation. Sometimes such an acceptance remained largely implicit, as when critics voiced resentment at the appropriation of Irish-born writers into the English canon. Usually, however, openness to Irish writers working in English was based on the idea – one again dating back to the beginning of the Revival – that certain Irish writers, despite their unfortunate choice of linguistic medium, were somehow blessed with a 'Gaelic note', an ineffable tinge of *Gaelachas* that could to some extent transcend language and thus at least in part redeem their literary efforts for the Gaelic nation. In his 1934 book *Prós na hAoise Seo*, Shán Ó Cuív stressed the survival of 'the Gaelic mind' (an aigne Ghaedhealach) among Irish country people even after the headlong language shift of the nineteenth century, and conceded that that racial memory had found and continued to find expression in *both* Irish and English: 'It is that mind that we find in the writings of Séamus Ó Dubhghaill and in the English-language writings of Gerald Griffin and Charles Kickham and other writers who did not have Irish.'[15] Kickham, a revered Fenian rebel as well as a very popular novelist, was believed by many to be particularly imbued with the right Gaelic stuff, a point underscored by T. Ó Murchadha in a 1931 essay in *Irisleabhar Muighe Nuadhat*:

> But God of Glory gave him extraordinary intellectual ability so that he was able to understand and reveal the Irish people with all their virtues and vices as honestly and as affectionately as a mother would describe her own child. That is why Gaels will have a fondness and a respect for him when they have forgotten Swift and people who call themselves 'Irish Writers' today (*IMN*, 1931, 49).[16]

The playwright T. C. Murray was another writer of English whom many Gaels felt to be Gaelic in all but language. For example, in a 1925 essay on 'Dráma Gaedheal' (The drama of the Irish), Seán Ó Ciarghusa wrote:

> Just as there is a 'brogue' in English as spoken in Ireland, there is T. C. Murray among the Abbey crowd. Although he is, I understand, from a predominantly English-speaking area, and although he writes in English, there is the scent of Ireland on his speech and on what he creates, and a bit of the breath of the Gaeltacht underlying them (*Sguab*, Jan. 1925, 264).[17]

An anonymous critic (probably An tAthair Mac Fhinn) reviewing the production of a translation into Irish of his play *The Spring* in 1939 made the same point more succinctly: 'All of the plays of Thomas Murray are in tune with the Irish language and with the Gaelic world' (*AA*, Mar. 1939, 5).[18]

At times this native quality could find expression in unexpected sources, as when Father Dinneen wrote of Oliver Goldsmith in 1928:

> Without any doubt, the Gaelic blood was in him; and we might as well take him to us as we would take a native poet even though he wrote his poems and all his literary work in English. There was undoubtedly a Gaelic vein in him (*Leader*, 15/12/28).[19]

Among other writers in the work of whom some Gaels at least detected various resonances of the Gaelic note were Yeats (*IP*, 15/8/39), 'Ethna Carberry' (Anna Johnston) (*Camán*, 18/2/33; *IS*, 11/5/29; *Ultach*, Apr. 1934, 5–6), Donn Byrne (*TCNÍ*, Dec. 1936, 284; *AA*, Jan. 1937, 7), James Stephens (*FL*, Apr. 1927, 15), Canon Sheehan (*IMN*, 1934, 8–12),[20] Peadar O'Donnell (*CT*, 8/8/36), Austin Clarke (*IBL*, Sept.–Oct. 1929, 113), and Daniel Corkery (*ACS*, 1/8/31).[21]

In fact, some in the movement saw it as but a short and logical step from the acknowledgement that an authentic native essence could survive the transition into English to the extension of the Gaelic *imprimatur* to writers who published mostly or exclusively in that language. While such a lapse from orthodoxy troubled some, other equally sincere Gaels had no problem taking this step and even going further, aware that once the concession had been made that writing in English could be seen as distinctively Irish, the debate could henceforth concern only the criteria for such inclusion in the national literary canon. The most articulate Gaelic proponents of the claim of Anglo-Irish literature to some national status were Daniel Corkery, León Ó Broin, Aodh de Blácam, P. S. O'Hegarty, and Riobárd Ó Faracháin. The best known and doubtless the most influential of these writers was Corkery. His 1931 book *Synge and Anglo-Irish Literature* is frequently dismissed for fostering an unduly restrictive definition of an authentic Irish literature in English as of necessity focused on the 'three great forces which, working so long in the Irish national being, have made it so different from the English national being'. These forces were, of course, 'The Religious Consciousness of the People . . . Irish Nationalism . . . and The Land.'[22] What is crucial here is that however controversial his elevation of these three themes into the touchstones for genuine Irish literature in English, he developed his arguments concerning them specifically to distinguish such a literature from a false or 'Ascendancy' Anglo-Irish literature, in the process acknowledging the right of at least some writing in English to be included in the Irish canon.[23]

Not surprisingly, some in the movement were puzzled by Corkery's deviation from adherence to a strict linguistic and literary apartheid. For example, in a 1931 piece on 'Daoine Áirithe' (Certain people), 'Sgéalaidhe' wrote with tongue in cheek: 'I was sorry to hear of the intellectual illness of Mr Daniel Corkery, now Professor of English in University College Cork. It led to weird imaginings, coming to climax in a book in English on John M. Synge' (*Féile na nGaedheal*, Nov. 1931, 3). More serious was 'Fergus', who, after listening to a 1937 Corkery lecture in English to the Keating Branch of the League in Dublin, felt compelled to remind the speaker of the dangerous error of his ways: 'Literature written in English is English literature, and we in Ireland are in its thrall' (*Leader*, 20/11/37).[24]

The majority of Corkery's colleagues seem, however, to have been more open to his act of cultural generosity in an often mean time, as was 'Colum:'

> The work before us is to create a literature; a literature that will show the spirit and mind of the Gaels; a literature of our own on which there will not be the flavor or the scent of Englishness. That is the road that is before us, and there are many holes and pits in which we are in danger of being injured. But we have a trustworthy guide in Daniel Corkery who will put us on our guard, and although he writes in English, that does not detract from the wisdom of his speech or the excellence of his counsel (*Leader*, 22/8/31).[25]

Most striking here is that 'Colum' makes no mention of the language of the books about which Corkery was offering such invaluable guidance. Similarly, in a 1931 review of Corkery's *Synge*, 'C. M.' praised his discussion of Irish writing in English for its thoroughly Gaelic perspective:

> We do not know another book with whose intellectual background we are more thoroughly in agreement. It makes one say with added conviction: Gaodhal mise is ní h-eol dom gur náir dom é [I am a Gael, and I do not know that that is any shame to me] (*Irish Monthly*, Oct. 1931, 659).

One of Corkery's most enthusiastic allies was León Ó Broin, who in a 1939 essay on 'Litríocht Náisiúnta i nGaedhilg' (National literature in Irish) agreed with Corkery's identification of the three major themes proper to genuine Irish literature and continued:

> There is, therefore, no doubt that it is important that Irish writers, whatever language they have, would reveal the people from whom they come to themselves in such a way that those people can recognise themselves in the literature.

While he was explicit that he felt 'much of what Irish people wrote in English in our own time' (a lán dár sgríobh Éireannaigh le n-ár linn féin i mBéarla) failed to meet Corkery's standards, he was equally clear that the problem was not solely linguistic. Rather, he worried that writers of Irish could be every bit as capable of exploiting their material in the service of a new stage Irishry: 'If writers of Irish are not vigilant, there is a danger that they will walk the same road, that they will imitate the standard of the writers from Ireland who write English' (*Guth na Gaedheal*, 1939, 23).[26] None of these ideas were new to Ó

Broin. In fact, he had preached real heresy in the pages of the Gaelic League's offical organ four years before the appearance of Corkery's book on Synge:

> We do not like the border between Six Counties of Ireland and the rest of the country. It is unnatural. But I fear many of us are in favour of that other great divide that was created the first day that Irish people who make use of English as a literary medium were called 'Anglo-Irish'. That also was an unnatural christening, one that did more harm to the ideals of *Gaelachas* than anything else we can think of (*FL*, Feb. 1927, 13).[27]

In a 1932 essay in *Outlook*, Aodh de Blácam came to the defence of Corkery against those who had criticised his book as bigoted and provincial. Taking an explicitly post-colonial stance from which he compared earlier Anglo-Irish writers with those of the Anglo-Indian establishment, he argued that times were changing in independent Ireland:

> In justice, be it said that many an 'Anglo-Irish' writer (I hate the word 'Anglo-Irish' except in its correct application to the eighteenth century ascendancy and Old Pale, both of which were admittedly only English-in-Ireland) – many a writer I say wishes to get into the heart of the historic people, and does not love the futile ascendancy pose (*Outlook*, 12/3/32).[28]

De Blácam's own *A First Book of Irish Literature* (1934) would deal with writers of both Irish and English – as well as Latin and Norman French – as a matter of basic principle, as he himself declared: 'Gaelic literature is the core of our heritage, but we have cause for pride and matter of study in the splendid Latin hymns that Irishmen made in olden times, and in the English writings of Goldsmith, Tone, Mitchel and the rest' (*New Irish Magazine*, Dec. 1934, 48).[29] Moreover, in an essay in *Studies* in this same year of 1934, de Blácam was willing to criticise Corkery quite sharply for not going far enough in his openness to some of his compatriots who worked in English. Commenting on a recent review essay Corkery had published in the same journal on several books dealing with Swift, de Blácam declared:

> He shewed as little sympathy for the Anglo-Irish as Lecky shewed for the Gael. If Lecky was partial, so was he. To dismiss Anglo-Ireland as unworthy of a Gael's study, however, is hurtful to Gaelic interests, seeing that a large part of Gaelic and Catholic thought was expressed, during two centuries, in English. The task of the just historian is to depict Irish history with the Gaeltacht as the core, but also to dissect the Anglicised sphere, recovering whatsoever belongs to the nation and discarding only what is alien through and through (*Studies*, Sept. 1934, 439).[30]

Of course, as the concluding sentence here makes clear, de Blácam was more than willing to discard some of what Irish people had written in English, particularly when those people seemed to have consciously rejected precisely those elements that could have redeemed their work for the nation. Thus of Yeats he wrote in 1930:

> The movement out of which his own work sprung was started by a revival of interest in the Irish language and the Gaelic tradition. To continue to work in that movement a deeper knowledge of the language and tradition were necessary; but neither was acquired. To be brief: Mr Yeats was stirred by some fragments of Gaelic tradition; but he never proceeded to become firmly seized by his subject. He was content to build up a phantasmagoria of his own, and to call it Gaelic. He moved away from reality, and lost Ireland in the Celtic twilight (*FMR*, Feb. 1930, 61).

P. S. O'Hegarty, a long-time cultural nationalist, as well as a historian, literary critic, and senior civil servant, felt that it was Corkery who had gone badly astray, lacking the commonsense and generosity to follow his own ideas to a more logical conclusion. Arguing in a 1932 review of *Synge and Anglo-Irish Literature* that once Corkery had conceded the possibility of an acceptably Irish literature in English he forfeited the right to try to formulate and impose any narrow definition of such a literature, O'Hegarty pulled no punches:

> Need I say more on this than that this theory of Mr Corkery's is wrong-headed and damnable. It is carrying bigotry and intolerance into literature. It is a denial of the Irish Nation. It is prejudiced, and in the real sense, ignorant. The Irish Nation includes all the people of this Island, Catholic and non-Catholic, Gael and Sean-Ghall, native and 'ascendancy'. An Irish national literature must include all of them, and an Irish 'cosmos' – a word beloved by Mr Corkery – must include all of them.

Nor was O'Hegarty in any way reluctant to state just how inclusive he himself was willing to be:

> For my part I think that work done by an Irishman in an Irish setting and with an Irish background, whether done in Irish or in English, is Irish literature, and I should use the term *Anglo-Irish* only as a convenient label, if it be used at all, and not as a definition. Maria Edgeworth, and Griffin, and Carleton, and Banim, and Allingham, and Lever and Lover, are all Irish literature, as Irish as Mr Corkery himself... English has become, in the course of time, a mother language here and we can, and do, express ourselves in it in a distinct and unmistakable way.

Then, after a brief and not all that convincing nod to right thinking, he continued in the same iconoclastic vein:

> We hope eventually to get back to Irish. But in the meantime and as things are we are expressing ourselves in English, and the feeblest beginning of that expression is as Irish literature as if it had been written in Irish . . . I throw the net wide, then. I claim as Irish Literature Molyneux, and Swift, and all those from Maria Edgeworth down to O'Casey, whom Mr. Corkery abolishes, and I claim as Irishmen of Letters Scotus Erigena, and Berkeley, and Sterne, and Hamilton, and Wilde, and a multitude of others. I deny in toto Mr Corkery's theories and propositions, explicit and implicit (*Dublin Magazine*, Jan.–Mar. 51–6).

O'Hegarty was also disappointed that de Blácam had not gone further in *A First Book of Irish Literature*. In full agreement with de Blácam's definition of Irish literature as 'literature written by Irishmen', and convinced that de Blácam 'has a better appreciation of literature than Mr Corkery, and his temperament is not so arid and hidebound', O'Hegarty nonetheless felt that de Blácam had missed an opportunity to dismantle the Corkery thesis, 'his arbitrary and narrow framework', as he called it. Needless to say, O'Hegarty himself felt no reservations about taking on the job. Having accused Corkery – and by implication de Blácam – of 'first getting a theory and then cutting up facts to fit it', he challenged his colleagues in the Irish-Ireland movement with a simple question: 'Why should Ireland not take pride in the fact that her sons can use the English language with an intensity that the English themselves cannot equal?' After the rather perfunctory claim that 'we shall use the Irish language with the same intensity some day', he returned with zest to his real theme:

> What we have given to literature in the English language is nothing accidental or transient, but something coming from the genius of the Race, which will go equally to literature in Irish when Irish has been schooled and fashioned to give full expression to the thoughts of what Berkeley called 'we Irishmen'.

Moreover, for O'Hegarty, this acceptance that Ireland was and would remain a bilingual country was only one aspect of his championing what we might now call the hybridity of Irish culture:

> There is something in Ireland, some friendly genius, something fierce and proud and unpredictable, which makes its own of every 'creed and race and clan', which works steadily through whatever material is available towards an Irish Nation, not a Gaelic Nation, but an Irish Nation (*Dublin Magazine*, Jan.–Mar. 1935, 64–6).

Yet however heterodox some of his opinions and however aggressive his rhetoric, O'Hegarty remained committed to his own liberal understanding of the Gaelic movement. It was the Gaels themselves who distressed him, as he acknowledged with exasperation in a piece on 'This Prejudice against English' in 1936:

> Again it is noticeable that a large body of national literature, poetry and drama in the English language is largely ignored by the promoters of Gaelicisation. The idea that this mass of material could be used to foster nationality and thus prepare the way for the Irish language, never appears to have entered their ultra-Gaelic heads (*Leader*, 5/9/36).

Riobárd Ó Faracháin was one prominent writer of Irish who went well beyond passive appreciation of the potential contribution literature in English could make in the campaign for a Gaelic Ireland. As Robert Farren, he published poetry and critical work in English to accompany *Fíon gan Mhoirt*, his 1938 short-story collection in Irish. Ó Faracháin's position on the significance of such creative work in English, spelled out most forcefully in his own summary of a 1931 lecture he delivered on 'The Gaelic Derivation of Anglo-Irish Literature', involved the familiar notion of an inherent *Gaelachas* in the work of some Anglo-Irish authors. But he broke with movement consensus when he asserted of the works of writers like Mitchel, Ferguson, Sigerson, Pearse, and Corkery: 'They are literature and they are national literature' (*ACS*, 26/12/31).[31]

Few, particularly among those O'Hegarty dubbed the 'ultra-Gaels' – often the thinkers most prominently associated with the movement in the public mind at the time – were willing to go anywhere near so far. More typical of the attitude of those Irish-Irelanders at least open to the charms and claims of Irish writing in English was the touchy and often contradictory ambivalence of Seosamh Mac Grianna.[32] On the one hand, he could see the question in the starkest confrontational terms, writing in 1926:

> First of all, let it be understood that there is no such thing as a bilingual race or a bilingual man. The Irish people are unilingual. No matter how many languages a man knows, one language rules the rest . . . The contest is then between Irish and Anglo-Irish, and one must triumph (*An Phoblacht*, 16/7/26).[33]

Yet at this very same time, he could also insist that there were 'really Irish' Anglo-Irish writers (*An Phoblacht*, 18/6/26)[34] – and he included them with writers of Irish as 'our writers', as opposed to the alien school of what he dubbed 'Clann Shaw' (*An Phoblacht*, 4/6/26). Among those of whom he approved were Kickham, Mitchel, Standish James O'Grady, Canon Sheehan,

Thomas McDonagh, Corkery, Joyce, O'Casey, and Liam O'Flaherty. But to add to the confusion – his as well as ours no doubt – he could elsewhere denounce two of the same writers, O'Casey and O'Flaherty, along with Brinsley McNamara and Patrick McGill,[35] as members of the 'The Frog-Spawn School of Irish Literature', a group of writers he saw winning foreign fame and fortune by vilifying and/or ridiculing their native land (*An Phoblacht*, 11/6/26).[36] Without apology, he could then, in a heated denunciation of An Gúm and the Free State's Censorship of Publications Act, elevate some of these very same 'Frog-Spawn' authors to the status of voice of the national conscience:

> Writers can only react to their environment. They are the historians of their people. As surely as the world will go on until worms eat the paper of the Censorship Bill so surely will the historians of the future go to James Joyce and to George Moore and to Liam O'Flaherty and to Patrick McGill for information about Irish life in the days in which those writers lived (*An Phoblacht*, 23/7/32).

At some level, Mac Grianna seems to have believed that these ambivalences could be resolved with an act of faith – or perhaps better, hope – writing in 1926, for example:

> Yet, although in worth and bulk it has the best claim to be called the national literature, Anglo-Irish literature can never fill that place permanantly. There is a gale unborn in the skies of tomorrow which will blow Anglo-Irish speech into the tongue of the English Empire (*An Phoblacht*, 2/7/26).

There were, then, meaningful differences of opinion among the Gaels concerning the proper place, if any, in the national canon for writing in English. Most, however, believed that the *sine qua non* for admission to this cultural inner sanctum was, if not possession of the Gaelic note itself, at least a passionate awareness of and pride in Irish identity and a loyalty to the national cause as defined in an author's own time and political circumstances. By these criteria, those in effect by which Corkery in his book on Synge distinguished 'true' or 'genuine' Anglo-Irish literature from 'Ascendancy' Anglo-Irish literature, many of the best-known Irish writers of English would not be eligible for Seamus Heaney's green passport.[37] Predictably enough, the writers of the heyday of the Ascendancy in the eighteenth century came in for particularly sharp criticism. In his 1938 essay on 'Éire na Gaedhilge nó Anglo-Ireland – Ciocu?' (The Ireland of the Irish language or Anglo-Ireland – Which one?), Pádraig Ó Siochfhradha dismissed Yeats's 'hard-riding country gentleman' as 'a people without talent, without culture, without accomplishments, except for intense pride and drinking and personal and political misconduct' (dream gan éirim gan chultúr gan tréithe, ach teasbach dearg is ól is mí-iomchur pearsanta is polaitidheachta) (*Bonaventura*, Autumn 1938, 17). Writing on 'Sgríbhneoirí Gall-Ghaedhealacha 1700–1800' (Anglo-Irish writers 1700–1800) in his *Stair na hÉireann*, Aodh Mac Dhubháin dismissed their claims to membership in the Irish nation so many of them despised:

> The eighteenth century was 'the golden age' of the Anglo-Irish writers in Ireland. They thought that they themselves were the nation, and they were proud of it accordingly. Almost all of them got their education in Trinity College. They had little respect for the native population of the country nor for their customs.[38]

Sergeant Tomás Morrisroe of the Gárda Síochána was considerably more generous toward the Ascendancy writers, but still saw them as fundamentally alien:

> During the eighteenth century the English colony in Ireland and the native Irish also were brought up according to English manners, cultivated the English language so much and to such good purpose that they outshone their English rivals during the same period in the excellences of their literary productions. Men like Goldsmith, Parnell, Swift, Burke, Sheridan, have shed lasting glory both to the country of their birth and on English letters. Nevertheless, writers such as these were, with all their excellences, did not express the heart and mind of the historic Irish race. Their works have undoubtedly an Irish flavour, but their souls did not drink in the traditional lore; they had, in a manner, cut themselves adrift from the historic current of Irish life. They spoke for the Pale and for the Ascendancy. The traditions they strove to perpetuate were English or Anglo-Irish rather than Irish traditions (*Iris an Ghárda*, 19/11/23).

Of the most prominent Anglo-Irish writers of the eighteenth century, even Swift found little favour with the Gaels, despite his deep involvement in the Irish politics of his time, his curious role as somewhat of a trickster figure in Irish folklore, and his probable acquaintance with contemporary Gaelic intellectuals like Seán Ó Neachtain and his Dublin-based literary circle. As we have seen, de Blácam and O'Hegarty were willing to claim him as Irish, but Corkery was far more sceptical, praising his 'large heart' and 'seeing mind' in *The Hidden Ireland*, but in general judging him, despite his good intentions and brilliance, as irretrievably Anglicised (*Studies*, June 1934, 210).

Goldsmith fared quite a bit better in Gaelic opinion. As we saw above, he was one of the writers of English in whose work a distinctive Gaelic note was detected, and he was discussed with respect and even affection by several leading Gaelic writers and critics of the period. For example, de Blácam declared that if Goldsmith had known Irish, he would have 'bent Irish prose to the range of modern thought', an idea that Seosamh Mac Grianna claimed as one of the factors that made him believe such a development was possible and that led him to turn away from English and to Irish as his linguistic medium.[39] Seán Ó Ciarghusa used Goldsmith's command of English as the standard against which to measure the accomplishments of Tomás Ó Criomhthain in *An t-Oileánach*.[40] And in perhaps the most impressive tribute to his eighteenth-century predecessor, Séamus Ó Néill in 1939 wrote *Poor Poll*, a short play in Irish about Goldsmith.[41] Of other Irish writers of English at the time like Sterne, Sheridan, Berkeley *et al.*, there were only passing references, if that, in the Gaelic literary discourse of the Free State years.

The nineteenth century saw the rise of an educated, English-speaking, and usually nationalist middle class throughout the country, the sort of people who would both create a demand for literature in English on Irish subjects and produce the writers to satisfy that demand. The considerable success of such writers, both in terms of popular acclaim and of the perceived status achieved by many of them as the legitimate voice of an awakening Irish Catholic nation, guaranteed that their work would attract serious and sustained attention from Gaelic intellectuals, many of whom had, after all, grown up reading and admiring their work. Of nineteenth-century Anglo-Irish writers, the most acceptable to the Gaels were, predictably, those of Gaelic, Catholic, and/or nationalist backgrounds. For this reason, Maria Edgeworth was in general dismissed rather perfunctorily, as she was, for instance, by Corkery in *Synge and Anglo-Irish Literature*. Rare to the point of non-existence was the language revivalist who would agree with the opinion of 'G.' on Edgeworth:

> Although she was not a Gael – she was born in England – she was not an Englishwoman to the people of this country, and her own life and everything she wrote showed the charity and the understanding that were in her heart for the people of Ireland (*IMN*, 1928, 98).[42]

Her contemporary, Lady Morgan, fared even worse. I have found no reference at all to her in the Irish-Ireland journals of our period. Not surprisingly, subsequent 'Big House' writers also failed to find favour with the Gaels, with Pádhraic Ó Domhnalláin writing of Somerville and Ross:

> We do not see in their work anything but jeering and mockery of Gaels, of their religious customs, of their patriotism, and of everything that is native to the Milesians [Gaels]. They themselves failed Ireland; they failed the religion of their ancestors, they failed their heritage for money and for sham nobility (*CB*, Mar. 1934).[43]

The Gaelic writers shared with virtually all of their fellow citizens in the Free State a deep respect for the patriotic contributions of nineteenth-century Protestant writers who committed themselves fully and openly to the national cause. Among such cultural and political nationalists who were praised by Gaels in our period were James Clarence Mangan (*Leader*, 6/12/30; 19/12/31), Thomas Davis (*An Phoblacht*, 30/7/26; 27/8/27), John Mitchel,[44] Samuel Ferguson,[45] George Sigerson (*FL*, 28/2/25; *Branar*, Mar. 1925, 50), and Standish James O'Grady (*An Phoblacht*, 14/1/27; 21/1/27; 4/2/27). The Trinity-educated Catholic Thomas Moore also retained the respect of most in the language movement, with 'Oisín' writing of him: 'It is my opinion that the people of this country never treated Thomas Moore fairly' (*Derry People*, 18/9/37).[46]

'Oisín' praised Moore for nurturing 'the proper spirit of Nationality' (spiorad ceart na Náisiúntachta), and saw him as a victim of his time, a time in which the idea of a literary career in Irish was beyond the imagination of even the most visionary members of his class and upbringing. This notion that patriotic Irish writers of the nineteenth century wrote English because a knowledge and true appreciation of Irish were denied them was as widespread as it was satisfying among cultural nationalists in the Free State. For example, T. Ó Murchadha in his essay on Kickham declared:

> But however much Irish-speakers want to revive the language of their ancestors, and however much bitterness they have in their heart against the people who always did it harm and who carry on that evil work still, they do not forget the true Gaels who tried to satisfy the desire of the Gaels for poetry and for prose stories when the doors of the bardic schools were closed forever, when the poets died off one after the other, and when the Irish language itself was banished from every city and village in Ireland. And indeed, those people have richly earned the love and respect of their fellow Gaels from the year 1848 on (*IMN*, 1931, 47).[47]

From this perspective, the fact that Kickham and his comrades wrote in English was a mere accident of history, and a rather superficial one at that, a point made by Piaras Béaslaí in a review of Tomás de Bhial's translation of William O'Brien's 1890 novel *When We Were Boys*: 'But in the condition in which this country was with regard to language, a great deal of literature that should have been written in the language of the country was written in the foreign language' (*IP*, 13/10/38).[48] Even more forthright was Ó Murchadha, who said of Micheál Breathnach's translation of Kickham's *Knocknagow*: 'We at last have this delightful story in the language most natural for it' (Tá ar fagháil againn fé dheire an sgéal aoibhinn seo 'san teangain 'nar dhual dó a bheith) (*IMN*, 1931, 49).

However problematic and contradictory, this belief that Kickham was, in effect, a Gaelic author in all but language had considerable currency at the time. Reviewing this same translation of *Knocknagow*, Tomás Ua Concheanainn wrote:

> Here is a book that was first written in English and that describes accurately and respectfully the life of rural people in Tipperary over one hundred years ago; and it is almost possible to say that there is not a turn of speech in it from start to finish that is not a Gaelic turn of speech (*CT*, 16/2/29).[49]

'An Léightheoir Comhthrom' saw Máirtín Ó Cadhain's translation of Kickham's *Sally Cavanagh* in virtually identical terms in 1932:

> The virtue of Kickham's books as material for translation is that it is not necessary to make any change in the events of the life of the people or in their thoughts. If anyone ever understood the mind of the people of Tipperary, Kickham did. It is, therefore, only necessary to put a Gaelic shape on the language to create a book that would be appropriate for people with Irish now (*TCNÍ*, Sept. 1932, 213).[50]

Similarly, commenting on Kickham's poem 'The Irish Peasant Girl' in *Oileáin Árann*, An tAthair Mártan Ó Domhnaill claimed: 'The thoughts and the spirit of the Gaels are in the original song, and it only needs the natural attire that suits it to make it truly Gaelic in every way.'[51]

Ó Cadhain himself drew attention to the Gaelic resonances in the work of William Carleton in a 1934 lecture to members of An Fáinne on 'Lucht Téisglinne Aithbheochana na Gaedhilge roimh Connradh na Gaedhilge' (The forerunners of the Irish language revival before the Gaelic League), a lecture of which *An t-Éireannach* reported:

> He informed them about how much Irish Carleton had (although he could not write Irish) and how the work of Carleton influenced the writers of Ulster – in Irish and in English – to the present day – for example, 'Máire' and Seaghán Mac Meanman and Peadar O'Donnell (*Éireannach*, 8/12/34).[52]

The anonymous reviewer of Gaelic titles for *The Irish Times* pondered what Carleton could have achieved had he written in Irish: 'For him it has been claimed that, if he had written in Gaelic – and he appears to have been an Irish speaker – he might have been the father of a great line of Gaelic novelists' (*IT*, 4/11/33). In the meantime, Carleton's work, like Kickham's, was seen as particularly suitable for translation into Irish: '*Fardorougha the Miser* is one of the best novels that poor Carleton left us, and it was a good thought on the part of Seán Mac Maoláin to translate it into Irish' (*TCNÍ*, Jan. 1934, 13).[53]

One of the things that appealed most to Gaels about these nineteenth-century writers was that they were safely dead and thus unable to protest at their conscription for a cause they might not have embraced had they known of it. What, for example, would Kickham have made of Ó Murchadha's opinion of where he would stand on the cultural politics of the Free State? Ó Murchadha wrote:

> What is most likely, if he were alive today, is that he would be working zealously to re-establish the dominance and the vigour of the old Ireland of the Gaels: Yes, – that he would be a Fanatic, according to the opinion of those who are content to see Ireland turning into an Anglicised country (*IMN*, 1931, 50).[54]

Living writers were far less pliable, but they were also far more present, and that presence demanded a response from those who saw themselves as the authentic literary voice of the new Ireland.

From the very outset of the revival, the most imposing writer of English with whom the Gaels had to engage was William Butler Yeats, whose universally acknowledged leadership of an 'Irish' literary renaissance made him a particular focus of fascination, frustration and anger. All of those emotions continued to be reflected in various combinations in comments on the poet throughout our period. As had always been the case, D. P. Moran's *The Leader* and Patrick T. Keohane's *Catholic Bulletin* treated Yeats with an almost irrational contempt right up to and beyond his death in 1939. Among many other things, various contributors to *The Leader* during our period called Yeats 'a West Briton' (16/8/24; 21/3/25), 'a Britisher, a bigot, and a bounder . . . one of the English breed in Ireland' (20/6/25), 'a distinguished businessman, a minor poet and a bounder' (14/7/28), and 'a man steeped in false history, false philosophy, pagan nonsense', a man whose 'spiritual progenitors' were 'the robber ruffians of the Reformation' (15/9/28). For *The Leader*, Yeats's 1923 Nobel Prize was 'a Norwegian tit-bits prize for poetry' (12/7/24).[55] *The Catholic Bulletin* was every bit as childishly scurrilous, calling Yeats 'a pensioner poet' and a 'neo-pagan' (Dec. 1923, 817, 819), 'one of the leading coryphants in the New Ascendancy movement' (Apr. 1924, 266), 'the Proud Pensionary' (July, 1925, 641), 'the mellifluous Mahatma' (Aug. 1925, 824), 'the moony Mahatma, the silly Swedenborgian, the yelping Yogi' (Nov. 1925, 1082), 'the sole and solitary extant specimen of the Mahatma school of versification, the great Auk of the London–Dublin Academy of Letters (Mar. 1938, 185), and 'this essentially English writer' (Mar. 1939, 183).[56]

If we sort through the puerile abuse, we can see that the principal charge these two publications levelled at Yeats was that he was alien in his religious/philosophical views and in his ethnic/political allegiance. In a 1923 editorial critical of the directors of the Central Catholic Library for sponsoring a lecture by Yeats, the *Catholic Bulletin* complained that 'the pension poet has long made it quite clear that he has no use for Christianity, and that he prefers, both on aesthetic and ethical grounds, if you please, the pagan past' (*CB*, Dec. 1923, 817). Nor was this charge of paganism limited to *The Leader* and the *Catholic Bulletin* alone. Writing in *An Tír* in 1932, 'Cormac' warned his compatriots of the sinister programme motivating Yeats and his followers:

> They have been working early and late for many a day, trying to bring about the triumph of their gospel, a gospel that is antithetical to the outlook of the Gaels and to the outlook of Catholics throughout the whole world (*Tír*, Dec. 1932, 6).[57]

In his introductory piece 'Why "The Irish Homeland" Is Here', the editor of this journal put Yeats, 'the high pontiff of paganism in this country', at the top of his list of adversaries to be fought in the name of true Irish culture (i.e. one 'Christian and Gaelic'):

> Imagine the long lackadaisical Yeats in his latest role: theologian, moral philosopher, aye – pope! . . . Catholics – the mere Irish – must see as Yeats sees, think as Yeats thinks, do as Yeats does! If the majority in this country object to the Paganism of Yeats and his school, they have no right to do so, that's what it comes to (*Irish Homeland*, Aug. 1925, 1).

As early as 1923, Pádhraic Ó Domhnalláin explained to readers of *Fáinne an Lae* why Yeats had opposed beginning sessions of the Free State Senate with a prayer in Irish: 'No one would expect anything different from him, for it is clear from his poetry that he adheres more to paganism than to Christianity' (*FL*, 22/12/23).[58] In forgiving mood on the occasion of the poet's death, the editor of the *Irish Rosary* still felt compelled to lament the 'serious limitations and grave defects of his work':

> For he was an exile from the God who has revealed truth and beauty at its highest *in facie Jesu Christi*. And while his poetry was incontrovertibly perfect in its expression, it lacked the illumination of the curtain-rise of Revelation (*IR*, Mar. 1939, 162–3).[59]

As a senator in the Free State legislature from 1922 to 1928, Yeats had a platform for views that scandalised and disgusted many cultural nationalists, who accused him of virtual treason to the new Gaelic Catholic state they wished to build. Moreover, many Gaels seem to have grossly exaggerated the poet's influence in the Free State's corridors of power, as when Risteárd Ó Foghludha, in a diatribe against 'An Táin Ghallda' (The Anglicised herd), called Yeats 'the bull of the herd, their prophet of great Allah' (tarbh na Tána, an té is fáidh aca d'Alla mór) (*FL*, 12/12/25), or when 'Cormac' traced Ernest Blythe's decision to subsidise the Abbey Theatre to the machinations of Yeats:

> The world knows that W. B. Yeats is the most significant person . . . in the affairs of the foreign culture in Ireland. He is the little god of the cultured foreigners in this country. It is he who will set you up or will break you according to his own wishes. If you are not willing to bow down to him and to accept the authority of himself and his followers, you will be broken and you will be crushed (*Tír*, Dec. 1932, 6).[60]

Perhaps the nastiest attack inspired by this paranoia about Yeats's political influence was that by Peadar Mac Fhionnlaoich in *An Phoblacht*. Having condemned the Free State Senate for providing a platform and publicity 'to a group of the planters and the Freemasons and the foreigners in Ireland who are most venemous in their opposition to everything Gaelic' (do dhream de na plandóirí agus na Saor-Saoir agus na gaill is nimhnighe in Éirinn in aghaidh gach rud Gaedhealach), he directed his fire at the man he saw as the worst of a very bad lot:

> Senator Yeats, for example: people who knew him always understood that he was a degenerate, that he had an excessively high opinion of himself and contempt for the Gaels of Ireland. At the time of the Black and Tans he was afraid to speak out loud for fear that it would be thought that he was on the side of Ireland. He would not even allow his friends to come into his house if they had any nationalist reputation for fear that the Black and Tans would be after him. But now he is a great man; a Senator and a statesman, and he can release his venom against the people of Ireland and he will get a column of publicity in every paper in Ireland (*An Phoblacht*, 4/9/25).[61]

Mac Fhionnlaoich was responding specifically here to Yeats's famous apotheosis of the Anglo-Irish in his 1925 Senate speech opposing a bill to prohibit divorce in the Free State. While Yeats as a politician was criticised for everything from objecting to prayers in Irish in the Senate chamber to denying the need for bilingual train tickets (*FL*, 12/7/24), nothing he said or did at the time aroused more Gaelic ire than did this single speech, which the *Catholic Bulletin* labelled 'the pestilent and premeditated pronouncement of Sen. W. B. P. Yeats' (*CB*, Sept. 1925, 926)[62] and 'the foul mass of the Pollexfen diatribe' (*CB*, Oct. 1925, 964), and of which D. P. Moran commented in *The Leader*: 'He is proud that he is not of the mere Irish; so are we' (*Leader*, 20/6/25).[63] For many Irish-Irelanders, this speech was the final confirmation that Yeats had betrayed the cause. Nowhere is this sense of Yeats as apostate more evident than in a 1925 essay by Seán Ó Ciarghusa:

> W. B. Yeats was boasting of the feats and accomplishments of his people in the Senate the other week. They were the cream of the countryside, he said, from Swift to Parnell. He was right. None of the Gaelic race could be at the top of anything in Swift's time, for if he showed his head, not to mention making any attempt to assert himself, that head would be lopped off him. And then when their hardships were removed, and ever since, instead of turning on the English and trying to throw off the intellectual, cultural, and philosophical domination, they have been currying favour with them and imitating them, with the English, no wonder, laughing at them the whole time. Even today, they have the whip up their sleeve, and we owe W. B. Yeats a debt of gratitude for showing us a bit of the crop of the whip. Seeing it might teach our people that it is high time for them to stop mimicking Yeats or competing with him in English, for as surely as tea comes from the East, the English language comes and will come from England, and Yeats and his company are the dealers who will provide it for us in Ireland. And along with the English language there will be, not surprisingly, everything that goes with it. Even the Faith, let us be on guard that the Faith of Patrick does not fade under the influence of Anglicisation (*Sguab*, July 1925, 384).[64]

The full Gaelic case against Yeats is there in Ó Ciarghusa's piece, but for language activists, the role of Yeats as an agent of Anglicisation was of particular significance. The global fame Yeats had won through the English language, coupled with his confident assertion of his own Irishness, made him a threat to almost everything the revival hoped to accomplish. 'Cormac' was blunt on this point in 1932: 'The Gaels must speak out strongly against these people [the followers of Yeats], and, in particular, against the attempt being made by Yeats to pretend that he has the authority to speak in the name of Ireland' (*Tír*, Dec. 1932, 6).[65] After reading an instalment of the poet's memoirs in 1936, Jeremiah Murphy, Professor of English at University College Galway and an active member of Taibhdhearc na Gaillimhe, was even more dismissive of Yeats's right to speak as *a*, much less *the*, Irish artist:

> If any man doubt the ability of our dominant *littérateurs* to express the genius of the Irish people in English, let him read the first part of Mr Yeats's Reminiscences, appearing in the *London Mercury*. They are certainly a revelation which at once disqualifies him from any claim to represent the Irish genius in literature. He has annihilated himself as a countryman of any country, for the English would repudiate a claim on them. And Mr Yeats is the acknowledged leader to whom all the rest do homage. Not that I think any less of Mr Yeats as a literary man! Certainly not! But Mr Yeats cannot henceforward get on the blind side of Ireland's Eye (*Gaedheal*, Jan. 1936, 3).

Yet despite all the anger and resentment, some of the more thoughtful Gaels were haunted by a sense of what could have been had they and Yeats been able to continue as allies in the cultural crusade they once seemed to have shared. Writing in 1933, de Blácam recalled:

> The poetry of the younger Yeats intoxicated us and we gladly acknowledged the claim of him who since has ceased, alas, to make it – Know that I would accounted be / True brother to that company / Who sang, to sweeten Ireland's wrong, / Ballad and story and rann and song (*Guth na nGaedheal*, 1933, 17).

He returned to this theme in a piece published the month after the poet's death:

> More and more with the years, he became the champion of Berkeley and Swift and the repudiator of the Gael. Those of us who have tried to find a synthesis, in which what is best in the Anglo-Irish should be given to the historic nation in its future growth, got no aid from him.

His conclusion was wistful: 'How great a man he would have been, how great a poet, had he been constant to the dream of his youth and to the fire that was kindled in him again by the deeds of the men of Easter Week!' (*Irish Monthly*, Mar. 1939, 209, 211).

Similarly, responding to a 1937 radio broadcast in which Yeats spoke slightingly of the language revival, an anonymous contributor to the Dundalk *Examiner* lamented:

> And notwithstanding his feeling for literature he seemingly could contemplate without sorrow or anger the disappearance of the language that first of all languages north of the Alps contained a whole body of literature: a literature in the translations and retellings from which he sought inspiration at the beginning of his literary life (*Examiner*, 9/10/37).

This acknowledgment of the Gaelic inspiration of some of the poet's work could lead to an appreciation of what he had accomplished as a genuinely Irish writer, a point made by 'Sliabh Bladhma' in 1934. Commenting on the fact that Yeats had been referred to in passing as an 'English poet' (file Gallda), 'Sliabh Bladhma' corrected what he saw as an unjust misconception: 'Now, very much of the best poetical work of W. B. Yeats is based on Gaelic lore and tradition . . . In this instance "Gallda" is wide of the mark. We must be thoughtful and just' (*Gaedheal*, 25/8/34).

Unfortunately, few were willing to go much further than that. One of them was the iconoclastic P. S. O'Hegarty, who at the beginning of our period said of Yeats that 'no poet of our time is so essentially or wholly a poet as Mr Yeats', and at its end unapologetically claimed him for the nation:

> I think that Ireland in the coming times will understand that the great Poet who worked for a national culture was during the whole of his life one of the most revolutionary influences in Ireland. He worked for the liberation of the spirit, and it is the spirit that moves the body (*Dublin Magazine*, July–Sept. 1939, 24).

Equally forthright was Séamus Ó Néill, who published his obituary tribute to Yeats in, of all places, *The Leader*:

> Whatever his failings, and like all men he had them, W. B. Yeats loved his Ireland . . . Yeats betrayed her not, and for one who was not of the ancient faith of Ireland, he came at times very near the vision, and his heart beat with the people and with understanding of them (*Leader*, 25/2/39).[66]

The Gaels found that other giant of Anglo-Irish literature, George Bernard Shaw, a much less troubling adversary, an attitude aided by his physical absence from the scene and, in their minds, his irrelevance to the national cause. The dominant Irish-Ireland response to Shaw was well summed-up in a 1923 piece on 'The Newer West Britons' in *The Leader*: 'In mentality and literary manner he is the most egregious anti-Irish Irishman now living on the planet of which he considers himself a citizen' (*Leader*, 22/9/23).[67] Shaw's work was also, of course, seen by Corkery in his book on Synge as a quintessential example of deracinated 'Colonial' literature.[68] Even more dismissive was Seosamh Mac Grianna, who wrote of the playwright in 1926:

> Joyce, O'Casey, O'Flaherty etc. are, it must be admitted, really Irish. But there is no such hope that Shaw can ever mean anything to us . . . Shaw is a complete alien, like his intellectual forebears, Wilde, Goldsmith, Sheridan, Burke, Steele and Swift. They are the writers of the West Britons. Their writings mean no more to Ireland's literary history than the campaigns of the Duke of Wellington and the campaigns of Kitchener and French mean to Ireland's military and political history.

None of this meant that Mac Grianna did not consider Shaw a major world writer. He was just not in any meaningful sense an Irish writer:

> Of course it is not suggested that Irish patriots should be total abstainers from Shaw. But we should read Shaw as we read Chesterton, or Papini, or Maeterlinck, or Ibsen or Dostoevsky, or any other modern foreign writer. The fact that he was

born in Ireland is the one fact of his life which should weigh least with us when reading him. Having absolved him of any duty toward the Irish nation, we can consider him impartially as a democratic thinker and a writer who adds writing of value to English literature (*An Phoblacht*, 18/6/26).

The Gaelic author who seems to have taken most interest in Shaw was Seán Ó Ciarghusa, in whose essays one occasionally finds positive remarks about him in passing. For example, discussing the origins of a series of educational proposals presented to the British government, Ó Ciarghusa with tongue-in-cheek pride commented:

Note that it is no witty and upstart Gael or sarcastic jokester the like of G. B. Shaw who proposed those things to the Government of England, but stolid, sensible, learned Englishmen who fully understand what they are saying.[69]

It is also worth noting that in a discussion of plays Stephen McKenna and himself had seen in London, Liam Ó Rinn mentions Shaw's *The Apple Cart*, O'Casey's *Juno and the Paycock*, the Belfast-born Shaw biographer Greer St John Irvine's *The First Mrs Fraser*, and, with a clear sense of both distinction and dismissal, 'another one by an English playwright' (ceann éigin eile le drámadóir Sasanach).[70] Once again, however, it was P. S. O'Hegarty who wrote the most positive assessment of Shaw as an Irish writer:

He is an Irishman, not by birth alone but by instinct, by equipment. Scratch him and you find the rebel. In May 1916, his was the first voice, in England or in Ireland, to be raised in defence of Ireland, and at every crisis he has been impelled, for all his mockery, to say the right thing and the bold thing. His feeling for England and for Englishmen varies from tolerant boasting to virulent dispraisement (*Irish Review*, 28/10/22).[71]

James Joyce seems to have shocked and baffled most Gaels as much as he did the majority of his English-speaking compatriots. This attitude was neatly summed up by Eoin Ua Mathghamhna in a 1924 essay on 'Obscenity in Modern Irish Literature': 'Mr James Joyce is apparently afflicted with a shameful mania, but, as his works are little read by sane folk, we need say nothing of him' (*Irish Monthly*, Nov. 1924, 569). The usually perspicacious 'Sliabh Bladhma' was downright condescending: 'Of James Joyce I know little beyond the fact that, according to his admirers, he has been evolving a new English language. The quotations, to me at any rate, suggest baby-prattle, which, of course, has its charm' (*Gaedheal*, 1/6/35).[72] Seán Ó Ciosáin felt that Joyce was the darling of an anti-national Irish pseudo-intelligentsia:

> They have long debates about 'the new language' being developed by James Joyce. According to them, that writer is the only Irishman who can reveal the soul of Ireland to Europe. Of course it does not matter if he succeeds in revealing that soul to the people of their own country. They are only barbarians (*Star*, 19/10/29).[73]

The Irish-Irelanders who engaged with Joyce's work most seriously were Liam Ó Rinn and P. S. O'Hegarty. In a 1929 piece on 'Séamas Seoighe / An Stíl Nua' (James Joyce / The new style), Ó Rinn commented on Joyce's stylistic experiments and his focus on the more sordid side of life, and then continued:

> Perhaps Mr Joyce is only following the lead of the painters who paint a pattern (if it is proper to call something that is meaningless a pattern) that is not like anything on earth and who say that it is a house and garden or snow on a mountain or a village. But if that is how it is – well, we will have to leave Mr Joyce and the painters and their followers and their constant arguments to the one being who understands them – the God of Glory (*Star*, 19/1/29).[74]

Reading *Ulysses* did not raise his opinion of Joyce at all. In a 1932 essay on the novel, he made clear that he began the book out of a sense of curiosity and finished it as an obligation. For Ó Rinn, the book was 'a dull, dry, detailed, lifeless, tedious account' (cuntas tur tirim mion-chruinn marbhánta leadránach) of the seamiest side of Dublin life as viewed by a person 'full of cynical bitterness' (lán de shearbhas shuiniciúil). While he was careful to note 'the amount of obscenity in it is hardly worth noticing if we think of its size and its bulk' (is ar éigin is fiú an méid salachair atá ann d'áireamh má chuimhnimíd ar a mhéid is ar a thoirt), his final impression of the book was entirely negative:

> This is a grim, gloomy book that leaves a bad taste in your mouth. If it were to be had for a half-crown, I do not think there would be any demand for it . . . Ulysses means one who hates. A fitting name – it seems that the author hates everything that the human race likes (*UIrman*, 17/12/32).[75]

O'Hegarty broke ranks once again to praise Joyce not only as an artist, but as an Irish artist:

> I make the assertion, after reading this [*Ulysses*], that Mr Joyce loves Ireland, especially Dublin. I do not mean that he does it politically, or in any 'wrap-the-green-flag' sense. But Ireland is all through him, and of him; and Dublin, its streets and its buildings and its people, he loves with the whole-hearted affection of the artist.

Nor was he concerned that his would be the minority position:

> Ireland at present will probably not love Mr Joyce. But Mr Joyce has done her honour. No Englishman could have written this book, even if one had the wit to conceive the plan of it . . . Wilde, Shaw, Moore, Synge, Joyce! Could a country provide five artists of this calibre, with certain common intellectual attitudes, if these did not really represent the mind of the country? (*Separatist*, 2/9/22).[76]

Despite O'Hegarty's inclusion of George Moore and Synge in his litany above, neither drew much comment from Irish-Irelanders during this period. Most Gaels at the time, if they thought about Moore at all, probably agreed with Moran's characterisation of him as 'the unconsciously comic old gentleman' (*Leader*, 27/9/30). A rare exception who devoted any attention to Moore was 'Sliabh Bladhma', who, writing of Moore's early enthusiasm for the Gaelic League, sounded a note that should by now be familiar:

> At the time, however, we expected things original and distinctive. We were fated to remain expectant . . . With the fuller Gaelic life he was not at home; he would not be a student – 'too old to learn Irish' – and could not be a simple worker . . . I think that at first he was entirely sincere, but wanted a share of hero-worship from the Gaels, while what they demanded was work and service. There is pathos as well as comedy in the tale of his quest of the Gaelic Ireland he never really reached (*Gaedheal*, 1/6/35).[77]

Synge, once the most hated Anglo-Irish figure among Irish-Irelanders, had, of course, escaped their malice the hard way, by dying in 1909. Nevertheless, he could still evoke strong reactions on occasion during our period. Obviously, the most sustained commentary on Synge's work by an Irish-Irelander at the time was Corkery's *Synge and Anglo-Irish Literature*, a work whose insightful discussion of Synge's plays has been overshadowed by the controversy concerning the author's definition of genuine Irish literature in English. But Corkery was not alone among the Gaels in discussing Synge's work with some sensitivity. For example, writing of *The Playboy of the Western World* in 1925, Muiris Ó Catháin acknowledged 'a strange beauty in the music of the dialect – every word hanging together like little crystal shells, humming in a gust of wind' (aoibhneas aisteach i gceol na canamhaine – gach focal ag crochadh le chéile mar bheadh sligirníní criostail agus iad ag siansán le sídh gaoithe), but then lamented that despite the haunting beauty of its language the play left Gaels with the sense 'that there is nothing of the Gael on stage . . . but pale ghosts with marble hearts and frozen blood, that there is nothing in the picture but a false Gaelic life under a foreign moon' (ná fuil den Ghaedheal ar an stáitse . . . ach taidhbhsí mílithe le croíthe marmair agus fuil reoidhte, ná fuil ins an phictiúir ach bréag-bheatha Ghaedhealach fé ghealaigh Ghallda). Again, the dominant note here was that of what could have been:

> O Spirit of Synge! You certainly belonged to us although you were not of us. There was some deficiency afflicting you so that you did not clearly understand the core of the Gaelic mind that you wanted to create in this drama (*Branar*, Apr. 1925, 63–6).[78]

Harder on Synge was 'Carraig', who compared his depictions of Irish-speaking islanders unfavourably with the account offered by Tomás Ó Criomthain in *An t-Oileánach*:

> Synge gave the world information about these people, he went among them, and there was little in their life that was concealed from him, but he forgot that they had a mind that the eye cannot examine, and he was not in sympathy with that mind. People liked what he wrote about them. Yes! People like an account of the barbaric tribes on the islands of the Southern Ocean. People are extremely fond of the unusual thing in literature (*Gaedheal*, Feb. 1937, 2).79

Somewhat surprisingly, the usually open-minded León Ó Broin had little use for Synge, calling *Playboy* 'outrageous and infamous . . . perversely fictitious . . . nefariously false', and after providing the facts of the situation on which the action of the play was based, continuing:

> Synge had only a superficial knowledge of the Irish language . . . Nevertheless he was not lacking in audacity, and he shamefully slurred the character of the people of this district. Synge may have been an excellent playwright but his offence against a nation's morals and ethics can never be forgiven (*FMR*, Jan. 1922, 17).[80]

But by far the most savage assault on Synge was that by Máighréad Ní Annagáin in 1924:

> Synge was foreign in name, in training, in outlook, and in race. He was, in fact, a fungus-like excrescence in the country, making his literary reputation by depicting any diseased spot he could find in the moral life of the Irish people. What he really gives us is a clear picture of the workings of his own diseased imagination (*Leader*, 25/10/24).

In another equally intemperate piece, again in English, in which she claimed to be presenting 'The Gaelic View', Ní Annagáin declared that given his ethnic and religious background, nothing that Synge could have done would have made him worthy of the title 'Irish writer', much less 'Gael', an ominous note to those who saw Gaelic culture as the legitimate inheritance of all Irish people:

> It does not necessarily follow that because one has learned Irish one has acquired the Gaelic mentality; this has to be born in one. If a person speaks French it does not necessarily follow that he is a Frenchman or has the French outlook and temperament, and there are a good many people about Dublin who can speak Irish after a fashion, but to us real Gaels they are foreigners (*Leader*, 6/12/24).[81]

Given all that she had done for the cause of cultural nationalism in general and for the language revival in particular, the Gaels' virtual silence regarding the work of Lady Gregory was ungrateful and churlish.[82] Nor was James Stephens, another longtime friend of the language, treated much better. Liam Ó Rinn paid him an affectionate if slightly patronising tribute in *Mo Chara Stiofán*:

> He is a lively, energetic man if there ever was one, just the sort you would think could create 'The Crock of Gold' and 'The Demi-Gods.' Listening to him and looking at him you would say that if he was not closely related to fairies and leprechauns he had spent a good part of his life in their company.[83]

But he was also the target of a sour criticism of his novel *Deirdre* by Eoin Ua Mathghamhna, who praised his 'delightful impishness, and that deep love of humanity which is constantly appearing beneath his mordant sarcasm', but went on to write of the novel: 'The opening pages and certain passages throughout the book – passages entirely unconnected with the story – will appear as sheer filth to all who hold an ideal of chaste manhood and womanhood' (*Irish Monthly*, Nov. 1924, 570).

More was involved here than Gaelic ingratitude towards old friends. There was a major difference between earlier Gaelic responses to Anglo-Irish writers and those voiced in the decades of the Free State. Earlier commentary had focused on writers whose use of English rather than Irish was the result not of choice but of circumstance, an understandable ignorance of a 'national' language neither taught nor valued in their formative years. Yeats, Moore, AE – even Synge – could be and were criticised for their various attitudes towards Irish, but even the most zealous Gaelic activists seem for the most part to have realised the absurdity of expecting them to engineer a midlife switch from a language over which they enjoyed full mastery and in which they had achieved considerable recognition, to one in which they would be rank beginners, and one which, moreover, lacked any significant modern literary discourse or even the ghost of a discerning audience. But by the 1920s and 1930s, largely if not exclusively as the result of the language movement itself, there had arisen in the country a new generation at least potentially capable of artistic expression in Irish. The battle over Anglo-Irish literature at this time had become one for the hearts, minds, and pens of this younger generation, a fact evident in León Ó Broin's 1927 essay on Irish literature in English:

> There is in Ireland at present, on the English language side, a group of writers who are far more capable and thousands of times more perceptive than the old crowd. That ability and that insight – the most effective part of them – come from the link they have with the Gaelic world (*FL*, Feb. 1927, 13).[84]

Here it may be instructive to examine in some detail the Gaelic response to two prominent members of this new literary generation so indebted to 'the Gaelic world', one a native speaker of Irish, the other a committed learner. Gaelic interest in the Aran-born Liam O'Flaherty was keen from the very beginning of his career, with critical response to his work in both languages being both more extensive and more thoughtful than that accorded the work of any other Irish author in English. Nor was there ever the slightest doubt about his potential significance for the development of modern prose literature in Irish, a point underscored in a 1930 editorial in *The Star*:

> It is, therefore, a great shame that a man like Liam O'Flaherty is writing English, a man in whom there is a natural talent for storytelling and who has a mastery of Irish. Irish would be the better for his writing in it, and his own work would be the better for being done in Irish.

The editor then went on to argue that writing in Irish would purge O'Flaherty's work of those elements in it that many of his compatriots found distressing:

> If Liam were writing in Irish, it would rein in his pen and it would eliminate the obscenity he puts into all of his stories now out of a desire to satisfy foul Englishmen. His stories would be better and stronger for the cleansing (*Star*, 22/2/30).[85]

It was doubtless this sordid side of O'Flaherty's depiction of Irish life that caused Mac Grianna to include him among 'the Frog-Spawn School of Irish Literature', although he also acknowledged the vigour of his prose. Likewise, León Ó Broin found himself 'a bit enraged' (roinntín ar buile) with O'Flaherty at times, but having discussed *The Informer* and *Mr Gilhooley*, he conceded:

> We can be certain of this much: O'Flaherty is a writer who understands his craft, who has an extraordinary writing talent, who has earned great fame as a literary man, and it is a great pity that he is not writing in Irish exclusively (*FL*, Feb. 1927, 14).[86]

Liam Ó Rinn was dismissive of the charge that O'Flaherty's work was 'terrible' (uafásach) and praised the sheer force of the writing in *Skerret* and another unnamed novel that fell afoul of the Free State censor:

> My eyes opened wide when I saw the strength that was in his style. One should not call the like of it writing, but rather a stormburst . . . It would be well worth their while for writers of Irish to make a study of the 'terrible' work of this 'terrible' person. I do not think that it is the 'immorality' of his books that entices the people of England to read them. Anything written in that powerful style in any language at all would be eagerly read (*UI*, 20/4/35).[87]

Many in the movement were delighted and proud when he brought these formidable skills to Irish, seeing his even partial enlistment in the cause as a harbinger of a genuine and wide-scale Gaelic literary revival in the not-so-distant future. Introducing O'Flaherty's story 'Bás na Bó' (The cow's death) in *Fainne an Lae* in 1925, Pádhraic Ó Domhnalláin wrote:

> There is a powerful story on another page of this issue. If we are not entirely mistaken we have a new writer who will raise Irish high in literary affairs. We think he is an artist to his fingertips. Is it not a fine thing for Irish to answer its critics? There is vigour in it yet, and it will surpass its rival in time. Take heed that it is not doing so already. If not, it is taking a healthy stretch, and when it takes on the competition in earnest, its strength will astound people (*FL*, 18/7/25).[88]

It is, moreover, worth noting that if Gaelic critics were thrilled at the prospect of first-rate work from a writer of O'Flaherty's stature, they nonetheless intended to hold that work to an appropriately high standard, albeit one at times more ideological than aesthetic. When O'Flaherty's play *An Dorchadas* (Darkness) premiered at the Abbey in March 1926, *Fáinne an Lae* ran two long reviews, one highly favourable and one quite negative. Pronouncing the work 'an artistic play that literature in Irish will be the better for having many more like it available' (dráma ealadhanta . . . go mb'fhearrde litríocht na Gaedhilge a lán eile dá shórt a bheith ar fáil), 'Noel' concluded: 'Irish language writers now have a guide in serious drama that they did not have until this time' (*FL*, 13/3/26).[89] 'Theo', on the other hand, denounced O'Flaherty's vision as morbid and un-Christian, explicitly linking it with that of Synge:

> The author is much mistaken if he thinks the people of the West live like that or have thoughts like that. It is the darkness of his own mind the author is revealing, I am afraid. His mind is playing tricks on him as Synge's mind played tricks on him when he wrote plays in the 'atmosphere' of the West (*FL*, 13/3/26).[90]

Writing in *An Sguab*, an anonymous critic stated that while the play dealt with challenging subject matter rooted in the bitterness of the Civil War, it was subject matter that the Irish had to face:

> If I am right in this opinion, the 'message' the author created must be that the person who would see the drama would care little no matter how bad an end overtook the people of Ireland young and old, for they deserved no good end. I praise him highly for how cleverly and precisely he put that message across. I can say nothing to the people to whom he put it across but – 'take that, and read and reread it as a lesson for your benefit' (*Sguab*, Apr. 1926, 64).[91]

Among those most impressed with the play was Pádraic Ó Conaire, who had always hoped his friend O'Flaherty would write more in Irish (*CS*, 29/3/27).

A recurrent theme in Gaelic discussions of O'Flaherty – and one that we will discuss in more detail later in this chapter – was the awareness that he could never hope for the level of recognition and financial success he had achieved through English should he ever decide to devote himself entirely or largely to Irish. In 1929, the editor of *The Star* argued for the necessity of financially meaningful literary prizes to encourage writers to use Irish. Noting that O'Flaherty 'was forced to turn to English to make a living by his pen', he continued:

> It would, perhaps, be too much to hope that Liam O'Flaherty would again turn to Irish as his literary medium, but it is evident from his case that the encouragement of writers in Irish must proceed for some time at least along the lines of offering substantial money prizes for their work (*Star*, 17/8/29).

Patrick Lynch expanded on this idea six years later in *Comhthrom Féinne*:

> It is all very well to say that Irish men of genius should write in Irish, but besides writing those men must also keep body and soul together, and the royalties from a book written in Irish would provide no man with even the elementary necessities of life. There are men contributing to the glories of English literature to-day like Liam O'Flaherty or Peadar O'Donnell who are as capable of writing in Irish as they are in the language of their adoption . . . Who doubts that Liam O'Flaherty is as capable of writing his masterpiece 'Famine' in his native language as he is of writing it in the beautiful though alien tongue he has had to adopt so that his book should reach a public willing to pay for what they read! (*Comhthrom Féinne*, Nov. 1938, 13).[92]

As editor of *The Bell* from 1940 to 1946, Seán Ó Faoláin was to become one of the harshest critics of the language movement and its literary ambitions. In editorials like 'The Gaelic and the Good' (Nov. 1941), 'Gaelic – The Truth' (Feb. 1943), and 'The Gaelic Cult' (Dec. 1944), he rang changes on a theme spelled out later in *The Irish* (1947): 'A literature, one feels, must justify itself on its literary merits, not a factitious appeal. An exclusively patriotic or nostalgic appeal in literature is disgusting.'[93] Yet as is clear from his memories of his own youthful involvement in the revival in Cork, his later cynicism was rooted as much in the disillusionment of the lapsed believer as in any rational analysis of the linguistic and ideological milieu of his young adulthood.[94] At a major turning point in his own life, Ó Faoláin took the Irish language very seriously indeed and committed himself wholeheartedly to mastering it and advancing it as the medium of a contemporary national and European literature. That others in the movement valued that early allegiance and lamented its passing is evident from the comments of Críostóir Mac Aonghusa in 1940:

> Peadar O'Donnell, Seán Ó Faoláin, Frank O'Connor, and Sean O'Casey are a great loss to the language. They gave their all embellishing English literature. They were tremendously successful, and their fame has spread throughout the world. But it is a sad story for the Irish language (*UCG Irisleabhar*, 1939–40, 33–4).[95]

Maurice Harmon has informed us that by the age of 17 Ó Faoláin spoke Irish 'fluently',[96] and in *Vive Moi!* Ó Faoláin himself states 'I was wearing my Fáinne in the summer of 1917.'[97] More important, at this very time he was also beginning to write fiction in Irish, with one of his very first stories, the mordant 'Teach' (House) from 1917, being a genuine pioneering effort to treat, in Irish, urban life with all its potential alienation and squalor. At any rate, whatever cynicism may later have coalesced around the symbol of the *Fáinne*, in its early days the organisation whose emblem it was prompted high ideals and rigorous standards with regard to both linguistic proficiency and ideological orthodoxy. For this reason, it required a good deal of nerve for the teenaged Ó Faoláin to praise the plays of the still distrusted if not actively loathed Synge in a May 1919 lecture to the Cork City branch of An Fáinne (*FL*, 17/5/19).

While Ó Faoláin's idealism faded with time, even in 1925, only a year before his dispassionate analysis of 'The Language Problem' in a series of contributions to the *Irish Tribune* (one of them asking 'Is the Irish Language Worth Reviving?'), Ó Faoláin published 'Deich mBliana d'Fhás i mBeatha Fhile / Dáibhidh Ó Bruadair: 1670–1680' (Ten years of growth in the life of a poet / Dáibhidh Ó Bruadair, 1670–1680) (*Éarna*, Mar. and Dec. 1925), an essay on the poet he would later make a symbol of everything wrong with Gaelic Ireland in the two centuries before the rise of Daniel O'Connell. In this piece, he saw Ó Bruadair as 'the most accomplished writer of the Gaelic poets in the seventeenth and eighteenth centuries' (an scríbhneoir is oilte d'fhilibh na Gaedhilge san tseachtmhadh aois déag agus san ochtmhadh aois déag), and praised his work for its 'truth' (fírinne) and 'seriousness' (dúthracht) (*Éarna*, Dec. 1925, 15).[98] It was also in 1925 that he published 'A Plea for Irish Scholarship', an essay that took its subject seriously, despite being marred by a puerile slap at an unnamed Corkery as one of 'the mass of the enthusiasts' who 'write in the superlative degree about Irish verse of no merit, too self-satisfied to instruct themselves' (*IS*, 14/11/25).

Moreover, he was in this same year still, albeit only briefly, engaging in an important literary debate with such enthusiasts within the movement as an insider, the clearest proof of his willingness, even eagerness, to claim that status being the fact that he chose to state his position in Irish in the official organ of the Gaelic League.[99] Significantly, in light of his later repudiation of Corkery's reading of the native tradition and his distaste for 'factitious' criteria, either 'patriotic or nostalgic', in lieu of rigorous intellectual and aesthetic standards for assessing literary merit, the only intramural Gaelic issue that seems to have fully caught his interest at the time was what he perceived as Seosamh Mac Grianna's provincial and uncritical praise of the eighteenth-century Ulster poets in his series 'Filí Móra Chúige Uladh' (The great poets of the province of Ulster) in *An t-Ultach*. Given Mac Grianna's aggressively sensitive temper as well as his mastery of his native Donegal Irish, one must again admire the courage of one who had learned the language in provoking him to certain battle on his own turf. And provocative Ó Faoláin was in an October 1925 letter to *Fáinne an Lae*:

> It is my opinion that the Gael should be as hard on himself as is the Englishman, but when I read essays in Irish like the one above [i.e. Mac Grianna's], it seems to me we are far too soft on ourselves at present . . . As I have said, the reason I am writing to you is because I see the Gaels everywhere taking this matter of the Irish language altogether too easily . . . If the rest of the learning of present day Irish speakers is that insipid . . . if that is the highest level at which they can live, I am afraid that the English who would say that a Gael is easily satisfied would be right.

He concluded his letter by pronouncing, unjustly, Mac Grianna's ideas mere 'propaganda' in which the author himself could hardly believe:

> But it is not possible for an essay in which something like that is said to have any effect, and if it were written in English, it would be like an essay on 'The Major Poets of the English' that tried to prove that Rudyard Kipling had never been surpassed as a poet (*FL*, 24/10/25).[100]

By the following year, he was blasting what he called 'The Gaoltacht Tradition' in the *Irish Statesman*, pontificating of this cultural heritage: 'As I have shown, it is not typical of the real Ireland: it has very little intrinsic value as a whole – it has its exceptions, of course – and it breeds a spirit of hopelessness and of fear of European learning' (*IS*, 24/4/26).[101] When a decade later he engaged in controversy over Corkery's vision of a vigorous but 'hidden' eighteenth-century Gaelic culture, Ó Faoláin was, in Gaelic eyes, a full-blown traitor, able to write in the 'Proem' to *King of the Beggars*, his 1938 biography of Daniel O'Connell: 'There is but small respect due to the end of the old order of Gaeldom, to that eighteenth-century collection of the *disjecta membra* of an effete traditionalism.'[102] Of Corkery's *The Hidden Ireland*, he declared:

> Its value is rather a negative value. Its value is to underscore the one thing with which we are here properly concerned – that chasm which was breaking apart the old world from the new, Gaeldom with all its irreality and make-believe from the modern democratic Ireland that, in the torment of slavery, presently opened its bloodshot eyes to a realisation of the state to which all that old Gaelic make-believe had reduced it.[103]

Nothing better illustrates his attitude at this time than the fact that he signed one of his essays during the controversy that ensued on publication of *King of the Beggars*, 'John Whelan (By youthful sentimentality Seán Ó Faoláin)' (*Leader*, 20/8/38).[104]

This controversy had been brewing for a good while. Ó Faoláin had aggressively contrasted his (and Frank O'Connor's) view of 'the national tradition' with that of Corkery in a letter to the *Irish Tribune* as early as 23 July 1926.[105] By 1936, the differences in opinion between Corkery and his former pupil-disciples had hardened into genuine antagonism, with Ó Faoláin writing in that year:

> To us the Irish fisherman and the Irish farmer and the Irish townsman is the result of about one hundred and fifty years struggle. And that, for history, is long enough for us. To us, Ireland is beginning, where to Corkery it is continuing (*Dublin Magazine*, Apr.–June 1936, 60–1).

Others were quick to see Ó Faoláin's attack on Corkery, and his attitude to the native tradition, as at once wrong-headed and self-serving, as did Aodh de Blácam:

> Are not all our representative writers almost all against the national ideal as we know it? Is not Daniel Corkery fighting a unanimous P. E. N. Club of authors, alone like Cúchulainn against the hosts? Yet, is not Corkery's doctrine that which was soul and body of the national tradition until to-day? On details, we differ with Corkery, but who will side with the opposition to him and pretend to be in the Irish and Catholic tradition? As Seán Ó Faoláin, an opponent of Corkery, says: 'Corkery is for a continuing Ireland, but we (he means the *literati*) are for a wholly new Ireland, a beginning Ireland.' Where is the 'continuing Ireland?' It seems to be that it must be sought in the Irish language, if anywhere (*Leader*, 25/4/36).

Another writer who followed Ó Faoláin's crusade against Corkery closely was 'Sliabh Bladhma', who in 1935 expressed his puzzlement over the identity of an 'S. Ó Faoláin' who had published an essay in the *Dublin Magazine*:

> I suppose there are not three or four writers named Seán Ó Faoláin. The Seán who writes tales in English nowadays, the Seán who published a book on Constance Markievicz last year, and the Seán who wrote in Irish a decade ago are probably one and the same. And probably S. Ó Faoláin who tries to decry the Gaelic poets (if not the whole nation) in the new number of the 'Dublin Magazine' is still Seán, but apparently disillusioned.

Struck by the 'pessimism and bonded spirit of the new Seán Ó Faoláin', he claimed to find it hard to believe in 'the identity theory', for 'the Seáns (*Seáiní*) differ utterly, in far more than language' (*Gaedheal*, 11/5/35). 'Sliabh Bladhma' was less amused by Ó Faoláin's criticism of Corkery in the article from 1936 cited above, writing in a piece entitled 'The Pale and the Gael:'

> Seán apparently still desires to put away the historic Irish nation and the Celtic world for a peculiar new patria that began about 150 years ago. In his present mood he may possibly be serious about it, but his attitude really recalls our old friend the fox that had lost his tail and tried hard to convince fellow-foxes of the advantages of his condition. Seán expresses concern for art and beauty but drops into the propagandism he professes to dislike.

'Sliabh Bladhma' could not, of course, be so easily outfoxed himself, and concluded with a sarcastic expulsion of Ó Faoláin from the Gaelic community:

> Seán Ó Faoláin – although he ignores Mr Corkery's Gaelic work – is good enough to admit that 'we know the value of the Irish tongue to extend our vision of Irish life, to deepen it and enrich it.' We do; and we know it means a great deal more than that. But enough of Anglo-Irish by-ways and theories (*Gaedheal*, May, 1936, 1).

Yet three months later, he could not resist another dig at 'Seán Ó Faoláin's Pale substitution for the historic Irish nation' (*Gaedheal*, Aug. 1936, 3). The following year, however, he acknowledged how bitter a loss Ó Faoláin was for the language and its literature:

> It is a pity that he could not go on writing as he began, in Irish, a pity that he lost the inspiration of the Gaelic League and produced the caricature of it that appears in his disappointing book on Constance Markievicz. His first faith would have carried him far; he might have become as noted as contemporary writers in Sweden, Norway, Poland, Finland, Chechoslovakia [*sic*], Bulgaria. Now he is apparently disillusioned and unhappy; and that spectral dwelling he tenants, grandiloquently termed the Irish Academy of Letters, does not help him (*Gaedheal*, Aug. 1937).[106]

After the publication of *King of the Beggars*, the debate intensified. For example, in his highly negative review of the book, Seán Ua Ceallaigh blasted Ó Faoláin's characterisation of O'Connell, wondering 'if it is proper for me to defile this journal with his boorish opinion at all' (má's dual dom an t-irisleabhar so do thruailliughadh le n-a thuairim dhroch-mhúinte i n-aon chor). Ua Ceallaigh went on to denounce the theories of Ó Faoláin and other intellectuals as growing out of 'pride and presumption and the ignorant authority that Gaels always detest' (uabhar is éirghe i n-áirde agus an t-ughdaras gan eolas is fuath riamh le Gaedhealaibh) (*CB*, Oct. 1938, 782). More savage yet was the editorial on 'The Genius of Irish Literature' in the same journal a few months later. Responding to a recent lecture by Corkery to the Civil Service Gaelic Society, the editor thundered:

> It is well known that the formative views of Mr Corkery are a persistent rock of offence to the residual dregs of the old Plunkett House Gang, and the pundits of the Outlanders' Academy of Literary Litter, who assembled at the call of Yeats and Shaw, and who have in more than one of their accessory elements taken pains to present themselves as dabblers in dirt, scholars in the sordid succession to the Sewage School of fifteen years ago. The offshoots of the Anglo-Irish slump [*sic*] are by no means without a sense of what the appointments of such professors of English as Daniel Corkery at Cork, or Dr Murphy at Galway, mean to our own Gaelic and Catholic nation of Ireland. English literature, even if English is still an official language of Ireland, is for Ireland a foreign literature, and its function is entirely subsidiary to the rapid development of fully Irish literature in the national language of the land (*CB*, Feb. 1939, 75–6).[107]

In a 1938 essay on 'Politics and Culture: Daniel O'Connell and the Gaelic Past', Michael Tierney pronounced Ó Faoláin's analysis of Gaelic culture in

King of the Beggars 'wholly wrongheaded', an opinion with which most of those asked to contribute 'Comments on the Foregoing Article' were in agreement. To be fair, Daniel Binchy and Gerard Murphy praised the biography itself, but they did reject the author's interpretation of Gaelic tradition, Murphy calling it 'a parody of history'. John Ryan wrote that Ó Faoláin's reading was based on 'an astounding misunderstanding of the historical situation'. Replying to his critics, Ó Faoláin seems to have been goaded into extremism in his rejection of Irish-Ireland orthodoxy: 'We used the Gaelic past as an excitement to inspire us; we never examined it; we are not able, when we do examine it, to see what it has to offer us in our present state' (*Studies*, Sept. 1938, 353–80).

By the late 1930s, even P. S. O'Hegarty could find Ó Faoláin irrationally radical in his opposition to a Gaelic orthodoxy with which O'Hegarty himself was often at odds. In his review of *King of the Beggars*, O'Hegarty called the book 'brilliant', but then continued:

> There are, however, certain things, fringes, so to speak, of his theme, which Mr Ó Faoláin exaggerates. He is in revolt against and is irritated with Mr Corkery's extremes, and he is unduly bellicose against the Gael . . . He does not understand at all that, were it not for the Irish language in the period after 1691, there might be no Irish People at all (*Dublin Magazine*, Oct.–Dec. 1938, 75).

By the end of our period, Ó Faoláin was, then, the enemy he was to remain in Gaelic eyes for the rest of his life, an ally of the movement that Risteárd Mac Maghnusa, with a confidence only tenuously grounded in reality, saw as doomed: 'The Seán Ó Faoláins are feigning blindness because they do not wish to see the inevitable end of the Anglo-Irish literary ascendancy which is approaching' (*Leader*, 4/2/39).[108]

Gaelic attacks on Ó Faoláin frequently linked him with his friend and fellow Corkman Frank O'Connor as 'the great twin brethren from Cork . . . the Leeside playboys' (*IBL*, Sept. 1939, 144). For example, in a 1937 letter to the *Irish Press*, Séamus G. Ó Ceallaigh wrote:

> The group represented by Mr A. de Blácam and Mr Corkery claim to speak on behalf of Gaelic Ireland, whilst the group represented by Mr O'Faoláin [sic] and Mr. O'Connor are inclined to sneer at the idea of a Gaelic Ireland and have got the idea into their heads that they are the real representatives of the Irish Nation although they write in English (*IP*, 22/4/37).

In a fairly balanced discussion of contemporary cultural debates in *Bonaventura* the following year, Thomas Barrington, having condemned 'the rabid traditionalists' for their attempt to associate *Gaelachas* with bigotry, bad manners, and insularity, continued:

> There are the literary men who would have us slaves to liberalism, more bad manners, and internationalism. These latter are the more dangerous enemies because they are the more able. The main attack from this quarter has come from Mr Ó Faoláin and Mr Frank O'Connor. They are agreed that the Irish nation began in 1800 AD (*Bonaventura*, Summer 1937, 121).[109]

More effective than any reasoned criticism of what Gaels saw as the pseudo-sophistication of Ó Faoláin and O'Connor was Seán Ó Ciosáin's satirical 1935 story 'An Bheirt Intleachtóirí' (The two intellectuals), a dead-on if not altogether just picture of two snobbish *poseurs* from the provinces who desert and betray their mentor, despise their country, worship James Joyce, and win acclaim for their work.[110]

Two other writers for whom the Gaels had some hope were Peadar O'Donnell and Seán O'Casey. O'Donnell, born in the Breac-Ghaeltacht (semi-Gaeltacht) near the Rosses of Donegal, could speak Irish and was a friend of Séamus Ó Grianna and Seosamh Mac Grianna. In an article by Patrick K. Lynch cited above, he was linked with O'Flaherty as a writer who should be urged to write in Irish, a hope that was doubtless encouraged when in a 1932 piece in *An Phoblacht*, O'Donnell himself wrote: 'I feel even in myself the need for the Gaelic medium to voice aspects of the life of the Ireland of to-day' (*An Phoblacht*, 23/7/32). Even his work in English won the approval of many Irish-Irelanders. Responding to O'Donnell's words quoted above, Séamus Ó Grianna went as far as he ever would in accepting some role for the English language in Irish cultural life:

> Those who do not understand the Gaeltacht and who have read the superb descriptions in *Islanders* and *Adrigoole*, will find it hard to believe that Peadar feels the need for any medium other than the one he has so far used in his writings (*An Phoblacht*, 6/8/32).

Similarly, in a 1936 review of Seosamh Mac Grianna's translation of O'Donnell's *Islanders* as *Muinntir an Oileáin*, 'Bóirne' wrote:

> There is no need to say much about this book . . . by Peadar O'Donnell, for everyone knows his work well. The account of the islanders here is fluid and simple as the author's narrative always is . . . He has not brought out clearly what is wretched in the nature of the poor, but rather the noble, agreeable qualities that are in the Gaels anywhere that remains like the island in question in the story (*AA*, Oct. 1936, 8).[111]

A Clongowes Wood schoolboy, Énrí Ó Féich, had been equally impressed by the same novel in its original English incarnation, writing: 'It is my opinion that one could not find another book that would give an account as accurate and as fine of the people and of their manners and customs' (*Clongownian*, 1929, 32).[112]

Like Ó Faoláin, O'Casey angered some Irish-Irelanders with his rejection of key elements of movement orthodoxy, in his case his vigorous criticism of 'compulsory' Irish in the pages of the *Irish Statesman* in late 1924 and early 1925.[113] But he was impossible to ignore once he left the Gaelic League fold for the Abbey stage and eventual world renown. In general, Irish-Irelanders did not like what they heard and saw from him on that stage and elsewhere. In 1924, D. P. Moran accused O'Casey of betraying the ideals to which he had once been committed: 'If Mr O'Casey does not hate Irish he certainly dissembles his love with great efficiency. He knows Irish, but a man might know a language and hate it' (*Leader*, 20/12/24). In a review of O'Casey's *Nannie's Night Out* the same year, Máire Nic Shuibhne (Mary MacSwiney, sister of the martyred Lord Mayor of Cork, Terence MacSwiney), accused the playwright of currying favour with 'the anti-Gaelic, anti-Republican pseudo "Intellectuals"', and hoped he would return to his earlier enthusiasms: 'Seán Casey [*sic*] is, I am told, a young man. He ought to be an Irishman. Is he going to continue to prostitute a promising talent instead of writing something which would make *Ireland* proud of him, now and in the future' (*An Phoblacht*, 18/10/24).[114] Four years later, with O'Casey now an established playwright after the success of his Dublin trilogy, *The Leader* again blasted him as an apostate: 'He gave us our Irish coward, our Irish trickster, our loafer, our street woman, but, if I remember rightly, he has not given us any character to illustrate our good points . . . Such plays are very depressing and hinder, not help, our nation' (*Leader*, 11/2/28). In an interesting reading of his early work that would doubtless have shocked O'Casey himself, Seán Ó Ciarghusa accused him of pandering to the bourgeoisie:

> It seems that the tendency among English-language dramatists in Ireland at present is to present the 'slums' on stage. I myself do not like dramas of that sort. The poor people of the 'slums' do not frequent the theatre, and in my opinion it is not right, – it is certainly not courteous – to deliberately present themselves and their life as a source of amusement to the arrogant, smug rich people who eat chocolates and make fun of them in comfort.[115]

It was, however, the 1935 Dublin premier of *The Silver Tassie*, the play Yeats had in 1928 so high-handedly rejected for the Abbey, that drew most comment from cultural nationalists. This play had won some support from Gaels at the time of its rejection, although one might wonder whether support for a play by O'Casey which they had not yet seen was not just another way to have a slap at Yeats. In a highly favourable review of the Gate Theatre's production of Dennis Johnston's *The Old Lady Says No!*, another play turned down by the Abbey, the anonymous critic for *The Star* wrote: 'The plays of Seán O'Casey benefited the [Abbey] Theatre a great deal, but when he sent his most recent creation, "The Silver Tassie", to them they did not think it worth putting on stage. They trampled on it' (*Star*, 13/7/29).[116]

There were, however, other opinions. Many Gaels would probably have agreed with Máire Ní Chróinín when, in a 1931 letter to *The Leader*, she wondered why Irish-Irelanders cared about the Abbey or O'Casey at all:

> They have nothing to do with us, and they never did. And whether the 'Silver Tassie' is put on the Abbey stage or not, it is next to nothing the Gaels of Dublin will have lost. There is plenty of obscenity in the 'Silver Tassie' and I hope that it will never be seen on stage in this ancient capital city (*Leader*, 18/1/30).[117]

If anything, attitudes hardened after the play was actually produced at the Abbey in 1935. In her review for *The Leader*, Nuala Moran ('N.') dismissed the play altogether:

> Go to the 'Silver Tassie' at the Abbey – and yawn your head off. Because you will be bored by an exceedingly stupid play, undeniably anti-Christian in sentiment but utterly unconvincing and ridiculous. It has no merit as a play – even as an immoral one. It is just an hysterical jumble of blasphemy, despair and hopelessness (*Leader*, 24/8/35).[118]

In September 1935, An tAthair Séamus Ó Ceallaigh proposed a motion at a Gaelic gathering in Tourmakeady, County Mayo, 'asking the Government to put a stop to dramas like "The Silver Tassie" and to put a stop to the subsidy they are giving to the theatre that produces a drama like that' (ag iarraidh ar an Riaghaltas stop a chur le drámaí ar nós 'The Silver Tassie' agus stop a chur leis an deóntas atá dá thabhairt acu do'n amharclainn a léirigheas dráma mar sin) (*Éireannach*, 7/9/35).[119]

Yet for all the anger directed at O'Casey throughout our period, Gaels also felt towards him that other emotion we have seen on several occasions with regard to Irish people who moved from cultural and linguistic nationalist circles to fame as writers of English. Regret for what might have been can be heard, albeit faintly, in one of the most intriguing Gaelic responses to O'Casey. 'Gaedhilg Shuionn [*sic*] Uí Chéasaí' (The Irish of Seán O'Casey) is in most respects a rather savage verbal caricature of the playwright by Micheál Ó Maoláin, O'Casey's one-time room-mate and the supposed model for Seamus Shiels in *The Shadow of a Gunman*. Among the boasts Ó Maoláin puts in the mouth of his conceited and bombastic Ó Céasaí is one concerning his previous contributions to cultural nationalism (*FL*, 22/5/26).

Of the two Irish writers of English whom the Gaels held in highest regard at the time, one was entirely predictable, the other quite a bit less so. Daniel Corkery had earned the gratitude and respect of cultural nationalists as the author of first-rate fiction of an unimpeachably Irish cast, as one of the chief theorists of the Irish-Ireland movement, as a writer willing to use Irish for some of his own creative and critical work, and as a committed and effective controversialist in both Irish and English. Commenting on Corkery's diverse achievements up to 1924 in an essay entitled 'Voice of Gaeldom / Daniel Corkery', 'Sandrach' wrote:

> Mr Corkery . . . speaks out of Gaeldom as out of his native environment. He brings to his criticism a sound scholarship; he has studied foreign and classic literature with earnest thoroughness and applies his knowledge fruitfully to the exposition of Gaelic; but if he knew nothing of foreign culture, he would still be Daniel Corkery and have something to say. He is *éigse Fáil* [Irish learning] articulate for a moment in the *Béarla* [English language].

Of his early fiction, poetry, and plays, 'Sandrach' declared: 'The remarkable quality of these first fruits of his genius was their authentic traditional character. Although he wrote in English, readers seemed to be seeing into the world of the Gaelic singers' (*SF*, 8/11/24). Pádhraic Ó Domhnalláin agreed, writing of Corkery the following year in a glowing full page review of *The Hidden Ireland*: 'Is he not himself the heir of the poets and the storytellers and the historians who clung to the learning and literature of their country however much turbulence and violence there was during their time' (*FL*, 28/2/25).[120]

Seán Ó Ciarghusa was another critic who found the genuine Gaelic note in Corkery, writing of his plays:

> It is, therefore, difficult to communicate what the innate quality of the Gaels is, but it is, I think, in 'An Pósadh' by 'An Craoibhín' [Douglas Hyde], in 'Ó Failbhe Mór' and in 'An Bunán Buidhe' by Daniel Corkery – although those last two were originally composed in English.[121]

More tongue-in-cheek was Ó Ciarghusa's praise of Corkery in his 1937 essay 'The War on the Pale', an essay prompted by a Corkery lecture to the Keating Branch of the Gaelic League in Dublin:

> Only that I knew Domhnall Ó Corcora to be an Irish-Irelander, and even with that knowledge, until he had written 'The Hidden Ireland', I should have felt like

> thinking him the worst living enemy of the Irish language he wrote English so beautifully and, by so doing, placed it on so high a pedestal in Ireland (*Leader*, 20/11/37).[122]

More serious was Aodh de Blácam, who, in a 1930 article on 'A Catholic's Library / The Books of Daniel Corkery', wrote of *The Hidden Ireland*: 'Every young Irish writer who counts for anything acknowledges himself indebted to this wonderful book.' Of Corkery himself he declared: 'Unlike the Abbey writers, he had made the real living Gaelic tradition vitally his own . . . He is the greatest of our realists; his reality is the truth' (*FMR*, Feb. 1930, 62).[123] In his praise of Corkery the previous year, 'Cúl Báire' may have crossed the line into linguistic heresy: 'There is only one Daniel Corkery. Daniel does not write in a foreign language. It is in English he has his thoughts and he reveals those thoughts to us beautifully and delightfully' (*UI*, 28/6/34).[124]

In a 1929 essay on 'Domhnall Ó Corcora mar Dhrámaidhe' (Daniel Corkery as a dramatist), 'S. Ó M.' wondered whether Corkery might be too impressive a human being to be a fully successful creative writer. He began his essay with lavish praise: 'Daniel Corkery has the quality of high imagination more strongly than does any other Irish writer of our time.' But he then went on to qualify that praise:

> Despite that (or, perhaps, because of that) he is not the best dramatist or story writer that we have. He inspires noble, gentle, sorrowful thoughts in the reader's mind; but the people he creates in his books are not of the human race.

His explanation of this paradox offers striking confirmation of Corkery's status in the cultural nationalist movement as one of those 'souls who barely wear a bodily covering, the superb men who, like the Alps, are high above the human race' (anama gurab ar éigin go bhfuil clúdach colna ortha, na sáir-fhir atá, ar nós na n-Alp, go h-árd os cionn an chine dhaonna):

> Every character in his books is a remarkable person. He tries to bring them down so that ordinary people would understand them. He fails. Let him try to bring the ordinary people up on the ladder of poetry to the noble ones. There is no other way, and that is his craft (*Nation*, 16/11/29).[125]

There were, in fact, very few serious criticisms whatsoever of Corkery from the Irish-Ireland movement, with even de Blácam and O'Hegarty, who disagreed with him at times, treating the man and his ideas with considerable respect. This consensus must have made the attacks of Ó Faoláin and O'Connor seem all the more inexplicable, even inexcusable. Both of his former pupils directed a good deal of criticism at Corkery over the years.

Here it should suffice to give a sense of the substance and tone of their attacks on the man who had introduced them to both the Gaelic tradition and literature itself. Writing in 1936, Ó Faoláin was abusively dismissive of Corkery and his work:

> Corkery's so-called Hidden Ireland of the 18th century is, thus, nothing but a racket, an attempt on the part of a number of semi-literate remnants of that effete, good-for-nothing, thick-headed aristocracy of the old Gaelic world to bamboozle the common people into supporting further a dead thing that had repeatedly betrayed them.

Then, having discussed the rise of Irish democracy under O'Connell, he continued:

> We have lost a good deal in the process – almost lost our language, certainly lost all facility in it. Prof. Tierney, writing in English, like Prof. Corkery, writing in English, suggests that to write in the English language is to feel less Irish. Less Gaelic, yes. But you cannot have it both ways. You cannot hammer a modern people out of helotry, as a dozen men from O'Connell to Griffith did, and still complain that you are not in every respect what you were in the time of Columbanus (*II*, 23/6/36).[126]

O'Connor used the occasion of the Abbey Theatre Festival of 1938 to launch an attack on Corkery's 'standards', in the process rejecting out of hand Corkery's three criteria for authentic Irish literature and defending the contributions of Yeats, Lady Gregory, *et al.* to a national literature in English. (*II*, 10/8/38).

Another writer about whom the Gaels were enthusiastic despite his writing in English was the playwright T. C. Murray. We noted above that he was seen as one of those in whose work could be detected an unmistakable 'Gaelic note', and this was an idea to which various writers returned throughout our period. Discussing 'The Gaelic Element in Gaelic Drama' in 1928, 'D. Ó D.' wrote:

> At this time of day there is no need, from the national point of view, to compare the genius of Murray with that of Synge and his disease-minded associates. Better far one Murray than a thousand Ibsens or Tchekovs, even though such a man be not born in a generation (*Leader*, 25/2/28).

In a review in *Ar Aghaidh* ten years later, An tAthair Mac Fhinn all but dismissed the playwright's use of English as a mere accident of history:

> And as for the dramas of T. C. Murray, there is no doubt but that they are truly suitable for the Irish language. Although they were first written in English, they deal with the Gaelic world and the Gaelic mind. There is no other Irish dramatist in whom there is the same native quality and the same nature. Even the speech in them, is not a great deal of it made up of Irish language constructions? (*AA*, Jan. 1938, 1).[127]

Writing of Micheál Ó Siochfhradha's translation of Murray's *Aftermath* in 1926, Seán Ó Ciarghusa lamented the fact that an Irish author of Murray's background and calibre was still writing in English, and continued: 'In my opinion, the emigration of the Gaelic learned class is nothing in comparison to those of them who stayed writing in English, and I am confirmed in that opinion by seeing T. C. Murray's *Aftermath* produced in the Abbey' (*Sguab*, Jan. 1926, 508).[128] As we saw above, other Gaelic literary figures were to make the same complaint about writers like O'Flaherty, O'Casey, O'Connor, and Ó Faoláin in the years to come. The problem facing those dedicated to creating a significant modern literature in Irish was not, then, a lack of available talent. There seemed to be more than enough gifted Irish writers, even writers able to use the language with some fluency, to satisfy the growing readership for work in Irish. The problem was that that Gaelic readership had a good bit more growing to do in both numbers and sophistication before it could offer writers of Irish either meaningful critical or worthwhile financial support.

In the present, however, there was a significant Anglophone audience at home, and a potentially enormous readership in Britain, Australia, Canada, and the United States, where the achievements of Yeats, Synge, Joyce and O'Casey were interesting readers even outside the diaspora in the work of Irish authors. There was, of course, nothing new about the resulting literary brain drain, as Father Dinneen, himself an admirer of English literature, made clear in 1925:

> I myself would say, although I regret criticising the English language, that we have for a long time now been losing too much wealth and work by cultivating English-language literature, and that the result we have from it is not worth what we have lost (*Leader*, 11/4/25).[129]

'Ardmel' was even more forceful on this point, writing of Irish writers of English after hearing Corkery lecture at a Kickham Commemoration in Tipperary:

> In England and America, these twin teams of penmen have got their audience. It was always so . . . It would be strange if it were otherwise. These people are all really

> English. It is as English literature that any work they have done will be judged. There never has been, and in all likelihood there never will be, any genuine Anglo-Irish Literature worthy of separate existence, neither [sic] English nor [sic] Irish (*CB*, Nov. 1928, 1125).

Corkery himself agreed, believing that the decision by writers to appeal to what he in his book on Synge called 'foreign suffrage' had from the start rendered the majority of Irish writing in English irrelevant to Ireland.[130] But now the danger was far greater. Not only might the lure of that large audience continue to pervert Irish literary expression in English, but it could also seduce a whole generation of bilingual Irish authors to abandon the native language of their country for the enticements of metropolitan fame and fortune. 'Lagan' offered a variant on this opinion in a 1936 essay opposing state aid to Irish writers of English:

> There is the plea that Irishmen of the George Bernard Shaw type might remain in Ireland if they were assured of a reading public here. Well, if they wrote Irish they would be welcome; but otherwise they are in their natural habitat where they are. For that matter those of them who have achieved fame can afford to live pretty much where they like, and they seem to choose England (*Leader*, 28/3/36).[131]

The dangers of compromising – not to mention betraying – an Irish vision to win a foreign reputation were stressed again and again throughout our period, nowhere more forcefully than in D. P. Moran's *Leader*. In 1926, Moran himself wrote:

> The prospect of an audience amongst 200,000,000 English speakers stimulates men of commercial talent to pander to the tastes of the time and is a temptation to a man of real genius. We can get on without that temptation; and there are many men now writing dirt for the English market who would be better off in soul and body if they remained digging potatoes (*Leader*, 18/9/26).

Seán Ó Ciosáin agreed, writing more specifically of Irish playwrights in 1930: 'If an Irish dramatist wants to gain money and fame, he must create people who will appeal to the English or to the Americans. The *stage-Irishman* has gone, but even if he has, we have a person as bad in his place. We have the *Informer*' (*Star*, 8/3/30).[132] Liam Ó Rinn was characteristically more broad-minded in a 1937 essay in which he pointed out that there was good reason for Irish writers of English to seek an audience abroad:

> As for writers of English, we have no small number of them, but since it is a fact that the average Irish person thinks every penny spent on books is money wasted, I wonder if we have the right to call them ours – if it were not for the English they could not survive, a fact so true that many of them live in England (*II*, 8/9/37).[133]

More typical of the Gaelic consensus was the attitude of the usually more enlightened 'Sliabh Bladhma', who wrote in the same year: 'Authors who write for a more or less imaginary England, and try to lay down the law for the rest of us, illuminate nothing. The strength and hope of Ireland are in the folk as a whole, and in *Gaelachas* in action' (*Gaedheal*, Aug. 1937, 1).

Of course *Gaelachas*, even at its most active, could not of itself put food on the table, and writers, even writers of Irish, had to eat. According to some, however, such writers did not need, nor should they want, much more than that, a point emphasised by an anonymous contributor (probably the editor, Tomás Ó Máille) in *An Stoc* in 1926:

> It is true – alas – that there is not remuneration for writers of Irish. As for money, it is not possible to compare the Irish language and the English language. There are a million English-speakers for every five hundred Irish-speakers. Let there be no expectation of money . . . but money will not inspire the writers to do the great work before them. If love of country will not inspire them, and if the condition in which Ireland is will not urge them to do it, our hope for Irish will be a hope in vain (*Stoc*, Mar. 1926, 6).[134]

From this point of view, the Gaelic writer's renunciation of financial, popular, or critical success (or any combination of the three) was proof of the kind of otherworldly idealism so typical of the Gael. Writing of Pádraic Ó Conaire two years after his premature death in abject poverty, Tomás Ua Concheanainn and Liam Ó Buachalla declared:

> When Pádraic Ó Conaire gave his love and his affection to the literature of the Irish language, he cast from him the ease and the wealth he would certainly have had if he had stooped to writing English as so many other Irish people had done before him. Where is the person among us who would cast from him, of his own free will, the wealth and the luxury of the world as he did? (*Stoc*, Dec. 1930, 11).[135]

'An Giolla Dubh' boasted of a living author who was making the same sacrifice, writing of Séamus Ó Grianna in 1936: 'Writers of Irish cannot survive by the work of their pens in the world as it is now. If "Máire" wrote in English he would be talked about. He could do it extremely well, but he would not.' Of Ó Grianna's work in Irish he wrote: 'They are all stories that, had they been written in English, would have had the fops of the country trying to shake the author's hand' (*Gaedheal*, Feb. 1936, 3).[136] It was doubtless the implied criticism that he lacked the courageous self-sacrifice and defiance of these writers that in 1927 provoked Liam O'Flaherty to such a vigorous, even abusive defence of his decision to write in English:

> I don't write for money. If I wanted to write for money I could be a rich man now. I am a good craftsman and I am cunning enough to understand the various follies of mankind and womankind. In fact, if I ever get so hard up that I'll lose my self-respect, I'll start a religious paper in the Irish language and make a fortune on it (*IS*, 17/12/27).[137]

Was there, then, to be a strict if informal apartheid that denied full rights of cultural citizenship to Irish writers who by necessity or choice used the English language? 'Sliabh na mBan' seems to have hoped so, writing in a 1922 essay on 'Responsibility':

> First and above all, writers who can write Irish well should make the resolution to do their serious, ambitious writing henceforth in Irish only . . . The complement, too, to that holds, namely, that writers who cannot write Irish should leave it to Irish writers to give us the books of national importance and appeal we shall all now be looking out for (*Leader*, 21/4/22).

Fortunately, this was an opinion of the rigid if not lunatic fringe. Most Gaels felt writers of English could serve the cause in some way, if not in their own words, then through translation into the language they should have been using anyway. There was, of course, nothing new about this idea of translating Irish writers into Irish. But as we have seen on more than one occasion, questions one would have thought long settled continued to be posed and debated as if brand new throughout our period. In 1931, Máirtín Ua Flaithbheartaigh felt it necessary to point out how logical a step it was to provide new reading matter on Irish topics by translating works with which an Irish audience would feel an immediate kinship and familiarity:

> Would it not be proper to translate first the books in English in which there is the spirit of the Irish language? We ourselves have men who wrote in English and who made a name for the Celts in English literature. What about William O'Brien, Canon Sheehan, Daniel Corkery, and many others? What about a translation of 'When We Were Boys' or 'The Blindess of Dr Gray?' Anyone who read them in English will read them eagerly in Irish (*AA*, July 1931, 3).[138]

Many at the time repeated another old idea, that the most authentically national work by Irish writers of English would actually be improved by translation into the language in which it was believed they would have been written but for the language shift set in motion by colonial oppression. Predictably enough, the plays of T. C. Murray were seen as particularly appropriate for translation, with 'D. Ó D.' writing of Máire Ní Shíothcháin's translation of his play *Birthright*: 'I would only say that the Irish language is more appropriate for this drama than the English' (*Leader*, 22/2/30).[139] An anonymous critic expanded on this idea in his 1936 review of Seosamh Mac Grianna's translation of Peadar O'Donnell's *Islanders*: 'It is a story that is predisposed to the Irish language, and in the hands of that master craftsman Seosamh Mac Grianna, the book is almost better told in Irish' (*CT*, 8/8/36).[140] And of the same writer's translation of Donn Byrne's *Hangman's House*, 'Bóirne' stated: 'This story is more fitting for the Irish language than for English, and therefore, instead of losing any of its beauty in the translation, it comes into its own' (*AA*, Jan. 1937, 7).[141]

Given this favourable attitude, a fair amount of literary work in English by Irish writers was brought into Irish in our period. Along with the titles by Kickham, Murray, O'Donnell, and Byrne mentioned above, we also have Gaelic versions of contemporary works like Daniel Corkery's *The Threshold of Quiet* (tr. Micheál Ó Floinn, 1933);[142] Canon Sheehan's *Glenanaar* (tr. Tomás de Bhial, 1933); *The Graves of Kilmorna* (tr. Domhnall Ó Grianna, 1932), *My New Curate* (tr. Pádraig Ó Corcardha, 1939) and *Lisheen* (tr. Séamus Ó Grianna, 1939); Pádraic Colm's *A Boy in Eirinn* (tr. Niall Johnny Ó Domhnaill, 1935) and *Castle Conquer* (tr. Niall Johnny Ó Domhnaill, 1939); Shan F. Bullock's *The Loughsiders*, tr. Niall Johnny Ó Domhnaill, 1935); Maurice Walsh's *The Key above the Door* (tr. Seán Mac Maoláin, 1936); Seamus Mac Manus's *A Lad of the O'Friels* (tr. Nioclás Tóibín, 1933) and *The King of Ireland's Son* (tr. Niall Ó Domhnaill, 1939); Donn Byrne's *Hangman's House* (tr. Seosamh Mac Grianna, 1936) and *Messer Marco Polo* (tr. Seán Mac Maoláin, 1938); and Annie M. Smithson's *Her Irish Heritage* (tr. Tadhg Ó Rabhartaigh, 1939). From the work of Irish writers from the past, we have the Lilliput section of Swift's *Gulliver's Travels* (tr. Donnchadh Ó Laoghaire, 1936); Goldsmith's *The Vicar of Wakefield* (tr. Seán Ó Ciosáin, 1931); Wolfe Tone's *Autobiography* (tr. Pádraig Ó Siochfhradha, 1932); Carleton's *Fardorougha the Miser* (tr. Seán Mac Maoláin, 1933); John Boyle O'Reilly's *Moondyne* (tr. Conchubhar Ó h-Argáin, 1931); Kickham's *Sally Kavanagh* (tr. Máirtín Ó Cadhain, 1932);[143] and less predictably, Bram Stoker's *Dracula* (tr. Seán Ó Cuirrín, 1932).[144]

As we saw in the previous chapter, many translators at the time turned their attention to theatrical works on the simple principle expressed by an anonymous reviewer of a 1925 production of Micheál Ó Siochfhradha's translation of Murray's *The Aftermath*: 'Until there are writers in the country who will be able to write dramas in Irish, it is very fortunate that we have something like this' (*II*, 15/12/25).[145] T. Rafferty made the same point a few years after after seeing a translation from Colum performed by An Comhar Drámaidheachta in the Peacock Theatre: 'Fiachra Éilgeach's translation shows beyond shadow of doubt that borrowing, especially from Anglo-Irish sources, is the most profitable for the Comhar at present' (*IS*, 9/3/29). Moreover, this kind of work was actively encouraged by groups like An Comhar and Taibhdhearc na Gaillimhe who were desperate for appealing and accessible scripts to fill their increasingly ambitious production schedules. For example, in April 1931, An Taibhdhearc offered a prize of £2 for translations of plays, and suggested, among other titles, Shaw's *Plays Pleasant*, *Three Plays for Puritans*, and *John Bull's Other Island*, as well as plays by Synge and Yeats. (*CT*, 11/4/31).[146] Among Irish plays translated into Irish at the time were Goldsmith's *She Stoops to Conquer* (tr. Piaras Béaslaí, 1929); Sheridan's *The School for Scandal* (tr. Micheál Ó Siochfhradha, 1932);[147] Yeats's *Cathleen Ni Houlihan* (tr. Seán Ó Conchubhair, 1937); Synge's *Riders to the Sea* (tr. Seán Tóibín as *An Mhuir*, 1923; tr. Domhnall Ó Ríoghardáin as *Maicne Mara*, 1933; tr. 'Brian an Iasgaire' as *An Mhuir*, 1933; tr. Séamus Ó Séaghdha and Tomás Ó Muircheartaigh as *Muir na Cinneamhna*, 1938); *In the Shadow of the Glen* (tr. Risteárd Ó Foghludha, 1923); and *Deirdre of the Sorrows* (tr. Liam Ó Briain, 1931); Lady Gregory's *Hyacinth Halvey* (tr. Micheál Ó Droighneáin, 1930); Alice Milligan's *The Last Feast of the Fianna* (tr. Risteárd Ó Foghludha, 1928); Shaw's *Saint Joan* (tr. Pádraic Mac Fhionnlaoich, 1937) and *Arms and the Man* (tr. Micheál Mac Liammóir, 1931); Pearse's *The Singer* (tr. Liam Ó Briain, 1936); Pádraic Colm's *Betrayal* (tr. Risteárd Ó Foghludha, 1925); Murray's *Maurice Harte* (tr. An tAthair Tomás Ó Gallchobhair, 1937),[148] *Aftermath* and *Autumn Fire* (both tr. Micheál Ó Siochfhradha, 1930), *Birthright* (tr. Máire Ní Shíothcháin, 1931), *Spring* (tr. Séamus Mac Cormaic, 1933), *The Pipe in the Fields* (tr. Risteárd Ó Foghludha, 1937), *A Stag at Bay* (tr. Peadar Mac Fhionnlaoich, 1938), and *Sovereign Gold* (tr. Máirtín Ó Direáin, 1939); Lord Dunsany's *A Night at the Inn* (tr. Aodh Mac Dhubháin, 1932); Lennox Robinson's *The Whiteheaded Boy* (tr. Seosamh Mac Grianna, 1935); Corkery's *The Yellow Bittern* (tr. Risteárd Ó Foghludha, 1927) and *Resurrection* (tr. Pádraig Ó Domhnaill, 1930); Paul Vincent Carroll's *St Francis and the Wolf* (tr. Seán Ó Neachtain, 1938); Maura Molloy's *Summer's Day* (tr. Pádhraic Óg Ó Conaire, 1938), and several plays by Father M. H. Gaffney, translated by Áine Ní Fhoghludha.[149]

Yet despite this not unimpressive engagement by some Gaels with the work of their compatriots writing in English, many in the movement continued to see the ongoing and often acclaimed attempt to create a national literature in what they insisted was a foreign language as a dangerous temptation if not a hostile conspiracy. This idea was developed most clearly by Micheál Mac

Liammóir of all people in a 1924 essay in which he conceded that the majority of Irish writers expressed themselves in English and continued:

> as long as English, and writers of English, are able to satisfy the literary needs of the most discerning people in the country, and as long as all who have power and strength and are involved with a new literary movement in the country are devoting themselves to English, the Irish language will be weak and ineffectual (*Sguab*, Sept. 1924, 173).[150]

Less temperate was 'Mac', who in a 1927 poem entitled 'To Certain Anglo-Irish Writers' declared:

> Your vaunted 'culture' still we spurn / Whose home on British ground is set. / For still the Gaelic flame will burn – / We are not all West Britons yet! / Your alien culture take elsewhere / Ye little gods of Merrion Square! (*An Phoblacht*, 18/3/27).

But even so cultured and liberal a writer as Liam Ó Rinn could see Anglo-Irish literature in this light. Responding to the recent publication of *Ancient Irish Tales* by the American Celticists Tom Peete Clark and Clark B. Slover, he stated:

> You would sometimes think that there was nothing in the Irish language or in the literature of the Irish language but things there specifically to benefit the English language . . . The writer of English is like a ravenous wolf seeking material for a book, and he does not care where he finds it (*II*, 4/12/36).[151]

It was, however, Seosamh Mac Grianna who offered the most succinct and memorable expression of the ambivalent fascination Irish writing in English held for the Gaels when, discussing the work of Standish James O'Grady as 'about the best of the Irish Renaissance crowd', he hastened to add 'but the trail of the serpent is over them all' (*An Phoblacht*, 4/2/27).[152]

EIGHT

AT THE COW'S RUMP OR IN THE NATIONAL THEATRE?

ISSUES IN GAELIC DRAMA[1]

No institution of Anglo-Irish culture more troubled the Gaels than did the Abbey Theatre, whose successes at home and abroad could seem to legitimate the claim that a genuine Irish literature might find adequate expression in the English language. Writing to the *Irish Independent* in 1935 in his capacity as president of the Gaelic League, Peadar Mac Fhionnlaoich was only restating movement dogma when he attacked the Abbey in the following terms:

> The Abbey Theatre at its best was never an exponent of Irish national ideals. At its worst, it is intolerable, and must be swept aside . . . As to the Abbey itself, I am inclined to echo the prayer that I heard an embittered old farmer utter on hearing of the death of his landlord: 'A speedy race down with him' (*II*, 21/8/35).[2]

On the other hand, some more optimistic Gaels tried to convince themselves that the Abbey was already dead, or at least gratifyingly moribund. As early as November 1923, D. P. Moran pontificated: 'Of course, the Abbey Anglo-Irish theatre was a blind-alley job, and when it got so far it stopped. The Abbey movement is as dead as the Kiltartan dialect' (*Leader*, 17/11/23). No less an authority than Daniel Corkery, himself of course an Abbey playwright, argued in a 1928 essay that 'the annals of the Abbey Theatre confirm what has been said of the creative spirit: that movement has become a withered branch' (*Guth na nGaedheal*, 1928, 7).[3] In an anonymous 1934 review of a production at Taibhdhearc na Gaillimhe, the critic saw the end of Irish drama in English as a necessary and desirable corollary of the language revival: 'With the growth of the Gaelic movement it can safely be said there is no future for Anglo-Irish drama' (*CS*, 13/3/34). And in a strikingly wishful essay in *Láimhleabhar Drámaidheachta*, Aindrias Ó Muimhneacháin, having acknowledged that the Abbey was 'the only national dramatic movement in English that ever took a meaningful hold on the people of Ireland' (an t-aon ghluaiseacht amháin drámuíochta i mBéarla a fuair aon ghreim le héifeacht ar phobal na hÉireann), continued:

> Most likely that movement itself has exhausted its period of significance, and as an indication of that, note that that same group is already drawing on plays in Irish as a support. They must feel a gap opening between themselves and the public, and they must think that these plays in Irish will serve as a bridge for them lest the public will not support them.[4]

However appealing, Ó Muimhneacháin's notion that Abbey audiences yearned for entertainment in Irish was to say the least idiosyncratic. Gaels were far more likely to be appalled by how keen Dublin audiences were for the fare served up at the Abbey. The primary Gaelic objection to the Abbey repertoire was, of course, linguistic, as will be discussed in some detail below. But other Irish-Ireland critics lambasted the theatre on religious, moral, political and class grounds. Many of these objections coalesced around the conviction that the Abbey, despite its origins in a movement created to 'show that Ireland is not the home of buffoonery and easy sentiment',[5] had itself spawned its own breed of marketable stage-Irish stereotypes. In a 1931 piece, Geraldine Dillon, a member of the board of directors of Taibhdhearc na Gaillimhe, wrote:

> The flood of Abbey plays, except for the well-reorganized [sic] exceptions, are poor and written from a decidedly superior point of view. The 'funny Irish' touch about them is sufficient to account for the extraordinary audience which the Abbey has acquired which makes it impossible to me, at any rate, to go to a play there (*CT*, 12/9/31).

The previous year, 'Delta' had pronounced the new Abbey caricatures even more harmful than the originals because they bore the *imprimatur* of an explicitly 'national' Irish cultural institution: 'Bad as the stage Irishman may have been, it would seem that the Abbey Irishman is immeasurably worse. Both should be remorselessly banished from Ireland' (*IR*, Mar. 1930, 227). In 1931, Donn Piatt indicted the Abbey for its treatment of the West of Ireland, claiming Abbey writers had made the heartland of the Gael 'a land of Romance, of Playboys, of Blind Rafterys, of Arran [*sic*] Islanders, of Kiltartanese' (*IP*, 9/12/31). As early as 1926, Maoghnus Ó Domhnaill saw the Abbey as eager to satisfy an audience of 'tourists' – foreign and domestic – and warned: 'If the Abbey continues to cater for the stalls, the time is not far off when "Paddy Whack" will re-appear on the stage to tickle the ribs of the stalls with his shillelagh' (*An Phoblacht*, 17/9/26).[6] A decade later, Micheál Ó Maoláin felt that the Abbey had created a new caricature of the Irish even more insidious than 'Paddy Whack', writing on the occasion of Yeats's death: 'The "Stage Irishmen" that used to be seen on the stages here in Dublin a half century ago were fine, purely Gaelic men next to the scoundrels they have in the Abbey Theatre' (*IP*, 4/2/39).[7]

In 1935, Tomás Ó Cléirigh inveighed against the anti-national cynicism of the Abbey, stating:

> The dramas they have would amaze you – almost all of them deal with rural life, and not only that, but the most famous of them deal with the Gaeltacht itself! I was absolutely unable to understand that until an Irish speaker explained to me that those dramas are by no means produced from love of us but rather from a wish to annoy us and mock us.

Ó Cléirigh went on to lament that even worse than the Abbey's contemptuous treatment of ordinary Irish people was the fact that the Irish government itself provided the theatre with the funds 'to go over to America and to make a laughing stock there of the people of this country, etc., etc.' (chun dul anonn go hAimeirica agus staicín áiféise a dhéanamh ann de mhuinntir na tíre seo 7rl. 7rl).[8] Again and again, Irish-Irelanders railed at the Free State authorities for underwriting the creation and propagation of this new, homegrown Stage Irishman, as when, in 1926, the editor of the *Irish Homestead* asked:

> What right has the Government to give the Abbey authorities £1000 of the Irish people's money to enable them to carry on their work of degrading us? Are we to pay for the luxury of having ourselves held up as a drunken, besotted, immoral people? . . . Filthy people will seek filthy things – and find them. We must take care we do not pay them to do so (*Irish Homestead*, Apr. 1926, 4).

In 1939, the Ard-Fheis of the Gaelic League, with Éamon de Valera in attendance and speaking in opposition, passed a motion calling on the government to end the subsidy to the Abbey and spend the money instead on the promotion of drama in Irish.[9]

It was, of course, the Abbey's perceived contempt for the Irish language that most angered those in the language movement with an interest in theatre. The Galway West deputy Josie Mongan raised this point in a Dáil debate on the Abbey subsidy in 1937. Having claimed he had never heard a word of Irish in the Abbey, he continued: 'We have been listening to Handy Andy and his likes long enough. We ought to have something really Irish [lit. Gaelic] in their place' (*CT*, 6/11/37).[10] It had, of course, always been a fundamental tenet of the language movement that any Irish national drama with a legitimate claim to the name would have to be in Irish – even though the language had absolutely no native tradition of theatre. And throughout our period the Gaels made sure this article of faith was not forgotten, calling on a regular basis for an authentic Irish drama in Irish. Indeed D. P. Moran saw the creation of such a drama as essential to the success of the language movement itself, writing in 1923:

> If Irish is to progress, we must have an Irish theatre . . . If Dublin, the capital of Ireland, cannot keep up an Irish theatre, with actors who are willing to act out of love of the language, Irish-Ireland may as well put up its shutters (*Leader*, 1/9/23).

The policeman S. de Búrca was even more ambitious, writing in 1933: 'If we had the likes of Shakepeare in Ireland, the language would be in no danger' (*GR*, Mar. 1933, 414).[11] But it was perhaps the editor of *An t-Éireannach* who best captured the more deliberate and determined Gaelic sense of what had to be done in this area: 'There is one loss or lack in Irish-language literature – and that loss is more noticeable at present than it ever has been before. We have a noble Poetry; we have a fine, poetic Prose; but we have no Drama at all' (*Éireannach*, 7/7/34).[12] Such an awareness was naturally a central motivation for the work of An Comhar Drámaidheachta, which, in a 1927 promotional circular, stated: 'It will be our duty to create an art of the stage and forms of acting that will be in tune with the spirit and qualities of our race.'[13]

Implicit in these words from An Comhar Drámaidheachta itself was the idea that the theatre had an ideological as well as aesthetic significance. Commentators throughout our period stressed that an active and vibrant Gaelic stage could provide another effective barrier against foreign, particularly English, influence and all its attendant corruptions. For example, in 1924 'Theo' declared:

> A well-developed Irish theatre would form a considerable barrier against the incursions into Irish literature of the soulless rationalistic philosophy of the continent and the materialism of England. Our traditions and our tastes will be spared from the calamity of being merely adaptations of English and continental standards (*Leader*, 20/2/24).

By the end of our period, Seán Feehan hoped that, in Galway at least, Taibhdhearc na Gaillimhe could perform just that function: 'A Gaelic theatre performing regularly, frequently and well, would at least provide an antidote open to everybody. It would be at least one Gaelicising force cutting into all the anglicising forces which threaten to overwhelm the City of the Tribes' (*CB*, Aug. 1938, 653).

That this was not solely the opinion of philistine ideologues is evident from a 1935 essay by Gearóid Ó Lochlainn, one of the Gaelic theatre's most sophisticated and accomplished writers, actors, and directors. With the challenge of the cinema foremost in his mind, Ó Lochlainn wrote: 'But for just that reason, the need is greater for normal, truly Gaelic theatres in the country that will be a protective barrier against the tide of Anglicisation.'[14]

There were, however, many in the language movement with little or no aesthetic interest in the theatre at all. The majority opinion among the Gaels who devoted any thought to the question seems to have been that the stage was, and should be, primarily an adjunct to the classroom or the lecture platform. Of course, such an attitude drew sharp criticism from some dedicated to the theatre as an art form, as when Micheál Mac Liammóir ('Taibhdhearc') wrote in a 1928 essay in *An Stoc* that was reprinted in the programme for the opening night of Taibhdhearc na Gaillimhe:

> I hope that they will come to us, not only because of the great respect they have for the language of St Patrick and St Brigid, but because they want to go to the theatre, and because it is a natural thing, in Galway, to go to the theatre in Irish, just as it is natural, in Seville, to go to it in Spanish . . . To make an exclusively educational medium of the Theatre would be a misuse. On the other hand, to make it merely a medium of entertainment and revelry would be to pervert the main object of the theatre, an object that most people, alas, do not understand. The main object of the theatre, as we understand it, is to teach the public about beauty and life through drama (*Stoc*, Aug.–Sept. 1928, 4).[15]

León Ó Broin saw little room for compromise with the philistines the following year:

> And above all, there must be an immediate divorce between the people who believe in the drama for the drama's sake and the people who are interested in the drama because it is Gaelic drama or because the Irish language is the medium of expression used (*Star*, 20/7/29).

But theirs was definitely the minority opinion, with the majority taking for granted that plays should be primarily audio-visual aids for language instruction. Particularly explicit on this point was an anonymous drama critic for *An t-Éireannach*, who wrote in 1935: 'The language is more important than drama, and is it not to advance the language that plays are produced in Irish?' (*Éireannach*, 30/3/35).[16] But many others shared a more moderate version of the same opinion. For example, in 1923 the Gaelic editor of the *Irish Independent* wrote:

> The theatre is a great help to any cause that uses it properly, and there are few causes that it would benefit more greatly now than the cause of the Irish language itself . . . The play entirely in Irish would provide material to the student for practice in speech and in reading as well (*II*, 23/7/23).[17]

'S. Ó R.' offered a more detailed expression of the same idea a decade later, arguing:

> There are few methods of teaching Irish that are as important as the drama, for in it one finds the events of the day and other things embodied in forceful, fluent speech . . . Educators and the learners could benefit most from the drama. They could see the history of our country brought back to life; they could see the ancient culture of the Gaels; and they could hear the musical Irish language being spoken from the stage elegantly and properly, fluently and richly (*Muimhneach*, Apr. 1933, 75).[18]

The Gaelic editor of the Dundalk *Examiner* was even more enthusiastic about the pedagogical potential of the stage, writing in 1937: 'There is absolutely no better way to advance the speaking of Irish among the public than to put a great number of plays in Irish on the stages throughout the country' (*Examiner*, 22/5/37).[19] Even Pádraic Ó Conaire, usually so dismissive of the tendency to see all literary work in Irish as raw material for textbooks, could support this view of drama, stating in the preface to his play *Caitlín na Clúide*: 'For people learning a language there is no better way to be found than to read plays, if the living speech just as it is spoken is in the play.'[20]

Given such attitudes, it was predictable enough that the schools would become one of the most dependable and productive allies in the campaign for a Gaelic drama in the Free State years, especially after the formation in February 1934 of Cumann Drámaidheachta na Scol (The schools' drama society). The extraordinary success of this organisation and its annual drama festivals, with strong support from the state's Department of Education, seems to have made the production of plays in Irish a major activity all over the country.[21] At the society's first festival, in Dublin in 1934, 28 plays were produced (*IP*, 18/10/34); in Galway in 1937, there were 40 plays, attended by 5,000 children (*IP*, 7/3/37); and at the 1938 festival, again in Dublin, the number of plays performed was up to 50 (*IP*, 18/10/38). As well as fostering theatrical activity in the schools of Connacht, Craobh an Iarthair (The western branch) of Cumann Drámaidheachta na Scol was responsible for the publication of the valuable *Láimhleabhar Drámaidheachta*, edited by Proinnsias E. Ó Súilleabháin and containing not only programme information for the 1938 festival, but also several essays on drama by recognised authors like Micheál Breathnach, Douglas Hyde, Gearóid Ó Lochlainn, and An tAthair Eric Mac Fhinn.[22]

Another intriguing initiative in Gaelic drama was the rise of local groups in various Gaeltacht areas, although some of these seem to have come together for short periods of time or even single performances.[23] By far the most substantial and long-lived was Donegal's Aisteoirí Ghaoth Dobhair. Performing for the first time on 10 January 1932, they seem to have quickly made a name for themselves in the Donegal Gaeltacht, so that their founder and most important playwright, Eoghan Mac Giolla Bhríghde could write in 1933: 'I would also like to say that more interest is being taken by the people here in plays in the native language than in the other kind, for the hall is quickly filled when we have performances' (*IP*, 1/5/33).[24] By 1937, they could boast no fewer than 87 performances, and their work had attracted the attention of leading figures in the national movement, so that, for example, Gearóid Ó Lochlainn travelled to direct the company in August of that year (*IP*, 1/9/37).[25]

As had always been the case since the production of the movement's first plays at *feiseanna* and at the Oireachtas, the Gaelic League continued to play an important role in the staging of plays in Irish. During our period, local Gaelic League branches throughout the country offered the occasional play, with Dublin predictably taking the lead in such theatrical activity.[26] By far the most active of the League groups in the capital was the Keating Branch, whose members in 1933 revived the languishing drama group that had been such a force in Gaelic drama in Dublin in the early years of the twentieth century. The Keating company seems to have quickly re-established its reputation among Dublin's theatre-going Gaels, so that in 1936 'Playgoer' could write: 'They have produced in all some 20 plays, including several new plays and a number of new translations, and have built up a useful company of young actors, most of whom show great promise' (*Leader*, 10/10/36).[27]

In a 1935 piece praising a performance by the Keating players in the Peacock, an anonymous contributor to *An t-Éireannach* wrote:

> It is clear that it would be of benefit to drama in Irish if other branches of the League would get productions like this going in the public theatres. If half the branches in Dublin did the like it would be possible to produce plays in Irish for a week every month, and they would doubtless be well attended provided that the productions were good (*Éireannach*, 30/3/35).[28]

Nowhere near half of Dublin's League branches were ever involved in the production of plays, but several did follow the Keating Branch onto the stage, the most important of them being Craobh Moibhí, whose members were addressed on the subject of drama by Aindrias Ó Muimhneacháin at their inaugural meeting in 1932 (*II*, 21/9/32), and Craobh na gCúig gCúigí, famous for the number of Protestants who belonged (*IP*, 15/2/38). Local League-sponsored *feiseanna*, large and small, were even more important for bringing Gaelic drama to the public, especially in the provinces. These *feiseanna* often staged plays as a feature of their programmes, and some of the larger festivals scheduled a downright intimidating array of dramatic offerings. For example, in 1934, 42 theatre groups were represented at the Dublin Feis, the League's largest cultural festival while the Oireachtas was suspended (*Camán*, 10/2/34), and the following year there were over 70 plays entered in its competitions (*Camán*, 9/2/35).[29] The 1934 Feis Charman in Enniscorthy, County Wexford was even larger, with no fewer than 90 Gaelic plays actually produced there (*Camán*, 9/6/34).[30]

None of these dramatic ventures was, however, to have anywhere near the impact of An Comhar Drámaidheachta in Dublin or Taibhdhearc na Gaillimhe in Galway. Nor was any to receive anything like the financial support provided these groups by the state, or anywhere near the attention focused on them by the Gaelic press. An Comhar Drámaidheachta evolved from Piaras Béaslaí's earlier company Na hAisteoirí (thus explaining why commentators often called the group Na h-Aisteoirí in reviews and reports in their early years). On its first managing committee sat Béaslaí himself along with Gearóid Ó Lochlainn, Pádraig Ó Siochfhradha, Risteárd Ó Foghludha, and Liam Gógan. From the autumn of 1923 until 1930, An Comhar played at first in the Abbey and then in the Peacock. In 1924, the company, like the Abbey players themselves, received a state subsidy, largely, no doubt, due to the advocacy of the Free State's Minister for Finance Ernest Blythe, a long-time and unswerving supporter of the Gaelic stage throughout his entire professional life. From 1930 to 1934, An Comhar performed in the new Gate Theatre, where they worked with Micheál Mac Liammóir, before returning to the Peacock for the rest of our period.[31]

From the start, An Comhar was a different and far more ambitious venture in Gaelic drama, with the board deciding at its very first annual meeting, with Ó Siochfhradha in the chair, that it would stage plays in Irish on two successive nights each month from October to April with the possibility of adding a Sunday matinee as well (*FL*, 19/4/24). *Fáinne an Lae* offered immediate editorial encouragement to An Comhar on its foundation, drawing attention to the fact that one could join the group for £1 with admission to all productions as a membership benefit (*FL*, 10/11/23). This subscription scheme was also touted by An Comhar itself in its programmes from October 1927 on, with the group's secretary urging the occasional patron to become a regular member: 'We would like to see, through the buying of the [membership] cards, that our friends are determined to stand by us and that they have confidence in us for the upcoming season.'[32]

In 1936, An Comhar embarked on a more ambitious project, undertaking to act as what was in effect a co-ordinating umbrella body for Gaelic drama nationwide, with special emphasis, of course, on Dublin.[33] Among the goals An Comhar had in mind with this initiative were:

> (a) the supply of suitable plays at low prices; (b) the supply of costumes at low prices; (c) to make provision for regional directors; (d) to secure public funds to

> assist the regional dramatic societies; and (e) to encourage authors to write plays (*IP*, 26/5/36).[34]

By 1937, when the policy was officially endorsed by the board of An Comhar, the following Gaelic League branches had affiliated themselves with the scheme: Craobh an Chéitinnigh, Craobh Moibhí, Craobh na gCúig gCúigí, Craobh Liam Uí Mhaolruanaidhe, Craobh na nGárdaí, and Craobh Thomáis Dáibhis. In addition, the players of Cumann Gaedhealach na h-Iolsgoile at Trinity College, Dublin, and Cumann Gaedhealach na Stáitsheirbhíse had also joined. From the start, An Comhar encouraged the participation of theatre groups from the schools in the scheme, and in the first year they arranged productions at the Peacock by four different student companies.[35] In general, this initiative was well received. For example, An tAthair Mac Fhinn welcomed it enthusiastically in *Ar Aghaidh*, declaring:

> We are glad to see that there is a proper 'Comhar' Drámaidheachta [dramatic 'partnership'] this year . . . That basically means that a strong dramatic movement has been established in Dublin and that it is being kept going by people who are co-operating for the good of the drama and for the good of the Irish language (*AA*, Nov. 1936, 3).[36]

An Comhar was, however, from quite early in its career to be a lightning rod for controversy, a situation due in no small part to its Dublin base far from the *Gaeltachtaí* and its enjoyment of taxpayer largesse from the Cumann na nGaedheal government of the Free State. Nevertheless, optimism prevailed at first as many Gaels looked forward to being able to see well-produced plays in Irish on a regular basis in a real theatre in the national capital.[37] *Fáinne an Lae* offered the group a warm welcome after its first performance in November 1923: 'This work of Na hAisteoirí is a great step forward for the Irish language, and great credit is due to them for that' (*FL*, 17/11/23).[38] Many were also sympathetically aware of the difficulties and responsibilities facing An Comhar and of the courage with which the group met them, as is evident from a 1930 piece on Gaelic theatre by 'R. Ó. P.':

> They are a little band who work during the day in shops and offices. They do not have the free time to practise their acting except in the evening. The acting could be improved – if they had free time for it. More suitable plays could be had – if they had time to look for them. They are doing excellent work. And – no thanks to their critics – they are succeeding (*An Phoblacht*, 25/1/30).[39]

In its early days, even the *Irish Statesman* could applaud the company and lend them encouragement, as when the paper's critic 'Feste' wrote in January 1924:

> The progress of the language movement is marked by the crowded houses at the Abbey Theatre when Na h-Aisteoirí give a Gaelic night once a month. Full houses are drawn and [Thomas] Macdonagh's dream of a living Gaelic drama seems in the way to be realised (*IS*, 26/1/24).

Seán Ó Ciarghusa went beyond plausibility in his praise of the group in 1927, writing: 'As to the actors, I may as well say at once that An Comhar Drámaidheachta are as good as I hope to see in my time. They play at once with the artlessness of amateurs and the art of professionals' (*Leader*, 12/11/27).[40] An Comhar member and playwright León Ó Broin expressed an insider's pride when he declared in a 1928 essay: 'What an Comhar Drámaidheachta has done is almost a miracle since it was begun in 1923' (*Inis Fáil*, Dec. 1928, 25).[41] For 'I. G.', proof of An Comhar's achievement over the years could be seen in the heightened expectations of its audiences, so that by 1938 he could write:

> The time is now gone when I would have to say that it was a duty for every Gael to 'help' An Comhar. At present, the productions of An Comhar are worth attending for the sake of the production itself, without thoughts about 'nationalism' or 'the cause of the Irish language' bothering you. You will get your money's worth (*Comhthrom Féinne*, Nov. 1938, 11).[42]

Many who attended the performances of An Comhar were more ambivalent, so that even favourable reviews could get in the odd dig at the company, as did 'P. Ó C.' in a 1931 piece on An Comhar's production of a Gaelic version of Molière's *Le Bourgeois Gentilhomme* as *An Geocach Duine Uasal*:

> Hitherto, the poor critic who did not want to hurt the Theatre of the Gaels with censure and who respected the truth was in a real predicament. The question he would ask himself after seeing a production was 'Is there anything that it is possible to praise?' and not 'Is there anything that it is possible to find fault with?' as is usual with every other critic (*Nation*, 6/12/31).[43]

It was Cearbhall Ua Dálaigh who most succinctly expressed such a sense of (often very) qualified optimism when he wrote in the same month: 'But however weak the work of the drama is, one hopes that the movement is not regressing' (*CB*, Dec. 1931, 605).[44]

Many in the movement were – or stategically claimed to be – outraged at An Comhar's receipt of a subsidy from the Free State government. Of course, as with every aspect of public life in the Free State, politics was a significant factor here in the attitude of some in the anti-Treaty camp towards a subsidy initiated by a pro-Treaty government, a point underscored by an anonymous contributor to *Ar Aghaidh* (probably An tAthair Mac Fhinn) in 1936: 'Somehow the people of Dublin have not supported An Comhar from the first day. The greatest cause for that was politics, because certain people did not wish to help a scheme set up by the Government of the Free State' (*AA*, Nov. 1936, 3).[45] Whether political rancour was the main source of resentment against An Comhar and the subsidy is now unclear. What is obvious, however, is that such resentment ran deep. In May 1929, 'An Scríobhnóir', the regular Gaelic columnist for *Honesty*, disingenuously raised the question of the subsidy: 'Perhaps this is a good expenditure of money and perhaps it is not.' But he then immediately struck what was to be his habitual note whenever he turned his attention to An Comhar:

> To tell the truth we are not too satisfied at all that a thousand pounds could not be used far more effectively for the language of the country than for giving a little tiny group a chance to go on stage once or twice a month (*Honesty*, 26/5/29).[46]

The following year the gloves were off, so that in April 1930 he could write: 'But to give six hundred pounds of this country's money every year to a little group with not a soul supporting them but themselves and no good coming from it – we are very much against that and we hope it will be ended at once' (*Honesty*, 26/4/30).[47] He returned to this theme a few months later:

> But it is a strange thing that a little group like that can get a subsidy from the State Treasury, with nothing to show as a result but complaining. Would it not be better to spend that money on some organisation from which some benefit would accrue to the Irish language (*Honesty*, 15/11/30).[48]

Micheál Ó Maoláin shared this view of An Comhar as a rather petulant elitist clique on whom money was being scandalously wasted. Writing in his regular 'Leathanach na Gaedhilge' (The Irish language page) column in *Nationality* in 1931, he proclaimed:

> It is a strange thing that it is possible to spend £600 a year out of the State Treasury on so small a group. The Gaels of this city are not supporting An Comhar Drámaidheachta; they do not trust them, and it is no help for anyone to be trying to fool the Gaelic World that the Irish-speakers of Dublin are behind them . . . An Comhar Drámaidheachta is nothing but Window Dressing (*Nationality*, 28/3/31).[49]

At one of the Gaelic League's weekly street rallies in Dublin in 1933, the following resolution, moved by Ó Maoláin and seconded by Peadar Mac Fhionnlaoich, was carried unanimously:

> That it is the opinion of this gathering that the Government is wrong not to provide money for Gaelic plays in the Gaeltacht, while money is being given to An Comhar Drámaidheachta in Dublin and to An Taibhdhearc in Galway, and to the Abbey Theatre in Dublin (*Tír*, May, 1933, 8).[50]

Despite its perceived link in this resolution with An Comhar, and – far worse the Abbey – Taibhdhearc na Gaillimhe received gentler treatment from the Gaels. In part, this leniency was due to the simple fact that An Taibhdhearc worked at a safe remove from the scrutiny of Dublin activists and critics, but another, more positive factor was a fairly general excitement at the thought of having a real Gaelic theatre in the Irish city with the closest ties to a flourishing Gaeltacht. According to Ernest Blythe, it was this excitement that kept Mac Liammóir involved with An Taibhdhearc, despite an attractive offer from An Comhar in the capital. Writing to Séamus Ó Beirn in 1930, Blythe stated:

> He [Mac Liammóir] said that he was very tempted to accept the offer which would be personally convenient for him, but that he recognised that the work which was being done in Galway was fundamentally more important than any work that could be done in Dublin.[51]

In addition, the foundation of An Taibhdhearc inspired a legitimate local pride among those in the language movement in Galway and the West in general, a pride evident in the comments of a *Connacht Tribune* correspondent in the month before the first performance at the theatre: 'The opening of the new theatre will be perhaps the most important event in the history of the language movement in the West of Ireland' (*CT*, 25/8/28). When An Taibhdhearc did open with Mac Liammóir's *Diarmuid agus Gráinne*, Tomás Ó Máille pronounced it 'a historic occasion' (ócáid staireamhail) and hoped that 'God willing, that Theatre will play a great role in the history of the revival of the Irish language from now on' (*Stoc*, Oct. 1928, 4).[52] Most Galwegians with an interest in drama, the revival, or both, seem to have agreed that An Taibhdhearc almost immediately lived up to such lofty expectations. For example, in a 1929 letter to An Taibhdhearc the UCG professor Liam Ó Buachalla said 'the foundation of Taibhdhearc na Gaillimhe is the greatest thing ever done for the Irish language' (bunú Taibhdheirc na Gaillimhe an rud is mó a rinneadh ar shon na Gaedhilge riamh).[53] An anonymous contributor to the *Connacht Tribune* went even further, praising the theatre for not only bringing quality Gaelic entertainment to Galway, but also for helping to heal the divisions of the Civil War:

> It is not only that the Stage of the Taibhdhearc dissipated much of the sadness and loneliness, yes, and the strife that was doing damage and separating Gaelic friends

> from each other, but it also increased and bound love of country and language closely and firmly among us (*CT*, 5/4/30).[54]

Nor was appreciation of the Galway theatre's accomplishments limited to the city itself or even the West. In a 1938 essay, Seán Feehan called An Taibhdhearc 'Ireland's Real National Theatre' and continued: 'From every material point of view, i.e., staging, costuming, lighting, and as regards acting and producing as well, the Theatre has revolutionised in the Galway area the conception of an "Irish play"' (*CB*, Aug. 1938, 651).[55]

It must have been frustrating for members of An Comhar Drámaidheachta to compare how graciously the Galwegians were usually treated by commentators – even their state subsidy went for the most part unchallenged – to the rough handling they so regularly received from critics. Perhaps prompted by such envy, An Comhar's president, Tadhg Ó Scanaill, speaking at the group's annual general meeting in 1938, claimed that it was An Comhar that had inspired what Gaelic theatrical activity there was anywhere in Ireland, including Galway. His comments drew a magisterial response from An Taibhdhearc:

> It was the judgment of the Society that the President of An Comhar is a bit astray in his wits to say such a thing, when it was clear to the world that it was in Connacht, beyond any other place in Ireland, that the movement has expanded and grown and that it is in Galway in particular that the roots of drama are (*IP*, 11/6/38).[56]

Apart from the subsidy, what were the main complaints directed at An Comhar Drámaidheachta and, to a much lesser extent, at Taibhdhearc na Gaillime? Predictably enough, much of the criticism focused on the artistic shortcomings inherent in an entirely amateur enterprise. We have already seen how a reviewer for *An Phoblacht* sympathetically drew attention in 1930 to the challenges facing the part-time players of An Comhar. Many Gaelic critics were nowhere near as patient or understanding, and grumbles about the overall quality of An Comhar's productions were common throughout our period. Particularly galling was the actors' frequent failure to have their lines off by heart, what 'Scrúdóir' in one review tactfully called 'the lapse of memory on the part of the players' (*Star*, 7/12/29). 'R. Ó P.' was caustic in a review the following year, writing of An Comhar's actors:

> Some of them [were] carrying themselves unnaturally, because their minds were focused entirely on the dialogue that they had not fully memorised, or that did not come fluently to them. A weak voice projection (but not on the part of the 'the prompter' behind!), awkward acting – a clear sign that the majority had not rehearsed the drama well (*An Phoblacht*, 25/10/30).[57]

Frank O'Connor felt that unlearned lines were a regular feature of plays in Irish in Dublin. Reviewing a Gaelic translation of T. C. Murray's *Birthright* in the Peacock, O'Connor wrote sarcastically:

> That actors should come on with only the haziest notions of their lines, stumble, stammer and pick themselves up, allow the angel of silence to draw a long sigh from the audience between challenge and response – that one was prepared for (*IS*, 22/2/30).

It seems that on some nights the prompter may have been one of the hardest working members of the company, as during a 1929 production of Béaslaí's *An Danar* at the Abbey, a production that, according to 'Scrúdóir', put 'constant strain on the resources of the prompter' (*Star*, 9/2/29). Béaslaí was no better served two months later when An Comhar produced the premiere of his new play *An Bhean Chródha*, a production of which 'Scrúdóir' wrote:

> No doubt the slip-shod memorising of their parts by the players accentuated this defect [occasional unintelligibility and incoherence], and more than once 'position' on the stage was sacrificed in order to keep in ear-shot of an over-worked prompter (*Star*, 13/4/29).[58]

On the other hand, 'D. Ó D.' probably felt that one actor he singled out in a 1927 Comhar production should have relied more on his prompter, however overworked: 'I don't like for any actor, however famous, to use books to read his part from' (*Leader*, 26/3/27).[59]

Knowing one's lines does not, of course, in itself lead to high dramatic art, and the quality of acting was often inconsistent or worse in many of An Comhar's productions, a fact that troubled an anonymous critic for *An Phoblacht* in 1930: 'Some of the Actors do not have good voice projection, others are clumsy and hesitant on the stage. I am afraid that most of them do not get the necessary instruction or practice in acting' (*An Phoblacht*, 22/2/30).[60] Far less charitable was Frank O'Connor, who wrote of the previous Comhar production the same year that the perfomers 'acted as in a secondary school production of Shakespeare', and concluded:

> The great fault of the players at the moment is inadequate production. Only one or two of the company have any real conception of acting technique, and the plays are a succession of slight errors, false starts, awkward or repeated gestures and over-emphasis, while no attempt is ever made at securing a broad general effect (*IS*, 18/1/30).[61]

Every bit as harsh was 'A. F.' in a piece on An Comhar the previous year:

> I am compelled to admit that the performances given from month to month in the Abbey Theatre are somewhat depressing . . . In nearly every performance there are marks of carelessness that seem to me to indicate something very like contempt for the audience, and a notion that people should pay for their seats at the Comhar Drámaidheachta performances and be quite content to merely hear Irish spoken from the stage (*Star*, 26/1/29).

Even more stinging was Seán Ó Meadhra, who wrote of An Comhar's production of Liam Ó Briain's translation of Synge's *Deirdre of the Sorrows*:

> That the house was packed for a week merely suggests that the Gaedhilgeoirí [Irish speakers] of this town are as lacking in taste as the players and were getting what they wanted. If most of these players are actors, then a tin whistler outside a pub is a musician – and funny enough, both expect to get money by it (*Ireland To-Day*, Nov. 1937, 75).[62]

For some, there had been no meaningful improvement even by the very end of our period, as is clear from the dismissive comments of an anonymous critic in *The Leader*: 'Gaelic acting standards are deplorably low . . . It is rare indeed to meet a player whose Irish is good, and who has the talent, training and experience to enable him to make effective use of it on stage' (*Leader*, 27/5/39). Even Ernest Blythe, one of the most committed and, in his days as Minister for Finance, most generous champions of Gaelic drama, felt compelled to face distasteful facts as our period closed:

> In general, dramatic performances in Irish are crude and clumsy and of a standard that would infallibly empty the theatre completely if lack of artistic quality were not partly neutralised by the draw of the language. As far as I can judge, most of those associated with the staging of Irish plays have no higher ambition than to give a passable amateur performance (*Leader*, 16/12/39).[63]

Nevertheless, on the whole, most Gaels seem to have been willing to wait while actors worked on their craft, and optimistic assessments of their progress outnumbered negative judgments throughout the Free State years. In 1924 Peadar Mac Fhionnlaoich wrote of An Comhar: 'I am delighted that the actors are succeeding so well. I do not say they are without fault, but there is time enough to point out their faults to them. Praise youth and it will come, and we greatly need drama' (*SF*, 2/2/24).[64] In the same year, 'Feste' offered a startlingly positive opinion of the work of An Comhar:

> The Gaelic players closed their season on May 5th. Month by month they have given us a night of Gaelic drama, and not only have most of the performances been

> extremely enjoyable, but the actors have so much improved their art that the last performances might be compared without hesitation to all but the very best work among professional players at the Abbey (*IS*, 17/5/24).

In a 1931 review of a production by An Comhar under the direction of Micheál Mac Liammóir, 'P. Ó C.' stated: 'What was most noticeable at this performance was how the company's acting is improving. Almost every one of them is progressing very well' (*Nation*, 2/5/31).[65] Even Frank O'Connor could rather grudgingly admit in a 1930 review that 'a certain improvement was noticeable in the production and acting' (*IS*, 5/4/30).[66]

For most Gaels interested in drama, the solution to this problem was for once simple enough to envision, but far more difficult to achieve. Actors learn by acting, and the sporadic short runs of plays in Irish – often only a night or two – provided little opportunity for learning, much less perfecting their skills. Such was certainly the opinion of Piaras Béaslaí, who in a 1928 letter to Ernest Blythe spelled out the difficulties frustrating members of An Comhar:

> It is our strong opinion that it is not possible for us to accomplish more, as long as we are confined to seven productions a year, and that there will be no further growth or progress in the work. Instead, the people will grow tired of us, and there is a danger that the acting itself will get a bit rusty unless we get more scope to develop it.[67]

Responding to a series of lectures on theatre sponsored by An Comhar in 1926, 'Aodh Éigeas' sounded a similar note:

> The Irish plays have been on for only one night a month. That means that the players have only a 'first night' of every play they stage after all their trouble, and with no chance of correcting inevitable slips of dialogue, etc. first nights reveal (*Leader*, 3/7/26).

Gearóid Ó Lochlainn shared this concern in an essay three years later: 'Playing one night in the month means no less work of preparation than playing for an entire week, and one night a month on the boards is of very little value in training to actors who are learning their business' (*Star*, 13/7/29).[68] And in his previously quoted harsh assessment of the state of Gaelic drama in 1939, Blythe called for the professionalisation of the Gaelic stage, asserting:

> Nothing less will do than a theatre in which plays in Irish will be performed six nights a week during forty weeks in the year and in which the artistic standard attained will not be below that which is usual in the Abbey Theatre and the Gate Theatre (*Leader*, 16/12/39).[69]

There was, however, a far greater sin in Gaelic eyes than bad memory or a wooden stage presence, and many felt that the actors of An Comhar committed that sin in public on a regular basis. Even a glance at reviews from the period shows an at times almost obsessive concern with the quality of the performers' Irish, a particularly sore point given the pedagogical importance assigned to the drama by so many at the time. A few of the abundant examples of this linguistic fixation should suffice. No one faced the basic question at issue more forthrightly than did 'Scrúdóir', who wrote in 1930:

> The old Gael will have little respect for an excellent drama unless the Irish in it is good and unless the actors can do justice to the author's or the translator's speech. People who will go to plays in Irish are more concerned with linguistic matters than with dramatic matters. Is the goal of An Comhar dramatic matters or linguistic matters? There are people who will say that they have neither of those two goals, or if they do, that they are trying to bring both sides with them – without satisfying either. This is a question that will have to be settled before any worthwhile result comes from the work of the Aisteoirí (*Star*, 5/4/30).[70]

An anonymous critic for *An t-Éireannach* felt the answer to this question was obvious enough, as he made clear in a favourable 1935 review of a performance by the Keating Branch:

> No one should take part in a play that is performed in public or in private unless he knows the speech properly. The language is more important than the drama, and is it not to advance the Irish language that plays in Irish are performed? That is not what many people think. The language does not matter to them if the acting is good, something that makes a mess of things (*Éireannach*, 30/3/35).[71]

The frustrations of the average Gaelic theatre-goer with bad Irish on stage were summed up by 'D. Ó D.', who complained in a 1927 piece:

> There is nothing at all that more disgusts an audience than weak and broken Irish. If an actor undertakes to play a part he should have that part properly, and if he is not a native speaker, he should practise the sounds intensively (*Leader*, 19/2/27).[72]

An tAthair Mac Fhinn offered a similar assessment of the problem in 1934, writing of Gaelic actors: 'The Irish must be well spoken, for there is nothing that more annoys the audience than to be trying to understand bad Irish, and it is truly difficult to understand it' (*AA*, Dec. 1938, 2).[73] The problem was to be a persistent one, with Hannraoi Ó Headhra writing from the perspective of the other side of the footlights in 1938: 'It would be more than difficult for an actor to do good acting if he has to be thinking about the Irish when he is speaking' (*Leader*, 9/4/38).[74]

Nor was the Irish of the actors always up to standard even in the Gaelic West. For example, after a meeting of An Taibhdhearc's board in May 1930, the secretary wrote of a recent production of Lady Gregory's *Hyacinth Halvey* in translation: 'Hy [*sic*] Halvey very bad – Mac Glla [*sic*] Cionnaith and Capt. Paor from Rinn Mór had bad Irish. Gill very bad as usual.'[75] At a 1932 meeting of the board of An Taibhdhearc, with the theatre now in existence for four years, 'there was a discussion of the speech and pronunciation of the actors on the stage, and it was suggested to the director that he make a great effort to get the best speakers of Irish for the parts in the plays.'[76] Of course, even the most intensive search could not find competent actors with good Irish if they did not yet exist, and even if the supply seems to have been better than it was in Dublin, this problem was to plague An Taibhdhearc for years to come. In a 1935 review in *An t-Éireannach*, 'Eoghainín' wrote:

> Among the majority of the actors the old fault of An Taibhdhearc's actors could be noticed. They have a truly bad accent. That weakness in speech, or better in pronunciation, is responsible for the smothering of the speech when deep emotion or passion comes into the voice (*Éireannach*, 15/6/35).[77]

Many commentators were, however, aware that good Irish on stage might well be wasted on many in the audience. A distressing and limiting reality for playwrights, producers and performers in our period was the frequently acknowledged fact that a not insignificant percentage of any audience outside the Gaeltacht might not be able to follow much of what was being said on stage. In his essay in *Láimh-Leabhar Drámaidheachta*, Douglas Hyde stressed that authors, directors and actors should never forget the linguistic limitations of their audiences:

> If they do not understand the speech everything is ruined. The actors will come with fine Irish in their mouths, and that Irish will not be understood, and when it is not understood it would be better for them to be silent. I cannot make this point too strongly, and if I only had once piece of advice to give to authors and performers of plays it would be – TAKE CARE THAT YOU WILL BE UNDERSTOOD.[78]

He really need not have worried that his theatrical colleagues would – or could – lose sight of this problem. Only a few months before the first performances by An Comhar Drámaidheachta in 1923, Éamonn Mac Giolla Iasachta anticipated Hyde's counsel, advising actors: 'It would be better to speak too slowly than too quickly as long as we are relying on people who are learning the language – or, better, trying to bring them in and encourage them' (*Sguab*, Sept. 1923, 227).[79] Having attended a 1934 student production of a play at Maynooth, Brian Mac Tréinfhir conceded: 'It is not easy to find suitable plays in Irish, and I do not believe that the audience understood too well the Irish in *Aiséirghe Dhonncha*. And what good is performing a play in a language that is not understood?' (*IMN*, 1932, 84).[80]

Other commentators praised the efforts of some theatre practitioners to accommodate their audiences, as did Nuala Moran in a 1937 review of Micheál Ó Siochfhradha's *Aon-Mhac Aoife Alban*: 'It speaks well for the author's technique when I say that I should imagine anyone with even a slight knowledge of Irish would be able to follow the play with interest' (*Leader*, 27/3/37).[81] Two months later, 'Eilis' suggested that An Comhar have an 'announcer', who would provide 'an outline of the play in English for the benefit of those who came to help despite a small knowledge of Irish' (*Leader*, 15/5/37).[82] In Galway, where it was often then and afterwards assumed that audiences would be far more likely to have the language, the editor of the *Connacht Sentinel* acknowledged that there were problems in this regard even in the West, praising An Taibhdhearc for its achievements despite this formidable linguistic obstacle:

> Handicapped as it is by having to produce plays in a language with which the vast majority of the people are not familiar, the Irish theatre of to-day as typified by Taibhdhearc na Gaillimhe is making remarkable progress (*CS*, 15/2/38).

When non-Gaeltacht audiences did appear able to follow plays with reasonable ease it was often seen as a point worthy of comment, as when an anonymous reviewer wrote of a performance of Mac Liammóir's *Lúlú* at the Taibhdhearc: 'A large number of school children from the city attended the matinee on Sunday. The manner in which they followed the plays shows that they thoroughly understood the dialogue' (*CS*, 5/11/29). And in this case children held the advantage over most adults, since they encountered the language daily during the school year. It may well have been their experience in Free State schools that won the seminarians in a Maynooth audience the following commendation in 1932:

> It is a cause for pride how well this little drama was performed and listened to. It was easy to see that the audience was taking great interest in it. You would think that they were amazed because they were able to follow the events of the play so easily (*IMN*, 1932, 79).[83]

An adult audience for a Taibhdhearc production in Galway won similar praise from an anonymous critic in 1935: 'It was clear, however, that every member of the audience that was there had Irish on the tip of his tongue, because of the way they followed everything that was said in the play' (*CT*, 22/6/35).[84] It is, then, easy enough to understand the frustration experienced by Ernest Blythe at the end of our period when he wrote:

> Up to the present it may safely be said that no dramatist writing in Irish has ever had a good audience to judge his work, that is to say, an appreciative and critical audience which would neither abuse the play on principle nor excuse it on principle. The result is that the Gaelic playwright has had to work, as it were, in the dark, without his natural stimulus and without feeling the stir of artistic emulation (*Leader*, 16/12/39).[85]

For some, an obvious solution to this problem was to take the show on the road, bringing drama in Irish to people with Irish, the residents of the Gaeltacht. This was not, of course, a new idea. Both Thomas MacDonagh and Pádraic Ó Conaire had called for touring companies well before independence, and Ó Conaire continued to explore this idea in our period. Moreover, he seems to have convinced Liam O'Flaherty of the importance of such a venture, for in a 1927 letter to the *Irish Statesman* O'Flaherty wrote:

> I consulted Pádraic Ó Conaire and we decided that drama was the best means of starting a new literature in Irish. I became fearfully enthusiastic. The two of us went to Dublin and entered a hall where some fellows were holding a Gaeltacht Commission. We put our scheme before them for a travelling theatre and so on. I guaranteed to write ten plays. They thought we were mad (*IS*, 17/12/27).[86]

More to the point, earlier that same year Ó Conaire himself wrote that An Comhar Drámaidheachta had originally intended to use some of its state subsidy for tours in the Gaeltacht (*CS*, 29/3/27).[87] This idea seemed self-evident to one 'Sgoláire Anoir', who, in a 1933 review of a play on the battle of Aughrim performed at the Tourmakeady Gaelic college in the Mayo Gaeltacht, stated:

> The audience is the most important part of any play . . . I am delighted by any effort at all for the Irish language, and everyone understands how important the drama is to teach and spread the language. But if it is a good, genuine Gaelic drama that is wanted, have the people of the Gaeltacht for an audience (*Camán*, 16/9/33).[88]

Micheál Mac Liammóir, who was so successful in staging quality Gaelic productions in both Galway and Dublin, seems to have shared this opinion, writing in a 1931 essay on 'Aisteoirí do'n Ghaedhealtacht' (Actors for the Gaeltacht) that the most genuinely appreciative audience for plays in Ireland was not to be found in the cities, but in the small towns and villages, and that for plays in Irish, the natural audience was in the Gaeltacht. The challenge was to bring the plays to these people, a challenge Mac Liammóir felt should not be all that daunting:

> It could not be difficult to provide the Gaeltacht something better than *Maria Martin* or *Desert Song* . . . Could it be too difficult to get hold of three good plays, ten actors, a director, a stage designer, an electrician, a portable lighting system, a couple of swathes of curtain, some canvas, and a stage carpenter who understood his craft? (*IP*, 16/10/31).[89]

Another professional man of the theatre who believed that such a travelling company was essential was Frank Dermody. In a 1933 piece he stressed the urgency of getting on with the work before it was too late, writing of Gaeltacht people:

> They understand Irish. They have an enormous interest in drama. Unless something is done now to provide them with entertainment, soon those foreign travelling actors who are so plentiful at present will be seen pushing into the Gaeltacht and performing the rubbish most of them usually do (*IP*, 19/9/33).[90]

In its detailed 'Scéim chun Feabhas a Chur ar Freastal Lucht Éisteachta agus chun Méadú ar Fághaltaisí an Taibhdheirc' (Scheme to improve audience attendance and to increase the income of An Taibhdhearc), the theatre considered the possibilty of touring the Conamara Gaeltacht and the Aran Islands with 'a play or two that would not involve much cost' (dráma nó dhó nach mbeadh mórán costais a baint leo).[91] And in another plan the following year, there was consideration of an even more ambitious touring schedule that would take the Taibhdhearc players to every Gaeltacht in the country.[92]

For J. J. Hayes, such travelling Gaelic companies could do far more than merely provide an evening's entertainment. They could heal a profound rift in the Irish psyche. In a 1932 article in *Outlook*, Hayes lamented the 'hyphen in our Anglo-Irish outlook', which 'symbolises what may be styled our transitory state of mind.' He believed that the establishment of 'a resident Community theatre group' performing in Irish in 'every town in the country' and of 'professional touring companies going out from the larger cities' would create a situation in which 'the hyphen in the descriptive adjective will remove itself and carry with it the prefix which still lingers to confuse the issue' (*Outlook*, 30/1/32).

Other Gaels were more interested in a bricks and mortar approach to building a solid Gaelic drama movement. Until the opening of Taibhdhearc na Gaillimhe in 1928, Gaelic drama had no permanent home anywhere in Ireland, and it was to lack such a home in the national capital throughout our period. On this point the Galwegians could, perhaps a bit smugly, sympathise with their counterparts in Dublin, as did Liam Ó Briain in a 1929 letter to *The Star*:

> The Comhar of Dublin have no theatre, no staff, no 'props' of their own; in other words, no material nucleus around which to grow. The trouble is mainly there.

> Galway has more of the mustard-seed of development because it has a home (*Star*, 15/6/29).

Outside Galway, Gaelic companies continued to make do as wandering players renting for brief periods whatever space they could. Not surprisingly, complaints about the inadequacy of those shifting spaces were constant and often caustic, with the Peacock – 'Amharclann na nGaedheal' (The theatre of the Gaels) as Béaslaí rather grandiloquently called it – coming in for particular abuse, like that from 'D. Ó D.' in 1930: 'I don't know why so wretched a little place would be christened "Amharclann na nGaedheal". But most likely Gaels are involved with nothing but poverty, and I fear that that misfortune will follow them forever' (*Leader*, 18/1/30).[93] If not quite that long, Gaelic actors and their audiences did have to suffer in and with the Peacock as a regular venue for the rest of the decade and beyond, provoking Nuala Moran to comment in 1938:

> The Gaelic actors grouse about the inadequacy of the 'Peacock' stage, but I think it is time that the audience indulged in a grouse or two. Here is mine: Will the players please remember not to drop their voices because, with the noise of the gear-changing of the buses outside in Abbey Street, we find it very difficult to hear, and often lose the drift of the whole dialogue for a time (*Leader*, 5/2/38).

The following year, 'Ar Aghaidh' discussed the discomforts of the Peacock as the cause of what he called 'the Peacock cramp', and called for 'a real home for Gaelic theatre' (*Leader*, 26/8/39).[94]

Many had long been in agreement, for without their own space Gaelic actors could never have adequate control over their rehearsal and production schedules, and Gaelic audiences might never enjoy their efforts in some comfort. Gearóid Ó Lochlainn laid out the facts with particular clarity in 1929:

> The launching of the Comhar in 1923 was an ambitious attempt to advance Gaelic drama from the phase of sporadic performances in small halls to that of regular and efficient productions in a properly equipped theatre – in other words, to found a permanent Gaelic stage.

That vision had not, of course, been realised, and Ó Lochlainn drew attention to the result of that failure by comparing 'the more or less faulty productions of the Comhar in Dublin' to 'the excellent opening performances of the Galway Gaelic Theatre' (*Star*, 13/7/29).[95] In March 1933, 'Mac Coinnigh' issued a forceful call to readers of the *Irish Press* to demand such a theatre for Dublin: 'Until we have a theatre of our own it is not possible to make any progress with regard to the productions. It is useless for us to be trying to establish a permanent dramatic movement without our having a permanent theatre' (*IP*, 6/3/33).[96] Within a fortnight, the officers of An Comhar Drámaidheachta itself declared, in a letter to the *Irish Press*, 'that the movement has made so much progress that it can no longer be served by the accommodations available to it' (go bhfuil an ghluaiseacht imthighthe comh fada san chun cinn nach féidir freagairt dí leis na córacha atá 'na líon) and that the first necessity was 'to establish a fully Gaelic theatre' (amharclann lán-Ghaedhilge do chur ar bun) (*IP*, 20/3/33). Nobody, however, was more succinct on this point than was Daniel Corkery in a 1939 lecture at the revived Oireachtas: 'A Gaelic theatre was urgently necessary. A dramatic movement without a theatre was the equivalent of a language movement without a dictionary' (*II*, 7/11/39).

Those recommending either the creation of travelling companies for the countryside or the acquisition of permanent home theatres in the cities were, however, forced to face a crucial and often embarrassing question throughout our period. If a play in Irish were produced, would an audience come? Few would have shared Ernest Blythe's rather Olympian indifference to this question as expressed in a letter to Liam Ó Briain:

> With regard to the Taibhdhearc, the attendance would not bother me – for some years at any rate. When I first began going to the Abbey Theatre, there would hardly be fifty people present any given night, with all the English-speakers there are in Dublin.[97]

Rather, most Gaels would doubtless have agreed with Seán Ó Ciarghusa when he underscored the importance of attracting an audience:

> And now as to our Irish dramatic audiences in Dublin and the other cities and towns. It goes, or should go, without saying that an appreciative audience is an indispensable part of even a Shakespeare drama, but yet, in Ireland, we seem to blame first the dramatists and secondly the actors for the poverty of our Irish dramatic material. As emphatically as I can, I want to shift some of the blame elsewhere. It is the want of an Irish audience more than the want of either Irish dramatists or Irish actors that is responsible for the want or the poverty of Irish drama (*Leader*, 12/11/27).

One experienced Gaelic dramatist and actor who also wanted to shift some of the blame here was Piaras Béaslaí, who in a 1929 article on An Comhar Drámaidheachta stated:

> It is, however, necessary to remind our critics that neither playwrights nor players can make a successful dramatic movement without a sympathetic public. The audiences are as necessary an ingredient to the success of a dramatic production as

players, producers or scenery. It is hardly too much to say that upon the support accorded by the public to this new experiment of An Comhar depends the future of the Gaelic drama in Dublin (*Star*, 5/10/29).

In general, it seems that rural and Gaeltacht areas, starved for much of anything else to do, particularly in the winter, could be trusted to provide a good audience when players came to town. In the cities, where the overwhelming majority of Gaelic plays were produced, the situation was altogether different. It was the rare review of a play in Irish that did not comment on the size of the audience, either with satisfaction or, more often, with disappointment, sometimes bitter. Here again a few of the more forceful of such observations from throughout our period will have to suffice.

There were always optimists among Gaels interested in the theatre, people who saw the tide finally turning in favour of what they insisted was a genuine national theatre in the national language. For instance, as early as 1926 a critic for the *Irish Independent* wrote: 'The Irish-language Aisteoirí are making progress, and their audience is gradually growing' (*II*, 12/1/26).[98] In 1928, the author of the 'Current Events' column for *The Nation* was far more optimistic, writing: 'From every angle the cause of the Irish Drama has made strides. The public has eagerly attended: the house was often during the winter full to overflowing' (*Nation*, 19/5/28). By the 1930s, other commentators also felt that the problem of attracting audiences for plays in Irish was well on the way to being solved, and not just by bringing in captive audiences of students, a point stressed by a reviewer for the *Irish Independent* in 1933: 'The theatre was filled to the door, and it was not just schoolchildren who were there but all kinds of people, and everyone enjoyed the performance immensely' (*II*, 7/2/33).[99] The following year, Máire Ní Aodhacháin noted that growing public interest was creating new challenges for An Comhar: 'There is such a demand for plays in Irish in the city that it is difficult for An Comhar Drámaidheachta to get a theatre as often as they would like' (*Guth na nGaedheal*, 1934, 14).[100] By 1938, a few critics had convinced themselves that theatre in Irish was now a fully established feature of the cultural life of Dublin, ready and able to hold its own with its English-language competitors, a belief expressed by 'Ar Aghaidh' in *The Leader*:

Are the Gaelic speakers of Dublin being attracted to the Gaelic theatre? They are. After years of patient and sometimes heartbreaking work, the time has come when the influence of the stage on the revival movement can no longer be denied. The time has arrived when Gaelic drama must be given a fair chance to compete with Anglo-Irish drama . . . During the season under review [1937–8] it was the rule rather than the exception to have to turn away Irish speakers from the Peacock (*Leader*, 4/6/38).[101]

Some in Galway were equally encouraged by audience support for An Taibhdhearc, as was, for example, a critic for the *Connacht Sentinel* who wrote of a 1933 production of Molière's *Les Fourberies de Scapin*: 'There was a record number present which was an indication of the growing popularity of these Gaelic players in Galway. Many people saw the performance standing up' (*CS*, 7/3/33). The following year, a critic for the same paper was inspired by the attendance at an original play in Irish to engage in a bit of civic chauvinism:

> The play played to packed audiences for five nights and might have gone on longer. The capacity of the hall is something over 300. That means that between 1,500 and 1,600 people witnessed the play – one in ten of the population. In no other city in Ireland has such a proportion of the population ever gone to see a play in Irish. A demonstration has been made last week that drama of quality in Irish has a very large, growing and appreciative public in Galway district among rich and poor alike (*CS*, 13/3/34).[102]

In his letter resigning as artistic director this same year, Frank Dermody could feel he was leaving the theatre on a high note, writing: 'The theatre has been, in my opinion, distinctly a success in Galway. It has now a very large appreciative public when it has a good show to offer.'[103]

Yet contemporaneous with such positive assessments – and outnumbering them by a fair margin – were complaints about the indifference or worse of Irish speakers towards the Gaelic dramatic movement, an attitude condemned by 'Teachtaire' in 1930:

> However much noise we make about the Irish language, the group attempting to establish Gaelic drama is getting little help from us. We are always complaining about how little Irish is heard around us, and when we have an opportunity to hear it from the stage, we do not think it worth our while to go to hear it (*FL*, Mar. 1930, 2).[104]

In a piece in *The Star* the same year, 'Scrúdóir', having drawn attention to how small the Peacock was and how few performances of Gaelic plays were performed there in any given season, continued:

> There are thousands of Irish speakers in Dublin who have a good bit of money to spend on the theatre. And that being the case, why are there so many empty seats in the Theatre of the Gaels [The Peacock]; what does it mean; and what is the cure for it? (*Star*, 22/2/30).[105]

In 1936, another critic posed the same question after attending a performance at the Peacock:

> Where was Irish-Ireland last Monday night when An Comhar Drámaidheachta opened its fourteenth season in Dublin at the Peacock Theatre? I counted about 25 people in the audience at 8 o'clock, but a few others strolled in late . . . And this on a *First Night* of a new season when the little theatre should have been crowded to the doors and a buzz of Gaelic chatter should have been heard out in Abbey Street till the curtain rose and silenced it. Why it should have been the occasion for a regular re-union of Gaels! (*Leader*, 10/10/36).

The following year 'S. Ó M.' reckoned there were not often many more than that in the seats, writing:

> How many thousand Irish speakers are there in Dublin to-day? Yet what of the audiences for Gaelic plays in the chief city of the Irish Nation? In the Peacock Theatre of 100 seats it is not an unusual thing for the Gaelic players to play to 50, 40, 30, aye, and sometimes only 20 people (*Leader*, 12/6/37).

Even after 1938, the year some, as we have seen, saw as a true milestone in the development of a reliable audience for drama in Irish, a contributor to *The Leader* could offer a far more guarded assessment of the situation, attributing whatever apparent increases in attendance there had been to price-cutting promotions and, more importantly, to the consolidation of Dublin's more active Gaelic drama groups under the general auspices of An Comhar:

> The attendance at Irish plays is always very small. There have often been performances in the Peacock which were attended by not more than 40 or 50 people. The full houses of the last year or two have been secured by the special effort under which tickets have been sold to groups at specially low rates, and by having the season's performances given by several different companies of players, each of which has had its following of relatives and personal friends and possibly of jealous rivals. There has been no increased attendance of the ordinary playgoers who, without being canvassed or being drawn by personal acquaintanceship with an actor, roll up to pay their shillings at the door (*Leader*, 27/5/39).[106]

Nor were such playgoers regularly rolling up to the doors of An Taibhdhearc in the kind of numbers suggested by the authors of some of the enthusiastic reports of audience support quoted above. In the first year of An Taibhdhearc's existence, a critic for the *Connacht Sentinel* was already worried about Galwegians' apathy toward this well-publicised new venture:

> The Taibhdhearc last evening was far less than half full, and on Sunday evening the attendance was as bad. Yet the price of admission was low, the plays were worth witnessing, if only for the beauty of the settings, and the acting was of a kind rarely

witnessed outside Dublin. In the words of the poet, 'What do the people want?' (*CS*, 23/4/29).

For a speaker at the awards ceremony of the western branch of Cumann Drámaidheachta na Scol in Carraroe, the question remained valid in 1937, as a report in the *Connacht Tribune* makes clear: 'He made reference to the work of An Taibhdhearc and how few people come to see the dramas there' (*CT*, 24/4/37).[107] The following year, Seán Feehan offered a balanced perspective on An Taibhdhearc's attempts to build an audience:

> At times, I could not help being discouraged by the smallness of the audiences, but on these occasions it was consoling to recall that other and better theatres in immensely bigger centres of population have had to go through severe crises as regards attendance. Other times it has received splendid support. On the whole it cannot complain of the way Galway has supported it (*CB*, Aug. 1938, 652).

Which way was it with Gaelic drama then – 'splendid support' or 'severe crises as regards attendance?' The records of An Comhar Drámaidheachta and Taibhdhearc na Gaillimhe should provide us with a more objective sense of audience support in Dublin and Galway than do any of the subjective and impressionistic assessments cited above. An Comhar certainly monitored its attendance closely. After all, ticket sales were, apart from the subsidy, virtually the only source of revenue available to the group. For example, in the budget estimate for the 1928–9 season, the expected subsidy was £600, while ticket sales were projected at £300, and programme advertisements at a mere £10.[108] Of course perceptions of how full a theatre is depend to a large extent on how full it can be. In the years from 1930 to February 1934, An Comhar played in the *c.*400-seat Gate Theatre, a space that from any realistic point of view it could never hope to fill. Therefore, while audiences may have looked thin on the ground in the Gate, there were actually a fair number present on most nights, an average of 108 in 1931–2, and a robust 277 in 1932–3.[109] In the 1935–6 season, split between the small Peacock and Torch Theatres, average attendance fell precipitously to 52 per performance, rising slightly to 58 in the Peacock the following season.[110] To some extent, the excellent attendances reported for 1937–8 by several writers above were the result of the Peacock's 102-seat capacity, a number that An Comhar regularly exceeded with an average audience of 105 in 1937–8, and a respectable 92 in 1938–9.[111] In terms of raw numbers, attendance at the Gate was 1945 in 1931–2, and 2,219 in 1932–3.[112] In the 1935–6 season, An Comhar drew 1,032 patrons; in 1936–7, 3,201 attended; and in 1937–8, 4,202 saw the plays.[113] Even given the high kinship quotient likely in any audience for what were still, after all, amateur theatricals, these numbers should not have been terribly discouraging. They have, at any rate, never been bettered.[114]

Neither An Comhar nor An Taibhdhearc was willing to leave something as crucial as audience recruitment and development to chance. An Comhar was particularly active in this regard in the capital.[115] As we have seen above, from its very first season in 1923, the company offered special benefits to supporters who, for a £1 subscription fee, were issued 'Comhar-Chártaí' (membership cards) entitling them to a ticket for each play throughout the season.[116] This scheme was to become a permanent feature of the group's audience outreach campaign, with attention being called to it, for example, in a 1933 piece on An Comhar in the *Irish Press*: 'The Comhar-Chárta is a great convenience for every kind of theatre seat can be had for a far lower price and it involves other privileges' (*IP*, 18/8/33).[117] Some idea of the nature of those benefits was provided in promotional notices in An Comhar's programmes, like this one from October 1927 headed 'An bhFuilir id Bhall Den Chomhar?' (Are you a member of An Comhar?): 'We want you to join us. You will be able to assist drama and you will get added benefit from the plays, lectures, etc. we have.'[118] The benefits were spelled out in greater detail in programmes the following year:

> Comhar-chártaí can be had for £1 apiece (pro rata as the year passes). If you have a card you can attend every production during the season and reserve a seat anywhere in the house you wish. In addition, you will be allowed to participate in the work of the annual general meeting, etc.[119]

To make attendance easier for those who did not join for the season, the board of An Comhar arranged that tickets for any night's performance could be booked through Clery's, the popular Dublin department store.

An Taibhdhearc developed a similar fundraising and audience-building strategy, introducing a membership scheme in 1929 by which for a fee of £1, the subscriber would get two tickets for every production and a vote in elections for the theatre's board.[120] In 1936 An Taibhdhearc introduced its own 'Cártaí Comhaltais' (Membership cards) with a sliding scale of £1 for admission to all plays in a season for one; £1 15*s*. for two; £2 5*s*. for three; and £2 10*s*. for four members of the same household' (i gcóir an líontighe céadna). Students and soldiers – along with the city's secondary schools, University College Galway was just a short walk away, and the Irish Army's Irish-speaking First Battalion was based nearby – were admitted for half-price on the second night of all productions (*CT*, 3/10/36).[122]

Many active in the dramatic movement itself were, however, aware that the best way to draw audiences was to give them something new they wanted to see. There was considerable concern at the time that a steady diet of translations – and it was not until the 1927–8 season that original plays for the first time outnumbered translations on An Comhar's season schedule[123] – was driving audiences away, or at the very least providing them with little incentive to spend an evening in the theatre. Critics on occasion pointed out the close link between worthwhile new plays and large audiences, as did 'Ball Geal' in a 1932 piece on An Comhar:

> It is obvious that the Gaels of Dublin will support any band of Aisteoirí who will produce Irish plays. And if the Comhar had a lean season last year, all the blame must rest with themselves . . . Insipid foreign dramas that never appealed to Irish sentiment were staged, and, what was worse, were accepted as contributions to the literature of drama, though they will never be utilised as an asset to revive national drama in Ireland (*Leader*, 5/11/32).[124]

Reservations about the quality of the Gaelic dramatic repertoire were even more generally held and expressed than were complaints about the quality of Gaelic acting. In fact, early in our period D. P. Moran found it all but impossible to sort out which of these two problems bore the greater responsibility for the failure of Gaelic drama to attract audiences and spread the language:

> Again, in Irish drama the output and performances have been very poor. Here supply must create demand. If we had good plays and good players, people who understand Irish would flock to them and many people who didn't know Irish, or knew very little of it, would go . . . We have seen some passable Irish plays; we have seen many rather ridiculous performances; but we never saw a first-class Irish dramatic performance (*Leader*, 21/3/23).

Six years later, 'A. F.' was also wondering whether bad plays inspired bad acting or bad acting made for bad plays:

> Until there is in existence a fair number of good plays in the language, the establishment of a regular Irish theatre can hardly be seriously contemplated. But more plays and better players could, I am convinced, be obtained if Gaelic drama had the prestige that would be given it by the existence in Dublin of a really competent company of Irish players (*Star*, 26/1/29).

Others felt that such a 'really competent company' could never evolve from actors forced to perform the mediocre and worse scripts that then comprised the majority of the Gaelic repertoire. The author of the 'Affairs of State' column in *The Star* made this point forcefully in 1929:

> No industry or ability on the part of actors and actresses can compensate for a poor play, and it is to be hoped that when next the Comhar comes before the public it will bring better dramatic fare. The putting on of really good plays, well produced and competently acted, is vital to the future of the Comhar (*Star*, 9/11/29).

The following year, Frank O'Connor offered the following sarcastic suggestion in the *Irish Statesman*: 'Somebody has recently made an anthology of Worst Poems. An anthology of Worst Plays might confidently rely on rich picking from amongst the plays written in Irish' (*IS*, 18/1/30).[125] More moderate and sympathetic was Canon J. Vaughn, the president of St Flannan's College in Ennis, County Clare, who wrote in 1936:

> In regard to Irish plays . . . it is true to say that they do not come up to the standard, either in conception, outlook, or technique. There is a very restricted repertoire and those wishing to stage Irish plays are hampered by the narrow range from which the selection must be made (*Clare Champion*, 26/12/36).[126]

From the north of the country came a similar assessment the following year, when 'Oisín' stated:

> The people of this country are not that keen about the Irish language. They need plays that would be worth performing in any language at all and in any country at all, and it is now high time for us to make the like available in place of defective, meaningless, and senseless little plays. Those things are doing nothing but damage to the language (*Derry People*, 1/5/37).[127]

We have already seen how some felt that this shortage of worthwhile scripts could be remedied most quickly and effectively through translation, and how a respectable number of translations, some of them quite good, were prepared and produced during our period. For most Gaels, however, what was most wanted were challenging and engaging original plays in Irish. Repeatedly, commentators urged writers to turn their talents to the stage. Again, a few of the many examples of such calls for new plays will have to suffice here. In 1924, 'S. Ó N.' saw the lack of new plays as the greatest challenge facing An Comhar Drámaidheachta, writing: 'As we look at the programme an Comhar has laid out for this season, it is clear that the people have already seen and seen again the majority of the plays' (*Iris an Gharda*, 7/1/24).[128] Considerably less patient was 'Gaedhilgeoir' in a similar complaint a few months later:

> Another thing that is causing us problems is the scarcity of plays in Irish and the fact that of the few of them there are there are fewer still suitable for performance, since the majority were written for another world altogether . . . If speakers of English can put hundreds of things on the stage, speakers of Irish should be able to create a couple of suitable plays (*Cork Weekly Examiner*, 10/5/24).[129]

In 1926, León Ó Broin tried to rally his fellow Gaels with a call to action: 'It is not possible to say this too often: plays, plays, and more plays is the best and most appropriate battle cry for the young person at present' (*FL*, Dec. 1926, 4).[130] In 1934, Colm Ó Domhnaill noted that only one of An Comhar's six productions for the 1933–4 season involved an original play, but then went on to explain that the problem was not so much that there weren't *any* new plays, but that there weren't any *good* new plays:

> It is not that original plays in Irish are not being written by authors at present, but that it is very difficult altogether to perform the plays that are being written. The reason for that is the authors' ignorance of stage 'Technique' and the Dramatic method (*Comhthrom Féinne*, May 1934, 40).[131]

Nor would the members of An Comhar itself have necessarily disagreed with this complaint. In his annual report on the 1937–8 season, An Comhar's secretary Proinsias Ó Sithigh acknowledged: 'There is a great shortage of good plays and there will be until something is done to encourage the writers.'[132]

To provide such encouragement, many in the movement turned to tried and trusted methods in use from the beginning of the literary revival, sponsoring competitions and offering prizes for new plays. Various Gaelic League *feiseanna* – the most important, as we have seen, the Dublin Feis and County Wexford's Feis Charman – continued to sponsor drama competitions during our period.[133] On a national level, the Oireachtas of 1922, at which nine plays were performed, had a single competition, for a short translated play (*Misneach*, 4/2/22), and there were three competitions, for full-length plays, one-acters and short translations, in 1924.[134] In the Civil War year of 1923 there was no Oireachtas as such, but during the week of the League's annual Ard-Fheis, Béaslaí's play *Bean an Mhilliúnai* and An tAthair Tomás Ó Ceallaigh's opera *Sruth na Maoile* were performed, apparently to very little audience enthusiasm.[135] When the Oireachtas was revived in 1939, drama competitions were again on the programme, and, according to a report in *The Leader*, they attracted a fair amount of interest:

> Twenty-three short plays and nine full-length plays were entered for the competitions, and the majority were good. There were a couple of original plays. The authors attempted all kinds of subject matter, from historical events to the affairs of our own time (*Leader*, 7/10/39).[136]

In a piece on the Oireachtas competitions in the same paper the following month, a reporter called the drama competitions 'perhaps the most successful section of the literary part of the Oireachtas', and praised the judges for their refusal to accept less than quality work (*Leader*, 18/11/39). He should not have been surprised, for the judges involved were some of the most experienced and accomplished figures in the Gaelic literary and dramatic movement, with Liam Ó Briain, Frank Dermody, Micheál Mac Liammóir, and Gearóid Ó

Lochlainn reading the short plays, and Daniel Corkery and Ó Lochlainn the full-length works (*IP*, 29/9/39).[137]

An Comhar Drámaidheachta itself also offered prizes (*dúthrachtaí* as they called them) for 'the best plays performed for the first time during the season [1932–3]' (na drámaí is fearr dá léireóchaí go nua le linn an tséasúir). According to a report in the *Irish Press*, these prizes were intended 'to encourage authors [to write] new plays and to urge them not only to write more plays but also to put more polish on their work' (chun misneach do chur ar ughdaraibh drámaí nua [do scríobhadh] agus chun iad do bhrostughadh chun ní h-amháin tuilleadh drámaí do scríobhadh acht chun iad do bhrostughadh chun breis slaicht do chur ar a saothar). The winner of the Craobh Óir (Golden branch) for a full-length play was Gearóid Ó Lochlainn for *Na Gaduithe*. Mac Liammóir's *Lúlú* won the Craobh Airgid (Silver branch), the prize offered for the best short play, while the Craobh Umha (Bronze branch) for a translated play went to Máiréad Ní Ghráda for *Micheál*, her version of a work by Tolstoy (*IP*, 12/10/34). The winner of the prizes for 1933–4 were Mac Liammóir for *Diarmaid and Gráinne* (full-length play) and Liam Ó Briain for his translation of a play by Robert Brennan as *Oidhche Mhaith a Mhic Uí Dhomhnaill*. Since no original one-act play had been produced during the season the Craobh Airgid was not awarded (*An Phoblacht*, 20/10/34).

As the result of discussions at its annual general meeting in December 1936, An Comhar decided to try another approach to generate new plays, founding a group called An Sgiath (The shield) 'to hasten and improve the supply of suitable plays in Irish, and to work for the benefit of the authors' (chun soláthar drámaí oireamhnach i nGaedhilge do bhrostú agus d'fheabhasú, agus na h-ughdair do chur ar a leas). Membership was open to anyone who had had an original or translated play in Irish produced. In addition to its primary role as a catalyst for the writing of new plays, the group also undertook, among other things, to propagandise for Gaelic drama and to assist playwrights in dealing with performance rights, royalties, etc. (*IP*, 20/1/37).[138]

In 1938, the Abbey itself sponsored its first Gaelic drama competition, offering a prize of £50 for one-act plays in Irish. In an interview with the *Irish Press* concerning the prize, Ernest Blythe, now a member of the Abbey's board, stated: 'We feel that in view of the National language policy and so on, the Abbey would not be doing its share if it did not produce a certain number of plays in Irish.' Blythe was cautiously optimistic about the eventual success of the new direction for the Abbey represented by this prize: 'Complete Gaelicisation of the Theatre is too far ahead to be considered at the moment – apart from the general trend toward the use of Irish. But, even now, most of our audiences would understand Gaelic plays' (*IP*, 19/2/38).[139] This was not a new idea for Blythe, who had written Liam Ó Brian in 1936 that at a meeting of An Comhar

> I threw out the suggestion that they should seek co-operation with the Abbey but it fell on deaf ears. My reason for bringing it up was that I have come to the conclusion that if the Abbey Theatre is to fulfil any permanent purpose in the country it must gradually put itself in position to produce Irish plays equally as well as English plays. The first step would be to begin to add a few good Irish speakers to the Company and to give an odd production of an Irish play in the Peacock. Further developments would depend on circumstances.[140]

Moreover, he came to believe that the use of Irish could revitalise the Abbey as well as legitimate its claim to be a national institution. Speaking at the Abbey Theatre Festival in August 1938, he was reported as saying:

> In the old days the Abbey had been in the main current of the national movement, but since the passing of the Treaty it has seemed to me at times that they were slipping a little into the slack water. He believed that this work of theirs for the Irish language would bring them back again to the main current of national life and give them fresh enthusiasm and support (*IT*, 20/8/38).[141]

Another fundamental unresolved question in our period concerned what kind of original plays were most appropriate for the Gaelic stage as it played its part in restoring to the nation its long-threatened Gaelic heritage. From early in the movement, some Gaelic writers had attempted strikingly ambitious plays, usually dealing with historical subjects, and often calling for large casts, elaborate costumes, and frequent set changes, even in one-acters. Experience had, however, convinced others with an interest in theatre that they should set themselves more modest goals, focusing on short comic plays.[142] For example, in 1932, Geraldine Dillon, a member of the board of An Taibhdhearc, wrote of Galway audiences: 'They will not come to see even the best of the Anglo-Irish rural plays. They think they are grim, and they do not like anything sad' (*IP*, 8/9/32).[143] According to An tAthair Mac Fhinn, Dublin audiences were no different: 'There is no longer any doubt that Irish-speakers like comic plays; they don't have half as much interest in a tragedy or a historical play.' He then went on to call for the Gaelic writer to give his audiences a 'proper comedy' (geandráma foghanta), presumably because he felt that most of what passed for comedies on the Gaelic stage were too insubstantial and frivolous to merit the title (*AA*, Mar. 1938, 5).[144] This was certainly the view of an anonymous contributor to the *Irish Press* who, responding to the same play that had prompted the comments in *Ar Aghaidh*, Micheál Breathnach's *Cor in Aghaidh an Chaim*, stated: 'Many attempts have been made to write comedies in the national language. Although we have plenty of farces (buffoonish plays) in it as the result of those efforts, very few true comedies have yet been composed' (*IP*, 16/2/38).[145]

One positive development arising from this focus on comedy was the effort to create a Gaelic pantomime, the genre that eventually, in particular under the guidance ofTomás Mac Anna at the Abbey, was to attract from the late 1940s through the 1970s the largest audiences plays inIrish would ever enjoy. Actually, comsidering how popular Christmas pantomimes in English were in Irish theatres, it is surprising how long it took Gaels to cultivate the genre, a point emphasised by Gobnait Ní Dhubhghaill in 1934:

> Is it not high time for the theatre owners to be thinking about producing a pantomime in Irish? Of the younger generation, some have a little Irish and some have a good deal, and even the ones with a little have enough to understand a pantomime in Irish.

Ní Dhubhghaill also had a suggestion as to where the subject matter for such a pantomime could be found: 'It would not be difficult for someone to put one of the adventures from folklore into the form of a pantomime' (*IP*, 27/11/34).[146] Cearbhall Ua Domhnaill, on the other hand, was far more sceptical about whether the genre could ever be sufficiently decontaminated of its alien origins to be viable in Irish:

> The usual pantomime in Dublin would suit any city at all in England. Ireland is altogether forgotten, and as for the Irish language, no one living ever heard a song in that language at the pantomime. The pity of the matter is that people take a very great interest in this thing that is English in spirit to the marrow. It was often said that it is a great shame that we do not have a Gaelic pantomime, but the people who say that are usually thinking of a production in English (*IP*, 22/12/31).[147]

It was An Taibhdhearc that proved Ua Domhnaill's fears groundless when at Christmas 1937 it produced Micheál Eoghan Ó Súilleabháin's *Súgradh na mBláth* (The game of the flowers) with original music by Poppy Ní Chuaráin. Both the *Irish Press* and the *Irish Independent* welcomed Ó Súilleabháin's initiative, with the *Independent* declaring:

> Micheál Óg Ó Súilleabháin, who is the author of short plays in Gaelic, may be remembered for them in the far-off years to come, but he will certainly be remembered by the fact that he is the originator and author of the first all-Gaelic pantomime produced in Éire. It is an event which deserves to be termed notable (*II*, 3/1/38).[148]

The following season An Taibhdhearc produced another pantomime, *Tóraidheacht an Ghiolla Deacair* (The pursuit of the difficult lad) by Jeremiah Murphy and S. Ó Neachtain. Of this show, An tAthair Mac Fhinn wrote: 'This play surpassed everything else so far with regard to attendance and what was paid at the door. And it was not only Gaels who were present, a good number of people without Irish came' (*AA*, Mar. 1939, 6).[149] Dublin's first attempt at the genre seems to have been Nessa Ní Shéaghdha's 'Robinson Crúsó', produced by Ní Séaghdha's family at their home in Dundrum at Christmas 1938 (*Leader*, 31/12/38).

As should have been obvious from the plays discussed throughout this book, Gaelic playwrights did not by any means limit themselves to farce and comedy. As early as 1923, Gearóid Ó Lochlainn, having acknowledged a general preference in favour of light entertainment on the part of Irish theatregoers, argued that popular taste need not limit the ambitions of Gaelic dramatists: 'Without a doubt there should be room and scope for the comic play also in any Gaelic theatre, but it is not healthy for a nation to be dependent solely on comedy for intellectual sustenance' (*II*, 10/4/23).[150] Particularly forceful on this point was 'Noel', who, in a published debate on drama in *The Leader* in 1928, proclaimed:

> The only essential of a Gaelic drama, in my consideration, is that it should be Gaelic in its medium of expression. If the language used by the dramatist is Irish, it does not matter a rap whether the story told, the philosophy advocated, the mode of approach to the plot and the form of the play are as far removed from Gaelic ideas and conceptions as Dublin is from Buenos Ayres (*Leader*, 11/2/28).

More than a few Gaelic playwrights were, as we have seen in previous chapters, willing to follow this approach, in the process stretching the language to fit new plotlines, themes, and genres. One 'C. Fh.' could be seen as speaking for all Gaelic dramatists of this pioneering stripe when he wrote in the UCG annual *An tIrisleabhar* for 1934–5:

> It was the speech, its energy, and the music of the speech that the Gaels always held in esteem. Because of how fluent and flexible the Irish language is, and because of how quick the Gaelic mind was, it would be easy to reveal the most complex and clever events with the help of speech alone (*Irisleabhar*, 1934–5, 27).[151]

With such a view of the language quite general among literary Gaels it was logical that they should see the new medium of radio as ideal for bringing drama in Irish to a wide audience. And the new Irish broadcasting service founded in 1926 by a government committed to a policy of language revival and eager for material in Irish on its schedule was a willing partner in the venture. Even before the station began broadcasting, León Ó Broin, a playwright, sometime secretary of An Comhar Drámaidheachta, and a civil servant in the Department of Posts and Telegraphs by which the service would be run, expressed optimism about the future co-operation between the theatre movement and the station.[152] For once, things went right, and plays were broadcast, often 'remote' from the theatre in which they were being performed, on a fairly regular basis throughout the 1930s. The majority of these plays were, however, works written for the stage rather than specifically for radio, a problem that troubled broadcasting professionals. As a result, the director of the station, writing to Liam Ó Briain of An Taibhdhearc in July 1935 to arrange for a series of transmissions from the theatre, added a handwritten postscript to his formal letter: 'Is there any chance of the ideal i.e. a short play especially written for radio production?'[153]

To realise this ideal, the station organised a competition the following year for genuine radio plays, spelling out clearly in a publicity announcement what was wanted:

> What a radio play is is a play written and contructed so that it could be produced in accordance with the specific facilities and demands of broadcasting. A stage play adapted for radio by making use of sound effects would not be appropriate for this contest (*Éireannach*, 15/2/36).[154]

The Gaelic League itself was thinking along these lines, establishing a subcommitee for radio under the chairmanship of Aindrias Ó Muimhneacháin to deal with issues relating to the medium, and in 1936 publishing a booklet entitled *An Gaedheal agus an Radíó*.[155] For this sub-committee, radio drama was of pre-eminent importance:

> The first resource we would suggest is drama because in drama, more than anything else perhaps, is found a way to express the hopes and the desires, the sorrows and the joys of any race. That is especially true with regard to plays that deal with the life of the period in which they are being performed; and those are the plays that are best and most appropriate for the radio.[156]

The pamphlet went on to stress that radio plays were quite different from dramas written for the stage, and that this new genre should be carefully cultivated by Gaels. Judging from the broadcast schedules published in the newspapers of the time, this challenge evoked a not insignificant response.

Other forms of dramatic performance explored by Irish speakers in our period included mummers' plays,[157] a marionette show,[158] and ballets.[159] There had, of course, been a few musical plays or 'operas' in Irish before independence, with An tAthair Tomás Ó Ceallaigh's *Eithne, nó Éan an Cheoil Bhinn* (Eithne, or the bird of the sweet music) the most sucessful, having been given a full production at the Oireachtas in 1909. Ó Ceallaigh continued to pursue his interest in this genre at the beginning of our period, collaborating with the musician Geoffrey Molyneux Palmer on *Sruth na Maoile*, a work based on the story of the children of Lir and staged at the Gaelic League's Ard-Fheis of 1923, where it lost the disastrous amount of £165 5*s.* 4*d.*[160] Ó Ceallaigh, again in collaboration with Palmer, also wrote what he variously called a '*light* opera in Irish', 'a comic or ballad opera in Irish', or 'an heroic farce set to music', but this work, written in the end in English with the working title 'Grania Goes', was never performed or published.[161] With Ó Ceallaigh's premature death in 1923, the genre lost its most visible and potentially influential enthusiast. Nonetheless, there were further attempts to develop musical theatre in Irish. In 1928, an 'operetta' entitled *An Bhainis* (The wedding) by one An tAthair Ó Cathail was performed to a full house in Castlepollard, County Kerry by 'the local choral class.' Among those in attendance was Lord Longford, who stated rather implausibly that 'the Operetta was comparable to anything in English or any other language' (*Kerryman*, 3/3/28). And in the Peacock in 1935, An Comhar Drámaidheachta produced *An Craipí Óg* (The young croppie), a work translated from the English of Maurice Kane (Muiris Ó Catháin) and arranged as a brief musical play by Gearóid Ó Lochlainn.[162]

Others called for more work of this kind, as did Joseph M. Crofts, who, having recalled the earlier work of Ó Ceallaigh, wrote in 1932: 'In Irish history, there are countless themes which might serve as subject-matter for Gaelic Opera' (*Leader*, 11/6/32). Four years later, one 'Éistightheoir', with radio in mind, suggested Gaelic writers try their hand at musical theatre: 'There is no shortage of true musicians in this country, and it would be possible to create Gaelic musical dramas' (*II*, 6/3/36).[163] Alfred Dennis was amazed that so little had been done by Irish-speakers in this area:

> We are supposed to be a musical people, but it is surprising what little development there has been in musical plays in Irish. Language enthusiasts are very formalistic in their outlook and rather cold-blooded in their application of the language to modern life (*FMR*, Mar. 1937, 174).

When the Oireachtas was revived in 1939, the sort of musical play for which a prize was offered was considerably more modest than had been Ó Ceallaigh's *Sruth na Maoile* in 1923:

> A one-act musical play . . . with no fewer than two characters and no more than four. A conversational link can be put with the songs or the verses. The performance of the whole thing to last around twelve minutes.[164]

Many Gaels were keenly aware of the growing influence in Ireland of the new dramatic medium of the film. For example, Micheál Ó Maoláin told the annual Comhdháil of the Gaelic League in 1937 that

> the young people of to-day knew much more about cinema stars than they did about many other persons and things. Some time ago he met a little girl from Skibbereen who knew more about Mae West than she did about O'Donovan Rossa (*IP*, 1/4/37).

Nor was Ó Maoláin's concern here in any way idiosyncratic. As early as 1923, Micheál Ó Gríobhtha had sounded an alarm for readers of *An Sguab*:

> The screens of the country are filled every night in the year by foreign pictures shaped by a foreign mind. Anglicisation is still in progress, and it is the same as conquest. The conquest being imposed on us by pictures is stronger than any conquest ever imposed on us with big guns; we do not flee from the pictures, but rather take them and their subtle treachery to our hearts. I believe a conquest is being imposed on us by the pictures that could not be imposed on us by the penal laws (*Sguab*, June 1923, 172).[165]

Even as progressive and broad-minded a writer as Liam Ó Rinn could find the movies a potential threat to both the national psyche and soul. Discussing 'Nimh na bPictiúirí' (The poison of the pictures) in 1929, he stated:

> It is bad enough that the pictures are doing damage to *Gaelachas*, but if they were as Gaelic as they are Foreign I would be as much against them as I am now. For it is not only *Gaelachas* they are harming, but everything in the form of civilisation in this country or in any other country, even if it were in the middle of Africa. They are injuring the person as a person, and they should be stopped (or improved) throughout the world, or the human race will soon have no more judgment or intellect than that ape from which we descended long ago, if Dean Inge is right (*Star*, 19/10/29).[166]

Yet along with this fear of the movies went a sense of the positive potential the new medium held for the Gaelic revival, and several influential activists called for the creation of an Irish-speaking film industry. No one dealt with the subject more perceptively and imaginatively than did Ernest Blythe. Long a champion and patron of Gaelicising the stage, Blythe attached the same importance to winning the screen for the language. Indeed with time he came to see the Gaelic theatre as a training ground for those who would build first a new Gaelic cinema and then an Irish-language television service. Writing in 1938 on 'The Need for Irish Films', he asserted: 'Now that the talkie has achieved a position of almost universal appeal and almost unrivalled influence, the position of Ireland without even the beginning of a film industry of its own is truly deplorable.' Particularly deplorable was the ongoing erosion of the Irish language through the influence of imported English and American movies:

> It must have become obvious some time during the last four or five years to everyone who gave a thought to the question that there is no possibility whatever of restoring the Irish language to general use or even of preserving it where it still survives, if we have no films in Irish.

Blythe also insisted that the Gaels come to terms with the future importance of television while there was still time to win the medium for the language:

> In another ten years the progress of television may have modified the importance of the film as we know it to-day. It is not that the film will disappear, but that it will be merged in a new art in which the broadcasting of the shadows of living figures will be combined and will alternate. Television will have a national side to it, perhaps a strongly developed national side, and will to that extent counteract certain of the influences of the screen. It must be clearly borne in mind, however, that unless we have first a film industry of our own, we shall find ourselves unable to transmit a television programme which is decently Irish (*Leader*, 17/12/38).[167]

The following year he returned to this theme in an essay on 'The Need for a Fully-Fledged Gaelic Theatre':

> But perhaps the greatest service which a professional theatre could render would be to make possible the production, later on, of films in Irish and also the giving of attractive television programmes in Irish when the time for inaugurating a service in this country arrives.

Developing this idea more than two decades before Irish television became a reality, Blythe continued:

> If we had a television station in Ireland to-morrow any plays that might be broadcast from it in Irish would be ill-done, but with the help of a good Gaelic-speaking repertory company television could be made a great instrument for the restoration of the language (*Leader*, 16/12/39).[168]

Many cultural nationalists welcomed Irish works like Thomas Cooper's War of Independence film *The Dawn* (1936) and Donal O'Cahill's *The Islandman* (1938) – a film that despite its title and Blasket setting was not based on Ó Criomhthain's book – or the Irish-American Robert Flaherty's classic *Man of Aran* (1934). But however gratifying they found these early attempts to deal with Irish life in a way that eschewed shamrockery and stage-Irishism, Gaels could never accept the idea of an Irish national cinema in the English language, whether spoken or in subtitles. Several critics were explicit on this point in their reviews of Flaherty's film on its premiere in Dublin. The editor of *An t-Éireannach*, who quite liked the movie, neverthless commented:

> The people of Aran were forced to abandon their own language and speak a foreign language that was unnatural to themselves and to anyone who was listening to them . . . Why would the people of Aran not have their native language as well as their clothing and customs? (*Éireannach*, 23/6/34).[169]

Other Gaels felt the film's use of English far outweighed whatever excellences it possessed. An anonymous critic in *An Camán* said that he had heard good things about the film, but still believed it presented a distorted picture of the islanders on linguistic grounds: 'The Irish language is the most interesting talent and characteristic to be noticed on Aran: and now it will go around the world that English is in use in the westernmost bit of Ireland' (*Camán*, 19/5/34).[170] One 'Aongus Óg' felt Flaherty's choice of language for the movie was a cynical commercial decision made at the expense of an honest depiction of the islanders to the outside world. Writing four months after the film's release, he stated:

> Another thing that dishonoured this island was the picture *Man of Aran* that was made there. I never saw that picture being shown, but even if I did not, I heard that it was English that was in it . . . Another thing, it was a Yank who was in charge of it, and, of course, he knew that the picture would earn much more by putting English in it (*Éireannach*, 7/9/35).[171]

By far the most outspoken and dismissive critic of the film was Pádraig Ó Briain, who wrote in *An Phoblacht*:

> This picture will be shown widely throughout the world. It will be judged, and we will be judged, in the world's towns. What will the other races have to say except that we have been beaten, that we are insignificant little Englishmen . . . English is the language of Aran, the language of the West of Ireland at last, the language of all of Ireland . . . The world thinks that we have been laid low, defeated as a result of this, defeated by ourselves. And the world will mock us, as it has often done already (*An Phoblacht*, 19/5/34).[172]

It is, however, the official Gaelic League response, as voiced in a resolution passed by the Executive Committee of the organisation, that best sums up the movement's radically ambiguous and opportunist response to the the movie. Having heard criticism of the absence of Irish in the film and a proposal that the government should require film companies to use some Irish in every picture made in the country, the committee passed a motion from Seán Óg Ó Ceallaigh

> praising the excellent effort made by Robert Flaherty in showing to the world in his picture the courage of Gaels and the hardships they endure, and in showing how

little the Government of the Saorstát had done for these Gaels, and condemning strongly the wrong done the Islanders and to our national language by having the actors speak English (*II*, 14/5/34).

When a short film entirely in Irish was finally produced, most Gaels quickly – and honestly – realised and admitted that language alone could not guarantee a successful cinematic experience. Produced by Robert Flaherty himself, involving several cast members from *Man of Aran*, and enjoying a state grant of £200, the short *Oidhche Sheanchais* (A night of storytelling), a filmed record of a storytelling session, opened in Dublin in March 1935 to mixed reviews at best in the cultural nationalist press.[173] The most favourable response was, surprisingly, in the satirical monthly *Dublin Opinion*, whose anonymous reviewer wrote: 'Every word in this notable little pioneer film was in Irish. It was short, lasting about ten minutes, but the glimpse was there of what might be done in this medium, the fore-gleams of the things that will yet be done.' Having pointed out 'a slight suggestion of staginess which we find hard enough to pin down to details and which may, therefore, only have existed in our imagination', this critic went on to ask:

> And, in any case, what does it matter? You can't expect a film-industry in Irish to spring out, like Minerva, fully armed. What matters is that a beginning has been made and a notable beginning. It is a thought-provoking thing this harnessing of the Cinema, of all things, to the task of re-establishing our ancient language (*Dublin Opinion*, Apr. 1935, 56).

The cinema correspondent for *The Irish Times* was also fairly generous towards the film after attending a private screening:

> One had forgotten the action which the Irish story-teller brings naturally into his work. Ó Dioráin [the storyteller in the film] tells his story not only with his voice, but with his hands and the expression on his face, and can hold the attention even of those who do not know a word of Irish. It is all done very naturally (*IT*, 15/12/34).[174]

Far less enthusiastic, and for that reason more representative, was the response of the anonymous author of the 'Annseo agus Annsúd' (Here and there) column in the *Connacht Tribune*. Having acknowledged that he was pleased to hear Irish spoken on screen, he nonetheless confessed that he found the film disappointing for several reasons, including its brevity and the distracting mannerisms of the title character. Far more important, however, was the movie's general mediocrity and reliance on the uncritical support of those committed to the language cause:

I would say that no one would take any interest at all in it if it were not Irish that was being spoken in it. There is entirely too much of that connected with the Irish language. People think that for interest to be taken in something it is enough for it to be Gaelic, books being in Irish, people speaking Irish, etc. But as well as a thing's being Gaelic, they should also look to it that it is good (*CT*, 11/5/35).[175]

Several writers commented on the film's lack of success in drawing and holding an audience. According to a columnist in *An t-Éireannach*, the scheduled Dublin run of a fortnight had been shortened to a week due to lack of audience enthusiasm:

It is a source of disappointment how little interest the public took this past week in the first Irish-language picture shown in Dublin. *Oidhche Sheanchais* was shown in two picture houses in the city, but the paltry attendance during the week proved that the majority of the public have little appetite for Irish or for *Gaelachas* although it is imagined that the spirit is growing stronger among us (*Éireannach*, 30/3/35).[176]

Alfred Dennis directed his criticism at language activists themselves, writing that 'the complete failure of the alleged Gaels to support the first all-Irish talkie is a sufficient indication of their real attitude' (*FMR*, May, 1935, 225). The regular film correspondent of the *Irish Independent*, 'J.A.P.', was even harsher:

The first all-Gaelic film, 'Oidhche Sheanchais', has not been supported in Dublin. I announce the indisputable fact with keen regret. It is a disgrace to the Gaedhilgeoirí in the Irish capital that, instead of long queues outside the two picture theatres that are showing it, those two cinemas have been almost empty since this film was first screened . . . There is something rotten in the Gaelic State of Denmark! (*II*, 23/3/35).

The Gaelic League was so troubled by the failure of *Oidhche Sheanchais* that it devoted time at its 1936 Comhdháil to a discussion of how to convince the government that funding of future Irish-language films would not be a similar waste of taxpayers' money.[177]

There was also some criticism of the movie precisely because it was in Irish, or at least in a particular kind of Irish. In a dismissive review in *The Blueshirt*, an anonymous critic saw the film as an attempt to impose Connacht Irish on Munster schoolchildren, writing:

It is said that this film cost a great deal of money. Nothing good will come of its like. The story is not engaging, the speech is not clever, and without any doubt the story is not suitable in any way at all for the schools in Munster, and if our opinion is worth anything, we would say that there will not be much respect for the Connacht dialect when this film has made the circuit of Ireland (*Blueshirt*, 9/2/35).[178]

Micheál Ó Maoláin attacked the film nearly two years before its premiere on grounds more parochial than provincial, wondering why the Conamara *seanchaí* Seáinín Tom Ó Direáin had been given the starring role over the many qualified Aran storytellers (*IP*, 3/11/33). A more disturbing criticism of the language of the film was that it was too difficult for many in the audience. This point was explored by 'Díoltóir Brat' in 1935: 'In the mind of many Gaels, the greatest faults with that picture were that the Irish was too complicated and too difficult for them; and, that the actors lacked vigour and energy' (*Gaedheal*, 4/5/37).[179]

For others, however, *Oidhche Sheanchais* was simply not an enjoyable movie – even for the scant few minutes it ran. We have already encountered criticism of some of the film's weaknesses in the reviews from *The Blueshirt* and *An Gaedheal* quoted above. Similar shortcomings were discussed at greater length in the previously cited review from *An t-Éireannach*:

> The picture itself is not without fault, and that is the opinion of the average person. In the first place, if the Government wanted to provide a Gaelic picture in Irish, they should have gone about it right and put a good example of a picture before the public – a picture with action that would help the audience to understand what was going on.

For this reviewer, the movie didn't move enough: 'The actors in this picture should not have been as stiff and dead as they were' (*Éireannach*, 30/3/35).[180] P. Mac Cionnaith agreed, criticising the movie for 'a lack of action' (easba gníomhartha) (*Belvederian*, 1935, 87). Looking back on the film in August 1939, Annraoi Saidléar wrote: 'Money was lost on that because it was not a picture that would lure a crowd. The public is accustomed to excellent pictures, and nothing else will do the job.' After suggesting several possibilities for appealing Irish films, he concluded with a damning implicit comparison with the subject and style of *Oidhche Sheanchais*:

> Let us not cling to the kind of '*Gaelachas*' that is nothing but old-fashionedness that is endured for the sake of people who want to show contempt for the new – and make martyrs of themselves and of their fellow human beings. Let there be brightness and pleasure (*Echo*, 8/5/37).[181]

The experiment was not to be repeated in our period, so that for even those Gaels open to the appeal of the cinema, movies remained a subject of conversation rather than creation.

For many, however, discussions of contests and prizes, pantomimes, operas, and movies were frivolous distractions from the crucial question of where authentic Gaelic drama should be sought. 'S. Mac P.' set out the problem with stark clarity in 1936: 'We have, therefore, the first reason for this lack of plays, that is, those who have Irish do not have the actor's craft, and few of those who have this craft have Irish' (*IP*, 7/12/36).[182] The dichotomy spelled out here should sound more than a little familiar, for it is, of course, merely another version of the central ideological debate of our period – whether the native speaker of Irish or the educated learner should have primacy in the language movement. As a highly public venture whose direction, leadership and financing seemed very much up for grabs, the theatre attracted keen attention from partisans of both camps in this intramural *Kulturkampf*. Once again, it was Séamus Ó Grianna who most forcefully and abrasively advanced the right of the native speaker to take the lead in all aspects of theatrical work in the language:

> But the first drama one of them [native speakers] will write, even if it is but a disorganised, shapeless, unfinished thing – and even if they have no place to stage it but in a cowshed at the cow's rump with a candle in a porter bottle for lighting – it will have a virtue that the plays in the Abbey Theatre do not have. It will be a natural start and it will evolve with time (*FL*, Nov. 1929, 7).[183]

In another editorial in *Fáinne an Lae* the same month, he began calmly enough: 'No group has yet succeeded in awakening the interest of the public in drama in Irish – because the people who have Irish do not have the opportunity, and the people who have the opportunity do not have Irish.' But he then hit his usual stride on the way to a typically categorical and bruising conclusion:

> But are there any plays at all in store for us in this country? It is unlikely there will be for some time. But whenever the drama comes, it will have to come *from the west*. The drama will have to come from the place where Irish is spoken naturally by the people. I will, of course, be told that the people of the Gaeltacht have no knowledge of that craft. I admit that. But however bad they are, they are as good as the crowd that has been in the Abbey Theatre for the past five years. In the first place, they don't rely on Liverpool Irish (*FL*, Nov. 1929, 1).[184]

He was no less abusive the following month, writing of An Comhar: 'They and their plays were a great public disgrace. It is bad enough for us that the Gaeltacht is vanishing without a flock of genuine Yahoos without mouth or tongue stammering on stage and trying to convince us that they have the language of our ancestors' (*FL*, Dec. 1929, 1).[185]

As usual, Ó Grianna had vociferous allies to back him up in this campaign. In his lengthy essay on 'Dráma Gaedheal', Seán Ó Ciarghusa asked and answered the fundamental question here: 'What is Gaelic drama?' Ó Ciarghusa wrote:

> The first characteristic is, of course, that the drama be in Irish. That is it should be written, or at any rate censored by a native speaker. For dialogue is the life-blood of the drama, and no mere learner of any language can be sure of his dialogue in it . . . Moreover, it is part of the function of our infant drama to teach Irish (Shakespeare taught all the world English), and it is highly desirable that only native Irish should be spoken on our stage (*Leader*, 5/11/27).

An anonymous critic asked the same question of his colleages more pointedly in a 1933 review of plays at the Munster Feis: 'Do they know that it is useless for us to rely on plays in Irish from English-speaking Ireland unless the Gaeltacht provides the good example first?' (*Camán*, 23/9/33).[186]

Ó Grianna was to find his staunchest supporters among the writers who contributed to *An t-Éireannach*, a paper that did, after all, boast that it was the voice of the Gaeltacht. In a 1934 essay in the paper, Gearóid Ó Cuinneagáin, himself a learner, shared Ó Grianna's outrage at state support for An Comhar Drámaidheachta while no effort was being made to root Gaelic drama in its native soil:

> It enrages me to think that the Government is bestowing a thousand pounds a year on an acting company in Dublin called 'An Comhar Drámaidheachta' in the hope that a dramatic branch will grow on the tree of Gaelic literature. And God sees the kind of Irish most members of An Comhar have! And the people with Irish in the West (And I am not forgetting Taibhdhearc na Gaillimhe) – there is not a red ha'penny being tossed to them to encourage them to take an interest in the drama (*Éireannach*, 17/11/34).[187]

In January 1936, 'Na Printíseacha' quoted with approval the remarks of An tAthair Mac Fhinn, who, speaking after the performance of a play in Conamara, stated that 'however much praise is going to people who are doing their best here and there throughout English-speaking Ireland, you could not be expecting real drama in Irish except from the people of the Gaeltacht' (*Éireannach*, 4/1/36).[188] Mac Fhinn expressed the same opinion in a 1937 review of the published version of An tAthair Pádhraic Mac Aodha's play *Peadar a' tSléibhe*: 'If Irish-language drama is to make genuine progress, that progress will have to come from the Gaeltacht' (*AA*, May, 1937, 8).[189]

Given the obvious centrality of fluent speech in drama, and the regular criticisms of the lack of such fluency on the part of too many Gaelic actors, even most learners were willing to concede that trained native speakers would be the ideal people to develop a native dramatic art. For example, in 1926, Gearóid Ó Lochlainn, who had more hands-on experience with the Gaelic stage than anyone, with the possible exceptions of Micheál Mac Liammóir and Piaras Béaslaí, pondered the practical consequences of this situation:

> Our most native dramatists live in An Ghaedhealtacht, but they don't know much about stage technique. If a committee of An Comhar would make it its business to teach as well as it could – by booklets, etc. – that technique, something might come of it. Indeed, if the dry bones, so to say, of dramas were sent from Dublin to known writers in An Ghaedhealtacht, they might come back clothed with flesh and blood, the Irish origins of which there would be no mistaking or disputing (*Leader*, 10/7/26).

Béaslaí was in general agreement here, declaring in a 1935 radio broadcast: 'An effort should be made to assist Irish writers in the Gaeltacht with advice and encouragement to produce simple, easily-acted plays of an original character' (*II*, 13/6/35).[190] This kind of openness represented by the learners Ó Lochlainn and Béaslaí – the latter, of course, English-born – seems to have fallen on the deaf ears of native speakers and their allies, of whom only a few cared about theatre anyway. Once again, the internal civil war within the language movement derailed what could have been one of the most exciting and influential experiments undertaken in Irish during a pivotal period when there was significant, perhaps even widespread, official and popular support for the extension of Irish if not for its genuine revival as the language of the nation.

The frustration such failure engendered in those who took both the language and the drama seriously was perhaps best expressed by Máiréad Ní Ghráda, a woman who was involved with An Comhar Drámaidheachta from its start in 1923, and who was to become one of the very few playwrights in Irish to ever write work likely to last. Speaking on 'Drámaíocht sa gCathair' (Drama in the city) over the radio in 1937, Ní Ghráda stated:

> With regard to drama in Irish we must admit that the biggest gap is yet to be filled. We have no Gaelic Theatre. And when I say that, I do not mean the house or the performance hall. Not at all. What I mean is the combination of the three things necessary in Theatre, that is: the plays, the actors, and the audience.[191]

One can sympathise with her exasperation, but one must also acknowledge that if there was failure, it was not for want of thought or effort. And on a few rare occasions over two decades, the Gaels of our period may well have brought Ní Ghráda's dramatic trilogy together more often and imaginatively than they have managed to do in any corresponding period since.

NINE

TAKING STOCK, TAKING CHANCES

The thought of beginning to Gaelicise Yeats's theatre in the very year of his death must have seemed to the more vindictive among the Gaels a marvellous stroke of poetic justice. Even the more forgiving must have taken some real satisfaction at the thought of hearing Irish from the same stage from which had been spoken what many felt were the blasphemies of Synge, O'Casey, and other Irish writers of English. Those Gaels of a literary bent should also have been encouraged by the steady, if on the whole undistinguished, growth of a modern literature in Irish, a literature that had existed in only the most rudimentary aspirational form only forty years earlier. Much had, then, been accomplished for the language and its literature in the first two decades of independence, even if a natural impatience with the pace of that accomplishment often obscured the fact. In this chapter we will try to take advantage of our six decades remove from the hopes and disappointments – not to mention the personal animosities – of the time to see how the Irish-Ireland literary revival stood in 1939.

As was noted in the introduction, the provision of a modern literature in Irish had been a central goal of the language movement from its beginning in the days of the Society for the Preservation of the Irish Language. It could well be argued that the extraordinary emphasis on this goal so early was premature and possibly even counterproductive for a movement with so many more pressing problems to resolve. Nevertheless, there were many who were ready to judge the new state's commitment to the re-Gaelicisation project and indeed the success of the language movement itself in terms of the ability of both to work together for the creation and publication of a genuine contemporary literature in the national language.

The most immediate result of this attitude was the demand that the new state assume at once the leading role in the provision of books in Irish of all kinds for all kinds of readers. A little over two years after the Free State came into official existence in December 1922, Seán Ó Ciarghusa discussed the need for substantial state involvement and investment to make Gaelic publishing economically viable on a significant scale, stating:

> The Irish language will never get its due until books in Irish are at least as cheap as books in English, and they will not be until the State comes to the assistance of Irish in every way and pays for publishing it in the same way it is paying for teaching it (*Sguab*, Feb. 1925, 291).[1]

At this very time, the Free State's Minister for Finance, Ernest Blythe, was formulating a scheme to create just such a publishing agency under the auspices of the Department of Education. That scheme came to fruition in 1926 as An Gúm, which immediately became the single most important and controversial force in Gaelic literature.[2]

Over the years, voices critical of An Gúm, some of them those of the most accomplished and influential Gaelic writers of their time, have tended to dominate discussion of the agency's work.[3] Many of those voices and their real and/or imagined grievances have been considered in detail above. Here, it is important to note that many equally committed and respected language activists and writers were genuinely excited by and grateful for the work An Gúm was doing. In 1928, T. Mac Artáin argued that while the early Gaelic League had made a major contribution as a publisher of Irish, both the quantity and quality of League publications had declined dramatically over the years, and that it was a cause for celebration that An Gúm had stepped into the breach so created: 'It is the Government that is taking this work in hand from now on. It is praiseworthy work, and work that will benefit the country's literature' (*Tír*, June, 1928, 6).[4] Writing in 1929, 'T. F.' was enthusiastic in his praise of what An Gúm had already accomplished:

> From the day An Gúm took up their work two years ago, they have put out more books of every kind in Irish than came out in the same period of time for forty years. Before this, writers of Irish used to complain that no one bought books in Irish and that those who wrote them could not take on the cost of publishing them. No Irish-language author serious about the work will have that excuse from now on (*Star*, 23/11/29).[5]

León Ó Broin, a civil servant who had worked for An Gúm, offered his positive assessment of the agency to readers of the *Capuchin Annual* in 1935 in a lengthy contribution followed by 'comments on the foregoing article' by other authors, and by his own *ceangal*, or final thoughts, in which he wrote:

> If we look first at the most obvious result of the Gúm's activities we can see that it has certainly fulfilled its function as a machine for turning out books: turning down books in Irish might not unfairly be described as a function of the commercial houses before the Gúm got going. I have no reason to suspect, however, that at any time since the beginning quality was needlessly sacrificed for quantity: on the

> contrary, the influence of the editors, from my own experience, has been steadily directed towards improving the standard of writing (*CA*, 1935, 142).[6]

And in a previously quoted 1937 piece in *An Ráitheachán*, 'An Sagart' proclaimed: 'Gaelic has never been flung so broadly on the waters of the world during even our Golden Age' (*Ráitheachán*, Mar. 1937, 11).

He had a point. Whatever the quality of An Gúm's offerings – and we have heard plenty on that subject – the quantity of books produced was a very tangible fact. According to An Gúm's report for 1930–1, the agency had, in its first five years, evaluated 389 manuscripts, publishing 103 with a total sale of 70,000 (*IP*, 23/11/32). The following year's report listed 135 publications (out of 445 submissions), with sales of 90,000 copies (*IP*, 8/8/33).[7] Speaking to Cumann Gaedhealach na Stát-Sheirbhíse in November 1934, the Fianna Fáil minister responsible for An Gúm, Tomás Ó Deirg, reported that according to his most recent statistics, 234 titles had been published with sales of approximately 180,000 (*IP*, 17/11/34).[8] By 1936, those figures had increased to 305 titles (61 textbooks and 284 'general' works, 144 of them translations) with sales of 250,000. Moreover, the agency had an additional 240 manuscripts in varying stages of the publication process (*IP*, 3/9/36).[9] The following year, An Gúm published 85 titles, an increase of 100 per cent over the yearly average since its foundation, bringing the total number of titles issued to 389, 100 of them novels (18 original and 82 translated) (*IP*, 2/4/37; *Bonaventura*, Summer 1937, 171). In a piece on 'A State-Fostered Literature' in 1938, León Ó Broin offered the following summary of An Gúm's work to that date:

> In that period, it has succeeded by hard unremitting toil and the judicious use of public money, in putting over 500 volumes on a market (and selling over 300,000 copies of them) which, if there had been no State intervention, would not have seen so many Irish books in four times as many years (*Irish Monthly*, Feb. 1938, 126).[10]

There can be no doubt that Ó Broin was right here. Readers of Irish had never had so much and such varied reading matter to choose from. And if the native state was doing its duty for the language in the schools and, after 1926, through An Gúm, what really serious complaints could there be for those who had so long campaigned for precisely such state involvement in the language and cultural revival? That there were profound concerns is evident from some of the general overviews of the contemporary linguistic and cultural climate offered by Irish-Irelanders. In 1926, the year of An Gum's foundation, Tadhg Ó Donnchadha wrote:

> The Irish language suffers from a lack at present. It is a great lack, for it hurts the language, holding it back when it has an urgent need to go forward. That lack is a

> shortage of writers. There are now a great number of young people who can read Irish. But what is there out there for them to read? . . . There is a need for good writers – people who will write entertaining things for us in Irish. If it is not possible to provide appealing reading matter for those with Irish, we might as well write 'Finit' to the history of the native language forever (*Tribune*, 19/3/26).[11]

An Gúm did not change things all that much in the eyes of many. Séamus Ó Grianna weighed in on the topic the year after An Gúm came on the scene: 'Do we have many books? Books that would entice a reader to read them for the story – as they read a story in any other language? Are there a dozen such books from one end of Ireland to the other today?' (*FL*, Oct. 1927, 1).[12] T. F. O'Rahilly had no trouble answering such a question, writing in a scathing indictment of the Gaelic movement in 1929:

> We have no newspapers in Irish, no periodicals fit for adults, hardly any attempt to provide reading matter for people once they leave school, no attempt to make Irish the language of a single town (though we talk glibly of making it the language of the entire country), school books written by people who do not themselves know Irish, Irish taught by people who do not themselves know Irish, Irish to a very large extent treated as non-existent by the Church (*Star*, 25/5/29).

An Gúm itself was seen by some as one of the biggest problems facing the language and its literary aspirations. The most forceful exponents of this position were the brothers Séamus Ó Grianna and Seosamh Mac Grianna. Ó Grianna, who regularly referred to the agency as 'An Mug', wrote in 1932:

> I looked on the Gúm as a friend of mine estimated a new patent razor he had bought. 'It is very handy', said he. 'It pares my nails, and sharpens my pencil, and cuts my tobacco. It will do everything but shave.' Well, my opinion of this 'literary department' was that it could do something with everything except literature (*An Phoblacht*, 6/8/32).[13]

In the same year, Mac Grianna lampooned what he felt to be the stifling bureaucracy of An Gúm:

> Now, I am the sort of man who would work for the devil if he paid me for it. But in Ireland even the devil is beggarly. No man worked harder for An Gúm than I did: no man is poorer at the end of it all. They had an amazing way of making every little trifle the subject of a dozen or so official documents. I was in mortal terror of leaving my hat behind in the office, lest I should have to fill several forms of application for its return, and lest there should be a separate file opened for it by the secretary, perhaps a separate department, a 'Roinn um Seanhatai' [Department of old hats] (*An Phoblacht*, 23/7/32).[14]

The following week he was even more dismissive:

> The Gúm must go, with its committee of doubtful credentials, and its swarm of merely ordinary civil servants. It is underselling the other Irish publishers. It is wasting the taxpayers' money to the extent of £20,000 a year . . . Bury the Gúm. Then on to something honest, impartial, intelligent, creative and Gaelic (*An Phoblacht*, 30/7/32).[15]

The brothers were members of a large and very vocal faction critical of what Brian O'Neill called 'the Gaelic Grub Street' (*Irish Workers' Voice*, 7/1/33). For example, Micheál Mag Ruaidhrí, an important language figure since the early days of the Gaelic League, wrote in 1929:

> There is no more difficult work at present than reviewing books in Irish, especially the books that have come from the Department of Education. That Department has put out a good number of books over the past little while. But it must be said about most of them that the Irish language would be better off had they never been published at all. It is certain that more harm than good will come as a result of publishing them (*Tír*, Dec. 1929, 6).[16]

Three years later, an anonymous contributor declared:

> The naked truth should be told and not hidden. Thousands of pounds of this country's money have been spent for five years on putting out books whose bulk is greater than their value. It can truthfully be said that there are not a half-dozen books in all that could be called literature, because the work was done by writers who did not have proper Irish and did not understand what literature is (*Tír*, Sept. 1932, 4–5).[17]

In what he called a 'dispassionate' survey of An Gúm's activities the same year, the poet and short story writer Riobárd Ó Faracháin stated:

> But even if it worked on a system compatible with Christian humanism a Government department should not be entrusted with the day to day publishing of books. Because books which are books are living things, and civil service which is civil service is very nearly a dead thing; inertia being a sign of the inanimate, and absence of choice, of slavery (*Bonaventura*, Summer 1937, 170).

And in 1939, *The Leader* contemptuously wrote off what some felt was An Gúm's greatest accomplishment: 'The Gúm's miserable six-hundred volumes does [*sic*] not represent even an apology for the beginning of a supply of books' (*Leader*, 5/8/39).[18] In a 1934 essay, Peadar Mac Fhionnlaoich summed up his objections to An Gúm:

> An author will not put up with restrictive rules, and excessive interference. And if he has an independent mind, his writings will not please An Gúm or the people behind An Gúm .... I have had some dealings with An Gúm that showed that it is not possible for a writer with an independent mind to do work for An Gúm (*Gaedheal*, 1/12/34).[19]

His was, of course, precisely the accusation levelled against the agency by Ó Grianna and his brother Seosamh, and many others shared the opinion. In a 1932 letter to *An t-Ultach*, Donn Piatt, who published his own work to escape An Gúm's control, blasted the pettiness of the agency's rules and the vindictiveness of its current editors towards those like Ó Grianna, Mac Grianna, and himself who had been critical of it.[20] In his 1934 book *Prós na hAoise Seo*, published by a commercial house, Shán Ó Cuív divided Gaelic authors into three groups: the dead, those 'who were cultivating the language before the State began giving assistance to writers' (a bhí ag saothrú na teangan sar ar thosnaigh an Stát ar chabhair a thabhairt do sgríbhneoirí), and 'those whose work is being edited and published by the Government' (an chuid díobh go bhfuil a saothar á chur i n-eagar agus a fhoillsiú ag an Rialtas). He then pointed out how this last group was required to consent to any changes the editors requested, and concluded: 'For that reason it is not possible to be certain that it is the work of the author himself that we have at all when we are reading a book from the Government.'[21] Writing in 1935, 'Cnuasaire' attacked An Gúm's editors as both 'dishonest' (mí-ionraice) and incompetent (*Ultach*, June 1935, 6–7).[22] More dispassionate was Máiréad Ní Ghráda, who wrote the same year:

> When An Gúm was founded, we hoped that a stream of literature would spring up in a current towards us. We thought the workers of An Gúm would be there to sift that stream so that it would be a well of true literature and so that the people would be able to draw from that well, and quench their thirst for literature. But it was not long until our hope was dissipated. An Gum's workers made the well, but all that sprung up was a trickle (*II*, 11/10/35).[23]

Less dramatic but more widespread than such accusations of bad faith and ineptitude were criticisms of An Gúm for lengthy delays between commission / acceptance and publication, and for failing to properly publicise titles when they appeared. Doubtless the lengthiest – and most notorious – delay in An Gúm's history was that inflicted on Seosamh Mac Grianna's novel *An Druma Mór*, a work An Gúm had in hand in 1933, but refused to publish until 1969![24] While no other Gaelic author endured a wait anywhere near so long, many saw their careers adversely affected by the dilatory pace of An Gúm's publication schedule, and their frustration was shared by readers, as is clear from the comments of Father Lawrence Murray in a 1930 editorial note in *An t-Ultach* commenting on a report that An Gúm had a backlog of books awaiting publication:

> That is good news, but a new book has not been given to us for a good while now, and we are waiting for some production from the writers. It is a great pity that publication involves so much delay, when the writers are being urged on (*Ultach*, Nov. 1930, 1).[25]

In an editorial note entitled 'What Is the Matter with the Gúm?' in *The Star*, a paper that was, one should remember, strongly supportive of the Cumann na nGaedheal government that had created and was at the time responsible for the agency, Micheál Mac Suibhne was blunt in his criticism:

> No book has been issued by the Gúm for a considerable time back and many people interested in Irish publications are beginning to wonder if the editorial staff have become tied up in their own red tape . . . We hope the Gúm authorities will stir themselves and bear in mind at all times that their job is to cater for the general Irish reader (*Star*, 14/6/30).[26]

Another regular columnist for *The Star*, 'B. Ní M.' seems to have felt An Gúm lost interest in its books once they were published, arguing that

> more of An Gúm's books would be read if readers of Irish knew their like were in print. It is every bit as necessary for Coiste na Leabhar [The Book Committee] to publicise their books as it is for the ordinary publishers, and perhaps more necessary (*Star*, 14/6/30).[27]

The situation did not improve with time, and in 1937, 'Sliabh Bladhma' vented his exasperation on this point:

> I think the 'Gúm' ought to do much more for its authors: widely circulating interesting notes about them and the books, for example – the original books, and the proportion of translation worth having. It does not seem to make the most of its resources and opportunities (*Gaedheal*, May, 1937, 1).

An Gúm could, of course, only publish what was being written, and much of that was, at least in the opinion of several critics, rarely good, often abysmal. Complaints about the paucity of engaging reading matter continued throughout the 1930s.[28] For example, in 1933, Margaret Gibbons declared: 'There is no educated reader of our modern Irish language publications but will agree with me, I think, in classifying the majority of them as literary failures' (*Irish*

Monthly, Apr. 1933, 195).[29] The following year, 'Student' acknowledged 'the fact . . . that there are at present very few writers of Irish who can produce original books worth publishing', and continued:

> Most of those who set about writing novels have neither the imagination to paint the lives of wholly fictitious characters nor the sense to write the rather interesting semi-biographical stories of which every person, who has any literary gift at all, and is not smothered in self-consciousness or fear of the criticisms of neighbours and relatives, can produce at least one . . . The position, therefore, is that the Gúm's output of worthwhile original work is so small as to be of little immediate importance (*UI*, 21/4/34).[30]

The following year, 'Oisín' offered a radical response to this problem:

> It would be far better not to print a word of Irish than to write something that the people would not read if it were in English. Not only will it sicken and discourage the Gaels, but it will give the enemies of the language a chance to attack it (*Derry People*, 24/7/37).[31]

And in 1939, the man most responsible for the existence of An Gúm, Ernest Blythe, expressed his reservations about the success of the agency in providing appealing reading matter in Irish:

> But its four hundred and eighty-three titles in the general literature class represent a very inconsiderable contribution towards the furnishing of an Irish library when it is remembered that at least ten thousand books in Irish are urgently required to give the average reader a chance of finding in the National language a sprinkling of books which he will read, not out of a stern sense of duty but for pleasure or information. With less than five hundred works for adults available in Irish the normal young person has no chance of finding week by week a book which is really to his taste (*Leader*, 16/12/39).[32]

While this question of An Gúm's work and success was, of course, a crucial one, some in the movement seemed willing to argue endlessly over whether their Gaelic bookshelves were half-empty or half-full, in the process losing sight of the larger goals to which they were supposedly committed. There were, however, a good number of their colleagues in the mid-1930s who wanted to keep those goals – the restoration of the language and the creation of a modern literature in Irish – front and centre in a united Irish-Ireland crusade. Foremost in this regard was An Comhchaidreamh, the inter-university organisation of students and graduates that from its foundation in 1935 attracted an impressive array of what would become the leading Gaelic scholars, writers and activists of the future.[33]

To realise the vision of a revitalised and visible movement that could connect with ordinary Irish people in a way unknown for more than two decades, such idealists believed it would be essential to recreate the zestful camaraderie and sense of shared purpose that had enabled their predecessors and their own younger selves to overcome such formidable obstacles and accomplish such valuable and tangible results. For many of them, there was no more potent symbol of that lost sense of common mission than the national Oireachtas, last held, with disappointing results, in 1924, in the immediate aftermath of Civil War. Accordingly, they set about reviving the festival as soon and as impressively as possible. There had, of course, been gatherings in Dublin called *Oireachtais* in 1931 and 1932, although these festivals seem to have been forgotten within a couple of years of their occurrence.[34] Even at the time of their celebration there was ambivalence about their status. For example, in an announcement of the upcoming event in 1931, it was referred to simply as 'Seachtmhain na Samhna' (November week), since it would occur in that month in conjunction with other Gaelic League functions (*II*, 31/10/31). Yet in a piece in the same paper a few weeks earlier entitled 'Féile na Samhna / Iarracht Nua ag an gCoiste Gnótha' (The November festival / A new effort by the Executive Committee), Shán Ó Cuív had written: 'The Executive Committee is making an attempt to revive the Oireachtas after its being absent for seven years. This attempt is like a new beginning' (*II*, 2/10/31).[35] An editorial in the very first issue of the *Irish Press* proclaimed:

> It is a great support for any group of people who share the same purpose to come together in one place to reinforce each other through talk and conversation. It was, therefore, a good idea to get the Oireachtas going again. It would be possible to encourage literature there; we would get to know each other well again so that it would be like the gathering together of an army (*IP*, 5/9/31).[36]

And the following month, a contributor to the same paper wrote of the upcoming gathering as the revived Oireachtas and 'this spear head of Gaelic cultural movement' (*IP*, 31/10/31). On the other hand, another contributor to the paper shared the uncertainty about just what the festival was and what it should be called. In a piece entitled 'Oireachtas na nGaedheal / Oireachtas Nuadh' (The Oireachtas of the Gaels / A new Oireachtas), this writer said with premature optimism that 'it is, therefore, timely and delightful to hear that the Oireachtas of the Gaels is being revived'. But he then went on to incorporate the event with Seachtmhain na Samhna. Still, he clearly had the highest hopes for the future of this new festival, whatever it was called: 'And every year after this it is to be hoped that the best from the *feiseanna* and the finest Gaels will be seen competing in Dublin' (*IP*, 17/10/31).[37]

Others were considerably more guarded in their expectations. For example, in his previously quoted piece on the upcoming festival, Shán Ó Cuív qualified his enthusiasm by writing: 'This Oireachtas will not be of the same kind as the ones there used to be previously. What is planned by the Executive Committee for this coming month is not unlike a *feis* (*II*, 2/10/31).[38] Opening the 1931 assembly at the Mansion House, Peadar Mac Fhionnlaoich invoked the first Oireachtas in 1897, doubtless both to give historic weight to the occasion and to lower overheated expectations of what could be accomplished in current conditions: 'The gathering present then was not large, but the Oireachtas grew, and he hoped that it would grow again because of this new effort' (*II*, 3/11/31).[39] Things did not look all that different from London, where *Féile na nGaedheal* in one piece referred to the festival as 'an Oireachtas of a new character', and in another gave some idea of the diminished nature of this novelty:

> Musical, dramatic, and dancing competitions will be the great features of the new Oireachtas in Dublin, November 2–7. With the Roinn Oideachais [Department of Education. i.e., An Gúm] and other schemes, the old necessity for literary competitions is not felt (*Féile na nGaedheal*, Nov. 1931, 4–5).

In fact, there were no literary competitions that year, although two prizes ('shields' / *sgiatha*) were awarded for dramatic performances.[40] Only modest expectations could explain the usually demanding Micheál Ó Maoláin's positive assessment of the 1931 'Oireachtas:' 'The Oireachtas this year succeeded better than it was at first thought it would . . . This is a good beginning, and we hope that this coming Oireachtas will have better success' (*Nationality*, 14/11/31).[41]

It didn't, despite the continued enthusiasm of its organisers and backers. Even the old ambivalence about whether the gathering merited the title 'Oireachtas' persisted, with Ó Cuív, for example, writing: 'Seachtain na Samhna is not far from us now, and if the Oireachtas of last year is to be surpassed the branches and the schools must begin at once to prepare for the competitions (*II*, 27/9/32).[42] Ó Cuív was well aware of the difficulties facing the festival, whatever one chose to call it. In a piece entitled 'An t-Oireachtas', he wrote: 'What has been decided is to weave the *feiseanna* and the Oireachtas together so that there would be a Supreme-oireachtas. It is, however, difficult to do that' (*II*, 16/2/32).[43] On the positive side, this 'Oireachtas' did offer several literary prizes. But despite these competitions, the 'Oireachtas' of 1932 seems to have inspired little enthusiasm, so that Seán Ó Ciarghusa all but dismissed it as an irrelevant failure:

> You would think this past week that people were beginning the work for the Irish language – and that a feeble beginning – instead of celebrating the day of the language's triumph as they should have been doing, and as they could have been doing if the Gaels backed up their words with deeds (*Leader*, 12/11/32).[44]

At any rate, the League decided to cut its losses the next year, cancelling the 'Oireachtas' for reasons that could not be ignored:

> It was clear to the Committee because of last year's Oireachtas that there were two major faults that it would be difficult to fix, i.e. a shortage of competitors in the principal contests, and a lack of proper support from the public (*Camán*, 14/10/33).[45]

Instead, a special conference (*comhdháil*) would be held in November 1933 to discuss the coordination of *feiseanna* with a more ambitious Oireachtas to be held in 1934.[46] In the meantime, the Dublin Feis stepped into the gap, offering far more comprehensive and successful festivals than had either of the so-called 'Oireachtais' of 1931 and 1932.[47]

This failure turned out, however, to be no more than a temporary setback. In January 1933, the League issued an appeal over the signatures of Mac Giolla Bhríde as president and Seán Óg Ó Ceallaigh as secretary, declaring: 'The League wishes to undertake its work again with enthusiasm, and, therefore, it has decided to have the Oireachtas in operation again' (*Tír*, Jan. 1933, 9).[48] Two months later, another influential Gael, the League secretary's father, Seán Ua Ceallaigh, emphasised the crucial issues at stake here in a speech to Feis Chorcaighe:

> The League should revive the Oireachtas and give big prizes every year, prizes that it would be an honour for a learned person to win, as is done at the Eisteddfod. Unless that is done, the Irish language will feel the effect: its movement will be stiff, weak, and sluggish, and we will have 'An Gúm's' rubbish and 'official' Irish instead of literature (*Camán*, 26/8/33).[49]

Aware from bitter recent experience that enthusiasm and high hopes were no guarantee of even modest success, most in the movement felt caution was in order. The Oireachtas projected for 1934 was accordingly cancelled.

The idea was, however, too good and too important to lie fallow for long, and by 1936 public calls for the revival of a genuine Oireachtas along the lines of the pre-independence festivals were again being heard.[50] In an essay in May of that year, an anonymous contributor wrote of the Oireachtas:

> No other institution in the land can set so high and true a guiding standard for the language, music, art, dress and cultural traditions of the Gael. The temporary lapse of the Oireachtas has been a sad loss to our national culture – social, intellectual and physical – and hence its restoration is all the more urgent and desirable (*CB*, May, 1936, 387).

Similar appeals continued to be heard the following year. For example, writing in 1937, 'Sliabh Bladhma' declared:

> The loss of the great central rally, the League Oireachtas, is deplorable. Its revival is essential, and ought not to be difficult. If there can be successful Feiseanna in the country, why not a worthy festival, literary and social, in Dublin? . . . We could have a record assembly next year. It would lead to new life in the League, in Gaelic Ireland, and in the Ireland that is gradually being Gaelicised (*Gaedheal*, Oct. 1937, 1).

Serious work was obviously going on behind the scenes. In November 1937, the *Irish Independent* reported that the League's Executive Committee had approved a resolution from Aindrias Ó Muimhneacháin 'that an attempt be made to put the Oireachtas in operation again in 1938, or as soon as is possible' (go dtabharfar fé'n Oireachtas a chur ar siubhal ath-uair in 1938, nó an túisge is féidir é) (*II*, 15/11/37).[51] By the following month, a sub-committee had been formed and had met with all the other leading Gaelic organisations 'to examine the possibility of revival' of the Oireachtas (*IP*, 13/12/37). And in January 1938, the Executive Committee of the League announced that 'arrangements are being made to hold the next Gaelic League Oireachtas next year' (*IP*, 17/1/38).[52] The announcement was greeted enthusiastically, with 'Boyle Roche's Bird', for example, exulting: 'What a stimulus to creative Gaelic talent those annual assemblies were! And what added opportunities have we not to hand to-day to emulate and even surpass the former triumphs!' (*Gaedheal*, Jan. 1938, 6).

This time around, the Gaels wanted to get things right. From the start, there was a willingness to face the difficulties involved. In January 1938, 'G. Mac R.' wrote that if the proposed festival were to be no more than a glorified *feis*, even one as large and successful as the Dublin Feis, it was not worth the effort or the risk of humiliating failure (*II*, 21/1/38).[53] 'Sean-Ghaedhilgeoir' agreed the following month, emphasising the need for the formation of 'The United Gaelic Front' (An Fronta Aontuighthe Gaedhealach) (*II*, 9/2/38).[54] In April 1938, the editor of the Enniscorthy *Echo* stressed that both Gaelic unity and a significant financial commitment (*c.*£10,000) would be necessary to make the new Oireachtas a success (*Echo*, 9/4/38). It seems those responsible for actually providing the money and doing the work were paying attention to such warnings and counsels. At any rate, it was a united Gaelic front that met at the Mansion House in April 1938 to adopt the following resolution:

> It is the opinion of this great meeting of all the Gaelic groups in Dublin that the Oireachtas should be revived again soon and celebrated every year from now on . . . We ask all the Gaels of the country to join us in a single organisation in this attempt to make of the Oireachtas a great national Institute to promote and develop culture, language, literature, music, drama, etc. (*Leader*, 16/4/38).[55]

With what was clearly a considered commitment thus made, the Gaels quickly lined up to support the initiative, with the emphasis now more on what could be accomplished than on the danger of failure. This optimism is evident in the words of what must be a League press release in the *Irish Independent* in October 1938: 'There is no need to mention how necessary it is for something great like the Oireachtas to go on annually in Ireland. It is clear, also, that the right time has come to undertake the like' (*II*, 10/11/38).[56] Seán Ó Ciarghusa was even more exuberantly confident: 'Well done, Gaels! It is joyful news that the Oireachtas is to be celebrated again. May the attempt succeed, and, of course, it will succeed' (*Leader*, 3/12/38).[57]

In 1939, the League issued an official *Athchuinghe* or 'Appeal' for support for the Oireachtas, beginning with a brief survey of its previous accomplishments and significance, as well as an acknowledgement of the damage its absence had caused: 'That work which had been a source of inspiration to the Gael and an impetus to the language revival was gone, and there was a consequent disintegration of the whole Irish-Ireland movement.' Announcing that a three-day Oireachtas would be held in Dublin in November 1939, the authors of the appeal, Micheál 'Eoghan' Ó Súilleabháin and León Ó Dubhghaill, pledged that along with its business and social components, the Oireachtas would showcase 'the best demonstrations of music, singing and other aspects of Gaelic culture' (na taisbeántaisí is fearr is féidir . . . ar cheol, amhránaidheacht, agus gnéithe eile de chultúr Ghaedhealach).[58] In what must have been another League press release – an identical text appeared in at least two major papers – the focus was on the more literary side of the upcoming festival:

> The disappearance of the Oireachtas for a number of years was a national calamity, and its revival is most desirable. It is hoped that this 'great convention of the Gaels' will again be a rallying centre of a great movement and a source of inspiration. Authors, poets, musicians, and dramatists will find a new field for their activities, and it is hoped that the winning of the various competitions connected with the Oireachtas will mean more to them than the value of prizes offered (*Cork Weekly Examiner*, 14/1/39).[59]

It is, of course, the literary side of the Oireachtas that is most relevant to this study. Unlike the 'Oireachtais' of 1931 and 1932, this festival would begin to restore literature to the prominent if not pre-eminent position it had occupied in the now near-legendary assemblies of the past. Many, therefore, must have shared the satisfaction of Caoimhín Ó Conghaile when he saw the proposed list of literary competitions for the upcoming Oireachtas:

> The progress to be seen in the Literary Section is wonderful and pleasing. One can see there that the Committee understands that we are living a new life and that the thoughts, manners and behaviour of that life must be expressed in Irish if it is to leave the domain of the books and take its proper place as the everyday language of the whole country (*GR*, Feb. 1938, 355).[60]

'A. R. D.' had equally high hopes for these competitions, confident that all the work of state, schools, press, and individual writers since the last Oireachtas of 1924 meant that the 1939 gathering could surpass anything previously accomplished, even in the golden days of the movement:

> Since the Oireachtas was last held, writers of Irish – the old writers as well as the new writers – have had a remarkable opportunity to get good experience of writing Irish in the form of prose, or poetry, or drama.

He was, therefore, not surprised when advance word from the literary adjudicators for the Oireachtas indicated that the turnout of competitors was gratifyingly large and the quality of the submissions correspondingly high (*II*, 13/10/39).[61] Yet in the following month, 'P. Ó C.' had obviously heard a diametrically different version of the adjudicators' reactions to the literary submissions, writing of the judges: 'They were not all that satisfied with the efforts in the literary competitions. That is odd' (*II*, 6/11/39).[62]

In fact, while more ambitious than the festivals of the early 1930s, the Oireachtas of 1939 sponsored a rather disappointing range of literary competitions. There were nine in all: for 'a short story for boys' (gearr-scéal do bhuachaillí); for a 5,000 to 7,000 word essay 'on any contemporary subject' (ar aon ádhbhar nua-aimseardha); for 'a marching song' (amhrán máirseála); for 'a light-hearted song' (amhrán suairc); for 'a comic song on contemporary events' (amhrán grinn ar chúrsaí nua-aimsire); for a ballad of around 48 or 60 lines 'on some historical event that occurred in Ireland' (ar eachtra éigin staireamhail a thárla i nÉirinn); for poetry (iarracht filidheachta); for 'a short one-act play to be performed in 30 to 45 minutes' (gearr-dhráma aon-ghníomh – le léiriú i dtuairim 30 go 45 neomataí); and for 'a full-length play' (dráma ilghníomh). There were no competitions for novels, collections of short stories, biographies, or full-length works on literature, history, politics, science, etc.[63]

Nor were the entries for these contests all that impressive. There were only seven contenders for the short-story prize, none of whom was felt worthy of an award. Five competed for the essay prize, won by Pádraig Ó Fionnghusa. The ballad contest drew eight entries and was won by Peadar Ó hAnnracháin. The drama competitions, possibly because they offered the richest prizes, were more popular, with 23 vying in the one-act category eventually won by 'A. Ó S.', with the future Trinity Celtic scholar David Greene and his wife Síle taking second prize; while nine submitted full-length plays, with the award going to Seán Ó Conchubhair.[64]

In the final analysis, the Gaels do seem to have been satisfied with what the Oireachtas had accomplished. First of all, it had actually taken place, and that at a time of considerable tension and uncertainty throughout Europe and in Ireland itself. Second, it had proved that it could attract enough support – institutional, financial, and personal – to convince both fence sitters and outright sceptics of its future viability. Perhaps the most considered and just judgment on the achievement of the Oireachtas of 1939 was that offered by *The Leader*:

> The Oireachtas was, at the very least, a cheerful and heartening episode in a struggle which has in recent years been marked by the appearance of new difficulties and dangers which the pioneers of the language movement scarcely foresaw. It may well prove to have been more than an episode or than the first episode of a long national series and may come to be looked back upon as the first step in a new national forward move (*Leader*, 18/11/39).[65]

It was certainly in this light that one of those pioneers of the movement, Pádraig Ó Siochfhradha, saw the future of the revived Oireachtas a week before it actually opened:

> Our dream is to make the Oireachtas a national institution which will cater for the spread of Irish as a spoken tongue, and the development of our literary and musical heritage, including art and other aspects of Gaelic culture . . . With that idea in view it is intended to widen the scope of the Oireachtas next year and to include within its plan activities not covered by this year's programme (*II*, 24/10/39).

The future was to vindicate Ó Siochfhradha's optimism for the Oireachtas, as it quickly became, and has remained, one of the most important catalysts for literary experimentation and achievement in the Irish language.[66]

But even if this first revived Oireachtas did not itself inspire writers to memorable efforts, 1939 was neverthless a year of real promise for those interested in Gaelic literature, with two books in particular standing out, one at the time and one more in retrospect. The one that generated the most enthusiasm in 1939 was Liam Ó Rinn's memoir of his friendship with Stephen McKenna, a work that broke major new ground in its unassuming, matter-of-fact approach to the discussion of the most sophisticated, up-to-date, even arcane topics in a clear and elegant Irish prose style. Critics as one understood precisely what Ó Rinn had achieved in *Mo Chara Stiofán* and greeted the book with unequivocal excitement. León Ó Broin called it 'so outstanding a book in Irish – it must beyond all doubt be one of the six best works written in our time – that it would be nothing short of a national tragedy if it did not run into many editions quickly.' Ó Broin then went on to discuss Ó Rinn's triumph in more detail:

> Liam Ó Rinn has produced a first-rate book, a book that is so superbly good in every way that it will supply the subject of conversation in literary circles for a long

time. What is perhaps most admirable is the author's refusal to shirk difficulties: he discusses abstruse topics with a clarity, precision, a depth of expression, and variety of phrase that is quite rare in our literature. To be believed this book must be read (*Irish Monthly*, June 1939, 435).[67]

No less enthusiastic was Liam Ó Briain, who wrote:

It is the most important, the most stimulating book that has appeared in Irish for many years. For fresh, vigorous, thought-provoking literary and linguistic criticism of the whole field of modern Irish writing, no book like it has ever appeared in the language . . . Liam Ó Rinn has given us, not only an indispensable adjunct to the 'Journals of Stephen McKenna' but a *vade mecum* which should be in the hands of all aspirants to Gaelic authorship (*Dublin Magazine*, Oct.–Dec. 1939, 87–8).

In his review, 'R. Ó F.' focused on the literary lessons that could be learned from the book:

But the greatest source of benefit to be had from it is the opinions and counsels in it concerning the cultivation of the Irish language in general and about the composition of literature in particular. It is unlikely that there has yet been published in Irish a long, probing commentary on an author's problems that could be compared with it for wisdom and breadth of knowledge . . . This book will benefit the Irish language in many ways. I offer Liam Ó Rinn heartfelt praise for that and I thank him for the pleasure I got from reading the book (*II*, 25/4/39).[68]

For these and other reasons, the reviewer for *The Leader* pronounced Ó Rinn's work a major milestone in the literary revival:

It may prove to some extent to be caviare to the general public, but anyone who has tried to write Irish, even in the humblest way, will find it of absorbing interest. For the student or the native speaker who intends to write it will be absolutely indispensable as indeed it will also be for all University professors of Irish and all interested in Scholarship in relation to modern Irish. Whether the book has a wide circulation or only a small enthusiastic circulation we prophesy that it will have a great influence on Irish literature in the future (*Leader*, 8/4/39).[69]

I have quoted at length from these contemporary critics to underscore their shared conviction that *Mo Chara Stiofán* was the highest achievement to date of the intellectual and critical side of the revival, irrefutable proof of the depth, subtlety and sophistication of which the language was now capable in 1939 in the hands of a serious and erudite man of letters. This sense of how far the language and its literature had, at least on one occasion, come was in no way invalidated by the tragically premature death of Ó Rinn himself at the age of 56 in 1943, however devastating was the loss of what he might, and probably would, have contributed to the movement in the future.[70]

The year 1939 also saw the appearance of another book that in retrospect marked an even more important moment in the literary revival, the publication of Máirtín Ó Cadhain's first book, the story collection *Idir Shúgradh agus Dháiríre.* The native-speaking Conamara native Ó Cadhain could hardly have been more different from the Dublin learner Ó Rinn. Whereas the latter supported the Treaty and spent his entire professional life working with and for the language in the Free State bureaucracy, Ó Cadhain first came to public notice as a firebrand organiser for the pressure group Muinntear na Gaedhealtachta, as a collector of Conamara folklore, and as a member of the outlawed Irish Republican Army who was to spend most of the Second World War interned by the same de Valera government that paid Ó Rinn's salary. Yet for all their differences, the two men shared a profound belief in the capacity of the Irish language to serve as the medium for a literature every bit as modern and adventurous as any in the world. The seeds of Ó Cadhain's extraordinary future accomplishment as one of Ireland's finest twentieth-century writers in either Irish or English were not immediately obvious to all in his 1939 debut, and *Idir Shúgradh agus Dáiríre* attracted far less attention in and immediately after our period than did *Mo Chara Stiofán.*[71] Yet even before the book appeared, some were aware that a powerful new voice had arrived on the scene. For example, in the 1934–5 edition of the UCG publication *An t-Irisleabhar,* Micheál Ó Flaithfhile wrote: 'There is one man who wrote a few short stories and who has little to learn. He is a master of the craft of story-telling. I am speaking of Máirtín Ó Cadhain' (*Irisleabhar,* 1934–5, 43).[72]

As Europe and the world faced war and Ireland prepared for an understandable if uninspiring neutrality in its own 'Emergency' years, those involved in the Gaelic revival could feel a genuine sense of accomplishment and renewed confidence as our period drew to a close in 1939. The independent state regularly affirmed its commitment to an active policy of re-Gaelicisation, and its schools continued to produce a significant number of graduates reasonably competent in the language. To serve this growing readership, books of many if by no means all kinds were appearing from An Gúm in numbers that would have been difficult to conceive in 1922. Liam Ó Rinn had shown the linguistic command and originality of which a dedicated learner was capable, while Máirtín Ó Cadhain gave promise that a native-speaker with unparalleled mastery of his medium could have something new and challenging to say through it. Certainly Gaelic readers were right to look forward to important new work not only from Ó Rinn and Ó Cadhain, but from those who would be inspired and instructed by their example. Plays in Irish, both original and translated from several languages in addition to English, were being staged regularly and frequently in Dublin, where the Abbey was now preparing to perform in Irish as a central component of its mission as the national theatre. In Galway, a national Gaelic theatre, An Taibhdhearc, had been in successful operation for more than a decade. And there were even the first stirrings of an interest in Gaelic films.

More immediately encouraging was the recent success of the revived Oireachtas, a festival whose organisation involved a level of co-operation that many must have felt augured well for the end of the sterile factionalism and acrimony that had so handicapped the movement, and driven away so many real and potential allies, in the years following the Civil War. This sense of a new page being turned was perhaps best expressed by C. B. Mac Séamuis in a celebratory piece on the 1939 Oireachtas:

> No one was questioned about the colour of his old school tie. His credentials were not examined with regard to the games he played or the dances he did. The only recommendation that mattered for anyone was that he be in favour of the Irish language and everything connected with the Irish language. It is my prayer that it will continue like that and that the Oireachtas and the broad-mindedness that goes with it will not be thwarted. May the Oireachtas be a social body free and clear of narrow-mindedness. May it leave behind fault-finding and slander. May its doors remain wide open. May it be ready to welcome everyone who is willing to walk even a piece of the road with it (*II*, 17/11/39).[73]

Maybe under the warm influence of Oireachtas fellowship the odd Gaelic lamb could join his leonine counterpart for a walk down this Hibernian yellow-brick road, but could Séamus Ó Grianna and Liam Ó Rinn, or Micheál Ó Maoláin and León Ó Broin, take that stroll while enjoying a friendly difference of opinion about font or the Gaeltacht? Would a judge at the 1939 Oireachtas have had the confidence to award a prize to either Art Ó Riain's *Lucht Ceoil or* Seán Ó Ruadháin's *Pádhraic Mháire Bhán* instead of resorting to the spineless compromise of having two winners, as did the the actual judges of An Gúm's 1931 contest for a novel in Irish? And, far more important for the future of the revival and its literature, after all the venom and pettiness of the past two decades, how many of the plain people of Ireland outside the movement itself would still care?

Notes

Introduction

1 An tréimhse ina bhfuilimíd anois, ón mbliain 1921 go dtí 1950 nó 1960 béidir, áirmheófar í sa stair mar thréimhse ullmhúcháin is atharúcháin chó fada leis an nGaedhilg de. Leis an obair go léir atá ar siúl againn, mar scoileanna, san arm, sa Ghárda Síochána agus mar sin, ag múineadh is ag foghlaim, ag ceapadh téarmaí, ag aistriú achtanna is orduithe oifigiúla, leabhra teicniciúla is úrscéalta, nílimíd ach ag Gaelú na tíre is ag cur na teangan féin in oiriúint don tsaol a bheidh ag ár sliocht ar ball nuair ná beidh éinne ag déanamh iongnadh dhí ná ag cuimhneamh uirthi in aon chor toisc í bheith chó nádúrtha leis an aer.

2 In a piece on the upcoming 1924 Oireachtas (which would be the last held until 1939), Éamon Ó Donnchadha touched on the damage the Civil War had inflicted on the language movement: 'At this time the year before last a split occurred between the Gaels who held authority in this country. That split occurred and the people went astray. They became bewildered and confused. Hardship and poverty, grief and death came so that they cannot be blamed for their lack of interest in national affairs' (An taca so athrú 'n-uiridh d'éirigh scoilt idir an dream Gael a bhí i gceannas na dúthaighe seo. Do thárla an scoilt sin, gur baineadh an pobal dá dtreoir. Tháinig mearathal is tré chéile ortha. Tháinig an cruadhtan agus an bhochtaineacht, an brón agus an bás, i dtreo nach locht ortha a neamhshuimiúlacht i ndálaibh náisiúnta). He went on to hope that the language movement could provide the inspiration that would reunite all Irish nationalists around a common goal, a hope fairly widely shared at the time (*II*, 20/6/24). See, for example, 'Language Basis of Unity', *II*, 26/9/25. These issues are a central theme of Aindrias Ó Muimhneacháin's *Dóchas agus Duainéis* (Hope and trouble) (Corcaigh: Cló Mercier, n.d.).

3 See Maurice Manning, *The Blueshirts* (Toronto: University of Toronto Press, 1971).

4 See the comments of Éamon Ó Donnchadha in 'An t-Oireachtas Seo Againne' (Our Oireachas), *II*, 20/6/24.

5 Fásfaidh teanga náisiúnta le gach aos dár n-óige d'oiliúint tríd an nGaedhilg. Chuige sin ní fuláir litríocht Ghaedhilge do shaothrú a bheidh freagrach do gach easnamh saoghail a bheidh orainn ón óige anuas. Tiocfaidh an fás san go nádúrtha don teangain agus raghaidh borradh agus scóp di fé mar leathnófar í i gcúrsaí léighinn na hóige. Éireóchaidh lucht léighinn i ndiaidh a chéile chun litriocht oiriúnach do cheapadh innti d'aois a gcomhaimsire. See also the comments of Daniel Corkery, 'Stair Litríocht na Gaoluinne' (The history of literature in Irish), *FL*, 17/3/23. By 1929, even with An Gúm in operation, some still felt the demand for books in Irish was outstripping the supply. See, for example, 'Notable Works from English into Irish / Great Undertaking', *II*, 9/7/29. Six years later, the Head Librarian for County Dublin could complain that with the increasing demand for books in Irish, 'the supply is very inadequate' (*IT*, 19/9/35). See also 'An Leastar', 'Ó Chonndae Chorcaighe / Ganntanas Leabhar Gaedhilge / Gearán á Dhéanamh' (From County Cork / Shortage of books in Irish / Complaint being made), *II*, 7/6/39.

6 Teaspeánaid sin go léir, in aindeoin cannrán lucht suaibhreois, go bhfuil léigheamh agus scríobhadh na Gaedhilge ag dul chun cinn in aghaidh an lae. Is fíor, gan éan agó, ná fuil comórtas ar bith idir lucht foghlumtha an lae indiu agus na seanfhondúirí atá á chailleamhaint [*sic*] againn ón tseachtmhain go chéile, acht is mór an nidh an oiread san den bhfíor Ghaedhilg a bheith againn fé bhuanchló sár ar éag ár bprímh Ghaedhilgeoirí.

7 An síol a chuirtear san Earrach ní thig bláth air go dtige teas an tSamhraidh. Is é a dhálta sin ag litridheacht na Gaedhilge é. Támuid ag teacht comhgarach de Shamhradh na litridheachta do réir a chéile agus deagh-chomhartha ar an tséasúir sin é go bhfuil oiread de scríbhneoirí maith sa chuibhreann a bheir uchtach dúinn uilig go mbeidh foghmhar maith trom ann amach annso.

8 Eoin Mac Néill, quoted in 'Gaelic Literature / Rising Out of Academic Stage, Says Dr Mac Néill / Expressive of Modern Ireland', *Star*, 3/5/30. See also Peadar Ó Dubhda ('Cú Chulainn'), editorial note, *An t-Ultach*, Apr. 1930, 4.

9 Donn Piatt, *Stair na Gaedhilge* (The history of the Irish language) (Áth Cliath: Cló na Saoirse, [1933]), 4. Tá oiread brí sa teanga, tá oiread litridheacht innte, tá oiread uaisleacht innte go mbeidh sí as contabhairt an lá a bhéas an tSaoirse againn gan chontabhairt, an lá a n-imtheóchaidh an rud is Gallda in Éirinn córus sóisealda na nGall, córus chapatail.

10 For a more guarded view, see the comments of Micheál Breathnach in a paper read to the annual

convention of the Association of Secondary School Teachers in April 1931: 'The language was growing and spreading from year to year, and although some useful, creditable works had been written and published, there was room for more and better literature. The works recently published in Irish were limited in scope, and some of them were not of much literary value' (*Nationality*, 18/4/31). See also, 'W. L.', Cúrsaí Thomáis / Úirsgéal Gaedhilge' (Thomas's affairs / A novel in Irish), *II*, 26–27/12/27.

11 In December 1930, the Gaelic League passed a motion from Aindrias Ó Muimhneacháin urging An Gúm to reissue League publications that had gone out of print. See 'An Coisde Gnótha' (The executive committee), *FL*, Dec. 1930, 5.

12 Ba mhisneamhail an rud é 'An Gúm' do chur ar bun agus in aimhdheoin na gconnstaicí go léir a bhí sa tslighe air, níl dabht ar bith ná go bhfuil obair mhaith dá déanamh aige. Don chéad uair ó cuireadh Connradh na Gaedhilge ar bun táthar ag soláthar leabhar oireamhnach don choitchiantacht. Is mór an chéim chun cinn é sin agus do b'olc ó dhuine ar bith gan an chreideamhaint is dual do thabhairt dos na daoine go raibh sé de mhisneach agus d'fhís acu an gléas so do cheapadh. See also 'Matters of Moment / Ag Soláthar na Leabhar' (Supplying the books), Editorial, *II*, 5/12/31.

13 Pádraic Ó Conaire tried, and was rewarded with a hard life and a penniless death. See the bitter editorial note by Maoghnus Ó Domhnaill entitled 'Scríbhneoirí' (Writers) in *Fáinne an Lae*, 18/4/31. For another pessimistic view of the possibility of a literary career in Irish, see Seosamh Mac Grianna, 'Litridheacht Ghaedhilge / Ní Furas do Scríbhneoirí Bheith Beo' (Literature in Irish / It is not easy for writers to stay alive), *II*, 16/7/34.

14 Cad na thaoibh ná cabhruighean Gaedhil a bhfuil neart airgid aca le scríbhneoirí Gaedhilge na linne seo? Furmhór ár scríbhneoirí ní féidir leo costas clóbhualta leabhar d'íoc – agus níl aon tuarastal le fághail de bharr aistí nó scéalta a scríobh'. Bhíodh cáil mhór ar Éireannaigh sul ar deineadh measíní [*sic*] cló i n-aon chor mar gheall ar an méid leabhra do scríobhaidís. Acht bhíodh congnamh le fághail ag ughdaraibh an tseantsaoghail. . . . Atá daoine ann a mheasas go ndéanfaidh riaghlóirí na hÉireann gach nídh un litridheachta agus leabhra a chur ar fághail acht sin rud nach féidir leo a dhéanamh. Ní íocfaidh siad-san ar 'litríocht' a chur ar fághail. Three years later, León Ó Broin could argue that it was actually the writers who were failing the readers, rather than the other way around: 'There is no reason in the world that writers of Irish should be dejected and gloomy today. There exists a reading public for them – a public that will increase as the literature increases' (Níl aon réasún ar domhan le go mbeadh sgríobhnóirí na Gaedhilge fá dhubhrón is fá dhuairceas an lá atá indiu ann. Tá pobal léightheoireachta ann dóibh – pobal a mhéadóchas de réir mar mhéaduigheas an litridheacht) (*II*, 16/11/25). Ó Broin was, however, aware of the special circumstances of those who chose to write in Irish and of their need for financial support: 'Money must be allocated to writers. The best mettle in them will not be had until it is coaxed from them with money. Without that money, our writers will not do much. They have to live and for the majority of them living means hard work from dawn to dusk. If they spend time, energy, and intellect on the writing of Irish let them be well paid' (Caithfear airgead do chur i n-áirithe do sgríobhnóirí. Ní bhfaighfear an miotal is fearr ionnta go meallfar uatha é le h-airgead. Gan an t-airgead sin, ní mórán a dhéanfas ár sgríobhnóirí. Caithfid maireachtáil agus do'n fhurmhór aca cialluigheann maireachtáil obair chruaidh ó dhubh go dubh. Má chaithid am, fuinneamh agus inntleacht le sgríobhnóireacht Ghaedhilge íoctar go maith iad). In a 1928 editorial, Séamus Ó Grianna apologised to readers of *Fáinne an Lae* that there was not more and better work in the paper, adding: 'But we are reluctant to be constantly asking people to write when we don't have a penny to give them as wages' (Acht tá leisg orainn a bheith ag síor-iarraidh ar dhaoinibh sgríobhadh agus gan aon phighinn againn le tabhairt dobtha mar luach saothair) (*FL*, Jan. 1928, 4).

15 Ní leor leath-chéad nó céad leabhar do chur amach i naon bhliadhain amháin. Caidé an mhaitheas na leabhair seo d'fhoillsiú má fágtar gan ceannach gan léigheamh iad . . . caidé an tairbhe don náisiún a lán leabhar do chur i gcló má fhanann siad chomh fada san i seilbh na foillsightheoirí agus go ndéanfar dearmad glan díobh am éigin amach annso? Mag Ruaidhrí estimated the potential market for books in Irish at two to three thousand, and felt that if An Gúm had not created a thousand new readers, and buyers, of books in Irish, it had failed in its primary responsibility.

16 Muna dtabharaidís cuidiú do scríobhnóirí na nua-Ghaedhilge, bheadh sé fánach aca bheith ag súil le litridheacht mhóir. Rachadh sé i dtairbhe do na scríobhnóirí dá ndéantaí iad féin agus a saothar liteardha do mheas, mar 'ní bhíonn saoi gan locht'.

17 Caithfidh an fear atá i n-ann leabhar a sgríobh', caithfidh sé greim a fhághail le h-ithe cosamhail le duine ar bith eile. Ar an ádhbhar sin caithfidh sé dul 'na h-oifige agus an lá a chaitheamh annsin ar obair a bhfuil na céadtaí á déanamh agus a bhfuil na céadtaí i n-ann a déanta. He felt one solution would be for the state to subsidise three or four of the finest Gaelic writers so that they would not have to earn a living except by their pens. He then continued: 'If three or four of those were free, every one of them could conceive and write two books a year' (Dá mbíodh cead na coise le triúr nó ceathrar aca sin thiocfadh le gach duine aca dhá leabhar a chumadh agus a sgríobh' sa' bhliadhain).

18 His remarks provoked the following outraged comment from 'A Viewer' in the *Catholic Bulletin*: 'It is well to have this official declaration – after fourteen years' costly experience – for the information of authors, translators, and overburdened taxpayers, who have been deceived into thinking that publishers have been making fortunes out of Gaelic publications' (*CB*, Mar. 1936, 210). Commenting on Ó Deirg's address, Daniel Corkery observed: 'Writing books to that tune can only be an act of self-sacrifice and not a means of livelihood, unless the writer submits himself to the limitations imposed by "an Gúm".' Corkery was here being quoted by William John McCausland, in '"Readers – not Writers – Are Lacking:" Literature, Irish and Anglo-Irish Reviewed', the *Irish People*, 29/2/36.

19 He published the same story again under a different title in *Fianna: The Voice of Young Ireland*, Feb. 1936, 60.

20 'Barra Ó Caochlaigh', Letter to Coiste an Oireachtais, 30 Sept. 1924, NLI MS 11,501. The request was refused due to lack of funds. The stories in question were among those published by An Gúm as *An Tost agus Scéalta Eile* (The silence and other stories) in 1927.

21 Is dearbh ná tiocfaidh aon fhás fé litríocht na Gaedhilge go dtí go mbeidh caoi níos fearr ag na scríbhneoirí ar thora a machtnaimh is a saothair do thabhairt amach fé sholus an lae. Ní foláir nó tá mórán scríbhte ag cuid mhaith aca agus go dtabharfaidís dúinn é mara mbeadh a chostaisí atá an chlódóireacht agus a chumhainge atá marga na leabhar Gaedhilge.

22 Is léar dúinn má mhaireann an Ghaedhilg go ndéanfar an chuid is mó den obair le leabhra. Ní sgríobhann aoinne leabhar maith gan spreagadh éicint a fháil. Caithfidh aghaidh an phobail a bheith air, caithfidh sé moladh nó cliú d'fháil, ach rud níos mó ná sin, caithfidh sé duais nó luach saothair a fháil. Sé airgead na leabhar an íocaidheacht a fhaghas sé agus dá mhéid an díol a bhíos ar leabhra seadh is fearr dó é. In a 1926 review of Pádhraic Ó Domhnalláin's *Ar Lorg an Ríogh* (In search of the king), 'A. Ó D.' wrote of his fellow Irish speakers: 'They should understand that it is their duty, not only to speak the language, but also to buy the Irish-language books and papers regularly and to read them . . . If there is good demand for the books in Irish, that will inspire the writers and encourage them to continue with the cultivation of the new literature' (Ba cheart dóibh a thuisgint go bhfuil sé de dhualgas ortha, ní h-amháin an teanga a labhairt, ach na theannta san na leabhair agus na páipéirí Gaedhilge do cheannach go féilteamhail agus iad do léigheamh . . . Má bhíonn glaodhach maith ar na leabhraibh Gaedhilge, déanfaidh sé sin na sgríobhnóirí do spreagadh agus do mheanmnú chun dul chun cinn le saothrú na nualitridheachta) (*IMN*, 1926, 85).

23 See, for example, 'Oireachtas, 1923 / Na Comórtaisí Liteardha' (Oireachtas 1923 / The literary competitions), *FL*, 20/1/23; 'Comórtais Liteardha' (Literary competitions), *FL*, 13/10/23; 'Oireachtas, 1925 / Clár na gComórtaisí Liteardha' (Oireachtas, 1925 / List of the literary competitions), *FL*, 1/11/24. One can get a good sense of the financial problems of the Oireachtas in the early years of the Free State in the minutes of the Gaelic League's Coiste an Oireachtais (Oireachtas committee), NLI MS 11,501. As late as 1929, Liam S. Gógan was petitioning the Gaelic League for the prizes he had won at the final, 1924 Oireachtas. He was told that the prizes could not be given since the Oireachtas of 1924 had lost £600. See also Donncha Ó Súilleabháin, *Scéal an Oireachtais, 1897–1924* (The story of the Oireachtas) (BÁC: An Clóchomhar, 1984), 41–57.

24 See the programmes: *Connradh na Gaedhilge / Seachtmhain na Samhna (Samhain 2-7adh) / Clár na gComórtas a bhéas ar siubhal i dTigh an Ard-Mhaoir, Áth Cliath fé choimirce Choiste Gnótha Chonnradh na Gaedhilge* (The Gaelic League / November week {2–7, November} / List of the competitions that will take place in the Mansion House, Dublin, under the auspices of the executive committee of the Gaelic League); *Connradh na Gaedhilge / Seachtmhain na Samhna, 1931 / Comórtaisí Amhránuidheachta, Ceoil, Rinnce agus Drámaidheachta* (The Gaelic League / November week, 1931 / Competitions in singing, music, dancing, and drama); and *An tOireachtas, 1932 / Clár na gComórtas a bhéas ar siubhal i dTigh an Ard-Mhaoir, Áth Cliath fé choimirce Choiste Gnótha Chonnradh na Gaedhilge.* Neither of these events is considered an Oireachtas in the official history of the Gaelic League, Proinsias Mac Aonghusa's *Ar Son na Gaeilge: Conradh na Gaeilge 1893–1993: Stair Seanchais* (For the Irish language: The Gaelic League 1893–1993: A history (BÁC: Conradh na Gaeilge, 1993). We shall return to this subject in chapter nine.

25 See the programmes, *Aonach Tailteann 1924: Revival of the Ancient Tailteann Games / Dublin 2nd–18th August* (BÁC: Aonach Tailteann, [1924]); *Leabhar Tailteann (Aonach Tailteann 1928/ Souvenir Program* (BÁC: Ard-Chomhairle Aonach Tailteann [1928]); and *Tailteann Games June 29–July 10, 1932 / Daily Programme / Tuesday, July 5th.* The winners of the 1928 and 1932 prizes are listed in these programmes. For the winners of the 1924 awards, see 'Irish Literary Awards / Tailteann Competitions', *II*, 16/10/24.

26 The competitors in this competition are listed in Mac Niocláis, *Seán Ó Ruadháin*, 186–7.

27 See 'An Roinn Oideachais / Fógra do Sgríbhneoirí Gaedhilge / Sgéim Gearr-Sgéal' (Department of education / Announcement to writers / A scheme for short-stories), *Gaedheal*, 4/8/34. Actually, this was not really a competition as such. Rather, An Gúm was offering to pay from £5 to £10 for every story of between 2,000 and 5,000 words it accepted for

publication. And for once, quality, not quantity, would be given precedence: 'But it is according to the quality and value of the story itself as literature and not according to the length of the story that payment will be measured' (Ach ní do réir faid an sgéil a tomhaisfear an íocaidheacht ach do réir feabhais agus fiúntais an sgéil féin mar litridheacht).

28 See 'Toradh na gComórtaisí Liteardha' (The result of the literary competitions), *Gaedheal*, 15/12/34. In what must have been a helpful innovation for the writers, the judges offered a one paragraph review of all entries.

29 See 'Prize Scheme Welcomed / Noted Gaelic Authors and Encouragement of Original Writing', *IP*, 6/1/37; 'Na Printíseacha', 'Litir Aniar' (A letter from the west), *Éireannach*, 6/2/37. The competition drew 13 entries. See 'Thirteen Original Gaelic Novels', *IP*, 7/1/38. The winning novel was *Ceol na nGiolcach* (The music of the reeds) by Pádhraic Óg Ó Conaire.

30 See 'Gradam do'n "Chraoibhín" / Duaiseanna d'Ughdaraibh / Saothair Nua-Cheaptha' (An honour for 'An Craoibhín' / Prizes for authors / Original works), *IP*, 15/12/36; 'Awards for Literature / Meeting of Academy of Letters: Tribute to Dr Hyde', *IP*, 27/5/37; 'An Leabhar a Bhuaidh Duais an Chraoibhín' (The book that won Duais an Chraoibhín), *IP*, 18/11/38; and '"Duais an Chraoibhín" / Connachtach do Ghnóthuigh' (A Connachtman won), *IP*, 21/8/39. In the Máirín Ní Mhuiríosa Papers (NLI MS 26, 784) is a typewritten list of the winners to 1940.

31 Is fíor – agus 'sé ár léan é – nach bhfuil luach saothair maith do sgríbhneoirí Gaedhilge. Maille le hairgead ní féidir an Ghaedhilg agus an Béarla a chur i gcomórtas le n-a chéile. Tá milliún Béarlóir ann in aghaidh gach aon cúig céad Gaedhilgeoir. Ná bíodh ár súil le hairgead . . . An obair mhór atá roimh na sgríbhneoirí, ní spreachaidh an t-airgead chuige iad. Muna spreachaidh an grádh tíre chuige iad, agus muna mbrostuighe an chaoi a bhfuil Éire chuige iad beidh ár súil le Gaedhilg mar a bhí súil Uí Dhubhda le hArd na Ríogh.

32 I ndiaidh ar dtearnadh le cúig bliadhna déag ar fhichid chum ár dteanga do theagasc do mhuinntir na tíre seo, tá sé le rádh gur theip glan orainn go dtí seo léightheoirí Gaedhilge do dhéanamh den chuid is mó de na daoine a d'fhoghlaim an Ghaedhilg. Colm Ó Murchú ('Taube') had made this point in 1920. See 'Taube', 'Comhacht an Leabhair / An "Fáinne" agus Gaedhilg Bhriste / Leigheas an Sgéil' (The power of the book / The 'Fáinne' and broken Irish / The remedy for the matter), *IF*, Aug. 1920, 12. Donnchadh Ó Frighil wrote in *An Tír* in 1930: 'We have failed altogether for the past thirty years to make the learners of the language into readers of Irish' (Theip glan orainn léightheoirí Gaedhilge a dhéanamh de lucht foghlama na teangtha le deich mbliadhna fichead anall) (*Tír*, Oct.–Nov. 1930, 5).

33 Ceann de na rudaí is mó a chuireas éadóchas orainn i nÉirinn indiu iseadh an dóigh a ndéantar failligthe i léightheoireacht na Gaedhilge . . . An té a d'fhág an Ghaedhealtacht, nó a chomhnuigheas ann go fóill, ní duine é, de ghnáth, a cheannóchadh agus a léighfeadh leabhra Gaedhilge. An té a d'fhoghlaim an Ghaedhilg, agus nach bhfuair an teagasc a chuirfeadh go cíocrach sanntach é ar lorg tuilleadh eolais as a stuaim féin, ní féidir é d'áireamh mar léightheoir Gaedhilge. In a letter to *FL* in 1923, Donn Piatt was critical of the libraries for not showing more interest in Gaelic books (*FL*, 8/9/23). That this was an important point is made clear by the comments of the Gaelic editor of *II*, who, in a piece on 'Leabhair agus Leabharlanna' (Books and libraries) stressed the importance of library sales for Gaelic authors, since readers were unlikely to buy many books in Irish, given that such books were often uninteresting and poorly produced (*II*, 28/8/26).

34 Níl an Ghaedhilg acht ag sciorta beag díobh sin, agus tá teanga eile, an Beurla, aca go léir. An sciorta beag a bhfuil an Ghaedhilg aca, níl acht fíor-bheagán díobh a n-iúl ar í léigheamh acht ar éigean. Rud eile, tá blas an Bheurla agus blas litridheachta an Bheurla imthighthte go smior i ngach aon dream sa tír agus ní bhfuighidís blas ar aon litridheacht eile acht í faoi láthair. Idir so, súd agus súd eile, ná bíodh aon iongna ar aoinne má fhágtar pé leabhar Gaedhilge foillseóchar go fóill beag – agus ní h-eadh acht go fóill fada – má fhágtar gan ceannach iad. Ar aon tslighe, ná bíodh aoinne ag coinne le scannradh cíochrais ar dhaoine chúcha. On a more cynical note, Ó Ciarghusa had written the previous year that a significant percentage of what small Gaelic readership there was would fall away 'if they weren't afraid that it [Irish] will survive as a living language and that one will not be able to get a job without it' (muna mbeadh eagla ortha go mairfidh sí [an Ghaeilge] i n-a teangain bheo agus ná beidh post oibre le fághail ag duine i n-a h-eughmais) (*Leader*, 26/9/31).

35 Writing in *The Father Mathew Record* the previous year, an anonymous contributor was optimistic, declaring: 'We have had a wonderful growth of the literature and there must be a great increase in the number of readers' (Tá fás iongantach ar an leitridheacht aguinn agus ní foláir go bhfuil méadú mór ar líon ár n-aos léighimh) (*Father Mathew Record*, Feb. 1936, 75). Indeed in 1929, a contributor in *II* claimed that 'the demand for Irish literature is far ahead of its supply'. Recalling a visit to the library of a secondary school where he noticed the well-stocked shelves of books in English and the single shelf of works in Irish, he reports the explanation of the school's headmaster: 'The students want ever so much reading matter in Irish . . . but we cannot give it to them for it is not to be got' (*II*, 9/7/29). On the other hand, addressing fellow librarians in a 1930 essay, Séamus Mac Gamhna bluntly questioned

whether libraries should be expected to stock books in Irish no one ever read. See Mac Gamhna, 'Leabhra Gaedhilge ins na Leabharlannaibh Puibhlidhe' (Books in Irish in the public libraries), *An Leabharlann*, Dec. 1930, 69. Riobárd Ó Faracháin saw different problems and challenges, some of them rooted in the quality of the new crop of books: 'I have not attempted any appraisal of the original books; many of them, of course, would have no chance of reaching print if they were written in English; but there is the necessity of encouraging writers who may improve' (*CA*, 1935, 177–8).

36 He added: 'Even those who do read Irish books don't seem to me to do more than skim them'.

37 Liam Ó Rinn, *Mo Chara Stiofán* (BÁC: Oifig an tSoláthair, 1939), 174–5. Mar sin bíonn gá ag scríbhneoirí cearta le léitheoirí cearta . . . Ach rud nua, dar liom, cuid mhór d'obair athdhéanta litríocht na Gaeilge a chur ar an léitheoir – a thaispeáint gur comhoibritheoir don scríbhneoir an léitheoir agus oiread gá leis is atá leis an scríbhneoir chun an litríocht san a dhealbhadh nach féidir leis an teanga maireachtaint dá héagmas. In a 1929 piece in *The Star*, Ó Rinn stated that the Irish people in general were not readers (*Star*, 17/8/29). See also 'Fear Faire' (Ó Rinn), 'Leabhra Gaedhilge do sna Daoine Óga' (Books in Irish for the young), *UIman*, 28/5/32. Ó Broin agreed with this point in a 1935 essay in *The Capuchin Annual*. See Ó Broin, 'Contemporary Gaelic Literature', *CA*, 1935, 122. (But see also his 1925 piece on 'Leabhra agus Lucht Léighte' (Books and readers) in *II*, in which he argued that the readers were out there, but were for the most part reading English because books in Irish were poorly publicised and often shoddily produced (*II*, 16/11/25). 'A. de B.' (Aodh de Blácam) felt that Gaelic readers were, in general, more educated and discerning than the average reader of English. See 'A. de B.', 'Pádraig Ó Conaire: Is He a European Master?' the *Irish Tribune*, 6/9/26. For various laments about the lack of a Gaelic readership, see 'Beatha Barra, 7c.', *IR*, January, 1923, 74; Peadar Ó Dubhda, Editorial Note, *An t-Ultach*, Aug. 1929, 1; ''Na Gunnaí Móra' / Daltaí an Choláiste Ghaillmhigh de'n Ollscoil / Ag Soláthar Scríobhnóirí' ('The big guns' / The students of University College Galway / Providing writers), *IP*, 21/11/33; 'Sarsfield' (P. S. O'Hegarty), 'What's Wrong with Irish-Ireland?' *Leader*, 18/7/36; and 'An nDíolaid Asta Féin?' (Do they pay for themselves?), *IP*, 13/5/37. In a letter to the editor of *An Tír*, Liam Ó Raghallaigh blasted the complainers, saying the readers would be there if there were anything worth reading (*Tír*, Aug. 1930, 11). In a review of T. F. O'Rahilly's edition of *Dánta Grádha* (Love poems) in *Studies*, the Jesuit Micheál Mac Craith wrote of an odd opinion held by some in the language movement: 'You would think they were of the opinion that reading harms speech in some obscure, mysterious, incomprehensible way. Urging the likes of them to read any Irish, however excellent, is like talking to a rock' (Is é is dóigh leo, dar leat, go ngoilleann an léigheamh ar an gcaint, ar chuma dhoiléir, dhiamhair, dho-thuigse éigin. Comhrádh le cairrig is eadh bheith ag tafaint ar a leithéidí aon Ghaedhilg, dá fheabhas, do léigheamh) (*Studies*, Sept. 1926, 502).

38 Is beag duine aca atá i dtaithighe leabhar Gaedhilge. Ar an ádhbhar san is saothar dochamhlach leo ceann aca do léigheamh. Is ar éigin atá céad duine in Éirinn go bhfuil sé 'na gcumas píosa Gaedhilge do léigheamh chomh tapaidh agus a léighfidís píosa Béarla. Ní fhéadfadh an scéal bheith ar a mhalairt de chuma. Níl páipéir Ghaedhilge ann ach roinnt mhíosachán beag agus níl puinn leabhar ar fáil. Is amhlaidh atá na daoine ag tabhairt failligh e ins an beagán [*sic*] leabhar Gaedhilge atá ann toisg go bhfágann a ghanna-chúise agus táid gach aoinne gan taithighe aige ar a leithéidí do léigheamh. In an essay in *An Stoc* shortly before the creation of An Gúm, 'Tadhg' argued that the problem was that there wasn't much in Irish worth reading: 'Writers of books in Irish complain that some of the new booklets and books are not bought, because they have neither shape nor form, but are insignificant and slipshod' (Bíonn casaoid ag lucht sgríobhtha leabhar Gaedhilge a rádh nach gceannuighthear cuid de na leabhráin agus de na leabhra nua, mar nach mbíonn cuma ná caoi ortha, ach iad gan bhrígh, gan chruinneas) (*Stoc*, Oct.–Nov. 1925, 1). Yet in the very same month, León Ó Broin questioned such a view, seeing it as fodder for 'enemies of the language' (naimhde na teangan): 'We have a certain amount of modern literature, but I would put the blame for the lack of readers on the bad habit we have given to the Irish language public. We always put too many obstacles in front of them. A book was written, it was put on the market badly finished, and it was then forgotten' (Tá a bheag nó a mhór de nua-litridheacht againn, ach chuirfinn locht an easbaidh léightheoirí ar an droch-nós atá tugtha againn do'n phobal Gaedhilge. Chuireamar i gcomhnuí an-iomarca connstaicí rompa. Sgríobhadh leabhar, cuireadh ar an margadh go mí-shlachtmhar é agus rinneadh dearmad annsin air). For Ó Broin, the problem of a Gaelic readership would solve itself over time: 'I do not agree with those who say that the public must precede the writer. That is an unnatural opinion. What is wanted is to educate the public in reading Irish and to give the writer full freedom of mind, soul, and style' (Ní réidhtighím leo seo a deir go gcaithfidh an pobal do theacht roimh an sgríobhnóir. Tuairim mí-nádúrtha an tuairim sin. Is éard a theastuigheas: an pobal d'oiliúnt chun léightheoireachta Gaedhilge agus lán tsaoirse aigne, anama is nós sgríobhtha a bhronnadh ar an sgríobhnóir). To which he added: 'At first it would also be necessary to pamper him' (I dtús báire theastóchadh, freisin, 'peataireacht' do dhéanamh air) (*II*, 16/11/25).

39 Dá mhéid chainnt a deirtear, ámhthach, 'sé mo thuarm go bhféadfaimíd go léir teacht ar aon fhocal i dtaobh na litridheachta. I gcúrsaí na Gaoluinne, ní'l aon cheist is tábhachtaighe ná is mó le rádh ná í. Má bheidh an litridheacht go maith ní baoghal do'n teangan agus ní baoghal do'n náisiúin. Rachaidh siad ar aghaidh uatha féin agus is feáirrde agus is glainede a labharfar an Ghaedhilg freisin. He continued: 'We are then resolved that literature will be our prime concern from now on, and we would all like to advance that question in the way we believe would best benefit the nation' (Táimíd socair air annsin gurbh'í an litridheacht a bhéas mar phríomh-chúram orrainn feasta, agus ba mhaith linn go léir an cheist sin do chur ar aghaidh ar an gcuma a chreidimíd is fearr a rachaidh i dtairbhe do'n náisiúin).

40 Tuigeadh cách gur fánach an obair teanga na nGaedheal do aithbheodhadh mar urlabhra bocht iargcúlta gan léigheann gan litridheacht. Mura bhfuilmíd chum litridheacht bhreágh mhaordha do chumadh 'sa nua-Ghaedhilg, bfhearr i bhfad dúinn cur suas do'n ghnó agus an Béarla do ghlacadh chugainn agus a bhfuil de shaidhbhreas intleachta le fághail ann.

41 He wanted Gaels 'gach intleacht oilte atá ag éirghe chughainn do bhréagadh chun scríobhnóireachta i nGaoluinn, agus léightheoireacht nodh agus scéaluíocht nodh do chur innte gur bhfiú le lucht léighte na Gaoluinne iompáil ón mBeurla chúcha agus go leanfaidís dá léigheadh ó aois a scoluíochta amach.

42 Deirtear go mbadh iad saighdiúirí na Gaedhilge na múinteoirí. Má seadh, siad na taoisigh, na sgríbhneoirí. Má thogruigheann na sgríbhneoirí treoir a dhéanamh do chlanna Gaedheal leanfa lucht na Gaedhilge iad. Má thugann na sgríbhneoirí aire dá ngnó agus má thugann siad treoir agus léargus agus pléisiúr dá lucht léighte mar thugas sgríbhneoirí gach teangan do lucht a léighte, ní hí an Ghaedhilg a rachas ar ceal. Má's maith leis na sgríbhneoirí Gaedhilge é tiocfa sí in uachtar in Éirinn. An lá a thiocfas sí in uachtar arís beidh deireadh le galldachas agus le Gaill in Éirinn. In another editorial the previous month, Ó Máille wrote: 'It is the writers who sustain the Irish language and who give guidance to the people, and it is not possible to go forward without them' (Siad na sgríbhneoirí a chothuigheas an Ghaedhilg agus a thugas treoir don phobul agus ní féidir dhul chun cinn gan iad) (*Stoc*, Feb. 1926, 1). See also 'Tadhg Ó Cianáin' (Liam Ó Rinn), 'Revival of Irish', *YI*, 17/6/22.

43 Ní mhairfidh teanga ar bith gan litridheacht ar a cúl. Tá litridheacht ag fás i nGaedhilg do réir a chéile. An nua-litridheacht so againne níl sí ach mar bheadh páiste ann go fóill. Fásfaidh sí do réir a chéile mar fhásas gach ní beo agus rachaidh i bhfeabhas le cleachtadh.

44 An easbaidh litríochta so fé ndeara do dhaoine gan aon tora do thabhairt ar an nGaedhilg; 'sí fé ndeara an leisce, agus an mhí-dhúthracht, agus an fuar-chrábhadh atá imthighthe i bfeidhm ar dhaoine. Dá mbeimís agus litríocht mhór thábhachtach dhá saothrú againn, ba scannradh leat an deithneas a bheadh ar Bhéarlóirí na tíre an Ghaedhilg do chur chúca féin láithreach!

45 Ní mhairfidh an Ghaedhilg mura mbí litridheacht mhór innte agus sin taobh istigh de fiche bliadhain. Ó Duibhir was here echoing the dire warning of Eoin Ó Searcaigh in 1924: 'A language in which there is not the salt of literature will not have a long life' (Teanga ar bith nach bhfuil salann na litridheachta innti ní bheidh saoghal fada aici). As we will see, Séamus Ó Grianna was one leading Gael who felt too much emphasis was being placed on literature too early. Peadar Mac Fhionnlaoich also warned his colleagues in An Fáinne, a group whose members had pledged to speak only Irish to each other and to others who knew the language, that they should not allow their interest in literature to make them lose sight of their main goal of advancing the spoken language. See Mac Fhionnlaoich, 'Buadha an Fháinne i mBaile Átha Cliath' (The successes of An Fáinne in Dublin), *IF*, Aug. 1922, 4–5; and 'An tAodhaire', 'An Fáinne / Obair Ghasra Átha Cliath' (An Fáinne: The work of the Dublin branch), *ACS*, 31/10/31.

46 Ach pé adeirfidhe mar gheall ar an sgeul, má tá Gaedhilg nádúrtha na ndaoine uait ceannuigh an leabhar so.

47 D'fhéadfí bheith dian go leor ar an leabhar so meireach feabhas na Gaedhilge ann – maithfear go leor dó thar a chionn san. For further examples of this attitude, see 'Déaglán', 'Leabhar Nua' (A new book), *FL*, 11/11/22; Tomás Ó hAodha, Review of *Solus an Ghrádha* (The light of love) by Pádhraic Óg Ó Conaire, *FL*, 20/10/23; 'C.', 'Leabhra Nua' (New books), *FL*, 15/12/23; and Peadar Mac Fionnlaoich ('Cú Uladh'), 'Leabhra Nua', *FL*, 18/7/25.

48 Ar an ádhbhar san is gnáthach linn go minic bheith sásta le leabhartha agus gan de chúis againn le go mbeimís sásta leo ach go bhfuil a bheag nó a mhór de dheagh-Ghaedhilg ionnta – leabhartha ná cuirfí cló ortha go deo dá mba in aon teangan eile a sgríobhfí iad.

49 Níor chóir go mbeadh sé riachtanach, nuair a bheidhfí a' déanamh léirmheasa ar leabhar, trácht ar an chineál Gaedhilge atá innti. Acht as siocair go bhfuil Gaedhilg agus Gaedhilg ann, caithfidh duine amharc ar an taoibh sin den sgéal. In fact, in a 1927 letter to Muiris Ó Droighneáin, who was then gathering information for his *Taighde i gComhair Stair Litridheachta na Nua-Ghaedhilge ó 1882 Anuas* (Research for a history of literature in modern Irish from 1882 on), Ó Grianna stated that he wrote his novel *Mo Dhá Róisín* (My two Róisins) as the result of his belief 'that it is high time for us to make an attempt to write stories that would be read for the stories and not to be always thinking about grammar,

idiomatic expressions, and poems with nothing in them but sounds' (gur mithid dúinn iarraidh a thabhairt sgéaltaí a sgríobhadh a léighfidhe mar mhaithe le sgéaltaí agus gan a bheith "choidhche" smaoitiughadh ar ghramadach, ar cora cainnte agus ar dhántaí nach rabh ionnta acht fuaimeanna). See *Féile Rann na Feirste 17ú–19ú Samhain 1989 / Séamus Ó Grianna ('Máire') Comóradh Céad Bliain* (The Rannafast festival, 17–19 November 1989 / Séamus Ó Grianna ('Máire') centenary commemoration), the program for a series of event honoring the hundredth anniversary of Ó Grianna's birth. Whatever the private beliefs that motivated his fiction, as a critic and as one of Ireland's most scathing satirists of the twentieth century, he saw literature – and just about everything else – as entirely secondary to a native command of the spoken language, as is evident in a 1931 essay in *Iris an Fháinne*: 'There is no value at all in the [technical] terms or in the schools or in the books or in the literature (if we had the like), except in their own place. And what place do they have? The place the top bit of thatch has on a house' (Níl maith ar bith ins na téarmaí nó ins na sgoltacha nó ins na leabharthaí, nó ins an litridheacht {dá mbeadh a leithéid againn} níl maith ar bith ionnta, acht i n-a n-áit féin. Agus goidé an áit atá aca? Tá, an áit a bhíos ag dlaoidh mhullaigh ar theach) (*IF*, Apr. 1931, 1).

50 See also 'Pádraig', 'Reviews of Current Literature / Onncail Seárlaí', *Star*, Oct. 1930, 43; and Liam Ó Rinn, 'Saothrú na Gaedhilge / Cé'ca Is Usa a Dhéanamh' (The cultivation of Irish / Which is easier to do?), *UI*, 21/4/34.

51 Go dtí seo is fíor-annamh a gheibhmís úr-sgéal i nGaedhilg gur fiú úr-sgéal thabhairt air chor ar bith. Ar a laghad de, caithfear a admháil go bhfuil beagán den leanbhacht ag baint le cuid acu. Ní léighfidhe iad fá choinne an sgéal a bhí ionnta, acht amháin fá choinne an Ghaedhilg a fhoghluim asta. Ba chuma le furmhór na ndaoine go dtí seo caidé bhíodh i leabhar dá mbeadh an fhíor-Ghaedhilg bhinn bhlasta ann . . . Ba cheart dos na sgríbhneoirí cuimhneamh air sin, agus leabharthaí a sgríobhadh ní amháin fá choinne lucht foghlumtha na Gaedhilge acht fá choinne lucht a léighte, mar adeirfá, fosta.

52 Tá laige bhunúsach ag baint le mór-chuid de'n litríocht a cumadh i nGaedhilg ó thosnuigh an aithbheochaint. Níor scríobhadh an litríocht san d'éan ghnó chun smaointe a bhí ag borradh is ag brúchtghaíl i gcroidhthibh na n-ughdar. Is amhlaidh a bhí na h-ughdair ag scríobhadh ar son na teangan féin, d'fhonn í a chleachtadh agus a chraobhscaoile. Bhí daoine ag scríobhadh gur beag a bhí le rádh aca, ach amháin go raibh d'ádh an tsaoghail ortha bheith 'na nGaedhilgeoirí.

53 I dtosach báire ba bheag duine taobh amuigh de'n Ghaedhealtacht a bhí ábalta an Ghaedhilg a léigheamh nó a thuigbheáil. Na daoine 'sa Ghalltacht a léigheadh Gaedhealg, mic léighinn a bhí ionnta nó daoine a bhí suim mór acu i gcúis na teangadh. Bhí na daoine seo dúthrachtach agus bhí siad réidh rud ar bith a dhéanamh mar mhaithe do'n Ghaedhilg nó mar mhaithe d'á n-eolas féin ar an teangaidh. Dá bhfeicfeadh siad rud ar bith i nGaedhilg léighfeadh siad é le feabhas a chur ar a gcuid Gaedhilge agus bheadh siad sásta leis . . . Ach nuair a bhí siad ag sgríobhadh na Gaedhilge bhí mórán acu agus ba cuma leo an rabh sgéal le h-innse acu nó nach bhfuil [*sic*]. Sgríobh siad i nGaedhilg agus sgríobh siad gan sgéal, gan ádhbhar. Bhí siad sásta fhad a bhí Gaedhealg mhaith ann. He added that those writers who continued to churn out work that no one would read if they wrote in English were doing great harm (*dochar mór*) to the language. He developed these ideas in much more optimistic fashion two years later: 'There is literature to be found in Irish, although there is not much writing being written in it that would suit the people of this century. The writers are not to blame for that; the people are. I am not saying that the new books in Irish are better than or as good as the books being published in French or in English, but they are ten times better than the foolishness the writers of English in this country offer as modern literature' (Tá litridheacht le fághail 'sa Ghaedhilg cé nach bhfuil mórán de'n sgríbhneoireacht a d'fhóireadh do mhuinntir na h-aoise seo dá sgríobhadh innti. Ní ar na sgríobhnoirí atá an locht sin ach ar na daoine. Ní abraim go bhfuil leabharthaí nua na Gaedhilge níos fearr nó comh maith leis na leabharthaí atá d'á gcur amach 'san Fhrainncis nó 'sa Bhéarla ach tá siad deich n-uaire níos fearr 'ná an amaidigh atá mar nua-litridheacht ag lucht sgríobhtha an Bhéarla 'sa tír seo) (*Derry People*, 25/2/39).

54 See, for example, P. J. Devlin, 'Pádraic Ó Conaire: As I Knew Him', *An Ráitheachán* (The quarterly), Sept. 1936, 27–30. Ó Conaire placed much of the blame for the sorry state of Gaelic letters on an abdication of responsibility by the Gaelic League. See, for example, 'Scríobhnoirí agus a gCuid Oibre: An Easba Misnigh Atá Orra?' (Writers and their work: Is it lack of courage that is afflicting them?), *Old Ireland*, 28/2/20. He was by no means alone in the opinion that the League was not doing all it could to advance the cause of a native literature. See, for example, the 1931 *ACS* editorial by Maoghnus Ó Domhnaill in which he wrote: 'In cultural affairs, great work is being done by the people of the League for Gaelic music and Gaelic dances' (I gcursaí cultúra is mór an obair atá á déanamh ag lucht an Chonnartha mar mhaithe leis an gceol Gaedhealach is na rinncí Gaedhealacha) (*ACS*, 19/9/31). Literature is conspicuously absent from this list.

55 Ins an Bhéarla tá litridheacht agus leabharthaí scoile, agus ní mheasgtar an dá chuid le chéile. Tá 'Hamlet' ag lucht na litridheachta, agus tá 'Ned put his leg in the tub' ag na páistí. Ba chóir go mbeadh an rud céadna i nGaedhilic agus go n-aithneóchaidhe an

difear atá eadar an rud a scríobh an t-Athair Peadar 's daoine mar é, agus litridheacht na bhfear mór a tháinig romhainn. Immediately preceding these words Ó Grianna dismissed the artistic importance of his own work, writing: 'If Irish progresses, literature will be written in it yet. And then the speech of people like myself and Father Peter who wrote books for schools will be superceded (Má thig an Ghaedhilic ar aghaidh sgríobhfar litridheacht innti go fóill. Agus annsin scadfar a chainnt ar dhaoiní mar mé féin agus an t-Athair Peadar a scríobh leabharthaí fá choinne sgoltach).

56 Ó Conaire, 'Scríobhnoirí agus a gCuid Oibre', in *Aistí Phádraic Uí Chonaire* (The essays of Pádraic Ó Conaire), ed. Gearóid Denvir (Indreabhán: Cló Chois Fharraige, 1978), 165. Do'n aos óg a sgríobhtaí na leabhra, do'n aos óg a foillsightí iad – ach bhí dul amudha eile ar na daoine a bhí i mbun na h-oibre. Ba dhóigh leat orra, agus ar a gcuid oibre, gur páisdí amháin a bhí i n-Éirinn, páisdí de réir inntleachta, cuma cé'n aois bhí aca. Ní raibh aon cheapadh aca go raibh na páisdí sin ag éirghe suas n-a bhfearaibh agus ina mnáibh agus nach sásóchadh an lón aigne céadna iad agus iad ag éirghe suas is do shásuigh nuair bhíodar óg. This essay originally appeared in *Old Ireland*, 28/2/20. See also Ó Conaire, 'Páisdí Sgoile: Bhfuil Siad ag Milleadh Nuadh-litridheacht na Gaedhilge' (Schoolchildren: Are they ruining modern literature in Irish?), in *Aistí*, 80–1. This essay originally appeared in *An Claidheamh Soluis*, 17/2/17. In a 1928 review in *An Stoc* of Éamonn Mac Giolla Iasachta's novel *Cúrsaí Thomais*, 'L.' wrote: 'I recommend to readers of *An Stoc*, except for the boys and girls, to get this book. Thanks be to God – if it is not a sin for me to say that in this case – there is a book available at last that is not suitable as a school book' (Molaim do léightheoirí an Stuic, ach amháin na buachaillí agus na cailíní – an leabhar seo fhághail. Buidheachas do Dhia – mura peacadh dhom é rádh sa gcás seo – tá leabhar ar fághail sa deireadh nach bhfuil feileamhnach mar leabhar sgoile) (*Stoc*, Feb. 1928, 3). In a 1928 review of *Geantraighe* (Laughter-provoking music), Seán Ó Ciarghusa's collection of humorous stories, Séamus Ó Grianna paid a similar tribute to Ó Ciarghusa: 'Stories must be written that will be read as I read *Geantraighe* – sitting smoking my pipe and not thinking at all about the fact that the stories were written in Irish. Pádraic Ó Conaire was the first man who ever succeeded in making me read a story in Irish for the sake of the story and in making me forget that I was reading Irish. "Cloch Labhrais" {Ó Ciarghusa} played the same trick on me' (Caithfear sgéaltaí a sgríobhadh a léighfear mar léigh mé 'Geantraighe' – mé 'mo shuidhe ag caitheamh mo phíopa agus gan mé ag smaoitiughadh ar chor ar bith gur i nGaedhilg a bhí na sgéalta sgríobhtha. Pádruig Ó Conaire an chéad fhear ariamh ar éirigh leis a thabhairt orm sgéal Gaedhilge a léigheamh mar mhaithe leis an sgéal agus dearmad a dhéanamh gur Gaedhilg a bhí mé a léigheamh. D'éirigh le "Cloch Labhrais" an cleas céadna imirt orm' (*FL*, Oct. 1928, 8). One influential writer who felt that little had changed over two decades was Ciarán Ua Nualláin, who in a 1937 essay urged writers of Irish to remember from time to time that there were a few adults left in the country (*Hibernia*, Nov. 1937, 24). It is beyond ironic that in 1937, *The Irish Times*, in an editorial critical of the teaching of Irish in Free State schools (a favourite theme in the paper since independence), linked the failure of the educational system in this regard with the fact that it was impossible to find any of the works of Ó Conaire, 'the only modern writer of Irish who is worthy to be enrolled in the canon of literary creators', in the Dublin bookshops (*IT*, 16/10/37).

57 See, for example, T. Mac Artáin, 'Nua-Litridheacht na Gaedhilge / Saothar Scríbhneoirí Óga a Rachas ar Sochar dár d'Teangaidh' (Modern literature in Irish / The work of young writers that will benefit our language), *Tír*, June 1928, 6; and '£150 d'Ughdair na Gaedhilge! (£150 for Irish-language authors!), *IP*, 3/9/32. That writers were sensitive to the need for schoolbooks is evident in 'Focal don Oide' (A word to the teacher) with which Risteárd Ó Luineacháin introduced *Greann agus Gáire* (Fun and laughter), his collection of brief comic tales: 'Many a teacher has been complaining for a while about the lack of suitable books in the primary schools and in the intermediate schools. It is the national teachers who have complained most, and indeed they did not do so without cause. Their greatest need for a long time has been for stories for their students that would be short and enjoyable and simple, and here am I now trying to do a little something to remedy that deficiency' (Is mó oide a bhí ag gearán le tamall i dtaobh easba leabhar oireamhnach ins na bun-scoileannaibh agus ins na meadhon-scoileannaibh. Na hoidí náisiúnta is mó a dhein an gearán san agus go deimhin, ní gan chúis a dheineadar é. Sgéalta dá gcuid scoláirí a bheadh gairid taithneamhach simplidhe an t-easnamh is mó a bhí ortha le fada, agus seo anois mé ad' iarraidh beagáinín a dhéanamh chun an easnaimh sin do leigheas). See Ó Luineacháin, 'Focal don Oide', in *Greann agus Gáire* (BÁC: Brún agus Ó Nóláin, Teor., [1923]), v.

58 On the other hand, Shán Ó Cuív offered a strong dissent from this position in his 1936 book *The Problem of Irish in the Schools*: **'The schools alone cannot save the language**. Their efforts must be sustained by the use of Irish in the public life of the country and by a movement among the adult population to make Irish speakers of the men and women of to-day. Until Irish is used as a living language, both inside and outside the schools, its continued existence will be in danger even though everybody has learnt it.' See Ó Cuív, *The Problem of Irish in the Schools* (Dublin: Browne & Nolan, 1936),

11. For a more jaundiced view of the Gaelicising mission of the schools, see the opinions of 'Querist' in *The Irish Statesman* in 1923: 'With the advent of self-government Gaelic comes into all Irish schools. The children will all learn Gaelic in a fashion. Perhaps Geoffrey Keating would be puzzled by a modern Gaelic conversation, and no doubt the first generation will talk in a variety of dialects which would make Gaelic angels weep listening from Tír na nÓg' (*IS*, 29/9/23). Far more negative was *The Irish Times*, admittedly a publication, like *IS*, much less than enthusiastic about the agenda of the language movement at this time. In a 1937 editorial on 'Living Gaelic', the paper pronounced the educational policy of the state a failure in its attempt to revive the language: 'Nearly everybody in the Free State, beneath the age of thirty to-day, has studied Irish at school; but how few read it and how far fewer speak it?' (*IT*, 16/10/37).

59 Adrian Kelly, *Compulsory Irish: Language and Education in Ireland 1870s–1970s* (Dublin: Irish Academic Press, 2002), 10. The topic of Irish in the schools has been the subject of considerable and on occasion heated discussion and analysis. In addition to Kelly's study, see Donald Harman Akenson, *A Mirror to Kathleen's Face: Education in Independent Ireland 1922-1960* (Montreal: McGill-Queen's University Press, 1975), 35–61; Norman Atkinson, *Irish Education: A History of Educational Institutions* (Dublin: Allen Figgis, 1969), 159–62; Seán Farren, *The Politics of Irish Education 1920–1965* (Belfast: The Queen's University of Belfast, Institute for Irish Studies, 1995), 106–28; 142–52; and Séamas Ó Buachalla, *Education Policy in Twentieth Century Ireland* (Dublin: Wolfhound, 1988), 253–63; 341–56.

60 Tá breis daoine i n-ann an Ghaedhilg do léigheamh go h-áirithe i measc an aosa óig agus muna mbeidh na leabhair oireamhnacha ann is deacair dóibh puinn feabhasa do chur ar a gcuid Gaoluinne agus fós is deacair do'n sprid Ghaodhlach leathnú má bhíonn an dramhuigheal litridheachta a thagann ó chathrachaibh Sasana i n-uachtar sa tír seo i gcomhnuidhe.

61 Tá lucht reachta leabhra i mBaile Átha Cliath a' cur a gcraicinn díobh ar an saoghal deiridh seo ag iarraidh an sluagh a riar le leabhra beaga Gaedhilge. Sluagh na bhfoghlainntidhe [*sic*] agus na bpáistí sin iad is mó atá a' fághail aire. Ní féidir a rádh fá n-a lán acu ach an muileann atá a' síor-mheilt go meileann sé mín agus garbh. Is dócha go dtoghfar aisti an garbh ar ball agus nach bhfanfa ach an sgoth.

62 Ó cuireadh tús le Connradh na Gaedhilge tuairim dá fhichead bliadhan ó shoin is iongantach an méid leabhra a sgríobhadh le cuidiú a thabhairt do ghluaiseacht na teangadh. Támuid ag súil le nualitridheacht mhór mar thoradh ar an fhorfhás seo. Ní air sin ba mhaith liom a thrácht ach ar a thábhachtaighe a's atá na leabhra seo do lucht foghlumtha na Gaedhilge. Ar na leabhra seo tá ár seasamh ar fad beagnach leis an teangaidh a mhúineadh ins an sgoil.

63 Ba mhaith liom a chur in úil ná fuilim sásta in aon chor leis an saghas leabhar Gaedhilge atá ag teacht amach le deunaí, nó bédir gur bhfearr dhom a rádh ná fuilim sásta toisc gan saghas áirithe bheith á gcur i gcló. Leabhair i gcóir scoileanna iad go léir nach mór, leabhair chun Gaedhilg a mhúine asta. Dar liom tá ár ndóithin den tsaghas san againn. See also Ó Rinn, 'Staid na Gaelge [*sic*]' (The state of the Irish language), *IF*, July 1923, 35; and Ó Rinn, 'Na Scoileanna / Feis Bhaile Átha Cliath' (The schools / The Dublin feis), *UIrman*, 11/6/32.

64 Tá leabhair Ghaedhilge líonmhar go maith le déanaí agus dá mbeadh a gcáilíocht chó mór lena líonmhaireacht ba mhaith an bhaill orainn é. Leabhair scoile a bhfurmhór. Níl ach roinnt bheag acu san go mbeadh aon mhola mór ag dul dóibh fiú amháin mar leabhair scoile. In a 1925 essay in *The Irish Ecclesiastical Record*, Father Paul Walsh wrote: 'The Irish-reading buying public do not support literature; anything more ambitious than a school-book has but little chance of paying for itself' (*IER*, July–Dec. 1925, 104). See also 'Senex', 'Is the Gaelic League Too Old?' *Leader*, 30/10/26. 'Senex' wrote that the Gaelic literature of the time consisted of 'Irish geographies and ranns and songs by parish priests which should be buried away in some of the Carnegie libraries for a couple of centuries.'

65 Féach an bhail atá ar an scríobhnóireacht 'sa Ghaedhilg fé láthair. Furmhór mór na leabhar do foillsigheadh i nGaedhilg le dachad bliadhan anuas tá teilgean na cainnte ró-shimplidhe ar fad ionnta. Tá an suarachas agus an leanbhuíocht cainnte chomh fairsing sin i gcuid aca gur cheap magaidh agus fonmhóide iad dá mba i n-aon teangain eile do scríobhthaí iad . . . Bhí leabhair dá leithéid seo an-oireamhnach do lucht foghlumtha na teangan ach anois ó tá Gaedhilg, a bheag nó a mhór di, ag cách ins na scoileanna, agus ag mórán leasmuigh dhíobh, ní dhéanfaidh a thuille de'n tsaghas seo leabhar ach droch-mheas do tharraingt ar an dteangain.

66 Ag freasdal ar scoláirí scoile atá an chuid is mó des na sgríobhnóirí fé láthair. Dá bhithín sin is gann é an saothar pinn gur fiú litridheacht nó iarracht lag ar litridheacht do thabhairt mar ainm air.

67 Ó Broin seems to have used the Soviet comparison in a favorable sense. Máirtín Ó Cadhain famously denounced the agency with a similar comparison in 'Irish Prose in the Twentieth Century', in *Literature in Celtic Countries*, ed. J. E. Caerwyn Williams (Cardiff: University of Wales Press, 1971), 147.

68 In May 1932, Liam Ó Rinn wrote: 'With things as they are, it would be little use for a person to write a book in Irish at all if it were not for An Gúm, for to tell the truth there is no demand worth speaking of for any book, whatever font is in it, except when it is put on a syllabus' (Agus an scéal mar atá ba bheag an mhaith do dhuine leabhar Gaedhilge do scríobhadh

in aon chor mara mbeadh an Gúm, mar chun na fírinne innsint ní bhíonn éileamh gur fiú trácht air ar aon leabhar, pé chló bhíonn ann, ach amháin nuair a cuirtear ar chlár oideachais é). See Ó Rinn, 'Leabhra Gaedhilge do sna Daoine Óga' (Books in Irish for young people), *UIrman*, 28/5/32.

69 Sgéilín 'seadh é a sgríobhadh i gcóir leanbhaí sgoile acht mise i mbannaibh go gcuirfidh eachtraí Chóilín áthas agus aoibheall ar dhaoine nach leanbhaí.

70 'Sé an rud is mó atá ins na sgéalta ná eachtraí, ach eachtraí a gcuirfeadh, ní h-amháin buachaillí, ach daoine fásta suim ionnta.

71 Leabhar é a bhéarfadh sásamh agus taithneamh do gach aoinne is cuma óg nó fásta dhó agus mholfainn go speisialta do mhúinteoiribh é chur ar fághail dá scoláirí. Earlier in the review, he wrote: 'Our critics often reproach us for how few original books in Irish are available, and how little substance there is in anything new that comes. If for no other reason, this new novel will be welcomed' (Is minic mar achmhusán ag lucht ár gcáinte é a luighead bun-leabhar Gaedhilge atá le fághail, agus a luighead téagar a bhíonn in aon nidh nua a thagann. Mura mbeadh aon rud eile ach san sa scéal fearfar fáilte roimh an úirscéal nua so).

72 Seán Ó Ciarghusa was concerned that some writers, however good their intentions, were challenging their learner-readers too much, in the process driving them away from the language. In a short 1926 sketch, he has a wise old man say: 'Wanting to teach us the language, they throw us in a deep hole . . . It is no wonder if we aren't reading Irish . . . Indeed that we hate it' (D'fhonn an teanga do mhúineadh dhúinn caithid isteach i bpoll doimhin . . . sinn . . . Nidh nach iongnadh má táimíd gan bheith ag léigheamh na Gaedhilge . . . Seadh, agus gráin againn uirthi) (*II*, 20/9/26). Guilt must have seemed a glut on the market to many.

73 Ó Conaire was ahead of his time in many ways. For example, in 1917 he began promoting the idea of a Gaelic book club whose thousand members would comprise the nucleus for the kind of predictable audience that would make publication in Irish economically feasible. The project failed in the inauspicious political and military climate of the time, publishing just one book, Liam Ó Rinn's story collection *Cad Ba Dhóbair Dó* (What almost happened to him). An Ridireacht was called 'a fine tool' (uirlis bhreágh) for the promotion of literature in Irish in a Gaelic editorial in *II*, 2/2/24. See also 'Taobh de'n Obair' (A side of the work), Editorial, *II*, 2/1/24. For a discussion of An Ridireacht Liteartha, see Gearóid Denvir, 'Aguisín II [Appendix II]: An Ridireacht Liteartha', in *Aistí Phádraic Uí Chonaire*, ed. Denvir, 271–9. This book also contains several essays by Ó Conaire explaining and promoting the scheme.

74 Art Mac Gréagóir, *Stair na nDéise* (BÁC: ODFR, 1938), x–xi. Nuair a bhíos ag sgríobhadh an leabhair chuadhas an-fhada leis an simplidheacht ar eagla go gcuirfinn isteach cora cainnte a thabharfadh droch-mhisneach do dhaoine óga . . . Nuair a chuaidh Liam [Ó Míodhacháin] sa léigheamh chuir sé ar a mhalairt de thuairim mé. Tá sean-teanga na h-Éireann ró-uasal, dar leis, chun go ndéanfaidhe aon éagcóir uirri d'iarraidh í do chur i n-oireamhaint do sna daoine ná fuil sí aca. In a 1929 review, An tAthair Micheál Mac Craith urged Gaelic writers not to give in too easily to 'the handicap of readers of Irish' (bacaidheacht lucht léighte na Gaedhilge). See Mac Craith, Review of *An Rábaire Bán* by Nioclás Tóibín, *Studies*, Mar. 1929, 149.

75 Dráma go mbeidh an cló Rómhánach ann agus an Litriú Simplí ann agus an sean-chló comh maith leo; dráma a bheidh simplí go leor do lucht foghlumtha na Gaedhilge, cruaidh agus casta go leor do mhacaibh léighinn na hOllscoile, spéiseamhail go leor do'n chléireach atá i ngrádh agus don fheirmeoir atá i ndíg, soiléir go leor do scoláirí móra na hEuropa; dráma nárbh fhéidir le héinne é léiriú ar árdán ná é léigheamh ós ard.

76 Baineann an Gúm go speisialta le leabhra a meastar a bheith oiriúnach mar théacs-leabhra ins na Meadhon-Sgoileanna. Taobh amuich dhíobh san, ámhthach, d'fhéadfí glacadh le leabhra eile chum foillsithe a measfí tairbhe fá leith do bheith ionnta do lucht foghluma na Gaedhilge.

77 Alan Titley discusses the importance of this stamp of approval in *An tÚrscéal Gaeilge* (The novel in Irish) (BÁC: An Clóchomhar, 1991), 90.

78 It is interesting that in a series on Irish universities in 1938, the playwright and future Gaelic novelist, poet, and general man of letters, Séamus Ó Néill, commented on the poor quality of what often passed for 'literature' in Irish libraries, criticised the philistinism of the state censorship, and wished his compatriots read more. He did not, however, directly confront the question of how literature was taught in the universities, nor did he specifically comment on language issues. See Séamus Ó Neill, 'Córas Léighinn / Iol-Sgoileanna na h-Éireann / Cothughadh na Litridheachta' (A system of learning / The Irish universities / The promotion of literature), *II*, 5/7/38.

79 See *University College Dublin: Calendar for the Session 1933–1934* (Dublin: Browne & Nolan, 1933), 194–7. See also the UCD calendar for the next year's session, where the general course had added Ua Laoghaire's *Séadna*, Pádhraic Ó Domhnalláin's *Conamara*, Cormac Ó Cadhlaigh's *Cormac Mac Airt*, and Ó Grianna's *Cioth is Dealán*, the only work of contemporary fiction on the list.

80 *Coláiste na hOllsgoile, Gaillimh / Riaghalacha ag Baint le Grádhaimh agus Réimeanna Oideachais 1933–1934* (University College Galway / Rules regarding degrees and educational courses) (Dublin: Alex Thom, n. d.), 10–11, 47. One can wonder whether this curriculum had anything to do with the lack of

student literary activity in Irish lamented by Seán Ó Mocháin in the 1925–6 edition of UCG's *University Annual* (p. 10). Ó Mocháin felt that, despite Galway's unique advantage of university resources and an adjacent Gaeltacht, the students of both Dublin and Cork were ahead of his *alma mater* in this regard.

81 *Coláiste Ollsgoile Corcaigh: Féilire / Calendar 1934–1935* (Corcaigh: Cló Ollsgoile Chorcaighe, n. d.), 86–8, 125. Seán Ó Faoláin commented in 1926 on the deficiencies of the university Irish curriculum of that year, writing of the BA texts in one of the 'constituent colleges': 'As literature, which they purport to be, the bulk of them are incredibly ridiculous.' See Ó Faoláin, 'The Language Problem 2. – Irish – An Empty Barrel?' *Irish Tribune*, 16/7/26.

82 Tiocfaidh sé [prós na Nua-Ghaeilge] sa deire, ach b'fhéidir go mbainfidh sin leath-chéad bliain dínn. Obair láighe atá ghá dhéanamh ag gach aon sgríobhnóir an lae indiu, ag glanadh an bhealaigh roimh na sgríobhnóirí tásgúla atá le teacht amach annseo. Níl ann ach má sábháiltear an teanga. Má sábháiltear, is cinnte go mbéarfar Turgénef Gaolach agus Puiscín Gaolach, cé nár rugadh fós iad.

83 Nua-theanga iseadh an Ghaodhluinn ameasg teangthacha na h-Eorpa. Sí an Rip Van Winkle ameasg na dteangthacha í. Tá rian na cian-aostachta uirthi... Ach caithfimíd-ne úire agus neart na h-óige a chur innti, a sean-ghéaga a shíneadh is a lúbadh, agus an dearg-fhuil a chur ag rith n-a cuisleanna airís. Caithfimíd leitridheacht úr-nua a shaothrú innti. Ní h-amháin san. Ach caithfimíd, ar an am gcéadna, sibhialtacht úr-nua d'ár gcuid féin a bhunú sa tír seo.

84 He stated that if Irish writers could create 'fíor-litríocht . . . do'n phobul in ionad baoise shuaraigh gan mhaith, cá bhfios dúinn ná go dtiocfadh an lá fós a mbeidh Éire ar na náisiúin is mó cultúir is léighinn san Euroip.' See also Mac Liammóir, 'An Misneach Nua sa Litríocht' (The new courage in literature), *Sguab*, Sept. 1924, 72–3.

85 Tá beárna mhór fhairsing gearrtha amach ag an aimsir idir an seana-shaol Gaolach agus an saol nua atá istigh indiu, ach is féidir an dá shaol a réidhteach agus do thabhairt le chéile i litríocht na Gaoluinne, an té a thuigeann iad araon agus ealadha na litríochta a bheith aige de dhúthchas.

86 For a contemporary discussion of the pros and cons of this Gaelic fondness for pseudonyms, see 'Scríbhneoireacht gan Ainm / Dhá Thaobh an Sgéil' (Anonymous writing / The two sides of the story), *II*, 6/5/22.

CHAPTER ONE

Maimed from the Start

1 Ní rabh aon turtóg ó d'fhágfá an Ghaedhealtacht i do dhiaidh nach rabh oide sgoile ina luighe uirthí, agus ardteastas ina luighe ar a bhrollach . . . I dtaca le lucht an Mhug de, níor fágadh fear beo aca. Agus maidir le lucht an 'Oideachais', bhí cuid aca ina luighe . . . ar thaobh na gcnoc agus a gcuid fola 'ag cur dath níos deise ar na sléibhte.' Tháinig díthreabhach nach rabh airde do ghlúine ann, Státseirbhíseach, a bhíodh mar chrann cosanta ag an chló Rómhánach, tháinig sé an tslighe agus mhairbh gallóglach mór ruadh as Fánaid le smuig an duine bocht.

2 For a discussion of Ó Grianna's troublous tenure as editor of *Fáinne an Lae*, see Ó Muimhneacháin, *Dóchas agus Duainéis*, 115–26; and 'Máire mar Eagarthóir ar *Iris an Fháinne* agus *Fáinne an Lae*' (Máire as editor of *Iris an Fháinne* and *Fáinne an Lae*), in *Jonneen Khordaroy Answers Critics: Léachtaí Cuimhneacháin ar Shéamas Ó Grianna, 'Máire' (1889–1969)* (Jonneen Khordaroy answers critics: Commemorative essays on Séamas Ó Grianna, 'Máire' (1889–1969), ed. Nollaig Mac Congáil (BÁC: Coiscéim, 1992), 140–52.

3 Annsin ar ndóighe tá mé searbh. Bíonn siad ag cur síos domh nach bhfuil agam acht an t-aon phort amháin, mar tá ag síor-chainnt ar an nGaedhealtacht . . . Agus dá mhéad fearg a gcuirfidh mé ar na sgearracháin dhobhránta a bhfuil a gceann sa spéir aca cionn is gráinín beag 'Gaedhilge' a bheith aca, dá mhéad sin is amhlaidh is fearr liom é.

4 Má's duine léir caolradharcach 'Máire' agus má's fíor a n-abruigheann sé, caithimís uainn í mar Ghaedhilge. Sa diabhal leis an tír, leis an teangaidh agus le nósacha ár gcinidh. Fuadach an chait ar an domblás a ndearnadh go n-uige seo. Bhí na speabhraoidí a' gabháil d'á bhfuair bás ar ár son! Tugamaois cuireadh do Shasana athghabháil a dhéanamh ar an tír seo ar an toirt. As early as 1924 an anonymous contributor to *FL* commented of Ó Grianna: 'Séamus is given to the truth, and that is usually bitter, and there is usually contention and sharp argument where he is giving out' (Séamus atá tugtha do'n bhfírinne a bhíonn searbh, agus is gnáth treasnuigheal agus géar-aighneas mar a mbíonn sé ag cur de) (*FL*, 17/5/24).

5 Lil Nic Dhonncha, Letter to Geoffrey Palmer, 4 Oct. 1922, Tomás Ó Ceallaigh Papers, NLI MS 8129 (6). Palmer must have been a sympathetic listener. In a letter to him the following year, An tAthair Tomás Ó Ceallaigh, his collaborator on musical plays in Irish, wrote:

> Last year, in August, I was in Wales. I had actually written some lines of an historical (!) comedy with present day characters. That evening I got the Irish paper and learned of Collins's death. I then lost all heart for it. Really one's enthusiasm is at such a low ebb just now that one hardly wants to do anything. The audience for the opera, for instance, is mostly in jail!

See Ó Ceallaigh to Geoffrey Molyneux Palmer, 11 May, 1923, Ó Ceallaigh Papers, NLI MS 8129 (3).

6 Do rinne mo bheirt cainnt ar an gcló Rómhánach, ar an gcló Gaodhlach, agus ar an Litriú Simplí, agus

ní raibh siad ar aon aigne i n-aon cheist díobh. Do thrácht siad ar an 'Ghaodhluinn' is ar 'Gaeluinn', ar 'Gaedhilg', 'Gaedhealg', agus 'Gaedhilge', agus ní dhearn siad dearmad ar 'Gaelge' ná ar 'Gayling Blea Clee'... agus bhí muinntir síothchánta Mars agus a mbéil ar leathad aca, ag féachaint orra.

7 In the same issue of the paper, see also Ó Rinn's 'A Worn-Out Old Man' (Seanduine Claoite), the story of a bitter and rigid old man whom Ó Rinn uses as a symbol of the League at the time. Niall Buidhe Mhac an tSacanaigh offered his own comic take on the League and its problems a decade later in 'Sgilí-Bhaigil Dae Cúl Dan' (An imaginary island) and 'Connradh na Sgilí-Bhaiglise' in *Dundalk Examiner* for 6 Aug. 1938, and 8 Oct. 1938, respectively. 'Sgilí-Bhaiglise' was an imaginary language in need of revival.

8 Chualas féin cainteóir a cur de ag tionól d'fháinneacha i mBláth Cliath mar seo. 'Nuair a bhéadh an cainteóir dúthchais deireannach básuighthe d'éireóchadh Cathaoirleach an Fháinne agus déarfadh sé "Rachaimíd ar aghaidh anois".' Agus b'fhéidir dó an ceart a bheith aige mar nach mbeidh rath ná rathamhnas ar a' 'nGaedhilg nó' chuns bhéas duine de'n dream eile os cionn talamhana.

9 In a groundbreaking 2002 doctoral thesis, Brian Ó Conchubhair has shown definitively that some of the debates over font and orthography had much broader implications in both an Irish and European context. See Ó Conchubhair, 'Meath na hEorpa: An Athbheochan mar Aisfhreagra na hÉireann' (The decline of Europe: The revival as Ireland's response), Unpublished PhD thesis, NUIG, 2002.

10 See Séamus Daltún, 'Scéal Rannóg an Aistriúcháin' (The story of the translation section), and Éamonn Ó hÓgáin, 'Téarmaí Teicniúla sa Ghaelige: Caighdeánú agus Ceapadh le Céad Bliain anuas' (Technical terms in Irish: Standardisation and creation over the past hundred years), in *Teangeolas*, Winter, 1983, 12–26 and 27–33, respectively.

11 See Seán Ó Riain, *Pleanáil Teanga in Éirinn, 1919–1995* (Language planning in Ireland, 1919–1995) (BÁC: Carbad, 1994), 63–75. See also Éamon Ó Ciosáin, *An t-Éireannach, 1934–1937: Páipéar Sóisialach Gaeltachta* (*An t-Éireannach*: A socialist Gaeltacht paper) (BÁC: An Clóchomhar, 1993), 205–9.

12 As early as 1924, Ó Grianna had sworn undying opposition to 'Official Irish . . . Roman font or Simplifed Spelling, or wooden-leg Irish' (Gaedhilic Oifigeamhail . . . cló Rómhánach nó Leitriú Simplidhe, nó Gaedhilic choise maide) (*FL*, 19/1/24). In a 1928 review of the journal *An Tír*, Ó Grianna wrote: 'Now everyone has his own bête noire and mine is the Roman font. The black buck, the evil spirit, the thing I hate most' (Anois bíonn a bhête noire féin ag gach duine agus sé an cló Rómhánach mo cheann-sa. An boc dubh, an t-ainspiorad, an rud is mó a bhfuil gráin agam air) (*FL*, Apr. 1928, 8). In a more 'objective' piece a few months later, Ó Grianna raised twelve points in favour of the Roman font and then proceeded to demolish them all (*FL*, Nov. 1928, 5). See also his parable on the Roman typeface in 'Dot, H, Stá-Taire-Bhiseach' (Dot, h, Free State civil servant), *An t-Ultach*, May 1932, 1–3.

13 There is a copy of this letter in the Dinneen Papers, NLI MS 8625 (4).

14 See also Peadar Mac Fhionnlaoich, 'An Cló' (The font), *FL*, Sept. 1928, 7; 'Nótaí na Seachtmhaine' (Notes of the week), *ACS*, 19/3/32; and Mac Aonghusa, *Ar Son na Gaeilge*, 232–3. Mac Fhionnlaoich's seconder was Seán Mac Maoláin. Included in the approved motion were the words: 'That it is better for Irish that no great change be made in the type or spelling of Irish until the language is out of danger of death or destruction' (quoted by Maolmhaodhóg Ó Ruairc, *I dTreo Teanga Nua* (Towards a new language) (BÁC: Cois Life, 1999), 15. Tomás Ua Concheanainn mounted a one-man boycott of An Gúm, refusing to buy books in the Roman font. See Ua Concheanainn, Letter, *CT*, 10/5/30.

15 See Domhnall Ó Mathghamhna, *Sgéalta a Filí na Rómha* (Stories from the Roman poets) (BÁC: Brún agus Ó Nóláin, Teór., 1924); and Shán Ó Cuív, *Domhnall Donn agus Sgéilíní Eile* (Domhnall Donn and other little stories) (BÁC: Brún agus Ó Nóláin, Teór., 1929). Perhaps the most radical proposal with regard to font was that made by 'O'Mahony' in a letter to *II* (13/4/25), in which he argued for the adoption of a whole new alphabet on the model of the Cyrillic characters used in Slavic languages.

16 Dr Panini, *Irish Up-to-Date / Eeris (Eire + is)* (Dublin: C. J. Fallon, n.d.), 5.

17 Diarmuid O Murcu, *Bodaire n Coota Lachtna* (The churl in the grey coat) (Blaaclia: Bruun agus O Nualaen, Teor., [1935]), cover. Among other works by O Murcu in Eeris were *Clann Lir in Eeris* (Dublin: C. J. Fallon [1935]); *Minstrel of Eerish: Being Some of the Best Known Hymns and Songs Done into Standard Irish, with Originals* (Waterford: 'The Munster Express' Printing Works, n.d.); and *Irish in a Week by the Rational Method* (Waterford: The Munster Express Printing Works, [1937]). Working on the principle that 'Every Celt under seventy can acquire Eirish', O Murcu in *Minstrel of Eerish* gave his version of songs like 'Faith of Our Fathers', 'The Rose of Tralee', 'The Minstrel Boy', and 'Auld Lang Syne'. O Murcu also published a version of the Irish national anthem 'Amhrán na bhFiann' ('The Soldiers' Song') in Eeris in *The Leader*, 16/11/35 and in *Irish in a Week*, a book that also included, among other things, Eeris versions of the Lord's Prayer, the Hail Mary, Robert Emmet's speech from the dock, and 'Angels We Have Heard on High'.

18 He wrote that they needed 'a theacht go díreach anois agus mí a chaitheamh i gConamara agus mí eile a chaitheamh i nDún na nGall'. Panini responded in the same issue of the journal.

19 For more on the Keating Branch, see Mac Aonghusa, *Ar Son na Gaeilge*, 131–5.

20 For a discussion of this split, see Mac Aonghusa, 217–27; and Ó Muimhneacháin, *Dóchas agus Duainéis*, 135–58. See also Father Lawrence Murray's comments in his untitled editorial notes in the inaugural issue of *An t-Ultach* in Jan. 1924 (p. 4).

21 Fosgail 'Fáinne an Lae' do na canamhaintí go dtroididh an cath i n-ainm Dé. Níl acht amaidigh dúinn a rádh nach bhfuil an cath seo romhainn, nó nach bhfuil ádhbhar troda ar bith againn. Tá daoine ann adeir nach bhfuil difear ar bith eadar na canamhaintí. Ní h-amhlaidh. Ní aon chineál amháin Gaedhilce atá ó Chonamara go Rosa Tír Chonaill agus atá i gCúige Mumhan. Ní aon teanga amháin iad. Agus is amaideach an té a déarfas gurb eadh. Among those who said there were no real dialects in Irish was his own brother Seosamh (*IP*, 3/12/31).

22 Tá muintir na Mumhan cosamhail le Sasain ar dhóigheanna eile diomaite dá gcuid fuaimeannaí. Tá siad ag iarraidh cos-i-bpoll a chur le ar gcuid Gaedhilce inne. Immediately prior to this passage, Ó Grianna wrote with a startling disingenuousness: 'It is a sorry and sad story, with the number of enemies that the country and the language have, that we cannot come together among ourselves. There is no one in Ireland who more dislikes this kind of quarrel than myself, if I could do anything about it' (Is bocht agus is brónach an sgéal é, agus an méid namhad atá ag an tír agus ag an teangaidh, nach dtig linn a theacht le chéile i n-ar measc féin. Níl aon duine i n-Éirinn is lugha air an cineál seo bruighne 'ná mise, dá mbeadh neart agam air). The Ulstermen were also incensed by what they felt was the bias towards Munster Irish of Thomas O'Rahilly's groundbreaking academic study *Irish Dialects Past and Present* (1932). Much of the issue of *An t-Ultach* for Easter 1932 was devoted to critical articles on the book, among them pieces by Ó Grianna (writing as 'An t-Ollamh Cam Ó Léaraidhe') and Mac Grianna.

23 Caithfidh cogadh na gcanamhaint a bheith ann. Agus i n-ainm Dé, troidimís an cogadh sin mar ba dhúthcha de Ghaedhil a dhéanamh. Ní hionann canamhaint Leath-Chuinn agus canamhaint na Mumhan. Tá siad éagcosamhail le chéile ar achan dhóigh. Ní hionann blas daobhtha, ní hionann a gcuid tuam, ní hionann an ghramadach, ní hionann na cora-cainnte, ní hionann na smuainte, ní hionann an t-aigneadh nó an leagan amach atá aca . . . Ní abóraidh mise cé aca is fearr nó cé aca is measa. In a response published in *FL* the following week, Liam Ó Rinn called Ó Grianna's call for 'cogadh na gcanamhaintí' 'shameful' (náireach) (*FL*, 7/11/25).

24 Ba chóir do gach Ultach, agus do gach duine ar fud na tíre a thuigeas cad as Gaedhilc ann, nó ar mhaith leis Éire a fheiceáil saor agus Gaedhealach, ba chóir daobhtha iad féin a dhéanamh réidh fá choinne na troda seo. See also Ó Grianna, 'Litir ó Mháire', *FL*, 29/11/24; and 'Litir ó Mháire', *FL*, 14/2/25. In the *Examiner* three years later, 'Tuanach' urged the Ulstermen to call off their misguided war against their fellow Irish-speakers from Munster (*Examiner*, 4/5/35).

25 Shocróchadh sé an cuid is mó de ghnaithe 'standard' dá dtéighthidhe siar go dtí an Ghaedhilge a bhí ann sul a rabh difear ar bith eadar na canamhaintí. Ní féidir cur i n-éadan seo nuair atá an tsean-Ghaedhilg seo beo ag na mílte daoine go fóill. He expressed similar views in 'Sgríbhinní agus Seanchus' (Writings and traditional lore), *An Phoblacht*, 18/2/26. See also his review of Séamus Ó Searcaigh's *Foghraidheacht Ghaedhilg an Tuaiscirt* (The phonetics of Northern Irish) (*FL*, 5/6/26); and his essay 'An bhFuil na h-Ultaigh Searbh?' (Are the people of Ulster bitter?), *Ultach*, Feb. 1929, 5. 'Droichead Átha' took exception to Ó Grianna's review of Ó Searcaigh in *FL* (19/6/26), for which he was rewarded the following week with a crude and abusive reply from Ó Grianna (*FL*, 26/6/26).

26 Tá obair mhór déanta aca. Le leith-chéad bliadhain tá sé curtha i gcéill aca don chuid eile de Éirinn go bhfuil Gaedhilg aca. A Dublin Gael who had learned the Munster dialect turned a sardonic eye on bigoted speakers of the other dialects in a 1926 letter to the *Irish Independent*:

> As a Dublin man I was interested enough in the language some years ago to start learning it, and with some slight amount of application I acquired a certain proficiency in it as taught in the city. Imagine my consternation when I found lately Connacht and Ulster men saying, and going a long way towards proving, that what I had learned was not Irish (*II*, 26/2/26).

27 Muimhnigh a bhí ionnta, agus ba mhaith leo sean-Ghaedhealg na nUltach agus na gConnachtach a *thrampáil* faoi n-a gcosaibh agus 'Gaoluinn' bhriste bhearnach na Mumhan do leitheadú thríd Éirinn . . . Má éirigheann leo tá deireadh le teangaidh na nGaedheal. In 1929, Ó Grianna, in a diatribe against An Gúm, claimed that even Munster Irish was being slighted by the agency: 'Some of them have the Irish of the province of Leinster, others have the Irish of the province of Government; and some have I don't know what kind of Irish unless it is the Irish of the province of Liverpool!' (Tá Gaedhilg Chúigeadh Laighean ag cuid aca, Gaedhilg Chúigeadh Riaghaltais ag cuid eile, agus cuid aca nach bhfuil fhios agam goidé an cineál Gaedhilge atá aca mur' Gaedhilg Chúige Liverpool!) (*FL*, Feb. 1929, 6). The last bit was probably a dig at the Liverpool-born Piaras Béaslaí.

28 Ní fhuil iarraidh agam-sa ar bhás na Gaedhilge, ach b'fhearr liom míle uair an teanga do bheith marbh 'ná an chanamhain atá níos cosamhla le droch-Laidin i mbéal briotacháin 'ná le Gaedhilg, – í do bheith ina 'standard' ins an tír. Responding to Mac Meanman, Louis Walsh wrote: 'He has no interest in literature. If

the best book ever written were put in front of him, the first thing he would do would be to count the number of "double n's" there were or should be in it!!!' (Ní chuireann sé aon tsuim i litridheacht. Dá gcuirfidhe ós a chomhair an leabhar a b'fhearr a scríobhadh ariamh, isé an chéad rud a dhéanfadh sé ná an méid 'n dúbailte' a bheadh ann, nó ar cheart a bheith ann, a chuntas!!!) (*Tír*, Aug. 1932, 5).

29 In a 1926 letter to the editor of the *Irish Independent*, a writer calling himself 'Lead Pencil' made a similar point, arguing that the triumph of Munster Irish would inevitably mean the death of true Irish and the emergence throughout the Gaeltacht of some form of English. He wrote:

> You, 'Pyoun Loo', [another *II* correspondent whose pseudonym, here spelled phonetically according to the Munster pronunciation, means 'Lead Pencil'] say that Munster Irish will be all over the country yet, that is to say, that Irish will be blown out of it as well as English, for the two, Munster Irish and Irish, cannot live together, because Munster Irish is daily growing closer to English. You will have to kill Irish first (Deir tú, a 'Phyoun Loo' go mbeidh an Ghaoluinn ar fud na tíre go fóill, sin le rádh, go mbeidh an Ghaedhealg siabtha as chomh maith leis an Ainglis, ná ní féidir de'n dá chuid, Gaoluinn agus Gaedhealg, mairstin i gcuideachta a chéile, cionnus go bhfuil an Ghaoluinn ag éirighe níos comhgharaighe do'n Ainglis in aghaidh an lae. Caithfidh tú an Ghaedhealg a mharbhadh ar dtús) (*II*, 3/2/26).

See also the letter by 'Peann Luaidhe' (another 'Lead Pencil') on the same page of this issue of *II*.

30 He wrote 'go bhfuil fuath, tarcuisne, agus gráin ag na Muimhnighibh atá i seirbhís an tSaor-Stáit ar na h-Ultaighibh. Na h-Ultaigh do sheasuigh i n-aghaidh Sean-Ghall agus Nuadh-Ghall ní b'fhaide 'ná dream daoine ar bith eile i n-Éirinn! . . . Na h-Ultaigh bhochta ar díoladh sé cinn dá gcuid conndaethe ionnus go mb'fhusa na trí cinn a congbhuigheadh a smachtughadh a's a cheannsughadh.'

31 Goilleann sé orainn uilig i gCúige Uladh a fheiceáil go bhfuil daoiní ar an taobh seo den Bhóinn atá i n-ainm a bheith ag sábháil na Gaedhilge, agus gurab é rud a chuireas sé mí-shásadh agus fearg ortha – i n-áit lúthgháire a chluinstin go bhfuil taobh tíre i gCúige Uladh nach bhfuil ag na daoiní go fóill ann acht Gaedhilic. Chuala mé ar an chluais is bódhaire agam daoiní ag déanamh áthais gur mhaith an cuidiughadh Rialtas na Sé gCondae leis an Ghaedhilic a mharbhadh sa Tuaisceart.

32 Agus a Mháire an bhfuil fhios agat goidé an scéal a chuala mé go minic ar an chluais is bodhaire agam? Tá, go bhfuil fíor-bheagán Gaedhilgeóirí an taobh ó dheas den Bhóinn nár mhaith leo an chríoch mairstin go bhfághadh Riaghaltas Bhéal-Feirste an teangaidh a mharbhadh i gCúige Uladh.

33 Is fearr an t-imreas ná an t-uaigneas agus níor mhisde liom féin iomarbadh d'fheiscint, nó do chloisint – idir na h-ughdair Thuaidh agus Theas féachaint an ndúiseóchadh coigeadal a dteangach léightheóirí na Gaedhilge as an dtrom-shuan n-a bhfuilid.

34 Tá níos mó scríobhnóirí Gaedhilge againn, nó mar atá ag Cúige ar bith eile, agus in a dhiaidh sin, tá Gaedhilge ár gCúige ag fághail bháis. 'Tuige? 'Tuige an bhfuil Gaothluinn na Mumhan ag brúghadh amach ár nGaedhilge féin as na sgoileannaibh? Is cuma faoi'n dtuige. 'Sé an leigheas atá uainn agus tá sé againn faoi dheireadh. Cumann Liteardha Mhic Éil an leigheas. See also the comments on the marginalisation of Connacht Irish by 'Tadhg' in 'Urlabhraidheacht / An Fhiadhnaise Fhírinneach' (Articulation / The true evidence), *Stoc*, Feb. 1928, 5: and by 'Soc Rat Éis', in 'Dhá Locht' (Two faults), *Ultach*, June 1934, 2 and 4.

35 Ní le droch-mheas ar Ghaedhilg na Mumhan adeirim sin. Tá meas mór agam uirthi san áit a mbadh cheart di a bheith .i. i gCúige Mumhan.

36 Ach má éirigheann le Micheál agus na Connachtaigh eile atá ag cabhrú leis, níl aon dabht ná go bhfaghfar réidhteach ar Chaighdeáin na Gaedhilge . . . Beidh Corcaighigh óga agus Ciarraighigh óga agus Déisigh óga ag dul go Connacht agus tabharfaid leo canamhaint Chonnachta, agus measfar an chanamhaint sin le canamhaint na Mumhan agus réidhteoid ar ball an cheist tubaisteach sin atá ag déanamh clampair agus díobhála do chúis na Gaedhilge le dachad bliain anuas.

37 Tá canamhaint Chonnachtach ann agus mar sin ní thuigfidh na Muimhnigh a lán den chaint atá ann, ach beidh scans acu eolus do chur ar fheabhas na cainnte atá acu thiar.

38 See Ó Rinn, *Mo Chara Stiofán*, 70.

39 Piaras Béaslaí, *Cúigeachas*, in *An Sgaothaire agus Cúig Drámaí Eile* (The blowhard and five other plays) (BÁC: Muinntir C. S. Ó Fallamhain i gcomhar le hOS, 1929). In the comic story, 'Tuisleann Saoi Féin' (Even a sage stumbles) by P. Mac Suibhne, a policeman stationed on the Aran Islands, Gárdaí from different counties create confusion as they argue over the different local Gaelic names for plants they are monitoring under an act regulating harmful weeds (*GR*, Oct. 1937, 1225–6).

40 This writer, 'Uí Laoghaire', was even willing to concede the superiority of the western dialect to his own: 'Notwithstanding my natural prejudices, I fail to see how Munster Irish even at its best – is superior to Connacht Irish. As a language, or dialect, viewed from any standpoint, it is, if anything, inferior.'

41 Is náireach an sgéal é i dtír chomh beag leis an tír seo againne, a bhfuil a cuid de'n Ghaedhilge comh caol agus atá sé, is náireach an sgéal le n-aithris é go mbéadh Gaedhil dealuighthe ó n-a chéile i gcúis na teangan. Shílfeá ó'n gcainnt a bhí ar Chonnachtaigh,

ar Mhuimhnigh agus ar Ultaigh le goirid go mba teanga iasachta gach canamhaint de chanamhaintí na Gaedhilge agus go mba é a ndualgas droch-mheas a chaitheamh ortha. Is dóigh go mb'fhearr le cuid aca Béarla féin a labhairt ná é a bheith le rádh go labhróchaidís i gcanamhaint Gaedhealtachta ar bith eile.

42 Is mithid dúinn smaoitiughadh gur mó Éire 'ná cúigeadh ar bith dá cuid, agus leabhar a mheas ar a feabhas nó ar a h-olcas is cuma c'as a dtig sí.

43 Thárluigheann sé gurb' í Gaedhealg Chúige Mumhan atá againn féin acht aon duine a bhfuil tuairm neamh-spleádhach aige agus ná fuil cumhangaigeantach caithfidh sé admháil ná fuil Gaedhealg Chúige Mumhan ná Gaedhealg Chúige Connacht ná Gaedhealg Chúige Uladh níos fearr ná a chéile i ngach aon slighe. Tá rudaí maithe ag baint le gach aon cheann ná fuil le fághail sna ceannaibh eile, ach níl aon dabht ná go bhfuil an iomarca cainnte agus an iomarca ráiméise ar siubhal mar gheall ar chúigeachas agus ar chanamhaintí.

44 Máire Ní Ghuairim, *Ceol na Mara* (BÁC: Brún agus Ó Nuallain, [1938]), 5. As an saothrú ar na canamhaintí a thiocfaidh na blátha ar ball. Tá an obair ar siubhal i n-aghaidh an lae ós comhair ár súl, agus beidh an rath air le congnamh Dé. Tugaimíd fá ndeara draoidheacht nó taithneamhaigheacht fá leith do bheith ag baint le gach 'abhainn' dena haibhnibh sin. Draoidheacht na calmachta i gcuid an Tuaiscirt; draoidheacht na fearamhlachta i gcuid an Deiscirt; draoidheacht na banamhlachta i gcuid an Iarthair. Ní fada a bheadh duine ag gabháil d'ár litridheacht nua go bhfeicfeadh sé an méid sin, agus is saidhbhride an teanga iad go léir.

45 I n-ainm an áidh, a cháirde, dearcaidh ar an námhaid atá agaibh araon, an Béarla. Agus ná bíodh sé le rádh libh i ndiaidh bhur mbáis nach rabh oiread céille agaibh agus go gcuirfeadh sibh bhur nguailleacha le chéile. Agus i n-áit a bheith ag iarraidh leabharthaí Gaedhilge agus rudaí Gaoluinne a scríobhadh, gur b'é rud a bhí sibh ag troid fá easair fhoilimh.

46 Is iad na sgríobhnóirí a dheinean teanga liteardha de theangain labhartha. An chanúint is mó agus is fearr a sgríobhtar siní an chanúint a bhíon mar theangain liteardha i gcomhnuidhe ins gach tír. Agus is mar sin a bheidh an sgéal againn in Éirinn leis, mara gcuirtear an teanga chun báis le rialacha chun na sgríobhnóirí a chosc ar a dteangain féin a sgríobhadh.

47 Tá sí ag fás cheana féin. Is mian le gach scríbhneoir fónta scríobh ar chuma go dtuigfidh cách é agus mar sin toghan sé an chaint a thuigfidh cách agus seachnan sé an doiléracht. As should be evident from his own rather peculiar orthography, Ó Rinn was not a man who shirked controversy.

48 Gidh go bhfuil limistéirí i n-Éirinn 'n-a labhartar an Ghaedhilg de ghnáth ní dócha go bhfuil aon áit is mó labhartar í le fíor-bháidh ná i gCathair Átha Cliath, dá Ghallda mar chathair é agus dá fhaid ó'n nGaeltacht. Connachtaigh, Muimhnigh, Ultaigh agus Laighnigh ná fuil i dtaobh le h-aon chanúint amháin des na trí cinn atá againn – iad so go léir ag déanamh cuidrimh le n-a chéile sa chathair seo agus a rogha canúna ar a bheola ag gach n-aon díobh. De bharr an chuidrimh sin, tá canúint nua ag fás de réir a chéile – 'canúint Átha Cliath'.

49 An tAthair Gearóid Ó Nualláin discusses Father Lehmacher in his autobiography *Beatha Duine a Thoil* (To each his own) (BÁC: OS, 1950), 274–5.

50 In a 1930 editorial in *An Stoc*, Ó Máille lamented the state of the language: 'As things now stand, every province, every county, every district, and I could say every parish, is trying to establish a dialect for itself' (Mar tá an sgéal fá láthair, tá chuile chúige, chuile chonndae, chuile cheanntair agus dá n-abrainn é, chuile pharóiste ag iarraidh canamhain a chur ar bun dó féin). He argued that if something were not done soon, revivalists should resign themselves 'to allowing Irish to be made into a couple of score or a couple of hundred languages' (cead a thabhairt . . . cúpla sgór nó cúpla céad teanga a dhéanamh den Ghaedhilge) (*Stoc*, June 1930, 6). Ó Máille was, of course, a native speaker of Conamara Irish with a profound knowledge of the resources of that dialect, as is evident from his 1936 book *An Béal Beo* (The living language). Others Gaels, among them Ó Grianna, favoured the creation of a Gaelic 'Academy', but neither the Gaelic League nor the state was ever able to bring any such institution into fruitful existence. See, for example, 'A Gaelic Academy / League Decides in Favour of the Proposal / Finance the Difficulty', *II*, 4/4/29; and 'Acadamh Liteardha' (A literary academy), *Blueshirt*, 15/12/34.

51 Quoted in Ó Muimhneacháin, *Dóchas agus Duainéis*, 54.

52 In a particularly nasty line from a 1934 appeal for financial support, *An Gaedheal* evoked the spectre of Ireland's becoming 'a mongrel community of abject half castes' (*Gaedheal*, 21/7/34). Equally troubling were the comments of Conor Mac Doal in a 1926 piece in the *Irish Tribune*, in which he argued that what was most important in determining a person's Irishness was an acceptance of the national past and of 'a future that shall be its continuation':

> Biologically it means acceptance of the Dominant type as the type to which progeny shall conform. Those who want to be Irish and yet to retain a nation foreign to the Irish Dominant are doomed to failure, not because the race will persecute them, but because their grafting is incomplete (*Irish Tribune*, 24/12/26).

53 Ní cóir go mbéadh deacracht dá laighead Gaedhealachas agus gach a mbaineann leis do chiallú. Tuigimíd go léir go bhfuil dhá chineál saoidheachta ag iarraidh buaidh do bhreith ar a chéile i nÉirinn i láthair na h-uaire seo – saoidheacht na nGaedheal agus saoidheacht na nGall. Tá an lámh i n-uachtar ag na Gaill go fóill, agus isé is

Gaedhealachas ann gach ní dá bhfuil ag teastáil le deireadh a chur le réim na nGall ar intinn agus ar anam mhuinntear uile na hÉireann.

54 Caithfear síbhialtacht amháin a bheith sa dtír agus gan dhá cheann a bheith ann fá mar atá anois . . . Nuair a bheidh tailte a sinnsear ag Gaedhil arís agus na déantúisí áiteamhla ar siubhal aca, agus cultúr amháin – an fíor-Ghaedhealachas ag ár ndaoinibh – annsan beidh rath Dé orainn agus a lámh linn. See also 'M. na M.', 'Nead na Gaedhilge / Suas leis an nGaedhilg' (The nest of the Irish-language / Up with Irish), *The Cross*, Dec. 1932, 338.

55 See also his views as developed in 'An Gaelachas', Enniscorthy *Echo*, 2/5/31; and in 'Dualgas an Dá Chumann' (The duty of the two organisations), *An Ráitheachán*, Sept. 1936, 45–7.

56 Má éirigheann an mhuinntir seo cleachtach ar Liberalism agus Tolerance, dhá chaoi i n-Éirinn le sglábhuidheacht a rádh, ní bhéidh mórán Gaedhilge ná Gaedhealachas a déanamh buadhartha dhóibh.

57 Tugtar 'Gaedhealachas' ar an tsaghas creidimh sin a bhíonn ag dream amadán áirithe go mbíonn Éire Shaor Ghaedhealach uatha. 'Facismo' a tugtar ar a chomh-shaghas de chreideamh san Iodáil. The writer of this piece was involved in a controversy with 'Brian Dubh', who in a piece in *FL* in July 1926 (p. 1) had warned his fellow Gaels of the dangers of Italian fascism. See also the comments of 'Brian Dubh' in the Dec. 1926 issue of *FL* (p. 6). One could also feel uneasy about remarks made by Peadar Mac Fhionnlaoich in an address to the Gaelic League critical of the Irish government for not doing enough for the language: 'There were many points that Herr Hitler or Signor Mussolini could give them so far as the nationalisation was concerned' (*II*, 31/3/37). In an unpublished MA thesis at UCG, Gearóidín Uí Nia briefly discusses An tAthair Eric Mac Fhinn's anti-Semitism. His prejudices do not, however, seem to have had any significant effect on his work as editor of *Ar Aghaidh*. See Uí Nia, *An tAthair Eric Mac Fhinn agus Ar Aghaidh*, Tráchtas i gcomhair MA, Coláiste na hOllscoile, 1994. Gaelic fascism is discussed by Éamon Ó Ciosáin in *An t-Éireannach*, 88. Needless to say, the left-wing *An t-Éireannach* was consistently anti-fascist.

58 In an essay on 'The New Education' in 1926, Seán Ó Faoláin called the attempt to restore 'a Gaelic Outlook' through the schools 'interesting', 'dangerous', and 'very necessary', and then went on:

> In other words, to induce the Gaelic viewpoint, it has been necessary to make sacrifices. Is the bargain a good one? It is a fair question . . . for nobody in Ireland is likely to want a Gaelic viewpoint if there is the slightest fear that this viewpoint does not imply the enlargement of the mind as fruitful, and one may well hope more fruitful than that induced by the old system we have rejected (*Irish Tribune*, 9/4/26).

At this stage in his life, Ó Faoláin was only mildly pessimistic about the possibilities that this venture could – or should – succeed.

59 In a 1937 essay in *Ireland To-Day*, Niall Sheridan, a close friend of Brian Ó Nualláin, was scathing in his attack on 'the current professional revival of Gaelic culture', seeing it as 'characterised by a humourless Calvinistic bigotry that is completely un-Irish' (*Ireland To-Day*, June 1937, 62).

60 Tá mé ag gabháil rudaí a rádh nach dtaiteónaidh le cuid mhór Gaedheal. Déarfar, tá eagla orm, nach Gaedheal mé. Thiocfadh leis a bheith fíor agus níl mé ag gabháil a shéanadh . . . Níl mé sanntach ar an dóigh sin. Leis an fhírinne a dhéanamh, tá mé i bhfad ó bheith cinnte 'cad is Gaedheal ann'. Nuair a tchím cuid de na daoine ar crochtar an t-ainm sin leóbhtha bheir sé i mo cheann macasamhail an ruda a dubhairt an Franncach fá na fir agus na madaidh: 'plus je vois les Gaedhil, plus j'aime les Gaill'.

61 Gaedheal mise. Nach uasal sin? Gaedheal im chroidhe, Gaedheal im mheoin, Gaedheal óm sheacht sinnsear Gaedheal. Gaedheal mise agus mé 'ghá mhaoidheamh. A slán fá'n domhan uile cineadh Gaedheal a shárughadh.

62 Ní Gaedhil aon chuid aca ó nach labhraid teanga Gaedheal, nuair nach lán a meon de ghrádh Gaedheal, de chultúr Gaedheal agus d'eolas ar Ghaedhil.

63 Ó tháinig an Béarla go hÉirinn tá deifríocht an domhan idir Éireannach agus Gaedheal. Uaireannta is fearr go mór an t-Éireannach ná an Gaedheal. Tá Éireannaigh mhaithe ann. Éireannaigh do tógadh sa Ghalltacht, agus do raghaidís i gcontabhairt bháis ar son a dtíre agus tá Gaedhil ann, do tógadh sa Ghaeltacht agus do dhíolfaidís a n-anam ar son airgid.

64 See, for example, Seán Ó Dúnaighe, *Inghean an Ghearaltaigh* (Fitzgerald's daughter) (BÁC: Muinntir Dollard, Teo., n.d.), 8.

65 Na daoine atá i n-Éirinn fá láthair, ní 'Gaedhil' iad ach measgán de Ghaedhil, Lochlannaigh, Normánaigh, Sasanaigh, Albanaigh, Breathnaigh agus eile . . . Tá muid chomh maith i dteidiol Gaedhil a thabhairt orainn féin – an méid againn a labhruigheas Gaedhilg agus a chreideas i náisiúntacht na nGaedheal – agus tá fear thall i dteidiol Sasanach do ghairm de: eisean go bhfuil fuil na mBreathnach, na Rómhánach, na n-Angles, na Sacsanach, na Jutes, na nDanar is na Normánaigh ann gan fuil na bhFranncach, na n-Éireannach is na n-Albanach do rádh. Dá bhrígh sin, gidh gur tearc 'Gaedheal' – má tá duine – atá beo indiú, deirimíd gur Gaedhil sinn toisg go bhfuil an teanga Gaedhilge agus síbhialtachas na sean-Ghaedheal gan a bheith marbh ar fad i n-ár measg. In a note to Éamonn Mac Giolla Iasachta, the editor of *An Sguab*, concerning this essay and dated 28 Dec. 1923, Ó Broin commented: 'I think it likely that there will be a row because of that. If so, all the better!' (Is dóigh liom go mbeidh raic mar gheall air

sin. Má bhíonn, is amhlaidh is fearr é!) The note is in the Edward MacLysaght Papers, NLI MS 8560 (9).

66 Ba cheart do gach Éireannach ar an lá so an cheist seo do chur air féin cad é an stáid i dtaca le gach a mbaineann le Gaedhealachas. Is Gaedhil sinn nó is Gaill sinn. Ní'l a thuilleadh díospóireachta sa sgéal. Ní thig le duine a rádh gur Gaedheal é má tá cos leis i gcúrsaí Gaedhealachais agus san am céadna an chos eile i n-umar na haimléise, sé sin i salachar claon-tréithre na nGall. In 1926, the editor of *An Lóchrann* stressed that the re-Gaelicisation of the country – a process in which language was *sine qua non* – was the preeminent duty of all wanting to call themselves Gaels: 'There is no higher goal for the nation than the re-Gaelicisation of our people, and anyone who puts anything else ahead of that IS NOT A GAEL. That's all there is to it' (N'il aon chuspóir eile is aoirde náisiúntas ná ath-Ghaedhealú ár ndaoine agus aon duine chuireas aon rud eile roimh an rud san NÍ GAEDHEAL É. Sin é iomláine an scéil) (*Lóchrann*, July 1926, 60).

67 In an essay entitled 'An Muimhneach nó Cad is Muimhneach ann?' (The Munsterman or what is a Munsterman?), 'An Grabaire' satirised the essay by 'C.', particularly with regard to its views on marriage. Indeed, 'An Grabaire' specified that a true Munster person should on no account ever leave the province (*Muimhneach*, Feb. 1933, 33 and 35). 'C.' politely took issue with this satire the following month (p. 63).

68 Tá an t-am ag teacht go luath nach bhféadfaidh fear óg gan Gaedhilg a rádh go bhfuil sé ní h-é amháin i n-a Ghaedheal, acht 'na Éireannach; óir ní bheidh aon Éireannach 'na Éireannach (acht an taobh thall de'n Teorainn mhí-ádhamhail b'fhéidir) nach mbeidh teanga a shinnsear aige – a bheag nó a mhór dí. Given his own ethnic background, it seems odd that Hyde would stress the ancestral nature of the Irish language here. In the context of Hyde's remarks, it is interesting to look at what the Gaels wanted from the national broadcasting service as outlined in *An Gaedheal agus an Radio* (BÁC: Fóchoisde an Radio, Connradh na Gaedhilge, 1936), esp. 8–9, 21. On 29 June 1937, Radio Éireann broadcast a conversation between Peadar Ó Donnchadha and Sighle Ní Dhonnchadha on the topic 'Gaedheal nó Eireannach?' (Gael or Irishman?) (*IP*, 29/6/37). Six months later, Risteárd Breathnach and Bairbre Ní Chonaire took to the airwaves to discuss 'the pertinent question of whether Gaelic culture is really culture and to what extent it contains from its origins the essentials of true culture' (*IP*, 25/12 and 27/12/37).

69 Huh! . . . tusa ag tabhairt Éireannaigh ort féin is gan Gaedhilg agat. Ní chreidim gur Éireannach tú chor ar bith.

70 See the discussion of Gaelic debates on this topic in the period immediately prior to independence in my *Prose Literature of the Gaelic Revival*, 464–71.

71 Shán Ó Cuív, *Prós na hAoise Seo* (BÁC: Brún agus Ó Nóláin, Teór., [1934]), 37. Bíonn nós machnaimh ag cine seachas cine eile, agus deir lucht eolais na haigeantachta gur saghas sgátháin teanga, agus go nochtann sí dhúinn nós machnaimh na ndaoine a labhrann í . . . Agus d'fhéadfí a chruthú go bhfuil nós machnaimh leo féin ag lucht labhartha na Gaedhilge chomh maith. An aigne Ghaedhealach a thugaimíd ar an nós machnaimh sin. In a 1928 piece in *The Leader*, 'Noel' had written: 'There is no such thing as a Gaelic mind: there is a Gaelic language and the form of thinking which that language compels' (*Leader*, 11/2/28). Actually, it is difficult to conceive of a better definition of what Gaels at the time meant by the 'Gaelic mind' than that given here by 'Noel'.

72 Ní h-iongnadh ar bith é gur sa teanga náisiúnta is mó a bhraithimíd anam agus spiorad na tíre seo againn-ne mar 'sí an teanga a thugas an léargus is soiléire dúinn ar aigne agus ar mheon na ndaoine. 'Sí an teanga náisiúnta an gléas a thugas léargus dúinn ar anam agus ar chroidhe ár ndaoine agus ó bheith ag múnlú mheon agus leagan amach an náisiúin múnluigheann sí freisin meon agus intinn na ndaoine féin. The title of his lecture was 'Sí an Ghaedhilg a Chothuigheas Spioraid na Náisiúntachta' (It is Irish that sustains the spirit of nationality.)

73 Tá daoine ann a deireann agus a chreideann gurb ionann Gaedhilg agus Gaedhealachas de bhrígh, dar leó, nach féidir do'n té a mbíonn Gaedhilg ar a theangan gan Gaedhealachas a bheith na chroidhe. Gidh go nglacaim leis an dtuairim nach Gaedheal go Gaedhilgeóir ní aontuighim go bhfuil an Gaedheal-achas is dual do Ghaedheal i gcroidhe gach naon a bhfuil roinnt Gaedhilge aige indiu . . . rud gan anam iseadh Gaedhilg gan Gaedhealachas.

74 Níl sa teangain féin ach cuid den Ghaedheal-achas agus má's tábhachtaighe dhúinn an t-anam ná'n corp nár chóir go mba thábhachtaighe dhúinn anam an Ghaedhealachais ná a chorp; nó go mbeidís ar chomhthábhacht dúinn ar a luighead de. See also the anonymous letter agreeing with his views in *II*, 18/11/38.

75 Among the debates at Rockwell College in Cashel, County Tipperary in 1936 was one on the following topic: 'It is in English that the gospel of Freedom has been proclaimed in Ireland for the past two hundred years, proving that it is possible to be Gaelic without the Irish language' (Is as Béarla a craobhscaoileadh soisgéal na Saoirse i n-Éirinn le dhá chéad bliadhain anuas i gcruthamhnas duit gur féidir bheith Gaedhealach gan Gaedhilg) (*Rockwell Annual*, June 1936, 87).

76 Compare his comments on the 'innate' Gaelicism of Micheál Mac Liammóir (*Gaedheal*, Apr. 1936, 1).

77 Uaireannta, ní bhím cinnte an ionann an chiall atá againn uilig do'n fhocal 'Gaedhealachas'. Sé an chiall atá leis i mo bharamhail féin an córus Gaedhealach agus an dearcadh náisiúnta a ba mhian le Gaedhil a chur i n-áit an sibhealtacht Ghallda atá 'san tír seo i láthair na h-uaire.

78 Go deimhin, ní réabhlóididhe é, ná nuareachtóir. Is ar thaobh na SEAN-NIDHTHE a sheasann sé. Is caomhnaidhe é, is conserbháididhe ó dhúthchas é. Níl aon dream daoine sa tír is mó thuilleann an ainm sin ná muinntir an Ghaedhealachais. Sé is cuspa dhóibh an sean-chreideamh, an tsean-teanga, an tsean-leitridheacht Chríostaidhe, an sean-chultúr agus an tsean-nósmhaireacht, iad san do chosaint agus do chaomhnadh is do bhuan-choimeád. It was precisely this attitude that drew the ire of Micheál Ó Donnabháin (Frank O'Connor) in a 1933 essay in which he wrote with exasperation of some Gaels: 'Almost nothing matters to them except the thing that came to them from antiquity; instead of opinions and insight, instead of understanding and sense, literature is nothing but antiquity, antiquity, antiquity, and without a doubt that is a poor intellectual medium for a person who wants to write about the great world as do the writers of any other country' (Ba chuma leo annsan gach rud beagnach ach an rud a tháinig chúcha le sinnsireacht; i nionad tuairmí is léirmheas, i nionad tuigsiona is céille, ní'l sa litríocht ach sinnsireacht, sinnsireacht, sinnsireacht, agus gan amhras is suarach an gléas inntleachta é sin do dhuine gur mhaith leis an saol mór do bhreacadh fé mar a dhineann sgríobhnóirí aon tíre eile é) (*Leabharlann*, Dec. 1933, 132).

79 Ar ndóigh nuair a thráchtar ar an gcultúr Gaedhealach, is gnáthach le cuid againn an ceann a chraitheadh nó tosuighe ar an ngáire. Creideann go leor gurb ionann an cultúr Gaedhealach a thabhairt ar ais agus chuile rud dár bhain le seanbhéasgnaidheacht na tíre a thabhairt ar aghaidh ath-uair. Go deimhin, tá mórán idir dlighthe, nósanna agus eile a mb'fhiú iad a thabhairt ar ais láithreach; b'fhearrde agus b-uaislede an tír iad. Mórán eile agus ní fhéadfaidhe iad a thabhairt ar ais. Ach ní mór dhúinn eolus cruinn a chur ar na sean-rudaí sin, ní mór dhul ar ais ortha leis an oideamhlacht (inspiration) atá riachtanach le go mbéidh cuma, cruth agus blas an Ghaedhealachais ar an saoitheamhlacht a thiúbhramaid ar aghaidh.

80 Tá rudaí eile riachtanach seachas an teanga féin, ach a bhaineann go dlúth léi, chun deilbh agus cruth Gaedhealach a thabhairt ar dhuine .i. níor mhór dó bheith líonta d'oideas béil, de chultúir agus d'fheallsúnacht agus de spioraid na nGaedheal a tháinig roimhe . . . Is leis na neithe sin agus leis an nGaedhilg a deintear Gaedheal de leanbh. Ní Gaedheal é gan iad – ná Éireannach féin. Duine d'fhoghlmóchadh [*sic*] Gaedhilg agus ná faghadh aithne na neithe eile tríthe is 'na teannta ní bheadh sa Ghaedhilg dó ach forra-chroiceann a bheadh ag tuitim de gach tráth. Ní thabharfadh an Ghaedhilg féin an sásamh ná an líonadh d'á aigne is gádh d'aigne duine agus ní raghadh sí i ngreim 'na nádúir ná 'na inntleacht agus ní shuidhfí an Gaelachas insa chathaoir órdha 'na anam. He published the same article the following month in *FL*, 5/12/25.

81 Taobh amuich de roinnt beag Gaedheal níl staid na náisiúntachta sroiste ag aon dream eile i nÉirinn. Is cuma cé mhéid Sasannach nó 'Neamh-rialtach' nó 'Státaire' atá marbh ag aon duine sa tír seo, ní Gaedheal dá bhrí sin é maran Gaedhilgeóir d'á thoil é agus mara bhfuil sé ar n-a líonadh d'eolas agus de bhéascna a chine agus a thíre 'na theannta san agus grádh aige do na neithe sin.

82 Cad is brígh le Gaedhealachas? Teanga uasal na nGaedheal do chur dá labhairt agus an Cultúr Náisiúnta a ghabhann leis do bhunú go seasamhach i gcroidhthe na Mac Léigheann. Cuid ana-mhór de'n chultúr sin iseadh an nósmhaireacht Ghaedhealach – na rinncí Gaedhealacha, an ceol Gaedhealach agus na cluichí Náisiúnta.

83 Is é is tuigthe as Gaedhealachas ná teanga, cultúr, béaloideas, cluichí is rinncí Gaedhealacha a chleachtadh is saoirse na hÉireann mar chuspóir náisiúnta. Breathnach asserted: 'Éireannach ar bith atá i bhfábhar lán-Ghaedhealachais fé mar a mhínigh an Coiste Gnótha é is a dheineann a dhícheall an méid is féidir leis de a chleachtadh is cóir é d'áireamh ina fhíor-Ghaedheal'. Compare an earlier formulation of such a definition by Pádhraic Ó Domhnalláin in 'Creideamh Chonnradh na Gaedhilge' (The faith of the Gaelic League), Editorial, *FL*, 24/10/25; and 'Tuairimí Gaedheal' (The Opinion of Gaels), *An Camán*, June 1932, 1. It is interesting to note that Seosamh Mac Grianna came to feel that, whatever its legitimate accomplishments, the League had little understanding of 'the Gaelic mind' (intinn Ghaedhealach) (*IF*, Apr. 1928, 21).

84 Art Mac Ganna, 'Réamh-Rádh' (Preface), in *Ár Rinncidhe Fóirne: Ten Irish Figure Dances (Leabhrán a h-Aon)* (BÁC: Coimisiún an Rinnce, 1939, 3. See also 'Seo agus Siúd / Comh-Chumann Gaedheal' (This and that / An alliance of Gaels), *Nation*, 28/4/28.

85 See also Seórsa Gabhánach Ó Dubhthaigh (George Gavan Duffy), 'The Irish Language and Irish Games', in *Leabhar Tailteann (Aonach Tailteann 1928 / Souvenir Program)* (BÁC: Ard-Chomhairle Aonach Tailteann, n.d.), 37; and Pádraig Ó Meadhra, 'An t-Iománaidhe Óg' (The young hurler), *An Fiolar .i. Irisleabhar Scoile na Mainistreach .i. Cnoc Sheosaimh i dTuaiscirt Éile (Mt St Joseph's College, Roscrea)*, 1935, 17–20.

86 See Marcus de Búrca, *The GAA: A History of the Gaelic Athletic Association* (BÁC: Cumann Lúthchleas Gael, 1980), 179–81.

87 Agus 'sí an teanga uirlis na h-aigne; níl san rinnce acht caitheamh aimsire. Níl cead leis ag lucht imeartha cleas lúith na nGaedheal dul ag feuchaint ar cleasa lúith na nGall ná a gcluithchí á n-imirt [*sic*] acht níl aon chosg leó teanga na nGall do labhairt agus do thaithighe agus do chothughadh chum a dtoile. See also Seán Mac Eachain, 'Sense, Nonsense and the Gaelic Ideal', *Leader*, 24/3/23; and Liam Ó Briain, 'Will the Gaelic League Survive?' *Star*, Dec. 1930, 81.

88 See also 'Frills', Editorial, *Star*, 23/11/29; 'Kilts and Jigs', Editorial, *Star*, 29/3/30; and Micheál Ó Maoláin, 'Leathanach na Gaedhilge' (The Irish-language page), *Nationality*, 3/10/31. It should be noted that *The Star* was the semi-official organ of the Cumann na nGaedheal government to which republican activists and members of the new Fianna Fáil party were so bitterly opposed. Those in the Government – and they were many and influential – who were suspicious of Republican influence in the Gaelic League regularly used the paper to criticise the League and undermine its position as a national icon. Blythe, in particular, had come to see the League as an ignorant enemy of the Free State. His opposition to the League's crusades over games and dancing was not, however, entirely political. As early as 1923 he had attended an event sponsored by the Trinity College Gaelic Society at which G. A. Duncan had lashed out at the pseudo-Gaelicism of kilts and the like. In response, Blythe stated that while he agreed on the whole, he felt the students should understand the origin of the problem: 'Conditions as they existed two decades ago, and the desperate struggle to save something at least from the wreckage, had been the root cause of Pseudo-Gaelicism. The result was that they attached ridiculous importance to dances and games.' T. F. O'Rahilly was also present and added the typically biting comment that 'under this cult everyone could pose as a Gael in 24 hours by the simple expedient of giving an order to a tailor for a kilt' (*Weekly Freeman*, 17/11/23).

89 Tá tuairim ag daoine gur comhartha galldachais 'dress suit' do chaitheamh, nó bata siubhail d'iomchar, gan aoinní eile d'áireamh. Is mór an t-iongnadh nach ndeirtear linn ár méaracha d'oibriú i n-áit sgeana is forcanna. Nach é an cás céanna é? An dúil mhallaighthe seo i ngaedhealachas nach gaedhealachas – aineolas is mí-shibhialtas bun agus bárr di. Despite their shared distaste for 'Gaelachas na gCos', Ó Broin and 'Tadhg Gaedhealach' ended up in a vigorous debate over the existence of a 'Gaelic mind' in the March and May 1923 issues of *An Sguab*. (There was no issue in April of that year).

90 An té nach eol dó a theanga féin agus gur cuma leis na taobh níl na chaint i gcoinne cluichí gallda ach fasduím. Nach tábhachtaighe teanga ná cluiche. Táimíd bréan den a lán tírghrádh atá á chlos againn.

91 The official text of the ban reads in its English version: 'Any member who plays, attends or helps to promote Rugby, Soccer, Hockey or Cricket thereby incurs automatic suspension from membership of the Association.' See Cumann Lúthchleas Gaedheal (Gaelic Athletic Association), *Treoraí Oifigiúil / Official Guide* (BÁC: Ard-Chomhairle an Chumainn, 1956), 57. The ban was lifted in 1938, only to be re-imposed a year later. See also de Búrca, 168–70.

92 Hanly, 275. Hanly had chapters on 'National Folklore and Nationality', 'National Dancing and Nationality', and 'National Athletics and Nationality.'

93 P. J. Devlin, *Our Native Games* (Dublin: M.H. Gill, n.d.), 49. Later in the book, Devlin wrote:

> We cannot call a player a Gael simply because, living in the midst of Gaelic games, he condescends to partake of their enjoyments, no more than we can accept a man as an Irishman from mere accident of birth. There must be a spirit of Gaelicism or an active sense of nationality to deserve either title (p. 73).

One could almost think that Devlin was here refuting Leopold Bloom's famous definition of Irishness in his argument with the Citizen (a character partially modelled on GAA founder Michael Cusack) in Joyce's *Ulysses*.

94 Phil O'Neill ('Sliabh Ruadh'), *Twenty Years of the GAA 1910–1930: A History and Book of Reference for Gaels* (Kilkenny: Kilkenny Journal, 1931), 276.

95 Rud eile ná bíodh aon bhaint agaibh le rinncí gallda. Táimíd go léir an-dhian ar Dhiarmuid Mac Murchadha ós rud é gurbh é siúd an céad dhuine a thug cuireadh dos na Sasannaigh teacht go h-Éirinn. 'Diarmuid na nGall' a ghlaodhaimíd air ach is ionann agus 'Diarmuid na nGall' eile an t-Éireannach 's cuma cé h-é atá ag taobhú le geáitsí iasachta agus le nósanna na nGall.

96 See also his columns in *The Land* for 19/5/23, and 26/5/23; as well as P. Ó Faodhagáin, 'Rinnce Gaedhealach' (Gaelic dancing), *SF*, 17/11/25. Some actually felt that the League was helping destroy native dances by introducing and sponsoring an ersatz style of Irish dancing and pretending it was traditional. See, for example, Seán Ó Toghdha, 'Traditional Irish Dances / Their Correct Forms / Instructions Made Clear by Diagrams', *IC*, 17/1/25.

97 The editor concluded by arguing that the League should be 'let die' since 'its day and its work are done'. In the letters column for 5 Apr. 1930, all of the correspondence on this topic took exception with the views of the editor.

98 Thug Dia deich n-aitheanta dhúinn agus thug an Eaglais sé cinn dúinn ach dfág Dia agus an Eaglais ár saor-thoil againn . . . Ach níorbh fholáir leis an gConnra dul ní ba shía ná Dia agus an Eaglais agus dá réir sin tar éis roinnt aitheanta eile do cheapa dhúinn, do shocruigh sé ar ár saor-thoil do bhaint dínn. 'Cóilíon na haitheanta so go léir no ní leigfar duit an Ghaedhilg dfoghluim' . . . Do cuireadh ar bun saghas creidimh nua agus Olifeur Cromwell mar cheann dofheicse uirthi! A Chromwell naofa, guidh orainn, i slí is ná géillfimíd do chlainn Bhéelsebub, eadhon, Waltz, Fox-trot, Jazz, Soccer, Rugby, Guinness, Power, Sciorta Gearr, Beethoven, agus Súirghe ar Staighre. To get some flavor for the debate as conducted by the other side, see Cathal Ó Tuathail, 'Ní bhFaighidh an Connradh Bás ar Ordú an

Riaghaltais' (The league will not die at the Goverment's command), *FL*, Apr. 1930, 1; and Angus MacDonald, 'A New Language Movement Needed – To Co-Operate with the Government', *An Phoblacht*, 17/7/30.

99 He said the League's mission was 'intinn na ndaoine a dhéanamh láidir agus spiorad an neamh-spleadhachais a chur ionnta, agus é sin a dhéanamh tré ár dteanga féin a bheith beo athuair agus tré n-a cur i n-úsáid go h-éifeachtach ó chionn go cionn na hÉireann . . . Tugaim fá ndear go bhfuil an conta-bhairt ann go bhfuil an Connradh ag éirghe níos cumhainge gach aon bhliadhain. Tá rúin dá gcur i bhfeidhm ó bhliadhain go bliadhain i n-aghaidh a lán rudaí, agus is lugha an méid saoirse fágtar ag na Connrathóirí bliadhain ar bhliadhain.'

100 He said that 'indiu, cheapfadh aoinne go raibh an Connradh amuigh le deireadh a chur ar fad le saoirse tríd na rúin atá i bhfeidhm i n-aghaidh an ruda seo agus an ruda siúd.'

101 Tá urmhór na nGaedheal fíor-thuirseach den dream beag daoine sin nach dtig leo ní is fearr a dhéanamh 'ná 'rúin' a chur i bhfeidhm agus 'riaghalacha' a cheapadh, ionnas, tré a gcuid 'rún' is 'riaghalach' go mbéidh caoi aca daoine nach bhfuil ins an Chonnradh a choinneáil as, agus daoine atá ins an Chonnradh a dhíbirt as. See also 'Cormac', 'Dreamanna Poilitidheachta / Cuid de na Neithe a d'Fhág an Connradh fá Chúpla Mí de Bhéal na hUaighe' (Political groups / Some of the the things that left the League within a couple of months of the grave's edge), *Tír*, Nov. 1933, 4 and 6.

102 Is íontach an chiall atá ag cuid de na daoine do 'Ghaedhealachas'. Mur ndéanaidh tú seo, mur gcuiridh tú leis an riaghal sin, má glmí tú a léitheid sin, ní 'Gaedheal' thú, agus níl tú ar shon an Ghaedhealachais. Is dóigh liom go bhfuil i bhfad bar-raidheacht riaghalacha ag Connradh na Gaedhilge . . . Ba mhaith le lucht Chonnradh na Gaedhilge tír shaor Ghaedhealach a bheith againn arís: Buidheachas do Dhia gur dúil gan fághail sin daobhtha go fóill, nó b'fhearr liom comhnuidhe i n-áit ínteacht eile ná ins an tír shaor Ghaedhealach sin, óir tá mé ag déanamh gur bheag saoirse a bhéadh inntí. In the April 1934 issue of *An t-Ultach*, an anonymous contributor ridiculed the League for banning just about every-thing except the use of English (*Ultach*, Apr. 1934, 6).

103 See also the criticism of the 'negative puritanism' of many Irish-Irelanders in Uinsion de Barra, Letter, *IP*, 4/12/36.

104 'Sé an chuid is measa de'n scéal ná an méid raiméis cainte atá déanta mar gheall ar rud nach fiú tráithnín, an chaint ar fad, dar ndóigh, tríd an mBéarla go bhfuilimíd go léir chomh bréan de mar dh'eadh, agus na daoine gur cuma leo Gaedhilg agus gach a bhaineas léithi ag fonomhaid fé na Gaedhlaibh. See also the attack on the humourless rigidity of many Gaelic Leaguers by Riobárd Ó Faracháin in 'bhFuil Féith an Ghrinn i nGaedhealaibh?' (Do Gaels have a sense of humour?), *Outlook*, 12/3/32.

105 In an 'autobiographical' essay in *Comhthrom Féinne* in 1934, one of Brian Ó Nualláin's many comic alter egos, 'Brother Barnabbas', wrote: 'I was also told not to jazz, the thing being foreign and erotic, and three-quarters of the very word being composed of letters quite unknown to the old Irish' (*Comhthrom Féinne*, Jan. 1934, 12–13).

106 'Jazz' seems to have been the term used for contemporary popular music of all kinds. Irish-Irelanders gave no indication whatsoever that they knew anything at all about jazz *per se* or could even identify any of its contemporary masters. In such a climate, Liam Ó Rinn was a relief in that his dislike of jazz was at least not based on moral objections. See Ó Rinn, *Turus go Páras* (BAC: ODFR, 1931), 17.

107 Dá mbéadh fhios ag máithribh na tíre céard is damhsa Gallda ann, badh fhearr leó a n-ingheanacha a fheiceál sínte marbh faoi n-a gcosaibh sar a leigfeadh siad dóbhtha dul in a leithéide d'áit. For young men, the threat was to their virility, athletic prowess, and sanity! A speaker at the 1927 convention of the County Dublin Board of the National Athletic and Cycling Association asserted: 'Jazzing had become a mental disease, and before long many of their athletes would be found in the asylum at Grangegorman. Jazzing, at its present rate, would mean good-bye to athletics for the young men of the country, and that inside five years' (*II*, 22/3/27). The group of poets who gathered together as Dámh-Sgoil Mhúsgraidhe Uí Fhloinn published a whole page of poems on jazz in the issue of *An Muimhneach*, Mar. 1933 (p. 59).

108 The note of snobbery here is interesting. 'Sliabh Bladhma' drew a somewhat similar distinction between English high culture and the debased English amuse-ments adopted by the Anglicised Irish in 'Europe and Ireland' (*Gaedheal*, 20/10/34).

109 In the same journal three years earlier Cormac Breathnach had called Irish-speakers with no loyalty to broader Gaelic ideals 'semi-Gaels or jazz Gaels' (breac-Ghaedhil nó jazz-Ghaedhil) (*Camán*, June 1931, 7).

110 Measaim mar sin fhéin, gur admhúghadh é ó mhuintir na h-Éireann go bhfuil a ré mar náisiún caithte an lá a bheidh tóir foirleathan acu ar an 'jazz' agus an 'swing' agus a leithéidí.

111 Ó díbrigheadh Giúdaigh as an nGearmáin amach tháinigeadar go dtí an tír seo 'na sluaighte, agus anois tá na mílte díobh i mBláth Cliath agus ní amháin iad a bheith ann ach greim daingean docht aca ar go leor leor dhen tráchtáil agus de na siopaí. Is leo ar fad nach mór na h-amharclainn, agus na tighthe pictiúirí. He went on to fanatasise some kind of Pan-Jewish cultural imperialism: 'What interest would Jews who are allied with the big Jews in England have in anything to do with the nationality of this country?' (Cé an tsuim a chuirfeadh Giúdaigh atá coimh-

cheangailte le Giúdaigh mhóra i Sasanna – cé an tsuim a chuirfidís-sean i n-aon nídh a bhainfeadh do náisiúntacht na tíre seo?). To be fair, as Éamon Ó Ciosáin points out in his study of the paper, the anti-semitism that was such a pervasive element in the atmosphere of the time was rare in *An t-Éireannach*. See Ó Ciosáin, 187.

112 Is mian leo briseadh go deo ar chomhacht na nGiúdach is ar chomhacht na n-Aimeriocánach; is mian leo an Almáin bheith ina carn nirt agus ina lóchrann eolais idir Sasana Nuadh agus Asia . . . An rud is mian le hAlmánach sé bhaineann sé amach. But see also Risteárd Ó Glaisne, *Cearbhall Ó Dálaigh* (Má Nuad: An Sagart, 2001), 27, 69. In 1925 Father Dinneen published a short comic tale entitled 'Albanaigh agus Iúdaigh' (Scots and Jews), the point of which was that the former were more miserly than the latter. Dinneen made the following authorial comment in the narrative: 'It is not that I am saying that either side has earned that bad reputation. I don't know, but at any rate they do have that reputation' (Ní hamhlaidh adeirim go bhfuil an droch-ainm sin tuillte ag aon taobh aca. Ní fheadar ach tá an ainm son ortha ar aon chuma) (*Leader*, 25/7/25). For a curious half sympathetic, half-bigoted Gaelic view of the Jews, see 'Osraidhe', 'Na hIúdaigh / A Stair agus a dTréithe' (The Jews / Their history and their characteristics), *Hibernia*, Apr. 1939, 22–3. 'Osraidhe' claimed that after 1919 the Jews 'almost made another Sodom of Berlin' (is beag nach ndeárna na hIúdaigh Sodom eile de Bherlin). Dermot Keogh provides an authoritative discussion of ambivalent Irish attitudes towards Jews in our period in *Jews in Twentieth-Century Ireland* (Cork: Cork University Press, 1998), 54–152.

113 See Lil Conlon, *Cumann na mBan and the Women of Ireland, 1913–1925* (n.p., 1969); and Carol Coulter, *The Hidden Tradition: Feminism, Women and Nationalism in Ireland* (Cork: Cork University Press, 1993).

114 William Ferris, *The Gaelic Commonwealth: Being the Political and Economic Programme for the Irish Progressive Party* (Dublin: Talbot Press, 1923), 106. He concluded: 'We entertain no doubt as to what the result will be.' Patrick Murray has noted how threatening and distasteful supporters of the Treaty and the Free State found the aggressive activism of Republican women. See Murray, *Oracles of God: The Roman Catholic Church and Irish Politics, 1922–1937* (Dublin: University College Dublin Press, 2000), 88–9.

115 Father Patrick Dinneen, 'Queen of the Hearth – essay on womanhood in 15 sections', Patrick Dinneen Papers, NLI MS 8623 (11), 7 of the 'Woman at the Hearth' section. The punctuation in these quotations is that of Father Dinneen. In a brief, undated and unpublished piece of a play in English among his papers in the NLI, Dinneen created a female protagonist who belongs to 'The Association for Women's Rights', distributes a pamphlet entitled *Women and Social Progress*, and neglects husband and family. See Dinneen Papers, NLI MS 8623 (19).

116 Dinneen, 'Queen', 6–7 of 'The Education of Women' section. Immediately before the passage quoted here, Dinneen had written: 'The typical woman, however, is the mother, and it is the functions and requirements of motherhood that should in the main regulate the course of education.' He went on to claim that while girls rarely distinguish themselves in mathematics, the classics, logic, philosophy, or the physical and natural sciences, they are good at vernacular and modern languages.

117 Dinneen, 'Queen', 5 of the 'Motherhood' section. In the 'Authority in the Family' section, Dinneen wrote: 'As then not even the most extreme feminists claim for the wife supreme authority it must follow that this authority resides in the husband and that to him is due the obedience of the wife and of the entire family' (p. 2).

118 Dinneen, 'Queen', 3 of 'The Spirit of Rivalry' section. In a 1928 lecture to the Catholic Truth Society with An tAthair Gearóid Ó Nualláin in the chair, Séamus Ó Searcaigh declared of the women of the golden age of Irish Christianity:

> The women of Ireland were not like many of the women of the present with regard to children. The married woman understood that it was her duty to bring children into the world, and if she had the misfortune that God did not give her children, she was an object of great pity (Níor chosamhail mná na hÉireann sa mhéid a bhaineas le clainn le mórán de mhnáibh na h-aimsire seo. Thuig an bhean phósta gurbh'é a dualgas clann a thabhairt chun tsaoghail agus dá mbeadh sé de mhí-ádh uirthi nach gcuirfeadh Dia clann chuici ba mhór an díol truaighe í).

He also stated: 'He [God] created man and He created woman, and he left it in the nature of woman to bear children and to bring them into the world. She is the fountain of life' (Chruthuigh Sé [Dia] an fear agus chruthuigh Sé an bhean agus d'fhág Sé de nádúir sa mhnaoi clann a ghiúlan agus a thabhairt chun tsaoghail. Tobar na beatha í) (*Tír*, Nov. 1928, 5). On the other hand, on 16 Sept. 1936, Cáit Ní Chonchubhair debated Tomás P. Ó Laochdha in Irish on Radio Athlone on the topic 'Women in Industry' (*IP*, 16/9/36); and on 29/1/37, *IP* published a report on a radio debate between Treasa Nic Aodháin and Áine Ní Cheanainn on 'Saoirse na mBan' (Women's freedom).

119 See *Gill & Macmillan Annotated Constitution of Ireland with Commentary*, ed. J. Anthony Foley and Stephen Lalor (Dublin: Gill & Macmillan, 1995), 116–23. See also Tim Pat Coogan, *Eamon De Valera: The Man Who Was Ireland* (New York: HarperCollins, 1993), 494–8. The constitutional prohibition against divorce also appeared in article 41. De Valera was by no means idiosyncratic or isolated in his belief that

Catholic social principles demanded political recognition in a predominantly Catholic state. See, for example, 'Ollamh Fódla', 'Cuing an Phósta' (The marriage bond), *Sguab*, Oct. 1924, 193; and An t-Athair Pádraig Mac Giolla Cheara, *Foras Feasa ar Theagasc na h-Eaglaise* (Basic information about the teaching of the Church) (BÁC: ODFR, 1937), 267–77.

120 An t-Athair Pádraig Mac Giolla Cheara, *Teagasc Morálta na h-Eaglaise* (BÁC: OS, 1938), 112. Gidh go mbíonn cead ag mnaoi obair a dhéanamh agus posta a líonadh taobh amuigh de'n tigh, is é amharc i ndiaidh obair an tighe agus cúram na cloinne an dualgas a d'fhág dlighe na nádúra uirthí. In a 1932 piece on St Brigid, 'Giolla Bhríghde' had urged Irish women to adopt the saint as their role model: 'Let them stick to the old Gaelic customs that were established when the Faith was bright and strong in the heart of the Gael. Let them give the back of their hand to shameless pagan women abroad who want to restore the reign of paganism' (Claoidhidís le na sean-nósanna Gaodhalacha a bunuigheadh nuair a bhí an Creideamh geal láidir i gcroidhe an Ghaodhuil. Tabhraidís druim lámha le mnáibh mínáireacha págánacha thar lear ar mhaith leo réim na págántachta do chur i bhfeidhm arís) (*Hearthstone*, Feb. 1932, 250).

121 Terence Brown, *Ireland: A Social and Cultural History, 1922 to the Present* (Ithaca: Cornell University Press, 1985), 62. Brown's chapter on 'An Irish Ireland: Language and Literature' (pp. 37–61) provides an interesting though quite one-sided and limited discussion of this attitude among Irish-Irelanders at the time.

122 Níl ionainne ach cine beag daoine, ceithre milliún againn nó mar sin, agus sinn caithte ar oileán beag amuigh i lár na fairrge móire mar a bhfuil na céadta milliún Béarlóirí ar gach taobh dínn.

123 In a 1924 piece on 'Cúrsaí na mBúraigh' (News of the Boers), 'An Chú Mhall' wrote:

> Incidentally, that is an important question that is making the leaders of South Africa lose sleep at night, the question of the black people, the brown people (that is, the Indians and the Malays), and those 'coloured' people, but since it is something of a sort that does not in any way concern us here in Ireland, there is no need to say anything more about it (Dála an sgéil, sin ceist thábhachtach atá ag baint codladh na hoidhche ó lucht stiúrtha na h-Aifrice Theas ceist na ndaoine ngorm, na ndaoine ndonna (.i. na h-Indiaigh agus na Malays) agus na ndaoine 'ndathaighthe' úd, ach ós rud é nach bhfuil aon rud dá shaghas ag déanamh cúraim dúinn annso i nÉirinn ní gádh a thuille do rádh mar gheall uirthi) (*Sguab*, 5/31/24).

In *Mo Bhealach Féin* (My own way), Seosamh Mac Grianna discusses the sufferings of Blacks, pronounces them far greater than those experienced by the Irish, and then, with startling paternalism, suggests himself as a potential saviour of the race! See Mac Grianna, *Mo Bhealach Féin* (BÁC: OS, 1970 [1940]), 97–101.

124 Ní droch-eolus go dtí eolus ar dhroch-léightheoireacht, mar is féidir na droch-leabhair do léigheamh i ganfhios agus tá a leithéididhe go raidhseamhail i n-ár dtimcheall, agus ní headh na leabhair amháin atá go holc tá cuid de sna páipéarthaibh go dona go mór mór cuid de sna páipéarthaibh seachtmhaineamhla. Dinneen was speaking more as a Catholic moralist than as a Gaelic activist in these essays in *The Leader*, as is evident from his criticism of contemporary non-Catholic novelists in English in October 1925 (*Leader*, 31/10/25). See also his essays in *The Leader* for 3 June 1922; 18 Nov. 1922; 6 Jan. 1923; 28 Nov. 1925; and 14 Apr. 1928.

125 See also the 1925 *II* editorial on 'A National Duty': 'Not all of England's battalions in the worst days of repression could inflict upon Ireland a greater degradation than now threatens her from the dissemination of indecent literature, unnatural doctrines, and objectionable dances' (*II*, 20/4/25).

126 Tá an Béarla againn. Ba mhór ár meas air. Anois támuid ag éagcaoin fá'n bhail atá sé 'thabhairt orainn . . . Dubhairt Tone, beannacht Dé le n-anam, dubhairt sé gur bh'í Sasain íde gach uilc i nÉirinn. Fad is bhéas meas againn ar Shasain agus ar theangaidh na Sasana, bhéadh sé comh maith againn iarraidh a thabhairt teine a fhadódh le loch le n-a shamhailt go dtiocfadh linn cúl a thabhairt do dhroch-sgríbhinní. Responding to an essay by An Athair Seán Mac Craith in *Fáinne an Lae* in 1926, in which the author had in the same way juxtaposed English corruption and the innate purity of the Irish language, one 'Péintéir' suggested Mac Craith read *Cúirt an Mheadhon Oidhche* (The midnight court) as an antidote to his 'untruthful rhetoric' (retoric neamhfhíreannach), and continued:

> Seán Mac Craith thinks immoral literature will be cleaned out of the country if the Irish language is made the dominant language here again. How does he know? There is little the Irish language could not do if it were challenged to, and I think it would be easy for it to do the work of immorality as well as any language at all. If the people conduct themselves immorally when they have Irish in future, who will say that they won't get an opportunity to have an immoral literature in Irish as bad as, or worse than, the 'smutty sniflets' they get in the English papers at present (Ceapann Seán Mac Craith go nglanfar litríocht mhí-mhorálta as an tír má cuirtear an Ghaedhilg in uachtar arís inti. Cá bhfios dó? Is beag obair nach bhféadfadh an Ghaedhilg a dhéanamh dá gcuirtí uirri é agus measaim-se go mbfurasta dhí obair an mí-mhorálais do dhéanamh chó maith le teangaidh ar bith. Má bhíonn na daoine droch-iompartha nuair a

bhéas an Ghaedhilg acu cé adéarfas nach bhfuighe siad caoi ar litríocht mhí-mhorálta bheith acu san nGaedhilg chó holc leis na 'smutty sniflets' a gheibhid ins na páipéirí Gallda faoi láthair, nó níos measa) (*FL*, 15/5/26).

In a review of Feardorcha Ó Conaill'a *Giotaí as Cúirt an Mheadhon Oidhche* (Excerpts from *The Midnight Court*) in *IMN*, 'S. Ó S.' praised Merriman's poem and regretted that Ó Conaill had left out most of the funniest bits (*IMN*, 1929, 130). So much for a monolithic Maynooth prudery. In a witty letter to the *Irish Statesman* in 1928, 'Mac Neasa' wondered whether 'the good things in Irish' like the *Midnight Court* were to be abolished under the Censorship Act, or 'do they think that we who read Irish may read anything?' He commented that if the act exempted speakers of Irish, 'I can guarantee that within twelve months every civilised person in Ireland will be an Irish speaker' (*IS*, 15/9/28). In a 1932 essay in *Outlook* Donn Piatt wrote: 'It is possible to Anglicise Ireland through the medium of Irish, just the same as it could, conceivably, have been possible to Prosletise through the medium of Irish. Irish words can be used to express any class of ideas' (*Outlook*, 13/2/32). Piatt felt that the work of Gaeltacht writers would be the best defence against the insidious threat of 'the presumptive re-Gaelicised-in-language-but-not-in-ideas Ireland'.

127 The priest's advice was 'má tá focal nó líne nó leathanach ann a moitheochadh tú cotadh nó náire 'ghá léigheadh díthe, tarraing an luaidhe ghorm trasna fríd'. The author pronounced this 'as good advice as I ever got about writing (ar chomhairle comh maith agus fuair mé riamh fá ghnoithe sgríbhneóracht). Other prominent Gaelic writers who were criticised on moral grounds were Pádraic Ó Conaire, Seán Ó Caomhánaigh, León Ó Broin, and Tomás Ó Criomhthain. For Ó Conaire, see 'Comhghall', Letter, *Standard*, 6/4/29, and An tSiúr Éibhlín Ní Chionnaith, *Pádraic Ó Conaire: Scéal a Bheatha* (Pádraic Ó Conaire: The story of his life) (Indreabhán: Cló Iar-Chonnachta, 1995), 373–4, 387. For Ó Broin, see 'P. Ó D.' (probably Peadar Ó Dubhda), 'Leabhraí Nuadha' (New books) *An t-Ultach*, Nov. 1929, 2. For Ó Criomthain, see Breandán Ó Conaire, 'An tOileánach i gCló' (The islandman in print), in *Tomás an Bhlascaoid* (Tomás of the Blasket), ed. Ó Conaire (Indreabhán: Cló Iar-Chonnachta, 1992), 270–3, 281. The case of Ó Caomhánaigh will be considered separately.

128 An té chuireas roimhe bheith i n-a scríbhneóir i n-Éirinn, chead aige an fhírinne lom a scrúdughadh is a innse. Ná seachnadh sé an nídh tá míothmhar, má tá sé riachtanach a scrúdughadh . . . A bhfocal amháin, innseadh an scríbhneóir an fhírinne go deó fá na h-Éireannaigh is cuma comh searbh is bhéas sí. Acht ná cuireadh an fhírinne i n-éadóchas é. Tá sé daonna lochtach. Daoine na h-Éireannaigh. Tá claonta uilig an duine acú is tá tréithe maithe uilig an duine acú. Consistency was not always a hallmark of the thinking of even those Gaels who thought most. For example, Nollaig Mac Congáil has shown how Seosamh Mac Grianna shared some of the narrow puritanical nationalism of his time. See Mac Congáil, 'Seosamh Mac Grianna', in *Rí-Éigeas na nGael: Léachtaí Cuimhneacháin ar Sheosamh Mac Grianna* (The chief poet of the Gaels: Commemorative lectures on Seosamh Mac Grianna), ed. Mac Congáil (BÁC: Coiscéim, 1994), 144. See also the discussion of wholesome native art and foreign 'filth' (salachar) in Mac Grianna's unfinished novel *Dá mBíodh Ruball ar an Éan* (If the bird had a tail) (BÁC: An Gúm, 1992 [1940]), 85–87.

129 For a full discussion of state censorship in independent Ireland, see Michael Adams, *Censorship: The Irish Experience* (University: University of Alabama Press, 1968).

130 See, for example, 'Current Topics', *Leader*, 5/2/27; and Peadar Mac Fhionnlaoich, 'Teachtaí Dála / Labhraidís an Ghaedhilg' (Dáil deputies / Let them speak Irish), *Tir*, Jan. 1933, 2.

131 Arae tá gaol chomh gairid sin idir an dá chúis go mba chóir go raghaidís ar aghaidh le chéile lámh ar láimh. Dá fheabhas a éirigheann leis an ngluaiseacht nua is eadh is feileamhnaighe a bhéas an ithir i gcóir úirsíoltacht na Gaedhilge. Agus, do'n láimh eile isí an Ghaedhilg an cliath cosanta is fearr – ní abraimíd an t-aon cliath cosanta amháin – a shábhálas sinn sa deire ar an tuile millteach seo atá ag bagairt ar aigne an náisiúin.

132 The evidence therefore qualifies somewhat Maurice Goldring's assertion that 'one of the most powerful weapons in the armoury of the defenders of the tribe was censorship, which was as much a defence of Ireland's cultural borders as a religious and moral decision'. See Goldring, *Pleasant Is the Scholar's Life: Irish Intellectuals and the Construction of the Nation State* (London: Serif, 1993), 169. It was not only AE and *The Irish Times* that were critical of aspects of the censorship law. See, for example, 'Clearing the Air', *Honesty*, 3/12/27; 'The Censorship Bill', Editorial, *Star*, 26/1/29; Patrick Dinneen, 'An Litridheacht agus an Dlighe' (Literature and the law), *Leader*, 22/1/27; 'Editorial Notes / Crime and Censorship', *GR*, Mar. 1930, 309–11.

133 Editorial notes, *An t-Ultach*, Aug. 1928, 4. See also Murray, 'Droch-Dhamhsaí agus Droch-Pháipéir / 'Bhfuil Muid Dáiríribh Ann?' (Bad dances and bad papers / Are we serious?), *FL*, July 1928, 3.

134 Sean-cheist í sin atá á plé leis na bliantaibh, ach is deacair focal a cheapadh a chuirfadh cosc le salachar fé chló agus ná cuirfadh cosc le clódóireacht eile san am gcéadna. See also 'Na Páipéaraí Gallda', *An t-Ultach*, Mar. 1931, 8.

135 Bu thuigsionaighe agus bu ghrinne pobal na hÉireann nuair nach raibh ach beagán leabhar – agus an beagán sin go maith – dhá léigheadh aca.

Chothuigheadh sin agus a mbéal-oideas féin . . . gur bhfeairrde iad é agus go raibh a shliocht orra, dá chionn sin . . . Ní mór, dar linn, an chriathar oibriú ar a lán téacs-leabhra atá ar úsáid i sgolta na hÉireann fá láthair. Cé a déarfadh go bhfuil baol ar a bhfuil díobh ann feileamhnach do Ghaedheala óga? He had begun this editorial by stating that virtually all (rí-fhurmhór) of the books then being published were suffused with 'worldliness and triviality' (saoltacht agus suarachas).

136 Isé an Ghaodhluinn an t-aon sgiath cosanta amháin atá aici, an t-aon mhúr amháin i gcoinnibh an namhaid. America féin, dá mhéid a cómhacht, cuid de impríocht na Sasannach is eadh í. Óir, níl de chultúr aici ach amháin cultúr na Sasannach. Speaking in Rathfarnham in the same year, Éamon de Valera called on the Irish to erect 'the wall of the language' (fál na teangan) against the threat of foreign corruption. See 'Sgeula na Seachtaine / E. de Bhaléra agus an Ghaedhilg' (The week's stories / E. de Valera and the Irish language), *FL*, 6/9/24.

137 Cad tá le tairgsin ag an Eoraip dúinne nach bhfuil againn féin? . . . Is minic a casadh linn go rabhamar ró-oileánach, go rabhamar cumhang-intinneach, agus nár mhaith linn aon dearcadh bheith againn, taobh amuigh de cheithre coirnéal na hÉireann. Ach má's amhlaidh a bhí, cad a chailleamar dá chionn soin? Má d'fhanamar oileánach féin, is feairrde sinn go mór fada é, óir d'éirigh linn saoidheacht phágánta na mór-thíre do sheachaint.

138 James Devane, *Isle of Destiny: The Clash of Cultures* (Dublin: Browne & Nolan, [1937]), 244. See also Devane, 'Four Irish Myths', *Ireland To-Day*, June 1936, 9–20. In its inaugural editorial in 1923, *An Gaodhal* also vowed to avoid 'any narrow line', and instead 'to endeavour to assimilate and mould to the Gaelic idea what we find best in the development of the world at large. It will be no part of our aim to take any course which will tend to shut out this country from the eyes of the world' (*Gaodhal*, 20/10/23). That Irish might be deliberately used to isolate the country from foreign influences was deeply troubling to George Thomson. See his views as quoted by Seán Ó Lúing in the preface to *Gach Orlach de Mo Chroí: Dréachta* (Every inch of my heart: Writings), ed. Ó Lúing (BÁC: Coiscéim, 1988), 4–5.

139 Mac Niocaill was much less enthusiastic about even the greatest treasures of English culture: 'To the people who flourished Shakespeare in their faces they would say that they were going to save their tongue if it killed Shakespeare and every other body.'

140 He went on: 'It is true that in an Irish-speaking Ireland we might have to do without much of the fourth or fifth rate stuff with which the country is flooded at present, but this is a loss which few of us would bemoan.'

141 Níor ghéill muinntear na hÉireann ariamh do Shasain i gcúrsaí creidimh; ní ghéillfidh siad anois d'ainchríostamhlacht na Rúise.

142 Dr Panini, *Irish Up-to-Date*, 7. See also 'P. H.', 'Intinn an Phápa – Mí Eanáir / An Cath i n-Aghaidh an Ainchreidimh' (The Pope's intention – January / The battle against unbelief), *TCNÍ*, Jan. 1935, 1–3. In a favourable piece on the labour leader James Larkin, Muiris Mag Uidhir did note that Larkin was guilty of 'things no one who is loyal to the faith of our race would do' (rudaí nach ndéanfadh aoinne atá díleas do chreideamh ár gcinidh), among them his fascination with the Soviet Union (*Tír*, June 1932, 3). Seán Ó Ciarghusa was sharply critical of socialism in his essay 'Mats' (i.e. Maths), *Leader*, 7/10/33. See also 'Finnéigeas', 'Bolséibheachas na Rúise – Námhaid na Náisiún Beag' (Russian Bolshevism / The enemy of the small nations), *Hibernia*, Jan. 1937, 15.

143 Shán Ó Cuív, 'An Saol sa Rúis' (Life in Russia), in *Deora Áthais agus Dréachta Eile* (Tears of joy and other writings) (BÁC: OS, 1937), 127–9. He wrote 'nách aon "neamh ar talamh" an Rúis ach gnáth-thír 'n-a gcaitheann daoine maireachtaint ar nós daoine ins gach tír eile, agus nách athrú chun leasa na ndaoine gach athrú dá dtáinig ann le tamall anuas.' See also Ó Glaisne's discussion of the views of Ua Dálaigh in *Cearbhall Ó Dálaigh*, 70–1. Pádraig de Barra offered a not entirely negative view of the Soviet Union in 'Coraí Cine Rúise' (The situation of the Russian race), *IMN*, 1931, 66–79.

144 Liam Ó Rinn, 'Roimhrá' (Preface), in Ivan Turgenev, *Dánta Próis* (Prose poems), tr. Ó Rinn (BÁC: ODFR, 1933), 9. He wrote of 'daoine áirithe go bhfuil glactha acu le naofacht na maoine príobháidighe mar phrinsiobal agus gur fuath leo dá réir sin an iarracht atá á dhéanamh ag muintir na Rúise ar a ngnó féin do riaradh contrárdha don phrionsiobal san.' See also the account of his discussion of capitalism and socialism with Stephen McKenna in *Mo Chara Stiofán*, 139.

145 Micheál Mac Craith, CI, 'De Thoradh na Sochaidheachta (i.e. Socialism) (Concerning the consequences of socialism), in *Deora Drúchta Camhaoire* (Dewdrops of dawn) (BÁC: M. H. Mac an Ghoill agus a Mhac, 1928), 37–9. Is móide gach lá ghá chur na luighe ar na gnáth-dhaoine é, a riachtanaighe atá sé ceangal na gcúig gcaol do chur ar na mór-ghustalaigh, i dtreo go bhfaghfar a rádh gan scáth nach amháin nach aon tsochaidiú oll-choitcheann theastaigheas ón bpobal, acht nach gábhadh dhóibh sochaidiú leath-rannach féin.' In 'Meón na Críos-taíochta agus an Tír Dhúchais' (The spirit of Christianity and the native land), Mac Craith again condemned both crass capitalist materialists and those on the left 'who would set the people adoring the idol and the false god of the State' (a chuirfeadh na daoine ag adhradh íodhail is dé bhréige an Stáit) (*Deora Drúchta*, 49–63).

146 See *Gill and Macmillan Annotated Constitution of Ireland*, 128–9. This section and section three, recognising the other religious denominations 'existing in

Ireland at the date of the coming into operation of this Constitution', were removed by a referendum in 1972 that approved of the fifth amendment to the document. The change was supported by 84.4 per cent of those who voted. See *Gill and Macmillan Constitution*, 209–14. See de Valera's remarks on the installation of Douglas Hyde as the first president of Ireland in *CB*, July 1938, 548; the full text is available in *Speeches and Statements by Éamon De Valera*, ed. Maurice Moynihan (Dublin: Gill & Macmillan, 1980), 353–4. For an insight into the climate of Catholic political thought at the time that would have influenced de Valera, see An tAthair Pádraic Mac Giolla Cheara, *Díon-Chruthughadh an Chreidimh nó Apologetic* (Apologetics) (BÁC: ODFR, 1936), 155, 182, 192–3.

147 There was nothing new in this belief, of which An tAthair Peadar Ua Laoghaire was a particularly forceful advocate. See O'Leary, *Prose Literature*, 19–27.

148 Is léir do chách an dlúthbhaint atá idir an Ghaedhilg agus an creideamh agus ar an ádhbhar san ní gádh aon tagairt do dhéanamh do'n cheist sin. Má imthigheann an teanga beidh an creideamh i mbaoghal. Is amhlaidh atá nádúr an díchreidimh sa Bhéarla.

149 Tá cion ar an gCreideamh, tá meas ar an Maighdean Muire, tá urramh do Phádraig naomhtha, tá grádh d'Íosa Críost, – tá siad laistigh de'n Ghaoluinn; tá siad fighte, fillte, geinte go dlúth i spioraid na Gaoluinne. Ach a mhalairt ar fad de thréithibh is eadh a bhaineann leis an mBéarla . . . Gaedheal dá fheabhas ná fuil ag cabhrú leis an nGaoluinn, tá sé ag cabhrú leis an nGall. Is léir don tsaoghail go bhfuil an Gall i gcoinnibh Dé agus i gcoinnibh an Chreidimh, i dtreo, an Gaedheal úd atá 'na Ghall, nach fuláir nó gur dall é, nó gur namhaid do'n Chreideamh agus do Dhia na Glóire é. Ó Nualláin's faith in the link between Catholicism and *Gaelachas* remained unshaken. See his autobiography, *Beatha Duine a Thoil*, 68–9, 200.

150 Má tá litridheacht le scríobhadh i n-Éirinn, le bheith na fíor-litridheacht, caithfidh sí bheith Gaedhealach. Is ionann sin a rádh go gcaithfidh sí bheith Catoiliceach. In a 1929 piece on 'Ár nOighreacht' (Our birthright), 'Giolla Brighde' stated succinctly: 'In the mind of the Irish speaker, Gael and Catholic are one and the same' (Ionann Gaedheal agus Caitliceach i n-intinn an Ghaedhilgeora) (*Standard*, 23/2/29). For other examples of this widespread attitude, see An tAthair S. Mac Leanacháin, 'An Creideamh agus an Ghaedhilg' (The faith and the Irish language), *Standard*, 29/6/29; 'Our Irish Sermon', *IC*, 22/2/30; and 'An Blascaod Mór / Saoghal ar an Oileán' (The Great Blasket / Life on the island) (*Standard*, 15/6/34), this last the thoughts of Peig Sayers as written down by her son Micheál Ó Gaoithín.

151 Ba í an Ghaedhilg, i ndiaidh grásta Dé, an cuidiú ba treise dá raibh ag an Chreideamh ó briseadh ar Ghaedhealaibh . . . Isí an teanga is sciath-chosanta don Chreideamh agus don Náisiúntacht. Ní móide go mbéadh Éire ina tír Chatoilicigh indiu murab é teanga na Gaedhilge. Isí an Ghaedhilg a las spiorad an Chreidimh i gcroidhe na nGaedheal le cúig céad déag bliadhain agus isí a choinneochas an Creideamh sin láidir neartmhar a fhad is bhéas focal den teangaidh sin dá labhairt ar bhántaibh Fáil. Gillian McIntosh discusses the importance of this event in 'Acts of "National Communion": The Centenary Celebrations for Catholic Emancipation, the forerunner of the Eucharistic Congress', in *Ireland in the 1930s: New Perspectives*, ed. Joost Augusteijn (Dublin: Four Courts Press, 1999), 83–95. On the other hand, Peadar Mac Fhionnlaoich saw a different message in the public celebrations of the centenary of Emancipation: 'The great celebration we had going on this past week showed how Catholic we are in Dublin and throughout the Free State; but it also showed how foreign we are and how poor we are in national characteristics' (Thaisbeáin an ceileabhradh mór do bhí ar siubhal againn an tseachtmhain seo caithte comh Catoiliceach is támaoid i mBaile-Átha-Cliath agus ar fud an tSaor-Stáit; ach thaisbeáin sé fosda, comh coigcríochach is támaoid, agus comh bocht is támaoid i dtréithe Náisiúnta) (*Nation*, 6/7/29).

152 Tá a fhios ag an tsaoghal anois gur tír Chatoiliceach Éire, agus gur tír í a bhfuil a teanga náisiúnta aici, teanga bhí dá labhairt go moch is go mall le moladh agus buidheachas a thabhairt do Dhia . . . Ní baoghal don Chreideamh i nÉirinn má mhaireann an Ghaedhilg slán.

153 Acht ní chríochnóchad an aiste seo gan seo do rádh: cuimhnighimís gur b'í an chuid is Gaedhealaighe dár n-aigne an chuid is dlúithe Catoiliceachas. See also Pádhraic Ó Domhnalláin ('An Connachtach Bán'), 'Meón na nGaedheal' (The mind of the Gaels), in *Na Spiadóirí agus Sgéalta Eile* (The spies and other stories) (BÁC: Brún agus Ó Nualláin, Teor., n.d.), 99–102.

154 Art Ó Riain, *Lucht Ceoil* (Musicians) (BÁC: ODFR, 1932), 245. Cuimhnigh go raibh an creideamh chomh fighte fuaighte sin i saoghal na nGaedheal nárbh fhéidir gan é bheith le fagháil i ngach rud. In a review of *Lucht Ceoil* in *IR*, the anonymous critic said the novel was characterised by 'true Catholicism and true faith' (fíor-chatoiliceacht agus fíor-chreideamh), and that it was 'a sound, healthy novel' (úrsgéal slán folláin) (*IR*, Feb. 1933, 160). The novel does, however, present a Catholic priest as snobbish and rather un-Christian (p. 217). But then again, he is English!

155 Tá tréith amháin ba mhaith linn a thraoslú dhó go speisialta. 'Sé rud é ná feallsamhnacht Chatoiliceach a bheith fighte isteach ins na scéalta aige . . . Is fáilteach linn so go mór-mór óir do cuireadh ar ár súilibh dúinn go borb le déanaighe gur baoghal do nuadh-litridheacht na Gaedhilge a tumadh i n-iomar na saluigheachta as ucht a leanta de lorg shleamhain an Bhéarla.

156 Is dóigh nach bhfuil teanga eile beo is mó a bhfuil cráibhtheacht agus creideamh ag baint léi ná mar atá le teanga na Gaedhilge mar labhartar í ó lá go lá.

157 Seán Ó Ruadháin, *Pádhraic Mháire Bhán nó An Gol agus an Gáire* (Pádhraic Mháire Bhán, or weeping and laughter) (BÁC: ODFR, 1932), 9. Ach tá oighreacht amháin ag an nGaedheal nach dtuigeann sé féin an tairbhe atá ann, is é sin creideamh láidir agus dóchas daingean. Duine ar bith a bhfuil sin aige is duine saidhbhir é bíodh i ndán agus go bhfuil sé ag dul ó theach go teach ag iarraidh na déirce, agus an té atá gan é . . . go bhfóiridh Dia na Glóire é.

158 Séamas Mac Conmara, 'Glóire Dé agus Onóir na hÉireann' (The glory of God and the honour of Ireland), in *Saol agus Saothar Shéamais Mhic Chonmara* (The life and work of Séamas Mac Conmara), ed. Seán Mac Cionnaith (BÁC: Coiscéim, 1988), 15. Mothuighimid ins an dá rud atá cóimhcheangailte i ngluaiseacht na Gaedhilge – an tsaoidheacht agus an béaloideas atá de dhíth orainn le náiseán úr a chur ar bun, agus an Ghaedhilg atá mar bhéadh ina taisgeadán don tsaoidheacht sin – mothuighimid tréith amháin go sonnruightheach. 'Sí tréith í sin báidh as cuimse aca leis an chreideamh chaitliceach. Ta an bháidh sin chómh láidir agus chómh buan agus chómh h-uile láithreach ionnta ina mbeirt a's go gcaithfeá a rádh nach tréith atá innte ach cuid bhunadhasach riachtanach . . . 'Sé a bhfuil mé 'á mholadh gléas úr ár gcosnuighthe féin a bheith againn, síothlán nó gléas sgagtha, mar a déarfá, a chuirfeadh cúl ar bhunadhas a bhfuil olc agus a bhéarfadh cead coise do bhunadhas a bhfuil maith. Ach sin go díreach an rud a dhéanfadh an Ghaedhilg dá mbíodh sí againn . . . Sin thuas an Ghaedhilg agus í ina sciathchosanta againn ar an tsaoghal mhór. Mac Conmara's was a broad-minded and inclusive definition of Irishness. For example, the protagonist of *An Coimhthigheach* (BÁC: OS, 1970 [1939]) regards members of the Orange Order as Irish despite their religion and politics (pp. 79–80).

159 Dlúthaigh Pádraig ár dteanga agus ár gCríostaidheacht i n-aon ghléas do-scaoilte amháin, agus snaidhm na naoimh agus na h-éigse i n-a chéile iad rith na gcúig gcéad bliain a tháinig 'n-a dhéidh sin. Ó Dubhda was campaigning to have the Gaelic League make the teaching of Catholic doctrine and prayers an official part of its programme.

160 See, for example, Brown, 80–106; F. S. L. Lyons, 'The Minority Problem in the 26 Counties', in *The Years of the Great Test 1926–1939*, ed. Francis MacManus (Cork: Mercier, 1967), 97–103; Julian Moynihan, *The Anglo-Irish: The Literary Imagination in a Hyphenated Culture* (Princeton: Princeton University Press, 1995), 198–210.

161 Tá daoine annseo go bhfuil obair mhór déanta aca ar son na Gaedhilge agus ar son náisiúntachta na hÉireann i gConnradh na Gaedhilge agus i ngluaiseachta eile i nÉirinn. Is aca-san atá an t-eolas maith chomh cáirdeamhail a's a bhíos na Gaedhil leo i gcomhnuidhe. Anois nuair nach mbéidhimíd deighilte ó'n a chéile mar gheall ar phoilitigheacht, ní fheicimse ádhbhar imris nó easaontais ar bith idir Protastúnaigh agus Caitlicigh Rómhánacha. Éireannaigh go léir sinne; Gaedhil go léir sinne.

162 Éamon Ó Ciosáin discusses Gaelic and Republican suspicion of Protestant cultural nationalists like Seán Beaumont and Ernest Joynt in *An t-Éireannach*, 67.

163 Creidim go bhfuil sa troid seo atá Connradh na Gaedhilge a dhéanamh rud is mó 'ná troid idir dhá theangaidh. Tá an Connradh ag iarraidh sibhialtacht ársa ár dtíre a choinneáil beo. Troid atá ann idir an tsibhialtacht a thoisigh Pádraig i nArd Mhacha agus an tsibhialtacht a thoisigh Martan Lútar, sibhialtacht atá ann go fóill, agus a bhfuil a toradh le feiceáil againn indiu féin.

164 Ní chuirim síos annseo aoinnídh i n-aghaidh creidimh ar bith; ní bhainim leis an tslighe chráibhtheachta atá ag duine ar bith; ní chuirim i n-aghaidh aon chreidimh mar chreideamh diadha. See also Seán Ó Ciarghusa's 'Liúteir' (Luther), *Leader*, 18/10/30; and 'Beurla na nGall' (The English of the English), *Leader*, 14/2/31.

165 Teastuigheann Poblacht uainn ar son iomlán na hÉireann. Agus, ó tá mórán daoine in Éirinn nach Catoilicigh ní theastuigheann aon dlighe nó riaghal uainn a chuirfeas isteach ortha siúd ach oiread le cách. Stát Catoiliceach a bhéas ann sa' chéill go mbeidh furmhór na ndaoine Catoiliceach. Agus ceart agus cóir aca sa' Stát. Ní rachamaoid níos fuide ná sin. Ní leigfear do'n Róimh cur isteach orrainn ach oiread le Sasanaibh. Mac Fhionnlaoich invoked the Protestant nationalist Thomas Davis (1814–45) in support of his views.

166 Dá mbeadh Tone i n-a bheatha faoi láthair, bhéadh creideamh Gallda aige, an mbéadh? Bhéadh air éisteacht le hioman Catoiliceach dhá sheinnt i bPáirc an Chrócaigh, cé gur cluiche i gcóir an náisiúin go h-iomlán a bhéadh ar siubhal. Cé gur Catoiliceach mé féin tá ard-mheas agam ar gach Gaedheal, cuma fá n-a chreidimh. Tá deighilt mhór idir creideamh agus náisiúntacht, agus a thúisge a thuigfeas cách é sin is amhlaidh is fearr é. Mag Uidhir responded that he used the term as did native speakers, who referred to anyone non-Catholic, wherever born and raised, as 'Gall' (an English person or foreigner). He added that he hoped it would be understood that 'it was not from any narrow-mindedness or ill-will towards anyone that people who are not Catholics are said to be of the "English religion" in places in Ireland' (nach le caol-intinneacht ar bith ná droch-mheon ar éinne a tugtar 'An Creideamh Gallda' ar daoine nach Caitilicigh iad, in áiteacha in Éirinn) (*Éireannach*, 14/3/36).

167 Tá náisiúntacht eile ann, ámh, seachas an náisiúntacht phoiliticeach. Tuigimidne, Fáinnigh, murab ionann agus daoine eile, gurb í an náisiúntacht

spioradálta an náisiúntacht is buaine agus is daingne . . . B'fhéidir nach misde a rádh gurb ionann brí do'n fháinne s'againne agus d'fháinne an phósta. Comhartha ceangail eadrainn seadh é, 'nó go scarfaidh an bás ó chéile sinn'.

168 The League's Craobh na gCúig gCúigí ('Branch of All [lit. Five] Provinces') was jokingly referred to as the 'Branch of the Five Protestants' because of the prominent role played by Protestants in its activities. In a 1934 piece in *An t-Éireannach*, Séamus Ó Néill urged his fellow Gaels to try to Gaelicise Northern Protestants and to educate them to a proper national outlook: 'They had that before and some of them have it still; why would they not all have it again?' (Bhí sin acu roimhe agus tá sé ag cuid acu go fóill, cad chuige nach mbeadh sé acu uilig arís?) (*Éireannach*, 23/6/34). On the other hand, many Irish-Irelanders supported the protests against the appointment of a Protestant as the county librarian for Mayo. To give them credit, however, they for the most part stressed the inadequate linguistic qualifications of the Protestant candidate, who did not know Irish. For a discussion of this whole episode, see J. J. Lee, *Ireland 1912–1985: Politics and Society* (Cambridge: Cambridge University Press, 1989), 161–7; and Murray, *Oracles of God*, 131–3, 255–7.

169 In a piece in *Sinn Féin* in 1924, Ó Grianna defined what he meant by a native speaker:

> There is only one meaning for native speaker. That is, the person whom the midwife who will put on his first garment cajoles in Irish. The person whose mother will soothe him to sleep with Gaelic music. The person who hears nothing but Irish in his youth. The person whose lungs and the rest of his vocal apparatus will grow in keeping with the sounds of Irish. There is the native speaker for you! (Níl acht aon chiall amháin le cainnteoir dúthchais. Sé sin an té a gcuirfidh an bhean-ghlúin an chéad chideóg air agus í ag blanndar leis i nGaedhilic. An té a chealgfas a mháthair un suain le ceol Gaedhilge. An té nach gcluineann acht Gaedhilic i n-a óige. An té a bhfásfaidh a sgeadamán agus an chuid eile dá ghléasaraidhe cainnte ag cur le tuaimneannaí na Gaedhilge. Sin agat an cainnteoir dúthchais!) (*SF*, 5/7/24).

In 1929, he offered a surprisingly tongue-in-cheek definition:

> A person who has Irish from the cradle – provided (1) that the person who cared for him while he was in the cradle and for five years after he left the cradle had good Irish. (2) That the cradle not be over two and a half feet. (3) That two and a half feet be long enough for the child, that is, that he can stretch himself in it (Duine a bhfuil an Ghaedhilg aige ó'n chliabhán – acht (1) Gaedhilg mhaith a bheith ag an té a rinne freastal air fad is bhi sé sa chliabhán agus ar feadh chúig mbliadhan i ndiaidh é an cliabhán a fhágáil. (2) Gan an cliabhán a bheith ós cionn dhá throigh go leith ar fad. (3) An dá throigh go leith sin a bheith fada go leor ag an leanbh, sé sin é bheith ábalta é féin a shíneadh ann) (*FL*, Jan. 1929, 4).

170 Is fada ó chuaidh mise i n-éadóchas fá Ghaedhilic Chúigeadh Uladh . . . Ní shílfear a dhath dár gcuid Gaedhilice feasta, nó do chuid na Mumhan, nó Chonnachta. 'Sí Gaedhilic Bhaile Átha Cliath a bhéas ann feasta. Agus leoga sin féin an donán ar thús cadhanaidheachta. Ní leas-ainm ar bith Gaedhilic coise-maide uirthí. Acht tá an chos-mhaide ag tarraingt orainn. See also Ó Grianna, 'Acadamh Gaedhealach', *CB*, June 1927, 636–8. In this piece Ó Grianna argued that if native speakers came together, they could sort out the dialect controversy in fairly short order. He stated that it was the learners who were most aggressively attached to the particular dialects they had acquired. Indeed he went so far as to say that much of his previous opposition to Munster Irish was due to his having mistaken what learners claimed was Munster Irish for the real thing.

171 Nach deacair dúinn a aidhmheáil gur ag an dóirnéalach gharbh ghlas atá an Ghaedhilic agus nach againne . . . Acht tá siad ag imtheacht, mar Ghaedhil. Agus imtheacht an t-srotha 'na mhuilinn chuca. Ár seacht mallacht go rabh leó féin agus le na gcuid fuamann agus cor-cainnte. In his October 1929 'As na Ceithre h-Áirdibh Fichead' (From all points of the compass) column, he called for the application of Swift's 'modest proposal' to Gaeltacht children, writing of the contemporary Gaeltacht: 'There are still native speakers there, and nothing can be done for the language until they are all dead' (Tá cainnteóirí dúthchais annsin go fóill agus ní féidir a dhath a dhéanamh ar son na teangtha go mbídh siad uilig marbh), *FL*, Oct. 1929, 2).

172 Dá mbíodh gléas cainnte ag na cainnteóirí dúthchais, ba doiligh do na sgoláirí agus do na h-ughdair agus do na h-ollamhain an árd-réamh atá aca a choinneál. Is fearr a mbás a leigin den ocras 'ná gléas a thabhairt dóbhtha ealadha-mhagaidh a dhéanamh dínn . . . na micilíní agus na seáiníní agus na taidhgíní beaga sgallta. Is beag a bhéarfadh orm mo sheacht mallacht a chur ortha. In a 1931 dialogue in *The Leader* between a linguistic purist and a more flexible Irish-speaker, Piaras Béaslaí gives the purist the following Ó Griannesque line: 'I'd rather see Irish decently dead than see the fine vigorous language of the Gaeltacht degenerate into a kind of "pidgin talk"' (*Leader*, 5/12/31).

173 Cainnteóirí dúthchais! Gheall ar Dhia leat agus bíodh trí spaideóg chéille agat anois féin go fuar. Déanamh go bhfuilmid-inne 'gabháil a dhéanamh aithris ar chuid uasgán Thírchonaill agus Chonamara, agus an chuid is mó aca gan de 'chultúr' aca acht oiread le madadh. A bhean chléibh, tá cuid aca agus níl focal Béarla i n-a bpluic. See also Ó Grianna,

'Leitir ó Mháire', *FL*, 14/2/25. When the then-editor of *FL*, Pádhraic Ó Domhnalláin, cut bits from this letter, Ó Grianna wrote in blasting the decision (*FL*, 21/2/25). In a 1928 piece in *The Leader*, 'Mughdorn' adopted a tone Ó Grianna must have enjoyed, writing: 'I am only joking, but the Native Speaker is a bit of a nuisance. It would be pleasant to be learning Irish only for him. You think you know the language till you meet him; then you find you don't, and you are disgusted with yourself.' He then went on to discuss the social failings of 'poor, old, tattered' and illiterate native speakers, concluding: 'In fact, your amour propre wouldn't let you consult the like of him at all only for your love of Irish' (*Leader*, 30/6/28).

174 Ní rabh rún ar bith agam i m'óige rud ar bith a sgríobhadh. Mheas mé (rud a mheasaim go fóill) nach rabh sé ionnam litridheacht éifeachtach a chruthughadh. Acht nuair a chonnaic mé an cineál Gaedhilge a bhí dá sgríobhadh, cuid de ag daoiní nár mhó ná go rabh an 'chéad leabhar' foghlumtha aca, dar liom go dtaisbeánainn an difear a bhí eadar Gaedhilg agus Gaedhilg. Ó Grianna, Letter to Muiris Ó Droighneáin, 20/10/27, quoted in *Féile Rann na Feirste 17ú–19ú Samhain 1989: Séamus Ó Grianna ('Máire') Comóradh Céad Bliain*, 12.

175 Ní maith liom rud mar seo a rádh fá dhaoiní atá ar a ndícheall. Ní abórainn é ach oiread le sin, murab é go bhfeicim le mo shúile cinn go bhfuil an lá a' teacht a gcaithfidh an cainnteóir dúthchais a ghabháil un spáirne leis an mhuintir a d'fhoghluim a gcuid Gaedhilge, go gcaithfidh sé cath dian díbhirceach a dhéanamh ag cosnadh na h-oighreachta a fágadh aige. Ó Grianna launched a full-scale attack on 'the scholars' (na scoláirí) in this piece, stating:

> They know in their hearts that they do not have Irish as we have it and that they will not unless they are remade all over again. They know that it is like mashed potatoes in their mouths compared to how it is with us. And they also know that if the Irish of the Gaeltacht becomes dominant they themselves will be objects of ridicule (Tá fhios aca istuigh i n-a gcroidhe nach bhfuil an Ghaedhilg aca mar tá sí againne agus nach mbíonn go ndéantar arais iad. Tá fhios aca go bhfuil sí mar bheadh brúightín i n-a mbéal le taobh mar tá sí againnne. Agus tá fhios aca fosta má thig Gaedhilg na Gaedhealtachta 'un cinn go mbeidh siad féin 'na n-ealadha-mhagaidh).

176 Mur bhfuilmuid dáríribh fá'n Ghaedhilg cad chuige i n-ainm na hÉireann, i n-ainm ár sinnsear, i n-ainm na fírinne, i n-ainm fiúntais, agus i n-ainm Dé, cad chuige nach leigimuid díthe bás a fhagháil go suaimhneach agus gan bheith 'silíneacht uirthi mar támuid? Tá sé dona go leor í bheith le rádh linn gur leigeamar a bás. Acht nach measa míle uair an bhúistéaracht atámuid a dhéanamh uirthi? See also his satirical piece 'Nuair a Bhí Mise i m'Aire Oideachais' (When I was Minister for Education), in which he confronts an embodied 'Official Irish' (Gayling Ifigool) in a government office (*An Phoblacht*, 22/12/28). When 'Aodh Dubh' wrote to *FL* to complain that Ó Grianna's 'bitter and venomous' (géar, nimhneach) writing was hurting those doing their best to learn and advance the language, Ó Grianna responded with a parable about a soft-skulled man hurt in a faction fight at a fair. The moral was that he should never have entered the fray if he was unfit for it (*FL*, Mar. 1929, 7).

177 Thig le uasgán ar bith na Phagocytes a ghríosughadh. Acht níl cumhacht ar an domhan le cainnteoir dúthchais a dhéanamh de dhuine. Slug sin, a ghiolla mhóir na mór-chéimeann agus na gann-Ghaedhilge. Níl liaigh ar an domhan a chuirfeadh an faobhar ar do theangaidh atá ar mo theangaidh-sa, mur' ndéanadh an Rúisíneach úd é a bhíos ag gabháil do na monkey glands. B'fhéidir dá mbaintí glands as sean-duine de chuid na Gaedhealtachta agus a gcur ionnat go ndéanfadh sé maith duit.

178 Níl fhios agam an síleann siad gur 'Cultúr Gaedhealach' an rud atá aca. B'fhéidir go síleann. Deirtear go síleann an préachán dubh gur geal atá sé . . . Níl fhios an rabh aon teangaidh eile ariamh ar an domhan a bhí comh breágh leis an Ghaedhilg? Nó aon teangaidh eile ar fágadh a sábháil i muinighín an cineál dobhrán agus caimleóirí atá ag teacht i dtír ar an Ghaedhilg?

179 Nach bhfuil fhios ag Dia is ag an tsaoghal nach bhfásann litridheacht sa Ghaedhealtacht? Ar ndóighe níl Béarla ag duine ar bith aca sin. Níl céim aca. Níl duine ar bith aca ag teagasg san ollsgoil . . . Bíodh ciall agat. Tá gnoithe na Gaedhealtacht' socair. Ní thugann duine ar bith áird anois uirthi.

180 In a 1922 review of Mac Maoláin's *An Bealach chun na Gaedhealtachta ('The Road to the Gaeltacht' Phrase Book)*, Seán Mac Eachain called Mac Maoláin

> an inspiration to all the aspirants to Gaelic as a man who has learnt Irish so successfully that he can speak it better than the best natives and write it as good as the best. If you do not believe me, you can ask Fionn Mac Cumhaill and Séamus Ó Grianna, our finest Ulster speakers and writers. Poor Séamus, who is now in prison, admitted that Seán Mac Maoláin could write a purer Irish even than himself or Fionn (*Leader*, 9/6/23).

In another review of the same title, the critic said of Mac Maoláin that 'he is admitted to speak as good an Irish as the best speakers in the Rosses, the best district in Donegal' (*UIrman*, 26/5/23). See also Pádraig Ó Baoighill, 'Scríbhneoir as Glinnte Aontroma' (A writer from the Glens of Antrim), *Feasta*, Oct. 1988, 86–8. Mac Maoláin's father was a native speaker.

181 Nuair nach rabh dath ar bith le gnódhadh ar an Ghaedhilg, adeirthidhe nach rabh 'á canstain ach muinntear na gcroc [*sic*] 's na gcladach shiar. Anois ó d'athruigh an saoghal cineál beag, táthar ag cur i n-umhail dúinn nach bhfuil Gaedhilg na gcroc 'suas-chun-dáta' go leor.

182 Mar sin de, má's mian le duine ar bith sgéal Gaedhilge a fhághail a bhfuil fior-bhlas na Gaedhilge air, agus é mar bhéadh sé ar maos ins an Ghaedhealachas, faghadh sé sgéal a sgríobh duine de mhuinntir na Gaedhealtachta ins an Ghaedhealtacht, fá dtaobh de mhuinntir na Gaedhealtachta. He did then slip in one other qualification: 'After that, all that is needed is for the person who wrote the story to be able to write a story' (I n-a dhiaidh sin, ní'l ach a'n rud amháin de dhíth .i. an té sgríobh an sgéal a bheith i n-inmhe sgéal a sgríobhadh).

183 In a 1926 piece in *The Leader*, 'Bricriu' shared his similarly low opinion of Gaelic League 'scholars' who boasted of their knowledge of a literature 'of which they know as little as an illiterate Norfolk agricultural labourer knows of Shakespeare, Wordsworth or Walter Pater' (*Leader*, 13/2/26).

184 Seaghán Mac Meanman, *Peinsean Shean-Mháire Ní Ruadháin* (Old Máire Ní Ruadháin's Pension) in *Trí Mhion-Dráma* (Three short plays) (BÁC: ODFR, 1936), 31–59.

185 Anns an Ghaedhealtacht a chaithfidh siad a theacht chun tsaoghail ná ar scor ar bith a chaithfidh siad an bainne a dhiúil a chothóchas spiorad an Ghaedhil anntú [*sic*]. He says he has only known one person who has done so. One wonders whether he had Mac Maoláin in mind.

186 He also wrote:

> We may be warped by the uneven conflict, but to us all the people of the Pale are brutal, unintelligent, and rather untidy. They have some technical skill – God knows it is not a lot – but no philosophy, no gift for distinguishing essentials from details, no grip of fundamentals.

See also his essay 'Fian-Litridheacht' (Literature of the Fianna), *IF*, Apr. 1926, 19–20.

187 Seosamh Mac Grianna, 'Pádraic Ó Conaire', in *Pádraic Ó Conaire agus Aistí Eile* (Pádraic Ó Conaire and other essays) (BÁC: OS, 1936), 26. Nach mb'fhéidir gur shamhail Pádraic an t-am sin go rabh an Ghaedhilg ag imtheacht, agus go dtiocfadh an lá nach mbéadh fágtha ach pearóid de Ghall-Ghaedheal a mbéadh Gaedhilg bhriste aige, mar chomhartha gur mhair an tsean-teanga uasal ariamh? For discussion of Mac Grianna's on occasion ambivalent attitude to the primacy of the Gaeltacht in independent Ireland, see Diarmaid Ó Doibhlin, 'Gnúis Dó Féin' (One of a kind), and Pól Ó Muirí, 'Seosamh Mac Grianna', in *Rí-Éigeas na nGael*, ed. Mac Congáil, 73 and 91–3, respectively.

188 Is mór an gar, ar ndóighe, an nua-Ghaedhilg a bheith 'ghá scathadh fhéin amach ó chainnt na Gaedhealtachta. Rath nó bláth ní bhéadh uirthí choidhche, dá bhfanadh sí i gceangal le h-urlabhra an ghramscair nach bhfuil 'aon tabhairt suas ceart' ortha. Ach, ar an droch-uair, ní féidir díthe sin a dhéanamh gan a scathadh fhéin amach ó'n Ghaedhilg a bhí ariamh ann go dtí ar na mallaibh. It is possible that this is once again Ó Grianna, who on occasion called himself 'dóirnéalach' (a rustic) and was fond of pseudonyms throughout his career.

189 Agus sí an fhírinne í gur rud gan bhrigh, gan bheodhacht, gan anam, an 'nua-Gaedhilg'. Ní'l cosamhlacht dá laighead aici le fior-Ghaedhilg ach amháin an chosamhlacht atá ag cnámhlach scabtha an duine mhairbh le corp folláin foirbhthe an duine bheó. See also 'Cormac', 'An Saoghal Fódlach / "An Ghaedhilg Oifigiúil": Croiceann Gaedhealach ar Chnámha Gallda' (The Irish world / 'Official Irish:' A Gaelic skin over English bones), *Tír*, Jan. 1930, 3.

190 He wanted an organisation 'chum na teangan agus a tréithe a chosaint ar na feallthóirí atá ar a tí agus ar a tóir; ar na daoine a bhrisfeadh agus a raobhfadh í agus a stracfadh as a chéile í agus ná fágfadh brígh ná fuinneamh inte; na daoine a fhágfadh gan teas fola ná cneasa í acht í d'fhágaint go liobarsach leadhbach againn gan croidhe ná cuisle dá cuid féin aici.' See also 'Tadhg Gaedhealach', 'Ithir Úr na Gaedhilge' (The new soil of the Irish language), *Sguab*, Jan. 1924, 63–5. In this piece, 'Tadhg' offered the following advice: 'If a person wants to pick up Irish properly, he will have to go on his knees to the speaker who has pure Irish' (Más maith le duine an Ghaedhilg a thabhairt leis go ceart, caithfidh sé dul ar a ghlúine go dtí an chainteoir a bhfuil an Ghaedhilg ghlan aige) (p. 64).

191 In a 1932 address to a Gaelic League audience, Peadar Ó Máille suggested that the bog, the mountain, and the shore were precisely where many in authority wanted the native speaker to stay:

> At present he was only a stranger in his own country; he was worse off than the red man in the 'reservations' in America. The red man got a grant from the Government, but the poor native speaker is expected to live on kelp, carrageen moss, and a commission (Ní raibh ann fá láthair ach strainnséar ina thír féin; bhí sé níos measa 'ná an fear dearg ins na 'reservations' i Meiriceá. Fuair an fear dearg deóntas ón Rialtas, ach bhíthear ag súil go mairfeadh an Gaedhilgeoir dúthchais bocht ar cheilp, charraigín, agus choimisiún) (*II*, 14/5/32).

192 Sílim féin go mba cheart dligheadh a bheith ann le duine ar bith de'n tseort sin a 'sgríobhfadh' leabhar agus gan an teanga go maith aige féin a shacadh isteach sa bpríosún go lobhadh a chnámha. Tá sé dona go leor ag an teangaidh a bheith ag fágháil bháis ach b'fhearr go mór fada leigean dí bás nádúrtha a fhágháil ná a *marbhú* mar atáthar a dhéanamh fá láthair . . . Is é mo bharamhail féin nach ceart 'Gaedhilgeoir dúthchais' a thabhairt ar dhuine ar bith ach ar an t-é a mbadh í an Ghaedhilg a ghnáth-theanga go raibh sé fásta suas, agus ní h-é sin amháin ach ní abróchainn gur Gaedhilgeoir ceart dúthchais é munar chleacht sé an teanga i n-a dhiaidh sin féin gach am dá raibh faill aige, agus, i n-a cheann sin, munar

chaith sé tamall gach bhliadhain imeasg Gaedhilgeoirí i n-áit nach air aon Bhéarla a labhairt.

193 Rud a chuireas an-iongantas orm-sa i gcomhnaidhe a éascaidhe is bhíos sé ag daoine nár rugadh le Gaedhilg leabhra sa teangain sin a scríobhadh. Tá cuid díobh i n-ann leabhra a chur ar an margadh 'chaon dara mí. 'Irish while you wait', mar déarfá. Maidir le léightheoirí ní chuireann an cheist sin imnidhe ar bith ortha, agus tuige a gcuireadh? Tá airgead fairsing do réir cosamhlachta. See also his piece 'An Teanga a Ghlanadh / Cuidiú do Uachtarán an Fháinne / Gaedhilg na Leabhra' (Purifying the language / Help for the President of An Fáinne/ Book-Irish), *II*, 6/6/39.

194 Níl ciall nó réasún ag an té deir gur cheart áird ar bith a thabhairt ar an mhuintir a bhfuil Gaedhilge aca. Ba chóir go mbéadh fhios ag an tsaoghal mhór anois nach féidir do dhuine ciall ar bith a bheith do Ghaedhilge aige má thig leis a chomhrádh a dhéanamh inntí. Duine ar bith a dtig leis teanga a labhairt ní thuigeann sé í. Acht an té a bhfuil Gaedhilge aige agus nach dtig leis a labhairt déanfaidh sé a chomhrádh i dteangaidh éigint eile agus béidh an Ghaedhilge cruinn cuachta i n-a chloiginn agus í ag éirghe níos neartmhaire achan lá.

195 Ní fheicim-se féin ach maistíní 'n Bhéarla / Ná dream na nó-Ghaeluinne cóirighthe, / In aibid, i státa, i gcóiste, i n-árus, / Gach boc ag gabháil thart ar a mhótor. / Gach cigire saidhbir le Béarla is le Gaeluinn / Nó práchas le ndéanfadh a chomhrádh. / 'S na leomhain bhochta tréith ar leabaidh an fhéidh / 'S an coinín i n-árus an leomhain. Séamus P. Ó Mórdha's 1939 story 'Comrádaí' (Comrades) is a tale of two friends, one a Donegal native speaker, the other a Dubliner who has gone to the Donegal Gaeltacht to learn the language. Years later, the Dubliner, a fervent language activist, has a comfortable government job while the native speaker is living in Glasgow (*Comhthrom Féinne*, Mar. 1939, 2–3). See also the ironic 'How to Write a Gaelic Book' by 'Lomaire', an essay ostensibly inspired by a desire to rebuff 'the destructive attitude of native speakers towards the literary attempts of non-natives' (*An Phoblacht*, 5/2/26).

196 Pádraic Ó Conaire, 'Joseph Conrad agus Smaointe faoi Litridheacht' (Joseph Conrad and thoughts about literature), in *Aistí Phádraic Uí Chonaire*, 212. Cuma cé'n cine dár dhíobh é, leagan agus dúthchas na Gaedhilge bhíos ar chainnt gach duine ar mhair a shinnsir i nÉirinn le trí chéad bliadhan, abair, bíodh is gur focla Béarla thagas óna bheal . . . An bharamhail bhréagach sin atá i gceist agam is mó a rinne dochar do sgríobhnóireacht na Gaedhilge le achar fada. Luigheadh sí san uaigh feasta le Conrad.

197 Ná héistimís leis an ndream adeireann 'ní féidir le haoinne litridheacht do cheapadh i nGaedhilg acht le cainnteoir dúthchais, le Gaedhilgeoir ón gcliabhán'. Ná géilleadh do chainnt den tsórt soin. Fuair Poilíneach bás an lá fá dheireadh do cheap úir-scéalta feidhmeamhla i mBéarla cé nár labhair sé Béarla go haois fir dó. Seán Ó Floinn also invoked the spirit of Conrad in defence of learners of the language (*IS*, 7/2/25). See also Dinneen, 'Sources of Error in Irish', *IR*, Dec. 1930, 916–21. Daniel Corkery believed that the success of Conrad's work as literature proved that writers could produce true art in an acquired language. See Patrick Maume, *'Life That Is Exile'*, 121–2. Eoin Ó Searcaigh made an identical point using Patrick Pearse as an example (*II*, 14/1/32).

198 Béidh gár agus gleáradh i dtimcheall do chluas in aghaidh gach focal nach mbéidh 'dúthchais' do na 'dúthchasachaibh' seo; agus mur n-airigheann tú an chúmhacht ionnat féin neamh-shuim do chur ann san uile, fuaim agus fothram agus gártha uathbhásacha gráineamhla mar bhus eadh é, agus oibriughadh leat gan áird dá laghad air, is fearr dhuit gan tosúghadh, acht fanacht go socair san mbaile. Go dtí go bhfághair a dheimhin ionnat féin nach bhfuil ins an lucht 'dúthchais' seo ach ceithearn agus cóisir agus cos-mhuintir, gan eolas gan tuigsin gan teagasg gan mhúnadh, ní'l aon gnaithe agat ag smaoineamh ar Gaedhilge do dhéanamh ar mhodh ar bith fhoileamhnach do'n lá aniú. In a vigorous defence of learners in 1929, Seosamh Mac Cormaic asked: 'Who are the people on whom the most money has been spent to publish their books? Aren't they from the Gaeltacht, south, west, and north?' (Cérbh'iad na daoine ba mhó ar caitheadh an t-airgead ortha le n-a gcuid leabhar d'fhoillsiú? Nár den Ghaedhealtacht díobh, theas, thiar is thuaidh?). He then went on to criticise these Gaeltacht writers for their pig-headed obsession with their own dialects and spelling systems to the detriment of the revival of Irish as a true national language) (*Tír*, Nov. 1929, 12).

199 'Cuilinn' was particularly grateful to O'Reilly for his criticism of what 'Cuilinn' called 'one of the greatest enemies which confront the Irish revival at present . . . this curse of dialects'. 'Cuilinn' was, however, quick to acknowledge the importance of educated and tolerant native speakers in the literary movement: 'We wish, however, to have it clearly understood that we do not underestimate the value of the spoken language to a writer, for who can write perfectly a language he cannot speak freely.' 'Cuilinn' also acknowledged the injustice of having native speakers ashamed of their Irish in the company of those with '"book" Irish', but was exasperated by the type of native speaker 'who thinks everything is "quare" unless he heard it from his ancestors, and above all the so-called "native speaker" who, having despised Irish all his life, now wishes to have a foremost place in the movement because it happens to be fashionable.' See also 'P. de B.'s' review of O'Reilly's book in *II*, 25/5/25, a review to which O'Reilly responded in *II*, 1/6/25. O'Reilly himself

might well have been amused by H. O'Hara's comic but commonsensical 1936 essay 'If You Are in the Gaeltacht to Learn Irish / There Are Certain Things You Must Not Do.' O'Hara warned his readers not to expect 'that every native speaker has got a silver tongue or any sort of teeth' (*II*, 15/8/36).

200 'Sé mo thuairim fhéin nach dtiocfaidh mórán litridheachta as an Ghaedhealtacht – nach dtiocfaidh go leor, ar scor ar bith, chun an Ghaedhilg a shábháil. Níl na cainteóirí dúthchais go h-iongantach fairsing anois, agus tá an mhórchuid acu ró bhocht le smaoitiughadh a dhéanamh ar cheisteannaí liteardha. Chan fhaca muinntir na Gaedhealtachta mórán de'n tsaoghal. Murray himself pretty much gave up writing in Irish after the 1920s, in part because of criticism from native speakers, Ó Grianna particularly. See Mac Giolla Chomhaill, *Lorcán Ó Muireadhaigh: Sagart agus Scoláire* (BÁC: An Clóchomhar do Éigse Oirialla, 1983), 42–3. Ó Grianna had, for example, criticised his Irish in a letter to *An t-Ultach* in Aug. 1927.

201 Agus má's leamh aindeiseach a sgríobhann muid-inne a d'fhoghluim an Ghaedhilg mar theanga iasachta, de thairbhe an ghrádha a bhí againn díthe agus do'n tír, nach dtaisbeánfaidh sé do'n dream a leanfas muid na lochtanna a bhí orainne, 'sa' chruth a's go mbeidh siad i ndán a seachnadh? . . . Sin a bhfuil muid ag éileamh dúinn féin, a chainnteóirí dúthchais! Is fada sinn ó bheith ag dúil go sgríobhfaidh muid a choidhche mar bhéadh cainnteóirí dúthchais ionann. Anois! Ná bígidh dian orainn! Níl muid ach ag iarraidh cabhrach oraibh. Cuidighidh linn! He continued: 'Níl muid ag iarraidh ár nGaedhilg bhriotach mhanntach a chur i n-áit mur gcuid Gaedhilge ar chor ar bith. Níl éad againn oraibh, gidh go bhfuil rud agaibh nach mbeidh againn go deo agus ár seacht n-díthcheall a dhéanamh!' If the native speakers were unmoved by his plea, he asked of them the favour Robert Emmet had asked of the people of an unfree Ireland, 'the charity of your silence' (p. 4).

202 In a letter to the folklorist James Delargy congratulating him on his recent PhD, the Scotsman J. G. McKay recalled the resistance he had received as a learner of the language when he had begun his own research in Scots Gaelic: 'Besides, I was looked upon as presumptuous beyond words for daring to attempt anything Gaelic (not being a native speaker).' See James Delargy Papers, Box 5, NUIG. The letter is dated 31 Dec. 1934.

203 Má leigtear leo is ar thaobh amháin bhéas na cainnteoirí dúthchais, agus is ortha amháin is cóir meas do bheith ag cách, agus is dóibh amháin is cóir an uile phinginn dá bhfuil i nÉirinn do thabhairt. Agus fós má leigtear leis an dream dí-chéillidhe sin praiseach a dhéanamh de chúis na Gaedhilge, is ar an taoibh eile ar fad cuirfear na daoine a d'fhoghlaim an Ghaedhilg. Ní bheidh cead aca labhairt ós cionn a n-anála i láthair na gcainnteoirí dúthchais, ná rud ar bith eile a dhéanamh ach dóigheanna do shíorfhagháil chun na cainnteoirí dúthchais i n-áiteacha áirithe do choimeád ins na postaí a fuaradar go bog furas de bhárr na h-oibre a rinne lucht foghlama na Gaedhilge.

204 Acht is baoghalach anois go mbíonn duine nó dhó de na cainnteoirí dúthchais á cheapadh go bhfuil saghas naomhthachta nó diadhachta ag gabháil leo féin maidir leis an nGaedhilg . . . Is dóigh leo nach ceart d'aoinne acht dóibh féin baint leis an nGaedhilg agus bíd ag fonomhaid fé na daoinibh a bhíonn a d'iarraidh í fhoghluim is í shaothrú. Nuair a gheobhaid bás imtheochaid pé diadhacht nó pé daonnacht atá ag gabháil leo. Ní fhanfaidh a gcuirp san aer cúig troighthe os cionn na talmhan ar nós corp Mhachmaid, agus ní dhéanfaidh sé aon mhaitheas do mhuinntir na hÉireann dul ar oilithreacht chucha d'fhonn tuinnte bheag de'n Ghaedhealachas a thabhairt leo abhaile.

205 An té nach féidir leis aon rud eile a dhéanamh ach magadh fé'n duine nár labhair an Ghaedhilg i dtús a h-óige deirim leis gur námha dár dtír agus dár dteangan é.

206 Tá an nádúr céadna ag an bheirt Éireannach pé aca Gaedhilg nó Beurla a dteanga dhúthchais. Mar sin de má éirigheann leis an mBeurlóir an Ghaedhilg d'fhoghluim i dtreo go bhfuil sí ar a thoil aige agus má bhíonn aon fhéith sgríobhnóireachta aige déarfainn gur féidir le na leithéid litridheacht Ghaedhilge do chumadh is do sgríobhadh. See also 'Na hÉireannaigh agus an Béarla' (The Irish and the English language), *Dundalk Examiner*, 26/9/31.

207 Ach tá dream áirithe ann a bhfuil cuma ortha gur fuath leo agus gur beag aca aoinne atá ag foghlaim na Gaedhilge . . . Dá mbéadh cumhacht ag na nua-uaisle cultúrdha seo, ní leigfidís d'aoinne peann a chur ar pháipéar le n-a smaointe a nochtadh. Sé an port atá aca nach ceart d'aoinne aon rud a scríobhadh ach an cainnteoir dúthchais. Má tá post le líonadh dar ndóighe ceannairc i gcoinibh sibhialtacht agus béascna na hÉireann é do thabhairt d'aoinne ach don Ghaedhilgeoir ó dhúthchas is cuma cad iad na tréithe eile atá in easnamh air. Responding to a piece in *IP*, 'Dubliner' lashed out at the apotheosis of the Gaeltacht in an essay entitled 'Language Movement Myths' in *The Leader* in 1935:

> The complacent remark that the Gaeltacht has 'a civilisation and a culture higher than anything that exists elsewhere' is almost too ridiculous for discussion. Thatched roofs, mud walls, oil-lamp illumination, non-existent plumbing and hopeless sanitation are poor evidences of high civilisation (*Leader*, 17/8/35).

Séamus Ó Néill shared Ó Nualláin's preference for satire as a way of deflating the pretensions of some native speakers. In his 1932 sketch 'M.B. B. Ch., B.A.O.', he creates a Gaeltacht bore who insists he knows more about medicine than do mere physicians! (*Ultach*, Sept. 1932, 7).

208 Más maith le muintir na Gaeltachta gan an Ghaedhilg do leathadh mar ba chóir, ní féidir dúinne a chur fhiachaint ortha é dhéanamh . . . Mara ndeineadh dea-shompla na Galldachta iad do spriocadh chuige is eagla liom ná déanfaidh éinní eile é. Isé is ceart dúinne sa Ghalldacht a dhéanamh ná rún daingean diongmhálta do ghlacadh istigh 'nár gcroidhe an Ghaedhilg d'aithbheochaint sa Ghalldacht pé olc maith an Ghaedhilg sin – pé aca béarlagar gránna nó a mhalairt í – agus pé rud a dhéanfaidh an Ghaeltacht ná ná déanfaidh. See the similar views expressed by 'Deisceart' in a letter to *II*, 30/10/26). Peadar Ó Dubhda offered an interesting perspective on this question in a 1925 piece in *An t-Ultach* entitled 'Gaedhilg na h-Éireann' (The Irish of Ireland): 'If it is a great advantage to the writer to have a language he has known all his life at his command, I think it is a great obstacle in the way of the movement for a literary language' (Má's mór an áis do'n sgríbhneoir teanga ó'n gcliabhán bheith ar a thoil aige dar liom gur cloch-i-mbéal-oibre é ar ghluaiseacht na teangadh liteardha) (*Ultach*, May 1925, 5).

209 Tá daoine eile le fagháil agus is léir ó n-a gcuid chainnte gur mhaith leo gobán a chur i mbéal gach aoinne nár thug an Ghaedhilg ó'n gcliabhán leis, agus gurab é a dtuairim nach ceart leigint d'á leithéid tabhairt fá scríobhadh na teanga i n-aon chor . . . Leanaimís de labhairt na Gaedhilge, má's Gaedhilg bhriste bhacach féin í, agus beidh an lá linn . . . Aoinne go raibh sé de mhisneach aige agus de bhuan-tseasmhacht ann an Ghaedhilg d'fhoghluim, tá creideamhaint mhór ag dul dó agus ní cuibhe ná cóir d'aoinne bheith ag tromaidheacht ar a leithéid mar gheall ar bhacaighe a chuid Ghaedhilge . . . 'Mol an óige agus tiocfaidh sí', agus ní fearr rud a dhéanfadh muinntir na glan-Ghaedhilge agus na bhfocal searbh ná an chomhairle sin do leanamhaint.

210 Ar aon dóigh, ní aontuighim dubh bán ná riabhach leis an ndearcadh atá ag daoinibh áirithe ar an gceist, sé sin, nach cóir d'aoinne ach do'n chainnteoir ó dhúthchas dul ag sgrí na Gaedhilge. 'Glan as ár linntibh' an fáilte a chuireann an dream so go h-iondual roimh an sgríobhnóir óg ó'n nGalltacht a dheineann iarracht ar a chuid smaointe do bhreacadh síos ar pháipéar i nGaedhilg. Caithfear a chur i dtuigsint do sna daoinibh seo ná fuil cirt aontseilbhe ag aon dream ar leithligh sa tír seo ar an dteangain ná ar sgrí na teangan. In 1927, 'Tadhg' urged readers of *An Stoc* to work for a broad and radical understanding of the Gaeltacht:

> The Gaeltacht means justice for the poor in Ireland. The Gaeltacht means turning away from English and the foul storytelling that follows English from the west and from the east. The Gaeltacht means the proper life, the virtue every Christian desires (Is ionann Gaeltacht agus cothrom do na bochta in Éirinn. Is ionann Gaeltacht agus cúl a bheith curtha ar an mBéarla agus ar an mbréine sgéalaidheachta a leanann an Béarla anoir agus aniar. Is ionann Gaeltacht agus an saoghal cóir, an buadh a shanntuigheas gach Críostaidhe).

Using such a definition, he believed that all Irish people could claim Gaeltacht citizenship: 'The Gaeltacht is the inheritance of speakers of Irish, those in the east as well as those who had the native language from the cradle, those in exile as well as those of us comfortable at home' (Is dual do'n lucht labhartha Gaedhilge an Ghaeltacht, do'n chuid aca atá thoir chó maith leis an gcuid aca a thug an teanga dhúthchais leo ó'n gcliabhán, do'n chuid aca atá ar an deoraidheacht chó maith linn-ne atá ar ár sástacht san mbaile) (*Stoc*, May 1927, 4). In 1936, Bríd Ní Neachtain ('Brighdín Béasach') provoked a controversy when she suggested in a letter to *An t-Éireannach* that native speakers wear some badge to distinguish themselves from those members of An Fáinne who had learned the language (*Éireannach*, 11/1/36). Her proposal drew an angry response in defence of learners from 'Fáinneoir' (*Éireannach*, 25/1/36). In this same issue of the journal, Micheál Ó Maoláin stated that after listening to wearers of the *fáinne* speaking English in the Abbey Theatre, he went home, took the pin out of his coat, 'and I tell you that the like of it will not be seen in it again soon' (agus deirim-se leat nach bhfeicfear a leithéid ann go luath arís). In his richly informative and provocative book *Athbheochan na hEabhraise: Ceacht don Ghaeilge?* (BÁC: An Clóchomhar, 1999), Muiris Ó Laoire suggests that the revival of Hebrew actually benefited from the absence of native speakers to belittle and discourage those struggling to learn what was to become the modern Hebrew language. See Ó Laoire, *Athbheochan*, 207, 219, 225. The Gaels of our period were certainly aware of what the Jews had accomplished in the Holy Land.

211 Riobárd Ó Druaidh, 'Editor's Preface', in Fearrgus Ó Nualláin, *Laidean tre Ghaedhilg I. / Dlúth-Aistriúchán / Solúidí agus Gluaiseanna* (Latin through Irish I. / Literal translation / Examples and glosses) (Rathfarnham: The Language and Literary Guilds, [1924]), 5–6.

212 Ó Broin continued:

> This, in effect, means that we begin our literary revival, so far as our literate native-speaker-writers are concerned, with an enormous advantage. If we could only increase their number, discipline them, and get them to learn how to find something to say!

See also his comments on this subject in 'A State-Sponsored Literature', *Irish Monthly*, Feb. 1938, 125–31. In his autobiography *Just Like Yesterday* (Dublin: Gill & Macmillan, n.d.), Ó Broin claimed that his own children were 'more or less native speakers of Irish' (p. 105).

213 Agus cé acu dream acu is tábhachtaighe i ndeire na dála? Muireach na Gaedhilgeoirí léigheannta ní

bhfuigheadh na foghluimtheoirí foghluim in ao' chor, agus in eugmais lucht foghlumtha na Gaedhilge bheadh sé chomh maith ag an dream eile an obair do thabhairt suas ar an bpointe. Ní neart go cur le céile, sin bun agus barr an scéil, agus tuigimís é.

214 See also Editorial, *An Róimh*, Summer, 1923, 1; and Cearbhall Ua Dálaigh, 'Nua-Litridheacht na Gaedhilge, 1920–1930' (Modern literature in Irish, 1920–1930), *CB*, June 1931, 609–11.

215 Más beo-theanga í an Ghaedhilg – agus is minic sinn dubh san aghaidh ó bheith á chur san 'na luighe ar namhadaibh an teanga – caithfimíd a thuiscint go gcaithfidh fás do theacht innte agus nach ealaidhe dhúinn i gcomhnuidhe bheith dár gciapadh féin i dtaobh cionnus chuirfeadh Seana-Pheats Teaimí in Iarthar Chorca-Dhuibhne Gaedhilg ar smaointe áirighthe. Ní hamhlaidh atáim ag rádh nách ceart ana-shuim do chur sa tseanduine chéadna ach ní ceart dul thar cailc leis an sgéal. He continued: 'We have too many pedants, and not enough of a sense of humour' (Tá an iomad *pedants* againn, agus gan ár ndóthain *sense of humour* againn).

216 Beidh an cainnteóir dúthchais ann mar chosantóir don theangaidh bheó. Sgríobhfaidh an bheirt seo leabhair mhóra bhréaghtha ab' fhiú 'litridheacht' a thabhairt mar ainm daobhtha.

217 Agus lucht foghluma na Gaedhilge agus tar éis an tsaoghail is foghlumthóirí ár bhfurmhór, gheobhaidh siad ann fuinneamh agus áilneacht na beó-Ghaedhilge fé mar a labharthar í fós i nGaedhealtacht Thír Chonaill chomh maith le cur síos léir taithneamhach ar ghnáth-shaoghal na ndaoine.

218 Bhí spiorad na náisiúntacht' mar bhéadh deascaidh ann i gConnradh na Gaedhilge. Chuir an deascaidh sin oibriughadh ann. Bhí an t-aer ar crioth na bliadhanta úd agus dar leat go gcuirfeadh lasóg dá laghad le theinidh é. Bhí meas ag cainnteoirí dúthchais agus ag lucht foghluma ar a chéile. Achan chuid aca go minic faoi chumaoin ag an chuid eile. Agus meas aca araon ar Éirinn. An lá a buaileadh na Gaedhil d'imthigh an spiorad sin as Connradh na Gaedhilge. Tiocfaidh sé arais nuair a smaoiteachas muinntir na hÉireann nach ar mhaithe le philology nó le folk-lore ba chóir a bheith ag saothrughadh na Gaedhilge acht ar mhaithe le Ireland a nation.

219 Annsin beidh an leabhar seo úsáideach ag páistí ins an Ghalltacht. Leis an fhírinne a rádh is fusa toiseacht le leabhar beag mar seo 'ná le Gaedhilic chasta na gcainteóir dúthchais. As a chéile a ghníthear na caisleáin, agus do réir a chéile a fhoghluimthear teanga. Mar sin de, ba chóir a bheith buidheach do na múinteóirí a scríobhas leabharthaí den chineál seo.

220 Ádhbhar áthais do dhuine an Ghaedhilg a bheith aige as a leanbhuidheacht acht chan ádhbhar mórtais é. Ní rabh neart ag duine ar bith againn ar a theacht 'un tsaoghail san áit a dtáinig sé. Níor cuireadh ceist ort-sa ar mhaith leat solus a' lae a fheiceáil i Ráth Maoinis nó orm-sa ar mhaith liom a fheiceáil i Rosaibh Thír-Chonaill . . . Nuair atá mé ag cainnt ar mhuintir na Gaedhealtachta tá mé ag smaoitiughadh ortha mar seo. Tá an Ghaedhilg aca. Is aca atá sí. Agus caithfear úsáid a dhéanamh daobhtha leis an teangaidh a sgabadh ar fud na hÉireann. He went on to argue that the native speaker was not more important than other Irish citizens as a human being, but he did have a special claim on the nation 'because of the precious jewel he has' (mar mhaithe leis an t-seóid luachmhair atá aige). Ó Grianna was, however, unable to resist a dig at the new Free State establishment: 'Any simpleton will learn the things the "learned" people boast about. It is possible to make a professor or a doctor or a lawyer of a native speaker. But it is not possible to go into the cradle when the day of the cradle is over' (Foghluimeochaidh uasgán ar bith na rudaí a mbíonn lucht an 'léighinn' ag déanamh mórtais asta. Is féidir ollamh nó dochtúir nó dlíghtheoir a dhéanamh de chainnteoir dúthchais. Acht ní féidir a ghabháil sa chliabhán nuair a théid lá an chliabháin thart) (p. 2).

221 Tá na mílte de dhaoiní fiúntacha fearamhla sa tír – daoine nach bhfuair an Ghaedhilg ó ghlún a máthara acht a chuaidh siar 'na Gaedhealtachta gach faill is áiméar dá bhfuair siad, agus d'fhoghluim an Ghaedhilg. Daoine nach raibh éad i n-a gcroidhe. Daoine atá buidheach beannachtach go bhfuil an Ghaedhealtacht ann. Tà na mílte aca seo sa tír agus is maith an rud go bhfuil.

222 Is maith an rud an Ghaedhilg a fhoghluim. Is breagh an obair atá déanta ag an mhuintir a d'fhoghluim í. Ó Grianna's considered opinion on the topic is perhaps best summarised in a 1929 piece in which he wrote: 'All the Irish in Ireland is worthless except for what there is in the Gaeltacht and for the Irish of people who learned it from native speakers' (Ní fiú cnaipe gan súil a bhfuil de Ghaedhilg i nÉirinn acht an méid atá ins an Ghaedhealtacht agus ag daoiní a d'fhoghluim í ó na cainnteoirí dúthchais) (*FL*, Nov. 1929, 1). Ó Grianna's brother Seosamh added a caveat to his defence of the learner in a 1932 piece in the Enniscorthy *Echo*:

> Having bad Irish is not the worst fault a person could have. It is far worse to have an non-Gaelic mind . . . It does not matter if there are people who have bad Irish. Those are people who are learning. But for God's sake let them understand that they are learning and not teaching (Ní h-é an locht is measa a thiocfadh le duine a bheith air droch-Ghaedhilg a bheith aige. Is measa i bhfad intinn neamh-Ghaedhealach a bheith ag duine . . . Is cuma daoiní a bheith ann a bhfuil droch-Ghaedhilg acú. Sin daoiní atá ag foghluim. Acht a gheall ar Dhia tuigeadh siad gur ag foghluim atá siad agus nach ag teagasg) (Enniscorthy *Echo*, 13/2/32).

See also his praise of some writers who had learned the language in 'Sgríbhneoirí Gaedhilge agus an

Gúm' (Writers of Irish and An Gúm), *An Phoblacht*, 10/9/32. Like his brother, however, he believed that such writers had to go to the Gaeltacht and immerse themselves in the Irish spoken there. See 'Goidé Tá d'easbaidh orrainn?' (What do we lack?), *An t-Ultach*, May 1924, 5; and 'Murcha agus Mánas', *An Camán*, 3/9/32.

223 After a rancorous meeting of writers to discuss the formation of Cumann na Scríbhneoirí (The writers' club), Niall Ó Searcaigh complained about Ó Grianna's comments during the session and said that while Ó Grianna on occasion spoke of peace between native speakers and learners, his actions were always those of a belligerent. See Ó Searcaigh, 'Sgríbhneoirí Gaedhilge' (Writers of Irish), *An t-Ultach*, July 1939, 4.

224 Déanfar feidhm do'n Ghaedhealtacht, dar ndóighe . . . Déanfar feidhm do na Gaedhilgeoirí dúthchasacha le blas agus ceart na teangan d'fhághail uatha agus cibé ar bith méid sean-litridheacht atá ar a meabhar leo fós. Ach cumfar canamhain nua agus litridheacht nua agus is i mBaile-Átha-Cliath cumfar iad. See also Mac Fhionnlaoich, 'Tuairisgí agus Tuairimí' (Reports and opinions), *An Phoblacht*, 7/5/26.

225 Dála an scéil, is iomdha duine do dhein agus is iomdha duine atá ag déanamh mioscaise idir an Ghaedhealtacht agus an Ghalldacht bíodh gur gan fhios dó féin é . . . I n-ainm na Gaedhilge agus i n-ainm na céille, tuigeadh an dá thaobh dínn a chéile agus do n-a chéile, agus ná bíodh an teanga d'á cailleamhaint eadrainn.

226 Anois is mór an náire agus an díth-dhearcaidh iarraidh a thabhairt dhá chuid a dhéanamh de lucht na Gaedhilge agus iad a chur i n-adharca a chéile. Duine ar bith a thuigeas an sgéal tá fhios aige nach féidir an Ghaedhilg a shábháil gan an Ghaedhealtacht. Agus rud eile: gan an Ghalltacht. Tá an dá dhream riachtanach. Ba bheag an chabhair an Ghaedhilg d'Éirinn dá bhfanadh sí a choidhche i gcúl na gcnoc thiar sa phurtach. Agus is beag a chabhair a ndéanfaidh muinntir na Galltachta mur' dtéighidh siad siar agus an Ghaedhilg atá sa phurtach a tharraingt ortha agus a mhór a dhéanamh díthe. Tá an dá dhream comh riachtanach agus tá cosa agus cloigeann ag duine. To be fair, it should be admitted that this writer's loyalties were with the native speakers. He saw only twenty or so people stirring up suspicion between Gaeltacht people and learners. He also bitterly attacked the Free State government for wanting to save everything in the Gaeltacht except the native speakers.

227 Acht tá an comhrac a' druidim linn. Agus caithfidh muintir na Gaedhealtacht' an droch-mheas atá aca ar a' chunamar cháidheach seo a thabhairt le fios don tír.

CHAPTER TWO

The Real and Better Ireland

1 Myles na gCopaleen, *An Béal Bocht no An Milleánach: Droch sgéal ar an Droch-shaoghal* (The poor mouth or the fault-finder: A bad story about the bad life) (Áth Cliath: Cló Dolmen, 1964 [1941]), 45. Níl aon ní ar an domhan so co deas no co Gaelach le fíor-Ghael fíor Ghaelach a bhíonn ag caint fíor-Ghaeilge Ghaelaí i dtaobh na Gaeilge Gaelaí.

2 An tAthair Mártan Ó Domhnaill, *Oileáin Árann* (BÁC: Muinntir C. S. Ó Fallamhain, Teo., i gcomhar le hOS, 1930), 41–2. Is ró-ghearr le fíor-Ghaedhilgeoir an tamall chaithfeas sé imeasg daoine atá chomh fíor-Ghaedhealach, ní i dtaobh na Gaeilge amháin, acht ar gach uile slighe. Acht le congnamh Dé, gheobhamuid faill ar theacht ar ais go h-Inis Meadhon agus ar thamall beag do chaitheamh imeasg muinntire an oileáin seo i nGaedhealtacht na Gaedhealtachta.

3 Tá in an nGaeltacht – agus annsúd amháin – nidhthe fé leith, mar atá saoidheacht is síbhialtacht is béal-oideas is fíor-thréitheachas chine Gaedheal. Nidhthe iad so atá fighte fuaighte leis an dteangain; go deimhin is iad beatha na teangan iad, agus an té ná súghann isteach leis an dteangain iad mothuightear easnamh ann; mar gidh go mbí an Ghaedhilg aige ní bhíonn an mheón Ghaelach ann. Is ins an nGaeltacht amháin is féidir an meón sin a gheineadh is a chothú.

4 See also his essay 'Goidé Tá d'Easbaidh orrainn?' *An t-Ultach*, May 1924, 5–6.

5 Agus cé hiad lucht na Gaeltachta? Sliocht uasal Gaedheal atá go beó bocht ag fullang an-smacht Gall le céadta blian . . . Daoine iad a bhfuil aca an t-aon bhuntús amháin ar arbh fhéidir stát Gaelach a thógaint.

6 Tá an náisiún Gaedhealach beó indiu dhá réir, ach má tá is sa nGaedhealtacht atá sí beó. Is cumhang é a limistéar, ach is treiseamhail iad a tréithe. An Ghaedhealtacht an t-aon chuid den Stáit seo ar fiú freastal dí, má séard atá ar intinn mhuinntire na hÉireann an náisiún Gaedhealach aithbheódhú. Dá mbéadh Éire aontuighthe amáireach agus dá mbéadh sí saor ó chladach go cladach, ní bhéadh aon cheart aici náisiún a thabhairt uirthi féin marach an Ghaedhealtacht a bheith aici. 'Sa nGaedhealtacht amháin atá ceart oighreachta an náisiúin. Ua Flaithbheartaigh was adamant on this point, writing at the conclusion of his essay: 'I began with the culture of the Gaeltacht as national culture. There will be no other culture in Ireland. Any other literature or any other culture, however good, do not belong to this country' (Thosuigh mé le h-éigse na Gaedhealtachta mar éigse náisiúnta. Ní bheidh aon éigse eile i nÉirinn. Litridheacht ar bith eile nó éigse ar bith eile, dá fheabhas iad, ní leis an tír seo iad) (p. 21).

7 Rev. E. Cahill, S. J., *The Framework of a Christian State: An Introduction to Social Science* (Dublin: M. H. Gill, 1932), 666.

8 Pádhraic Óg Ó Conaire, *Solus an Ghrádha* (BÁC: Muintir Dollard, 1923), 120. Sin iad anois clann na bhfíor-Ghaedheal ar dhíbir Cromaill a sinnsear ó mhachairí míne na Mídhe . . . Ach cuireadar fútha annseo i gcolbha an chladaigh, agus imeasg na gcnoc agus bhunuigheadar an Creideamh agus an t-Sibhialtacht Ghaedhealach, a theip ar na sgriosadóirí a mhilleadh. Seadh, chuireadar fútha annseo agus choinneadar an Creideamh agus tréathra uaisle na nGaedheal beo brioghmhar; agus is duine aineolach ar dheagh-thréathra na nGaedheal, duine nach gcaithfidh tamall cois chladaigh is cnoc ar imeall na fairrge thiar. See also Ó Conaire, *Seoid ó'n Iarthar Órdha* (Gaillimh: Ó Gormáin, Teach na Clódóireachta, 1933 [1924]), 33.

9 He also had a dig at the patriotic pretensions of the Gaeltacht: 'One would like to remind over-enthusiastic Irish revivalists that it was the English-speaking East, Midlands, and South that fought and won our recent struggle for independence, while the Gaeltacht remained more or less comatose.'

10 Devane did also concede that

> there is a sense in which the Gaeltacht myth is true. If one says in our western province live the speech, imagery, symbols, metaphors, the idiom, the lore, the moulds in which for two thousand years and more the Irishman cast his thoughts; that somehow or other that tradition and that speech must be incorporated in our life, or our life and struggle for a thousand years is meaningless – in that sense, the Gaeltacht myth is not a myth (p. 17).

See also the comments of Máirín Nic Eoin on the fallacy of the West as the soul of the Irish nation in *An Litríocht Réigiúnach* (Regional literature) (BÁC: An Clóchomhar, 1982), 62.

11 Is é chúis nár thréigeadar sin an Ghaedhilg mar dho dhein muintir eile na tíre, mar nár ionnsuidh Crommell ná a shíolrach iad. Agus ba é chúis nár ionnsuidh mar nárbh fhiú leo é. Ní raibh aca aon chreach le fagháil san áit . . . An bochtanas mar sin, do shábháil an Ghaedhilg san nGaedhealtacht. Perhaps the most balanced judgment on this question was that of Séamus Ó Searcaigh, who in a lecture at University College Dublin on emigration from the Gaeltacht, stated: 'The people who live in the Gaeltacht are no worse nor better than any other group in the country' (Ní measa agus ní fearr an dream a mhaireas sa Ghaedhealtacht 'ná dream ar bith eile sa tír) (*Tír*, Apr. 1928, 5).

12 Is cruaidh an saoghal atá ag muinntir Chonamara. Is cruaidh sin. Ní mór dhóibh bheith ag rómhar agus ag tochailt a bpúicín talmhan ó mhaidin go faoithin; bheith go síor ag treabhadh agus ag forsadh ar fhairrge ar fhraoch, chun greim a mbéal do bhaint amach . . . Acht tá rud amháin aca nach bhfuil go coitcheannta ag sibhialtacht an lae indiu, faraoir, seód nach féidir le talamh dá bhreághthacht ná airgid dá mhéid do cheannach – síothcháin anama i nDia.

13 Micheál Ó Gríobhtha, 'An tSrúill', in *Cathair Aeidh* (BÁC: ODFR, 1937), 107. Is ionann dealbhas sa dúthaigh seo nó dún i nbhur dtimcheall chun urchóid an tsaoghail do chongbháil abhfad amach uaibh. Tá an tsubháilce annso fós; níl ádhbhar an pheacaidh ann.

14 Ní mór an t-aimhreas air ná go mb'aoibhne do na Gaedhealaibh a dfan beatha na naomh aca, ó'n láimh go dtí an mbéal, nó fiú amháin faoi ghorta agus faoi dhuadh, i n-a n-iasgairibh i dTír Chonaill ná dóibh siúd a fuair gradam i gcúirteannaibh na h-Eórpa.

15 Seán Ó Ciosáin, 'Móna', in *Sgéalta cois Laoi* (Leeside stories) (BÁC: ODFR, 1935), 39. Bhí saghas éada agam leo – bhí meon chómh díreach san acu. Gan dabht bhí a dtrioblóidí féin ortha. Iad i gcomhnuidhe ag faire ar an aimsir mar sí is mó a chasann an mí-ádh nó a mhalairt 'na dtreo – iad ag iomrasgáil le cruadhtan éigin i gcomhnuidhe, ach 'na dhiaidh san gan aon chastacht aigne acu. Bíonn gach aon rud 'na dhubh nó 'na gheal acu munab ionann is lucht intleachta go mbíonn fiche gné ar gach dath acu.

16 Cé go bhfuil an chuid is mó de na daoinibh bocht sa gceantar sin ní bhíonn gruaim ná buaidheart ariamh ortha, bíonn siad méidhreach áthasach ó dhubh go dubh. Sé mo bharamhail nach bhfuil dream daoine faoi luighe na gréine atá chomh sona sonasach leis na daoinibh bochta sin . . . Ní bhíonn siad ag casaoid ná eile acht iad i gcomhnuidhe lán-tsásta leis an mbail a chuir Dia ortha.

17 Éamon de Valera, 'The Ireland that We Dreamed Of', Radio Broadcast, 17 Mar. 1943, in *Speeches and Statements*, ed. Moynihan, 466–69.

18 See for example, the descriptions of comely maidens, athletic youths, and wise elders in the following Gaelic stories and novels: Tadhg Saor Ó Séaghdha's 'Draoidheacht na Gaedhilge', in *Dhá Sgéal*, 55; Diarmuid Ua Laoghaire's *An Bhruinneall Bhán* (BÁC: ODFR, 1934), 104; Seán Ó Ciarghusa's *Bun an Dá Abhann* (BÁC: ODFR, 1933), 71 and 83; 'Fionn' Mac Cumhaill's *Tusa a Mhaicín* (BÁC: COÉ, [1922]), 1; Úna Bean Uí Dhíosca's *Cailín na Gruaige Duinne* (BÁC: ODFR, 1932), 79; and Nioclás Tóibín's *An Rábaire Bán* (BÁC: C. S. Ó Fallamhain, Teo. i gcomhar le hOS, 1928), 7.

19 Ní fear sanntach Gael na Gaeltachta. Ní maith leis bheith ina thocaidhe ramhar bodamhail. Tá sé sásta leis an mheasaracht. Má tá a spleotán beag préataí agus coirce ag teacht 'un cinn go deas agus gan an aicéad a theacht orrtha tá sé ar a sháimhín suilt an bhliadhain sin. Má tá muiseog mhaith phréataí aige, cruach de mhóin tirim agus an cíos agus an gearradh díolta níl i nÉirinn féin fear níos lugha mairg. Mac Pháidín did, however, point out how close to the edge such people lived, always a single bad crop season from real distress.

20 De Blácam could hardly have been more in tune with de Valera's thinking as reflected in the Constitution. He continued:

Above all, we have the parochial life which safeguards nations. Never let it be broken up by high industrialism, the employment of masses of workers by anonymous and soulless companies, or the transference of young womanhood from the home to the degrading machine-room (p. 525).

21 Both Blythe and Ó Rinn used this pen name, Blythe in *The Star* and Ó Rinn in *United Ireland* and the *United Irishman*, but I doubt very much this is either of them.

22 Tá an Gaedheal tugtha, de dhúthchas, don tsaol tuaithe. Taithneann sé leis; réidhtíonn sé leis. 'Sé an saol is fearr agus is uaisle amuigh é. Ní féidir é shárú, an té go mbíonn treó oiriúnach air, sé sin, dóithin tailimh aige dá chothú; stoc is gus dá réir aige; é saor ó fhiacha agus ó ghlaedhta doghlantha [*sic*], agus é ag maireachtain fé ghnaoi Dé is fé ghreann na gcomharsan. Saol duine uasail, an saol san, gan aon agó.

23 Ba ghráin chroidhe leis an nGaedheal, béascna bréige na sráide i gcómhnuidhe riamh. Saoghal saonta na tuaithe atá dá léiriú n-a litríocht féin. B'ait leis, cuideachta a dhéanamh leis an nádúr rúnda i n-uaigneas na tuaithe, agus a bheith ag feallsúnacht in' aigne féin ar na h-iongantaisí go léir á leathadh n-a thimcheall. D'árduigh san a aigne chun Dé na n-uilechómhacht.

24 Ach anois tá an Renaissance imthighthe – marbh – agus dá bhrígh sin tá an dá nóta san ag teacht thar n-ais arís chun gach aon litriocht i nEuróip agus i nAimeriocá. Dá chomhartha san, an litriocht is fearr a deineadh le nár linn féin, d'fhéadfá an focal san 'Ceanntarach' (Regional) do thabhairt uirthi. 'Sé aigne na ndaoine gcomónta is mó atá i gceist i litríocht den tsaghas san. It is interesting to note that in this piece Corkery confessed surprise that Irish novelists in English such as Seamus O'Kelly, Darrell Figgis, and Edward MacLysaght (Éamonn Mac Giolla Iasachta) had hitherto dealt more, and more profoundly, with the theme of the land than had writers of Irish.

25 Caithfear gan faillighe a thabhairt sa Ghaedhealtacht. Níl fás i ndán do litridheacht na Gaedhilge muna ndeintear í phréamhú san ithir is dual dí.

26 Tá focal Béarla a fheileas go maith dho lucht cosanta na feallsamhnachta sin – an focal 'snob', nach bhfuil aon aistriúchán air, go bhfios dom-sa, sa nGaedhilge ná i n-aon teangaidh eile, agus ar thug sgríobhnóir Sasanach sainmhíniú air: 'duine a bhfuil omós aige dho rudaí suaracha agus a theasbáineas an t-omós sin ar bhealach suarach'.

27 Tá géar-ghádh go fóill le n-a lán leabhar a bhaineas le saoghal na ndaoine i nÉirinn. Tá súil agam nach ndéanfaidh scríbhneoirí na leabhar seo dearmad de rud atá an-tábhachtach in mo thuairimse; sé sin: nach leor léightheoireacht den chineál céadna do sholáthar do lucht léighte na Gaedhilge i gcómhnaidhe. Tá saoghal amháin, saoghal ciúin simplidhe sa Ghaedhealtacht, cuir i gcás, agus is iomdha sin rud atá le scríobhadh fá'n saoghal sin fós, gan na rudaí céadna do shíor-rádh ina thaoibh. Is cuma a chiúine agus a shimplidhe is tá saoghal na ndaoine sa Ghaedhealtacht, is féidir le sár-ughdar ádhbhair a dhóthain a fhagháil ann le aistí agus le scéalta a scríobhadh a mbéidh cuimhne ortha go cionn i bhfad. Addressing secondary teachers in 1936, Proinnsias Ó Cinnéide also noted how narrow was the range of contemporary writing from the Gaeltacht (*Association of Secondary Teachers, Ireland / Official Year Book and Diary*, 1937–8, 85).

28 Pádhraic Óg Ó Conaire, *Ceol na nGiolcach* (BÁC: OS, 1939), 199. He called them 'dream . . . nach bhfuair cothrom na Féinne ariamh ó lucht pinn a mheas gurab acu féin a bhí an léargus ceart. A lán dár sgríobhadh fútha is le háibhéil is fiodmhagadh é. Cuireadh caint ina mbéal nár smaoinigh a gcroidhe ariamh air.' In Mac Giolla Iasachta's *Cúrsai Thomáis*, the narrator acknowledges the faults of rural people, but is critical of the depictions of them by some modern writers (p. 40).

29 Titley, *An tÚrscéal*, 231.

30 Níl mórán scríbhneoirí i gCúige Uladh a bhfuil fonn ortha saothar a chur ortha féin le leabhar a scríobhadh ach ar an bheagán atá, tá Seaghán Mac Meanman ar an ughdar is fearr nochtas saoghal na ndaoine sa Ghaedhealtacht go simplidhe nádúrdha.

31 Ó Cuív, *Prós na hAoise Seo*, 36.

32 Níor chruthaigh Dia, acht Parthalán Mac an Dubhda, scríobhnóir, agus Feidhlimidh Ó Casaidhe, file – beirt de mhuinntir Bhaile Átha Cliath . . . Tá siopaí ar an phortach anois, agus tá bus-ticket agus cigarette agus daily mail le fagháil ann. Tá daoine coitcidheanta ar an phortach sin indiu. See Breandán Ó Conaire, *Myles na Gaeilge: Lámhleabhar ar Shaothar Gaeilge Bhrian Ó Nualláin* (The Irish-language Myles: A handbook on the Irish-language work of Brian Ó Nualláin) (BÁC: An Clóchomhar, 1986), 9–12.

33 Seán Joyce, *Eachtra Múinteora* (BÁC: Muinntir C.S. Ó Fallamhain, Teo., i gcomhar le hOS, 1929), 71. Ní h-amháin go mbíodh Gaedhilgeóirí na tíre seo bocht, acht bhíodh siad fá dhroch-mheas ag lucht saidhbhris agus ag lucht léighinn is Laidne, nach mbíodh 'fhios acu céard cáll, ocras ná tart, agus ag rádh go mba dream leisgeamhail na Gaedhilgeóirí. Ní daoine leisgeamhla Gaedhilgeóirí an Iarthair, acht daoine beodha sgiobtha, fad-bhreathnuigheacha, glan-intinneacha a shaothruigheas greim a mbéil go cneasda le allus a gcnámh.

34 Colm Ó Gaora, 'An Truisle', in *As na Ceithre hÁirdibh: Cnuasach Gearrscéal* (BÁC: OS, 1938), 101. Bhí fir as gach áird ag cur an bhóthair tharta go tréan. Iad leath-chromtha agus a gcosa leath-lúbtha, mar bhéidís cithréimeach – ó chruadh-obair na bliana. Leath-ghuala árd ortha – an ghuala dheas ar dhuine,

nó an ghuala chlé ar dhuine eile. Bheadh 'fhios ag duine le breathnughadh ortha an ciotach nó deiseal a d'oibrighdís ó dholbha na ngualann sin. Chuir obair chruaidh na láighe nó tarrngáil na gcliabh sa riocht seo iad. Siubhal mall roighin ag na mnáibh. Shaoilfeá go rabhadar ag ceapadh go rabhadar faoi ualach indiu féin. Compare the comments of Tom O'Flaherty in his English-language story 'Coming Home':

> The Gaeltacht is oftentimes charged with laziness by superior persons from other parts of Ireland who themselves failed to make a living out of good tillage and pasture land, but if any one of these critics had to rear a family of from ten to fourteen children on sixteen or twenty four acres of Aran Mor or the other two islands in the chain he would have a different story.

See O'Flaherty, 'Coming Home', in *Aranmen All* (Dingle: Brandon, 1991 [1934]), 155.

35 Séamus Ó Grianna, *Caisleáin Óir* (Sráid Bhaile Dhúin Dealgan: Preas Dhún Dealgan, 1924), 69. Maidín gheimhridh bhí ann. Bhí sé ag toiseacht a chasgairt an t-sneachta a bhí curtha le seachtmhain. Bhí gaoth nimhneach pholltach ag teacht 'na séideáin anuas ón Eargal agus í ag gabhail go dtí an croidhe ins an triúr ban a bhí ag spágáil leó fríd a t-sneachta, ar a mbealach 'na Clocháin Duibh agus beairtíní stocaí ar a ndroim leó. Bhí Caitlín Chonaill agus a ceann 's a cosa buailte ar a chéile leis an aois agus leis an ualach, a' dá chuid le chéile.

36 Mar phionós a cuireadh an saothar ar an cine daonda sa tosach; ach is amhlaidh a iompuigheann sé chun aoibhnis agus chun beannachta do'n té a chlaoidheann go fonnmhar leis. Téidheann sé chun sochair dá aigne agus dá chorp; is fearrde a shláinte é; is uaisle de a mheon é; ní bhfaghan buairt ná imní aon lom air chómh fada agus a thugan sé a aigne go h-iomlán d'á ghnó.

37 Mhúsglóchadh an leabhar seo do mheanma agus do smaointe ar gach rud dá bhfuil uasal foghanta i nádúr na nGaedhilgeóirí chois fhairrge. Thiubharfadh duine fá deara an t-simplídheacht, uaisleacht, agus an grádh atá aca do Dhia – is mó a mbuidheachas Air nuair atá ádhbhar na céasachta go láidir aca.

38 Mhair an tsaoidheacht Ghaedhealach d'aindeoin ansmacht Gall. Bhí an Creideamh agus an Náisiúntacht fighte fuaighte ina chéile, agus an teanga mar ór-shnáithe agá gcómh-cheangal le chéile i gcómhnaidhe.

39 Ní dóigh liom go bhfuil aon áit eile i nÉirinn a bhfuil oiread ómóis is cheana aca ar an Maighdean Bheannuighthe – cé mór é sin in gach áird de'n tír – is tá i nÁrainn. Ar na trí hoileáin caithfear Inismeadhoin a chur sa' gcéad áit ... Ní dóigh liom gur caitheadh cúig nóiméad ariamh i saoghal duine as Inismeadhoin gan ainm Mhuire dá luadh i bpaidir nó i mbeannacht eicínt aige.

40 Tá annso agus i n-áiteannaibh mar é an síol is luachmhaire do'n náisiún so agus do'n domhan bhraonach má's maith linn an saoghal simplidhe, neamh-urchóideach a ghabháil chughainn féin arís.

41 Sé an bun-smaoin a rithfeadh tré intinn an léigh-theóra ná an t-simplidheacht, saoidheacht agus neamh-urchóid atá i bhfolach i muinntir na Gaedhealtachta.

42 Seán Mac Maoláin, *Gleann Airbh go Glas Naíon* (BÁC: OS, 1969), 67. Dá mhéid dár thaitin maise na tíre liom, ámh, níor thaitmhí liom í ná na daoine féin agus a ndóigheanna. Idir óg agus aosta, bhí muintir an bhaile mar a bheadh teaghlach mór amháin ann, agus iad chomh maith dá chéile agus a bheadh lucht aon chlainne in áit ar bith.

43 Aindrias Ó Baoighill, *An t-Airidheach* (BÁC: OS, 1939), 5–6. Daoine córa carthannacha bunadh Mhín an Fhéidh. Is annamh a chluintear fá bheirt ar bith aca a bheith ag tabhairt droch-chomhursanachta dá chéile. Nuair a bhíos an saoghal ag cur cruaidh ar aon duine aca cuidigheann an chuid eile aca leis ... Ghní siad céad gar eile de'n chineál chéadna, ó cheann amháin de'n bhliadhain go dtí an ceann eile; acht ní chluin an saoghal iomrádh ar bith ar an gharaidheacht sin, agus b'fhearr leo gan mise ná aon duine eile a bheith ag cainnt uirthi.

44 Seosamh Mac Grianna, *An Druma Mór*, 19. Agus a gceart féin a thabhairt dóibh, is cuma goidé an gus a bhí iontu, ní raibh fear ar bith ag maíomh air féin go raibh teach nó talamh nó toice ní b'fhearr ná fear eile aige. Dhearcadh siad ar na buanna a bhí as broinn le duine, agus na buanna a chruinnigh sé ag teacht i gcrann dó. Mac Grianna was rather more dispassionate in a 1926 piece in *An t-Ultach* entitled 'Comhrádh as an nGaedhealtacht' (A conversation from the Gaeltacht), in which he acknowledged that the very word 'Gaeltacht' in the title could alienate some readers, but that he was convinced of the potential richness of Gaeltacht settings for contemporary literature in Irish (*Ultach*, May 1926, 2). See also the albeit undeveloped reservations about Gaeltacht art, painting in this case, expressed by the protagonist of his unfinished novel *Dá mBíodh Ruball ar an Éan*, 35–6. For a discussion of the powerful influence exerted on Gaelic writers by the ideological and literary expectations of their revivalist readership, see Proinsias Mac Cana, 'Strac-Fhéachaint ar Nua-Litríocht Ghaeilge Uladh' (A glance at modern Ulster literature in Irish), in *Fearsaid: Iris Iubhaile an Chumainn Ghaelaigh, 1905–1956* (Béal Feirste: Cumann Gaelach na hIolscoile, 1956), 49–50.

45 An náisiúntaidhe ceart – an t-é go bhfuil a thnúth le Éire Ghaodhlach – is amhlaidh is taca leis an gcreideamh é. Go deimhin, ní réabhlóididhe é, ná nua-reachtóir. Is ar thaobh na SEAN-NIDHTHE a sheasann sé. Is caomhnaidhe é, is conserbháididhe ó dhúthchas é. Níl aon dream daoine sa tír is mó thuilleann an ainm sin ná muinntir an Ghaedhealachais. Sé is cuspa dhóibh an sean-chreideamh, an tseana-theanga agus an tsean-leitridheacht Chríostaidhe, iad

san do chosaint is do chaomhnadh is do bhuanchoimeád. See also the description of the grandmother in Pádraig Ó Siochfhradha's *Caibidlí as Leabhar Mhóirín* (Chapters from Móirín's book) (BÁC: COÉ, 1934), 17.

46 An tAthair Seoirse Mac Clúin, *Róisín Fiain na Mara* (BÁC: Brún agus Ó Nóláin, Teór., 1924), 96–7.

47 Is é rud a chialluigheann sean-aimsireacht ná nidhthe d'á mbítí ag tagairt nuair a tugtaoi i bhfochair a chéile cois na teine ins na hoidhcheanntaibh fada geimhridh ag scoruidheacht fad ó . . . Ní bhfuighthear deagh-labhairt agus deas-bhéulacht i n-aon áit eile in Éirinn fé láthair acht sa Ghaedhealtacht.

48 The author acknowledged that 'the shocking economic depression' of the Gaeltacht had caused some to lose pride in and hope for the language, and that 'the Gaeltacht is merely the linguistically fortunate part of rural Ireland'.

49 Is cleas ag Gallaibh an focal san 'sean-aimsireacht', óir tuigtear dóibh má thagann náire ar Ghaedhealaibh roimis, gur beag an mhoill a bheidh ortha drom láimhe do thabhairt le n-a dteangain agus le n-a sinnsear . . . Tá an náisiún Gaedhealach chómh lag-bhrígheach san fé láthair nach féidir tárrtháil do thabhairt uirthi gan dul siar go dtí sean-shaoghal. Is ionann san agus a rádh go gcaithfear an nua-náisiún Gaedhealach do chothú le 'sean-aimsireacht' go mbeidh sé inghníomha.

50 The adjective 'sean-aimseardha' (old-fashioned) is invariably used as a term of praise in the prose of the period.

51 Cuireann sé iongantas ortha, nuair a théighid go dtí an Ghaedhealtacht, a fhágáil amach go labhrann fear an tighe, nach bhfuil ábalta Gaedhilg – ná Béarla, acht oiread, tá seans, – a léigheadh, go labhrann sé Gaedhilg gan dearmad ar bith innti . . . An sgéalaidheacht agus an amhránaidheacht cois teine a choinnigh an Ghaedhilg glan, gan mheath, i rith na gcéadta bliadhain atá caithte, nuair fágadh í gan saothrú.

52 Ach tugaimís aire nach é bheidh aca Gaedhilg a bheidh 'na teangain nua agus gan ar iompar aici ach gramadach agus litriú agus foghraíocht agus í scartha le stair, le blátha urlabhra, le béal-oideas na mílte blian agus le coidreamh meoin agus tuiscionna na ndaoine ó dtánamair.

53 Agus tá daoine . . . ann, lucht na glan-Ghaedhilge do lorg – sluagh nach suarach – agus táim i n-amhras nach eol do'n bhformhór mór aca gur tobar fíor-Ghaedhilge 'Béaloideas' agus an té a chleachtfadh a thart a thraochadh ann ó am go h-am nár ghádh dhó bheith ar lag-Ghaedhilg feasta. See also the awareness of folklore as an incomparable linguistic resource in 'Adhbhar Cainte agus Leabhra' (Subject matter for talk and books), Editorial, *Stoc*, Oct. 1926, 4).

54 Is gábhadh é shaothrughadh i n-Éirinn mar go bhfuil an Ghaedhilg níos fearr agus níos glaine san mbéaloideas ná in sna leabhraibh fós.

55 Is baoghalach linn go bhfuil bunadhas d'á mbíonn ag cainnt air an náisiúntacht agus an Gaedhealachas nach dtuigeann an gaol atá ag na rudaí seo leis an bhéal-oideas – nach féidir an tír a ath-Ghaodhalughadh gan an béal-oideas agus an cultúr a bhaineas leis a thabhairt arais chomh maith. Na sean-scéaltaí, na sean-amhráin, na sean-phaidreacha agus na sean-fhocla, taisbeánann siad aigne agus tréathra na sean-Ghaodhal dúinn; agus má's maith linn a bheith fíor-Ghaodhalach, má's maith linn an tuigbheál Gaodhalach agus an dearcadh-amach Gaedhalach a bheith againn i gceart, caithfidh-muinn bheith suighte air an tsean-bhéaloideas.

56 Muna mbíonn againn mar sin ach na focail fhuara Gaedhilge is tanaidhe trochailte an cineál gaedhealachais a bhéas againn d'á thoradh. He wrote that folklore offered insights into 'stair aigne na ndaoine gurbh í a dteanga í le himeacht na mílte blian . . . neithe d'fhás as an dteangain agus gur cuid d'á treallamh agus d'á maise iad agus gur rud bocht scriosta maol í d'á n-éaghmais . . . An bhféadfadh aoinne a cheapadh go mbeadh Gaedhealachas againn gan iad-san?'

57 Bhíomair fé sglábhuigheacht aigne. Bhí dhá shlighe chun gach aon rud a dhéanamh, an tslighe Ghaedhealach a chleacht ár seacht sinnsir romhainn agus an tslighe ghallda. Ní raibh aon *initiative* 'sa litríocht againn. Ba chuma cé'n ábhar sgéil a bhí againn ní raibh ach aon fuirm amháin 'nár cheart é innsint – fuirm an tseanchaidhe. Muna raibh sé 'sa bhfuirm sin ní raibh 'sa sgéal ar fad ach béarlachas agus dubhradh go raibh an té a cheap é ag cabharughadh le Seán Buidhe i ngallú na tíre. In a 1932 piece on the Eucharistic Congress, the Jesuit Seán Ó Muirthile saw such 'medievalism' as a virtue: 'There is as it were a rim around the West of Ireland in which the spirit of the Middle Ages is still alive' (Tá mar a bheadh imeall timcheall Iarthair na hÉireann i n-a bhfuil spiorad na Meadhon Aois beo fós) (*TCNÍ*, Nov. 1932, 259). On the other hand, in a 1937 essay on Gaelic poetry in *An Gaedheal*, 'Craiftine' wrote: 'That is the tragedy of poetry in Irish – lack of growth, excessive regard for folklore, reluctance to leave the old thing, the constant backward look. But that is a fault that relates to us as a race' (Sin é tragóid na filíochta Gaoluinne – easbadh fáis, an ró-chion ar an mbéaloideas, an leisce chun an sean-rud d'fhágaint, an síor-fhéachaint siar. Ach is locht é sin a bhaineann linn mar chine) (*Gaedheal*, June 1937, 3). See also the comments of Máirtín Mac Niocláis on the constrictive effect of an obsession with folklore on writers from the Gaeltacht in *Seán Ó Ruadháin*, 50–8.

58 Father Patrick Dinneen, 'Nósa agus Béasa ár Sinnsear' (The customs and manners of our ancestors), in *Leabhar Tailteann*, 41. Is maith is fiú dhúinn na sean-nósa is na sean-bhéasa do chothughadh is d'aithbheodhchaint. Acht ní mór dhúinn gluaiseacht leis an aimsir agus cruth an tsaoghail atá á

chaitheamh againn do chur ar an gcothughadh is ar an aithbheodhchaint.

59 Seán Ó Ciarghusa, 'Teangthacha na dTuath' (Rural languages), in *Ar Mo Mharanadh Dam* (BÁC: ODFR, n.d.), 75–6. Gan amhras, is iomdha nídh sa mBeurla d'fhoghanfadh dúinn agus go mór-mhór an t-eolus go léir do bhí an teanga sin a bhailiú an fhaid do bhí an Ghaedhilg bhocht i n-a cime fé ghlas. Téighimíd go dtí an Beurla fé dhéin an eoluis sin agus fé dhéin aon nidhthe eile atá ann agus ná fuil dá cuid féin ag an nGaedhilg. Ach, na nidhthe nach leis an mBeurla iad ach leis an nGaedhilg, mar atá, an Ghaedhilg féin agus a mbaineann léi d'fhilidheacht agus d'fhiannaidheacht agus de shoilbhreacht agus de bheuloideas nGaedheal, téighimíd fé n-a ndéin go dtí an áit i n-a bhfuilid, is é sin, an Ghaedhealtacht agus an Ghaedhilg féin.

60 An focal san 'béal-oideas' cuireann sé déistean orm uaireannta . . . Cuireann an tseana-scéalaíocht i gcuimhin dom i gcomhnaí go bhfuil an Ghaedhilg ar leabaidh a bháis, go bhfuil sí ag fáil bháis in éineacht le seanóirí na Gaeltachta. An dream dílis atá ag bailiú an bhéal-oidis samhluím iad am' aigne leis na hársadóirí bhailíonn iarsmaí beaga chun a gcur ar a gcumas léargus éigin do bheith acu ar shaolta is ar shíbhialtachtaí atá fé chlúdach féir nó gainmhe leis na cianta . . . Tar éis gach ní do rá i dtaobh an bhéal-oidis, tá sé chó túr is chó craptha leis an sean-aois agus, ar nós na sean-aoise arís, is mairg a bheadh ag brath ar ábhar dóchais d'fháil ann. Mothuím am' chnámha gur ní é ná fuil is ná beidh go brách aon fhás ann.

61 Is dóigh liom go mb'fhiú dúinn úsáid a dhéanamh de sgéaltaí na ndaoiní ins an leitridheacht úir atá le cumadh againn do'n dream Gaedheal atá le teacht. On the other hand, he stated: 'And I also think that every group of people always had a complete education, except for Imperialists and the people of the big machines' (Agus sílim fosta go rabh oideachas iomlán ag achan dream daoiní ariamh, acht lucht Impireachta agus lucht inneall mór). For his own paean to men like Micheál Ruadh, see 'Eoin Rua', *IF*, Apr. 1925, 5–7. For a brief discussion of the influence of folklore on Mac Grianna's writing, see Nollaig Mac Congáil, 'Réamhrá', in *Seosamh Mac Grianna / Iolann Fionn: Clár Saothair* (Seosamh Mac Grianna / Iolann Fionn: Bibliography) (BÁC: Coiscéim, 1990), 1–2; Liam Ó Dochartaigh, 'Mac na Míchomhairle: Smaointe ar *Mo Bhealach Féin* (The erring son: Thoughts on *Mo Bhealach Féin*), *IMN*, 1974, 60–72; and Ó Dochartaigh, '*Mo Bhealach Féin*: Saothar Nualitríochta' (*Mo Bhealach Féin*: A work of modern literature), *Scríobh* 5 (1981), 242–3.

62 Mac Grianna, *Mo Bhealach Féin*, 157. Ach ní thiocfadh liom smuaintiughadh ar chuid targaireachta Cholm Cille dá h-aithris i n-áit ar bith acht ag teinidh mhónadh i gcuideachta a rabh achan duine ag tuigbheáil an duine eile inntí, agus sgáth millteanach na gcnoc amuigh, agus an Fhairrge Mhór ag greadadh na mbreac-chreagach, agus sean-turas thall udaidh agus uaigneas fíochmarach an domhain os ceann leabaidh na naomh.

63 Níl leabhar ná tráchtas is iomláine náisiúntachas ná an béaloideas; go mór-mhór in Éirinn. Chítear an aigne Ghaedhealach agus nósmhaireacht an fhíor-Ghaedhealachais ins na sean-sgéalta. Chítear leithleachas an Náisiúntachais Ghaedhealaigh fé mar a bhí an leithleachas sin ceaptha ag Dia agus sar ar truailligheadh le Gallaibh é . . . Má's buan d'aithbheóchaint an bhéaloidis, ní baoghal don Ghaedhealachais. He was, however, concerned that some cultural nationalists lacked a proper understanding of the national heritage:

> They understand everything involved with *Gaelachas*, except the one necessary thing – that the essence of *Gaelachas* is not to be found in the traditional culture of our ancestors itself, but in the way that traditional culture accepted St. Patrick. (Tuigeann siad gach rud a bhaineas le Gaedhealachas ach an t-aon rud is riachtanaighe – nach i nósmhaireacht ár sean ann féin atá fíor-bhuaidh an Ghaedhealachais le fagháil, acht sa tslí in ar ghlac sí le teachtaireacht an Tailginn (p. 31).

The Very Rev. E. J. Cullen, C. M., believed of Irish oral tradition that 'even her pagan folklore teaches character and high ideals', adding 'unlike the folklore of Greece and Rome, though the folklore of both these latter countries is the heritage of Europe' (*IER*, Oct. 1933, 340).

64 Siad na tagarthaí, na samhlaoidí, na smaointe, na taidhbhrithe, na sean-fhocail, na h-abairtí seo ó'n nGaedhealtacht an smior agus an smúsach atá sa Ghaedhilg féin. Siad a dheineann cine fé leith de Ghaedhealaibh, a nochtann leithleachas – an taca láidir sin fé náisiúntas – a scarann Gaedhil ó chine nach ionann tagarthaí, taidhbhrithe, ná smaointe dóibh.

65 Is insan mbéal-oideas, insna sean-fhoclaibh agus insna dánfhoclaibh is soiléire a nochtar dúinn meóin agus aigne na nGaedheal agus eagna is feallsamhnacht na ndaoine a chuaidh romhainn. Ní fios cé cheap an chuid is mó de sna dánfhoclaibh, acht tá fhios againn go bhfuil tuairimí ár sinnsir ionnta agus a bhfeallsamhnacht. See also Conchubhar Ó Ruairc, 'Cultur Gaedhealach / Ná Bac leis an Aistriúchán' (Gaelic culture / Don't bother with translation), *Standard*, 16/4/37.

66 Ar nós an teangan agus na staire is rud beo é gur gádh é chleachtadh go laethiúil chun go maireadh sé ar aon chor. Is é feidhm aicionta dhóibh a triúr ná eolas a bheith ag daoinibh ortha. Ní le cur i gcás gloine iad, ná fé ghlas i n-iarsmalainn, mar dhéanfaí le hiarsmaí marbh an lámh-shaothair a dhein ár sinnsear.

67 Nach bhfuil aon ionntaoibh againn as na daoinibh atá luaidhte le bheith ar Choimisiún an Bhéaloideasa as an tslighe oibre chleachtuigheann siad; gur dóigh

linn gur fearr an scéim d'oibriughadh ar mhaitheas na Gaedhilge i measg an phobail i n-ionad í oibriughadh ar mhaitheas na n-ollamhan.

68 See also Gearóid Mac Eoin, 'Folklore Does Not Belong to Cranks and Professors', *Hibernia*, June 1937, 18. For a criticism of this nature directed personally at James Delargy, see 'Cearnac' [*sic*], Letter, *II*, 29/10/28.

69 Máirtín Ó Cadhain, 'An Chré Mharbh' (The dead clay), in *Ó Cadhain i bhFeasta*, ed. Seán Ó Laighin (BÁC: Clódhanna Teoranta, 1990), 154. Ó Cadhain blasted 'an t-ólagón duileargúil, an crónach Meán-Aoiseannúil atá ag diúl gach smior dóchais as an gcine.' This essay was originally delivered as a lecture to Cumann na Scríbhneoirí on 11 Feb. 1950.

70 An Cumann le Béal-Oideas Éireann, Printed circular, 1927, in the James Delargy papers (box 2, folder 2), NUIG. Tá an béal-oideas a bhí ag ár sinnsir ag dul chun báis i n-aonacht leis na sean-daoine atá ag imeacht uainn i n-aghaidh an lae. Ní bheidh fáil ar é bhailiú agus é chur ar bun-choimeád don náisiún muna ndeintear an obair le n-ár linn-ne agus ins na deich mbliana seo chugainn.

71 Henry Morris, *Oidche Áirneáil i dTír Chonaill* (Sráid-Bhaile Dhúin Dealgan: Preas Dhún Dealgan, [1924]), 1. Tá coim na hoidhche ag teacht anuas go dubh dorcha ar sgéalaidheacht i dTír Chonaill. Cé gur líonmhar flúirseach an méid de Chinéal Chonaill a bhfuil Gaedhilg ó'n chliabhan aca go seadh, cha bhíonn sgéalaidheacht aca a choidhche níos mó mar a bhí ag a sinnséir ariamh anall. He regretted that in future such fireside sessions would be dominated by small talk about the weather, politics, and the ephemerata of daily news reports. In a 1931 article on the use of recording technology to collect folklore, Séamus Ó Néill approached the question with a touch of rare optimism. Having told of watching with sadness an old *seanchaí* leave a recording session, he commented: 'But although it is hard for me to suppress that fit of sorrow, from the sorrow came hope, for I thought that perhaps his sort would arise again' (Ach ainneoin gur dhoiligh damh an racht bróin sin a mhúchadh, as an bhrón tháinig dóchas, óir smaoinigh mé go mb'fhéidir go n-éireóchadh a sheórt-sa arís) (*II*, 8/10/31). More realistic was Séamus Ó Conaill, who in a 1933 lecture at University College Dublin stressed that while the Irish language would doubtless outlive traditional folklore, 'it is not possible to keep folklore alive. There is nothing to do but put it in safe keeping' (ní féidir béaloideas do chimeád beo. Níl le déanamh ach é chur i dtaisge) (*II*, 27/4/33). 'Y.O.' offered a cynical perspective on the theme, writing in a review of *Béaloideas* that it was a good thing the collectors were at work, for 'in another generation our national schools and the modern Gaelic taught in them will have obliterated the ancient Gaelic mentality' (*IS*, 31/8/29).

72 That he, and doubtless many like him, were concerned about the negative effect on the national image being generated by ignorant versions of traditional material is evident from his next sentence:

> We are not yet in a position to form an accurate judgment of its merits, but of this we are certain, that the nonsensical rubbish which passes for Irish folklore, both in Ireland and outside, is not representative of the folklore of our Irish people.

Delargy was a true missionary, contributing pieces to various papers and journals large and small, and taking his gospel on the road in lectures throughout Ireland.

73 Ba bhreá an rud dá ndeineadh gach Contae eile i n-a bhfuil an Ghaedhilg beo ann fós aithris ar Chontae an Chláir. There are two additional points of interest here. First of all, the writer insisted that the children would need help to do this work correctly, taking care to write down everything just as they heard it, without any attempt to 'correct' it in any way. Second, the writer seems to have had no interest in traditional material preserved in the English language. Even more dismissive of folklore in English was 'Gréasuidhe Poill a' Chlaidhe' (probably An tAthair Eric Mac Fhinn). See, for example, 'Litir Aniar / Gnoithe an Chomhairle Conndae' (A letter from the west / County council affairs), *Éireannach*, 8/12/34.

74 Tá eagla orm go mbeadh sé ró-dhéidheannach nuair a thuigfidh na riaghalthóirí seo atá orrainn luachmhaireacht na seoide atá i bhfolach sa nGaedhealtacht. Badh chóir go gcuirfidhe daoine tuigsionacha ag bailiughadh agus ag cuardach i ngach aon áit díobh so ar fhan an Ghaedhealg beo ionnta; agus fuireach ag bailiughadh agus ag bailiughadh agus ag líonadh leabhar uatha.

75 Ó Domhnaill, *Oileáin Árann*, 178. 'Sé an truagh é go bhfuil an oiread sin de bhéaloideas agus de shean-sgéaltaibh inspéise ár dtíre caillte cheana. Acht gidh gur mar sin atá, is ádhbhar áthais agus muinghine dúinn go bhfuil buidhean beag, d'á laighead iad, a bhfuil dúil aca i mbéaloideas agus atá ag cur chun an méid de is féidir d'fhagháil, do chur ar bhuanchuimhne agus mar sin do shábháil.

76 Among less predictable Gaels enthusiastic about the preservation of folklore were Pádraic Ó Conaire and Cearbhall Ua Dálaigh. See, for example, Pádraic Ó Conaire, 'Dualgas an Oide / Obair Mhór' (The duty of the teacher / Great work), in *Iriseoireacht Uí Chonaire* (Ó Conaire's journalism), ed. An tSr. Eibhlín Ní Chionnaith (Béal an Daingin: Cló Iar-Chonnachta, 1989), 190–1. Pádraigín Riggs discusses the influence of the oral tradition on Ó Conaire's own fictional narrators in *Pádraic Ó Conaire: Deoraí* (BÁC: An Clochomhar, 1994), 167. For Ua Dalaigh, see 'Ne Periant / Lucht Cnuasta an Bhéal-Oideasa' (Ne Periant [Let them not perish] / Folklore collectors), *Nation*, 30/5/31.

77 Curiously enough, there were no competitions involving folklore when the Oireachtas was revived in earnest in 1939.

78 See Ó Muimhneacháin, *Dóchas agus Duainéis*, 71.

79 The editor of the journal had been approached by Sergeant T. D. Mac Morrisroe of Galway, who, at the request of Douglas Hyde and Eoin Mac Néill, was collecting folklore in the West. The editor said he would welcome such material for publication and would give prizes, and then commented: 'Nothing is more to be deplored than the passing into oblivion of our ancient monuments, both in stone and in literature . . . and we know of no better custodians of what remains than the Gárda Síothchána.'

80 *An Lóchrann* did take note of the new situation following the appearance of *Béaloideas*, but stressed that it would continue to publish folk material (*Lóchrann*, Feb. 1930, 2). Indeed, when the journal suspended publication in December 1931, the editor specifically urged that its readers continue to collect folklore and submit it to the other Gaelic journals (*Lóchrann*, Dec. 1931, 4).

81 Cuirtear sean-amhráin chugainn, sean-sgéalta, fiannaigheacht nó sean-chainteanna ar bith eile . . . tá go leor freisin de sheanchas a' baint le áiteacha anonn is anall ar fud na tíre nár cuireadh ar pháipéar i mBéarla ná i nGaedhilg go fóill. Ní mór a leithéid a sgríobh síos a fhad 's tá fághail air. Druididh isteach, a sgríbhneoirí.

82 In addition to folktales, the Gaelic journals published an enormous amount of other traditional material. Proverbs seem to have been particularly popular. Religious folklore – prayers, blessings, and the like – also attracted considerable interest in the journals, and An tAthair Donnchadh Ó Donnchadha published a booklet on *Seanchas an Chreidimh* (The folklore of the faith) (BÁC: M. H. Mac Ghuill agus a Mhac, 1923). Miscellaneous categories of traditional material published in journals of the period include games, riddles, fairy beliefs, calendar customs – including some submitted by Micheál Mac Liammóir to *Fáinne an Lae* (1/5/26) – keens, charms and cures, crafts, the making of *poitín*, place-name lore, prophecies, and various *pisreoga* or 'superstitions'. In September 1939, the *Journal of the Royal Society of Antiquaries of Ireland* published Seán Ó Súilleabháin's 'Adhlacadh Leanbhaí' (The burial of children), a scholarly discussion of *cillíní*, burial places set aside for unbaptised infants (*JRSAI*, 69 (3), 143–51).

83 See, for example, Ó Ruadháin, *Pádhraic Mháire Bhán*, 87–8, 102–22, 174–6; 226–39. Writing to *II* in response to an article by Ernest Blythe that was critical of his novel (*II*, 28/3/33), Ó Ruadháin stated: 'What I wanted was to describe the life and the customs and the manners and the qualities of the people as well as I could' (Ba éard a bhí uaim-se saoghal agus nósa agus béasa agus tréithe na ndaoine a chur síos chomh maith agus d'fhéadfainn) (*II*, 4/4/33). See also the comments of Máirtín Mac Niocláis in *Seán Ó Ruadháin*, 62, 64–5, 86–7.

84 See, for example, Ua Laoghaire, *An Bhruinneall Bhán*, 31–5, 99–101, 220 (this one thematically relevant).

85 See Ó Gallchobhair, *Cáitheamh na dTonn*, 86–90, 169–98, 199–208. 'Céile Sheáin Mhóir' (The wife of Seán Mór) is unusual for its happy ending with husband, mermaid-wife, and children living together as sea creatures.

86 In his *An Bealach chun na Gaedhealtachta ('The Road to the Gaedhealtacht' Phrase Book)* (Belfast: Coisde Mhodha na Ráidhte, n.d.), Seán Mac Maoláin provided a substantial collection of traditional idioms favoured by Donegal native speakers, and he expanded the list in *Cora Cainnte as Tír Chonaill* (Idiomatic expressions from Donegal) (BÁC: ODFR, 1933).

87 The purpose of many of the little stories in *Clocha Sgáil* is to explain proverbs.

88 In his brief preface, Ó Criomthain states that he has given an explanation of every place name on the islands as well as any history connected with it and added: 'No place is a Gaeltacht without this being done' (Ní Gaedhealtacht aon áit gan so do bheith déanta).

89 Actually, Ó Gaora virtually ignored folk traditions in his book, concentrating instead on what we should perhaps call social history and material culture. He was criticised for ignoring the folklore connected with his subject in an otherwise favourable review of the book by 'P.B.', *IP*, 31/3/38.

90 Tomás Ó Máille, 'Réamh-Fhocal', in Séamus Mac Con Iomaire, *Cladaigh Chonamara* (BÁC: OS, 1938), ix–xi.

91 Ní dóigh liom go raibh an scéal san i gcló riamh fós; is amhlaidh do chuala-sa ó shean-duine sa bhaile é.

92 Ní'l ainmneacha na ndaoine a gcuala mé na sgéalta seo uatha agam ach is i gCois Fhairrge a chuala mé iad.

93 Sean-scéilín seo a chuala mé ó shean-duine atá suas le deich mbliana agus ceithre fichid.

94 Sin sgéal a fuair mé ó shean-fhear atá ina chomhnuidhe annseo.

95 Fuaireas an t-eolas seo ó shean-mhnaoi sa gcomhursanacht. *II* frequently published retellings of folktales without identifying the original informant in any way.

96 In the preface to *Pota Cnuasaigh (An Chéad Chuid)*, Murray wrote: 'I have selected these stories from the large number taken down during the last ten years from Omeath speakers, most of whom are now dead.' His intention in compiling the collection was not, however, to collect folklore for scholarly analysis, but rather to 'help supply the deficiency of text books in Ulster Irish for National Schools' (p. 2).

97 See, for example, Ó Roithleáin, 'Teagasc Bhríghde ar a Leas do'n Pheacach' (Brigid's good advice to the

sinner), *CT*, 28/1/30; and Ó Roithleáin, 'Tarbh Fiadhain an tSléibhe' (The wild bull of the mountain), *CT*, 17/6/30. In a 1931 piece in *II*, Micheál Óg Mac Pháidín created a glowing pen portrait of a Donegal storyteller and retold one of his tales. He did not, however, feel the need to give the man's name (*II*, 3/12/31). On the other hand, in a piece on anonymous heroes in 1929, one 'Cairbre Lifechair' insisted that traditional tales and songs, while a communal treasure, were the creations of individual artists:

> We have a way of speaking in which we always refer to the folklore of the people as if the people had but a single mind. Let there, however, be no misunderstanding about the fact that it was a particular person who thought up every folktale and every old tune that there is (Tá sé de nós cainnte againn bheith a' síor-thagairt do bhéal-oideas na ndaoine amhail is dá mba ná beadh acht aigne amháin 'ges na daoine. Ná bíodh aon phioc d'á mhearthal orainn, ámhthach, ná gur duine áirithe a cheap gach sean-scéal agus gach sean-phort d'á bhfuil ann) ('An Saighdiúir gan Ainm / Dearmad sa Scéal' [The soldier without a name / A mistake in the story], *II*, 12/12/29).

98 In a review of Seoighe's *Sgéalta Chois Teallaigh*, 'G. de P.' was obviously a bit confused about Seoighe's methodology: 'The rest are short stories of the countryside and the sea; some of those are true stories, it would seem' (Scéalta gearra tuaithe agus mara an chuid eile, fíor-scéalta cuid díobh-san, do réir deallraimh) (*Nation*, 23/11/29).

99 See Ó Míodhacháin, *Eachtraí Pháidín Turraoin: Aith-Innsint ar Shean-Sceulta* (The adventures of Páidín Turraoin: A retelling of old stories) (BÁC: COÉ, n.d.).

100 Ó Muimhneacháin, *Béaloideas Bhéal Átha an Ghaorthaidh* (The folklore of Ballingeary), 144.

101 Scríobhaidís síos an scéal nó an rud eile díreach mar adeir an duine é, is cuma é bheith ceart nó mí-cheart, slachtmhar nó mí-shlachtmhar.

102 See also his comments in the same journal earlier that year (2/2/32) and in the following year (27/6/33).

103 Ní ceart leigint do dhuine ar bith nach bhfuil eolas ceart aige ar Ghaedhilg na h-áite toiseacht a chruinniú béal-oidis i n-áit ar bith.

104 Séamus Ó Duilearga, 'Réamhfhocal', in Seán Ó Súilleabháin, *Láimh-Leabhar Béaloideasa* (BÁC: An Cumann le Béaloideas Éireann, 1937), i. Beidh an leabhrán so – an chéad cheann dá shaghas i nGaedhilg – beidh sé i n-a ádhbhar gríosuithe agus i n-a fhuarán eolais agus comhairle do lucht bhailithe béaloideasa, do sgoláiribh na teangan agus na litridheachta, agus do'n méid de chine Gaedheal nár thréig an rud ba dhúthchas tráth do'n náisiún go hiomlán – 'Seanchas Éireann'. In his review of the *Láimhleabhar* in *II*, Gearóid Mac Eoin wrote:

> An English translation of the handbook is an urgent want. Folklore in English districts is as valuable as in the Gaeltacht and is far more exposed to the ravages of time. The translation would be useful, too, for English and Scottish workers, as well as for those who are trying to collect the abundant Irish materials spread throughout the American continent (*II*, 16/11/37).

Máirín Nic Eoin has commented that the headings in the *Láimh-Leabhar* could almost serve as a table of contents for Gaeltacht autobiographies! See Nic Eoin, *Litríocht Réigiúnach*, 34.

105 Ó Súilleabháin, 'Comhairle do'n Bhailitheoir', in *Láimh-Leabhar*, iii–v.

106 *Scéim agus Ceistiúchán le h-Aghaidh Stair Paróiste* (A scheme and questionnaire for parish history) (Béal Átha na Sluagh: Coláiste Sheosaimh Naomhtha, Páirc Ghearrbhaile, 1929), a handbook prepared for the most part by An tAthair Eric Mac Fhinn to assist those interested in working on the history of parishes in the diocese of Clonfert, County Galway, urged such people to collect folklore. See pp. 20, 23. For Mac Fhinn's involvement in this book, see Gearóidín Uí Nia, *An tAthair Eric Mac Fhinn agus Ar Aghaidh*, 62. In 1937, the Free State Department of Education announced that it intended to compile 'lists of words and idioms dealing with the ordinary life of the Gaeltacht' (liostaí focal agus leaganacha cainnte a bhaineas le gnáth-shaoghal na Gaedhealtachta). The department also suggested some areas of interest, such as 'religion' (creideamh) and 'local place name lore' (dinnseanchas na h-áite). See 'Scéim Nua / Foclóir de Chainnt na Gaedhealtachta' (A new scheme / A dictionary of Gaeltacht speech), *IP*, 19/5/37.

107 Seán Ó Ciarghusa, 'Iarsma an Uilc' (The consequence of evil), in *Geantraighe: Scéalta Beaga Grinn* (Laughter-provoking music: Little humorous stories) (BÁC: Muinntir C.S. Ó Fallamhain, Teo., i gcomhar le hOS, 1928), 93–6. Ó Ciarghusa originally published the story as 'Ag Lorg an Léighinn Dúinn / Iarsma an Uilc' (As we were seeking learning / The consequence of evil) in *II*, 28/7/25.

108 Micheál Ó Siochfhradha, 'An Turus' and 'An Corp', in *Seo Mar Bhí* (BÁC: COÉ, [1930]), 28–33, 34–9.

109 In Séamas Mac Giubúin's [*sic*] 'An Baile Seo Againne' (This townland of ours), it is the informant who is bull-headed and rather arrogant (*An Chearnóg*, Mar.–Apr. 1924, 5–6). In 'Slán leis an Áirneán' (Farewell to the night visiting) by Tomás Ó Colmáin, a *seanchaí* tells the narrator about the visit of a circus elephant to County Mayo.

110 Ach ná bíodh mearughadh ort, a léightheoir, fhad agus a mhairfeas deór biotáilte i mbun gloine, ná éireochaidh na fir sin as an obair uasal seo. Má's duine liath thú nó ionndaire na ceithre scór, ná síl teiceadh nó dul i bhfolach ortha. Agus nuair a thig siad, bíodh scéal réidh agat daobhtha, nó más fearr leat sin, dhá leithscéal, óir is ionann dhá leithscéal

agus scéal. Bíodh sin agat agus ní baoghal duit. See also the mock folktale 'Cúrsaí Báis: Sean-Scéal Suairc Soilbhir Sruth-Bhriathrach Seafóideach Siamsamhail Scannruighteach Scaolmhar Scléipeach Saothamhail Suimeamhail So-Léighte' by Myles's brother Ciarán Ua Nualláin in the *New Irish Magazine / An Sgeulaidhe*, Aug. 1934, 43–4. In 1935, 'Pilibín Ó Neachtain' satirised the contemporary Gaelic fascination for folklore in his column 'Leitreacha do Mhol ó Thuaidh' (Letters to the North Pole) in *An t-Éireannach*. His narrator writes to a friend taking up residence at the North Pole urging him to set to work immediately to collect 'the folklore of the Arctic Circle' (Béal-Oideas an Chearcaill Arctaigh). The narrator also tells of how the local schoolmaster corresponds on folklore with colleagues around the world, including one who is researching 'the folklore of the sausage' (Béal-Oideas an Isbín) with a Doctor Sauerkraut. 'Pilibín' also parodied the folktale, publishing a story that begins 'There was once a widow and she had three sons' (Bhí baintreach ann uair amháin agus bhí triúr mac aici), and commenting: 'Let it be noticed that this is a widow who lived her life according to the Highest Laws of Folklore; she would not be satisfied with two sons, and the potato garden would not be big enough to feed the fourth one' (Tugtar fá deara gur baintreach í seo a chaith a saoghal de réir Dlighthe an Bhéal-Oideasa is Áirde; ní bheadh sí sásta le beirt mhac; agus ní bheadh garrdha na bhfataí sáthach fairsing leis an gceathramhadh duine a chothú) (*Éireannach*, 6/4/35).

111 Tomás Bairéad, 'Folach na Fiannaidheachta' (The hiding of lore about the Fianna), in *Cumhacht na Cinneamhna* (BÁC: ODFR, 1936), 131–45. The story does provide an excellent depiction of the difficulty of transcription from oral narration (pp. 137–9). For a discussion of the influence of traditional storytellers on Bairéad himself, see Niall Ó Murchadha, 'Gearrscéalaíocht Thomáis Bairéad, 1893–1973' (The short stories of Tomás Bairéad), *IMN*, 1991, 162–89.

112 Máirtín Ó Cadhain, '"Fóide Cnapánacha Carracha Uachtar an Bhaile"', in *Idir Shúgradh agus Dáiríre* (BÁC: OS, 1975 [1939]), 109–16. Tradition bearers are also important characters in the following stories: Micheál Ó Gríobhtha, 'An tSrúill', in *Cathair Aeidh*, 89–125; Tomás Laoi, '"Cairní"', *Bonaventura*, Winter 1938, 175–84; 'Cóil Pheadair Éamuinn', 'Máirtín Ceannuidhe' (Martin the merchant), *CB*, Dec. 1939, 808–10. In Mac Grianna's *An Druma Mor*, local people are amazed outsiders would ever be interested in their *seanchas* (pp. 102–3). The sense of traditional skills being scorned in favour of innovations from the outside world was also the theme of the melancholy anonymous story 'Máirtín Figheadóir' (Martin the weaver), which traces the decline and death of a country weaver unable to compete with the more fashionable clothes available in the Galway shops (*Stoc*, Dec. 1929, 4).

113 Ealuíon ann fhéin é bailiú seo an bhéaloidis – go mór mór an chaoi le ceistiúchán a dhéanamh ar na seanchaidhthe. Ní h-annamh nach bhfeileann an cheist díreach beag ná mór. Ní mór leath-bhord a thabhairt, teach timpeall air – teacht, mar déarfá ar thaobh na gaoithe de'n tseanchaí.

114 Dála an sgéil, má tá sgéalta le fáil ar leath-choróin nó coróin, nárbh fhearr dhon Riaghaltas airgead an dole a chaitheamh le iad a cheannach ná an t-airgead sin a sgaipeadh i n-aisge? He noted that the tradition bearers believed 'that the teacher is making a pile of money on the stories' (go bhfuil an múinteoir ag déanamh cairn airgid ar na sgéalta).

115 Cé go bhfuil seanchuidhthe na Gaedhealtachta fial flaitheamhail faoi n-a gcuid béaloidis ní cheapaim féin go bhfuil sé ceart ná cóir a bheith a diúl seanchais uatha gan luach saothair eicínt a thabhairt dóibh i n-a leabaidh. 'Sliabh na mBan' expressed the idea more pithily in 1931, praising the work of collectors in preserving lore that would otherwise perish, but continuing: 'But that does not mean that it is right or proper to leave the old Irish-speaker with no profit for his Irish and his work except for a puff of tobacco' (Acht ní fhágann sin gur ceart ná cóir an sean-Ghaedhilgeoir d'fhágaint gan de thairbhe a choda Gaedhilge agus a shaothair aige acht gal tobac) (*IP*, 19/9/31).

116 See also the views of Cormac Breathnach: 'Some of the Irish books in the schools are merely anglicising pupils. We should have national folk-lore instead of "Humpty-Dumpty" and "Little Red Riding Hood"' (*II*, 5/9/28).

117 This information is from the typescript of a September 1977 talk entitled 'Schools Mss.' broadcast on Radio Éireann by Séamas Ó Catháin. The typescript is now among the James Delargy Papers, NUIG MS G16, box 2. See also Seán O'Sullivan, 'Introduction', in *Folktales of Ireland*, ed. O'Sullivan (London: Routledge & Kegan Paul, 1966), xxxv. Also among the Delargy papers (MS G16, box 1) is a copy of one of the questionnaires circulated to the teachers involved in the project, indicating all of the data that should be collected to make this a sound scholarly undertaking. For an idea of how rich was the harvest from a single school, albeit one in an area justly famous for its storytellers, singers, and, later, writers, see *Rann na Feirsde: Seanchas Ár Sinsear* (Rann na Feirste: The traditional lore of our ancestors), ed. Conall Ó Grianna (Rann na Móna: Cló Cheann Dubhrann, 1998).

118 Diarmuid Ó Giolláin, *Locating Irish Folklore: Tradition, Modernity, Identity* (Cork: Cork University Press, 2000), 135. Not all in the movement were convinced about the success of the scheme, however. In a 1939 *Irish Independent* piece entitled 'Justice Says Much Folklore Spurious / Schools Collection', which called into question the supposed educational value of the schools folklore project, Judge Louis J. Walsh

claimed that parents were manufacturing 'traditional' lore for schoolchildren fearful of punishment because they had nothing authentic to contribute! (*II*, 3/4/39).

119 Ní fheadramar, leis, ná go mbadh dheas leis an lucht éisteachta seanchaidhe, nó scéalaidhe, dh'innsint scéil le linn sosa anois agus arís. Anál na Gaedhealtachta, oiread agus is féidir é, do thabhairt isteach san amharclainn, d'fhóghanfadh sé do idir aisteóiríbh agus do'n chuid eile againn. Storytellers had performed regularly at the Oireachtas prior to its suspension in 1924.

120 See also Pádhraic Ó Domhnalláin, 'An Craolóir' (The broadcaster), in *Dréachta* (BÁC: OS, 1956 [1935]), 31.

121 Dar linn pé leitríocht Ghaedhilge a sgríofar feasta i n-Éirinn muna beidh sí Gaedhealach agus muna mbeidh a préamhacha bunuithe greamaithe i leitríocht agus i mbéaloideas na Gaedhilge, ní bheidh innti ach rud leamh neamblasta gan áird. See also 'A Venerable Heritage / Irish Folklore a National and Cultural Asset of Highest Value' (report of a Delargy lecture in Rathmines, Dublin), *Star*, 23/11/29. For other examples of a similar belief in the centrality of folk modes of thought and style in the development of a modern literature in Irish, see 'Máire de. B.', 'Béaloideas na nGaedheal i gCúrsaí Léighinn agus Cultúir' (The folklore of the Gaels in educational and cultural matters), Dundalk *Examiner*, 30/7/32; An tAthair Seán Ó Catháin, 'Im' Leabharlainn Dom', *TCNÍ*, Nov. 1936, 259–60; Nioclás Breathnach, 'Tábhacht an Bhéaloidis' (The importance of folklore), *IP*, 8/3/37; 'Óráid ó'n Aire Oideachais' (A speech from the Minister for Education), *IP*, 22/2/38; Conn Ó Ruairc, 'An Dúthchas Gaedhealach / An bhFuil Sé i mBaoghal a Chaillte?' (The Gaelic heritage / Is it in danger of being lost?), *Leader*, 2/7/38.

122 Is beag do bhí le foghlaim ag Gaedhealaibh fá dtaobh do scéalta ná do scéalaidheacht agus is amaideach an mhaise dhúinne é bheith a' leanstan nós scéalaidheachta an Anglo-Sacsan. Is fearr abhfad dúinn 'leanmhain go dlúth do chlú ár sinnsear'.

123 Budh géar-riachtanas leis [.i. an béaloideas] chun dath agus blas a chur ar chainnt an dreama nua so atá ag éirghe suas i nÉirinn, agus chun a bheith 'na mhaise agus 'na adhbhar agus 'na inspioráid i gcúrsaí litridheachta, agus ealadhan, agus drámaidheachta agus a leithéid eile ag an gcine seo againn-ne feasta, fé mar bhí sé 'na chuid de shaoghal anma agus inntleachta ag ár sinnsear, go dtí seo. See also Ó Siochfhradha, 'Pictiúirí Cuimhne' (Pictures in the memory), *Bonaventura*, Summer 1938, 11–26.

124 Ó Cuív, *Prós na hAoise Seo*, 9. Is ar an mbéaloideas san is ceart an leitríocht nua do bhunú, air sin agus ar shaothar na bhfilí agus na n-ughdar próis a chuaidh romhainn, agus go dtí go mbeidh samplaí maithe den bhéaloideas againn ós gach dúthaigh sa Ghaeltacht ní bheidh tosach ceart déanta againn ar an dteangain do shaothrú i gcúrsaí leitríochta. Beidh an béaloideas 'na thaca againn agus 'na cheangal idir prós agus filíocht ár sean. See also his essay 'Dúil sa Léann' (Enthusiasm for learning), in *Deora Áthais*, 73.

125 Tá tréithe áirighthe ag baint le gach gluaiseacht liteardha an domhain agus is ar na tréithe sin a bhraitheann a n-idirdhealbhughadh ó n-a chéile. Anois caithfidh na tréithe sin a bheith ar fagháil i ngach gné litridheachta a saothruightear i gceanntar áirighthe má réidhtigheann an gné sin leis an ghluaiseacht liteardha atá suas san gceanntar sin. Tá na tréithe sin ar fagháil san mbéaloideas mar níl ann acht meón an chineadh a saothruigheann an litridheacht do bheith dhá fhoillsiughadh san tslighe is simplidhe ó thaobh an chultúir dhe. Uime sin réidhtigheann drámaí atá bunuighthe ar an mbéaloideas do'n ghluaiseacht liteardha i nÉirinn.

126 For Ó Tuathail, see 'Drámaí Gaedhilge / Léigheacht do Lucht an Fháinne i nDún Dealgan' (Plays in Irish / A lecture to the members of An Fáinne in Dundalk), *Dundalk Examiner*, 20/12/30; for Ó Dubhda, see 'Value of Folklore / Dr Duilearga [*sic*] Speaks to Teachers at Dundalk', *Examiner*, 26/3/38.

127 Ngúgí wa Thiong'o, *Decolonising the Mind: The Politics of Language in African Literature* (London: James Curry, 1986), 7.

128 Gheobhaidh scríbhneoir Gaedhilge a bhfuil mian aige litridheacht a thabhairt dá lucht léighte rudaí ins na sean-scéaltaibh a chuirfeas craiceann agus bláth ar a shaothar ach úsáid cheart a bhaint as.

129 For Mac Grianna, see, for example, 'Bíonn Súil le Muir acht ní Bhíonn Súil le hUaigh' (The one who goes to sea may return, but there is no return from the grave), 'Slóighte na bhFiann' (The hosts of the Fianna), and 'Taisgidh an Úcaire' (The fuller's treasure), all in *An Grádh agus an Ghruaim* (BÁC: OS, 1929); and 'Bruidhean Dhroim an Uaignis' (The fairy dwelling of Droim an Uaignis), in *Pádraic Ó Conaire agus Aistí Eile* (BÁC: ODFR, 1936). For Ó Grianna, see, for example, 'Sagart Éamoinn Sheáin Oig' in *Cioth is Dealán* (Dún Dealgan: Preas Dhún Dealgan, 1926. For Ó Cadhain, see '"Mac Rí na nDeachmann"' (The son of the king of tithes), in *Idir Shúgradh agus Dáiríre*. For a detailed discussion of Ó Cadhain's use of folklore in his later work, see Gearóid Denvir, *Cadhan Aonraic: Saothar Liteartha Mháirtín Uí Chadhain* (Lone bird: The literary work of Máirtín Ó Cadhain) (BÁC: An Clóchomhar, 1987), 171–228. On the other hand, Diarmaid Ó Crualaoich has written of how Ó Grianna and other Ulster writers, were all but smothered by a tradition few of them were willing to explore creatively. See Ó Crualaoich, 'Conallaigh ag Scríobh faoi Thír Chonaill' (Donegal people writing about Donegal), *IMN*, 1990, 31–50.

130 Atá mianach seol (plots) go fairsinn flúirseach sa gcríoch úd Thuadh-Mhumhan. Gabhann an t-údar chuige cuid de na seolta sin, go gcrochann sé iad, is go

dtugann sgód dá shaoilsin ar mhuir na samhlaidheachta. Tugann sé leath-bhord annseo is annsiúd dó ar a mhian, agus cruthuigheann sé go bhfuil in don an bád a ghabháil cho paitionta le sean-iondúir dá fheabhas. See also the similar remarks of the book's anonymous reviewer in *II*, 14/6/26. This critic called the collection 'a voice from the Gaeltacht' (guth ó'n nGaedhealtacht). In his preface to the collection, Ó hAodha says that he found most of his material in and around Miltown Milbay, County Clare, and identifies his father and mother as major sources. He also tells of how he got one from his mother, wrote it down, read it to her, and then revised it with her help until he got it right, upon which she commented: 'It is now like a story you would read in a book' (Is cosamhail anois le scéal a léighfeá i leabhar). See Ó hAodha, 'Brollach', in *An Figheadóir* (BÁC: Brún agus Ó Nóláin, n.d.), 5–9.

131 Nollaig Mac Congáil, 'An Traidisiún Béil i Saothar Sheagháin Mhic Mheanman' (The oral tradition in the work of Seaghán Mac Meanman), in *Éigse 1988: Seán Bán Mac Meanman*, ed. Séamus Ó Cnáimhsí (BÁC: Coiscéim, 1988), 17. Mac Congáil writes of Mac Meanman 'go gcuireann sé an t-eolas faoi [an "Hidden Ireland" dá chuid scéalta] inár láthair ar an dóigh chéanna a bhfuair sé é óna chuid oidí múinte, mar atá, na seanchaithe, oidhrí dlisteanacha an traidisiúin bhéil.' See also Séamus Ó Cnáimhsi, 'Seán Bán Mac Meanman', in *Scríbhneoireacht na gConallach* (Donegal writers), ed. Mac Congáil (BÁC: Coiscéim, 1990), 84, 89–90.

132 Seaghán Mac Meanman, 'Réamhrádh', in *Fear Siubhail a's a Chuid Comharsanach agus Daoine Eile* (BÁC: ODFR, 1937 [1924]), n.p. In his preface to *Indé agus Indiu*, which he called 'the second part of "An Fear Siubhal a's a Chuid Comharsanach"' (an dara roinn d' 'Fhear Siubhail a's a Chuid Comharsanach'), he stated that there was 'a good foundation of truth' (bun maith fírinne) to every story, and that some were in fact true. See Mac Meanman, 'Réamhrádh', in *Indé agus Indiu* (BÁC: Muinntir C. S. Ó Fallamhain i gcomhar le hOS, 1929), n.p. For other examples of stories of this type, see Séamus Maguidhir, 'Gearrán Bán Dhubh-Choill' (The white gelding of Dubh-Choill) and 'Domhnall Dualbhuidhe' (Domhnall with the blonde curly hair), in *Dhá Chrann na Marbh* (BÁC: OS, 1939), 73–8; 95–110; Peadar Ó Dubhda, 'Scéal an tSean-Fhidileora' (The story of the old fiddler), in *An t-Óganach Ceann-Órdha agus Scéalta Eile* (The golden-headed youth and other stories) (BÁC: OS, 1939), 87–124. In a brief introductory note in *Sgéalta Chois Teallaigh*, Tadhg S. Seoighe states that some of his stories were based on personal experience and others on tales heard from *seanchaithe* when he was young.

133 For other stories dealing more seriously with issues of class consciousness in rural society, see Seaghán Mac Meanman, 'Rothaidhe an tSaoghail' (The wheel of life), in *Indé agus Indiu*, 83–104; Micheál Ó Gríobhtha, 'Criostíona', in *Cathair Aeidh*, 257–301; and Máirtín Ó Cadhain, 'Culaith le Cois', in *Idir Shúgradh agus Dáirire*, 47–69.

134 In an appreciation of the work of Pádraic Ó Conaire in UCG's *University Annual*, 'Caoilte Mac Ronan' [*sic*] acknowledged the challenges that would face authors attempting to write frankly of Gaeltacht life:

> Those who can forgive brutality in Maupassant and worldliness in Gautier, who can tolerate innuendo in Wilde and irreverence in Shaw, who can condone on the plea of art all that might offend moral sensitiveness, are prepared to be shocked beyond measure by the veriest suggestion of anything debatable in a writer of Gaelic (UCG *University Annual*, 1922–3, 10).

On the other hand, in 1937 the UCD graduate Tomás P. Ó Siadhail worried that some Gaelic writers – in particular those from Ulster – were too eager to explore the dark side of life:

> There is another quality that I notice in prose in modern Irish – a quality that that prose would be better off with less of – the excessive gloominess and sadness . . . If that continues, it is not long until writers of the Irish language will be as gloomy as some of the authors in England at present, people like Aldous Huxley who cannot look at a living man laughing without seeing the skull behind his face in their minds (Tá tréith eile a bhraithim i bprós na Nua-Ghaedhilge agus tréith gurbh fhearrde an prós sin gan oiread de bheith ann, an duairceas agus an brón thar meadhon . . . Má leantar de, ní fada go mbeidh sgríobhnóirí na Gaedhilge chomh duairc le cuid de sna h-úghdair atá i Sasana fé láthair, daoine mar Aldous Huxley nach dtig leo féachaint ar fhear bheo agus é ag gáire gan an cloigeann taobh thiar dá aghaidh d'fheicsint 'n-a n-aigne) (*AA*, Oct. 1937, 7).

135 An fear a bháidh na Máilligh gan uair na h-aithrighe a thabhairt dhóibh ní bhfuair sé féin ná a mhac uair na h-aithrighe 'na dhiaidh sin nuair a bádhadh sa gcuan céadna iad. Bhí Dia na Glóire ag dearcadh anuas ortha agus bhuail sé buille ortha chomh tobann is bhuail siad féin ar na fir nár thuill é.

136 Seán Ó Ciosáin, 'Cad Dubhairt an File?' (What did the poet say?) in *Sgéalta cois Laoi*, 63–74.

137 Pádhraic Ó Domhnalláin, 'An Chónra', in *An tIolrach Mór: Díoghluim Gearr-Sgéal* (The great eagle: A collection of short stories) (BÁC: Brún agus Ó Nualláin, Teór., n.d.), 30–4. In a Mylesian satirical jab at the eagerness of some Gaeltacht people to cash in on the language, *Dublin Opinion* in 1933 published 'Income Tax Return from Resident in the Fíor-Ghaeltacht (Respectfully imagined by Our Grangegorman Correspondent' [Grangegorman is a mental asylum]. Among the items declared are:

Eight Irish-speaking children at £2 each . . . Profits on boarding teachers during Irish Courses . . . Fees for tuition of Irish to Captains of French trawlers . . . Publisher's Royalties on Book . . . Article in *Irish Press* on 'Ireland's Cinderalla – the Gaeltacht' (*Dublin Opinion*, Oct. 1933, 253).

138 Is minic a bhíos sé ráidhte gurb iad sgoth na nGaedheal a ghabhas thar sáile. Ní hé sin ár mbaramhail ná brighthin ár sgéil ach gurb iad sgoth na nGaedheal a fhanas sa mbaile le ceart a sheasamh d'Éirinn. Father Dinneen held a diametrically different opinion:

> For it is not the people of least importance; the people of least strength; of least intellectual ability; of least diligence and loyalty, it is not they who have been leaving us for years past and who are leaving us even now, but the finest of the young men and the young women; people of ability and knowledge; people of diligence and civilisation; people of learning and good upbringing (Mar ní hiad na daoine ba lugha tábhacht; na daoine ba lugha neart is fuinneamh; ba lugha éirim aigne; ba lugha dúthracht is dílse, ní hiad soin a bhí ag imtheacht uainn le sna bliadhantaibh is atá ag imtheacht anois féin uainn, acht togha na n-óigfhear is na n-ógbhan; lucht éirim is eolais; lucht dúthrachta is sibhialtachta; lucht léighinn is tabhairt suas) (*CA*, 1930, 47).

In Seán Ó Ruadháin's *Pádhraic Mháire Bhán*, Irish migrant labourers are compared to the 'Wild Geese', the aristocratic patriot-exiles of Irish history.

139 Má leanaid do'n táirim seo atá fútha beidh ar rialtas bac a chur orra.

140 Shaoil gach duine ar chuir an cheist buaidhreadh air go mbéadh fuascladh na ceiste seo ar láimh cómh luath géar agus gheobhadh Éireannaigh réim i stiúradh na tíre. Saoileadh, ar ndóighe, nach mbéadh fiachadh ar bith feasta ar Chlannaibh Gaedheal imtheacht thar tuinn le gléas beo a bhaint amach . . . Mealladh gach duine a rabh an bharamhail sin aige, óir i n-áit laghdú a theacht ar an Imirce as Éirinn isé an rud a mhéaduigh sé le sé nó seacht de bhliadhantaibh.

141 Dhíbir Cromail an Gaedheal go sliabh is go riasg. Ach na Cromailíní beaga atá ar an saoghal anois ní fhágfaidh siad ar shliabh ná ar riasg é: tá siad dá dhíbirt de'n sliabh agus dá dhíbirt anonn thar sáile – anonn go dtig diabhail, áit ar dhiúltaigh a athaireacha roimhe a dhul ach nach bhfuil goir aige-sean a dhiúltú anois.

142 Ní bhíonn mórán am agam ag obair ó mhaidin go faoithin. Sin mar tá an sgéal annseo ag gach duine, a' síor-choimhlint agus a' rith i gcomhnuidhe, mar bheadh teine ar a gcraiceann.

143 Cá mhéad duin' ariamh a dearn an t-Oileán Úr duine saidhbhir de? Fíor bheagán. Ach is iomdha duine a mharbh sé agus a chuir sé 'n dramhlais. Tá mé cinnte dá mbéadh droichead trasna fairrge móire san am i láthair go mbéadh na mílte Éireannaigh ar sodair anall, ach mar tá siad, níl a'n phighinn aca. See also, 'Unemployment in America / Warning to Intending Irish Emigrants', *Clare Champion*, 24/11/28, in which the writer quotes the following passage from 'a young lady who left Cork some time ago writing from New York': 'This city is overrun with coloured people, and you know, they work very cheap, and that is why there is so much unemployment and small wages in all the institutions.'

144 In Seaghán P. Mac Éinrí's 'M'Oncail Seaghán' (My Uncle Seán) (UCG *University Annual*, 1925–6), a returned Yank who has failed in the States and who returns home as a shabby merchant sailor is snubbed by his poor but hard-working Galway brother, whom, mercifully, he does not recognise (pp. 32–4, 42).

145 Seán Ó Dálaigh ('Common Noun'), 'Is Giorra Cabhair Dé ná an Doras', in *Clocha Sgáil* (BÁC: Muinntir C.S. Ó Fallamhain i gComhar le hOS, 1930), 44–5; and Criostóir Mac Aonghusa, 'Cladóir', *IP*, 17/2/36.

146 In 'Ag Filleadh Abhaile' (Returning home) by the Jesuit A. Ó Conaill (*TCNÍ*, Feb. 1933), a young woman returns from England having lost her faith. Her mother and sister pray for her, and one night she dreams of Christ's passion and repents.

147 Ar nós na gcéadta eile níorbh fhada a bhí Pádraig imithe ó aer ghlan diadhanta a bhaile dhúchais go raibh sé ag dul síar diaigh ar ndiaigh ó chleachtadh a chreidimh. Ní raibh sé ag déanamh, dár ndóighe, ach géilleadh do sprid na tíre, sprid na fuaire i neithibh spioradálta.

148 Less exemplary is the behaviour of a returned Yank in Séamus Ó Dubhghaill's 'Baile na Scairte / Siopa na Croise' (Baile na Scairte / The shop at the crossroads) who becomes a greedy shopkeeper and a landlord's bailiff. See Ó Dubhghaill, 'Baile na Scairte', in *Beartín Luachra* (BÁC: M. H. Mac an Ghoill agus a Mhac, Teo., 1927), 7–20. Even more despicable is the returned American of Micheál Ua h-Eibhrín's 'Creachadh Mhuinntire Bhaile an Toim' (The robbing of the people of Baile an Toim) (*Standard*, 2/3/29), a man who cheats the people of an Irish village out of their money by promising them a fortune from Wall Street investments. See also the crudely materialistic returned Yank villain in Micheál Ó Gríobhtha's *Lorgaireacht* (Detective work) (BÁC: Muinntir Alex Thom agus Comh., i gcomhar le hOS, 1927), 26, 29. 44. On the other hand, in Eoghan Mac Giolla Bhríghde's play *An Fealltóir* (The traitor), the United States is praised for its political freedom, and as a place where an Irish rebel can continue his work for the cause. See Mac Giolla Bhríghde, *An Fealltóir* (BÁC: OS, 1939), 18. Perhaps the most idiosyncratic of the complaints about returned Yanks is the one recorded by Tomás Ó Criomhthain in *Allagar na h-Inise*, claiming that people back from America set a bad example for those at home by working too hard!

See Ó Criomhthain, *Allagar na h-Inise*, ed. Pádraig Ua Maoileoin (BÁC: OS, 1977 [1928]), 33.

149 Dream eile atá ag bascadh Gaedhealachais go mór sa nGaedhealtacht iseadh na Ponncáin . . . Tagann siad abhaile feistighthe, gallda, neamh-thuilleadh mbuidheach, teann in airgead, mórán meas acu ar Mheiriocá agus beagán tuigsiona agus níos lú ná sin de mheas ar a dtír féin . . . 'Cé'n mhaith a rinne Éire dhom-sa ariamh?' adeir an streabhóg ghléasta agus canamhain uirthí a chuirfeadh fonn múisg ar bhundún leice. See also 'Sean-Sgoláire', 'An Franncach agus an Caife' (The Frenchman and the coffee), *An Fiolar*, 1931, 4.

150 Má fheiceann tú fear feolach beathuighthe, éadaigh éagsamhla ioldaithte air, léar-scáil bóthair ag gobadh aníos as a phóca, spéacláirí móra cruinne adharc-imeallacha air, é ag féachaint faoi agus thairis agus ag tabhairt faid agus leithid na sráide leis, tig leat buille-fá-thuairim a thabhairt ar cérb as é. 'Tréan-Dorn' made a clear distinction between the native-born American, a fairly decent sort, and the *Poncán*, writing of the latter:

> That is a man who is by right an Irishman and who goes to America to earn his living. He puts together a little bit of money, forty pounds perhaps, but he would let on to you that he had a king's ransom. He is given to 'big talk', to bombast, and to exaggeration (Fear é sin atá 'na Éireannach ó cheart agus ghabhas go dtí an tOileán Úr le greim a bhéil a bhaint amach. Cruinnuigheann sé glac beag airgid, dachad punt, b'fhéidir, ach bhuailfeadh sé isteach id aigne duit go raibh carn ríogh aige. Tá sé tugtha do'n 'chainnt mhór', do'n bhladhmann, agus do'n áidhbhéil).

151 Bhí gach aoinne sa chómhursanacht bodhar aige le cuntaisí na tíre thall – an t-slighe in a deintear gach aon rud ann, fiú amháin cabáiste do bheiriú – ní fhéadfadh an tsuarach so teacht suas leo thall i gceann céad blian. Annsan an méid airgid a bhí le fághail, na postanna breaghtha gan bheith amuigh fé shioc ná fé bháistig, sa phludar ná sa phortach. In Séamus Ó Maolchathaigh's 'Eachtra Shéimín Paor' (Jamey Power's adventure), a woman returns home from the US quiet and without airs. See Ó Maolchathaigh, 'Eachtra Shéimín Paor', in *As na Ceithre hÁirdibh*, 195. In 'An Punncán / Iongnaí Saoghail i Meirice' (The Yank / Wonders of life in America) by 'Móin Ruadh' (*II*, 30/6/33), the returned Yank talks about the scale of agriculture in the United States and the machines used by farmers, but he is not presented as a foolish blowhard, nor is he put in his place by those to whom he is speaking. In Seán Ó Ciarghusa's 'Buile ar Bhuile, nó an Puncán i bPonc' (Blow for blow, or the Yank in a fix) (*Sguab*, Nov. 1923, 33–4), the returned Yank is a dupe, but not on account of his nationality. Indeed, he has admirable characteristics, being able to speak Irish for example. Reviewing a Dublin production of *Grádh na Spréidhe* (The love of the dowry), Máirtín Ó Direáin's translation of T. C. Murray's *Sovereign Gold*, the anonymous critic (probably An tAthair Mac Fhinn) found the actor playing the American 'one of the quietest and most sensible Yanks we ever saw on the stage or anywhere else' (ar dhuine de na puncáin is ciúine agus is ciallmhaire dá bhfacamar ariamh ar an ardán nó in áit ar bith eile), and offered the following advice to the actor playing the part: 'It wouldn't hurt for him to show some vigour and boldness and humbug' (Níor mhiste dhó spreacadh agus dánuidheacht agus cur-i-gcéill a chleachtadh) (*AA*, Mar. 1939, 5).

152 Táim ar aigne trí lá do chaitheamh i gColáiste na Tríonóide mar a bhfuil na sean-láimsgríbhinní áilne úd – tá a fhios agat, na cinn do sgríobh Dubhghlas de h-Íde agus na sean-ionndúirí eile go léir – agus ní rachad abhaile gan iad do thuisgint. A substantial and somewhat self-important American woman reporter is the protagonist of the comic story 'Eachtraí na Mná Móire' (The adventures of the big woman) by 'E. Ó N.' (*II*, 28/10/26), but she is really neither pompous nor overbearing.

153 Och . . . bhí a fhios agam go maith nach raibh ionnta acht stáblaí nuair a chonnaic mé ceann an asail amuigh as an bhfuinneóig. In the anonymous anecdote 'An Bheirt' (The two people) in the same issue of *An Stoc*, a dying Irishman in the US wants to send £200 home to his mother. When he mentions his intention, the doctor and lawyer at his bedside immediately claim £100 each in fees. The Irishman changes his letter to his mother, informing her that he is dying like Christ, surrounded by two thieves (*Stoc*, Nov. 1929, 10).

154 Seán Ó Cearbhaill, *Scéilín is Caogadh le Léigheamh, le Meabhrú agus le hAth-innsint* (Fifty-one little stories to read, memorise and re-tell) (BÁC: COÉ, 1934), 25–6.

155 Ó Ciarghusa was responding to a story by Seán Ó Cuill, entitled 'An Nathair Nimhe agus an Gunna Mór' (The poisonous snake and the cannon) (*FL*, 28/6/24), in which an Irishman on the American frontier is attacked by a snake that bites his gun. He throws the weapon away, but finds it again years later, swollen with the poison to the size of a cannon. Séamus Mac Aodha's 'Oidhche 'san Tuaisceart Fiadhán' (A night in the wild north) is a straightforward adventure tale about Irishmen in Canada (*Camán*, 20/1/34).

156 Citizen de chuid a' domhain! D'amharc mé síos a' tsráid. Chonnaic mé mo citizen bocht eadar bheirt chonstabla agus iad á bhreith leó 'na beirice siocair 'a bheith de mhianach ann an fód a sheasamh ar shon onóra Bhreifne.

157 Annraoi Saidléar, *Oidhche sa Tábhairne: Dráma Aon-Mhire* (BÁC: OS, 1945). There is also a happy ending, after many perilous adventures, to Éanraoi Ó Gráda's 1933 story 'An t-Eachtránaidhe Beag' (The

little adventurer), in which a young Irishman gone to Australia to search for gold ends up a successful family man in Melbourne (*Camán*, 14/1, 21/1, and 28/1/33). In 'Oidhche Nodlag' (Christmas eve) by Seán Ó Conaill, a priest in danger of freezing to death in Canada is brought into a house where he can give an Irish family what they most want – a chance to hear Mass (*Standard*, 8/12/39).

158 He does, however, return to the United States himself.

159 Séamus Maguidhir, *Fánaidheacht i gContae Mhaigh Eo* (BÁC: An Gúm, 1994 [1944]), 7. The essays that comprise this book originally appeared in *An t-Éireannach*. In Séamus de Bhilmot's unpublished play *Casadh an Rotha* (The turning of the wheel), the arch-villain was, according to Frank O'Connor's review of a Dublin performance, a returned Yank who betrays the Irish at Kinsale in 1601. At any rate, he must surely be the earliest such character in Gaelic literature. His descendants, right to the present, are every bit as despicable. See O'Connor, 'At the Peacock', *IS*, 26/10/29.

160 Ní dóigh liom go bhfaca mé ariamh dráma is mó do thaithnigh liom idir ádhbhar agus aistidheacht agus eile. Is fada mé 'ghá rádh go bhfuil ádhbhar drámaí 'sa nGaedhealtacht, agus drámaidhthe leis, agus nach gábhadh puinn ceapadóireachta chum an t-ádhbhar do chur i n-oireamhaint do'n ardán. Fiadhnaise fírinne mo thuairime ar 'Cor i n-Aghaidh Chaim' agus ar Mhicheál Breathnach.

161 *Tart*, performed at Taibhdhearc na Gaillimhe in November 1939, was set in 1950.

162 Máirtín Ó Cadhain, *An Phléasc*, ed. Gearóid Denvir, in *Macalla*, 1983, 1–21. See also 'University Notes / UCD Dramatic Club to Produce Play by Spiddal Man', *IP*, 25/12 and 27/12/37.

163 In 1932, Ó Cathaláin published a story entitled '"An Ridire Bóthair" / An Stroinséir agus an Fear Saidhbhir' ('The knight of the road' / The stranger and the rich man), on which this play was presumably based (*II*, 26/9/32).

164 Séamus de Bhilmot, *An Casán agus Múchadh an tSoluis: Dhá Dhráma Aon-Mhíre* (BÁC: ODFR, n.d.).

165 An tAthair Pádhraic Mac Aodha, *An Broc Dubh: Dráma Trí Gníomh ó Chonamara* (Gaillimh: Ó Gormáin agus a Chomh, Teach na Clódóireachta, 1936). The tragic death of a whole boatload of fishermen is the subject of Séamas Ó hÉilidhe's unpublished one-act radio play, *Na Crogaí Nua* (The new thole-pins). See 'C. Ua D.', 'Dráma Radió', *IP*, 17/3/34.

166 D'fhágfá i do dhiaidh é sin i lár na farraige. Muise, furasta a aithinte gur bobarún thú. Cá bhfios nach ciste atá istigh ann agus nach é ár saibhreas a dhéanfadh muid as. Dar príosta, caithfidh sé go bhfuil éadáil eicínt ann agus an bhlaosc a chuireadar air. B'fhéidir gur iontu sin a stuáileanns siad an t-ór dhá chur sna soithigh ó Shasana go Meiriceá anois. See also the short story based on this incident, 'Bás Mí-Fhortúnach Sheáin Uí Neachtain' (The unfortunate death of Seán Ó Neachtain), *An Stoc*, Sept.–Oct. 1929, 11–18.

167 For example, Nollaig Mac Congáil has shown that it was the Blasket books that inspired Séamus Ó Grianna's autobiographical writings, as well as his 1942 book on his own native place, *Rann na Feirste*. See Mac Congáil, 'Réamhrá', in *Máire – Clár Saothair*, 37. Ó Grianna had begun publishing autobiographical material as early as 1916, but it was 1929 before he turned to the genre in earnest. The first of his two autobiographical works, *Nuair a Bhí Mé Óg* (When I was young), appeared in 1942; the second *Saoghal Corrach* (Troubled times) in 1945. See Mac Congáil, *Máire – Clár Saothair*, 77–9. Gearóid Denvir has argued that the influence of the Blasket books on Ó Grianna was by no means entirely positive. See Denvir, 'Litríocht agus Pobal' (Literature and community), in *Litríocht agus Pobal* (Indreabhán: Cló Iar-Chonnachta, 1997), 44–5. It is worth noting that one of the very first Gaeltacht autobiographies was written in 1926, predating *An tOileánach* by three years, but was not published until 1968. This work was the schoolmaster Diarmaid Ó hÉigeartaigh's *Is Uasal Céird* (It is a noble occupation), ed. Stiofán Ó hAnnracháin (BÁC: Foilseacháin Náisiúnta Teóranta, 1968). Francis Mac Manus spoofed the popularity of the Blasket translations in 1938, writing of 'the language of Brighid, Columcille and Dr Hyde': 'In this language you will achieve fame if you are a native of one of Ireland's foreign possessions, the islands off the western coast, if you can be Civilly Servantish, and if you have a good English translator' (*Hibernia*, Nov. 1938, 3).

168 In the Dec. 1934 issue, there was a cartoon of two islanders walking on a beach. The first says to his companion: 'You're livin' an extraordinary sort of life this while past! What's come over you?' The other man responds: 'I have to keep findin' things to do that'll make good readin' in me autobiography' (*Dublin Opinion*, Dec. 1934, 351).

169 See 'An t-Oileánach', Editorial, *IP*, 2/7/32. A section of Ó Criomhthain's manuscript of the book superimposed over a map of the Blaskets used to appear on the back of the Irish £20 note. A portrait of Yeats was on the front of the bill.

170 Is leasc le daoine leabhartha na Gaedhilge do mholadh ar eagla go bpreabfadh an fear thall chúcha agus go n-abróchadh ná raibh ionnta acht dreabhghail gan mhaith. Acht ní heagla liomsa an leabhar so 'An t-Oileánach' do chosaint ós cómhair an tsaoghail.

171 Adubhairt 'An Seabhac' gurab é 'An t-Oileánach' an leabhar do b'fhearr d'á dtáinig as an Ghaedhealtacht. Adeurfainn-se gurab é an leabhar is fearr d'á dtáinig as Éirinn le n-ár linne é. See also Aodh de Blácam's high praise for Flower's translation in the *New Irish Magazine*, Nov. 1934, 3; and the assertion

by 'G. M.' (perhaps Gerard Murphy) that *An t-Oileánach* was 'undoubtedly one of those three or four good books which have been written in Irish since the beginning of the revival movement' (*IBL*, Mar.–Apr. 1935, 49).

172 'Sé seo an leabhar Gaedhilge is fearr a léigheas le fada, agus leabhar nach bhfuil a leithide le fáil ach é. 'M. Ó M.' felt the book was worthy to be a classic of world literature: 'It is the most important book published by An Gúm and it is equal to books of its sort that live and will live in the literature of the world' (Sé an leabhar is tábhachtaighe a clóbhuaileadh fé Choisde an Oideachais agus tá sé ar aon dul le leabhraibh dá shórt a mhaireann is a mhairfidh i litríocht an domhain) (*Standard*, 14/9/29).

173 Tá an tsaoirse ag maidneachan orainn fé dheire thiar thall agus má's maith é is mithid ach ní bheidh an tsaoirse, lán-tsolus na saoirse againn go dtí go mbeidh sprid an Oileánaigh, creideamh an Oileánaigh, teanga an Oileánaigh agus dóchas do-chlaoidhte an Oileánaigh go daingean docht i meón agus i gcroidhe na nGaedheal. In his essay on the Blasket books in *Bonaventura*, Thomas Barrington wrote: 'It is not argued that the Blasket culture should of necessity become the culture of Ireland . . . It is argued that the Blaskets throw out some hope that all Dubliners, for example, will ultimately be saved from their present cultural damnation' (*Bonaventura*, Summer 1937, 120–1).

174 Ach dar ndóigh éireochadh duine ar bith tuirseach de t'réis roinnt de a léigheamh arae sé an rud céadna atá ann ó leathanach go chéile gan mórán eachtraí ná athrú suidhimh . . . Leabhar maith gan amhras ach ná téighimís thar teorainn leis an moladh. In a series on 'Prós-Ughdair na 20mhadh Aoise' (Prose authors of the twentieth century) in *Our Boys*, the anonymous author wrote of Ó Criomhthain's book: '"The Islandman" is a work worthy of praise, but it is hardly worth all the praise that has been given to it' (Is ionmholta an saothar é 'An t-Oileánach', ach is ar éigean is fiú é an moladh go léir a tugadh dó) (*Our Boys*, 31/1/35).

175 Sé is fearr de chuid an 'Ghúim' é agus ní dóigh liom go bhfuil thar cupla leabhar i nua-litríocht na Gaedhilge is fearr ná é. Ach ar a shon san ní sár-leabhar é . . . Ní bheidh sé ar chlasaigí na Gaedhilge . . . Caithfear admháil mar sin ná fuil i leabhar Thomáis ach ábhar comónta ná fuil aon bhuaine ag baint leis i gcúrsaí leitríochta.

176 D'aithin siad an litridheacht . . . san OILEÁNACH. Chan eadh amháin sin, ach rinne siad standard agus cúl taca na Litridheachta de'n leabhar. Nár bh'í an leabhar ba mhó de chuid na nua-Ghaedhilge í? Nach rabh sí ionchurtha le litridheacht ar bith de chuid an lae indiu i mBéarla nó i nGaedhilg? He called it 'cunntas seanduine a bhfuil cuimhne mhaith aige agus feallsamhnacht atá comh simplidhe coitch-eannta agus nach cheart feallsamhnacht a thabhairt uirthi . . . Ní árd-litridheacht é mar chunntas agus níl samhlaidheacht ar bith ann.

177 Ta píosaí sa leabhar seo agus ní thuigim cad chuige ar cuireadh i gcló iad. Is lugha 'ná sin a thuigim cad chuige a samhailtear gur litridheacht iad. Acht ba mhaith liom an méid seo a rádh leo: Féadaidh siad an t-airgead a chaitheamh ar choib-leoracht acht ní éireochaidh leo choidhche a chur i gcéill don phobal gur a' gréasuidheacht atá siad.

178 Tá an scéal san *Oileánach* acht is beag a bhfuil de litridheacht ann . . . Agus is ait linn dream atá i nainm a bheith coidreamhail go maith le na bhfuil de litridheacht ar fuaid na cruinne agus i gcúpla áit eile a bheith chomh beag tuisciona i dtaobh cúrsaí leabhar deighscríobhnóireachta agus litridheachta. He continued: 'Perhaps it would be a good and profitable thing if people were to read a book before they reviewed it' (B'fhéidir go mbadh mhaith is go mbadh thairbheach an rud é dá léigheadh daoine leabhar sar a ndeinidís léirmheas air). See also the positive review of this title by 'M. Ó M.', a review in which he did, however, stress that Ó Criomhthain was not an educated writer (scríobhnóir oilte) and that he lacked the tricks of the trade (cleasa lucht leabhar) (*Standard*, 26/1/29).

179 Comhartha de'n saoghal nua atá ag éirí in Éirinn is eadh an leabhar so, agus comhartha leis de'n cheangal atá idir saoghal ár aimsire [*sic*] féin agus an tsean-shaoghal atá ag sleamhnú uainn. Préamh de'n bhuinne nua 'Fiche Blian ag Fás.' In a highly romantic review in *The Standard*, 'S. Ó F.' (not Ó Faoláin) pronounced the book 'remarkable' (*Standard*, 6/5/33).

180 Cuireann san i gcuimhne dhom gur beag má tá aon leabhar againn ó mhná na Gaeltachta, rud fhágann go bhfuil an iomad fearúlachta sa Ghaedhilg chlóbhuailte – bfearra de í roinnt de rian deiliceálta na haigne banda bheith uirthi. Agus is dócha gurb é sin cúis go dtaithneann 'Peig' chó mór liom . . . Is fearr le mná, do ghnáth, bheith ag caint ar dhaoine ná ar rudaí . . . Déarfainn go bhfuil an ceart acu. Is inspéise go mór an t-ainmhí bocht ar a nglaotar an duine ná a bhfuil sa chruinne le chéile lasmuich de.

181 See, for example, 'N. Ní D.', 'Ban-Ughdar ó'n mBlascaod' (A female author from the Blaskets), *IP*, 7/8/36; 'Woman Wins Gaelic Literary Award', *IP*, 24/7/37 (the main front-page headline story for that day); and 'An Tiaracht', 'Duais an Chraoibhín le Bronnadh ar Pheig Saors' (The Craoibhín Prize to be bestowed on Peig Sayers), *IP*, 27/7/37.

182 Blythe seems to have liked *Peig* better than he had *An tOileánach*. See his review in *II*, 30/6/36. 'Seathrún' also had high praise for *Peig* in his review of the book for the *Irish Catholic* (22/8/36). On the other hand, Ó Rinn seems to have felt Peig's next book, *Machtnamh Seanamhná*, was exactly the sort of disappointment 'An Stad' had feared it could be. His *II* review was on the whole positive, but he also acknowledged: 'This book is, not surprisingly, not

half as interesting as the book she wrote about her own life' (Níl an leabhar so leath chó h-inspéise leis an leabhar do scríobh sí ar a saol féin, ní nach iongnadh), *II*, 22/12/39. Unlike Ó Rinn, the anonymous reviewer for the *Irish Catholic* preferred the book to *Peig* (*IC*, 21/12/39).

183 Thomas Barrington had noted in 1937 that 'each book was inspired by a visitor to the island'. But he also insisted: 'They were not aliens these visitors; they came to steep themselves in the island culture, and succeeded to a great extent.' Therefore, while the books are 'the result of the clash of two separate cultures', they also 'come from a tradition that was uninterrupted', and it is to this cultural integrity that they owe their 'purity' (*Bonaventura*, Summer 1937, 118).

184 See Seán Ó Ciarghusa, 'Gaedhilg an Oileáin' (The Irish of the Island), *Leader*, 17/8/29; and 'Athair Altroma Litridheachta' (A literary foster-father), *IP*, 31/12/36, and 'S. Ó C.' (possibly Ó Ciarghusa again), 'Brian Ó Ceallaigh', *Standard*, 8/1/37. See also the revealing comments of one native speaker who attempted to keep a diary without the support of a sympathetic outsider in Micheál Ó Conaill, *Fá Sgáth Shléibh' Eachtgha: Cinn Lae* (In the shadow of Slieve Aughty: A diary) (BÁC: ODFR, 1937), 40–1. In *An Litríocht Réigiúnach*, Máirín Nic Eoin comments on the role played by Ní Chinnéide and other outsiders (pp. 64–5), and speculates on how easy it theoretically could be for an outsider to generate a Gaeltacht autobiography: 'All that was necessary was an enthusiast or two and a talkative old person who was willing to tell the public about the great events of his life and the customs of the culture from which he came' (Níor ghá ach díograiseoir nó dhó agus seanduine cainteach a bhí sásta imeachtaí móra a shaoil agus nósanna an chultúir ar de é a insint don phobal) (p. 32).

185 Níl aon sgéal amháin air aon bheirt dá [bhfuil] air an saoghal. Leis-sin, an Té atá a sgríobh a sgéal-féin, má's gádh dho doll a lorag cabhartha ar sgéal chách cuirfidhsion amach as a sgéal féin é, agus ní bheidh a sgéal féin ná sgéal aoinne eile aige. The letter is in the Ó Criomhthain Papers, NLI MS 15,785. In another letter in this file, again undated and with no correspondent identified, Ó Criomhthain says he has read 'a bit of every book' (smut do gach leabhar) he has been given, and continues: 'Seán [most likely his son] says that the fisherman [Pierre Loti's *Pêcheur d'Islande*, in English translation] is the nicest of them; I also think so' (Deir Seán gur bé an t-iasgaire an ceann is deise aca, is dóil liom-sa leis é).

186 'An Seabhac', 'Ón Eagarthóir', in Tomás Ó Criomhthain, *Allagar na hInise*, xi. Is guth ón nGaeltacht féin an leabhar seo – an Ghaeltacht sin atá balbh, tláth, gan cumas ar í féin a chur in iúl ná a scéal féin a phlé chun an saol amuigh a chur ar buaireamh le himní chun a fuascailte.

187 Ní haon díoghbháil saoghal mhuinntir an oileáin a chur i niúil do na Béarlóirí i dtíorthaibh eile agus annso i nÉirinn féin. Tá furmhór muinntir na tíre seo dall ar a leithéid [saol mhuinntir an oileáin] a bheith ann i naon chor agus ar chuma éigin tabharfaidh sé taithneamh dóibh fé mar a thabharfadh cuid de na leabhair a scríobhadh i dtaoibh réigiún nimigcéineamhail na umhúrdha. I do not know this final word, but context makes its meaning obvious. I have translated it here as 'earth'.

188 Agus tá tuisgint doimhin ar shaol na Gaeltachta le fáil sa leabhar . . . Leabhar é mar a chéile a mbéidh fonn a léighte ar dhuine ar bith – as Gaillimh go Berlin – a dteastuigheann uaidh eolas a chur ar an saol agus ar na daoine le n-a mbaineann an Ghaedhilge bheo. Compare Mac Fhinn's attitude toward Pádhraic Óg Ó Conaire's novel *Ceol na nGiolcach*: 'But, however good the story, the best part of the book is the insight it gives into the life of Conamara' (Ach, dá fheabhas é an sgéal, 'sí an chuid is fearr dhen leabhar an léargus atá innti ar shaoghal Chonnamara) (*AA*, Dec. 1939, 4).

189 Fear é Tomás Ó Criomhthain nach bhfuil mórán dá leithid fágtha. Tá tuisgint mhaith aige agus croidhe mór, agus tá sé stuama. Casadh orm daoine mar é, is dóigh, ach ní fhéadfadh aon duine aca a leithide seo de leabhar a scríobh ná leabhar ar bith. Is i ngeall ar sin go mba cheart dúinn buidheachas mór a ghlacadh le Tomás. Seán Mac Giollarnáth certainly saw his informant Peadar Mac Thuathaláin as an individual, stressing that he was more of a creator of new narratives than a recounter of old ones. See 'Peadar Mac Thuathaláin, An Seanachaidhe', in *Peadar Chois Fhairrge*, 9. On the other hand, for the same reason, 'Carraig' was unimpressed with Mac Thuathaláin's storytelling and felt that he was no true *seanchaí* (*Gaedheal*, Apr. 1937, 3).

190 For an appreciation of Ó Criomhthain as a self-conscious literary craftsman, see Pádraig Ó Héalaí, 'An Bheathaisnéis mar Litríocht' (The autobiography as literature), *Léachtaí Cholm Cille* I (1970), 34–40.

191 Corruíodh an saol Gaelach go mór ar fhoillsiú an 'Oileánaigh' is 'Fiche Blian ag Fás.' Go deimhin tá daoine ann ná fuil tagtha chucha féin fós ón taom feirge do ghaibh iad toisc gur dhein Muiris Ó Súilleabháin, le barr neamh-urchóideachta, an fhírinne d'innsint i dtaobh muintir na Gaeltachta, sé sin, nach naoimhíní dóibe is plástair iad ná bréag-uaisle ach gnáth-dhaoine mar atá ag teacht ó aimsir Ádhaimh anuas.

192 Tomás Ó Criomhthain, Microfilm of NLI MS G1020 (*An tOileánach*). Deireadh an sgéalaidhe fadó, taréis sgéal a rádh dho – sinné mo sgéal-sa, agus má tá bréag ann bíodh. Se-seo, mo sgéal-sa, agus ní'l bréag 'na chorp – sé, laom na fírinne. Ba bhreágh liom an leabhar do bheith na n'dóid aige 'macaibh-léighinn' na h-Éireann agus thar lear.

193 See Seán Ó Coileáin, 'An tOileánach: Ón Láimh go dtí an Leabhar' (The Islandman: From the hand to the book), in *Tomás Ó Criomhthain, 1855–1937*

(Céiliuradh an Bhlascaoid 2), ed. Máire Ní Chéileachair (An Daingean: An Sagart, 1998), 25–43; Ó Coileáin, 'Tomás Ó Criomhthain, Brian Ó Ceallaigh agus an Seabhac' (Tomás Ó Criomhthain, Brian Ó Ceallaigh and An Seabhac), in *Tomás an Bhlascaoid* (Tomás of the Blasket), ed. Breandán Ó Conaire (Indreabhán: Cló Iar-Chonnachta, 1992), 233–65; Breandán Ó Conaire, 'An tOileánach i gCló' (The Islandman in print), in *Tomás an Bhlascaoid*, 266–82; Máiréad Nic Craith, *An tOileánach Léannta* (The learned Islandman) (BÁC: An Clóchomhar, 1988), 104–5; 115–16. The most extensive and detailed discussion of the bowdlerisation of Ó Criomhthain's text is James Stewart's '*An tOileánach* – More or Less', *Zeitschrift für Celtische Philologie* 35 (1976), 234–63. The full text of *An t-Oileánach* is finally available, as edited by Seán Ó Coileáin (BÁC: Cló Talbóid, 2002).

194 When his friend rejoins him, Tomás says that it is the women who should be ashamed: 'The hussy that was giving out to me, the baptism of her child was nearer than her wedding afterwards, and of course that was what was driving her and that she was revealing' (An Ráibéard do bhí a tabhairt na cainnte dhamsa, ba thiubhaisge a baiste nó a pósa na dhiaidh sin, ⁊ darnó bé-sin an fuaghdar do bhí chumhche ⁊ agus do bhí aici á thiosbáint).

195 Bé críoch agus deire sa m'beart é, nár mhór an luach do bfhiú a raibh do bhalcaisí air a seisear pantalóg, ⁊ pé tuirse do bhí oram dimthhigh sé dhíom, mar do thugadh an seisear fhéin fré-cheile go minnic, ⁊ ba có-lústa na seasamh iad nua a d'tóin as a g'crúghann, ⁊ go lan mhinnic cuid dá gcorp le feisceint, nár shaighnáil an ghrian rísin roimis-sin go dti an uair-seo. All quotations in this paragraph are from the microfilm of the original manuscript in the NLI. The text of *Allagar na h-Inise* as published in 1928 also omitted passages that treated sexuality with a similar matter-of-fact earthiness. Some of these have now been published by Pádraig Ua Maoileoin in Ó Criomhthain, *Allagar II*, ed. Ua Maoileoin (BÁC: Coisceim, 1999), 3, 108, 110–11, 114, 141–2, 147. For a comprehensive discussion of Ó Criomhthain's treatment of women in his books, see Angela Bourke, 'Na Mná trí Shúile Thomáis' (Women through the eyes of Tomás), in *Tomás Ó Criomhthain*, ed. Ní Chéileachair, 101–22. The young island women Éibhlín Ni Shúilleabháin and Eibhlís Ní Shúilleabháin depict social life among their contemporaries on the Great Blasket as quite lively and relatively unrepressed. See *Cin Lae Éibhlín Ní Shúilleabháin* (The diary of Éibhlín Ní Shúilleabháin), ed. Máiréad Ní Loingsigh (BÁC: Coiscéim, 2000), 7, 34, 148; Eibhlís Ní Shúilleabháin, *Letters from the Great Blasket*, ed. Seán Ó Coileáin (Cork: Mercier Press, n.d.), 47–8. See also the memoir by Seán Ó Criomhthain, the son of Tomás, in *Leoithne Aniar* (A breeze from the West), ed. Pádraig Tyers (Baile an Fheirtéaraigh: Cló Dhuibhne, 1982), 74–5, 123. Éibhlín's diary was from 1923, and was serialised in the Enniscorthy *Echo* in 1931; Eibhlís's letter, addressed to George Chambers and telling of Redemptorist attempts to put an end to easy socialising between the sexes on the island, was written in 1932.

196 Nioclás Tóibín, 'An Grádh agus an t-Airgead' (Love and money), in *Oidhche ar Bharr Tuinne agus Scéalta Eile* (BÁC: Cualacht Oideachais na hÉireann, n.d.), 46–51.

197 An tAthair Seán Ó Gallchóir, 'Séamus Ó Grianna', in *Scríbhneoireacht na gConallach* (Donegal writing) ed. Nollaig Mac Congáil (BÁC: Coiscéim, 1990), 101. Tá an grá seo cumhachtach – mar a bheadh aicíd ann. Tá sé geanmaí, maoithneach, rómánsúil. Tugann cúinsí an tsaoil orthu scaradh lena chéile . . . Ag deireadh an scéil ní thig bláth ar ghrá. Tig deireadh duairc brónach ar scéal a ngrá. See also Mac Congáil, *Léargas ar 'Cith is Dealán' Mháire* (Insight into 'Cioth is Dealán' by Máire) (BÁC: Foilseacháin Náisiúnta Teoranta, 1982), 84–97.

198 Séamus Ó Grianna, *Caisleáin Óir* (Sráid Bhaile Dhúin Dealgan: Preas Dhún Dealgan, 1924), 164. Fuair mé buaidhreadh agus brón agus léan agus leathtrom an t-saoghail ó shoin de thairbhe na h-oidhche céadna; agus 'na dhiaidh sin 's uilig, rachainn i gcionn an iomláin arais agus arais ar chuantar oidhche amháin eile de chineál na h-oidhche udaigh, ar chuantar amharc amháin fhághail ar an dá shúil ghlinne dhubh-ghorma udaigh, ar chuantar breith in mo láimh ar a méara geala tanaidh snuighte, ar chuantar aon phóg amháin fhághail ó na béilín meala a bhí chomh fuar le bior éireógaighe agus chomh dearg le caor chaorthainn. Ernest Blythe was sharply critical of the timid immaturity with which love between supposed adults was treated in two award-winning Gaelic novels of the time, Art Ó Riain's *Lucht Ceoil* and Seán Ó Ruadháin's *Pádhraic Mháire Bhán*, writing: 'They are both in a way love stories, and it would appear that the authors were afraid to discuss the passionate or the emotional side of love. They were even too timid to discuss courtship' (Sgéalta grá iad araon i slí agus de réir deallraimh bhí eagla ar na hughdair cur síos ar pháisiún ná ar mhaoithneachas an ghrá. Bhíodar ró-chuthail le cur síos fiú amháin ar an suiríocht) (*II*, 28/3/33). Ó Ruadháin responded in a letter to *II* (4/4/33) saying he only included the love interest 'to attach the thing to it, you might say' (leis an rud a ghreamú dhe, mar adéarfá). Nor, he added, was he interested in passion, as English authors would have been.

199 See, for example, Ó Grianna, *Caisleáin Óir*, 89, 96, 191.

200 Ó Grianna, 'Anam a Mháthara Móire', in *Cioth is Dealán*, 94. Bhí sé féin agus Nábla an Mhuilteóra luaidhte le chéile ar feadh na mbliadhantach. Shíl achan duine go mbéadh siad ag n-a chéile. Ach ní mar shíltear ach mar chinntighthear. Bhí an Muilteóir

Bán 'na shuidhe go te san am, agus gléas air cruth maith a chur le n-a nighin. Agus chan de lámha folamha a bhí gnoithe ag fear ar bith a ghabhail a dh'iarraidh Náblann air.
201 Diarmuid Ó Duibhne, *Cliamhain Isteach* (BÁC: ODFR, 1933), 37. An t-airgead! Agus do dhíolfá mé ar airgead? Níor dhíol mo shean-athair mo mháthair ar airgead nuair a fuairis í le pósadh; agus dá mairfeadh sí ní díolfaí mise ar airgead.
202 Seaghán Mac Meanman, *Athrughadh Intinne*, in *Trí Mhion-Dráma*, 96. Bhal, ní bhfuighidh Bidí an seans. Glacfaidh mé féin é! Fear nach bhfuil luime na láimhe nó airc airgid air sin an fear is fearr! In her review of Mac Meanman's published plays, 'M. Ní Dh.' commented on the note of misogyny in them, adding 'that is a bad Gaeltacht custom and one that it is apparently difficult to get rid of' (droch-nós na Gaedhealtachta é sin agus is deacair fagháil réidhte leis, is dóiche) (*II*, 28/7/36). Micheál Breathnach offered a quite different take on this theme in his unpublished play *Íodhbairt* (Sacrifice), in which, in the words of a critic reviewing the Taibhdhearc na Gaillimhe production, an old man 'sacrifices his liberty so that a young neighbour may marry his sweetheart' (*IT*, 25/11/39).
203 Éamonn Mac Giolla Iasachta, *Toil Dé* (BÁC: ODFR, 1933), 115.
204 Peig Sayers, *Peig .i. A Scéal Féin* (BÁC: Clólucht an Talbóidigh, Tta., 1936), 177–8. Bhí gach aoinne aca ró-mhaith d'fhear domh-sa dá mbeinn seacht nuaire níos fearr ná mar a bhíos . . . Níl aithne ná eolas agam ar mhuinntir an Oileáin . . . ach tá aithne agus eolas maith agat-sa ortha, agus an rud is maith leat-sa 'sé is maith liom-sa. Raghad pé áit a déarfaidh tú liom.
205 Tomás Ó Criomhthain, *An t-Oileánach*, 161. Do bhreac sí amach do'n mbeirt aosta cad é an oibliogáid a leanfadh an té ná pósfadh duine béal-dorais ach a cheanglóchadh le dream eile bhí i bhfad ó bhaile agus ná beadh cabhair ná congnamh le fagháil uatha lá an ghádhtair. See also the comments of Tomás's son Seán on matchmaking in an interview with Pádraig Tyers in *Leoithne Aniar*, 124–5.
206 Ó Criomhthain gives us the words he sang in his manuscript, but Ó Siochfhradha cut the text of the song from the 1929 edition. He also omitted Tomás's account of his singing and the audience's response to it, one of the most beautifully and movingly understated passages in the entire work. Tomás tells us: 'This is the song I sang at my own wedding, and I sang nothing else . . . You would think no one else in the house had a tongue until it was finished' (Is sé-seo an t-amhrán a dúbhart air ma phósa fhéin, agus ní dubhart ach' é . . . Ní cheapfá go raibh aon teanga an son duine eile sna tigh, beag ná mór, nua go raibh sé críochnaighthe). For a detailed discussion of the song Ó Criomhthain sings and its treatment in different versions of his book, see Cathal Ó Háinle, 'Tomás Ó Criomhthain agus "Caisleán Uí Néill"', *IMN*, 1985, 84–109.
207 Muiris Ó Súileabháin, *Fiche Blian ag Fás* (BÁC: Clólucht an Talbóidigh, 1933), 261. Tá talamh go leor agus an talamh is fearr aige, tá na céadta caorach ar na cnuic aige agus gan trácht ar airgead a bheith sábhálta aige.
208 A Shéamuis Uí Cholmáin . . . má cheapann tú go bpósfainn fear bacach cosamhail le Mac Uí Mhurchadha, tá dearmad ort. Is fearrde dhuit bheith díomhaoin ná bheith ag déanamh droch-ghnó. In *Mian na Marbh*, Tadhg Ó Rabhartaigh noted that there was an ongoing change in the Gaeltacht away from matches based primarily on financial considerations (p. 104). Nevertheless, the parents of a young woman in the novel marry her off to a well-off, much older man (pp. 111–12). Their daughter reluctantly accepts the match (p. 119).
209 Peig Sayers, *Machtnamh Seanmhná* (BÁC: OS, 1980 [1939]), 109. She also tells of a woman who walks out on her husband. When she returns after forty years, he refuses to let her into the house (pp. 37–9). In his account in *Leoithne Aniar*, Ó Criomhthain's son Seán tells of how an islandman tricked his son into marrying an ugly woman by pointing out to him a more attractive one as the woman he has chosen for him. According to Seán, the young man did not realise the deception until he was at the altar, by which time it was too late to do anything about it (p. 54).
210 Ó Criomhthain, *An tOileánach*, 158. Cé gur bheirt fhear iad ná raibh rogha ná díogh ortha thar n-a chéile féach gur dhein an cailín rogha mór do dhuine aca.
211 In the same book, the abduction of a woman by the Molly Maguires at the beginning of the matchmaking season results in her death (pp. 83–4).
212 Seán Ó Ciarghusa, 'Trí Scéalta Grádha', in *Geantraighe*, 66–72.
213 Ó Dálaigh, '"Mian Mic a Shúil"', in *Clocha Sgáil*, 1–14.
214 She is finally reconciled with her father whom she sees again after her daughter unwittingly defeats her sister's daughter in an Irish-dancing competition in Dublin!
215 Séamus Maguidhir, 'Dhá Chrann na Marbh', in *Dhá Chrann na Marbh*, 9–26.
216 Tomás Bairéad, 'Rún na Mná Duibhe', in *An Geall a Briseadh*, (BÁC: ODFR, 1952 [1932]), 67–78.
217 There is also, of course, a failed marriage in Art Ó Riain's 1932 novel *Lucht Ceoil*, but it is not a major thematic element in the book. Rather, the desertion of his family serves primarily to make the villain more villainous, and his long-suffering wife more saintly.
218 An tAthair Mac Fhinn agreed, writing in his review of *Peig* that there were too many references to drink: 'I would hardly believe that drink has such an important place in the life of the Kerry Gaeltacht' (Ar éigean a chreidfinn go bhfuil ionad chomh tábhachtach sin ag an ól i saoghal Gaedhealtachta Ciarruidhe) (*AA*, Aug. 1936, 1).

219 See also the references to drink in *Letters from the Great Blasket*, 47–48; in *Cin Lae Éibhlín Ní Shúilleabháin*, 82, 84 (entries for 9 and 11 Aug. 1923); and in *Leoithne Aniar*, 33, 42, 46–7, 94–5, 97, 121–2. The references in *Leoithne Aniar* are from a memoir by and interviews with Seán Ó Criomthain.

220 Ó Criomthain, *An t-Oileánach*, 135. Do bhí cúis agam bheith cráidhte: an bád a bhí i n-éineacht linn imithe abhaile agus criú mo bháid-se agus leaghadh chubhar na h-abhann ortha, triúr dritheár aca craosálta le digh, fear aca i bpríosún, beirt eile bhí innti ná feaca i rith an lae ná fós.

221 Ó Criomhthain, *Allagar na h-Inise*, 266–7. Cromadh ar phuins a theannadh leo nó go rabhadar bog-shúgach go maith. Bóthar an rí suas a bhuaileadar, bean ag titim, bean ag éirí, beirt ag amhrán, beirt ag gol, agus cé go raibh an bóthar réidh agus gan aon achrann ann ní rabhadar ag dul chun cinn, mar is amhlaidh a bhíodh tamall suas acu agus tamall eile le fánaidh. This passage did not appear in the 1928 edition; the orthography is that of Ua Maoileoin's 1977 edition. See also Ó Criomhthain, *Allagar II*, ed. Ua Maoileoin, 67.

222 Ó Súileabháin, *Fiche Blian ag Fás*, 81–2. Do ghlaoidh fear ar ghallún agus fear eile riamh agus choidhche nú go rabhadar caoch ar meisce . . . Is gearr anois gur thosnuigh na hamhráin ar fuaid an tighe agus círín dearg ortha ag an ól mar is gnáthach le na leithéidí.

223 Sayers, *Peig*, 47. Do bhí dúil mhalluighthe ag gach aoinne aca sa bhraon.

224 Mac Meanman, 'An Cailín Seo agus an Cailín Udaidh Eile', in *Indé agus Indiu*, 71. Is cuma caidé deir sagart nó ministéir ní thiocfadh le dadaidh níos deise bheith ar clár i dtráthaibh an tráthnóna 'ná buideal cárta a's é lán d'uisge bheatha bhuidhe . . . Má amharcann tú thríd an bhuideal ar an tsolas 'tchidhfidh tú na néalta ómra atá thart fá chladaighibh Í Bhreasail agus Tír na h-Óige, agus na gatha órdha a thig aniar ó'n ghréin nuair atá sí ag 'ul i bhfarraige.

225 B. N. Lóiste, *Cathal faoi Ghealltanas* (BÁC: ODFR, n.d.).

226 Temperance was one of the principal themes of Dinneen's weekly column in *The Leader* in the summer of 1923. See his columns of 7, 14, 21, 28 July; and 4 Aug. See also other columns by him in the same journal for 21 June 1924; 22 Aug. 1925; and 31 Mar. 1928. Among his papers is an undated typescript headed 'T. A.' (i.e. Total Abstinence), in which he wrote:

> At the present time I believe that a total abstinence movement – total abstinence from alcoholic drinks – if carried on vigorously and on a national scale would result in benefits for the nation of a lasting character and furthermore that such a movement is absolutely necessary if we are to save the nation from the depths of degradation into which it is fast sinking (NLI MS 8623 (folder 9)).

In a 1923 piece in *The Father Mathew Record*, Seán Ua Ceallaigh ('Sceilg') delivered a virtual temperance sermon, going so far as to see this virtue as an element of true Gaelicism. See 'Sciath na Measardhachta' (The shield of temperance) *FMR*, July 1923, 5.

227 Ó Dálaigh, 'Lomadh an Luain Ort', in *Timcheall Chinn Sléibhe*, 118.

228 Bairéad, 'An Stiléara', in *Cumhacht na Cinneamhna*, 15–26.

229 'Toradh na Dílseachta agus na Foighde' (The result of loyalty and patience), in *An Chraobh Chumhra* (The fragrant branch), ed. Máirtín Ua Flaithbheartaigh (Gaillimh: Ó Gormáin agus a Chomh., 1934), 67–74.

230 Mac Meanman, 'An Cheud Mheisge agus an Mheisge Dheireannach', in *Fear Siubhail*, 1–15.

231 Ó Rabhartaigh, *Mian na Marbh*, 145–6. O, 'Chathail, a dhearthháir; 'sé an faisián is malluighthe é dár thóg aon fhear óg chuige féin ariamh. 'Sí'n deoch ughdar gach uilc, agus is agam-sa atá a fhios sin, faraor! . . . Mo chomhairle duit, a mhic, coinneáil amach ó'n dígh. Dá mbeadh a fhios agat an bhail a thug an deoch orm-sa, a mhic, cha leigfeá aon deór daoithe ar chlasaidhe d'anála le do lá.

232 Pádhraic Óg Ó Conaire, *Ceol na nGiolcach*, 241. Nár fhága mé seo muna mbuaileann náire mé nuair a léim an *Connacht Champion*: daoine ag troid is ag súiteach ag teacht abhaile ó shochraidí; iad ag caitheamh cloch; agus bíonn corrdhuine acu a oibríos miodóg! Ní call dúinn milleán a chur ar Shasana faoi seo, agus ní call dúinn, ach an oiread, a bheith fanacht le *Home Rule* le deireadh a chur leis. Another neighbour supports the banning of *poitín* at the wake, quoting a letter from a son in America on the need for Conamara people to change some of their ways (p. 244). When there is no drink at the wake, some of the local people decide not to attend (pp. 248–9). In *Éan Cuideáin* (1936), Ó Conaire depicted an unscrupulous *poitín* maker who is cursed by the mother of a young man whose life he has ruined. Few of his neighbours attend the moonshiner's funeral. See Pádhraic Óg Ó Conaire, *Éan Cuideáin* (BÁC: OS, 1970 [1936]), 96–100.

233 Peadar Mac Fhionnlaoich, 'An Fiadhach', in *An Cogadh Dearg agus Scéalta Eile* (BÁC: Cú Uladh agus a Chuid, n.d.), 43–8.

234 An tAthair Casáin, 'Gleann an Uaignis', in *An Londubh agus Scéalta Eile* (BÁC: ODFR, 1937), 49–59.

235 Pádhraic Ó Domhnalláin, 'Dubhshlán Fear Éireann!' and 'Clú an Pharóiste', in *An tIolrach Mór*, 5–21, 89–98. In 'An Litir' in the same collection (pp. 116–21), we are introduced to a rural blacksmith who detests both greed and violence

236 Seaghán Mac Meanman, 'Tús Sgéil as an Leabhar Thuas', in *Fear Siubhail*, 42–53; and 'Oidhche Mhór i bhFad ó Shoin', in *Indé agus Indiu*, 1–15.

237 Micheál Ó Siochfhradha, 'Loch an Pheidléara', in *Seo Mar Bhí*, 101–3. Ó Siochfhradha says he heard this story from his father.
238 Ó Dálaigh, 'Lomadh an Luain Ort', in *Timcheall Chinn Sléibhe*, 117–23.
239 See 'Fionn' Mac Cumhaill, *Tusa a Mhaicín* (BÁC: COÉ, n.d.), 53, 59, 80, 84–5.
240 See Mac Giolla Iasachta, *Cúrsai Thomáis*, (BÁC: An Clóchomhar, 1969 [1927]), 42, 77–9, 111, 114, 138, 140–1.
241 Ó Conaire, *Éan Cuideáin*, 30–1.
242 Ó Conaire, *Ceol na nGiolcach*, 231–3, 260–7.
243 Ciarán Ua Nualláin, *Oidhche i nGleann na nGealt* (BÁC: OS, 1939), 141–4.
244 Mac Aodha, *An Broc Dubh*, 34–5. She then married the brother!
245 See Ó Criomthain, *Allagar*, 154, 164; Sayers, *Machtnamh*, 29. In Shán Ó Cuív's comic play *Troid*, the plot is based on the confusion that arises when a travelling tailor asks for 'tred' [thread], and the farmer in whose house he is staying thinks he is looking for *troid* [a fight]. See Ó Cuív, *Troid*, in *Troid agus an Bhean ón dTuaith* (A fight and the woman from the country) (BÁC: ODFR, 1931), 15–16.
246 Ní Ghráda, *An Udhacht* (BÁC: OS, 1935). This subject is also treated comically in Micheál Ua h-Eibhrín's 'Udhacht Shéamais Ruaidh' (Séamas Rua's will), *Standard*, 7/9/29. For a more edifying view of the honesty of Irish country people, see Father Dinneen's story 'An Udhacht do Loisceadh' (The will that was burned), *Leader*, 31/1/25.
247 Ó Conaire, *Seoid ó'n Iarthar Órdha* (Gaillimh: Ó Gormáin, Teach na Clódóireachta, 1933), 128–30.
248 Mac Conmara, *An Coimhthigheach*, 13.
249 Seoighe, 'Adhlacadh agus Aiséirghe Shean-Mhícil', in *Sgéalta Chois Teallaigh*, 30–6.
250 There is also a great deal of unedifying Gaeltacht behaviour in the stories told by Peadar Mac Thuathaláin in *Peadar Chois Fhairrge*. See, for example, 19, 22, 24, 33–5 (where a character manhandles a priest), 89–91, 143, 148.
251 See Ó Criomhthain, *Allagar*, 70–71, 180–1, 325. His son Seán also refers to thefts of turf in *Leoithne Aniar*, 71.
252 Ó Criomhthain, *Allagar*, 303–4. 'Cá bhfios díbh nach amhlaidh a bhuailfeadh long i gcoinne na cloiche a thabharfadh bhúr ndóthain díbh fé mar a bhuail an *Quebra* [*sic*]', arsa Micheál [Séamas in 1928 edn], 'gur mhaireamar trí bliana d'á deascaibh'. 'Ach ní bhuaileann árthaí mar sin i gcomhnaidhe an uair a bhíonn ganntar leo', arsa Micil [Séamisín in 1928 edn]. See also p. 201; and Ó Criomhthain, *Allagar II*, 28 and 65.
253 Lá ar na mháireach ba bhreá leat féachaint uait síos ar an gcaladh agus na trághanna, binnsí móra do chláracha annso agus annsúd, agus an naomhóg is lú go raibh seilg aice do bhí as cionn céad clár aice. – Dar fia, adeireadh fear, gur maith é an cogadh. – Dhera, dhuine, adeireadh fear eile, má fhanann sé ann beidh an t-oileán so 'na Thír-na-nÓg againn. See Ó Súileabháin, *Fiche Blian ag Fás*, 214–15. See also pp. 216, 231. On the other hand, Ó Súileabháin also tells of the generosity of the islanders towards the survivors of shipwreck (p. 239). For other accounts of the importance of wrack to the islanders, see the memoir by Seán Ó Criomhthain in *Leoithne Aniar*, 32, 58. Ó Criomhthain does say that though the islanders believed shipwrecks were a gift from God, they were concerned about the crews and prayed for those drowned. Compare Tom O'Flaherty's depiction of Aranmen's excitement about seawrack in his story 'Wrack' in *Aranmen All*, 111–24, esp. p. 112. Outsiders were at times shocked that Blasket Islanders could, because of fish prices and wrack, have found the First World War more relevant to them than the War of Independence. See Máirín Nic Eoin, 'Éirí Amach 1916 agus Litríocht na Gaeilge' (The Easter Rising of 1916 and literature in Irish), *IMN*, 1985, 47–8.
254 See, for example, the depictions of such shopkeepers in Ó Grianna's *Caisleáin Óir* or Pádhraic Óg Ó Conaire's *Ceol na nGiolcach*, as well as in Ó Criomhthain's *Allagar na h-Inise*.
255 Ó Siochfhradha, 'Mar Baisteadh Maidhc', in *Seo Mar Bhí*, 16 21.
256 Mac Meanman, *Cad Chuige nach dTabharfainn?* in *Trí Mhion-Dráma*, 9–27.
257 Ó Gríobhtha, 'Criostína', in *Cathair Aeidh*, 257–301.
258 Mac Meanman, 'Bláthach Préataidhe agus Salann', in *Fear Siubhail*, 54–71.
259 Ó Grianna, 'Sagart Éamoinn Sheáin Óig', in *Cioth is Dealán*, 7–34.
260 Ó Cadhain, 'Culaith le Cois', in *Idir Shúgradh agus Dáirire*, 47 70.
261 Ó Ruadháin, *Pádhraic Mháire Bhán*, 42. Duine a raibh buidéal bainne leis, duine a raibh buidéal tae leis, agus duine a mb'éigean dó a ghreim aráin a ithe tur. Na daoine a raibh arán plúir leó ní raibh scáth ná eagla ortha agus thoisigheadar ag ithe ós comhair a raibh ann, mar bheidís ag déanamh gaisce . . . Ach bhí tuilleadh ann nach raibh aca ach an t-arán buidhe, agus é sin féin déanta leis an uisce, agus tuilleadh fós a bhí i muinighín an 'bhacstí' agus chuaidh siad-san i bhfolach comh-fhad's bhíodar ag ithe. In a 1937 essay in *Bonaventura*, Diarmuid Ó Duibhne claimed that such class distinctions were absent in the uncorrupted Gaeltacht of the past:

> The farmer and the labourer were friendly and well disposed towards each other. The labourer would take as much interest in the farmer's affairs as would the farmer himself. The two would be seen going to fair and market together. They would never call each other anything but 'Seán' and 'Domhnall' . . . There was no distance or dissension between them (Bhíodh an feirmeoir

agus an fear oibre muinnteardha báidhiúil le chéile. Bheadh an fear oibre ag cur an oiread suime i gcúrsaí an fheirmeora agus bheadh an feirmeoir féin. Chífí an bheirt ag dul go dtí aonach agus margadh le chéile. Ní raibh sa bheirt riamh ach 'Seán' agus 'Domhnall' . . . Ní bhíodh deighilt ná easaontas eatortha) (*Bonaventura*, Summer 1937, 98).

Séamus Mac Cuaige felt the Gaeltacht was still cheerfully classless. Having commented on the contentedness of the people despite their poverty, he continued: 'But when everyone is in the same condition, they never think about that. They don't complain but are always fully satisfied with the station to which God assigned them' (Acht nuair a bhíos gach duine ar an gcéadna ní smaoinigheann siad ariamh ar sin. Ní bhíonn siad ag casaod ná eile acht iad i gcómhnuidhe lán-tsásta leis an mbail a chuir Dia ortha) (*Gearrbhaile*, Jan. 1927, 5).

262 See, for example, Ó Criomhthain, *Allagar*, 46, and *passim*. See also Sayers, *Machtnamh*, 21.

263 Ó Siochfhradha, 'Ciall Cheannaigh', in *Seo Mar Bhí*, 1–4.

264 Seán Mac Thorcail, *Slis de'n tSean-Mhaide: Dráma Grinn* (BÁC: ODFR, 1936).

265 See, for example, Mac Giolla Iasachta, *Cúrsaí Thomáis*, 39.

266 See, for example, Micheál Ó Griobhtha, *Briathar Mná* (BÁC: Muinntir C.S. Ó Fallamhain, Teo., i gcomhar le hOS, 1928), 108.

267 See, for example, Ua Laoghaire, *An Bhruinneall Bhán*, 45–50.

268 See, for example, Mac Conmara, *An Coimhthigheach*, 37, 145–6.

269 O'Flaherty's stories in Irish usually appeared in an English version as well. For a discussion of the relationship and differences between the Gaelic and English versions, see William Daniels, 'Introduction to the Present State of Criticism of Liam O'Flaherty's Collection of Short Stories: *Dúil*', *Éire/Ireland*, Summer 1988, 122–34. O'Flaherty was not the first Gaelic literary figure to write of animal life, Pádraic Ó Conaire already having published 'Sealgaire Oidhche' (A night hunter) in *New Ireland* (31/8/18) and 'An Comhrac san Fhásach' (The fight in the wilderness) in the *Irish Independent* (22/12/24).

270 An tAthair Casáin, O.M. Cap., 'An Londubh', in *An Londubh*, 7–21.

271 Ó Cadhain, 'Leathtromadh na Cinneamhna', in *Idir Shúgradh agus Dáirire*, 33–45

272 There were also a few stories in Seán Ó Dálaigh's *Clocha Sgáil* with titles like 'An Fireád agus an Fiolar' (The ferret and the eagle), 'Banbh an Fhiolair' (The eagle's piglet), and 'Díoghaltas an Mhada Ruaidh' (The revenge of the fox) that suggest they are animal stories. In fact, they are about people and their dealings with animals. While Tomás Bairéad's story '"Is É Dia a Rathaíos"' (It is God who gives success) in his 1932 collection *An Geall a Briseadh* is also a primarily a story about people, Bairéad, who was later to write true animal stories, does have a sheep as a principal character here, and does attempt to give us an insight into what passes through the animal's mind. See Pádhraic P. Ó Ciardha, 'Ainmhí agus Duine: Léamh ar Ghearrscéalta Thomáis Bairéad' (Animal and person: A reading of the short stories of Tomás Bairéad), *IMN*, 1976, 39–46; and Ó Murchadha, 'Gearrscéalaíocht Thomáis Bairéad', *IMN*, 1991, 172–4.

273 Mac Meanman, *Peinsean Shean-Mháire Ní Ruadháin*, in *Trí Mhion-Dráma*, 59. Ní fhuil splannc nó splaideóg chéille aige! Bhí sé ins an targairneacht go ngoilfeadh an Gaedheal ar uaigh an Ghaill, agus is fíor é. Ní bhfuighidh mé pighinn ruadh!

274 An tAthair Liam Ó Beirn, 'An Lios' (The fairy fort), in *Seo Siúd* (Gaillimh: Ó Gormáin agus a Chomh., Teach na Clódóireachta, 1934), 62. Tá cuid againn ceart go leór – madraí bhfuil daba acu. B'fheáirrde an domhan (Sasanach) é, agus b'fheárr dúinn féin é, dhá ndéanadh an chuid eile againn soláthar saoghalta ins na hOileáin. Glanamuis amach ar chómhairle lucht na céille!

275 Ó Gallchobhair, *Caoineadh an Choimhighthigh*, in *Cáitheamh na dTonn*, 24. Ba é an saoghal nach rabh rannta cothrom! Buachaillí breághtha ag imtheacht i mbéal a gcinn agus bodaigh, nach salóchadh a mbéal ag caint le daoine bochta, ag gabháil thart ina sáith den tsaoghal!

276 Speaking at a meeting of the Gaelic Teachers' Association in Dublin, Micheál Ó Maoláin reported that an islander had told him 'that the Congested Districts Board [under British rule] did more for the people of Aran than the present government had done altogether' (*II*, 2/2/29).

277 Father Patrick Dinneen, 'Bhirgil agus Maecenas' (Virgil and Maecenas), in *Aistí ar Litridheacht Ghréigise is Laidne* (Essays on Greek and Latin literature) (BÁC: Muinntir C.S. Ó Fallamhain, Teo., i gcomhar le hOS, 1929), 102. Níl tír fá'n spéir níos áilne ná níos saidhbhre 'ná tír na hÉireann. Le déidheannaighe agus le roinnt mhaith de bhliadhantaibh bhí bruigheanta ar siubhal eadrainn, i dtreo go rabhamar ag déanamh failligh i saothrughadh an tailimh agus go rabhamar ag éirghe mío-shásta le n-ár dtír dúthchais agus fonn ar ár n-aos óg í thréigean. Is mithid dúinn claoidhe léi agus feidhm do bhaint aiste agus bruigheann is coimheascar do shéanadh.

278 In *The Prose Literature of the Gaelic Revival*, I ascribed the uneasiness of Irish language writers with regard to folk beliefs and superstitions to a blend of Catholic orthodoxy and distaste for what they saw as a cynical manipulation of such material by Irish writers of English from Yeats to Seamus MacManus. Angela Bourke's masterful analysis of the significance of folk beliefs in the tragic events surrounding the killing of Bridget Cleary by her own husband in 1895

has, however, convinced me that Gaelic discomfort with traditional fairy lore was only part of a wider and deeper Irish fear of being seen by the outside world as primitive, benighted, and unfit for self-government on the eve of the twentieth century. See Bourke, *The Burning of Bridget Cleary: A True Story* (London: Pimlico, 1999).

279 Mrs de Valera was the author of several fairy plays for children both in and after our period. For Ó Gríobhtha, see *Bean an Bhrait Bháin* (BÁC: Muinntir C.S. Ó Fallamhain, teo., i gcomhar le hOS, 1928). For Mac Liammóir, see *Oidhche Bhealtaine: Dráma Beag le haghaidh Leanbhaí* (May Day eve: A little play for children) (BÁC: ODFR, 1932). On a more serious level, highly literate characters discuss parallels between Irish folk beliefs and spiritualism in Mac Liammóir's story 'Dúchas an Uilc' (The nature of evil) in *Lá agus Oidhche* (Day and night) (BÁC: C.S. Ó Fallamhain, teo., i gcomhar le hOS, 1929), 13–14, 17–18.

280 Béaslaí, 'Deimhniú an Sgéil', in *As na Ceithre hÁirdibh*, 7–17.

281 Mac Meanman, 'Tús Sgéil as an Leabhar Thuas', in *Fear Siubhail*, 42–53. In Aindrias Ó Baoighill's novel *An t-Airidheach*, superstitions are presented objectively as the beliefs of 'old people' (sean-daoine) (pp. 29, 91).

282 Ó Broin, 'Cruitín an Chóta Dhuibh', in *An Rún agus Scéalta Eile* (BÁC: ODFR, 1932), 53–66.

283 Ó Criomhthain, *Allagar*, 337. Seadh, pé nósanna atá glan leo níor ghlan nósa na nDaoine Maithe fós leo agus d'á dheascaibh sin dob' éigeant beirt de mhná scoth-aosta do sholáthar i gcomhair na h-oidhche chun go mbeadh an naoidheanán le fagháil ar maidin. Bhí teine mhór ann. Bhi biadh agus deoch ann. Do fuair an bheirt bhan faireacháin píp an duine aca agus tarrac ar thobac a chur ionnta – agus do réir m'aithne ortha ba mhó an costas do lean an dá phíp ná airgead baistighe an leinbh. Ó Criomthain does, however, provide the natural explanation for apparently 'supernatural' events in *Allagar* (pp. 46–7, 245, 307–8). Compare the ambivalent comments of Eibhlís Ní Shúilleabháin, Tomás Ó Criomhthain's daughter-in-law, in two letters to George Chambers, one from 1931, the other from 1932. In the former, she stated: 'We believe in fairies here; that's why we are so interested in fairy tales.' In the latter, she wrote: 'Old men and women say that you should not be in the strand when the sun is gone down entirely. I am sure they used be afraid of fairies.' See Ní Shúilleabháin, *Letters*, 48, 64. In an interview with Pádraig Tyers in *Leoithne Aniar*, her husband Seán recalls: 'The place was awash in superstitions' (Bhí an áit ar snámh le piseoga) (p. 132; see also pp. 48, 134). In an autobiography from the other end of the country, the Donegal native speaker Niall Mac Ghiolla Bhríghde debunks the belief in spirits. See *Dirbheathaisnéis Néill Mhic Ghiolla Bhríghde* (The autobiography of Niall Mag Giolla Bhríghde), recorded and edited by Liam Ó Connacháin (BÁC: Brún agus Ó Nualláin, Teór., [1938]), 41–2.

284 In 1934, the Wexford branch of An Fáinne held a doubtless tongue-in-cheek debate between Donnchadh Ó Laoghaire (pro) and his son Donnchadh Óg (con) on the topic 'Do fairies exist or not?' (An bhfuil sidheogaí ann nó nach bhfuil?) The *II* report on the debate (13/12/34) does not, alas, mention which side won. The following year, the Mullingar branch of An Fáinne debated the existence of ghosts. Again, we are not told which side prevailed (*II*, 3/1/35).

285 Ó Súileabháin, *Fiche Blian ag Fás*, 179. Féach anois, arsa mise, gur mairg a bheadh gan foidhne agus is é mo mhór-thuairim gur mar seo a deintear púcaí do mhórán ar an oileán so. In his sister Éibhlín's diary entries from 1923 there are several stories about how gullible people were fooled into believing in supernatural occurrences. See, for example, 126, 134, 152, 162–3. In Seán Ó Dálaigh's *Timpeall Chinn Sléibhe*, superstitions were presented as common, but comical, in the West Kerry Gaeltacht (pp. 56–8).

286 Ó Cinnéide, 'Fear Misnigh', in *Eithneacha an Ghrinn: Cruasacht Scéalta* (Kernels of humour: A collection of stories) (Gaillimh: Ó Gormáin Teach Clódóireachta, 1924), 13–22.

287 Ó Domhnalláin, 'An Taidhbhse', in *Na Spiadóirí*, 59–63.

288 Ó Conaire, 'Ar Lorg Troda' (Looking for a fight), in *Fearfeasa Mac Feasa* (Indreabhán: Cló Chonamara, 1983 [1930]), 101–9.

289 Ó Nualláin, 'An t-Áirseoir', in *As na Ceithre hÁirdibh*, 263–77.

290 Ó Dálaigh, 'Breac Beannuighthe Thobar Mhíchil', in *Clocha Sgáil*, 24–33.

291 Ó Dálaigh, 'An Sagart agus an Amhailt' and 'Garsún agus an Sluagh Sidhe', in *Timcheall Chinn Sléibhe*, 131–9; 140–6.

292 Ó Riain, 'Radharc na Fírinne', in *An Tost agus Sgéalta Eile* (BÁC: Muinntir Alex Thom i gcomhar le hOS, 1927), 64. Géilleann na dúile go léir do thoil an Stiúrthóra san: glór na fairrge fíochmhaire, monabar na dtonn mbeag sa loch, torann uathbhásach na tóirthnighe, tá an uile cheann aca fé n-A smacht. Is Dó a cantar ceól na cruinne, agus éisteann reanna neimhe nuair árduigheann Sé A lámh. An duine amháin a loiteas an chliaruidheacht, agus an focal céadna aige do loit ar dtús í: *Non Serviam*! See also the more sophisticated treatments of this passivity in the face of a divinely ordained destiny in Niall Ó Domhnaill's story 'Bás a's Beatha' (Death and life), in *Bruighean Feille* (A treacherous fight) (BÁC: ODFR, 1934), 143–50; in Seosamh Ó Torna's story 'Oidhche Churtha an Chluig Siar' (The night to put the clock back), in *Cois Life* (Liffeyside) (BÁC: ODFR, 1936), 90; and in Seán Mac Maoláin's novel *Éan Corr* (Odd man out) (BÁC: OS, 1937), 185–6, 201.

293 Cormac Ó Cadhlaigh, *Eagna an Ghaedhil* (BÁC: Brún agus Ó Nóláin, Teór., 1925), 73. Má tá aon tréith seachas a chéile de thréithibh an Ghaedhil is ionmholta, is í tréith í ná an mhuinighin agus an ionntaoibh a bhíonn aige i gcomhnuidhe a Dia na Glóire, moladh go deó leis. Pé anacra ná pé buairt a luigheann anuas air, bíonn an dóchas go láidir 'na chroidhe, mar tuigeann sé go mbíonn Rí na gComhacht ós a chionn dhá chumhdach is dá choimeád.

294 Domhnall Ó Conchubhair, 'Dé Bheatha Toil Dé' (Welcome to the will of God), in *Duanaire Dúithch' Ealla*, ed. Seán Ua Cadhla (BÁC: ODFR, 1932), 96. Chun ár leasa do thigheann gach díth mar thárla / Acht foidhne 's fad-fhulang bheith againn dá bhárr san: / Mar cúiteochaidh Dia ró-fhial go leor linn, / Mar b'ionann ar talamh – i bhFlaitheas na Glóire, / Dé bheatha toil Dé, 's a réir go ndeárnaidh.

295 An rud atá i mbéalaibh na ndaoine seo taisbeánann sé nach bhfuil siad ag dúil le chuid mhór 'san t-saoghal seo agus go bhfuil siad toilteanach cibé chuireas Dia rompa a ghlacadh. 'Toil Dé go rabh déanta.' D'fhéadfainn a rádh gurb' é sin riaghail agus sgéal a mbeatha. Is cuma anró, nó ocras nó an bás féin, má thig an droch-bhail ortha ní ag gearán atá siad. 'Sé deirtear i gcómhnaidhe d'aimhdheoin comh cruaidh is tá a gcás, 'Toil Dé go rabh déanta.' See also the views of 'D. Ó D.' in his essay on the Eucharistic Congress in 1932:

> Offer sympathy to an Irish-speaker for the greatest loss that could happen to him, and the answer you would get would be 'Christ's Passion was worse.' The Gael accepted willingly every hardship it was God's will to send him. 'A hundred welcomes to the the will of God' (Déan comhbháidhe le Gaedhilgeoir fá'n gcaillteanas bu mhóide do tharlóchadh dhó agus sé an freagra gheobhfá 'Bu mhó Páis Chríost ná é.' Do ghlac an Gaedheal go toileamhail le gach fulaing bu thoil le Dia do chur chuige. 'Céad fáilte roimh thoil Dé' (*Far East*, June 1932, 133).

296 Sayers, *Peig*, 249. Daoine bochta ab'eadh sinn ná raibh eolas ar rachmas ná ar éirghe i n-áirde an tsaoghail againn. Ghlacamair leis an sórt saoghail a bhí againn 'á chleachtadh; ní rabhamair ag tnúth le n-a mhalairt. Thug Dia, moladh go deo leis! cabhair dúinn. Is minic a thugamair fé ndeara an t-Árd-Mháighistir Naomhtha a bheith i bhfábhar dúinn, mar is mó scríb agus ruathar a bheir ar ár ndaoine ar an bhfairrge, agus gan dul as aca ach le nA chabhair. See also *Peig*, 77, 109, 135, 137, 168, 208, 248, 250; and *Machtnamh Seanamhná*, 15, 31, 62, 129, 139.

297 Ó Criomhthain, *An tOileánach*, 217. See also *Allagar*, 101, 106, 112, 220, 298. Pádraig Ó Héalaí discusses the importance of *toil Dé* for Ó Criomhthain in 'Na hOileánaigh agus a dTréithe' (The islanders and their traits), in *Tomás an Bhlascaoid*, 171–3. In addition, see Ní Shúilleabháin, *Letters*, 34, 80; and the comments of Seán Ó Criomhtain in *Leoithne Aniar*, 38. See also *Dirbheathaisnéis Néill Mhic Ghiolla Bhríghde*, 121, 124, 125. One of the subheadings of the section 'Piseogacht agus Draoidheacht' (Superstition and magic), in Ó Súilleabháin's *Láimh-Leabhar Béaloideasa* is 'Toil Dé' (p. 61).

298 Maguidhir, 'Ba Toil Dé é' (It was God's will), in *Dhá Chrann na Marbh*, 29–43.

299 Mac Giolla Iasachta, *Toil Dé*, esp. 166, 263, 308, 314.

300 Ó Grianna, 'Grásta ó Dhia ar Mhicí', in *Cioth is Dealán*, 81.

301 Ó Broin, 'An Bhrighdeach', in *Ag Stracadh leis an Saol agus Scéalta Eile* (Struggling with life and other stories) (BÁC: Muinntir C. S. Ó Fallamhain, Teo., i gcomhar le hOS, 1929), 64. This story has an urban setting.

302 Ó Nualláin, 'An Hata', in *Tighearna an Tailimh agus Sgéalta Eile* (The landlord and other stories) (BÁC: Clólucht an Talbóidigh, Teór., 1923), 27. This story has an urban setting.

303 Breathnach, 'Daoine Gaoithe', in *Trom agus Éadtrom* (BÁC: COÉ, n.d.), 26. Cuma cé'n áit 'na mbím gheibheann na 'daoine gaoithe' amach mé, agus 'sé tá socruighthe agam anois ná mo thoil do chur le toil Dé sa scéal le súil nach mbeidh Sé ródhian orm Lá an Luain agus a bhfuil á fhulaing agam ar an saoghal so. This story has an urban setting.

304 Chan ceart dúinn bronntanais Dé do chur i n-achrann le chéile, acht iad do bheith ag cuideadh le chéile. An té a tharcuisigheann buadha Dé 'na bhráthair, ní chóimhlíonann sé toil Dé ann féin.

305 'Fág fé Dhia é', adeirtear le gach aon rud. B'fhéidir go b'shin an locht is mó atá orra, go bhfágtar an iomarca fé Dhia. Caithfear an teagasc eile a chur i bhfeidhm orra .i. 'gur maith le Dia congnamh d'fhagháil.'

306 O'Flaherty, 'Going Away', in *Aranmen All*, 137. See also p. 141. There is also a rather inchoate questioning of God's will in Micheál Ó Conaill's *Fá Sgáth Shléibh' Eachtgha*, 41–2.

307 Needless to say, Ó Cadhain's fellow radical leftist Peadar O'Donnell had litle use for such passivity, writing in the London journal *Guth na nGaedheal* in 1930: 'Yes, resistance is mighty but rebellion is little. That phase of thought where institutions that oppress and hurt are looked on as a part of life to be endured and softened but not torn down, holds the field to-day.' O'Donnell did, however, hope and believe that acceptance would ultimately give way to a revolt that would unite the Gaeltacht peasant and the resident of the Dublin slum: 'Call, voices in at the roots of the Gaedhealtacht; courage yet Gaels for there is a day hurrying towards us.' For a comparison of O'Donnell's attitude toward Gaeltacht passivity with that of his friend and fellow Donegal native, see my essay 'The Donegal of Séamus Ó Grianna and Peadar O'Donnell', *Éire/Ireland*, Summer 1988, 135–49.

O'Donnell's 1933 play *Wrack* is particularly interesting in this regard.
308 Diarmaid Ó Doibhlin, 'Gnúis dó Féin', in *Rí-Éigeas na nGael*, ed. Mac Congáil, 60. Is í an tréith is láidre a bhraithimse ar nua-litríocht na Gaeilge sna blianta tosaigh, an ceiliúradh buan atá inti, thuaidh is theas, sna Blascaodaí agus sna Rosa, ceiliúradh rialta buan ar ghnéithe den saol Gaelach – saol a bhí, ainneoin na n-ainneoin, i ndiaidh teacht slán, ainneoin ansmacht Gall agus neamart Gael, ainneoin scoileanna náisiúnta, ainneoin bochtanais, imirce agus gorta.
309 In his review of the novel for *FL*, 'Tadhg' wrote: 'But we don't much like the setting of the story. We do not think it is natural . . . Most of the people involved here never accepted the life of the people of the West, and it is no use trying to convince readers that they did' (Ach ní mó ná go maith a thaithnigheas suidheamh an sgéil linn. Níl sé nádúrtha, dar linn . . . Níor ghlac furmhór an dreama atá i gceist aige le saol na nIartharach ariamh agus ní cabhair féachaint a chur in a luighe ar léightheoirí gur ghlac) (*FL*, 22/7/22).
310 Ó Conaire, *Seoid ó'n Iarthar Órdha*, 201. Ba mhaith liom geábh a thabhairt ar fud an domhain go cinnte, ach sin a' méid. B'fhearr liomsa an gleann is uaignighe san Iarthar, ná an áit is áilne i n-aon tír sa domhan. Sílim féin nach bhfuil daoine fá ghréin Neimhe mar na créatúir bhochta lághacha sin, a bhfuil cómhnuidhe orra ar imeall cladaigh, agus i gcuasa cnoc, gidh nach bhfuilid gan a lochta féin. Is cuma sin. Tá an bháidh agus an ghnaoidheamhlacht ag rith leó. I have dealt in some detail with this theme in the fiction of Pádhraic Óg both in and after our period in *Déirc an Dóchais: Léamh ar Shaothar Phádhraic Óig Uí Chonaire* (Indreabhán: Cló Iar-Chonnachta, 1995). See also Titley, *An tÚrscéal Gaeilge*, 297.
311 Úna Bean Uí Dhíosca, *Cailín na Gruaige Duinne*, 6–7. Go dtí an nóiméad sin is dócha nár chreid mé amach is amach go raibh ár dteanga féin dá labhairt fós ag cuid de mhuintir na hÉireann. Sháruigh sé a bhfaca tú riamh! Nárbh' shin é an cruthú gur náisiún fé leith Éire? Nárbh' fhéidir linn an t-éitheach dearg do thabhairt don dream adéarfadh a mhalairt? . . . Thuig mé nach raibh muintir na hÉireann ina n-ainmhidhthe allta mar a dubhairt m'oncal. She later realises she could never live in the Gaeltacht after she experiences its darker side, particularly through her marriage with a land-obsessed and brutish Gaeltacht man.
312 Titley, *An tÚrscéal*, 267. Ar shlí an-simplí ar fad léiríonn *Bean Ruadh de Dhálach* agus *Le Clap-Sholus* an chodarsnacht a dhein dhá leath, ní hamháin de mhianta Mháire, ach d'idéal lucht páirte na Gaeilge i gcoitinne a lorgaigh slánú spioradálta imeasc aicme dearóile boichte nach mbeidís riamh sásta dul ina haice ach i rith geal-luachair an tSamhraidh. Is é sin le rá, gan drandal a ghearradh, idéal teanga amháin a bhí riamh san dlúthphobal ainnis caillte, agus ní idéal sóisialta, ná cultúir (sa chéill is leithne), ná slí mhaireachtana, ná saoil. See also pp. 240, 251, 253–4.
313 Ó Criomhthain, *An tOileánach*, 265. Do scríobhas go mion-chruinn ar a lán dár gcúrsaí d'fhonn go mbeadh cuimhne i mball éigin ortha agus thugas iarracht ar mheon na ndaoine bhí im' thimcheall a chur síos chun go mbeadh ár dtuairisc 'ár ndiaidh, mar ná beidh ár leithéidí arís ann. See also Sayers, *Peig*, 250. Ó Grianna stressed the same idea with regard to the eponymous hero of his *Micheál Ruadh*, 49.
314 Quoted by Breandán Ó Conaire, in *Myles na Gaelige*, 94.
315 Brian Ó Nualláin, provisional advance publicity memo for the third (1964) edition of *An Béal Bocht*, quoted by Ó Conaire in *Myles na Gaeilge*, 71.

CHAPTER THREE

Bringing Mohammed to the Mountain

1 Mara bhfuil an Ghaedhluinn 'na h-urlabhra oireamhnach cum gach ealadhain dá aoirde, cum gach smaoinimh dá uaisle do theagasg agus do chur i gcéill, ní móide gur cheart í chothú. Agus is neamhthairbheach an bheart aga ná airgead do chaitheamh léi, mar tá an bás i ndán dí; agus má tá, ba chóra, dob' fhearr an chiall, agus ba dhaona leigint do an rud bocht bás a dh'fhagháil ar a suaimhneas, gan a bheith á suathadh agus á buaidhreamh 'na túighlaethibh. Acht tá sí ábalta ar gach cúram dá bhféadfaí a chur uirthe a dhéanamh, agus ar a dualgas a chomhall, dá bhfuigheadh sí a ceart. Agus ní bhfuighidh sí bás. Nár leigidh Dia go bhfuighidh.
2 Caithfimíd teisbeánadh do chách go bhfuil an Ghaedhealg atá ar theangaidh na ndaoine ábalta ar ghnáth-chúrsaí saoghal an lae indiu a dhéanamh mar tá an Béarla i Sasain, an Fhraincis sa Fhrainc, an Ghearmáinis sa Ghearmáin, an Spáinnis sa Spáin, agus an Eadáilis san Iodáil.
3 Mac Néill, 'An Réamh-Rá', in Mac Clúin, *Róisín Fiain na Mara*, 6. Má's maith libh an Ghaoluinn a bheith beo, cuirigí ag obair í, cuirigí annró uirri agus oraibh féin, na fágaigí ina suan sámh í, beirigí amach sa tsráid í, bainigí saothar aisti, ná bíodh cead aici staonadh ó aon saghas oibre atá foghainteach do mhuinntir na hÉireann.
4 Má's amhlaidh go bhfuil an Ghaedhealg le bheith ina ghnáth-theangain againn is gádh í a shaothrú go mbeidh sí fóirsteanach do chúrsaí an tsaoghail mhóir idir scríbhneóireacht, oideachas, agus cúrsaí gnótha. Go dtí seo is beag iarracht atá déanta, nó ní mór le rádh é chun neithe a bhaineas leis an saoghal mór a láimhsheáil tríd an nGaedhilg.
5 Is greannmhar an dream iad mórán de Ghaedhealaibh. Ní h-áil leo trioblóid ná saothar de aon sórt, ach go mór-mhór is leasg leo léigheamh de chineál ar bith géar ná dian do dhéanamh ar aon rud, ach mur bhfeicid agus mur mbeirid ar 'chuile rud go breágh réidh sásta, gan saothar gan díthcheall, tá

fearg orthú ar áit na mbonn, fearg agus iongantas . . . 'Fat iz he dhrivin' at at all?' adéarfa siad! Mar bhudh eadh, caithfidh sé go bhfuil sé ar báinidh, nó as a chéill ar chuma eicínt, agus gan sinne d'á thuigsint! See also, 'Aodh', 'Litridheacht na Gaedhilge' (Literature in Irish), *CB*, October, 1926, 1073–1074; and 'Micheál Óg', 'Creideamh Ár Sinnsear i nGaedhilg Ár Sinnsear' (The faith of our ancestors in the Irish of our ancestors), *Hibernia*, Mar. 1937, 15.

6 Caithfimid gan ár súile dhúnadh ar rud ar bith. Caithfimid bheith ag síor-chuardach. Cé'n fáth dhúinn bheith ag creathadh ós cóir déithe bréige na n-amadán is na bhFilistíneach? Cé'n fáth dhúinn umhlú do chlaoin-bhreith an ghramhasgair ainbhfiosaigh, do bhréagchrábhadh na mbúistéirí is na bhfuinnteóirí?

7 He wanted Gaelic writers 'dearmad a dhéanamh ar feadh tamaillín ar na fataí agus ar na fódaibh móna is ar Nóra bhig ag dul go dtí an tobar agus ar Phádhraic Óg ag bligh na mbó, is ar Shean-Bhrighid ag gol agus coróin Mhuire 'na glaic aici, agus ar an sagart caomh cneasta ag dul síos an bóithrín drúchta.'

8 Toirmisgeann an aithne seo orainn cabhair ar bith a thabhairt de leabharthaibh mar 'Phrátaí Mhichíl Thaidhg' agus 'Ag Séideadh agus ag Ithe', agus 'Cloich Cheann Fhaolaidh' nach bhfuil brigh ná tábhacht, ná sugh ná seamhair ionntú. Orduigheann sí dúinn, nuair a chuireas duine ar bith rud i nGaedhilg atá a fhios aige nach léighfeadh duine dá mbeadh sé i mBéarla, iarraidh a thabhairt air, agus é a ithe ó chnámhaibh loma, agus gan a chuid béalastánachta a léigheadh, ann an dóigh nach leigfeadh an eagla dó níos mó 'dhochar a dhéanamh. Of the three books mentioned here, the first was by Séamus Ó Dubhghaill, the second by Father O'Leary, and the third by Séamus Ó Searcaigh. In a brief editorial comment on the article, Father Lawrence Murray chided Mac Grianna for choosing to make his case by citing books published a fair number of years earlier.

9 Ach nach sílfeá ar a gcuid gearr-sgéal uilig, nach rabh rud ar bith i n-Éirinn taobh amuigh de'n Ghaedhealtacht ar bh'fiú trácht air? Bhí a n-umhail uilig ar shaoghal na Gaedhealtachta . . . Agus lean siad de'n ghnáthas sin gur mhinic a dubhairt mé nach mbéadh meas ar an Ghaedhilg mar ghnáth-theanga na tíre go ndéanfadh na sgríbhneóirí dearmad glan de'n Ghaedhealtacht agus a n-aghaidh a thabhairt ar na bailte móra. See also Ciarán Ua Nualláin's satiric take on the subject in 'Mo Sheacht Mallacht Ortha / Na Daoine sin Atá ag Ithe a Ruball Féin sa Tír seo' (My seven curses on them / Those people who are eating their own tails in this country), *Hibernia*, Sept. 1937, 26.

10 Ní scríobhnóir oilte tá fhios agat go fear cathrach, nó go fear a' bhaile mhóir. Má's i ndán dúinn litríocht Ghaedhilge bheith againn ní mór d'fhir a' bhaile mhóir fioghar na maitheasa a chur orra féin is tosnú a' tál.

11 Sé an rud is géire a theastuigheann uatha ná drámaí ar an nua-shaol a bhun-cheapfar sa Ghaedhilg féin – drámaí, cuir i gcás, a léireóchaidh saol cathrach na linne seo, nó an saol intliúil, nó gluaiseacht an tsaoil mhóir.

12 Tá a leithéid de scríbhneóracht a dhíoghbháil orrainn i litridheacht na Gaedhilge mar chan ionann saoghal na ndaoine i mbailtí móra na tíre seo agus saoghal ciúin simplidhe mhuinntir na Gaedhealtachta; agus, ar an droch-uair dúinn féin, bhféadfaidhe gur líonmhaire na daoine a chuireas spéis 'san chineál seo scríbhneórachta. Typically more pragmatic was Máirtín Ó Cadhain, who in 1934 pointedly proclaimed: 'Irish will not be saved in the Gaeltacht, but only as it will come back in English-speaking Ireland, because the people of the Gaeltacht will not be willing to be made into a group apart, separated out from the rest of the country' (Ní shábhálfar an Ghaedhilge sa nGaedhealtacht, ach amháin de réir mar thiocfas sí ar ais sa nGalldacht, óir ní bheidh muinntir na Gaedhealtachta sásta go ndéanfaoi dream fá leith díobh agus iad deighilte amach ón gcuid eile dhen tír) (*Éireannach*, 25/8/34). This belief that Gaeltacht people should and would resist being made the inmates of a linguistic and cultural reservation was by no means unique to Ó Cadhain, or to native speakers for that matter. See, for example, Liam Ó Rinn ('Coinneach'), Letter, *IS*, 14/12/29.

13 Má leathan an Ghaedhilg i n-aon chor is ós na cathrachaibh agus go mór-mhór ó B'l'á Cliath a leathfaidh sí amach ar fuaid na tíre. Agus is amhlaidh a thiocfaidh athrú chomh mór san uirri gur ar éigin a bheidh Gaedhilgeoirí an lae indiu ábalta ar í thuiscint, abair, i gceann céad blian.

14 Má tá Árd-Éigse sa Ghaedhilg i ndán dúinn san aois seo déarfainn gur ó'n áit ar a dtugtar an Ghalltacht fé láthair a thiocfaidh sí. 'Sé mo bharamhail é gur mó de bheodhacht inntine agus de bheodhacht spioradálta atá le braith indiu agus le blianta beaga anuas sa Ghalltacht. Mara mbéadh a mhéid suime a chuireann muinntir na Galltachta sa Ghaedhealtacht, is beag a cloisfí uaithe cor ar bith. See also Ó Siadhail's similar comments in his lecture to An Comchaidreamh in Rosmuc three years later (*AA*, Oct. 1937, 7).

15 Tá na húdair Ghaedhilge i gcoitinne ró-thugtha do shaol na tuatha do phínteáil dúinn. Rud nua dhúinn údar a bheith againn go bhfuil grádh aige do shráideanna cathrach agus ná féachann ar an tuaith ach mar fhéachann na cathruitheóirí uirthi. Is bréan liom cúrsaí iascaigh is feirmeoireachta, agus déarfainn gur bréan le muintir na tuatha féin cuntaisí ortha – gur fearr leo go mór fada na scéalta ina dtráchtar ar shaol shíor-atharuitheach is ar shoillse na gcathrach.

16 Is féidir teanga a bheith ró-chomhgarach do'n chré. An Ghaedhilg, fé mar a labhairtear í, go mór-mhór isna ceanntair sin go raibh scoileanna litríochta ar cheal ionnta san ochtmhadh aois deug, déarfainn go bhfuil sí ró-chomhgarach do'n chré.

17 Anois tá an Ghaedhilg ag dul tré mhuilleann an tsaoghail nua seo, agus caithfear í do léiriú agus do réidhteacht go cothrom, oireamhnach i gcóir gach riachtanais a bhaineann le cúrsaí saoghail an lae indiú . . . Caithfear sean-fhocail do chuardach, agus focail nua do cheapadh nó do ghoid; caithfear na canúintí go léir do mheasgadh mar do dhéanfaí le bainne i ndabhach, agus, i gceann tamaill, an t-uachdar do bhaint díobh, agus an cuigeann do dhéanamh, agus, tréis iad a chasadh agus a shuathadh go maith, an t-im a ghabháil chughainn mar theanga na hÉireann uile.

18 Agus má oir an Ghaoluinn don Ghaedheal; má bhí a dhíol de theangain innte uair, don liacht glaodhach a bhí uirthi, ba chóir go n-oirfeadh sí dhó anois ach í leathadh agus í lúbadh le hoireamhaint an tsaoghail nua . . . Tá bearna mhór fhairsing gearrtha amach ag an aimsir idir an seana-shaol Gaolach agus an saol nua atá istigh indiu, ach is féidir an dá shaol do réidhteach agus do thabhairt le chéile i litríocht na Gaoluinne, an té thuigeann iad araon agus ealadha na litríochta do bheith aige de dhúthchas. See also Micheál Ó Donnabháin (Frank O'Connor), 'An Gúm', *An Leabharlann*, Dec. 1933, 132.

19 In his preface to his dictionary, Dinneen wrote: 'The wide and varied assortment of Irish words and phrases here presented will afford ample material for an extensive use of the language and for its application to social, commercial, scientific and literary pursuits.' See Dinneen, 'Editor's Preface', in *Foclóir Gaedhilge agus Béarla / An Irish-English Dictionary: Being a Thesaurus of the Words, Phrases and Idioms of the Modern Irish Language*, new edn, revised and greatly enlarged (Dublin: Irish Texts Society, 1927), viii.

20 Ní dóigh liom féin go dtiocfaidh an prós ceart nó go mbeidh an Ghaedhilg in úsáid coitchcannta ar fud na hÉireann sna cathracha, sa traen, sa tram, san amharclainn, sna sgoileanna, sna coláistí, imeasg na ndaoine ag díol is ag ceannach ar an margadh.

21 Ó Cuív, *The Problem of Irish in the Schools* (Dublin: Browne & Nolan, 1936), 11.

22 Is minic a cuirtear i n-aghaidh na Gaedhilge go minic [*sic*] ná féidir í a mhúnlú ná í a chur i gcóir do cheisteanna an lae indiu. Tá roinnt de'n fhírinne annsan, 'sa mhéid ná fuil an Ghaedhilg do réir mar labhartar indiu í – cainnt na ndaoine, mar adeirtear – ná fuil sí i n-oireamhaint do cheisteanna na h-aimsire seo. Ach dearmad 'seadh é a rádh ná féidir í a chur i n-oireamhaint . . . Adeirid feallsamhnaigh ná féidir argóint a dhéanamh i n-aghaidh na rud a thárla, agus féach gur tráchtadh i nGaedhilg shimplí shoiléir, suas le cúig céad bliain ó shoin, ar stair, ar fheallsamhnacht, ar leigheas, ar réalt-eolas agus ar dhiadhacht.

23 Agus n'íl fáth ná leathsceul ag litridheacht na Gaodhluinne i dtaobh bheith chomh tanaidhe, triuchalta san acht easbaidh focal agus dá bhrígh sin, nó dá bhárr, easba smaointe . . . Táid na focail ann, do'n chuid is mó de, acht iad do lorg, iad d'fhagháil, agus iad do riaradh. As na foclaibh iomdha, úsáideacha sin fásfaidh litridheacht uasal, acfuinneach chughainn seachas litridheacht baothairí agus bodachán.

24 Hanly, 50.

25 Ó Cléirigh, *Aodh Mac Aingil* (BÁC, ODFR, n.d.), 91–2. Fhaid a bhí an Ghaedhilg faoi chois is beag an bhaint a bhí aici le beatha an náisiúin. D'ísligh sí céim i dtreó is nach raibh gádh aici ach le gnóthaí talmhan agus iascaigh. Tagann de sin go bhfuilimíd chum deiridh d'oireasbaidh focal a d'fheilfeadh do shaoghal an lae indiu agus is iomdha focal agus leagan cainnte a bhí ag Mac Aingil agus a leithéidí a thiocfadh isteach go h-áiseamhail anois agus dfhéadfaoi do chur ag fóghaint don tír uile. In a Nov. 1923 letter to Éamonn Mac Giolla Iasachta, the editor of *An Sguab*, Seán Mac Giollarnáth praised him for his willingness to tackle the terminology challenge: 'It is necessary work also, if we want to bring the language out of the glass house in which it has been for many a day' (Is riachtanach an obair í freisin, má's mian linn an teanga a thabhairt amach as an dtig ghloine 'na raibh sí le fada'n lae) (Edward MacLysaght papers, NLI MS 8560 {8}).

26 Cómhartha nirt teangan é bheith ar a cumas focail atá uaithi a tharaing isteach chúici agus a smachtú d'réir a reachta féin. Ní h-aon cómhartha laige é easbaidh focal a mhothú, acht cómhartha beódhachta agus beatha. He did, however, stress that Irish should not draw too heavily on the resources of English.

27 Seoirse Mac Tomáis, 'Fógra' (Announcement), in *Alcéstis le h-Eurípidés*, ed. Mac Tomáis (BÁC: ODFR, 1932), n.p. Maidir le téarmaí teichniúla, isé mo thuairim gur maith an bhail ar an nGaodhluinn, i gcúrsaí litríochta ach go h-áirithe, ná fuil le fáil innte ach an beagán díobh. Má bhíonn téarma éigin i n-easnamh, caithfear an chiall do chur i n-iúl go mín macánta le cainnt shimplí, ní a raghaidh chun tairbhe don mhúinteoir agus don mhac léighinn araon; ach, má bhíonn an iomarca aca le fáil, is ró-fhuiriste dhúinn ceal eolais do cheilt fé chainnt léigheannta . . . An méid díobh dob éigin dom a cheapadh, do mheasas gurbh fhearra dhom iad do thógaint ón Laidin, ar nós an Bhéarla agus na Frainncise agus a lán teangthacha nach iad, ná dul siar go dtí an tsean-Ghaodhluinn dá n-iarraidh, mar gur mó tábhacht, dar liom, iad do bheith so-thuisciona ná glan-Ghaodhluinn do bheith ortha.

28 Caithfimíd glacadh ó'n mBéarla agus ó theangthacha iasachta eile. Luigheann sin le tuigsint. Tá'n Ghaedhilg gan saothrú leis na céadta bliadhain . . . Ní mór na céadta focal a thabhairt isteach i nGaedhilg na haimsire seo chun a cur i n-oireamhaint do'n tsaoghal atá anois ann. Sin é díreach an baoghal. Sin fáth gur ceart dúinn bheith aireach caomhnach. Sin cúis gur ceart ár sean-sgríbhinní do chur ar fágháil agus gur cheart do gach éinne a bhfuil faoi cur le litridheacht na Gaedhilge staidéar a dhéanamh ortha.

29 See also 'Leabhar Tábhachtach (An important book)', Review of *Cuirp-Eolas*, *II*, 7/11/27.

30 In 1922 Gógan seems to have been willing to go even farther, suggesting that most of the words required were already in the language. See Gógan, '"Words, Words, Words!" (*Hamlet*)', *An Reult*, May 1924, 20–2.

31 See Ó Súilleabháin, *Scéal an Oireachtais*, 178–9.

32 This series ran in *An Stoc* until May 1929.

33 That there was some demand for such a book is clear from a letter to *II* from 'Earnest Student' (7/6/23): 'The scope of conversation in Irish seems to be limited to rural life. I have attended classes, and bought phrase books, but none of them proved of much use to me in my daily occupation, which is that of a clerk in a city office.' Office life was the topic of 'Scríbhneoirí agus an Oifig / Tuairim de Maupassant' (Writers and the office / de Maupassant's opinion) by 'Noel', *II*, 19/8/29; and a few sketches by Seán Ó Ciarghusa in *The Leader*, including 'Tar Éis na Nodlag' (After Christmas) (14/1/33); 'Is Cuideachta Beirt' (Two is company) (3/10/33); and 'Caith Uait na Páipéirí!' (Throw away the papers!) (15/4/33). Ó Ciarghusa also wrote several pieces for *The Leader* in the 1930s dealing with commuters and other Dubliners riding the city's buses and trams.

34 See An tSiúr Bosco Costigan and Seán Ó Curraoin, *De Ghlaschloich an Oileáin: Beatha agus Saothar Mháirtín Uí Chadhain* (Of the grey stone of the island : The life and work of Máirtín Ó Cadhain) (Béal an Daingin: Cló Iar-Chonnachta, 1987), 44–5.

35 For a brief survey of this division of the civil service, see Séamas Daltún, 'Scéal Rannóg an Aistriucháin' (The story of the translation division), *Teangeolas*, no. 17 (Winter 1983), 12–26; as well as the discussion of its work in Michael Cronin, *Translating Ireland: Translation, Languages, Cultures* (Cork: Cork University Press, 1996), 153–6. Less impressed by the contribution of Rannóg an Aistriucháin is Maolmhaodhóg Ó Ruairc, who feels that the new State missed an opportunity by not drafting its legislation primarily in Irish rather than merely providing Irish versions of the laws as written and passed in English. See Ó Ruairc, *I dTreo Teanga Nua*, 24.

36 For a discussion of the work of this committee, see Cathal Ó Háinle, 'Ó Chaint na nDaoine go dtí an Caighdeán Oifigiúil', in *Stair na Gaelige, in ómós do Pádraig Ó Fiannachta* (The history of the Irish language: In honour of Pádraig Ó Fiannachta), ed. Kim McCone, Damien McManus, Cathal Ó Háinle, Nicholas Williams, and Liam Breathnach (Maigh Nuad: Roinn na Sean-Ghaeilge, Coláiste Phádraig, 1994), 772–3. In a brief note at the beginning of *Téarmaí Staire is Tír-Eoluíochta*, Tomás Ó Máille and Tadhg Ó Donnchada are thanked for their help in preparing this booklet. An Coiste Téarmaíochta disbanded in December 1939 because of the war. It was revived in 1968 and continues its work to this day. Father Lambert McKenna was to draw extensively on the work of both Rannóg an Aistriucháin and An Coiste Téarmaíochta for his *Foclóir Béarla agus Gaedhilge* (1935). See Ó Háinle, 'Ó Chaint na nDaoine', p. 774.

37 Ua Ceallaigh, *Taistealuidheacht no Cúrsa na Cruinne* (BÁC: M. H. Macanghoill is a Mhac, Teor., 1931), 4. Ní gábhadh a rádh gur iomdha focal is ainm neamh-choitchianta a thagas treasna ar ughdar le linn mór-thurais mar soin is gan a samhail fós 'san Ghaedhilg toisc gur beag feidhm a baineadh as ár teangain dúthchhais le ciantaibh. Chuireas na focail is na hainmneacha úd i gcomhairle na n-ughdar Gaedhilge is cliste ar mo lucht aithne, agus tá toradh ár gcomhairle uile annso, pé olc maith é.

38 Tá daoine an-eólach ar fuaid na hÉireann a cheapas nach féidir trácht ar ealaidhean agus ar chruaidhcheisteanna mar é tré Ghaedhilg, acht dá mbeadh an dream seo sa láthair ag éisteacht leis na léigheachtaí thuigfidís gur féidir teanga na nGaedheal a lúbadh, a shníomhadh agus a chasadh chun gach smaoineamh dá dhoimhne agus gach ealadhan dá úire a nochtadh innti chomh maith le aon teanga eile beó agus níos fearr ná cuid mhaith aca.

39 See also his 'Déanamh an Domhan' (The making of the world), a heavily glossed discussion of geology that commenced serialisation in *An Stoc* in Aug. 1923; and his essays 'Sgéal na mBeóg' (The story of the microbes) in *An Branar*, June 1925, 183–90); and 'Teas na Réalt' (The heat of the stars) in UCG's *University Annual* for 1924–5. The former essay includes terms like *beóg-lacht* ('vaccine'), *fiodán fromhtha* ('test tube'), and *galar-shaorsacht neamhghníomhach* ('passive immunity'). The latter piece concludes with a glossary of words like *solsgarachán* ('spectroscope'), *soltomhas réaltach* ('stellar photometer'), *teintomhas* ('pyrometer'), and *teastomhas* ('thermometer').

40 The piece in *II* for 28/1/26 was by 'Sean-Éireannach'; that for 7/8/28 (in English) by the veteran language activist and television pioneer E. E. Fournier d'Albe; and the series in *The Leader* by Seán Ó Ciarghusa. See also Ó Ciarghusa's 'An "Television" So' (This television), *IP*, 7/2/38.

41 The contributions by 'Ceannabhán' appeared in the 'Smaointe ar Rudaí Reatha' (Thoughts on current affairs) column to which he was the most frequent, important, and versatile of several contributors. Another regular contributor to *II*, one 'Goibhniu', wrote on music. See for example, *II*, 1/10/26 and 6/2/31.

42 Predictably enough, textbooks were, as we will see immediately below, a prime focus of activity in this area. For examples of Gaelic appeals for appropriately up-to-date school books in Irish, see 'Educationist', 'Learning through Irish? / Is it Practicable Yet? / Few New Text Books', *II*, 27/9/24; 'Easba Teucs-leabhar' (A lack of textbooks),

Editorial, *II*, 2/6/26; and 'Cúrsaí Téacs-Leabhar i nGaedhilg' (The textbook situation in Irish), Letter, *II*, 30/6/33.

43 Ní'l aon chainnt teicneamhail annso; ní'l focal ann nach bhfuil i n-úsáid 'san nGaedhealtacht.

44 Is mór an sólás do'n mhúinteoir ar deireadh thiar thall nach measfar é do réir éifeachta a chuid ceacht, ná toradh scrúdaighthe acht fá mar chabhruigh sé le na páistí Ríoghacht a nAthar Síorruidhe do bhaint amach (p. 118).

45 Ó Dubhdha, 'Turas Gaedhilgeóir go Lourdes', in *Cáith agus Grán*, 84–94.

46 Agus atá sé buille luath ag Gaedhilgeoirí go fóill brat na léir-mheasdórachta i gcúrsaí litríochta a ghabháil chucu. Is námha í an cheard gan í fhoghluim, adeirtear. Ní chuimhnigheann léightheoirí Gaedhilge na haimsire seo ar an seanfhocal sin ar éigean. Léirmheasadóirí 'chuile mhac an aoin bheo díobh!

47 Maidir leis na tuairimí atá aige i dtaobh na saothar ar a bhfuil cur síos déanta aige, is cuibhe dhúinn cuimhneamh nach bhfuil an léirmheastóireacht acht ag tosnú fós in Éirinn, agus go mórmhór go bhfuil sé ana dheacair breitheamhntas ceart do thabhairt ar sgríobhnóir 'na ré féin. D'á bhithín sin ní cóir bheith ag súil le breith do-earráideach ó aon léirmheastóir, acht fáilte do chur roimh pé tuairm atá aige má thaisbeánann sé go bhfuil aon bhunadhas cuibhseach creideamhnach léithe. Mar sin is eadh a chuirfear an léirmheastóireacht chun cinn agus a déanfar an litridheacht do shaothrú. There was also concern that in the absence of criticism in Irish of literature in Irish the void was being filled by criticism of that literature in English.

48 Ach i dtaobh na Gaedhilge, níor tosnuíodh i gceart fós ar aon díospóireacht a dhéanamh sa Ghaedhilg féin ar chúrsaí leitríochta. Táid na hughdair mhóra 'na dtost. Tá teanga nua á ceapadh ag cuid aca agus is dócha go gceapann cuid eile go bhfuil ardleitríocht á ceapadh aca féin. B'fhéidir go bhfuil, leis, ach gan é bheith de rath ar na léightheoirí an ardleitríocht san d'aithint. Ach ar aon chuma táid siad so go léir róbhruidiúil chun a smaointe do nochtadh i dtaobh na leitríochta, má tá aon smaointe aca 'na taobh.

49 Fá láthair ní fhághann leabhar ach moladh nó leamh-mholadh de ghnáth: dá ghéire dá mbíonn cáineadh ag teastáil, ní déantar é ach uair as an gcéad. Tá sé seo do-thuigthe nuair a chuimhnighimíd go bhfuil beagnach gach duine a thuigeas an sgéal ar aon inntinn faoi a dhonacht is tá cuid den Ghaedhilg atá dá scríobhadh indiú. Má tá feidhm ar bith le lucht léirmheasa ba cheart go bhféadfadh siad a innsint dúinn cé na leabhra a bhfuil maith ionnta agus cé na cinn nach bhfuil . . . Tar éis machtnamh fada a dhéanamh ar an gceist b'fhacthas dom gurab easbaidh eolais ar na riaghalacha a bhaineas le deaghscríobhtha nó deagh-stíl is cionntach in sna lochta seo go léir beagnach.

50 On the other hand, 'Celt' was surprisingly optimistic about the future of Gaelic criticism: 'Take him all in all, however, the native Irish critic is more hopeful than the non-native. He has, or should have, at any rate, his future in front of him.'

51 Ba mhaith liom go ndéanfaí léir-mheas réasúnta ar an saothar a foillsighthear; ach bheadh súil againn le congnamh ón léir-mheas i n-ionad táinsimh. An deacracht is mó, b'fhéidir, a bhaineas le léir-mheas Gaedhilge, go bhfuilmíd gan caighdeán seasmhach liteardha. Ó Deirg believed, 'It is high time for us to establish an independent court to settle every question involving literature' (Is ró-mhithid dúinn cúirt neamh-spleadhach a bhunú le gach ceist a bhaineas le litridheacht a shocrú). In a letter to the same journal the previous year, Pádhraic Ó Gallchobhair deplored the state of Gaelic literary discussion and wrote: 'Unless books of this sort [that is books from An Gúm] are reviewed, and reviewed accurately, rigorously, fairly, the language will be corrupted day by day' (Muna ndéantar léirmheas agus léirmheas cruinn, cruaidh, cóir, ar leabhra den tsórt seo [.i. leabhra an Ghúim] beidh an teanga dá truailliú ó ló go ló) (*Tír*, Dec. 1932, 8).

52 Sgéim dúthchasach léir-mheastóireachta atá uainn. Chuige sin ní foláir aghaidh a thabhairt ar bhuntréithe na litríochta dúthchais go neamh-bhalbh, agus ná coisgeadh aon bhaoth-bhoige ná ró-mhaoithneachas sinn.

53 Even so sophisticated a writer as León Ó Broin could argue in 1924 that a truly objective and honest assessment of writing in Irish could do more harm than good by discouraging those doing their best to produce reading matter in the language (*II*, 1/1/24).

54 Ní móide go bhfuil sé cóir dí-mholadh a dhéanamh ar leabhar Gaedhilge ar bith ar an saol atá ann. Ach na dhiaidh sin caithfear a ceart a sheasamh don teangain.

55 Peata beag millte mí-riaghalta a bhí innti. Níor measadh go nuige seo scríbhinní na nua-Ghaedhilge de réir chaighdeáin ar bith a chuirfeadh ar aon dul le scríbhinní na nua-theangthach eile iad, agus dá dheascaibh sin is ana-dheacair teacht ar aon bhreitheamhnas cruinn ciallmhar ar nua-litríocht na Gaedhilge ó thosach na h-aithbheochana anuas.

56 Caidé mar ghníthear léirmheas i n-Oileán na Naomh? Tá sin furasd a innse. Caitheann tú suas pighinn. Má thuiteann sí agus an chearc ar uachtar cáinfidh tú an leabhar. Anois, foscail an leabhar seo áit ar bith is léigh leat go bhfágha tú (a) dearmad cló (b) dearmad 'sa litriú (c) canamhaint nach dtaitneann leat (d) droch-Ghaedhilg cheart (e) 'droch-Ghaedhilg' do réir baramhla atá agat féin. Scríobh léirmheas ar na lochtaí annsin, is tá leat. Má thig an chláirseach ar uachtar mol an leabhar is cuir i gcomórtas í le Dante nó le rud ínteacht eile nár léigh tú ariamh. MÁ'S CARA DUIT A SCRÍOBH AN LEABHAR FAN AG CAITHEAMH PIGHNEACH GO

DTARAIDH AN CHEARC AR UACHTAR. He added: 'Do not write books yourself or vengeance will be inflicted on you for your reviews' (Ná scríobh leabharthaí tú féin nó imreofar díoghaltas ort as do chuid léirmheas). See also 'An Dóirnéalach' (Ó Grianna?), 'Béarlachas agus Ciotachas' (Anglicism and clumsiness), *An t-Ultach*, Dec. 1934, 1–2.

57 In 1923 de Blácam worried that the obsession with the language itself could stifle the creative impulse in would-be Gaelic writers. See de Blácam, 'Cosc ar Deagh-Scríobhadh', *FL*, 8/12/23). More than a decade later, he could still describe Gaelic criticism as 'uneven, not to say jumbled', and declare: 'A great national work it is, to re-establish Gaelic criticism' (*Irish Monthly*, Oct. 1935, 681). In a 1937 review, Liam Ó Buachalla divided readers of Gaelic literature into three types: learners, those who read for pleasure and enlightenment, and 'those who read it to find faults in it. This last group cannot read a line without feeling spite or disgust because of the spelling of the words, idioms, diction, vocabulary, grammar, etc.' (iad-san a léigheas í le lochtaí fhagháil uirthi. An dream deireannach seo, ní thig leo líne a léigheamh gan olc nó déistin a theacht ortha de bharr leitrighthe na bhfocal, corra-cainteanna, teilgin, sanas, graiméar, 7rl). (*Éireannach*, Feb. 1937, 7).

58 'Ní'l mórán maith' ins an sgéal, ach tá sgoith na Gaedhilge ann. Tá na cora cainnte go flúirseach ar gach aon leathanach de.' Sin agaibh an léir-mheas is coitchianta ar leabharthaí úra Gaedhilge.

59 In his review of Seaghán Mac Meanman's *Fear Siubhail*, Eoin Ó Searcaigh also said virtually nothing about the book's literary qualities, concentrating instead on illustrating 'the sweet flowing Gaelic which is his' (*Leader*, 31/1/25).

60 Tá cuid de'n lucht léirmheasa nach mbíonn sásta tuairim a thabhairt air phíosa scríbhneórachta gan a fhagháil amach i dtús ama cén cúige arb as do'n scríbhneoir. Tá daoine eile ann a mbíonn an tuairim acu gur fearr i bhfad go bhfuigheadh an Ghaedhilg bás ná go dtosóchadh na daoine a d'fhoghluim an Ghaedhilg ag scríobhadh leabharthach. Is beag duine a ghníos iarracht air leabhar a léirmheasadh mar ghníthear a leithéid i litridheacht tíortha eile. Easbaidh eolais air na riaghalacha simplidhe coitcheannta a bhaineas le léirmheastóireacht is cionntach leis na lochtaí seo uilig.

61 Ná leigtear d'aoinne, ach dam-sa agus do mo cháirde, meoin, inntleacht, éirim aigne, spiorad ná meisneach a bheith aige. Is againne atá an t-eolas go léir; is againne atá an ceart; aoinne nach bhfuil ar aon aigne linne, ní ceart aon chaidreamh a dhéanamh leis; namha don Ghaedhilg agus do Ghaedhealachas é. 'Aengus' added: 'All of this is a sign of spiritual and mental slavery' (Comhartha sclábhaidheachta anama agus aigne an méid seo go léir). In his column in the inaugural issue of *An Tír*, 'Aengus' stated his own intention to review books fairly and objectively, and stressed the need for such criticism in Irish (*Tír*, Mar. 1928, 3). His intentions were praised by Ó Grianna in a review of the new journal (*FL*, Apr. 1928, 8). In 1931, Seán Ó Ciarghusa made the same point with tongue in cheek. He first commented on the general spitefulness of many of his colleagues, and then illustrated his point by analysing Hamlet's famous 'To be or not to be' soliloquy according to the rigid linguistic criteria favoured by Gaelic critics (*Leader*, 26/12/31). Those whose work was criticised rarely suffered in silence. For example, in a 1937 article in *An t-Ultach* entitled 'Léirmheas ar an Léirmheastóir' (A review of the reviewer), Seaghán Mac Meanman responded to a negative review of his *Trí Mion-Dráma* by Séamus Ó Néill by labelling the reviewer 'this buck' (an boc seo) and a petty, bitter, mean-hearted enemy' (namhaid bheag shearbh chumhang-chroidheach) (*Ultach*, Jan. 1937, 3).

62 Is gnáthach cúpla focal a scríobh fé leabhra nua chun a chur a n-úil do'n phobal go bhfuil a leithéidí ar an margadh. Má's leabhar maith é agus go mór mór má's leabhar é ó pheann ughdair a bhfuil clú na scéaluidheachta air cheana féin ní gádh a thuille a rádh.

63 Bhéadh an méid céadna eolais – nó bfhéidir a thuilleadh – fáighte agat ach dul agus breathnughadh isteach i bhfuinneóig aon tsiopa leabhar.

64 That Mac Liammóir was aware that he was challenging Gaelic orthodoxy in this essay is evident from the letter dated 5 June 1923 he wrote to the editor of *An Sguab*, Éamonn Mac Giolla Iasachta: 'You probably will not agree with the opinions I have expressed. I am not certain that I agree with them entirely myself. But it came into my head to write them, and if it does nothing but anger someone I will have done something' (Ní dócha go n-aontóchaidh tú leis na tuairimí atá nochtuithe agam. Nílim cinnte go n-aontuighim féin leo ar chuile bhealach. Acht tháinig sé 'mo cheann a sgríobha, agus muna ndéanann sé acht fearg chur ar dhuine éigin beidh rud eicínt déanta agam) (MacLysaght Papers, NLI MS 8560 {3}).

65 Corkery also had a great deal to say on literature in Irish in articles and reviews he published in English throughout our period. Moreover, as Alf Mac Lochlainn has shown in a recent article on a 1925 letter from Corkery to Art Ó Riain, his advice to young writers was both aesthetically informed and broadminded. See Mac Lochlainn, 'Corkery's Advice to a Young Writer', *Éire-Ireland*, 35, 1–2 (Spring–Summer, 2000), 219–25.

66 This was the text of a lecture delivered by Breathnach to a convention of secondary school teachers. Reports of lectures in Irish on literary topics appeared with some regularity in the journals of the period, often including sections of the text. Literary lectures in Irish were also heard regularly on Irish radio. Often these consisted of broadcasts of 15-minute lectures to An Fáinne.

67 Ua Laoghaire was the most popular subject of critical essays during our period.

68 In a 1929 piece, Ó Rinn called for the creation of a monthly periodical to review all books in Irish and other books of importance in any language. He felt such a periodical would, among other things, foster the growth of a critical vocabulary in Irish.

69 See also the comic essays on literature written by Ciarán Ua Nualláin, the brother of Brian Ua Nualláin: 'Amhras i gCúrsaí Litridheachta / Bristear ar an Suaimhneas Mharbhthach' (Uncertainty in literary affairs / Let the deadly quiet be broken), *IP*, 2/8/38; 'When the Reader Groans – The Author Has Slipped', *II*, 21/4/39; and 'An Uadhacht / Fuasclann Sé Gach Fadhb / Cabhair do Scríbhneoirí' (The will / It solves every problem / Help for writers), *II*, 25/7/39.

70 Má tá tábhacht ar bith i n-ár laetheanta, má tá rud éigin thar caithcamh aimsire i n-ár mbeatha, cad déarfaimíd faoi'n t-é a mholann iad is a dheineann árd-shagart le págántacht de féin ós cóir an phobail? Má's fíor ní ar bith faoi'n gceist seo, sé gur árd-thábhachtach an duine an léirmheastóir; go bhfuil freagarthacht mhór air . . . Úsáideamair an focal 'árd-shagart' ó chianaibhín. Ba chóir go mbéadh an léirmheastóir 'na árd-shagart, gan amhras; ach chuige sin níor mhór naomhthacht beatha is glaine chroidhe, is an smaoineamh is an gníomh uasal a thogha amach mar chuspóir. Seadh, is níorbh olc an t-ullmhú, i dteannta neithe eile, caibideal de'n Tiomna Nua le h-aghaidh an lae. It was above all for its high moral tone that Mac Clúin's book was praised by one reviewer. See C. Edwards, 'Thoughts on Irish Literature / The High Road', *II*, 9/12/28.

71 He did, however, wonder, why Mac Clúin had nothing to say about newer writers like Mac Grianna and Mac Liammóir. Shán Ó Cuív agreed with 'Brian Dubh' both about the book's heavy reliance on English sources and on its importance as a pioneering contribution (*II*, 25/10/26). Seaghán Mac Meanman was entirely unimpressed by the book, charging that Mac Clúin must have written the book in English and then produced a 'bricklaying translation'. See Mac Meanman, Letter to Muiris Ó Droighneáin, 3 Jan. 1928, quoted in Ó Droighneáin, '"Bricklaying Translation!"' *Feasta*, May 1964, 7. Mac Clúin denied the charge in a letter to Ó Droighneáin dated 11 Feb. 1928 and quoted in the same essay.

72 Ag cur an leabhair seo le chéile dhom séard a bhí uaim ná cur síos a dhéanamh, i nGaedhilg shimplidhe, ar sgríbhinní ughdar áirithe na Gaedhilge le hionchas go músglóchthaí suim an léightheora i n-ár litridheacht féin agus go dtabharfaí congnamh éigin chun deagh-litridheacht a aithneachtáil agus a mheas . . . Giotaí Gaedhilge a thaithnigh liom féin is mó atá sa chnuasach seo agus dá bhrigh sin is beag cáineadh a bhéas le tabhairt faoi deara ins na tuairimí atá nochtuighthe agam in a dtaobh. Ó Raghallaigh also published *Litridheacht na Gaedhilge* (BAC: Brún agus Ó Nualláin, Teor., n.d.) as a kind of companion to *An Léirmheastóir*. The former is very much a school reader, with excerpts taken from writing in Irish since the start of the revival.

73 Tá a fhios agam gur dána an mhaise damh leabhar a sgríobhadh ar nua-sgríbhneoirí na Gaedhilge. Tá a fhios agam nach mbéidh aon-duine dá bhfuil beo indiu de na sgríbhneoirí sin sásta leis an mhéid atá ráite agam fá n-a shaothar liteardha. Ach ní le fonn na hughdair a shásamh ach le fonn ciudiú leis an aos óg a mbéidh ortha stuidéar a dhéanamh ar a saothar a thug orm an leabhar a chur i gcionn a chéile. Tá a shúil agam nach bhfuil éagcóir déanta agam ar ughdar ar bith. Má tá, ní le mailís ach de dhíoghbháil dearcaidh a rinneas í.

74 Ó Searcaigh's book was savaged by Seán Ua Ceallaigh ('Mogh Ruith') in his review for the *Catholic Bulletin*:

> Without going so far as to state that there may not be some area in the country where this strange diction will pass muster, one may say with safety that it will be regarded generally as sorry stuff indeed. That there should be even a seeming need for a production of this kind with a National University in our midst this quarter of a century is truly a depressing reflection. Whether a book which would bristle with inspiration, but will be searched in vain for an edifying thought, will bring lustre to the University Degree or render a distinct disservice to Irish composition is for those who may read it to judge (*CB*, Jan. 1934, 61).

Ó Searcaigh held a doctorate from UCD. Writing in *The Leader* a few months later, 'Ultach' blasted Ua Ceallaigh for what he felt to be an ignorant review and called instead for 'constructive literary criticism of the work of Gaelic authors . . . at this period of the growth of our native literature' (*Leader*, 5/5/34). The reviewer for *The Leader*, 'Conall Gulban' praised Ó Searcaigh's book as 'a notable contribution to constructive and scholarly Gaelic criticism' (*Leader*, 11/11/33).

75 Toisc an aithne a bhí agam ortha, do bhí tomhas agam chun a saothair do mheas ná beadh ag an té ná feacaidh riamh iad 'na shúilibh cinn, agus nár airigh riamh a nglór agus ná raibh aon eolas aige i dtaobh a n-éirim aigne agus na dtréithe a bhí ionnta ó dhúchas agus ó oiliúint agus ón saol a chaitheadar, ach pé méid a gheóbhadh sé ós na sgríbhinní d'fhágadar 'na ndiaidh.

76 Is maith an bhail orainn a gcuid saothair bheith againn chun sinn a chosaint ar an sgríbhneoireacht éireochaidh as an saoghal nua atá ann anois nuair is líonmhaire iad lucht foghluma na Gaedhilge ná na daoine a labhrann an teanga go nádúrtha. Is mór an chontabhairt don teangain an saoghal nua san.

77 He called Pádraic Ó Conaire 'príomh-ughdar Gaedhilgeoirí an iarthair . . . agus príomh-sgéalaidhe na Nua-Ghaedhilge' (p. 44).

78 Isé gnó an staruidhe litridheachta, ag cur síos dó ar ré fé leith, ughdair na ré sin d'áireamh, agus cunntas do thabhairt ar a mbeatha, mar aon leis an oighreacht d'fhágadar againn. Agus a chur leis sin tuairisc éigin ar na 'gluaiseachta' is mó dár thárla san litridheacht cor na ré sin. Nuair a théigheann an staruidhe thairis sin ní bhíonn aige acht tuairmidheacht, agus tá a fhios ag an saoghal nach 'lia fear ná tuairim.' Beidh a thuairim ag cách is cuma cad déarfaidh an staruidhe. Agus an té go dteastuigheann tuairim uaidh, léigheadh sé féin an litridheacht agus cheapadh sé a thuairim féin di. Nach chuige sin a scríobhtar stair litridheachta? Reviewing the book for *An t-Ultach*, Séamus Ó Néill regretted Ó Droighneáin's unwillingness to share his opinions regarding the work of the authors he discussed (*Ultach*, July, 1937, 3).

79 All of these were published by An Gúm. In addition, he edited an annotated anthology of poetry by Keating, Haicéad, Ó Bruadair, and others as *Duanarán re 1600–1700* (An anthology of poetry of the period 1600–1700) (BÁC: C.S. Ó Fallamhain, Teor., 1935); and a school text of eighteenth-century poetry, *Scoth-Dhuanta maille re Cumair-Scéal ar Bheatha a n-Ughdar agus Gearra-Ghluais Acarthach* (Major poems with concise biographies of their authors and a convenient short glossary) (BÁC: Brún agus Ó Nualláin, Teor. [1933]). For the most part Ó Foghludha offered little if anything in the way of literary criticism, preferring instead to sketch historical contexts and provide notes explaining difficult words and phrases.

80 Rud nua é seo ag léirmheasaidhe a thráchtann an [*sic*] litridheacht Ghaedhilge. Ard-mholadh nó dian-cháineadh an gnáth-rud agus is minic gur baoth a bhíd. Ach tá slaitín tomhais ag Piaras agus tomhaiseann sé filidheacht gach duine de na scríobhnóirí dá réir. In his positive review in *II* (26/9/33), Shán Ó Cuív disagreed with some of Béaslaí's ideas, but acknowledged his authority and hoped his work would stir debate. Seán Ó Ciarghusa also praised Béaslaí highly, although he did question whether Béaslaí felt criticism of Irish needed to be in Irish (*Leader*, 4/11/33). Incidentally, Ó Ciarghusa's own critical work as collected in his book *Ar Mo Mharanadh Dom* was praised by Ó Cuív as 'an attempt to cultivate the Irish language to express ideas on literary matters' (iarracht ar an nGaedhilg do shaothrú chun smaointe do nochtadh ar chúrsaí leitríochta) (*II*, 24/3/33). In a 1932 essay on '"Clann Lóip" / An Daor-Chlann agus na Filí' ('Clann Lóbuis' / The rabble and the poets) (*II*, 16/5/32), Béaslaí discussed in erudite fashion the seventeenth-century satire *Pairlement Chloinne Tomáis* (The Parliament of Clan Thomas).

81 Déarfadh sé, ós rud é ná fuil nós fáis na Gaeilge socair ar fad mar atá nós fáis an Bhéarla, nár dheacair dúinn an Ghaeilge a mhúnlú de réir ár dtoile. B'é a shíor-ghearán gur claonadh chun Béarlachais pé claonadh atá inti chun na hiasachta agus, in ionad bheith ag cur ina choinnibh sin, gurb amhlaidh a leanaimid lorg an Bhéarla amhail is dá mb'é 'an chaighdeán daonna' é. Both McKenna and Ó Rinn felt it was essential that Gaels explore and cultivate the resources of Dinneen's dictionary to enrich the language (pp. 80, 97–8, 106).

82 Taibhsítear dom go bhfuil tabharthaistí móra nó tabharthaistí maithe á ndiomailt ag scríbhneoirí Gaeilge le corp easpa machnaimh. Samhlaím iad le fear gur mhaith leis bean uasal d'fháil le pósadh. Nuair a théann sé chuici chun í bhuachtaint dó féin bheireann sé leis, i dteannta cumhacht iomlán a intleachta is draíocht uile a phearsan, an coinleach féasóige atá ag fás le seachtain agus an coiléar is an ciarsúir nár níodh le ráithe.

83 Smaointe an ní is mó atá de dhíth orainn, smaointe agus stíl láidir chumhachtach; soiléire a choimeád ina lán-dúiseacht ag tabhairt aire do chaint. Dar liom is fearr formhór na bhfógraí tráchtála mar scríbhneoireacht ná formhór na gclasaicí. Féach orthu! Caint díreach a thugan buille sa tsúil duit is a théann isteach it inchinn, a leanann it chuimhne, a chlingeann it thaibhrithe, a mheallann an t-airgead as do phóca.

84 Is déine-de an obair a chaithfidh scríbhneoirí Gaeilge dhéanamh gan aon mhórlitríocht nua-aimseartha bheith againn fós agus dá bhrí sin gan aon chabhair a bheith le fáil acu mar a bhíonn le fáil ar iomad slite ag ábhar scríbhneora Bhéarla. Níl éinne ann, cuir i gcás, chun breith do thabhairt ar a gcéad-iarrachtaí. See also Ó Rinn's essays 'Prós Rithimiúil' (Rythmic prose), *IP*, 17/4/39; and 'Ag Ceapadh Rann' (Composing verses), *IP*, 23/5/39.

85 Ní mór an léitheoir is mian linn (agus is ró-riachtanach dúinn) a thréineáil . . . nó go mbeidh sé chomh maith san go mbeidh áthas air (go coinníollach) díreach mar gheall ar an deacracht a bhaineann le nuacht: Ná déanadh sé, Ó ná déanadh choíche, i bpéin an pheaca mharfaigh, ná déanadh sé go brách ar aon chúinnse bolathú chuige, á rá, 'Go hait: crua-chaint.' Abradh sé, le mionghháirí ardghlóracha, 'Míle buíochas le Dia, seo rud éigin chun faobhar a chur ar ár meabhair;' bíodh sé ar buile chun dul i ngleic leis an ní atá nua aduain, agus is deacair a thuiscint.

86 McKenna called for 'ní is mó go mór tábhacht i láthair na huaire ná aon tsórt litríochta a scríobhtar le L mór is a luaitear le hanáil choiscthe, sé sin, togha stuif le léamh ar nithe a dteastaíonn ó ghnáthdhaoine síbhialta den fhichiú aois bheith ag léamh trácht orthu. Le déithe is ard-ollaimh a bhaineann litríocht agus san aois seo is cosúla le caint na nuachtán an ní a dhéanfadh teanga, agus ní mór roinnt mhaith truiféise bheith ann, ach nach truiféis draíochta é, bíodh a fhios agat, ná fós truiféis phiseog ná truiféis sean-scéalta tuatha, ach Garvice-íocht is a leithéid . . . An Ghaeilge ná beadh inti ach Dante, dhamnódh sí í féin; Charles Garvice mo rogha den bheirt.' See also pp. 176–7.

87 Nuair adeirtear an focal beannaithe sin 'litríocht' is mó duine chuimhníonn i gcéadóir ar Hómér is ar Dhante, ar Shakespeare is ar Dhostoievski. Dá mbeadh ceathrar dá samhail sin againn dob oirearc an tabhartas ó Dhia iad, ach monuar! is annamh a chítear a gcomh-ghile sin de réalta i gcuanta na spéire liteartha. Le linn a n-uireasa chaoineadh áfach, fiafraímis dínn féin an iad an sórt údar iad do réifeadh ród romhainn is do riarfadh ár gcás. Is éigean dúinn an ní is feas do chách d'admháil, eadhon, nach iad na húdair mhór-uaisle is mó thaithíonn formhór na ndaoine i gcrích ar bith. Dá mbeadh Shakespeare Gaelach againn níor mhór dúinn Edgar Wallace Gaelach leis. See also pp. 12–13.

88 Dar leo, is amaideach do chreidte iad na sgéalta sidhe agus san am chéadna léighid siad go fonnmhar sgéalta nach bhfuil bun ná bárr leo. Furmhór na ndaoine, bainid siad feidhm as leabhar mar do bhainfidís feidhm as biorán suain – chun codladh do chur ortha féin.

89 Féachaidh féin an scubhadh [*sic*] a bhíonn ortha [na daoine óga] chun na 'Buffalo Bills' agus na 'Secston Blakes', siúd is nach mbíonn ionnta san acht droch-Bhéarla is gan pioc de dheallramh na fírinne ag bainnt leo. Budh dhána an mhaise dhom é, is dócha, moladh do lucht scríobhtha na Gaedhilge aithris a dhéanamh ar 'Buffalo' agus ar 'Secston', acht dá luaithe déanfar é 'seadh is fearr an dul bheidh ag an nGaedhilg ar bhuadhchaint ar an mBéarla. This was an ongoing concern for Breathnach. See 'Scríobhnóirí na Nua-Ghaedhilge' (The writers of Modern Irish), *Dundalk Examiner*, 25/4/31. That Breathnach had an accurate sense of what Irish readers were interested in is evident from various reports on library circulation. See, for example, 'Galway's Good Taste / Work of County Library / Cultivation of Gaelic / Popular Authors', *II*, 19/10/36; and '"Wild West" Fiction Is Most Popular', *IP*, 6/9/38. For a general discussion of what the Irish were reading in the 1930s, see Elizabeth Russell, 'Holy Crosses, Guns and Roses: Themes in Popular Reading Material', in *Ireland in the 1930s*, ed. Augusteijn, 11–28.

90 Tá muid ag iarraidh barraidheacht ar an ghnáthdhuine agus ag nochtadh nach bhfuil aithne ar dhúthchas an duine againn má iarrann muid air leabharthaí a cheannach agus a léigheadh siocair amháin gur leabharthaí Gaedhilge iad, gan a fhiafruighe dínn féin an léighfeadh sé iad dá mbeadh siad i mBéarla. Tá sé soilléir dá mbeadh leabharthaí Gaedhilge comh suimeamhail aige agus atá leabharthaí Béarla, go léighfeadh sé iad.

91 Go dtí ar na fíor-mhallaibh is beag a sgríobhadh acht fá choinne lucht foghlumtha na Gaedhilge. Caithfear a ghabháil giota níos fuide 'un tosaigh. Caithfear an uile chineál rudaí a sgríobhadh a mbíonn suim na ndaoiní ionnta. Caithfear sgéaltaí a sgríobhadh a léighfear mar léigh mise 'Geanntraighe' – mé 'mo shuidhe ag caitheamh mo phíopa agus gan mé ag smaoitiughadh ar chor ar bith gur i nGaedhilg a bhí na sgéalta sgríobhtha.

92 Ádhbhar léightheórachta do'n phobal atá uainn. Tá an iomad trácht ar an litridheacht, sé sin má dhallann an trácht sinn maidir le neithe a sholáthar a chabhróchaidh le gnáth-bheo-theanga náisiúnta a dhéanamh de'n Ghaedhilg. See also, 'Grafan', 'Tá Ádhbhar Scríobhnóirí Ann!' (The makings of writers exist!), *IP*, 19/4/32.

93 Cé gur dhána an gnó damh-sa tabhairt fé n-a leithéid, do bheartuigheas ar dhíchillín mo chroidhe do chur le iarracht chun sgéal do chumadh 'n-a mbeadh eachtraí agus beodhacht innste, agus olcas agus maitheas; do chuireas rómham scéal do chumadh ná caithfeadh an léightheoir uaidh sul a mbeadh a leath léighte aige. Ní fios dam ar éirigh liom; is é an léightheoir an breitheamh.

94 Gan aon fhiacail do chur ann, 'Deadwood Dick' Gaedhealach atá sa scéal. The anonymous critic for *The Leader* (14/11/25) also invoked Deadwood Dick in his laudatory review of the book. Reviewing Ó Gríobhtha's historical novel *Briathar Mná* (A woman's word) for *II* (23/7/28), 'M. Ua M.' praised the author for once again creating 'something new in literature in Irish' (rud nua i litridheacht na Gaedhilge).

95 In his preface (p. 4), Ó Gríobhtha was explicit that he wrote to edify as well as amuse his readers.

96 He had serialised some of the novel in *An Sguab* in 1924.

97 There were also at least two stories with Native American protagonists: Éanraoi Ó Gráda's 'Séamus Gnóthach' (Busy James) (serialised in *An Gaedheal* from 4/8/34 to 18/8/34); and the schoolboy Pádraig Ó Riain's 'Glór an Iarthair Thuaidh' (The voice of the Northwest) (*The Rock*, Autumn and Winter 1936).

98 See Ó Dubhshláine, 'Scéal Úirscéil: *Fánaí*, Seán Óg Ó Caomhánaigh, 1927' (The story of a novel: *Fánaí*, Seán Óg Ó Caomhánaigh, 1927), *Léachtaí Cholm Cille* 19 (1989), 93–128.

99 Titley, *An t-Úrscéal*, 98.

100 Ní dheaghaidh aon staon ar an gcoimheascar eatartha. Níor ghaibh aon náire eisean. Níor thaithighe leis mná ghá dhiúltughadh . . . Lé n-a raibh de neart innte do bhuail sí lé na dhá dorn isteach sa fiaclaibh é. Níor dhein seisean ach leamhgháire fé na hiarracht. Thug sé seáp eile ar í do chlaoidheachtaint. Screuch sí.

101 Shílfeá mar sin, go mbeadh na céadta daobhtha seo á scríobhadh i nGaedhilg. Shílfeá ar mhaithe leis an phobal a mhealladh le leabharthaí Gaedhilge a léigheadh go mbeadh níos mó aca ann ná de shaghas ar bith eile. Ua Nualláin was hard on the translated detective novels published by An Gúm, calling them 'translations no one reads because they have already read them in English' (aistriúcháin nach léigheann aoinne siocair go bhfuil siad léighte cheana i mBéarla aige).

102 Tá an 'Gúm' ag cur Gaedhilge ar scéalta bleachtaireachta – agus níl beirt ar aon aigne i dtaobh ciaca

moladh nó cáineadh ba cheart a thabhairt do'n iarracht so. Is beag duine, ámh, a thuigeann stair an scéil lorgaireachta, ná a smaoinigh seal ar a thréithe, siúd is gurab é an braith-scéal an saghas litríochta is mó a bhfuil éileamh air fé láthair. Ó Brolcháin provided a brief history of the genre in his four broadcasts, published as 'An Lorgaireacht' (Detective work) (8/5/39); 'An Chéad Scéal Lorgaireachta' (The first detective story) (12/8/39); 'Sherlock Holmes: Árd-Bhleachtaire na Litríochta' (Sherlock Holmes: The great detective of literature) (18/8/39); and 'Braith-Scéalta na Linne Seo' (Contemporary detective stories) (25/8/39).

103 Tá deas-Ghaoluinn air, ach 'na dhiaidh sin scéal ní ba Ghallda ná é níor léigheas riamh. Níl ann ach cur síos ar an gcuma a bhíonn daoine mí-ámharacha dá ngéar-leanúint ag lucht an dlí: ach níl sé ró-mhaith mar scéal lorgaireachta féin, óir tuiteann a lán rudaí amach i rith an scéil ná tuiteann amach ar an saol dáiríribh. Shilling Shocker iseadh é a gheobhadh buachaill scoile ar na siopaí i Sasana aon lá sa tseachtain. Republicans would obviously have had little affection for detectives at this time.

104 'An Duine Marbh ar an tSráid / Mistéir na Cathrach' (The dead person on the street / An urban mystery) by 'Cian-Éisteoir' is not a true detective story, but rather tells how an innocent man is cleared of a crime for which he has been imprisoned after a friend reads of his arrest and is able to clear up the misunderstanding (*II*, 30/7/31). Another aspect of the criminal justice system of the time was the subject of 'Caidreamh Beirte sa Tréan / An Crochaire' (A relationship between two people in the train / The hangman) by 'Cnáib', a story dealing with the English hangman the Irish government employed for executions (*II*, 22/9/28).

105 See, for example, pp. 105, 141–2.

106 The play was first produced by An Comhar Drámaidheachta in the Gate Theatre in 1923 under the direction of Micheál Mac Liammóir, and won Craobh Órdha an Chomhair Drámaidheachta for 1932–3.

107 The play has never been published. It was performed by An Comhar Drámaidheachta at the Abbey Theatre in 1925. See the positive review by 'Oscar', who saw the play as 'the first attempt . . . to produce a play not based on action on an Irish-language stage' (an chéad iarracht . . ar chluiche 'neamh-ghníomhach' do léiriú ar stáitse Gaedhilge) (*FL*, 14/11/25). See also, 'Dráma Nua Eile / Gáirí agus Greann in Amharclann na Mainistreach' (Another new play / Laughs and humour in the Abbey Theatre), *II*, 3/11/25; and 'Current Affairs', *Leader*, 7/11/25. For another language parable, see C. B. Mac Séamuis's story 'Sgéal an Bhréidín / Dream Daoine a Bhí in Oileán Beag san Am a Chuaidh thart' (The story of the homespun cloth / A group of people who were on a small island in the past), *II*, 21/8/39. *Tart* (Thirst), another unpublished play set in the future, deals with the coming of prohibition to Ireland in 1950! See 'Galway Gaelic Theatre / Three New Plays', *IT*, 25/11/39.

108 The schoolboy M. Ó Raghallaigh offered another picture of the future in his dream story 'Éire mar a Bhéas Sí i gcionn Seascadh Bliadhan' (Ireland as it will be in sixty years) (*The Rockwell Annual*, June 1936, 70). His Ireland of the 1990s is an imperial power, ruling, among others, England, the United States, and Egypt. In addition, there are no more schools, all necessary information being implanted by a surgical procedure.

109 In addition to the surgical solution to the challenges of education noted above, M. Ó Raghallaigh's people of the future travel in self-propelled personal vehicles that move on tracks.

110 De thoradh a shíor-thadhaill le hiolsadhas inneall do thárla rud gur ar éigin leómhfad a luadh. Thárla claochlódh damanta istigh i gcroidhe agus in aigne an fhir. Do théaltuigh a thoil. Do chalcuigh a mheabhar chinn. Do thráigh féith na filidheachta agus do dhoirchigh solas an chreidimh agus an ghrádha aige. Fuair an meicneachas treise ar an ndaonnacht aige. Do réir mar chuaidh a thréithe Gaedhil i mbádhadh connacthas airdheanna an innill 'na n-ionad. 'Sa deire níor chreidte go raibh sé 'na dhuine ná 'na inneall acht idir a bheith eatorra.

111 Brúighfear nósa bhur sinnsear fé chois ag Duinneall na bhfaisean. Crosfar dráma agus ceol oraibh ag Duinneall an tSoin-mheaisín. Bainfidh Duinneall Státaire bhur saoirse dhíbh. Bainfidh scoith na nDuinneall – Duinneall Saighdiúir – bhur mbaill bheathadh dhíbh. Agus mar bhárr donais ní fhágfaidh Duinneall Feallsamh bhur n-anam spioradálta agaibh. Ó Torna ends with a moral for his own troubled time and ours: 'Duinneall seeks total power. He is a dictator who surpasses Hitler and Stalin. No weapon wounds him except for the weapon he does not believe exists. The weapon of truth will defeat him' (Loirgeann Duinneall ollchomhacht. Is déachtóir é a sháruigheann Hitler agus Stalin. Ní dheargann arm air acht amháin an t-arm ná creideann sé a bheith ann. Arm na fírinne is ea a chlaoidhfidh é).

112 Ní bhaineann an cogadh so linne . . . agus ní mian linne baint leis. Táimíd ghá fhóghairt don domhan uile, agus go h-áirithe dos na tíortha atá ag troid, ná fuilimíd agus ná beimíd ar aon taobh, an fhaid ná cuirfear cath orainn. Má tá báidh ag Éireannaigh le h-aon taobh aca nó má tá fuath aca d'aon taobh aca isé a mbuac gan an bháidh sin ná an fuath san do nochtadh. Béal iadhta, obair dhíchealllach, agus muinighin as Dia – sin í mo chomhairle-sa dhíbh.

113 In 1940, Máiréad Ní Ghráda published *Manannán* (BÁC: OS, 1940), the tale of a mysterious new planet given the name of the Irish sea god after its discovery by an Irish astronomer. Éamon Ó

Ciosáin sees this as the first science fiction book in Irish ('Máiréad Ní Ghráda agus a Saothar Liteartha', in Ní Ghráda, *An Triail / Breithiúnas: Dhá Dhráma*, ed. Ó Ciosáin (BAC: OS, 1978), 179. He has a point, given that Ó Riain's *An Tost* was published with other stories that were not science fiction.

114 Ó Nualláin, 'An Hata', in *Tighearna an Tailimh*, 19–42.

115 Ó Cuirrín, 'Beirt Dhéiseach' (Two men from the Decies), in *Beirt Dhéiseach, mar atá Sceul Nua-Cheaptha agus Trí Sceulta arna dTiontódh ó Theangthacha Eile* (Two men from the Decies, that is an original story and three stories translated from other languages) (BAC: OS, 1936), 1–33. In his diaries, Seosamh Mac Grianna outlined ideas for a series of 'Stories of Wealth', one of which was to be set in South Africa and deal with prospecting for diamonds.

116 Ó Broin, 'An Rún', in *An Rún*, 7–21.

117 An tAthair Casáin, 'An Seirbhíseach Foghanta Dílis', in *An Londubh*, 87–99.

118 The play was produced by An Comhar Drámaidheachta at the Abbey Theatre in 1925.

119 In Mac Liammóir's 'Caitlín', a young man on vacation in Conamara is visited in a dream by a comforting vision of his sister, who is in Paris. On awakening, he is given a telegram informing him she has just died (*Misneach*, 31/12/21).

120 Ó Nualláin, 'An Sprid', in *Tighearna an Tailimh*, 85–101.

121 For a discussion of this story, see Pádraig Ó Croiligh, 'Éifeacht an Ghnímh – Staidéar Éadomhain ar an Scéal "Dhá Chroí Cloiche" le Seosamh Mac Grianna, i gCló ar *Humanitas*' (The significance of the act – A quick study of the story 'Dhá Chroí Cloiche' by Seosamh Mac Grianna, published in *Humanitas*), *IMN*, 1970, 7–12.

122 Tig linn b'fhéidir, úirscéalta a cheapadh a chuirfidh síos ar shaoghal na Gaedhealtachta indiu, acht is follus go dteipfidh glan ar a lán de sna leabhartha a thráchfaidh tar saoghal na cathrach. Bíonn so ann i gcúrsaí úirscéal – go mbaineann buaidh agus cómhacht an leabhair go dlúth le cainnt na ndaoine féin. Agus ó thárla nár chrom lucht na gcathrach ar a gcúrsaí do phléidhe as Gaedhilg go nuige seo, ní thiocfadh a bheith go mbeidh blas na fírinne ar a mbreacfaidh úghdair.

123 Is éachtach an éirim a bhíonn ag daoinibh óga ins an tsíbhéaltacht nua so againn . . . Tá a rian air, tá na bailtí móra agus na cathracha ag fás, acht is soiléir nách fás sláinteamhail é . . . Nuair a bheidh tailte a sinnsear ag Gaedhil arís, agus na déantúisí áiteamhla ar siubhal aca, agus cultúr amháin – an fíor-Ghaedhealachas ag ár ndaoinibh – annsan beidh rath Dé orainn agus a lámh linn.

124 Na daoine go léir, idir óg agus aosta, a' dul is a' teacht gan stad gan sos. A ghnaithe féin ag gach aon duine, solus na catha i súilibh na bhfear agus na mban. Mar feictear go mbíonn troid mhór neamh-fhuilteach ar siubhal i gcomhnuidhe i n-a n-aignidh agus n-a gcroidhthibh . . . Na páisdidhthe beaga féin, ní fhéadann siad gan bheith aosta roimh a n-am, tréigeann an solus a súla óga, agus an gáiridhe a gcroidhthe bochta, mar bíonn an chathair mhór, ar nós fathaigh gan trócaire, i n-a dtimcheall i gcomhnuidhe, agus a forann neamh-cheolmhar i n-a gcluasaibh.

125 Ó Conaire, quoted by An tSiúr Éibhlín Ní Chionnaith, in *Pádraic Ó Conaire: Scéal a Bheatha*, 396. An Census / Ag taispeáint cén drochbhail atá ar an tír. Ní hé méid na ndaoine atá i gceist agam ach an imirce go dtí an baile mór agus an saol atá iontu siúd. / Lobhadh an duine sa chathair. / Specialisation. See also, Ó Conaire, 'I Londain / Smaointe agus Eile' (In London / Thoughts, etc.), *CS*, 13/9/27; and 'Na Muca / Imnidhe agus Aithmhéala' (The pigs / Anxiety and regret), *CS*, 2/3/26.

126 See, for example, Seamus Deane, '*Mo Bhealach Féin*', in *The Pleasures of Gaelic Literature*, ed. John Jordan (Dublin: Mercier Press, 1977), 52–61; Declan Kiberd, '*Mo Bhealach Féin*: Idir Dhá Thraidisiún' (*Mo Bhealach Féin*: Between two traditions) in *Scríobh* 5 (1981), ed. Seán Ó Mordha, 84–93; and Liam Ó Dochartaigh, '*Mo Bhealach Féin*: Saothar Nualitríochta' (*Mo Bhealach Féin*: A work of modern literature), in *Scríobh* 5, 240–7.

127 Mac Grianna, 'Pádraic Ó Conaire', in *Pádraic Ó Conaire*, 15–16. Agus an té a chuaidh fríd Lonndain . . . fríd thoit agus cheó a bheir dubhlán ghrian na glóire – fríd dhaoiní tanaidhe gruamdha tostacha nach bhfuil feóil nó fuil ar a gcnámha nó machtnamh i n-a n-intinn; an té a chonnaic an abhainn mhór a rabh uisge seal inntí agus deallramh ar a h-ucht – an té a chonnaic í agus í ramhar le salachar agus an t-aer os a ceann ramhar le salachar . . . an té a chonnaic urraim an dlighidh, agus faillighe an dúthchais – an té a chonnaic adhradh na ngníomh agus dí-mheas na h-intinne a chuireas maise ar an ghníomh; an té a bhí i Lonndain, le sgéal fada a dhéanamh goirid, tuigeann sé an buaidhreadh intinne nach socruigheann go sochruighidh féar na h-uaighe é. In a 1926 piece on the Gaeltacht, he compared urban people to ants (*Ultach*, May 1926, 2).

128 Oidhche amháin ag dul suas a luighe domh, agus mé ag meabhrughadh go mór fá mo chroidhe, fuair mé colmán 'n-a sheasamh os ceann m'fhuinneóige. Bhí sé cosamhail le teachtaire ó shaoghal eile, saoghal fairsing a rabh sgáilí air agus contabhairt ann, saoghal a mheallfadh thú mar bhéadh ceól a chluinfeá i bhfad uait agus a dheas duit, saoghal an tsluagh sídhe . . . B'fhéidir gurbh' é an dúthchas é, b'fhéidir gurbh' é an oileamhain é, acht is é an chéad rud a rinne mé iarraidh a thabhairt an colmán sin a cheapadh. Ba sin an uair a bhí an seomra cumhang. Bhí sé comh cumhang agus go roinnfeadh an colmán a chnámha air acht go bé gur fhosgail mé an fhuinneóg. Thug sé léim fhada anonn trasna na sráide . . .

Mhair an léim fhada sin a bhí comh huasal le tuinn, mhair sí i m'aigneadh ó shoin agus cnap bróin i n-aice léithe. See Oilibhéar Ó Croiligh, 'Idir Dhá Cheann na h-Imní – Bealach Mhic Grianna' (On the horns of a dilemma – Mac Grianna's way), *IMN*, 1967, 12–25.

129 Ó Séaghdha, 'Draoidheacht na Gaedhilge', in *Dhá Sgéal*, 66. Ba rígh-mhinic mo cheann 'n bhulla báisín acu ó bheith ag feuchaint ortha ag gabháil tharm; is go deo na ndeor ní chloisfá duine ag beannú do'n duine eile. Rud eile a thugas fé ndeara leis, ná bíodh aon fhonn gháiridhe ar cheachtar acu.

130 Bhí an áit beo beithidheach le daoiní agus iad uilig fá dheifre, ag teacht agus ag imtheacht 'acha'n chasán. Bhí 'acha'n chineál daoiní annseo, ó dhuine liath go leanbh, agus a bhuaidhreadh féin ar 'acha'n dhuine. Bhí buachaillí óga agus cailíní ag gabháil thart le Cathal agus iad ag caint agus ag gáiridhe, agus ag déanamh grinn . . . Ba dheas a bheith sa bhaile anocht . . . agus nár dheas a bheith ag éisteacht le comhrádh laghach a mháthara, le taoibh a bheith ag éisteacht leis an tormán uathbhásach seo ag búirthidh ina chluasa ó mhaidin go meadhon-oidhche!

131 Ó Domhnalláin, 'In Ospidéal', in *Dréachta*, 20. Níorbh fhios dom go raibh sé tinn chor ar bith. Ach bheadh do chomharsa béil dorais in uachta báis, b'fhéidir, i mBaile Átha Cliath is ní bheadh a fhios agat é. Ní coimhthíochas go coimhthíochas Átha Cliath!

132 Is maith mar a chuireann an t-ughdar síos ar an saoghal 'sa chathair, agus ar a uaignighe bhíonn an fear tuatha go minic ann. Actually, at one point in this novel Ó Baoighill paints an interesting picture of urban diversity in his description of people in line outside a Dublin cinema (pp. 42–3).

133 Tá na sluaighte 'n-a dtost i mBaile-Átha-Cliath, agus ní fhuil cóirnéal sráide a seasuigheann tú ann nach mbuailtear leat fir agus mná ag cuartughadh déirce. Tá muinntir na tuaithe, 'tchítear damh, an-tugtha do theacht 'na cathrach agus is mór an truaigh é. Má tá siad bocht 'san tír beidh a sheacht n-oiread bochtaineachta rompa má fhágfar ar sráid an bhaile mhóir iad i muinighin na déirce.

134 Badh cheart iad do choimeád i bhfad amach ós na cathracha mar deineann na cathracha dradairí agus spriosáin díobh. Sa Ghaedhealtacht atá an chuid is fearr do mhuinntir na tuaithe . . . Badh cheart muinntir na tuaithe a chosaint ar na cathracha agus badh cheart tosnú leis an nGaedhealtacht.

135 Sa chathair bíonn na sluaighte daoine ag gabháil mar seo is mar siúd; a chúram féin ag gach duine aca. Bíonn gach saghas duine ann: an duine bocht, an duine saidhbhir, amadáin, lucht chéille, lucht na calaoise, lucht na macántachta. Budh dhóigh le duine gur i n-áit dá leithéid do b'usa dhó dlúth-mhachtnamh do dhéanamh ar an gcine daonna agus air féin fá leith. Acht ní mar sin atá. Téigheann na sluaighte tar bhrághaid, acht ní thuigeann tú a gcúrsaí agus ní thuigfir go bráth . . . Is maith agus is tairbheach an rud an chathair do bheith ann; acht ní miste do dhuine ar uairibh an chathair do thréigean agus dul ó n-a cuid fothraim. Dinneen offered a less favourable view of the city in 'Laghdughadh na gCatoiliceach le Céad Bliadhan Anuas' (The decline of the Catholic population over the past hundred years), *Standard*, 20/7/29.

136 Ní'l sárughadh lucht Bhaile Átha Cliath le fagháil i n-aon chathair eile ar chneastacht, ar shibhialtacht, ar mhuinnteardhas. Moreover, he praised them for 'the savouriness of their speech, particularly when they speak their native language' (blastacht a gcuid cainnte, go mórmór nuair a labhraid 'na dteangain dúthchais), presumably acknowledging thereby the potential for an acceptable, even pleasing, new dialect – Dublin Irish. The following month, Dinneen published another article with the significant title 'Meas is Cion ar Bhaile Átha Cliath' (Respect and affection for Dublin), in which he wrote that everyone loves Dublin (*Leader*, 12/11/27). Seán M. Ó Fiathcháin also found Dubliners pleasant and cheerful people. See his 'Muintir na Cathrach / Tá a Saol Dian ach Táid Geal-Gháiritheach' (The people of the city / Their life is hard, but they are light-hearted) (*Hibernia*, June 1937, 11). That Dinneen himself was comfortable writing about contemporary urban life in Irish is evident from stories like 'An Chulaith Bhaistidh' (The baptismal clothes) (*Leader*, 23/3/24) and 'An Fáinne nár Aimsigh an Chuideachta' (The ring that the company did not find) (*Leader*, 7/5/27), with their middle-class Dublin settings far removed from the circumstances of everyday life in the Gaeltacht.

137 Ní Ghráda, 'Sos Comhraic', in *An Bheirt Dearbhráthar*, 31–50.

138 Ó Domhnalláin, 'An Lánamhain Óg fá'n Tuaith', in *An tIolrach Mór*, 187–97.

139 Ó Cléirigh, 'Sa gCathair Dom', in *Seoidíní Cuimhne*, 37–8. Uch! Na leacracha cruadha agus na pianta a tháinic i mo chosa dá mbárr agus ba mheasa ná an méid sin féin gíoscán damanta agus scréachadh mí-nádúrtha na riancharr. Ní fhéadaim a thuigsint cén chaoi gcuireann muinntir oilte na cathrach suas le n-a leithéid de bharbaracht mar táim-se cinnte nach gcloistear ar an taoibh seo de gheataí Ifrinn a leithéid eile de thormán. Chuala le déidheannaighe go bhfuil airgead sa scéal agus creidim é, mar 'sé an t-airgead céadna atá i mbun agus i mbárr gach uilc . . . Ina dhiaidh sin a's uile, taithnigheann an chathair go seoid liom agus maidir le muinntir na cathrach, ní éirighim-se tuirseach choidhche de bheith ghá dtabhairt fá deara.

140 Nic Ghabhann, *Mágh Ealta Éadair* (BÁC: Máire Ní Raghallaigh, n.d.), 49. Féachamuis ar Chuan Átha Cliath anois – agus ar an leath-chearcall de shoillsí atá timcheall air – ó dheas, thoir, agus ó thuaidh . . . Nach gceapfá gurab í Tír na n-Óg atá romhat amach i n-ionad Bhaile Átha Cliath – cathair dhraoidheachta i leabaidh ceann-chathrach saoghalta!

141 Ó Rinn, *Turus go Páras*, 16–17. See also pp. 69–70. Dar liom níl aon uair is fearr a fhéachann cathair ná an uair a bhíonn na sráideanna mar a bheidís ina lasair o sna lampaí go léir agus na daoine ag siúl timpall agus iad ag caint is ag gáirí go geal is go meidhreach. Chíonn tú sráid leath-dhorcha agus solus ag lonnra o thithe is o shiopaí anso is ansúd ann. Síos an tsráid sin leat go haireach agus go heaglach. Braitheann tú mar a bheadh mistéir ann.

142 These pieces were accompanied by a glossary.

143 Proinsias Mac an Bheatha was of the opinion that Mac Grianna may have been considering compiling a book of urban sketches in 1932. See Mac an Bheatha, 'Seosamh Mac Grianna', in *Seosamh Mac Grianna agus Cúrsaí Eile* (Seosamh Mac Grianna and other matters) (BÁC: Foilseacháin Náisiúnta Teoranta, 1970), 21–2. In his diaries, Mac Grianna jotted down notes for what was apparently to be a novel entitled 'The Streets of Dublin'. (The novel was in all probability to be written in Irish. For some reason, Mac Grianna kept his diaries in English.) Among his notes for this project from 1934, one finds: 'The Ideas of Dublin: The Free Stater, the Fianna Fáiler, The Republican and new Communist, The Trade Unionist; the official Communist; the fierce localism; The Invaders – Corkmen – up Tipperary' and 'The Rhythm of Dublin: slow work; many rings. The Anglicisation of Dublin: the philosophical workingman; the Southrow.' In addition, he included a list of 'Experiences which may be worked in' and 'conversations'. He saw the 'motif' of this work as 'the attempt of a man to avoid spiritual death. The clash and conflict of two sets of ideas – barbarian and civilisation.' Some of this material was included in his unfinished novel *Dá mBíodh Ruball ar an Éan*, which will be discussed below.

144 See also Father Dinneen's 'Ceoltóirí Sráide' (Street musicians) (*Leader*, 3/1/25), and 'Ceol Sráide' (Street music) by 'Mac Casnaidh' (*Redemptorist Record*, May–June 1939, 179).

145 Tá filidheacht ins an chathair. Is deas í 'sa lá agus is aoibhinn 'san oidhche í. Ag siubhal na sráide dom, smuaintighim go bhfuil mé ag dul thart leis an bhocht agus leis an tsaidhbhir, leis an tighearna agus leis an cheannaidhe, leis an oibridhe atá i ndubhshráithe an domhain, leis an chainnteóir, leis an fhile, leis an chearrbhach, agus leis an ghadaidhe. Bím ag dul thart leis an ghol agus leis an gháire, leis an ghrádh agus leis an fhuath. He saw the city as 'fárus a sgiobadh ó shuaimhneas marbhthach an domhain. Croidhe dúithche agus fuil agus galar agus léigheas dúithche. Nead i lár fásaigh; solus ins an rae-dorcha; glór i bhfad uait i gciúineas oidhche.'

146 Tá an bhoichtíneacht agus an saidhbhreas fá choiscéim dá chéile i mBaile Átha Cliath. Cor ar thaobh do láimhe deise nó ar thaobh do láimhe chlí amach as na sráideannaí is breaghtha agus tá tú i lár na mbocht-shráideann – na 'slums'. Tá an chathair mar bhéadh ubhla a mbéadh trí cheathramha de lobhtha.

147 A rosier picture of the life of newsies can be found in 'Giolla na b-Pápeur Nuachta / Saoghal Greannmhar' (The newspaper boys / A pleasant life) by 'Sean-Éireannach', *II*, 9/12/27; and 'Buachaill Óg na bPáipéar / Géar-Shúileach Géar-Intinneach Deagh-Bhéasach' (The young paper boy / Sharp-eyed, keen-witted, well-mannered) by Seán Ó Laoghaire, *II*, 28/5/34.

148 For a brighter picture of life among the urban working class, see Seosamh Ó hAodha's sketch of workers enjoying a sunny bank holiday Monday in 'Saoghal na Cathrach / Lucht Oibre Bhaile Átha Cliath / Gliondar Croidhe ortha' (The life of the city / The workers of Dublin / Enjoying themselves), *II*, 8/6/39.

149 Ó Cinnéide does present an interesting pen sketch of Eccles Street as a bucolic oasis in the city.

150 Bairéad, 'Ceo an Chroí', in *An Geall a Briseadh*, 232–46.

151 See Bairéad, *Gan Baisteadh* (BÁC: Sáirséal agus Dill, 1972), 240.

152 Bairéad, 'Cáit a' Mheadhoin-Oidhche' and 'Costas an Ghirrfhiaidh', in *Cumhacht na Cinneamhna*, 7–11, 103–115. Niall Ó Murchadha has pointed out that fewer than a quarter of Bairéad's short-stories deal with the city, where he was living while he was writing them. See Ó Murchadha, 'Gearrscéalaíocht Thomáis Bairéad, 1893–1973', *IMN*, 1991, 163.

153 Ó Faracháin, 'Truaghán Mná', in *Fíon gan Mhoirt*, 49–53. Fé scáil an ocrais do rugadh í; i dtigh cumhang, salach do tógadh í. An anál do shúghadh sí isteach ina scamhóga níor threise ar an mbeatha 'ná ar an mbás innte . . . Gorta – salachar – anródh – b'shin iad do dáileadh di.

154 Ní Dhochartaigh, *Seamróg na gCeithre nDuilleog*, 40–1. Ní bhíonn cathair ar bith 'sa domhan gan boichtíneacht mar sin innti, siocair go mbíonn gach uile sheórt daoine bailighthe innti: daoine a bhíos ró-fhallsa le h-obair a dhéanamh agus gur bh'fhearr leobhtha i bhfad an airc agus an anás nó saothar ar bith a chur orra féin. Daoine eile gur mhian leobhtha slighe bheatha a bhaint amach, ach ní bhíonn obair nó turastal le fághail go h-oireamhnach aca, daoine eile gur bhfearr leobhtha gaduidheacht agus feall-tacht ná lá oibre a dhéanamh go h-ionnraice. By contrast, he sees Gaeltacht poverty as the result of foreign oppression. León Ó Broin offered a slightly unusual perspective on the theme in 'An Sean-Lead insan g-Caifé / An Té Atá Thíos' (The old fellow in the cafe / The person who is down) (*II*, 27/11/23), a picture of a shabbily dressed old man trying to maintain the dignity of his former situation in life.

155 An tsaoghal, freisin, bhí ins an gcathair; bhí sé beo; bhí rud éigin ar siúbhal innte i gcómhnaidhe . . . Sluaighte daoine ag spáisteóireacht, ag teacht agus ag imtheacht gan stad . . . ins an oíche, na soillse, ag cur

loinnreach an ómra ar an uile nídh agus ag athrughadh deallraibh na háite go gceapfá gur cathair na sidhe bhí ann. His sister sends him money to enable him to return to the farm, but he decides to stay in the city.

156 Tá a h-athchuinghe agus a lorg aici sa deireadh; ba í ba chionntach le gach aon rud . . . Ó'n lá pósadh sinn . . . bhíodh sí i gcomhnuidhe ag guidhe Dé go mbeidhmís bocht fé bhfuighmís bás.

157 Mac Meanman, 'Rothaidhe an tSaoghail', in *Indé agus Indiu*, 83–104.

158 Another interesting story involving university life is Micheál Ó Siochfhradha's 'Ní Bhíonn Saoi gan Locht' (The wise man is not without fault), in which among other things we share the disillusionment of an idealistic student when he learns there are professors 'with no interest in teaching and students with no interest in learning' (gan fonn teagaisc ortha agus aos léighinn gan fonn léighinn) (Enniscorthy *Echo*, 23/4/32).

159 This brief summary is from a report on the performance of the play by An Comhar Drámaidheachta in the Abbey Theatre in 1926 (*Irish Tribune*, 8/10/26). The play has never been published.

160 In Ailbhe Ó Monacháin's 'An Sean-Mháilidh Ní Ghuidhir' (The old Molly Maguire), a law student contemplates, though he does not commit, suicide as the result of a drinking problem (*Ultach*, May, 1938, 6). 'Fionn' Mac Cumhaill wrote of a suicide in Donegal during the Famine in *Na Rosa go Bráthach*, 10.

161 Tóibín, 'Teoiní agus Tighthe Lóistín', in *Teoiní agus Tighthe Lóistín agus Dhá Scéal Eile* (Tony and lodging houses and two other stories) (BÁC: COÉ, 1923), 24. Bhí an bhean – bean a dheallruigh go raibh tonn mhaith dá h-aois caithte – ag siubhal 'n gcoinne. Bhí fear 'na fochair – fear breágh óg. Bhí maidrín ar a bhaclainn aige. D'fhéachadar air. Ba é Teoiní a bhí ann . . . D'éirigh idir Theoiní agus a mhuintir an ghráin agus an fuath sin a dhein iad a dheighilt go h-eug.

162 Ó Gríobhtha, 'Cról', in *Cathair Aeidh*, 61–2.

163 Ó Broin, 'Is Fearr le Dia Mná', in *Ag Stracadh leis an Saol*, 100–7; Thomson, 'Éirí an tSaoghail' and 'An Leanbh Tabhartha', in *Gach Orlach de Mo Chroí*, ed. Ó Lúing, 56–66, 78–85. Neither of Thomson's stories was published during our period.

164 Ó Dubhda, 'An Toil 's an Taithighe', in *Thríd an Fhuinneoig*, 69–76.

165 Mac Maoláin, 'Taisce Dhomhnaill Dhuibh', in *As na Ceithre hÁirdibh*, 145–59.

166 Ó Dubhda, 'Idir Am Luighe agus Am Éirghe', in *Cáith agus Grán*, 74–5.

167 See 'Drámaí Gaedhilge / Bille Breagh san Abbey' (Plays in Irish / A fine bill at the Abbey), *II*, 12/2/25. On the other hand, while he appreciated the play as 'something new' (rud nua) and 'an attempt to move beyond the usual matter' (iarracht ar éirghe as an ngnáth-chúrsa), the anonymous reviewer for *An Branar* found the play philosophically superficial (*Branar*, Mar. 1925, 47.

168 Mura bhfuil sé dia-mhaslach agam, is minic a shamhail mé, dá dtigeadh le duine aithne a chur ar Chríost gurb é rud a gheobhadh sé amach nach bhfuil an Muirthileach éagcosamhail Leis. In his essay 'Éagosc an tSagairt: Staidéar ar Úrscéal le Séamus Mac Conmara' (The distinguishing mark of the priest: A study of a novel by Séamus Mac Conmara), Micheál Ó Duibhir sees Mac Conmara's protagonist as an 'alter Christus'. See Ó Duibhir, 'Éagosc an tSagairt', *IMN*, 1969, 53–61.

169 Thuig sí gurbh é seo an luach saothair a gheall Dia dó ar son na híodhbartha millteanaighe a rinne sé uair amháin ar A shon-san – luach saothair nár den tsaoghal seo agus nach mbéadh daoiní dall-intinneacha an tsaoghail seo ábalta a thuigbheáil.

170 Coga isea an gnó . . . agus isiad gliocas agus airgead na h-airm troda a mbaintear úsáid asta sa gcoga san. An té ná tuigeann i gceart conus feidhm a bhaint as an dá ghleus san, buailtear ar lár é gan trua gan trócaire. An duine do leigfeadh don charthannacht nó don trua é chur óna ghnó a chur chun cinn, bhéadh sé chó maith aige cur suas don chluiche ar fad! See also pp. 21, 22, 23.

171 Dar ndóigh, ní'l éan rud le maitheamh duit agam, a chailín ó! Eadrainn féin, an dtuigeann tú, ní deurfainn ná go raibh cuid mhaith den cheart agat!

172 'Brionglóid', in *An Chraobh Chumhra*, 75–8.

173 Ní uaigneas go dtí an t-uaigneas a bhíos orm agus mé im' aonar imeasc na mílte móra ar shráideanna geala na Baibiolóine Móire. Is cuma mé annsin – dar liom féin – nó braoinín beag, mar deurfá, i lár an aigéin, gan cara, gan comráda, gan duine ar m'aitheantas, im' ghoire ná im' ghaobhar.

174 Ó Nualláin and Ó Nualláin, *Sean agus Nua*, 87–103.

175 Ní Dhochartaigh, *Seamróg na gCeithre nDuilleog*, 14. Ach in aindeoin na n-iongantas go léir, b'uaigneach is ba dhólásach croidhe Chaitríona i measg na gcoimhthigheach . . . Ba dhúranta mí-nádúrtha an dream iad go léir.

176 Duine a chaitheann a shaoghal 'g obair thart fá chathair, sin a' té a chuirfeas spéis ins an eachtra a bhfuil fúm-sa innseacht dó. Chan do mhuintir na tuaithe é, ná 'sé a' choitchinnteacht leobhtha-san é! Duine mise a rugadh agus a tógadh ins an chathair, áit a chaithfeas muid aithne a chur ar dhuine sul a labhrann muid leis. Cha dtig linn bheith muinteardha le choimhthigheach, ach an oiread, go dtig duine aoindheach i láthair a bhfuil aithne aige ar a' bheirt againn agus a chuirfeas in aithne d'á chéile sinn. Má's coimhthigheach ná deóraidhe thú, a chailleach, seachain a' chathair agus tionntuigh d'aghaidh ar a' tuaith!

177 Ó Domhnalláin, 'Dhá Litir', in *Oidhre an Léighinn*, 69–74.

178 Bairéad, 'Imnidhe an Ghrádha', in *Cumhacht na Cinneamhna*, 149–56.

179 Ó Gríobhtha, 'An Teine Chnámh', in *Cathair Aeidh*, 128–55. See also Donn Piatt's comic story 'An

bhFuil Leigheas ar an nGrádh?' (Is there a cure for love?) (*IP*, 17/11/32).
180 Ó Broin, 'Fear na Beirte Ban', in *An Rún*, 88–97.
181 Ó Broin, 'Mairg a Phósfadh' and 'Troid na gComharsan', in *An Rún*, 67–76, 77–87. For a much less political satire, see 'An Tuarasgabhálaidhe', 'An Bhuinreacht Nuadh / Céadshúil ar an gCáipéis' (The new Constitution / A first look at the document), *An Bolgán Béiceach / Galway's Annual Explosion* (UCG student 'rag mag'), 1936, 3.
182 Ó Broin, 'An Ganndailín', in *Ag Stracadh leis an Saol*, 72–4.
183 Ó Broin, 'Sgéal na Gamhna Buidhe', in *An Rún*, 22–32.
184 Bhí sé mar 'rún' eadortha go rabhas im' 'native speaker' – rud nárbh fhíor – ach do chuir san mo cháil ó bhaoghal ionsuithe ó dhaoine fiosracha.
185 Little dramatic sketches with urban settings also appeared from time to time in journals of the period. See, for example, 'Sliabh Ruadh', 'Ag Cur i gCóir do'n Saoire' (Getting ready for the holidays), *II*, 20/6/29; Pádraig Ó Bróithe, 'An Cuaird: Dráma do Gharsúnaibh' (The visit: A drama for children), *An Óige: A Bright Bi-Lingual Monthly*, Oct. 1930, 5 and 7; and the anonymous 'Sin í an Cheist' (That is the question), UCG *University Annual*, 1930–1, 25–6. This last play is set in 'Seomra na mBan' at UCG and in a lodging house in Salthill near the city, and spoofs, among other things, Gaelic affairs at the university. Life at UCG was also the subject of the story 'Fuath agus Grádh' (Hatred and love) by 'Tadhg na Buile' in which two bosom buddies at the university batter each other bloody over a young woman they later decide is unworthy of their attention (*University Annual*, 1927–8, 45–6)
186 Nára fada gur maol abheid siad. Gach óinseach díobh ad' iarraidh ógánaigh a dhéanamh de féin! Is gearr go dtosanóid ar bhristí do chaitheamh! The play was performed by An Comhar Drámaidheachta in the Abbey in 1929.
187 This play was never published, but see the synopsis in the programme for 4 and 5 Nov. 1929 in the Taibhdhearc na Gaillimhe Papers, NUIG.
188 Ó Broin, *Siamsa Gaedheal* and *Rogha an Dá Dhíogh*, in *An Mhallacht agus Drámaí Eile* (The curse and other plays) (BÁC: ODFR, 1931), 18–36, 37–84. The former was produced by An Comhar Drámaidheachta in the Abbey in 1928; the latter by the same company in the Abbey the previous year.
189 Tá dream beag i mBaile Átha Cliath a choimeádann an clú dhóibh féin, agus éad ortha chun éinne eile go bhfuil clisteacht ann. Níl cothrom le fagháil ag ughdar nua.
190 Proinnsias Mac Casarlaigh's short unpublished radio play, *Éagcóir* (Injustice), also dealt comically with the mishaps of urban lovers. See 'Dráma Nua a Craoladh' (A new play that was broadcast), *IP*, 26/8/38.
191 Bairéad, 'An Reillig', in *Cumhacht na Cinneamhna*, 29–34.
192 Ó Nualláin, 'Cúig Phíosaí Óir', in *Dia Diabhail agus Daoine*, 51–8.
193 Ó Domhnalláin, 'Deagh-Nodlaig?' in *Oidhre an Léighinn*, 140–8. In 'Reggie: Buile nó Togha Céille –' (Reggie: Madness or the best of sense –), Pádraic Ó Conaire offers a tongue-in-cheek perspective on the dangerous psychological effects of learning Irish as an adult (*CS*, 10/8/26).
194 In an anonymous 1929 essay in *The Leader* entitled 'An Untilled Field for Dramatists', the author wrote:

> We are sure that they [members of the Ascendancy] have very many good points and that notwithstanding much apparent bitterness and sourness, are lovable enough to those who sympathise with them as kindred and understand them from the inside. They offer a great chance to dramatists, and it would be a good and wholesome thing if that chance were adequately taken, and taken without delay (*Leader*, 16/3/29).

Doubtless this advice was being directed towards Irish writers of English, but it could also be applied to writers of Irish, with the caveat that few Gaels would have had – or admitted – a kindred or inside connection with the gentry.
195 Ar thaobh amháin de bhí uaisleacht agus cumhacht agus saidhbhreas agus uaibhreas, agus ar an dtaobh eile bochtanas agus ísle, cráidhteacht agus cráibhtheacht. Is minic cheana a mhasluigh sé i ngníomh agus i smaoineamh an dream sin de thuataigh. Tuige nach raibheadar ar aon nós leis an drong ar shíolruigh seisean uatha, muinntir Shasana? Tuige nach raibh brígh agus fuinneamh agus dul-ar-aghaidh ionnta? . . . Tuige nach gcuirfidís déantúisí ar bun agus cathracha móra, agus iad féin a thabhairt i gceist ar an saoghal? Dá gcreideamh amháin bhíodar dúthrachtach, don chreideamh sin a bhí ghá gcoinneál, dar leis san, gan feidhm, gan éifeacht . . . gramaraisc thuatach, chuirfidís déistin ar dhuine.
196 Ó Domhnalláin, 'An Leaghadh', in *Na Spiadóirí*, 71–4.
197 Bairéad, 'Mná Caointe na Linnseach', in *Cumhacht na Cinneamhna*, 93–100
198 Ó Ciarghusa, 'Dualgas', in *Geantraighe*, 57–9. See also 'Caisleán na h-Áirde' (The castle on the height), in *An Chraobh Chumhra*, 19–28. In Seán Ó Ciosáin's 'Móna', the title character is a sincere if confused Anglo-Irishwoman unclear about the place of her people in Irish society. See Ó Ciosáin, 'Móna', in *Sgéalta Cois Laoi*, 31–50.
199 Más fíor dam . . . tá rian an náisiúin, meon na nGaedheal, ar Phrodasdúnacht agus ar Chaitliceacht na hÉireann chomh maith.
200 Ó Dubhda, 'Chun Glóire a Ríogh agus Onóra a dTíre!' in *Cáith agus Grán*, 67–70. In Ó Dubhda's 1923 story 'An Smál ar an bPictiúr' (The stain on the picture), the narrator tells his friend he can't see an

ugly line defacing the landscape, only to be answered: 'You are dull-witted. Isn't that where the border line between Ulster and Leinster is?' (Tá tú dall-inntinneach. Nach annsin atá líne teorainteach Uladh agus Laighean?) (*Sguab*, May 1923, 150–1).

201 Ó Ciarghusa says he is here recalling a visit he made to Belfast on 12 July 1914. Micheál Ó Maoláin's 'Cuaird go Béal Feirste / Mór-Obair na Comhdhála / Beann Mheadagáin / Na Fir Órdha agus an Aos Óg' (A visit to Belfast / The great work of the Congress / Cave Hill / The Orangemen and the young) (*II*, 18/4/32) was prompted by his attendance at a Gaelic League convention held in Belfast, and doesn't tell us all that much about the North.

202 Bairéad, 'Saidhbhreas na gCon', in *An Geall a Briseadh*, 113–23.

203 Ó Dubhda, 'An Dá Sheift', in *Thríd an Fhuinneoig*, 16–21. In Ó Ciarghusa's *Onncail Seárlai*, one of the characters is an Orangeman who always goes berserk on the 12th of July.

204 Nic Mhaicín, 'Scilling', in *As na Ceithre hÁirdibh*, 135–41.

205 Ó Dubhda, 'Séadna (ar an aimsir seo)', in *Cáith agus Grán*, 38–41.

206 Ó Ciarghusa, 'Golf', in *Geantraighe*, 60–5. There were also several essays in Irish on this sport.

207 Ó Dubhda, 'An Bonn Malluighthe', in *An t-Ógánach Ceann-Órdha*, 147–62.

208 Tá iarracht déanta ag an ughdar ar na gnéithe is gránamhla de'n t-saoghal daondha a chur sa litridheacht Ghaedhilge – i gcupla ceann de na scéaltaí. Baineann sé úsáid as an ádhbhar sin a bhíos ag cuid dhe na scríobhnóirí Béarla mar Ó Flaithbheartaigh nuair is áil leo rud taithneamhach a thabhairt do'n lucht-léighte cam-inntineach i Londun. Deirfinn gur masla ar dhaondacht 's ar Chríostaidheacht mhuinntir na h-Éireann iad seo.

209 Tá a n-ionad uile go léir beagnach suidhte i gcúl-shráideanna Bhaile Átha Cliath. Acht ní h-é sin d'fhágas iad gan blas agus teilgean na Gaedhealtachta bheith ortha . . . Ag cur síos don sgríbhneoir ar lucht na gcúl-shráideanna ní ar a gcuid droch-nósa ar fad a bhí sé ag cur síos – thug sé amach a chunntas ortha go nádúrach agus is maith an nídh é sin mar baineann sé blas na sgríbhneoirí Gallda d'á chur síos. The book inspired 'Bricriu' to take a particularly iconoclastic stance in his review for *An t-Ultach*:

> But would you not think from all their short stories that there was nothing at all in Ireland worth talking about outside the Gaeltacht? All of their attention was on the life of the Gaeltacht . . . And they continued that practice so that I have often said that Irish would not be considered the habitual language of the country until the writers forgot the Gaeltacht altogether and turned to face the towns (Ach nach sílfeá ar a gcuid gearr-sgéal uilig nach rabh rud ar bith i n-Éirinn taobh amuigh de'n Ghaedhealtacht ar bhfhiú trácht air? Bhí a n-umhail uilig ar shaoghal na Gaedhealtachta . . . Agus lean siad de'n ghnáthas sin gur minic a dubhairt mé nach mbeadh meas ar an Ghaedhilg mar ghnáth-theanga na tíre go ndéanfadh na sgríbhneoirí dearmad glan de'n Ghaedhealtacht agus a n-aghaidh a thabhairt ar na bailte-móra) (*Ultach*, Aug. 1935, 5–6).

210 Tuar é sin ar iompáil na Gaedhilge ar na bailtí inead 'nar riachtanach í ghreamú go préamhacha nua. An leabhar is mó le rádh a tháinig ón nGúm le fada.

211 Bhí seó daoine ar fuaid an bhaill, cuid aca ag teacht amach tar éis an chéad léiriú bheith thart, agus a thuille aca ag fanacht 'na streillín fhada le hathoscailt na ndóirse. Bhí cailín bocht agus seál timcheall uirthi aniar ag rádh 'Gráinne Mhaol' dóibh. San am gcéadna bhí bean an atúrnae ag fáscadh a láimhní uirthi tar éis bheith ag cuardach dá tuicéad. Nuair stad an t-amhrán chonnaic Mícheál an lámh 'á síneadh amach chuige. Do sleamhnuigh sé raol isteach 'sa láimh gan fiú féachaint uirthi.

212 Tá scríbhneoirí ann agus dar leat nár bhreághtha leo rud ná bheith ag tabhairt mion-chúnntais ar dhaoine a bheadh 'na leithéid de chás. Acht má's duine thú féin, a bhráthair, a bhí it naoi truagha lá, tú ar easba misnigh agus gan súil le fóirithint agat, níorbh' aoibhinn leat na cúrsaí sin a tharrac anuas arís. Scaoilfead tharm mar scéal é.

213 More positive was Ernest Blythe, who, reviewing the collection for *II*, called it 'one of the most important books that has been published lately' (ceann de's na leabhraibh is tábhachtaí dár foillsigheadh le déanaí), and praised Ó Faracháin as 'an heir to Pádraic Ó Conaire' (oidhre ar Phádraic Ó Conaire) (*II*, 31/1/39). See also the positive reviews of the book by 'P. B.' (probably Béaslaí) in *IP*, 15/12/38; and by 'C.' in *Bonaventura*, Spring 1939, 169–70.

214 Labour activism was the subject of an unpublished play from the period, Proinnsias Ó Casarlaigh's *An Stailc*. This play was first performed by An Comhar Drámaidheachta in the Peacock, 19–22 Dec. 1939. See 'Nua-Dhrámaí ag an gComhar' (New plays by An Comhar), *IP*, 20/12/39.

215 Mara mbeadh a laighead aga do bhí fágtha ní cuirfí i gcló in aon chor é. Maran féidir leat aon nídh do scríobhadh ach briolla brealla gan deallramh na fírinne air, gheobham duine eile a dhéanfaidh an gnó dhúinn. In ainm an Ríogh tabhair iarracht ar scéalta d'fhéadfadh a bheith i gceist do cheapadh. Cailleadh Charles Garvice agus ní háil linn aon oidhre air. The writer-protagonist is himself an admirer of O. Henry and his technique.

216 Úirscéal is eadh é nach bhfuil mórán dá shórt againn san nGaedhilg. Saoghal na cathrach agus saoghal na ndaoine a bhfuil cómhnuidhe ortha innti agus thart uirthi a léirightear ann. An té a bhfuil uaidh eolas a chur ar an saoghal sin, seo é an leabhar chuige.

217 An leabhar seo an sompla is deise – muna

mbéadh an cló Gallda – a chonnaiceas fós de Ghaedhilge Bhaile Átha Claith. Ní le magadh atá mé ar chor ar bith, ach lom dáiríribh. Bhéadh fhios agat ar bhealach eicint nach duine de mhuintir na Gaeltachta, ar nós 'Máire' nó Páraic Óg Ó Conaire, a sgríobh an leabhar, ach ní fhágann sé sin ná gur sgéal deas é i n-a bhealach féin. A dissenting voice was that of Blythe, who saw neither Ó Riain's novel nor Ó Ruadháin's as 'a source of hope . . . for the person hoping that a strong growth will come in the new literature in Irish' (cúis dóchais . . . do'n té atá ag dúil le fás láidir do theacht i nua-litridheacht na Gaedhilge) (*II*, 28/3/33). Of the two he preferred *Pádhraic Mháire Bhán*.

218 It is, perhaps, little wonder that 'S.' felt the novel required a particularly vigorous suspension of disbelief: 'In our opinion, the author allows his imagination too much free reign in places so that you are convinced that the age of the Fenian tales is still with us' (Dar linn go leigeann an t-ughdar dá shamhluigheacht imirt ró-mhór air i n-áiteacha ionnus go gcuirtear i n-a luighe ort ré na fiannaidheachta a bheith linn fós). 'S.' did, however, praise Ó Riain for his treatment of city life (*IMN*, 1933, 62).

219 Titley, *An tÚrscéal*, 163–4.

220 Féach, a mhic ó . . . beidh an cineadh daonna gan ceann ar bith i gcionn céad bliadhain má leanann sé mar atá. Teaspáin dom aoinne a dheineann machtnamh dá chuid féin fé láthair. Ní dheineann aoinne . . . Céad bliadhain ó shin, nuair a bhíodh cearduithe ag déanamh rud éigin le n-a dhá láimh, dob éigean dó a chiall agus a thuigsint féin do chur ag obair. Bhí a rian air, bhí pearsantacht éigin ag baint le toradh a shaothair, rud éigin a theaspáin duit gur *duine* do dhein é . . . Deirtí liom, nuair a bhíos ar scoil, go mbíonn an cineadh daonna ag foghluim i gcomhnuidhe, go mbíonn breis eolais ag gach glúin dá dtagann seachas an ghlúin a bhí roimpi. Fastaoim, a mhic ó! B'fhéidir gur mar sin a bhíodh an scéal, ach is fada an lá ó b'eadh. See also pp. 27–8, 284–6.

221 Dob iongantach mar do múscluigheadh agus mar do corruigheadh na smaointe ionnam ar feadh an dá lá san. Do shamhluighinn uaireannta gur chuma nó neamh ar an saoghal so an mhainistir, bhí an tsíothcháin chomh doimhin agus na húrnuithe chomh coitchianta san ann. Uaireannta eile, ba léir dom gur laochradh do-chlaoidhte na manaigh agus go raibh comhacht éigin ag imtheacht uatha amach, comhacht a bhí ag dul i bhfeidhm ar an saoghal i ngan fhios dó – díreach mar sheomra úd na holl-chomhachta do chonnac cois Sionainne tráth, seomra ciúin ná raibh ach fear amháin ag obair ann; ach d'fhéadfadh seisean solus do thabhairt d'Éirinn go léir, nó an tír d'fhágáil fé dhorchadas, mar ba mhaith leis.

222 It is hardly surprising that the anonymous reviewer for *IR* found the novel an edifying read: 'There is true Catholicism and true faith to be found in this book. It is a sound and wholesome book, and we greatly need its like' (Tá fíor-chatoiliceacht agus fíor-chreideamh le fagháil san leabhar so. Úrsgéal slán folláin 'seadh é agus tá a leithéid ag teastáil uainn go géar) (*IR*, Feb. 1933, 160). For a far more formulaic treatment than Ó Riain's of the reformation of a criminal through penance, see the anonymous 'Dhá Oidhche Nodlag' (Two Christmas nights) (*Standard*, 10/12/37), in which an escaped murderer hides in a church, prays for forgiveness, and dies in peace there.

223 Bhí dúil nimhe agam a fhiafruighe dhe cad é an saghas éadaigh a chaitheadh na hAspuil nó cad iad na gairme beathadh a bhíodh aca, ach do bhrúghas fúm. Caitheann gach aoinne géilleadh dá bhacaighe féin; agus ní raibh de bhacaighe san Athair Harfleur ach an iomad galántachta, agus an méid sin féin ar mhaithe le n-a phobul, dar leis.

224 Goldring, *Pleasant Is the Scholar's Life*, 76.

225 In addition, there is a bridging of the class and social divide in the novel in Stiana's friendship with the Traveller Braon.

226 Ní abraim gur cheart dom Mícheál d'fhágáil ach cuirim a mhilleán ar an gcuma ina raibh an saoghal Fódlach. Is beag an cuimhneamh a bhí agam an lá phósas Mícheál go dtiocfadh sé chun baile dom mallacht do chur air. Ach amhail a lán eile in Éirinn an t-am úd, go mór mór na mná, ní raibh mo chiall cheart agam. Bhí sé buailte isteach im aigne dá bhfanainn i bhfochair Mhíchil go gcaillfinn mo mheabhair ar fad. Ní hé gur dhubhairt mé sin liom féin, ach bhí rud éicint dom thiomáint uaidh.

227 Chuireadh sé scannradh mo chroidhe orm dearcadh ar an bhfuinneóig mar thagadh fonn nimhneach orm mé féin a chaitheamh amach dá bhféadfainn í shroichint. Chuireadh an leanbh ins na tríthíbh dubha guil mé. Uair amháin shíl siad go ndéanfainn droch-bheart éicint dá bhfágadh siad an leanbh agam . . . An comhrac aigne ba mheasa cuireadh riamh ar dhuine bhí sé le fulang agam. Luigheas annsin mar a bhéadh dealbh chloiche ach bhí gach uile ribe dem' ghruaig ina sheasamh, croiceann mo chinn tarraingthe mar a bhéadh croiceann ar dhroma, codladh driúlach orm ó bhonn go baitheas agus fionnadh crith ar mo chuid feola. An deamhan a bhí istigh ionam thosuigh sé dom' spochadh – 'Tacht é; cuir do dhá láimh fá n-a mhuineál agus bain an anál as, bhéarfaidh sin fuascailt duit.' Indeed it takes several paragraphs before she even tells the reader whether the baby is a girl or a boy.

228 O! a shagairt, an dtearn aon duine eile de shíol Éabha an gníomh atá déanta agam-sa? . . . Ní dhearn. Ní dhearn. Nach iongantach nach dtig teine ó Neamh agus an domhan a bhfuil mé ag siubhal air a lasgadh. Fan uaim, a shagairt; na nach bhfuil eagla ort roimhe na deomhain agus na diabhail atá astoigh ann mo cholainn. Na nach bhfuil eagla ort go gcríonfaidh do lámh go dtí an ghualainn má leagann tú orm í?

229 D'imthigh an dreach álainn de'n loch. Tháinig gruaim – smúid – rinn uirthi. Thoisigh scáileogaí

beaga confadhacha a dh'éirghe daoithe. Ní rabh iarraidh ar bith aici orm; chuir sí cuil uirthi féin, ar eagla go mbeinn ag brath a cuid uisce shoineannta a shalughadh le mo chnámhaibh malluighthe.

230 B'fhéidir, a shagairt, nach bhfuil mo chinneamhaint comh dona sin. Nach bhfuil sé ráidhte go dtógann Uan Dé peacaidh an tsaoghail, an chuid is truime agus is duibhe acu? Tá teinte tréana i bPurgadóir. B'fhéidir nach bhfuil sé peacach agam a bheith ag smuaintiughadh go nglanfadh siad an smál roimh Lá an Luain. A Mhuire mhuirneach, as béalaibh Ifrinn agraim thú, mé a chosaint ar do Mhac mhillteanach. In the same year Mac Grianna's collection appeared, Father Dinneen published a story entitled 'An Té a Dhein an Éagcóir / "Odisse quem Laeseris"' (The person who committed an injustice / 'To hate whom you have hurt'), in which a first-person narrator tells of his hatred for a man he had wronged. His story ends with the Latin proverb of the title and the following reflection from the narrator: 'I hate the person I wronged; and I want nothing but to eliminate him and everything involving him, for fear he would inform on me and that I would lose whatever respect the public has for me' (Is fuath liom an té gur dheineas éagcóir air; agus ní'l uaim acht é fein agus a mbaineann leis do bhaint as, ar eagla go scéithfeadh sé orm agus go gcaillfinn cibé meas atá ag an gcoitchianntacht orm) (*Leader*, 1/8/25, 609).

231 Ó Laoire, 'Tart an Anama agus Deoch na Colla: Forbairt Théama an Choimhthís i Saothar Sheosaimh Mhic Grianna' (The soul's thirst and the body's drink: The development of the theme of alienation in the work of Seosamh Mac Grianna), in *Rí-Éigeas na nGael*, ed. Mac Congáil, 99.

232 I ndiaidh a dul thart ar leath na h-Éireann ní thug an t-astar dada i mo cheann ach an cumhnglach. Bhí mé i bpríosún. B'ionann 's an cás agam é, i mo sheomra beag annseo nó eadar dhá cheann na tíre. Chuaigh mé a luighe agus gruaim orm, agus bhíthear 'ghá aidhbhsiughadh domh go rabh rud éighinteacht éagsamhalta i ndán domh gan mhoill. Kiberd discusses what he sees as Joycean themes in *Mo Bhealach Féin* in '*Mo Bhealach Féin*: Idir Dhá Thraidisiún', *Scríobh* 5, 224–39.

233 See Eoghan Mac Éinrí, 'An Éifeacht Fhiliúnta' (The poetic significance), in *Rí-Éigeas na nGael*, ed. Mac Congáil, 117–34.

234 Bhí m'astar déanta. Bhí bród orm. Dá gcuireadh aon duine ceist orm goidé an fáth a bhí leis an tsiubhal, bhéadh obair agam freagra a thabhairt air. Ba é mo bhealach féin é. Neartuigh sé m'intinn agus chruadhaigh sé mo cholann. Bhí méid ann; bhí sé deacair; agus ní thabharfadh an-diabhail ormsa ariamh an rud a bhí beag agus a bhí furast a dhéanamh . . . Tá an saoghal uilig taobh thall den sgáth bheag focal a chuir muid air, agus ní h-ionann ciall thall annsin agus abhfos, an áit nach bhfuil muid ach ag siubhal le gnás agus le comhairle, mar bhéadh daill ag déanamh an eólais dá chéile. B'fhearr liom siubhal ins an rae dorcha ná a bheith dall.

235 Ní feasach domh-sa cé'n dara cearn a rachaidh mé, ach tá a fhios agam go dtiocfaidh na hiongantais chugam agus gan mé ag dúil leó. Tá an saoghal mór lán den fhilidheacht ag an té dar dual a tuigbheáil, agus ní thráighfidh an tobar go deó na ndeór; agus a fhad agus mhairfidh mise béidh mé ag déanamh an eólais chun an tobar seo do Chlannaibh Gaedheal.

236 Thráigh an tobar ins an tSamhradh, 1935. Ní sgríobhfaidh mé níos mó. Rinne mé mo dhícheall agus is cuma liom.

237 See Antain Mag Shamhráin, 'Nóta faoin Saothar' (A note about the work), in *Dá mBíodh Ruball ar an Éan*, ed. Mag Shamhráin, 91–5.

238 Ba í an mhéin rúin sin a thug orm gan a theacht i n-éifeacht ariamh. Ba í an mhéin chéadna a thug orm a bheith ag dúil le bliadhanta go mbéinn 'mo sheasamh os ceann an tslóigh. Corr-uair ba laoch mé, corr-uair ba naomh mé, agus corr-uair ba file mé, agus go minic ba mé mian-reatha gan chuma a bhí comh do-cheansa le gaoith.

239 Ar fheall an saoghal ort ariamh, ins an dóigh ar chaill tú do chuid airt ar feadh tamaill, ins an dóigh a rabh tú seal mar bheitheá i n-Ifreann?

240 Níor bhac 'Laochraidh na Saoirse' leis na daoiní a bhí as obair ar chor ar bith. Ba bhreóidhteacht a bhí ar an dream seo, dar leó, agus ba chóir a gcur i bpríosúin faoi shúile 'dochtúirí oibre.' Ba é a ndearcadh go raibh an Chumannacht ag teacht, agus go gcaithfidhe comhar agus caradas a dhéanamh eadar na daoiní a bhí ag obair agus a rabh fiúntas na tíre 'n-a mbun.

241 Sé an creideamh náisiúnta atá agam acht an creideamh a fhógair Éamon de Bhaléra cúig nó sé de bhliadhantaibh ó shoin – gurbh' fhearr liom Éire fé smacht Gaill agus an Ghaedhealg d'á labhairt inntí ná Éire saor agus an Ghaedhealg i n-éag. . . Is gránda liom poilitidheacht ar fad. Má tháimse ar Sheanad an tSaorstáit, táim ann chun buille do bhualadh ar son na Gaedhilge má's féidir liom é. In a 1924 piece in *An Sguab*, 'Tadhg Gaedhealach' wrote: 'The whole Gaelic world now knows that the Irish language does not have a truer or more far-seeing friend at home or abroad than Éamonn Mac Giolla Iasachta' (Tá a fhios ag an saoghal Gaedhealach anois ná fuil cara níos fíre ná níos fad-cheannaighe ag an Ghaedhilge amuigh ná i mbaile ná Eumon Mac Giolla Iasachta) (*Sguab*, Dec. 1924, 231).

242 Táim ar an Seanad le trí bliadhna agus gheobhainn a rádh gur dheineas mo dhícheall chun cúis na Gaedhilge do chur chun cinn ar feadh na h-aimsire sin. Ba í an Ghaedhilg mo chéad chúram sa Seanad i gcomhnuidhe.

243 Is an-tsuimeamhail ar fad mar chuireas an t-ughdar síos ar shaoghal agus ar shaothar an Fheilméara i nÉirinn sa gcuid seo de'n leabhar. Go deimhin is ar éigin riamh a léigheas i naon úrsgéal trácht ar chúrsaí Feilméarachta chomh maith

fírinneach leis ach amháin, b'fhéidir in 'Wet Clay' Shéamuis Bhoithtléir Cheallaigh agus 'The Gael' a sgríobh Mac Giolla Iasachta.

244 Cearbhall Ua Dálaigh was more muted in his enthusiasm for Mac Giolla Iasachta's novel: '*Cúrsaí Thomáis* is not an extraordinary or heroic achievement, but even so, it is a very readable book, and it can be considered as one of the best novels that has come out in the past ten years' (Ní h-éacht ná gaisce *Cúrsaí Thomáis*, acht mar sin féin leabhar an-shoiléighte atá ann, agus ní miste é d'áireamh ar cheann des na h-úirscéalta is fearr d'á dtáinig amach le deich mbliadhna anuas) (*CB*, May 1931, 504).

245 Titley, *An tÚrscéal*, 186. Tá *Cúrsaí Thomáis* ar cheann de fhíor-bheagán úrscéalta Gaeilge, agus úrscéalta Éireannacha d'aon saghas, a mbraitheann tú uaisleacht na hoibre agus dínit an tsaothair ann. See also Seán Ó Tuama, 'Úrscéalta agus Faisnéisí Beatha na Gaeilge: Na Buaicphointí' (Novels and autobiographies in Irish: The high points), *Scríobh*, 5, 150–1; and Gearóid Denvir, 'Litríocht agus Pobal: Nualitríocht na Gaeilge agus an Tradisiún' (Literature and community: Modern literature in Irish and the tradition), in *Litríocht agus Pobal*, 45. Pádraig Ó Croiligh was less taken with the novel, seeing it as a missed opportunity, an unsuccessful hybrid of literary novel and account of rural life. See Ó Croiligh, 'Scáil Úirscéil: Sracfhéachaint ar "Cúrsaí Thomáis" le Éamonn Mac Giolla Iasachta' (The shadow of a novel: A glance at 'Cúrsaí Thomáis' by Éamonn Mac Giolla Iasachta), *IMN*, 1969, 77–89.

246 Dá mhéid a sgaoilim-se lem' theanga ar gach aon cheist eile brughaim fúm nuair a bhíonn cúrsaí an chroidhe i gceist. Nós iseadh é sin, go deimhin, atá ag Éireannaigh mar aon leis na Franncaigh agus maidir leis sin de, le náisiúin na Laidne uile is dócha, a thugthacht a bhímid chun a bheith osgailte agus cainnteach i dtaobh gnáthchúrsaí ár saoghail agus san am chéadna a chúlántacht a bhímid i dtaobh na nidhthe tábhachtacha agus na nidhthe doimhinne a bhaineann leis an taobh istigh dínn.

247 Creid uaim é, is gairid ná beidh leanbhaí ag leithéidí Caitlín má tá an chontabhairt ann go ndéanfaidhe rabhadh puiblí díobh mar a dheineadh di siúd. Agus annsan do bheimís chomh dona as a's atá an chuid eile den domhan.

248 Bhí braon den fhuil ghorm innti. Bhí leanbh dubh aici. Bhíos im' gheilt nuair a chonnaiceas é. Dubhairt sí liom go ndéanfadh sí anaoid uirthi féin, agus do bhádhaigh sí í féin an oidhche chéadna.

249 Ach san am céadna do bhraitheas fuinneamh agus brigh ionnam agus fonn orm dul chun cinn rud beag sa saoghal, agus go mór mór fonn orm a bheith gairid dí ar feadh an lae ó mhaidin go h-oidhche – ní dheirim-se ar feadh na h-oidhche, mar ní dóigh liom go raibh aon droch-smaointe im' aigne 'na taobh, cé go mbíodh an dúil úd taobh thiar ann gan dabht: fear óg a bhí ionnam dar ndóigh.

250 Bhí rud beag fallsaer orm. Ach cuimhnigh ar conus mar a bhí mo chúrsaí an uair sin, agus, rud eile, bean an-dhathamhail ba dheadh Peig; ní raibh uirthe ach gúna oidhche; fear óg ba dheadh mise.

251 Ach níl Tomás sásta gan aithris a dhéanamh ar an aicme gránda úd, na scríbhneoirí salacha, mí-náireacha, atá comh flúirseach fé lathair . . . Bíonn gearán géar le clos ó am go h-am sa tír seo 'gainne i dtaobh droch-leabhar ó Shasana, agus, dar ndóigh, tá cúis leis. Ach is mithid dúinn aire mhaith a thabhairt do na leabhraí a cuirfear amach sa' bhaile as so amach . . . Ba fhearr liom go mór fada an leabhar do mholadh ná é do cháineadh; ní'l a mhalairt de rogha agam an turus so, ámhach, ach a rádh go bhfuil súil agam go mba fada uainn an lá a gcuirfear i gcló leabhar gaedhealach eile dá leithéid.

252 Molaim do léightheóirí an *Stuic* – ach amháin na buachaillí is na cailíní – an leabhar seo fhághail. Buidheachas do Dhia – mura peacadh dhom é rádh sa gcás seo – tá leabhar ar fághail sa deireadh nach bhfuil feileamhnach mar leabhar sgoile.

253 Ní h-é amháin nach bhfuil aon scríbhneoir Gaedhilge eile ionchurtha leis, acht ní tháinig úirscéal Béarla ar bith amach i n-Éirinn le dhá bhliain, go bhfios domh, atá ar na gaobhair dó . . . B'fhéidir gurbh'é an leabhar seo tús an Renaissance Gaedhilge. See also the positive review by 'D.A.B.' (Daniel A. Binchy?) in *IS*, 24/12/27; and the brief favourable review by 'I. H.' of the English translation in the same journal (7/12/29).

254 Léighfidh a lán daoine 'Toil Dé' le fonn is le pléisiúr. Iarracht an-mhacánta iseadh é ar úrscéal ceart do thabhairt dúinn i nGaedhilg . . . Tréith eile ba dhóbair dom a dhearmhad, an ilghnéitheacht atá ann: feirmeoireacht, polaitíocht, cogadh, grádh, saol daoine bochta (gach duine lán-bheo agus a phictiúir sa cheart), comórtas Rugbí, vamp, an Dáil, an Seanad etc. Úrscéal a bhaineann le n-ár n-aimsir féin chó dlúth san nárbh fhéidir é shuidheamh in aon aimsir eile.

255 Níl aon smaoineamh ná feallsúnacht mar bhun leis an leabhar. Ní chruthuíonn sé ná ní thugann sé iarracht ar aon seóraí dá chuid féin do chruthú dhúinn i dtaobh cúrsaí beatha na ndaoine ná cúrsaí na tíre.

256 Ach féach a mhic ó, teastuigheann uainn gan focal do chloisint i dtaobh poilitidheachta go deo arís. Caithimís uainn mar sgéal é. Táim bréan de. Caithfidh mé an chuid eile dem' shaoghal ag cur cleite id stocaí más maith leat.

257 Chomh siúrálta a's atá féar ag fás in Éirinn is treise an bhanamhlacht ná an phoilitidheacht in Anna. Earlier in the novel, the mother had told her husband that were it not for him she would have opposed the Treaty. She says that Anna's problem is that she has no one to provide her with 'good counsel' (deagh-chomhairle) (p. 176).

258 Fágaimís mar sin iad: maran líontighe soilbhir iad is líontighe dlúithte iad, líontighe a bhíonn ag

obair as láimh a chéile, agus ná géilleann don éadóchas a ghoilleann ortha. Agus dar ndóigh, ní cóir dhúinn ár misneach do chailleamhaint toisg aon duine amháin, ná beirt ná triúr, dá thaithneamhaighe dá fheabhas iad, a bheith imthithe uainn. Buidheachas le Dia, do bhí an ceart ag an Athair Feargus: tá deigh-fhir agus deigh-mhná leis, in Éirinn fós; agus a ndóthaint oibre le déanamh aca in ath-thógaint na hÉireann.

259 Más rud é go bhfuilir chun leanamhaint den bhfeirmeoireacht beidh rud éigin ag teastáil uaim seachas fear oibre fuinneamhail. Sé rud atá in easnamh orm féin ach eolas ar ealadhain an curadóireachta a's mar sin de. Caithfidh tú do chéim a bhaint amach agus eolas ar an modh is déanaighe do thabhairt abhaile leat. Áirighim uaim é a's mé ad' iarraidh feabhas do chur ar chúrsaí na háite.

260 Ní den náisiún Gaedhealach iad, dar leó féin – sin mar a bhí an sgéal aca deich mbliadhna ó shoin sar ar cuireadh an réim nuadh i gcrích in Éirinn ach go háirithe. Droch-mheas a bhí aca ar na Gaedhil a dheineadh treabhadh agus fuirseadh dóibh chun iad a choimeád in uachtar. Ba dhóigh leat gur mí-nádúrtha an aigne seo i sean-Ghaedheal cé gur ion-tuigthe i nGall é, ach is amhlaidh nach fuirist an Gaedheal d'aithint ó'n nGall i measg uaisle na hÉireann.

261 Do bhí an dream san fíor-Ghallda ina n-aigne, ach mar sin féin do thugaidís Éireannaigh ortha féin d'aimhdheoin an ghráin a bhí aca ar Ghaedhil na hÉireann. Ní shéanfainn ná go raibh grádh aca d'Éirinn, leis, ina slighe féin: grádh áiteamhail mar a bhíonn ag Sasanach, cuir i gcás, dá chonntae féin. Sasanaigh ba dheadh iad i meon a's i gcroidhe, agus ní raibh sa ghrádh san ina dhiaidh sin ach grádh do sna tailtí breághtha fairsinge a bhí aca in Éirinn, don bhfiadhach, don lámhaigh, don iasgaireacht agus don spórt go léir a bhí le fagháilt aca innti.

262 Do bhí deire ar fad le réim na dtighearnaí talmhan in Éirinn . . . Ní raibh a gceacht foghlumtha go hiomlán aca, ámhthach. Níor thugadar an oiread san fuatha, b'éidir, do Chlanna Gaedheal a's do thug sar ar dibrigheadh iad ach do theip ortha glan an cuspóir agus an fuinneamh a bhí taobh thiar den éirighe amach do thuigsint agus bhíodar dall i gcómhnuidhe ar cad is Gaedhealachas ann.

263 Ní fheadar cad tá ag teacht ar an saoghal in ao' chor. Na daoine is saidhbhre a's is creideamhnaighe im' pharóiste ag taobhú leis an gramasg!

264 Dá luighead é a shuim i ngnáth-obair an Oireachtais do bhí aon cheist amháin leathismuigh de chúrsaí na talmhan inar chuir Máirtín an-spéis: do theastuigh uaidh go mbeadh fíor mhuinteardhas idir Éire agus Sasana, muinteardhas a bheadh bunuithe ar ionannas gradaim, mar ba cuibhe agus dhá náisiún ársa neamh-spleádhacha i gceist.

265 Ba mhar a chéile na habairtí cruinne eolgasacha a bhí á rádh chomh fuinneamhail san ag Máirtín Mac Cárthaigh agus béarlagar fir ghuirm ó chríochaibh na hAifrice.

266 Ó Gaora, 'An tÓráididhe Gasta', in *As na Ceithre hÁirdibh*, 111–20.

267 The play was performed in Taibhdhearc na Gaillimhe in 1938. The 'special reporter' for *IP* wrote of the play's Galway premiere:

> The applause was something more than the usual cheers which any new play might provoke. It was appreciation of a significant portent in the life of the modern Gaelic drama . . . There was almost an atmosphere of victory in the now famous western theatre when the final curtain dropped on the latest and perhaps the most important contribution to the real national drama (*IP*, 31/1/38).

268 Ach cé thug na h-órduithe? Saighdiúirí gairmeamhla a chaith a saoghal le pleananna báis is fola. Ach anois nuair ná fuil aon mhaith le n-a bpleananna cad a dheinid . . . Téigheann siad taobh thiar den arm agus imreann siad bás ar bhantracht is ar chlann na saighdiúirí. Cogadh! Troid ghlórmhar ar son do thíre! Agus ceapann na daoine úd ná fuil aon eisceachtaí ann . . . gur féidir leó daoine d'fhagháil chun a n-órduithe gránna do chur i ngníomh. Ceapann siad go bhfuil sé cómh h-éasgaidh do dhuine a mheóin atharú agus atá sé a chuid éadaigh.

269 Do sheas Tusa it' aonar tráth. Tuigfidh Tusa mo sgéal. Tuigfidh Tusa é. Seán Ó Conchubhair's unpublished play *Taidhbhreamh* (A dream) deals with a vision seen by a young gypsy woman in her cell on the eve of her execution. The play was first produced by An Comhar Drámaidheachta at the Peacock, 7–11 Dec. 1937. See 'Ar Aghaidh', 'At the Peacock Theatre', *Leader*, 18/12/37.

270 Níl ach dhá ní le déanamh má's maith linn an Ghaedhilg a bheith 'na teangain náisiúnta againn arís – an Ghaedhilg a thabhairt anuas trí chéad bliain nó an saol a chur siar an méid sin aimsire. Ní deacair dhéanamh amach cé'cu den dá ní sin a déanfar. Fearacht Mhahomet agus an sliabh fadó, tá an saol so ró-dhaingean ar a bhonnaibh agus is baoghalach gurb í an Ghaedhilg a chaithfidh gluaiseacht aniar má's maith léi teangmháil leis. Anois is í an litridheacht an bóthar, an t-aon bhóthar, a chaithfidh an Ghaedhilg gabháil sa ghluaiseacht sin aniar. Is í an litridheacht an chré 'na bhfásfaidh an Ghaedhilg nó go mbeidh an méid sin fáis atá sí chun deire déanta aici, agus is í leis, an chriathar trí na sgagfar gach aon ní nua a thiocfaidh agus a chaithfidh teacht innte le linn an fháis sin.

CHAPTER FOUR

'Wellspring of Nationality'

1 Nic Ghabhann, *Mágh Ealta Éadair*, 15. Glacaigidh misneach. An sean-Náisiún Gaedhealach seo a bhfuair na mílte bás ar a shon, béidh sé i n-a

Náisiún Gaedhealach go bráth. An tír a sheas fód ar feadh naoi gcéad mbliadhan i n-aghaidh na náimhde a chonnaic sibh ag teacht i n-a coinne, seasfaidh sí fód go deire sgríbe. Músglaigigh bhur misneach, a chlann ó!

2 Michael Collins, 'Advance and Use Our Liberties', in *The Path to Freedom* (Cork: Mercier Press, 1968 [1922]), 35.

3 Níl daoine ar talamh na cruinne is lugha eoluis i dtaobh seanchais agus staire a dtíre ná muinntear na h-Éireann. Tá ceachtanna móra i ngach aon ghiota dhe ach teacht isteach ortha.

4 Ach cia mhéad duine a chuireas suim dá laighead i stair na tíre nuair amháin a bheir sé cúl a chinn do'n Sgoil nó do'n Choláiste? Agus rud is náirighe ná sin, cia mhéad duine a bhfuil beagán nó a mhórán eolais aige ar an stair, ach nach bhfuil aige ann ach rud tur marbh – rud gan sugh gan seamhair? Nach dtiocfadh tabhairt ar na daoine dúil a chur i stair na tíre; agus, do réir a chéile, nach dtiocfadh tabhairt ortha móthachtáil goidé comh h-álainn oirdhearc uasal le n-a dtír féin?

5 Chum cabhrú le foillsiú leabhar nach úirscéalta i nGaedhilg, tá an Roinn Oideachais ag tairisgint roinnt áirithe de dheontaisí speisialta ó £150 go £250 an ceann d'úghdair a scríobhfaidh leabhair ar ádhbhair áirithe fé na mír-chinn seo leanas ach na h-ádhbhair a bheith ceaduighthe ag an Roinn:

(1) Stair gluaiseachta éigin poilitidheachta nó comhdhaonnachta a bhí ann le déidheannaighe;

(2) Beathfhaisnéis ar Éireannach mórchliú;

(3) Staidéar ar ghné nó ar thréimhse áirithe de stair litridheachta na Gaedhilge. Deontaisí Speisialta i gcomhair Leabhar nach Úirscéalta i nGaedhilg.

6 Is maith gur scríobh Tomás Ó Cléirigh an leabhar seo i nGaedhilg. Mairg nach ndéanann an Gúm daoine a bhéadh eolach ar an obair a chur a scríobhadh leabharthach de'n chineál seo.

7 Seo mar a thuigim-se an scéal. Níor bh'ionann ar fad stáid na mban agus stáid na bhfear. Má bhí an ceann ag duine aca ar an duine eile is ag na fearaibh do bhí sé. Acht ní h-amhlaidh do choimeád na fir aon chomhacht aca dóibh féin; níor choimeádadar acht ainm na comhachta. Níor theastaigh uatha pribhléidí a bhaint de na mnáibh acht ba bhreágh leo do chur i n-iúl do'n t-saoghal ar fad gur aca féin do bhí an barr ceannais. N-a dhiaidh sin, ba dheas leo soghluistí do bhronnadh ar a gcuid ban an tráth bhídís go ciúin cneasta. Ba shuarach leo intinn na mban agus a macántacht agus dá bhrigh sin choimeádadar an chomhacht aca féin, agus deirim-se libh gur beag an t-athrú atá tagtha ar an saoghal ó shoin i leith.

8 Among other groups that regularly sponsored history lectures were Cumann Gaelach na Stát-Sheirbhíse and Cumann na Sagart nGaedhealach. See, for example, *An Chléir: Tuarascbháil Chumainn na Sagart nGaedhealach* (The clergy: The report of the Association of Gaelic Priests) 1937–8, 33.

9 Atá Rialtas an tSaor Stáit ar tí craoláin a chur ar bun. Cuimhnighdís ar an nGaedhilg, ar stair na hÉireann, ar shaoidheacht na Banban . . . Sé an craolóir cliste líomhtha a mhúinfeas na táinte amach annseo, fearacht seanchaidhthe na hÉireann i n-allód. Many of these broadcasts were of lectures delivered to An Fáinne.

10 Níl ach dhá leigheas ar na scannánaibh: – iad do ruagadh ar fad (agus ní mórán a chaillfimís), nó pictiúrí Gaedhealacha d'fhagháil in a mbeadh cultúr agus náisiúntacht agus spiorad ár dTíre. Agus an oiread sin ádhbhar atá againn ó stair ioldaithte, bhríoghmhar ár ndaoine, ó shaoghal na Gaedhealtachta agus na gcathrach, ó áilneacht éadan na tíre agus meoin na nGaedheal.

11 Is féidir ádhbhar sgannáin atá níos fearr ná 'Catherine the Great' nó 'The Chess Player' dfhághailt ó'n ár stair féin. Dé fáth ná beadh sgannán de 'Chath Chluain Tarbh' agus an t-aighneas a d'imthigh roimhe do nochtadh? Ní foláir nó go mbeadh sé cómh maith le 'Nibelung' a rinne Lang. In ionsuidhe Luimnighe agus i bpléascadh na n-arm i mBaile an Fhaoite tá ádhbhar a bheadh oiriúnach do 'Eisenstein' féin.

12 Is truagh gan tuille drámaí d'á leithéid seo againn – drámaí a bheadh bunuighthe ar stair na tíre, idir stair thuata agus stair eaglaise.

13 Cúis bróid do lucht an Choláiste a fheabhas a h-aistrigheadh agus a léirigheadh – agus a héisteadh! – an dráma iongantach so. Tá súil agam go spreagfaidh sé duine éigin chum ádhbhar dráma a bhaint as stair nó litridheacht na hÉireann, chum go bhfeicimíd go fóill righthe agus naoimh ar na léiriú ar an árdán go maordha mórdhálach.

14 Tá ádhbhar dráma i ngach blúire de stair na h-Éireann. Dá léireóchtaí ar árdán dráma gurbh ádhbhar dó 'Beann Borb' cuir i gcás agus dá gcloisfimís arís Eoghan Ruadh Ó Néill ag spreagadh a shaighdiúirí . . . Nó fós dá gcloisfimís rosc catha na Gaedhna [*sic*] bhFiadhna ag 'Fontenoy' . . . buailfí isteach 'nár n-aigne cuimhne ár seacht n-aithreacha romhainn agus is beag duine ná beadh fuath aige do ghramaisc an Bheurla – rud níos fearr músclóchthaí 'nár gcroidhthe cion ar an dteangain aoibhinn ba dual do Phádruig, Bhrighid agus do Cholumcille.

15 'Siad an t-aos léighinn agus an t-aos foghluma is mó a bhainfeadh tairbhe as an drámuíocht. Chífidís stair ár dtíre aithbheodhaithe; chífidís cultúr ársa na nGaedheal; agus chloisfidís an Ghaedhilg bhinn d'á spreagadh ó'n árdán le binneas agus le ceart, le blas agus le fluírse.

16 Tá's againn conus a labhrann na daoine atá anois ann agus cad is dóichí a dhéanfidís agus adéarfidís ina leithéid seo no ina leithéid siúd de chás agus conus a déarfidís é. Tá eolas agus tá taithí againn ar 'atmosféir' an tsaoil atá anois ann ach níl ár ndóithin eolais againn fós ar chúrsaí na haimsire atá imithe chun 'atmosféir' no 'atmosféirí' na haimsire sin do shamhlú dhúinn féin.

17 *An Gaedheal agus an Radió*, 10. Ní hionmholta an rud dráma staireamhail ón sean-aimsir do thoghadh mar ní féidir a leithéid sin do léiriú gan éide agus feisteas a bhainfeadh le linn-ré an dráma féin, chun an saoghal an-aithnidh sin do chur in iúil don lucht éisteachta. Riobárd Ó Faracháin, who worked in Irish radio for many years, introduced a discussion of the challenges facing Gaelic playwrights interested in dramatising Irish history in his short story 'An Feall Gránna' (The ugly betrayal) in *Fíon gan Mhoirt*, 41.

18 Tomás Mac Eochaidh, 'An Gníomh-Amhrán agus an Mion-Dráma Ceoil', in *Láimh-Leabhar Drámaidheachta*, ed. Proinnsias E. Ó Súilleabháin (BÁC: Brún agus Ó Nualláin, Teor., n.d.), 32. I gcóir an ghníomh-amhráin soláthruigheann tú amhrán a bhfuil eachtra nó scéal ghá aithris ann agus léirigheann tú an scéal sin chómh maith is fhéadas tú. I gcóir an mhion-dráma ceoil ceapann tú féin an scéal nó an eachtra, agus annsan soláthruigheann tú na hamhráin is fearr oireas do'n scéal agus is fearr a léireochas é do'n lucht-éisteachta. Ní thig leat ach aon amhrán amháin a chur sa ngníomh-amhrán; sa mhion-dráma ceoil níl teora leis an méid amhrán is féidir a chur ann, ach ar aon choingheall amháin – go gcaithfidh siad uile baint a bheith aca le heachtra an dráma.

19 See 'Lucht Buaidhte na nDuaiseann, Féile an Iarthair, 1938' (The prize winners, the Festival of the West, 1938), in *Láimh-Leabhar Drámaidheachta*, 43; and Donncha Ó Súilleabháin, *An Cumann Scoildrámaoíchta, 1934–1984* (The Schools Drama Association, 1934–1984) (BÁC: An Clóchomhar, 1986), 20. In 1925 Seán Óg Ó Haonghusa published his poem 'An Tableau Gaodhlach' (The Gaelic tableau) about 'the historical production' (an stair-léiriú) at Feis Charman in Wexford (*FL*, 20/6/25). Irish Historical Productions, Inc., with help from Micheál Mac Liammóir and Hilton Edwards, put on 'The Pageant of the Celt' in Soldiers' Field in Chicago. Mac Liammóir provided the narrative, while 1,000 actors and 500 singers presented scenes from Irish history from 1700 BC to the Easter Rising of 1916. See 'Pageant of the Gael / Chicago Exiles React [*sic*] History of Irish Race', *An Phoblacht* 22/9/34.

20 Tá a lán á rádh le déidhnaighe gur righin an teacht é ag an scríbhneóir Gaedhilge atá chum scéalta a cheapadh dhúinn ar nidhthe a thárla in Éirinn do réir an tseanchais, fé mar a rinne Bhaitéir Scott sa Bhéarla i dtaobh galldacht na hAlban, agus R. L. Stephenson [*sic*], agus mar atá déanta insa Bhéarla ag Standish Ó Gráda, agus ag an mnaoi uasail sin Nic Mhághnuis. Is righin an teacht é gan amhrus, acht ní mór dúinn beagáinín foidhne bheith againn.

21 Ní mór an chabhair dúinn fíora loma fuara na staire chun sean-eachtraithe do shamhlú dhúinn féin mar fhéachadar fadó don mhuintir a bhí páirteach ionta no do chonnaic iad, no do chuala trácht ortha go luath tar éis iad do thárlachtaint. Tagann an t-úrscéalaí agus cuireann sé feoil ar an gcnámharlach. Séideann sé anam isteach ann agus cuireann sé ar ár gcumas maireachtaint tríd an scéal go léir fé mar a bheimís nár mbeathaidh le linn é thuitim amach. Go deimhin is mó duine gan d'eolas aige ar an stair ach an méid fuair sé as úrscéalta is drámaí staire. See his account of his own attempt to write a historical story in *Peann agus Pár*, 163–4. Cearbhall Ua Dálaigh recommended that Gaelic writers turn to historical fiction for stylistic reasons. Specifically, he suggested that writers follow the example of Scott and Sigrid Undset (*CB*, June 1931, 609).

22 Caithfear a admháil go bhfuil stair na h-Éireann gan scríobh fós. See also Aodh de Blácam, 'Stair' (History), *FL*, 28/6/24.

23 Seana-ghearán agam iseadh gan stair na hÉireann a bheith againn fós i nGaedhilg. Níl againn acht roinnt leabhra beaga suaracha staire nár dteangain féin agus aistrithe ón mBéarla iseadh a leath is dóich liom.

24 Agus ceist agam ar sgoláiribh Gaedhilge ár gcómh-aimsire. Cad chuige nach bhfuil le fagháil uatha cunntas maith beacht ar an dá Aodh mór, beatha a mbéadh ann an t-ádhbhar nua as na láimhsgríbhinnibh, agus mar sin de, a tháinig as ceilt san Spáinn, i nÉirinn agus i Sasanaibh i rith na h-aimsire atá caithte ó'n uair do chéad-cheap Ó Cléirigh an leabhar bunúsach? Sin rud atá a dhíth go géar ar léightheoirí. Ní moladh atá ag dul do sgoláirí na hÉireann gan sreath leabhra ar laochaibh Gaedhil san módh nua agus san spiorad nua a bheith le fagháil an t-am seo de'n lá.

25 Níor scríobhadh stair na tíre i gceart fós agus ní scríobhfar i gceart choidhche í nó go mbeidh an t-eólas go léir ag daoinibh, mar bíodh is go gcloisimíd go leor trácht ar chathannaibh agus ar ghluaiseachtaí ní thuigimíd saoghal ná meón na sean-Ghaedheal ná na smaointe a bhíodh 'na gcroidhe . . . Do b'ionann na cathanna agus na gluaiseachtaí agus uachtar an uisce a bhí á chorruighe is á shuathadh ag an anaithe acht maidir leis na rudaí a bhí fé'n uisce féin, maidir leis na rudaí a mhothuigh na daoine comónta is an saoghal a chaitheadar táimíd beagnach dall ortha. See also Manus O'Donnell (i.e. Maoghnus Ó Domhnaill), 'Read Your History', *An Phoblacht*, 29/10/26.

26 'Sé an t-ainm atá ar an leabhar ná 'Sgeul na h-Éireann' agus má's sgéal cogadh, clampar, agus trioblóid amháin, sgéal na h-Éireann, tá an sgéal san tugtha dúinn ag an Athair Pádraig. Ach ní mar sin a bhí, tá taobh eile leis an sgéal, agus ní thráchtann sé thar an taoibh sin ar chor ar bith . . . Mar sin tar éis an leabhair bheith léighte aca, ba dhóigh le páistibh gur fíor an rud atá curtha 'nár gcoinne le naimhdibh ár dtíre nach rabhamar de shíor ach ag clampar agus ag troid. See the similar views expressed by An tAthair Eric Mac Fhinn in 'Local history', *Studies*, June 1931, p. 278.

27 Do mheasas féin tamall ná bíodh de chúram ar na daoinibh a bhí ar an saoghal fadó ach bheith ag

lámhach agus ag marbhú a chéile ó cheann ceann na bliana; níor chuimhnigheas riamh go raibh mná ann an uair sin, ná páistí, ná lucht oibre ach righthe agus saighdiúirí ar fad . . . Is mó spéise a chuireann na scoláirí (agus na múinteoirí leis, tá eagla orm) i gcúrsaibh cogaidh ná mar a chuirid i gcúrsaibh síothchána agus gnótha. In a 1930 essay on 'Eagnaidheacht an Staireolais' (The science of history) in the same paper, 'Taistealaidhe' argued that a disproportionate emphasis on warfare in a nation's history was a sign of the failure of Christianity to take deep root in that nation (*II*, 30/6/30).

28 Go dtí le deireannas 'séard a bhí 'sa' stair a múintí scéal na righthe a tháinic i gcomhairle na tíre, agus faoi na cathanna a thugadar, lá a mbreithe, lá a mbáis, agus mar sin de. Ach is iondamhail go ndéantar iarracht anois ar an sean-tsaol idir uasal agus íseal, a mbéasa agus a ngníomhartha agus a smuainte, cúrsaí cogaidh agus cúrsaí síothcháin, a chiallú do'n tsaol nuadh.

29 Leis an saghas sin staire do theagasc do thuigfeadh na leanbhaí an árd-chéim a fuair Éire tráth, agus an tábhacht a bhaineas le n-ár dteangain náisiúnta agus le n-ár sean-nósmhaireacht.

30 An chuid is tábhachtaighe dhen stair – agus an chuid is lugha a mbíonn tagairt fhéin dó ins na gnáthleabhra fá stair na hÉireann, abair sa naomhadh aois déag – saoghal muinntire na tíre: a gcuid nósa, a gcuid smaointe, na neithe a thaithnigh leo, an bealach a mairidís – na rudaí beaga seafóideacha féin a chuirfeadh laethannta a óige i gcuimhne dhon deoraidhe. Ó bhéal-aithris na sean atá na neithe sin le foghluim. See also An tAthair Mac Fhinn's review of Ó Cléirigh's *Aodh Mac Aingil*, *AA*, June 1936, 7.

31 Is iomdha gné de shaoghal an náisiúin nach léar don té a scríobhas cunntas ar chúrsaí poilitidheachta amháin. Ní léar dó intinn ná meon na ndaoine a choinnigh an béaloideas luachmhar beo. Ní léar dó an fheallsamhnacht a bhí taobh thiar de sheanchus agus de chreideamh do-chlaoidhte an Ghaedhil. Níor thuig sé gur buaine dúthchas an chinidh 'ná na neithe beaga amaideacha ar chuir sé féin suim ionnta.

32 Cuireann an béal-oideas ar an eolas muid, ní hé amháin fá eachtraí loma na staire, ach fá aigne agus croidhe agus smaointe ár sean agus ár sinnsear.

33 See his editorial 'The Importance of Irish Popular Traditions', *Béaloideas*, June 1931, 103–4. Henry Morris also discussed the importance of folklore for an understanding of the history of the common people in any country in his 'Focal do'n Léightheoir' (A word to the reader), in *Oidhche Áirneáil i dTír Chonaill*, ii–iii. See also Seán Ó Súilleabháin, 'Na Daoine Comónta / A Stair Dá Scríobh!' (The common people / Their history being written!), *IP*, 20/4/38; and Conchubhar Ó Ruairc, 'Béaloideas na dTighthe / Stair is Ceárduíocht' (The folklore of the houses / History and craftsmanship), *Standard*, 22/7/38.

34 Dinneen, 'Stair Phoblacht na Rómha' (The history of the Roman Republic), in *Aistí ar Litridheacht Ghréigise is Laidne*, 62. Do ghéill a lán léightheoirí do sna scéaltaibh sin; agus is mór an mhaise ar an stair iad a bheith 'na fíor-thosach; mar an méid díobh nár thárla do ceapadh iad tré ghrádh do Phoblacht na Rómha agus chum an choitchianntacht do theagasc. Tá scéalta dá leithéid ag baint le tíorthaibh eile agus le tír na hÉireann chomh maith céadna.

35 Nic Ghabhann, *Mágh Ealta Éadair*, v. Níl aon nidh is buaine – ná is iontaobhtha, ar a bhealach féin – ná'n béal-oideas. Innstear sgéalta faoi'n dúthaigh cois teine, díne i ndiaidh díne. Cuirtear leo, nó baintear asta, acht fanann bunús na sgéalta gan athrú. Fíortar na sgéalta, uaireannta. It should, however, be noted that she herself seems too willing to accept the historical veracity of folk material. See, for example, pp. 9 and 20.

36 Ó Siochfhradha, 'Réamh-Rádh', in *Triocha-Chéad Chorca Dhuibhne*, xiii. Ba mhór go léir an tsuim a bhí im liostaí ag na daoine gur léigheas dóibh iad agus ba gheall le bheith ag tabhairt na marbh beo as an uaigh dóibh é an méid tuarasgabhála agus seanchais a múscluigheadh le cuimhne a n-ainmneacha. Do tuigeadh dom gurab 'in gné den bhéaloideas dob fhiú a chuardach agus a chur síos – stair agus saoghal na ngnáth-daoine tuaithe ins na bailte fearainn – agus é choimeád mar eolas do gach glúin dá dtiocfaidh.' See also Máirtín Ó Cadhain, 'Sgéaluigheacht Chois-Fhairrge' (The storytelling of Cois Fhairrge), *Béaloideas*, June 1933, 86.

37 For a brief discussion of Murray's extensive use of folklore in his historical work, see Mac Giolla Chomhaill, *Lorcán Ó Muireadhaigh*, 81.

38 See Nollaig Mac Congáil, 'An Traidisiún Béil i Saothar Sheagháin Mhic Mheanman', and Séamus Mac Giolla Uain, 'Saothar Sheáin Mhic Mheanman agus Patrick McGill: Gné d'Oidhreacht Áitiúil Pharóiste Inis Caoil' (The work of Seán Mac Meanman and Patrick McGill: An aspect of the local heritage of the parish of Inis Caoil), in *Éigse 1988: Seán Bán Mac Meanman*, ed. Ó Cnáimhsí, 14–19, and 21–30, respectively.

39 Domhnall Ó Súillebháin, *Beatha Dhomhnaill Uí Chonaill* (BÁC: ODFR, 1936), 254–75. At the start of this chapter, Ó Súillebháin wrote:

> We have here some of that sort of thing that we encountered, both prose and poetry. I would have had more of them also if it were not that the manuscript where I had them and that I made around the year 1900 had not gone missing without a trace (Tá againn annso cuid den tsaghas san a bhuail linn, idir prós agus filidheacht. Bheadh a thuille, leis, agam díobh mar mbeadh gur imigh an scríbhinn mar a rabhadar agam, agus a dhéanas tuairim na bliana 1900, chun fáin gan a tuairisc) (p. 254).

Reviewing the book for *II* in 1937, 'C. Mac M.' wrote: 'The really valuable portion of this new life of

O'Connell relates to the stories, legends, and poems that grew up around the folk legend of him' (*II*, 9/3/37). The author's use of folklore about O'Connell was also praised by Seán Ó Faoláin in his review of the book (*IT*, 13/2/37).

40 For his awarness of the problematic nature of some of his sources, see Ó Domhnaill, *Oileáin Árann*, 9, 96, 102, 180, 200. For his naive acceptance of those sources, see *Oileáin Árann*, 60, 62–3, 67, 85, 145–7.

41 In an unsigned 1936 piece on 'Dána and St Brigid', the author (probably W.P. Ryan) states: 'We ought not allow romance and folk-lore to obscure for us the many fascinating issues raised by old Irish history' (*Féile na nGaedheal*, Nov. 1926, 4).

42 Ní go dtí le goirid, pé brí fáth a bhí leis, a luigheamar isteach ar stair na hÉireann do sgrúdú go healadhanta, cruaidh-aigeantach. I gcruthamhnas ar sin, níl againn le déanamh ach ár leabhragáin sa mbaile do chuartú. Cá bhfuil na himleabhair mhóra chliútúla sin a bhíos le feiceál go coitchianta ar leabhargáin lucht léighinn is cultúir i dtíortha eile? Tá leath-dhosaen nó dosaen leabhar againn gur féidir linn a rádh le méid áirithe cinnteacht' ina dtaoibh go bhfuil fíor-eolas ar stair ár sean ionnta agus nach fabhail-sgéalta nó liostaí de chatha mórfhuaimneacha. Le goirid a sgríobhadh na leabhra sin. In 1925, Tomás Ó Máille wrote to Alice Stopford Green asking her permission to translate her forthcoming *History of Ireland to the Norman Conquest*. See Ó Máille, Letters to Green, 19 and 26 Mar. 1925; Alice Stopford Green Papers, NLI MS 10,457 (7).

43 Tá suim nua dá chur i seanchas na hÉireann anois, ach is eagal liom dá mhéid dá bhfuiltear a dhéanamh, gurab annamh chuirtear pioctúir fíor ar an tsaoghal atá thart os cómhair scoláirí. Shílfeá ó mhórán de na leabhraibh seanchais atá ar fagháil nach raibh locht de lochtaibh an chinidh daonna ar ár sinnsear, gur dhaoine iad a chaith a saoghal go deaghmhóideach cráibhtheach, gur naoimh thug iad féin suas go h-iomlán do Dhia an mhór-chuid aca. Bhí naoimh ina measc gan amhras, ach bhí daoine ann i ngach aois nár ghéill d'aitheanntaibh Dé mar bhí i ngach tír eile. Measaim gurab é cuspóir badh cheart bheith ag an tseanchaidhe pioctúir a thabhairt ar an tsaoghal atá thart eadar maith is olc. He himself, however, saw little that was not noble in the history of his country.

44 An anonymous writer in the same paper offered an explanation of the Irish tendency to idealise the national past:

> British propaganda maligned us and maligned our ancestors. We met that propaganda by describing ourselves and our ancestors as wronged and long-suffering angels. Neither view is correct, and it is imperative that a correct picture should be obtained, because history, instead of being something entirely useless, is essential for every people (*UIrman*, 28/12/34).

45 On rare occasions the quest for a more objective stance could lead to a startling iconoclasm, as when in 1929 'An Droighneán Fionn' pictured the social class that included the royalty and heroes of Irish legendary history as parasites, writing of the treatment of the poor in standard histories: 'There is no mention of the ones who paid the piper and who were obliged whether they wanted to or not to support by the sweat of their brows Cú Chulainn, Feargus Mac Róigh, Niall of the Nine Hostages, Dáithí and the rest of the plunderers' (Ní luaidhtear iad seo a d'íoc an píobaire agus ar cuireadh orthu Cú Chulainn, Feargus Mac Róigh, Niall-Naoi-nGiallach, Dáithí agus an chuid eile de na sgriosadóirí a bheathughadh air an neamh-chead dóbhtha fhéin as allus a malacha) (*Ultach*, Feb. 1929, 2). His views provoked responses from Father Murray and Seosamh Mac Grianna in the issue of *An t-Ultach* for June 1929.

46 Ní h-é cuspóir an tseanchaidhe feabhas a chur ar shaoghal an lae indiu ná grádh athardha a dhúiseacht i n-intinn na n-óg, ná seanmóir a chur síos ar olcas an tsaoghail atá thart. Tiocfaidh gach ceann aca sin de bhárr a shaothair má bhíonn intinn an léightheora ag claonadh 'un na h-uaisle agus an mhaitheasa, ach ní mar gheall ar chuspóir an tseanchaidhe é, ach mar gheall ar fhírinne an phioctúra atá tugtha aige.

47 As an staraidheacht seadh tiocfaidh chughainn arís an mhuinighin agus an dóchas náisiúnta úd a bhí beo in Éirinn nuair a bhí an teanga náisiúnta dá labhairt coitianta sa tír. Tugaimís eolas cruinn dár scoláirí óga ar ré órdha an chreidimh agus an léighinn, nuair a bhí meas ar ár dtír dhúthchais ar fuaid na hEorpa. Mar is in aithbheócaint na spride a bhí beo in Éirinn an uair sin atá slánú agus tógáil an náisiúin indiu.

48 Dinneen, 'Réamhrádh', in *Scéal na hÉireann don Aos Óg: Cuid a hAon* (BÁC: Brún agus Ó Nualláin, Teor., [1932]), 3. Ní foláir nó raghaidh léigheamh is breathnughadh an scéil sin chum suime do pháistibh scoile; gríosóchaidh sé iad chum foighne, chum féile, chum carthannachta; gríosóchaidh sé iad chum cródhachta is chum meanman; chum dílse do thír a ndúthchais is do theagasc na naomh.

49 Ní haon mhaith aire do thabhairt do 'litir' staire agus gan aire do thabhairt dá 'spiorad' . . . Is fearr bréag bhlasta spriocfaidh na daoine chun grádh thabhairt dá dtír ná fírinne thur fhágfaidh ina Seoiníní iad.

50 Tá an Stair chóir a bheith comh tábhachtach leis an Ghaedhilg í féin. Bun-chloch amháin de'n Náisiúntacht an Stair, mar tá sí i Sasain, 'sa' Ghearmáin, 'san Fhrainc, fiú ins na Stáit Aontuighthe.

51 Seosamh Ó Greanna [*sic*], *Léigheacht ar Crois-Bhealaigh i Stair na h-Éireann* (BÁC: Sinn Féin Ard-Chomhairle, 1924), 15.

52 Cuireann sé crith ar na sean-daoine a bheith ag léigheadh staire, go mór-mór an chuid aca nach bhfuair mórán oideachais, mar bíonn faitchíos ortha

go dtiocfaidh an lá nuair a bhéas ar an mac sin acu fhéin dul amach ar son na tíre.

53 Hanly, *The National Ideal*, 123.

54 Is minic a dubharthas – agus dob'fhíor é – go mbeimís dall ar stair na hÉireann go dtí go mbeadh taobh na nGaedheal de ar fáil againn. An fhaid a bhíomair ag brath ar an dtaobh eile, an taobh a sgríbh daoine iasachta nár thuig aigne ár muintire agus a chuir a n-innsint féin ar gach ní dá bhfeacadar, níor fhéadamair fíorbhreith a thabhairt ar aon rud dár thuit amach sa tír seo ó fuair na Gaill an lámh uachtair ann. Seosamh Mac Grianna was contemptuous of the claims of Anglo-Irish historians – among whose number he seems to have included Eoin Mac Néill! – writing in 1933: 'That is the attitude the Anglo-Irishman always has, that all knowledge and everything good is on the other side of the water, and that that is how it always was. No man at all with that attitude can write Irish history' (Sin an dearcadh atá ag an GhallGhael i gcónaí, gur ar an taobh eile den uisce atá gach eolas agus ollmhaitheas, agus gur mar sin a bhí riamh. Ní féidir d'fhear ar bith a bhfuil an dearcadh sin aige stair na hÉireann a scríobh) (*Camán*, 14/1/33). In 'Comhairle don "Droighneán Fionn"' (Advice to 'An Droighneán Fionn'), he did, however, recommend works in English by Alice Stopford Green and P. S. O'Hegarty as truthful accounts of Irish history (*Ultach*, Jan. 1929, 3).

55 Anois an té a scríobhfas stair na h-Éireann mar is ceart a sgríobhadh, tá mórán le foghluim aige, agus le n-a chois sin, caithfidh sé na téadaí dubháin-ealla a shníomh amadáin a shíl go rabh eolas aca ar stair, caithfidh sé iad a sguabadh as a bhealach. Agus os cionn gach uile nidh caithfidh sé an difear atá eadar náisiúntacht agus saoirse a thuigbheáil.

56 Seosamh Mac Grianna, *Na Lochlannaigh* (BÁC: OS, 1938), 8. Mur' as an Ghaedhealtacht an t-ughdar, is deacair dó tuigse ar bith a bheith aige ar an chineál Gaedheal a bhí ann tá míle bliadhain ó shoin.

57 Creidim gur iomdha marc a chaill mé ar scoil cionnus nach dtiocfadh liom suim a chur i gcuid de 'Stair na h-Éireann.' Níor chuir mé riamh suim i stair na Sasannach i n-Éirinn, agus ní bhuaidhirfinn mo chionn leis na daoine a d'éirigh 'níos Éireannaighe 'ná na h-Éireannaigh iad féin' – más fíor é . . . Acht ní chuala mé ainm Branaigh nó Tuathalaigh ariamh 'ghá luadh nár éirigh mo chroidhe. B'iad san na daoine cearta – na daoine sheasaigh ar son na saoirse.

58 Niall Ó Domhnaill, *Beatha Sheáin Mistéil* (BÁC: ODFR, 1937), 281–4.

59 See Mac Congáil, 'Seosamh Mac Grianna', in *Rí-Éigeas na nGael*, ed. Mac Congáil, 151–2; and 'Réamhrá', in *Seosamh Mac Grianna / Iolann Fionn: Clár Saothair* (BÁC: Coiscéim, 1990), 27.

60 Mac Grianna, *Mo Bhealach Féin*, 10.

61 Mac Grianna, *Léigheacht*, 3.

62 Bhí cumhacht níos treise ar a chúl 'ná poilitidheacht ar bith. B'í an Ghaedhealg agus an spiorad a mhúscail sí ar fud Éireann an chumhacht sin. Ní thug sí ach leath-bhealaigh sinn go fóill. Bhéarfaidh sí iomlán an bhealaigh sinn go cuan na Saoirse ach Éire Ghaedhealach a bheith ar uachtar, an Éire Ghaedhealach sin ar briseadh uirthi le linn Eoghan Ruaidh Uí Néill agus Phádraic Sáirséil.

63 Surprisingly enough, *An Lóchrann* offered MacManus's book as first prize in a competition for the collection of folklore in 1927 (*Lóchrann*, June 1927, 151).

64 Nic Ghabhann, *Mágh Ealta Éadair*, vi. Níor bhacas mórán leis na leabhra staire do sgríobhadh i mBéarla amháin – cuid acu d'ár thugas seársa tríotha nílid iontaobhtha, cuid eile, is ar shaoghal na nGall sa tír seo is mó a chuirid síos.

65 Tá sí chomh dlúth-cheangailte sin le stair na tíre – nár mhór duit í chun fíor-sgéul na hÉireann a thuisgint i gceart. See also 'U.A.', 'Leabhar Nua [A new book] / The Story of the Irish Race', *Misneach*, 17/6/22. Interestingly enough, An tAthair Mac Fhinn wrote of Ernest Joynt's *Histoire de l'Irlande des origines à l'État Libre* (A history of Ireland from the start to the Free State) that it had 'the two qualities . . . a historian needs most, a Gaelic outlook and a charitable Christian outlook' (an dá thréith . . . is mó a theastuigheas ón staruidhe, dearcadh Gaedhealach agus dearcadh carthannach Críostuidhe) (*AA*, Dec. 1936, 7). 'L. Ó B.' (probably Liam Ó Briain) praised Joynt's book as 'an accurate, balanced account of Ireland from the side of the Gaels' (cunntas cruinn comhthrom ar Éirinn ó thaobh na nGaedheal de) and said that it should be translated at once into Irish and English (*CT*, 1/2/36).

66 Hanly, *National Ideal*, 125.

67 Mac Gréagóir, 'Réamh-Rádh', in *Stair na nDéise*, viii. Nach é an díombáidh agus nach truagh an sgéal é ná fuil aon mhaith sa leabhar so don chuid is mó ar fad de sna daoine is fearr a mbeadh tuigsint aca sa nGaedhilg atá ann, sin iad lucht na tuatha d'airigh an Ghaedhilg mar bheo-theangain ó n-a n-óige. Nach ait an t-oideachas a fuair muintir na Gaedhilge nuair a caithtear leabhar Gaedhilge d'aistriú go Béarla chun go bhféadfadh cainnteoirí maithe Gaedhilge aon tairbhe do bhaint as.

68 Ó Siochfhradha, 'Réamh-Rádh', in *Triocha-Chéad Chorca Dhuibhne*, xviii.

69 See Finnín Ní Choncheanainn and Ciarán Ó Coigligh, *Tomás Bán* (BÁC: Conradh na Gaeilge, 1996), 146–147. Reviewing the book in *An Róimh*, Maitiú Ó Cathail called it 'the best example we have yet been given in Irish for writing about history' (an eisiompláir is fearr a tugadh dúinn fós 'sa nGaedhilg i gcóir scríobhnóireachta faoi'n stair) (*Róimh*, Summer 1923, 23).

70 There are several exceptions, among them Sligo ('the Castlebar Races', the great Irish–French victory in County Mayo [!] in 1798); Leitrim (turf and bogs); Roscommon ('the people' [na daoine]); Offaly

(Clonmacnoise); Meath (Tara); Longford ('grazing land' [talamh feurach]); Cavan (roads), and Fermanagh (canals).

71 In his review of the book for *AA*, An tAthair Mac Fhinn pronounced it the best textbook available on the period in either Irish or English (*AA*, Nov. 1939, 8).

72 Séamus Ó Ceallaigh published a series of essays in English on 'Famous Women in Irish History', in *Our Girls* in 1930, 1931, and 1932. Máire Ní Churráin published a series of brief biographical pieces on famous Irishwomen of the past in *Mother and Maid* in 1932. Among her subjects were 'An Inghean Dubh', the mother of Aodh Ruadh Ó Domhnaill; Éibhlín Dubh Ní Chonaill (the author of 'Caoineadh Airt Uí Laoghaire'); and the famous queen Gormfhlaith of Viking times.

73 Ua Concheanainn, *Laochra Gaedheal*, 133. Acht sé lom-chlár na fírinne a rádh nach raibh na fir a throid ar son na hÉireann ariamh gan neart oighrí a fhágáil i n-a ndiaidh. An dá luath is bhíodh laoch leagtha ar lár, bhíodh duine is duine eile d'á chineadh nó d'á bhunadh féin, réidh chun seasadh go tailceach i mbearnain an bhaoghail. Their strategy was applauded by the critic who reviewed the book for *II*:

> I think that that is the best way to tell the story of Ireland to the young – to give them the lives of the most famous saints and soldiers and kings so that there will be a link among all the chapters, and to do that in the form of a story instead of a history (Is dóich liom gurab é sin an tslighe is fearr chun scéal na h-Éireann d'innsint don aos óg – beatha na naomh agus na saighdiúirí agus na ríghthe is mó cáil a thabhairt dóibh i dtreo go mbeidh ceangal idir gach caibidil agus an méid sin do dhéanamh i bhfuirm sgéil in ionad staire) (*II*, 19/3/23).

74 Is minic a chluin tú daoine ag cainnt ar mhuintir na h-Éireann agus a rádh: 'Bíonn an croidhe san áit cheart i gcomhnaidhe ag an t-sluagh, acht díolann na fir-ceannuis iad.' Sílim féin nach rabh a croidhe san áit cheart ariamh ag an t-sluagh agus nach mbíonn go deo. Am ar bith a dteárn Éire cleas éifeachtach ar bith rinne sí de bhrígh de go rabh fear éifeachtach amháin ann a rinne a chomhairle féin agus thug ar an t-sluagh géilleamhaint dó. See also Ó Grianna, *Feara Fáil*, 126.

75 Níor chall do dhuine puinn aimsire do chaitheamh ag gabháil do sheanchas na hÉireann chun a thuiscint gur *daoine* do dhealbhuigh é agus nach *policies* . . . Byron, sílim, a chas d'achmhusán linn: 'The Irish dearly love a lord.' Ghéillfinn dó, ach déarfainn gur umhluigheamair do thighearnas aigne agus anama chomh minic is dheineamair don teidiol. B'fhuiriste ainmneacha a luadh a léiróchadh mar ghreamuigh taoisigh poilitidheachta áirithe samhluidheacht na ndaoine i dtreo gur coinnigheadh cuimhne ortha le breis agus céad blian.

76 Mac Clúin, *An Litríocht*, 21. Conus is féidir tuairim fiúntach bheo a bheith ag an léightheóir muna bhfuil an bheatha bheo i leathanaigh an leabhair, is fórsaí beo an chroidhe daona? Ní déarfar go bhfuil an stair is fearr is féidir i *The French Revolution* le Carlyle . . . ach ná fuil an scéal dian-chomhachtach? Is ná fuil na caragdaeirí móra ag borra ós ár gcóir le brí is fuinneamh beatha?

77 Tuigeann an t-ughdar an poinnte tábhachtach so .i. gur fearr stair aon aoise do chomhcheangailt le h-aghaidh na ndaoine óg, le h-ainm duine mhóir éigin do mhair agus d'oibrigh ins an aois sin; cuir i gcás Colm Cille, Brian Bóraimhe, Eoghan Rua Ó Néill agus arl. See also 'Peann', 'Stair mar Ádhbhar Léighinn ins na Scoileanna Náisiúnta' (History as an academic subject in the National Schools), *An Chearnóg*, June 1923, 1. One cultural nationalist who wanted to go beyond the biographical obsession was Thomas McGreevy, the poet and future director of the National Gallery of Ireland, who in 1924 called for the compilation of 'a Gaelic Encyclopedia, a compendium of all the known facts about Gaelic Ireland . . . about our great men and women, our buildings, our sculptures, our work in precious metals, our literature, our science, our religion', all to be written in 'unpretentious but intelligible prose' (*SF*, 8/11/24).

78 Ua Concheanainn, *Laochra Gaedheal*, 57. I n-a dhiaidh seo mheas Brian go gcuirfeadh sé Maolseachlainn as ceannas ar fad. Leis sin a thabhairt chun críche rinne sé rud éigin nár cheart dó a dhéanamh, agus caithfear é cháineadh as ucht go ndeárna.

79 Ó Fallamhain, *Gearr-Stair*, 11. Bhí an t-éirghe i n-áirde i mBrian agus ní raibh sé sásta fanacht mar bhí sé. Ba mhian leis bheith i n-a Áird-Rígh. Throid sé le muintir Chonnacht agus le Rígh Laighean agus sa deireadh b'éigin do Mhaoileachlainn Mór, an t-árd-rí géilleadh dhó san mbliadhain 1002.

80 Mac Énrí, *Sár-Laochra Éireann*, 34.

81 Ó Siochfhradha, *Stair-Sheanchas Éireann: Cuid 1*, 66, 71. Do chonnacadar gur tré lámh-láidir do dhein Brian árd-rí dhe féin agus ná raibh aon cheart eile aige. Do thuigeadar nár ghábhadh aon cheart a bheith aca féin dá mbeadh an neart aca. Is mar sin do thosnuigh na ríghthe cúige ag troid le chéile agus ag creachadh na tíre féachaint cé'ca duine díobh a bheadh 'na Árd-Rí.

82 Ó Grianna, *Feara Fáil*, 25. Tháinigh an fear a bhí 'dhíoghbháil. Chuaidh Brian Bóroimhe i gceannus na tíre mar Árd-righ agus ghéill an chuid eile dó.

83 Breathnach, *Cúrsaí na hÉireann*, 62. 'Séard a chuir sé roimhe ná cinidheacha na hÉireann do shnadhmadh agus do dhaingniú le chéile i n-aon náisiún láidir amháin. Breathnach never really blames Brian for the incessant anarchic power plays that followed his death. In his *Eacthraí Móra ó n-Ár Stair*, Pádraic Ó Conaire notes the constant competition for the kingship after Brian, but does not present it as a result of his usurpation (p. 42).

84 Ua Concheanainn, *Laochra Gaedheal*, 165. Ní'l duine againn a rachfas go dtí roilig mhór Ghlais Naoidheain agus a leagfas a rinnrosg ar an mhóir-leacht-chuimhne atá i bhfuirm cruinn-túir ós cionn a uaighe nach mbogfaidh an croidhe i n-a chliabh, agus nach n-abróchaidh leis féin, déanfar dearmad ar lochta an laoich laochamhail agus coinnightear a mhór-ghníomhartha agus a mhóir-éachta i gcuimhne Gaedheal go héag. Nothing whatever was said about the Liberator's alleged marital infidelities. Gaelic historians were just as adept at sidestepping the moral issues raised by the conduct of Parnell. Of those who discussed Parnell, Ó Siochfhradha admits that the rumours spread about his relationship with Katherine O'Shea were confirmed, but makes no further comment on the issue. Ó Súilleabháin simply states that disagreement arose among members of his party with regard to his leadership, but never says why.

85 Breathnach, *Cúrsaí na hÉireann ó Chath Chionn-tsáile anall go dtí 1921*, 133. Ó bunuigheadh Saor-stát Éireann (1922) tá a lán déanta ag ár Riaghaltas féin leis an nGaedhilge d'aithbheodhchaint.

86 Dinneen, *Scéal na hÉireann*, 106. Cuireann an connradh soin an treo céadna ar Éirinn is mar atá ar Chanada acht go mbeadh cuanta áirithe fá réir chabhlaigh na Breataine i n-aimsir síothchána agus an cósta ar fad le linn chogaidh. Dinneen noted that the Treaty gave the six counties in the north the right to opt out of the Free State, and that they did indeed exercise that right. He also commented briefly on the Civil War itself.

87 Ó Siochfhradha, *Stair-Sheanchas Éireann: Cuid II*, 169. Is deacair áireamh a dhéanamh ar an droch-thoradh a tháinig den dtroid mhí-ádhmaraigh seo. Do deineadh deighilt gan leigheas idir an dream ba dhílse d'Éirinn. Do cuireadh síol fala agus droch-amhrais ameasc Gaedheal; do marbhuigheadh agus do lámhachadh mór-chuid de na fearaibh dob fhearr sa tír sa Chogadh Cathardha, agus ins an milleadh a thárlaidh do deineadh diomáiste thar áireamh ar chuid agus ar ghnó na tíre. As another indication of his attempt at objectivity, he comments on the accomplishments of the pro-Treaty Cumann na nGaedheal government of 1922 to 1932, and notes that the victorious anti-Treaty Fianna Fáil party removed the oath of fidelity to the British crown from the Free State constitution, and retained land annuities payments to the British Exchequer, two major promises of their election platform in 1932. It is worth noting here that a surprising number of these school histories were published by commerical presses, although their market was obviously the schools, schools controlled throughout our period by one or the other of the two main parties that emerged from the Civil War.

88 Is fíor le rádh gur bé an stráinséar a theasbáineadh dúinn chomh measamhail 's ba cheart dúinn a bheith do stair 's do áiteachaibh staireamhla atá thart timcheall orainn.

89 Mothóidh siad mar a bhéadh sruth na staire ag rith tríotha féin agus go bhfuil sé de dhualgas ortha agus gur rud nádúrtha dhóibh claoi go dlúth le gach aon rud a bhaineann lena dtír féin.

90 Is minic a deirtear gur truagh gan stair Ghaedhlach againn. Stair a neosfadh, insan teangan náisiúnta, sceul na h-Éireann i leith leis an náisiún Gaedhlach féin. Gan amhras tá saothar speisialta deunta ag scoláiribh áirithe, ach an stair phobalta as Gaedhilg ní dócha go scríobhfar í go dtí go mbeidh saothrú deunta ar an dtuath-sheanchas, nó dúthaigh-eolas, roimh ré. Ar an bhfoirgneamh sin, béidir, tógfar fíor-stair náisiúnta ar ball.

91 At least one critic, 'M. Ó D.', questioned the rationale of this scheme on the grounds that the counties themselves were relatively late colonial impositions on Irish geography (*II*, 26–27/12/38).

92 See Diarmuid Breathnach and Máire Ní Mhurchú, *1882–1982: Beathaisnéis a Ceathair* (BÁC: An Clóchomhar, 1994), 118.

93 Seaan [*sic*] Ó Cadhla's *Cathair Phort Láirge agus na Déise / A Gael's Guide to Waterford and the Déise Country*, originally published in 1917, was reprinted in a new and revised version in 1927.

94 Mac Gréagóir, 'Réamh-Rádh', in *Stair na nDéise*, vi–vii.

95 In his review of *Ros Comáin*, Séamus Ó Néill took the author to task for his uncritical acceptance of legendary material as valid history (*IP*, 28/12/38).

96 Acording to the same article, there was also 'a drama of a period of Dublin history' at this feis. See also the report of a lecture by R. Dudley Edwards in ''Sa Mheadhon-Aois / Cathair Bhaile Átha Cliath / A Córus Riaghaltais' (In the middle ages / The city of Dublin / Its system of government), *IP*, 8/3/38.

97 There is an unpublished typescript of the pageant in NLI. It is divided into seven 'episodes', dealing with, among other events, 'the rape of Dervorgilla', 'the Judas of the Gael' (Diarmuid Mac Murchadha), the trial of Robert Emmet, and 'Easter, the City in Dawn.' In his 'Focal ó'n Údar' (A word from the author) in the programme for the performances, Mac Liammóir said that he and Hilton Edwards were of the opinion 'that it is not right, in a work of this kind, to adhere too much to historical exactitude with regard to the people dealt with in the drama' (nach bhfuil sé ceart, i saothar de'n chineál seo, bheith ag iarraidh claoi an iomarca le beachtuíocht stairiúil maidir le gníomharthaibh na ndaoine a bhfuil trácht orra sa dráma) (pp. 7–8).

98 Father Dinneen contributed a series of essays on Irish saints to the *Father Mathew Record* in 1932.

99 Among the Irish saints dealt with in this series were St Columbán (by Dóirín Nic Aodha, 1936); St Iarlaith (by An tAthair Pádraig Mac Aodha, 1936); St Breandán (by An tAthair Eric Mac Fhinn, 1937); and St Brigid (by An tAthair Mac Aodha, 1937). There were also lives of non-Irish saints in the series. See

also the brief question and answer piece on St Flannán in *The Clare Champion*, 3/2–10/2/23; and 'Ceann-Droma', 'Gobnait Naomhtha i mBaile Mhúirne' (St Gobnait in Ballyvourney), *IP*, 11/2/32.

100 Anecdotes from the lives of Irish saints were also regular features of the 'Do'n Aos Óg' column in *II*. There was also a more substantial piece on Lawrence O'Toole for adults in *II* (16/11–17/11/38).

101 For Ua Dálaigh, see 'Dúthchas na Dlighe / Conus a Cuireadh i bhFeidhm ar Ghaedhil é' (The heritage of the law / How it was enforced on Gaels), *Nation*, 31/1/31. See also the report of Gógan's lecture to UCD's Cumann Liteardha on 'Fir Éireann' (The men of Ireland) in *II* ('Our Ancestors/ Invaders from All over Europe / A Very Mixed Collection', 10/12/28).

102 In a letter to *II* (25/2/27), de Cheabhasa asserted that early Irish law and polity gave considerable recognition to women's rights. He was here engaging in the contemporary debate about whether women should serve on juries in the Free State.

103 It is worth noting that in their history textbooks, Ó Siochfhradha questioned this scheme, and Breathnach rejected it.

104 Ó Mathghamhna, 'Aguisín' (Appendix), in *Inis Atlaint: Scéal a Chéad-Cheap Platón 'san Ghréigis* (Atlantis: A story first composed by Plato in Greek) (BÁC: Brún agus Ó Nualláin, Teor., [1935]), 78. An cúntas do-bheireann na sean-ughdair ar gach gabháltas d'á ndearnadh ar Éirinn, baineann sé le heachtraíbh a thárla gan gó; ach thárladar chómh fada san roimh ré nár fhanadar i gcuimhne na ndaoine ach ar chuma neamh-shoiléir, mar bheadh taidhbhridhthe.

105 See, for example, 'Crois Imríne Mainistreach Lios Laichtín' (The carved cross of the Monastery of Lios Laichtín) (*Inis Fáil*, Dec. 1928), 'Cloigthighe na h-Éireann' (The round towers of Ireland) (*Inis Fáil*, Dec. 1929), 'The Ardagh Chalice: Dating a Gaelic Masterpiece' (*Nationality*, 25/4/31), 'Aoiseanna Óir na hÉireann / Órnáidí Óir' (The golden ages of Ireland / Gold ornaments) (*IP*, 5/10/31), 'Cailís Ard-Achaidh / Príomh-Sheod Eochairistic Éireann' (The Ardagh Chalice / The prime eucharistic treasure of Ireland) (*IP*, 26/6/32); 'St Patrick's Vision / The Problems Considered: Who Was Victoricus? Where was Silva Focluti?' *Standard*, 12/11/32. See also Pádhraic Ó Domhnalláin, 'Dán-Sgoil Chonnacht' (The Connacht school of art), *Standard*, 3/8/29 (on medieval Irish metalwork).

106 Hunger strikes were an emotionally charged issue in 1923, with the tactic being used on a wide scale by Republicans imprisoned by the Free State authorities.

107 See also Diarmuid Ua Laoghaire, 'Naomh-Abstal na h-Éireann / Duadh a Chuid Oibre' (The saint-apostle of Ireland / The difficulty of his work), *II*, 12/3/28; Risteárd Ó Foghludha, 'Tobar Phádraig i n-Áth Cliath' (St Patrick's Well in Dublin), *IP*, 4/5/32; Murt Ó Dubhghaill, 'Ar Las Pádraig an Teine Úd na Cásga Ariamh / Breith na Staraidhthe', *IP*, 7–8/4/39; and Peadar Ó Dubhda's story 'Brighid agus a Geall' (Brigid and her promise), *IP*, 30/1/32.

108 See also 'Naomh Feichín / Aspal Chonamara' (St Feichín / The apostle of Conamara), (*CT*, 29/1/31). This was a different St Feichín, based at Ballysodare, County Sligo. The missionary activities of Columbanus were discussed by Sighle Ní Chinnéide in a lecture at UCC summarised in the *Irish Press* as 'Columbanus ar an Mór-Roinn' (Columbanus on the continent), *IP*, 6/4/38. The bilingual *Nótaí Staire*, published by the Mercy Convent in Carlow (in 1935?) deals almost entirely with European history, but the two pages of chapter seven tell of 'Obair na Manach nGaodhalach' (The work of the Irish monks) on the Continent.

109 Mac Fhionnlaoich, 'Cnoc Maolrúnaidhe', in *An Cogadh Dearg*, 52–9.

110 See also the anonymous 'Eriúgena', in *Féile na nGaedheal* (May 1928, 1), whose author may well have also been Ryan.

111 Mac Craith, 'Peadar ó Eirinn (Petrus de Hibernia) Oide Múinte Tomás N. Acuin' (Peter from Ireland [Petrus de Hibernia] The tutor of St Thomas Aquinas), in *Deora Drúchta Camhaoire*, 8–20.

112 See also, 'Aengus Céile Dé', *Nation*, 1/12/28.

113 Ó Domhnalláin, 'An tOileán Úr' (America), in *Dréachta*, 49–52.

114 Morris, *Oidhche Áirneáil*, 44–7; Tomás Ua Concheanainn agus a Bhean, *Inis Fáil: Sgéalta faoi Árd Righthe na h-Éireann* (Ireland: Stories about the high-kings of Ireland) (BÁC: Brún agus Ó Noláin, n.d.), 33–47; and Séamus Ó Grianna, *Sraith na Craobhrua* IV (Sráid Bhaile Dhún Dealgan: Preas Dhún Dealgan, [1927], 39–43. See also 'Do'n Aos Óg / Bás Chormaic agus a Adhnacal' (For the young / The death of Cormac and his burial), *II*, 28/1/33. There were, of course, stories about other Irish kings in *Inis Fáil* as well, among them Conn Cétchathach and Niall Naoi nGiallach. There is also a story about Conn by 'S. E. B. C.' entitled 'Comhairle ag Dul Amugha / Géarrcúis [*sic*] Mná' (Advice going astray / A woman's shrewdness) in *II*, 25/2/29.

115 In the programme for the first production of the play by Taibhdhearc na Gaillimhe in May 1933, we are told of the author: 'He spent most of his life around Limerick and in Dublin. He served a long prison sentence in 1921. He wrote the play around 25 years ago, but it has not been produced until now' (Thart timcheall Luimnigh agus i mBaile Átha Cliath is mó a chaith sé a shaoghal. Chaith sé téarma fada i bpríosúin i mbliain a 1921. Cheap sé an Dráma suas le 25 bliana ó shoin acht níor tugadh deis a léirighthe dhó go dtí anois). The programme is among the Taibhdhearc na Gaillimhe Papers, NUIG. Frank Dermody discussed the ambitious nature of An

Taibhdhearc's production of this play involving more than 50 characters in 'An Dráma is mó Fós' (The biggest play yet), *IP*, 12/5/33.

116 See also the short, catechism-like question and answer piece 'Cath Cluain Tairbh' (The battle of Clontarf) (*Clare Champion* 13/1 to 27/1/23).

117 Mac Grianna, *Na Lochlannaigh*, 112. B'fhearr an fear Maoilsheachlainn Mór ná aon fhear acú, agus ní bhfuair sé maitheamhnas ar a shon sin le naoi gcéad bliadhain. Acht an té bhéarfas a cheart dó, aidmheóchaidh sé go rabh sé ar shaighdeoir chomh h-éifeachtach agus thóg Éire ariamh, agus go mb'fhéidir nár thóg sí a leithéid eile.

118 Mac Grianna, *Na Lochlannaigh*, 112–13. See also 23–6, 107–10.

119 Mar chúnntas stairiúil ar ré na Lochlannach in Éirinn ní fiú an leabhar so do chóimhreamh. 'E.' was more impressed, praising Mac Grianna's 'talent for narration and imagination' (buadh innste agus samhlaidheachta), and saying that if Mac Grianna's opinions were unorthodox, they were also well researched (*Bonaventura*, Autumn 1938, 201). See also Breandán Delap, *Úrscéalta Stairiúla na Gaeilge* (Historical novels in Irish) (BÁC: An Clóchomhar, 1993), 46.

120 See Proinsias Mac an Bheatha, 'Seosamh Mac Grianna', in *Seosamh Mac Grianna agus Cúrsaí Eile*, 50.

121 Ó Muirí, 'Seosamh Mac Grianna', in *Rí Éigeas na nGael*, ed. Mac Congáil, 90–1. Tá tábhacht leis an dearcadh atá ag Mac Grianna ar an stair. B'fhéidir gur chóra a rá nach leabhair staire a scríobh sé ach cuntas pearsanta ar an stair. Creidim go bhfeiceann muid sna leabhair seo iarracht le stair na hÉireann a mhíniú ó dhearcadh phobal na Gaeltachta.

122 Mac Grianna, *Na Lochlannaigh*, 121. Tá seo ar ghníomh comh h-éifeachtach agus tá i gcurnas daoiní saoghalta, agus bheir sé le fios dúinn cibé feasbhaidh eolais nó uirnéis a bhí ar ár gcuid sinnsir, gur mhillteanach na fir iad, agus nach bhfuil ionainn féin ach márlaí a bhfuil táilliúir ag cur maise orainn, agus páipeáir ag coinneáil agra chinn ionainn.

123 Ó Gríobhtha, 'An t-Ubhall Óir', in *Cathair Aeidh*, 211–56.

124 Ó Siochfhradha, *Cath Chluana Tarbh* (The battle of Clontarf), in *Muir, Tuath agus Cathair* (Sea, land and city) (BÁC: COÉ, 1938).

125 Ó Domhnalláin, 'Bí i do Thost', in *An tIolrach Mór*, 182–6. Peadar Ó Dubhda's 'Scrios na Lochlannach' (The Vikings' devastation) tells of a Norse raid on a monastery in County Louth (*Standard*, 29/8/31).

126 Béaslaí, *An Danar: Dráma Trí Mír* (BÁC: Muinntir C. S. Ó Fallamhain, i gcomhar le hOS, 1929), 30. Is mairg don té fhanann n-a allmhurach san tír i n-ar tógadh é. Ní san Lochlainn do rugadh sinn-ne ná ár n-athracha féin, ach i nÉirinn. Táimíd i n-ár gcomhnuidhe imeasg na nGaedheal, tá caidreamh againn leo leis na ciantaibh, agus is feárrde sinn é. Bhí mórán againn le foghluim uatha. Ní hiongnadh meas againn ortha.

127 Béaslaí, *An Danar*, 56. Maith an sgeul sinn a bheith réidh leis an dtionnsgalóir buile sin. Beidh an seana-shaoghal socair againn feasta, fé mar bhíodh sul ar chuir Olaf isteach orainn . . . Go ndeinidh Dia trócaire ar a n-anmannaibh. In his brief preface to the play, Béaslaí said that he took pains to avoid mistakes with regard to what little was known of the history of the period, but added: 'It was not, however, history that concerned me most. I just wanted a world, a time, and a place that would be suitable for the story of Olaf and Inga' (Ní stair na seanchaidheachta ba mhó a bhí ag cur cúraim orm, áfach. Ní raibh uaim ach saoghal, am agus ionad a bheadh oireamhnach do sgéal Olaf agus Inga) (p. 3). The play was very favourably received.

128 There is a synopsis of the play in the programme in the Taibhdhearc Papers, NUIG.

129 Ó Domhnalláin, 'Freagra an Danair', in *An tIolrach Mór*, 70–4.

130 Má meastar an leabhar seo mar sgéal abróchainn go bhfuil an iomarca cur síos ann faoi stair na haoise sin . . . Ach má's 'beatha' ughdarásach é caithfear é do mheas dá réir sin. Amannta tóigeann an tAth. Benedict caisleáin staireamhla ar chaol-fhiadhnaise; amannta eile ní thig leis a bharramhail féin do cheilt orainn. Among essays on Ua Tuathail published in the period were S. Mac Amhlaoigh's 'Duais-Aiste' (Prize essay) (*Standard*, 3/1/31); An tAthair Aindrias Ó Fearghail's 'Lorcán N. Ua Tuathail / Fíor Easbag agus Fíor-Naomh' (St Lawrence O'Toole / True bishop and true saint), a sermon delivered at the Jesuit Church in Dublin's Gardiner St (*IC*, 12/11/32); and two brief biographical pieces for young readers that appeared in *An Gaedheal Óg*, the Gaelic supplement to *Our Boys* (*Gaedheal Óg*, 10/11/38, and 26/10/39).

131 Ó Domhnalláin, 'An Éiric', in *Na Spiadóirí*, 82–4; and 'An Cíos', in *Oidhre an Léighinn*, 30–4.

132 Ó Dubhda, 'Bás an Bhrúsaigh', in *Thríd an Fhuinneoig*, 98–102. In June 1924, the Gaelic League branch in Ennis, County Clare performed a play by 'a local Gaelic Leaguer' entitled *An Bheansidhe* (The banshee), dealing with 'an old legend of Quin Abbey' (*Clare Champion*, 14/6/24).

133 There is a synopsis of the play in the programme in the Taibhdhearc Papers, NUIG.

134 There is a synopsis of the play in the programme in the Taibhdhearc Papers, NUIG.

135 Saidléar, *Éibhlín Talbóid: Dráma Thrí Mír don Aos Óg*, in *Ceithre Drámaí* (Four dramas) (BÁC: ODFR, 1934), 47–67. In his preface, Saidléar says he based the play on a poem by Thomas Davis ('Emmeline Talbot'), and makes no claim to historical accuracy (p. 47). There is an interesting debate in the play on the possibility of an alliance between the so-called 'Old English' and the native Gaels (pp. 63–4).

136 Ó Domhnaill, 'Oidhche Ruadh Leitir Catha', in *Bruighean Feille*, 67–131.

137 Ó Domhnalláin, 'Rí Bréige', in *Oidhre an Léighinn*, 127–30.
138 Mac Grianna, 'Creach Chuinn Uí Dhomhnaill', 112.
139 *Ibid.*, 124. A laochraidh, tá creach eile romhainn. Siubhailfimíd Inis Fáil ó mhuir go muir. Ar mur gclí libh; go Deasmhumhain.
140 See Mac Grianna's comments on Standish James O'Grady's novel *The Flight of the Eagle* in 'A Book for Brave Boys', *An Phoblacht*, 14/1/27; and *Mo Bhealach Féin*, 172. See also Liam Lillis Ó Laoire, 'Tart an Anama agus Deoch na Colla', in *Rí-Éigeas na nGael*, ed. Mac Congáil, 113–14.
141 Mac Grianna, 'Creach Chuinn Uí Dhomhnaill', 117. Bhí na daoiní a mhair an t-am sin fial ós cionn gach nidh, agus bhí siad onórach. Ní rabh an mhíníneacht intinne ionntú atá sa dream beag atá indiu ann, acht bhí a ndubh dubh agus a ngeal geal.
142 Mac Grianna, 'Dúil gan Fhagháil', in *Pádraic Ó Conaire agus Aistí Eile*, 148–52.
143 Ó Domhnalláin, 'Airgead an Abba Bháin', in *Oidhre an Léighinn*, 65–8. Ó Domhnaill was also the topic of the 'Do'n Aos Óg' column in *II* (12/6/29 and 22/6/29).
144 See Séamus Ó Grianna's account of his unorthodox way of inspiring his students' pride in Ó Néill and Ó Domhnaill in 'Lá Oirdhearc an Átha Bhuidhe' (The renowned day of the Yellow Ford), *FL*, Jan. 1929, 1–2.
145 See also 'Máire Mhilis Bhreágh / Buadhairt an Ghrádha' (Sweet, beautiful Mary / Love's anguish), *IP*, 5/10/34.
146 Ó Domhnalláin, 'Oidhre an Léighinn', in *Oidhre an Léighinn*, 7–10; and 'An Torc Fiadhain', in *An tIolrach Mór*, 132–40.
147 Surprisingly, Ó Domhnalláin had a low opinion of Patrick Sarsfield. See 'An Fealltóir!' (The traitor!) and 'An Ding' (The wedge), in *Oidhre an Léighinn*. In a 1923 letter to Éamonn Mac Giolla Iasachta, Seán Ó Gruagáin wrote that he had adapted an Italian story, 'La Piccola Vedetta Lombarda', giving it a setting in the Ireland of Sarsfield. The story had, however, been submitted to *FL* during the War of Independence and lost. See Seán Ó Gruagáin, Letter to Mac Giolla Iasachta, 8 Sept. 1923; Mac Lysaght Papers, NLI MS 8560 (6).
148 Bairéad, 'Ciarán Cathach', in *Cumhacht na Cinneamhna*, 81–9.
149 Ó Dubhda, *Brian* (BÁC: ODFR, 1937), 138–9.
150 Mac Eochaidh himself provided a synopsis of the play for *Láimh-Leabhar Drámaidheachta*, 32. He also said he had worked seven songs into the play, with 'Slán le Pádraic Sáirséal' (Farewell to Patrick Sarsfield) being the most important of them.
151 The play was originally serialised in *Ar Aghaidh* from Nov. 1931 to July–Aug. 1932.
152 An smaoineamh sin atá laistiar de'n dráma, go réidhteóchaidh an dá dhream le chéile dá leigtí leo agus gan bheith 'ghá mbrostú i n-aghaidh a chéile, tá sé chomh fíor indiu agus a bhí sé trí céad bliadhan ó shoin. Agus is baoghlach nach réidhteóchthar ceist na sgoilte choidhche go dtí go dtuigfear sin.
153 The plot summary here is from O'Connor's review, in which, among other jibes, he wrote: 'The play was acted with appropriate naiveté except perhaps by Gearóid Ó Lochlainn and Tadhg Mac Firbisigh, who deserve censure for introducing an alien atmosphere of dramatic intelligence.' The play was reviewed more kindly in *II* (21/10/29), although the anonymous critic pronounced it 'unbelievable' (do-chreidte). The unnamed reviewer for *An Phoblacht* (19/10/29) saw the play as 'an effort at expressionism, illustrating the continuity of Irish history . . . an imaginative fantasy having several strongly dramatic situations.' 'S.' also praised de Bhilmot for his ambitious attempt to break new ground in his review for *The Standard* (26/10/29).
154 At the Oireachtas of 1922, there was only one entry in the competition for the novel. This work, which I have been unable to identify, dealt with the time of Sarsfield and received high praise from the adjudicators for its Irish, but very mixed reports otherwise. See 'Comórtais an Oireachtais' (The Oireachtas competitions), *Misneach*, 7/1/22.
155 Sílim nach raibh scóip ná fairsingeacht go leor ag an ughdar annseo . . . Ba mhaith liom an fear a rinne 'Creach Chuinn Uí Dhomhnaill' . . . a fheiceál agus faill aige réim mhór páir a bheith fá n-a láimh. D'fhéadfadh sé úirscéal staireamhail claisiceach a dhéanamh.
156 See Delap, *Úrscéalta Stairiúla*, 46–51. Interestingly enough, it was in a review of Taylor's book that an anonymous critic asked: 'When will his life and his story be written in Irish?' (Caidé go sgríobhtar a bheatha agus a eachtra as Gaedhilg?) (*FL*, 5/4/24).
157 Nollaig Ó Muraile, 'Caithréim Eoghain Rua Uí Néill' (The triumphant career of Eoghan Ruadh Ó Néill), *IMN*, 1972, 97. See also Niall Ó Dónaill, 'Seosamh Mac Grianna', in *Scríbhneoireacht na gConallach*, ed. Mac Congáil, 115.
158 Cé go bhfuil cur síos ar an stair ann, is ar éigin fhéadfadh duine a rá gur leabhar staire é. Sgéal is ea é atá bunuithe sa stair. In a 1933 column on Ulster writers in *United Ireland*, Liam Ó Rinn commented perceptively on the book, 'I think it is a pity that he did not make it into a novel. If he had, I think that it would be better organised. In my opinion, we see too many individual trees, but we do not see the forest' (Is truagh liom nár dhein sé úrscéal de. Dá ndeineadh measaim go mbeadh sé cruinnithe le chéile níos fearr. Chímíd an iomad de sna crainn ar leithligh, dar liom, ach ní fheicimíd an choill) (*UI*, 16/9/33).
159 Mac Congáil, 'Seosamh Mac Grianna: Rí-Éigeas na nGael, 1900–1990', in *Rí-Éigeas na nGael*, ed. Mac Congáil, 152–3. In 'Comhairle do "Droighneán Fionn"', Mac Grianna explicity states that the period

of history in which Irish people could take unadulterated pride ended in 1652 (*Ultach*, Jan. 1929, 3).

160 Mac Grianna, *Eoghan Rua Ó Néill* (BÁC: OS, 1931), 5. Tairgim an leabhar seo a scríobh Gael fá Ghael do 'Ór-shliocht álainn ársaidhe Chobhthaigh Chaoilmbreágh.'

161 Mac Grianna, *Eoghan Rua Ó Néill*, 114. Ach tháinig sé leis na blianta, an rud a raibh sé ag dúil leis fad ó; bhí teachtairí ag teacht ó Shéarlas na Sasana ag iarraidh síothú, agus bhí teachtairí ag teacht ón Phápa agus ón Róimh anoir. Bhí Éire ina cuid den Euraip i súile na náisiún fá dheireadh. See also 13–14, 20, 33–4, 66, 79, 87, 123, 184.

162 Mac Grianna, *Eoghan Rua Ó Néill*, 124. Níl ainm ar bith agam is fearr ná diabhal saolta fá choinne an té sin a chuireas críoch idir Ultaigh agus Laighnigh, agus nach dtugann Éireannaigh orainn uilig mar an gcéanna.

163 *Ibid.*, 123.

164 *Ibid.*, 86. See also 115, 209–10.

165 *Ibid.*, 197. Tá dream Albanach in a gcónaí i gCúige Uladh, agus beidh cuid acu ansan i ndiaidh an chogaidh, is cuma cá fhad a mhairfeas sé. Cuir i gcás go raibh muid a dh'aon-taoibh leo an lá a thiocfadh Cromall anall.

166 Mac Grianna, *Léigheacht*, 10.

167 See also his discussion of such enemies in *Mo Bhealach Féin*, 172–3. Reviewing the book in *ACS*, 'Tír-Eoghain' focused on the richness of Mac Grianna's Irish (*ACS*, 7/11/31). In his review for *Outlook*, Riobárd Ó Faracháin also drew attention to the excellence of Mac Grianna's prose, writing of the author that 'the heir of the ancient storytellers has come among us speaking their stately, vigorous vernacular' (go bhfuil oighre na sean-scéaluidhe tagtha 'nár measc agus a gcanamhain mhaordha, bhríoghmhar dá labhairt aige) (*Outlook*, 9/1/32). Cathal Ó Háinle discusses Mac Grianna's conscious attempt to draw on the resources of the Irish literary tradition as a counterweight to the obsession with contemporary folk speech in 'Friotal Fileata: Tionchar an Dúchais ar Fhriotal Sheosaimh Mhic Grianna' (A poetic speech: The influence of native tradition on the speech of Seosamh Mac Grianna), *Rí-Éigeas na nGael*, ed. Mac Congáil, 1–28.

168 See Nollaig Ó Muraile, 'Caithréim Eoghain Rua Uí Néill', *IMN*, 1972, 91–2.

169 Mac Grianna, *Eoghan Rua Ó Néill*, 212–13. Cailltear Éire nó ná cailltear, bíodh na glúin a bhí le teacht i ndaoirse nó i saoirse, bhí deabhaidh ní ba mhó ná sin le socrú an lá sin. Bhí an chinniúint ina suí ag an tSiúir, ag breathnú cad é mar rachadh fiacháil na fearúlachta. Aigesan a bhí sé le dearbhú nach bhfeiceadh an tSiúir ná an tSionainn é, nach gcanfadh bard go deo é, sna haoiseanna ceocha a bhí le theacht, gurbh fhearr an fear bodach de Mhuintir Chromail ná rogha agus rí-laoch Chlanna Néill. Sheasaigh sé ansin . . . agus chan fear tíre ná creidimh ná fear sonais an chine daonna a bhí ann, ach fear comhraic agus Gael, ag fanacht leis an ionsú a d'fhiachfadh dúchas agus oiliúin.

170 See Mac Congáil, *Seosamh Mac Grianna: Clár Saothair*, 53; and Delap, *Úrscéalta Stairiúla*, 52–3.

171 The novel certainly has its share of vicious Protestant Yeomen and drunken and brutal British soldiers – one attempts to rape a young Catholic woman and is killed by her female friends. But it also has some decent Protestants, and even some of the British are disgusted by the injustices inflicted on the Irish, often through the perversion of the legal system.

172 'D. M.' compared the book to Canon Hannay's *The Northern Iron* or S. R. Keightly's *The Pikemen*, but added that Mac Maoláin's novel was superior, 'since he makes us aware that Irish was vigorous and alive in a good many places in Counties Antrim and Down at that time' (óir cuireann sé ar ár súile dúinn . . . go raibh an Ghaedhilg bríoghmhar beo i gcuid mhaith áiteach i gCo. Aondroma agus i gCo. an Dúin ins an am sin) (*Ultach*, Jan. 1939, 7).

173 It is worth noting that the suicide of the mentally unbalanced spy at the novel's end leaves his Gaelic foes and his victims guiltless of his death.

174 Ó Dochartaigh, 'Bliadhain na bhFranncach', in *Creach Bhaile an Teampaill*, 77–118.

175 Ó Domhnalláin, '"Ní Abróchad"', in *An tIolrach Mór*, 84–8.

176 Ó Dubhda, 'Capall an Ríogh', in *An t-Ogánach Ceann-Órdha*, 125–45.

177 Maguidhir, 'Dáithí na Miodóige', and 'Mairtir Óg na Muaidhe', in *Dhá Chrann na Marbh*, 47–70; 143–50.

178 Ó Domhnalláin, 'Ar Fud an Domhain, in *An tIolrach Mór*, 165–81.

179 Ó Domhnalláin, 'Carraig Mhic Fhaltair', in *Oidhre an Léighinn*, 16–21.

180 Ó Dubhda, 'Réamonn Ropaire' and 'Coiléir, an Ropaire', in *Thríd an Fhuinneoig*, 121–33; 134–40.

181 Ua Murchadha, 'An Broiceallach Ua Buachalla', in *Sean-Aimsireacht*, 47–8.

182 Maguidhir, 'Dhá Chrann na Marbh', in *Dhá Chrann na Marbh*, 9–26.

183 A Charraig an Aifrinn! Chonnacais dearg-ár, creach, agus anfhorlann dá n-imirt le chéile ar Ghaedhealaibh bochta. Chonnacais lom dá léirscrios agus támh dá dtreascairt; acht in aimhdheoin an bhaoghail báis, a bhí ann dóibh, mhothuighis led ais an sagart beannuighthe gona phobul cheusta agus iad ag agallamh an Dé a thúirling chúca anuas ar chlár t'uchta.

184 Ó Conaire, 'An tAifreann Binn 'ghá Rádh', in *Eachtraí Móra ó n-Ár Stair*, 81–2.

185 Ó Dubhda, 'Caisleán Dhúin Mhathghamhna', in *Thríd an Fhuinneoig*, 77–83.

186 Ó Domhnalláin, 'An tSochraid', in *Oidhre an Léighinn*, 59–64.

187 Mac Grianna, 'Codladh an Mháighistéara', in *An Grádh agus an Ghruaim*, 51–7; 'Séamus Mac Murchaidh', in *Pádraic Ó Conaire agus Aistí Eile*, 155–226. Mac Grianna had, of course, included an essay on Ó Doirnín in his essay series, 'Filí Móra Chúige Uladh' (The great poets of the province of Ulster), in *Pádraic Ó Conaire agus Aistí Eile*, 68–76.
188 Ua Murchadha, 'Cearbhall Ua Dálaigh' and 'Gliocas Aodhagáin Uí Rathghaile', in *Sean-Aimsireacht*, 40–41, 50–2. Ua Murchadha also included a story about Jonathan Swift, 'Déin Swift i dTeannta' (Dean Swift in a fix) (pp. 52–4), in which Swift is outwitted by a servant. There is a fair amount of folklore in Irish about Swift. See, for example, Diarmuid a' Choitir, 'Dean Swift is a Ghiolla' (Dean Swift and his servant) (Enniscorthy *Echo*, 25/3 to 1/4/33).
189 In his essay 'Teangthacha na dTuath', Seán Ó Ciarghusa pondered the lack of Gaelic interest in the events of 1782 and 1798. See Ó Ciarghusa, 'Teangthacha', in *Ar Mo Mharanadh Dam*, 8.
190 He saw them as 'tranglam agus meascán de "ál gach crána coigcríche", "all-thuirc chlaon" do thraoch Gaedhil fé mhór-smacht agus a dh'imir tíorántas agus cos-ar-bolg ar "clann righthe, maca míleadh, dragain fhíochtha is gaiscidhigh."'
191 Is fíor gurb eol dom an dúthaigh seo. Is ann do rugadh is do tógadh mé, agus tá mo shliocht préamhuighthe go daingean i dtalamh na tíre. Do chaitheas na bliadhanta thar lear, agus níl éin chion ag na Gaedhealaibh orm, toisg gur ghabhas páirt le na namhaidibh – le cúis Dé, a mheasas a rádh – ach is fearr a thuigimse iad ná mar a thuigeann éan captaen Gallda nó éan bhúistéir ó Lúndain. See also 72, 78.
192 Ach do rugadh na Gaill úd i nÉirinn, leis. Shughadar isteach an t-aer céadna, chonnaiceadar taitneamh na gréine ar na bántaibh céadna ... Ach is móide mo dhóchas féachaint ortsa, a Mháiréad – ortsa do tógadh imeasg na nGall. Comhartha an nua-shaoghail óig i nÉirinn tú! Do shínis do lámh chugham anall. Do bhuaidh an fhuil Ghaedhealach ionnat ar an bhfuil Ghallda.
193 Cad chuige go gclaoidhfinn leis an dtír bocht deireóil seo? Níl éan dul agam ar ghlóir ná ar réimeas ann, níl éin bhreith agam ar nithe éifeachtacha dhéanamh a raghaidh chun leasa na ndaoine. Níl annso ach annró is bochtaineacht. Ach tá fórsaí ann is treise ná an réasún. Ní leigfadh mo chroidhe dhom an tír seo thréigint, agus an talamh fhágaint fé sna bodaigh Ghallda do bhain dinn é. Munar féidir liom iad do ruagairt is féidir liom staincín a dhéanamh ortha. See also 38–40.
194 Nach bhfuil fhios agat go maith nach bhfuil uasal ná íseal anois ann? Támuid uilig 'nár sglábhuidhthe. Flatha, iarlaí, támuid uilig i n-umar na h-aimléise ó fuair na Gaill an bhuaidh orainn. The play was published by An Gúm in 1946. The poet Peadar Ó Doirnín is also a character in this play. The young woman's father is delighted with the success of his plot after Mac Murchadha's arrest, an arrest that will mean his certain execution.
195 See Mac Eochaidh, 'An Gníomh-Amhrán', in *Láimh-Leabhar Drámaidheachta*, 31; and 'Annseo agus Annsúd' (Here and there), *CT*, 11/3/39. See also *An Craipí Óg: Ceol-Dráma Gearr* (The young croppy: A short musical drama), tr. Muiris Ó Catháin, and arranged as a musical play by Gearóid Ó Lochlainn (BÁC: n.p., n.d.). There are only two pages of text in a four page booklet. The piece was performed by An Comhar Drámaidheachta in the Peacock Theatre in Feb. 1935.
196 See Ó Cadhain, *'Páipéir Bhána agus Páipéir Bhreaca'* (BÁC: An Clóchomhar, 1969), 15.
197 Nioclás Tóibín's translation of P. Kehoe's play *When Wexford Rose* as *'Nuair d'Adhnamar an Gleo'* ('When we stirred up the fight') was performed regularly at *feiseanna* in Wexford in the 1930s.
198 Is ar éigin atá aon ré i stair na h-Éireann is lugha a cuirtear eolas indiu uirri 'ná an 19adh aois. Ní thaith-nigheann sgéal le h-éinne nuair nach bhfuil ann ach an brón agus an ghruaim agus síor-bhriseadh chatha. Agus tar éis fuasgailt chreidimh d'fhagháil i dtús na h-aoise, cad eile a thárla ach gorta, imirce, bánú na tíre agus éirghe amach suarach na bhFíníní i 1867, agus annsan fás agus meath an 'Party' gan mhaith.
199 Domhnall Ó Grianna translated M. Bodkin's Emmet play *True Man and Traitor* as *Fear Fíor agus Fealltóir* (BÁC: ODFR, 1935). See also Proinnsias Ó Súilleabháin, 'Bean Tighe Emmet' (Emmet's house-keeper), a short essay about the heroic Ann Devlin (*IP*, 26/6/36).
200 Pé breithiúnas a déantar ar shaothar Dhomhnaill Uí Chonaill is binn le Gaedhil a ainm seachas taoiseach ar bith eile b'fhéidir i rith na h-aimsire ó do cailleadh Brian Bórumha. There was a debate at Maynooth on 'Aodh Ó Néill, nó Domhnall Ó Conaill, cia'cu a b'fhearr?' (Aodh Ó Néill or Daniel O'Connell, which was better?). The O'Connell side won (*IMN*, 1929, 83–5). In a 1937 contest sponsored by the *Irish Catholic*, O'Connell was selected as the third greatest 'hero' (*laoch*) in Irish history, following Aodh Ó Néill and Patrick Sarsfield. See 'Seathrún', 'Laochas na hÉireann' (Irish heroism), *IC*, 30/12/37.
201 See, for example, 44, 118–19. For a more doc-trinaire attitude to O'Connell as 'that fully Anglicised Irishman' (an tÉireannach lán Ghallda úd) who did 'far more than a man's share to spread the English language and to bring the Irish language into disrepute' (breis mór agus cion fir chum Béarla a mhéadú agus drochmheas a tharrac ar Ghaedhluinn), see Pádraig Ó Briain, 'Nár Feicidh Éire Páipéar Gallda Arís! / Bás gan Sagart Chúcha!' (May Ireland never see an English paper again / Death without a priest to them!), *An Phoblacht*, 8/9/34. See also the discussion of Cearbhall Ua Dálaigh's attitute to O'Connell at this time in Ó Glaisne, *Cearbhall Ó Dálaigh*, 67–8.

202 He believed 'go ndearna Parnell níos mó ar son na hÉireann 'ná mar a rinne aon Gaedheal roimhe ná ó n-a linn i leith, ach amháin Domhnall Ó Conaill.' There is a bit of ambivalence in one of Ó Catháin's sentences in the review, but he does seem to regard Parnell as worthy of the title *Gaedheal*. See also the high praise of Parnell's patriotism – attributed to the influence of his family's Irish gatekeeper – in Pádhraic Ó Domhnailláin's 'Oide Pharnell' (Parnell's tutor), in *Oidhre an Léighinn*, 111–13; and the following essays on Parnell by Dinneen in *The Leader*: 'Beirt Duine Uasal agus Iarrthóir' (Two noble people and a beggar) (24/11/23), 'Tréithe Pharnell' (Parnell's traits) (1/12/23), 'An Té Chuir Eagla ar Mhuinntir Shasana' (The person who frightened the people of England) (8/12/23), and 'Daoine Móra i gCompráid le Chéile' (Great people compared to each other) (15/12/23), in which O'Connell also figured. Ó Broin himself discusses the book – and its disappointing sales figures – in his autobiography *Just Like Yesterday*, 113.

203 Níor Ghaedheal Parnell 'n-a chroí ná 'n-a aigne. Níor Ghaedheal de réir foluíochta nó de réir oiliúna é. Ach ar a shon-san, níor cheart d'aoinne é mheas 'n-a eachtránaí gur tharla dhó taobh na nGaedheal do ghlacadh 'sa troid nua a bhí ag tosnú le linn teacht in aois fir dó.

204 There is a curious hint of incest in the relationship between mother and son. See, for example, 94–5.

205 Do cuireadh oiread sin suime sa scéal gur dalladh gach taobh leis an dtábhacht do bhraitheadar a bheith ann. Do cheap na Gaedhil dá bhfaigheadh Feargal an bhuaidh go mbeadh deire go deo le an-smacht na dtighearnaí talmhan; agus do mheas na Gaill dá bhfaigheadh Seon an bhuaidh go mbeadh deire le droch-mhúineadh agus le tógaint chinn na nGaedheal. Reviewing the novel for *An Tír*, 'Lorcán' perceptively criticised as a major weakness in it the reduction of the class and economic struggles of nineteenth-century Ireland to a fistfight. He also saw the Big House mother as an implausible monster (*Tír*, Nov. 1929, 6–7). But see Vera Kreilkamp's discussion of 'monstrous women' in *The Anglo-Irish Novel and the Big House* (Syracuse: Syracuse University Press, 1998), 184–7.

206 Ó Ciarghusa stresses the support of the local priest for these men. See 203 and 329.

207 Is í mo ghuidhe ná beidh aon achrann ná cúis achrainn idir Ghaedhealaibh agus Gallaibh ann i gcionn tamaill mar ná beidh na Gaill ann chuige. Commenting on the book in *An Gaedheal*, 'Carrig' praised the author's historical research, but said he lost control of his complex plotline and that 'Seán Ó Ciarghusa failed entirely to attend to this composition and to tie and weave the story together properly' (gur theip glan ar Sheán Ó Ciarghusa friotháilt ar an gceapadóireacht so agus an scéal do shnaidhmeadh agus d'fhigheadh n-a cheart' (*Gaedheal*, Jul. 1937, 3). In an anonymous review in *TCNÍ*, the critic denied that the book was a novel in any meaningful sense, seeing it as a series of episodes or 'slim threads that are holding the pictures together' (caol-shnaithí atá ag coinneáil na bpictiúirí le chéile). Nevertheless, he liked the book, and saw dipping into it at random as 'a quiet cure' (ciúin-leigheas) for the stresses of contemporary life! (*TCNÍ*, Nov. 1934, 261–2). Alan Titley sees *Bun an Dá Abhann* as the representative Gaelic novel of the 1930s (See *An tÚrscéal Gaeilge*, 48), and writes that it is 'of the many Irish-language pretenders the most legitimate heir to Charles J. Kickham's *Knocknagow*, a book that is both a communal and a historical work' (an t-oidhre is dlisteanaí ar fad de *phretenders* iomadúla na Gaeilge ar *Knocknagow* Charles J. Kickham ar saothar pobail agus stairiúil in éineacht é) (p. 359).

208 Under the *nom de plume* 'Muirghein', Ó Gallchobhair published the novel along with two short stories and a play in *Cáitheamh na dTonn*.

209 Nach éachtach an tubaist a bhíonn ar a lán daoine, agus ar mhór-chuid de náisiúnaibh an domhain, ná féadann aire a thabhairt dá ngnó agus dá náisiún féin, agus gan bheith ag cur isteach ar dhaoinibh eile, ar náisiúnaibh eile, agus '"ghá dtabhairt chun creidimh" mar dheadh!'

210 Dá mba mé a bheadh ag riaghlú an náisiúin, is é an chéad ghnó a dhéanfainn ná a mbeadh de bhitheamhnachaibh ann a chnuasach le chéile, agus iad a chomáint isteach i gcró, agus lainncisí a chur fútha, i gcás go mbeadh aithne ortha i dteannta smacht a bheith ortha.

211 See, for example, pp. 231, 244.

212 See, for example, pp. 52–3, 72, 144.

213 Gadaidheacht agus fealltacht agus creachadh, sin é atá ar siubhal faoi bhrat uasal na Breataine . . . Tá sibh fá mheas go deimhin ag foghlaidhthe eile, ach tá na céadta mallacht ag éirghe suas in bhur gcoinnibh ó gach tír in ar leag sibh cos – san Afraic, san Asia, agus san Eoraip.

214 An cuimhin leat eachtra an fhir san soiscéal, an fear a fuair an péarla luachmhar? Dhíol sé a raibh aige leis an bpéarla cheannach. 'Sé a fhearacht sin agam-sa é. Déan an rud céadna thusa agus bhéarfa sé sólás croidhe dhuit. Caith i leathtaoibh uait gach ní a thagann idir thú agus Toil Dé a dhéanamh, agus beidh an péarla luachmhar agat-sa freisin. Note Bartlaí's perverse misreading of the concept of 'God's will' (*toil Dé*) during their argument (pp. 112–15).

215 An raibh iongantas ar bith oiread deifre a bheith ar na daoine óga ag imtheacht – ag imtheacht ó ansmacht agus ó thiorántacht?

216 Ó Ciarghusa, 'Dráma Gaedheal' (The drama of Gaels), in *Ar Mo Mharanadh Dam*, 133–4. See also Hanly, *National Ideal*, 163–4.

217 Tá an Tadhg so Dhiarmada chómh ciallmhar san nách beag ná go bhfuil sé in a 'automaton' agus tá an saoghal chómh socair séimh sin aige go bhféadfá a

rádh go bhfuair Diarmuid 'Utopia' sa leabhar, pé áit na bhfuil sé sin leasmuich de chlúdach an leabhair.

218 In this light one may wonder if there is any irony in the comments of the 'D. Ua L.' (most likely Diarmuid Ua Laoghaire), who reviewed the book for *II*: 'There is discussion in this book of the prudent things "Tadhg Ciallmhar" did, of the way he became rich although he started with very little. There was no craft he was not skilled at' (Tá cur-síos ins an leabhar seo ar na rudaí stuamdha a ghníodh 'Tadhg Ciallmhar', ar an dóigh ar éirigh sé saidhbhir agus gan aige ach an fíor-bheagán. Ní raibh céard ar bith nach raibh sé oilte air) (*II*, 8/10/35). Ua Laoghaire certainly showed a keen appreciation of the social stigma that accompanied poverty in rural nineteenth-century Ireland in his story 'Ba Mhairg a Bheadh Bocht / An Breitheamh' (It would be a pity to be poor / The judge) (*II*, 26/3/29). Alan Titley says of the novel, 'There is no better example to be found in literature in Irish of "the Protestant work ethic"' (Níl solaoid a sháraithe i litríocht na Gaeilge le fáil ar an 'eitic oibre Phrotastúnach'). See *An tÚrscéal Gaeilge*, 352. But he adds that it is also an accurate depiction of one aspect of Irish rural life in the nineteenth century (p. 354).

219 Ó Nualláin, 'Tighearna an Tailimh', in *Tighearna an Tailimh*, 1–12.

220 Ó Grianna, '"Faoi na Fóide is Mé Sínte"', in *Cith is Dealán*, 110–21. In 1933, the editor of *An Camán* suggested as the subject for an Irish movie an eviction in Donegal that drove a family to emigrate to Australia. He felt that if such a film were successfully shot in the Donegal Gaeltacht, it 'might have big human values' (*Camán*, 3/6/33).

221 Ó Dubhghaill, 'Baile na Scairte / Siopa na Croise', in *Beartín Luachra*, 7–20.

222 Mac Meanman, 'Peadar Fheidhlimidh na nDartán', in *Indé agus Indiu*, 16–38.

223 Mac Meanman, 'Micheál Cordáin', in *Indé agus Indiu*, 39–54.

224 'Nuair a Las na Teinte ar Árd na Coilleadh', in *An Chraobh Chumhra*, 79–87.

225 Bairéad, 'Costas an Ghirrfhiaidh', in *Cumhacht na Cinneamhna*, 103–15.

226 Ó Cuív, 'Pluais an Mhóránaigh', in *Deora Áthais*, 140–7.

227 Ó Cuív, 'Bean fé Bhrón', in *Deora Áthais*, 148–55.

228 Maguidhir, 'Bánughadh Bhaile an Mhullaigh', in *Dhá Chrann na Marbh*, 113–26. There are two unpublished stories in English among Father Dinneen's papers in the NLI. One, 46 pages long, deals with a small farmer living in the shadow of eviction by a landlord and 'his retinue of furies.' The other, set during the time of Whiteboy activity, is only 15 pages long and incomplete. See Dinneen Papers, NLI MS 8623 (20) and (21).

229 Ó Conchubhair, *Conncas: Dráma Dhá Ghníomh*, in *Duanaire Dúithch' Ealla*, ed. Seán Ua Cadhla, 73–94.

230 The excitement generated by the events on which this play was based were still recalled in our period. See, for example, Ó Grianna, *Caisleáin Óir*, 113–16, and *Dirbheathaisnéis Néill Mhic Ghiolla Bhríghde*, 78–89. For a recent discussion of the episode, see Seán 'Ac Fhionnlaoich, *Scéal Ghaoth Dobhair* (The story of Gweedore) (BÁC: Foilseacháin Náisiúnta Teoranta, 1983), 115–22. Áine Nic Ghiolla Bhríde discusses the importance of the historical plays of Mac Giolla Bhríghde for local drama in Donegal in 'Drámaíocht i nDún na nGall' (Drama in Donegal), in *Scríbhneoireacht na gConallach*, ed. Mac Congáil, 204.

231 Socair, socair! Tá eagla orm go ndóirtfidh sibh fuil go fóill. A cháirde dílse, ní dhéanfaidh seo gnoithe. Caithfidh sibh bheith foighdeach. Sin teagasg na h-Eaglaise Naomhtha.

232 Faraor! Tá sé mar a bhíodh na sagairt i n-aimsir na géar-leanamhna – ar a seachnadh agus cúiteamh maith le fagháil ag an té a dhéanfadh feall ortha.

233 The story of a Famine death is also recounted in Pádhraic Ó Domhnalláin's 'An tIolrach Mór' (The big eagle), in *An tIolrach Mór*, 63. Nóra Ní Chearnaigh's 'An Naomhóg' tells the story of the religious relic of the title from the early Christian period to the time of the Famine on Achill Island (*Standard*, 6/7/29).

234 Chuaidh Cathal isteach ina háit, agus chuir sé gogán a bhí leis isteach thar béal an choire. Leis sin beireadh greim taobh thiar ar an chorp a bhí ar a dhruim agus tarraingeadh amach ón choire go garbh é. Chuaidh sé chúig nó sé choiscéimeanna amach agus thuit sé. The quote here is from the text of the story as published in *An Grádh agus an Ghruaim*, 85.

235 In his discussion of the proselytising activities of the Protestant Achill Mission, Maguidhir states that it would be difficult to be too harsh towards those who gave up their Catholic faith for food. See *Fánaidheacht i gContae Mhaigheo*, 155–7. In *Fa Sgáth Shléibh' Eachtgha*, Micheál Ó Conaill is unwilling to condemn those who stole to feed themselves during the Famine (p. 51).

236 Ins an am san bhí an oiread san sceimhle agus scannraidh agus uathbháis agus allthachta ar na daoine ar fuaid na dúithche trí uireasbaidh bhídh agus tríd an ndroch-aicíd do tháinig ortha d'á dheascaibh, i gcás dá mbuailidís um a chéile ar an mbóthar ná raibh de mhisneach aca beannughadh d'á chéile; agus ní mó ná do chuireadh aoinne puinn suime, nídh nár bh'iongnadh, i ngnó a chomharsan.

237 Ó Gríobhtha, 'Sciúrd, an Peata Sionnaigh', in *Cathair Aeidh*, 156–205.

238 The Famine represented 'an saoghal do chuir Dia chun Éireannach, ag baint triallach asta agus ag feuchaint cia'cu dílseacht nú meathtacht, neart nú laige, a nochtfuidhe 'n-a gcreideamh.'

239 Ó Domhnalláin, 'An Gabha Nua', in *An tIolrach Mór*, 147–55.

240 Ó Cuív, 'Caint agus Gníomh', in *Deora Áthais*, 17–20.
241 Ó Dubhghaill, 'Bliain na bhFinianach', in *Beartín Luachra*, 21–8.
242 Cathain is cóir bás a imirt? Cad é an riaghail ina chóir? Cad é an dlighe 'na cóir? A Bhráithre, de bhrígh a dhéine é, de bhrígh a uaisle é, de bhrígh a bhuaine é, ní cóir é úsáid ach in aghaidh na guaise is déine agus is uaisle agus is buaine . . . Sé is riaghail dó ná riachtanas – riachtanas atá imighthe thar smacht agus thar leigheas agus thar réim reachta.
243 Ó Domhnaill, 'Ar Scáth na Croiche', in *Bruighean Feille*, 155–246.
244 Bíonn na fealltóirí ann; ach, mar sin féin, bíonn fir ós a gcoinne sin ann le díoghaltas 'imirt ortha, agus, dar mo choinsiasa! is trom an cúiteamh a bhainfear as na fealltóirí an iarraidh seo.
245 Ní thearn mise ach mo dhualgas. Is maith atá 'fhios agam caidé atá i ndán domh. Má tá, chan náire ach bród a bhéas orm, ag dul i n-áirde ar an chroch domh. D'fhág Carey fealltach smál trom ar chliú Éireannach, ach b'fhéidir nach mbéadh an smál sin comh dubh gránda nuair a bhéas sé nighte le fuil a' Dálaigh.
246 Ó Domhnalláin, 'Nimh do'n Mhadadh', in *Ar Lorg an Ríogh*, 74–85.
247 Bairéad, 'An Crochadóir nár hÍocadh', in *An Geall a Briseadh*, 179–97.
248 Maguidhir, 'Ba Toil Dé É', in *Dhá Chrann na Marbh*, 29–43.
249 See, for example, Éilín Ní Ghráinne, 'Beathaisnéisí an Bhlascaoid mar Fhoinse don Stair Shóisialta' (The Blasket autobiographies as a source for social history), *IMN*, 1983, 33–60. The historical reliability of such sources is, of course, another question. See, for example, Cathal Ó Háinle, 'Stair agus Scríbhneoireacht Chruthaitheach i Saothar Uí Chriomhthainn' (History and creative writing in the work of Ó Criomthain), in *Tomás an Bhlascaoid*, ed. Ó Conaire, 329–53; and Pádraig Ó Héalaí, 'An Bheathaisnéis mar Litríocht' (The autobiography as literature), *Léachtaí Cholm Cille* I (1970), 35–6. For the value of Séamus Ó Grianna's Donegal fiction in this regard, see Tomás Ó Fiaich, 'Saothar Mháire mar Fhoinse don Stair Shóisialta' (The work of Máire as a source for social history), *LCC* 5 (1974), 5–30. Micheál Ó Conghaile mines the literature of Conamara as a rich source of social and cultural history in *Conamara agus Árainn 1880–1980: Gnéithe den Stair Shóisialta* (Conamara and Aran: Aspects of the social history) (Béal an Daingin: Cló Iar-Chonnachta, 1988).
250 Dá siubhalóchadh duine do mhair roimh an gábhatar síos suas ar fuaid na hÉireann fé láthair deirfeadh sé nár bh'é an cine céadhna sin i n-aon chor. Tá an sult is an scléip imthighthe as na daoinibh. Níl siad chómh fáilteach roimh dheoraidhthibh is bhíodar, mar sa' droch-shaoghal bhíodh eagla orthu rómpa, agus ní leagfaidís isteach i n-aon chor iad. Chuaidh an scannradh agus an tsainnt sin i n-achrann ionnta agus is deacair é ruaigeadh amach.
251 Ua Ceallaigh, *Taistealuidheacht*, 171.
252 Moladh go deo ó Ghaodhlaibh le Fíníní Éireann! Níor mhair riamh fir dob'fhearr ná iad. Ní móide go mairfidh. Críostaidhthe glana daingne, fir thuisgeanacha mór-eolais, Gaodhail mhaithe dhílse, naimhde dána fearamhla – b'shin iad na Fíníní. Ua Duinnín says that the Fenians saw their defeat as 'God's will' (*toil Dé*).
253 Ó Domhnalláin, 'An Naoú Aois Déag', in *Dréachta*, 114–28.
254 Tá cuid aca anso ná creideann gur dhein aon ghlúin Gaedheal a leath-oiread agus tá déanta aca féin cheana! Ach nách maith an scéal iontaobh mhór a bheith ag daoinibh asta féin.
255 Delap, *Úrscéalta Stairiúla*, 40. Bhí próiséas na staire beo beathach ag tús na haoise seo agus dhiúltaigh úrscéalaithe na linne do dheorantacht na staire imigéiniúla mar thoradh.
256 Rud eile: D'ainneoin an scéal a bheith neachoitianta go leor ghlacas col leis toisc é bhaint le Seachtain na Cásca agus an troid in aghaidh na nDubhchrónach. Mheasas gur ró-uiriste scéal den tsórt san do cheapadh ó tharla go raibh an saol lán d'eachtraí in aimsir an choimheascair.
257 Delap, *Úrscéalta Stairiúla*, 62.
258 Ó Broin, 'Cúrsaí Toghacháin', in *Ag Stracadh leis an Saol*, 85–99.
259 Ó Cadhain, '"Idir Shúgradh agus Dáiríre"', in *Idir Shúgradh agus Dáiríre*, 1–18.
260 See also Mac Grianna's brother Séamus's two essays on the same customs involving local bands in *An Phoblacht*. There are few differences between the two essays, both of which are titled 'An Droma Mór' (*An Phoblacht*, 16/5/25 and 4/6/26).
261 Rud iontach agus ábhar machnaimh dhá dhream in aghaidh a chéile, go háirid dhá dhream a bhfuil aithne mhaith acu ar a chéile. Ní bheadh gar a rá le ceachtar acu go raibh ceart, dá laghad é, ag an taobh eile . . . Agus dá mhéad aithne go bhfuil ag an dá dhream ar a chéile, sin is mar is díbhircí in aghaidh a chéile iad . . . Nuair a bhíos a leithéid de bhruíon ar cois bhéarfadh sé ort smaoineamh nach raibh sa Chríostúlacht ach aisling file agus, cár bith fáth ar cuireadh chun an tsaoil muid, gur dual dúinn go brách a bheith ar ár ndúdhícheall ag cur smaicht ar a chéile.
262 A dissenting voice was that of Mac Grianna, who was cynical about those who boasted of their service in Easter Week. See *Mo Bhealach Féin*, 35–6. For an overview of Gaelic treatments of the Rising, see Máirín Nic Eoin, 'Eirí Amach 1916 agus Litríocht na Gaeilge' (The Easter Rising of 1916 and literature in Irish), *IMN*, 1985, 38–61.
263 Ó Cuív, 'Luan Cásga', in *Deora Áthais*, 14–16.
264 Mórag Ní Néill, 'An Fhuinneog', in *As na Ceithre hÁirdibh*, 203–13.

265 Ní Ghráda, 'An Chrann', in *An Bheirt Dearbhráthar*, 200. Gach glún dá dtiocfadh bheadh de dhualgas ortha a neamh-spleadhachas a chur i n-úil le neart airm nó go mbainfí amach saoirse na hÉireann. Do scaip an scamall d'á aigne agus nochtadh dó an rud a bhí le déanamh aige.

266 Ó Ciarghusa, 'Gaedheal gan Cam', in *Geantraighe*, 109–22. Stories in which the Rising plays a background or merely peripheral role include the anonymous 'Dílis go h-Éag' (Loyal to death), set in the Rocky Mountains (*Our Boys*, 15/4/37) and Tadhg Ó Murchadha's school story 'Turas an Mheadhon-Oidhche' (The midnight trip) (*TCNÍ*, June 1939, 27–33).

267 Máirtín Mac Niocláis discusses the historical basis for this fictional ambush in *Seán Ó Ruadháin*, 71. Alan Titley points out that in this novel Ó Ruadháin celebrates both a traditional rural way of life and the political movement that put an end to it, without ever seeming to be aware of this radical contradiction. See Titley, *An tÚrscéal Gaeilge*, 251.

268 Máiréad Ní Ghráda was even more unorthodox in her story 'An tSochraid', in which she viewed the War of Independence through the eyes of a young RIC man at a comrade's funeral. See Ní Ghráda, 'An tSochraid', in *An Bheirt Dearbhráthar*, 157–64.

269 Éireannaigh ab eadh na póilíní agus níor lugha-de a misneach iad a bheith 'na dtuarastalaigh ag an namhaid. Mo thruagh nár stealladh solas an tír-ghrádha isteach 'na gcroidhe i n-am!

270 Ní gábhadh an t-aithreachas . . . Ní raibh aon leigheas agaibh air . . . Bhíos-sa ar an dtaobh chontrálta. While most of de Paor's Black and Tans are predictably drunken, cowardly brutes, the author does on occasion present a more positive view of some members of that force. See, for example, pp. 116, 156.

271 According to Séamas Céitinn, Ó Dubhdha was opposed to all violence, even that in the service of Irish independence, and was never himself involved in the physical force movement. See Céitinn, 'Peadar Ó Dubhda: An Scríbhneoir Gaeilge' (Peadar Ó Dubhda: The Irish-language writer), in *Peadar Ó Dubhda: A Shaol agus a Shaothar* (Peadar Ó Dubhda: His life and his work), ed. Aodh Ó Cearra and Céitinn (BAC: An Clóchomhar, 1981), 29–30.

272 Is cinnte nár bh'fiú d'aon fhear ar thalamh ghlas na h-Éireann cos nó lámh a chorrú ar son cuid de mhuinntir na tíre seo, acht san am chéadna is maithte dóbhtha seo nach n-aontóchadh linn. Tá sclábhaidheacht seacht gcéad blian taobh thiar d'á n-ainbhfiosacht, bíodh fhios agat, agus ní ró-fhurusta é sin a ruaigeadh asta i gcupla mí nó i gcupla bliadhain. Béidh na daoine seo ceart go leor i ndéidh tamaill nuair a tchífeas siad an chuid a bhfuil an sean-spiorad ionnta.

273 Liam Ó Rinn lauded the novel in his review for *II* (22/6/37), calling it 'a tragedy' (traigide), 'a new genre in Irish' (genre nua sa Ghaedhilg), and 'a little jewel' (seod beag), writing: 'I have been waiting for a long time for the writer who could give us something like this, and I think we have him at last' (Is fad mé ag feitheamh leis an scríbhneoir fhéadfadh a leithéid a thabhairt dúinn agus measaim go bhfuil sé againn fé dheireadh).

274 Ó Broin, 'An Gé Balbh', in *Ag Stracadh leis an Saol*, 41–7.

275 An tAthair Casáin, '"Duine de'n Mhuinntir Bheag So"', in *An Londubh*, 75–86.

276 Béaslaí, *An Fear as Buenos Aires*, in Béaslaí, *An Sgaothaire agus Cúig Drámaí Eile* (BÁC: Muinntir C.S. Ó Fallamhain, Teor., i gcomhar le hOS, 1929). The play was performed by An Comhar Drámaidheachta in the Abbey Theatre in 1928.

277 The same story was published in *An Phoblacht*, 15/6 to 29/6/33.

278 '"Ní'l Grádh Níos Mó"', in *An Chraobh Chumhra*, 9–17.

279 Ó Domhnaill, 'Muiris', in *As na Ceithre hÁirdibh*, 39–52.

280 The same story was also published in *An Phoblacht*, 17/8/29.

281 The same story was published in *An Phoblacht*, 10/1/31.

282 Breathnach, 'Seilg an Ghasraidh', in *Trom agus Éadtrom*, 48–52.

283 Ó Ciarghusa, 'Liaimín', in *Geantraighe*, 17–27.

284 Ó Dubhda, 'Luigheachán gur Theip Air', in *Cáith agus Grán*, 42–5.

285 Ó Siochfhradha, 'Glóire Bhaile an Phludaigh', 'An tÉitheach', and 'Ceol 'nár Chleachtamair', in *Seo Siúd*, 22–7, 71–6, and 86–92.

286 Mac Meanman, 'Bláthach Préataidhe agus Salann', in *Fear Siubhail*, 54–71.

287 Ó Gríobhtha, 'An Sprid', in *Cathair Aeidh*, 84–8.

288 Ó Finneadha, 'Is Fearr Stuaim ná Neart', in *As na Ceithre hÁirdibh*, 55–63.

289 'Dar a bhfaca mé riamh! Sin an léine a chailleas sa chogaidh mhór. Orm-sa a bhí sí ó shoin', arsan Sasanach agus é sásta leis féin.

290 Níor lean ach an dáréag de'n tsaighdiúireacht. Marbhuigheadh cuid aca. Bhí an céad ar a sochraid – ag máirseáil.

291 Ó Cuív, *Cúirt na Dála*, in *Cúirt na Dála agus Sgéal Eile* (BÁC: Brún agus Ó Nóláin, Teor., n.d.), 6–15. In Mac Giolla Iasachta's *Toil Dé*, the justice of Sinn Féin courts, in which the protagonist's father is a judge, is stressed, but it is also acknowledged that intimidation played a role in their success (p. 89).

292 Ó Nualláin, 'Sála Salacha', in *Dia Diabhail agus Daoine* (BÁC: COÉ, 1922), 35–43. The couple's maid is, despite her presumed ability to speak Irish and her Gaelic surname, a British spy. When found out, she flees the country.

293 Bairéad, 'An Dath a d'Athraigh', in *An Geall a Briseadh*, 127–40.

294 Ó Gaora, 'An Díoghaltas', in *As na Ceithre hÁirdibh*, 67–75.
295 Ó Nualláin, 'An Chrois' and 'An Díomhaointeas', in *Dia Diabhail agus Daoine*, 44–50, 82–9.
296 Ó Nualláin, 'An Dúnmharú', in *Tighearna an Tailimh*, 109–20.
297 Ó Grianna, '"Faoi na Fóide is Mé Sínte"', in *Cioth is Dealán*, 110–21.
298 Mac Meanman, 'Tuilleadh Duilleog Amach as Leabhar Radaire' and 'Ná Leig Sinn i gCathuighthibh nó i n-Achrann', in *Indé agus Indiu*, 55–67, 106–22.
299 Ó Siochfhradha, 'An t-Éitheach', in *Seo Mar Bhí*, 71–6.
300 Mac Meanman, 'Duilleoga Amach as Leabhar Radaire', in *Fear Siubhail*, 72–81.
301 Bairéad, 'Teach Ósta na dTans', in *An Geall a Briseadh*, 33–50; 'An Balbhán Bocht', in *Cumhacht na Cinneamhna*, 49–56.
302 Mac Maoláin, 'An Fear Faire', in *Ceannracháin Cathrach*, 153–77.
303 Ó Torna, 'Sinnsear Cloinne', in *Cois Life*, 7–31.
304 Ó Cuív, 'Malairt Smaointe', in *Deora Áthais*, 21–2.
305 Béaslaí, 'Deimhniú an Sgéil', in *As na Ceithre hÁirdibh*, 7–17.
306 Ó Gaora, 'An Ruathar' and 'An Piobaire Dall', in *As na Ceithre hÁirdibh*, 79–86, 89–97.
307 Ó Faracháin, 'Braighdeanas', in *Fíon gan Mhoirt*, 9–14.
308 Lá na sochraide bhí brat Shasana thart ar chónra an Ruarcaigh fearacht na gcónraí eile. Agus an mhuintir nár bheannaigh dhó tugadh griosáil dóibh!
309 Cuireadh fleasc bláthann ar uaigh Shcoirse agus cárta a raibh scríobhtha air: – 'I ndíl-chuimhne ar mhac dhílis, agus i gcomharthacht bhróin ó n-a shean-chómhrádaidhthe.'
310 Apparently Ní Ghráda herself did not a have a very high opinion of her own stories. This is her only published collection, and henceforth virtually all of her creative work would be in drama. See Éamon Ó Ciosáin, 'Máiréad Ní Ghráda agus a Saothar Liteartha' (Máiréad Ní Ghráda and her literary work), in Ní Ghráda, *An Triail / Breithiúnas: Dhá Dhráma*, 178.
311 Bhí luas croidhe agus meidhbheán cinn air, agus bhí greim reatha 'na chliathán, ach bhí árdú meanman air, agus bhí aoibhneas 'na chroidhe nár bhraith sé a leithéid ann le fada an lá. He had made his fortune dealing in motor vehicles and airplanes, one of his customers being the British War Office.
312 He does, however, have a conversion experience through which he comes to realise the heroism of his erstwhile enemies and decides he can no longer oppose the wishes of the Irish people.
313 Béaslaí does not comment in the work on his decision to write it in English.
314 Ó Broin, *Rogha an Dá Dhíogh*, in *An Mhallacht agus Drámaí Eile* (BÁC: ODFR, 1931), 37–84. The play was performed by An Comhar Drámaidheachta at the Abbey in 1927.
315 In Pádhraic Óg Ó Conaire's novel *An Fraoch Bán* (Gaillimh: Ó Gormáin, Teach na Clódóireachta, 1927), a Gaeltacht farmer scandalises his son and the young man's Dublin nationalist friends by his willingness, at the height of Treaty negotiations, to settle for 'something less than the Republic, anything that would raise the price of livestock' (rud níos lú ná Poblacht, rud ar bith a dhaorsóch' an t-eallach) (p. 21).
316 This report said that the play would be performed 'after the next production', but it seems never to have reached the stage.
317 There is a synopsis of the play in the programme in the Taibhdhearc Papers, NUIG. See also 'Galway Gaelic Theatre / Three New Plays', *IT*, 25/11/39. Siobhán Ní Bhrádaigh, with reference to Pádraig Ó Siadhail, believes that Máiréad Ní Ghráda's play *Stailc Ocrais* (Hunger strike), though not produced until 1962, had been submitted to the Abbey as early as 1939, but held back because of its controversial theme of the hunger strike. See Ní Bhrádaigh, *Máiréad Ní Ghráda: Ceannródai Drámaíochta* (Máiréad Ní Ghráda: Dramatic pioneer) (Indreabhán: Cló Iar-Chonnachta, 1996), 50–1, 54–5.
318 This play was produced by An Comhar Drámaidheachta in the Peacock Theatre in 1938.
319 Do dheinis do dhícheall dúinn – do mhíle dícheall. Ná bíodh aon mhairg ort. Do sheasuighis led' dhualgaisí agus do sheasuigheamar-na le n-ár ndualgaisí. Tá dualgas éagcórach ar thaobh éigin. Nach cuma cé'n taobh anois, ach buailfimíd le n-a chéile san áit úd ná bíonn ar éinne dualgas cam d'fhreastailt. This play was produced by An Comhar Drámaidheachta as *Dia 'á Réidhteach* (Being settled by God) in the Gate Theatre in 1931. The critic for *II* said that the incident on which the play was based took place in Tralee in December 1920 (*II*, 23/4/31). The play as performed by the Civil Service Dramatic Society was broadcast on Radio Éireann on 5 Dec. 1938. See 'Radio Programmes', *IP*, 5/12/38. In his review of the play, An tAthair Eric Mac Fhinn rejected on moral grounds the justification for killing prisoners advanced in the play (*AA*, Dec. 1933, 3).
320 He saw the Irish during the Civil War 'i ngreim scornaigh ina chéile, ag marú a chéile agus ag dúnmharbhú a chéile níos nimhní agus níos fraochta ná rinne na Sasanach marú ar cheachtar acu le cúpla céad bliain.'
321 See also his essays 'An Saoghal Ait Seo' (This strange world) (*Free State*, 6/5/22), 'Pictiúirí Beaga' (Little pictures) (*Free State*, 5/7/22), 'Nótaí Cois Slighe' (Notes in passing) (*Free State*, 8/7/22), as well as his tribute to the recently killed Michael Collins in 'Ár Laoch, Ár nGiolla Mear' (Our hero, our spirited lad) (*Free State*, 29/8/22).

322 Ní Ghráda, 'An Díthreabhach' and 'Máthair an tSaighdiúra', in *An Bheirt Dearbhráthar*, 69–88, 89–106.

323 Ó Broin, *An Mhallacht*, in *An Mhallacht agus Drámaí Eile*, 5–17; de Bhilmot, *An Casán*, in *An Casán; agus Múchadh an tSolais*, 3–14. Ó Broin's play was performed by An Comhar Drámaidheachta in the Abbey in 1927; de Bhilmot's by the same group in the Gate in 1931. The discussion here, however, is of the published text of Ó Broin's play. As originally performed, *An Mhallacht* was set in Poland and dealt with the 1925 revolt of Pilowski. See 'D. Ó D.', 'Na hAisteoirí', *Leader*, 26/11/27; and 'T. O'R.', 'The Gaelic Players', *IS*, 12/11/27. In his review, 'D. Ó D.' wrote that the play did not move those present and suggested it would be more effective for Irish audiences if the setting were changed to the Irish Civil War. Whether or not this advice is what motivated Ó Broin, he did make the change.

324 Dhearmadamar go raibh mná na beirte sin ann, go raibh máithreacha agus clann aca a' déanamh truaighe dhóibh, agus ag tabhairt a míle mallacht ar an dream d'fhuadaigh uatha go deo iad. Tá an mhallacht san fós orainn. Mallacht fola na bhfear agus mallacht caointe na mban.

325 Imtheóchaidh Colm uaim amáireach nó athrú amáireach ag troid ar son Éireann. Tuige a bhfuil Éire chomh craosach sin, chomh mí-fhoighneach sin go gcaithfidh sí plúr na bhfear d'alpadh, nach féidir léi an ghlún seo do leigean thairsti.

326 Seosamh Mac Grianna and Séamus Ó Grianna, *Saoirse nó Suaimhneas?* in Mac Grianna, *Ailt*, ed. Nollaig Mac Congáil (n.p.: Coiste Foilsitheoireachta Chomhaltas Uladh, 1977), 1–12. The play was originally published in the issues of *Poblacht na hÉireann* for 18 and 25 May, and 1 and 8 June 1922. The brothers present the majority of the local Donegal Gaeltacht people as highly unsympathetic to the Republican position in their materialistic eagerness to reap the benefits of peace regardless of any compromises involved. Local Republicans are seen as demoralised until an uncompromising female firebrand whose fiancé has been killed by the English steels the resolve of the anti-Treaty officer discouraged by the prospect of fighting former comrades. Also worth noting is the unambiguously heroic view of de Valera propagated by the authors.

327 Níor mheas mé ámh, go rabh na hÓglaigh dáiríribh sa troid go háithrid i dtús an charaghail. Cha rabh fonn troda ortha. Chosain siad iad féin agus sin a rabh ann. Agus bhí fhios aca go maith go rabh na Sasanaibh taobh budh thiar do na Státairibh, na mílte atá annsiúd ins an Pháirc agus ins an churrach ag feitheamh go foighideach an mbeadh aon chall dobhtha méar do chur sa mhéaróig. Cailleadh an troid ach cár cailleadh an chúis.

328 Ní Ghráda, 'An t-Oifigeach', in *An Bheirt Dearbhráthar*, 167–81.

329 Mac Clúin, 'Troma-Cosach, Brónach, Mall' (Heavy-footed, sorrowful, slow), in *Róisín Fiain na Mara*, 77. Mo léan go bhfuilimíd tagtha go dtí san, go bhfuil réasún is aragóint is comhacht mórálta caithte i leath-taoibh, is gurab é an gunna meathta an breitheamh suidhte sa chathair breithiúntais; go bhfuil daoine ag sléachta, ag tabhairt adhra dhó, is é 'na dhia árd.

330 Breathnach, *Cuimhne an tSeanpháiste*, 216. Níl ar intinn agam cur síos a dhéanamh ar an dochar a rinne an Cogadh Cathartha ná ar na drochiarsmaí a d'fhág sé ina dhiaidh. B'fhearr liom brat mór dubh a ligean anuas ar an dtréimhse sin agus é a chur as mo chuimhne ar fad dá bhféadfainn é.

331 Among Father Dinneen's papers are two copies of an undated allegorical story in English dealing with the triumph of a queen named Gadelica. The story has no specific temporal setting. See Dinneen Papers, NLI MS 8623 (17) and (18).

332 The book was also serialised in *IP* beginning 22/10/32.

333 There was also an essay in English by Shán Ó Cuív about the movement's first paper, *Fáinne an Lae* (*II*, 8/7/26). In addition, in 1932 'Dún Buidhe' published 'Sean-Chloigeann / Cúis Aighnis i mBaile Bheag' (An old skull / The cause of a dispute in Ballybeg), a comic tale about a Gaelic League travelling teacher in the early days of the movement (*II*, 29/8/32).

334 See also Séamus Ó Néill's discussion of Gaelic enthusiasts in nineteenth-century Ulster in 'The Hidden Belfast', *IR*, May 1937, 351–4.

335 There is also a report of a similar lecture he delivered on pioneers of the movement in *II*, 24/1 and 29/1/36. See also 'An Guirtín Ard', 'Céad Éigin Dráma (Some hundred plays), *IP*, 3/4/33 (a brief survey of the ten-year history of An Comhar Drámaidheachta), a group whose even shorter history had been the subject of an essay by León Ó Broin (*IS*, 7/4/28), and a letter in response by Piaras Béaslaí (*IS*, 28/4/28).

336 Ní Dhubhgháin's focus was very much on religious issues. Reviewing the book for *IP* (30/12/38), 'B. Mac D.' praised Ní Dhubhgháin for giving a balanced view of the practices of the Inquisition. See also Pádhraic Ó Domhnalláin's translation of a book by Nicholas Weber as *Stair Choitcheann na Ré Críostaidhe i nDá Imleabhar* (BAC: ODFR, 1932).

337 Thomson ('Seoirse Mac Laghmainn'), 'Réamhrádh', in *Breith Báis ar Eagnuidhe: Trí Comhráidhte d'ár Cheap Platón (Apologia, Criton, Phaedon)* (A death sentence on a sage: Three dialogues by Plato [Apologia, Crito, Phaedon]) (BÁC: Muinntir C.S. Ó Fallamhain, Teor., i gcomhar le hOS, 1929), 7–16.

338 Ó Nualláin and Ó Nualláin, 'Clódius na mBan', in *Sean agus Nua*, 5–27.

339 Ó Domhnalláin, 'Napoléon agus an Fealltóir', in *Oidhre an Léighinn*, 79–83.

340 Ó Domhnalláin, 'Bás Mharat', in *Oidhre an Léighinn*, 114–21.
341 Bairéad, 'An Chláirseach Bhinn', in *Cumhacht na Cinneamhna*, 59–70.
342 Ó Nualláin and Ó Nualláin, 'Togha agus Rogha' in *Sean agus Nua*, 28–51.
343 The play was performed by An Comhar Drámaidheachta at the Peacock Theatre in 1939.
344 The play was performed at Taibhdhearc na Gaillimhe in 1936.
345 Do bhí ag Gaedhil i nÉirinn na cúig gnéithe nó ádhbhar gur díobh náisiúntas iomlán – (1) Pobal d'aon-dúthchas nó d'aon fhuil .i. comh-aontas cinidh. (2) Pobal aon-teangan – an Ghaedhilg a bhí 'na h-aon teangan choitchinn ag an gcineadh uile. (3) Comh-ionannas cuimhne is traidisiún maidir le stair, cultúr is nós. He included two other elements as well: '(4) A land theirs by ancient hereditary right' (Fearann dá sean-cheart dúthchais), and '(5) Political freedom and authority over that land, that is, a State' (Saoirse phoiliteamhail agus uachtaránacht ar an bhfearann san .i. Stát). He did, however, add: 'It is not necessary that they all be present in every case' (Ní gádh iad uile a bheith ar fagháil i ngach cás). Compare the impassioned comments of 'Sean Ghall' in 'The National Ideal in Irish History – I', *CB*, June 1923, 394–5.
346 Nic Ghabhann, *Mágh Ealta Éadair*, 35. Dá leanadh na Sasanaigh do'n tsean-chreideamh, nó dá nglacadh na hÉireannaigh leis an nua-chreideamh, tá gach deallramh go mbéadh a mhalairt de sgéal le hinnsint faoi Bhaile Átha Cliath – agus faoi Éirinn.
347 Ó Criomhthain, *Allagar na h-Inise*, 336. He lamented 'gnáth-bhéas ag muinntir na h-Éireann riamh deighilt ó chéile le linn aon rud cóir do bheith le fagháil aici.' See also Ó Criomhthain, *Allagar II*, ed. Ua Maoileoin, 80, 87, 97.
348 In his biography of St Lawrence O'Toole, An tAthair Benedict acknowledged Irish disunity after the Battle of Clontarf, but pointed out that much of Europe was in chaos at the time. See *Lorcán Naomhtha Ua Tuathail*, 1–2.
349 Mac Gréagóir, 'Réamh-Rádh', in *Stair na nDéise*, ix. Múineann an stair dúinn ceacht oireann do chúrsaibh na h-aimsire seo. Féach an díoghbháil a dhein an mhioscais agus na troideanna gan gádh ó am go h-am. Dá ndéanadh daoine beag agus mór marnadh air sin, thabharfadh sé congnamh dóibh bheith go foighdeach agus go carthannach le n-a chéile. See also 'B. Ó F.', 'Smaointí / Cogadh agus Éachta' (Thoughts / War and great deeds), *Plain People*, 30/4/22; and 'An Droighneán Fionn', '"Pro Fide et Patria"', *An t-Ultach*, Feb. 1929, 2–3.
350 Mac Grianna was not entirely critical of that disunity. There is more than a bit of Ulster pride in his discussion of how Brian Bóruma never conquered the Uí Néill and so never really unified Ireland. See *Na Lochlannaigh*, 85. Mac Grianna seems to have believed that it was the Vikings who brought internal dissension into the native Irish polity. See 'Comhairle do "Droighnean Fionn"', *An t-Ultach*, June 1929, 3. For his brother's view of Irish disunity at this time, see *Feara Fáil*, 24–5. Unlike Seosamh, Séamus saw Brian as a necessary and heroic figure.
351 Mac Grianna, *Eoghan Rua Ó Néill*, 121. An té a choinneodh fir Éireann a dh'aontaoibh an uair seo, chuirfeadh sé gad ar ghainimh. See also Mac Grianna and Ó Grianna, *Saoirse nó Suaimhneas?* in Mac Grianna, *Ailt*, ed. Mac Congáil, 9.
352 Úna Bean Uí Dhíosca, *An Seod Do-Fhaghála*, 16–17. Bheadh buaidhte ag seirbhísigh Dé muna mbeadh an t-éad a bhí ag na taoisigh dá chéile.
353 Dá mbeadh taoiseach ar nós Gándhi in Éirinn againn ní fada go bhfeicfeadh an saoghal neart iongantach míorbhúilteach na comhachta spiridéalta atá ag náisiúin a sheasann ar a gceart go cródha agus a chuireann a muinghin i nDia mar a rinne na hÉireannaigh nuair a throid siad gan airm ar son a gCreidimh.
354 Maidir le hÉirinn. Ní raibh arm againn le linn Dhomhnaill Uí Chonaill agus nárbh' ionghantach an spioraid a bhí sa náisiún agus nárbh' ionghantach an bhuaidh, buaidh gan droch-iarsma. Nach bhfuil ceithre airm againn i n-Éirinn faoi láthair agus an chúis misnigh dhúinn iad? Dá luighead arm a bhíos ag náisiún iseadh is fearr agus is sabháilte dhí. Ní sgiath ar bith arm ach tuar tubaiste géire. Tá ár muinighin sa gclaidheamh soluis – **spiorad na ndaoine**.
355 Úna Bean Uí Dhíosca, *Cailín na Gruaige Duinne*, 22. Rinne mé mo dhícheall gan smaoineamh ar an gcogadh ach theip orm. Dubhairt mé uair ar bith a bhí sé de dhánaidheacht agam é rádh, go raibh an cogadh glan díreach i gcoinne na Críosduidheachta, agus cibé scéal é nach raibh baint ná páirt ag Éirinn leis. Bhí mé i mbruighin le chuile dhuine dem mhuintir.
356 *Ibid.*, 23. Bhí an ceart aige ar bhealach ach do réir mar thuigim an scéal anois ní raibh an ceart ar fad aige. Má's maith linn íodhbairt a dhéanamh ar son ár dTírín dílis is breagh é sin agus tiocfaidh maitheas as, ach má dhéanamuid daoine eile d'íodhbairt dá n-aimhdheoin dearg tiocfaidh droch-fhuil agus mioscais agus fuath ag borradh aníos as ifreann as, maraon leis an maitheas. Dá ndéanadh an Piarsach agus a chomh-Ghaedhil iad féin d'íodhbairt ar son na hÉireann gan cogadh fuilteach a chur ar bun idir Éireannaigh agus Sasanaigh ní bheimís in iomar na haimléise mar atá muid i láthair na huaire. In an essay on Éibhlín Nic Niocaill, the woman believed by some to have been the love of Pearse's life, 'L.' wrote of Pearse's death:

> What it meant in the national order I had to face with a sadly divided mind: acclaiming his heroism, yet loathing all war as an abomination, whatsoever its ends: bringing new problems and curses in its train, even when seemingly successful: a pitiful commentary altogether on Christian humanity (*Féile na nGaedheal*, Nov. 1938, 6).

357 Úna Bean Uí Dhíosca, *Cailín na Gruaige Duinne*, 84. Dá olcas é cogadh na nÉireannach in aghaidh na Sasanach ba seacht míle measa cogadh idir Gaedhealaibh. Cad é an mhaith bheith ag caitheamh an mhilleáin ar aon taobh amháin? Bhí an mhilleán ar an dá thaobh.

358 Delap, *Úrscéalta Stairiúla*, 163–4.

359 Ó aimsir Phádraig Naomhtha i leith agus ósna haoiseanna roimis sin, is beag trácht ná raibh baint ag daoine ó Eirinn le tíorthaibh eile. Nuair a tugtar fé stair a mhúineadh ní mór cuimhneamh air sin chun suim na macléighinn 'na dtír féin do mhúsgailt agus stair na tíre seo do cheangal de stair na tíortha eile sin i dtreo gur fearr a tuigfí cad is stair ann.

360 For just two examples of the former attitude, see Peadar Mac Fhionnlaoich, 'Tuairisgí agus Tuairimí' (Reports and opinions), *An Phoblacht*, 31/7/25; and Tadhg Ó Cearbhaill, 'Cogadh na Síothchána ar Ghallaibh / Gandhí, Taoiseach na nIndiach' (The peaceful war against the English / Ghandi, leader of the Indians), *IP*, 24/10/34. Examples of the latter attitude are too obvious to require mention here.

361 Ó hAnnracháin, *Machtnamh Cime*, 49. Nách mór an truagh ná féadfaí fola-thachtadh a thabhairt dóibh féin anois. Nách fada scaoileann Dia leo, agus a bhfuil d'éagcóraibh déanta aca ar a lán den chine daonna.

362 Beidh fuaim do philéar i gcluasaibh namhad do shinnsear agus beir mar dhealg i mbeo ionnta. Beidh sgannra roimh d'urchar agus déarfar go bhfuil draoidheacht id' láimh. In ionad Stiana tabharfar Nána ort agus beidh Nána Sahib i mbéalaibh daoine. See Ó Séaghdha, *Stiana*, 121 for his hatred of the English; 48, 53, 56 for his solidarity with the oppressed; and 158 for the passage quoted.

363 See Ua Ceallaigh, *Taistealuidheacht*, 26, 32–3, 126–8, 131, 171.

364 Mac Fhionnlaoich, *Bliadhain na h-Aiséirghe*, 6. Le linn an ama chéanna bhí Sasan ag dul i neart agus i dtreis ar fud an domhain, iad ag briseadh na gclathacha teorann ar chiníocha laga ag gabháil a dtíortha; ag cur iomaire le hiomaire agus páirc le páirc san Impireacht Mhór. See also his condemnation of European imperialism in 'Tuairisgí agus Tuairimí', *An Phoblacht*, 26/6/25.

365 Ó Lochlainn, *Na Fearachoin*, 30. Ní fios dúinn deireadh an scéil ag an gcine daonna. B'fhéidir gur ag útamáil romhainn mar chréatúirí bochta baotha dalla a bhéimíd go deo. Ach an lá ná beidh fir ann a sheasóchaidh agus a dhéanfaidh troid i gcoinne an uilc agus na h-éagcóra tá an cine daonna damnuithe go bráth.

366 Ó Broin, *An Oíche Úd i mBeithil*, 7–8. Ní heol dúinne aon tslí chun síocháin a bhunú ach saoirse a bhaint de dhuine nuair a nochtas sé a mhí-shástacht le rud éigin, le hocras, cuir i gcás, nó le cánacha troma, nó le hiarracht ar an ngrá atá aige dá dhéithe féinig a mhúchadh ina chroí.

367 Ó Domhnalláin, 'An Naoú Aois Déag', in *Dréachta*, 116. Ní foláir a rá, ámh, nach de rinn chlaidhimh tríd is tríd do rinne Eorpaigh iad féin d'árdú ó íochtar go huachtar an domhain. Do chuidigh an bua do rith lena mbéascna leo chun a dhéanta. Do tuigeadh go raibh an treoir iontu, go raibh éirim iontu seachas éirim chun troda, gur ghlac a lán leo agus a riaradh uime sin.

368 Is fearra dhúinn féachaint a bhfad siar ná bheith ag cuimhneamh agus ag camhrán ar ar thuit amach na bliadhanta so ghaibh tharainn.

369 Ó Cuív, 'Aondacht na hÉireann', in *Deora Áthais*, 121–2. An deighilt atá ann fé láthair tá a préamhacha fite go daingean i stair na hÉireann agus i stair Shasana. Ní raibh fíor-aondacht poilitíochta i nÉirinn riamh . . . Do bhí aondacht seachas aondacht poilitíochta againn, ámhthach. Do bhí teanga agus nósanna agus síbhialtacht againn a dhein tír ar leithlig d'Éirinn.

370 Mac Gréagóir, 'Réamh-Rádh', in *Stair na nDéise*, ix. Múineann an stair dúinn ceacht oireann do chúrsaibh na h-aimsire seo. Féach an díoghbháil a dhein an mhioscais agus na troideanna gan gádh ó am go h-am. Dá ndéanadh daoine beag agus mór maranadh air sin, thabharfadh sé congnamh dóibh bheith go foighdeach agus go carthannach le n-a chéile.

371 Ó Cadhain, *'Páipéir Bhána agus Páipéir Bhreaca'*, 41.

CHAPTER FIVE

'Rebuilding Tara in our Mental World'

1 Eimar O'Duffy, *King Goshawk and the Birds* (New York: Macmillan, 1926), 98. Having pointed out the author's membership in the Gaelic League, León Ó Broin wrote of this novel in 1927: 'I myself think that this book is one of the finest, most original, and most vigorous pieces of writing that I have read for many a day. It reminds one of Swift.' (Dar liom féin go bhfuil an leabhar seo ar na sgríbhinní is fearr agus is úire agus is fuinniúla dár léigheas le fada an lá. Cuireann sé Swift i gcuimhne dhuit) (*FL*, Apr. 1927, 15).

2 Níl rud ar bith i sean-litridheacht iarthar na hEorpa gur fiú cur i gcomparáid le sean-litridheacht na nGaedheal.

3 Sé tuairim scoláirí mór-cháile ná fuil sárú na h-eipice sin ar litridheacht an domhain.

4 Má tá aon chomhartha cuncais níos mó ná chéile ar Éireannaigh is é sin go bhfuil a bhformhór aineolach ar shean-litríocht áluinn a dtíre. Ní h-amháin go bhfuil an choitiantacht gan eolas uirri, ach, fiú tá roinnt d'ár sár-scríobhnóirí Gall-Ghaelacha, agus pé breac-eolas atá acu siúd uirri, claon-eolas iseadh san féin: Mar, ó thárla ná tuigid an teanga ina bhfuil sí scríobhtha, níl de choidreamh acu léi ach tré chlaon-aistriúchán ar ghiotaí beaga, scartha, fánacha.

5 See, for example, An tAthair Pól Breathnach, 'Cath Cula Dremne' (The battle of Cul Dremne), *IMN*, 1926, 3–11; Breathnach, 'Brussels 6131 x 6133 (Ff. 74–80)', (a story about Niall Noígiallach), *IMN*, 1932, 43–52, and *IMN*, 1933, 34–41; Máiréad Ní Ghráda, 'Táin Bó Geanainn', *Lia Fáil: Irisleabhar Gaedhilge Ollsgoile na hÉireann*, 1927, 49–78; Douglas Hyde and T. Ó Caomhánaigh, 'Cuireadh Mhaoil Uí Mhananáin ar Fhionn Mac Cumhaill agus Fianaibh Éirionn' (The invitation of Maol Ó Manannáin to Fionn Mac Cumhaill and the Fianna of Ireland), *Lia Fáil*, 1930, 87–114; Gearóid Ó Murchadha, 'Bás Oisín' (The death of Oisín), *An Reult*, Mar. 1922, 11–14; 'C. Fh.', 'Fuil agus Foghluim' (Blood and learning), *An t-Irisleabhar*, 1934–5, 15–23. The Gaelic columns of the daily papers of the time also published occasional popular essays on the early literature. There were, in addition, radio broadcasts of lectures on the early literature.

6 See O'Leary, *Prose Literature*, 223–5.

7 A particular and persistent sore point was the inability or unwillingness of many scholars to use modern Irish as a working language. When a scholar did use Irish, as did Kathleen Mulchrone in the introduction to her 1934 edition of *Caithréim Cellaig* (The triumphant career of Ceallach) for the Medieval and Modern Irish Series, it was worthy of notice (*IT*, 14/4/34).

8 Mara gceannuítear leabhair mheán-Ghaedhilge is ar na heagarthóirí is ceart a mhilleán do chur do ghnáth. Is do scoláirí, do lucht scrúdtha seana-chnámha na Gaedhilge, do dhaoine ná cuireann suim in áilleacht is i míne an tseana-phróis go minic a chuirid na leabhair seo in eagar ... Níl ionta dhó fé láthair ach lumber (dá mhéid maoidheamh aige astu) agus beidh san amhlaidh faid a bheidh na scoláirí ag brath ar dhéithe an árd-léighinn agus gan suim acu sa duine comónta.

9 Many at the time were insistent that native scholars should play a much larger role in this work than had hitherto been the case. For example, in a 1926 review of Séamus Ó Searcaigh's *Foghraidheacht Ghaedhilge an Tuaiscirt* in *The Leader*, Lughaidh Ó Cléirigh stated: 'It has long been a reproach to Irish scholarship that the field has been in the almost exclusive possession of foreign scholars (*Leader*, 14/8/26). See also 'A. Ó C.', 'Sgoláireacht sa Ghaedhilg / Fuighleach Oibre le Déanamh' (Scholarship in Irish / More work to be done), *Standard*, 19/10/34. In a 1925 essay in *The Leader*, Father Dinneen acknowledged the paucity of Irish Catholic involvement in Gaelic literary scholarship in comparison with what foreigners and Irish Protestants had contributed. It is, however, clear that while he valued the academic achievements of Irish Protestants in the study of early Irish culture, he still saw it as in some way rooted in an alien prespective (*Leader*, 17/10/25).

10 Information is from the programme for the 1924 Oireachtas in the minutes of Coiste an Oireachtais (The Oireachtas Committee), NLI MS 11,558.

11 Hanly, *National Ideal*, 139. See also Conchubhar Ó Ruairc, 'Foillsiú na Láimhsgríbhinní' (The publication of the manuscripts), *Standard*, 21/1/38.

12 Ach nár cheart, ar an uair seo de'n lá, na sean-scéalta d'aistriú go díreach ó shean-Ghaedhilg go nuadh-Ghaedhilg. Is náireach aineolus na ndaoine 'na dtaobh, agus is náireach, freisin, ná fuil an obair seo déanta ag lucht léighinn. Ní thiocfaidh áilneacht nó fairsinge i litridheacht na nuadh-Ghaedhilge go mbeidh ádhbhar agus blas agus gaois na scéalta so ar eolus ag an aos foghluma. Tomás Ó Cléirigh praised what he saw as the selfless zeal of Welsh academics in the work of making sound scholarly texts available to a more general audience. See 'Ins an mBreatain Bhig' (In Wales), in *Seoidíní Cuimhne*, 150.

13 An feadh a leanfar de bheith ghá haistriú go Béarla beidh litríocht ár sinnsear gan rian ar bith d'fhágaint ar litríocht Ghaedhilge na linne seo, agus ní bheidh inti do lucht labhartha agus scríbhte na Gaedhilge ach mar atá cnámha seana-Laidne nó Sanscrit, rudaí go bhfuil deannach is dusta na n-aois ortha, gan éinne ag cur suime ionta ach scoláirí mór-léighinn atá na céadta míle amach ó mheon is ó chroidhe na ngnáth-dhaoine. He had also discussed the need for such modernisations in 'A Literary Standard for Irish', *Leader*, 7/11/25; and 'Focal nó Dhó', *Freeman*, 7/7/28.

14 Mac Grianna, 'Ár nDúthchas – Ár gCinneamhaint', in *Pádraic Ó Conaire*, 186–7. An chéad rud atá riachtanach an tsean-litridheacht a chur i gcló, agus litriughadh an lae indiu uirthí, agus gan míniughadh ar bith i mBéarla uirthí. Annsin í a chur roimhe gach cinéal eile oideachais i sgoltacha agus i gcoláistí, imeasg sagart agus ollúna agus sgríbhneoirí. There were rare dissenting voices. See, for example, 'Theo', 'Contemporary Literature / The Growth of Irish Drama', *Leader*, 20/12/24. When Liam Ó Rinn argued for the modernisation of the earlier literature, Stephen McKenna disagreed, stating that he was by nature predisposed to favour modern over older literature and that he felt 'that what the Irish language (and the people of Ireland) lacked was modern ideas' (gurb é a bhí de dhíth ar an nGaeilge {dála muintir na hÉireann} ná smaointe nua-aimseartha). In addition, he expressed a strong suspicion that, while such modern versions would enrich the language and its literature to some extent,

> because of the translators being so Anglicised Anglicism would take precedence instead of being relegated to the inferior position; because the fabric, the colour, and the subject matter of the translation being ancient, the Anglicism would have a truly Gaelic veneer and would seem divinely ordained (toisc na haistritheoirí a bheith chomh Gall-aigeanta, go mbeadh an Béarlachas fé onóir in ionad é bheith in áit an bhacaigh mar atá; toisc gréasán, dath, is mianach an aistrithe a bheith seanda, go mbeadh snó fíor-

Ghaelach ar an mBéarlachas agus é mar a bheadh sé naomh-ordaithe.)

See Ó Rinn, *Mo Chara Stiofán*, 162–3.

15 She expressed the hope 'gur gearr eile go bhfoillseófar sa nGaeilg na sgéalta, na haistí, agus na bloghanna litridheachta a cuireadh i gcló le fiche blian i dTréimhseacháin Iasachta, cuir i gcás, sa *Revue Celtique*, san *Zeit. für Celt. Phil.*, agus i *Silva Gadelica*. B'fheileamhnaighe agus ba chiallmhaire go mór leagan nua-aimseardha do chur ar ár sean-sgéalta ná bheith ag aistriú leamhas liteardha an lae indiú.' A rare, but biting, dissent from Gaelic orthodoxy on this issue was registered by Nuala Moran ('N.'), who wrote in *The Leader* in 1936:

> Dr Douglas Hyde spoke and suggested that too much attention has been paid to modern Irish and that we should go back to the ancient sagas. I don't agree. I think the ancients have had their day and should be let rest in peace. Let us get on with something new and up-to-date. Well and good, let the interested student by all means go back to the past for study and inspiration but why try and drag the Gaels of 1936, *en masse*, back along the dusty well-trodden road to live in the past again? (*Leader*, 23/5/36).

Interestingly enough, Moran herself wrote a satirical piece in English entitled 'Old Warriors', in which the statues of Cú Chulainn and Lord Nelson converse in the main hall of Dublin's General Post Office at midnight on Easter Sunday, 1935. Cú Chulainn is presented as fond of whiskey, angry at being confused with Fionn by young Dubliners, and outraged that some thought he had married Medb (*Leader*, 4/5/35).

16 Ní gádh dhúinn feasta bheith a' brath ar innsintí Béarla Standish O'Grady, Eleanor Hull, Joyce, agus a leithéidí eile chun an Fhiannuidheacht do thuigsint. Agus ní a' lochtú a saothar san atáim, acht aistriúcháin iad, agus i n-aistriúchán ar sheana-sgéaltaibh is minic nach léargus fírinneach a tugtar acht tuairim neamh-chruinn an aistrightheora. It is worth noting that as early as 1934 a correspondent for *IT* was hoping that Ó Cadhlaigh would some day undertake the modernising of tales of the Fianna for young readers (*IT*, 13/7/34). This reporter was writing in response to a lecture by Ó Cadhlaigh on 'Women in the Fenian Tales' (Na Mná sa bhFianuidheacht) delivered at the Celtic Congress held in Dublin that year.

17 He urged An Gúm 'chun ár seana-litríocht go léir ó thosach ré na meán-Ghaedhilge anuas, do chur in eagar agus do mhíniú i nGaedhilg na haimsire seo, agus chun i d'aistriú go Gaedhilg na linne seo (nuair is gá é agus sa mhéid gur gá é agus an t-aistriúchán bheith ana-dhlúth, mar a deirtear – dfonn atmosféir na meán-aoise do chimeád slán).'

18 'Táin Bó Cuailngne [*sic*]', *AA*, Nov. 1938, 2. Ní aistriú lom ar an tsean-téacs ar leith é. An sean-sgéal a chur ar faghái1 do Ghaedhilgeoirí an lae indiu atá rún ag an sgríbhneoir a dhéanamh. Is fearr de cheart oighreachta atá acu ar an sgéal sin ná ag na scholars seo bhíos a' caint is a' sgríobh i mBéarla faoi'n sean-sgéal sin. Agus ní bheidh beann feadóige ar móin ag an sgríobhnóir ar na scholars úd ná ar a bpór má bhaineann a dhaoine féin, na Gaedhilgeoirí ó dhúthchas, taithneamh as a shaothar. His modernisation will be discussed in detail below.

19 Seán Ua Ceallaigh, 'Réamhrádh', *Rudhraigheacht* (BÁC, M. H. Macanghoill agus a Mhac, Teor., 1935), v–vi. B'éigin cuid de chainnt Úathaighe d'fhágaint ar lár, fé mar b'éigin a dhéanamh uair eile le cuid de ghníomharthaibh Clainne Tuireann tar éis a dtroda 'san Domhan Toir. 'San saoghal so féin, ní leomhfaidhe dhúinn gach nidh d'á ndearna saighdiúiridhe tar éis Cogaidh Deiscirt Afraice, cuir i gcás, nó le linn na gCogadh Mór ar fuaid na hEórpa le céadtaibh bliadhan, do nochtadh i leabhar scoile. Is iomdha droich-iomchur a bhíonn i sna longphortaibh uile ar chúlaibh machaire an áir.

20 Pádraig Ó Siochfhradha, 'Réamhrádh', *Tóraidheacht Dhiarmada agus Ghráinne* (Baile Átha Cliath: COÉ, n.d.), vi. D'fhágas a dó nó a trí de neithe ar lár as an téacs d'fhonn gomadh oireamhnaighe an scéal le léigheadh i rangaibh.

21 Tomás Ó Máille, 'Réamh-Fhocal', *Mac Dathó: Innsean Nua* [A new version] (BÁC: COÉ, 1924), 7. Mar is léar don léightheoir ar an gcéad amharc, ní hé a aistriú díreach as an meadhon-Ghaedhilg a rinne mé ach a innsean mar innseochaidhe a leithéid anois. Lean mé go dlúth don tsean-innsean i n-áiteacha (An Comhramh); i n-áiteacha eile, chuir mé athrú mór air.

22 Dá fhad siar uainn ré na sean-litríochta tá rud éigin sa litríocht sin a shoillsíonn anuas tré na cianta chughainn. Braithimíd tréithe áirithe innte a mothuíotar i gcoitinn níos léire ná mar is féidir iad a thuigsint fé leith. See also 'Sean-Ghaedheal', 'Sean-Litridheacht na Teangan' (The ancient literature of the language), *II*, 17/9/25.

23 Séamus Ó Grianna, *Saghaol Corrach*, ed. Niall Ó Dónaill (BÁC: Mercier Press, 1981 [1945]), 87. Cá huair a tchífimid an lá nach leigtear do mhac léighinn ar bith i nÉirinn amharc ar Shakespeare ar Horace nó ar Chicero go bhfoghluimighidh sé an *Táin* agus na Laoithe Fianaidheachta agus an Mheadhon-litridheacht ar tús? See also the similar ideas of his brother Seosamh Mac Grianna as expressed in 'Prós na Gaedhilge' (Irish language prose), *IP*, 7/11/31.

24 Is é 'Iliad' na h-Éireann é. Tagann sé anuas chughainn ó cheartlár na ré 'La Tène.' Tá blas na págántachta nó blas na Déiomchuairde go tiugh ar an Táin. Síolruigheann príomh-phearsain a fóirne ó Thuatha Dé Danann. Is beag má tá baint ar bith leis an Táin ag aon tír eile seachas Éire amháin – litríocht dhúthchasach amach is amach iseadh é. M. Mac D. Pléimionn of Rockwell College in Cashel, County Tipperary, had obviously learned this lesson well, writing in a 1934 essay in his school magazine *The Rock*: 'In the early prose we will also find the Gaelic

mind in its natural state unaffected by foreign domination' (San t-sean-phrós leis, seadh gheibhimíd an aigne Ghaedhealach 'na chuma nádúrtha féin gan cur isteach air le smacht coigcríocach) (*The Rock*, Summer 1934, no pagination). Seán Ó Ruadháin also insisted on a lengthy oral transmission of the heroic tales in a lecture to An Fáinne in Dublin (*II*, 13/10/34). On the other hand, with characteristic energy, Seosamh Mac Grianna argued the idosyncratic theory that the pre-Christian Irish had had books that were destroyed by the early clerics. He believed that among these lost books was a manuscript version of the *Táin*. What survived in the later oral tradition was, in Mac Grianna's view, based on this written exemplar. See Mac Grianna, 'Clanna Míleadh i n-Éirinn' (The children of Míl in Ireland), *Camán*, 14/1/33.

25 An sgríbhneoir nach eol dó an litridheacht a ghabh roimhe, ní bheidh agus ní féidir go mbeadh aon toradh ar a shaothar. Bheirim 'sean-chuimhne liteardha' ar an litridheacht sin a ghluais roimhe, agus 'sé adeirim, an té nach bhfuil oilte ar an sean-chuimhne sin, bíodh gur duine meabhrach éirimeamhail é, ag cur gad um ghainimh atá sé, má thugann sé fá litridheacht a chumadh.

26 Tá fotha na nua-litridheachta ins an sean-litridheacht agus mara dtógtar an foirgneamh nua ar na fotha san ní bheidh innti ach fás coimthigheach.

27 Ó Rinn, *Mo Chara Stiofán*, 20. Cheap sé gurbh fhiú go maith do scríbhneoirí staidéar a dhéanamh uirthi, ní chun aithris a dhéanamh ar stíl is ar abairtí, ach chun iad a spriocadh chun stíl Ghaelach dá gcuid féin a shaothrú, chun abairtí nua a bheadh chomh gonta leis na sean-chinn a chumadh de réir mhúnlaí dúchasacha, chun go mbeadh falla cosanta acu in aghaidh an Bhéarlachais, chun go mbeadh na sean-údair acu mar chúl mhachnaimh is mar thobar inspioráide fé mar atá Shakespeare, Milton, is iliomad údar eile ag scríbhneoirí an Bhéarla.

28 Seán Ó Ciarghusa, 'Do Thionntódh Teangan' (Concerning the translation of languages), in *As Mo Mharanadh Dam*, 73. Na saghasanna litridheachta atá i n-easnamh orainn táid le fagháil nó tá meur ar eolus chúcha go háirighthe le fagháil, in san sean-Ghaedhilg dá mbeadh sé de chéill againn dul dá lorg, nó aosóg na Gaedhealtachta do mhúineadh chun dul dá lorg.

29 Má tugtar an tsean-litríocht dúinn – dlúth-aistriú uirthi ar a gcimeádfar blas seanda uaisleacht na meán-aoise – oibreoidh anál na sean-litríochta ar an nua-litríocht i slí is ná beidh sí breac le focal chéirde fé mar a bhíonn mórán den Bhéarla a scríobhtar agus fós i slí is go meallfar ár scríbhneoirí chun caint chomhgarach ghonta do chleachta agus chun có-fhocail chomhachtacha sholus-bhríomhara, a mbeidh pictiúir nach mór iomlán i ngach ceann aca, do cheapa.

30 Dá ndéanfaidhe sin, bhéarfaidhe aithne agus eolas do lucht cothuighthe na teangan ar mheon agus ar nósmhaire na sean agus fós ar mhianach litridheachta na Meadhon-Ghaedhilge. Is dócha, freisin, go mba thairbhe don nua-theangain é, focla agus cora cainnte na Meadhon-Ghaedhilge a mbeadh úsáid agus maise leo a shníomh isteach sa nua-theangain. He did, however, add that 'this work requires intelligence and taste' (Ní mór, ámhthach, cloigeann agus blas chun na h-oibre seo).

31 Father Shaw was reported as saying 'gurbh' é a thuairm féin gur túisce a sochróchtaí an cheist seo dá mbeadh lucht scríobhtha na Gaedhilge réidh prós na sean-litridheachta do ghlacadh mar bhunús na teangan liteardha i n-ionad bunús canamhna áirithe do ghlacadh.'

32 Agus tá súil agam go maitheóchthar dhom an rud a dubhairt mé nuair a bhí an leabhar léighte agam: 'Tá ceithre thruaighe na scéaluidheachta ann', arsa mise. 'Gaoluinn i mbéal Chú Chulainn an ceathramhadh truaighe, agus an truaighe is mó.'

33 Brian Ó Nualláin ('Myles na gCopaleen'), a student of earlier forms of the language, played with this idea by writing in Middle Irish. See his comic piece 'Pisa Bec oc Parnabus / Extractum o Bhark i bPrograis' (A little piece of Barnabas's / Extract from a work in progress), *Ireland To-Day*, Feb. 1938, 138 and 165. See also Breandán Ó Conaire, *Myles na Gaeilge*, 4–9.

34 Cormac Ó Cadhlaigh, *An Fhiannuidheacht* (BÁC: ODFR, 1937), 473. Is é ní bheartuigheas a dhéanamh, don chéad dul síos, ná an Fhiannuidheacht go léir, idir laoithe agus scéalta, do chnuasach is do chruinniú is do riaradh ar chuma gur bh'uiriste don mhac foghluma teacht ortha go léir le chéile i n-aon leabhar amháin agus go bhféadfadh sé a fhoghluim agus a thuiscint ó n-a léigheadh ca huaisleacht agus ca laochas ba dhual dár sinnsear Gaedheal agus ca smaointe do bhíodh aca dhá spreagadh is dá ngríosadh chun beatha uaisle do chleachtadh.

35 Tomás Ua Concheanainn agus a Chéile, *Eamhain Macha / Cú Chulainn agus Ridirí na Craoibhe Ruaidhe* (BÁC: Brún agus Ó Nóláin, Teor., n.d.), 5. Níl aon chailín ná aon bhuachaill i nÉirinn nár cheart dóibh a bheagán nó a mhórán eolais a bheith aca ar na sgéalta sin, mar ní féidir a rádh le fírinne, go bhfuil aon oideachas ná aon tabhairt-suas ceart, ar aon Ghaedheal, is cuma cé hé ná cé hí, nach bhfuil eolas aige ar shean-sgéalta na Craoibhe Ruaidhe. That the young were seen as a particularly important audience for modernisations and adaptations of heroic literature is evident from calls for authors to develop such work as an important sub-genre of Irish children's literature. See, for example, M. Breathnach, 'Leabhra go bhFuil Gádh leo 'san nGaedhilg' (Books that are needed in Irish), *II*, 10/8/22; and 'Ceannabhán', 'Leabhra Gaedhilge do'n Aos Óg' (Books in Irish for the young), *II*, 13/2/25.

36 Seán Ua Ceallaigh, 'Réamhrádh', *Trí Truagha na Scéaluidheachta* (BÁC: M.H. Mac Ghoill agus a

Mhac, Teor., 1932), iv. Thug Mochaomhóg a mhallacht ar Lairgnéan, rí Chonnacht, toisc gur bhain a ríoghan de'n naomh a dhíl-éin .i. ceathrar clainn Lir, is gur cailleadh iad d'á dheascaibh . . . Mar a chéile, do mhallaidh Cathbhadh draoi an Eamhain de chionn mac nUisnigh do mharbhadh inte, agus adubhairt fós ná beadh an Eamhain ag éinne d'á shliocht ó'n bhfionghail sin amach go deireadh an bhrátha. Mhallaidh Ruadháin an Teamhair nidh ba dhiadhnaighe. Tá a rian orainn, agus is dual dúinn machtnamh air.

37 Ua Ceallaigh, 'Réamhrádh', *Rudhraigheacht*, iv. Is truagh gan an caidreamh céadna idir Ultaibh is Corca Dhuibhne le diadhnaighe. An muinnteardhas a nascadh an uair d'adhlacadh Brian Bóirmhe, a mhac, agus mac a mhic i nArd Macha leigeamair do dhream iasachta a ropadh le n-ár linn féin, pé fada gairid a bheidh an scéal amhlaidh.

38 Glacaimís chughainn d'á bhrigh sin an Fhiannaidheacht. Glacaimís chughainn í mar adhbhar scéalaidheachta, mar adhbhar oideachais, mar adhbhar drámaidheachta. Ní suarach a bhfuil le foghluim againn uaithi. Misneach, uaisleacht aigne, fíor-charadas, deagh-laochas – iad san an Foghmhar atá le baint againn-ne indiu, an Foghmhar atá mar thoradh ar an síol bheag úd a cuireadh i dtalamh fad fadó nuair a bhí an t-Earrach i n-Éirinn áin.

39 An tAth. Tomás Ó Cillín, 'Preface', in *Artúraidheacht*, 3. Ní raibh an Fhiannaidheacht agus diabhlaidheacht i n-aon teach ariamh. Ó Cillín continued: 'These nights of story were nights of sinlessness; no evil thoughts, no calumny, no detraction could co-exist with the narration of these tales.' The stories in question here were not only Irish tales of Cú Chulainn and Fionn, but also Arthurian stories.

40 Ó Cadhlaigh, *Fiannuidheacht*, 493.

41 Mac Grianna, *Na Lochlannaigh*, 140. Chuir méin agus gníomharthaí Chúchulainn neart ins an Phiarsach, agus b'fhéidir go gcuirfeadh an fhírinne agus an uaisle agus an áilneacht atá san Fhiannaidheacht neart i nGaedhil, lá is fuide anonn ná indiu, agus gur mhian linn gan feall a dhéanamh agus gan bréag a shamhailt linn. See also his essay 'Fian Litridheacht' (The literature of the Fianna), *IF*, Apr. 1926, 19–21, and his comments in *Léigheacht ar Crois-Bhealaigh i Stair na h-Éireann / Turning Points in Irish History*: 'Once the thoughts of the young men of Ireland were directed to the literature of the Gael, ranging from the sagas with their chivalrous and independent spirit, to the passionate cry of a Keating or an Eoghan Ruadh for the rights of his race, the development of a prouder manhood was inevitable' (p. 14).

42 An té a chum an sgéal seo, thuig sé an dearcadh a bhí ag na Fianaibh. An dearcadh a bhí ag Éirinn nuair ba gheall le tír í. Nuair a bhi sí ceann-ard, bródamhail, borb agus nach rabh eagla uirthí amharc ar tír ar bith eadar an dá shúil. Ins an am sin bhí muinighín ag Éirinn as súiste Ghuill . . . Na fir a sheasuigh go daingean i n-a n-aghaidh [na Sasanaigh] chreid siad uilig sa t-súiste. Aodh Ó Néill, Aodh Ruadh Ó Domhnaill, agus ó sin aniar go dtí Cathal Brugha. I have changed a pronoun in the penultimate sentence above, from the third person singular feminine *i n-a h-aghaidh* to the third person plural plural *i n-a n-aghaidh*. The nearest plausible antecedant for the pronoun is *na Sasanaigh* (the English).

43 Indeed he wanted Tara to become 'the titular seat at least of the Government of a free people . . . the spiritual capital of the race'.

44 Má bhí na sean-Ghaedheal [*sic*] chomh h-uasal sin agus gur cheapadar Cúchulainn, badh chóir go mbeimís-ne chomh h-uasal agus go gcreidfimís go raibh Cúchulainn ann. Séamas Ó h-Éamhthaigh expressed the same basic idea more temperately in 1934 when he wrote of the Fianna:

> Undoubtedly half of what is told about them is not true, but that is no proof that they did not live, rather quite the opposite . . . Although we have no precise knowledge about what kind of people they were or when they lived, it is true that they did live, and it is true that all the Irish people respected and honoured them . . . (Gan amhras ní fíor leath a bhfuil innste mar gheall ortha, ach ní cruthú nár mhaireadar é sin, ach a mhalairt . . . Bíodh is ná fuil eolas againn go cruinn ar cad é an saghas daoine a bhí ionnta ná cathain a mhaireadar, is fíor go rabhadar ann, agus is fíor go raibh urraim agus onóir dóibh ag muinntir na h-Éireann go léir . . .)

In a rather surprising acknowledgement that the presence of roving bands of armed young men could be a mixed blessing, Ó h-Éamhthaigh continued: '. . . although they had reason enough to complain' (cé go raibh adhbhar gearáin go leor aca) (*Clongownian*, 1934, 128).

45 Séamus G. Ó Ceallaigh, 'Heroes of the Gael – No. I – Cuchulann [*sic*]', *Camán*, 2/7/32; 'Heroes of the Gael II. – Fionn Mac Cumhall [*sic*]', *Camán*, 13/8/32; and Famous Women in Irish History – XIX / Macha: Erin's Great Pre-Christian Queen', *Our Girls*, May 1932, 104–5.

46 See, for example, Peadar Ó Dubhda, 'An Mealladh chun na gCnoc' (The enticement to the hills), in *Cáith agus Grán*, 107–8; 'Thríd an Fhuinneoig', in *Thríd an Fhuinneoig*, 9; and *Brian*, 94–5, 109–10. For a slightly more sceptical view, see 'An Mhealladh chun na gCnoc', *Cáith agus Grán*, 109–10. 'Maonas' seemed to share Ó Dubhda's usual belief in a historical Cú Chulainn. See his piece 'Sliabh gCuilinn', Dundalk *Examiner*, 31/12/32.

47 See Micheál Ó Siochfhradha, *Stair-Sheanchas Éireann: Cuid 1*; and Proinnséas Ó Súilleabháin, *Stair na h-Éireann ó Aimsir Naoimh Pádraig go dtí an Lá Indiu*. A 1932 editorial writer in *IP* wondered, apparently seriously, whether an ancient grave recently discovered in County Cavan could be that of Conall

Cearnach (*IP*, 10/9/32). One can assume that this whole question was treated from a more scholarly perspective by Tadhg Ó Donnchadha in his lecture series at UCC in 1922. For example, his topic for 24 June of that year was 'the social and historical aspects of the saga' (*Cork Weekly Examiner*, 27/5/22). See also the anonymous essay 'Mar do Tharla Fianna Éireann ann / Sár-Eachtraí na Fiannaidheachta agus Innsint na Staire' (How the Fianna of Ireland came to be / The great adventures of the Fianna and the historical account), Dundalk *Examiner*, 3/12/32, for a fairly well-informed overview of what had been published on the Fianna at that time.

48 Is deacair aon iontaoibh a bheith againn as béal-oideas nó stair atá chomh seanda sin, mar ní gnáthach uachtar na fírinne i mbéalaibh na sluagh. B'fhéidir go raibh fear ann fadó d'arb ainm Cúchulainn agus gur dhein sé a lán gníomhthara [*sic*] gaisce acht is cinnte nach bhféadfadh aon fhear beo na neithe atá ráidhte 'na thaobh san do dhéanamh. Is dócha pé sgéul é go raibh a leithéid sin d'fhear ann a rinne a lán ar son a Chúige agus go mbíodh a ghníomhthara gaisce mar adhbhar chainnte ag na daoinibh agus bhíodh gach duine ag cur aguisín leo go dtí gur ceapadh gur fáthach a bhí ann 'sa deire.

49 Ní aontuighim go h-iomlán leis an ughdar agus é ag moladh subháilcí na nGaedheal do réir mar atáid le fagháil 'sna sgéalta. Is fíor gur mhór leis an bhFéinn i gcomhnaidhe fearúlacht agus misneach agus dílse. Ach do réir mar thuigim na sgéalta, subháilcí 'nádúrtha' ab' eadh iad san. Ní raibh aon tuisgint aca do shubháilcí críostúla, mar atá umhluíocht agus fulaing agus ceannsacht... Mar sin, ní dóigh liom gur ceart aird a thabhairt ar 'mhoráltacht' na sgéalta, agus dearmhad a dhéanamh ar an bpágántacht atá ionnta.

50 Admhuimíd go bhfuil tréithe barbruithe sa tsean-litríocht, ach ar gach leathnach, chítar dúinn go bhfuil míneas agus uaisleacht taobh leo. In the preface to his school text *Ór-Chiste Fiannuíochta* (A treasury of literature about the Fianna), Tadhg Ó Donnchadha explicitly drew attention to how the Fenian lore of Munster, unlike that of Leinster, emphasised Fionn's duplicity, 'deceit in his heart; betrayal of trust; hounding the person who would cross him; concealing his anger and his hatred and waiting for a chance to wreak vengeance' (cealg i n-a chroidhe; feall ar ionntaoibh; tóir ar an té a thiocfadh crosta air; a fhearg is a fhala do cheilt agus fanamh-aint le caoi chun a dhíoghaltas a bhaint amach). See 'Réamhrádh', in *Ór-Chiste Fiannuíochta* (BÁC: COÉ, n.d.), xi. Yet Ó Donnchadha made plain that he had put together this book 'to disseminate knowledge about the past of Ireland and the Irish language among the young and to thereby increase their affection for our ancestors and our native land' (chun eólus ar sheanaimsireacht na hÉireann is na Gaedhilge a scaipeadh i measc an aosa óig, agus go méadófar dá dhruim sin a gcion ar ár sinsear is ar ár dtír dhúthchais) ('Réamhrádh', xvii). He never addressed the possibility that the young Gaelic reader might not find the Munster Fionn all that one could want in an ancestor.

51 Is é bun-smaoineamh na dtuairimí seo uile agam ioná gurbh iongantach ar fad an chosúlacht atá idir rudaí áirithe i sean-litridheacht na Dé-Scéaluíochta agus na Craobh-Ruaidhe agus rudaí áirithe mór-thábhachtach i sean-scéalta an tsean-Bhíobla . . . An féidir mar sin, maidir le roinnt de sna tréithe atá in ár sean-litridheacht-na gurb é atá ins na tréithe sin ioná iarsmaí scéalta an tsean-fhír-Chreidimh – creideamh an tsean-Bhíobla. Doubtless influenced by the pseudo-historical scheme of *Lebor Gabála Érenn*, Ó Catháin saw these parallels as due to the Gaels' ultimate origin in Mesopotamia. He was willing to go so far as to trace the roots of Trinitarianism to the Irish Mythological Cycle and to see echoes of the Incarnation of Christ in the tale of Cú Chulainn's birth. In his mind, all of these similarities proved the ancient Irish were preordained to accept Christianity in due time. Parallels between the heroic literatures of Ireland and Greece were discussed by Father Dinneen in 'Filidheacht Hóiméir agus Sean-Scéalta na hÉireann' (The poetry of Homer and the ancient stories of Ireland), *Leader*, 26/12/25. 'T. Ó M.' (doubtless Tomás Ó Máille) discussed the connections between the ancient Irish tales and the Icelandic sagas in 'Sgéalaidheacht na Lochlannach' (The storytelling of the Vikings), UCG *University Annual*, 1927–8, 19–22.

52 Caithfimíd dírigheacht agus uaisleacht na Féinne a shaothrú ionainn féin agus caoine is ródhacht Chonchulainn, agus an sean-chreideamh a mhúin Pádraig dúinn a shuidhiú go daingean 'nár gcroidhe. The schoolboy Aghuistín Ó hAodha, writing in the *Catholic University School Annual* in 1924, stated that the nobility and high principles of the Fianna made the Irish acceptance of Christianity that much easier (*CUS Annual*, Summer 1924, 18).

53 W. P. Ryan, 'Cuchulainn', *Dublin Magazine*, Mar. 1925, 509–10.

54 Prímh-sgéal na hÉireann – *Iliad* na hÉireann, mar a thugtar air uaireannta – an sgéal is uaisle agus is éachtaighe, ní h-amháin de sgéaltaibh na hÉireann, ach de sgéaltaibh mórdha Iarthair na hEorpa ar fad. He added 'that the Homer or the Virgil had not come to organise that great literature, to link together the disconnected bits, to smooth over the rough patches and to bestow on their descendants the finished epic of the Celtic world' (nár tháinig an Homer nó an Virgil chun an mhór-litridheacht sin do ghléasadh, chun na giotaí sgaoilte do chómhnasgadh, na h-aimhréidhte do réidhteach agus laoidh-sgéal críoch-nuighthe an domhain Cheiltigh do bhronnadh ar a shliocht).

55 He wrote 'nach mbíonn, go minic, aontacht 'sa sean-sgéal. Ní bhíonn gníomhartha an duine bunuighthe ar a phearsantacht go h-iomlán, is minic nach dtagaid le n-a cháilidheacht. Cuireann an

"deus-ex-machina" – geasa, draoidheacht, nó déithe – cuireann sin go léir isteach ar an nduine, ar shlighe nach mbíonn ann ach "ailleagán na cinneamhna".'

56 Na sgéalta is fuide d'á bhfuil 'sa bhFiannaidheacht agus 'sa Ruaidhridheacht, níl ionnta ach gearrsgéalta ceangailte le chéile. Níor bhac Gaedhil ariamh, do réir deallraimh, le forfhás pearsanachta a léiriú. Agus d'fhág san a sgéalta gan d'aondacht ionnta ach gur do'n laoch chéadna a thárluigheadh na h-eachtraí go léir. The anonymous reviewer of Seán Ua Ceallaigh's *Eachtraidheacht* for *The Nation* was critical of 'excessive exaggeration and bombast' (an iomad áiféise agus ritheadh seama) in the narrative of Cú Chulainn's fight with Fer Diad, and wished Ua Ceallaigh had retold the tale 'in a more moderate form of the craft' (i bhfuirm a bheadh do réir mheasardhachta na céirde) (*Nation*, 12/5/28).

57 In 1927, Aodh de Blácam, having called the Fenian literature 'the national literature *par excellence*', continued 'but, like Ireland's own being, it is incomplete, thwarted, still awaiting completion'. His hope was that the work would be resumed in his own time:

> The work of the poets of 'Duanaire Finn', however, has not been resumed, and neither in prose nor verse has that great dream of our forefathers, which filled the place names of Ireland with romance and men's hearts with exultation, found lasting embodiment. If ever the work is done, in Fenian prose mingled with Ossianic verse, Ireland will possess a book comparable to 'Don Quixote' and the Odyssey. Are we to leave our fathers' works unfinished? (*IR*, Jan. 1927, 5, 7–8).

58 Cá bhfios ná gur i n-ár ndiaidh agus nach romhainn atá ré an Shakespeare nó an Dante Ghaedhealaigh? Dá mbeadh an ceart i n-a cheart suidhte ó aimsir na Tána i n-Éirinn, cia deurfaidh nach fadó bheadh sceulta agus eachtraí na Tána fighte i n-aon dán áluinn amháin; dán a bheadh ionchurtha leis an Iliad nó leis an gCoimeidia nó le drámaibh Shakespeare?

59 James Stephens to James Pinker, 6 Nov. 1918, *Letters of James Stephens*, ed. Richard J. Finneran (New York: Macmillan, 1974), 240–1.

60 The distinction was not always maintained by contemporary *seanchaithe*. Thus in 'Sgéal – "Cúchulainn"' (A story – 'Cú Chulainn') by Dómhnall Ó Colcháin, Cú Chulainn is a member and later leader of the Fianna (*GR*, Dec. 1928, 1223–5).

61 There are two Fenian tales in this collection and one story about Cormac Mac Airt. Morris was careful to identify his sources in 'Clár an Leabhair agus Lucht Inniste na Sgéal' (The table of contents and the narrators of the stories) (pp. iv–v).

62 There are two Fenian tales and one Ulster Cycle tale in this collection. Like Morris, Mac Giollarnáth was careful to identify his informants in 'An Ceathrar Sgéalaidhe' (The four storytellers) (pp. xiii–xxvi).

63 There is one Fenian tale in this collection. No informant is named.

64 For example, *An Stoc* offered prizes for folktales submitted to the journal. In a 1927 editorial, Tomás Ó Máille called attention to these prizes, writing:

> These old stories, in particular the Fenian stories, are becoming rare. When stories of that sort were reasonably common around twenty years ago no one thought much of them, particularly people learning Irish. Just as with the Irish language itself, it is only when the stories have all but disappeared that people will value them. (Tá na sean-sgéalta seo, go háirithe an Fhiannaidheacht, ag éirghe gann. Nuair a bhí a leithéidí réasúnta fairsing tuairim 's fiche bliadhain ó shoin ní raibh aon mheas ortha, go háirithe ag lucht foghluma na Gaedhilge. Sé fearacht na Gaedhilge féin acu nuair nach mbeidh siad ar éigin le fagháil sin í an uair a bhéas meas orthu) (*Stoc*, Jan. 1927, 4).

65 See *An tOireachtas, 1932 / Clár na gComórtas a bhéas ar siubhal i dTigh an Árd-Mhaoir.*

66 Fuighleach na bhFiann a bhí 'san bhothóig seo ar fhosgadh an tsléibhe an oidhche adaí. 'Sé; agus bhí siad i ndeireadh a réime. Bhí siad fá thocht, agus ceineamhaint ag luighe go trom orthu. Acht bhí Osgar i gcath Ghabhra arais; bhí Goll ar an charraig mara fá phianaigh, ag tabhairt dubhshlán Chloinne Baoisgne go fóill; bhí Diarmaid ag teicheadh le Gráinne agus fárus oidhche acu i mBroinn-na-Sliabh; chaill Oisín Niamh-Chinn-Óir indé, agus anocht bhí Feidhlimidh Rudhraighe faoi chian dó.

67 See the favourable review of Ó Cionnfhaolaidh's translation in 'Leabhra Nua' (New books) *FL*, 17/11/23; and of Ó Gallchobhair's in 'Im' Leabharlainn Dom' (In my library), *TCNÍ*, Feb. 1934, 35–6.

68 See, for example, Mac Grianna, 'A Book for Brave Boys' (*An Phoblacht*, 14/1/27), 'Books for the Home' (*An Phoblacht*, 21/1/27) and 'A Footnote to the O'Grady Reviews' (*An Phoblacht*, 4/2/27). In a 1939 review of Tomás Ó Gallchobhair's translation of O'Grady's *The Coming of Cuchulain*, an anonymous critic wrote that 'a uniform edition of the works that he based upon early Irish mythology is much to be desired in Gaelic' (*IT*, 9/12/33).

69 Pádraic Ó Conaire offered simplified retellings of these same tales in *Trí Truaighe na Sgéalaidheachta: Aith-Innseacht Shimplidhe do'n Aos Óg* (The three sorrows of storytelling: A simple retelling for the young), ed. Micheál Ó Maoláin (BÁC: Brún agus Ó Nóláin, Teor., [1924]).

70 As professor of Irish at UCG, Ó Máille had devoted a good deal of thought to the early literature. See, for example, the 51-page 'dissertation' on 'the outstanding characters of the Red Branch Saga' among his papers, NUIG MS G 1108.

71 In another of his books for children, *Mór-Thimcheall Éireann ar Muir* (Around Ireland by sea),

ed. Micheál Ó Maoláin (BÁC: Brún agus Ó Nóláin, Teor. [1925]), a Conamara boy falls asleep and in a dream travels around Ireland in the curragh of Manannán Mac Lir.

72 Volume IV (1927) included 'Bran Fhinn Mhic Cumhaill' (Fionn Mac Cumhaill's Bran) and two tales from the so-called Historical Cycle or Cycle of the Kings. Volume V (1928) contained eight Ulster Cycle stories, including how Cú Chulainn got his name and the fight between Cú Chulainn and Fer Diad. Volume VI (1930) had two Fenian tales as well as some poems about the Fianna. All of these booklets were published in Dundalk by Preas Dhún Dealgan.

73 These versions began on 8 Jan. 1927 and ran with interruptions to 29 Feb. 1928. Instalments included a 'foclóir' (glossary) and were predictably bowdlerised.

74 This series began with 'Bás Chonchubhair Mhic Neasa' (The death of Conchubhar Mac Nessa) in the inaugural issue of the magazine on 15 Sept. 1938; the final piece in our period was the fourth instalment of a retelling of the Fenian story *Tóruidheacht an Ghiolla Dheacair* in the issue for 7 Dec. 1939. The series ran on into 1940.

75 Micheul Ó Cionnfhaolaidh, *Eolas ar Éirinn* (BÁC: Muinntir Dollard, 1923).

76 Ó Grianna, 'Cúchulainn i nDeabhaidh Lainne', in *Feara Fáil*, 3–12.

77 Seán Ó Cathasaigh, 'Brolach' [*sic*] (Preface), in *Táin Bhó Cuailngne arna hiomlánú agus arna heagar as iomad seantéacs agus arna gléasadh faoi chulaith nuaGhaedhilge* (*Táin Bó Cuailnge*, completed and edited from many ancient texts and prepared in a Modern Irish version), unpublished MA thesis, UCG, 1943, i. Isé an rún a bhí agam ar dtús agus mé ag foillsiú sleachta den Táin ar 'Ar Aghaidh' leagan chó simplí agus ab fhéidir a chur ar fáil ionnus go dtuigfeadh seaniondúir ar bith é ach gluais bheag a bheith aige leis a réidheóchadh thar dhiamhairí na seanaimsire é. Sin é an rún a bhí agam agus mé ghá ullamhú ina thráchtas ina dhiaidh sin ... Is í an Ghaedhilge amháin fheileas de chulaith don Táin. An méid de bhlas na seanaimire d'fhága mé ar an leagan seo ní móide nó isé a leas é; agus, thairis sin, ní díth ná dochar a dhéanfas sé do Ghaedhilge na linne seo, comhábhar den tseanGaedhilge chur d'uige inti. Ó Cathasaigh based his modernisation on Ernst Windisch's edition of the text from the *Book of Leinster*, adding: 'I adopted the method Joseph Dunn adopted, that is, to complete the story from other versions as was appropriate' (Ghlac mé an modh a ghlac Joseph Dunn, sé sin, an sgéal iomlánú as leaganacha eile do réir mar d'fheil). He also used other editions of different redactions of the *Táin* or of sections of the *Táin* then available, all of which he noted in his bibliography.

78 'Táin Bó Cuailngne [*sic*]', *AA*, Nov. 1938, 2. Likewise, the thesis included a two-part glossary spanning 45 pages (pp. 299–344).

79 Ó Cathasaigh, *Táin*, iii.

80 Thug Cúchulainn sídhe faoi agus mheil agus chuimil sé idir a lámha é, bheartuigh sé é agus d'fháisg sé é, cheangail sé é agus bhrúigh sé é agus chroith sé é gur sgaoth sé a chainneabhar uile go raibh an t-áth scrabailte lena chac agus go raibh aer na cheithre haird truaillithe dá dheannachar. For Cú Chulainn's *ríastrad*, see Ó Cathasaigh, *Táin*, 36, 150–1; for the episode with the women, see pp. 62–3; for various references to Medb's sexuality, see pp. 80, 171, 291. To be fair, none of these passages was among those serialised in *AA*, but they indicate Ó Cathasaigh's commitment to producing a faithful modernisation at a time when most were far more squeamish in their approach to the material.

81 See also his 'Seilg Sléibhe gCuilinn' (The hunt on Slieve Gullen), *An Lóchrann*, Mar. 1926, 35–6. In his review of *Guaire an Oinigh*, the editor of *The Leader* praised Ó Cadhlaigh for putting the needs of the general reader of Irish ahead of those of

> the desiccated pundits who were annoyed because he did not delay its issue for fifteen or twenty years in which he wrote obscure notes on unimportant constructions and searched the manuscripts for alternative readings of every uncertain line in the poems (*Leader*, 23/9/39).

82 Ó Donnchadha modernised his texts a bit for the benefit of his student audience. In the words of Aodh de Blácam, who reviewed the book for *IP*, 'he dropped the antiquated words and he wove a thread of Modern Irish through the verses here and there' (d'fhág sé na focla seannda ar lár agus d'fhigh sé snáth na nua-Ghaedhilge fríd na bhéarsaí annso is annsiúd). Interestingly enough, de Blácam disagreed with this approach, but acknowledged 'Torna's work will help bring the pieces back into the memory and onto the tongue of the young people of the present' (go gcuideóchaidh saothar Thorna leis na píosaí a tharraingt ar ais ar chuimhne is ar theangaidh aos óg na h-aimsire seo) (*IP*, 11/12/33).

83 Ó Siochfhradha's scholarship won high praise from the anonymous reviewer of his editions in *IP*, 13/10/39. A similar scholarly approach characterises his edition of *Bruighean Eochaidh Bhig Dheirg* (The quarrel of Eochaidh Beag Dearg) (BÁC: COÉ, n.d.), in the preface to which he discusses in some detail the various manuscripts and scribes, and sets out his methodology for the preparation of school editions of this sort.

84 See, for example, 'Sean-Éireannach', 'Eachtra Sléibhe Cuilinn' (The adventure of Slieve Gullen), *II*, 17/12/25; 'Sceulaidhe', 'Fianna Éireann as Baile / Cleas na mBan' (The Fianna of Ireland away from home / The women's trick), *II*, 25/11/30; 'Caoilte Mac Rónáin', 'Fionn Mac Cumhaill ar Aonach Tailtean' (Fionn Mac Cumhaill at the Fair of Tailtiu), *IP*, 9/7/32; Nioclás Tóibín, 'Fionn Mac Cumhaill i mBrí' (Fionn Mac Cumhaill in Bray), *IP*, 30/3/36; Seán Ó

Ciarghusa, 'Ní Chleachtaídís an Fhiann Eacha go dtí sin!' (The Fianna did not use horses until then!), *IP*, 11/8/39; Séamus Ó Grianna, 'Sgríbhinní agus Seanchus' (Writings and discussion), *An Phoblacht*, 21/5/26; 'Bricriu', 'Lá Fhéile Phádruig' (St Patrick's Day), Enniscorthy *Echo*, 14/3/31; 'Niamh Chinn Óir', *Echo*, 15/8/31; Cáit Ní Dhonnchadha, 'Tóiríocht [*sic*] Dhiarmada agus Ghráinne', *Cork Weekly Examiner*, 29/4/33.

85 See also Ua Concheanainn, 'Cormac Mac Airt agus an Craoibhín Iongantach' (Cormac Mac Airt and the marvellous little branch), *Stoc*, Aug. 1925, 6; 'Cormac Mac Airt i dTír Tarngaire' (Cormac mac Airt in the Land of Promise), *Stoc*, Sept. 1925, 3; 'Cormac Mac Airt agus Manannán Mac Lir', *Stoc*, Oct.–Nov. 1925, 5; 'Niall Naoi nGiallach', *Stoc*, Oct.–Nov. 1925, 8; and 'Niall Naoi nGiallach agus a Dhearbhráithreacha' (Niall of the Nine Hostages and his brothers), *Stoc*, Dec. 1925, 2.

86 The latter simply glossed a few of the more obscure words.

87 Hanly, *National Ideal*, 161.

88 Ní mór ná gur dráma 'na lán-deilbh é an Táin: Méadhbh mí-shásta i gCruachan ag áireamh a maoin saolta – na teachtraí [*sic*] i gcúirt Rí Chuailnge agus an t-eiteach aige sin dóibh – bailiú na sluagh ag Méidhbh – an táin mhór. Tá féith láidir drámuíochta annsan agus is amhlaidh dos na sgéalta san go léir mar bhídís 'á n-aithris ós comhair righthe ag na báird, agus ní fada ó aithris aonfhir go haithris ag fóirnibh. 'Guaire' saw the adventures of the Fianna as particularly promising dramatic material (*Leader*, 17/11/28). See also the views of the Scots Gael R. Erskine of Marr in 'Decadence of Drama / What the Celts Accomplished / Another Revival?' *II*, 21/8/28.

89 Ó Cadhlaigh, 'Réamhrádh', in *Guaire an Oinigh*, 8. Má deintear scríbhneoir éigin Gaedhilge a bhogadh chun úirscéil nó chun dráma a scríobhadh ar Ghuaire feasta, as a bhfuil de scéaltaibh annso air, sin toradh maith ar an dtaghad a deineadh chun iad a thabhairt le chéile. In his review of *Guaire*, 'L. Ó B.' (probably León Ó Broin) wrote of Ó Cadhlaigh: 'He has had in mind, if we are to judge from the preface, that this collection may provide an ambitious novelist with the raw materials for a greater story than An t-Athair Peadar gave us in his *Guaire* or W. B. Yeats in *The King's Threshold* (*Irish Monthly*, Oct. 1939, 733). The linking of Ó Laoghaire's work with that of Yeats was not one of Ó Broin's more insightful moments.

90 On the other hand, Ó Conghaile was not alone in his opinion. See 'Éistightheoir, 'Úr-Dhrámaí don Radió / Saoghal an Lae Indiu' (Original plays for the radio / Modern life), *II*, 6/3/36.

91 Seán Ó Ciarghusa was amazed that no films based on Fenian tales had yet been made, 'and authors competing with each other composing absurd adventures for those same pictures' (agus ughdair ag iomadh le n-a chéile ag ceapadh eachtrai áiféise le h-aghaidh na bpictiúirí gceudna) (*Leader*, 13/5/33).

92 It is probable that Wall and 'Ogma' were thinking about English-language films. 'J. A. P.' certainly was, for although he had a silent film in mind, he suggested Yeats as the author of the subtitles. There were rare voices expressing reservations about the contemporary potential of the early literature. For example, in a piece on 'Literary Fiction and the Cinema' in 1935, 'Celt' wrote: 'Pictures would make Homer ludicrous. They actually do make the Irish Red Branch and Fenian Tales ludicrous. Father O'Leary told readers of his "Táin" that their imagination must supply the stage of the story' (*Leader*, 20/7/35). In a review of Mac Liammóir's *Diarmuid agus Gráinne* the following year, an anonymous critic stated:

> Despite the fact that the old stories portray the Fenians as human beings capable of experiencing a full gamut of human emotions, a mental picture of demigods is built up which it would be difficult for any stage players to portray. Perhaps in justice to the Taibhdhearc Fenians it should be said that if their characterisations did not coincide with our ideas the fault could have been ours (*CS*, 13/10/36).

93 Nioclás Tóibín, 'Conall Cearnach ar Chnoc Cailbhre', in *Oidhche ar Bhárr Tuinne*, 29. Adeirtear go raibh teachtaire ó gach náisiún ar domhan ann ar chuma éigin agus gurb é Conall teachtaire na nGaedheal – an treibh sin d'fhan dílis do Chríost ó shin riamh i leith agus gur dóigh go bhfanfaidh go deo agus choidhche.

94 See Ó Dubhda, 'An t-Ógánach Ceann-Órdha', in *An t-Ógánach Ceann-Órdha*, 7–52. Interestingly enough, speaking after a 1938 lecture by James Delargy in Dundalk, Ó Dubhda suggested dramatising some Irish folktales to interest adults in them, but then added he doubted adults would take any interest in Cú Chulainn or Fionn Mac Cumhaill (Dundalk *Examiner*, 26/3/38).

95 Two essayists wondered about Cú Chulainn's golfing skills in pieces about the possible Irish origins of the game. See Séamus Ó Néill, 'Golf i nÉirinn Fadó? / Cluiche Imríodh Cú Chulainn / Eolas ón "Táin" / Cosúil le Cluiche na hAimsire Seo' (Golf in Ireland long ago? / A game Cú Chulainn used to play / Information from the *Táin* / Like today's game), *II*, 18/1/32; and 'L. H.', 'Golf a Gaelic Game? / Cúchulain Holed Out at 200 Paces / But Scots Are the Great Pioneers', *II*, 11/11/35.

96 Nach mór an truaigh go bhfuiltear ag milleadh an oiread sin de scéalta Fiannaidheachta na hÉireann! Cé'n uair a scríobhfar dráma maith gaisgidheachta? Seo seans iongantach do'n scríobhnóir nua. She suggested Ibsen's *The Vikings in Helgeland* as a possible model. See also 'E. C.', 'The Gaelic Players', *IS*, 16/4/27.

97 See '"I Tumbled Headlong into Fairyland" / Children's Drama / Micheál Mac Liammhóir's [*sic*]

High Praise', Enniscorthy *Echo*, 26/5/34. As improbable as it may sound, *Tochmharc Eimhir* was apparently a play for children.

98 See 'Inishowen Gaels Foregather / Great Hosting at Carndonagh / Successful Eighth Annual Feis', *Derry People*, 19/6/37. Again, this seems to have been a play for young people. It was, at any rate, performed by a school group.

99 This tale had been retold in summary fashion by Séamus Ó Grianna in his 'Sgríbhinní agus Seanchus' column in *An Phoblacht*, 14/5/26.

100 See Ó Siochfhradha, *Aon-Mhac Aoife*, 6. 'L. Ó R.' (probably Ó Rinn) reviewed the play judiciously in *II*, writing of Ó Siochfhradha's source text: 'A great poet could make a marvellous drama from it. I praise Micheál's courage and I praise how well he succeeded – it would have been easy for him to lapse into insipidity, but he did not' (D'fhéadfadh ard-fhile dráma iongantach do dhéanamh de. Molaim misneach Mhíchíl agus molaim a fheabhas d'éirigh leis – b'uiriste dhó tuitim chun leamhais ach níor thuit) (*II*, 21/3/39).

101 Reviewing the published text of the play, 'An t-Iolar' praised the playwright's ambition but felt that his execution had fallen short of the mark: 'The picture painted here of the Red Branch Knights might be malicious in its failure to create any semblance of the epic grandeur of that noble heroic company . . . If the author had set out to write a satirical extravaganza, he could scarcely have done better' (*Standard*, 28/4/39).

102 Approximately 250 people took part in the three episodes of the pageant, the second of which dealt with St Patrick at Tara, and the third with the Battle of New Ross in 1798. See 'Wexford's Gaelic Festival / Preparations for Feis in New Ross', Enniscorthy *Echo*, 23/4/32.

103 The ballet was given a generally favourable review by 'P. T.' in *IP*, 15/11/37. The critic did, however, raise one interesting reservation: 'The choice of theme suffered from an initial handicap – our own conceptions of Cúchulain. He looms such a vast figure in our minds that only the scope of the Nibelung Ring can afford us a realisation of our preconceptions.' When the ballet was revived in the same venue the following year, 'L. C.' wrote:

> 'Doomed Cuchulainn' might be set as a milestone in the Irish Renaissance. Here, through a great traditional Irish figure, a primal conception of Irish heroism translated into music is united with the ballet, a form comparatively modern in Europe, and new in Ireland. Such an effort deserves nothing but encouragement (*IP*, 20/6/38).

There is a picture from the original production in *IP*, 17/11/37. 'P. T.' was able to comment on this subject again in 1939 in a report on a lecture demonstration on Irish ballet at the Peacock Theatre. Of the demonstration, he wrote:

> Here we had cosmopolitan ballet with no stress, as far as I could see, upon distinctively Irish values. Emer, Aoife and Cuchullain [*sic*] were not what they are in my own mind – beings set apart. They were really first cousins to the Sultan in Rimsky Korsakoff's Scheherezade (*IP*, 16/3/39).

See also C. Sharp, 'Our Gaelic Ballet', *Leader*, 2/7/38. The Irish language certainly would have played a very audible role had Máire Ní Chaisín's proposal for a Gaelic opera based on the *Táin* borne fruit (*IP*, 5/11/38).

104 A play for children entitled *Labhraidh Loingseach* was broadcast on Radio Éireann on 3 Mar. 1938 (*IP*, 3/1/38). See also the retelling of the story about this character by 'Goibniu', 'Suantraighe agus Geantraighe / Cleas an Cheoil' (Lulling music and laughter-provoking music / The art of music), *II*, 9/9/26.

105 The play was never published, but there is a synopsis in the programme for the production at the Gaiety in the Ó Ceallaigh papers, NLI MS 8129 (8). An tAthair Tomás Ó Láimhín discusses the opera and provides a plot summary in 'Notaí ar Cheol-Drámaí an Athar Tomás / *Sruth na Maoile*' (Notes on the musical dramas of Father Tomás), in *An tAthair Tomás Ó Ceallaigh agus a Shaothar* (An tAthair Tomás Ó Ceallaigh and his work), ed. Ó Láimhín (Gaillimh: Complacht Foillsighthe an Iarthair, Tóranta, 1943), 264–6. From Ó Láimhín's discussion, it does seem that much of the libretto had been written, in English, by Palmer, and translated into Irish by Ó Ceallaigh. Ó Ceallaigh's name did not appear on the program, an omission he noted in letters to Palmer, though he acknowledged his collaborator was not to blame for the slight.

106 Séamus Ó Conglinne, Letter to Geoffrey Molyneux Palmer, 1 Sept. 1923, in the Ó Ceallaigh papers, NLI MS 8129 (7).

107 In a letter to Palmer dated 12 May 1923, he had stated 'I think the thing should be done all in English or all in Irish', adding that he preferred to do the songs in Irish. See the letter in the Ó Ceallaigh papers, NLI MS 8129 (3).

108 Tómas Ó Ceallaigh to Palmer, 25 May 1923, *ibid.*

109 There is, however, a full text of the script in the Geoffrey Palmer Papers, NLI MSS 5239 and 5240. The handwritten score, with lyrics in English, is in the Palmer papers, NLI MS 5232 to 5237. Ó Ceallaigh's ideas about the opera can be studied in the letters among his papers in the NLI MS 8129.

110 Féachaidh libh . . . Cá méid daoine ins na táinte tighthe annsan shíos? Agus cá bhfios dúinn cé acu Oscar agus cé acu Oisín, agus iad fá dhraoidheacht ar nós Fhinn i gan fhios dóibh féin gur duine do mhuinntir Fhinn é.

111 Ó Gríobhtha, 'An Mhiúil', in *Cathair Aeidh*, 39–54.

112 This was described in the programme for the Aonach as 'a short arena drama which depicts Fionn Mac Cumhaill as a boy, leaving his tutors to seek his

future, and by his skill and valour winning the leadership of a band of youthful warriors'. While dialogue must have been a minor element of this pageant, what there was seems to have been in English. See 'S. Mac C.', '"The Coming of Fionn" Arranged by Messrs. Bewley and Séamas Mac Coll', *Leabhar Tailteann* (BÁC: Ard-Chomhairle Aonach Tailteann, n.d.), 139–49. Incidentally, given the prominence accorded athletics from the very inception of Aonach Tailteann, it is hardly surprising that in 1922 T. H. Nally offered Fionn as a role model, 'one of the greatest athletic figures in Irish history:' 'His real athletic achievements and warlike exploits, as attested by reliable historical records, were not by any means humanly impossible, but some of them, certainly, were such as would put the best of our modern athletic champions to shame.' See Nally, *Aonach Tailteann and Tailteann Games: Their Origin, History, and Ancient Associations* (Dublin: Talbot Press, 1922), 36.

113 This information is from the synopsis in the pantomime programme in the Taibhdhearc na Gaillimhe Papers, NUIG. In a piece in *The Leader* the previous month, Joseph D. O'Connor had asked 'Why not an Irish pantomime?' His suggested hero was Cú Chulainn (*Leader*, 7/1/39). In 1931, the Taibhdhearc had staged a brief dialogue between St Patrick and Oisín as part of their St Patrick's Day programme. See the minutes of the directors' meeting for 2 Mar. 1931 in the Taibhdhearc Papers.

114 The Fianna were also the heroes of several plays for children like Sinéad Bean de Valera's *An tUbhall Órdha* (The golden apple) (published in *The Catholic Bulletin* in April 1939) and of other plays produced but never published, among them *Niamh Chinn Óir* and *Laoi Oisín* (The lay of Oisín), performed at Feis Charman in 1934 (Enniscorthy *Echo*, 26/5/34).

115 In the Feb. 1934 issue of *An t-Ultach*, Ó Néill published an excerpt from *Cath Finntrágha* with the note: 'It is on this passage from "Cath Finntrágha" that I based the play "Buaidh an Ultaigh".' (Ar an ghiota seo de 'Cath Finntrágha' a bhunaigh mé an dráma 'Buaidh an Ultaigh.') See Ó Néill, 'Cath Fhinntrágha', *An t-Ultach*, Feb. 1934, 2–3. One of the judges, Aodh de Blácam, called the play 'the best Gaelic drama he had ever seen' (an dráma Ghaedhilge a b'fhearr dá bhfaca sé ariamh), and commented that the author had made better use of the literature than any other Gaelic playwright (*II*, 12/3/35). The play is never named in this report, but it could only be Ó Néill's. See also Cathal Ó Baoighill, 'Dráma ar Fheabhas' (An excellent drama), *An t-Ultach*, June 1934, 8. The text of the play was first published in serial form in *The Examiner* between 15 Dec. 1934 and 2 Feb. 1935. It was broadcast over Radio Éireann on 17 June 1937 (*IP*, 17/6/37).

116 In a rather startling passage in the minutes of a meeting of An Taibhdhearc's board on 27 July 1929, we read:

> S. Ó B. [Séamus Ó Beirn] told Blythe that it was the opinion of "everyone" here that MLM should not be on stage. Deir D. Ó Cbr. (D. Ó Conchubhair) that he would not go to watch him again and that other people had told him the same thing. – Mac Glla [Seán Mac Giollarnáth] that he did not understand the part of Diarmuid in his own play so that he was like 'a fop from Piccadilly' (Dubh. S. Ó B. le Blaghd gur bé tuairim 'chuile dhuine' annseo nár cheart MLM a bheith ar an ardán. Deir D. Ó Cbr. nach rachadh sé ag breathnú air arís agus gur ubhairt [*sic*] daoine eile an rud céadna leis. Mac Gllá nár thuig sé páirt Dhiarmada 'na dhráma féin, go rabh sé ar nós 'gaigín as Piccadily' [*sic*].

See Taibhdhearc Papers, NUIG Add. MS 58. The reviewer for *An Phoblacht*, 'Mac Duach', also had reservations about Mac Liammóir's acting, finding his Diarmuid a bit 'melodramatic' and 'self-conscious' (*An Phoblacht*, 15/9/28). We can get some idea of Mac Liammóir's attention to detail in this production from the notes he entitled 'Prímh Gluaiseachtaí [*sic*] an Dráma' (The main movements of the drama), a series of 349 blocking instructions for the play, accompanied by diagrams illustrating the more complicated movements. At the end of these notes, he wrote: 'The end, thanks be to God' (A chríoch sin, a bhuíochas mór le Dia). Nor was he afraid to spend money to achieve the effect he wanted. The minutes of the Taibhdhearc directors' meeting for 25 Aug. 1928 state that Gráinne's wig (*perruque*) cost no less than eight guineas. On the other hand, while impressed with the set design and lighting, 'Mac Duach', in the review quoted above, felt the costumes were not all they could be:

> A few of the costumes left a good deal to be desired, but lack of funds is no doubt responsible for this. However, some of the men's attire bordered perilously on the ridiculous, and Fionn Mac Cumhal's [*sic*] elegant dorsal decolletage made laughter obliterate passing events whenever a full back view was presented.

All information above is from the Taibhdhearc na Gaillimhe Papers, NUIG.

117 Níl eagla ar bith ar Mhicheál Mac Liammhóir [*sic*] an 'simile' agus an 'metafor' a tharraingt ar féin agus sin mar is fearr liom é . . . Mothóchaidh tú fíor-anál na sean-aimsire ar an dráma seo. Thuig an t-ughdar i gceart an dlúth-cheangal a bhí eadar saoghal na ndaoine i n-allód agus iontaisí na cruinne.

118 Ní treise í an dubh-ghaoth adtuaidh ná mo mhian-sa. Ní treise iad tonnta glasa na fairrge agus iad ag léimnigh in áirde faoi sholas na gealaighe, ná mo mhian-sa. Níl rud ar bith faoi'n ngréin, a Dhiarmuid, atá cho láidir le mo mhian-sa.

119 Le n-a toil féin 'seadh tháinig sí, a Aonghuis, le n-a toil fíochmhar féin. Toil láidir i mnaoi áluinn . . . nach treise é, a Athair, agus nach uathbhásaighe é sin, ná rud ar bith eile faoi luighe na gréine?

120 Tá trom ualach ar mo chroidhe i ngeall ar áilleacht na mná seo. Tá a ceann crochta go hárd maordha aici, agus má's ciúin caomh é a glór, nach bhfuil magadh is fonóid an domhain iomlán le léigheamh 'na béal is 'na súile.

121 Sgaoil díom, a Ghráinne. Cé go bhfuil mílseacht na meala in do chorp, is nimhneach an mhílseacht í, agus feicim drithle na nimhe faoi do shúil. In an intriguing note in a 1933 review of the Dublin production of the play, 'M.' wrote:

> There is endless scope for drama in the story of 'Diarmuid and Gráinne', but a more faithful keeping to the old folk tale would give gorgeous material for a somewhat Shavian play, in which an ardent and romantic young woman pitched on a very conventional young man to play Romeo to her Juliet, or perhaps I should say Naoise to her Deirdre, and was sold a pup (*UI*, 4/11/33).

122 Tagann sgannradh ar shúile Fhinn. Filleann sé an clóca 'na timpeall. Téighid amach le chéile. Diarmuid sínte i lár an stáitse agus fir na Féinne ar a nglúna 'na thimpeall i bhfuirm corráin. Tost.

123 A play titled 'Gráinne of the Ships' was submitted to Taibhdhearc na Gaillimhe in 1939, but was rejected and returned to the author. See the minutes of the directors' meeting for 21 Dec. 1939 in Taibhdhearc na Gaillimhe Papers, NUIG Add. MS 63.

124 Dates here are dates of production.

125 Mac Fhionnlaoich lectured on *Fled Bricrend* (Bricriu's feast) to An Fáinne in Dublin on 18 Nov. 1931 (*IP*, 17/11/31). He also published a poem from *Buile Shuibhne* with accompanying glossary in *An Phoblacht* in 1926. See 'Tuairisgí agus Tuairimí', *An Phoblacht*, 2/4/26. In a prefatory note, Mac Fhionnlaoich wrote: 'It appears that there was trouble and strife in Ireland at that time – just as there is now.' (Do réir cuma bhí suathadh agus buaidhreadh in Éirinn an uair sin féin – díreach mar atá anois.)

126 Mac Fhionnlaoich, 'An Cogadh Dearg', in *An Cogadh Dearg*, 25. Ní mheasann sé an oiread do eachtraibh na bhFiann ó shoin is do mheasfadh tráth; deir sé gur mó na heachtraí do thuiteann amach in ár n-aimsearaibh féin.

CHAPTER SIX

Flawed, Failed, Forgotten?

1 Bhí mé trí bliadhana go leith ag obair don Ghúm. Is é an chuimhne atá agam air go rabh mé mar a bhéinn i bpríosún, agus lucht mo choimheádta ag déanamh úsáide de riaghalacha an phríosúin ar gach dóigh a mb'fhéidir le masla agus easonóir agus anró a thabhairt domh. See also Mac Grianna, *Mo Bhealach Féin*, 8; 'Murchadh agus Maghnus', *An Camán*, 27/8/32; and 'An Gúm / "Ceárdcha Litridheachta"' (An Gúm / A 'literary workshop'), Dundalk *Examiner*, 3/9/32.

2 See also Ó Grianna, *Saol Corrach*, 234–43. Ar feadh bliana ina dhiaidh sin bhí mearbhlán i mo cheann agus bhí cruit orm. Bhí crampaí i mo mhéara agus mé ag cailleadh amharc na súl. Agus bhí mo chuid Gaeilge briste brúite bearnach. In a bitter letter to *An Phoblacht* in Aug. 1932, Ó Grianna explained why he had turned to translation:

> I am writing Irish for exactly twenty years. Of that period I have spent eighteen years at original work (in one form or another) and two years at translation. In 1928 I had published four original books. In 1929 I wrote what I consider by far my best work – *Innis Beannach*. What happened it? Where is it? Lying under a heap of dust in the company of tailors' bills and income-tax demands. That is my answer to anyone who asks why I gave up original work and took to translation (*An Phoblacht*, 6/8/32).

Ó Grianna's lecture to An Fáinne on 'Aistriughadh' (Translation) was broadcast on 2RN on 19 June and 3 July 1928 (see 'Broadcasting' for those dates in *II*).

3 Two translators who claimed to enjoy their work for An Gúm were León Ó Broin and Seán Mac Maoláin. See Ó Broin, 'Contemporary Gaelic Literature', *CA*, 1935, 132; and Mac Maoláin, *Gleann Airbh go Glas Naíon*, 156–62.

4 Máirtín Ó Cadhain, 'Irish Prose', in *Literature in Celtic Countries*, 150.

5 O'Leary, *Prose Literature*, 355–99.

6 There were also on occasion competitions for translation at regional *feiseanna*. See, for example, 'Prizes for Drama Translations / Feis Chonnacht Competitions', *CT*, 11/4/25.

7 See Mac Niocláis, *Seán Ó Ruadháin*, 109.

8 *Ibid.*, 188.

9 Ní cheapfar fíor-litríocht go deo le hordú, ach is féidir mórán a dhéanamh ar a son ina dhiaidh sin féin. Ach tá cineál litríochta nó saothar litríochta ann, agus is féidir daoine a chur á oibriú – cuirim i gcás aistriúcháin ar gach teanga choimhthíoch.

10 Ná deinimís brí beag de leabhraibh a haistrigheadh ó theangthachaibh iasachta. Mara mbeadh iad ní bheadh fhios againn ná gur saghas éigin beithidhigh an Francach nó an Spáinneach nó an Síneach. Níl aon-tseilbh na háilleachta is na huaisleachta againn féin. Níl aon chine de chineacha sibhialta na talmhan ná fuil áilleacht éigin fé leith ina gcuid litríochta acu. Chun go gcuirfimís eolas uirri ní mór dúinn na leabhair ina bhfuil sí do chur i nGaedhilg. Saibhreó [*sic*] sí an Ghaedhilg agus neartó [*sic*] sí léi. Ó Rinn urged Gaelic translators not only to turn their attention to contemporary European literature, but also 'to attempt languages from every group: Slavic, Semitic, Mongolian, etc., so that they could draw the fresh water of every literature from its own well instead of drawing it from the stream of English' (túirt fé theangthacha a bhaineann le gach grúpa: Sclábhach, Semiteach, Mongólach, etc., i dtreo go bhfeudfid

fior-uisce gach litríochta do tharang glan amach as a tobar féin in ionad é tharang as sruthán an Bheurla). See also Ó Rinn, 'Litríocht na Gaeilge / An Bhfuil Aon Tóir ag Gaedhilgeoirí ar Léitheoireacht?' (Literature in Irish / Do Irish-speakers have any interest in reading?), *Star*, 17/8/29.

11 Comhartha ar bheodhacht teangtha an dóigh a dtig léithe a dul féin a chur ar adhbhar atá i dteangaidh eile . . . Is beag rud is riachtanaighe le beodhacht a chur i nua-litridheacht na Gaedhilge 'ná aistriúcháin mhaithe ar shaothar na mór-ughdar i tíorthaibh eile.

12 S. Labhrás Ua Súilleabháin, 'Roimh-Rádh' (Preface), in *An Brón-Chluiche Macbeit do scríobh William Shakespeare* (The tragedy Macbeth by Shakespeare), trans. Ua Súilleabháin (Dublin: Cahill & Co., [1925]), 3–4.

13 See also 'Not Literature but Books', Editorial Note, *UIrman*, 18/6/32.

14 Ní fheicim aon tslí eile chun a ndóthain leabhar Gaedhilge do chur ar fáil 'sa Ghalltacht agus 'sa Ghaeltacht dos na daoine óga a bheadh ábalta ar iad do léigheamh ach amháin dul ar aghaidh leis an aistriúchán. Blythe was willing to go even further, claiming that the translations were the best work An Gúm had produced. See also Blythe's comments in the Irish Senate as summarised in 'Seanad Proposals to Develop Language', *II*, 11/4/35.

15 Tuigimíd go bhfuil an propaganda ar siubhal chun cosc do chur le haistriúchán, acht go dtí go mbeidh scríobhnóirí oilte ar fáil caithfimíd leanúint don aistriúchán.

16 Ó Broin, *Just Like Yesterday*, 67.

17 See also 'Affairs of State / Úr-Scéalta sa Ghaedhilg' (Novels in Irish), *Star*, 22/2/30; and 'Notes and Comments / Puny Efforts of An Gúm', *UI*, 4/1/36.

18 Ó Deirg's remarks were originally made at the Munster Feis in Killarney. Caidé an rogha atá againn seachas aistriúchán? An amhlaidh is ceart dúinn baint go mór ó uimhir na leabhar atá dá gcur amach againn anois, agus bheith ag brath ar an gcorr-leabhar fhoghanta i mbun-cheapadóireacht a gheibhmid anois agus arís chun nua-litridheacht na Gaedhilge a chur ar fáil?

19 The situation was exacerbated because many native speakers, like the two just named, were resentful not only of the politics of those running An Gúm, but also of the fact that many of them were newly minted civil servants who were not native speakers themselves. Donn Piatt expressed the suspicions, not to say the paranoia, of this group with characteristic bite: 'They tried to create an official dialect in order to discredit the speech of the Gaeltacht. They spent thousands of pounds to break the Irish language and to replace it with Blythe-speak' (Thugadar iarraidh canamhaint oifigeamhail a dhéanamh d'aon ghnó le caint na Gaedhealtachta do chur fá dhí-mheas. Thugadar na mílte púnt chun na Gaedhilge do bhriseadh agus an Bhlaghdais a chur ina háit) (*An Phoblacht*, 20/8/32).

In a bold response to this kind of animosity, one of the staunchest defenders of An Gúm, Liam Ó Rinn, disingenuously explained how working for the agency could benefit the native speaker. Writing of translation, Ó Rinn claimed that 'it disciplines the native speaker of Irish, and from that discipline will come the strength and the power that many of them lack' (cuireann sé smacht ar an nGaedhilgeoir dúchais agus as an smacht tiocfidh an neart agus an chomhacht atá de dhíth ar a lán acu) (*Star*, 17/8/29). On the other hand, Gaelic reviews in *The Irish Times* lamented the fact that some translators were attempting to impose their own dialects in works set outside of their native areas, leading to what one critic in 1935 called 'a chaos of idiom' (*IT*, 16/2/35). His objection here was to Seosamh Mac Grianna's translation of the Cork playwright Lennox Robinson's *The Whiteheaded Boy* into Ulster Irish.

That the questions raised during the debate about An Gúm's translation policy ultimately transcended the political and personal is perhaps most obvious when one notes that the same basic criticisms of the agency continued to be voiced, at times even more sharply, throughout the 1930s, well after Fianna Fáil had assumed control of it from Cumann na nGaedheal.

20 Tá claon ró-mhór againn chun aistriúcháin . . . Is maith ann é an t-aistriúchán ach tuigimís ná fuil ann ach líonadh beárnan. Is baoghal liom go raghaidh scríobhnóirí go bhfuil féith na cumadóireachta ionnta ag aistriú ar a mbog-stróic chun teacht ar airgead bog. Ta sé déanta cheana ag cuid aca. Is olc an comhartha é. Marbhófar an plannda bog óg eile mura mbítar i bhfad níos cineálta leis.

21 Deirtear go bhfuil a lán de na fir is fearr i gcionn phinn agus is fearr ag cumadóracht sgéalta, go bhfuil siad ag obair ar aistriúchán le tamall. Mór 'truaigh é seo, 'ná is cinnte go gcuirfidh sé sin isteach ar fhéith na scríobhnórachta atá ionnta cheana. B'fhearr i bhfad do litridheacht na teangadh leigint do na fir seo bheith a' gabháil do'n chumadóracht úr-nuaidh agus iad a dhíol as. An Gúm paid translators £1 per thousand words put into Irish, an amount that Ó Broin tells us 'kept the wolf from the door as my family began to arrive' (*Just Like Yesterday*, 67), and was seen by 'Sliabh Bladhma' in 1937 as tempting enough to lure writers from original work (*Gaedheal*, Feb. 1937, 1).

22 Má bhíonn ár scríbhneoirí Gaedhilge ag gabháil don aistriúchán de shíor is ró-bhaoghalach go raghaidh féith na bun-scríbhneoireachta ar ceal ar fad ionta, pé méid di, beag ná mór, ná fuil múchta ionta fós. Tá a n-aigne dhá múnlú ag obair an aistriúcháin le fada i slí is ná féadfaidh siad ar ball aon tsaghas eile oibre dhéanamh fiú amháin má chuireann siad chuige. His solution to this problem as outlined in this essay was for the Gaelic writer to alternate between translation and original work:

If he were to do so, the translation and the original writing would assist each other, the former teaching him how to give the latter the proper form and shape and finish, the latter teaching him how to inject the proper rhythm and the natural music of the Irish language into the former (Dá ndeineadh sé amhlaidh bhéadh obair an aistriúcháin agus obair na bun-scríbhneoireachta ag cabhrú le n-a chéile aige, an chéad obair ghá mhúineadh dho conus fuirm cheart agus crot agus slacht do chur ar an dara hobair, agus an dara hobair ghá mhúineadh dho conus rithim cheart agus ceol nádúrtha na Gaedhilge do chur sa chéad obair).

23 Nach mór idir é [*Peig*] agus an drabhuigheall aistriúchán a thagann chughainn ó'n nGúm. Nárbh'fhearr go mór fada cuid de'n airgead a caithtear ar ghnó gan tairbhe a chur ar leath-taoibh do sgríobhnóirí ó'n nGaedhealtacht. Dá ndeintí sin ní bheadh na bunscéalta chomh gann agus táid. Even before the foundation of An Gúm, Éamonn Mac Giolla Iasachta was worried about such a development, telling a contributor who had offered a translation of an O. Henry story to *An Sguab* in 1923: 'We would prefer something a person would compose himself . . .' (Bfearr linn rud a cheapfadh duine é féin . . .). He did, however, continue: ' . . . but a good translation is better than something new that is wretched' (. . . ach is fearr aistriú maith ná rud nuadh suarach). The letter, dated 10 Dec. 1923, is in the Edward McLysaght Papers, NLI MS 8560 (9).

24 An mhuinntir a deir go bhfuil mórchuid 'nea-réaltachta' ag baint le hobair aistriúcháin chomhairleóchainn dóibh an fhoidhne do chleachtadh. Ní in aon lá amháin a tógadh an Róimh ná níor chlos riamh gur fhás litríocht náisiúnta in aon deich mbliana amháin . . . Obair mhillteach mhór teanga a bhí dhá leigint i bhfailligh ar feadh trí chéad blian d'athmhúnlú ar nós go mbeadh sí inniúil don obair a dheineann gnáth-theangthacha sibhialta na hEorpa agus san ar shlí ná brathfaí aon mhí-nádúrthacht ná nea-réaltacht sa chuma ina ndéanfa sí an obair.

25 Is iongantach an méid aistriúcháin atá á dhéanamh ach ní hionann san is í [an Ghaeilge] bheith ag fás as an gcomhacht dúthchais atá inti. Níl ann ach mar bheadh leigheas an dochtúra don leanbh bhreoite nó congnamh inealltóirí iasachta chun oibreacha móra chur ar bun do náisiún bheag a bheadh chó lag san tar éis na daoirse gur ró-dheacair dóibh éinní fónta dhéanamh uatha féin.

26 The quotation here is from the essay as published in Ó Ciarghusa, 'Do Thionntódh Teangan' (Concerning translation), in *Ar Mo Mharanadh Dam*, 49. Is baoghal liom go bhfuilid ann daoine adeurfadh ná fuil tairbhe, ach a mhalairt, do'n Ghaedhilg in san tionntódh. Gur dochar, dar leo, agus nach sochar, thiocfadh dí as. Ní fheadar féin ach is dóigh liom go gcaithfimíd an tionntódh a dheunamh pé 'ca olc maith liom é, nó pé 'ca olc maith dúinn nó do'n Ghaedhilg é mar ná fuil dul uaidh againn.

27 See, for example, O'Leary, *Prose Literature*, 405–8.

28 Rud amháin a dheinean an sciam seo ag an Rialtas aistrighean sé a lán téarmaí atá de dhíth oruinn sa Ghaedhilg agus beidh na téarmaí seo go léir go nádúrtha ag na leanbhaí.

29 Déanfaidh an t-aistriúchán maitheas le lúth agus láidreacht a chur sa teangaidh agus le sompla a thabhairt d'ár sgríbhneoirí ar an gcineál litridheachta atá dhá sgríobhadh i dteangacha eile ach taobh amuigh de sin níl aon tairbhe ann.

30 Gléas maith is eadh an t-aistriúchán chun ceárd na sgríobhnóireachta do mhúineadh do sna sgríobhnóirí óga má tá féith na sgríobhnóireachta ionnta. Tá fhios againn go léir gur chaith Shakespeare na bliadhanta fada ag deisiú seana-dhrámaí sár ar cheap sé dráma as a stuaim féin. Ó Ciosáin went so far as to assert, 'The Translation Department is the most important department under An Gúm' (Roinn an Aistriúchán an Roinn is tábhachtaighe fén nGúm). He did, however, express concern about the kind of books the agency was choosing for translation, preferring that 'simple country stories in which there is vigorous speech and a suitable plot' (sgéalta simplidhe tuatha go bhfuil cainnt bhríoghmhar ionnta agus plot oireamhnach) be chosen over books like *At the Villa Rose* and *Dr Jekyll and Mr Hyde*.

31 Measaim ná beidh aon letríocht againn a dféadfimíd a chur i gcomórtas le letríochta móra an domhain godi go mbeidh somplaí againn nár dteangain féin chun an cheárd dfoghlaim asta, sé sin, aistriú ar chuid desna hoibreacha móra uaisle agus ar anachuid ar fad desna hoibreacha ná fuil cho mór ná cho huasal.

32 Tá rud amháin déanta ag an Súilleabhánach uasal, agus togha rud é: Tá talamh úr briste aige – briste in Éirinn! Tá taisbeánta aige go bhfuil sé in a am againn, dá fhaide de ló é, éirghe ós cionn an chothroim litridheachta atámuid do chongbháil leis na ciantaibh, agus rud eicínt níos áirde d'aimsiúghadh, agus féachaint ar deireadh thiar a bhféadfamuis dóchas féin do chur ar bun go dtiocfamuis suas lá eicínt le cothrom litridheachta an domhain in a mairimid. See also the brief but positive anonymous review of the translation in *II*, 14/12/25.

33 Ó Ciarghusa, 'Do Thionntódh Teangan', in *Ar Mo Mharanadh*, 66. But he also expressed reservations on this same point. See p. 60.

34 Ua Dálaigh reprinted this essay as a section of his survey of 'Nua-Litridheacht na Gaedhilge, 1920–1930' for the *Catholic Bulletin* in June 1931 (pp. 605–11). Tá meirg tréis teacht ar an nGaedhilg ó bheith amuigh fé spéir le fada agus an droch-shíon ann. Ní thiocfaidh linn í do chur ag obair ar ár dtoil féin gan a bheag nó a mhór de'n aistriúchán. Is fada ó tráchtadh ar ghnáth-chúrsaí léighinn 'sa nGaedhilg, agus sin a bheir di bheith go ciotach agus go tuathach indiu. Tá géar-ghádh leis an aistriúchán; cuirtear Gaedhilg ar

leabhartha feallsamhnachta, ar leabhartha staire, ar leabhartha ealadhna, agus ar leabhartha léighinn, ar scéalta, ar eachtraí, agus ar dhánta. Bídís go léir ann, agus a thuille má's féidir.

35 Ní'l litridheacht ar bith 'sa Ghaedhilg is fiú a léigheamh. Ní'l sgríbhneóir ar bith Gaedhilge againn ar fiú sgríbhneóir a thabhairt air. Taobh thall den fhairrge Ghaedhealaigh atá gach rud a bhfuil tairbhe ar bith ann. Is fusa léightheóirí a fhághail do dhroch-Ghaedhilg nó do Ghaedhilg mhaith. Tá fiche fear nach dtig leis litridheacht a sgríobhadh a dtig leis aistriughadh a dhéanamh.

36 Cibé duine nó daoiní a chéad-mheabhruigh ar ár litridheacht a chur chun cinn tré aistriúchán deirfinn go rabh na smaointí cama céadna aca 's bhí ag lucht-foghlumtha-ceoil-tré-opéra. Ní fhásfaidh ceachtar de'n dá nidh seo as an iasacht.

37 Tá mórán leabharthaí Gaedhilge 'á gcur amach ag an Riaghaltas ar na mallaibh acht níl ins an mhór chuid aca acht aistriúcháin ó'n mBéarla agus ó theangthacha eile. Dar liomsa nach bhfásann litridheacht i choidhche amach as aistriúcháin, agus nach dtéigheann na leabharthaí seo a táthar a chur [*sic*] amach anois chun tairbhe na teangtha ar fud na tíre. Má thig fás ar bith as an nGaedhilg caithfidh sé 'theacht go nádúra, agus do réir mo thuairim-se níl rud ar bith comh mí-nádúra le sgéal Gaedhilg a chluinstin ná a léigheamh agus dubhshraithe an sgéil leagtha i Londuin, i mBerlin, nó i bpríomh Chathair na Frainnce. In a 1933 essay in a professional journal for librarians, Micheál Ó Donnabháin (Michael O'Donovan, i.e. Frank O'Connor) discussed at some length what he called 'the fundamental unreality' involved with much of the translation being done into Irish. See Ó Donnabháin, 'An Gúm', *An Leabharlann*, Dec. 1930.

38 See Ó Rinn, *Mo Chara Stiofán*, 125–6.

39 Not all were so concerned. For instance, Ernest Blythe wrote in 1931:

> In the Galltacht . . . there must be made available great masses of reading matter to suit all tastes. The quantity that is required can only be obtained in time by translation. Therefore, we must translate English novels and detective stories in much greater numbers than had been thought of heretofore (Blythe, quoted by Mac Niocláis, in *Seán Ó Ruadháin*, 111).

See also the editorial opinions expressed in 'Notes and Comments', *UI*, 10/11/34. The anonymous reviewer of Mac Grianna's translation of *The Nigger of the 'Narcissus'* for *TCNÍ* felt that renderings from English need not be a problem if the source text was chosen with care and discrimination: 'If we must have translation from English, we will have no problem as long as we are given the best work the great writers of that language did' (Má's éigean dúinn bheith i dtaobh le haistriúcháin ón mBéarla, ní gearánta dhúinn an fhaid a tugtar dúinn an saothar is fearr d'ár dhein scríobhnóirí móra na teangan san). (*TCNÍ*, Apr. 1934, 3). In fact, he argued that there might well be less Béarlachas in translations because those doing the work were more on the lookout for it than were those involved in creative work.

40 Ó Ciarghusa, 'Do Thionntódh', in *Ar Mo Mharanadh*, 58–9. Níor mhór dúinn go léir, mar sin, scríobhnóirí agus léightheoirí mar atáimíd, ceurd nó ealadha an tionntuighthe do thuigsint chun go bhféadfaimís an Beurlachas d'aithint agus do sheachaint . . . Má's fiú an Ghaedhilg í do thárrtháil, tárrtháiltear do réir a glaine agus a córach í. Ní beag de'n 'Brogue' Beurla againn gan 'Brogue' Gaedhilge i n-a teannta.

41 Furast' aithinte gur Béarlachas – fíor-dhearg-Bhéarlachas – é an tionntúchán seo ó thús deire go tosuigh . . . Dar liom níl rádh-cainnte ó thosach go dtí deire an leabhair, a bhfuil Gaedhilge cheart dhúthchasach ann . . . Is geall é an tionntúchán seo le bréidín is bróga úr-leathair a chur ar dhubh-chneasach agus féachaint annsin le cur i gcéill gur Árannach é. In *An Stoc* the following month, 'E. Ó N.' criticised Ó Cadhain for not providing specific examples of the shortcomings of this translation. He was also disgusted with Ó Cadhain for attacking the work of a devoted Gael so soon after his death. Ó Cadhain defended himself and provided the desired examples in the July–Aug. issue of the journal. Risteárd Ó Foghludha was aware of the flaws in Ó Conaill's translation, writing in a tribute to the recently deceased Ó Conaill in *Catholic University School Annual* that he had read the text of the translation three or four times before it was published and told Ó Conaill he adhered too closely to the English, a criticism with which Ó Conaill agreed (*CUS Annual*, Summer 1930, 16). Seosamh Mac Grianna shared Ó Cadhain's low opinion of Ó Conaill's translation. See his letter in *United Irishman*, 20/8/32. Interestingly enough, Ó Cadhain's own 1932 translation of Kickham's *Sally Cavanagh* had its own problems, the first draft having been returned to Ó Cadhain by An Gúm as it was almost twice the length of the original! See Mac Niocláis, *Seán Ó Ruadháin*, 114.

42 Ó Ciarghusa, 'Do Thionntódh', in *Ar Mo Mharanadh*, 60. He saw the threat posed by translation as 'eagnaidheacht na ceud teangan a bheith bun os cionn le heagnaidheacht na dara teangan, – í Gallda i n-áit bheith Gaedhealach, Págánach i n-áit bheith Críostaidhe. Is nimh i bhféitheachaibh na dara teangan tionntódh ó n-a leithéid agus nach fios cad é an fhaid siar iarsma sluigthe na nimhe aici.' Among specific translations criticised on moral grounds were Tomás Ó hEighneacháin's version of Martínez-Sierra's *Los Pastores* as *An Bheirt Aodhairí* (see 'Léightheoir Comhthrom', 'Am' Leabharlainn Dom', *TCNÍ*, May 1933, 118); Niall Ó Domhnaill's rendering of H. Rider Haggard's *She* as *Ise* (see 'S. Ó C.', 'Am' Leabharlainn Dom', *TCNÍ*, Sept. 1933, 213); Tadhg Ó Cúrnáin's version of Jack London's *White Fang* as *Mac an Mhactíre* (see 'S. Ó C.', 'Im' Leabharlainn

Dom', *TCNÍ*, Apr. 1937, 93–4); Seosaimhín Bean Mhic Néill's *Finnsgéalta ó India* (see 'A Novice', 'Gleanings', *CB*, Sept. 1933, 725; and *Bean an Iasgaire*, Gearóid Ó Lochlainn's translation of T. H. Stafford's play *The Fisherman's Wife* (*IP*, 25/3/39). On the other hand, Liam Ó Rinn liked *Ise* (see 'Saothrú na Gaedhilge / Eachtra le Rider Haggard / Aistriú Eile le Niall Ó Domhnaill' (The cultivation of the Irish language / An adventure by Rider Haggard / Another translation by Niall Ó Domhnaill), *UI*, 14/10/33), and in 1932 Mrs Mac Néill's work was praised in *IMN* for introducing Gaelic readers to 'that populous race that is so incomprehensible to us, but that is as human and straightforward as ourselves with regard to the love it has for freedom and the loyalty with which it stands up for its rights (an chine líonmhar san atá chómh dothuigse sin dhúinn-ne, acht atá chómh daonda díreach linn féin maidir leis an ngrádh atá aca don tsaoirse agus leis an ndílseacht le na seasann siad a gcirt) (p. 64). Mrs Mac Néill does not identify her sources, but we can assume that none of the four tales in the book were actually translated from any Indian language. See *Finnsgéalta ó India* (Fables from India), trans. Seosaimhín Bean Mhic Néill (BÁC: COÉ, [1933]). In his *Briocht-Scéalta na h-Aráibe: Cuid a h-Aon* (Magical stories of Arabia) (BÁC: Alec Tom agus a Chuid, n. d.), Seán Óg Ó Caomhánaigh was more forthcoming, informing us that he was working 'from an English translation' (ó aistriú Béarla).

43 Níl aon doicheall agam roim aistriúchánaibh ó theangthachaibh eile. Ach tá gach aon doicheall agam roim *standards* ó litríocht eile do chur i n-uachtar ar na *standards* atá cheana féin sa litríocht againne . . . Ach má thugaimíd, de dheascaibh neamh-thuigsiona a bheith againn ar na h-aistriúcháinibh sin, faillighe sa nós dúthchasach; má dheinimíd aithris ortha; má thugaimíd an díghnit bhréige sin go bhfuil an domhan go leor tuirseach dí isteach sa Ghaedhilg, is beag seans a bheidh againn ar chlassicí do scríobhadh innti.

44 Anois níl dochar leabhar a aistriughadh as teangaidh go dtí teangaidh eile. Ní dochar Gaedhilg a chur ar leabhar Gearmáinise ná ar leabhar Frainncise ná ar leabhar Béarla. Níl acht a oiread agus tá dochar Gearmánach nó Franncach nó Sasanach a theacht a chomhnaidhe go hÉirinn. Acht má thig a bhfuil de Ghearmánaigh ins an Ghearmailte nó de Fhranncaigh ins an Fhrainc, nó a bhfuil de Shasanaigh i Sasain, má thig siad a chomhnaidhe go hÉirinn ní bhéidh áit ag Éireannach ar bith i n-a thír dhúthchas. Indeed he felt that French was far closer in spirit to Irish than was English. See his review of An tAthair Bendict's translation of the autobiography of St Teresa, *An t-Ultach*, Dec. 1926, 9.

45 Nuair a sgaip Roinn an Oideachais leabhra an Ghúim sa nGaedhealtacht, níor dhonaide an rud é na leabhra, ach ba dhonaide é an t-aos óg a bheith ag léigheamh faoi agus a' súghadh isteach tréithre daoine agus dúithche nár thuigeadar i nGaedhilge nár luigh leó. Ní feairrde éigse na Gaedhilge na tionntódha nó na haistriúcháin.

46 Is fíor go bhfuil beart mór leabhar aistrighthe ón mBéarla anois le tréimhse fada, i dtreo go ndéarfadh duine go bhfuilimíd múchta ag an Sasanachas. Níl ins na leabhraibh seo ach nósanna iasachta agus meon iasachta. For other examples of this concern, see Liam Ó Rinn, 'Cumann na Scríbhneoirí / Tuille Tuairimí' (The Writers' Association / More opinions), *FL*, 25/3/22; 'Our Review Table', *CT*, 20/1/34; 'Prós-Litríocht na Gaedhilge / Fás na Linne Seo' (Prose literature in Irish / Contemporary growth), the report of a lecture by P. Ó Cinnéide to a convention of secondary school teachers in Limerick, *II*, 15/4/36; and Conchubhar Ó Ruairc, 'Cultúr Gaedhealach / Ná Bac leis an Aistriúchán' (Gaelic culture / Don't bother with translation), *Standard*, 16/4/37. On the other hand, some Gaelic translators were praised specifically for their ability to transcend this difficulty. In a 1923 review of Pádraig Ó Cadhla's translation of *Alice in Wonderland* as *Eibhlís i dTír na nIongantas*, Tomás Ua Concheanainn wrote: 'You could say Pádraig Ó Cadhla takes this little girl in hand, and with the magic wand of the Irish language, he makes her so Gaelic that you would swear that she had been living in the Ring Gaeltacht from the beginning of time' (Tógann Pádraig Ó Cadhla an cailín beag seo eidir lámhaibh, mar adéarfadh, agus le slaitín dhraoidheachta na Gaedhilge déanann sé chomh Gaedhealach í is go dtiubhradh an leabhar go raibh sí in a comhnuidhe i nGaedhealtacht na Rinne ó thús ama) (*Studies*, Mar. 1923, 152). See also Seán Ó Ciarghusa ('Marbhán), 'Eibhlís i dTír na nIongantas', *An Sguab*, Nov. 1922, 37–8; and Liam Ó Rinn, 'Leabhair Nua' (New books), *YI*, 2/12/22. Ó Ciarghusa felt that Ó Cadhla had improved Carroll's work by making it more virile! He wrote:

> I would not say but that the Gaelic one is better than the English one. There is virility, or strength or some force, in it that is not in the English. Was it not Dr Henebry who said that Irish was a language of men and not of fops? Whoever said it, this 'Eibhlís' makes you remember it. (Ní deirim ná gur deise an rud Gaedhlach ná an rud Gallda. Tá fearamhlacht, nó neart nó éifeacht éigin, ag baint leis ná fuil sa mBeurla. Nárbh é an Dochtúir de hIndeberg adubhairt gur teanga bhfear agus nach teanga ndailtíní an Ghaedhilg? Pé duine adubhairt é, cuireann an 'Eibhlís' seo ag cuimhneamh air thú) (p. 38).

47 On the other hand, only four of An Gúm's 15 short story collections were translations, a fact that reflects the fondness of Gaelic authors for a literary form for which native speakers felt they had legitimate indigenous models in the folklore, and for which all writers of Irish found willing publishers in the various Gaelic periodicals. It should, however,

also be remembered that scores of translated short stories were published at this time.

48 For example, while Pádhraic Ó Domhnalláin may have translated the French of Maupassant or Mérimée into Irish for his collection *Sgéalta Eorpacha is Eile* (European stories and others) (BÁC: M. H. Mac an Ghoill agus a Mhac, 1927), he hardly worked with the stories of Jokai in Magyar or Kallas in Estonian. The title page of this collection merely tells us that it was Ó Domhnalláin who 'did' (rinne) these stories in Irish. There are also stories by Uilenspiegel, Chekov, and Lamberts-Hurrelbrinck, among others, in this book. On the back of the title page of his version of Erich Kastner's *Emil und die Detektive* (BÁC: ODFR, 1937), Seán Mac Giollarnáth wrote: '*Emil agus na Lorgairí* is a translation of *Emil and the Detectives*, and the Irish version was compared with the original *Emil und die Detektive*' (Aistriú é 'Emil agus na Lorgairí' ar 'Emil and the Detectives' agus cuireadh an leagan Gaedhilge i gcomparáid leis an mbunleagan 'Emil und die Detektive'). Mac Giollarnáth's ability to impart a Gaelic quality to his work was praised by Flannan O'Flaherty: 'Yet so well has Seán Mac Giollarnáth done his work, that Emil might have been a boy from Connemara on a visit to Dublin' (*IP* 19/7/38).

49 The editorial staff of An Gúm complied a list of titles to be translated, although writers could also submit translations of works not on the list. See Seán Ó Ciosáin, 'Leabhair Ghaedhilge / A Cheataighe Atá an Gléas Oibre Atá ag an nGúm fé Láthair / Ladar na Sár-Scoláirí / Cionnus Toradh níos Fearr d'Fháil gan Breis Duaidh do Chailliúint leis' (Books in Irish / How awkward An Gúm's system is at present / The intervention of the great scholars / How to get more benefit without wasting more effort), *Star*, 1/3/30; 'Caoimhghín', 'My Home Estate', *Féile na nGaedheal*, May 1938, 7–8 and Mac Niocláis, *Seán Ó Ruadháin*, 111–12.

50 Sgéal clúmhail é, agus is iomdha duine a bhfuil sé léighte aige. Cad chuige, mar sin, a aistriú go Gaedhilg? Bíodh agus go mbíonn an fhírinne searbh, is fíor an méid seo – agus leanfaidh sé fíor go ceann tamaill – nach léighfidh an duine coitcheanta, an gasúr scoile, cuirim i gcás, sgéal i nGaedhilg, má's féidir leis lámh a leagadh go héasgaidh ar an mbun-sgéal i mBéarla.

51 Na daoine go dtaithneann 'thriller' an uathbháis leo bainfid aoibhneas as an leabhar so. Iarracht é, is dócha, ar an 'Aos Óg Aerach' do chur ag léigheadh na Gaedhilge, ach ní dóigh liom féin go n-éireochaidh leis an iarracht, mar is túisce leis an aos óg gcéadna a leithéid de leabhar a léigheadh i mBéarla agus is anfhuirist é fhághail. Is truagh lucht scríobhtha na Gaedhilge bheith ag cur aimsire amú le haistriúcháin den tsaghas so.

52 See, for example, *Óráid Caointe Pheiricléis* (The speech lamenting Pericles) (BÁC: Brún agus Ó Nóláin, [1930]); *Vera Historia: Scéal Ainspianta a Chéad-Cheap Lucian san Ghréigis* (True history: A grotesque story originally composed by Lucian in Greek) (BÁC: ODFR, 1931); *An Tarna Philippica .i. M. Tulli Ciceronis in M. Antonium Philippicarum, Liber Secundus* (BÁC: ODFR, 1932); *Saoghal-Ré na nGracchi* (The life of the Gracci) (BÁC: ODFR, 1933); *Démostenés agus Cicero: Tuairisc a mBeathadh* (Demosthenes and Cicero: An account of their lives) (BÁC: ODFR, 1935); and *Inis Atlaint: Scéal a Chéad-Cheap Platón 'san Ghréigis*. *Inis Atlaint* is a translation of *Crito*.

53 'Seoirse Mac Laghmainn' (Thomson), trans., *Breith Báis ar Eagnuidhe: Trí Cómhráidhte d'ár Cheap Platón (Apologia, Criton, Phaedón)*. In his papers, some of which have been published posthumously by An tAthair Pádraig Ó Fiannachta, Thomson left translations of dialogues by Plato and a four-volume typescript of a translation he did with the UCG classics professor Máiréad Ní Éimhthigh of Augustine's *Confessio*. See Ó Fiannachta, ed., 'Fuíoll Léinn Sheoirse Mhic Thomáis, I, II' (The scholarly remnants of George Thomson, I, II), *Léachtaí Cholm Cille* 18 (1988), 162–82. In addition, in a note he made on the manuscript of *Fiche Blian ag Fás*, Thomson wrote:

> I made a translation of the Odyssey which was accepted for translation, but withdrew it with the intention of re-writing it in collaboration with Maurice [Muiris Ó Súileabháin]. I also translated half of Augustine's *Confession* (rejected [doubtless by An Gúm] because I was not a Catholic); Plato's Symposium; Republic i–ii; and various smaller things. And I wrote a Greek Grammar and a *Tosnú na Sibhialtachta* [The beginning of civilisation] (based on lectures at University College Galway). They were also rejected, the first because of my spelling, the second because I was suspected of believing in the Darwinian theory. (Thomson, quoted by Ó Fiannachta, in 'Fuíoll Léinn Sheoirse Mhic Thomáis, III', *IMN*, 1988, 160, n. 1).

54 Cormac Ó Cadhlaigh, trans., *De Bello Gallico. Leabhar a Dó* (BÁC: Brún agus Ó Nóláin, 1922). In 1932, Seán Ó Ciarghusa published 'Teagasc ó'n nGréig' (Lessons from Greece), a collection of ethical maxims from authors like Pericles, Thucydides, Socrates, and Xenophon in Irish translation in *The Leader* (10/9/32). Ó Ciarghusa also published a collection of such quotes from Latin authors (*Leader*, 18/11/39), and on occasion similar miscellanies from various other languages. See *Leader*, 24/9/32, and 16/3/35.

55 Liam Ó Rinn, trans., *Dánta Próis* (BÁC: ODFR, 1933). Some of these translations first appeared in *The Star* in the summer of 1929.

56 An tAthair Gearóid Ó Nualláin, 'An Fiosrú' (Tolstoi) and 'Síon agus Sneachta' (Pushkin), in *Dia, Diabhail agus Daoine*, 1–34, 62–81. In *An Síoladóir: Irisleabhar Chumainn na Sagart nGaedhealach*

(Summer 1922), Seumas Ó Súildhubháin translated a story by Tolstoi under the title 'Mac an Diabhail agus an Caisnín Aráin' (The devil's son and the slice of bread). The translation was accompanied by the following note: 'The Russian Tolstoi first composed this, and the Kerryman S. Ó S. put it into Irish (An Rúiseánach 'Tolstoy' do chéad-cheap é seo, agus an Ciarruidheach S. Ó S. do chuir Gaedhilg air). This must be the same 'S. O. S.' who published 'An Peacach Aithrigheach' (The repentant sinner), 'a retelling of a story by Tolstoy' (aith-innsint ar scéal le Tolstoy) in *An Branar* in May 1925 (pp. 140–4). There was no indication in either journal whether S. Ó S. was working from the original. On the other hand, the anonymous translator of 'An Crann Nodlag' by 'Dostoebhegi' [*sic*] in the *Cork Weekly Examiner* stated that his version was 'from the original Russian' (ón mbun-Rúisis). This translation commenced serialisation 23 June 1923. Micheul Ó Cionnfhaolaidh published a story 'from Russia' (ón Rúis), 'Bainríoghain Speireat' (Queen of Spades) in *The Examiner* (30/7/32), but it is highly unlikely he was working from the Russian. There was also a story by Pushkin in Domhnall Ó Mathghamhna's *Slabhra Nóiníní .i. Cnósach de Ghearr-Sgéalta ar a bhFuil Deasgán de sna Sgéilíní is Mó Cáil d'Ár Cumadh ar Roinn na hEorpa* (Daisy chain, i.e. A collection of short stories in which there is a selection of the most famous stories composed on the Continent of Europe) (BÁC: COÉ, [1934]). Cearbhall Ua Dálaigh translated stories by Chekhov in *The Nation* (3/8/29; 31/8/29; 7/9/29; 23 and 30/10/29). (He may also have translated others by Chekhov as well as one by Dostoevsky {*Nation*, 14/12/29}). In addition, he translated work from French and German. See Ó Glaisne, *Cearbhall Ó Dálaigh*, 66. Ó Glaisne does not indicate whether Ua Dálaigh knew Russian.

57 Maighréad Nic Mhaicín, *Gearrscéalta Tcheckov: Cuid a hAon* (BÁC: OS, [1939]), and *An Silín-Ghort: Dráma Grinn i gCeithre Ghníomh* (BÁC: ODFR, 1935). Nic Mhaicín lived for a time in the Soviet Union and was a fluent speaker of Russian. One of Gogol's plays was translated by George Thomson and Aodh Mac Dhubháin as *An Cleamhnas Cliste* (The clever marriage arrangement) and performed at Taibhdhearc na Gaillimh in December 1931. There were also translations of Chekhov's *An Béar* (The bear) by Risteárd Ó Foghludha in 1923, and of his *Cúrsaí Cleamhnais* (Matchmaking matters) by Muiris Ó Catháin in 1933, but neither of these translators was working from the original Russian.

58 Ó hEighneacháin translated Sierra's *La Mujer del Heroe* and *Los Pastores*, and Quintero's *El Centenario*. The first two were first produced at Taibhdhearc na Gaillimhe in 1929 and 1931, respectively, the third by An Comhar Drámaidheachta in the Gate Theatre in Dublin in 1934. All three were later published by An Gúm. In Oct. 1936, *An Diabhal is Alcarez*, a translation by Ó Cadhain of a Spanish play I have not been able to identify, was first performed by An Taidhbhearc.

59 Liam Ó Rinn was delighted with Ó Buachalla's translation of this children's classic by Carlo Lorenzini. See his review, 'Leabhar do Leanbhaí / Scéal Maith ón Iodáilis / Cleachtar an Dánaíocht!' (A book for children / A good story from the Italian / Let us be bold!), *UI*, 15/9/34. Carlo Goldoni's *Il Burbero Benefico*, as translated by Maoghnus Ó Domhnaill, was staged by Taibhdhearc na Gaillimhe in Dec. 1935, and later published by An Gúm. Liam Ó Rinn's serialised (and incomplete) translation of 'Romeo agus Giulietta (from the Italian)' (ón Iodáilis) ran in *The United Irishman* from 7 July to 17 Nov. 1923. No author's name was given for this story. The polyglot Ó Rinn ('Tadhg Ó Cianáin') also translated a short story from the German of Carl Busse as 'An Feallaire Mná' (The treacherous woman) in *Young Ireland*, 29/4/22, and another from the Portuguese of Eça de Queiroz.

60 Among the more significant were Pádraig Ó Moghráin's translations of Thomas Mann's *Herr und Hund* as *Mé Féin agus Mo Mhadadh* (Myself and my dog), of Hans Dominik's *John Workmann* as *Seán Workmann* and of Wilhelm Hauff's *Die Karavane* as *An Carabhán* (The caravan); and Máire Ní Chinnéide's *Scéalta ó Ghrimm* (Stories from Grimm). Tadhg Ó Donnchadha published a collection of translations of German poems as *Fíon Gearmánach: Iarrachtaí Aistriúchán ón Ghearmáinis* (German wine: Translated pieces from the German) (BÁC: Muinntir C.S. Ó Fallamhain, Teo., i gcomhar le hOS, 1930), writing in his preface: 'Scholars from Germany have done so much for the language and literature of Ireland, that it is shameful for us Gaels how little interest we take in the language and literature of Germany' (Tá an oiread san déanta ag sgoláirí ón Ghearmáin ar son teanga agus litríocht na hÉireann gur náire dhúinne, ár nGaedhil, a laighead suime a chuirimíd i dteangan agus litríocht na Gearmáine) (p. v). Gearóid Ó Lochlainn's translation of a play by Arthur Schnitzler as *An Cheist Chinneamhnach* (The fateful question) was performed by An Comhar Drámaidheachta in the Abbey Theatre in May 1924. In July 1939, Donn Piatt began translating Goethe's *Faust*. There are 46 typewritten pages of the text in his papers in NLI MS G 1077.

61 The former was first performed by An Comhar Drámaidheachta in the Abbey Theatre on 15 Dec. 1924, and revived regularly thereafter; the latter was first performed by An Comhar in the Peacock Theatre on 25 Apr. 1939.

62 Among Ó Foghludha's translations from the French were *Fiche Gearr-scéal* (Twenty short stories) (1930), *Maria Chapdelaine* (1933), Louis Hémon's classic novel of Québec, and a host of short stories in the Gaelic journals and papers. Among other important titles brought into Irish from the French were Alexandre Dumas' *La tulipe noire* (tr. Máire Nic

Aodháin), Mérimée's *Colomba* (tr. Cormac Ó Cadhlaigh), About's *Le roi des montagnes* (tr. Cormac Ó Cadhlaigh), Bédier's *Tristan et Iseult* (tr. Donn Piatt), Bordeaux' *La robe de laine* (tr. Donn Piatt), René Bazin's *La terre qui meurt* (tr. Séamus Ó Grianna), and Daudet's *La belle Nivernaise* (tr. Nioclás Tóibín). Another major Gaelic Francophile was Liam Ó Briain, who taught the language at UCG and translated several French plays for the Taibhdhearc in that city, among them Ghéon's *La parade du pont du diable* and *La merveilleuse histoire du jeune Bernard de Menthon*, Molière's *Le dépit amoureux*, and Fauchois' *Prenez garde à la peinture*. For an idea of how highly Ó Briain valued French literature, see 'The Irish Revival and Modern Languages', UCG *University Annual*, 1928–9, 15–18. Ó Briain called the French 'a sister Celtic race, whose most fundamental qualities are largely identical with the most fundamental of our own' (p. 17).

63 One can safely assume that truly exotic material was not translated from the putative originals. I have in mind stories like 'Ag Súil le Breith 'san Pú-Ha-La / Aistriú ó'n Sínis' (Expecting a birth in Pú-Ha-La / A translation from the Chinese) by Seán Ó Ciarghusa (*II*, 21/7/22); 'Tír an Bhrothail' (The land of the heat), an 'adaptation' (ath-innsint) by 'T. C. L.' of a Turkish story by Mehmet Sadi, *Branar*, June 1925, 191–6; 'An Daonnacht thar Gach Nídh / Sceul ó Thír na h-Araibe' (Humanity above all / A story from Arabia) by 'Hassan' (*II*, 18/8/27); 'Scéal Seapánach' (A Japanese story) by Pádhraic Ó Domhnalláin (*IP*, 14/2/38); and 'Triad' by Gearóid Mac Eóin, said to be an adaptation 'from the Arabic of Abulbeca, c. 1175 A.D.' (ó Araibís Abulbeca, timcheall 1175 A.D.) (*Hibernia*, Apr. 1937, 4). Ó Domhnalláin says of his piece 'An Féileachán / Scéal Suimeamhail Seapánach' (The butterfly / An interesting Japanese story) (*II*, 15/8/35), that it had been told to him by a Japanese man. Other Gaelic translations from less familiar languages (or, perhaps more accurately in some cases, from existing English translations from them) include 'Tar Chugainn san Earrach' (Come to us in the spring) 'Sceul Seiceach le Gabriella Preissora' (A Czech story by Gabriella Preissora) (*YI*, 11/3–15/4/22); 'An Ortha' (The charm), 'a retelling of a story by the Turkish author Nedjdet' (ath-innsint ar scéal a scríobh an t-údar Túrcaise Nedjdet) by 'T. C. L.' (*Branar*, May 1925, 116–25); 'Na Ceithre Séasúir' (The four seasons), 'an adaptation of an old Bohemian story' (claon-aistriughadh ar shean-sgéal Bothaemach), by Seán P. Mac Énrí (UCG *University Annual*, 1926–7, 49–51); 'Aoighe Aon-Oidhche' (An overnight guest), 'a story by the Czech, Jan Neruda' (scéal leis an Czech, Jan Neruda), by Cearball Ua Dálaigh (*Nation*, 24/9/29). In 1925, Antoin Mac A' Bháird produced a version of *The Rubáiyát of Omar Khayyám*, no doubt based on Edward Fitzgerald's translation. There had also been previous Gaelic translations of this text. See O'Leary, *Prose Literature*, 374.

64 Ó Briain's translation was performed at Taibhdhearc na Gaillimhe, 19–22 May 1938, the first production of one of Shakespeare's plays in Irish. See 'Was Shakespeare a Fascist? / Play that Created Riots / Coriolanus Produced in Galway', *CS*, 17/5/38. The only other full-length Shakespearean play translated in our period was Ua Súilleabháin's *Macbeth* noted above. In 1934, there was a performance of something called *Julius Caesar* in Irish at Coláiste Chaoimhín in Dundalk, concerning which there was the following rather cryptic note in the local paper, *The Examiner*: 'It should be said that every one of the actors took his own part of the drama and translated it into Irish by himself' (Is ceart a rádh gur thóg gach duine des na h-aisteoirí a pháirt féin den dráma, agus gur chuir sé Gaoluinn air, uaidh féin) (*Examiner*, 13/1/34). Four years later, Coláiste Moibhí presented 'a musical play based on *Julius Caesar*' (cluiche adhbhachta bunuithe ar 'Julius Caesar') (see 'Leus Nua ar Thréithre Chaesar –' (A new light on Caesar's character), *IP*, 14/11/38). In 1930, Diarmuid Ó Duibhne broadcast an 'excerpt' (sliocht) from *The Merchant of Venice* on 2RN (see 'Broadcasting', *II*, 26/8/30). In 1937, Liam Ó Laoghaire presented scenes from *Hamlet* in Irish over Radio Éireann (see 'Radio Programmes / Shakespeare in Irish', *IP*, 2/12/37).

65 Parts of this translation were originally serialised in *An t-Eaglaiseach Gaedhealach*, commencing in Sept. 1924. There was also an Irish translation of this text made by a Baptist woman, 'H. G.', in Edinburgh in 1838. Ninety-five pages of it were published in Dublin and London under the title *Gluaiseachd an Oilithrigh nó Turas an Chriosduighe ó'n t-Saoghal so chum an t-Saoghal le teacht fá samhlughadh aisling. Aistrighthe ó Mbhéarla* [*sic*] *Eoin Bhunian* (The pilgrim's progress or the Christian's journey from this world to the world to come in the manner of a dream. Translated from the English of John Bunyan). The rest of the work, though completed in manuscript, seems never to have been published. See 'S. Ó C.', 'An Irish Translation of Bunyan', *IBL*, July–Dec. 1928, 118. Joynt himself pronounced this earlier translation by 'H.G.' 'bad with regard to speech, and spelling, and grammar' (go dona idir chainnt, agus litriú, agus gramadach). See Joynt, 'Réamh-Rádh' (Preface), in John Bunyan, *Turas an Oilithrigh fá shamhail aislinge* (The pilgrim's journey in the manner of a dream), tr. Joynt (BÁC: Alec Thom agus a Chuid, Teor., 1928), 4. A partial translation by 'J. D. R.' of Milton's *Paradise Lost* as 'Mar a Cailleadh Parrthas' (How Paradise was lost) was serialised in *United Ireland* commencing 30 June 1934.

66 Ó Ruadháin's version of *David Copperfield* is the only Gaelic translation that has been the subject of detailed study. See Mac Niocláis, *Seán Ó Ruadháin*, 122–47.

67 See *Pegasus nó an Capall Sgiathánach* (Pegasus or the winged horse) (BÁC: COÉ, n. d.) and *Tír na n-*

Óg nó an Bosca Iongantach (BÁC: COÉ, n. d.). These two minor stories by Hawthorne were clearly meant as school texts, not as serious reading for those interested in literature.

68 Seamus Heaney, 'A Shooting Script', in *The Haw Lantern* (London: Faber & Faber, 1987), 45. Ballantyne's novel *The Coral Island* was translated by Micheál Ó Catháin as *An t-Oileán Corghruanach* and published by An Gúm in 1939.

69 Three of his novels were translated into Irish, *The Cask* by Diarmuid Ó Súilleabháin as *An Soitheach*, *Sir John Magill's Last Journey*, and *The Pit-Prop Syndicate* both by Seán Mac Maoláin, the first as *An Uaigh sa Choillidh*, the second as *Comhlucht na Maide Mianach*.

70 His *Autobiography of a Super-Tramp* was translated by Colm Ó Gaora as *Féin-Scríbhinn Fíor-Shreothaidhe*.

71 His *The Kang-He Vase* was translated by Seán Mac Maoláin as *An Crúiscín Síneach*.

72 Four of his novels were translated into Irish in our period: *She* (trans. Niall Ó Domhnaill as *Ise*), *Marie* (trans. Niall Ó Domhnaill as *Máire*), *The Heart of the World* (trans. Niall Ó Domhnaill as *Croidhe na Cruinne*), and *The People of the Mist* (trans. Aodh Mac Seághain as *Cineadh an Cheó*).

73 Four of his books were brought into Irish in our period: *At the Villa Rose* (trans. Micheál Ó Gríobhtha as *Sa Villa Rose*), *Clementina* (trans. Micheál Ó Súilleabháin as *Cleimintín*), *The House of the Arrow* (trans. Pádraig Mac Giolla Bhríghde as *Teach na Saighde*), and *Parson Kelly*, co-authored with A. Lang (trans. Niall Ó Domhnaill as *Ministir Ó Ceallaigh*).

74 Her *Comin' Thro' the Rye* was translated by Seosamh Mac Grianna as *Teacht Fríd an tSeagail*.

75 His *The Farmer's Wife* was translated by Pádhraic Óg Ó Conaire as *Bean an Fheilméara*.

76 His *Boy Hunters of the Mississippi* was translated by Tomás Page as *Na Sealgairí Óga*.

77 His *The Wreck of the Grosvenor* was translated by Seosamh Mac Grianna as *Báthadh an Ghrosvenor*. In an essay on An tAthair Gearóid Ó Nualláin, Damien Ó Muirí compares translations by Mac Grianna and Ó Nualláin of the opening paragraph of this novel, adding Ó Nualláin's notes about what translation decisions he made and why. See Ó Muirí, 'An tAthair Gearóid Ó Nualláin: Gramadóir Nua-Aoiseach' (An tAthair Gearóid Ó Nualláin: A modern grammarian), *Léachtaí Cholm Cille* XVI (1986), 209–10.

78 Is minic a mholas ar na leathanaigh seo go bhféachfadh Coiste na Leabhar le haistriúcháin ó theangachaibh eile seachas an Béarla a chur ar fagháil. Más é cuspóir a chuir An Coiste rómpa leabhair a sholáthar a tharraiceochaidh an pobal le Gaedhilge a léigheamh, is beag tairbhe leabhair Bhéarla d'aistriú.

79 Ó Rinn, *Mo Chara Stiofán*, 125–6, 165.

80 Nach bhfuil sé i n-am againn agus thar am, príomh-leabhraí Frainncise, Laidne, Almáinise, Spáinnise, agus a leithéide a bheith ar fáil sa nGaedhilg? Sibh-se, a sgríneoirí, a bhíos ag saothrú na leabhar, nach léir daoibh na beárnaí sa bhfál?

81 Déanfa sé maitheas dúinn féin agus don Ghaedhilg aithne do chur ar mhuintir na hEorpa, ar a nósa, ar a meon, ar a gcroí is a n-anam tríd an aistriúchán. Tá a lán litríochta ar fuaid na hEorpa nár haistríodh go Béarla riamh agus an méid di atá le fáil sa teangain sin b'fhearr é theacht chughainn trí n-ár dteangain féin agus ár ndath dúthchais féin air.

82 To accomplish this goal, Blythe suggested the creation of a 'Publication Board' with a 'permanent translation staff' like the one at Dáil Éireann.

83 See Liam Ó Rinn, 'Roimhrá' (Preface), in Ivan Turgenev, *Dánta Próis*, trans. Ó Rinn, 9–25.

84 See Micheál Ó Droighneáin, trans., 'Risí Niál' (Njal's saga), *Stoc*, Mar. 1928, 2; and 'T. Ó M.' (doubtless Tomás Ó Máille), 'An Tóir / Sgéal Lochlannach' (The pursuit / A Norse story), UCG *University Annual*, 1924–5, 46–52. The serialisation of Ó Droighneáin's translation commenced in this issue; it did not appear in every subsequent number. 'T. Ó M.' published an essay on 'Sgéalaidheacht na Lochlannach' (The storytelling of the Norse) in the 1927–8 issue of the same journal (pp. 19–22), a piece in which he argued that the Icelandic achievement in prose narrative was due in part to contact with Ireland and the Irish between the eighth and the eleventh centuries.

85 Ó Nualláin, *Laidean tré Ghaedhilg*, 6. Of course, contemporary educational thought still saw the classics as *sine qua non* of a liberal education. Father Dinneen in particular wished to ensure that Irish speakers would be every bit as comfortable in their knowledge of the classics as their Anglophone compatriots. See, for example, his regular weekly columns on classical authors in *The Leader* from Jan. to May in 1926, as well as 'Tacitus, Stairidhe na h-Impireachta' (Tacitus, historian of the Empire), *IP*, 12/1/32; and 'Sár-Dhán na nGréagach' (The great poem of the Greeks), *IP*, 16/1/32. Dinneen incorporated much of the material from the essays in *The Leader* into *Aistí ar Litridheacht Ghréigise is Laidne* (1929). See also 'Prometheus fé Chuibhreach', 'Hóiméar: An Raibh a Leithéid Ann?' (Homer: Was there any such person?), UCG *University Annual*, 1932–3, 32–4.

86 Ba mhaith linn a mhola don Chomhar beirt nó triúr go bhfuil eolas fóirleathan acu ar leitríocht na hEorpa do cheapa chun liost a dhéanamh amach de dhrámaí oiriúnacha Béarla, Fraincise, Spáinnise, etc. agus ansan iad do chur á n-aistriú ag daoine.

87 Moreover, he felt that there would be real cultural benefits from such work: 'If we want to get to know the peoples of Europe, there is no better way than to translate into Irish some of the best dramas the people of the Continent have created' (Más áil linn aithne do chur ar chineadhacha na hEorpa níl slí is fearr chuige ná cuid de sna drámaí is fearr dár cheap lucht na mór-tíre d'aistriú go Gaedhilg).

88 Ní fuláir an obair a chongbháil ar siubhal ó mhí go mí, acht ní bhacfar le tionntódh ná le claonaistriúchán chomh luath is bheidh ár ndaothain bunchluichí maithe Gaedhilge ar láimh againn. Go dtí san, ní cannrán a dh'oireann dúinn ó Ghaedhilgeóirí acht obair, rud is déistin le n-a lán, mar is eól dúinn.

89 That the interest of one important Gaelic theatre figure was primarily in the performance possibilities of translated drama is evident from Piaras Béaslaí's thoughtful and perceptive prefatory remarks to his translation of Goldsmith's *She Stoops to Conquer*. See Béaslaí, 'Don Léiritheoir' (To the director) and 'Réamh-Rádh' (Preface), in Oliver Goldsmith, *Ísliú chun Buadha*, trans. Piaras Béaslaí (BÁC: OS, n.d.), 5, 9–12. *Ísliú chun Buadha* was first performed by An Comhar Drámaidheachta at the Peacock Theatre on 1 Dec. 1929. It is also worth noting that at least one anonymous critic felt that, despite Béaslaí's best efforts, the play was irrelevant to Irish life (*II*, 2/12/29). The review drew a dissenting letter from Pádraig Ó Bróithe in the same paper the following day.

90 Chomhairleóchainn dóibh, áfach, gan bun-dráma do chur le chéile go dtí go mbeidh roinnt mhaith drámaí iasachta aistrighthe aca nó léighte go cúramach is go staidéartha aca . . . Caithfimíd dul a' tóruigheacht drámaí maithe iasachta: drámaí Gearmáinise, Frainncise, Iodáilise, etc. See also the 'advice' (comhairle) offered to prospective translators on the last page of An Comhar Drámaidheachta's playbill for 7 Mar. 1927: 'It is the opinion of the Membership of An Comhar that Irish speakers who intend to translate plays should avoid plays in English and turn to other languages' (Is é tuairim Comhaltais an Chomhair gur ceart do Ghaedhilgeóirí, atá ar aigne drámaí do thionntódh, cluichí i mBéarla do sheachaint agus a n-aghaidh do thabhairt ar theangthacha eile). This programme is among the materials dealing with An Comhar Drámaidheachta donated to the NLI by Pádraig Ó Siochfhradha.

91 Go cinnte, is ceart cuidiú lesna drámathóirí Gaodhalacha agus tús áite a thabhairt dá gcuid saothair má bhíonn aon mhaitheas i n-éan chor ann. Is beag a bhfuil ann díobh fé láthair, ámh, agus dá bhrí sin beifear i dturtaoibh le roinnt mhaith aistriúchán go ceann i bhfad fós chun clár na bliana do líonadh . . . Ach fiú amháin dá mbéadh flúirse bun-drámaí Gaedhilge le fáil ba cheart slí éigin d'fhágaint ar an gclár i gcomhnuí d'aistriúcháin ar dhrámaí foghanta ó thíorthaibh eile. Ní feabhas go comórtas.

92 *An Gaedheal agus an Rádió*, 10. D'fhonn an bheárna a líonadh, chun go mbeadh fagháil againn ar dhóthain bun-drámaí oireamhnacha i nGaedhilg, níor mhisde drámaí d'aistriú ó theangthachaibh eile . . . Ní bheadh san méid sin, dar ndóigh, acht líonadh beárnan, go dtí go mbeadh fagháil againn ar bhun-drámaí oireamhnacha d'ár gcuid féin.

93 Caithfear 'dul ar an árdán', bíodh is ná fuil againn de dhrámaibh chuige acht aistriúcháin.

94 Ní thógfainn ar an gComhar ceann amháin ó'n iasacht a thabhairt dúinn, nó dhá cheann, b'fhéidir, dhá mbéadh an saoghal ag dul dian ortha, acht déarfainn go ndeachadar ró fhada leis an scéal nuair do líonadar an clár ar fad le déantús an fhir thall . . . Rud eile dhe, ní raibh ceachtar de na trí drámaí a chuaidh go ró-mhaith le meón is le hintinn Ghaodhal. An Strainséir a thiocfadh go Bláth Cliath agus rachadh go dtí léiriú an Chomhair le súil go bhfeicfeadh sé Dráma Náisiúnta na hÉireann bhéadh dul amú air agus díombáidh arae ní raibh de Ghaodhlachas ann an oidhche fé dheire acht an teanga amháin.

95 Is é mo bharamhail féin d'á mhéid aistriúchán d'á ndéanfaí, d'á mhéid brath d'á mbeadh ag drámathóiribh ar shaothar na gcoigríoch, d'á mhéid aithris d'á ndéanfaí ar an duine thall, gur b-amhlaidh go mba laige an fás a bheadh ar an dráma Ghaedhealach féin. Tomás Ó Cléirigh had argued in a 1927 letter to the *Irish Independent* that the work of writers like León Ó Broin himself was already making translation irrelevant: 'It is time to put an end to translation, and it will be for the best if Piaras and León and the other little group that is trying to promote original dramas succeed in putting an end to the age of translation' (Is mithid deire do chur leis an aistriúchán, agus má éirigheann le Piaras agus le León agus leis an dream beag eile atá a d'iarraidh bun-drámaí do chur chun cinn, deire do chur le ré an aistriúcháin mar sin is fearr é) (*II*, 9/3/27).

96 Ní cuibhe bac a chur le drámaidhe agus é ag soláthar adhbhar dráma pé áit is mian leis, ach de bhárr an cheada san tá dualgaisí ansan. Níor chóir dó-san dul thar lear ag lorg adhbhair go mbeidh an Náisiún go láidir agus go fíor-Ghaedhealach.

97 Acht ní h-í sprioc obair na Gaedhilge ár dteanga féin do bheith againn agus aigne iasachta le nochtadh tríthi. Do b'fhearr dhúinn fé seacht ár n-aigne féin do choimeád gan truailliú agus an teanga Ghaedhilge do chaitheamh uainn. The production in Irish of this British First World War play provoked a lively controversy. See, for example, '"Journey's End" to be Produced at Taibhdhearc na Gaillimhe', *CT*, 17/10/31; 'War Play in Irish / "Journey's End" Given at Galway Theatre', *IP*, 5/11/31; 'Taibhdhearc na Gaillimhe / "Deireadh an Aistir" Well Produced', *CT*, 7/11/31; Sighle Ní Chinnéide, 'Taibhdhearc na Gaillimhe – Cad Is Fiú í?' (Taibhdhearc na Gaillimhe – What is it worth?), *IP*, 2/12/31; Liam Ó Briain, 'An Taibhdhearc: Bunadhas an Dráma' (An Taibhdhearc: The origin of the drama) *IP*, 11/12/31; and G. Dillon, 'Motives of the Irish Theatre', *CT*, 12/9/31. The play was every bit as controversial on its revival. See '"Journey's End" / A Great Production / Trench Life during Great War, *CS*, 1/12/36 (virtually a word for word repeat of the original 1931 review!) and '"Deireadh an Aistir" / Aisteoirí an Ghárda ar Ardán na Péacóige' ('Deireadh an Aistir' / The Gárda actors on the Peacock stage),

IP, 9/3/38 (a very negative review of the decision to translate and produce such a play). See also the similar but more subdued criticism of the translation of Eden Phillpott's *The Farmer's Wife*, a translation not even the Irish of Pádhraig Óg Ó Conaire could adequately Gaelicise (*IP*, 12/3/38).

98 Is clos dom go bhfuil cogadh dearg mí-thrócaireach ar siúl idir na daoine atá i mbun Taidhbhdhearc na Gaillimhe, toisc – más fíor a gcloisim – go gceapann furmhór an Choiste gur gallda, i.e. bárbardha an rud é drámaí iasachta ar bith d'aistriú. At the meeting of An Taibhdhearc's board on 12 Oct. 1929, a letter was read from Seán P. Mac Énrí dissenting from pro-translation ideas expressed by Micheál Mac Liammóir in the *Connacht Tribune*. Mac Énrí was recorded as stating: '99% of Ctee of opinion foreign plays unsuitable – only plays of merit and of standard classical language a dhéanamh feasta [be done from now on]'. See Taibhdhearc na Gaillimhe Papers, NUIG Add. MS 58.

99 Níl amhras ar bith nach maith an chiall do lucht an Chomhair, agus do gach dream eile dá sórt, drámaí iasachta chur ar an stáitse mar, má léirítear go maith iad, beidh siad ar fheabhas mar phátrún do lucht ceaptha drámaí, ghá spriocadh le a [*sic*] ndícheall a dhéanamh. See also Micheál Breathnach, 'Scríobhnóirí na Nua-Ghaedhilge', Dundalk *Examiner*, 25/4/31. Breathnach, himself a successful Gaelic playwright, did, however, continue:

> Translation is a good thing in many ways, but a national drama will never be established on translation . . . Translation gives us examples and teaches us the craft of drama, but in the end is like a prop for a child who would be beginning to walk (Is maith an rud an t-aistriúchán ar a lán bealach ach ní bunóchthar drámaidheacht náisiúnta go deo ar aistriúchán . . . Tugann an t-aistriúchán somplaí dúinn agus múineann sé céirdine na drámaidheachta dúinn ach níl ann sa deireadh ach fé mar a bheadh taca ag páiste bheadh a' túisighe ar siubhal a dhéanamh).

100 Is ar an lucht éisteachta is mó a chaithfeas An Comhar Drámaíochta smaoineamh agus caithfidh siad drámaí do léiriú a thaithneóchas le n-a bhfurmhór. Muna bhfuil níos mó drámaí nua-cheaptha á léiriú sé'n fáth atá leis gur fearr go mór leis an bpobal drámaí iasachta maithe ná drámaí dúthchasacha tuatacha.

101 See 'Feadhmannach', 'Na Drámaí Gaedhil / Aistriúcháin is Fearr Linn' (The drama of Gaels / We prefer translations), *IP*, 6/2/33. To be fair, of the nine most popular plays, five were originals, including Béaslaí's *An Bhean Chródha* and *An Danar*, An tAthair Tomás Ó Ceallaigh's *An Foghmhar*, and Liam O'Flaherty's *Dorchadas*. The most popular original Gaelic play was Micheál Ó Siochfhradha's *An Ball Dubh*. The preference of Gaelic audiences for translations of comedies was discussed by an anonymous reviewer of An Comhar's production of *Les Fourberies de Scapin* in 1931:

> Of the dramas from other languages put into Irish, the comic ones succeeded well when they were produced. The old life and the simplicity of those dramas better suits the Irish language and performance and our audience than do the joyless dramas of this time, with their incomprehensible ideas (Na drámaí ó theangthaibh eile gur cuireadh Gaedhilg ortha d'éirigh go maith leis na cinn mheidhreacha nuair a léiríodh iad. Is fearr oireann an sean-shaol agus simplíocht na ndrámaí sin don Ghaedhilg agus don léiriú agus dár lucht éisteachta ná mar oireann drámaí duairce na haimsire seo agus a gcuid smaointe do-thuigse) (*II*, 17/11/31).

In the same month, and no doubt prompted by the same production, Seán Ó Ciarghusa proposed Molière as an ideal model for Gaelic dramatists because of his humour, his colloquial speech, and the fact that he wrote when French theatre was just beginning to evolve (*Leader*, 28/11/31). At least seven of Molière's plays were performed in translation by either An Comhar Drámaidheachta, Taibhdhearc na Gaillimhe, or both, in our period. Moreover, at least two plays, *Le Bourgeois Gentilhomme* and *Le Médecin malgré lui* were translated twice.

102 The play, *An Mhíorbhúilt*, was translated by the Rev. G. M. Cussen, who was working from Rev. M. H. Gaffney's English translation of the text. A short story by this Portuguese writer was translated by Liam Ó Rinn as 'An Bhean Chíoch' (The wet nurse) and serialised in *Young Ireland* from 18 Feb. to 4 Mar. 1922.

103 For a list of the plays, translators, and dates and places of production, see Pádraig Ó Siadhail, *Stair Dhrámaíocht na Gaeilge*, 168–79, 191–7. Ó Siadhail feels that translations made little real contribution to the development of Gaelic drama because they failed to attract the interest of audiences. See xiv and 122.

104 Cad chuige nach n-aistrighthear príomh-sheodanna litridheacht na Breathnaise go Gaedhilge? Níorbh iongnadh go mbeadh cineál comhcheangail agus comhbháidhe eadar a litridheacht-sa agus ár litridheacht fhéin, ná isé meon na gCeilteach a nochtuighthear ionnta araon.

105 See, for example, Máirtín Ua Flaithbheartaigh, 'Aríst!' (Again!), *AA*, June 1937, 1–2; 'Nuaidheacht / Ollamh i b-Príosún / Iarratas ó Mhic-Léighinn' (News / A professor in prison / An appeal from students), *II*, 21/6/37; and Ernest Blythe, 'From Wales / National Movement', *Bonaventura*, Spring 1938, 191–2. Lewis was called 'one of the clearest thinkers and most distinguished writers in the Principality' in *The Leader* (26/8/39), but here again the focus was on his work as politician and activist. The poet, playwright, novelist, and critic Saunders Lewis was one of the founders and an early president of the Welsh

nationalist party Plaid Cymru. In a 1936 action protesting the English military presence on Welsh soil, he helped burn down aircraft sheds at the RAF bombing school at Penyberth in Carnarvonshire. He and his two comrades were arrested, convicted, and imprisoned. See Ned Thomas, *The Welsh Extremist: A Culture in Crisis* (London: Victor Gollancz, 1971), 52–63. A picture of the three men with the caption 'An Triúr Laoch – Y Tri Gwron' (The three heroes) appeared as an illustration with the *Ar Aghaidh* piece of June 1937. Incidentally, given Blythe's staunch opposition to what he saw as nationalist extremism during his time as a cabinet minister in the early years of the Free State, the lack of condemnation in his treatment of the Lewis case is striking.

106 Ba cheart go mbéadh fhios ag an dream Gaedhealach annso i nÉirinn go bhfuil cáirde thar lear aca, gur chóir go ndéanfaí aith-mhuinntearas eatorra, gur féidir leó siúd cabhrú linne 'san troid so na Gaedhilge agus gur féidir linne cabhrú leó. Nach í an Ghaedhilge ár gcomh-theanga – nach Gaedhil sinn araon?

107 Cruthuigheann sé go bhfuil Gaedhil na h-Éireann agus na h-Alban a' cur aithne agus eolais ar a chéile agus nach bhfuil siad 'séanadh a ngaol le chéile. Agus tuige a séanfadh? Nach muid féin a chéile . . . 'Sé mo shúil nach fada go gcuirfeadh an dá Ghaedhealtacht aithne agus eolas níos fearr ar a chéile, agus go dtiocfaidh an lá nuair a bhéas gach aon dream aca ag oibriú i n-aon bhun amháin ar son oighreacht na nGaedheal idir teanga, ceol agus a ngabhann leo. In a 1925 lecture to the Edinburgh branch of the Scots National League, Art Ó Briain stated:

> We had hoped that by mutual help the crisis in our two movements might be made to coincide, and that a federation of interests of the two remaining Gaelic nations would secure success for both . . . But alas many – we might say the majority – amongst both our peoples have long since fallen victims to the wiles of English strategy + propaganda which has successfully driven a wedge between us (from the handwritten text of the lecture in the Art Ó Briain papers, NLI MS 8417).

A humorous break from all this high earnestness was provided by Niall Buidhe Mhac a' tSacánaigh, who in 1938 wrote a comic piece in which Irish-Scots Gaelic unity was pledged in a public house. See Mac a' tSacánaigh, 'Connradh-Duilisg' (A Dulse League), *Ultach*, Easter 1938, 5–6.

108 Piatt, *Stair na Gaedhilge*, 12. Piatt was working on the principle that 'náisiún amháin Gaedhealach a bheadh i n-Éirinn agus i n-Albainn ach gur b'é an Béarla' (p. 11). In November of the same year, he was suggesting Irish writers look to Scots Gaelic for ideas and inspiration. See Piatt, 'Litir ó Iarthar na Frainnce' (A letter from the west of France), *IF*, Nov. 1924, 14.

109 Ar na laethibh deiridh seo nuair atá rian agus blas an Bhéarla ar chuile rud is maith an rud go bhfuil litridheacht fhíor-Ghaedhealach ann atá, in a thaca sin, gan a bheith Éireannach agus in a bhfuighidh an t-Éireannach smaointe nuadha agus leathnughadh eólais. In this same issue of *FL*, Caitlín Nic Ghabhann, writing on 'Litridheacht na Gaedhilge' (Literature in Irish), said that Gaels must strive to reclaim their full linguistic and literary heritage, including that part of it given expression in Scots Gaelic.

110 Tá Gaedhilg bhreagh sa leabhar so, cé go bhfuil cuid den chainnt beagán doiligh a thuigbheáil ag an té nach dearn stuidéir ar chuid Gaedhilge na hAlban. Mar sin féin, thuigfeadh Éireannach ar bith brigh na cainnte.

111 See, for example, Annag Nic Iain, 'Na Beanntan Gorma' (The blue hills), *Béaloideas*, June 1933, 46–50; J. G. McKay, 'Nighean Righ na Frainge' (The daughter of the king of France), *Béaloideas*, June 1934, 292–8; Nic Iain, 'Sgeulachd a' Ghamhna Dhuinn' (The legend of the brown calf), *Béaloideas*, Dec. 1936, 257–69; McKay, 'Báillidh Lunnainn' (The London bailiff), *Béaloideas*, Dec. 1938, 226–32; McKay, 'Uisdean Mór Mac Gille Phádruig', *Béaloideas*, June 1939, 36–7. See also McKay, 'Scottish Gaelic Parallels to Tales and Motifs in *Béaloideas*, vols I and II', *Béaloideas*, Dec. 1931, 139–48; and 'G. Ó M.' (Gerard Murphy), Review of *Orain Ghaidhlig le Seonaidh Caimbeul* (Gaelic songs by Seonaidh Caimbeul), ed. J. L. Campbell, *Béaloideas*, June 1937, 147–8.

112 'Abrach' was a fervent Pan-Gaelic enthusiast, writing: 'You, Gaels of Éire, have given us a noble example in this matter. May we, Scottish Gaels, follow it, and may success attend the efforts of both branches of our race.'

113 Calum Mac Gilleathain, 'Leabhraí Nua / *Mar Chonnac-sa Éire*', *AA*, Jan. 1938, 8; and Mac Gilleathain, 'Leabhraí Nua / *Triocha-Céad Chorca Dhuibhne, Cuid a I*', *AA*, May 1939), 7. See also Mac Gilleathain's 'Bárdacht Uilleam Rois' (The poetry of William Ross), an essay on the poetry of Ross prompted by the publication of a new edition of his work. This essay appeared in *AA*, Mar. 1938, 6–7.

114 For a list of his essays in this journal, see Ó Ciosáin, *An t-Éireannach*, 251. The periodicals to which Mac Gilleathain contributed had strong Galway affiliations. In 1937, Mac Gilleathain wrote to Agnes O'Farrelly in Scots Gaelic expressing his disappointment that ties between Ireland and Gaelic Scotland were so weak, but added 'with diligence we will put a bridge across the North Channel' (le dìcheall ni sinne drochaid a chur air Sruth na Maoile). His letter, dated 20 July 1937, is in the O'Farrelly Papers, NLI MS 21,853.

115 See, for example, the letter published in the issue for 22 Feb. 1936; and 'A Alba' (From Scotland), a brief essay by 'C. H.', in the issue for 16 May 1936.

116 Mac Dhunléibhe did not deal with the South African government's treatment of the many African languages spoken in the country. It is worth noting that the Scots Gaelic poems, 'Alba fo Dhaorsa' (Scotland in bondage) and 'Carnaich Ghlinne Comhan' (The stony ground of Glen Comhan), both by 'Crois Tara' from Glasgow, were published in *Republican Review* in Dec. 1938 and Jan. 1939 respectively.

117 On the other hand, Donald McPherson did welcome the translation into Irish by Seán Tóibín of Neil Munro's Anglo-Scottish novel *John Splendid*, writing in the *Journal of the Cork Historical and Archaeological Society* in 1931:

> For numerous reasons the two main branches of the Gaelic language have tended to become more different. One reason is the lack of a common popular literature. The translation into Irish of this popular Scottish novel is a step towards unification (p. 56).

118 Rev. Gerald O'Nolan, *Trí Sheoda ó Alban* (BÁC: COÉ, 1922). Ó Nualláin dedicated the book 'to the Gaels of Scotland' (do Ghaodhlaibh na h-Alban), and wrote in the introduction: 'If I have not adhered too closely to the Scottish here and there, I hope I will be forgiven' (Murar leanas ró-dhlúth de'n Albanais annso is annsúd, tá súil agam go maithfar dhom é).

119 Ba dhual dúinn spéis do chur i litríocht na gCeilteach seachas litríocht na hÉireann. Mholfainn do lucht riartha oideachais na hÉireann leabhra Ceilteacha a scaipeadh fríd na scoltacha. Mholfainn do scríbhneoirí Gaedhilge a bhíos ag aistriú bun-oibreacha an domhain go Gaedhilg, príomhscéalta na Breataine do tharraingt chuca agus Gaedhilg do chur ar eachtraí Artúir Rí agus eile. Ghlacfadh na leabhra Ceilteacha leis an Ghaedhilg níos fearr ioná leabhra na dTeutonach – cuir i gcás – agus 'na theannta sin, thaithneochadh siad le léightheoirí na hÉireann. De Blácam stressed that England's appropriation of the Arthurian material was an act of cultural imperialism: 'Let it not be thought the English had anything to do with the stories of Arthur, except that they have possession of the country in which those adventures took place' (Ná meastar go bhfuil aon bhaint ag na Sasanaigh le scéalta Artúir acht amháin go bhfuil seilbh aca-san ar an tír 'nar dearnadh na heachtraí úd).

120 Five short poems translated from the Welsh by Icerg appeared in *IMN* 1932, 13, 38, 52, 56, 65. See also, 'Líonadh na Taoide' (The flowing tide) and 'Cú Aodha Uí Bhuirgheasa' (The hound of Aodh Ó Buirgheasa), *IMN*, 1933, 12, 30–1; and 'Dolly na Feirme Luime' (Dolly of the barren farm) and 'An t-Ubhall Buidhe' (The yellow apple), *IMN*, 1934, 21–24, 37. 'An t-Ubhall Buidhe' is the only translation for which Icerg provided his source, stating that it was 'based on "Yr Apal Melyn", originally composed by Eifion Wyn' (ath-aithris ar 'Yr Apal Melyn' – Eifion Wyn do chéad-cheap).

121 See 'Torna', 'An Seanabhaile' (The old home), *Cork Weekly Examiner*, 28/1/22; 'Eoin', *Cork Weekly Examiner*, 25/3/22; and 'Codladh nó Dúiseacht, Ciaca' (Asleep or awake, which), *Cork Weekly Examiner*, 15/4/22.

122 This translation was reprinted in Ó Cléirigh's 1937 collection *Seoidíní Cuimhne* (pp. 155–66). In the school text *Scéilíní i gCóir na bPáistí*, we find 'a story from Wales' (scéal ó'n mBreatain Bhig), but no original source is identified.' See 'Scéal ó'n mBreatain Bhig / Éad' (Jealousy), in Proinnséas Ó Súilleabháin, *Scéilíní i gCóir na bPáistí*, 34–6. There was also an anonymous translation of a poem from Welsh, under the title 'Mí na Bealtaine (ón mBreathnais)' (The month of May {from the Welsh}) in *AA*, May 1933, 4. The author of the original was also not given. In December 1938, *TCNÍ* published 'Éan Shain Máirtín' (St Martin's bird), an anonymous translation of a poem written by Odo, 'a Welsh priest' (sagart Breathnach), in 1219. Seven of Pádraic Ó Conaire's stories were translated into Welsh by David Myrddin Lloyd and Tomás Ó Cléirigh under the title *Ystoriau Byr o'r Wyddeleg* (Short stories from the Irish) (Llandysul, Gwasg Gomer, 1934). In his preface to this volume, Lloyd made clear that Ó Conaire's were stories worthy of translation, writing:

> In his work can be found the best gallery of portraits of the Irish people of which I know, and the easiest opening into the mystery of this people as they are today . . . He wrote the language of his day, avoiding every convention and style that he did not see as a help to his purpose and his modern mind, but at the same time, his work has a dignity and his personal style gives a zest to the everyday sayings of his countrymen. (Yn ei waith fe geir yr oriel orau y gwn amdani o bobl Iwerddon, a'r agoriad hwylusaf i gyfrinach y bobl hyn fel y maent heddiw . . . Ysgrifennai yn iaith ei ddydd, gan ymwrthod a phob defod ac arddul na welai eu bod yn help i'w bwrpas a'i feddwl modern, ond ar yr un pryd y mae i'w waith urddas, a rhydd ei arddul bersonal flas i ymadroddion bob dydd ei gydwladwyr.)

123 For the play, see 'Gairm Phádraig' (Patrick's calling), *Féile na nGaedheal*, May 1931, 6. The translator was not identified. For the story, see Tadhg Ó Séaghdha, 'An Píobaire ón Sliabh (Sgéal ó Bhreatain na Frainnce)' (The piper from the mountain {A story from Britanny in France}) *AA*, Dec. 1931, 5–6. In 1930, Rev. M. McGrath published a comparative study of a traditional prayer in Irish, Welsh, and Breton. See McGrath, 'A Medieval Night Prayer', *IR*, Jan. 1930, 34–43, and Feb. 1930, 97–103. 'Caitríona' published a story entitled 'Bainphrionnsa na Briotáine' (The princess of Brittany), set in Brittany in 'the distant past' (sa tsean-aimsir ar fad) in *II*, 7/8/26; 'Siubhlóir' retold a tragic story of Breton fishermen lost at sea that he had read in a French paper in *II*, 10/10/30: and 'Duibhneach' published 'Bruidhean an

Riogh Uabhraigh / Sean Sgéal ó Bhreatain na Frainnce' (The palace of the proud king / An old story from Brittany) in *The Standard*, 6/6/31.

124 Níl cine Ceilteach ar bith ann, ach tá dreama Ceilteacha ann nó Ceiltigh; sé sin le rádh dreama a raibh teangthacha Ceilteacha, agus nósa Ceilteacha aca. See also the letters on this topic from Osborn Bergin and 'C. D.' in the *Irish Statesman* for 3 Nov. 1923.

125 Dubhairt cheana gurbh obair chruaidh obair an aistriúcháin . . . Ní féidir aon riaghalacha do leagadh amach ina chóir. An riaghal a bheadh oiriúnach in áit ní dhéanfaidh sí ach an obair a lot in áit eile. Ní leor don aistritheoir eolas maith a bheith aige ar dhá theangain gan a mheon féin do lúbadh nó go mbeidh sé ar aon dul le meon an bhun-údair. Ní mór do iarracht éigin d'fhéith na filíochta agus na healadhnachta bheith ann. Is annamh a dheineann sé an gnó abairt d'aistriú focal ar fhocal. Na habairtí is simplí ar domhan is minic gur gádh iad do chasadh is do lúbadh i dtreo go mbeidh deallramh nádúrtha chó maith le deallramh liteardha nea-leamh ortha agus i dtreo go mbeid in oiriúint do sna habairtí rómpa agus ina ndiaidh.

126 Ar ndóigh tá sé níos deacra leabhar 'aistriú go Gaedhilge ná mar tá leabhar bunadhasach a sgríobh i nGaedhilg ar an ádhbhar céadna. Dá fheabhas é an leabhar agus a chulaith féin air, a chabhail, a chnámha agus a chorp idir fuil is feóil, is amhlaidh is deacra fós é aistriú.

127 Ó Ciarghusa, 'Do Thionntódh Teangan', in *Ar Mo Mharanadh*, 60. Baoghal aca nach suadh ach saor an tionntuightheoir . . . agus gur milleadh maide i na theannta sin go minic é, ná deineann ach culaith de'n dara theangain do chur ar chabhail na ceud teangan, – saothar nach fearrde crot ná cabhail an dara teangan é.

128 Má bhíonn tú ad iarraidh bheith ro-chruinn déanfir feall ar spiorad na bun-oibre (agus is uaisle an spiorad atá sa bhfocal ná an focal féin) agus beidh t'iarracht mí-thaithneamhach don léitheoir – agus don bun-údar, leis, má thuigeann sé Gaedhilg.

129 Ó Rinn, *Turus go Páras*, 44–5. Tá aistriú agus aistriú ann . . . agus maran féidir do dhuine dlúth-aistriú do dhéanamh gan rud is leimhe ná liomonáid do dhéanamh den Bhurgundy is fearr sa bhun-obair bfearra dho triail do bhaint as an mbun-obair do chlaon-aistriú.

130 Dá suidhfeá síos agus leabhar Béarla nó Fraincis a léigheamh agus machtnughadh in d'aigneadh agus in do chroidhe orthaí, agus í a scríobhadh i nGaedhilg ins an dóigh, dar leat, a b'fhearr a dtuigfeadh an Gaedheal a deis cainnte agus a smuaintiughadh agus a teas, déanfá aistriughadh maith. See also his comic dialogue 'Murcha agus Mánas', *An Camán*, 27/8/32.

131 Is é gnó an aistrightheóra na focail d'infhiúchadh nó go n-imthighid na focail as a chuimhne agus go bhfanann na bun-smaointe amháin aige, agus na smaointe do nochtadh annsan ina chuid focal Gaedhilge féin . . . Ar an scéal do thógaint le chéile, nach dócamhlach é saothar an aistrightheóra?

132 Isé fé ndear cuid mhór den deacracht a bhaineann le leabhar d'aistriú ná a bheith de riachtanas ar an aistritheoir, toisc gur aistriú an ainm a tugtar ar an obair a bhíonn ar siúl aige, bheith ag briseadh a chroidhe ag iarraidh an cubhrán d'aistriú chó maith leis an substaint. In a perceptive 1933 review of Pádhraic Ó Domhnalláin's translation *Stair Choitceann na Ré Críostaidhe*, An tAthair Micheál Mac Craith discussed three ways that the translator could go about this task:

> He could filter the thoughts of the original author through his mind, and then put them into conversational Irish speech. He could put the constructions and words into noble, rich, literary Irish. Or he could follow the original author as closely as possible so that the constructions and even the words of that author would exert too much influence, not only on the style but also on the choice of words of the translator. It seems to me that Pádhraic chose the second method, and I would say that he was entirely successful (D'fhéadfadh sé smaointe a bhun-údair do scagadh trí n-a aigne, agus, annsan, caint chomhráiteach Ghaedhilge do chur orra. D'fhéadfadh sé Gaedhilg uasal, shaidhbhir liteardha do chur orra, idir leagana agus focla. Nó d'fhéadfadh sé claoidh chomh dlúth san le n-a bhun-údar go n-imreóchadh a leagana agus fiú féin a fhocal so tionchur ró-mhór ní h-amháin ar scríbhghne acht ar thogha focal fós an tionntóra. Sé chidhtear domhsa gurbh é an dara ní chuir Pádhraic roimhe; agus, tríd is tríd, déarainn [*sic*] gur éirigh leis) (*Studies*, Sept. 1932, 495–6).

133 Cormac Ó Cadhlaigh, 'Nóta', in Sophie de Séjur, *Aindeise Shiobhán*, trans. Ó Cadhlaigh (BÁC: Muinntir C. S. Ó Fallamhain, Teo., i gcomhar le hOS, 1928), n.p. Ins an aistriú seo deineadh atharú ar ainmneachaibh daoine is áiteanna agus port ceóil, d'aon ghnó chun go gcuirfí crot Gaedhealach ar na sgéalaibh.

134 Shán Ó Cuív, 'Réamhrádh', in Ó Cuív, *Troid agus An Bhean ón dTuaith*, 3.

135 León Ó Broin, *Labhartar Béarla Annseo* (BÁC: OS, n. d.).

136 Máiréad Ní Ghráda, *An Udhacht* (BÁC: OS, 1935), 5.

137 Tóibín did not identify the source of his work, calling it simply 'an adaptation of a French play' (aith-leagaint ar dhráma Fraincíse). See Tóibín, *An Dubh 'na Gheal: Dráma Trí n-Amharc* (Ceatharlach: Muintir an 'Nationalist', n. d.). On the other hand, Jeremiah Murphy was opposed to such transpositions of foreign plays to Irish settings, writing in 1936:

> It is assuredly an excellent thing to translate from Russian a story about Ivanoff in the Gaelic, provided that you still call him Ivanoff in the Gaelic; but, if you translate, if you change Lord Monkhurst into Pádraig Ó Briain, I wonder if

you are doing good or harm. By making him drink Guinness instead of Benedictine, you may make him more dramatic, but you won't change his attitude towards life unless you rewrite the whole story. Yet is that not what some of our excellent translators, with 'wonderful tongues of Irish' are doing? (*Gaedheal*, Jan. 1936, 3).

138 Seán Ó Ciarghusa chose to stress the positive aspects of this bilingualism for the would-be Gaelic translator:

> Whatever about foreign languages, there are few countries where two languages are spoken as fluently and easily as are Irish and English by the Gaels I am discussing [i.e., the translators of An Gúm]. If it is possible to translate English deftly into Irish I would say they will do it (Pé mar atá i dtaoibh na dteangacha iasachta, is beag tír a bhfuil aon dá theanga chomh líomhtha, pras aca agus atá an Ghaedhilg agus an Beurla ag na Gaedhil a luaidhim [.i. aistritheoirí an Ghúim]. Má's féidir an Beurla d'aistriughadh go slachtmhar go Gaedhilg adeurfainn go ndéanfaid sin é) (*Leader*, 16/1/32).

That such work was by no means easy even for those with a sound knowledge of both languages is evident from the remarks of Father Dinneen in an undated draft of an essay on English–Irish translation:

> The deep chasm that separates modern Irish from modern English renders translation from either language into the other a difficult task. The difficulty of translating English into Irish is much greater than that of translating Irish into English chiefly because Irish has remained undeveloped for some centuries.

This draft is among the Dinneen Papers, NLI MS 8623 (15).

139 Is beag duine ar m'eolas go bhfuil go leor Frainncise ná Gearmáinise ná Spáinnise ach chó beag aige chun aon aistriú bunúsach do dhéanamh, agus an fíor-bheagán go bhfuil roinnt bheag de theanga éigin aca san níl go leor Gaedhilge aca. One wonders how the usually acute Liam Ó Rinn could state in 1929 that 'I cannot, off-hand, name two even minor Irish writers who do not know at least three languages. That is more than can be said for Anglo-Irish writers' (*IS*, 14/12/29).

140 As we have already seen, Ernest Blythe was also, for practical reasons, in general agreement on the need for widepread translation from English.

141 In his report of a meeting of the UCD Cumann Gaedhealach in 1934, Shán Ó Cuív summarised an interesting argument by Piaras Béaslaí that in earlier periods those who translated work into Irish were scholars working from a comfortable knowledge of their source languages and 'as a pastime or from love of learning and the work' (mar chaitheamh aimsire nó mar chion ar an léighean agus ar an obair). Béaslaí went on to argue that some translating in his day were not scholars, 'but slaves in literary affairs' (sglábhaithe i gcúrsaí sgríbhneoireachta) (*II*, 19/1/34).

142 See 'Forward Policy for Irish Needed / What a Thoroughgoing, Intelligent Government Could Do / Fitting the Language for Modern Needs / The Part of Wireless and Television', *UI*, 7/7/34. From Oct. 1930 to July 1931, 'Ag Faire na hÉanlaithe' (Watching the birds), a translation by 'D. Ó D.' of Rev. P. G. Kennedy's 'The Lure of Birdwatching' was serialised in *The Far East*.

143 See Ó Rinn, 'Saothrú na Gaedhilge / Leabhair do Leanbhaí' (The cultivation of the Irish language / Books for children), *UI*, 19/5/34.

144 See 'Modernising the Irish Language', *UI*, 12/5/34.

145 See Ó Rinn, *Mo Chara Stiofán*, 50–1. See also Ó Rinn, '"Cleimintín" / Scéal Breá do Bhuachaillí Óga' (*Clementine* / A fine book for young boys), *UI*, 3/8/35, and the 1932 letter from An Gúm's publication officer to Séan Ó Ruadháin quoted in Mac Niocláis, *Seán Ó Ruadháin*, 153. Among the lightest forms of reading translated were the American comic strip 'Henry', which ran in *IP* as 'Eachtraí Éinrí' (The adventures of Henry), and the translated advertisements that ran in Irish periodicals from time to time, most notably in *An Sguab*, whose editor, Éamonn Mac Giolla Iasachta, insisted that all advertising material in the journal be in Irish.

146 See 'Oighreacht ó'n Athair Peadar' (A bequest from Father Peter), Editorial, *II*, 28/4/23; 'Delta', 'Recent Books by Irish Priests', *IR*, Jan. 1927, 74–8; 'L. Mac G.', 'Leabhair Nuadha' (New books), *IMN*, 1934, 90; Ó Rinn, 'Oibreacha Oile [*sic*] an Athar Peadair' (The complete works of Father Peter), *UI*, 23/2/35; and 'Bláithíní Shain Proinnsiais' (The flowers of St Francis), *IP*, 5/9/36. Some important translations of religious work were done at this time, among them D. Ó Súilleabháin's rendering of sections of the *Confessio* of St Augustine as 'Faoisdíní Naoimh Augustín' (The confessions of St Augustine), in *An Síoladóir* in the spring and summer of 1922; An tAthair Benedict's translations *Beathafhéinscríbhinn Naoimh Treasa leis an Leanbh Íosa* (The autobiography of St Teresa of the Child Jesus) (Coillte Mágha: Siúracha Lughaidh Naomhtha, n. d.), and *Teachtaireacht ó'n tSiúr Bheannuithe Treasa* (A message from Blessed Sister Teresa) (BÁC: Ua Cathail agus A Bhuidheann, [1923]); An tAthair Cainneach's *Guthanna Neamhdha* (Heavenly voices) (from St Francis of Assisi and two of his disciples) (BÁC: Clólucht an Talbóidigh, 1926) and *Seoda Spirideálta nó Roinnt Smaointe Tógtha a Sgríbhinníbh Phróinséis Naomhtha de Sales* (Spritual treasures or some thoughts taken from the writings of St Francis de Sales) (BÁC: Clólucht an Talbóidigh, 1924); Cormac Ó Cadhlaigh's translation of Pope Leo XIII's encyclical *Rerum Novarum* as *Stáid an Lucht Saothair* (The state of the workers) in the *Irish Tribune* from 10 September

to 24 Dec. 1926; Séamus Ua Séaghdha's *Sgríbhiní Naoimh Phádraig* (The writings of St Patrick) (Dublin: Association for Promotion of Christian Knowledge, 1932); Pádraig Ó Móráin's version of St Alphonsus Liguori's *Cuarta ar an tSacraimint Rónaomhtha agus ar an Maighdin Mhuire Bheannuighthe in aghaidh Gach Lae den Mhí* (Visits to the Blessed Sacrament and to the Blessed Virgin Mary for every day of the month) (BÁC: Cló-Lucht an Talbóidigh, [1934]); Conn Ó Mongáin's translation of the same saint's *An Mhaighdean Ghlórmhar* (BÁC: M. H. Mac Ghoill agus A Mhac, 1936); An tAthair Tomás Ó Gallchobhair's *Críost an Uile* (*Christ Is All* by Rev. John Carr, C.SS.R.) (BÁC: ODFR, 1936); *Beatha Íosa Críost* (The life of Jesus Christ), translated by Pádraig Ó Baoighealláin and An tAthair Pádraig de Brún from the Greek New Testament (BÁC: Comhartha na dTrí gCoinneal, 1929); and two renderings of Francis of Assissi's *Fioretti*, one by An tAthair Caoimhghín Ó Súilliobháin as *Bláithíní Shain Próinnsiais* (The little flowers of St Francis) (BÁC: Clólucht an Talbóidigh, 1936); and one by Seán Ó Muirthile as *Flóisíní Shain Proinsias* (BAC: ODFR, 1936). The former had previously been serialised in the *Irish Catholic* in 1922 and 1923. In addition, Maoghnus Ó Domhnaill edited *An Bheatha Chrábhaidh* (The pious life), an early seventeenth-century Irish translation by Filip Ua Raghallaigh of *An Introduction to the Devout Life* by St Francis de Sales (BAC: OS, 1938). Aodh de Blácam's 'Golden Priest', dealing with an episode in the life of Saint Oliver Plunkett, was translated by Gearóid Mac Spealáin (*Redemptorist Record*, Sept.–Dec. 1939). There were also, of course, more functional religious translations like An tAthair Tadhg Ó Cúrnáin's, *Mion-Mhíniú ar an dTeagasg Críostaidhe: Aistriú ar an Leabhar Béarla Manual of Religious Instruction do sgríobh an tAth. Pádraig Paor* [*sic*] (A detailed explanation of Christian doctrine: A translation of the book in English *Manual of Religious Instruction* by Father Patrick Power) (BÁC: Maunsel agus Roberts, [1923]); Brian Seoighe's translation of Mother Loyola's *Leabhar Beag ar an bhFaoisdín le h-Aghaidh Páistí* (A little book on confession for children) (BÁC: Cló-lucht an Talbóidigh, n. d.); and Liam Ó Rinn's edition of An tAthair Peadar Ua Laoghaire's *Eochar na bhFlathas: Leabhar Úrnaithe Caitlicí maraon leis na hEipistilí is na Soiscéil* (The key to Paradise: A book of Catholic prayers together with the epistles and the gospels) (BÁC: Clólucht an Talbóidigh, Tra., n.d.). From Apr. to Dec.1922, the *Catholic Bulletin* serialised a translation into Irish of the Maynooth *Catechism*. In 1934 and 1935, *II* ran translations of the epistles and gospels for each week's Sunday Mass.

147 See Ó Rinn, *Mo Chara Stiofán*, 98–9.

148 See Ó Rinn, '"Rí na gCnoc" / Saothrú Stíle Liteardha' (*The King of the Hills* / The cultivation of a literary style), *UIrman*, 25/3/33; and 'Notes and Comments', *UIrman*, 31/12/32.

149 Má bhíonn tú tuirseach is gur mian leat roinnt uair a' chluig do chaitheamh go pléisiúrtha is go neathairbheach níl slí is fearr chuige ná ceann acu, sliocht sleachta inchinne Edgar Allan Poe do tharrac chughat.

150 Ó Rinn, *Mo Chara Stiofán*, 87.

151 Is dóigh liom go dtuigim anois cad chuige a dheineann ughdair Ghaedhilge aistriú ar leabhair Bhéarla den tsaghas úd ar a dtugtar sgéalta bleachtaire. Sé fáth is tuairim liom ná fuil aon úrsgéalta eile glan mórálta ach iad. For objections to detective fiction on moral grounds, see An tAthair Eric Mac Fhinn, 'Leabhraí Nua / Fá agus Faoi' (New books / Fá agus Faoi [two forms of an Irish preposition]), *AA*, Oct. 1934, 7–8; and 'E.', 'New Books / Léirmheasa' (Reviews), *Bonaventura*, Autumn 1938, 202. On the other hand, the anonymous reviewer of Niall Mac Suibne's translation of General Sir William Butler's *Red Cloud* as *Néal Dearg* saw this 'Red Indian story' as 'wholesome, heroic, Christian . . . quite in harmony with the Irish mind.' See 'Reviews / Books in Irish', *CB*, June 1936, 521.

152 For a lengthy positive review of this translation, see 'T. W.', 'Reviews / The Small Fields of Carrig', *Star*, 18/1/30.

153 Ní haon díobháil saol mhuintir an oileáin a chur in iúl do na Béarlóirí i dtíortha eile agus anso in Éirinn féin.

154 Interestingly enough, Liam Ó Rinn wasn't sure that it mattered all that much whether translations were actually read or not, as long as they were there to be read. Writing in 1922, at a time when there was little translated work available in Irish, he stated:

> I often said long ago that some attempt should be made to translate important books, some of the big, bulky books we see in the National Library, for example. Although no one would read them, they would be there as a source of hope and as a witness that this language of ours that has not been cultivated for three hundred years is not just a *patois*. (Is minic aduart fadó gur cheart iarracht éigin a thúirt ar leabhair tháchtacha d'aistriú, cuid desna leabhra móra toirtiúla a chímíd sa Leabharlainn Náisiúnta, cuir i gcás. Bíodh is ná léfadh puinn daoine iad do bhedís againn mar abhar dóchais, agus mar fhianaise nách 'patois' ar fad an teanga so againn nár saohraíodh le trí chéad blian). (*YI*, 4/11/22).

On the other hand, in an admittedly impressionistic and unscientific sampling, Seán Ó Ciarghusa visited a library and examined the circulation figures for Gaelic books, finding that while the three most popular titles (at 38, 34 and 27 borrowings) were original works, seven of the next nine were translations: Dickens's *A Tale of Two Cities* (19), Maurice Walsh's *The Key above the Door* (19), Doyle's *The Adventures of Sherlock Holmes* (18), Stoker's *Dracula* (17), Mason's *At the Villa Rose* (16, tied with an original title), and

Ben Hur (15, tied with an original title). See 'I Leabharlainn Dam' (In a library), *Leader*, 15/4/39.
155 See Titley, *An tÚrscéal Gaelige*, 291–2; Máirín Nic Eoin, *An Litríocht Réigiúnach*, 31–2; Mac Niocláis, *Seán Ó Ruadháin*, 111–14; and Delap, *Úrscéalta Stairiúla na Gaeilge*, 11, 54–5.

CHAPTER SEVEN

'The Trail of the Serpent'

1 Aon rud a déantar i mBéarla is le hAnglo-Ireland é, ag saothrú is ag déanamh 'traidisiún' dhó agus ag cur gnéithe éagsamhla maise is cultúra air agus á bhuanú 'na stáid náisiúnta . . . Cuirimís i n-iúl dóibh ná fuil ciall ná éifeacht le tighthe leath-bhealaigh, ná fuil ann dóibh ach fanacht i mbun Béarla agus Anglo-Ireland nó dul ar fad le Gaedhilg agus le náisiúntas dá réir. Tuigidís ná fuil aon Ghaedheal ann ach an té théigheann ar fad leis an dara rud.' See also 'Luimneach', 'Our "Literary Revival"', *The Leader*, 21/11/25.
2 See, for example, Niall Ó Searcaigh, 'Scríbhneoirí Gaedhilge', *An t-Ultach*, July 1939, 4.
3 Ó Donnchadha wrote 'gur sa teanga dhúthchais a ceapfar is a líomhnófar an teachtaireacht san. Is tríd an teanga dhúthchais is tríthi sin amháin, a fhéadfam casadh siar orainn fhéin agus breith ar aigne ár sinnsear chun *entwickelung* [*sic*] nó treorú nua a thabhairt don oighreacht léighinn is leitríochta atá factha againn uatha.
4 Is sa Ghaoluinn amháin a gheibhtear tuairisc chruinn dhílis ar sheanchas ár sean. Is i litríocht na Gaoluinne a gheibhtear tuairm ar mheon agus ar spriodáltacht ár gcine, an meon agus an spriodáltacht do lean gach glún díobh ó linn go céile. For another perspective on this quintessential post-colonial issue, see Ngúgí wa Thiong'o, *Decolonising the Mind*, xii, 24–33, 87, 93–4. Discussing a new Kenyan school syllabus for world literature, Ngúgí calls Yeats and Synge the 'British and Irish' representatives, apparently unaware that there is an indigenous Irish literary tradition (p. 99).
5 His comments drew strong opposition from the editor of *IS*, George Russell ('AE'), in the same issue. The thoughtful Gaelic response to AE was perhaps best formulated by 'Sliabh Bladhma' in 1938: 'Mr George Russell, to the Gaelic view, is a puzzle. Some of his utterances on *Gaelachas* have been thoughtful and penetrative, some grudging and almost petulant – as from time to time in his rather unfortunate "Irish Statesman"' (*Gaedheal*, May 1938, 1). See also 'Sliabh Bladhma', 'George Russell and the Gael', *An Gaedheal*, Aug. 1935, 1.
6 Nach truaighbhéalach an sgéal é nach dtuigeann sé sin agus a gcomh-chleasuidhthe go bhfuil a ré thart sa tír seo agus nach mbeidh baint olc, maith ná donaidhe ag an aos óg atá ag éirghe suas anois le na ngeátsaí ná le duaiseanna le h-aghaidh 'litridheachta'!
7 In a 1936 review of Stephen Gwynn's *Irish Literature and Drama*, de Blácam blasted Gwynn for asking whether members of the Irish Academy of Letters 'should . . . co-opt members whose writings they cannot read [i.e. those writing in Irish]?' De Blácam wrote: 'Is there any other land in which persons profess to be the exponents of the national literature while ignorant of the national language? Surely the answer to Mr Gwynn's question is that all Academicians ignorant of Irish should resign' (*IP*, 12/5/36). For other criticisms of the Academy, see 'An "Irish" Academy', Editorial, *Standard*, 3/9/32; 'The New "Academy"', Editorial, *Standard*, 24/9/32; 'Irish Academy of Letters – Unwelcome and Unauthorised / Brilliant Lecture by Rev. P. J. Gannon, S.J. / Devastating Critique of Mr Yeats' Project', *IC*, 19/11/32.
8 Ní abraim go bhfuil leabharthaí nua na Gaedhilge níos fearr ná comh maith leis na leabharthaí atá d'á gcur amach 'san Fhrainncis nó 'sa Bhéarla ach tá siad deich n-uaire níos fearr 'ná an amaidigh atá mar nua-litridheacht ag lucht sgríobhtha an Bhéarla 'sa tír seo.
9 Do chuir an Céitinneach, uair, dream áirithe sgríbhneoirí i gcomórtas leis an bpriompallán, an daol salach úd a chaitheas a shaoghal ar an gcarn aoiligh. Is béas leo seo áilleacht agus uaisleacht an duine a fhágáil ar leathtaobh, agus pé salachar nó uirísleacht atá ann a léiriú go cruinn. Is eól dúinn go bhfuil Éireannaigh d'á leithéid ann i láthair na h-uaire . . . I mBéarla, ar ndóigh, a cumadh an litridheacht sin. What is most striking about these moral denunciations of Anglo-Irish literature is how marginal a role language plays in them.
10 Lynd's next sentence was: 'Standish O'Grady was as necessary to the preparation of the ground for the Irish literature of the future as was Douglas Hyde.'
11 Is fearr go mór fada an iarraidh a rinne na daoine a d'fhéach sa teangaidh Bhéarla le saoghal na hÉireann a nochtadh ina gcuid scéalta sa naomhadh haois déag 'ná mar atá déanta againne go fóill in ár teangaidh fhéin. See also Corkery's praise of some contemporary Irish novels in English – Darrell Figgis's *The Children of Earth*, Edward MacLysaght's *The Gael*, and Séamus O'Kelly's *Wet Clay* – for being closer to 'the old Gaelic world' (an sean-saoghal Gaodhlach) than were novels written in Irish (*FMR*, Nov. 1924, 242). Some Gaelic critics pointed out how writers of Irish had been influenced by Anglo-Irish authors. For example, in a 1927 review in *IMN* (p. 102), A. Ó D.' suggested that Séamus Ó Grianna had been influenced by Abbey playwrights, while An tAthair Seán Ó Catháin saw Corkery's English-language fiction as a model for the stories of Seán Ó Ciosáin in *Sgéalta Cois Laoi* (*TCNÍ*, Mar. 1936, 66). More recently, in *An Litríocht Réigiúnach* (p. 188), Máirín Nic Eoin has discussed the influence of nineteenth-century Anglo-Irish novelists on Ó

Grianna, while in *An tÚrscéal Gaeilge* (p. 448), Alan Titley has commented on the effect his reading of Patrick MacGill's *Children of the Dead End* had on Ó Grianna's autobiographical writings.

12 Later in the piece, de Blácam challenged writers of Irish: 'It remains to be seen whether the writers of Gaelic will yet show themselves as intellectually alert as the writers of English.' See also 'An Cullach', 'An Dá Sheod in Easnamh / Slacht agus Uaisleacht' (The two missing gems / Polish and nobility), *II*, 6/3/24.

13 Is fearr (agus fágaim fuigheall mór molta uirthe nuair a deirim seo) – is fearr atá litridheacht 'un cinn i mBéarla na hÉireann 'ná tá sí 'sa Ghaedhilg.

14 Na giotaí beaga nó na leabhra beaga a cumadh le deich mblianna [*sic*] fichead anuas is suarach le rádh iad i gcomórtas le leabhra fiúntacha atá le fagháil sa mBéarla. Maille le mianach agus méid, le háille agus slacht, ní féidir a cur [*sic*] i gcomórtas le leabhra an Bhéarla atá dhá sgríobhadh ag Éireannaigh agus dhá léigheadh go fonnmhar ag Éireannaigh. In 1939, Seán Ó hÉigeartaigh, the son of P. S. O'Hegarty and the future founder of the publishing firm Sáirséal agus Dill, sparked a debate in the *Irish Press* when he asked what he apparently meant to be a rhetorical question at a meeting of An Comhchaidreamh in Rann na Feirste in the Donegal Gaeltacht: 'Are we to abandon Burke and Swift and Davis and Mitchel; are we to cast aside Yeats and Shaw and Moore and Russell (An bhfuil muid le Burke agus Swift agus Moore agus Mitchel a thréigeadh; an bhfuil muid le Yeats agus Shaw agus Moore agus Russell a chaitheadh ar leathtaoibh?). His audience, however, responded vigorously in the affirmative (*Leader*, 19/8/39). Among those who took sides in the debate in *IP* were M. J. MacManus, Peadar Mac Fhionnlaoich, Peadar O'Donnell, and Íde Ní Choindealbháin. Éamon de Valera himself was drawn into the debate when he spoke to the Trinity College Gaelic Society on 30 Oct. 1931, with Seán Ó hÉigeartaigh in the audience. De Valera said he had not followed the debate, but added he saw no need to defend Yeats and Shaw because he did not think anyone was attacking them (*IP*, 31/10/39). Ó hÉigeartaigh himself explained his remarks in a letter to *IP* in which he rejected any narrow ethnic criteria for membership in the Irish nation and said that he had wanted to provoke debate about 'the place of the Anglo-Irish in the Ireland of the future' (áit na nGall-Ghaedheal 'san Éirinn atá le teacht). In that Ireland, he believed Irish people of all backgrounds would use Irish as their means of communication, oral and written (*IP*, 1/9/39).

15 Ó Cuív, *Prós na hAoise Seo*, 37. Is í an aigne sin a gheibhmíd i sgríbhinní Shéamais Uí Dhubhghaill agus i sgríbhinní Béarla Gerald Griffin agus Charles Kickham agus sgríbhneoirí eile ná raibh an Ghaedhilg aca. Ó Cuív added that not all writers of Irish were possessed of this Gaelic mind: 'We have Irish language writings now in which the Gaelic mind has not been revealed, but rather the mind that goes with the language of the English' (Tá sgríbhinní Gaedhilge againn anois agus ní hí an aigne Ghaedhealach atá nochtaithe ionnta, ach an aigne a ghabhann le teanga na Sacsan).

16 Ach thug Dia na Glóire éirim aigne thar an gcoitcheanta dhó, agus thug Sé an croidhe breagh Gaedhealach san dó ionnus go raibh sé i n-inmhe muinntear na h-Éireann agus gach subháilce agus dubháilce d'ár bhain leo do thuisgint agus do nochtadh chomh cneasta grádhmhar agus a chuirfeadh máthair síos ar a leanbh féin. Sin é an chúis go mbeidh cion agus meas ag Gaedhealaibh air nuair a bheidh dearmhad déanta aca ar Swift agus ar dhaoinibh a thugann an ainm 'Sgríobhnóir Gaedhealach' ortha féin indiu. Ó Murchadha said that were Kickham alive in 1931, he would be a Gaelic Leaguer. See also 'Sliabh Bladhma', 'From Kickham to Hyde', *An Gaedheal*, 3/11/34.

17 Dála mar atá an 'Barróg' i mBéarla na h-Éireann, tá Tomás C. Ó Muireadhaigh ar dhruing na Mainistreach. Cé gur ó'n mBreac-Ghalldacht do Thomás, fé mar thuigim, agus bíodh gur i mBéarla a scríobhann sé, bíonn boladh na h-Éireann ar an gcaint agus ar an gceapadóireacht aige, agus iarracht d'anál na Gaedhealtachta fútha.

18 Tá drámaí uilig Thomáis Uí Mhuireadhaigh rithteach leis an teangaidh agus leis an saoghal Gaedhealach. See also the review of the Gaelic version of Murray's *Birthright* in *The Nation*, 22/2/30.

19 Bhí an Gaedhealfhuil ann gan aon amhras; agus ní miste dhúinn uile é ghlacadh chughainn geall leis mar ghlacfaimís file dúthchais cé gur i mBéarla do scríobh sé a chuid dán agus a shaothar liteardha uile. Bhí féith Ghaedhealach ann gan amhras.

20 Canon Sheehan seems to have been as popular among the Gaels as he was among Irish readers in general. For example, An tAthair Mánus Mac Aisín wrote in 1926: 'There has been nothing in the past thirty years that has done more to make the cause of Ireland known in the world than the books of the Canon' (Ní'l aon rud ins na tríochadh bliadhan atá gabhtha tarainn is mó a dhein cúis na h-Éireann a chraobhsgaoileadh sa domhan ná leabhair an Chanónaigh) (*An Róimh*, Summer 1926, 13–23). Of course the Gaels doubtless appreciated Sheehan's own movement orthodoxy as reported by Pádraig Ó Cadhla: 'He said that he would prefer to all he had written to have been able to write one little story in Irish' (Dubhairt sé gurbh' fhearr leis ná an méid go léir a bhí scríobhtha aige go mbeadh sé in a chumas aon scéilín beag amháin a scríobhadh i nGaedhilg) (*Sguab*, Mar. 1924, 105).

21 For Corkery, see also Seán Ó Ciarghusa, 'Dráma Gaedheal', in *Ar Mo Mharanadh Dam*, 106. In a piece on 'Our Bards and Critics', 'Sliabh Bladhma' wrote: 'In Gaelic and Anglo-Irish fields (that show more or less Gaelic impulsion) we are richer than we often

think' (*Gaedheal*, Oct. 1936, 1). On the other hand, in 1925 Máighréad Ní Annagáin was contemptuous of 'the long-haired and side-whiskered poetasters who hung around the edge of the Gaelic movement, acquiring enough Irish to give their work "a Celtic note"' (*Leader*, 3/1/25). For Clarke, see Liam Gógan's laudatory poem 'Iar bhFilleadh Aibhistín Uí Chléirigh, File' (On the return of Austin Clarke, poet) in *Dánta agus Duanóga* (Poems and little verses) (BÁC: Muinntir C. S. Ó Fallamhain, Teo., i gcomhar le hOS, 1929), 49.

22 Daniel Corkery, *Synge and Anglo-Irish Literature: A Study* (Cork: Cork University Press, 1931), 19.

23 Patrick Maume is entirely right when in his biography of Corkery he states: 'In analysing *Synge and Anglo-Irish Literature* it must be remembered Corkery was not condemning Synge but assessing him as a model for future writers'. See Maume, *Life that is Exile*, 114. See also viii–ix.

24 See also 'A nDubhairt Domhnall Ó Corcara' (What Daniel Corkery said), *Nation*, 25/10/31; and '"A Gigantic Vested Interest" / Prof. Corkery's Lecture to Dublin Gaelic League Branch', *IP*, 13/11/37.

25 Sé an obair atá romhainn ná litríocht a cheapadh; litríocht a theasbáinfidh meon is meanma na nGaedheal; litríocht dhár gcuid féin nach mbeidh blas ná bolath an Ghalldachais uirthi. Sin é an bóthar atá romhainn agus is iomdha poll is slug ann gur baoghal dúinn dul d'ár mbascadh ionnta. Ach tá treóraidhe muinghíneach againn i nDomhnall Ó Corcardha a chuirfidh ar ár bhfaire sinn, agus cé gur sa mBeurla a scríobhann sé ní bhaineann san ó ghaois a chainnte ná ó fheabhas a chomhairle.

26 Níl aon agó mar sin ná gur tábhachtach é go ndéanfadh sgríobhnóirí na h-Éireann, pé teanga a bhíos aca, go ndéanfaidís an mhuinntir óna dtagann siad do nochtadh dóibh féin ar chuma gur féidir leis an muintir sin iad féin d'aithint sa litríocht . . . Mara mbídh sgríobhnóirí na Gaedhilge san áirdeall, tá baol ann go siubhalfaidh siad an bóthar céanna, gur ag déanamh aithris a bhéas siad ar chaighdeáin na sgríobhnóirí ó Éirinn a sgríobhas Béarla.

27 Ní maith linn an teórainn atá idir Sé Conndaethe d'Éirinn agus an chuid eile den tír. Tá sé mí-nádúrtha. Ach is eagal liom go bhfuil a lán againn fabhrach go leor don deighilt mhóir eile san do rinneadh an chéad lá do tugadh 'Gall-Ghaedhil' ar Éireannaigh a bhain feidhm as an mBéarla mar áis litríochta. Baisteadh mhí-nádúrtha ab eadh é sin, freisin, a rinne i bhfad níos mó dochair do chuspóirí an Ghaedhealachais ná éinní eile gur féidir linn cuimhneach air.

28 He continued: 'The attack on Corkery, then, reduces itself to the outcry of the pro-smut party, and the folly of an Ascendancy pose.' For another example of de Blácam's thinking about Anglo-Irish literature, see 'Roddy the Rover' (de Blácam), 'Seen, Heard and Noted / Six Good Writers – Some Irish Prose Models', *IP*, 7/8/33.

29 See also 'M. C.', 'Mr. de Blácam on the Anglo-Irish Writers / The "Academy" School and the Gaelic Tradition', *IT*, 10/11/31. 'M. C.' confessed that

> knowing that he has professed adherence to the curious doctrines preached by Mr Daniel Corkery in his 'Synge and Anglo-Irish Literature' a couple of years ago, I was fearful that his comments on the so-called Anglo-Irish writers would drive me to an insensate fury.

But he then admitted that on reading de Blácam's book he was pleasantly surprised:

> On the subject of the Anglo-Irish writers I find that Mr. de Blácam's judgments are not only sober and considered, but reasonable, though naturally biased by his fondness for Gaelic literature and the new school of writers in English which claims to derive therefrom.

30 Corkery responded angrily in the next issue of the same journal: 'I do not, however, cry Nazi at Mr de Blácam as he does at me. I leave him to his confessor' (*Studies*, Dec. 1934, 619).

31 Litridheacht iad agus litridheacht náisiúnta iad. Ó Faracháin's views as expressed in this lecture were criticised by Maoghnus Ó Domhnaill in 'Nótaí na Seachtaine / Cúrsaí Litridheachta' (Notes of the week / Literary affairs), *ACS*, 12/12/31.

32 It is interesting to note that in a review of Mac Grianna's story collection *An Grádh agus an Ghruaim*, 'T. Ó R.' wrote:

> This book by Seosamh Mac Grianna, *An Grádh agus an Ghruaim*, is attempting what Carleton did for Tyrone in his own time, what Donn Byrne did for Newry, and for one group of people in Ireland before the Great War, and what Corkery is doing for Cork and for Kerry at present (An leabhar so le Seosamh Mac Grianna, tá sé ag 'ul i gcionn an rud a rinne Carleton do Thír Eoghain ina am féin, a rinne Donn Byrne do Iubhar Cinn Trágha, is do dhream amháin i nÉirinn roimh an Chogadh Mhór is atá Ó Corcora a dhéanamh do Chorcaigh is do Chiarraidhe fá láthair) (*Tír*, Mar. 1930, 3).

33 Compare the view of 'Sliabh Bladhma': 'One may have a Gaelic outlook on life and art, or one may have an English outlook, but a position between the two is artistically an impossibility' (*Gaedheal*, 26/1/35).

34 In *An Bhreatain Bheag*, Mac Grianna wrote of the English-language writings of Caradoc Evans that there was so much of the flavour of Welsh (blas na Breathnaise) on his English that there was no other writer 'who made so clear to English-speakers what Welsh was like' (a thug le tuigbheáil do lucht an Bhéarla cá leis an rabh an Bhreathnais cosamhail) (p. 142).

35 For MacGill, see also Liam Ó Rinn, 'Saothrú na Gaedhilge / Aicmí nár Scríobhadh Ortha Fós' (The cultivation of the Irish language / Groups not yet written about), *UI*, 2/6/34.

36 He repeated this charge that Anglo-Irish writers had sold out to London publishers in *An Bhreatain Bheag* (p. 147).

37 See Seamus Heaney, 'An Open Letter', in Field Day Theatre Company, *Ireland's Field Day* (London, Hutchinson, 1985), 25.

38 Mac Dhubháin, *Stair na hÉireann*, 346. Sé'n ochtmhadh céad déag 'aois-órdha' na sgríbhneoir nGall nGaedhealach i n-Éirinn. Mheasadar gurb iad féin an náisiún agus bhíodar bródamhail as, dá réir. I gColáiste na Tríonnóide a fuaireadar bunáite go léir a gcuid oideachais. Ba bheag é a meas ar shean-bhunadh na tíre ná ar a gcuid nósa.

39 See Oilibhéar Ó Croiligh, *Bealach Mhic Ghrianna: Treoir don Leabhar 'Mo Bhealach Féin' le Seosamh Mac Grianna* (Corcaigh: Cló Mercier, 1972), 14.

40 Seán Ó Ciarghusa, 'Teangthacha na dTuath', in *Ar Mo Mharanadh Dam*, 40–1.

41 The text of the play was published in *An t-Ultach*, July 1939, 1–3, 8. It was first produced by An Comhar Drámaidheachta at the Peacock in Dec. 1940 with the title *'Ní Chuireann Siad Siol' nó 'Poll Bocht'* ('They do not plant seed' or 'Poor Poll'), and published under that title by An Gúm in 1945. In a 1937 essay on 'Guth na nDaoine' (The voice of the people), Brighid Ni Redmond [*sic*] wrote of the eighteenth century:

> The works of the English writers in Ireland in this period were famous. *The Vicar of Wakefield* and *The School for Scandal* will be read until English has vanished from the earth, but they were written in the English language. Their fame among the learned is very great, as is their reputation among the English, but we have no business with them. They are not national authors (Is mór le rádh oibreacha na nóghdar [*sic*] Sasanach in Éirinn le linn na haoise seo. Léighfear 'Vicar of Wakefield' agus 'The School for Scandal' go dtí go mbéidh an Beurla imthighthe as an saoghal, ach is sa teangain Bheurla do sgríobhadh iad. Ba mhór é a gclú sa léigheamh, ba mhór é a gcáil i measc na Sasanach. Ach níl aon ghnó againn dhíobh. Ní úghdair náisiúnta iad) (*IR*, May 1937, 386).

In a 1926 letter to *II*, Micheál Ó Maoláin was critical of plans for the Government to purchase Goldsmith's house, saying the money should be spent on Gaelicisation (*II*, 13/1/26).

42 Gé nár Gaodhal í – is i Sasana do rugadh í – níor Gall í do mhuintir na tíre seo agus do thaisbeáin a beatha féin agus gach do scríobh sí an charthanacht agus an tuigsint do bhí na croidhe do mhuintir na h-Éireann.

43 Ní fheicimíd i n-a saothar siúd acht sgige agus magadh fá Ghaedhil, fá n-a nósa crádhbha, fá n-a dtír-ghrádh, agus fá gach nidh bu dhual do chlainn Mhílidh. Do thréigeadar féin Éire, do thréigeadar creideamh a sinnsir, do thréigeadar a ndúthchas ar son airgid is ar son uaisleacht' bréige. Writing of the authors' novel *The Real Charlotte* the previous year, Ó Domhnalláin attacked Violet Martyn (i.e. 'Martin Ross') for betraying her compatriots by holding them up to ridicule, and continued: '*The Real Charlotte* will in future be used to lash the people of the Big Houses' (Bainfear feidhm as 'The Real Charlotte' lá níos fuide anonn ná indiu le lucht na dtighthe móra do lasgadh) (*CB*, June 1933, 512).

44 Ó Grianna, in particular, was an admirer of Mitchel. See *Saoghal Corrach*, 18–23.

45 See Ó Domhnalláin, 'Éire agus an Armhairc' (Ireland and Brittany), in *Dréachta*, 117.

46 'Sé mo bharamhail nach dtug muinntear na tíre seo comhthom na Féinne do Thomas Moore ariamh. See also Father Dinneen, 'Litridheacht agus Ceol / An Bhaint Atá Aca le n-a Chéile' (Literature and Music / Their connection with each other), *Tír*, July 1930, 4; and An tAthair Mártan Ó Domhnaill, *Oileáin Árann*, 281. For a more negative view of Moore, see W. Stockley, 'Moore's Claim as Anglo-Irish National poet', *Dublin Magazine*, Oct.–Dec. 1939, 14–20.

47 Ach d'á mhéid an fonn a bhíonn ar Ghaedheal-góiribh teanga ár sinnsear d'aithbheóchaint, agus d'á mhéid searbhas a bhíonn 'na gcroidhe i n-aghaidh na ndaoine a dhein dochar dí riamh agus a leanann ar an droch-obair fós, ní dheineann siad dearmhad ar na fíor-Ghaedhil a dhein iarracht ar dúil na nGaedheal san fhilidheacht agus ins na sgéaltaibh próis do shásamh nuair a dúnadh doirse na ndámh-scol go deo, nuair d'imthigh na filidhe i ndiaidh a chéile ar sluagh na marbh agus nuair a díbreadh an Ghaedhealg féin as gach cathair agus sráid-bhaile d'Éirinn. Agus go deimhin, is sár-mhaith atá grádh agus meas a gcomh-Ghaedheal tuillte ag na daoine sin ó'n bhliain 1848 i leith.

48 Ins an stáid a bhí ar an tir seo maidir le teangaidh, scríobhadh mórchuid litridheachta sa teangaidh iasachta ar chóir a scríobhadh i dteangaidh na tíre.

49 Seo leabhar a sgríobhadh i mBéarla i dtosach báire, agus a chuireas síos go beacht agus go hurra-manta ar shaoghal muinntire na tuaithe i dTiobruid Árann ós cionn leathchéad bliadhain ó shoin; agus is beag nach féidir a rádh nach bhfuil aon leagan cainnte innte ó n-a thosach go dtí n-a deireadh nach bhfuil i n-a leagan Gaedhealach.

50 S'é buaidh leabhar Kickham mar adhbhar aistriúcháin nach gádh aon atharú a dhéanamh ar chúrsaí saoghal na ndaoine ná ar a gcuid smaointe. Má thuig aoinne riamh meon muinntir Thiobraid Árainn do thuig Kickham é. Ní gádh más eadh ach crot Gaedhealach a chur ar an gcainnt chun leabhar a cheapadh a bheadh oireamhnach do lucht na Gaedhilge anois.

51 Ó Domhnaill, *Oileáin Árann*, 192. Tá smaointe agus spioraid an Ghaedhil 'san mbun-amhrán, agus ní theastuigheann uaidh acht an chulaith nádúrtha

fheileas dó le n-a dhéanamh fíor-Ghaedhealach ar gach uile slighe. He translated one stanza into Irish.

52 Chuir sé i n-iúl an méid Gaedhilge a bhí ag Carleton (bíodh is nach raibh sé i ndon an Ghaedhilge a scríobh) agus an chaoi a ndeachaidh saothar Carleton i gcionn ar sgríobhnóirí Chúige Uladh – Gaedhilge agus Béarla – go dtí an lá indiu – cuir i gcás, 'Máire' agus Seaghán Mac Meanman agus Peadar Ó Domhnaill.

53 Tá *Fardorougha the Miser* ar na húirsgéaltaibh is fearr dár fhág Uilliam bocht Carleton againn agus ba mhaith an cuimhneamh ag Seán Mac Maoláin Gaedhilg a chur air.

54 'Sé is dóighche, dá mbeadh sé 'na bheathaidh anois, go mbeadh sé ag obair go dian chun sean-Éire na nGaedheal do chur fé réim agus fé lán-tseol arís: Seadh, – go mbeadh sé 'na Fanatic, de réir tuairm na ndaoine atá sásta le Éire d'fheisgint ag iompáil 'na tír ghallda.

55 In 1924 *Fáinne an Lae* ran a front page cartoon of Yeats being welcomed back to Ireland by Caitlín Ní Uallacháin (Kathleen Ni Houlihan), who says in Irish, 'And you have brought the Nobel Prize home to Inisfree' (Agus thugais duais Nobel abhaile leat go hInis Fraoigh), to which the poet responds: 'Pardon me, Madame, I don't understand a word you say' (*FL*, 27/9/24).

56 In a brief dramatic skit in the *Irish Rosary* entitled 'Crowns and Palavers at Tara – 1935 AD', Maurice Leahy offered a spoof of Yeats as 'Jupiter Firbolg' (*IR*, Dec. 1935, 911–15).

57 Tá siad ag obair go moch déidheannach le fada an lá ag iarraidh an tsoiscéil atá aca a chur ar uachtar, soiscéal atá bun-os-cionn le dearcadh na nGaedheal, agus le dearcadh na gCatoiliceach ar fud an domhain uile.

58 Ní bheadh aoinne ag súil le'n a mhalairt uaidh-sean óir is iontuigthe ó'n a chuid filíochta gur mó a chlaoidheas sé le págántacht ná le Críostaidheacht.

59 In a 1934 essay on 'The Celtic Element in the Poetry of W. B. Yeats', the Jesuit celticist Father Francis Shaw wrote: 'And if its oriental or pseudo-oriental basis be denied, we must admit that Mr. Yeats's "dream-world" is nothing more than "private, personal and literary" and that, as far as things Irish are concerned, it has no "external validation"' (*Studies*, June 1934, 276).

60 Tá a fhios ag an tsaoghal gurab é an Dr W. B. Yeats an té is mó le rádh . . . i ngnóithe ghall-chultúir i nÉirinn. Eisean an dia beag ag Gaill an chultúir sa tír seo; eisean a chuirfeas ar do bhonnaibh thú, nó a bhrisfeas thú, do réir mar is mian leis féin. Muna bhfuil tú sásta sléachtadh dó agus glacadh leis an chaighdeán atá aige féin agus a lucht leanamhna, brisfear thú, agus bascfar thú.

61 An Seanadaidhe Yeats, cuir i gcás: thuig daoine go rabh aithne aca air i gcomhnuidhe, gur duine meathta do bhí ann, go rabh tuairim thar barr aige air féin agus droch-mheas aige ar Ghaedhil Éireann. In aimsir na dubh-chrónach bhí faitchíos air labhairt ós ard ar eagla go measfaidhe go rabh sé ar leith Éireann. Ní leigfeadh sé dá cháirdibh féin teacht ina thoigh má bhí aon cháil náisiúntach ortha ar eagla go mbeadh na dubh-chrónach ar a thóir. Ach anois is fear mór é; Seanadaidhe agus fear-stáit, agus is féidir leis an nimh do leigint le muintir na hÉireann agus gheobhaidh sé colamhain puiblidheacht i ngach páipéar in Éirinn.

62 The 'P.' here stood for Pollexfen, the name of the poet's mother's family. Moran and other *Leader* writers often used it to emphasise Yeats's exotic foreignness.

63 See also Father Dinneen's essay 'Ag Maslughadh na gCuradh nach Maireann' (Insulting the heroes who are no longer alive), *Leader*, 19/2/27.

64 Bhí W. B. Yeats ag maoidheamh gaile agus gaisce a chinidh sa tSeanaid an tseachtmhain eile. B'iad plúr-scoth na tíre iad, adubhairt sé, ó Swift go dtí Parnell. Bhí an ceart aige. Ní fhéadfadh duine de'n chineadh Gaedheal bheith n-a scoth, – plúr ná eile – i n-aimsir Swift, mar do scothfaidhe an ceann de dá nochtadh sé a cheann, ní áirimhimíd aon iarracht do dhéanamh ar é féin do chur i n-iúl. Agus annsin nuair tógadh an brácа díobh agus riamh ó shoin, i n-ionad iompódh ar an Sasannach agus iarracht do dhéanamh ar an forlámhas inntleachta agus saoidheachta agus eagnaidheachta do bhaint de, ag sodar i n-a dhiaidh, agus ag aithris air, bhíodar agus é, nídh nárbh iongna, ag plámas leo nó 'ghá lascadh do réir mar oir, agus ag clith-mhagadh fútha i gcomhnuidhe. Indiu féin, tá an fhuip suas a mhuinchille aige agus tá ár mbuidheachas ag dul do W. B. Yeats i dtaoibh chos na fuipe do nochtadh beagáinín. Í d'fheiscint, b'fhéidir go múinfeadh sé d'ár muintir gur mithid dóibh stad de bheith ag aithris ar Yeats ná ag iomáidh leis i mBéarla, mar chomh siúralta agus tagann té ó'n Domhan Thoir, go dtagann agus go dtiocfaidh an Béarla ó Shasanna, agus gurb iad Yeats agus a chomhluadar na ceannaidhthe riarfaidh orainn i nÉirinn é. Agus le cois an Bhéarla, beidh, nídh nach iongna, a ngabhann léithi. Fiú an Creidimh, seachnuighmís ná tréigfeadh Creideamh Phádraig a dhath fé anál an Ghalldachais. See also 'Grattan agus Yeats', Editorial, *II*, 22/8/25.

65 Caithfidh na Gaedhil labhairt go láidir i n-éadan na dreama seo, agus, go h-áirithe, i n-éadan na h-iarrachta atá á dhéanamh ag an Dr. Yeats a chur i gcéill go bhfuil ughdarás aige labhairt i n-ainm na h-Éireann.

66 He also called Yeats 'among the foremost of the great English romantic poets'.

67 See also 'The "Irish Statesman" / The New Imperial Push – and Mr. Shaw!' *Éire*, 6/10/23; Hon. R. Erskine V. Marr, 'Tongues / National and International', *Cork Weekly Examiner*, 27/10/28; 'Current Affairs', *Leader*, 1/11/30; 'Shaw and Yeats and Their Tribe', Editorial, *CB*, Sept. 1933, 693–6.

68 Corkery, *Synge and Anglo-Irish Literature*, 19. See also Corkery's review of Shaw's *Collected Plays*, in

which he pretty much ignores the question of Shaw's Irishness (*IP*, 11/9/31).

69 Ó Ciarghusa, 'Teangthacha na dTuath', in *Ar Mo Mharanadh Dam*, 35. Tugtar fé ndear nach aon dosaire deas cainnteach Gaedhil ná fear adhbhachta agus searbhais do leithéid G. B. Shaw do mhol na nidhthe sin do Riaghaltas Shasana ach Sasanaigh stuamdha, ciallmhara, léigheannta, do thuig go maith cad a bhíodar a rádh. See also Ó Ciarghusa's essays 'Lucht Cainnte' (Speakers), *Leader*, 30/7/32; and 'Cluasaidheacht' (Eavesdropping), *Leader*, 8/9/34.

70 Ó Rinn, *Mo Chara Stiofán*, 72. In Seaghán Mac Meanman's story 'An Cailín Seo agus an Cailín Udaidh Eile', there is at one point an impassioned discussion among the characters of the work and ideas of Shaw. See Mac Meanman, *Indé agus Indiu*, 72–3. In Riobárd Ó Faracháin's 'Truaghán Mná', the protagonist has seen and enjoyed Shaw's *Candida*. See Ó Faracháin, *Fíon gan Mhoirt*, 49. On the other hand, Ó Faracháin himself wrote of Shaw in 1937:

> I don't believe Shaw matters so very much. Maybe he did many grand things for sincerity and common-sense and so on . . . As a writer I don't think he wears well. He has two qualities in his prose: speed and clarity; they make him an exceptional journalist. I doubt if there is much else to him (*Bonaventura*, Winter, 1937, p.221).

See also the spoof by Nuala Moran ('N.') entitled 'Back to Methusaleh' and set in the Gate Theatre during a three-night run of Shaw's play of this title (*Leader*, 8/11/30).

71 The editor of the *Irish Tribune* shared O'Hegarty's respect for Shaw's willingness to defend the men of 1916 (*Irish Tribune*, 26/11/26).

72 The following year the editor of *An Gaedheal* wrote: 'We looked up Mr Joyce's writings and find that they are written in what must have been the language of Dean Swift in the closing years of his life' (*Gaedheal*, Mar. 1936, 2).

73 Bíonn díospóireachtaí fada acu ar an 'dteangain nóidh' atá dá saothrú ag James Joyce. Sé an sgríobhnóir sin dar leo an t-aon Éireannach amháin gur féidir leis anam na hÉireann do léiriú don Euroip. Is cuma dar ndóigh an éirigheann leis an anam céadna do léiriú do mhuintir a dtíre féin. Níl ionnta san ach fir bolg. 'Fir Bolg', which I here translate as 'barbarians', were mythical early settlers of Ireland who were displaced by the Tuatha Dé Danann, in their turn supplanted by the Gaels. See also the little dig at Joyce in 'Enemy Mechanised Music', Editorial, *An Camán*, 18/11/33.

74 B'fhéidir ná fuil an Seoigheach ach ag leanúint lorg na bpinteóirí a phéinteálann pátrún (más ceart pátrún do thabhairt ar rud ná bíonn bun ná barr air) nach cosúil le héinní ar talamh agus adeir gur tigh is gáirrdín é nó sneachta ar shliabh nó sráid-bhaile. Ach más mar sin atá – bhail, caithfimíd an Seoigheach agus na pinteóirí agus a lucht leanúna agus a gcuid síor-argóintí dfágáint fén éinne amháin a thuigeann iad – Dia na Glóire. Ó Rinn added a brief parody – in Irish! – of Joyce's style.

75 Leabhar dúr duairc é seo fhágann droch-bhlas ad' bhéal. Dá mbeadh sé le fáil ar leath-choróinn ní dóigh liom go mbeadh puinn éilimh air . . . Fuathuitheoir an brígh atá le *Ulysses*. Ainm oiriúnach – gach ní thaithníonn leis an gcineadh daonna is fuath leis an údar é do réir dheallraimh. See also Ó Rinn's comments on Joyce in *Turus go Páras*, 22 (he did not buy a copy of *Ulysses* while there); and in *Mo Chara Stiofán*, 65–6 (where he and McKenna discuss the questions Joyce's work raises with regard to morality in literature). Ó Rinn was, however, able to have some fun with Joyce's work, as when, in a letter to the *Irish Stateman*, he commiserated with another reader baffled by *Ulysses*: 'Samhluighthear mihi que Jamesy enjoys seine páirt as buachaill báire du monde western. In andere verbis measaim dass ille est pulling la jambe de gach mug qui íocann drei ou sex guineas for etwas ná fuil si bon que Esperanto agus that ist fortasse worse als Volapuk' (i.e., It seems to me that Jamesy enjoys his role as the playboy of the western world. In other words I think that he is pulling the leg of every mug who pays three or six guineas for something that is not as good as Esperanto and that is much worse than Volapuk) (*IS*, 13/7/29). The letter was addressed 'don Editor du Staatsmann Hibernicus' and signed 'Wilhelm O Rinn.' Joyce was also discussed, quite seriously, in Micheál Mac Liammóir's short story 'Dúchas an Uilc' in *Lá agus Oidhche*, 10. This story was originally published under the title 'Aonghus Ó Cruadhlaoich' in *FL*, 15/12/23.

76 In a 1930 essay, 'Séanó' wrote: 'The Irishman Joyce is an Irish Ireland type in his experimenting with the English language; but he has no check on him as the Irish or Breton writer has from the standard of the language of the people' (*FMR*, June 1930, 223). For other Irish-Ireland views of Joyce, see 'Editorial / The Aesthetes and the Censorship', *CB*, Mar. 1927, 232–40; 'Editorial', *CB*, June 1927, 565–70; 'Editorial', *CB*, Oct. 1928, 988–92; 'Mr Gwynn Forgets Irish Writers', *Star*, 19/7/30; Donn Piatt, 'Native Ireland Sixty Years Ago', *Outlook*, 16/4/32; 'Enemy Language', *Camán*, 18/11/33; 'Freagra ó "Dr Panini" / Irish Up-to-Date' (An answer from 'Dr Panini'), *Camán*, 2/12/33; Criostóir Mac Aonghusa, 'Cúrsaí Liteardha na Gaedhilge' (Irish language literary matters), UCG *Irisleabhar*, 1939–40, 33.

77 Although not much discussed by the Gaels, Edward Martyn, always a fervent supporter of the Gaelic League both morally and financially, fared better than did his cousin Moore. See, for example, 'Gaedheal Maith ar Lár' (A good Gael fallen), *II*, 8/12/23; 'Current Affairs', *Leader*, 15/12/23; 'Current Affairs', *Leader*, 27/9/30.

78 A Sprid Synge! ba linn tú go deimhin cé nár dhínn tú. Bhí ceal éigin ag goilliúint ort nár thuigis go

soiléir lár croidhe na h-aigne Gaedhealaighe a bhí fút a chruthú ins an dráma so. Ó Catháin continued:

> It is not excuse enough for Synge and his like that he studied the Gaelic mind in the real Gaeltacht. It is as if he came on a visit to a beautiful, noble house by the shore and had to go in the back door and judge the beauty of the house in the servant's cold, empty little back room, and with no one to welcome him but the Hag of Beare grumbling in the corner. And poor Synge would not understand her (Níor leor de leathscéal do Synge ná dá leithéid gur dhein sé stuidéar ar an aigne Ghaedhealaigh ins an bhfíor-Ghaedhealtacht. Is ionann scéal dó agus dá dtagadh sé ar chuaird chun tighe áluinn uasail cois trágha agus go mbeadh air dul isteach 'on dorus tiar agus áilneacht an tighe do mheas i gcúl-sheoimrín fuar, follamh an tseirbhísigh agus gan éinne ann roimis ach Cailleach Bhéara ag cannrán sa chúinne. Agus cha dtuigfeadh Synge bocht í).

79 Do thug Synge eolas do-n saoghal ar na daoine seo, chuaidh sé in a measg, agus ba bheag a bhí i n-a saoghal a bhí ceilte air, ach do dhearmhad sé go raibh aigne aca nach féidir leis an súil a chíoradh agus ná raibh comhbháidhe aige leis an aigne sin. Tugadh taithneamh do'n mhéid a scríobh sé n-a dtaobh. 'Seadh! Tugtar taithneamh do chuntas ar threabhacha barbardha na n-oileán 'san Aigéan Theas. Is ró-annsa le daoine an nídh suaithinseach sa litríocht. On the other hand, the English synopsis found in the programme for a 1933 performance of a Gaelic translation of *Riders to the Sea* at Taibhdhearc na Gaillimhe begins:

> This little masterpiece of J. M. Synge should have an especial appeal for Westerners in that it portrays so faithfully the hardships of life along the coast, and the ceaseless struggle for existence of those who depend for their livelihood on the sea.

The following year An Taibhdhearc performed Liam Ó Briain's translation of Synge's *Deirdre of the Sorrows*.

80 Ó Broin addressed members of An Fáinne on Synge in 1928, a lecture broadcast over 2RN (*II*, 21/2/28). In *Just Like Yesterday*, Ó Broin confesses to a fondness for Synge's *Playboy* (p. 72).

81 It is clear from another of Ní Annagáin's essays that she saw the Gael as invariably a Catholic (*Leader*, 15/11/24).

82 For example, Lady Gregory took a real interest in the work of Taibhdhearc na Gaillimhe, allowing them to produce plays of hers in translation without charge, and returning royalties when they were sent to her. See the letter (in English) from Lady Gregory to An Taibhdhearc dated 21 Feb. 1929 in Folder 2/1–13; and the the minutes of Taibhdhearc meetings for 25 Feb. 1929 and 16 May 1930 (Add.MSS 22 and 75, Taibhdhearc na Gaillimhe Papers, NUIG). For a favourable comment in passing on Lady Gregory, see 'A. Ó L.', 'Leabhra ar an mBord', *GR*, Mar. 1938, 493.

83 Ó Rinn, *Mo Chara Stiofán*, 118. Fear beo bríomhar é má bhí a leithéid riamh ann, díreach an saghas ba dhóigh leat a fhéadfadh 'The Crock of Gold' agus 'The Demi-Gods' a chumadh. Déarfá is tú ag éisteacht leis is ag féachaint air, mura raibh dlúth-ghaol aige le sióga is le leipreacháin, gur thug sé cuid mhór dá shaol ina gcuideachtain. Ó Rinn also commented on Stephens's interest in Irish (p. 117). In a 1922 lecture to the Dublin Metropolitan School on 'Irish Literature Seen through the European Literary Situation', Stephens began his plea for the Irish to assume a more European outlook with the words: 'Learn the Irish language they must; talk like Irishmen they must . . .' (*Weekly Freeman*, 18/2/22). Two years later, speaking to the Trinity College Gaelic Society, Stephens declared 'that the Gaelic culture was the only barrier we had to put between us and Anglicisation' (gurb í an chultúr Ghaelach an t-aon chlaidhe amháin a bhí againn le cur idir sinn agus an Galldachas) (*II*, 11/11/24). For Stephens's fascination with early Irish narratives at this time, see Joyce Flynn, 'The Route to the Táin: James Stephens' Preparation for His Unfinished Epic', *Proceedings of the Harvard Celtic Colloquium* 1 (1981), 125–44.

84 Tá, ar thaobh an Bhéarla, i nÉirin faoi láthair, sgata sgríobhnóirí atá i bhfad níos cumusaighe agus na mílte uair níos inntleachtúla ná an sean-dream. Tagann an cumas agus an inntleachtúlacht – an chuid is éifeachtaighe dhe – ón gceangal atá eatorra agus an saol Gaedhealach. See also Proinnsias Ó Cinnéide, 'Cumann na Meán-Múinteoirí, Comhdháil na Cásga, 1936 / Prós-litríocht na Gaedhilge – An Riocht Atá Anois uirthe' (The Assocation of Secondary Teachers, Easter Convention, 1936 / Prose literature in Irish – Its present state), *Association of Secondary Teachers, Ireland / Official Year Book and Diary, 1937–8*, 89.

85 Is mór an náire mar sin go bhfuil fear mar Liam Ó Flaithearta go bhfuil féith na scéalaidheachta ann agus an Ghaedhilg ar a thoil aige ag scríobhadh sa' mBéarla. B'fhearrde an Ghaedhilg é bheith ag scríobhadh inti agus b'fhearrde a chuid oibre féin é bheith ghá déanamh sa Ghaedhilg . . . Dhá mbeadh Liam ag scríobhadh sa Ghaedhilg chuirfeadh sé srian le n-a pheann agus leigfeadh sé ar lár an gháirseamhlacht a chuireann sé i ngach scéal leis anois d'fhonn Sasanaigh bhréana do shásamh. B'fhearrde agus ba threiside a scéalta an glanadh.

86 Is féidir deimhin do dhéanamh den méid seo, gur scríobhnóir Ó Flaithbheartaigh go bhfuil tuisgint aige ar a chéird, go bhfuil féith neamh-choitchianta sgríobhnóireachta ann, go bhfuil ard-chliú saothraighthe aige mar fhear litríochta, agus gur míle truagh nach i nGaedhilg amháin a bhíos sé ag sgríobhadh.

87 Leath mo shúile orm nuair a chonnac an neart a bhí ina stíl. Ní scríobhadh is ceart a thabhairt ar a leithéid ach réabadh stoirme . . . Ba mhaith ab fhiú do

scríbhneoirí Gaedhilge staidéar do dhéanamh ar obair 'uafásach' an duine 'uafásaigh' seo. Ní dóich liom gurb í 'mí-mhoráltacht' a chuid leabhar a mheallann muintir Shasana chun iad do léigheamh. Éinní a scríobhfaí sa stíl neartmhar san i dteangain ar bith léighfí é le fonn.

88 Atá sgéal cumasach ar leathanach eile de'n eagrán seo. Muna bhfuil dul amudha mór orainn atá sgríobhnóir úr againn a árdóchas an Ghaedhilg go hárd i gcúrsaí litridheachta. Dánaidhe é, go barra a mhéar, dar linn. Nach breagh ó'n nGaedhilg freagra a thabhairt ar lucht a cáinte? Atá spionnadh innti dólam agus sgothfa sí a hascath leis an aimsir. Seachnaimís nach bhfuil sí dá sgothadh cheana féin. Muna bhfuil, atá sí ag baint searradh na sláinte aisti féin agus ar chromadh dí ar an gcoimhlinnt dá ríre chuirfe a brígh iongantas ar dhaoine.

89 Tá treoir ag sgríbhnóirí Gaedhilge i dtrom-dhrámuíocht anois nach raibh aca go dtí seo.

90 Is mór an dul amú atá ar an ughdar má cheapann sé gur mar sin a mhaireann muinntir an Iarthair ná más smaointe den tsórt sin a bhíos acu. Dorchadas a aigne féin atá á léiriú ag an ughdar, tá faithchíos orm. Tá a intinn ag imirt cleas air mar d'imrigh intinn Singe cleas air agus é ag scríobh dráma in 'atmosphere' an Iarthair. O'Flaherty never lost his idiosyncratic identification with the West of his birth. See, for example, his letter to the editor of the *Irish Statesman* defending the Gaeltacht against Oliver St John Gogarty's charge, made in the Free State Senate, that it was 'decadent'. The letter concluded disingenuously: 'I am not quite sure, but I am almost positive that not one single character in *Ulysses* comes from the West of Ireland' (*IS*, 10/3/27). It should be noted that Gogarty himself seems to have only attracted the attention of Irish-Irelanders for what they felt was his hostility to the language in the Free State Senate.

91 Má tá an ceart agam sa tuairim seo ní fuláir nó ba é an 'múineadh' do cheap an t-ughdar, acht, an t-é chífeadh an dráma. go mbadh ró-bheag leis críoch d'á dhonacht do bhreith ar mhuintir na h-Éireann idir óg agus sean, mar nárbh' aon deagh-chríoch do bhí tuillte aca. Molaim é go h-ard a chlisteacht, bheachtacht, do chuir sé an múineadh sin abhaile. Ní'l le rádh agam leis an mhuintir ar chuir sé abhaile orra é acht – 'bíodh san agaibh, agus léigheadh agus ath-léigheadh é mar cheacht bhur leasa dhíbh.' 'Cleite' also praised the play for its honesty and force:

> If one judges 'Darkness' as a symbol of the new art, it is a good play, a powerful play. The dialogue is forceful and vigorous and the play keeps hold of the audience's interest throughout. Indeed that interest becomes so sharp at times that it distresses the mind a bit (Má bhreithnítear 'Dorchadas' do réir fáthchomhartha na nua-ealadhnaidheachta, dráma comhachtach iseadh é. Tá an t-agallamh go bríomhar fuinneamhach agus coinnigheann an cluiche greim ar an tsuim ag an lucht éisteachta tríd síos, arae, téigheann an tsuim sin chomh mór i ngéire ar uairibh go ngoilleann sé ar an aigne beagán).

'Cleite' concluded by welcoming O'Flaherty's '"áirithidheacht" nó "realism"' as an important new development in writing in Irish (*II*, 2/3/26). For a discussion of the controversy over *Dorchadas*, see Ó Broin, *Just Like Yesterday*, 70; and Ó Siadhail, *Stair Dhrámaíocht na Gaeilge*, 65.

92 In 'Slán le Scéalaidhe' (Farewell to a storyteller), his tribute to Pádraic Ó Conaire, Tomás Ó Cléirigh commented that, unlike another Galway writer, Ó Conaire did not sell out to English. There can be little doubt he had O'Flaherty in mind. See Ó Cléirigh, 'Slán le Scéalaidhe', in *Seoidíní Cuimhne*, 130.

93 Sean O'Faolain, *The Irish* (West Drayton: Penguin, 1947), 130.

94 See O'Faolain, *Vive Moi!* (Boston: Little, Brown, 1963), 138–42.

95 Caillteanas iongantach don teangaidh iseadh Peadar Ó Domhnaill, Seán Ó Faoláin, Proinnsias Ó Conchubhair agus Seán Ó Cathasaigh. Chaitheadar a ndúthracht ag cur snais ar litridheacht an Bhéarla. D'éirigh leo thar cionn, agus tá a gcáil faoi'n saoghal mór. Ach is bocht an sgéal ag an nGaedhilg é.

96 Maurice Harmon, *Sean O'Faolain: A Critical Introduction* (Notre Dame: University of Notre Dame Press, 1966), xv.

97 O'Faolain, *Vive Moi!*, 132. See also Maurice Harmon, *Sean O'Faolain: A Life* (London: Constable, 1994), 39–41, 43–5, 63–4.

98 The essay on Ó Bruadair was an excerpt from his MA thesis for the Department of Irish at UCC, where he did the Honours Course in Irish, including lectures in Old and Middle Irish, as one of his minor concentrations. See Harmon, *Sean O'Faolain: A Life*, 46–7. In 1926, Ó Faoláin published an essay in English entitled 'An Irish Dominican Poet (Pádraigín Haicéad, 1600–1654)' (*IR*, Jan. 1926, 52–9).

99 As late as April 1926, *Iris an Fháinne* listed Ó Faoláin as one of those giving lectures to the Cork branch of the organisation (*IF*, Apr. 1926, 26).

100 Is é mo thuaraim go mbadh cheart go mbeadh an Gaedheal chomh cruaidh air féin agus atá an Gall, ach nuair a léim aistí as Ghaedhilg de'n tsaghas san thuas [aiste Mhic Grianna ar na filí Ultacha] tuigtear dom go bhfuilimíd a bhad [*sic*] ró-bhog orainn féin fá láthair . . . Má tá an chuid eile de léigheann Gaedhilgeoirí na haimsire seo chomh leamh sin . . . má's é sin an chéim is aoirde ar féidir leo maireachtaint air, is baoghal liom go beadh an ceart ag an Gall adeirfeadh gur fuirist an Gaodhal do shásamh . . . Ach ní féidir aon éifeacht do bheith in aiste adeireann a leithéid sin: agus dá mbadh as Beurla a bhi sé dob ionainne agus aiste ar 'Filí Móra na nGall' ag d'iarraidh [*sic*] a chruthú nár buadhadh riamh ar Rudyard Kipling mar fhile. His comments drew angry rebuttals from both Mac Grianna (*FL*, 21/11/25) and his brother

Séamus (*FL*, 31/10/25). In a comment on Corkery's review of Thomas O'Rahilly's edition of *Laoithe Cumainn* (*IS*, 22/8/25), Ó Faoláin was critical of what he saw as an undue fascination with eighteenth-century Gaelic poetry in preference to superior literature from other periods. It should, however, be noted that his remarks on Corkery himself were quite temperate in this piece: 'Even Daniel Corkery, who has probably done more than anyone of his period to give a true picture of the eighteenth century he loves so well, has sacrificed the main body of Irish literature to the nearer portion . . .' (*IS*, 5/9/25).

101 Needless to say, his comments precipitated an immediate debate in the letter columns of *IS*. Among those involved were Úna Bean Uí Dhíosca, Frank O'Connor and Seosamh Mac Grianna. While conceding a little to Ó Faoláin, Mac Grianna remained, as usual, a Gaeltacht partisan.

102 O'Faolain, *King of the Beggars* (Swords: Poolbeg Press, 1980 [1938]), 21.

103 *Ibid.*, 27.

104 In a 1929 letter to Edward Garnett he wrote:

> I beg of you to understand that my father and mother tore the soil with their hands but I have torn myself out of their blighted, blinded, uncivilised, intolerant, shutminded tradition at no small cost to my nature and my immortal soul . . . have I not warned you I am an Anglo-Irishman now? (Ó Faoláin, quoted by Harmon in *Sean O'Faolain: A Life*, 90).

105 In this letter Ó Faoláin saw his cultural and political differences with Corkery as a battle between 'Mr Corkery's generation' and 'my own generation, which is not Mr. Corkery's generation'.

106 In his biography of Markiewicz, Ó Faoláin wrote of the League: 'The Gaelic League, for example, was a weird and wearisome hinterland.' See O'Faolain, *Constance Markievicz* (London: Sphere Books, n.d. [1934]), 78.

107 Corkery had beaten Ó Faoláin for the chair at Cork, a defeat Ó Faoláin took badly. See Harmon, *Sean O'Faolain: A Life*, 90–5. As a member of the Irish Academy of Letters, Ó Faoláin served regularly on the committee for the O'Growney Prize for writing in Irish. See Harmon, *Sean O'Faolain: A Life*, 105.

108 In his 1939 essay 'Our Critics Are at Fault', Ó Faoláin ignored Gaelic writers and critics altogether, discussing only Irish writers who worked in English (*IP*, 12/1/39). To be fair, he did discuss writing in Irish in other pieces like 'Songs We Should Sing' (*IP*, 1/6/37) and 'City Irish and Country Irish' (*IP*, 20/9/39), although most Gaels would have been horrified by many if not most of the opinions he expressed.

109 See also, 'Anglo-Irish Literature / Pleas for State Recognition / Bounty on Books', *II*, 1/2/36; Seán Ó Ciarghusa, 'The Hidden Ireland', *Leader*, 10/4/37; 'D.', 'Book Lore', *Féile na nGaedheal*, Aug. 1937, 6; 'Imtheachta na nGaedheal / An Irish-Ireland Commentary / A Position Made Clear', *Cork Weekly Examiner*, 8/10/38. On the other hand, O'Connor was praised lavishly by M. K. McNevin for his literary bilingualism in 'Impressions of the Cork Conference', *An Leabharlann*, Sept. 1933, 8–9. It was probably O'Connor's barbed (though doubtless usually accurate and just) reviews of Gaelic plays in the *Irish Statesman* that won him the most enemies among the Gaels. See, for example, his heated exchange of letters with the playwright Séamus de Bhilmot and others in *IS* in late 1929 and early 1930. We will return to this subject in the next chapter.

110 Ó Ciosáin, 'An Bheirt Intleachtóirí', in *Sgéalta cois Laoi*, 75–84. O'Connor defended himself against some Gaelic charges against him in a letter in Irish to *IP* published under the title '"Renegades" an Acadaimh Nua' (The renegades of the new Academy) (*IP*, 23/9/32). Gaels must, however, have been outraged by his 1928 *IS* review of Séamus Ó hAodha's poetry collection *Uaigneas* (Loneliness), where he wrote:

> Modern Irish is a desert so far as literature is concerned. It seems extraordinary that of the number of books published in Irish during the past ten years, scarcely one can be said to have any literary value whatever (*IS*, 17/3/28).

On the other hand, in a review in 1932, P. S. O'Hegarty called O'Connor's novel *The Saint and Mary Kate* 'a real addition to Irish literature' (*Dublin Magazine*, Oct.–Dec. 1932, 70). In his centennial history of the Gaelic League, Proinsias Mac Aonghusa points outs that O'Connor was still involved with the League as late as 1962, only four years before his death. See Mac Aonghusa, *Ar Son na Gaeilge*, 323.

111 Ní gádh mórán a rádh faoi an leabhar seo le Peadar Ó Domhnaill, mar tá eolas maith ag cách ar a shaothar. Tá an cur síos annseo ar mhuinntir an oileáin go réidhe simplidhe, mar is gnáth le cur síos an ughdair a bheith i gcomhnaidhe . . . Ní hé an rud atá suarach i nádúr na mbocht atá tugtha amach go soiléir ach na tréithre uaisle saoitheamhla atá insna Gaedhil in áit ar bith atá fágtha mar an t-oileán atá i gceist 'sa sgéal.

112 'Sé mo thuairim ná féadfaí leabhar d'fhagháil a thiubhrfadh [*sic*] tuarasgabháil chomh cruinn agus chomh breagh leis ar na daoinibh agus ar a mbéasaibh agus nósaibh.

113 His principal opponent in this debate was Liam Ó Rinn, who argued that urban poverty was a problem that had to be faced on its own dreadful terms and that poor children had just as much right to their national heritage as did the better-off members of their generation (*IS*, 24/1/25). O'Casey responded to Ó Rinn two weeks later, beginning with a childish jibe about his choosing to write in Irish (*IS*, 7/2/25).

114 See also 'S. L.', 'The Insincerity of Sean O'Casey', *An Phoblacht*, 19/2/26; and Manus O'Donnell (Maoghnus Ó Domhnaill), 'The Shadow of a Dramatist / Drams and Dramas', *An Phoblacht*, 24/9/26.

115 Ó Ciarghusa, 'Dráma Gaedheal', in *Ar Mo Mharanadh Dam*, 132. De réir deallraimh, is é fuadar atá fé dhrámadóiribh Beurla i nÉirinn fé láthair ná saoghal na 'slums' do léiriú ar an ardán. Ní thaithnigheann drámai de'n tsórt liom féin. Ní thaithigheann muinntear bhocht na 'slums' an amharclann agus ní ceart, – agus ní cneasta go h-áirighthe – dar liomsa, iad féin agus a saoghal do léiriú d'aon ghnó mar adhbhar suilt do dhream sotlach, sásta an tsaidhbhris a bhíonn ag cogaint seaclait agus ag deunamh grinn díobh ar a sógh. On the other hand, 'Emer' wrote of *The Plough and the Stars* in 1927 that it was 'great . . . coarse, crude and dismal, but . . . very true to the life in the slums' (*Leader*, 1/10/27). According to Joseph Holloway's diaries, Pádraic Ó Conaire initially thought *The Shadow of a Gunman* was 'a revue not a play', and in 1925 was capable of drunkenly 'railing against O'Casey's plays not being drama'. See *Joseph Holloway's Abbey Theatre: A Selection from the Unpublished Journal 'Impressions of a Dublin Playgoer'* ed. Robert Hogan and Michael J. O'Neill (Carbondale: Southern Illinois University Press, 1967), 216, 244. On the other hand, in 1927, Ó Conaire expressed sympathy with O'Casey over the troubles he was having with Abbey audiences who disliked *The Plough and the Stars* (*CS*, 8/3/27). In 1930, the request of a Mrs McDermott to rent its theatre from Taibhdhearc na Gaillimhe for an O'Casey play was rejected. In the minutes for the meeting of 17 Apr. 1930, the secretary added parenthetically that the board acted 'properly' (le ceart). See Taibhdhearc Papers, NUIG Add. MS 58.

116 Dhein cluichí Sheáin Uí Chathasaigh mórán maitheasa do'n Amharclainn, ach nuair a chuir sé a cheapachán deiridh, 'An Cuaichín Airgid', chúcha níor bhfiú leo é chur ar an stáitse. Ghabhadar de chosaibh ann.

117 Ní bhainid linn agus níor bhaineadar riamh linn. Agus pé 'cu a cuirfear an 'Silver Tassie' ar ardán na Mainistreach nó ná cuirfear, is ró-shuarach a bheidh caillte ag Gaedhil Bhaile Átha Cliath. Tá go leor salachar sa 'Silver Tassie' agus tá súil agam ná feicfear go bráth ar ardán é sa phríomh-chathair ársa so.

118 In another piece the following year, Nuala Moran wrote:

> Neither do we deny that O'Casey's unpleasant characters are true to Irish life. They are. Human nature being what it is, we Irish are as capable of making beasts of ourselves as another nation. But why can our native writers only see our bad side? Why harp always on our weaknesses? (*Leader*, 6/6/36).

119 The motion was passed with 'only one person, a visitor, opposing it' (duine amháin, cuairteoir, i n-a choinne).

120 Nach eisean féin oighre na bhfile is na sean-chaidhthe is na staraidhthe a chlaoidh le léigheann agus litridheacht a dtíre dhá mhéid corraíghle agus anfhorlainne bhíodh ann le'n a linn.

121 Ó Ciarghusa, 'Dráma Gaedheal', in *Ar Mo Mharanadh Dam*, 106. Is deacair a chur i n-iúl cad is dúthchas Gaedheal mar sin ann ach ta sé, is dóigh liom-sa, in 'An Pósadh' ('An Craoibhín'), in 'Ó Failbhe Mór' agus in 'An Bunán Buidhe' (Domhnall Ó Corcra) – cé gur i mBeurla do ceud-cheapadh an dá cheann deireannacha sin.

122 See '"A Gigantic Vested Interest"', the report of this lecture in *IP*, 13/11/37. See also Shán Ó Cuív's lengthy and laudatory review of *The Hidden Ireland*, *IR*, June 1925, 409–15. In 1918, Corkery himself defended his use of English against the insistence of his friend Terence MacSwiney that he should write exclusively in Irish. See Maume, 66. But he was later to dismiss his own work in English as 'part and parcel of English literature', and to say of *An Doras Dúnta* (The closed door): 'This play of mine in Irish I reckon as having more significance than all that I have done in English.' See Maume, 124, 126.

123 See de Blácam, *Gentle Ireland: An Account of a Christian Culture in History and Modern Life* (Milwaukee: Bruce Publishing Co., 1935), 145–7. See also 'Feste', 'Gaelic Plays at the Abbey', *IS*, 23/2/24.

124 He was reviewing Micheál Ó Floinn's translation of *The Threshold of Quiet* as *Log an Chiúnis*.

125 Ta tréith na h-ard-íomáighneachta ag Domhnall Ó Corcora níos treise ná ag aon scríobhnóir Éireannach eile d'ár linn . . . D'á aimhdheoin sin (nó, b'fhéidir, d'á bharr sin), ní h-é an drámaidhe ná an scéalaidhe is fearr againn é. Beódhann sé smaointe arda, mionla, dubhacha i n-aigne an léightheóra; acht na pearsain a chruthuigheann sé i n-a chuid leabhar, ní de'n chine daonna iad . . . 'Duine ann féin' is eadh gach duine i n-a chuid leabhar. Deineann sé iarracht ar iad do thabhairt anuas chun go dtuigfeadh an choitchianntacht iad. Teipeann air. Tugadh sé fé'n choitchianntacht do thabhairt aníos ar dhréimire na filidheachta chun na n-uasal. Ní fhuil aon tslighe eile ann, agus is í sin a chéard.

126 Actually in his piece in *II* (16/6/36), Tierney had been quite critical of Corkery.

127 Agus maidir le drámaí T. C. Uí Mhuireadhaigh níl aon aimhreas nach bhfuil siad fíor-fheileamhnach don Ghaedhilg. Cé gur i mBéarla a scríobhadh i dtosach iad sé an saoghal Gaedhealach agus an aigne Ghaedhealach atá i gceist ionnta. Níl aon drámadóir Éireannach eile ann a bhfuil an dúthchas agus an nádúr céadna ann. An chaint féin atá ionnta nach leaganacha Gaedhilge cuid mhór dí? Murray was, however, chided by Seán Ó Ciarghusa for saying nothing about the language in a 1922 lecture to the Catholic Truth Society (*Leader*, 21/10/22). On occasion, Murray shared his views on literature with Irish-Irelanders. See, for example, his 'The Twilight of Our Theatre' in *An Ráitheachán*, Sept. 1936, 7–8. Many of those cultural nationalists must, however, have been dismayed by his comments in 1937:

> Hapless circumstance has made of us an English speaking people and however passionately men may long for the ideal of a purely Gaelic-speaking, Gaelic-thinking Ireland, only those blinded by their own vision could reasonably look to its fulfilment. The whole trend of modern life is sufficient to extinguish the most ardent hope in that direction (*IP*, 13/4/37).

128 Dar liom-sa, ba neamh-nídh imirce na n-Éigeas nGaedheal seachas ar fhan díobh bheith ag scríobhadh Béarla, agus is láidrede ar an dtuairim sin mé 'Ath-Bharra' T.C. Uí Mhuirighthe d'fheiscint d'á léiriughadh san Mainistir.

129 Adéarfainn féin, cé gur olc liom an Béarla do cháineadh, go bhfuil an iomad maoine is saothar 'á gcailleamhaint againn le saothrughadh litridheacht an Bhéarla le sna ciantaibh, agus nach fiú an toradh atá againn aiste an méid sin cailleamhna.

130 Corkery, *Synge*, 23. See also Corkery, 'How She Stands', *Guth na nGaedheal*, 1928, 6–9; and 'The Colonial Branch of Anglo-Irish Literature', *IP*, 21/4/37. See also 'Hours of Interest / A Challenge to a Great Book', an anonymous essay defending *Synge and Anglo-Irish Literature* against hostile reviews (*FMR*, Feb. 1932, 83–5). Corkery discussed the decision of some Irish writers to seek an audience abroad with understanding and dispassionate clarity in 1931, the very year his *Synge* was published, writing:

> I think it is too lightly assumed that all such Irishmen as the late Donn Byrne, for instance, who take to writing for a non-native public do so entirely from monetary considerations. I think that the fact that they find themselves drawn towards an arena where criticism has long, long since found its feet, where it is stablilised, counts as much with them as the money or even fame. It is only writers themselves who understand what a help or a hindrance it is, that unknown, that unseen, yet half-comprehended public for whom one writes (Corkery, quoted by Maume, 117).

131 For similar expressions of the belief among Irish-Irelanders that Irish writers of English pandered to foreign audiences while writers of Irish sacrificed the rewards of fame and fortune for a higher cause, see 'An Irish Play / A Valuable Text Book for Students', *Clare Champion*, 8/11/30; and 'Editorial / The Pollexfen Peacock Parade', *CB*, Oct. 1932, 773–5. On the other hand, in a 1936 lecture to secondary schoolteachers, P. Ó Cinnéide suggested that An Gúm, instead of wasting money on translations, should fund generous prizes to entice Irish writers of English to produce work in Irish (*II*, 15/4/36).

132 Má theastuigheann ó dhrámadóir Éireannach airgead agus clú a thuilleamh, ní mór dó daoine a cheapadh a thaithneóchaidh leis na Sasanaigh nó leis na 'Meiriocánaigh. Tá an *stage-Irishman* imthighthe ach má tá féin, tá duine chomh holc leis againn in inead. Tá an t-*Informer* againn. In an interesting article in 1936, Frank O'Connor stated that Gaelic authors 'wrote for an entirely uncritical Government Department [An Gúm]', while 'the Irish writer who uses English had to write for the critical Anglo-American public, who considered his nationality a drawback' (*II*, 1/2/36). See also Ó Faoláin, 'Let Ireland Pride [*sic*] – In What She Has', *IP*, 2/4/37. Peadar O'Donnell argued that a primary reason Irish writers of English published abroad was because of the cowardice of Irish publishers when offered challenging material. See O'Donnell, 'Between Two Worlds', *Inis Fáil*, Mar. 1933, 34.

133 Maidir le scríbhneoirí Béarla ní beag a bhfuil againn díobh ach ós rud é go gceapann an gnáth-Éireannach gur airgead curtha amú gach pingin a caitear ar leabhra ní fheadar an ceart dúinn a rá gur linne iad – mara mbeadh na Sasanaigh ní fhéadfaidís maireachtaint, rud atá chó fíor san gur i Sasana chomhnuíonn a lán aca. He went on to say that the Anglo-Irish were, in his opinion, 'the only people in Ireland . . . who cultivate the arts (an t-aon dream amháin in Éirinn a chothuíonn na h-ealadhna), and the people without whom Irish painters, for example, could not even eke out what living they did in the Ireland of the time. Writing in 1923, 'Querist', who claimed to be in no way 'opposed to Gaelic', but rather 'filled with a spirit of reasonable scientific enquiry', offered what he doubtless believed to be an objective analysis of the situation:

> Now if a man of genius can choose whether he will write in a language spoken by three million people, few of whom have acquired a habit of reading, or in a language spoken by nearly two hundred million people, including his own countrymen, what language will he choose? (*IS*, 29/9/23).

One 'Fiach' saw Irish reluctance to recognise an Irish artist until he had won acclaim abroad as symptomatic of 'the political and mental slavery of a big proportion of our people and the Press which caters for them' (*An Phoblacht*, 27/11/25).

134 Is fíor – 'sé ár léan é – nach bhfuil luach saothair maith do sgríbhneoirí Gaedhilge. Maille le hairgead ní féidir an Ghaedhilg agus an Béarla a chur i gcomórtas le n-a chéile. Tá milliún Béarlóir ann in aghaidh gach cúig céad Gaedhilgeoir. Ná bíodh ár súil le hairgead . . . ach an obair mhór atá roimh na sgríbhneoirí ní spreacfaidh an t-airgead chuige iad. Muna spreacfaidh an grádh tíre chuige iad, agus muna mbrostuighe an chaoi a bhfuil Éire chuige iad beidh ár súil le Gaedhilg mar a bhí súil Uí Dhubhda le hArd na Ríogh. In a set of his lecture notes under the title of 'Éigse na h-Aimsire Seo – Sraith Nua 1928–1930' (Contemporary literature – NS 1928–30), Ó Máille wrote:

> There are people (like 'Brinsley McNamara') who increase the faults of the Irish for the sake of making a good, strong story. cf. The Playboy of

the Western World. Most likely it is not done out of malice, but only that they fail to create a good story without so much exaggeration. That is something that I call counting up the misery (Tá daoine {ar nós 'Brinsley McNamara'} a mhéaduigheas ar lochta na nÉireannach de ghrádh sgéal maith feidheamhail a dhéanamh amach. cf. Buachaill Imeartha Iarthair Dhomhan. Is dócha nach le mailís a déantar é ach amháin go cinneann se orrú sgéal maith a cheapadh gan an oiread sin áidhbhéil. Sin rud ar a dtugaimse comhaireamh na hanachana) (Tomás Ó Máille Papers, NLI MS G 1108).

135 Nuair a thug Pádraic Ó Conaire a ghnaoi agus a ghean do litridheacht na Gaedhilge, chaith sé uaidh an sógh agus an saidhbhreas a bheadh aige go cinnte dá mba rud é go gclaonfadh sé le sgríobhadh i mBéarla mar rinne go leor leor Éireannach eile roimhe. Cá bhfuil an duine sin in ár measg a chaithfeadh uaidh, do mhaol a mháinge féin, saidhbhreas agus iolmhaitheas an tsaoghail mar rinne seisean.

136 Ní féidir le scríobhnóirí Gaedhilge maireachtaint ar shaothar a phinn [*sic*] san saoghal atá anois ann. Dá scríobhadh 'Máire' i mBéarla do bheadh trácht air. Tig leis é dhéanamh ar fheabhas na cruinne, acht ní dhéanfadh . . . Sgéalta iad uilig agus dá sgríobhtai i mBéarla iad bheadh gaigíní na tíre ag iarraidh lámh a chrothadh leis an ughdar. 'An Giolla Dubh' also asked pointedly: 'Is there any other group of people inhabiting any country under the sun who would be content to make a civil servant – an automatic totter – of the best writer they had' (Bhfuil aon aicme eile daoine áitreabhtha in aon tír fé luighe na gréine a bheadh sásta stát-seirbhíseach – automatic totter – a dhéanamh de'n scríbhneoir is fearr aca). In 1936, Ernest Blythe worried that 'the talented young authors are having all enthusiasm squeezed out of them and are, in certain cases, apparently being driven over to the writing of English (*II*, 16/12/36).

137 In this letter he stated he had started writing in English because he wanted to express important ideas on politics to the Irish people, who could not or would not have read them had he published them in Irish. He also commented on his brief return to the writing of Irish in the mid-1920s, disingenuously comparing himself to George Moore in his role as saviour of Irish. Curiously enough, however, what seems to have stuck with him most about his play *Dorchadas* was

> the only remuneration I received was from an English Socialist who dislikes Irish and everything connected with nationalism of any sort in any place. He paid me twenty five pounds for the Gaelic manuscript, i.e. for my handwriting (*IS*, 17/12/27).

O'Flaherty was responding here to a brief comment by 'AE' to a letter writer from New York, who suggested O'Flaherty wrote in English because of the inadequacies of Irish as a vehicle of modern life. 'AE' rejected this idea, stating:

> Mr O'Flaherty probably desired to be published and read. We doubt if he could have found either publisher or readers for his realistic novel. At present the books for schools are the only books in Irish sure of a swift sale (*IS*, 19/11/27).

When two weeks later, Úna Bean Uí Dhíosca wrote a letter on this controversy, wondering whether O'Flaherty gave up writing in Irish because 'he was not competent' to do so or 'for monetary reasons as you suggest', 'AE' took the opportunity to clarify his previous comments:

> We did not suggest that Liam O'Flaherty wrote his tales in English for monetary reasons, but because he wished what he wrote to be published and read. Our correspondent should not insinuate a meaning which was not intended (*IS*, 3/12/27).

The comments of Bean Uí Dhíosca seem to have particularly annoyed O'Flaherty, provoking him to make two nasty and gratuitous comments about her surname and national allegiance in his letter of 19 November. She was defended by P. J. McDonnell, who took exception in terms worthy of Mac Grianna:

> Every conquered country has the misfortune to produce creatures of the O'Flaherty type – a swarm of toadies, flunkies and gombeen-men . . . Though not writing for money, he has the gombeen-man's instinct of knowing how it is to be got. Play down to the self-love of the English by blackening your own people (*IS*, 31/12/27).

138 Nár chóir leabhra Beurla a bhfuil spiorad na Gaedhilge ionntu aistriú ar dtús? Tá fir againn fhéin a sgríobh as Beurla agus a d'fhág aithne an Cheiltigh sa tSac-litríocht. Céard faoi Uilliam Ó Briain, faoi'n gCanónach Ó Síothcháin, faoi Dhomhnall Ó Corcordha nó faoi go leor eile nach iad? Céard faoi aistriúchán ar 'When We Were Boys' nó ar 'The Blindness of Dr Gray?' Duine a léigh sa' mBeurla iad is i n-a shean-rith a thiubhras sé aith-léigheamh sa' nGaedhilge orthu. Both Sheehan and O'Brien were translated into Irish in our period.

139 See also 'D. Ó D.', 'Na hAisteoirí / Deireadh le Ré Aistriúcháin' (Na hAisteoirí / An end to the age of translation), *Leader*, 26/3/27.

140 Sgéal a chlaonann leis an nGaedhilg is eadh é, agus fá lámhaibh an tsáir-chéardaidhe úd Seosamh Mac Grianna is ar éigin nach bhfuil innseacht níos fearr ar an leabhar san nGaedhilg.

141 Tá an sgéal céadna níos feileamhnaighe don Ghaedhilge ná don Bhéarla, agus dá bhrígh sin in áit tada dá maiseamhlacht a chailleadh sa tiontú is amhlaidh a tháinig ann dó.

142 *Desecration*, a play written by Jeremiah Murphy, translated into Irish by Tomás Ó Máille as *Milleadh* and performed at Taibhdhearc na Gaillimhe in 1934, was based on Corkery's story 'The Ploughing of Leaca-na-Naomh'.

143 For a discussion of Ó Cadhain's battle with An Gúm over this translation, and for Alan Titley's opinion of its importance, see An tSr. Boscó Costigan and Seán Ó Curraoin, *De Ghlaschloich an Oileáin*, 25–6. For other translations of Kickham, see Conchubhar Ó Muimhneacháin's Gaelic version of 'White Humphrey of the Grange' as 'Amhlaoibh Bán na Gráinsighe' in the *Irish Monthly*, Jan.–June 1933; and 'Eachtra Mháire Ní Mheachair sa Bhliain '98 a Thárla' (The adventure of Mary Meagher that happened in the year '98), *Irish Monthly*, Aug.–Sept. 1933.

144 In a 1939 essay expressing his appreciation of Irish writing in English, Liam Ó Briain suggested that the revived Oireachtas fund a competition for the best translation of 'twenty-odd of the poems most beautiful and filled with the national spirit . . . from the poetry of Yeats and his followers' (fiche éigin de na duanta is áilne agus is líonta den spiorad náisiúnta . . . as filíocht Yeats agus a lucht leanúna) (*Leader*, 30/12/39).

145 Go dtí go mbeidh sgríbhneoirí sa tír a bheidheas i ndon drámaí Gaedhilge a sgríobh is mór an gar a leithide a bheith againn.

146 At a meeting of the board of An Taibhdhearc on 30 Nov. 1929, 'the following plays were recommended (moladh na drámaí seo a leanas). The Bribe. The Building Fund. Spreading the News. The Siulear's [*sic*] Child. The Drone. Charlie's Aunt.' In 1931, an Taibhdhearc was considering staging translations of, among others, *Androcles and the Lion*, *Shuiler's Child*, *Autumn Fires* [*sic*], and *Riders to the Sea*. See Add. MS 22, Taibhdhearc na Gaillimhe Papers, NUIG.

147 A scene from Sheridan's *The Rivals* entitled *Comhrac Éinfhir* (Single combat) as translated by Piaras Béaslaí and Risteárd Ó Foghludha was performed at the Abbey in November 1928.

148 For the programme of the April 1934 production of this play by the Gaelic League of London, Murray himself prepared a synopsis of the plot in English. See T. C. Murray Papers, NLI MS 24,969.

149 Nioclás Tóibín's translation of P. Kehoe's *When Wexford Rose* as *'Nuair d'Adhnamar an Gleo': Éacht d'Éachtaibh a '98: Dráma Aon-Ghníomha* was a popular entertainment at *feiseanna* in Wexford in the 1930s. The play was published by An Gúm in 1936.

150 He wrote: Agus fhaid is bhéas an Béarla agus sgríbhneoirí an Bhéarla, in ann riachtainisí liteardha na ndaoine is mó tuigsint sa tír shású, agus an fhaid is bhéas a bhfuil de neart agus de láidreacht is de nuaghluaiseacht litríochta sa tír ghá dtabhairt féin do'n Bhéarla, beidh an Ghaedhilg go lag is go mí-éifeachtach.

151 Ba dhóich leat uaireanta ná raibh sa Ghaedhilg is i litríocht na Gaedhilge acht rudaí atá ann d'aon ghnó chun maitheas do dhéanamh do'n Bhéarla . . . Bíonn an scríbhneoir Béarla mar bheadh faolchú amplach ag lorg adhbhar leabhair agus is cuma leis cá bhfuighe sé é.

152 For a clear indication of his ambivalence toward O'Grady, see 'Standish Ó Gráda agus Stair na hÉireann' (Standish O'Grady and Irish history), *Humanitas*, Mar. 1930, 10–12.

CHAPTER EIGHT

At the Cow's Rump or in the National Theatre?

1 This chapter will not offer an analysis of individual plays, many of which have been discussed in relevant sections of the book. Nor is it intended as an institutional history of the Gaelic theatre, its financing, relations with the state, etc. for which see Pádraig Ó Siadhail's *Stair Dhrámaíocht na Gaeilge*.

2 There were, of course, some in the language movement who, with whatever reservations, appreciated the work of the Abbey. See, for example, 'Abbey Theatre Comes of Age / Work for the Nation / Tribute by Minister', *II*, 28/12/25 (the Minister in question was Blythe); León Ó Broin, 'An Dráma Náisiúnta' (The national drama), *II*, 31/5/26; 'W. X.', 'Gaelic Plays / The Aisteoirí', *Eaglaiseach Gaedhealach*, Dec. 1926, 99; 'Thespis', 'Amharclann na Mainistreach' (The Abbey Theatre), *Star*, 4/1/30. Both the Abbey and the Gate were spoken of favourably in a 1930 editorial in *The Star* entitled 'Enriching Dublin Life' (*Star*, 22/2/30), and by Gearóid Ó Lochlainn in 'Staid na h-Amharclainne i nÉirinn' (The state of the theatre in Ireland), in *Aistí Gaedhilge*, 50. In Riobárd Ó Faracháin's story 'An Feall Gránna' (The ugly betrayal), the protagonist is a fan of the Abbey. See Ó Faracháin, 'An Feall Gránna', in *Fíon gan Mhoirt*, 38.

3 He continued: 'Its writers were accustomed always to keep their eyes on Dublin rather than on Ireland; now, however, they have learned to keep their eyes on London.'

4 Is cosamhail go bhfuil ré a héifeachta caithte ag an ngluaiseacht san féin, agus dá chomhartha san, féach go bhfuil an dream céadna san ag tarrac drámaí Gaedhilge chúcha cheana féin. Ní foláir nó go mbraithid duibheagán ag teacht idir iad féin agus an pobal agus go measaid na drámaí Gaedhilge seo do bheith mar dhroichead acu ar eagla ná geobhadh an pobal i leith chúcha. In October 1939, the English Literature Society of UCD debated the motion 'that the Abbey does not fill the place of a national theatre'. Those supporting the motion stressed that 'the Irish language was necessary as a medium for the claim to national status' (*IP*, 25/10/39).

5 This quotation is, of course, from the original manifesto of the Irish Literary Theatre. See Lady Gregory, *Our Irish Theatre* (New York: Capricorn, 1965 [1913]), 9.

6 See also 'Muck-Raking in the Abbey', *An Phoblacht*, 19/2/26. The play condemned for

'vulgarity' here was O'Casey's *The Plough and the Stars*.

7 An 'stage Irishman' a bhíodh le feiceál leith-chéad bliadhan ó shoin ar na h-ardáin annseo i mBl' Áth Cliath ba bhreagh glan Gaedhealach na fir iad le h-ais na mbitheamhnach a bhíodh aca i nAmhar-clainn na Mainistreach.' Ó Maoláin was answered by 'L. D.' in a measured article entitled 'Sochar agus Dochar' (Benefit and harm) in the same paper within the week (*IP*, 8/2/39).

8 Tomás Ó Cléirigh, 'Sa gCathair Dom' (In the city), in *Seoidíní Cuimhne*, 39. Na drámaí a bhíos aca; chuirfeadh siad iongnadh ort – baint aca go léir, nach mór, le saoghal na tuaithe agus ní hé amháin sin ach na cinn is iomráidhte dhíobh, baineann siad leis an nGaedhealtacht féin! Bhí sé ag dul díom glan an méid sin a thuigsint go dtí gur mhinigh duine de na Gaedhilgeoirí dhom nach le grádh dúinn a léirightear na drámaí sin ar chor ar bith ach d'fhonn bheith ag spochadh asainn agus a bheith ag magadh fúinn. See also 'Tadhg Gaedhealach', 'Mo Shiubhalta' (My travels), *An Sguab*, Feb. 1926, 27.

9 In a 1936 letter to Liam Ó Briain, Ernest Blythe wrote: 'As it seems to me now, the best way to advance drama in Irish is to provide (slowly and carefully) a company with English and Irish for the Abbey Theatre.' See Blythe to Ó Briain, 2 Feb. 1936; Taibhdhearc Papers, NUIG MS T1/262 (1). De réir mar chídhtear dhom anois, sé an tslí is fearr le drá-muíocht Ghaedhilge do chur ar aghaidh, ná com-placht le Béarla agus Gaedhilg do sholáthair (go mall réidh) d'Amharclainn na Mainistreach. He added that he also wanted 'to establish a permanent company that would perform in Irish only in the Taibhdhearc' (complacht seasta nach léireóchadh ach tríd an nGaedhilg do bhunú sa Taibhdhearc). See also Blythe's remarks as quoted in 'Abbey Theatre Comes of Age', *II*, 28/12/25.

10 Tá muid sáthach fada ag éisteacht le Handy Andy agus a leithéidí. Ba cheart dhúinn rud eicínt fíor-Ghaedhealach a bheith againn ina n-áit.

11 Dá mbeadh leithéid Shakespeare in Éirinn níor bhaoghal do'n teangain.

12 Tá caill nó easbhaidh amháin ar litridheacht na Gaedhilge – agus is mó atá an chaill sin le sonnradh san am i láthair ná bhí ariamh go dtí seo. Tá Filidheacht uasal aoibhinn againn; tá Prós bhreagh fhileamhanta againn, ach, níl Dráma ar bith againn.

13 Quoted by Tomás Ó Cléirigh, 'Siamsaidheacht ag Gaedhealaibh' (Gaelic entertainment), *II*, 7/10/27. According to 'C. C.', the sort of spiritual harmony envisioned here, one created between actors and audiences by the use of the ancestral tongue on stage, was occasionally realised in our period. Writing of a recent performance by An Comhar in 1928, he stated:

> What struck us as important beyond all else was the secret unity of sentiment between author, actors and audience, because of the Irish medium of expression, the rightness, the real-ness, so to speak, of Irish in an Irish subject (*Nation*, 7/4/28).

A rare dissenting voice was that of P. Ó Suibhne, who wrote in a 1939 letter to the *Irish Press*:

> There is too much drama and acting and propa-ganda going on in this country at present . . . At any rate, a dramatic edifice cannot be built on an Irish-language foundation, something that does not exist, nor is there any enthusiasm for it. It is nothing but 'drama' for us to be pretending there is (Iomarca drámuíochta agus aisteoireachta agus propaganda atá ar siubhal 'sa tír seo fé láthair . . . Ar aon chuma ní féidir foirgneamh drámuíochta a thógaint ar bhonn Gaoluinne, rud ná fuil ann, ná sprid chuige ach oiread. Níl ann ach 'drámuíocht' bheith á leogaint orainn go bhfuil) (*IP*, 21/2/39).

14 Gearóid Ó Lochlainn, 'Staid na h-Amharclainne i nÉirinn' (The state of the theatre in Ireland), in *Aistí Gaedhilge*, 54. An tAthair Micheál Ó Murchadha felt this was work in which the Catholic Church should take a leading role. See 'Obair do Shagartaibh' (Work for priests), *IP*, 23/6/37.

15 Tá súil againn go tiocfa siad isteach chugainn, ní hé amháin i ngeall ar an meas mór atá acu ar theangain Naoimh Pádraic is Naoimh Brighid acht i ngeall ar gur mian leo dhul chuig an amharclainn, agus i ngeall gur nádúrtha an rud é, i nGaillimh, bheith ag dul chuig an amharclainn sa nGaedhilg, díreach mar is nádúrtha, i Sébhilla, dhul chuice sa Spáinnis . . . Gléas oideachais amháin dhéanamh den Amharclainn ní bheadh ann acht mí-úsáid. Ar an taoibh eile den sgéal, gléas siamsa is pléaráca amháin dhéanamh dhí, séard bheadh ann práchas dhéanamh de phríomh-chuspóir na hamharclainne, cuspóir nach dtuigeann an chuid is mó den phobal, faraoir. Sé príomh-chuspóir na hamharclainne, mar thuigeamuid an sgéal, eolas ar an áilneacht is ar an saol thabhairt don phobal thríd an dráma. Mac Liammóir went on to express his belief that Gaelic theatre would have to draw on the best models available to it in Europe to develop its own style, and his hope that an appreciative Gaelic audience would evolve in tandem with such a genuine and sophis-ticated dramatic movement. He was, however, clear that even more important than the emergence of a stylish native drama was the creation of 'a discerning audience for Drama in Irish' (lucht éisteachta tuigseanach i gcomhar Dráma na Gaedhilge). To get an idea of Mac Liammóir's commitment to quality productions at An Taibhdhearc, see his letters to Liam Ó Briain in the spring of 1928, Taibhdhearc Papers, NUIG MSS T1/3; T1/6; T1/7. Mac Liammóir was particularly insistent on the importance of artistic lighting. That Ó Briain was in full agreement is evident from a letter he sent at the same time to an official at the Department of Education (T1/14).

16 Is tábhachtaighe an teanga ná an drámaidheacht agus nach leis an nGaedhilge a chur 'un cinn a léirightear drámaí i nGaedhilge?

17 Cabhruíonn an t-amharclann go mór le cúis ar bith a dheineann úsáid de mar ba chóir agus is beag má tá aon chúis go raghadh sé níos mó chun tairfe dhó anois ná cúis na Gaedhilge . . . Bheadh an cluiche as Gaedhilge amháin mar ábhar cleachta do'n mac léighinn ar an gcainnt agus ar an léitheóireacht le chéile. See also 'Saothrú an Dráma' (The cultivation of the drama), Editorial, *II*, 15/11/24.

18 Is beag gléas múinte Gaedhilge atá chomh támhachtach [*sic*] leis an dráma, mar is ann a gheibhtear cúrsaí an lae agus cúrsaí eile nach iad ioncholnuighche [*sic*] i gcainnt ghonta bhlasta . . . 'Siad an t-aos léighinn agus an t-aos foghluma is mó a bhainfeadh tairbhe as an drámuíocht. Chífidís stair ár dtíre aith-bheodhaithe; chífidís cultúr ársa na nGaedheal; agus chloisfidís an Ghaedhilg bhinn d'á spreagadh ó'n ardán le binneas agus le ceart, le blas agus le flúirse.

19 Níl dóigh ar bith is fearr le labhairt na Gaedhilge a chur chun tosaigh ameasc an phobail ná neart drámaí Gaedhilge a chur ar na h-ardáin ar fud na tíre.

20 Pádraic Ó Conaire, 'Do'n Lucht Léighte agus Léirighthe é seo' (This is for the readers and performers), in *Caitlin na Clúide: Dráma Beag Trí-Mhír le Ceol agus Damhsai i gComhair an Aosa Óig* (Kathleen of the Chimney Corner: A little play for the young in three scenes with music and dances) (BÁC: Taisceadán Ádhbhar Léighinn do Sgoileannaibh Éireann, n.d.), 4. Do dhaoine atá ag foghluim teangan, níl aon bhealach níos fearr le faghail ná drámaí a léigheadh, mar bíonn an chainnt bheo san dráma díreach mar labhartar í. Ó Conaire always had a keen interest in drama. See Ní Chionnaith, *Pádraic Ó Conaire*, 446–7; and Riggs, *Pádraic Ó Conaire: Deoraí*, 56. The potential role of drama for language teaching was a frequent theme of 'S. Ó F.' in his regular book columns for *The Standard* throughout 1933. See, for example, his columns for 28/1, 25/2, 13/5 and 17/6/33.

There were some, like 'Theo', who felt that drama might well resolve the battle for dialect supremacy (*Leader*, 20/12/24). See also Feehan, 'Ireland's Real National Theatre', *CB*, Aug. 1938, 652; and Ní Chonceanainn and Ó Coigligh, *Tomás Bán*, 229–30. On the other hand, Shán Ó Cuív worried that the new Gaelic literature and particularly the drama, drawing as it did, at least in Dublin, its players from different Gaeltachtaí, was prematurely engaged in the suppression of dialect differences (*II*, 25/10/32). At times, the mix of dialects spoken by actors on stage seems to have caused problems. See 'D. Ó C.', 'An Taibhdhearc / Togha Dráma Grinn / "An Páistín Fionn"' (A fine comic play / The whiteheaded boy), *CT*, 9/3/35.

21 For the history of this organisation, see Donncha Ó Súilleabháin, *An Cumann Scoildrámaíochta 1934–1984* (BÁC: An Clóchomhar, 1986). No fewer than 4,000 people attended the Cumann's first festival in Dublin in 1934, 'and hundreds had to be turned away' (*II*, 23/6/34). State support included permission to use published plays as textbooks and to consider play rehearsals as part of the language curriculum. See 'Féile Náisiúnta Drámaidheachta' (A national drama festival), *IP*, 12/5/36. Eighty per cent of Irish schools were involved with the work of An Cumann in 1938, and 6,000 Dublin students attended the festival that year. Plays were judged by age group, with a special category for Gaeltacht schools. See '"An Fhéile ar Fhearr"' (The best festival), *IP*, 7/3/38. That school productions could be fairly ambitious is evident from the comments in *IP* on an upcoming performance of a Gaelic version of *Ben Hur* at the North Monastery in Cork City. See '"Ben-Hur" sa Ghaedhilg' (*Ben Hur* in Irish), *IP*, 30/1/37.

22 According to the favourable review by 'P. B.' (doubtless Piaras Béaslaí), this was seen as the first of many such handbooks, none of which, however, appeared (*IP*, 10/12/38).

23 This was an important development for many in the movement who worried about the lack of any theatrical tradition or interest in rural Ireland. See, for example, Micheál Ó Briain, Letter, *II*, 22/10/23.

24 Badh mhaith liom, fosta, a rádh go bhfuil níos mó suime á cur ag na daoiní annseo i ndrámaí san teanga dhúthchais ná a mhalairt, mar go mbíonn an halla líonta amach ar an tsúl nuair a bhíos léirighthe againn.

25 See also Eoghan Mac Giolla Bhrighde, Letter, *IP*, 1/5/33; 'I nGaedhealtacht Thír Chonaill / Léiriú Drámaí i nGaoth Dobhair' (In the Donegal Gaeltacht / Performance of plays in Gweedore), *IP*, 1/9/37; and 'Drámaidheacht i dTír Chonaill' (Drama in Donegal), *IP*, 20/12/37. Áine Nic Ghiolla Bhríde offers a longtime insider's perspective on the group in 'Drámaíocht i nDún na nGall' (Drama in Donegal), in *Scríbhneoireacht na gConallach*, ed. Mac Congáil, 203–10. See also Ó Siadhail, *Stair Dhrámaíocht na Gaeilge*, 151–4. In August 1936, another group from the Donegal Gaeltacht, The Derrybeg Players, broadcast three plays over Radio Athlone (*IP*, 25/8/36).

26 For the kind of enthusiasm a League branch's involvement could inspire in the provinces, see the 1938 report from Waterford by 'Rogha na nDéise':

> A long-felt want in Waterford Gaelic League circles was remedied when a miniature Gaelic theatre was officially opened on December 14th in the Gaelic League Hall to assist in the rapid development of Gaelic drama in the city . . . It is to be hoped that this initial venture of the Gaelic League in fostering drama in the city will receive the support it deserves from the Gaelic public of Waterford.

He saw this work as paving the way for 'a Comhar Drámaíochta for Waterford City and District' (*Leader*, 1/1/38).

27 The branch had been far less involved with drama in the immediate post-Civil War period. Its theatrical work in the 1930s was almost invariably well received.

28 Is follus gurbh é leas na drámaidheachta Gaedhilge é dá gcuireadh Craobhacha eile de'n Chonnradh léirighthe mar seo ar siubhal ins na h-amharclanna puiblidhe, dá ndéanadh leath na gCraobhacha atá i mBaile Átha Cliath féin a leithéid do b'fhéidir drámaí Gaedhilge do léiriú ar feadh seachtmhaine, gach mí de'n bhliadhain agus bheadh freastal maith ortha, gan aon aimhreas, acht na léirighthe a bheith go maith.

29 There was a falling off in numbers in the following years, doubtless due to the fact that most school groups were concentrating their efforts on the festivals organised in 1934 and after by Cumann Drámaidheachta na Scol. Of course, were it not for the Cumann, it is doubtful these *feiseanna* would have had anywhere near the number of plays they had, most of which were short works by school groups inspired and supported by the Cumann. Before the Cumann came on the scene the situation was far different. For example, in 1929 even a major provincial festival like Feis Chonnacht could have only two plays on its schedule (*Stoc*, June 1929, 2), while in 1933, the oldest of all provincial gatherings, Feis na Mumhan, had just four entrants for its drama competition, none of which was judged worthy of a prize (*Camán*, 7/10/33).

30 There had been 36 plays performed at the feis the previous year (Enniscorthy *Echo*, 17/6/33).

31 See Gearóid Ó Lochlainn, *Ealaín na hAmharclainne* (The art of the theatre) (BÁC: Clódhanna Teoranta, 1966), 31–7.

32 An Comhar Drámaidheachta, Programme for the 10 Oct. 1927 performance at the Peacock Theatre.

33 There was also a group calling itself Comhar Chorcaighe in Cork. The group was founded in 1933 by the Taibhdhearc na Gaillimhe producer/playwright/actor Aodh Mac Dhubháin. Its director in 1937 was Éamonn Ó Góilidhe (later well known at the Abbey as Edward Golden). For a positive assessment of their first season, see Kathleen Mulcahy, 'Intellectual and Artistic Life of Cork / Gaelic Drama', *Irisleabhar Chumann na gCéimithe i gCorcaigh*, June 1934, no pagination.

34 See also 'Sgéim Náisiúnta do'n Drámaidheacht', *IP*, 26/5/36; 'For Gaelic Drama / Proposal to Form a National League', *IP*, 26/5/36; 'Gádh na hUaire / Amharclann Ghaedhealach' (The need of the hour / A Gaelic theatre), *IP*, 11/10/37; and Ó Siadhail, *Stair Dhrámaíocht na Gaelige*, 72–3.

35 See 'An Comhar / Saothar na Príomh-Chathrach' (An Comhar / The work of the capital), *IP*, 29/5/37.

36 Is maith linn a fheiceál gur 'Comhar' ceart Drámaidheachta atá ann i mbliadhna . . . Is ionann é agus a rádh go bhfuil gluaiseacht láidir drámaidheachta bunaighthe i mBaile Átha Cliath agus go bhfuil sí dhá congbháil ar siubhal ag daoine atá a' comh-oibriú le chéile ar mhaithe leis an drámaidheacht agus leis an nGaedhilg. Actors from the civil service were praised highly in 'An Comhar Drámaidheachta', *AA*, Mar. 1938, 5.

37 Welcoming the performance of plays in Irish at the Gaiety Theatre in August 1923, the editor of the Connacht journal *An Chearnóg* wrote: 'Is the day far from us when there will be a Gaelic play going on for a week every month? May God grant that it not be long until it will pay producers of plays to put one on stage every night! (An fada uainn an lá nuair a bheidh dráma Ghaedhealach ar siubhal ann seachtmhain sa mí? Go dtugaidh Dia nach fada go n-íocaidh sé lucht léirighthe na ndrámanna ceann a chur ar an ardán gach oidhche!) (*An Chearnóg*, Aug. 1923, 4).

38 Céim mhór un cinn do'n Ghaedhilg saothar seo na nAisteoirí agus is mór an chreideamhaint atá ag dul dóibh dá chionn sin.

39 Gasra beag iseadh iad a bhíonn ag obair i rith an lae i siopaithe agus i n-oifigí. Níl d'uain aca a gcuid aisteoireachta do chleachtadh ach amháin um tráthnóna. D'fhéadfaí an aisteoireacht d'fheabhsú – dá mbeadh uain aca chuige. D'fhéadfaí drámaí níos oiriúnaighe d'fhagháil – dá mbeadh aga aca iad a chuardach, nó dá sgríobhfaí dóibh iad. Tá sár-obair á déanamh aca féin. Agus – gan buidheachas do lucht a gcáinte – tá ag éirighe leo. See also the similar awareness of the problems the group faced in 'Nótaí na Seachtaine / An Drámaidheacht' (Notes of the week / Drama', *ACS*, 28/5/32).

40 He added that 'considering that they have only one night a month on which to perform, and that, therefore, their every performance is, in reality, no more than a dress rehearsal, they are wonderfully good'.

41 See also Ó Broin's remarks on 'The Gaelic Drama in Ireland' delivered before the 1927 Celtic Congress, as reported in 'Co-Operation of Celtic Nations / An Urgent Necessity', *II*, 28/7/27.

42 Tá an t-am imighthe anois, nuair a bheadh orm a rádh go raibh sé de dhualgas ar gach Gaedheal 'cabhrú' leis an Comhar. I láthair na h-uaire, is fiú freastal ar léirighthe an Chomhair ar son an léirighthte féin, gan smaointe i dtaoibh 'náisiúntachais' nó 'cúis na Gaedhilge' bheith id bhodhradh. Geobhfaidh tú luach do chuid airgid.

43 Go dtí seo, bhíodh an léirmheasóir bocht nár theastuigh uaidh Amharclann na nGaedheal a loit le cáineadh agus go raibh urraim do'n fhírinne aige i gcruadhchás cheart. B'é ceist a chuireadh sé air féin tar éis dó léiriú d'fheiscint ná: 'An bhfuil aon rud ann gur féidir é a mholadh!' agus ní 'An bhfuil aon rud ann gur féidir locht d'fhagháilt air?' mar is gnáth do gach léirmheasóir eile. See also 'Teachtaire', 'An Comhar Drámuíochta', *FL*, Mar. 1930, 1–2. In a defence of the company against what he felt was

unjust criticism, Ó Lochlainn himself acknowledged that An Comhar's achievement did not always match its high ideals (*Star*, 5/7/30).

44 He included the work of An Taibhdhearc as well as An Comhar in his assessment.

45 Ar bhealach eicínt níor chuidigh muinntir Bhaile Átha Cliath leis an gComhar ón gcéad lá. Cúiseanna poilitidheachta is mó ba chionn-tsiocair leis sin, arae níor mhian le daoine áirithe cuidiú le sgéim a bhí curtha ar bun ag Riaghaltas an tSaorstáit.

46 B'fhéidir gur maith an caitheamh airigid é seo agus b'fhéidir nach eadh . . . Leis an fhírinne a dhéanamh nílmid róshásta chor ar bith nach bhféadfaí míle punt a chur i bhfad ní ba threise do theangain na tíre, ná deis a thiubhairt do dhream beag bídeach a dhul ar ardán uair nó dhó 'sa' mí. Ó Siadhail discusses how post-Civil War politics hampered the work of An Comhar in *Stair Dhrámaíocht na Gaeilge*, 60–2.

47 Ach sé chéad punt a bhronnadh gach bliadhain as airgead na tíre seo ar dhream beag nach bhfuil duine ná daonnda ar a gcúl ach iad fein, agus gan maitheas ar bith a' teacht as – támuid go mór in aghaidh sin agus tá súil againn go gcuirfear deireadh leis lom láithreach.

48 Ach is aisteach an rud é gur féidir le dream beag mar sin deontas airgid 'fhagháil as Cisde an Stáit, gan aon rud ach éagcaoin a spáint ar a son. Nár bhfearr an t-airgead sin a chaitheamh ar Chumainn éicin a dtiocfadh tairbhe éicin do'n Ghaedhilg as. See also 'An Sgríobhnóir', 'Clúid na nGaedheal', *Honesty*, 10/8/29; and 'BOH.', 'Stage and Screen', *Honesty*, 5/10/29.

49 Is aisteach an rud é gur féidir £600 'sa' mbliadhain as an gCisde Náisiúnta a chaitheamh ar dhream chomh beag sin. Níl Gaedhil na cathrach seo a' taobhachtáil leis a' gComhair-Drámuidheachta; níl aon mhuinighin aca asta, agus níl aon chabhair do'n duine i bhfus ná do'n duine thall bheith ag iarraidh dalladh mullóg a chur ar a' Saoghal Fódlach go bhfuil Gaedhilgeoirí Átha Cliath taobh thiar díobh . . . Níl 'sa' gComhar Drámuidheachta ach Feistiughadh Fuinneog. See also his comments in his *Nationality* columns for 14 Mar. and 4 July 1931; and the unsigned piece 'Cúrsaí Drámaíochta / Na Scoileanna laistiar den Ghluaiseacht' (Theatre affairs / The schools behind the movement), *Nation*, 29/6/35. In 1928, An Comhar was criticised by 'T. O'R.' for not expanding its inner circle of actors (*IS*, 12/5/28). Many involved with either An Comhar or An Taibhdhearc complained that state subsidies were too small. See, for example, Liam Ó Briain, 'Taibhdhearc na Gaillimhe', *IP*, 8/6/35; and Jeremiah Murphy, 'The Drama in Irish / Meeting the Cinema on Its Own Ground', *IP*, 4/5/37. With time, Ernest Blythe, the politician who created the first subsidies for An Comhar and An Taibhdhearc (and, of course, for the Abbey), came to believe that the subsidies should be increased significantly, with An Comhar and An Taibhdhearc combined receiving eight times what the Abbey was getting (*Leader*, 16/12/39).

50 The resolution stated 'gurab é tuairim an chruinnighthe seo nach bhfuil an ceart ag an Riaghaltas gan airgead a sholáthar le h-aghaidh drámaí Gaedhealacha sa Ghaedhealtacht, agus airgead dá bhronnadh ar an Chomhar Drámaidheachta i mBaile Átha Cliath, ar an Taibhbdhearc i nGaillimh, agus ar an Abbey Theatre i mBaile Átha Cliath.'

51 Ernest Blythe to Séamus Ó Beirn, 16 Oct. 1929, Taibhdhearc Papers, NUIG MS T 107 (1–5). It was always Blythe's belief that An Taibhdhearc could accomplish more for theatre in Irish than could be done in the capital. See, for example, 'Irish Drama in Galway / Minister for Finance and the New Theatre', *Freeman*, 8/9/28.

52 Má's le Dia, beidh baint mhór ag an Taibhdhearc sin le stair aithbheochaine na Gaedhilge feasta. See also 'Expansion in the Language Movement', *Camán*, 11/11/33.

53 Liam Ó Buachalla, Letter, 7 Oct. 1929, Taibhdhearc Papers, NUIG MS T1/92 (1–2). Ó Buachalla, a professor at UCG, was later to take an active role in the affairs of An Taibhdhearc.

54 Ní hé amháin gur sgaip Ardán an Taoibhdheirc [*sic*] lán de'n bhrón agus de'n uaigneas, seadh agus de'n imreas a bhí ag déanamh dochair agus ag sgaradh cáirde Gaodhal ó chéile; acht mhéaduigh sé, agus cheangail sé grádh tíre agus teangan go dlúth agus go docht inár measg. Actually, Pádraig Ó Bróithe had offered similar praise to An Comhar in 1925:

> When they first went on the boards, the world was troubled and there was bitterness in every Gaelic heart. They did their share to dissipate and to extinguish that trouble and that bitterness – that is one of the virtues of every kind of art (Nuair a chuadar ar na cláracha an cheud uair bhí an saoghal buaidheartha agus seirbhthean i ngach croidhe Ghaedhealach. Dheineadar súd a gcuid chun an bhuaidhirt agus an seirbhthean do scaipeadh agus do mhúchadh – sin buadh de bhuadha gach saghas ealadhan) (*FL*, 3/10/25).

55 We should not infer from all this praise that there were no problems at An Taibhdhearc. Feehan criticised the theatre for doing too many translations and for not having enough native-speaking actors. More significant was its own board's clearsighted assessment of the challenges facing the theatre in 1935, challenges that included a lack of funds, consequent paltry remuneration for actors and technicians, loss of talented performers, and a 'small and bizarre' playing space. See Taibhdhearc Papers, NUIG MS T1/262 (1–9). 'P. Mac Fh.' offers us a comic look at rehearsals at An Taibhdhearc in his story 'Ar Chúl Stáitse' (Backstage), *IP*, 26/10/36. One of the most accomplished Taibhdhearc actors, the future poet Máirtín Ó Direáin, also wrote a comic story about

actors, 'Tuitim an Aisteora!' (The actor's fall!), *IP*, 21/11/38. Other humorous stories in Irish about the profession and its practitioners were Pádraig Ó Bróithe's 'Lucht Drámuíochta a Fuair Bua / Muiris Aisteoir' (Theatre people who triumphed / Maurice the actor), *II*, 13/9/23; and Seán Ó Ciarghusa's 'Fás an Dráma agus a Stair / Rud ná Tuigeann Moltóirí' (The growth of drama and its history / Something adjudicators do not understand), *II*, 2/6/24.

56 B'é breith an Chumainn go raibh fóidín mearbhaill eicínt ag tigheacht ar Uachtarán an Chomhair agus a leithide de rud a rádh, nuair ba léir do'n tsaoghal mór gurab i gConnachta, thar áit ar bith eile i nÉirinn is mó atá borradh agus fás tagtha faoi'n ngluaiseacht agus gur i nGaillimh go h-áithrid atá fréamhacha na drámaidheachta. See also Michael Riley's piece 'Galway's Taibhdhearc' (*IP*, 28/6/39), in which he lauded the theatre while chiding Galwegians for not sufficiently appreciating it.

57 Cuid díobh agus gan iad á n-iomchar féin go nádúrtha, toisg a n-aigne do bheith dírighthe ar fad ar an gcaint ná raibh de ghlan-mheabhair aca, nó nár tháinig go líomhtha leo. Uchtach lag (ach gan é ag 'fear an chogarnaigh' laistiar!), aisteoireacht thuathalach – rian glan ar a bhfurmhór ná raibh an dráma cleachtaithe go maith aca. To be fair, he also praised the work of some of the actors and argued that it was an injustice to inexperienced actors to expect too much of them, and to the more skilled to force them to share the stage with the inept.

58 See also 'E. C.', 'The Gaelic Players', *IS*, 16/4/27; and 'Scrúdóir', 'An Comhar Drámaidheachta / Drámaí Sean agus Nuadh' (Plays old and new), *Star*, 10/5/30.

59 Ní maith liom féin aon aisteoir dá fheabhas é a cháil go mbeidh úsáid á dhéanamh le leabhra chun a pháirt do léigheamh as.

60 Tá cuid des na h-Aisteoirí agus níl uchtach maith aca, cuid eile agus bíd tuathalach triopallach ar an ardán. Is baoghal liom ná faghann a bhfurmhór an múineadh ná an cleachtadh is gádh san aisteoireacht. He went on to place the principal blame for these problems on the director, Piaras Béaslaí. See also the vitriolic criticism of Béaslaí by 'Arion' in 'An Comhar Drámuíochta', *Leader*, 25/1/30. Béaslaí was, of course, a bugbear of Republicans because of his service at high rank in the Free State army and his authorship of a very favourable biography of Michael Collins. Those on the other side of the political divide had a higher opinion of his theatrical work. See, for example, 'Na h-Aisteoirí / Drámaí Gaedhilge', *II*, 2/11/26. However, to be fair to both Béaslaí and contemporary critics, it should be said that some at the time were able to assess Béaslaí's very real talents and contributions more dispassionately, as did An tAthair Mac Fhinn: 'Piaras Béaslaí is the best if not the only Irish-speaker who has the dramatic craft. He is able to put the pieces together cleverly and artistically so that he has interesting, stageworthy plays' (Sé Piaras Béaslaí an Gaedhilgeoir is fearr – munab é an t-aon Ghaedhilgeoir amháin é – a bhfuil céard na drámaidheachta aige. Tá sé i ndon na píosaí a chur le chéile go cliste ealadhanta i gcaoi go mbeidh drámaí suimheamhla so-léirighthe aige) (*AA*, Nov. 1936, 3). Béaslaí was also paid an impressive compliment by 'A. Ó L.' in 1937: 'We can compare what he has done for drama in Irish with what Lady Gregory did for drama in English' (Thig linn an méid atá déanta aige ar son drámuidheachta na Gaedhilge a chur i gcomparáid leis an méid atá déanta ag Lady Gregory ar son drámuidheachta an Sacs [*sic*]-Bhéarla) (*GR*, Dec. 1937, 493).

61 See also O'Connor, 'At the Peacock', *IS*, 26/10/29. A Gaelic actor almost invariably exempt from such criticism was Gearóid Ó Lochlainn. See, for example, Frank O'Connor, 'The Peacock and the Moon', *IS*, 5/4/30; and 'Sár-Léiriú / An Lochlannach go h-Iongantach' (An excellent production / Ó Lochlainn wonderful), *II*, 17/10/31. Moreover, his Irish was also generally regarded as above reproach. 'Teachtaire', for example, wrote in 1930: 'A person listening to Gearóid [Ó Lochlainn] would think that this skilful actor spent his life in the Gaeltacht' (*FL*, Mar. 1930, 1).

62 But see his review of a production by An Comhar earlier the same year in which he wrote that 'no great care had been taken with the staging', and criticised the group for its 'inability to express *team work*', its 'undeveloped ability and lack of detached standards', but then went on to praise the performance for being '*alive* with a real spontaneity I miss in our professional theatres' (*Ireland To-Day*, Mar. 1937, 69). In another of his 'Theatre' columns that year, Ó Meadhra showed sympathy for the constraints under which An Comhar laboured while still drawing attention to the 'uneven production and utter lack of imagination and enterprise for staging and dressing, for which there is no excuse whatsoever'. In general, he seems to have felt that the actors were often too good for the shabby productions in which they too often found themselves (*Ireland To-Day*, June 1937, 71–2).

63 Blythe could be every bit as sharp with regard to the work of An Taibhdhearc, writing to Séamus Ó Beirn after seeing a play in Galway in 1929:

> The performance on Sunday night was somewhat better than the performance given by the Comhar Drámuíochta in Dublin, simply because the players had a much better command of Irish and spoke their lines with their natural expression. Apart from that I thought the performance showed greater faults and less finish than the ordinary performances in Dublin (Ernest Blythe to Séamus Ó Beirn, 25 July 1929, Taibhdhearc Papers, NUIG MST1/78 {2}).

See also Ó Siadhail, *Stair Dhrámaíocht na Gaeilge*, 121.

64 Is breagh liom go bhfuil ag éirghe comh maith sin leis na haisteoiribh. Ní dheirim go bhfuil siad gan locht ach tá sé in am go leor na lochta do chur in iúl dóibh. Mol an óige is tiocfaidh sí agus teastuigheann uainn go mór an drámuidheacht.

65 B'é ní ba mhó a tugadh faoi ndeara ag an léiriughadh so ná an feabhas atá ag teacht ar aisteoracht na foirinne. Ta gach duine aca nach mór ag dul ar aghaidh go h-ana-mhaith. Most Gaels were well aware of the professionalism and polish Mac Liammóir brought to drama in Irish. In 1929, Liam Ó Briain stated that much of the credit for the early success of An Taibhdhearc was due to Hilton Edwards and Mac Liammóir, 'to whom . . . it is entirely due that a much higher standard of production, staging and lighting was achieved there than had ever been seen on the Gaelic stage before' (*Star*, 15/6/29). The following month the editor of this same paper praised Mac Liammóir for his 'skill and knowledge of stagecraft' and his 'expert direction' (*Star*, 20/7/29). The board of An Taibhdhearc certainly made every attempt to retain his services even on a part-time basis when he left for Dublin to found and direct the Gate Theatre. See the correspondence between the board and Mac Liammóir in the Taibhdhearc Papers. After he left Galway, the rest of Mac Liammóir's distinguished career was, of course, to be spent at the Gate, although he did direct at An Taibhdhearc in the early 1930s, brought the company to the Gate, and never lost his affection for and allegiance to the Galway theatre. See, for example, his 1936 letter to Liam Ó Briain concerning royalties for a revival of *Diarmaid agus Gráinne* (Taibhdhearc Papers, NUIG MS T1/268).

66 He was, however, particularly hard on the Irish of most of the actresses.

67 Piaras Béaslaí to Ernest Blythe, 8 Aug. 1928, Ernest Blythe Papers, NLI MS 20,708. Isé ár dtuairim láidir nach féidir dúinn, an fhaid is bheimíd i dtaobh le seacht léirithe in aghaidh na bliana, iarracht is fearr ná san a dhéanamh, agus ná beidh a thuille fáis ná dul chun cinn san obair. In a ionad san is amhla d'éireoig [*sic*] na daoine tuirseach dinn, agus is baoghalach go dtiocfaidh saghas meirge ar na haisteoirí féin muna bhfaghaid siad níos mó scóip chun a saothair. See also León Ó Broin's question the following year: 'Would it not be expecting too much of human nature – even of Gaelic human nature – to hope that interest could be maintained in a theatrical movement which is before the public eye for only 21 hours each year?' (*Star*, 20/7/29).

68 See also his essay 'Staid na h-Amharclainne i n-Éirinn', *IP*, 22/4/35.

69 An Taibhdhearc also had problems in this area. In the May 1929 report of the secretary, Liam Ó Briain, he complained: 'Another thing – actors. It is difficult to get them. They must be given a rest after every production, and for most of them the second drama is not like the first; they don't have the same enthusiasm for it' (Rud eile dhe, aisteoirí. Deacair iad fháil. Ní mór sgíth thabhairt dhóibh thréis gach léirighthe agus ní hionann dá bhfurmhór an dara dráma agus an chéad cheann ní bhíonn an dúil chéadna aca ann) (Taibhdhearc Papers, NUIG Add. MS 75). In May 1929, it was decided that actors should be paid five shillings a week and fined a shilling for every rehearsal they missed (Minutes of board meeting, 10/5/29, Taibhdhearc Papers, NUIG Add. MS 22). (The previous year Blythe had met with members of the board and agreed that actors be paid, but specified 'very little' (fíor-bheagán) (Minutes of board meeting, 30/1/28, Taibhdhearc Papers, Add. MS 58). The creation of a permanent company was from early on a central goal at An Taibhdhearc. In a 1929 letter to Blythe, the group's then secretary, Séamus Ó Beirn, wrote:

> The Committee agrees with you that to achieve this [i.e. 'An Irish Theatre in Galway that will do credit to the Nation'] a number of whole-time actors must gradually be evolved and that such a Company when formed should except in holiday time give performances every week either in Galway or in any other part of Ireland and probably abroad. We recognise that this stock company is essential (Séamus Ó Beirn to Ernest Blythe, 31 July 1929, Taibhdhearc Papers, MS T1/102).

This hope remained alive throughout our period. See NUIG MSS T1/262; T1/284 (3–4); T1/286 (3).

70 Is beag an mheas a bhéas ag an sean-Ghaedheal ar shár-dhráma muna mbídh an Ghaedhilg go maith ann agus munar féidir le haisteoirí a cothrom do thabhairt do chainnt an údair nó an aistrightheora. Is mó í an bhaint atá ag cúrsaí teangain le daoine a raghas go dti drámaí Gaedhilge ná atá ag cúrsaí drámaíochta. An cúrsaí drámaíochta nó cúrsaí teangain an chuspóir atá ag an gComhar? Tá daoine ann adéarfas nach bhfuil ceachtar den dá chuspóir sin aca nó má tá nach bhfuil siad ach ag iarraidh an dá thaobh do thabhairt leo – gan ceachtar taobh do shásamh. Seo ceist a caithfear a réidhteach sul a dtiocfaidh aon toradh foghanta ar obair na nAisteoirí. Similar concerns had been raised the previous year by an anonymous contributor to the same paper in a piece on the Gaelic plays at Feis Charman:

> In future, however, we think that a better balance will have to be maintained between the Irish speaker and the actor. There are several other suitable fields at the Feis for the competitor who is solely an Irish speaker, but more consideration must be given to the claims of those potential actors and actresses who may never be able to appreciate the phonetic nuances of inter-dentals, liquids and nasals (*Star*, 8/6/29).

71 Ní ceart aon duine a bheith páirteach i ndráma a léirightear go puiblidhe ná go príomháideach gan an chainnt a bheith i gceart aige. Is tábhachtaighe an teanga ná an drámaidheacht agus nach leis an

nGaedhilge a chur 'un cinn a léirightear drámaí i nGaedhilge? Ní mar sin a cheapann go leor daoine. Is cuma leo an teanga, acht an aisteoireacht a bheith go maith rud a ghníos brochán de'n sgéal.

72 Níl éinní in ao' chor is mó a chuireann déistean ar lucht éisteachta ná Gaedhilg lag-bhriste. Má ghlacann aisteoir air féin páirt do ghabháil ba cheart an pháirt sin do bheith i gceart aige agus munar cainnteoir ó dhúthchas é bheadh sé ceart aige ana-thaithí a dhéanamh ar na fuaimeanna.

73 Níor mhór an Ghaedhilg a bheith go blasta aca mar níl éinní is mó a ghoilleann ar an lucht éisteachta ná bheith ag iarraidh droch-Ghaedhilg a thuisgint agus tá sé fíor-dheacair ar fad í thuisgint.

74 Badh dheacair, agus ba dheacaire fós d'aisteoir aistidheacht mhaith a dhéanamh má chaithfidh sé bheith ag cuimhneamh ar an nGaedhilg agus é ag cainnt.

75 Minutes of the meeting of 12 May 1930, Taibhdhearc Papers, NUIG Add. MS 58. Hy Halvey go han-dona – Mac Glla Cionnaith agus Capt. Paor as Rinn mór an droch-Ghaedhilge. Gill go han-dona mar is gnáth. See also the minutes of the meeting of 10 Feb. 1930, in which one of the student actors from UCG was said to have 'bad Irish' (droch Ghaedhilge).

76 Minutes of the meeting of 8 Sept. 1932, Taibhdhearc Papers, NUIG Add. MS 22. Bhí díospóireacht faoi cheist cainnte agus guth na h-aisteoirí [*sic*] ar an ardán agus moladh do'n fear [*sic*] léirithe dianiarracht a dhéanamh agus na cainnteoirí Gaedhilge is fearr d'fháil i gcóir na bpáirteanna sna drámaí.

77 Imeasg furmhór na n-aisteoirí bhí sean-locht aisteoirí na Taidhbhdheirce le tabhairt faoi ndeara. Bhí fíor-dhroch-bhlas aca. Sé an laigeacht sin sa gcainnt, nó sa bhfoghraidheacht a bfhearr a rádh, sé an laigeacht sin is cionntach le plúchadh na cainnte nuair a thaganns an tocht nó an paisiún sa nglór. He continued: 'When they try to speak quickly and loudly (I am not saying that they do not sometimes speak too loudly and too quickly), the sounds get tangled together so that a good deal of the speech is lost' (Nuair a fhéachann siad le labhairt go sgioptha agus go h-ard (ní dheirim nach labhrann siad ró-ard agus ró-sgioptha amannta) téigheann na fuaimeanna i n-aimhréidh 'n chéile i gcaoi go cailltear cuid mhaith de'n chainnt). His solution was to use native-speaking actors, although he did acknowledge they would be hard to come by. One native speaker whose acting seems to have been of a consistently high standard was Máirtín Ó Direáin. See, for example, 'Taibhdhearc na Gaillimhe', *Stoc*, Mar. 1929, 2; 'An Comhar Drámaidheachta', *AA*, Feb. 1938, 4; 'An Comhar Drámaidheachta', *AA*, Mar. 1939, 5. See also the tribute to Ó Direáin in *AA* for all his work in Galway on the occasion of his moving to Dublin (*AA*, Oct. 1937, 4).

78 'An Craoibhín Aoibhinn' (Douglas Hyde), 'Adhbhar i gCóir Drámaí Gaedhilge, Cá Bhfaightear é?' (Material for plays in Irish, where is it to be found?), in *Láimh-Leabhar Drámaidheachta*, 11. Muna dtuigeann siad an chainnt tá gach uile shórt millte. Tiocfaidh na haisteoirí agus Gaedhilg bhreagh i n-a mbéalaibh aca, agus ní tuigfear an Ghaedhilg sin, agus nuair ná tuigfear b'fhearr dóibh bheith i n-a dtost. Ní fhéadaim bheith ró-láidir ar an bpoinnte seo, agus muna mbeadh ach aon chomhairle amháin agam le tabhairt do lucht-cheaptha agus lucht-léirighthe drámaí budh é – TABHAIR AIRE GO DTUIGFEAR THÚ.

79 Do b'fhearr labhairt ró-righin ná ró-thapaidh an fhaid a's bhímíd ag braith ar lucht foghlumtha na teangain – nó d'iarraidh iad do thabhairt isteach agus misneach do chur ortha ba chirte a rádh.

80 Ní furasta drámaí feileamhnacha fhagháil i nGaedhilg agus an méid Gaedhilge a bhí i n*Aiséirighe Dhonncha*, ní chreidim gur ró-mhaith a thuig an lucht éisteachta í. Agus cé'n mhaith dráma a léiriú i dteangain nach dtuigtear.

81 Sometimes actors with good Irish must have felt there was no way they could win. When actors from Carraroe in the Conamara Gaeltacht performed in Dublin in 1936, some praised them for speaking more slowly in deference to their audiences, while others faulted them for not speaking as quickly as they would at home, prompting one member of the company to say: 'Since we came to Dublin everyone was telling us to speak slowly. Then, when we did that on stage, I was told to speak a bit more quickly' (Ó tháinigeamar go Baile Átha Cliath bhí chuile dhuine a' rádh linn labhairt go mall. Annsin, nuair a rinneamar é sin ar an ardán, dubhradh liom labhairt beagán níos sgiobtha) (*Éireannach*, 27/6/36).

82 The idea that audiences came to plays in Irish to 'help' is an interesting one. Audiences at Taibhdhearc na Gaillimhe were, and still are, provided in their programmes with a brief synopsis of the play to assist those 'with little Irish' (ar bheagán Gaeilge).

83 Cúis bróid a fheabhas a léirigheadh agus a h-éisteadh an dráma beag seo. B'fhuraist a fheiceáilt go raibh an lucht éisteachta ag cur an-spéise ann. Shílfeá go raibh alltacht ortha gheall ar iad bheith ábalta cúrsaí an Dráma a leanstan comh réidh sin.

84 An lucht éisteachta a bhí ann ámh ba léir go raibh an Ghaedhilge ar bharr a dteangan ag chaon duine acu, toisg an chaoi nar lean siad gach rud a dubhradh san dráma. In 1927, 'D. Ó D.' made the interesting suggestion that the unfamiliar rural life and themes so often depicted in Gaelic plays could be a factor in an urban audience's failure to fully understand what they were seeing and hearing on stage (*Leader*, 5/11/27).

85 An inadequate grasp of spoken Irish was not the only fault of Gaelic audiences that drew the attention, and sometimes the ire, of commentators in our period. They were also criticised for, among other things, lack of punctuality, talking during performances, and – a

failing they seem to have shared with patrons of the Abbey – a tendency to laugh too much and at inappropriate moments. In a 1925 piece in *An Sguab*, Seán Ó Ciarghusa directed a much more serious accusation against the audience for Gaelic plays in Dublin:

> Everyone must yield to his own handicap, but an Comhar Drámaidheachta must yield to the affliction of the audience and the critics as well, and the applause of the audience and the critics in Dublin cannot, I fear, be trusted in matters of *Gaelachas* (Is éigean do gach n-aon géilleadh d'á bhacaidheacht féin, ach is éigean do'n Chomhar Drámaidheachta géilleadh do bhacaidheacht na lucht éisteachta agus an lucht measta leis, agus an lucht éisteachta ná an lucht measta i mBaile Átha Cliath, ní muininghneach is baoghal liom, a nglór molta i gcúrsaidhibh Gaedhealachais (*Sguab*, Feb. 1925, 277).

86 See also O'Flaherty, 'Ag Casadh le Pádraic Ó Conaire' (Meeting with Pádraic Ó Conaire), *Comhar*, Apr. 1953, 3–6; and Ní Chionnaith, *Pádraic Ó Conaire*, 215–16. For an earlier version of the idea, see Ó Conaire, 'Drámaí', in *Aistí Phádraic Ui Chonaire*, ed. Denvir (p. 128), an essay originally published in *The Irishman*, 28/9/18. Aodh de Blácam also supported this idea just before our period. See de Blácam, *From a Gaelic Outpost* (Dublin: Catholic Truth Society of Ireland, 1921).

87 Actually, An Comhar was prohibited by the terms of its subsidy from performing outside Dublin. See Ó Lochlainn, 'Cáineadh nó Congnamh' (Criticism or help), *Star*, 11/1/30. It was doubtless due to this restriction that Ó Conaire did not expect An Comhar to serve this audience. Rather, he wanted the state to fund a separate full-time company to tour both the Gaeltacht and English-speaking Ireland.

88 An lucht éisteachta an chuid is tábhachtaighe dhe dhráma ar bith . . . Is breagh liom iarracht ar bith áit ar bith ar son na Gaedhilge, agus tuigeann chuile dhuine an tábhacht a bhaineas le drámaí le haghaidh teanga a mhúnadh [*sic*] agus a sgaipeadh. Ach má theastuigheann dráma Gaedheal [*sic*] maith i gceart bíodh muinntir na Gaeltachta mar lucht éisteachta agat.

89 Ní féidir go mbeadh sé deacair rud eicínt sholáthar do'n Ghaedhealtacht bheadh níos fearr ná Maria Martin ná an Desert Song . . . Ní féidir go mbeadh sé ró dheacair greim fháil ar trí drámaí, ar dheichneabhar aisteoirí, ar léiritheoir, ar fheisteoir-stáitse, ar eileictreoir, ar ghléas taistil soillseacháin, ar chupla sraith cúirtíní, ar roinnt canbháis agus adhmuid, agus ar shiúinéir stáitse a thuig a chéard?

90 Tuigeann siad an Ghaedhilge, tá spéis an domhain aca san drámuíocht. Muna ndéantar rud eicínt anois chun caitheamh aimsire a sholáthar dóibh, is gearr go bhfeicfear na h-aisteoirí taisdil Gallda sin atá chomh fairsing sin i láthair na h-uaire, ag brugh isteach san nGaedhealtacht féin agus ag léiriú an dríodair sin a bhíonns ag a bhfurmhór acu de ghnáth. He saw the provision of such entertainment as a duty (dualgas) for An Taibhdhearc. One member of An Taibhdhearc's board who hoped to see more touring in the Gaeltacht was Geraldine Dillon (*IP*, 8/9/32).

91 They had thought the idea through, picking potential venues and planning to send out an advance man to consult with local priests and teachers.

92 See 'Taibhdhearc na Gaillimhe / Scéim le h-Aghaidh Fuireann Seasta Aisteoirí', Taibhdhearc Papers, NUIG MS T1/286 (3). They projected visits of a week each to the Gaeltachtaí in Donegal, Mayo, Kerry, Cork and Waterford, and a three-week tour in County Galway. In addition, they hoped to perform in Dublin for three weeks and in Cork, Limerick and Wexford for a week each. Such a schedule, in addition to a 26-week programme in An Taibhdhearc itself, would have them on stage forty weeks a year. See also Taibhdhearc papers, MS T1/261

93 Ní fheadar ca na thaobh go mbaistfí 'Amharclann na nGaedheal' ar áitín chó suarach. Ach is dócha ná fuil ach bochtanas ag baint le Gaedhil agus is baolach go leanfaidh an mío-ádh san dóibh go deo na ndeor. See also 'An Comhar Drámaidheachta', *AA*, Dec. 1936, 3.

94 On the other hand, in a 1931 review of a performance by An Comhar at the Gate, 'C.' complained that he could not enjoy the show because the theatre was 'cold, very cold' (fuar, an-fhuar) (*Leader*, 21/3/31).

95 In a 1936 essay on 'The Gaelic Drama Movement / Difficulties Confronting It', Blythe discussed many of the challenges the amateur players of An Comhar were wrestling with, and praised An Taibhdhearc for 'gradually laying the foundation of an Irish equivalent of the Abbey Theatre'. Curiously, he never mentioned the fact that the Galwegians, unlike their colleagues in Dublin, had their own building (*Leader*, 30/5/36).

96 Go dtí go mbeidh amharclann d'ár gcuid féin againn ní féidir bheith ag iarraidh aon dul-chun-cinn do dhéanamh maidir le na léirithe. Tá sé fuar againn bheith ag iarraidh buan-ghluaiseacht drámuíochta do chur ar bun gan buan-amharclann bheith againn. He was immediately offered generous support from Galway by Liam Ó Briain in a piece entitled 'Gádh le h-Amharclann' (Need for a theatre), *IP*, 9/3/33.

97 Ernest Blythe to Liam Ó Briain, Taibhdhearc Papers, NUIG MS T1/289. (The letter is undated but is filed with material from late 1937 and early 1938 in the Taibhdhearc Papers at NUIG). Maidir leis an dTaibhdhearc, ba chuma liom an tinnreamh – go ceann roint bhlian ar aon chuma. Nuair a thosnuíos ar dhul go dtí Amharclann na Mainistreach ar dtúis is ar éigin a bhíodh caoga duine i láthair oíche ar bith agus a bhfuil de Bhéarlóirí i mB'leá-cliath.

98 Tá na h-Aisteoirí Gaedhilge dhul ar aghaidh, agus tá a lucht éisteachta a' méadú de réir a chéile.

99 Do bhí an t-amharclann lán go dorus, agus ní leanbhaí sgoile amháin a bhí ann ach gach aon tsaghas daoine agus do thaithin an léiriú go seoigh le gach éinne. Schoolchildren did, however, remain the most dependable audience for plays in Irish, a fact decried by An tAthair Mac Fhinn in a piece on An Comhar in 1936: 'When plays for schoolchildren are produced, the house is full of young people, but the adults even yet give little assistance to An Comhar Drámaidheachta' (Nuair a bhíos drámaí do pháistí sgoile dhá léiriú bíonn an teach lán le daoine óga, ach is beag an chabhair a thugas na daoine fásta fós féin do'n Chomhar Drámaidheachta) (*AA*, Dec. 1936, 3).

100 Tá a leithéid sin d'éileamh ar dhrámaí Gaedhilge sa chathair gur deacair do'n Chomhar Drámuíochta amharclann a fhagháil comh minic a's ba mhaith leobhtha é.

101 Indeed he claimed that the attendance could have been 50 per cent higher had there been sufficient seating in the Peacock.

102 In 1935, *The Connacht Tribune* congratulated An Taibhdhearc for the large listenership it was attracting for its monthly broadcast of plays on the radio (*CT*, 23/11/35).

103 Frank Dermody, Letter to Proinnsias O'Duffy, Deputy Secretary (Leas-Rúnaí), Dept. of Education, 11 Apr. 1934, Taibhdhearc Papers, NUIG MS T1/242. He continued that financial constraints kept the theatre from doing enough such shows, and urged that the subsidy be 'largely increased' so that An Taibhdhearc could 'give permanent engagements to actors . . . travel round Connacht, and have a larger staff and give more frequent performances in Galway'.

104 Dá mhéid fothraim atá á dhéanamh againn i dtaobh na Gaedhilge is lag an chabhair atá le fagháil uainn ag dream atá ad' iarraidh an dráma Gaedhlach do chur ar a bhonnaibh. Bímíd ag gearán i dtaobh a laighead Gaedhilge a bhíonn le cloisint i nár dtimpeal agus nuair atá caoi againn ar í chloisint ón stáitse ní fiú linn dul ag éisteacht léi.

105 Tá na mílte Gaedhilgeoirí i mBaile Átha Cliath ag a bhfuil screablach maith airgid le caitheamh ar amharclainn. Agus an sgéal amhlaidh cén fáth go mbíonn oiread suidheachán folamh i nAmharclainn na nGaedheal; cén chiall atá leis; agus cén leighis atá air. He returned to this theme two months later, claiming he had never seen the tiny Peacock full for An Comhar (*Star*, 5/4/30).

106 He saw a vicious circle at work, with poor audiences giving directors and actors little incentive to do good work, and shoddy productions – 'the almost universally low standard of Gaelic acting and production' – having little appeal for potential playgoers.

107 Rinne sé tagairt d'obair an Taibhdheirc agus a laighead daoine a thaganns ag breathnughadh ar na drámaí annsin. He went on to say that this would not be the case if An Taibhdhearc performed in the Gaeltacht. Speaking on the same occasion, An tAthair Mac Fhinn said that Galwegians would support plays about subjects meaningful to them.

108 'Meastachán don Chomhar Drámaíochta 1928–29' (Estimate for An Comhar Dramaidheachta), Blythe Papers, NLI MS 20,708.

109 See Ó Siadhail, *Stair Dhrámaíocht na Gaeilge*, 70; and '2,300 Duine i Láthair ag Drámaí an Chomhair' (2,300 people in attendance at the plays of An Comhar), *IP*, 23/5/33.

110 'Cuntas an Chisdeora 16adh Seiseon' (Treasurer's account 16th season), bound with programs donated to the NLI by Pádraig Ó Siochfhradha. This report provides comparative figures for the four seasons from 1935 to 1939.

111 'Tuarasgabháil an Rúnaí ar an obair a deineadh i rith an 15adh Seiseoin' (Report of the secretary on the work done during the 15th season), bound with programmes donated to the NLI by Pádraig Ó Siochfhradha.

112 See 'Criunniú Cinn Bliadhna an Chomhar Drámuíochta' (Annual meeting of An Comar Drámaidheachta), *Camán*, 27/5/33.

113 See 'Cuntas an Chisdeora 16adh Seiseon.' It is, of course, possible that some loyal Gaels purchased tickets to support drama in Irish but then did not use them. Such 'no-shows' may account for some of the discrepancy between the attendance statistics and some of the accounts of audience numbers from contemporary commentators. One such commentator who was untroubled by poor audiences at this point in the Revival was 'S. Mac P.', who wrote in 1937:

> At present things are tight enough for the English-language theatres, with everyone in the country a member of the 'potential audience'; and therefore is it any wonder that the plays in Irish do not have audiences as large as we might wish and they just struggling on without a theatre, without plays, without money? (I láthair na h-uaire tá an sgéal cumhang go leor ag amharclanna an Bhéarla agus gach duine sa tír 'na dhuine de 'potential audience'; agus dá réir sin an aon iongnadh é ná fuil an lucht éisteachta ag na drámaí Gaedhilge chomh mór agus ba mhian linn agus gan iad ach ag stracadh leis an saoghal gan amharclann, gan drámaí, gan airgead?) (*IP*, 11/1/37).

114 The records of An Taibhdhearc provide us with gate receipts rather than audience numbers. These figures do not provide a breakdown by ticket price, nor do they take into consideration season ticket sales. Furthermore, the figures given are sometimes for individual performances and sometimes for periods of several months. Thus while the information provided in the accounts can be quite detailed, it is difficult to translate it into precise estimates of audience numbers.

115 In this light, the accusation from 'Éinín' that An Comhar had ignored audience recruitment is not

fair. See 'Éinín', Letter, *Gaedheal*, 13/4/35. On the other hand, he was not alone in his view of An Comhar's indifference to the public. In 1929, 'Scrúdóir' had accused the group of 'the very obvious contempt . . . for the "Fates of Advertisement"' (*Star*, 9/3/29).

116 See 'An Dráma', Editorial, *FL*, 10/11/23. The price went up a shilling to a guinea the following year. See 'Lucht Drámuíochta i g-Comhairle' (Drama people in conference), *II*, 14/4/24.

117 Is mór an áis é an Comhar-Chárta mar gheibhtear gach sórt suidheacháin amharclainne ar luach i bhfad níos saoire agus tá pribhléidí eile ag gabháil leis. There was a change in the scheme in 1933 when it was decided that Comhar-Chártaí would cost a crown (5*s.*), and would entitle members to purchase booklets of tickets that would reduce the cost of the best seats to seven shows by a third (from 21*s.* to 14*s.*) and that of the cheaper seats by a half (from 14*s.* to 7*s.*). The tickets could be used for any performance. Members of the public who did not have Comhar-Chártaí could purchase these booklets for a less favourable discount. In addition, students could purchase their own booklets entitling them to attend seven shows for 5*s.* (a saving of 2*s.*). See the letter dated September 1933 sent to members of An Comhar and bound with programmes donated to the NLI by Pádraig Ó Siochfhradha.

118 An Comhar Drámaidheachta, Programme for the performance of 10 Oct. 1927, bound with programmes donated to the NLI by Pádraig Ó Siochfhradha. Is áil linn tú bheith orainn. Beidh ar do chumas cabhrú leis an drámuíocht agus gheobhair féin breis tairbhe as na drámaí, léigheachtaí, 7rl., a bhíos againn.

119 An Comhar Drámaidheachta, Programme for performance of 1 Oct. 1928, bound with programmes donated to the NLI by Pádraig Ó Siochfhradha. Tá comhar-chártaí le fagháil, £1 an cárta (agus níos lugha de réir mar bhéas an bhliain dhá caitheamh). Má bhíonn cárta agat beidh cead duit bheith ar gach aon léiriú d'á mbeidh ann i rith an tseisiúin agus suidheachán a chur i n-áirithe roimh ré i n-aon áit sa tigh is mian leat. Ina theannta san, beidh cead duit bheith páirteach i n-obair an chruinnithe chinnbhliana, 7c.'

120 Minutes of the meeting for 18 Feb. 1929, Taibhdhearc Papers, NUIG Add. MS 75.

122 In addition, a committee at An Taibhdhearc devised 'Scéim chun Feabhas a Chur ar Freastal Lucht Éisteachta agus chun Méadú ar Fághaltaisí an Taibhdheirc' (Scheme to improve audience attendance and to increase the income of An Taibhdhearc) that included the performance of specifically named plays of proven audience appeal and consultation with local teachers and the Department of Education to encourage student attendance at the theatre (Taibhdhearc Papers, NUIG MS T1/284). See also 'Sgéim Nua i dTaibhdhearc na Gaillimhe' (A new scheme at Taibhdhearc na Gaillimhe), *IP*, 6/11/37.

123 Ó Siadhail, *Stair Dhrámaíocht na Gaeilge*, 65.

124 On the other hand, in 1927 Seán Ó Ciarghusa wrote of An Comhar's audiences:

> They will continue to go whether the plays presented be good, bad, or indifferent. There is, therefore, no incentive to either dramatists or actors to strive to excel themselves. If they do excel themselves they will get the same perfunctory clap of applause as if they do the other thing, and the same perfunctory newspaper puff (*Leader*, 13/11/27).

His was, however, a minority opinion, although doubtless there were those in the movement who loyally performed what they saw as their (often painful) duty to attend the theatre and encourage the performers. And needless to say, few Gaelic actors would have agreed with his view of the unfailing benevolence of the critics.

125 He was speaking specifically of Pádraic Ó Conaire's *Bairbre Ruadh*. In another review of Gaelic plays, O'Connor wrote: 'I will do anything to prevent the performance of *An t-Athrú Mór* or *Heiricléas*, short of blowing up the theatre in which they are performed' (*IS*, 12/12/25). The former play was a bilingual propaganda piece by Felix Partridge from the early days of the Revival; the latter was a translation from our period by Gearóid Ó Lochlainn. See also Frank O'Connor, Letter, *IS*, 16/11/29.

126 He was explaining why the school had not performed a play in Irish for the feast of their patron saint that year.

127 Ní fhuil muinntear na tíre seo comh giallmhar sin ar an Ghaedhilg. Tá drámaí de dhíth ortha a b'fhiú a léiriughadh i dteanga ar bith agus i dtír ar bith agus is mithid dúinn anois a leithéid seo a chur ar fagháil i n-ionad drámaí beaga, lochtacha gan bhrigh, gan chéill. Ní fhuil na rudaí sin ach ag déanamh dochar do'n teangaidh. M. Ó Séaghdha felt the fault was primarily with authors afraid to challenge the low expectations of their audiences:

> Few dramas have yet been written in Irish that are worth performing at all. Until now the taste of the public has been kept low with straightforward, simple plays. If the author becomes serious for a minute, the audience expects that they will be in stitches the next minute and they are not disappointed (Is beag dráma atá scríobhtha fós sa Ghaodhluinn gur fiú é léiriú in aon chor. Go dtí seo tá blas an phobail coimeádta go h-íseal le drámaí díreacha simplidhe. Má éirigheann an t-ughdar dáiríreach ar feadh neomaite, bíonn súil ag an bpobal go mbeidís ins na tríthibh an céad neomait eile agus ní teiptear ortha) (*Quarryman*, Dec. 1937, n. p.).

128 Ag feuchaint dúinn ar an gclár atá leagtha amach ag an gComhar-drámaidheachta i gcomhair an

téarma so, 's léir go bhfuil urmhór des na drámaibh feicste agus ath-fheicste ag na daoinibh cheana.

129 Rud eile atá ag déanamh ceataighe dúinn ná gunna-cúiseacht [*sic*] drámaí sa Ghaoluinn agus as an mbeagán acu atá ann is beag arís díobh atá oireamhnach le léiriú anois, mar gur do shaoghal eile i bhfad a scríobhadh a bhfurmhór . . . Má's féidir le lucht an Bheurla na céadta rudaí do chur ar an ardán, ba chóir go bhféadfadh Gaedhilgeoirí cupla drámaí oireamhnacha do chumadh. He must have had in mind the plays of Hyde, Father O'Leary, Father Dinneen, Peadar Mac Fhionnlaoich, and others from the beginning of the Revival.

130 Ní féidir an rud seo do rádh ró-mhinic: drámaí, drámaí, agus tuille drámaí an rosg catha is fearr agus is feileamhnaighe do dhuine óg atá suas fa láthair. He wanted both original plays and new translations.

131 Ní h-amhlaidh ná fuil bun-drámaí Gaodhluinne á sgríobh ag na h-ughdaraibh fé láthair, acht is amhlaidh go bhfuil sé an-deacair ar fad na drámaí atá 'á sgríobh do léiriú. Easba eolais ag na h-ughdaraibh ar 'Technique' an stáitse agus ar an modh Drámuíochta is bun le sin. In 1936, Thomas Barrington called attention to the fact that the secretary of An Comhar Drámaidheachta had recently reported that only one play 'of any merit' had been submitted to the group that year (*IR*, July 1936, 521). See also 'A. Ó C.', 'Cheithre Drámaí Bunaidh' (Four original plays), *Standard*, 3/1/36; and 'Seathrún', 'Cúrsaí Drámaidheachta Gaedhilge' (Gaelic dramatic affairs), *IC*, 13/6/36.

132 'Tuarasgabháil an Rúnaidhe ar an obair a deineadh i rith an 15adh Seiseoin', 3 (bound with programmes donated to the NLI by Pádraig Ó Siochfhradha). One Gaelic writer who felt he was getting very little encouragement from Taibhdhearc na Gaillimhe was Micheál Breathnach, who complained in a Nov. 1929 letter that it had taken the theatre more than six weeks to comment one way or another on a play he had submitted. The previous month, he had demanded that the script be returned to him at once, adding: 'I do not think it is any wonder that drama in this country is not growing at all, since the person who tries to make plays available is not even treated honestly' (Ní hiongnadh ar bith, dar liom, nach bhfuil fás ar bith ag dul fé dhrámuíocht sa tír seo, arae ní bhíonn cneastacht féin le fagháil ag an té a bhíos iarraidh ar drámaí a chur ar fagháil). See Micheál Breathnach, Letters to Taibhdhearc na Gaillimhe, 13 Nov. 1929, and 31 Dec. 1929, Taibhdhearc Papers, NUIG MSS T1/117, T1/118. See also the 1941 letter from Séamus Ó Néill complaining about his treatment at the hands of An Taibhdhearc in *The Leader*, 13 Sept. 1941.

133 In 1931, the board of An Taibhdhearc voted to donate £4 to a *feis* in Galway to fund prizes for competitions for a translated children's play and for a play for adults (Minutes of the meeting for 2 Mar. 1931, Taibhdhearc Papers, NUIG Add. MS 22).

134 See 'Comórtais an Oireachtais', *Misneach*, 4/2/22; and Ó Súilleabháin, *Scéal an Oireachtais*, 184.

135 Seán Ó Ciarghusa wrote: 'The Gaels of Dublin are shamed forever with how few of them came to play or concert during the week. Where were they, or what did they prefer to do?' (Tá Gaedhil Bhaile Átha Cliath náirighthe go deo, a laighead díobh tháinig go dtí dráma ná Cuirim [*sic*] Ceoil i rith na seachtmhaine. Cá rabhadar; nó cad ab rogha leo?) (*Leader*, 4/8/23). 'Micheál na Téide' also referred to the attendance as 'shameful' (náireach) (*FL*, 10/11/23). See also 'Aithnighthear Cara i gCruadhtan' (A friend is recognised in hard times), Editorial, *Sguab*, Sept. 1923, 227–8.

136 Fritheadh 23 gearr-drámaí agus 9 drámaí ilghníomh le h-aghaidh na comórtaisí agus bhí a bhfurmhór go maith. Bhí cupla bun-drámaí ann. Thug na h-údair fé gach saghas adhbhair, ó eachtraí staire go dtí cúrsaí ár linne féin. Most of the plays submitted were tragedies (trom-drámaí).

137 A 'Ballet agus Míme Ghaedhealach' (Ballet and Gaelic mime show) were also performed in the Gaiety Theatre during the Oireachtas. See *An tOireachtas, Samhain 4adh–8adh Lá i dTigh an Ard-Mhaoir Baile Átha Cliath* (The Oireachtas, 4–8 Nov. in the Mansion House, Dublin) (a sort of publicity brochure in advance of the Oireachtas). There had also been drama competitions at the 'Oireachtais' of 1931 and 1932. Another important national festival that sponsored competitions for Gaelic drama was Aonach Tailteann, where in 1924 the prizes went to Micheál Ó Gríobhtha and Seán Ó Tóibín (*II*, 16/10/24), while in 1928 the gold medal was awarded to Piaras Béaslaí (*II*, 15/8/28). In 1932, Micheál Ó Siochfhradha won the first prize with the second going to Micheál Breathnach (*Tailteann Games, June 29–July 10, 1932 / Daily Programme, Tuesday, July 5th*).

138 See also 'Cumann do Dhrámadóirí / Iarracht Nua i nÁth Cliath', *IP*, 16/2/36. The members of the provisional committee of the group were Béaslaí, Pádraig Ó Bróithe, an author of plays for children, Máire Ní Chinnéide, Micheál Breathnach, and Tadhg Ó Scanaill.

139 He added: 'The Abbey, we feel, would not deserve its name of "National Theatre" unless it not only could but did produce works in Irish.' The competition drew 56 entries (*IP*, 15/6/38). In 1939, Radió Éireann sponsored a competition for radio plays in Irish, with Tomás Ó Laoi winning and Séamus de Bhilmot taking second prize (*IP*, 30/10/39).

140 Blythe, Letter to Liam Ó Briain, 28 May 1936, Taibhdhearc Papers, NUIG MS T1/266. Blythe had been appointed a member of the Abbey's Board of Directors in March 1935. By 1937, the board was giving serious consideration to the idea that plays in Irish should become a regular feature of the Abbey's schedule. See 'Gaelic Plays at the "Abbey" / Important Decision Meets with General Approval: Bilingual

Players', *IP*, 18/9/37. Among those supportive of such a venture were the actor Cyril Cusack and Frank O'Connor.

141 Compare the quite similar views expressed in 'Current Affairs / And the Abbey', *Leader*, 14/1/39. A few weeks earlier, the author of the 'Our Gael's Letter' column in the same paper wondered if the Abbey was serious about its new commitment to drama in Irish and stated that Gaels would have to insist that the Abbey 'gave the productions as much sympathetic attention as they give the plays in English' (*Leader*, 24/12/38).

142 Some of these goals could be very modest indeed. For instance, in 1929 T. J. Doorly called for 'more amateur theatricals' in Irish, with the first scripts to be bilingual (*Leader*, 25/2/29).

143 Ní thiocfaidh siad chun fiú amháin na cinn is fearr des na drámaí tuaithe Sacs-Ghaedhealacha d'fheiceál. Feictear dóibh go bhfuil siad dúr agus ní thaithnigheann aon nídh brónach leo. She added that Galway audiences best liked comedy and religious drama and did not have any appreciation for satire.

144 Níl aimhreas ar bith feasta nach drámaí grinn a thaithnigheas leis na Gaedhilgeoirí; níl leath oiread spéis aca i ngoldráma ná i ndráma staireamhail. See also 'An Comhar Drámaidheachta', *AA*, Jan. 1939, 3; and 'An Comhar Drámaidheachta', *AA*, Mar. 1939, 5.

145 Is iomdha iarracht atá tugtha ar gheandrámaí a scríobhadh sa teangain náisiúnta. Cé go bhfuil dóthain mhór de fhronnsaí (cluichí áilteoireachta) inti de thoradh na n-iarrachtaí sin is tearc fíor-gheandráma atá ceaptha fós. See also 'Bricriu', 'Léirmheas ar Leabhraibh / Drámaí' (Review of books / Plays), Enniscorthy *Echo*, 1/8/31. In his comic piece 'Drámaí Truagha' (Sorrowful plays), Seán Ó Ciarghusa tells of his efforts to write tragedy on the principle that 'the plays of the Gaels should be sad like the music of the Gaels' (badh cheart drámaí na nGaedheal a bheith brónach, dála ceoil na nGaedheal) (*Leader*, 2/12/39).

146 Nach mithid do lucht na n-amharclann bheith ag cuimhneamh ar phantomím Ghaedhilge do léiriú. Tá a bheagán nó a mhórán de'n Ghaedhilg ag an nglúin óig agus dá luighead an beagán san ba leor é chun pantomím Ghaedhilge do thuigsint . . . Níor dheacair do dhuine ceann d'eachtraí an bhéaloidis do chur i bhfuirm pantomím. In lieu of an original pantomime, she suggested that one of the shows in English be translated.

147 An pantomime a bhíonn i n-Áth Cliath d'oirfeadh sé do chathair ar bith i Sasana. Deintear dearmhad ar fad ar Éirinn agus maidir le Gaedhilg ní chuala aoinne beo amhrán sa teangain sin ag an pantomime ariamh. Sé truagh an sgéil go gcuirtear suim an-mhór sa rud seo a bhfuil aigne na nGall go smior ann. Minic adubhradh gur mór an náire é nach mbíonn pantomime Gaedhealach againn, ach na daoine adeir sin is ag cuimhneamh ar léiriú i mBéarla a bhíd.

148 See also 'Pantomím i gCóir na Nodlag' (A pantomine for Chrtistmas), *IP*, 11/12/37.

149 Sgoith an cluithche seo ar gach a raibh ann go dtí seo le tinnreamh daoine 's le n-ar íocadh ag an dorus, agus ní Gaedhilgeoirí amháin a bhíodh sa láthair, ach thagadh cuimse daoine gan Gaedhilge. Extra performances were added to accommodate those turned away.

150 Gan amhras ba cheart go mbeadh slí agus scóip don dráma suilt, leis, i n-aon amharclainn Ghaedhealaigh, ach ní foláir do náisiún bheith i dturtaoibh leis an sult amháin mar lón don aigne.

151 Is ar an gcaint, ar a brigh agus ar cheol na cainnte a bhíodh meas ag na Gaedhil. Mar gheall ar a líomhtha, so-lúbtha agus atá an teanga Ghaedhilge agus mar gheall ar a aibidhe agus a bhí an aigne Ghaedhealach, b'éasgaidh na heachtraí ba chasta agus ba chlisde a léiriú le congnamh na cainnte amháin. The use of tenses here is interesting.

152 See 'Plays in Irish / Promising Movement', *II*, 18/12/25.

153 Letter from Director of Radio Athlone to Liam Ó Briain, 26 July 1935, Taibhdhearc Papers, NUIG MS T1/256.

154 Sé is cluiche Radio ná cluiche do scríobhfaí agus do leagfaí amach i dtreo go bhféadfaí í léiriú do réir áiseanna agus éilithe speisialta an fhoirleatha. Cluiche amharclainne do cuirfí i n-oiriúint do'n radio tré úsáid do bhaint as fuaimiúlacht, ní bheadh sí oiriúnach i gcóir an chomórtais seo. In 1936, the station announced a plan to train native speakers as actors for radio plays. Those responsible were clearly aware of the challenges they faced:

> Experience has shown that in most cases the native speaker of Irish had no idea of the fundamental rules of radio acting. It is hoped, however, that with time and hard work these difficulties will be overcome and that it will be possible to provide listeners with first class Irish dramatic productions (*IP*, 17/7/36).

155 Not all Gaels were as thoughtful in their approach to this medium, with some feeling that if virtually all broadcasts were not in Irish, the station should be disbanded. See Mac Aonghusa, *Ar Son na Gaeilge*, 261.

156 Isé céad áis a mholfaimís ná an drámuíocht toisc go bhfaghtar caoi san drámuíocht, thar aon nidh eile, bféidir, chun léiriú do dhéanamh ar dhóchais agus ar mhianta, ar bhróin agus ar áthais aon chinidh. Tá san fíor, go speisialta, i dtaoibh drámaí a bhaineas le saoghal na linne ina mbíd d'á léiriú; agus sin iad na drámaí is fearr agus is oireamhnaighe don Radió. The pamphlet stated 'that our principal obligation is to truthfully express through the radio the character of the Gael and the Gaelic nation (gurab é príomhchúram atá orainn ná fír-léiriú do dhéanamh tríd an

Radió ar thréithíocht an Ghaedhil agus an náisiúin Ghaedhealaigh) (p. 21).

157 See 'Mumming in Irish Language / Novel Feature at Big Wexford Feis', *IP*, 17/5/37.

158 See 'A Gaelic Marionette Show', *Teacher's Work*, Apr. 1936, 324. The show was 'based on Gaelic Folklore'.

159 The ballets were, of course, 'Gaelic' in theme and musical accompaniment rather than in language. The group that created them, An Ceol-Chumann, made its first appearance at the Gate Theatre in 1936. Their Cú Chulainn ballet has been discussed above in chapter five. They also produced ballets based on Pearse's play *The Singer* (*II*, 20/11/37), on Hyde's play *Casadh an tSúgáin* (*II*, 5/11/38), and on a landscape by the painter Paul Henry with reference to poems by Pearse and Geoffrey Keating (*IP*, 7/11/39).

160 Letter from S. Mac Conglinne, secretary of the Gaelic League, to Geoffrey Molyneux Palmer, 1 Sept. 1923, Tomás Ó Ceallaigh Papers, NLI MS 8129 (7).

161 See the letters to Palmer of 12 Apr. 1920; 2 Oct. 1920; 21 June 1921; and 12 May 1923, Ó Ceallaigh Papers, NLI MS 8129.

162 See *An Craipí Óg: Ceol-Dráma Gearr*, tr. Muiris Ó Catháin (BÁC: n.p., n.d.).

163 Ní beag a bhfuil de fhíor-cheoltoirí sa tír seo, agus ba indéanta ceol-drámaí Gaedhealacha a chumadh.

164 *An tOireachtas: Clár na gComórtaisí* (The Oireachtas: Programme of the competitions), 5. Mion-radharc ceol-dráma . . . Gan níos lugha 'ná beirt a bheith ann nó níos mó ná ceathrar. Cead comhrádh ceangail a chur leis na hamhráin nó leis na bhéarsaí. Gabháil an iomláin do mhaireamhaint tuairim dhá neomat déag. The conditions for the competition said that this work should be 'light or comic' (aerach nó greannmhar). In the programme for the Oireachtas itself, the conditions for this competition had changed considerably. Readers were told that the play should last an hour, the theme should be 'Gaelic', and contestants could use existing songs and melodies if they wished. Despite a hefty first prize of £50, the competition only attracted one entrant and no prize was awarded. See *An tOireachtas: Samhain 4adh go 8adh, 1939* (The Oireachtas, 4–8 Nov. 1939), 20.

165 Breactar scáileáin na tíre gach oidhche sa bhliadhain leis an bpictiúir gallda a fuintear le aigne gallda. Tá an galldughadh ar siubhail fós agus is ionann é agus smachtughadh. Is treise go mór an smachtughadh atá á chur orainn le pictiúirí ná aon smachtughadh dá ndeárnadh riamh orainn le gunaí móra; ní theicimíd ó sna pictiúirí acht gabhaimíd le croidhe iad féin agus a gcuid sáimh-cheilge. Creidim go bhfuil smacht á chur orainn leis an gcinema ná féadfaí a chur orainn leis na dlíghthe pianamhla.

166 Tá sé dona go leor na pictiúirí do bheith ag déanamh díobhála don Ghaelachas ach dá mbeidís chó Gaelach is táid Gallda do bheinn chó mór ina gcoinnibh is táim anois. Óir ní don Ghaelachas amháin atáid ag déanamh dochair, ach do gach ní i bhfuirm sibhialtachta sa tír seo nó in aon tír eile, dá mb'é lár na hAifrice é. Táid ag lot an duine mar dhuine agus ba cheart deire do chur leo ar fuaid an domhain (nó iad fheabhsú) nó is ar éigin a bheidh an cine daonna ar ball níos aoirde meas is intleacht ná an t-apa úd óna shíolruíomair fadó, más fíor do Dean Inge. Ó Rinn did feel that the talkies were somewhat less dangerous than the silent films because at least the dialogue engaged the mind, while the silent screen stultified the viewers' intelligence and reduced them all to the lowest common denominator. One 'Sásta' took forceful exception to Ó Rinn's plan to ban all films from the Free State for five to ten years (*Star*, 26/10/29).

167 Blythe's article 'Gádh le Scannáin Ghaedhealacha' (Need for Gaelic films) in the 1940 issue of *Éire: Bliainiris Ghaedheal / Rogha Saothair Ghaedheal mBeo* (Ireland: A Gaelic yearbook / A selection of the work of living Gaels) is a translation into Irish of this piece. See also his thoughts on television as expressed in 'Trí Módha Léirighthe' (Three modes of performance), *IP*, 20/1/38) and in an undated letter to Liam Ó Briain, Taibhdhearc Papers, NUIG MS T1/289. The letter would appear to be from late 1937 or very early 1938.

168 Blythe was willing to go to extremes to finance such a scheme: 'If, for example, money could only be found for film production by abolishing our legations abroad, I think it would be wise to close every one of them.' In an address to the revived Oireachtas in 1939, Blythe called again for the production of films in Irish. See 'Oireachtas Leader Says Irish Must Be Used in Business', *IP*, 7/11/39; and 'An t-Oireachtas / Irish Not Safe Until –', *IP*, 9/11/39. In a piece in *II* on 16 Dec. 1936, Blythe lamented the fact that there was no reading matter in Irish on 'the development of television.' Nor was he the only visionary in this regard. An anonymous contributor to *An t-Éireannach* devoted an entire 1934 article to the need for the Irish state to develop broadcast facilities for television as had been done for radio (*Éireannach*, 30/6/34).

169 Cuireadh iallach ar mhuinntir Aránn [*sic*] a dteanga féin a thréigsint agus teanga coimhthigheach a labhairt a bhí mí-nádúrtha dhóibh féin agus d'aoinne a bhí ag éisteacht leo . . . Tuige nach mbeadh a dteanga dúthchais ag muinntir Árainne [*sic*], chomh maith lena bhfeisteas agus nósanna.

170 An Ghaedhilg an féith agus an tréith is suimeamhla atá le tabhairt fá deara in Árainn: agus anois rachaidh sé thríd an domhain go bhfuil an Ainglis i bhfeidhm san ghiob is fuide siar d'Éirinn. This column, 'An Fórum', was usually published under the name of Peadar Mac Fhionnlaoich, writing as 'Cú Uladh.'

171 Sin rud eile a chuir droch-mheas ar an oileán seo an pictiúr 'Fear Árainn', a rinneadh ann. Ní fhaca mise an pictiúr sin ghá thasbáint ariamh, acht mara bhfaca féin, chuala mé gurbh é an Béarla a bhí ann . . . Rud eile dhe badh Phuncánach a bhí na mháighistir air, agus, arnó, bhí a fhios aige siúd gur mhó go mór a shaothróchadh an pictiúr leis an mBéarla a chur ann. 'Sliabh Bladhma' stated that he had heard a great deal about the film, but had never seen it, adding, 'In Western Europe nowadays the films, like the novels, appear to constitute a vast entertainment industry, or to be regarded as stimulants, and I do not find them attractive' (*Gaedheal*, 17/11/34).

172 Taisbeánfar an pictiúir seo go fóirleathadúil fé an n-domhan. Measfar é agus measfar sinn i mbailtibh mhóra an domhain. Cad a bheidh le rádh age na cinnidheachaibh uile acht go bhfuil gabhtha orainn, gur Sasannaigh bheaga gan aird sinn . . . Béarla teanga Árainn, teanga Iarthair na hÉireann ar deire, teanga na hÉireann go léir . . . Táimíd ar lár, claoidhte dar leis an domhan dá bharra so, claoidhte againn féin. Agus déanfaidh an domhan fonóid fughainn, rud a dheineadar go minic cheana. 'Oisín' agreed, writing with the characters of *Man of Aran* clearly in mind: 'Since they could not speak English, they were made into mutes' (Nuair nach dtiocfadh leo Béarla a labhairt rinneadh balbháin daobhtha) (*Derry People*, 9/4/38).

173 Kevin Rockett discusses the film and some of the response to it in 'Documentaries', in Rockett, Luke Gibbons and John Hill, *Cinema and Ireland* (Syracuse: Syracuse University Press, 1988), 72–3. The entire text of the story as told in the film was published by the government as *Oidhche Sheanchais* (BÁC: Roinn an Oideachais, [1934]), and in *IP* on 9 Jan. 1935, and again on 15 Mar. 1935). The tale told by Ó Dioráin is a variant of 'Scian a Caitheadh le Toinn' (A knife that was thrown at a wave). See *Scian a Caitheadh le Toinn: Scéalta agus Amhráin as Inis Eoghain agus Cuimhne ar Ghaeltacht Iorrais* (A knife that was thrown at a wave: Stories and songs from Inishowen and a memoir of the Iorras Gaeltacht), collected by Coslett Ó Cuinn, edited by Aodh Ó Canainn and Seosamh Watson (BÁC: Coiscéim, 1990), 85.

174 Ó Dioráin was also singled out for special praise as 'a very fine natural actor' in another piece on the film in *IT* on 18 Dec. 1934. In the *IT* supplement on the events of 1934 quoted above, *Oidhche Sheanchais* was called 'an excellent little film' (*IT*, 23/1/35, supplement). 'A. Ó C.' felt that those who criticised the film failed to see it for what it was, not an amusement but an artistic attempt to preserve for posterity the performance art of a traditional storyteller (*Standard*, 26/4/35).

175 Ní déarfainn go gcuirfí suim dá laighead ann meireach gurab é Gaedhealg a bhí á labhairt ann. Tá an iomarca de'n rud sin ar fad ag baint leis an nGaedhilg. Ceapann daoiní gur leor earra a bheith Gaedhealach, leabhra a bheith i nGaedhilge, daoiní a bheith ag cainnt Gaedhilge ⁊rl. chun go gcuirfí spéis ann. Ach chomh maith le rud a bheith Gaedhealach ba chóir dhóibh freisin féachaint go bhfuil sé go maith. His next sentence was 'Even so, this picture is a step in the right direction' (Mar sin féin is coiscéim sa treo ceart é an pictiúir seo).

176 Is cúis díombuaidhe dhúinn a laighead 'e spéis is chuir an pobal ins an gcéad pheictiúr Gaedhilge a léirigheadh i mBaile Átha Cliath an tseachtmhain seo caithte. Bhí 'Oidhche Sheanchuis' dá léiriú i dhá theach peictiúir sa gcathair acht chruthuigh an freastal suarach a rinneadh ortha i rith na seachtmhaine gur blas searbh atá ag furmhór an phobail ar Ghaedhilge agus ar Ghaedhealachas bíodh is go bhfuil sé ceapaithe do'n spioraid a bheith ag neartú i n-ár measg.

177 See 'An tSeachtmhain' (The week), *Éireannach*, 20/4/35. The previous month the editor of *An t-Éireannach* had written of the state's involvement with this film:

> Since the Government went this far, they should have finished the job properly, and made the first attempt a worthwhile one . . . The Government has taken the first step, and we hope it is not the last one they take in this direction (Ó chaith an Riaghaltas an choinneal ba chóir go gcaithfidís an t-órdlach agus iarracht ar fóghnamh a dhéanamh de'n chéad iarracht . . . Tá an chéad chloch caithte ag an Riaghaltas agus ta súil againn nach í an chloch dheirionnach í a chaithfeas siad sa treo sin) (*Éireannach*, 30/3/35).

On the other hand, 'J. A. P.' blasted the state for its unimaginative and niggardly approach to the project, claiming that what the government wanted was 'something extremely pedagogical' and that it had treated Flaherty shabbily: 'And, incidentally, it is rather an insult to an artist like Flaherty to ask him to make such a cheap film' (*II*, 15/7/33).

178 Deirtear gur chosnuigh an scannán so mórán airgid. Ní bheidh aon tóra as a leithéid. Níl an scéal éirimiúil, níl an chainnt cliste, agus gan aon dobht [*sic*] níl an scéal oiriúnach in aon tslí in ao' chor do scoileanna sa Mhumhain, agus más fiú éinní ár dtuairim déarfaimís nach ró-mhór an meas a bheidh ar chanamhaint Chonnachta nuair a bheidh an scannán so tar éis cúrsa do thabhairt ar fud na hÉireann.

179 Dar le n-a lán Gaedheal, ba iad na lochtaí ba mhó ar an phictiúr sin 'ná go raibh an Ghaedhilg ró-chasta agus ró-chruaidh dóbhtha; agus, go raibh brígh agus fuinneamh na n-aisteoirí ar iarraidh. This writer did add that 'these are fixable faults; and, through their being fixed, Gaelic pictures will become better and more polished' (lochtaí ion-leighiste iad seo; agus, tré n-a leigheas, tiocfaidh barr feabhais agus slacht ar phictiúirí Gaedhealacha). The editor of *An t-Éireannach* also pointed out that few audience members who were not native speakers would be able

to understand the Irish in the film (*Éireannach*, 30/3/35).

180 Níl an peictiúr féin gan locht agus sin é tuairim an ghnáth-dhuine. Sa gcéad chás de ó ba leis an Riaghaltas peictiúr Gaedhilge Gaedhealach do chur ar fagh//áil ba chóir go rachaidís i n-a chionn i gceart agus sompla maith de pheictiúr a chur ós comhair an phobail – peictiúr gníomhach a thiubharfadh le tuigsint do'n lucht éisteachta céard a bheadh ar siubhal . . . Níor chóir go mbeadh na h-aisteoirí ins an bpeictiúr seo chomh roighin marbh agus a bhíodar. Even critics who liked the film commented on the inherently static nature of the subject matter – a storyteller sitting in a room and recounting a tale. See, for example, the generally positive *IT* columns cited above, all of which noted, if only to downplay, the lack of action in the picture. It is worth noting that in a 1928 article in *II*, 'Sean-Éireannach' criticised the movies for fostering passivity in their audiences, an attitude he contrasted with the active involvement of listeners at a traditional storytelling session (*II*, 6/11/28).

181 Cailleadh airgead air sin mar níor phictiúir é a mheallfadh sluagh. Tá an pobal i dtaithighe sár-phictiúirí agus ní dhéanfaidh aon nídh eile an gnó . . . Ná bímís ag claoidhe leis an sórt san 'Gaedhealachais' ná fuil ann ach sean-aimsireacht a fulaingtear ar mhaithe le daoine gur áil leo fuath den nuadh a theasbáint – agus mairtírigh a dhéanamh díobh féin agus dá gcomh-dhaonnaidhthe. Bíodh gealadh agus pléisiúir ann. In the brief preface prepared by the Department of Education for the published version of the story told in the film, we read:

> On the Aran Islands, the western limit of the Gaels, some of the customs practised by the people of Europe in the Middle Ages are still alive – and the talent for storytelling is one of those customs. The long, cold nights of winter are spent narrating stories and singing songs. Seáinín Tom Sheáin tells an old story that was an old story a thousand years ago (Ar Oileáin Árainn, teorainn thiar na nGaedheal, tá roinnt de na nósanna a bhain le muinntir na hEorpa sa meadhon-aois beo fós – agus tá buadh na scéal-aidheachta ar cheann de na nósanna sin. Is ag ríomhadh scéal agus ag gabháil amhrán a caithtear oidhcheannta fada fuara an gheimhridh. Innsigheann Seáinín Tom Sheáin sean-scéal a bhí 'na shean-scéal míle bliain ó shoin).

Liam Ó Laoghaire was to write in *Invitation to the Film* (1945) that 'the script which was foisted on [Flaherty] by our enlightened Department of Education was utterly devoid of any filmic content.' (Ó Laoghaire, quoted by Rockett in 'Documentaries', in Rockett *et al.*, *Cinema and Ireland*, 73. Writing in *Scéal na Scannán* (The story of the films), Proinsias Ó Conluain declared of *Oidhche Sheanchais* that it was

> the first film accompanied by a soundtrack in Irish, and the worst film that Flaherty ever allowed his name to be put on. Of course, the fault was not entirely his – there was little he could do with the £200 with which the Department of Education provided him (an chéad scannán a raibh fuaimrian Gaeilge ag gabháil leis agus an ceann ba mheasa dár cheadaigh Ó Flaithartaigh [*sic*] a ainm a chur leis. Ní hairsean ar fad a bhi an locht, ar ndóigh – ba bheag a d'fhéadfadh sé a dhéanamh leis an £200 a chuir an Roinn Oideachais ar fáil dó).

See Ó Conluain, *Scéal na Scannán* (BÁC: OS, 1953), 241.

182 Tá againn mar sin an chéad chúis do'n easba so drámaí, mar atá, iad san go bhfuil an Ghaedhilg acu agus fonn sgríobhtha ortha níl aon eolas acu ar chéird na h-aisteoireachta, agus iad san go bhfuil an t-eolas so acu, is beag díobh go bhfuil an Ghaedhilg acu.

183 Acht an chéad dráma a sgríobhfas duine aca, dá mba i ndán 's nach mbeadh ann acht rud sgaoilte gan chuma gan déanamh – agus nach mbeadh áit ar bith aca le n-a léiriughadh acht i mbóitheach ag tóin na bó, agus coinneal i mbuidéal pórtair mar sholus aca – beidh buadh aige nach rabh ag na drámaí a bhí i n-Amharclainn na Mainistreach. Tús nádúrtha a bhéas ann agus tiocfaidh as le linn na h-aimsire. See the strikingly similar views expressed by his brother Seosamh in 'An Dráma agus Nithe Atá Gaolmhar dó' (The drama and things related to it), *An t-Ultach*, Sept. 1924, 5–6.

184 Níor éirigh le dream ar bith go fóill a thabhairt ar an phobal suim a chur i ndrámaí Gaedhilge – ar an adhbhar an mhuintir a bhfuil an Ghaedhilg aca nach bhfuil an chaoi aca agus an mhuintir a bhfuil an chaoi aca nach bhfuil an Ghaedhilg aca . . . Ach anois an bhfuil drámaí ar bith i ndán dúinn sa tír seo? Ní móide go bhfuil go cionn tamaill eile. Acht ca bith uair a thiocfas an drámaidheacht caithfidh sí a theacht *aniar*. Caithfidh an drámaidheacht a theacht as an áit a bhfuil an Ghaedhilg dá labhairt go nádúrtha ag na daoiní. Déarfar liom ar ndóighe nach bhfuil eolas na céirde sin ag muintir na Gaedhealtachta. Aidmhighim. Acht dá olcas iad tá siad comh maith leis an dream a bhí i n-Amharclainn na Mainistreach le cúig bliadhna. Ins an chéad chás de níl siad i muinghin Ghaedhilg Liverpool. He was, of course, referring to An Comhar Drámaidheachta. For another of Ó Grianna's diatribes directed at An Comhar, see 'Clúid na nGaedheal' (The Gaels' corner), *Honesty*, 18/5/29.

185 Ba mhór an náire shaoghalta iad féin is a gcuid 'drámaí'. Tá sé dona go leor againn an Ghaedheal-tacht a bheith ag imtheacht, agus gan sgaifte de yahoos mhacánta gan béal gan teangaidh a bheith a' snagarsaigh ar ardán agus ag iarraidh a chur i gcéill dúinn gur teanga ár sinnsear atá aca.

186 An eol dóibh go bhfuil sé fuar againn bheith ag brath ar dhrámaí Gaedhilge ó'n nGalldacht mara dtugann an Ghaedhealtacht an deagh-shompla ar dtúis.
187 Cuireann sé ar mire mé smaoitiú go bhfuil an rialtas ag pronnadh míle punta gach bliadhain ar chumann rágaireachta i mBaile Átha Cliath a dtugtar 'An Comhar Drámaidheachta' air mar i ndúil a's go bhfágaidh [*sic*] ar chrann litridheachta na Gaedhilge craobh drámaidheachta; agus tchí Dia an cineál Gaedhilge atá ag an mhór-chuid de'n Chomhar! Agus muintir na Gaedhilge ins an iarthar (níl mé a ligean le dearmad Taibhdhearc na Gaillimhe) níl leithphighinn ruadh á theilgean chúca le n-a spriochadh chun suim a chur i ndrámaidheacht.
188 Dá mhéad moladh atá ag dul dho dhaoine ata a' déanamh a ndíchill annseo is annsiúd ar fud na Galldachta, ní fhéadfá bheith a' súil le dráma Gaedhilge dáiríre ach amháin ó mhuinntir na Gaedhealtachta.
189 Má tá forfhás ceart le teacht ar dhrámaidheacht na Gaedhilge, caithfe gur as an nGaedhealtacht a thiocfas sé. He did go on to say that he in no way meant to belittle or discourage the efforts of Gaelic acting companies in English-speaking Ireland.
190 A dissenting voice was that of 'B. S.', who, having criticised the Irish of some actors in a 1934 production by An Comhar Drámaidheachta, continued:

> It is not suggested that only native speakers, or people with Irish almost as good, should participate in the Comhar Drámuíochta productions. To make any such rule might throw the producer back on material which was too unsatisfactory from a histrionic point of view (*UI*, 22/12/34).

See also 'B. S.', 'Tragedy and Farce / Gaelic Players in the Peacock', *UI*, 26/1/35.
191 Máiréad Ní Ghráda, quoted by Ní Bhrádaigh, in *Máiréad Ní Ghráda*, 30. I gcúrsaí drámaíochta na Gaedhilge caithfimíd a adhmháil go bhfuil an bheárna is mó gan líonadh fós. Níl aon Amharclann Gaedhealach againn. Agus nuair a deirim é sin, ní hé an tigh nó an halla léirighthe atá i gceist agam. Ní hé i n-aon chor. Sé rud atá i gceist agam ná comh-cheangal na dtrí nidhthe atá riachtanach i nAmharclann, mar atá: na drámaí, na h-aisteoirí, agus an lucht éisteachta.

CHAPTER NINE

Taking Stock, Taking Chances

1 Ní bhfuighidh an Ghaedhilg a ceart go mbeidh leabhair Ghaedhilge chomh saor ar a laighead le leabhraibh Béarla, agus ní bheidh siad go dtiocfaidh an Stát i gcabhair i ngach aon tslighe ar an nGaedhilg agus díol as í chló-bhualadh sa tslighe chéadna agus atáthar ag díol as í mhúineadh. In 1922, Cumann na Scríbhneoirí drew up a series of proposals to present to the Dáil. Among them was: 'Support for authors with regard to their own writing £500' (Tacaidheacht le hughdaraibh i dtaoibh a gceapadóireachta féin £500) (*Misneach*, 29/4/22). Cumann na Scríbhneoirí, with Ó Rinn as secretary, held its first meeting after the outbreak of civil war in Cork in Feb. 1922. See 'Thall is Abhus / Sgeul Dóchais' (Here and there / A hopeful story), *Separatist*, 25/2/22.
2 See 'An Roinn Oideachais / Gúm chun Cabhruithe le Foillsiú Leabhar i nGaedhilg' (Department of Education / A scheme to assist with the publication of books in Irish), *FL*, 27/3/26. This announcement appeared in most of the Gaelic papers.
3 For an interesting perspective on An Gúm and its troubled relationships with Gaelic writers, see Alan Titley, 'An Scríbhneoir agus an Stát 1922–1982' (The writer and the state), *Scriobh* 6 (1984), 82–3.
4 Isé an Riaghaltas atá ag glacadh as láimh an obair seo feasta. Is ion-mholta an obair í a rachas ar sochar do litridheacht na tíre.
5 Ón lá a chuaidh Muinntir an Ghúim in éadan a gcuid oibre tá dhá bhliain ó shoin, tá níos mó leabhra Gaedhilge de gach cineál curtha amach acu ná ar tháinig amach sa sgathaimh céadna le dhá scór bliain. Roimhe seo do bhíodh scríobhnóirí Gaedhilge ag cleamhsán faoi nach raibh aon cheannach ar leabhra Gaedhilge agus nár fhéad lucht a scríobhtha dul faoi chostas a gclóbhuailte. Ní bheidh an leithsgéal sin feasta ag ughdar Gaedhilge ar bith go bhfuil fonn oibre dáiríribh air . . .. He continued a bit disingenuously: 'and who does not hate any working arrangement with which the Government is involved' (agus nach fuath leis aon ghléas oibre go bhfuil baint ag an Rialtas léi). In 1933, 'S. Ó F.' praised An Gúm for making its books available at bargain prices (*Standard*, 25/2/33).
6 He also wrote that

> the scheme has been conducted with a minimum of friction with either writers, the general public or the commercial houses. On the question of censorship, a sore matter with writers, it has never been found necessary to define, with any particularity, the circumstances in which it should be exercised. The few cases that have arisen have, I understand, been amicably settled. There is certainly no sense of dissatisfaction on this score among Irish writers in general (pp. 128–9).

On the other hand, in his autobiography *Just Like Yesterday*, Ó Broin acknowledged that An Gúm encouraged self-censorship by authors and provided some examples of how it worked (pp. 67–8). In his 'Ceangal', Ó Broin also wrote that he hoped for the writers' sake that there would be greater competition among publishers producing Gaelic books, adding that 'the machinery of the Gúm can be effectively used as a bargaining point in these cases of the commercial houses'. In the following year, 'Sliabh

Bladhma' urged the Gaelic League to get back into the publishing business, because 'it would be a healthy rival to the "Gúm", and it would be free of certain prejudices and limitations' (*Gaedheal*, Mar. 1936, 1).

7 In a piece in An *Tír* two months later, Ó Deirg said An Gúm had published 100 books with sales of 100,000 (*Tír*, Sept.–Oct. 1933, 6).

8 Things must have then slowed down a good deal at An Gúm, for in July 1935, the official count of books published by the agency was 235 (*IP*, 31/7/35).

9 See also 'An Sagart', 'Towards the Irish Revival', *Ráitheachán*, Mar. 1937, 11; and '400 Leabhra Gaedhilge' (400 books in Irish), *IP*, 2/4/37.

10 See also 'An Gúm / 290,000 Cóib a Díoladh' (An Gúm / 290,000 copies have been sold), *IP*, 28/10/38. Ó Broin himself reviewed some of An Gúm's new titles over the radio in February 1938 (*IP*, 12/2/38). See also the positive assessment of An Gúm's work by 'An t-Iolar' in 'Smaointe Reatha / An Gúm', (Current thoughts) (*Standard*, 28/7/39), a piece in which he questioned whether the newly revived Cumann na Scríbhneoirí had an anti-Gúm agenda.

11 Tá easnamh ar an nGaedhilg fé láthair. Easnamh mór iseadh é, mar deineann sé ceataighe don teangan, ghá coimeád chun deiridh, nuair atá dianghádh uirthi le dul ar aghaidh. Is é easnamh é sin ná uireasbha sgríbhneoirí. Tá anachuid daoine óga ann anois gur féidir leo an Ghaedhilg do léigheamh. Ach cad tá ann dóibh chuige? . . . Tá gádh le sgríbhneoirí maithe – daoine a cheapfaidh rudaí taithneamhacha dúinn san Ghaedhilg. Muran féidir adhbhar léightheoireachta go mbeidh blas air do sholáthar do lucht na Gaedhilge, tá sé chomh maith againn 'Finit' do sgríobhadh le stair na teangan dúthchais go lá an Luain. Ó Donnchadha went on to rebuke the writers for their laziness (*leisge*).

12 An bhfuil mórán leabhar againn? Leabharthaí a mheallfadh daoine 'un a léighte mar mhaithe le sgéal – mar léigheann siad sgéal i dteangaidh ar bith eile? An bhfuil duisín de na leabharthaí seo ó cheann go ceann na hÉireann indiu?

13 See also Nollaig Mac Congáil, 'Réamhrá', in *Máire – Clár Saothair*, 35–36; and the chapter 'Mé Féin agus Niall ag Coimhlint' (Myself and Niall competing) in Ó Grianna's autobiography *Saoghal Corrach*, 234–5. Peadar O'Donnell offered his support for Ó Grianna's view of An Gúm in 'Irish Artists', Letter, *An Phoblacht*, 23/7/32, as did Riobard Ó Faracháin in his reponse to Ó Broin's *Capuchin Annual* essay on 'Contemporary Gaelic Literature' (*CA*, 1935, 138–9).

14 An Gúm was not a particularly generous employer, paying by the word – at first £1 per thousand words for translations, £1 5*s.* per thousand words for original work, the rates for both kinds of writing being *lowered* by 5*s.* in 1932 – with a maximum payment of £50. Authors of original work were entitled to royalties; translators surrendered all rights to An Gúm on payment for their work. In addition it was the responsibility of the author to deal with copyright issues, reimbursing An Gúm if any penalties were incurred.

15 See also '"He Knows Everything"' (*UIrman*, 20/8/32); 'An Gúm / "Ceárdcha Litridheachta"' (An Gúm / 'A smithy for literature'), Dundalk *Examiner*, 3/9/32; and Mac Congáil, 'Réamhrá', in *Seosamh Mac Grianna: Clár Saothair*, 34–43.

16 Níl saothar is deacra ann san am i láthair 'ná leabhair Ghaedhilge do léirmheas, go mór mór na leabhair a tháinig ó Roinn an Oideachais. Chuir an Roinn sin cuid mhór leabhar amach le tamall beag anuas. Ach caithfear a rádh fá'n gcuid is mó díobh go mb'fheairrde an Ghaedhilg gan iad d'fhoillsiú ar chor ar bith. Is dearbh gur mó an dochar 'ná an mhaitheas thiocfas mar thoradh ar a bhfoillsiú. See also Mag Ruaidhrí, 'Litriú na Gaedhilge / An Dóigh ina bhFuiltear ag Lot ár dTeangadh' (The spelling of Irish / How our language is being destroyed), *Tír*, Oct. 1929, 4–5.

17 Is ceart an fhírinne lom a innsin, agus gan dul ar chúl sceiche leis. Caitheadh na mílte punt d'airgead na tíre le cúig bliadhain ar chur amach leabharthaí ar mhó a dtoirt 'ná a dtairbhe. Is féidir a rádh le fírinne nach bhfuil leath-dhuisín leabhar ar an iomlán a bhféadfaí litridheacht a thabhairt air, de bhrígh gur saothar sgríobhnóirí a bhí ann nach raibh an Ghaedhilge mar ba cheart aca agus nár thuig cad is litridheacht ann.

18 In another piece on the topic earlier in the year, this writer had stated that An Gúm's output 'ought to be increased at least tenfold.' See 'Current Affairs / Fewer Books', *Leader*, 11/3/39. See also Proinnsias Ó Cinnéide, 'Cumann na Meán-Múinteoirí', *Association of Secondary Teachers of Ireland / Official Year Book and Diary*, 1937–8, 81. In his 1938 essay on 'A State-Fostered Literature', Ó Broin asserted:

> I should say that the position of Gaelic literature will remain insecure until such time as there is in existence a collection of about five thousand works of quality to which new volumes are being added at the rate of at least one a day (*Irish Monthly*, Feb. 1938, 126).

19 Ní chuirfidh ughdar suas le riaghalacha cumhanga, agus barraidheacht cur isteach air. Agus má tá inntleacht neamh-thuilleamhnach aige ní shásóchaid a scríbhinní leis an Ghúm agus leis an dream atá taobh thiar de'n Ghúm . . . Bhí beagán roinnte agam féin leis an Ghúm a thaisbeáin nach féidir le scríobhnóir go bhfuil inntinn neamhspleadhach aige obair a dhéanamh do'n Ghúm. Mac Fhionnlaoich at one point ran his own press, Cú Uladh agus a Chuid, as a counter to An Gúm. As early as 1923, Seán Ó Ciosáin, in an address to a convention of vocational schoolteachers, had argued that literature could not be bought and that any scheme to do so might endanger the creativity of writers involved (*FL*,

16/6/23). Among the motions submitted to the Gaelic League's convention in 1933 was one from the Executive Committee asking for an independent inquiry into An Gúm, looking into the agency's choice of books, sales, etc. See 'Cúrsaí an Chonnartha / Rúin do'n Chomhdháil' (League affairs / Motions for the Congress), *Camán*, 15/4/33.

20 See Donn Piatt, 'An Gúm Arís' (An Gúm again), Letter, *Ultach*, Oct. 1932, 3. Piatt was praised by 'An Cleitire' for having the 'initiative' to publish his own works (*An Phoblacht*, 25/2/33). Piatt's press was Cló na Saoirse.

21 Ó Cuív, *Prós na hAoise Seo*, 10. Ar an adhbhar san, ní féidir bheith deimhin de gurab é saothar an ughdair féin a bhíonn againn i n-aon chor nuair a bhíonn leabhar ón Rialtas á léigheamh againn.

22 In his biography of Seán Ó Ruadháin, Máirtín Mac Niocláis discusses the often stultifying effect of An Gúm on writers of the period. See Mac Niocláis, *Seán Ó Ruadháin*, 163, 186. Tomás Bairéad recalled the prudishness of An Gúm's editors in his autobiography *Gan Baisteadh*, 19, 219, 240. Seosamh Mac Grianna's experience of Gúm censorhip is discussed in a 1932 essay 'Irish Artists, the Gúm, the People and So Forth' (*An Phoblacht*, 23/7/32). See also Mac Congáil, 'Réamhrá', in *Seosamh Mac Grianna: Clár Saothair*, 37. An Gúm's treatment of Seán Ó Caomhánaigh's 1927 novel *Fánaí* was discussed earlier in this study.

23 Nuair do bunuigheadh an Gúm bhi súil againn le sruth litridheachta do bhrúcht chugainn ina chaise. Bheadh oibridhthe an Ghúim ann, dar linn, chun an chaise sin do scagadh chun go mbeadh sí ina tobar fíor-litridheachta, agus chun go mbeadh neart don phobal tarrac as an dtobar san, agus an tart a bhí ortha chun na litridheachta do mhúchadh. Ach níorbh' fhada gur cuireadh scaipeadh ar ár ndóchas. Dhein oibridhthe an Ghúim an tobar ach níor bhrúcht chúcha ach an caol-sruth. She saw An Gúm's realisation of its failure to generate original work as motivating the emphasis on translation. See also Micheál Ó Donnachadha, 'Leabhair Ghaedhilge / Úir-Scéalta agus Aistriúcháin' (Books in Irish / New works and translations), *II*, 13/12/35.

24 The reason for holding the novel back was apparently fear of potential libel suits. See Mac Congáil, 'Réamhrá', in *Mac Grianna: Clár Saothair*, 37; Niall Ó Domhnaill, 'Seosamh Mac Grianna', in *Scríbhneoireacht na gConallach*, ed. Mac Congáil, 117; and Pól Ó Muirí, *Flight from Shadow*, 129.

25 Maith an scéal é, acht níor cuireadh leabhar nuadh amach chugainn le tamall maith anois agus sinne ag feitheamh le toradh éigin ó na scríobhnóirí. Is mór an truaigh go bhfuil an oirid sin d'fhadálacht ag baint leis an chur amach, agus an bruideadh bhíos ar na scríobhnóirí.

26 The editor wondered if the problem was 'a tendency on the part of the editorial staff to be more than meticulous in the work of editorship'. The editor repeated his criticism of 'the hold up of publications under the Gúm' two months later. See 'Stoppage of Irish Publications', *Star*, 2/8/30. 'Léitheoir Comhthrom' expressed his frustration with An Gúm's delays in the London journal *Féile na nGaedheal*, May 1932, 3.

27 She asserted 'go léighfí níos mó de leabhra an Ghúim dá mbeadh a fhios ag léightheoirí Gaedhilge a leithéide a bheith i gcló. Tá sé 'chuile órlach chó riachtanach ag Coiste na Leabhar fógraíocht do dhéanamh ar a gcuid leabhar agus atá ar na gnáthfhoillsightheoirí agus b'fhéidir níos riachtanaighe.' See also Aodh de Blácam, 'Literary Notes and Notions / Neil Munro in Irish', *Standard*, 25/7/31.

28 In her regular column in *The Star* in 1930, 'B. Ní M.' put some of the blame on An Gúm, claiming that with An Gúm paying them for even slipshod work, writers were now unwilling to submit material to journals that offered little or no compensation (*Star*, 19/7/30). For a far more optimistic perspective on the situation, see 'The Modern Gael', *Nation*, 15/3/30.

29 Having acknowledged An Gúm's 'life and death struggle to save the native idiom from extinction', she asserted that she had no individual authors in mind; rather 'I have in mind only the general recognition of the fatuousness of most of the printed matter – the "rameis" [*sic*] [nonsense] which is given to our children and to students of modern Irish in Ireland to-day, as literary pabulum.'

30 He also stated: 'Those who find fault with what the Gúm is doing have the wrong end of the stick altogether. What it is doing is very good and useful as far as it goes. Complaint should be made about what it is not doing.' Others felt that there was too much page filling and too little real writing going on in Irish. For example, in a July 1937 editorial in *An Gaedheal*, we read: 'A certain great writer said – "I hate the 'natural-born genius'." We have a flood of them in Irish. If there were fewer "geniuses" and more knowledge of the art of writing, we would be the richer for it' (Dubhairt scríobhnóir mór áirithe – 'Is fuath liom an "natural-born genius".' Tá tuile dhíobh 'sa Ghaoluinn againn. Dá mbeadh níos lugha 'genius' agus níos mó eolas ar an ealadhain scríobhnóireachta ba shaidhbhre-de sinn) (*Gaedheal*, July 1937, 2). Ó Rinn felt that readers should understand the conditions in which Gaelic authors were working, and so better appreciate what they had accomplished. He was, however, insistent that standards not be lowered for the cause:

> We should not disparage everyone who takes on this work, all but certain before time that he will not succeed in doing anything, but rather praise him highly because of his courage and then take his work and pass honest judgement on it (Gach éinne dhíríonn ar an obair seo agus é nach mór deimnitheach roimh ré ná héireoidh leis puinn

do dhéanamh, ní droch-mheas do chaitheamh air is ceart dúinn a dhéanamh ach é mholadh go mór mar gheall ar a mhisneach agus ansan a chuid oibre do thógaint agus breith mhacánta thabhairt uirthi) (*UI*, 8/12/34).

31 B'fhearr i bhfad gan focal Gaedhilge a cur i gcló 'ná rud a sgríobhadh nach léighfeadh na daoine dá mbeadh sé i m-Béarla. Chan é amháin go gcuirfidh sé samhnas agus droch-mhisneach ar na Gaedhil ach bheirfidh sé seans do naimhde na teangadh ionnsaighe a dhéanamh uirthi.

32 In a 1933 piece, Micheál Ó Donnabháin (Frank O'Connor) stated flatly that all librarians knew full well that An Gúm could never, under any circumstances, meet the needs of the Irish reading public, even if that public were willing to seek its information and entertainment in Irish in preference to English. See Ó Donnabháin, 'An Gúm', *An Leabharlann*, Dec. 1933, 130.

33 See 'Gluaiseacht 'sna hOllscoileanna' (A movement in the universities), *IP*, 15/3/38; and *An Comhchaidreamh: Crann a Chraobhaigh: Cnuasacht Aistí* (An Comhchaidreamh: A tree that branched out: A collection of essays), ed. Stiofán Ó hAnnracháin (BÁC: An Clóchomhar, 1985).

34 The 1931 festival was forgotten by some within a year. In a 1932 piece in *II* it was announced that 'tonight, in the Mansion House, Dublin, will be revived, after a lapse of eight years, the Oireachtas, the great social concourse of Gaeldom' (*II*, 31/10/32). See also 'An t-Oireachtas', *AA*, Aug. 1939, 4. No subsequent history of the Gaelic League makes mention of an Oireachtas in either 1931 or 1932, although in an essay on the contributions of Pádraig Ó Siochfhradha to the revival of the Oireachtas, Éibhlín Ní Chathailriabhaigh does call the 1932 gathering an Oireachtas. She says nothing of the 1931 festival. See Éibhlín Ní Chathailriabhaigh, 'Pádraig Ó Siochfhradha ("An Seabhac") agus Athbheochan an Oireachtais' (Pádraig Ó Siochfhradha {'An Seabhac'} and the revival of the Oireachtas), in *Oireachtas na Gaeilge, 1897–1997*, ed. Proinisas Mac Aonghusa (BÁC: Conradh na Gaeilge, 1997), 55–60.

35 Tá iarracht á dhéanamh ag an gCoiste Gnótha ar an Oireachtas d'aithbheochaint tar éis é bheith ar lár ar feadh seacht mbliain. Is geall le tosnú nua an iarracht so.

36 Is mór an taca d'aon dream daoine go mbíonn an aigne chéadna aca, agus is mór an taca dhóibh teacht ar aon láthair ag neartú ar a chéile tré chainnt agus tré chomhrádh. Ba mhaith an smaoineamh é dá bhrigh sin an t-Oireachtas do chur ar siubhal arís. Gheobhfaidhe caoi ann chun litridheacht a sporradh; do raghaimís i dtaithighe a chéile go mór i slighe is go mba chosamhail le tionól sluaighte airm é.

37 Is tráthamhail é mar sin, agus is aoibhinn le cloisint é, go bhfuiltear chun Oireachtas na nGaedheal do chur ar siubhal arís . . . Agus gach bhliadhain na dhiaidh seo tá súil go mbeidh plúr na bhfeiseann agus togha na nGaedheal le feicsint ag iomaidheacht i mBleá Cliath.

38 Ní bheidh an t-Oireachtas seo ar aon dul leis na ceannaibh a bhíodh ann roimhe seo. Ní mí-chosúil le feis an rud atá beartuithe ag an gCoiste Gnótha an mhí seo chughainn.

39 Níor mhór an cruinniú a bhí sa láthair an uair sin ach d'fhás an tOireachtas agus bhí súil aige go bhfásfadh sé ath-uair de bharr na h-iarrachta seo.

40 See *Connradh na Gaedhilge / Seachtmhain na Samhna (Samhain a 2–7adh): Comórtaisí Ceoil, Amhránaidheachta, Rinnce agus Drámaidheachta* (Gaelic League / November week {November 2–7}: Competitions in music, singing, dancing and drama).

41 D'éirigh leis an Oireachtas i mbliadhna níos fearr ná mar cheapadh ó thosach dhó . . . Tús maith an tús seo agus tá súil againn go néireochaidh níos fearr leis an Oireachtas seo chugainn. He did, however, feel that the Gaels had failed in their duty to support the festival. See also Ó Maoláin, 'Leathanach na Gaedhilge', *Nationality*, 9/4/32.

42 Ní ró-fhada uainn Seachtain na Samhna anois, agus má táthar chun buachtaint ar an Oireachtas a bhí ann anuiridh caithfidh na craobhacha agus na sgoileanna tosnú láithreach ar ullmhúcháin a dhéanamh i gcóir na gcomórtas.

43 Is é rud atá beartuithe ná na Feiseanna agus an t-Oireachtas d'fhigheadh isteach 'na chéile i slí go mbeadh Ard-oireachtas ann. Is deacair, ámhthach, é sin a dhéanamh.

44 Ba dhóigh leat an tseachtmhain seo caithte gur ag tosnughadh ar obair na Gaedhilge bhíothas – agus an tosnughadh lag – i n-áit bheith ag ceileabhradh lá buadha na teangan mar ba chóir go mbeifidhe, agus mar bheifidhe dá mbeadh gníomhartha na nGaedheal do réir a mbriathar.

45 Bhí sé soiléir do'n Choisde de dheascaibh an Oireachtais anuraidh, go raibh dhá locht móra gur deacair a leigheas .i. ganntanas iomadhthóiridhe i sna príomh-chomórtaisibh, agus níor fhreastal an pobal mar ba cheart. This festival, like the one in 1931, lost money that the League at this time could not afford. See also Peadar Mac Fhionnlaoich, 'An Fórum / An t-Oireachtas', *Camán*, 10/3/34.

46 See 'Ní Bheidh an t-Oireachtas ann i mBliadhna: Scéim Nua' (There will be no Oireachtas this year: A new plan), *IP*, 11/10/33; and Ó Cuív, 'An Chomhdháil / Sgéim Nua i gcóir na bhFeiseanna' (The congress / A new plan for the feiseanna), *II*, 22/9/33.

47 In September 1934, an anonymous contributor to *An Gaedheal* (probably Peadar Mac Fhionnlaoich) wrote: 'Since the Oireachtas has not been in progress for some years, it is for the most part at the Dublin Feis that the people of the city see the Culture and the quality of *Gaelachas* at present (Ó nach mbíonn an t-Oireachtas ar siubhal le roinnt bliadhan is ag Feis Átha Cliath is mó a feictear Cultúr agus gné an

Ghaedhealachais i láthair ag muintir na cathrach) (*Gaedheal*, 29/9/34).

48 Is mian leis an gConnradh tabhairt faoi n-a shaothar arís le fonn, agus, dá bhrigh sin, tá ceaptha aige an tOireachtas do bheith ar siubhal aige feasta.

49 Is cóir do'n Chonnradh an t-Oireachtas d'aithbheodhachtain agus duaise móra, duaise gur bh'onóir do shaoi a mbuadhachtain, do bhronnadh gach bliadhain fé mar dheintear ag an Eisteadfod [*sic*]. Muna ndeintear san beidh a rian ar an nGaedhilg: beidh a gluaiseacht go roighin leamh mall-triallach agus truflais an 'Gúm' agus Gaedhilg 'oifigiúil' againn i n-ionad litridheachta. Gaels were frequently urged to emulate the success of the Eisteddfod (and, less often, the Mòd). See, for example, 'Ceist an Oireachtais' (The question of the Oireachtas), Editorial, *II*, 18/12/37; 'Current Affairs / Revival of the Oireachtas', *Leader*, 14/1/39; 'Plans for Big Gaelic Festival in Dublin Next Month', *II*, 24/10/39.

50 This is not, of course, the place for a detailed historical analysis of the developments that led to the revival of the Oireachtas, for which see Mac Aonghusa, *Ar Son na Gaeilge*, 262–74; Mac Aonghusa, 'Athréimniú an Oireachtais' (The restoration of the Oireachtas), in *Oireachtas na Gaeilge*, ed. Mac Aonghusa, 65–80; and Éibhlín Ní Chathailriabhaigh, 'Pádraig Ó Siochfhradha agus Athbheochan an Oireachtais', in *Oireachtas na Gaeilge*, ed. Mac Aonghusa, 55–60.

51 Ó Muimhneacháin's plan was to revive the Oireachtas by instituting 'Féile Drámuíochta na gCraobh' (The drama festival of the branches [i.e. of the League]). He thought such a festival would lead to large-scale competitions and evolve into a true Oireachtas. See 'Ó Chúig Ardaibh na h-Éireann', *Gaedheal*, Nov. 1937, 7.

52 The League was insistent that it retain control of the Oireachtas.

53 He worried about possible competition from Aonach Tailteann.

54 See also Clem de Búrca, 'Cúis na Teangan / Aithbheochaint an Oireachtais' (The language cause / The revival of the Oireachtas), *II*, 29/11/37.

55 Isé tuairim an chruinnithe mhóir seo dena dreamanna Gaedhealacha uile i mBaile Átha Cliath go mba chóir Oireachtas Chonnradh na Gaedhilge d'aithbheodhchaint go luath airís agus a chomóradh gach bliain feasta . . . Iarraimíd ar Ghaedhil uile na tíre teacht linn d'aon-bhuidhin ins an iarracht so chun Institute mór náisiúnta a dhéanamh den Oireachtas chun cultúr teangan, liteardha [*sic*], ceoil, drámuíochta ⁊ aroile a chothú agus a fhoirbhiú. Among the groups involved in the revival of the Oireachtas were Comhaltas Uladh, An Fáinne, An Comhar Drámaidheachta, the Gaelic Society of UCD, the GAA, Feis Átha Cliath, and Cumann Drámaidheachta na Scol. See Proinsias Mac Aonghusa, 'Athréimniú an Oireachtais', in *Oireachtas na Gaeilge*, ed. Mac Aonghusa, 65–80.

56 Ní gábhadh a luadhadh a riachtanaighe atá sé rud mór de shaghas an Oireachtais do bheith ar siubhal go bliantúil in Éirinn. Is léir, leis, go bhfuil an tráth cóir tagaithe chun tabhairt fé n-a leithéid. This must have been a publicity release from the League, as it appears in the exact same wording in *Féile na nGaedheal*, Feb. 1939, 2.

57 Tar slán, a Ghaedheala! Sceul áthais an t-Oireachtas a bheith d'á chomóradh arís. Go n-éirighidh leis an iarracht, agus, dár ndóigh, éireochaidh. He continued: 'For, if it does not succeed, there is an end to Gaels and to Ireland' (Nó, mara n-éirigheann, tá deire le Gaedhealaibh agus le h-Éireann). See also 'E. Ó R.', 'Sean agus Nua / Cúis Mhór Dóchais agus Áthais do Ghaedhil / Aithbheochaint an Oireachtais' (Old and new / A Great source of hope and joy for Gaels / The revival of the Oireachtas), *II*, 10/11/39. 'Oisín' at first rather grudgingly noted the success of the 1939 festival, and said that instead of taking pride in what they had just accomplished, the Gaels should be ashamed it took them so long (*Derry People*, 18/11/39). Yet the previous year he had written: 'Is it not a great source of courage for Gaels that the Oireachtas is going to be reinstituted this coming year' (Nach mór an adhbhar misnigh do Ghaedhil go bhfuiltear leis an t-Oireachtas a athbhunadh 'sa bhliadhain seo chugainn) (*Derry People*, 10/12/38).

58 See Ó Súilleabháin and Ó Dubhghaill, 'The Oireachtas – An Appeal', in *An tOireachtas, 1939: Athchuinghe*, 4–6. Note how little emphasis there was on literature.

59 See also 'Current Affairs / The Oireachtas', *Leader*, 14/1/39.

60 Is iongantach agus is taithneamhach an dul ar aghaidh atá le feicsint san Roinn Litríochta. Chítear ann go dtuigeann an Coiste go bhfuil saoghal nua-aimsire á mhaireachtaint againn is go gcaithfear smaointe, nósanna is iomchar an t-saoghail sin do léiriú sa nGaedhilg má tá sí chun fearann do ghlacadh mar ghnáth-chainnt na tíre go leir. It should, however, be noted that not all were as interested in the literary side of the festival. In a 1939 editorial in *IP*, the goal of the Oireachtas was said to be 'to advance the Irish language and the music and dances of Ireland' (an teanga Ghaedhilge agus ceol agus rinncí na hÉireann do chur ar aghaidh) (*IP*, 1/11/39).

61 Ó'n uair a bhí an t-Oireachtas ann an t-am deireannach, bhí caoi faoi leith ag na sgríbhneoirí Gaedhilge – na sean-sgríbhneoirí comh maith leis na sgríbhneoirí nua – cleachtadh maith a fhagháil ar an nGaedhilg a sgríobhadh i bhfuirm próis, nó filidheachta, nó dráma. He gave credit to An Gúm as the chief catalyst for the creation of new literature in Irish, and he clearly saw greater things to come, writing of the contestants: 'The knowledge they gained this year will help them when the Gaelic Oireachtas runs other literary competitions (An t-eolas a fuair siad i

mbliana cabhróchaidh sé leo nuair bhéas comórtaisí eile liteardha ar siubhal ag an Oireachtas Gaedhealach). See also 'An t-Oireachtas', Editorial, *II*, 25/10/39.

62 Actually, he doesn't seem to have found it all that odd, instead blaming the problem on a usual suspect – An Gúm:

> One would think that there would be a certain number of skilled writers of Irish by now because of the work of An Gúm. But it is to be feared that the majority of them are using up their energy on translation so that the talent for original work is ruined from lack of practice.

'P. Ó C.' seems to have been a bit of a pessimist, having begun this essay with a gloomy assessment of the situation even with the Oireachtas itself in full swing:

> Destructive forces are at present putting a battle-ring around the Gaelic nation. Among those forces are radio, the movies, the newspapers and publications, new modes of travel, and on top of them all, the indifference of the public (Tá fórsaí millteacha a' cur fáinne catha ar an náisiún Gaedhealach i láthair na h-uaire. Ar na fórsaí sin tá an Radio, na scannáin, na nuachtáin agus foillsiúcháin, nua-chórus taistil agus mar bharr ortha sin go léir – neamh-shuim an phobail.

63 See *An tOireachtas: Clár na gComórtaisí*, 3; and *An tOireachtas: Samhain 4adh go 8adh, 1939*, 16–20. The prizes offered were fairly modest, with the most generous by far being the £30 first prize for a full-length play.

64 See the official programme, *An tOireachtas: Samhain 4adh go 8adh, 1939*, 16–20.

65 This writer also called the Oireachtas 'a great propagandist achievement' and wrote of its organisers: 'They achieved in fact a whole host of successes, but it may, perhaps, be said that the all-embracing success which attended their efforts was that they definitely revived the Oireachtas as an institution.' *The Irish Press* celebrated the opening of the Oireachtas with its main front-page headline on 6 Nov. 1939: 'Ta An t-Oireachtas Ar Siubhal (The Oireachtas Is in Progress) / President at Opening.' Even *The Irish Times* found the festival worthy of a fair amount of coverage. See, for example, 'The Oireachtas Revived / Enthusiasm at the Opening Meeting /Work for the Spread of the Language', *IT*, 6/11/39; 'Buadha an Oireachtais' (The triumphs of the Oireachtas), *IT*, 14/11/39; 'Oireachtas, 1939, Literary Awards / High Standard of Work Submitted', *IT*, 21/10/39; and 'The Oireachtas / Big Programme for Revival', *IT*, 24/10/39. The paper devoted a full page to the festival on 4 Nov. 1939, featuring a piece by Seán Beaumont entitled 'Litridheacht na Gaedhilge – Ceárd [*sic*] Atá i nDán dí?' with accompanying translation as 'Future of Irish Literature'.

66 It should also be noted that 1939 saw the revival of Cumann na Scríbhneoirí, a group that had been inactive longer than the Oireachtas itself. See Máirín Ní Mhuiríosa, 'Cumann na Scríbhneoirí – Memoir', *Scríobh* 5 (1981), 168–81.

67 *Mo Chara Stiofán* has only been reissued once, in 1957. The book is currently long out of print.

68 Ach sé sochar is mó atá le baint as, na tuairmí agus na comhairlí atá ann i dtaobh saothrú na Gaedhilge i gcoitchinne agus i dtaobh cumadh na litríochta go sonnradhach. Ní móide gur foillsigheadh fós i nGaedhilg trácht fada, fiosrach ar fhadhbanna ughdar do cuirfí i gcomhréim leis maidir le tuigsint agus foirleathadacht feasa . . . Foghanfaidh an leabhar so don Ghaedhilg ar mhórán slighte. Molaim Liam Ó Rinn ó chroidhe in a thaobh san agus bheirim buidheachas dó as ucht an aoibhnis do bhaineas as an leabhar do léigheamh.

69 See also 'Current Affairs / Liam O'Rinn [*sic*], Writer and Painter', *Leader*, 1/4/39. The author of this article saw Ó Rinn as 'the ideal journalist' and wrote: 'He will write with equal facility and verve about Gaelic dialects, French architecture, German songs, water-divining, painting, folk-lore, Russian poetry, gardening and fifty other topics.' As the title of this piece indicates, Ó Rinn was also a competent painter. 'T. Mac C.' told his readers that this was 'a new book that will gladden your heart, awaken thought in your mind, and arouse hope in your soul' (leabhar nua a chuirfidh gliondar ar bhur gcroí, a mhúsclóidh machtnamh i nbhur n-aigne agus a bhíogfaidh dóchas i nbhur n-anam) (*GR*, Aug. 1939, 1051).

70 Ó Rinn's career provides a neat symmetry for our period. At its close in 1939, he won Duais an Chraoibhín for *Mo Chara Stiofán*, while as early as 1917 his short story collection *Cad Ba Dhóbair Dó* was the first, and only, work published by An Ridireacht Liteartha, the book club it was hoped would revolutionise Gaelic publishing by insuring a predictable sale for the club's selections. Another promising Gaelic writer was lost to the movement with the 1936 death of Séamus Mac Conmara, whose posthumous novel *An Coimhthigheach* showed real potential. In the month before the 1939 Oireachtas, Ciarán Ua Nualláin wrote a laudatory piece on Seosamh Mac Grianna with the title 'Bhfuil Scríobhnóir Mór n-Ár Measc?' (Is there a great writer among us?) (*IP*, 9/10/39). Tragically, however, Mac Grianna's literary career had also already come to an end by this time.

71 Seán Mac Réamoinn, the author and broadcaster who was a leading figure in An Comhchaidreamh in the late 1930s, has written that Ó Rinn's book made a more powerful impression on him when he first read it than did Ó Cadhain's *Idir Shúgradh agus Dáiríre*. See Mac Réamoinn, 'Branar le cur' (Fallow land to be planted), *Comhar*, Oct. 1986, 14. Ó Cadhain's book seems to have attracted surprisingly little critical notice, although it was greeted enthusiastically by Nuala Moran in the editorial 'Current Affairs'

column in *The Leader*: 'We believe that the emergence of a new Irish writer with the heart and mind and skill of an artist is an event of national importance' (*Leader*, 27/4/40). See also 'Current Affairs / Outstanding Writer of Short Stories', *Leader*, 25/5/40.

72 Tá aon fhear amháin a sgríobh cupla gearr-sgéal agus is beag atá le foghluim aige. 'Sé an chaoi a bhfuil sé 'na mháighistir ar chéird na sgéalaidheachta. Máirtín Ó Cadhain atá mé a rádh. He went on: 'If Máirtín Ó Cadhain continues with the short-story, we will have a storyteller as good as old Pádraic Ó Conaire' (Má leanann Máirtín Ó Cadhain don ghearrsgéal beidh sgéalaidhe chomh maith le Sean-Phádraig Ó Conaire againn.

73 Níor ceistigheadh aoinne cad é an dath a bhí ar a shean-charabhat sgoile. Níor sgrúduigheadh a dhinn-tiúirí maidir leis an gcluiche a d'imir sé nó cad iad na rinncí nó na damhsaí a chleachtuigheadh sé. Ní raibh de theist ar aoinne ach go mbeadh sé i bhfábhar na Gaedhilge agus ar bhain leis an nGaedhilge. Sé mo ghuidhe gur mar sin a leanfaidh sé agus ná cuirfear isteach ar an Oireachtas is ar an leathan-aigeantacht a ghabhann leis. Bíodh an t-Oireachtas 'na chumann coidrimh saor is glan ó chaol-aigeantacht. Sgaradh sé de lochtúchán is spídiúchán. Fanadh a dhóirse ar dian-leathadh. Bíodh sé réidh chun fáiltiú roimh aoinne atá toilteannach fiú amháin cuid de'n bhóthar do shiubhal leis. These were exactly the high ideals set forth in the 'Focal Brollaigh' (Prologue) to the official Oireachtas programme, although it is interesting that the author of the prologue still saw the attacks of external enemies of the language and the *Gaelachas* it enshrined as more dangerous than the sterile wrangling of ostensible allies in the cause. See 'Focal Brollaigh', in *An tOireachtas: Samhain 4adh go 8adh, 1939*, 2–3.

Selected Bibliography

I. PRIMARY SOURCES

MANUSCRIPTS AND PAPERS

National Library of Ireland

Coiste an Oireachtais, Minutes (MSS 11,501, 11,558).

An Comhar Drámaidheachta, Programmes, 1924–31.

An Comhar Drámaidheachta, Documents Relating to, including letters, reports of the secretary and treasurer, etc., donated to NLI by Pádraig Ó Siochfhradha ('An Seabhac').

de Blaghad, Earnán (Ernest Blythe), Papers (MS 20,708).

Dinneen, Father Patrick (Pádraig Ó Duinnín), Papers (MSS 8623, 8625, G 722, G 827).

Green, Alice Stopford, Papers (MS 10,457).

Hutton, Margaret, Papers (MS 8611).

Hyde, Douglas, Papers (MSS G 561, G 1096).

Mac Giolla Iasachta, Éamonn (Edward MacLysaght), Papers (MS 8560).

Mac Liammóir, Micheál, 'The Ford of the Hurdles: A Masque of Dublin'. Unpublished typescript of a pageant presented at the Mansion House, Dublin, during Civic Week, 9–15 Sept. 1929. The programme for the pageant is bound with the text in NLI.

Mac Néill, Eoin, Papers (MS 10,881).

Murray, T. C., Papers (MS 24,969).

Ní Fhaircheallaigh, Úna (Agnes O'Farrelly), Papers (MS 21,853).

Ní Mhuiríosa, Máirín, Papers (MS 26,784).

Ó Briain, Art, Papers (MS 8417).

Ó Ceallaigh, Tomás, Papers (MS 8129).

Ó Criomhthainn, Tomás, *An t-Oileánach* (MS G1020)

——Papers (MS 15,785).

Ó Máille, Tomás, Papers (MSS. G1075, G1108).

Ó Riain, Art, Unfinished novel (MS G1149).

Palmer, Geoffrey Molyneux, Papers, including the musical score and libretto for the light opera *Grania Goes*, written in conjunction with An tAthair Tomás Ó Ceallaigh (MSS 5232, 5233, 5234, 5235, 5236, 5237, 5239, 5240)

Piatt, Donn, Papers (MS G1077).

James Hardiman Library, NUI Galway

Ó Duilearga, Séamus (James Delargy), Papers.

O'Flaherty, Liam (Liam Ó Flaithbheartaigh), *Dorchadas*, Typescript of play with some handwritten corrections and additions.

Taibhdhearc na Gaillimhe, Papers

Mac Grianna, Seosamh, Photocopy of typescript journal lent by Professor Nollaig Mac Congáil, NUI, Galway.

PERIODICALS

Academy of Christian Art Journal
Ar Aghaidh: Páipéar le Gaedhealachas, Litridheacht, Éargna agus Géilleagair
Association of Secondary Teachers of Ireland / Official Year Book and Diary
An Barr Buadh (supplement to *Irish Freedom*)
Béaloideas: The Journal of the Folklore of Ireland Society
The Belvederian
An Bhrídeog
An Birín Beo: Chun Cuspóirí Chonnradh na Gaedhilge do Chraobh-Scaoileadh agus chun Cath d'Fhógairt ar an nGalldachas
Blackrock College Annual
The Blueshirt
Blather
Bonaventura: A Quarterly Review
An Branar
An Camán: Teachtaire na nGaedheal is na nGaiscidheach: A Review of National Affairs: Athletics, Language, Literature, Art, Industry
The Capuchin Annual
The Castleknock College Chronicle
The Catholic Bulletin and Book Review
Catholic University School Annual
An Chearnóg
Chimney Corners: A Journal of Recreation for the Irish Home
An Chléir: Tuarascbháil Chumainn na Sagart nGaedhealach
The Christian Family
The Clare Champion, Thomond News, Galway Advocate
The Clongownian
Coláisde Mhíchíl, Baile 'n Sceilg, Co. Chiarraidhe
Comhthrom Féinne / The College Magazine
The Connacht Sentinel: A Mid-Weekly Evening Paper Circulating Throughout Southern Connacht
The Connacht Tribune and Tuam News
Cork Weekly Examiner and Weekly Herald
The Cross: A Monthly Magazine Conducted by the Passionist Fathers
The Derry People and Donegal News
The Dublin Magazine
Dublin Opinion: The National Humorous Journal of Ireland
The Dundalk Examiner and Louth Advertiser
An t-Eaglaiseach Gaedhealach / The Gaelic Churchman
Éarna: Irisleabhar fé Chúram an Scoil Cheilteach i gColáiste na hOllscoile i gCorcaigh
The Echo and South Leinster Advertiser (Enniscorthy)
Éire: Bliainiris Ghaedheal / Rogha Saothair Ghaedheal mBeo, 1940–1945.
Éire / The Irish Nation
Éire Óg / Young Ireland
An t-Éireannach / Guth na nGaedheal
The Examiner / An Scrúduightheoir (Dundalk)
Fáinne an Lae
The Far East / An Domhan Thoir: An Illustrated Monthly Mission Magazine

The Father Mathew Record: The Irish Home Journal / A Monthly Magazine of Irish Interests, for the Promotion of Temperance
Féile na nGaedheal (London)
Fianna: The Voice of Young Ireland
An Fiolar .i. Irisleabhar Scoile na Mainistreach .i. Cnoc Sheosaimh i dTuaiscirt Éile
The Freeman / An Saoránach
Fuaim na Mara: Irisleabhar Choláiste Mhic Phiarais
An Gaedheal
An Gaedheal Óg
An Gaodhal / The Gael
The Garda Review / The Organ of the Garda Síothchána
Gearrbhaile
Greann / Irish Fun in Fact and Fiction
Green and Gold: A Magazine of Fiction, etc.
Guth an Gharda
Guth na nGaedheal: An Occasional Magazine published by the Gaelic League of London
The Hearthstone: The Story Magazine of Ireland
Hibernia
Honesty: A Weekly Journal of Independent Criticism
Humanitas
Inis Fáil (ar n-a chur amach dos na macaibh léighinn i mBelmont, Tigh Lorcáin, Co. Bh'láth Cliath)
Inis Fáil: Published to Maintain a Sympathetic Contact between Irishmen Living Abroad
Ireland To-Day
Iris an Fháinne
Iris an Gharda
The Irish Booklover / An Leabhar-Chara Gaodhlach
The Irish Catholic
The Irish Ecclesiastical Record: A Monthly Journal under Episcopal Sanction
Irish Freedom / Saoirse na h-Éireann: An Organ of Uncompromising Republicanism
Irish Fun
The Irish Homeland
Irish Independent
The Irish Monthly: A Magazine of General Literature
The Irish People / Muinntear na h-Éireann
The Irish Press
The Irish Review of Politics, Economics, Art and Literature
The Irish Rosary
The Irish Storyteller: The Magazine of the People
The Irish Times
Irish Workers' Voice: Organ of the Irish Revolutionary Workers' Movement (later subtitles: *Organ of the Communist Party of Ireland* and *Weekly Organ of the Communist Party of Ireland, Section of the Communist International*)
An t-Irisleabhar, Ollsgoil na Gaillimh
Irisleabhar Chnuic Mhuire / Knock Shrine Annual
Irisleabhar Chorcaighe
Irisleabhar Chumann na gCéimithe i gCorcaigh / Cork Graduates' Club Annual
Irisleabhar Hibernia (Fribourg)

Irisleabhar Lorcáin Naomhtha (ar n-a chur amach do Chumann Lorcáin Naomhtha i mBelmont, Tigh Lorcáin, Áth Cliath)
Irisleabhar Muighe Nuadhat (ar na chur amach do Chuallacht Chuilm Cille)
Journal of the Cork Historical and Archaeological Society
Journal of the County Louth Archaeological Society
Journal of the Galway Archaeological and Historical Society
The Kerryman
The Land / An Talamh: A Weekly Journal Advocating the Interests of Unpurchased Tenants, Farmers, Traders, Irish-Ireland, United Ireland
An Leabharlann: Journal of the Library Association of Ireland
The Leader: A Review of Current Affairs, Politics, Literature, Art and Industry
Leaves / Billeoga: Political – Literary – Irish-Ireland Monthly: An Independent Monthly Journal of the Highest Standard
Lia Fáil: Irisleabhar Gaedhilge Ollsgoile na hÉireann
An Lóchrann: Páipéar Gaedhilge in Aghaidh Gacha Mí
Misneach
The Missionary Annals of the Holy Ghost Fathers
Molua: Irisleabhar Cuallachta Gríogóir, N. / Organ of the Association of St. Gregory
Mother and Maid
An Muimhneach: Irisleabhar le h-Aghaidh an Mhí
Mungret Annual
Naomh Ursula: Clochar Ursulíneach i nDurlas Éile
The Nation (Blueshirt)
The Nation: A New National Weekly Review (Fianna Fáil)
The National Student / The College Magazine
Nationality, Economic, Cultural, Political: An Organ of Opinion, Not of Party
The New Ireland Review
The New Irish Magazine / An Sgeulaidhe Nuadh
An t-Óglach: The Irish Army Quarterly
An Óige: A Bright Bi-Lingual Monthly
Our Boys
Our Girls / Ár gCailíní: The Magazine for the Girls of Ireland
Outlook
An Phoblacht
The Plain People / Na Daoine Macánta
The Quarryman
An Ráitheachán: The Gaelic Quarterly Review: A Magazine of National Thought and Action: Language – Pastimes – Music – Arts – Crafts – Literature – Customs – Folklore – Industry
The Redemptorist Record
The Republican
Republican Congress: Organ of the Committees of Workers and Small Farmers, working for the United Front against Fascism, and for the Irish Workers' Republic
The Republican File
Republican Review
An Reult: Irisleabhar na h-Ollscoile (arna chur amach do lucht an Chumainn Ghaedhealaigh i gColáiste na h-Ollscoile i mBaile Átha Cliath)
The Rock
The Rockwell Annual

An Róimh (Rome)
An Saorstát / The Free State
The Separatist: A National Political Weekly
An Sguab
Sinn Féin
An Síoladóir: Irisleabhar Chumainn na Sagart nGaedhealach
An Sléibhteánach / The Mountaineer: Irisleabhar Choláiste Chnuic Mhellerí
The Standard / An t-Iolar: A Journal of Irish Catholic Opinion
The Star / An Reult: A National Weekly Devoted to Politics, Economics and Social Affairs
An Stoc
Studies: An Irish Quarterly Review of Letters Philosophy and Science
The Teacher's Work: A Practical Journal of School Progress and Efficiency
Timthire Chroidhe Naomhtha Íosa
An Tír: Míosachán Gaedhilge
Tír na nÓg
The Torque (Davos, Switzerland)
The Tribune (*The Irish Tribune*)
Tús a' Phota (Aguisín do 'Ghearrbhaile' de Thoradh na Laetheannta Saoire)
An t-Ultach: Páipéar Míosamhail fá choinne Gaedheal Thuaisceart Éireann
United Ireland
The United Irishman (1923)
The United Irishman (1932–3)
The University Annual: University College Galway
Up and Doing: An Organ of the Lay Apostolate
The Weekly Freeman, National Press And Irish Agriculturist
The Wind Bag (An Bolgán Béiceach): UCG's Annual Explosion

BOOKS, PAMPHLETS AND ARTICLES

Aistí Gaedhilge (Irish Essays for Examinations) (Baile Átha Cliath: C. S. Ó Fallamhain, Teo., 1935).

Alphonsus Liguori, St., *An Mhaighdean Ghlórmhar*, trans. Conn Ó Mongáin (Baile Átha Cliath: M. H. Mac Ghoill agus a Mhac, Teor., 1936).

Aonach Tailteann: Baile Átha Cliath; 6adh-13adh Lughnasa, 1922 / Irish Race Olympics: A Revival of the Ancient Tailteann Games Which Will Be Held in Dublin, 6th–13th August (Baile Átha Cliath: Oifig Aonach Tailteann, [1922]).

Aonach Tailteann 1924: Revival of the Ancient Tailteann Games / Dublin 2nd–8th August (Baile Átha Cliath: Aonach Tailteann, [1924]).

Ár Rinncidhe Fóirne: Ten Irish Figure Dances: Leabhrán a h-Aon (Baile Átha Cliath: Coimisiún an Rinnce, 1939).

Bainne – le haghaidh na hóige (Corcaigh: An Bord Bainne do Cheanntar Chorcaighe, 1939).

Bairéad, Tomás, *Cumhacht na Cinneamhna* (Baile Átha Cliath: Oifig Díolta Foillseacháin Rialtais, 1936).

_____, *Gan Baisteadh* (Baile Átha Cliath: Sáirséal agus Dill, 1972).

_____, *An Geall a Briseadh* (Baile Átha Cliath: Oifig Díolta Foillseacháin Rialtais, 1952 [1932]).

Bean Riaghalta as Clochar na nUrsalach, Sligeach, *Eoluidheacht don Scoláire Óg* (Baile Átha Cliath: Oifig Díolta Foillseacháin Rialtais, 1936).

Bean-Riaghalta Clochar Lughaidh i Muineacháin, *Cuirp-Eolas* (Áth Cliath: M. H. Mac Ghuill agus a Mhac, Teo., [1927]).

Bean-Riaghalta i gClochar na n-Ursulach i Sligeach, *Macallaí ó'n bhFrainc: Corra-Cainnte, Ráidhte agus Sean-Fhocail i bhFraincis agus i nGaedhilg* (Baile Átha Cliath: Comhlucht Oideachais na hÉireann, Teor., n. d. [1936]).

Béaslaí, Piaras, *An Bhean Chródha: Dráma Cheithre Mír* (Baile Átha Cliath: Oifig Díolta Foillseacháin Rialtais, 1931).

_____, *Blúire Páipéir: Dráma Grinn Trí Mír* (Baile Átha Cliath: Oifig Díolta Foillseacháin Rialtais, 1938).

_____, *An Danar: Dráma Trí Mír* (Baile Átha Cliath: Muinntir C. S. Ó Fallamhain Teo., i gcomhar le hOifig an tSoláthair, 1929).

_____, *Earc agus Áine agus Scéalta Eile* (Baile Átha Cliath: Oifig an tSoláthair, 1946).

_____, *Éigse Nua-Ghaedhilge*, 2 vols. (Baile Átha Cliath: Comhlucht Oideachais na hÉireann, [1933]).

_____, *An Fear Fógraidheachta: Farsa Trí Mír* (Baile Átha Cliath: Oifig an tSoláthair, 1938).

_____, 'Réamh-Rádh', in Goldsmith, Oliver, *Ísliú chun Buadha* (*She Stoops to Conquer*), trans. Béaslaí (Baile Átha Cliath: Oifig an tSoláthair, n. d.).

_____, *An Sgaothaire agus Cúig Drámaí Eile* (Baile Átha Cliath: Muinntir C. S. Ó Fallamhain Teo., i gcomhar le hOifig an tSoláthair, 1929).

Beirne, Liam, *Seo Siud* (Gaillimh: Ó Gormáin agus a Chomh. Teach na Clódóireachta, 1934).

_____, *An Troid agus an t-Uaigneas* (Baile Átha Cliath: M. H. Mac Ghuill agus a Mhac, 1926).

'Beirt Déiseach', *An bhFeadair Tú So Dhom? .i. Dosaon Díospóireacht ó Radio Éireann* (Baile Átha Cliath: Oifig an tSoláthair, 1940).

Benedict, An tAthair, O. D. C., trans., *Beathafhéinscríbhinn Naoimh Treasa leis an Leanbh Íosa* (Coillte Magha: Siúracha Lughaidh Naomhtha, n. d.).

_____, *Lorcán Naomhtha Ua Tuathail* (Baile Átha Cliath: Muinntir C. S. Ó Fallamhain Teo., i gcomhar le hOifig an tSoláthair, 1929).

_____, *An t-Siúr Bheannuighthe Treasa leis an Leanbh Íosa* (Baile Átha Cliath: Muinntir Uí Chathail, Teo., [1924]).

_____, trans., *Teachtaireacht ó'n tSiúr Bheannuithe Treasa* (Baile Átha Cliath: Ua Cathail agus A Bhuidheann, [1923]).

Bráithre Críostamhla, Na, *Stair na hÉireann: Ceist is Freagra* (Baile Átha Cliath: M. H. Gill agus a Mhac, 1927).

Breathnach, Micheál, *Cor in Aghaidh an Chaim: Dráma Grinn Aon-Mhíre* (Baile Átha Cliath: Oifig Díolta Foillseacháin Rialtais, 1933).

_____, *Cuimhne an tSeanpháiste* (Baile Átha Cliath: Oifig an tSoláthair, 1966).

_____, *Cúrsaí na hÉireann*, 2 vols. (Baile Átha Cliath: Brún agus Ó Nualláin, Teor., [1935–6]).

_____, *Draoidheacht Chaitlín* (Baile Átha Cliath: Oifig Díolta Foillseacháin Rialtais, 1932).

_____, *Prós na Fiannaidheachta* (Baile Átha Cliath: Comhlucht Oideachais na hÉireann, Teor., n. d.).

_____, *Trom agus Éadtrom* (Baile Átha Cliath: Comhlucht Oideachais na hÉireann, Teor., n. d.).

Bunreacht na hÉireann (Constitution of Ireland) (Baile Átha Cliath: Oifig Díolta Foilseacháin Rialtais, n. d.).

Cahill, E., S. J. *The Framework of a Christian State: An Introduction to Social Science* (Dublin: M. H. Gill, 1932).

——, *Ireland's Peril* (Dublin: Published for An Ríoghacht {The League of the Kingship of Christ} by M. H. Gill, 1930).

Cainneach, An tAthair, O.S.F.C., trans., *Guthanna Neamhdha* (Baile Átha Cliath: Clólucht an Talbóidigh, Teoranta, 1926).

_____, *Seoda Spirideálta nó Roinnt Smaointe Tógtha a Sgríbhinnibh Phroinséis Naomhtha de Sales* (Baile Átha Cliath: Clólucht an Talbóidigh, Teoranta, 1924).

Carey, W. J., *Saidhbhreas Mháire Mhór. Greas Grinn Fuirseoireachta in Dhá Ghníomh*, trans. Liam Ó Míodhacháin (Baile Átha Cliath: Máire Ní Raghallaigh, 1927).

Carty, James, *Rang-Leabhar de Stair na hÉireann*, 4 vols, trans. Gearóid Mac Spealáin (Baile Átha Cliath: Muinntir C. S. Ó Fallamhain, 1936–8).

Casáin, An t-Athair, O. F. M. Cap., *An Londubh agus Scéalta Eile* (Baile Átha Cliath: Oifig Díolta Foillseacháin Rialtais, 1937).

Cnámha Aistí dos na Ranga is Aoirde le h-aghaidh Scrúdúchán Idir-Mheadhonach, Stát-Sheirbhíseach, Máithreánach agus Uile / Advanced Outline Essays in Irish Free Composition for Intermediate, Civil Service, Matriculation and Other Students (Baile Átha Cliath: P. Mac Gafraidh, n. d.).

Coláiste na hOllsgoile, Gaillimh, *Riaghalacha ag Baint le Grádaimh agus Réimeanna Oideachais, 1933-34* (Dublin: Alex Thom & Co., n. d.).

Coláiste Ollsgoile Corcaigh, *Féilire / Calendar, 1934–5* (Corcaigh: Cló Ollsgoile Chorcaighe, n. d.).

Collins, Michael, *The Path to Freedom* (Cork: Mercier Press, 1968 [1922]).

Connradh na Gaedhilge, *An Gaedheal agus an Radió .i. Leabhrán do thabhairt eolas do Ghaedhealaibh ar an fheidhm is acfuinn dóibh a bhaint as an Radió, agus ar an gceárdachas is riachtanach chuige sin* (Baile Átha Cliath: Fóchoisde an Radió, Connradh na Gaedhilge, 1936).

_____, *An tOireachtas [1939]: Clár na gComórtaisí*

_____, *An t-Oireachtas, 1932 / Clár na gComórtas a bhéas ar siubhal i dTigh an Ard-Mhaoir, Áth Cliath fé choimirce Choiste Gnótha Chonnradh na Gaedhilge*

_____, *An tOireachtas, 1939, Athchuinghe*

_____, *An tOireachtas: Samhain 4adh go 8adh, 1939*

_____, *An tOireachtas, Samhain 4adh–8adh Lá i dTigh an Ard-Mhaoir Baile Átha Cliath*

_____, *Seachtmhain na Samhna (Samhain a 2-7adh) [1931]*

Connradh na Gaedhilge (Craobh an Chéitinnigh), *'You May Revive the Irish Language . . . '* (Baile Átha Cliath: Craobh an Chéitinnigh de Chonnradh na Gaedhilge, [1937]).

Corkery, Daniel, *The Hidden Ireland: A Study of Gaelic Munster in the Eighteenth Century* (Dublin: M. H. Gill, 1924).

——, *Synge and Anglo-Irish Literature* (Cork: Cork University Press, 1931).

An Craipí Óg: Ceol-Dráma Gearr, trans. Muiris Ó Catháin, adapted as a musical play by Gearóid Ó Lochlainn (Baile Átha Cliath: n. p., n. d.).

Cumann Lúthchleas Gaedheal, Treoraí Oifigiúil / Gaelic Athletic Association, Official Guide (Dublin: Central Council of the Association, 1956).

de Bhilmot, Séamus, *Baintighearna an Ghorta: Dráma Aoin-Mhíre* (Baile Átha Cliath: Oifig an tSoláthair, 1944).

_____, *An Casán agus Múchadh an tSolais: Dhá Dhráma Aon-Mhíre* (Baile Átha Cliath: Oifig Díolta Foillseacháin Rialtais, n. d. [1931]).

_____, *'Grádh níos Mó:' Dráma Trí Mhír* (Baile Átha Cliath: Oifig an tSoláthair, 1947).

_____, *'San Am Soin, —': Dráma Ceithre Mír* (Baile Átha Cliath: Oifig an tSoláthair, 1944).

de Blácam, Aodh, *From a Gaelic Outpost* (Baile Átha Cliath: Catholic Truth Society of Ireland, 1921).

_____, *Gaelic Literature Surveyed* (Dublin: Talbot Press, 1929).

_____, *Gentle Ireland: An Account of a Christian Culture in History and Modern Life* (Milwaukee: Bruce Publishing Co., 1935).

de Brún, Pádraig, trans., *Aintioghoiné: Dráma le Sofoicléas* (Baile-Átha-Cliath: Ponsoinbí agus Gibbs, Clódh na hOllscoile, 1926).

_____, *Ataile: Dráma le Racine as Stair Ríghthe Iúda* (Baile Átha Cliath: Muinntir C. S. Ó Fallamhain, Teo., n. d.).

_____, trans., *Beathaí Phlútairc* (Baile Átha Cliath: Oifig Díolta Foillseacháin Rialtais, 1936).

_____, trans., *Íodhbairt Ifigéine: Dráma le Euripides* (Baile Átha Cliath: Oifig Díolta Foillseacháin Rialtais, 1935).

_____, trans., *Oidiopús i gColón: Dráma le Sofoicléas* (Mágh Nuadhat: Cuallacht Chuilm Cille, 1929).

_____, *Poiléacht: Dráma don Mhairtíreacht Chríostaidhe le Pierre Corneille* (Baile Átha Cliath: Ponsoinbí agus Gibbs, Clódh na hOllscoile, 1932).

_____, trans., *Rí Oidiopús: Dráma le Sofoicléas* (Mágh Nuadhat: Cuallacht Chuilm Cille, 1928).

de Buitléir, Éibhlín, *Bonn agus Forsgreamh na hÉireann* (*Structural Geography of Ireland*), tr. Micheál Breathnach (Baile Átha Cliath: Muinntir C. S. Ó Fallamhain i gcomhar le hOifig an tSoláthair, 1930).

de Lása, Liam, *Fotha Feasa* (Baile Átha Cliath: Comhlucht Oideachais na hÉireann, Teor., n. d.).

de Paor, Alín, *Paidí Ó Dálaigh* (Baile Átha Cliath: Comhlucht Oideachais na hÉireann, n. d.).

de Valera, Éamon, *Speeches and Statements by Éamon De Valera*, ed. Maurice Moynihan (Dublin: Gill & Macmillan, 1980).

Devane, James, *Isle of Destiny: The Clash of Cultures* (Dublin: Browne & Nolan, [1937]).

Devlin, P. J., *Our Native Games* (Dublin: M. H. Gill, n. d.).

Dinneen, Patrick, *Aistí ar Litridheacht Ghréigise is Laidne* (Baile Átha Cliath: Muinntir C. S. Ó Fallamhain, Teo. i gcomhar le hOifig an tSoláthair, 1929).

_____, *Scéal na hÉireann don Aos Óg: Cuid a hAon ó Thosach go Teicheadh na nIarlaí (1607)* (Baile Átha Cliath: Brún agus Ó Nualláin, Teor., 1932).

_____, *Teachtaire ó Dhia: Dráma Bhaineas leis an Droch-Shaoghal* (Baile Átha Cliath: M. H. Gill agus a Mhac, n. d.).

Ferguson, A. B. Ochiltree, *Sceul Ár dTíre*, translated and supplemented by Liam Ó Rinn (Baile Átha Cliath: Comhlucht Oideachais na hÉireann, Teoranta, [1923]).

Ferris, William, *The Gaelic Commonwealth: Being the Political and Economic Programme for the Irish Progressive Party* (Dublin: Talbot Press, 1923).

Foclóir Staire is Tír-Eoluíochta (Baile Átha Cliath: Oifig an tSoláthair, n. d.).

For-oideas Aigne-eolais do'n Aos Léighinn (Baile Átha Cliath: M. H. Gill agus a Mhac, 1932).

Hanly, Joseph, *The National Ideal: A Practical Exposition of True Nationality appertaining to Ireland* (Dublin: Dollard Printinghouse, 1931).

Joyce, Seán ('Loch Measca'), *Eachtra Múinteora* (Baile Átha Cliath: Muinntir C. S. Ó Fallamhain, Teo., i gcomhar le hOifig an tSoláthair, 1929).

Joynt, Ernest, 'Réamh-Radh', in *Turas an Oilithrigh fá shamhail aislinge (Pilgrim's Progress by John Bunyan)* (Baile Átha Cliath: Alec Thom agus a Chuid, Teor., 1928).

Kehoe, P., *'Nuair d'Adhnamar an Gleo:' Éacht d'Éachtaibh a' 98: Dráma Aon-Ghníomha* (*When Wexford Rose*), trans. Nioclás Tóibín (Baile Átha Cliath: Oifig Díolta Foillseacháin Rialtais, 1936).

Leabhar Tailteann (Aonach Tailteann 1928 / Souvenir Programme) (Baile Átha Cliath: Ard-Chomhairle Aonach Tailteann, n. d.).

Leamy, Edmund, *Píobaire Sídhe Ghleann Maoiliughra*, tr. Proinnsias Ó Brógáin (Baile Átha Cliath: Oifig Díolta Foillseacháin Rialtais, 1933.

_____, *Sidhe-Scéalta .i. Irish Fairy Tales*, tr. Brighid Ní Loingsigh (Baile Átha Cliath: Brún agus Ó Nualláin, 1936).

Lóiste, B. N., *Cathal faoi Ghealltanas (Dráma Grinn)* (Baile Átha Cliath: Oifig Díolta Foillseacháin Rialtais, [1936]).

_____, *Inbhear Náile* (Baile Átha Cliath: Oifig Díolta Foillseacháin Rialtais, 1936).

Luibhéid, Tomás, *An Biorán Suain* (Baile Átha Cliath: Oifig Díolta Foillseacháin Rialtais, 1937).

Mac Aodha, Pádhraic, *An Bhail a Thuill Sé: Dráma Cheithre Gníomh ó Chonnamara* (Gaillimh: Ó Gormáin, Teach na Clódóireachta, [1934]).

_____, *Brighidín ó Cheathramha-Ruadh* (Baile Átha Cliath: Séamas Ó Dubhthaigh agus a Chomh., Teor., 1932).

_____, *An Broc Dubh: Dráma Trí Gníomh ó Chonnamara* (Gaillimh: Ó Gormáin agus a Chomh., 1936).

_____, ed., *An Chaoi le Faoisdin a Dhéanamh* (Gaillimh: Ó Gormáin agus a Chomh., Teach na Clódóireachta, [1935]).

_____, ed., *Leabhrán Úrnaighthe na Ceathramhan Ruaidhe* (Baile Átha Cliath: Seumas Ó Dubhthaigh agus a Chomh. Teor., 1933).

_____, *Naomh Brighid* (Gaillimh: Ó Gormáin Tóranta, 1937).

_____, *Naomh Iarlaith* (Gaillimh: Ó Gormáin agus a Chomh., 1936).

_____, *Peadar a' tSléibhe: Dráma Trí nGníomh ó Chonnamara* (Gaillimh: Ó Gormáin agus a Chomh., 1937).

Mac Aonghusa, Criostóir, *Ó Ros Muc go Rostov* (Baile Átha Cliath: An Clóchomhar, 1972).

Mac Clúin, Seoirse, *Binn is Blasta* (Baile Átha Cliath: Brún agus Ó Nóláin, Teor., 1922).

_____, *An Litríocht: Infhiúcha ar Phrionnsabail, Fuirmeacha agus Léirmheastóireacht na Litríochta* (Baile Átha Cliath: Brún agus Ó Nóláin, Teor., n. d.).

_____, *Réilthíní Óir: Cuid a 1* (Baile Átha Cliath: Comhlucht Oideachais na h-Éireann, 1922).

_____, *Róisín Fiain na Mara* (Baile Átha Cliath: Brún agus Ó Nóláin, Teor., 1924).

Mac Con Iomaire, Séamus, *Cladaigh Chonamara* (Baile Átha Cliath: Oifig an tSoláthair, 1938).

Mac Conmara, Séamas, *An Coimhthigheach* (Baile Átha Cliath: Oifig an tSoláthair, 1970 [1939]).

_____, *Saol agus Saothar Shéamais Mhic Chonmara*, ed. Seán Mac Cionnaith (Baile Átha Cliath: Coiscéim, 1988).

Mac Craith, Micheál, *Deora Drúchta Camhaoire* (Baile Átha Cliath: M. H. Mac an Ghoill agus a Mhac, Teo., 1928).

Mac Dhubháin, Aodh, *Stair na hÉireann ó 1607 go dtí 1938 (Ó Chath Chionntsáile anall go dti foillsiú na Bun-Reachta, 1937)* (Baile Átha Cliath: Brún agus Ó Nualláin, Teor., 1939).

Mac Énrí, Micheál, *Sár-Laochra Éireann* (Baile Átha Cliath: Brún agus Ó Nóláin, Teor., n. d. [1924]).

Mac Énrí, Seaghán P., *Tuaith agus Cathair (Cuid a hAon)* (Baile Átha Cliath: M. H. Mac Guill agus a Mhac, Teor., 1926).

Mac Fhinn, P. E., *Naomh Breandán* (Gaillimh: Ó Gormáin agus a Chomh., 1937).

Mac Fhionnlaoich, Peadar, *Blian na hAiséirí* (Baile Átha Cliath: Coiscéim, 1992).

_____, *An Cogadh Dearg agus Scéalta Eile* (Baile Átha Cliath: Cú Uladh agus a Chuid, n. d.).

Mac Giolla Bhríde, Liam, *Gregoire agus Iom-Chlódh na Frainnce* (Baile Átha Cliath: An Tír, [1932]).

Mac Giolla Bhríghde, Eoghan, *An Fealltóir: Dráma Thrí nGníomh* (Baile Átha Cliath: Oifig an tSoláthair, 1939).

_____, *In Aimsir an Mháirtínigh: Dráma Staireamhail Cheithre nGníomh ag Léiriú an tSaoghail a bhí ag Muinntir Ghaoth Dobhair sa Bhliadhain 1889* (Baile Átha Cliath: Oifig Díolta Foillseacháin Rialtais, 1937).

Mac Giolla Bhríghde, Niall, *Dírbheathaisnéis Néill Mhic Ghiolla Bhríghde*, dictated to Liam Ó Connacháin (Baile Átha Cliath: Brún agus Ó Nualláin, Teor., [1938]).

Mac Giolla Cheara, Pádraic, *Díon-Chruthughadh an Chreidimh nó Apologetic* (Baile Átha Cliath: Oifig Díolta Foillseacháin Rialtais, 1936).

_____, *Foras Feasa ar Theagasc na h-Eaglaise* (Baile Átha Cliath: Oifig Díolta Foillseacháin Rialtais, 1937).

_____, *Leabhar Úrnaighthe* (Béal Feirste: Comhaltas Uladh, 1939).

_____, *Teagasc Morálta na h-Eaglaise* (Baile Átha Cliath: Oifig an tSoláthair, 1938).

Mac Giolla Iasachta, Éamonn ('M'), *Cúrsaí Thomáis* (Baile Átha Cliath: An Clóchomhar, 1969 [1927]).

_____, *The Gael* (Dublin: Maunsel, 1919).

_____, *Toil Dé* (Baile Átha Cliath: Oifig Díolta Foillseacháin Rialtais, 1933).

Mac Giolla Phádraig, Brian, *Dhá-Theangachas agus Sgoileanna na Tíre: Páipéar do Léigh Brian Mac Giolla Phádraig, O. S., M. A. os comhair Ard-Fheis na Múinteoirí, Cáisg 1921* (Baile Átha Cliath: Maunsel agus Roberts, Teo., 1922).

Mac Giollarnáth, Seán, trans., *Emil agus na Lorgairí* (Erich Kastner) (Baile Átha Cliath: Oifig Díolta Foillseacháin Rialtais, 1937).

_____, *Loinnir Mac Leabhair agus Sgéalta Gaisgidh Eile* (Baile Átha Cliath: Oifig Díolta Foillseacháin Rialtais, 1936).

_____, ed., *Peadar Chois Fhairrge: Scéalta Nua agus Seanscéalta d'Innis Peadar Mac Thuathaláin nach Maireann do Sheán Mac Giollarnáth* (Baile Átha Cliath: Oifig Díolta Foillseacháin Rialtais, 1934).

Mac Gréagóir, Art, *Stair na nDéise .i. Déise Mumhan, Dúthaigh Déaglán ó Thosach go dtí A. D. 1108* (Baile Átha Cliath: Oifig Díolta Foillseacháin Rialtais, 1938).

Mac Grianna, Seosamh, *Ailt: Saothar Sheosaimh Mhic Grianna, Cuid a Dó*, ed. Nollaig Mac Congáil (n. p., Coiste Foilsitheoireachta Chomhaltas Uladh, 1977).

_____, *An Bhreatain Bheag* (Baile Átha Cliath: Oifig Díolta Foillseacháin Rialtais, 1937).

_____, *Dá mBíodh Ruball ar an Éan* (Baile Átha Cliath: An Gúm, 1992 [1940]).

_____, *Dochartach Duibhlionna agus Sgéaltaí Eile* (Baile-Átha-Cliath: Cú Uladh, [1925]).

_____, *An Druma Mór* (Baile Átha Cliath: Oifig an tSoláthair, 1969).

_____, *Eoghan Ruadh Ó Néill* (Baile Átha Cliath: Oifig an tSoláthair, 1956 [1931]).

_____, *Filí agus Felons*, ed. Nollaig Mac Congáil (Cathair na Mart: Foilseacháin Náisiúnta Teo., 1987).

_____, *An Grádh agus an Ghruaim* (Baile Átha Cliath: Brún is Ó Nualláin, Teor., n. d. [1929]).

_____ (as Seosamh Ó Greanna), *Léigheacht ar Crois-Bhealaigh i Stair na h-Éireann / Turning Points in Irish History* (Baile-Átha-Cliath: Sinn Féin Ard-Chomhairle, 1924).

_____, *Na Lochlannaigh* (Baile Átha Cliath: Oifig an tSoláthair, 1938).

_____, *Mo Bhealach Féin* (Baile Átha Cliath: Oifig an tSoláthair, 1970 [1940]).

_____, *Pádraic Ó Conaire agus Aistí Eile* (Baile Átha Cliath: Oifig an tSoláthair, 1969 [1936]).

Mac Liam, Seoirse, *An Doras do Plabadh* (Baile Átha Cliath: Oifig an tSoláthair, 1940).

Mac Liammóir, Micheál, *Diarmuid agus Gráinne: Dráma Trí nGníomh* (Baile Átha Cliath: Oifig Díolta Foillseacháin Rialtais, 1935).

_____, *Lá agus Oidhche* (Baile Átha Cliath: Muinntir C. S. Ó Fallamhain Teo. i gcomhar le hOifig an tSoláthair, 1929).

_____, *Oidhche Bhealtaine: Dráma Beag le hAghaidh Leanbhaí* (Baile Átha Cliath: Oifig Díolta Foillseacháin Rialtais, 1932).

Mac Loingsigh, Éamonn, and Aindrias Ó Baoighill, *Fir Mhóra na hÉireann* (Sráid Bhaile Dúin Dealgan: Preas Dhún Dealgan, 1925).

MacManus, Francis, *Tóirthneach Luimnighe: Dráma Staireamhail i dTrí Radharcanna*, trans. Riobárd Ó Faracháin (Baile Átha Cliath: Brún agus Ó Nualláin, Teoranta, n. d. [1935]).
Mac Maoláin, Seán, *An Bealach chun na Gaedhealtachta ('The Road to the Gaedhealtacht' Phrase Book)* (Belfast: Coisde Mhodha na Ráidhte, n. d.)
_____, *Ceannracháin Cathrach* (Baile Átha Cliath: Oifig Díolta Foillseacháin Rialtais, 1935).
_____, *Éan Corr* (Baile Átha Cliath: Oifig an tSoláthair, 1937).
_____, *Gleann Airbh go Glas Naíon* (Baile Átha Cliath: Oifig an tSoláthair, 1969).
_____, *Iolar agus Sionnach* (Baile Átha Cliath: Oifig Díolta Foillseacháin Rialtais, 1938).
Mac Meanman, Seaghán, *Fear Siubhail a's a Chuid Comharsanach agus Daoine Eile* (Baile Átha Cliath: Oifig Díolta Foillseacháin Rialtais, 1937 [1924]).
_____, *Indé agus Indiu* (Baile Átha Cliath: Muinntir C. S. Ó Fallamhain Teo. i gcomhar le hOifig an tSoláthair, 1929).
_____, *Trí Mhion-Dráma* (Baile Átha Cliath: Oifig Díolta Foillseacháin Rialtais, 1936).
Mac Thorcail, Seán, *Slis de'n tSean-Mhaide: Dráma Grinn* (Baile Átha Cliath: Oifig Díolta Foillseacháin Rialtais, 1936).
Maguidhir, Séamus, *Dhá Chrann na Marbh* (Baile Átha Cliath: Oifig an tSoláthair, 1939).
_____, *Fánaidheacht i gContae Mhaigh Eo* (Baile Átha Cliath: An Gúm, 1994 [1944]).
Máire, an tSiúr, *Naomh Moinice* (Gaillimh: Ó Gormáin agus a Chomh., 1936).
Mac Cumhaill, 'Fionn', *An Dochartach* (Dundalk: Dundalgan Press, n. d.).
_____, *Is É Dia an Fear is Fearr* (Baile Átha Cliath: Comhlacht Oideachais na hÉireann, n. d.).
_____, *Maicín* (Dún Dealgan: Uilliam Tempest, Dún Dealgan Press, n. d.).
_____, *Na Rosa go Bráthach* (Baile Átha Cliath: Oifig an tSoláthair, 1952 [1939]).
_____, *Tusa a Mhaicín* (Baile Átha Cliath: Comhlucht Oideachais na hÉireann, n. d.).
Mhic Néill, Seosaimhín Bean, trans., *Finnsgéalta ó India* (Baile Átha Cliath: Comhlucht Oideachais na hÉireann, Teoranta, [1933]).
Morris, Henry ('Feargus Mac Róigh'), *Oidhche Áirneáil i dTír Chonaill* (Sráid Bhaile Dúin Dealgan: Preas Dhún Dealgan, [1924]).
_____, *Seanfhocla Uladh* (Baile Átha Cliath: Muinntir Ch. S. Ó Fallamhain, Teo. i gcomhar le hOifig an tSoláthair, 1931).
Mullen, Pat, *Man of Aran* (Cambridge: MIT Press, 1970 [1935]).
Nally, T. H., *Aonach Tailteann and Tailteann Games: Their Origin, History, and Ancient Associations* (Dublin: The Talbot Press Limited, 1922).
Nic Ailpín, Treasa, and Seán Ó Cuirrín, *Teagosc-Leabhar na Bheidhlíne* (Baile Átha Cliath: Brún agus Ó Nóláin, Teor., 1923).
Ní Airtnéide, Éibhlín, trans., *Críostóir Naomhtha agus Sgéalta Eile* (Baile Átha Cliath: M. H. Mac Ghuill agus a Mhac, Teo., 1923).
Nic Aodha, Dóirín, *Naomh Columbán* (Gaillimh: Ó Gormáin agus a Chomh., 1936).
Nic Ghabhann, Caitlín, *Eolaidhe na Cruinne: Leabhar Tlácht-Eolais* (Baile Átha Cliath: Brún agus Ó Nóláin Teor., [1924]).
_____, *Mágh Ealta Éadair* (*Dúthaigh Átha Cliath*) (Baile Átha Cliath: Máire Ní Raghallaigh, n. d.).
_____, *Tír-Eolas na hEorpa* (Baile Átha Cliath: Comhlacht Oideachais na hÉireann, Teoranta, 1923).
Nic Ghiobúin, Máire C., *Féichín Fobhair: Dráma um Mhiorbhailt* (Baile Átha Cliath: Oifig Díolta Foillseacháin Rialtais, 1936).
Ní Chinnéide, Máire, *Scéal an Tighe* (Baile Átha Cliath: Oifig an tSoláthair, 1952).
_____, trans., *Scéalta ó Ghrimm* (Baile Átha Cliath: Connradh na Gaedhilge, 1923).
Nic Mhaicín, Máighréad, ed., *As na Ceithre hÁirdibh: Cnuasach Gearr-Scéal* (Baile Átha Cliath: Oifig an tSoláthair, 1938).

Ní Dhéisighe, Searloit, *Paidreacha na nDaoine: Leabhar Cráibhtheachta ó'n tSean-Aimsir*, 2nd edn (Baile Átha Cliath: Clólucht an Talbóidigh, 1924).

Ní Dhochartaigh, Brighid, *Seamróg na gCeithre nDuilleóg* (Dún Dealgan: Preas Dhún Dealgan, n. d.).

Ní Dhubhghaill, C. M., *Ancient Irish Culture* (Dublin: Catholic Truth Society of Ireland, [1933]).

Ní Dhubhgáin, Laoise, *Aistí ar Stair na hEorpa* (Cuid a hAon) (Baile Átha Cliath: Brún agus Ó Nualláin, Teor., n. d.).

Ní Dhuibhir, Ális, *Míniú na Sean-Fhocal* (Dublin: An Coláiste Náisiúnta um Phost Oideachas / National Correspondence College Press, [1938]).

Ní Ghráda, Máiréad, *An Bheirt Dearbhráthar agus Scéalta Eile* (Baile Átha Cliath: Oifig an tSoláthair, 1939).

_____, *An Giolla Deacair agus Scéalta Eile* (Baile Átha Cliath: Comhlucht Oideachais na hÉireann, Teor. n. d. [1936]).

_____, *An Grádh agus an Gárda: Dráma Grinn Aon-Mhíre* (Baile Átha Cliath: Oifig Díolta Foillseacháin Rialtais, 1937).

_____, *Manannán* (Baile Átha Cliath: Oifig an tSoláthair, 1940).

_____, *Stailc Ocrais: Tragóid Stairiúil: Dráma Aonghnímh* (Baile Átha Cliath: Oifig an tSoláthair, 1966).

_____, *An Udhacht* (Baile Átha Cliath: Oifig Díolta Foillseacháin Rialtais, 1935).

Ní Ghuairim, Máire, *Ceol na Mara* (Baile Átha Cliath: Brún agus Ó Nualláin, [1938]).

Ní Shúilleabháin, Éibhlín, *Cinn Lae Éibhlín Ní Shúilleabháin*, ed. Máiréad Ní Loingsigh (Baile Átha Cliath: Coiscéim, 2000).

Ní Shúilleabháin, Eibhlis, *Letters from the Great Blasket*, ed. Seán Ó Coileáin (Boulder: Mercier Press / Irish American Book Company, n. d.).

Nótaí Staire: Meadhon-Scoil Leomhain, Clochar na Trócaire, Ceatharloch (n.p: n.p., n.d).

Ó Baoighealláin, Pádraig and Pádraig de Brún, ed. and trans., *Beatha Íosa Criost atá curtha i n-eagar as na Ceithre Soiscéil agus aistrighthe ón nGréigis* (Baile Átha Cliath: Comhartha na dTrí gCoinneal, 1929).

Ó Baoighill, *An t-Airidheach* (Baile Átha Cliath: Oifig an tSoláthair, 1939).

_____, *An Dílidhe* (Baile Átha Cliath: Oifig Díolta Foillseacháin Rialtais, 1932).

_____, *Sgéilíní na Finne* (Baile Átha Cliath: Muinntir C. S. Ó Fallamhain, Teo., i gcomhar le hOifig an tSoláthair, 1928).

Ó Broin, León, *Ag Stracadh leis an Saol agus Scéalta Eile* (Baile Átha Cliath: Muinntir C. S. Ó Fallamhain Teo., i gcomhar le hOifig an tSoláthair, 1929).

_____, *Árus na nGábhadh agus Sgéalta Eile* (Baile Átha Cliath: Cló Oifig Uí Mhathghamhna, 1923).

_____, *Béal na hUaighe* (Baile Átha Cliath: Muinntir Alex Thom i gcomhar le hOifig an tSoláthair, 1927).

_____, *An Clósgríobhaí: Dráma Grinn* (Baile Átha Cliath: Oifig Díolta Foillseacháin Rialtais, 1936).

_____, *Just Like Yesterday: An Autobiography* (Dublin: Gill & Macmillan, n. d.).

_____, *An Mhallacht agus Drámaí Eile* (Baile Átha Cliath: Oifig Díolta Foillseacháin Rialtais, 1931).

_____, *An Oíche Úd i mBeithil: Dráma Aoin-Mhíre* (Baile Átha Cliath: Oifig an tSoláthair, 1949).

_____, *Parnell: Beathaisnéis* (Baile Átha Cliath: Oifig an tSoláthair, 1937).

_____, *An Rún agus Scéalta Eile* (Baile Átha Cliath: Oifig Díolta Foillseacháin Rialtais, 1932).

Ó Bróithe, Pádraig, *Cinnte: Dráma Aon-Mhíre* (Baile Átha Cliath: Oifig Díolta Foillseacháin Rialtais, 1937).

_____, *Clann Lir agus Inghean an Ard-Ríogh* (Baile Átha Cliath: Brún agus Ó Nualláin, Teor., n. d. [1936]).

_____, *An Fobha: Mion-Dráma Oireamhnach do Bhuachaillí Scoile* (Baile Átha Cliath: Brún agus Ó Nualláin, Teoranta, [1938]).

_____, *Gaedhealg 'san Oifig / Irish in the Office: Office Dialogues in Irish with Pronunciation and Translation* (Dublin: Powell Press, n. d.)

_____, trans., *Pegasus nó An Capall Sgiathánach* (Nathaniel Hawthorne) (Baile Átha Cliath: Comhlucht Oideachais na hÉireann, Teor., n. d.).

_____, *Réidhteach na Ceiste: Dráma Aoin-Mhíre* (Baile Átha Cliath: Oifig an tSoláthair, 1951).

_____, trans. *Tír na n-Óg nó An Bosca Iongantach* (Hawthorne) (Baile Átha Cliath: Comhlucht Oideachais na hÉireann, Teor., n. d.).

Ó Cadhain, Máirtín, *Idir Shúgradh agus Dáiríre* (Baile Átha Cliath: Oifig an tSoláthair, 1975 [1939]).

_____, *'Páipéir Bhána agus Páipéir Bhreaca'* (Baile Átha Cliath: An Clóchomhar, 1969).

_____, *An Phléasc*, in *Macalla 1983*, ed. Gearóid Denvir, Máiréad Ní Dhúill, and Éibhlín Ní Scanláin (Gaillimh: An Cumann Éigse agus Seanchais, Coláiste na hOllscoile, 1983), 1–19.

Ó Cadhla, Seaan [*sic*], *Cathair Phortláirge agus na Déise / A Gael's Guide to Waterford and the Decies, new and revised edition* (Waterford: Waterford News, 1927).

Ó Cadhlaigh, Cormac, trans. *Aindeise Shiobhán* (Sophie de Ségur) (Baile Átha Cliath: Muinntir C. S. Ó Fallamhain. Teo., i gcomhar le hOifig an tSoláthair, 1928).

_____, *Cormac Mac Airt* (Baile Átha Cliath: Muinntir Alex Thom i gcomhar le hOifig an tSoláthair, 1927).

_____, *Cúntaisíocht* (Baile Átha Cliath: Brún agus Ó Nóláin, n. d.).

_____, trans. *De Bello Gallico: Leabhar a Dó* (Julius Caesar) (Baile Átha Cliath: Brún agus Ó Nóláin, Teor., 1922).

_____, *Eagna an Ghaedhil* (Baile Átha Cliath: Brún agus Ó Nóláin, Teor., 1925).

_____, *An Fhiannuidheacht* (Baile Átha Cliath: Oifig Díolta Foillseacháin Rialtais, 1937).

_____, *Guaire an Oinigh* (Baile Átha Cliath: Oifig an tSoláthair, 1939).

Ó Canainn, Pádraig, ed., *Diarmuid agus Gráinne, An Giolla Deacair, agus Bodach an Chóta Lachtna* (Baile Átha Cliath: An Preas Náisiúnta, [1939]).

Ó Caomhánaigh, Seán Óg, trans., *Briocht-Scéalta na h-Araibe: Cuid a h-Aon* (Baile Átha Cliath: Alec Tom agus a Chuid, Teoranta, n. d.).

_____, *Fánaí* (Baile Átha Cliath: Muinntir Alex Thom agus Comh. Teo. i gcomhar le hOifig an tSoláthair, 1928).

Ó Ceallaigh, An t-Athair Tomás, *An t-Athair Tomás Ó Ceallaigh agus a Shaothar, maille le Réamh-Rádh, Nótaí agus Eile*, ed. An t-Athair Tomás S. Ó Láimhín (Gaillimh: Complacht an Iarthair, Tóranta, 1943).

Ó Cearbhail, Seán, *Scéilín is Caogadh le Léigheamh, le Meabhrú agus le hAth-innsint* (Baile Átha Cliath: Comhlucht Oideachais na hÉireann, Teor., 1934).

Ó Ceit, Seosamh Th., *Maon: Úrchluiche dTrí nGníomh* (Baile Átha Cliath: Connradh na Gaedhilge, 1924).

Ó Ciardha, Séamus and Domhnall Ó Conalláin, eds. *De Bello Gallico: Leabhar V* (Julius Caesar) (Baile Átha Cliath: Comhlucht Oideachais na hÉireann, Teor., n. d.).

Ó Ciarghusa, Seán, *Ar Mo Mharanadh Dam* (Baile Átha Cliath: Oifig Díolta Foillseacháin Rialtais, n. d.).

_____, *Bun an Dá Abhann* (Baile Átha Cliath: Oifig Díolta Foillseacháin Rialtais, 1933).

_____, *Díoghlaim* (Baile Átha Cliath: Oifig an tSoláthair, 1947).

_____, *Geantraighe: Scéalta Beaga Grinn* (Baile Átha Cliath: Muinntir C. S. Ó Fallamhain, Teo., i gcomhar le hOifig an tSoláthair, 1928).

_____, *Onncail Seárlaí* (Baile Átha Cliath: Muinntir C. S. Ó Fallamhain Teo., i gcomhar le hOifig an tSoláthair, 1930).

Ó Cillín, Tomás, ed. *Artúraidheacht 'Thír-an-Áir'* (Áth Cliath: Comhlucht Oideachais na hÉireann, Teor., n. d.).

Ó Cinnéide, León, *Eithneacha an Ghrinn: Cruasacht Scéalta* (Gaillimh: Ó Gormáin Teach Clódóireachta, 1924).

Ó Cionnfhaolaidh, Micheul, *Eolas ar Éirinn* (Baile Átha Cliath: Muinntir Dollard, 1923).

_____, trans., *Fionn agus a Chuideachta* (Standish James O'Grady) (Baile Átha Cliath: Comhlucht Oideachais na hÉireann, Teoranta, 1923).

Ó Ciosáin, Seán, *Is Ait an Mac an Saol* (Baile Átha Cliath: Foilseacháin Náisiúnta Teoranta, 1973).

_____, *Cois Laoi na Sreabh* (Baile Átha Cliath: Foilseacháin Náisiúnta Teoranta, 1970).

_____, *Sgéalta cois Laoi* (Baile Átha Cliath: Oifig Díolta Foillseacháin Rialtais, 1935).

Ó Cléirigh, Tomás, *Aodh Mac Aingil agus an Scoil Nua-Ghaedhilge i Lobháin* (Baile Átha Cliath: Oifig Díolta Foillseacháin Rialtais, n. d.).

_____, *Seoidíní Cuimhne* (Baile Átha Cliath: Oifig Díolta Foillseacháin Rialtais, 1937).

Ó Colmáin, Micheál, *Clann Lir* (Baile Átha Cliath: Cló na gCoinneal, n. d.).

_____, *In Óige an tSaoghail: Sean-Sgéalta Gaodhalacha* (Baile Átha Cliath: Cló na gCoinneal, [1924]).

Ó Conaill, Micheál, *Cinéal Féichín agus Síol Anmachadha* (Baile Átha Cliath: Máire Ní Raghallaigh, 1932).

_____, *Fá Sgáth Shléibh' Eachtgha: Cinn Lae* (Baile Átha Cliath: Oifig Díolta Foillseacháin Rialtais, 1937).

Ó Conaire, Pádhraic Óg, *Anam Páiste* (Baile Átha Cliath: Muinntir Dollard, 1924).

_____, *Cara an Mhic Léighinn* (Baile Átha Cliath: Comhlucht Oideachais na hÉireann, 1924).

_____, *Ceol na nGiolcach* (Baile Átha Cliath: Oifig an tSoláthair, 1939).

_____, *Cóilín Ó Cuanaigh* (Baile Átha Cliath: Brún agus Ó Nóláin, 1923).

_____, *Draoidheacht na Farraige* (Gaillimh: Ó Gormáin, Teach na Clódóireachta, 1927).

_____, *Éan Cuideáin* (Baile Átha Cliath: Oifig an tSoláthair, 1936).

_____, *An Fraoch Bán* (Gaillimh: Ó Gormáin, Teach na Clódóireachta, 1922).

_____, *Mian a Croidhe* (Baile Átha Cliath: An Gaedheal-Comhlucht Taighde um Clódóireacht, Foilseóireacht, agus Tráchtáil, 1922).

_____, *Seoid ó'n Iarthar Órdha* (Gaillimh: Ó Gormáin, Teach na Clódóireachta, 1933).

_____, *Solus an Ghrádha* (Baile Átha Cliath: Muinntir Dollard, 1923).

Ó Conaire, Pádraic, *Aistí Phádraic Uí Chonaire*, ed. Gearóid Denvir (Indreabhán: Cló Chois Fharraige, 1978).

_____, *Brian Óg* (Baile Átha Cliath: Comhlacht Oideachais na hÉireann, [1926]).

_____, *Caitlín na Clúide: Dráma Beag Trí-Mhír le Ceol agus Damhsaí i gComhair an Aosa Óig* (Baile Átha Cliath: Taisceadán Adhbhar Léighinn do Sgoileannaibh Éireann, n. d.).

_____, *Eachtraí Móra ó n-Ár Stair*, ed. Micheál Ó Maoláin (Baile Átha Cliath: Taisceadán Adhbhar Léighinn do Sgoileannaibh Éireann, n. d.).

_____, *Fearfeasa Mac Feasa* (Indreabhán: Cló Chonamara, 1983 [1930]).

_____, *Iriseoireacht Uí Chonaire*, ed. An tSr. Éibhlín Ní Chionnaith (Béal an Daingin: Cló Iar-Chonnachta, 1989).

_____, *Mór-Thimcheall Éireann ar Muir*, ed. Micheál Ó Maoláin (Baile Átha Cliath: Brún agus Ó Nóláin, Teor., [1925]).

_____, *Sgéalta an tSáirsint Rua* (Baile Átha Cliath: An Preas Náisiúnta, n. d.)

_____, *Trí Truaighe na Sgéalaidheachta: Aithinnseacht Shimplidhe do'n Aos Óg*, ed. Micheál Ó Maoláin (Baile Átha Cliath: Brún agus Ó Nóláin, Teor., [1924]).

_____, *Ystoriau Byr o'r Wyddeleg*, trans. Tomás Ó Cléirigh and David Myrddin Lloyd (Llandysul: Gwasg Gomer, 1934).

_____, and Micheál Ó Maoláin, *Scéalta na mBard: Cuid a h-Aon (Cur Amach Muimhneach)* (Baile Átha Cliath: Brún agus Ó Nóláin, 1924).

Ó Concheanainn, Peadar, *Inis Meáin: Seanchas agus Scéalta* (Baile Átha Cliath: An Gúm, 1993 [1931]).

Ó Concheannain, An tAthair Tomás, *Naomh Proinnsias* (Gaillimh: Ó Gormáin Tóranta, 1938).

Ó Conchubhair, Domhnall, *Conncas: Dráma Dhá Ghníomh*, in Ó Conchubhair, *Duanaire Dúithch' Ealla*, ed. Seán Ua Cadhla (Baile Átha Cliath: Oifig Díolta Foillseacháin Rialtais, 1932), 73-94.

Ó Conchubhair, Tadhg, *Racaireacht Ghrinn na Tuaithe*, ed. Muintir 'An Lóchrann' (Corcaigh: Liam Ruiséal, 1924).

Ó Criomhthain, Tomás, *Allagar na hInise (ó 5.12.1918 go 1.1.1923)*, ed. Pádraig Ua Maoileoin (Baile Átha Cliath: Oifig an tSoláthair, 1977).

_____, *Allagar II*, ed. Pádraig Ua Maoileoin (Baile Átha Cliath: Coiscéim, 1999).

_____, *Bloghanna ón mBlascaod*, ed. Breandán Ó Conaire (Baile Átha Cliath: Coiscéim, 1997).

_____, *Dinnsheanchas na mBlascaodaí* (Baile Átha Cliath: Oifig Díolta Foillseacháin Rialtais, 1935).

_____, *An t-Oileánach*, ed. Seán Ó Coileáin (Baile Átha Cliath: Cló Talbóid, 2002).

_____, *An t-Oileánach: Scéal a Bheathadh Féin do Scríobh Tomás Ó Criomhthain*, ed. Pádraig Ó Siochfhradha (Baile Átha Cliath: Comhlucht Oideachais na hÉireann, 1929).

Ó Cuirrín, Seán, *Beirt Dhéiseach, mar atá sceul Nua-Cheaptha agus trí sceulta arna dtiontódh ó theangthacha eile* (Baile Átha Cliath: Oifig an tSoláthair, 1936).

_____, *Uimhrigheacht* (Baile Átha Cliath: Comhlacht Oideachais na h-Éireann, 1922).

Ó Cuív, Shán, *Cúirt na Dála agus Sgéal Eile* (Bleaclieh: Brún agus Ó Nóláin, Teor., n. d.).

_____, *Deora Áthais agus Dréachta Eile* (Baile Átha Cliath: Oifig an tSoláthair, 1937).

_____, *Domhnall Donn agus Sgéilíní Eile* (Baile Átha Cliath: Brún agus Ó Nóláin, Teor., 1929).

_____, *Niamh Chinn Óir: Comedi Aon Ghníomh* (Baile Átha Cliath: Máire Ní Raghallaigh, [1929]).

_____, *The Problem of Irish in the Schools* (Dublin: Browne and Nolan, Limited, 1936).

_____, *Prós na hAoise Seo* (Bleathcliath: Brún agus Ó Nóláin, Teor., [1934]).

_____, *Sgéalta ón Radió* (Baile Átha Cliath: Oifig Díolta Foillseacháin Rialtais, 1931).

_____, *Troid agus An Bhean ón dTuaith* (Baile Átha Cliath: Oifig Díolta Foillseacháin Rialtais, 1931).

Ó Curnáin, Tadhg, trans., *Mion-Mhíniú ar an dTeagasg Críostaidhe: Aistriú ar an Leabhar Béarla 'Manual of Religious Instruction' do Sgríobh An tAth. Pádraig Paor* (Baile Átha Cliath: Maunsel agus Roberts, Teo., [1923]).

Ó Dálaigh, Seán, *Clocha Sgáil* (Baile Átha Cliath: Muinntir C. S. Ó Fallamhain, Teo., i gcomhar le hOifig an tSoláthair, 1930).

_____, *Timcheall Chinn Sléibhe: Aistí agus Scéalta* (Baile Átha Cliath: Oifig Díolta Foillseacháin Rialtais, 1933).

Ó Direáin, Peadar, *Sgéalaidhe Leitir Mealláin*, ed. Seán Ó Mocháin (Baile Átha Cliath: Comhlucht Oideachais na hÉireann, Teo., 1926).

_____, *Sgéalta na n-Oileán* (Baile Átha Cliath: Muinntir C. S. Ó Fallamhain, Teo., i gcomhar le hOifig an tSoláthair, 1929).

Ó Dochartaigh, Micheál, *Creach Bhaile an Teampaill* (Baile Átha Cliath: Oifig Díolta Foillseacháin Rialtais, 1930).

Ó Domhnaill, Maoghnus, ed. *Beatha Gillasius Ardmachanus* (Baile Átha Cliath: Oifig an tSoláthair, 1939).

_____, ed. *An Bheatha Chrábhaidh ('De Theacht Isteach ar an mBeathaidh Chrábhaidh') San Proinsias de Sales do Scríobh i Laidin sa bhliadhain 1608, an tAthair Filip Ua Raghallaigh Bráthair Bocht d'Ord S. Proinsias, agus Gáirdian na mBráthar nÉirionnach i bPráig sa Bhohemia d'aistrigh go Gaedhilg sa bhliadhain 1670* (Baile Átha Cliath: Oifig an tSoláthair, 1938).

Ó Domhnaill, Mártan, *Oileáin Árann* (Baile Átha Cliath: Muinntir C. S. Ó Fallamhain i gcomhar le hOifig an tSoláthair, 1930).

Ó Domhnaill, Niall, *Beatha Sheáin Mistéil* (Baile Átha Cliath: Oifig Díolta Foillseacháin Rialtais, 1937).

_____, *Bruighean Feille* (Baile Átha Cliath: Oifig Díolta Foillseacháin Rialtais, 1934).

_____, *Forbairt na Gaeilge* (Baile Átha Cliath: Sáirséal agus Dill, 1951).

Ó Domhnalláin, Pádhraic, *Ar Lorg an Ríogh agus Sgéalta Eile* (Baile Átha Cliath: M. H. Mac Guill agus a Mhac, Teo., 1925).

_____, *Dréachta* (Baile Átha Cliath: Oifig an tSoláthair, 1956 [1935]).

_____, *An tIolrach Mór: Díoghluim Gearr-Sgéal* (Baile Átha Cliath: Brún agus Ó Nualláin, n. d.).

_____, *Oidhre an Léighinn agus Aistí Eile* (Baile Átha Cliath: Oifig Díolta Foillseacháin Rialtais, 1935).

_____, *Na Spiadóirí agus Sgéalta Eile* (Baile Átha Cliath: Brún agus Ó Nualláin, Teor., n. d.).

_____, trans., *Stair Choitcheann na Ré Críostaidhe i nDá Imleabhar: Imleabhar a hAon ó'n Tús dí chum Éirghe Amach na bPratústún (1–1517)* (Nicholas A. Weber) (Baile Átha Cliath: Oifig Díolta Foillseacháin Rialtais, 1932).

_____, and Tomás Ó Raghallaigh, *Bruth-Fá-Thír* (Baile Átha Cliath: M. H. Mac Ghuill agus a Mhac, Teo., 1923).

Ó Donnchadha, Donnchadh, *Seanchas an Chreidimh* (Baile Átha Cliath: M. H. Mac Ghuill agus a Mhac, Teo., 1923.

Ó Donnchadha, Éamon, *Gluais Matamaitice* (Baile Átha Cliath: Brún agus Ó Nualláin, Teoranta, [1935]).

_____, *Uimhríocht* (Baile Átha Cliath: C. S. Ó Fallamhain, Teo. i gcomhair le hOifig an tSoláthair, 1928).

Ó Donnchadha, Tadhg, *Filidheacht Fiannaigheachta* (Baile Átha Cliath: Comhlucht Oideachais na hÉireann, n. d.).

_____, ed. *Leabhar Cloinne Aodha Buidhe* (Baile Átha Cliath: Oifig an tSoláthair, 1931).

_____, ed., *Ór-Chiste Fiannuíochta* (Baile Átha Cliath: Comhlucht Oideachais na hÉireann, Teor., n. d.).

_____, 'Réamhrádh', in *Fíon Gearmánach: Iarrachtaí Aistriúchán ón Ghearmáinis* (Baile Átha Cliath: Muinntir C. S. Ó Fallamhain i gcomhar le hOifig an tSoláthair, 1930).

Ó Droighneáin, Muiris, *Taighde i gcomhair Stair Litridheachta na Nua-Ghaedhilge ó 1882 anuas* (Baile Átha Cliath: Oifig Díolta Foillseacháin Rialtais, 1936).

Ó Dubhda, Peadar, *Brian* (Baile Átha Cliath: Oifig Díolta Foillseacháin Rialtais, 1937).

_____, *Cáith agus Grán* (Baile Átha Cliath: Muinntir C. S. Ó Fallamhain Teo. i gcomhar le hOifig an tSoláthair, 1929).

_____, *Lá na Cúirte (agus Dhá Eachtra Eile)* (Oméith: Lucht Choláisde Bhríghde, [1924]).

_____, *An t-Ógánach Ceann-Órdha agus Scéalta Eile* (Baile Átha Cliath: Oifig an tSoláthair, 1939).

_____, *Thríd an Fhuinneoig* (Baile Átha Cliath: Oifig Díolta Foillseacháin Rialtais, 1936).

Ó Dubhghaill, Séamus, *Beartín Luachra* (Baile Átha Cliath: M. H. Mac an Ghoill agus a Mhac, Teo., 1927).

O'Duffy, Eimar, *King Goshawk and the Birds* (New York: Macmillan, 1926).

Ó Duirinne, Séamus, *Eachtra na Nádúire* (Baile Átha Cliath: M. H. Mac an Ghoill agus a Mhac, Teo., 1928).

Ó Dúnaighe, Seán, *An Crann Cuilinn* (Baile Átha Cliath: Oifig Díolta Foillseacháin Rialtais, 1933).

_____, *Inghean an Ghearaltaigh* (Baile Átha Cliath: Muinntir Dollard, Teo., n. d.)

_____, *Plúr na Gaedhilge* (Baile Átha Cliath: Comhlucht Oideachais na hÉireann, Teoranta, 1923).

Ó Fallamhain, Séamus, *Gearr-Stair .i. Gearr-Aithris ar Dhaoine Cáileamhla i Seanchas na hÉireann* (Baile Átha Cliath: Comhlucht Oideachais na hÉireann, Teoranta, [1922]).

Ó Faracháin, Riobárd, *Fíon gan Mhoirt: Cnuasach Gearr-Scéalta* (Baile Átha Cliath: Oifig an tSoláthair, 1938).

O'Flaherty, Tom, *Aranmen All* (Dingle: Brandon, 1991 [1934]).

Ó Flaithbheartaigh, Máirtín, ed., *An Chraobh Chumhra* (Gaillimh: Ó Gormáin agus a Chomh., 1934).

Ó Foghludha, Risteárd, ed., *Ar Bhruach na Coille Muaire: Liam Dall Ó hIfearnáin cct. [?]1720-1803* (Baile Átha Cliath: Oifig an tSoláthair, 1939).

_____, ed., *Carn Tighearnaigh .i. An tAthair Conchubhar Ó Briain, D. D.* (Baile Átha Cliath: Oifig an tSoláthair, 1938).

_____, ed., *Cois na Bríde: Liam Inglis, O. S. A., 1709-1778: A Chuid Filidheachta dá Chnuasach is dá Chur in Eagar ag Risteárd Ó Foghludha* (Baile Átha Cliath: Oifig Díolta Foillseacháin Rialtais, 1937).

_____, ed., *Cois na Cora .i. Liam Ruadh Mac Coitir agus a Shaothar Fileata* (Baile Átha Cliath: Oifig Díolta Foillseacháin Rialtais, 1937).

_____, ed., *Donnchadh Ruadh Mac Conmara 1715–1810*, 2nd edn (Baile Átha Cliath: Oifig Díolta Foillseacháin Rialtais, 1933).

_____, ed., *Duanarán ré 1600–1700* (Baile Átha Cliath: C. S. Ó Fallamhain, Teoranta, 1935).

_____, ed., *Eoghan an Mhéirín cct.* (Baile Átha Cliath: Oifig an tSoláthair, 1938).

_____, ed., *Pádraig Phiarais Cundún*, 1777-1856 (Baile Átha Cliath: Oifig Díolta Foillseacháin Rialtais, 1932).

_____, ed., *Scoth-Duanta maille re Cumair-Scéal ar Bheatha a n-Ughdar agus Gearra-Ghluais Acarthach* (Baile Átha Cliath: Brún agus Ó Nualláin, Teo., n. d.).

_____, ed., *Seán Clárach 1691-1754: A Shaothar Fileata agus Scéal a Bheathadh*, 2nd edn (Baile Átha Cliath: Oifig Díolta Foillseacháin Rialtais, 1932).

_____, ed., *Tadhg Gaelach: Ath-Eagar ar a Dhuanta Diadha agus ar a Chuid Amhrán maille re Mórán Nuadh-Eolais ar a Bheatha* (Baile Átha Cliath: Muinntir C. S. Ó Fallamhain, Teo. i gcomhar le hOifig an tSoláthair, 1929).

Ó Gallchobhair, Pádraig ('Muirghein'), *Cáitheamh na dTonn* (Baile Átha Cliath: Oifig Díolta Foillseacháin Rialtais, 1934).

Ó Gallchobhair, Tomás, trans., *Críost an Uile* (Rev. John Carr) (Baile Átha Cliath: Oifig Díolta Foillseacháin Rialtais, 1936).

_____, *Scéal an Bhíobla le Pictiúirí: An Tiomna Nua* (Father I. Schuster) (Mainistir Fhearmuighe: Coláiste Colmáin, 1933).

Ó Gaora, Colm, *Obair is Luadhainn nó Saoghal sa nGaedhealtacht* (Baile Átha Cliath: Oifig Díolta Foillseacháin Rialtais, 1937).

Ó Grianna, Conall, ed., *Rann na Feirsde: Seanchas Ár Sinsear* (Áth na gCoire: Cló Cheann Dubhrann, 1998).

Ó Grianna, Séamus, *Caisleáin Óir* (Sráid Bhaile Dúin Dealgan: Preas Dhún Dealgan, 1924).

_____, *Cioth is Dealán* (Corcaigh: Cló Mercier, 1976 [1926]).

_____, *Feara Fáil* (Dún Dealgan, Cló-Lucht 'An Scrúduightheoir, 1933).
_____, *Micheál Ruadh* (Sráid Bhaile Dhún Dealgan: Preas Dhún Dealgan, n. d.).
_____, *Sraith na Craobhrua*, vols. 4-6 (Dún Dealgan: Preas Dhún Dealgan, [1927-30]).
Ó Gríobhtha, Micheál, *Bean an Bhrait Bháin* (Baile Átha Cliath: Muinntir C. S. Ó Fallamhain, Teo., i gcomhar le hOifig an tSoláthair, 1928).
_____, *Briathar Mná* (Baile Átha Cliath: C. S. Ó Fallamhain Teo., i gcomhar le hOifig an tSoláthair, 1928).
_____, *Buaidh na Treise: 'Cogadh Gaedheal re Gallaibh'* (Baile Átha Cliath: Muinntir C. S. Ó Fallamhain Teo., i gcomhar le hOifig an tSoláthair, 1928).
_____, *Cathair Aeidh* (Baile Átha Cliath: Oifig Díolta Foillseacháin Rialtais, 1937).
_____, *De Dhruim na hAille .i. Dráma Dhá Mhír* (Baile Átha Cliath: Oifig Díolta Foillseacháin Rialtais, 1935).
_____, *Go mBeannuighthear Dhuit* (Baile Átha Cliath: Comhlucht Oideachais na hÉireann, n. d.).
_____, *Lorgaireacht* (Baile Átha Cliath: Muinntir Alex Thom agus Comh. i gcomhar le hOifig an tSoláthair, 1927).
Ó hAnnracháin, Peadar, *Machtnamh Cime* (Baile Átha Cliath: Oifig Díolta Foillseacháin Rialtais, 1933).
_____, *Mar Chonnac-sa Éire* (Baile Átha Cliath: Oifig an tSoláthair, 1937).
Ó hAodha, Séamus, *Aodhagán Ó Rathaille* (Baile Átha Cliath: Comhlucht Oideachais na hÉireann, Teo., n. d.).
_____, *Giolla an Amaráin: Dráma Ceithre Mhír* (Baile Átha Cliath: Oifig an tSoláthair, 1954).
_____, *An Luch Tuaithe: Dráma Grinn* (Baile Átha Cliath: Comhlucht Oideachais na hÉireann, Teor., n. d.).
Ó hAodha, Tomás, *An Figheadóir* (Baile Átha Cliath: Brún agus Ó Nóláin, n. d.).
Ó hAonghusa, T., *Games of the Gael / 'An Gaedheal Óg'* (Drogheda: *Drogheda Independent* Co., Ltd., 1923).
Ó hÉigcartaigh, Diarmuid, *Is Uasal Céird*, ed. Stiofán Ó hAnnracháin (Baile Átha Cliath: Foilseacháin Náisiúnta Teoranta, 1968).
_____, *Tadhg Ciallmhar* (Baile Átha Cliath: Oifig Díolta Foillseacháin Rialtais, 1934)
Ó hIfearnáin, Séamus, and Tomás Ó Breacáin, *Tír-Eolas agus Stair na h-Éireann* (Baile Átha Cliath: Comhlucht Oideachais na hÉireann, Teoranta, n. d.).
Ó hÓgáin, Seán, *Conntae an Chláir: A Triocha agus a Tuatha / Gairbh-Fhearann Luighdheach, le himtheacht na haimsire Tuadhmhumha, agus anois Conntae an Chláir* (Baile Átha Cliath: Oifig an tSoláthair, 1938).
_____, *An Fheilm* (Baile Átha Cliath: Oifig an tSoláthair, 1962).
_____, *Smacht: Dráma Aon-Ghnímh* (Baile Átha Cliath: Oifig an tSoláthair, 1962).
Ó hUiginn, Brian, *Scéalta na Maighdine Muire* (Áth Cliath: Brian Ó hUiginn, n. d.).
Ó Laochdha, Seosamh, *Muirthéacht na Frainnce* (Baile Átha Cliath: Muinntir C. S. Ó Fallamhain i gcomhar le hOifig an tSoláthair, 1930).
Ó Lochlainn, Gearóid, *Bean an Mhilliúnaí: Dráma i n-éan gníomh amháin* (Baile Átha Cliath: Clódhanna Gaedhealacha, 1923).
_____, *An t-Éirighe Amach: Dráma Éin-Ghnímh* (Baile Átha Cliath: Oifig an tSoláthair, 1944).
_____, *Na Fearachoin ('Fearachoin Groidhe ná Claoidhfeadh Céadta'): Dráma Trí Gníomh* (Baile Átha Cliath: Oifig an tSoláthair, 1946).
_____, *Na Gaduithe: Dráma Grinn i dTrí Gníomha* (Baile Átha Cliath: Oifig Díolta Foillseacháin Rialtais, 1935).
Ó Longáin, Seán, *Riobárd Emmet* (Baile Átha Cliath: Brún agus Ó Nualláin, Teor., [1937]).
Ó Luineacháin, Risteárd, *Greann is Gáire* (Baile Átha Cliath: Brún agus Ó Nóláin, Teor., [1923]).

Ó Máille, Tomás, *Mac Dathó: Innsean Nua* (Baile Átha Cliath: Comhlucht Oideachais na hÉireann, 1924).

_____, ed. *Micheál Mac Suibhne agus Filidhe an tSléibhe* (Baile Átha Cliath: Oifig Díolta Foillseacháin Rialtais, [1934]).

_____, *An t-Iomaire Ruadh* (Baile Átha Cliath: Comhlucht Oideachais na hÉireann, 1939).

Ó Maoláin, Micheál, *Chiefs of Éire, 222-1847 A.D.* (Dublin: Browne & Nolan, 1924).

_____, *Inis Ealga: Stair Beag na h-Éireann i gCóir an Aosa Óig* (Baile Átha Cliath: M. S. Ó Maoláin, Foillsightheoir Oideachais, n. d.).

_____, *Saoghal na Cathrach* (Baile Átha Cliath: M. S. Ó Maoláin, Foillsightheoir Oideachais, 1925).

_____, *Stair na h-Eorpa Thiar*, trans. Seán Ó Ruadháin (Baile Átha Cliath: M. S. Ó Maoláin, Foillsightheoir Oideachais, n. d.).

Ó Mathghamhna, Domhnall, trans., *Demostenes agus Cicero: Tuairisc a mBeathadh* (Plutarch) (Baile Átha Cliath: Oifig Díolta Foillseacháin Rialtais, 1935).

_____, trans., *Inis Atlaint: Scéal a Chéad-Cheap Platon 'san Ghréigis* (Baile Átha Cliath: Brún agus Ó Nualláin, Teor., [1935]).

_____, trans., *Oráid Caointe Pheiricléis* (Baile Átha Cliath: Brún agus Ó Nóláin, [1930]).

_____, trans., *Saoghal-ré na nGracchi* (Plutarch) (Baile Átha Cliath: Oifig Díolta Foillseacháin Rialtais, 1933),

_____, *Sgéalta a Filí na Rómha* (Baile Átha Cliath: Brún agus Ó Nóláin, Teor., 1924).

_____, *Slabhra Nóiníní .i. Cnósach de Ghearr-Sgéalta ar a bhFuil Deasgán de sna Sgéilíní is Mó Cáil d'Ár Cumadh ar Roinn na hEorpa* (Baile Átha Cliath: Comhlucht Oideachais na hÉireann, [1934]).

_____, trans., *An Tarna Philippica .i. M. Tullii Ciceronis in M. Antonium Philippicarum, Liber Secundus* (Baile Átha Cliath: Oifig Díolta Foillseacháin Rialtais, 1932.

_____, trans., *Vera Historia: Scéal Ainspianta a Chéad-Cheap Lucian san Ghréigis* (Baile Átha Cliath: Oifig Díolta Foillseacháin Rialtais, 1931).

Ó Meadhra, Pádraig, *Riobárd Emmet: Dráma Scol i gCúig Radharcanna* (Aonach Urmhumhan, Muinntear an 'Guardian', 1937).

Ó Míodhacháin, Liam, *Eachtraí Pháidín Turraoin: Aith-Innsint ar Shean-Sceulta* (Baile-Átha-Cliath: Comhlucht Oideachais na h-Éireann, Teor., n. d.).

Ó Monacháin, Ailbhe, tr. *Doinicíní an Domhain* (Baile Átha Cliath: Oifig an tSoláthair, 1939).

Ó Monacháin, Seosamh, ed., *Timire Aniar: Tomás Ó Mannacháin* (Baile Átha Cliath: Coiscéim, 1995).

Ó Mongaigh, Seoirse, *Slánlús* (Baile Átha Cliath: Comhlucht Oideachais na hÉireann, Teor., [1935]).

Ó Mongáin, Colm, *An Críostaidhe ar a Leas tré Bhrígh na n-Úrnaidhe-Mheanman: Comhairle do Mhuinntir na h-Éireann Úrnaidhe-Mheanman do Chleachtadh* (Baile Átha Cliath: Preas Dúndealgan, [1938]).

Ó Móráin, Pádraig S., trans., *Cuarta ar an tSacraimint Rónaomhtha agus ar an Maighdin Mhuire Bheannuighthe in aghaidh Gach Lae den Mhí* (St Alphonsus Liguori) (Baile Átha Cliath: Cló-Lucht an Talbóidigh, [1934]).

Ó Mórdha, An Choronail Muiris, *Tús agus Fás Óglách na hÉireann, 1913–1917*, trans. Liam Ó Rinn (Baile Átha Cliath: Oifig Díolta Foillseacháin Rialtais, 1936).

Ó Muimhneacháin, Conchubhar, compiler, *Béaloideas Bhéal Átha an Ghaorthaidh* (Baile Átha Cliath: Oifig Díolta Foillseacháin Rialtais, 1935).

Ó Murchadha, Micheál, *Leabhar Eoluis ar an gCreideamh* (Baile Átha Cliath: Oifig Díolta Foillseacháin Rialtais, 1931).

Ó Murchadha, Tadhg, *An Cliathán Clé* (Baile Átha Cliath: Oifig an tSoláthair, 1932).

Ó Murchú, Micheál ('Micheal Fionn'), *Caogadh Amhrán* (Baile Átha Cliath: Máire Ní Raghallaigh, [1936]).

_____, *Litreacha ó'n bhFrainnc* (Baile Átha Cliath: Oifig Díolta Foillseacháin Rialtais, 1935).

O Murcu, Diarmuid, *Bodaire n Coota Lachtna* (Blaaclia: Bruun agus O Nualaen, Teor., [1935]).

_____, *Clann Lir in Eeris* (Dublin: C. J. Fallon, [1935]).

_____, *Irish in a Week by the Rational Method* (Waterford: The Munster Express Printing Works, [1937]).

_____, *Minstrel of Eerish: Being Some of the Best Known Hymns and Songs Done into Standard Irish, with Originals* (Waterford: The Munster Express Printing Works, [1936]).

O'Neill, Phil, *Twenty Years of the GAA 1910–1930: A History and Book of Reference for Gaels* (Kilkenny: Kilkenny Journal, 1931).

Ó Néill, Séamus, *Buaidh an Ultaigh: Dráma Nua* (Baile Átha Cliath: Oifig Díolta Foillseacháin Rialtais, 1936).

_____, *Díolta faoi n-a Luach: Dráma Cheithre Radharc* (Baile Átha Cliath: Oifig an tSoláthair, 1946).

_____, 'Triúr nach Maireann', in *Fearsaid: Iris Iubhaile an Chumainn Ghaelaigh, 1906–1956* (Béal Feirste: Cumann Gaelach na hOllscoile, 1956), 31–4.

Ó Nualláin, Ciarán, *Oidhche i nGleann na nGealt* (Baile Átha Cliath: Oifig an tSoláthair, 1939).

_____, *Óige an Dearthár .i. Myles na gCopaleen* (Baile Átha Cliath: Foilseacháin Náisiúnta Teoranta, 1973).

Ó Nualláin, Fearrgus, *Laidean tré Ghaedhilg I. / Dlúth-Aistriúchán / Solúidí agus Gluaiseanna*, ed. Riobárd Ó Druaidh (Rathfarnham: The Language and Literary Guilds, [1924]).

Ó Nualláin, Gearóid, *Beatha Dhuine A Thoil* (Baile Átha Cliath: Oifig an tSoláthair, 1950).

_____, *Dia Diabhail agus Daoine* (Baile Átha Cliath: Comhlucht Oideachais na hÉireann, 1922).

_____, *Tighearna an Tailimh agus Sgéalta Eile* (Baile Átha Cliath: Clólucht an Talbóidigh Teo., 1923).

_____, trans., *Trí Seoda ó Albain (Three Folk-Tales): Translated from the Scotch Gaelic 'Na Daoine Sidhe is Uirsgeulan Eile'* (Baile Átha Cliath: Comhlucht Oideachais na hÉireann, Teoranta, 1922).

_____, and Fearrgus Ó Nualláin, *Sean agus Nua* (Baile Átha Cliath: Brún agus O Nóláin, [1923]).

Ó R., L., ed., *Eochair na bhFlathas: Leabhar Úrnaithe Caitlicí maraon leis na hEipistilí is na Soiscéil (an t-aistriú údarásach a dhein an tAthair Peadar Ó Laoghaire S. P. Canónach)* (Baile Átha Cliath: Clólucht an Talbóidigh, Tra., n. d.).

Ó Rabhartaigh, Tadhg, *Mian na Marbh* (Baile Átha Cliath: Oifig an tSoláthair, 1937).

Ó Raghallaigh, Críostóir, *Dúthracht* (Baile Átha Cliath: Brún agus Ó Nualláin, Teor., [1927]).

_____, *An Léirmheastóir* (Baile Átha Cliath: Brún agus Ó Nualláin, Teor., 1931).

_____, ed., *Litridheacht na Gaedhilge* (Baile Átha Cliath: Brún agus Ó Nualláin, Teor., n. d.).

Ó Raghallaigh, Tomás, *Dráma: Eachdhruim an Áir* (Gaillimh: Ó Gormáin, Teach na Clódóireachta, 1932).

Ó Raithbheartaigh, Toirdhealbhach, *Máighistrí san Fhilidheacht: Láimh-Leabhar ar na Filí Móra ó Chéitinn anuas* (Baile Átha Cliath: Oifig Díolta Foillseacháin Rialtais, 1932).

O'Rahilly, Thomas F., *Irish Dialects Past and Present* (Dublin: Dublin Institute for Advanced Studies, 1972 [1932]).

_____, *A Miscellany of Irish Proverbs* (Dublin: Talbot Press, 1922).

Ó Riain, Art ('Barra Ó Caochlaigh'), *Lucht Ceoil* (Baile Átha Cliath: Oifig Díolta Foillseacháin Rialtais, 1932).

_____, *An Tost agus Scéalta Eile* (Baile Átha Cliath: Muinntir Alex Thom i gcomhar le hOifig an tSoláthair, 1927).

Ó Riain, Liam P., *Cnámha Sgéal na nUghdar* (Baile Átha Cliath: An Press Náisiúnta, n. d.).

_____, *Feilm an Tobair Bheannuighthe* (Dúndealgan: 'An Sgrúduightheoir', 1936).

_____, *Gaedhealachas i gCéin* (Baile Átha Cliath: Oifig Díolta Foillseacháin Rialtais, 1933).

Ó Rinn, Liam, trans. *Dánta Próis* (Ivan Turgenev) (Baile Átha Cliath: Oifig Díolta Foillseacháin Rialtais, 1933).

_____, *Mo Chara Stiofán* (Baile Átha Cliath: Oifig an tSoláthair, 1939).

_____, *Peann agus Pár* (Baile Átha Cliath: Oifig an tSoláthair, 1940).

_____, *So Súd* (Baile Átha Cliath: Oifig an tSoláthair, 1953).

_____, *Turus go Páras* (Baile Átha Cliath: Oifig Díolta Foillseacháin Rialtais, 1931).

Ó Rónáin, An tAthair Maolmhuire, *Dún Laoghaire agus na Ceanntair Mágcuairt*, trans. Donnchadh Mac Aodha (Baile Átha Cliath: Oifig Díolta Foillseacháin Rialtais, 1936).

Ó Ruadháin, Seán, *Gearr-Sgéalta Grinn*, ed. Micheál Ó Maoláin (Baile Átha Cliath: M. S. Ó Maoláin, n. d.).

_____, *Pádhraic Mháire Bhán, nó An Gol agus an Gáire* (Baile Átha Cliath: Oifig Díolta Foillseacháin Rialtais, 1936).

Ó Séaghdha, Pádraig ('Conán Maol'), *Stiana* (Baile Átha Cliath: C. S. Ó Fallamhain Teo., i gcomhar le hOifig an tSoláthair, 1930).

Ó Séaghdha, Pádraig ('Gruagach an Tobair'), *Déanamh an Chleamhnais* (Corcaigh: Oifig 'An Lóchrann', 1926).

_____, *Fastuím* (Corcaigh: Oifig 'An Lóchrann', 1926).

Ó Séaghdha, Tadhg Saor, *Dhá Sgéal* (Baile Átha Cliath: Muinntir C. S. Ó Fallamhain Teo., i gcomhar le hOifig an tSoláthair, 1929).

Ó Searcaigh, Séamus, *Nua-Sgríbhneoirí na Gaedhilge* (Baile Átha Cliath: Brún agus Ó Nualláin, Teor., 1934).

_____, *Pádraig Mac Piarais* (Baile Átha Cliath: Oifig an tSoláthair, 1938).

Ó Siadhail, Seán, *Aistí Soisgéalacha* (Baile Átha Cliath: Oifig Díolta Foillseacháin Rialtais, 1937).

Ó Siochfhradha, Micheál, *Aon-Mhac Aoife Alban: Dráma Trí Mír* (Baile Átha Cliath: Oifig an tSoláthair, 1938).

_____, *An Ball Dubh: Drama Trí Mír* (Baile Átha Cliath: Muinntir C. S. Ó Fallamhain, Teo. i gcomhar le hOifig an tSoláthair, 1929).

_____, *Deire an Chunntais: Dráma Aon-Mhíre* (Baile Átha Cliath: Oifig Díolta Foillseacháin Rialtais, 1939).

_____, *Seo Mar Bhí* (Baile Átha Cliath: Comhlucht Oideachais na hÉireann, n. d.).

_____, *Stair-Sheanchas Éireann: Cuid I: Ó Thús Aimsire go 1609 AD* (Baile Átha Cliath: Comhlucht Oideachais na hÉireann, Teoranta, n. d.).

_____, *Stair-Sheanchas Éireann: Cuid II: Ó 1609 go 1933 AD* (Baile Átha Cliath: Comhlucht Oideachais na hÉireann, Teor., n. d.).

_____, trans., *Taoisigh Eorpa .i. 'The Makers of Europe' / Gearr-innsint ar Stair na hEorpa i gcomhair Scoláirí Meán-Scol* (E. M. Wilmot-Buxton) (Baile Átha Cliath: Oifig Díolta Foillseacháin Rialtais, 1933).

Ó Siochfhradha, Pádraig, *Caibilidí as Leabhar Mhóirín* (Baile Átha Cliath: Comhlucht Oideachais na hÉireann, Teor., 1934).

_____, ed., *An Seanchaidhe Muimhneach .i. Meascra de Bhéaloideas Ilchineál ó 'An Lóchrann' 1907-1913* (Baile Átha Cliath: Institute Béaloideasa Éireann, 1932).

_____, *Seanfhocail na Muimhneach* (Corcaigh: Cló-chualacht Seandúna, 1926).

_____, ed., *Tóraidheacht an Ghiolla Dheacair* (Baile Átha Cliath: Comhlucht Oideachais na hÉireann, Teor., n. d.).

_____, ed., *Tóraidheacht Dhiarmada agus Ghráinne* (Baile Átha Cliath: Comhlucht Oideachais na hÉireann, Teor., n. d.).

_____, *Triocha-Céad Chorca Dhuibhne .i. Tiomargadh ar a Log-Ainmneacha agus ar Sheanchas a Ghabhann leo san mar aon le Sloinnte agus Ainmneacha Daoine* (Baile Átha Cliath: Comhlucht Oideachais na hÉireann, Teor., do An Cumann le Béaloideas Éireann, 1939).

Ó Súildhubháin, Seumas, *Clann Lir de Thuatha Dé Danann* (Baile Átha Cliath: Comhlucht Oideachais na hÉireann, 1923).

Ó Súileabháin, Muiris, *Fiche Blian ag Fás* (Baile Átha Cliath: Clólucht an Talbóidigh, Tta., 1933).

Ó Súilleabháin, Diarmuid, *Cliamhain Isteach: Dráma Trí Mír* (Baile Átha Cliath: Oifig Díolta Foillseacháin Rialtais, 1933).

Ó Súilleabháin, Domhnall, *Beatha Dhomhnaill Uí Chonaill* (Baile Átha Cliath: Oifig Díolta Foillseacháin Rialtais, 1936).

Ó Súilleabháin, Proinnseas, ed., *Láimh-Leabhar Drámaidheachta* (Baile Átha Cliath: Brún agus Ó Nualláin, Teor., n. d.).

_____, *Scéilíní i gCóir na bPáistí* (Baile Átha Cliath: M. H. Mac an Ghoill agus a Mhac, Teo., n. d.).

_____, *Sgéal na h-Éireann i gCóir Páistí Scoile* (Baile Átha Cliath: Comhlucht Oideachais na hÉireann, Teoranta, [1922]).

_____, *Sidhe-Scéalta na mBráthar Grimm, Cuid a h-Aon* (Baile Átha Cliath: Alec Thom agus a Chuid, Teoranta, n. d.).

_____, *Stair na h-Éireann ó Aimsir Naoimh Pádraig go dtí an Lá Indiu* (Baile Átha Cliath: Brún agus Ó Nualláin, [1938]).

Ó Súilleabháin, Seán, ed. *Diarmuid na Bolgaighe agus a Chomhursain* (Baile Átha Cliath: Oifig Díolta Foillseacháin Rialtais, 1937).

_____, *Láimh-Leabhar Béaloideasa* (Baile Átha Cliath: An Cumann le Béaloideas Éireann, 1937).

Ó Torna, Seosamh ('Seán Sabháiste'), *Cois Life: Cheithre Scéalta* (Baile Átha Cliath: Oifig Díolta Foillseacháin Rialtais, 1936).

Ó Tuathail, Éamonn, ed., *Sgéalta Mhuintir Luinigh: Munterloney Folk-Tales* (Dublin: Irish Folklore Institute, 1933).

'Panini, Dr.', *Irish Up-to-Date / Eeris (Eire + is)* (Dublin: C. J. Fallon, n. d.).

Piatt, Donn, *Stair na Gaedhilge* (Áth Cliath: Cló na Saoirse, [1933]).

Ronan, Rev. Myles, ed., *Cuimhneachán Céad Bliadhan de Shaoirse Creidimh in Éirinn / Catholic Emancipation Centenary Record* (Dublin: The Literary Committee, 1929).

Ros Comáin (Stair na gConndae I) (Baile Átha Cliath: Oifig an tSoláthair, 1938).

Ryan, John, *Stair na hÉireann*, 3 vols, trans. Micheál Breathnach (Baile Átha Cliath: Connradh na Gaedhilge, n. d.).

Saidléar, Annraí, *Ceithre Drámaí* (Baile Átha Cliath: Oifig Díolta Foillseacháin Rialtais, 1934).

_____, *Misneach: Dráma Dhá Mhír* (Baile Átha Cliath: Muinntir C. S. Ó Fallamhain, Teo., i gcomhar le hOifig an tSoláthair, 1929).

_____, *Oidhche sa Tábhairne: Dráma Aon-Mhíre* (Baile Átha Cliath: Oifig an tSoláthair, 1945).

Saorstát Éireann / Irish Free State: Official Handbook, ed. Bulmer Hobson (Dublin: Talbot Press, 1932).

Sayers, Peig, *Machtnamh Seanmhná*, ed. Máire Ní Chinnéide, new edn by Pádraig Ua Maoileoin (Baile Átha Cliath: Oifig an tSoláthair, 1980 [1939]).

_____, *Peig .i. A Scéal Féin*, ed. Máire Ní Chinnéide (Baile Átha Cliath: Clólucht an Talbóidigh, 1936).

_____, *Scéalta ón mBlascaod*, collected and edited by Kenneth Jackson (Baile Átha Cliath: An Cumann le Béaloideas Éireann, 1968 [1938]).

Scéim agus Ceistiúchán le h-Aghaidh Stair Paráiste (Béal Átha na Sluagh: Coláiste Sheosaimh Naomhtha, Páirc Ghearrbhaile, 1929).

Sceulta Mhícil Uí Mhuirgheasa ó'n Rinn, ed. Séumas Ó h-Eochadha (Baile Átha Cliath: Comhlucht Oideachais na hÉireann, 1923).

Seáinín Tom Sheáin, *Oidhche Sheanchais: Sean Sgéal* (Baile Átha Cliath: Roinn an Oideachais, [1934]).

Seoighe, Brian, trans., *Leabhar Beag ar an bhFaoisdin le h-Aghaidh Páistí, Máthair Loyola do Scríobh* (Baile Átha Cliath: Cló-Lucht an Talbóidigh, Teor., n. d.).

Seoighe, Tadhg S., *Scéalta Chois Teallaigh* (Baile Átha Cliath: Comhlucht Oideachais na hÉireann, Teor., n. d.).

Souvenir Program for the Aeridheacht / Easter Week Anniversary 1916–1922 Commemoration at the Hermitage (St Enda's)

Sullivan, A. M., *Eachtra na hÉireann*, trans. Tomás de Bhial (Baile Átha Cliath: Oifig an tSoláthair, 1939).

Swift, Jonathan, *Eachtraí an Ghiolla Mhóir*, trans. Donnchadh Ó Laoghaire (Baile Átha Cliath: Oifig Díolta Foillseacháin Rialtais, 1936).

Tailteann Games June 29–July 10, 1932 / Daily Programme / Tuesday, July 5th

Téarmaí Eoluidheachta (Baile Átha Cliath: Oifig an tSoláthair, n. d.).

Téarmaí Staire (Baile Átha Cliath: Oifig an tSoláthair, 1934).

Thomson, George (Mac Tomáis, Seoirse), *Breith Báis ar Eagnuidhe: Trí Comhráidhte d'ár Cheap Platon (Apologia, Criton, Phaedon)* (Baile Átha Cliath: Muinntir Ch. S. Ó Fallamhain, Teo. i gcomhar le Oifig an tSoláthair, 1929).

_____, 'Fógra', in *Alcestis le h-Euripides*, ed. Mac Tomáis (Baile Átha Cliath: Oifig Díolta Foillseacháin Rialtais, 1932).

_____, 'Fuíoll Léinn Sheoirse Mhic Thomáis, I, II', ed. Pádraig Ó Fiannachta, *Léachtaí Cholm Cille* XVIII (1988), 162–82.

_____, 'Fuíoll Léinn Sheoirse Mhic Thomáis, III', ed. Pádraig Ó Fiannachta, *Léachtaí Cholm Cille* XIX (1989), 157–89; *Irisleabhar Mhá Nuad* (1989), 76–102.

_____, *Gach Orlach de Mo Chroí: Dréachta*, ed. Seán Ó Lúing (Baile Átha Cliath: Coiscéim, 1988).

_____, *Tosnú na Feallsúnachta* (Baile Átha Cliath: Oifig Díolta Foillseacháin Rialtais, 1935).

Titles (in Irish and English) of Civil Service Posts / Teidil (i nGaedhilg agus i mBéarla) Phostanna san Stát-Sheirbhís (n. p.: n. p, 1938).

Tóibín, Nioclás, *Ár gCúrsaí Féin* (Baile Átha Cliath: Brún agus Ó Nualláin, Teor., [1937]).

_____, trans., *An Dubh 'na Gheal: Dráma Trí n-Amharc* (Ceatharlach: Muintir an 'Nationalist agus Leinster Times', n. d.).

_____, *Oidhche ar Bharr Tuinne agus Scéalta Eile* (Baile Átha Cliath: Cualacht Oideachais na h-Éireann, n. d.).

_____, *An Rábaire Bán* (Baile Átha Cliath: C. S. Ó Fallamhain Teo., i gcomhar le hOifig an tSoláthair, 1928).

_____, *Róisín Bán an tSléibhe: Scéal Nua-Cheaptha* (Baile Átha Cliath: Cualacht Oideachais na h-Éireann, 1923).

_____, *Teóiní agus Tighthe Lóistín agus Dhá Scéal Eile* (Baile Átha Cliath: Comhlucht Oideachais na hÉireann, Teor., 1923).

Tone, Theobald Wolfe, *Beatha Theobald Wolfe Tone mar do frith 'na scríbhinní féin agus i scríbhinní a mhic*, trans. Pádraig Ó Siochfhradha (Baile Átha Cliath: Oifig Díolta Foillseacháin Rialtais, 1932).

Ua Ceallaigh, Seán, *Rudhraigheacht* (Baile Átha Cliath: M. H. Macanghoill agus a Mhac, Teor., 1935).

_____, *Taistealuidheacht no Cúrsa na Cruinne* (Baile Atha Cliath: M. H. Macanghoill is a Mhac, Teor., 1931).

_____, *Trí Truagha na Scéaluidheachta* (Baile Átha Cliath: M. H. Mac Ghuill agus a Mhac, Teor., 1932).

Ua Concheanainn, Tomás, agus a Chéile, *Eamhain Macha / Cú Chulainn agus Ridirí na Craoibhe Ruaidhe* (Baile Átha Cliath: Brún agus Ó Nóláin, Teor., n. d.).

_____, *Fianna Éireann* (Baile Átha Cliath: Brún agus Ó Nóláin, Teor., n. d.).

_____, *Inis Fáil / Sgéalta faoi Ard-Ríghthe na h-Éireann* (Baile Átha Cliath: Brún agus Ó Nóláin, Teor., n. d.).

_____, *Laochra Gaedheal* (Baile Atha Cliath: Oifig Díolta Foillseacháin Rialtais, 1922).

_____, *Seoda na Sean*, 1–4 (Baile Átha Cliath: Brún agus Ó Nóláin, Teor., n d.).

Ua Laoghaire, Diarmuid, *An Bhruinneall Bhán* (Baile Átha Cliath: Oifig Díolta Foillseacháin Rialtais, 1934).

_____, *Saothar Bliana: Aisde ar Chuireadóireacht agus ar Ghnóthaibh Feirmeach* (Baile Átha Cliath: Oifig Díolta Foillseacháin Rialtais, 1935).

Ua Laoghaire, Peadar, *Críost Mac Dé*, 1–2 (Baile Átha Cliath: Brún agus Ó Nóláin, Teor., [1923] and [1925]).

_____, *Sgéalaidheachta as an mBíobla Naomhtha*, 1–7 (Baile Átha Cliath: Brún agus Ó Nóláin, 1922–5).

_____, *Sgéalaidheacht na Macabeach*, 1–2 (Baile Átha Cliath: Brún agus Ó Nóláin, Teor., [1926]).

Ua Murchadha, Domhnall, *Rann-Scéalta, Scéalta Gearra, agus Paidreacha* (n. p.: n. p., n. d.).

_____, *Sean-Aimsireacht* (Baile Átha Cliath: Oifig an tSoláthair, 1939).

Ua Muireadhaigh, Lorcán (Father Lawrence Murray), ed., *Pota Cnuasaigh (An Chéad Chuid)* (Dún Dealgan: Oifig Sheagháin Uí Mhaitiú, 1923).

Ua Séaghdha, Séamus, tr., *Sgríbhiní Naoimh Phádraig* (Dublin: Association for Promotion of Christian Knowledge, 1932).

Ua Súilleabháin, S. Labhrás, trans., *An Brón-Chluiche Macbeit* (Shakespeare) (Dublin: Cahill, [1925]).

Uí Dhíosca, Úna Bean, *Cailín na Gruaige Duinne* (Baile Átha Cliath: Oifig Díolta Foillseacháin Rialtais, 1932).

_____, *An Seod Do-Fhaghála* (Baile Átha Cliath: Oifig Díolta Foillseacháin Rialtais, 1936).

University College Dublin, *Calendar for the Session 1933-34* (Dublin: Brown & Nolan, 1933).

_____, *Calendar for the Session 1934-35* (Dublin: Browne & Nolan, 1934).

Yeats, W. B., *The Senate Speeches of W. B. Yeats*, ed. Donald R. Pearce (London: Faber & Faber, 1960).

II. SECONDARY SOURCES

Akenson, Donald Harman, *A Mirror to Kathleen's Face: Education in Independent Ireland 1922–1960* (Montreal: McGill–Queen's University Press, 1975).
Atkinson, Norman, *Irish Education: A History of Educational Institutions* (Dublin: Allen Figgis, 1969).
Augusteijn, Joost, ed. *Ireland in the 1930s: New Perspectives* (Dublin: Four Courts Press, 1999).
Bourke, Angela, *The Burning of Bridget Cleary: A True Story* (London: Pimlico, 1999).
_____, 'Na Mná trí Shúile Thomáis', *Tomás Ó Criomhthain 1855–1937* (Ceiliúradh an Bhlascaoid), ed. Máire Ní Chéileachair (An Daingean: An Sagart, 1998), 101–22.
_____, 'Reading a Woman's Death: Colonial Text and Oral Tradition in Nineteenth-Century Ireland', *Feminist Studies* 21, 3 (Fall, 1995), 553–86.
Breathnach, Diarmuid, and Máire Ní Mhurchú, *1882–1982: Beathaisnéis* 1–5 (Baile Átha Cliath: An Clóchomhar, 1986–97).
_____, '"Who Were Those Guys?": Pearsana Chonradh na Gaeilge', in *Conradh na Gaeilge: Céad Bliain ag Obair* (Comhdháil an Chraoibhín 1993: Conference Proceedings) (Boyle: Comhairle Chontae Roscomáin, 1994), 46–78.
Breathnach, Pádraic, 'An Dá Phádraic (Ó Conaire)', *Feasta* June–July, 1972, pp. 3–7; and *Feasta*, Aug. 1972, pp. 3–6.
Calder-Marshall, Arthur, *The Innocent Eye: The Life of Robert J. Flaherty* (Baltimore: Penguin, 1970).
Céitinn, Séamas, *Craobh den Chonradh: Scéal Chraobh Dhún Dealgan de Chonradh na Gaeilge, 1899–1976* (Dún Dealgan: Coiste Mhuirtheimhne, 1980).
Céitinn, Seosamh, *Tomás Oileánach* (Baile Átha Cliath: An Clóchomhar, 1992).
Coogan, Tim Pat, *Eamon De Valera: The Man Who Was Ireland* (New York: HarperCollins, 1995).
Costigan, An tSr. Bosco, and Seán Ó Curraoin, *De Ghlaschloich an Oileáin: Beatha agus Saothar Mháirtín Uí Chadhain* (Béal an Daingin: Cló Iar-Chonnachta, 1987).
Cronin, Michael, *Translating Ireland: Translation, Languages, Cultures* (Cork: Cork University Press, 1996).
Daltún, Séamas, 'Scéal Rannóg an Aistriúcháin', *Teangeolas* 17 (Winter, 1983), 12–26.
Daniels, William, 'Introduction to the Present State of Criticism of Liam O'Flaherty's Collection of Short Stories: *Dúil*', *Éire-Ireland* 23, 2 (Summer, 1988), 122–34.
Deane, Seamus, '*Mo Bhealach Féin*', in *The Pleasures of Gaelic Literature*, ed. John Jordan (Dublin: Mercier Press, 1977), pp. 52–61.
de Búrca, Marcus, *The GAA: A History of the Gaelic Athletic Association* (Dublin: Cumann Lúthchleas Gael, 1980).
de Hae, Risteárd, and Bríghid Ní Dhonnchadha, eds, *Clár Litridheacht na Nua-Ghaedhilge, 1850–1936: I. Na Leabhra* (Baile Átha Cliath: Oifig Díolta Foillseacháin Rialtais, 1938).
_____, *Clár Litridheacht na Nua-Ghaeilge, 1850–1936:* III. *Prós i dTréimhseacháin* (Baile Átha Cliath: Oifig Díolta Foillseacháin Rialtais, 1940).
Delap, Breandán, *Úrscéalta Stairiúla na Gaeilge* (Baile Átha Cliath: An Clóchomhar, 1993).
de Mórdha, Mícheál, ed., *Bláithín: Flower* (An Daingean: An Sagart, 1998).
Denvir, Gearóid, *Cadhan Aonair: Saothar Liteartha Mháirtín Uí Chadhain* (Baile Átha Cliath: An Clóchomhar, 1987).
_____, *An Dúil is Dual* (Indreabhán: Cló Iar-Chonnachta, 1991).
_____, *Litriocht agus Pobal: Cnuasach Aistí* (Indreabhán: Cló Iar-Chonnachta, 1997).
_____, 'Peacaí an Fhiréin: Smaointeachas Mháirtín Uí Chadhain', in *Criostalú: Aistí ar Shaothar Mháirtín Uí Chadhain*, ed. Cathal Ó hAinle (Baile Átha Cliath: Coiscéim, 1998), 53–86.
_____, '*An Phléasc*: Nóta Mínithe', in *Macalla 1983*, ed. Gearóid Denvir, Máiréad Ní Dhúill, and

Éibhlín Ní Scanláin (Gaillimh: An Cumann Éigse agus Staire, Coláiste na hOllscoile, 1983), pp. 20–1.

de Val, Séamas S., *Donnchadh Ó Laoghaire Dhoire An Chuilinn: A Shaol agus a Shaothar* (An Daingean: An Sagart, 1997).

Fallon, Brian, *An Age of Innocence: Irish Culture 1930–1960* (Dublin: Gill & Macmillan, 1998).

Farren, Seán, *The Politics of Irish Education, 1920–1965* (Belfast: The Queen's University of Belfast, Institute of Irish Studies, 1995).

Garvin, Tom, *1922: The Birth of Irish Democracy* (Dublin: Gill & Macmillan, 1996).

Giltrap, Risteárd, *An Ghaeilge in Eaglais na hÉireann* (Baile Átha Cliath: Cumann Gaelach na hEaglaise, 1990).

Goldring, Maurice, *Pleasant Is the Scholar's Life: Irish Intellectuals and the Construction of the Nation State* (London: Serif, 1993).

Harmon, Maurice, *Sean O'Faolain* (London: Constable, 1994).

_____, *Sean O'Faolain: A Critical Introduction* (Notre Dame: University of Notre Dame Press, 1966).

Kearney, Colbert, 'Dónall Ó Corcora agus an Litríocht Angla-Éireannach', *Scríobh* 4 (1979), 138–51.

Kelly, Adrian, *Compulsory Irish: Language and Education in Ireland 1870s–1970s* (Dublin: Irish Academic Press, 2002).

Kiberd, Declan, 'Dónall Ó Corcora agus Litríocht Bhéarla na hÉireann', *Scríobh* 4 (1979), 84–93.

_____, '*Mo Bhealach Féin*: Idir Dhá Thraidisiún', *Scríobh* 5 (1981), 224–39.

Kreilkamp, Vera, *The Anglo-Irish Novel and the Big House* (Syracuse: Syracuse University Press, 1998).

Lee, J. J., *Ireland, 1912–1985: Politics and Society* (Cambridge: Cambridge University Press, 1989).

Mac an Bheatha, Proinsias, *An Earnáil agus an Ghaeilge* (Baile Átha Cliath: Foilseacháin Náisiúnta Teo., 1985).

_____, 'Seosamh Mac Grianna', in *Seosamh Mac Grianna agus Cúrsaí Eile* (Baile Átha Cliath: Foilseacháin Náisiúnta Teo., 1970), pp. 1–83.

_____, 'Seosamh Mac Grianna, Scéalaí (Cuid a Dó)', *An t-Ultach*, Jan. 1967, pp. 6 and 11.

Mac Aonghusa, Criostóir, 'Cathair na Gaillimhe sna Tríochaidí: Sliocht as Beathaisnéis', *Scríobh* 5 (1981), 211–23.

Mac Aonghusa, Proinsias, *Ar Son na Gaeilge: Conradh na Gaeilge 1893–1993: Stair Sheanchais* (Baile Átha Cliath: Conradh na Gaeilge, 1993).

_____, 'Máirtín Ó Cadhain: Fear Cúise ar Bhealaí Conspóideacha', *Scríobh* 3 (1978), 87–107.

_____, ed., *Oireachtas na Gaeilge 1897–1997* (Baile Átha Cliath: Conradh na Gaeilge, 1997).

Mac Cana, Proinsias, 'Strac-Fhéachaint ar Nua-Litríocht Ghaeilge Uladh', in *Fearsaid: Iris Iubhaile an Chumainn Ghaelaigh, 1905–1956* (Béal Feirste: Cumann Gaelach na hIolscoile, 1956), pp. 47–53.

Mac Congáil, Nollaig, ed., *Jonneen Khordaroy Answers Critics: Léachtaí Cuimhneacháin ar Shéamas Ó Grianna 'Máire' (1889–1969)* (Baile Átha Cliath: Coiscéim, 1992).

_____, 'Máire agus a Chuid Iriseoireachta', *Irisleabhar Mhá Nuad* (1988), 67–80.

_____, *Máire – Clár Saothair* (Baile Átha Cliath: Coiscéim, 1990).

_____, 'Nua-Litríocht na Gaeilge i bhFoirm Aistriúcháin', *Irisleabhar Mhá Nuad* (1992), 123–33.

_____, 'Ó Cadhain agus an Gearrscéal', *Scríobh* 5 (1981), 106–13.

_____, ed., *Rí-Éigeas na nGael: Léachtaí Cuimhneacháin ar Sheosamh Mac Grianna* (Baile Átha Cliath: Coiscéim, 1994).

_____, ed., *Scríbhneoireacht na gConallach* (Baile Átha Cliath: Coiscéim, 1990).

_____, *Seosamh Mac Grianna / Iolann Fionn: Clár Saothair* (Baile Átha Cliath: Coiscéim, 1990).

Mac Conghail, Muiris, 'Brian Ó Ceallaigh (1889–1936), Páirtí Thomáis Uí Chriomthain: Obair idir Lámhaibh', *Irisleabhar Mhá Nuad* (1989), 189–98.

Mac Craith, Máiréad, *An tOileánach Léannta* (Baile Átha Cliath: An Clóchomhar, 1988).

Mac Giolla Chomhaill, Anraí, *Lorcán Ó Muireadhaigh: Sagart agus Scoláire* (Baile Átha Cliath: An Clóchomhar do Éigse Oirialla, 1983).

Mac Murchaidh, Ciarán, 'Cóta Ioldathach an Irisleabhair', *Léachtaí Cholm Cille* XXIII (1993), 200–18.

Mac Niocláis, Máirtín, *Seán Ó Ruadháin: Saol agus Saothar* (Baile Átha Cliath: An Clóchomhar, 1991).

Mac Tomáis, Seoirse, *An Blascaod mar a Bhí* (Má Nuad: An Sagart, 1977).

Mag Shamhráin, Antain, 'Portráid den Stoirm: Úrscéal Deireannach Sheosaimh Mhic Grianna', *Oghma* 2 (1990), 41–6.

Manning, Maurice, *The Blueshirts* (Toronto: University of Toronto Press, 1971).

Matthews, James, *Voices: A Life of Frank O'Connor* (New York: Atheneum, 1983).

Maume, Patrick, *'Life that is Exile': Daniel Corkery and the Search for Irish Ireland* (Belfast: The Queen's University of Belfast, Institute of Irish Studies, 1993).

Mhac an tSaoi, Máire (as Máire Cruise O'Brien), *'An tOileánach'*, in *The Pleasures of Gaelic Literature*, ed. John Jordan (Dublin: Mercier Press, 1977), 25–38.

_____, 'Pádraig de Brún agus an Ghaeilge: Saol agus Saothar in Aisce?' *Léachtaí Cholm Cille* XXIII (1993), 140–60.

Murray, Patrick, *Oracles of God: The Roman Catholic Church and Irish Politics, 1922–1937* (Dublin: University College Dublin Press, 2000).

Ngúgí wa Thiong'o, *Decolonising the Mind: The Politics of Language in African Literature* (London: James Currey, 1986).

Ní Aimhirgín, Nuala, *Muiris Ó Súileabháin: Saol agus Saothar* (Má Nuad: An Sagart, 1983).

Ní Bhrádaigh, Siobhán, *Máiréad Ní Ghrádha: Ceannródaí Drámaíochta* (Indreabhán: Cló Iar-Chonnachta, 1996).

Nic Eoin, Máirín, 'Éirí Amach 1916 agus Litríocht na Gaeilge', *Irisleabhar Mhá Nuad* (1985), 38–61.

_____, *An Litríocht Réigiúnach* (Baile Átha Cliath: An Clóchomhar, 1982).

Ní Chéilleachair, Máire, ed., *Peig Sayers Scéalaí, 1873–1958* (Ceiliúradh an Bhlascaoid 3) (Baile Átha Cliath: Coiscéim, 1999).

_____, ed., *Tomás Ó Criomhthain, 1855–1937* (Ceiliúradh an Bhlascaoid 2) (An Daingean: An Sagart, 1998).

Ní Chinnéide, Máiréad, 'Na Mná i gConradh na Gaeilge', in *Conradh na Gaeilge: Céad Bliain ag Obair*, ed. Breandán Ó Conaire, (Comhdháil an Chraoibhín: Conference Proceedings, 1993) (Boyle: Comhairle Chontae Roscomáin, 1994), pp. 30–44.

Ní Chinnéide, Tríona, *Comhlucht Gaedheal na Gaillimhe, 1938–1988* (Gaillimh: Comhlucht Gaedheal na Gaillimhe, 1989).

Ní Chionnaith, An tSiúr Éibhlín, *Pádraic Ó Conaire: Scéal a Bheatha* (Indreabhán: Cló Iar-Chonnachta, 1995).

Ní Chnáimhin, Áine, *Pádraic Ó Conaire* (Baile Átha Cliath: Oifig an tSoláthair, 1947).

Ní Choncheanainn, An tSr. Finnín, and Ciarán Ó Coigligh, *Tomás Bán* (Baile Átha Cliath: Conradh na Gaeilge, 1996).

Ní Dhonnchadha, Aisling, *An Gearrscéal sa Ghaeilge, 1898–1940* (Baile Átha Cliath: An Clóchomhar, 1981).

Ní Ghráinne, Éilín, 'Dírbheathaisnéisí an Bhlascaoid mar Fhoinse don Stair Shóisialta', *Irisleabhar Mhá Nuad* (1983), 33–60.
Ní Mhuiríosa, Máirín, 'Cumann na Scríbhneoirí: Memoir', *Scríobh* 5 (1981), 168–81.
Ní Shé, Máiréad, 'Séamus Ó Néill: Saol agus Saothar', *Irisleabhar Mhá Nuad* (1987), 62–101.
Ó Bléine, Ruairí, 'Séamus Mac Conmara, Dochtúir agus Scríbhneoir', *An tUltach*, Oct. 1985, pp. 3–6.
Ó Buachalla, Breandán, '"Duileasc a Cuantaibh Cléire"', *Léachtaí Cholm Cille* XXII (1992), 8–25.
_____, 'Ó Corcora agus an Hidden Ireland', *Scríobh* 4 (1979), 109–37.
Ó Buachalla, Séamas, *Education Policy in Twentieth Century Ireland* (Dublin: Wolfhound, 1988).
Ó Cadhain, Máirtín, 'An Gearrscéal sa Ghaeilge', *Scríobh* 5 (1981), 100–5.
Ó Cearra, Aodh agus Séamas Céitinn, *Peadar Ó Dubhda: A Shaol agus a Shaothar* (Baile Átha Cliath: An Clóchomhar a d'fhoilsigh do Éigse Oirialla, 1981).
Ó Ciosáin, Éamon, *An t-Éireannach, 1934–1937: Páipéar Sóisialach Gaeltachta* (Baile Átha Cliath: An Clóchomhar, 1993).
_____, 'Máiréad Ní Ghráda agus a Saothar Liteartha', in Máiréad Ní Ghráda, *An Triail / Breithiúnas: Dhá Dhráma* (Baile Átha Cliath: Oifig an tSoláthair, 1978), 171–96.
Ó Ciardha, Pádhraic P., 'Ainmhí agus Duine: Léamh ar Ghearrscéalta Thomáis Bairéad', *Irisleabhar Mhá Nuad* (1976), pp. 39–46.
Ó Cnáimhsí, Séamus, ed., *Éigse 1988: Seán Bán Mac Meanman* (Baile Átha Cliath: Coiscéim, 1988).
Ó Coileáin, Diarmaid, 'An tÚrscéal sa Ghaeilge', *An t-Ultach*, June 1980, p. 23.
Ó Conaire, Breandán, 'Blas na hAoise', review of *Éan Cuideáin* by Pádhraic Óg Ó Conaire, *Comhar*, Jan. 1971, 19–20.
_____, *Myles na Gaeilge: Lámhleabhar ar Shaothar Gaeilge Bhrian Ó Nualláin* (Baile Átha Cliath: An Clóchomhar, 1986).
_____, ed., *Tomás an Bhlascaoid* (Indreabhán: Cló Iar-Chonnachta, 1992).
Ó Conaire, Peadar, 'Pádraig Óg Ó Conaire: A Shaol is a Shaothar Litríochta', unpublished MA thesis, UCG, 1988.
Ó Conchubhair, Brian, 'Meath na hEorpa: An Athbheochan mar Aisfhreagra na hÉireann', unpublished PhD thesis, NUIG, 2002.
Ó Conghaile, Micheál, *Conamara agus Árainn, 1880-1980: Gnéithe den Stair Shóisialta (Staidéar ar nualitríocht chruithaitheach Ghaeltacht na Gaillimhe agus Oileáin Árann, féachaint cén léiriú atá inti ar ghnéithe den stair shóisialta c 1880-1980 – mar aon lena tábhacht mar fhoinse chun stair shóisialta a mheas* (Béal an Daingin: Cló Iar-Chonnachta, 1988).
_____, ed., *Gaeltacht Ráth Cairn: Léachtaí Comórtha* (Béal an Daingin: Cló Iar-Chonnachta i gcomhar le Raidió na Gaeltachta, 1986).
Ó Conluain, Proinsias, *Scéal na Scannán* (Baile Átha Cliath: Oifig an tSoláthair, 1953).
_____, and Donncha Ó Céileachair, *An Duinníneach: An tAthair Pádraig Ó Duinnín: A Shaol, a Shaothar agus an Ré inar Mhair Sé* (Baile Átha Cliath: Sáirséal agus Dill, 1958).
Ó Corráin, Ailbhe, 'An tSamhlaíocht v. an Réaltaíocht i gCuid Scríobhnóireachta Shéamuis agus Sheosaimh Mhic Grianna', *An tUltach*, June 1982, pp. 36–40.
Ó Croiligh, Oilibhéar, *Bealach Mhic Ghrianna: Treoir don Leabhar 'Mo Bhealach Féin' le Seosamh Mac Grianna* (Corcaigh: Cló Mercier, 1972).
_____, 'Éifeacht an Ghnímh – Staidéar Éadomhain ar an Scéal "Dhá Chroí Cloiche" le Seosamh Mac Grianna, i gCló ar *Humanitas*, Meitheamh, 1930', *Irisleabhar Mhá Nuad* (1970), 7–12.
_____, 'Idir Dhá Cheann na hImní – Bealach Mhic Grianna', *Irisleabhar Mhá Nuad* (1967), 12–25.

Ó Croiligh, Pádraig, 'Scáil Úirscéil: Sracfhéachaint ar "Cúrsaí Thomáis" le Éamonn Mac Giolla Iasachta', *Irisleabhar Mhá Nuad* (1969), 77–89.

Ó Crualaoich, Diarmaid, 'Conallaigh ag Scríobh faoi Thír Chonaill', *Irisleabhar Mhá Nuad* (1990), 31–50.

Ó Crualaoich, Gearóid, 'Litríocht na Gaeltachta: Seoladh Isteach ar Pheirspictíocht ó Thaobh na Litríochta Béil', *Léachtaí Colm Cille* XIX (1989), 8–25.

Ó Dochartaigh, Liam, 'Fear Eile ón Pholainn', *Irisleabhar Mhá Nuad* (1980), 9–24.

_____, '*Mo Bhealach Féin*: Saothar Nualitríochta', *Scríobh* 5 (1981), 240–7.

_____, 'Seanphiseoga agus Nualitríocht: Sracfhéachaint ar Ghné Amháin den Aigneolaíocht i Nualitríocht na Gaeilge', *Irisleabhar Mhá Nuad* (1976), 59–70.

Ó Doibhlin, Breandán, 'An Dúchas: Téama na Dúchais i Litríocht na Gaeilge', *Irisleabhar Mhá Nuad* (1972), 9–35.

_____, 'Fear agus Finnscéal: Dála *An Druma Mór* le Seosamh Mac Grianna', *Irisleabhar Mhá Nuad* (1969), 7–20.

_____, 'An Grá sa Nuaphrós', *Léachtaí Cholm Cille* VI (1975), 117–25.

_____, 'Irish Literature in the Contemporary Situation', *Léachtaí Cholm Cille* I (1970), 5–11.

Ó Doibhlin, Diarmaid, 'Druma Mór an Imreasáin', *An tUltach*, Mar. 1971, pp. 14–16.

Ó Doibhlin, An tAthair Éamonn, 'Seán Mac Meanman: Scríbhneoir agus Scéalaí', *An t-Ultach*, Nov. 1963, p. 5.

Ó Domhnaill, Micheál, *Iolscoil na Mumhan ris a Ráidhtear an Tan Seo Coláiste na Rinne* (n. p.: n.p., n. d.).

Ó Donnchadha, Diarmuid, *Castar an Taoide* (Baile Átha Cliath: Coiscéim, 1995).

Ó Droighneáin, Muiris, 'Uch-Uch! . . . Amen – A Rí na bhFeart!' *An t-Ultach*, July 1971, pp. 7, 11.

Ó Dubhshláine, Tadhg, 'Ceapadóireacht an Chriomhthanaigh', *Léachtaí Cholm Cille* XXII (1992), 26–54.

_____, 'Scéal Úrscéil: *Fánaí*, Seán Óg Ó Caomhánaigh, 1927', *Léachtaí Cholm Cille* XIX (1989), 93–128.

_____, 'Tríocha Bliain ag Fás', *Léachtaí Cholm Cille* XXI (1991), 105–38.

Ó Duibhir, Micheál, 'Éagosc an tSagairt', *Irisleabhar Mhá Nuad* (1969), 53–61.

Ó Fiaich, Tomás, 'Saothar Mháire mar Fhoinse don Stair Shóisialta', *Leachtaí Cholm Cille* V (1974), 5–30.

_____, 'Stair Chumann na Sagart', *Irisleabhar Mhá Nuad* (1988), 108–24.

Ó Fiannachta, Pádraig, 'Creideamh an Bhlascaoid', *Léachtaí Cholm Cille* XXII (1992), 55–80.

_____, 'Mescéal Gaeltachta', *Léachtaí Cholm Cille* XXI (1991), 175–83.

Ó Flaithimhín, S. N., 'Monsignor Pádraig de Brún (1889–1960), Cathaoirleach Chomhairle na hInstitiúide (1940–1960)', *Irisleabhar Mhá Nuad* (1994), 10–32.

Ó Gaora, Piaras, 'Pádraig Óg Ó Conaire', *Comhar*, Sept. 1971, p. 15.

Ó Giolláin, Diarmuid, 'An Cultúr Coiteann agus Léann an Bhéaloideas', *Léachtaí Cholm Cille* XXIII (1992), 137–58.

_____, *Locating Irish Folklore: Tradition, Modernity, Identity* (Cork: Cork University Press, 2000).

Ó Glaisne, Risteárd, 'Iolann Fionn (Cuid a Dó)', *An t-Ultach*, Feb. 1971, pp. 5–6.

_____, 'Iolann Fionn (Cuid a Trí)', *An t-Ultach*, Mar. 1971, pp. 11–13.

_____, 'Micheál Mac Liammóir', *An tUltach*, July 1970, pp. 6–8.

_____, 'An Moinsineoir Pádraig Eric Mac Fhinn', *Irisleabhar Mhá Nuad* (1988), 125–43.

_____, 'Niall Ó Domhnaill (Cuid a Dó)', *An t-Ultach*, Jan. 1972, pp. 3–5.

Ó Gráinne, Diarmaid, 'Léirmheas Dhiarmada Uí Ghráinne ar *Cheol na nGiolcach*', *Feasta*, Mar. 1976, pp. 20–2.

Ó Háinle, Cathal, 'An Druma Mór: Athléamh', *Léachtaí Cholm Cille* (1989), 129–67.

_____, 'Ó Chaint na nDaoine go dtí an Caighdeán Oifigiúil', in *Stair na Gaeilge in Ómós do Pádraig Ó Fiannachta*, ed. Kim McCone, Damien McManus, Cathal Ó Háinle, Nicholas Williams, Liam Breatnach (Máigh Nuad: Roinn na Sean-Ghaeilge, Coláiste Phádraig, 1994), pp. 745–93.

_____, 'Seanchas Mháire', *Scríobh* 5 (1981), 248–57.

Ó Héalaí, Pádraig, 'An Bheathaisnéis mar Litríocht', *Léachtaí Cholm Cille* I (1970), 34–40.

Ó hAnnracháin, Stiofán, ed., *An Comhchaidreamh: Crann a Chraobhaigh: Cnuasach Aistí* (Baile Átha Cliath: An Clóchomhar, 1985).

Ó hAodha, Micheál, 'An tIasc Órga (Aiste Chuimhneacháin ar Mhicheál Mac Liammóir)', *Scríobh* 4 (1979), 188-96.

Ó hÓgain, Éamonn, 'Téarmaí Teicniúla sa Ghaeilge: Caighdeánú agus Ceapadh le Céad Bliain Anuas', *Teangeolas* 17 (Winter, 1983), 33.

Ó hUiginn, Ruairí, 'Tomás Ó Máille', *Léachtaí Cholm Cille* XXVII (1997), 83–122.

Ó Laoghaire, Diarmuid, 'An tAthair Donnchadh Ó Floinn – An Síoladóir', *Léachtaí Cholm Cille* XXIII (1993), 161–76.

Ó Laoire, Muiris, *Athbheochan na hEabhraise: Ceacht don Ghaeilge?* (Baile Átha Cliath: An Clóchomhar, 1999).

O'Leary, Philip, 'Castles of Gold: America and Americans in the Fiction of Séamus Ó Grianna', *Éire-Ireland* 21, 2 (Summer, 1986), 70-84.

——, *Déirc an Dóchais: Léamh ar Shaothar Phádhraic Óig Uí Chonaire* (Indreabhán: Cló Iar-Chonnachta, 1995).

_____, 'The Donegal of Séamus Ó Grianna and Peadar O'Donnell', *Éire-Ireland* 23, 2 (Summer, 1988), 135–49.

_____, ed. *Éire-Ireland: Special Issue: Translation*, Spring–Summer, 2000.

_____, *The Prose Literature of the Gaelic Revival, 1881–1921: Ideology and Innovation* (College Park: Pennsylvania State University Press, 1994).

Ó Muimhneacháin, Aindrias, *Dóchas agus Duainéis: Scéal Chonradh na Gaeilge 1922–1932* (Corcaigh, Cló Mercier, n. d.).

Ó Muircheartaigh, Aogán, ed., *Oidhreacht an Bhlascaoid* (Baile Átha Cliath: Coiscéim, 1989).

Ó Muirí, Damien, 'An tAthair Gearóid Ó Nualláin: Gramadóir Nua-Aoiseach', *Léachtaí Cholm Cille* XVI (1986), 200–29.

_____, 'Ó Gramhnaigh, Ó hIceadha, Ó Nualláin – Ollúna na hAthbheochana', *Léachtaí Cholm Cille* XXIII (1993), 44–88.

_____, 'Seosamh Mac Grianna agus *Wild Wales*', *Irisleabhar Mhá Nuad* (1976), 47–58.

Ó Muirí, Pól, *A Flight from Shadow: The Life and Work of Seosamh Mac Griana* (Belfast: Lagan Press, 1999).

Ó Muraile, Nollaig, 'Caithréim Eoghain Rua Uí Néill: *Eoghan Rua Ó Néill* le Seosamh Mac Grianna', *Irisleabhar Mhá Nuad* (1972), 81–97.

_____, 'Pól Breathnach (1885–1941), Sagart, Saoi is Seanchaí', *Léachtaí Cholm Cille* XXIII (1993), 89–120.

Ó Murchadha, Niall, 'Gearrscéalaíocht Thomáis Bairéad, 1893–1973', *Irisleabhar Mhá Nuad* (1991), 162–89.

Ó Murchú, Máirtín, *Cumann Buan-Choimeádta na Gaeilge: Tús an Athréimnithe* (Baile Átha Cliath: Cois Life, 2001).

Ó Riain, Seán, *Pleanáil Teanga in Éirinn 1919–1985* (Baile Átha Cliath: Carbad i gcomhar le Bord na Gaeilge, 1994).

Ó Ruairc, Maológ, 'An Aisling a Théann ar Strae: Nóta ar "Chaisleáin Óir"', *Irisleabhar Mhá Nuad* (1978), 92–100.

_____, *I dTreo Teanga Nua* (Baile Átha Cliath: Cois Life Teoranta, 1999).

Ó Sé, Diarmuid, 'Tomás Ó Rathile', *Léachtaí Cholm Cille* XXVII (1997), 177–210.

Ó Siadhail, Pádraig, *Stair Dhrámaíocht na Gaeilge 1900–1970* (Indreabhán: Cló Iar-Chonnachta, 1993).

Ó Siadhail, Seán, 'Caidé a d'Imigh ar Fhear na hAislinge?' *Irisleabhar Mhá Nuad* (1986), 134–52.

Ó Súilleabháin, Donncha, *An Cumann Scoildrámaíochta, 1934–1984* (Baile Átha Cliath: An Clóchomhar, 1986).

_____, *Scéal an Oireachtais, 1897–1924* (Baile Átha Cliath: An Clóchomhar, 1984).

Ó Torna, Caitríona, 'Cruthú Constráide agus an Turas Siar: An Ghaeltacht i dTús an Fichiú Aois', *Aimsir Óg* 2000, part 2, pp. 51–64.

Ó Tuama, Seán, 'Dónall Ó Corcora', *Scríobh* 4 (1979), 94–108.

_____, 'Úrscéalta agus Faisnéisí Beatha na Gaeilge: Na Buaicphointí', *Scríobh* 5 (1981), 148–60.

Ó Tuathaigh, Gearóid, '"Is do Chuala Croí Cine Soiléir"', *Scríobh* 4 (1979), 75–83.

'Peigí Rose', *Peigí ar 'Mháire'* (Baile Átha Cliath: Coiscéim, 1992).

Prút, Liam, 'Cúrsaí Aistriúcháin an Stáit', *Irisleabhar Mhá Nuad* (1996–7), 226–59.

Riggs, Pádraigín, 'Caint na nDaoine: An Chaint agus na Daoine, *Aimsir Óg* 2000, part 2, pp. 78–90.

_____, *Pádraic Ó Conaire, Deoraí* (Baile Átha Cliath: An Clóchomhar, 1994).

Rockett, Kevin, Luke Gibbons, and John Hill, *Cinema and Ireland* (Syracuse: Syracuse University Press, 1988).

Stewart, James, '*An tOileánach* – More or Less', *Zeitschrift für Celtische Philologie* 35 (1976), 232–63.

Thomas, Ned, *The Welsh Extremist: A Culture in Crisis* (London: Victor Gollancz, 1971).

Titley, Alan, 'An Náisiúntacht Ghaelach agus Náisiúnachas na hÉireann', *Aimsir Óg* 2000, part 2, pp. 34–49.

_____, 'An Scríbhneoir agus an Stát 1922–1982', *Scríobh* 6 (1984), 72–104.

_____, *An tÚrscéal Gaeilge* (Baile Átha Cliath: An Clóchomhar, 1991).

Tyers, Pádraig, ed., *Leoithne Aniar* (Baile an Fheirtéaraigh: Cló Dhuibhne, 1982).

Ua Maoileoin, Pádraig, 'An tAllagar', in *Iomairí Críche* (Baile Átha Cliath: Coiscéim, 1991), 105–23.

_____, 'An Criomhthanach', in *Ár Leithéidí Arís: Cnuasach de Shaothar Ilchineálach* (Baile Átha Cliath: Clódhanna Teoranta, 1978), pp. 61–70.

_____, 'An Criomhthanach agus a Shaothar', in *Iomairí Críche*, pp. 38–48.

_____, 'Peig Sayers', in *Iomairí Críche*, pp. 52–68.

_____, 'An Scríbhneoir agus an Béaloideas', in *Ár Leithéidí Arís*, pp. 9–26.

_____, 'Scríbhneoirí Chorca Dhuibhne', in *Ár Leithéidí Arís*, pp. 46-60.

Ua Súilleabháin, Seán, 'Osborn Bergin', *Léachtaí Cholm Cille* XXVII (1997), 150–76.

Uí Nia, Gearóidín, 'An tAthair Eric Mac Fhinn agus Ar Aghaidh', unpublished MA thesis, UCG, 1994.

Brief Biographies of Major Figures

(I have taken most of the information in these biographies from the five volumes of *Beathaisnéis: 1882–1982* by Diarmuid Breathnach and Máire Ní Mhurchú, to whom all students of the Gaelic Revival owe an enormous debt of gratitude.)

Bairéad, Tomás. Born Moycullen, Co. Galway, 1893. Native speaker. Member of the IRB and IRA. Did not take sides during the Civil War. Published five volumes of short stories, two in our period, and an autobiography. Died 1973.

Béaslaí, Piaras. Born Liverpool 1883 of Irish parents. Learned Irish in Kerry and was active for many years in the Keating Branch of the Gaelic League. Editor of *Fáinne an Lae* 1917–20. Central in the founding of An Fáinne. Member of the IRB and IRA, and a member of the first Dáil Éireann. Imprisoned during the War of Independence. Supported Treaty and served as major-general in the Free State army. Long active in Gaelic theatre, having founded Na hAisteoirí in 1913. Later a board member of An Comhar Drámaidheachta. Actor, director, and one of the most prolific and accomplished playwrights in the Irish language. Also wrote a novel, poems, short stories, translations, reviews, and literary criticism as well as *Michael Collins and the Making of a New Ireland* (1926). Died 1965.

Blythe, Ernest (de Blaghd, Earnán). Born near Lisburn, Co. Antrim, 1889. Father Church of Ireland, mother Presbyterian. Learned Irish as member of Gaelic League in Dublin and while working as farm labourer in West Kerry. Joined IRB and later IRA. Frequently imprisoned for subversive activities. Member of first Dáil. Supported Treaty and served in Cumann na nGaedheal governments as, first, Minister of Local Affairs and then Minister of Finance. One of the most aggressive voices against Republicans during the Civil War. A key figure in the creation of An Gúm and a major supporter of Gaelic drama both in Dublin and at Taibhdhearc na Gaillimhe. Also provided first state support for the Abbey Theatre, on whose board he served, 1941–72. Prominent in the revival of the Oireachtas in 1939. Died 1975.

Breathnach, Micheál ('Tóchar Máirtín', 'Clais an Aifrinn'). Born Belclare, Co. Galway, 1886. Native speaker. Educated Royal University of Ireland. Pro-Treaty. Teacher and school inspector. Author of humorous short stories, translations, textbooks, plays, an autobiography. Died 1987.

de Bhilmot, Séamus. Born Listowel, Co. Kerry, 1902. Learner of Irish. Educated UCC. Among the most adventurous Gaelic playwrights of the Free State period. Secretary of An Comhar Drámaidheachta from 1928 to 1931, and member, for a time chair, of the board of Taibhdhearc na Gaillimhe, 1935–8. After our period also wrote novels in Irish and English as well as short stories. Died 1977.

de Blácam, Aodh. Born London 1891 of a Northern Irish father and an English mother (christened Hugh Saunders Blackham). Learned Irish in Gaelic League classes in London. After moving to Ireland converted to Catholicism. Opposed Treaty and was briefly interned. Spent most of working life as a journalist, most notably as 'Roddy the Rover' for the *Irish Press*. Wrote prolifically in several genres on a wide range of topics, usually in English, but did publish reviews and essays on literature in Irish during the Free State years. Died 1951.

de Brún, An tAthair Pádraig. Born Grangemockler, Co. Tipperary, 1889. Learned Irish from Fr O'Growney's primers and at Coláiste na Mumhan in Ballinageary, Co. Cork. Trained as a scientist and mathematician at UCD (BA, MA), the Sorbonne, and Göttingen. Ordained after theological studies at the Irish College in Paris. Sympathised with anti-Treaty side in the Civil War. Poet and translator of world classics in Latin, Greek, French, and Italian. First chairman of the Dublin Institute for Advanced Studies in 1940 and later president of UCG. Died 1960.

Delargy, James (Ó Duilearga, Séamas). Born Cushendall, Co. Antrim, 1899. Learned Irish at school. Educated UCD. Among founders of the Irish Folklore Society in 1926 and editor of its journal *Béaloideas* for 46 years. A central figure in the development of the folklore archives now held at UCD. In our period he was not only a collector and scholar of folklore, but an activist who travelled the country lecturing on the need for its preservation. Died 1980.

Dinneen, Patrick, SJ (Ó Duinnín, Pádraig). Born near Rathmore, Co. Kerry, 1860. Native speaker. Educated Royal University of Ireland (BA, MA). Very active in the early days of the Gaelic League as a member of the Keating Branch. Editor, novelist, playwright and essayist, he is best known for his Irish–English dictionary of 1904 (greatly expanded edition, 1927). Pro-Treaty. During our period most of his literary energy went into journalism, producing a wide range of essays, often on surprising topics. Died 1934.

Gógan, Liam S. Born Dublin, 1891. Learned Irish in the Gaelic League. Educated UCD. Spent his working life at the National Museum of Ireland. Pro-Treaty. Best known as the author of six volumes of poetry between 1919 and 1966 – two in our period – he was the most accomplished and original poet in Irish during the Free State years. Also wrote essays in Irish and English on Irish antiquities and worked closely with Fr Dinneen on the 1927 dictionary. Served on the board of An Comhar Drámaidheachta for whom he also wrote an original play. Died 1979.

Hyde, Douglas ('An Craoibhín Aoibhinn'). Born Frenchpark, Co. Roscommon, 1860. Father a Church of Irleand rector. Learned Irish from people in his neighbourhood. Educated TCD (BA, LLD). Member of the Society for the Preservation of the

Irish Language, the Gaelic Union, and one of the founders of the Gaelic League in 1893. Served as first president of the League until 1915. Had also been a guarantor of the Irish Literary Theatre in 1899. One of the founders of the Irish Folklore Society in 1926. Collector, editor, and translator of folk material into English, as well as a poet, playwright, and historian of the language revival. First President of Ireland under de Valera's Constitution of 1937. Died 1949.

Mac Aodha, An tAthair Pádhraic. Born Tuam, Co. Galway, 1882. Native speaker. Educated Maynooth. Supported IRA in War of Independence; neutral in Civil War. Author of saints' lives, religious texts, and plays. Died 1938.

Mac Clúin, An tAthair Seoirse. Born Scarriff, Co. Clare, 1894. Learned Irish. An early visitor to the Blasket Islands, he was assisted by Tomás Ó Criomthain in the preparation of *Réilthíní Óir*, a compilation of expressions and scayings from the Kerry Gaeltacht (1922). His most important work in our period was *An Litríocht*, his survey of the art of literature. Died 1949.

Mac Conmara, Séamas. Born Newry, Co. Down, 1909. Learned Irish from bilingual parents. Educated QUB and Maynooth. Qualified as physician but never practised. Died in 1936 before his ordination as a priest. His only novel, *An Coimhthigheach*, was published posthumously in 1939 and won Duais an Chraoibhín in 1940.

Mac Cumhaill, Maoghnus ('Fionn Mac Cumhaill'). Born Leitir Chatha, Co. Donegal, 1885. Native speaker. Educated UCD (no degree). Lived in US for a time. Fine athlete, once winning a prizefight in Madison Square Garden. Fought in War of Independence. Opposed Treaty, but was not active in Civil War. Novelist, his *Sé Dia an Fear is Fearr* won a gold medal at the 1928 Aonach Tailteann. Died 1965.

Mac Fhinn, Pádraig Eric. Born Clontuskert, Co. Galway, 1895. received MA from UCD and PhD in theology in Rome. Lecturer in education at UCG. Editor of *Ar Aghaidh* for 40 years. Local historian, essayist, literary and dramatic critic. Died 1987.

Mac Fhionnlaoich, Peadar ('Cú Uladh'). Born Glenswilly, Co. Donegal, 1856. Virtually a native speaker, having learned Irish as a very young child. An early member of the Gaelic League and later president on two occasions, and one of the first writers of Donegal Irish to achieve recognition. Opposed Treaty and later named to Senate by de Valera. Author of plays, retellings of heroic tales, and, in our period, short stories and a history of the Easter Rising of 1916. Died 1942.

Mac Giolla Ceara, An tAthair Pádraig. Born Fanad, Co. Donegal, 1888. Native speaker. Educated Maynooth. Served as chaplain with British forces in the First World War. Delivered sermons in Irish at Eucharistic Congress of 1932. Author of works in Irish on the Catholic Church and its doctrines. Died 1956.

Mac Giolla Iasachta, Éamonn (Edward MacLysaght). Born Long Ashton, Somerset, England, 1887 of a Co. Clare family. Learned Irish as young adult in Gaelic League and from native speakers employed on his model farm in Clare. Educated Rugby, Oxford, UCC. Pro-Treaty. Served in Free State Senate, where he made the advancement of the Irish language his primary focus. Founded and edited the journal *An Sguab*, 1922–6. Lived for a while in South Africa, about which he wrote a book in Irish (published 1947). Novelist, diarist, and travel writer in Irish, he also wrote a novel in English and became best known for his work in that language as historian, chairman of the Irish Manuscripts Commission, expert on Irish family names, and Chief Herald of Ireland. Died 1986.

Mac Giollarnáth, Seán. Born near Ballinasloe, Co. Galway, 1880. As civil servant based in London studied Irish in the Gaelic League and also took the IRB oath. Returned to Ireland in 1908 and took over editorship of *An Claidheamh Soluis* from Patrick Pearse. Qualified as lawyer in 1920 and served as judge in the republican courts during the War of Independence and after under the Free State. Folklorist, translator, and author and translator of books on birds, his *Mo Dhúthaigh Fhiáin* (1949) deals with the folklore and natural history of Conamara. Died 1956.

Mac Grianna, Seosamh. Born Rinn na Feirste, Co. Donegal, 1900. Brother of Séamus Ó Grianna. Native speaker. Educated St Patrick's College, Drumcondra. Anti-Treaty. Fought in Civil War and imprisoned 1922–3. Attempted to live by pen as short story writer, novelist, historian, essayist, literary critic, and translator for An Gúm, later claiming that the effect of producing twelve translations for the agency (including works by Conrad and Peadar O'Donnell) had destroyed his creative spirit. His finest work, *Mo Bhealach Féin* (1940), is seen by many as the most significant literary work from the first 60 years of the revival. After a mental breakdown in 1935, he was institutionalised for most of the rest of his life and wrote no more. Died 1990.

Mac Liammóir, Micheál. Born London, 1899. Learned Irish in Gaelic League of London. Actor, director, designer and playwright, his greatest contributions to Gaelic theatre were made at Taibhdhearc na Gaillimhe, but he was also involved with An Comhar Drámaidheachta in Dublin. One of the co-founders of the Gate Theatre in Dublin. In addition to plays, he wrote short stories, poems, memoirs, essays, and literary and dramatic criticism in Irish and English. Died 1978.

Mac Maoláin, Seán ('Brighid'). Born Glenariff, Co. Antrim, 1884. Learned Irish from O'Growney's primers and in the Omeath and then Donegal Gaeltachtaí. Aligned himself with Séamus Ó Grianna and other native speakers in their dispute with learners of the language. Long-time member of the Gaelic League and of the editorial staff of An Gúm from 1932. In addition to novels, short stories and many translations, he wrote books on the language. Died 1973.

Mac Meanman, Seaghán. Born An Ceann Garbh, Co. Donegal. Native speaker. Educated University of London (correspondence degree). Made living as a teacher while writing short stories, plays and essays. Acerbic opponent of standardising the language and the adoption of Roman font, and a champion of Donegal Irish and the primacy of the native speaker in the revival. Died 1962.

Maguidhir, Séamus. Born Geesala, Co. Mayo, 1902. Native speaker. Travelling teacher for the Gaelic League. Fought in War of Independence. Local historian, essayist, and writer of short stories, he was a regular contributor to *An t-Éireannach*. Died 1969.

Murray, Fr. Lawrence (Ó Muireadhaigh, Lorcán). Born Dundalk, Co. Louth, 1883. Learned Irish. Educated Maynooth, but expelled and ordained in USA. One of the founders of the County Louth Archaeological Society. Founder and first editor of *An t-Ultach* and a key figure in the founding of Comhaltas Uladh as a semi-autonomous northern affiliate of the Gaelic League. Local historian, folkorist, editorial writer and essayist. Died 1941.

Nic Gabhann, Caitlín. Born Oldbridge, Co. Wicklow, *c.*1882. Learned Irish in London in the Gaelic League, of which she was an officer and whose plays she acted in. Worked in Ireland as traveling teacher for the League, also serving on Executive Committee and as vice-president, 1924–5. Active in An Fáinne. Believed to have entered a convent in 1928 or soon thereafter. Historian, essayist, author of plays for children. Date of death unknown.

Ní Ghráda, Máiréad. Born Kilmaley, Co. Clare, 1896. Learned Irish from native speakers in the neighbourhood and at school. Educated UCD (BA, MA). Member of the Gaelic League and the women's nationalist movement Cumann na mBan. Worked as secretary for Ernest Blythe during the Civil War and after. Important pioneer in the development of Irish radio as producer, writer, and broadcaster. Wrote one book of short stories and several plays, most notably *An Triail* (1964). Died 1971.

Ó Baoighill, Aindrias. Born Mulnamin, Co. Donegal. Learned Irish. Worked as travelling teacher for Gaelic League in Donegal. Novelist, storywriter, translator and essayist. Died 1972.

Ó Briain, Liam. Born Dublin, 1888. Learned Irish from O'Growney's primers, in school, and in Gaelic League. Educated Royal University (BA) and UCD (MA) and also studed in Germany and France. Taught French at UCD and UCG. Active in the Gaelic League, serving on the Oireachtas and Executive Committees in 1915. Took part in Easter Rising and imprisoned thereafter. Served as judge in republican courts during War of Independence. Pro-Treaty. In Galway took a leading role in the work of Taibhdhearc na Gaillimhe as board member, actor, and playwright, several of his translations from English and French being staged there. Died 1974.

Ó Broin, León. Born Dublin, 1902. Learned Irish at school and in Gaelic League. Member of Fianna Éireann. Imprisoned during War of Independence though not a combatant. Pro-Treaty and an officer in the Free State army. Career civil servant, played an important role in the development of Irish radio and, later, television. Briefly edited *Fáinne an Lae*. Leading member of An Comhar Drámaidheachta, for whom he wrote and translated plays. Member of Irish Folklore Commission. Prolific writer of short stories, playwright, biographer, historian, translator, and literary critic. Writing in English, he achieved recognition as authority on the Fenians and the Easter Rising. Died 1990.

Ó Bróithe, Pádraig. Born Dublin, 1897. Learned Irish at school and in the Gaelic League as a member of the Keating Branch and later Craobh Moibhí. Served in IRA during the War of Independence. Active in An Comhar Drámaidheachta from its inception in 1923. Most of his work was intended for children, but he did write two plays for adults in our period. Died 1949.

Ó Cadhain, Máirtín. Born An Cnocán Glas, Spiddal, Co. Galway. Native speaker. The most important writer of fiction in Irish in the twentieth century, although the majority of his work was done after our period. Educated St Patrick's College, Drumcondra. A committed republican, he was a member of the IRA and was interned by the Irish government for much of the Second World War. In our period he was best known as an activist and propagandist for the Gaeltacht, a leader in the pressure group Muinntear na Gaedhealtachta. He also collected folklore and began writing the short stories that were to become his greatest literary legacy. Eventually published six collections of stories, one posthumous, and three novels, two posthumous, as well as scores of essays on language, literature, and politics. Taught in TCD from 1956, appointed Professor of Irish 1969. Died 1970.

Ó Cadhlaigh, Cormac. Born Kinsale, Co. Cork, 1884. Learned Irish from O'Growney's primers and in the Gaelic League, for which he also worked as an organiser and teacher in summer language schools. Educated Royal University (BA, MA). Early visitor to Blasket Islands. Taught at UCC before being named Professor of Irish at UCD in 1932. Author of textbooks, translations, and important retellings of early Irish literature. Died 1960.

Ó Ciarghusa, Seán ('Leac Logha', 'Marbhán', 'Cloch Labhrais'). Born Kilmacthomas, Co. Waterford, 1873. Native speaker. As British civil servant moved frequently, but was active in the Gaelic League in London and Belfast. Novelist, storywriter, and essayist on a wide range of topics, literary and otherwise. Died 1956.

Ó Cléirigh, Tomás. Born Navan, Co. Meath, 1901. Learned Irish. Educated at UCD (MA in Celtic Studies). Published his thesis *Aodh Mac Aingil agus an Scoil Nua-Ghaedhilge i Lobháin*, a study of Franciscan intellectuals working in Irish in seventeenth-century Louvain, in 1936. Published essays on a wide range of topics in the 1930s. Died 1956.

Ó Conaire, Pádhraic Óg. Born Ros Muc, Co. Galway, 1893. Native speaker. Attended Pearse's Sgoil Éanna. Worked as travelling teacher for the Gaelic League for two decades. Member of the IRB and fought in War of Independence. Worked as translator in Dáil Éireann and as radio broadcaster. Author of seven novels, six between 1922 and 1939, two collections of short stories, and children's books, as well as many translations, most of plays. Died 1971.

Ó Conaire, Pádraic. Born Galway, 1882, but after mother's death in 1894 was raised by relatives in Rosmuc in the Conamara Gaeltacht and learned Irish there. Worked 1900–14 in the civil service in London, where he was active in the Gaelic League and began writing. Frequent winner of Oireachtas prizes in a range of genres from 1904 on. By the time of his return to Ireland most of his best work had been done. First Gaelic author to attempt to make a living with his pen. Pro-Treaty, but not active in Civil War. Socialist. Author of novels, stories, plays, and essays. At his best, one of the finest and most original writers the language has produced, but he often recycled his stories and did hack work for money. Died destitute in 1928.

Ó Criomhthain, Tomás. Born Great Blasket Island, Co. Kerry, 1855. Native speaker. Served as tutor for a series of scholars who visited the island, among them Carl Marstrander, Thomas O'Rahilly, Robin Flower, and Brian Ó Ceallaigh. Ó Ceallaigh was to urge him to keep a diary, eventually published as *Allagar na h-Inise* (1928), and to write his autobiography, eventually published as *An t-Oileánach* (1929). The latter is credited with inspiring the genre of Gaeltacht autobiography in Irish literature. It was awarded the prize for 'creative prose' at Aonach Tailteann in 1928. An English version by Flower was published in 1937. Ó Criomhthain also published a book on the place names of the Blaskets, a collection of his tales, and many pieces in contemporary journals and newspapers. Died 1937.

Ó Cuív, Shán. Born Macroom, Co. Cork, 1875. Parents were native speakers but raised him with English. Learned Irish as a child in the neighbourhood. One of the founders of the Keating Branch of the League and of Coláiste na Mumhan. Journalist and editor of *Glór na Ly* (1911–12) and of *Fáinne an Lae* (1926). Lifelong champion of a simplified Irish orthography (hence his spelling of his name, Seán Ó Caoimh in standard orthography). Author of works on language pedagogy, poems, stories, plays and literary criticism. Died 1940.

Ó Dálaigh, Seán ('Common Noun'). Born Baile an Ghleanna, Co. Kerry, 1861. Native speaker. Educated St Patrick's College, Drumcondra (one year). Schoolteacher in Dún Chaoin in the Kerry Gaeltacht. Also tutored scholars like Vernam Hull, Daniel Binchy, Osborn Bergin, and Thomas O'Rahilly in Irish. Essayist and storywriter. Died 1940.

Ó Deirg, Tomás (Derrig, Thomas). Born Westport, Co. Mayo, 1897. Son of native-speaking father, he spoke Irish from his youth. Educated UCG. Member of IRA. Imprisoned during War of Independence. Took anti-Treaty side in the Civil War and was again imprisoned, spending 40 days on hunger strike. Founder member of Fianna Fáil, and served as Minister of Education 1932–48, apart from a brief period as

Minister of Posts and Telegraphs in 1939. Government's most visible advocate and implementer of the policy of Gaelicisation. Died 1956.

Ó Domhnaill, Maoghnus. Born Annascaul, Co. Kerry, *c.*1900. Parents bilingual. Learned Irish at home and in school in Tralee. Studied for priesthood but left before ordination. Editor of *Fáinne an Lae/An Claidheamh Soluis*, 1930–2. Translator from French, Italian, English and Latin. After our period published a novel, a collection of stories, and a travel book on Italy. Died 1949.

Ó Domhnaill, Niall. Born Loch an Iubhair, Co. Donegal, 1908. Native speaker. Educated UCD. Anti-Treaty. Worked as civil servant, including for An Gúm. Author of short stories, reteller of tales from early Irish literature, historian, biographer, translator. His 1951 pamphlet *Forbairt na Gaelige* was to stir controversy for arguing that the Irish language would have to be saved from English-speaking Ireland and not the Gaeltacht. His greatest contribution was undoubtedly his *Foclóir Gaeilge-Bearla* (1977), the Irish–English dictionary that succeeded Dinneen's 1927 dictionary as the standard work in the language. Died 1995.

Ó Domhnalláin, Pádhraic. ('Darach Mac Eibhir', 'An Connachtach Bán'). Born Oughterard, Co. Galway, 1884. Native speaker. Taught in Coláiste Chonnacht in Tourmakeady, Co. Mayo, 1906–21. Joined IRA and spent time in prison. Long active in Gaelic League, he edited its official organ as *Misneach* in 1920 and as *Fáinne an Lae* 1922–5. Prolific author of essays and short stories. Died 1960.

Ó Donnchadha, Tadhg. ('Torna') Born Carrignavar, Co. Cork, 1874. Learned Irish in the local branch of the Gaelic League. Educated St Patrick's College, Drumcondra. One of the founders of the League's Keating Branch in Dublin. Editor of *Irisleabhar na Gaedhilge*, 1902–9. Appointed professor of Irish in UCC, 1916. Author of hundreds of poems, original and translated, as well as other translations, editions, and scholarly essays on literature. Had a keen interest in the other Celtic languages and literatures. Died 1949.

Ó Droighneáin, Muiris. Born Charleville, Co. Cork, 1901. Learned Irish at school. Educated UCC (BA, MA). His MA thesis, *Taighde i gcomhair Stair Litridheachta na Nua-Gaheilge ó 1882 anuas*, was published in 1936 and remains an important source of information on writers of the revival period. Schoolteacher and later lecturer in QUB. Died 1979.

Ó Dubhda, Peadar ('Cú Chulainn'). Born Hackballscross, Co. Louth 1881. Learned Irish in Gaelic League in Dundalk. Taught in Coláiste Bhríde in Omeath and in Clochaneely, Co. Donegal. Opposed to violence as a means to achieve political goals. Prolific author of children's literature, including plays, as well as a novel, short stories, and essays for adults. Passionate advocate of closer links between the language movement and the Catholic Church. Between 1943 and 1955 translated the entire Bible into Irish. Died 1971.

Ó Faracháin, Riobárd. Born Dublin, 1909. Learned Irish at school and in Gaelic League. Educated UCD (BA, MA). As Robert Farren wrote most of his literary work as poet, playwright and critic in English. His major Gaelic publication was the story collection *Fíon gan Mhoirt* (1938). Named a member of the Abbey Theatre board in 1940. Long active in radio, eventually becoming Controller of Programmes at Radio Éireann. Died 1984.

Ó Foghludha, Risteárd ('Fiachra Éilgeach'). Born Knockmonalea, Co. Cork, 1871. Native speaker. One of the founders of the Keating Branch of the Gaelic League. Most important for his editions of the work of eighteenth- and nineteenth-century Munster poets, he also translated stories and plays from French and English. Died 1957.

Ó Grianna, Séamus ('Máire'). Born Rinn na Feirste, Co. Donegal, 1889. Native speaker. Brother of Seosamh Mac Grianna. Educated St Patrick's College, Drumcondra. Anti-Treaty and fought in Civil War; interned 1922–4. Editor of *Fáinne an Lae*, 1926–9, eventually removed for scurrilous attacks on opponents. Vitriolic champion of the native speaker and of Donegal Irish, and opponent of An Gúm and its policies. Published nine novels (eight as books, one as newspaper serial, 13 collections of short stories, two autobiographies, seven translations, as well as other books and hundreds of editorials and essays. A scathing satirist, he was one of the two or three most important figures in the Gaelic movement in our period. Died 1969.

Ó Gríobhtha, Micheál ('Cos Obann'). Born Caherea, Co. Clare, 1869. While raised with English, heard Irish regularly at home and in the neighbourhood. As a civil servant under British rule, he moved frequently, but was active in the Gaelic League whenever possible. Lived in Dublin from 1913 and worked as civil servant in the Free State Department of Education, much of that time in An Gúm. Responsible for the official translation of de Valera's Constitution of 1937 into Irish. Writer of stories, novelist, playwright, and translator. His 1937 story collection *Cathair Aeidh* won Duais an Chraoibhín. Died 1946.

Ó hAnnracháin, Peadar. Born near Skibbereen, Co. Cork, 1873. Although both parents were native speakers he was raised with English and learned Irish from O'Growney's primers and reading Peadar Ua Laoghaire's *Séadna* with his father. Worked as a travelling organiser for the Gaelic League, and edited *An Lóchrann* 1907–8. A member of the IRA, he was frequently imprisoned in the years after 1916. Not active in the Civil War. Wrote poems and an autobiographical volume in our period, and later a novel, more autobiography, and a play. Died 1965.

O'Hegarty, Patrick S. ('Sarsfield'). Born Cork, 1879. Learned Irish in Gaelic League in London, where he lived from 1902–13, and in Ireland. member of IRB and editor of its paper *Irish Freedom*. Became disillusioned with violence after the 1916 Rising, although he sheltered his friend Michael Collins during the War of Independence. Supported Treaty. Free State civil servant and key figure in development of Irish radio. Historian and literary critic, virtually all of his work was done in English. Father of Seán Ó hÉigeartaigh, founder of the publishing house Sáirséal agus Dill. Died 1955.

Ó Lochlainn, Gearóid. Born Liverpool of Irish parents, 1884. Brought to Ireland at age of six months. Learned Irish as a child from a native speaker and in Gaelic League. Member of IRB. Studied acting with Frank Fay and joined the Fay Brothers' company. Also acted in Gaelic League productions in Dublin. In 1907 went to Denmark where he studied at the University of Copenhagen, worked with a film company, and submitted essays in Irish to *An Claidheamh Soluis*. With founding of An Comhar Drámaidheachta in 1923, he became one of the seminal figures in the development of drama in Irish as actor, producer, director, playwright, and translator of plays. Also acted in English, most notably at the Gate, of which he was one of the co-founders. Died 1970.

Ó Máille, Tomás. Born Muintir Eoin, Co. Galway, 1880. Native speaker. Awarded PhD at Freiburg for work with Rudolf Thurneysen. Also studied in Manchester, Liverpool, Baden, and Berlin. Professor of Irish at UCG. Fought in War of Independence in Conamara. Editor of *An Stoc*. Author of scholarly works on the language in Irish and English. Worked on Linguaphone Irish course in 1927–8. Died 1938.

Ó Maoláin, Micheál. Born Inis Mór, Aran Islands, Co. Galway, 1881. Native speaker. Active in Gaelic League there and after moving to Dublin. Member of IRB and lifelong labour activist, imprisoned after the Dublin lockout in 1913. Interned in Frongoch after 1916. Perhaps most famous as the one-time roommate of Sean O'Casey and possible model for Seumas Shields in *The Shadow of a Gunman*. Founder of Coiste na bPáistí, a group formed to send children of the urban working class to the Gaeltacht to learn Irish. Prolific essayist and controversialist. Died 1956.

Ó Muimhneacháin, Aindrias ('An M.O.'). Born near Keimaneigh, Co. Cork, 1905. Lifelong Gaelic League activist. Worked as organiser and travelling teacher. Served on Executive Committee for 40 years and for 25 as chairman of the Oireachtas, in whose 1939 revival he played a major role. Essayist. Died 1989.

Ó Néill, Séamus. Born Clarkhill, Co. Down, 1910. Learned Irish. Educated QUB (BA, MA), with further study on the Continent. Professional journalist, editor of *An t-Ultach* for two and a half years. Playwright, novelist, storywriter, and essayist. Best known for his novel *Tonn Tuile* (1947) dealing with the failure of a marriage. Died 1981.

Ó Nualláin, Brian ('Flann O'Brien', 'Myles na gCopaleen'). Born Strabane, Co. Tyrone, 1911. Native speaker (raised through Irish by parents). Brother of Ciarán, nephew of Gearóid. Educated UCD (BA, MA). Began writing in Irish in UCD student publications, in his own short-lived, self-published journal *Blather*, and in *Irish Press*, before winning fame with his *Irish Times* column 'Cruiskeen Lawn', intially written entirely in Irish, then bilingual, and finally all but exclusively in English. Best known for his novels in English, most notably *At Swim-Two-Birds* (1939). *An Béal Bocht* (1941), his parody of the Gaeltacht autobiography, is also a classic. Died 1966.

Ó Nualláin, An tAthair Gearóid. Born Dergmoney, Co. Tyrone, 1874. Uncle of Brian and Ciarán Ó Nualláin. Educated Royal University (BA) and Maynooth (MA), where he began learning Irish. Appointed to the chair of Irish at Maynooth 1909. Grammarian, author of short stories, translations, and an autobiography. Died 1942.

Ó Riain, Art ('Barra Ó Caochlaigh'). Born Thurles, Co. Tipperary, 1893. Learned Irish. Career civil servant. Novelist and short story writer, he was a pioneer of urban and science fiction in Irish. His *Lucht Ceoil* was co-winner with Seán Ó Ruadháin's *Pádhraic Mháire Bhán* of a prize for novels sponsored by An Gúm in 1931. Died 1968.

Ó Rinn, Liam ('Tadhg Ó Cianáin', 'Coinneach', 'Fear Faire'). Born Dublin 1886. Learned Irish in Gaelic League, in whose headquarters he worked for 13 years. Fought in Easter Week 1916, interned in Frongoch. Imprisoned again during War of Independence. His 1920 story collection *Cad Ba Dhóbair Dó* was the first and only selection of the book club An Ridireacht Liteartha and represented a major advance in the treatment of urban life in Irish. Pro-Treaty. Longtime member of the translation staff of Dáil Éireann, where he was able to give practical expression to his interest in standardizing Irish and increasing its vocabulary to deal with contemporary life. His best known work is *Mo Chara Stiofán* (1939), an account of his friendship and wide-ranging conversations with the Irish classicist Stephen McKenna. Skilled amateur painter, travel writer, translator, essayist, and the most sophisticated and perceptive Gaelic literary critic of his time. Died 1943.

Ó Ruadháin, Seán. Born Gweensalia, Co. Mayo, 1883. Native speaker. Lifelong teacher of Irish and Gaelic League activist, serving on Executive Committee. Also served as president of An Fáinne. Author of comic stories, was best known for his sole novel *Pádhraic Mháire Bhán*, co-winner with Art Ó Riain's *Lucht Ceoil* of a prize for novels sponsored by An Gúm in 1931. Translated *David Copperfield* and other titles from English. Died 1966.

Ó Séaghdha, Pádraig ('Conán Maol'). Born Gort Breac, Co. Kerry, 1855. Native speaker. Inspired to write for the first Oireachtas in 1897. One of the most important writers of the early revival, producing a novel, short stories, plays, short biographies, and essays. His principal contribution in our period was the posthumously published novel *Stiana* (1933). Died 1928.

Ó Searcaigh, Séamus. Born near Cionn Caslach, Co. Donegal, 1886. Native speaker. Education QUB (BA, MA, PhD). Worked as traveling teacher for Gaelic League and taught at Coláiste na Mumhan, Coláiste Chonnacht, and Coláiste Uladh, doubtless the only person to teach in the stronghold of all three dialects. Lecturer in Irish in UCD, 1933–55. In addition to his scholarly work on the language he collected folk material and wrote a book on modern Gaelic authors and a biography of Pearse. Died 1965.

Ó Siochfhradha, Micheál. Born near Dingle, Co. Kerry, 1901. Brother of Pádraig Ó Siochfhradha. Though not a native speaker in the strict sense, had a good knowledge of Irish from childhood as the result of hearing it regularly in his neighbourhood. Educated UCD. Earned living as teacher and school inspector. Leading member of An Comhar Drámaidheachta. Author of short stories, a history of Ireland, and plays, both translated and original. Died 1986.

Ó Siochfhradha, Pádraig ('An Seabhac'). Born near Dingle, Co. Kerry, 1883. Brother of Micheál Ó Siochfhradha. Though not a native speaker in the strict sense, had a good knowledge of Irish from childhood as the result of hearing it regularly in his neighbourhood. Lifelong Gaelic League activist, frequently on Executive Committee. Editor of *An Lóchrann*. Fought in War of Independence. Pro-Treaty but not active in Civil War. Member of An Comhar Drámaidheachta from its inception in 1923. One of the founders of the Irish Folklore Society and the Irish Manuscripts Commission. Editor of Tomás Ó Criomhthain's *An tOileánach*. Centrally involved in the revival of the Oireachtas in 1939. Novelist, storywriter, translator, adapter of tales from early Irish literature, specialist on place names, essayist. Died 1964.

Ó Súileabháin, Muiris. Born Great Blasket Island, Co. Kerry, 1904. After mother's death in 1905 was raised in an orphanage in Dingle until brought back to island by father in 1911, where he had to relearn his native Irish. Joined Gárda Síochána, the Irish police force, in 1927. As the result of encouragement from and with the help of George Thomson, he wrote his autobiography *Fiche Blian ag Fás* (1933), the translation of which as *Twenty Years A-Growing* appeared the same year. Also wrote plays, some for radio, pious stories rooted in his Catholic faith, an unpublished second volume of autobiography, and an unpublished novel. Died 1950.

Piatt, Donn. Born Rathmines, Dublin, 1905 of an American father and an Irish mother. Learned Irish from native-speaking nannies from Kerry. Educated UCD (BA, MA). Opposed Treaty and was later a supporter of de Valera's Fianna Fáil party. In addition to translations, he wrote poetry, literary criticism, histories of Gaelic Dublin, and of the Irish language. Died 1970.

Saidléar, Annraoi. Born Buttevant, Co. Cork, 1896. Learned Irish. Educated UCC (one year) and a training school for primary teachers in London. Spent working life as a secondary teacher. Active in Gaelic League, member of Executive Committee 1931–2. Playwright who wrote for both children and adults, as well as a scriptwriter for radio. Died 1976.

Sayers, Peig. Born Dún Chaoin, Co. Kerry, 1873. Married into Great Blasket Island 1892. At the urging of Máire Ní Chinnéide and Léan Ní Chonalláin, she dictated her life story to her son Micheál Ó Gaoithín. The result, *Peig .i. A Scéal Féin* (1936), won Duais an Chraoibhín in 1937. A further collaboration with Ní Chinnéide and Ó Gaoithín produced *Machtnamh Sean-Mhná* (1939). One of the most gifted storytellers of the twentieth century. Material from her was published in *Béaloideas* and other journals as well as in *Scéalta ón mBlascaod* (1938), edited by Kenneth Jackson. Died 1958.

Thomson, George (Seoirse Mac Tomáis, 'Seoirse Mac Laghmainn'). Born London, 1903. Learned Irish in Gaelic League in London and on Great Blasket Island, where he first went in 1923. Educated Cambridge University. Lectured on Greek literature through Irish at UCG 1929–34. Encouraged and helped Muiris Ó Súileabháin to write his autobiography *Fiche Blian ag Fás* (1933). Held chair of Greek at Birmingham from 1936 until his retirement in 1970. In addition to scholarly work in English on Greek language and literature, he edited Greek texts and wrote on pre-Socratic philosophy in Irish. Also wrote short stories in Irish not published until 1988. Died 1987.

Tóibín, Nioclás. Born Ring, Co. Waterford, 1890. Native speaker. Educated Model School (for teachers), Marlborough St., Dublin (two years). Worked as a Gaelic League organiser. Author of novels, short stories, plays, essays, many translations – including of Sherlock Holmes – and readers for children. Died 1966.

Ua Ceallaigh, Seán ('Sceilg', 'Mogh Ruith'). Born Valentia Island, Co. Cork, 1872. Raised with English in area where he heard a good deal of Irish spoken. Studied language at school and in Gaelic League, which he joined and worked for after moving to Dublin, eventually becoming president, 1919–23. One of the founders of the Keating Branch, in whose dramatic productions he acted. Also involved with newly founded Na hAisteoirí in 1911. Worked with Dinneen on the 1904 dictionary. Cabinet member in second Dáil with responsibility for education and Irish. Anti-Treaty and circled the globe on a republican publicity campaign in 1923. Elected president of Sinn Féin after de Valera left to form Fianna Fáil. Also involved with the by then moribund Society for the Preservation of the Irish Language, the publisher of several of his books. Biographer, playwright, editor, republican polemicist, and author of retellings of tales from early Irish literature. Died 1957.

Ua Concheanainn, Tomás. Born Inis Meáin, Aran Islands, Co. Galway, 1870. Native speaker. Emigrated to US and lived there and in Mexico before returning to Ireland in 1899. Briefly attended Boston College and took MA in accounting at Eastman School of Commerce in Poughkeepsie, NY. As first full-time organiser for Gaelic League played a central role in the organisation's explosive growth in the first decade of the twentieth century. Advance agent for Douglas Hyde's fundraising tour of America in 1905. Had little interest in politics apart from language issues. Essayist, translator, and, with his wife, the historian Helena Concannon, author of books for young readers. Died 1961.

Ua Dálaigh, Cearbhall. Born Bray. Co. Wicklow, 1911. Learned Irish in school, including a year at Coláiste na Rinne in the Waterford Gaeltacht. Educated UCD. Qualified as lawyer and was later to serve as Attorney-General, Chief Justice of the Irish Supreme Court, and President of Ireland. Active in Gaelic League, serving on Executive Committee, 1931–2. Irish language editor of *Irish Press*, 1931–40. Storywriter, translator, essayist, literary critic. Died 1978.

Ua Laoghaire, An tAthair Peadar. Born Liscarrigane, Co. Cork, 1839. Native speaker. Educated Maynooth. Generally credited for having with his novel *Séadna* (1904) established *caint na ndaoine* (the speech of the people) rather than *Gaeilge Chéitinn* (Keating's [seventeenth century] Irish) as linguistic medium for modern literature in the language. In addition to *Séadna*, he wrote plays, retellings of ancient tales, an autobiography, a translation of *Don Quixote* and the Bible, and hundreds of essays. While work by him did appear posthumously in our period, he was perhaps most important in the Free State years as the symbol of Munster's dominance over the other dialects. Died 1920.

Ua Nualláin, Ciarán. Born Strabane, Co. Tyrone, 1910. Brother of Brian, nephew of Gearóid. Native speaker (raised through Irish by parents). Educated UCD. Active in the League's radical Craobh na hAiséirí in the early 1940s and one of the founders and first editor of the long-lived weekly *Indiu* founded by the branch. Author of comic tales, a detective novel (1939), and a book of stories featuring the same sleuth (1944). Died 1983.

Uí Dhíosca, Úna Bean (Elizabeth Leech Dix, 'Breanda', 'Bláth Aitinne'). Born Dublin, 1880, of Church of Ireland parents. Educated in Switzerland and at Alexandra College in Dublin. Learned Irish in Gaelic League. Taught in Canada. Converted to Catholicism some time after 1923. Committed pacifist as well as nationalist, was opposed to use of violence in 1916, the War of Independence, and the Civil War. President of Irish section of War Resisters' International. Novelist, playwright, translator. Died 1958.

Index

Short Loan Collection